# Lecture Notes in Computer Science 3708

Commenced Publication in 1973
Founding and Former Series Editors:
Gerhard Goos, Juris Hartmanis, and Jan van Leeuwen

## Editorial Board

David Hutchison
  *Lancaster University, UK*
Takeo Kanade
  *Carnegie Mellon University, Pittsburgh, PA, USA*
Josef Kittler
  *University of Surrey, Guildford, UK*
Jon M. Kleinberg
  *Cornell University, Ithaca, NY, USA*
Friedemann Mattern
  *ETH Zurich, Switzerland*
John C. Mitchell
  *Stanford University, CA, USA*
Moni Naor
  *Weizmann Institute of Science, Rehovot, Israel*
Oscar Nierstrasz
  *University of Bern, Switzerland*
C. Pandu Rangan
  *Indian Institute of Technology, Madras, India*
Bernhard Steffen
  *University of Dortmund, Germany*
Madhu Sudan
  *Massachusetts Institute of Technology, MA, USA*
Demetri Terzopoulos
  *New York University, NY, USA*
Doug Tygar
  *University of California, Berkeley, CA, USA*
Moshe Y. Vardi
  *Rice University, Houston, TX, USA*
Gerhard Weikum
  *Max-Planck Institute of Computer Science, Saarbruecken, Germany*

T0189002

Jacques Blanc-Talon   Wilfried Philips
Dan Popescu   Paul Scheunders (Eds.)

# Advanced Concepts for Intelligent Vision Systems

7th International Conference, ACIVS 2005
Antwerp, Belgium, September 20-23, 2005
Proceedings

 Springer

Volume Editors

Jacques Blanc-Talon
DGA/D4S/MRIS, CEP/GIP
16 bis, avenue Prieur de la Côte d'Or, 94114 Arcueil, France
E-mail: jacques.blanc-talon@etca.fr

Wilfried Philips
Ghent University, Telecommunications and Information Processing (TELIN)
Sint-Pietersnieuwstraat 41, 9000 Ghent, Belgium
E-mail: wilfried.philips@ugent.be

Dan Popescu
CSIRO ICT Centre
P.O. Box 76, Epping, Sydney, NSW 1710, Australia
E-mail: dan.popescu@csiro.au

Paul Scheunders
University of Antwerp, Department of Physics
Groenenborgerlaan 171, 2020 Antwerp, Belgium
E-mail: paul.scheunders@ua.ac.be

Library of Congress Control Number: 2005932211

CR Subject Classification (1998): I.4, I.5, I.3, I.2.10

ISSN      0302-9743
ISBN-10   3-540-29032-X Springer Berlin Heidelberg New York
ISBN-13   978-3-540-29032-2 Springer Berlin Heidelberg New York

This work is subject to copyright. All rights are reserved, whether the whole or part of the material is concerned, specifically the rights of translation, reprinting, re-use of illustrations, recitation, broadcasting, reproduction on microfilms or in any other way, and storage in data banks. Duplication of this publication or parts thereof is permitted only under the provisions of the German Copyright Law of September 9, 1965, in its current version, and permission for use must always be obtained from Springer. Violations are liable to prosecution under the German Copyright Law.

Springer is a part of Springer Science+Business Media

springeronline.com

© Springer-Verlag Berlin Heidelberg 2005
Printed in Germany

Typesetting: Camera-ready by author, data conversion by Scientific Publishing Services, Chennai, India
Printed on acid-free paper      SPIN: 11558484      06/3142      5 4 3 2 1 0

# Preface

This volume collects the papers accepted for presentation at the 7th International Conference on Advanced Concepts for Intelligent Vision Systems (ACIVS 2005). The ACIVS conference was established in 1999 in Baden-Baden (Germany) as part of a large multiconference. ACIVS has maintained the tradition of its first edition of having 25-minute oral talks in a single track event, even though the number of participants has been steadily growing every year. The conference currently attracts computer scientists from more than 20 countries, mostly from Europe, Australia and Japan, but also from USA, Asia and the Middle East.

Though ACIVS is a conference on all areas in image processing, one of its major domains is image and video compression. A third of the selected papers dealt with compression, motion estimation, moving object detection and other video applications. This year, topics related to clustering, pattern recognition and biometrics constituted another third of the conference. The last third was more related to the fundamentals of image processing, namely noise reduction, filtering, restoration and image segmentation. We would like to thank the invited speakers Fernando Pereira, Marc Op de Beeck and Rafael Molina for enhancing the technical program with their presentations.

A conference like ACIVS would not be feasible without the concerted effort of many people and the support of various institutions. The paper submission and review procedure was carried out electronically and a minimum of 3 reviewers were assigned to every paper. From 200 submissions, 44 were selected for oral presentation and 46 as posters. A large and energetic Program Committee, helped by additionnal referees – listed on the following pages – completed the long and demanding reviewing process. We would like to thank all of them for their timely and high-quality reviews. Also, we would like to thank our sponsors Philips Research, Barco, Eurasip, the IEEE Benelux Signal Processing Chapter and the Flemish FWO Research Community on Image Processing Systems for their valuable support.

Last but not least, we would like to thank all the participants who trusted us in organizing this event for the seventh time. We hope they attended a stimulating scientific event and enjoyed the atmosphere of the ACIVS social events in the historic city of Antwerp.

July 2005      J. Blanc-Talon, D. Popescu, W. Philips and P. Scheunders

# Organization

ACIVS 2005 was organized by the University of Antwerp and Ghent University.

## Steering Committee

Jacques Blanc-Talon (DGA/D4S/MRIS, Arcueil, France)
Wilfried Philips (Ghent University, Ghent, Belgium)
Dan Popescu (CSIRO ICT Centre, Sydney, Australia)
Paul Scheunders (University of Antwerp, Antwerpen, Belgium)

## Organizing Committee

Wilfried Philips (Ghent University, Ghent, Belgium)
Paul Scheunders (University of Antwerp, Antwerpen, Belgium)

## Sponsors

ACIVS 2005 was sponsored by the following organizations:

- Faculty of Engineering Sciences, Ghent University
- Philips Research
- IEEE Benelux Signal Processing Chapter
- EURASIP
- Barco
- DSP Valley
- FWO Research Community on Image Processing Systems

The ACIVS 2005 organizers are especially grateful to Philips Research for providing the conference bags free of charge and for their financial sponsorship. They are also grateful to the FWO Research Community on Image Processing Systems for sponsoring some of the invited speakers and to Barco for providing a small present for the participants.

## Program Committee

Fritz Albregtsen (University of Oslo, Norway)
Philippe Bolon (University of Savoie, Annecy, France)
Don Bone (Mediaware Solutions, Canberra, ACT, Australia)
David Clausi (University of Waterloo, Canada)
Jean-Pierre Cocquerez (UTC, Compiègne, France)
Pamela Cosman (University of California at San Diego, La Jolla, USA)

Mihai Datcu (German Aerospace Center DLR, Wessling, Germany)
Jennifer Davidson (Iowa State University, Ames, USA)
Christine Fernandez Maloigne (Université de Poitiers, Chasseneuil, France)
Jan Flusser (Institute of Information Theory and Automation, Prague,
    Czech Republic)
Don Fraser (University of New South Wales, Canberra, Australia)
Georgy Gimel'farb (University of Auckland, New Zealand)
Daniele Giusto (University of Cagliari, Italy)
Christine Guillemot (IRISA, Rennes, France)
Fred Hamprecht (Ruprecht-Karls-University of Heidelberg, Germany)
John Illingworth (University of Surrey, Guildford, UK)
Jean-Michel Jolion (INSA, Villeurbanne, France)
Andrzej Kasinski (Poznan University of Technology, Poznan, Poland)
Ashraf Kassim (National University of Singapore, Singapore)
Nahum Kiryati (Tel Aviv University, Israel)
Richard Kleihorst (Philips Research, Eindhoven, The Netherlands)
Ullrich Koethe (University of Hamburg, Germany)
Murat Kunt (EPFL, Lausanne, Switzerland)
Hideo Kuroda (Nagasaki University, Japan)
Kenneth Lam (Hong Kong Polytechnic University, Hong Kong, China)
Bruce Litow (James Cook University, Townsville, Australia)
Brian Lovell (University of Queensland, Brisbane, Australia)
Pierre Moulin (University of Illinois at Urbana-Champaign, USA)
Mads Nielsen (IT University of Copenhagen, Denmark)
Edgard Nyssen (Vrije Universiteit Brussel, Belgium)
Marcin Paprzycki (Oklahoma State University, Tulsa, USA)
Jussi Parkkinen (University of Joensuu, Finland)
Fernando Pereira (Instituto Superior Técnico, Lisbon, Portugal)
Béatrice Pesquet-Popescu (ENST, Paris, France)
Matti Pietikäinen (University of Oulu, Finland)
Aleksandra Pizurica (Ghent University, Belgium)
Gianni Ramponi (Trieste University, Italy)
Thierry Ranchin (Ecole des Mines de Paris, Sophia Antipolis, France)
Murat Tekalp (University of Rochester, USA)
Frederic Truchetet (Université de Bourgogne, Le Creusot, France)
Dimitri Van De Ville (Ecole Polytechnique Fédérale Lausanne, Switzerland)
Peter Veelaert (Hogeschool Ghent, Belgium)

## Reviewers

Arnaldo Abrantes (ISEL, Lisbon, Portugal)
Fritz Albregtsen (University of Oslo, Norway)
Jesus Angulo (Ecole des Mines de Paris, Fontainebleau, France)
Gianluca Antonini (EPFL, Lausanne, Switzerland)
Alain Appriou (ONERA, Chatillon, France)

Hasan Ates (Sabanci University, Istanbul, Turkey)
Jean-Francois Aujol (ENST Paris, France)
Itay Bar-Yosef (Ben-Gurion University, Beer-Sheva, Israel)
Asker Bazen (University of Twente, Enschede, The Netherlands)
Philippe Bekaert (LUC, Diepenbeek, Belgium)
Abdel Belaid (LORIA, Vandoeuvre les Nancy, France)
Rik Bellens (Ghent University, Belgium)
Alia Benali (Ruhr University Bochum, Germany)
Hugues Benoit Cattin (CREATIS, Villeurbanne, France)
Thierry Bernard (ENSTA, Paris, France)
Jacques Blanc-Talon (DGA/D4S/MRIS, Arcueil, France)
Isabelle Bloch (Ecole Nationale Superieure des Telecommunications, Paris,
    France)
Leonardo Bocchi (University of Florence, Italy)
Philippe Bolon (University of Savoie, Annecy, France)
Don Bone (Mediaware Solutions, Canberra, ACT, Australia)
Patrick Bonnin (Universite de Versailles, Velizy, France)
Samia Boukir (Laboratoire L3i, Université de La Rochelle, France)
Elbey Bourennane (Le2i, Dijon, France)
Pierrick Bourgeat (CSIRO, Epping, Australia)
François Bremond (INRIA, Sophia Antipolis, France)
Alan Brooks (Northwestern University, Evanston, USA)
Jean Camillerapp (IRISA, Rennes, France)
Paola Campadelli (Università Statale di Milano, Italy)
Stéphane Canu (PSI, INSA, Rouen, France)
John Carter (University of Southampton, UK)
Antonio Castelo (University of Sao Paulo, Sao Carlos, Brazil)
Andrea Cavallaro (Queen Mary University of London, UK)
Jocelyn Chanussot (INPG, Grenoble, France)
Jean-Marc Chassery (INPG, Grenoble, France)
Chi-Fa Chen (I-Shou University, Kaohsiung, Taiwan)
Youcef Chibani (Université des Sciences et de la Technologie Houari Boumédiene,
    Algiers, Algeria)
Wojciech Chojnacki (University of Adelaide, Australia)
Bill Christmas (University of Surrey, Guildford, UK)
David Clausi (University of Waterloo, Canada)
Jean-Pierre Cocquerez (UTC, Compiègne, France)
Didier Coquin (ESIA, Annecy, France)
Pamela Cosman (University of California at San Diego, La Jolla, USA)
Daniel Cremers (Siemens Corporate Research, Princeton, USA)
Vladimir Crnojevic (University of Novi Sad, Serbia and Montenegro)
Wim d'Haes (University of Antwerp, Belgium)
Matthew Dailey (Sirindhorn International Institute of Technology, Thammasat
    University, A. Muang, Pathumthani, Thailand)
André Dalgalarrondo (DGA/CEV, Cazaux, France)

Frederic Dambreville (CEP, Arcueil, France)
Jennifer Davidson (Iowa State University, Ames, USA)
Steve De Backer (University of Antwerp, Belgium)
Johan De Bock (Ghent University, Belgium)
Martine De Cock (Ghent University, Belgium)
Arturo de la Escalera (Universidad Carlos III de Madrid, Leganes, Spain)
Patrick De Smet (Ghent University, Belgium)
Guy De Tré (Ghent University, Belgium)
Didier Demigny (IRISA, Université Rennes 1, Lannion, France)
Xavier Descombes (INRIA, Sophia Antipolis, France)
Ernst Dickmanns (Universitaet der Bundeswehr, München Neubiberg, Germany)
Sim Dong-Gyu (Kwangwoon University, Seoul, Korea)
Karen Egiazarian (Eguiazarian) (Tampere University of Technology, Finland)
Frédéric Falzon (ALCATEL, Cannes, France)
Guoliang Fan (Oklahoma State University, Stillwater, USA)
Joaquin Fdez-Valdivia (University of Granada, Spain)
Cornelia Fermüller (University of Maryland at College Park, USA)
Christine Fernandez Maloigne (Université de Poitiers, Chasseneuil, France)
Paul Fieguth (University of Waterloo, Canada)
David Filliat (DGA/DET/CEP, Arcueil, France)
Robert Fisher (University of Edinburgh, UK)
Markus Flierl (Swiss Federal Institute of Technology, Lausanne, Switzerland)
Jan Flusser (Institute of Information Theory and Automation, Prague,
    Czech Republic)
Don Fraser (University of New South Wales, Canberra, Australia)
Andre Gagalowicz (INRIA, Rocquencourt, France)
Jean Gao (University of Texas at Arlington, USA)
Patrick Garda (Université Pierre et Marie Curie, Ivry sur Seine, France)
Sidharta Gautama (Ghent University, Belgium)
Stefan Gehlen (Bochum, Viisage Germany)
Edouard Geoffrois (CEP, Arcueil, France)
Theo Gevers (University of Amsterdam, The Netherlands)
Anarta Ghosh (University of Groningen, The Netherlands)
Georgy Gimel'farb (University of Auckland, New Zealand)
Daniele Giusto (University of Cagliari, Italy)
Werner Goeman (Ghent University, Belgium)
Hilario Gómez Moreno (University of Alcalá, Madrid, Spain)
Valerie Gouet (INRIA Rocquencourt, Le Chesnay, France)
Emmanuele Grosicki (CEP, Arcueil, France)
Anne Guérin-Dugué (UJF, Grenoble, France)
Fredrik Gustafsson (Linkoping University, Sweden)
Fred Hamprecht (Ruprecht Karls University of Heidelberg, Germany)
Rudolf Hanel (University of Antwerp, Belgium)
Michael Harville (Hewlett-Packard Laboratories, Palo Alto, USA)
Tetsuo Hattori (Kagawa University, Takamatsu, Japan)

Janne Heikkila (University of Oulu, Finland)
Ernest Hirsch (ULP, Strasbourg, France)
Mark Holden (CSIRO ICT Centre, Sydney, Australia)
Rein-Lien Vincent Hsu (Identix Inc., Jersey City, USA)
Mark Huiskes (CWI, Amsterdam, The Netherlands)
Dimitris Iakovidis (University of Athens, Greece)
Khalid Idrissi (LIRIS–INSA–Université Claude Bernard, Villeurbanne, France)
John Illingworth (University of Surrey, Guildford, UK)
Maarten Jansen (TU Eindhoven, The Netherlands)
Jean-Michel Jolion (INSA, Villeurbanne, France)
Odej Kao (Universität Paderborn, Germany)
Andrzej Kasinski (Poznan University of Technology, Poland)
Ashraf Kassim (National University of Singapore, Singapore)
Yvon Kermarrec (ENSTB, Brest, France)
Ekram Khan (Aligarh Muslim University, Aligarh, India)
Nahum Kiryati (Tel Aviv University, Israel)
Richard Kleihorst (Philips Research, Eindhoven, The Netherlands)
Ullrich Koethe (University of Hamburg, Germany)
Andreas Koschan (University of Tennessee, Knoxville, USA)
Hideo Kuroda (Nagasaki University, Japan)
Mathias Kölsch (Naval Postgraduate School, Monterey, USA)
Olivier Laligant (Le2i Lab., Le Creusot, France)
Kenneth Lam (Hong Kong Polytechnic University, Hong Kong, China)
Ivan Laptev (INRIA, Rennes, France)
Alessandro Ledda (Ghent University, Belgium)
Alexander Leemans (University of Antwerp, Belgium)
Sébastien Lefèvre (University Louis Pasteur—Strasbourg 1, Illkirch, France)
Rongxin Li (CSIRO ICT Centre, Epping, Australia)
Chia-Wen Lin (National Chung Cheng University, Chiayi, Taiwan)
Stefaan Lippens (Ghent University, Belgium)
Bruce Litow (James Cook University, Townsville, Australia)
Brian Lovell (University of Queensland, Brisbane, Australia)
Hiep Luong (Ghent University, Belgium)
Evelyne Lutton (INRIA, Le Chesnay, France)
Siddharth Manay (Lawrence Livermore National Laboratory, USA)
Paul Manoranjan (University of New South Wales, Canberra, Australia)
Antoine Manzanera (ENSTA, Paris, France)
Maurice Margenstern (Université de Metz, France)
David Masip (Computer Vision Center, Bellaterra, Spain)
Basarab Matei (Université Paris Nord — Institut Galilée, Villetaneuse, France)
Sandrine Mathieu-Marni (ALCATEL Space, Cannes la Bocca, France)
Stefano Mattoccia (DEIS — ARCES — University of Bologna, Italy)
Gildas Menier (South Britanny University, Vannes, France)
Bernard Merialdo (Institut EURECOM, Sophia Antipolis, France)
Fabrice Meriaudeau (Université de Bourgogne, Le Creusot, France)

Maurice Milgram (Jussieu Université, Paris, France)
Luce Morin (IRISA, Rennes, France)
Pierre Moulin (University of Illinois at Urbana-Champaign, USA)
Adrian Munteanu (Vrije Universiteit Brussel, Belgium)
Mike Nachtegael (Ghent University, Belgium)
Mai Nguyen (University of Cergy-Pontoise, France)
Jean-Marie Nicolas (ENST, Paris, France)
Edgard Nyssen (Vrije Universiteit Brussel, Belgium)
Jean-Marc Odobez (IDIAP Research Institute, Martigny, Switzerland)
Jean-Marc Ogier (Université de La Rochelle, France)
Marc Op de Beeck (Philips Research, Eindhoven, The Netherlands)
Marcin Paprzycki (Oklahoma State University, Tulsa, USA)
Jussi Parkkinen (University of Joensuu, Finland)
Shmuel Peleg (Hebrew University of Jerusalem, Israel)
Fernando Pereira (Instituto Superior Técnico, Lisbon, Portugal)
Herbert Peremans (University of Antwerp, Belgium)
Jean-Christophe Pesquet (Univ. Marne la Vallée, Champs sur Marne, France)
Béatrice Pesquet-Popescu (ENST, Paris, France)
Sylvie Pesty (IMAG, Grenoble, France)
Maria Petrou (University of Surrey, Guildford, UK)
Sylvie Philipp-Foliguet (ETIS, Cergy, France)
Wilfried Philips (Ghent University, Belgium)
Massimo Piccardi (University of Technology, Sydney, Broadway, Australia)
Mark Pickering (Australian Defence Force Academy, Canberra, Australia)
Wojciech Pieczynski (Institut National des Télécommunications, Evry, France)
Matti Pietikäinen (University of Oulu, Finland)
Rui Pires (IncGEO vzw, Hasselt, Belgium)
Aleksandra Pizurica (Ghent University, Belgium)
Dan Popescu (CSIRO ICT Centre, Sydney, Australia)
Vlad Popovici (EPFL, Lausanne, Switzerland)
Jack-Gerard Postaire (University of Science and Technolgy of Lille (USTL),
    Villeneuve d'Ascq Cedex, France)
Geoff Poulton (CSIRO ICT Centre, Epping, Australia)
Mikhail Prokopenko (CSIRO, Sydney, Australia)
Georges Quenot (IMAG, Grenoble, France)
Esa Rahtu (University of Oulu, Finland)
Gianni Ramponi (Trieste University, Italy)
Thierry Ranchin (Ecole des Mines de Paris, Sophia Antipolis, France)
Paolo Remagnino (Kingston University, Surrey, UK)
Volker Rodehorst (Berlin University of Technology, Germany)
Joost Rombaut (Ghent University, Belgium)
Filip Rooms (Ghent University, Belgium)
Abdelhakim Saadane (Ecole Polytechnique de l'Université de Nantes, France)
Dimitri Samaras (Stony Brook, USA)
Manuel Samuelides (ONERA, Toulouse, France)

Gerald Schaefer (Nottingham Trent University, UK)
Hanno Scharr (Research Center Jülich, Germany)
Peter Schelkens (Vrije Universiteit Brussel, Belgium)
Paul Scheunders (University of Antwerp, Belgium)
Ivan Selesnick (Polytechnic University, Brooklyn, New York, USA)
Sheng-Wen Shih (National Chi Nan University, Puli, Taiwan)
Jan Sijbers (University of Antwerp, Belgium)
Olivier Stasse (CNRS/AIST, Tsukuba, Japan)
Duncan Stevenson (CSIRO, Canberra, Australia)
Gjenna Stippel (University of Cape Town, South Africa)
Dirk Stroobandt (Ghent University, Belgium)
Changming Sun (CSIRO Mathematical and Information Sciences, Sydney, Australia)
Eric Sung (Nanyang Technological University, Singapore)
Hugues Talbot (CSIRO Mathematical and Information Sciences, Sydney, Australia)
Albena Tchamova (Bulgarian Academy of Sciences, Institute for Parallel Processing, Sofia, Bulgaria)
Murat Tekalp (University of Rochester, USA)
Nikola Teslic (University of Novi Sad, Faculty of Technical Sciences, Novi Sad, Serbia and Montenegro)
Céline Thillou (Faculté Polytechnique de Mons, Belgium)
Emanuele Trucco (Heriot-Watt University, Edinburgh, UK)
Frederic Truchetet (Université de Bourgogne, Le Creusot, France)
Filareti Tsalakanidou (Aristotle University of Thessaloniki, Greece)
Dimitri Van De Ville (Ecole Polytechnique Fédérale Lausanne, Switzerland)
Patrick Vandewalle (EPFL, Lausanne, Switzerland)
Ewout Vansteenkiste (Ghent University, Belgium)
Peter Veelaert (Hogeschool Ghent, Belgium)
Thomas Vetter (Basel University, Switzerland)
Yulin Wang (Wuhan University of Technology, China)
Lance Williams (University of New Mexico, Albuquerque, USA)
Jing-Hao Xue (University of Glasgow, UK)
Zhen Yao (University of Warwick, Coventry, UK)
Jun Yu (Southern Methodist University, Dallas, USA)
Hongqing Zhu (Southeast University, China, China)
Vladimir Zlokolica (Ghent University, Belgium)

# Table of Contents

## Biometrics

## Classification and Recognition

## Content and Performance Characterization

## Image and Video Analysis

## Image and Video Coding

## Image and Video Segmentation

## Medical Applications

## Motion Estimation and Tracking

# Noise Reduction and Restauration

## Real-Time Processing and Hardware

# Video Pupil Tracking for Iris Based Identification

W. Ketchantang[1,2], S. Derrode[1], S. Bourennane[1], and L. Martin[2]

[1] Univ. Paul Cézanne, Institut Fresnel (CNRS UMR 6133),
Dom. Univ. de Saint Jérôme, F-13013 Marseille cedex 20, France
william.ketchantang@fresnel.fr
[2] ST Microelectronics, ZI Rousset BP 2, F-13106 Rousset, France
lionel.martin@st.com

**Abstract.** Currently, iris identification systems are not easy to use since they need a strict cooperation of the user during the snapshot acquisition process. Several acquisitions are generally needed to obtain a workable image of the iris for recognition purpose. To make the system more flexible and open to large public applications, we propose to work on the entire sequence acquired by a camera during the enrolment. Hence the recognition step can be applied on a selected number of the "best workable images" of the iris within the sequence. In this context, the aim of the paper is to present a method for pupil tracking based on a dynamic Gaussian Mixture Model (GMM) together with Kalman prediction of the pupil position along the sequence. The method has been experimented on a real video sequence captured by a near Infra-Red (IR) sensitive camera and has shown its effectiveness in nearly real time computing.

## 1   Introduction

Person identification from its iris is known to be one of the most reliable biometric technique, amongst face, fingerprint, hand shape, etc, based methods [1]. Iris texture is a relatively stable physical characteristic over years (and quite hard to falsify), that can be used even to guaranty high-level security access, by using a number of different iris signature [2,3,4].

Iris coding and comparison technics are relatively mature and show nice performances, in terms of both False Acceptance Rate (FAR) and False Rejection Rate (FRR). However, one major drawback in such iris identification systems comes from the eye acquisition procedure which needs a strict cooperation of the user in order to get a good quality image. Several snapshots of the iris are generally necessary to obtain a ready-to-process image. Examples in Fig. 1 show classical near IR iris acquisition problems obtained during enrolment, with blurred, noisy or defocused images. These problems are emphasized when using low-cost IR camera for large public applications. To increase the flexibility and to make the system more friendly, we propose to work on the entire sequence of images acquired by a camera during the enrolment, and to automatically select the "best workable image(s)" of the iris within the sequence before applying

J. Blanc-Talon et al. (Eds.): ACIVS 2005, LNCS 3708, pp. 1–8, 2005.
© Springer-Verlag Berlin Heidelberg 2005

the recognition procedure. The "best workable images" are images showing a clear iris (without degradations shown in 1) where partial occlusions provoked by eyelids and eyelash are small.

For this purpose, it is necessary to track the pupil along the sequence, in order to locate it efficiently and exactly, and to measure iris quality in the vicinity of the pupil. This problem is different from the -more studied- eye following problem in face sequence [5,6], typically encountered in driver attention level surveillance [7]. Such pupil sequences generally present images whose quality varies during time of acquisition, depending on the user motion:

– jerky motion of the user head resulting in quick and large scale translations of the pupil,
– translation of the user head along the optical axis resulting in both (i) scale variations of the pupil size and (ii) alternative focus and out-of-focus series of images.

Pupil tracking is a difficult problem also because of image degradations due to light variations and specular reflections in iris area (see white spots in the three images in Fig. 1). However, we can use some prior knowledge about the pupil which is approximatively circular and dark. In this context, the aim of the paper is to present a method for pupil tracking based on a GMM, which is dynamically and automatically updated along the time of acquisition. This method is combined with a Kalman filter to predict the pupil position in the next frame. The method has been experimented on a real sequence captured by an IR sensitive camera and has shown its effectiveness in nearly real time computing.

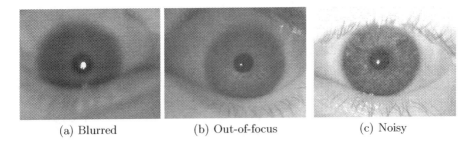

(a) Blurred          (b) Out-of-focus          (c) Noisy

**Fig. 1.** Three kinds of degradations encountered in iris IR image acquisition

This paper is organized as follows. In section 2, we describe the principles of the algorithm based on GMM and Kalman prediction of the pupil modeled by a circle. Section 3 presents experimental results on an iris IR sequence and section 4 draws conclusion and perspectives.

## 2   Pupil Tracking Algorithm

This section is devoted to the description of the tracking method, whose principle is presented in Fig. 2. The pupil is modeled by a circle, with center $C(x, y)$ and radius $R$ which vary along the sequence.

First, the pupil is detected and localized in the first frame, thanks to the Gradient Hough Transform (GHT) and the integro-differential operator detailed in [3]. The gray-level mixture of pixels inside the pupil is then modeled by a GMM whose parameters are learned by an EM algorithm (section 2.1). Pixels from white spots inside the pupil are thresholded and did not take into account in the mixture. In step 2, a Kalman filter is used to predict the box where the pupil has to be searched in the current image (section 2.2). If the pupil is not found in the predicted box, we simply copy both mixture and pupil parameters of previous image to the next image. Conversely, if the pupil is found in the box, we compute precisely the new pupil position $C_t$ and size $R_t$ (section 2.3), and update GMM parameters according to the new localized pupil at time $t$. This way the gaussian mixture of the pupil is updated dynamically along the sequence.

### 2.1   Parameters Estimation of the GMM

The gray-level distribution of pixels inside the pupil is modeled by a mixture of $M$ Gaussian distributions:

$$P(x/pupil) = \sum_{m=1}^{M} \alpha_m \, P_m(x \,|\mu_m, \sigma_m) \tag{1}$$

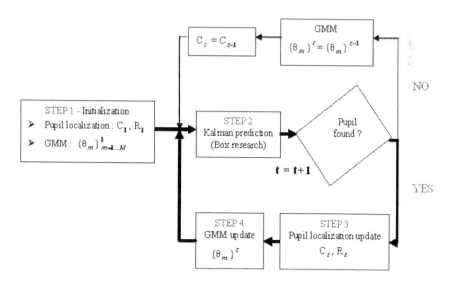

**Fig. 2.** Overview of the pupil tracking module

Hence, mixture parameters are defined by the $M$ means $\mu_m$, the $M$ variances $\sigma_m$ of the Gaussians $\mathcal{N}_m$ $(P_m(x/\mu_m, \sigma_m))$ and the $M$ relative weights $\alpha_m$ of each Gaussian in the mixture; $\theta_m = \{\alpha_m, \mu_m, \sigma_m\}$ and $\sum_{m=1}^{M} \alpha_m = 1$. These parameters are estimated thanks to the well-known iterative Expectation - Maximisation (EM) method [8,9], whose update equations are given by:

$$\theta_m^{old} = \theta_m^{new}$$

$$P(m \,|x_n, \theta_m) = \frac{\alpha_m^{old} \, P_m\,(x_n \,|\mu_m, \sigma_m)}{\sum_{m=1}^{M} \alpha_m^{old} \, P_m(x_n \,|\mu_m, \sigma_m)}$$

$$\alpha_m^{new} = \frac{1}{N} \sum_{n=1}^{N} P(m \,|x_n, \theta_m)$$

$$\mu_m^{new} = \frac{\sum_{n=1}^{N} x_n \, P(m \,|x_n, \theta_m)}{\sum_{n=1}^{N} P(m \,|x_n, \theta_m)}$$

$$\sigma_m^{new} = \frac{\sum_{n=1}^{N} (x_n - \mu_m^{new}) \, (x_n - \mu_m^{new}) \, P(m \,|x_n, \theta_m)}{\sum_{n=1}^{N} P(m \,|x_n, \theta_m)}, \qquad (2)$$

where $N$ is the number of pixels inside the pupil. This kind of model has been used successfully to track face or hand human skin in video sequences [10,11,7].

Thus, we get parameter values that maximise the pupil data likelihood. Due to local convergence of the EM procedure, good initial parameter estimates are important. For the first frame of the sequence, we implemented a K-means algorithm whereas, for other frames, we used parameter values estimated at previous frame, guarantying a convergence of EM in a few number of iterations since the pupil distribution is supposed to vary slowly between two consecutive images. Since the pupil area is dark and almost homogeneous, we take only two Gaussians. The number of EM and K-means iterations were respectively set to 10 and 5.

## 2.2   Kalman Prediction of Pupil Position

Kalman filter [12] is used to predict the position of the pupil center $C_{t+1}$ in next frame from its positions in previous frames. In general, the Kalman filter describes a system with a system state $X_t$ and a measurement model $C_t$ as follows

$$X_{t+1} = A\,X_t + W_t$$
$$C_t = H\,X_t + V_t \qquad (3)$$

where $W_t$ and $V_t$ denote respectively the model and measurement noises. They are supposed to be independent and their variance-covariance matrices are respectively $Q$ and $R$. $A$ and $H$ are respectively the transition and measurement matrices.

Kalman filter is one of the most popular estimation techniques in motion prediction because it provides an optimal estimation method for linear dynamic systems with Gaussian noise.

Filtering equations are given by

$$K_t = P_{t/t-1} H_t^T (R + H_t P_{t/t-1} H_t^T)^{-1},$$
$$P_{t/t} = (I - K_t H_t) P_{t/t-1},$$
$$X_{t/t} = X_{t/t-1} + K_t (C_t - H_t X_{t/t-1}), \qquad (4)$$

where $K_t$ and $P_{t/t}$ are respectively the Kalman gain and error covariance matrices at time $t$. Finally, prediction equations are given by

$$P_{t+1/t} = A P_{t/t} A^T + Q,$$
$$X_{t+1/t} = A X_{t/t}. \qquad (5)$$

As pupil moves slowly, we can assume that the first derivatives of position $(x_t, y_t)$ is constant. Then, $A$ and $H$ are defined through

$$A = \begin{pmatrix} 1 & 0 & \Delta T & 0 \\ 0 & 1 & 0 & \Delta T \\ 0 & 0 & 1 & 0 \\ 0 & 0 & 0 & 1 \end{pmatrix}, \quad H = \begin{pmatrix} 1 & 0 & 0 & 0 \\ 0 & 1 & 0 & 0 \end{pmatrix}, \qquad (6)$$

where $\Delta T$ is the time of frame acquisition ($\Delta T = 1/25s$) with as state vector $X_t(x_t, y_t, \dot{x}_t, \dot{y}_t)$ and measurement vector $C_t(\hat{x}_t, \hat{y}_t)$.

These equations allow us to predict the position of the pupil in next frame.

## 2.3   Pupil Parameters

We now search for the real position of the pupil center $C_t$ in a square box centered on the predicted position (predicted box : PB), with a side equal to $2 R_{t-1}$. We should use the method employed to determine the position of the pupil in the first frame.

We prefer to use the gray level distribution of pupil pixels modeled by a GMM to compute the center of mass of pixels $x_n$ $(C_t(\hat{x}_t, \hat{y}_t))$ with $P(x_n | \theta)$ lower than a given threshold.

$$P(j | \theta) = \sum_{m=1}^{M} \alpha_m P_m(j / \theta_m) \qquad (7)$$

$$\hat{x}_t = \frac{\sum_{j \in PB} x_j P(j | \theta)}{\sum_{j \in PB} P(j | \theta)}$$

$$\hat{y}_t = \frac{\sum_{j \in PB} y_j P(j | \theta)}{\sum_{j \in PB} P(j | \theta)}$$

If all pixels verify $P(x_n/\theta) < threshold$ then the pupil is considered lost in this frame, and tracking is delayed to the next frame.

As the pupil size also varies with time (due to translation of the head along the optical axis and to natural size variations), we also compute the pupil radius $R_t$ to have a tracking robust to scale changes. The radius $R_t$ is computed as follows

$$R_t = \underset{R}{Argmax} \left| \frac{\partial}{\partial c} \oint_c I(x,y)ds \right| \tag{8}$$

where $c$ is the edge of the circle which gets as radius $R$, and $I(x,y)$ is the gray level of pixels belonging to $c$. $R$ varies between $R_{min}$ and $R_{max}$.

## 3   Pupil Tracking Results

The algorithm has been coded in C++, on a Pentium IV (2.6 GHz) PC platform and performs tracking at approximately $f \simeq 16$Hz. Experimental results in Fig. 3 show the pupil tracking algorithm in action along an IR video sequence. Globally,

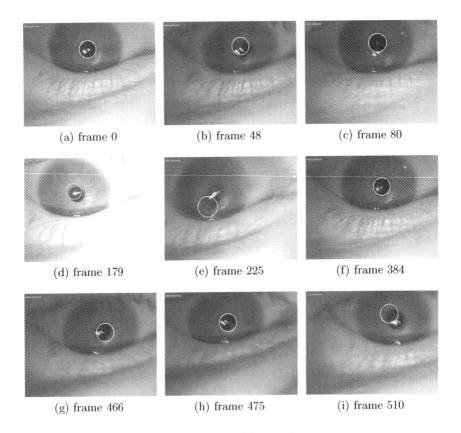

(a) frame 0             (b) frame 48            (c) frame 80

(d) frame 179           (e) frame 225           (f) frame 384

(g) frame 466           (h) frame 475           (i) frame 510

**Fig. 3.** Pupil tracking results

the method seems to be efficient and relatively robust to the image degradations mentioned in introduction. Indeed, our algorithm localizes correctly the pupil for not too fast eye motion, despite specular reflections (white spots). Even with out-of-focus images, the tracking algorithm manages to localize the pupil, provided that eye motion is slow (frame 475).

On the other hand, when pupil motion is quick and jerky, the algorithm does not localize it correctly (frames 48, 225 and 510) since the pupil position is not well predicted by Kalman filtering. This can be explained by the constant velocity hypothesis which is too strick and can not be assumed for all images in the sequence. When we take into account the velocity variations by integrating acceleration $(\ddot{x}, \ddot{y})$ in state vector, we verified experimentally that the performances and stability of the tracker decrease, because slow eye motion are not well predicted. In addition, our algorithm can loose the pupil when illumination variations are strong (frame 179). Indeed, an intensive illumination variation modifies considerably the pupil gray-level distribution, and the GMM is not able to update the model instantaneously.

An important point to note is that the algorithm is able to recover (frame 384) the pupil even if it was lost before (frame 225), as soon as the assumption on slow eye motion is verified.

## 4   Conclusion and Perspectives

In this paper, we have presented a method for tracking a pupil in an IR iris sequence of images. The pupil geometry is modeled by a circle and the pupil distribution by a mixture of two Gaussians. The pupil position is predicted according to a Kalman filter. The GMM allows a computation of the pupil center which is robust to illumination change, and the Kalman filter is used to predict the area where to search the pupil in the next frame. The results we obtained are really encouraging. Nevertheless, we can think of making the tracking more robust by taking into account brief jump of velocity in the state evolution equation. Thus, the constant velocity assumption of the Kalman filter will be applied in slow pupil motion, and modified in fast eye motion parts of the sequence. By selecting the best workable image(s) of the pupil along the sequence, we can expect to improve the recognition rates and identification.

## References

1. Ross, A., Jain, A.K.: Information fusion in biometrics. Pattern Recognition Letters **24** (2003) 2115–2125
2. Daugman, J.: High confidence visual recognition of persons by a test of statistical independence. IEEE trans. on PAMI **15** (1993) 1148–1161
3. Tisse, C.L., Martin, L., Torres, L., Robert, M.: Person identification technique using human iris recognition. In: 15th Int. Conf. on Vision Interface, Calgary, CA (2002) 294–299
4. Ma, L., Tan, T., Wang, Y., Zhang, D.: Efficient iris recognition by characterizing key local variations. IEEE trans. on Image Processing **13** (2004) 739–750

5. Sirohey, S., Rosenfeld, A., Duric, Z.: A method of detecting and traking irises and eyelids in video. Pattern Recognition **35** (2002) 389–401
6. Zhu, Z., Ji, Q.: Robust real-time eye detection and tracking under variable lighting conditions and various face orientations. Computer Vision and Image Understanding **38** (2005) 124–154
7. Zhu, Y., Fujimura, K.: Driver face tracking using Gaussian mixture model. In: Proc. of the IEEE Intelligent Vehicles Symp. (2003) 587–592
8. Dempster, A.P., Laird, N.M., Rubin, D.B.: Maximum likelihood from incomplete data via the EM algorithm. J. of the Royal Statistical Society **39** (1977) 1–38
9. Bilmes, J.A.: A gentle tutorial of the EM algorithm and its application to parameter estimation for Gaussian mixture and hidden Markov models. report tr-97-021, International Computer Science Institute, Berkeley, CA, USA (1997)
10. McKenna, S., Gong, S., Raja, Y.: Modelling facial colour and identity with Gaussian mixtures. Pattern Recognition **31** (1998) 1883–1892
11. Yang, J., Lu, W., Waibel, A.: Skin color modeling and adaptation. In: Proc. of the Third Asian Conf. on Computer Vision. Volume 2. (1998) 687–694 Lecture Notes In Computer Science - Vol. 1352.
12. Minkler, G., Minkler, J.: Theory and Application of Kalman filtering. Magellan Book Company, Palm Bay, FL, USA (1993)

# Three Dimensional Fingertip Tracking in Stereovision

S. Conseil[1], S. Bourennane[1], and L. Martin[2]

[1] Univ. Paul Cézanne, Institut Fresnel (CNRS UMR 6133),
Dom. Univ. de Saint Jérôme, F-13013 Marseille cedex 20, France
{simon.conseil, salah.bourennane}@fresnel.fr
[2] ST Microelectronics, ZI Rousset BP 2, F-13106 Rousset, France
lionel.martin@st.com

**Abstract.** This paper presents a real time estimation method of the three dimensional trajectory of a fingertip. Pointing with the finger is indeed a natural gesture for Human Computer Interaction. Our approach is based on stereoscopic vision, with two standard webcams. The hand is segmented with skin color detection, and the fingertip is detected by the analysis of the curvature of finger boundary. The fingertip tracking is carried out by a three dimensional Kalman filter, in order to improve the detection with a local research, centered on the prediction of the 3-D position, and to filter the trajectory to reduce the estimation error.

## 1 Introduction

Hand gestures are a natural and instinctive mean for humans to interact with their environment. They can be used to emphasize speech, to point or to manipulate objects in augmented environment, or to communicate with sign language. Over the past few years, there has been a growing interest in hand gestures recognition, thanks to the use of computer vision techniques [1].

Finger pointing is a simple gesture, well-fitted to replace the mouse. The finger is indeed a natural and very practical pointing device for Human Computer Interaction. Various assumptions have been used to ease fingertip detection and different configuration have been studied. Hence it is possible to determine the 3-D finger trajectory with a geometric model of the body, using a single camera and the detection of head and shoulders [2] or with a stereovision system and eye-to-fingertip pointing mode [3].

Other systems recognize 2-D trajectory with a single camera above the work plane. In the Digital Desk system from Crowley *et al.* [4] tracking is carried out on a single view by correlation with a fingertip template, but it is not robust to orientation and scaling changes. The resulting plane trajectory have been used for handwriting recognition with HMM [5]. In the EnhancedDesk system [6], several fingers are tracked in one view, with a two-dimensional Kalman filter for each finger. The detection of the fingertips is carried out thanks to an infrared camera and a normalized correlation. Finally two-dimensional trajectories (square, circle, triangle) are recognized using HMM.

J. Blanc-Talon et al. (Eds.): ACIVS 2005, LNCS 3708, pp. 9–16, 2005.
© Springer-Verlag Berlin Heidelberg 2005

Segen and Kumar [7] use two cameras to determine the 3-D direction pointed by the finger. Strong curvature points are detected on the boundary of the hand region and used to classify three hand gestures. They apply this system to a computer game interface and a navigation software. The use of the disparity obtained from a stereoscopic pair has also been studied by [8], but the computation of a disparity map is computationally expensive.

In this paper, we focus on fingertip tracking for pointing gestures. Two calibrated cameras are used to compute 3-D fingertip trajectory, but errors in the fingertip localization and the absence of synchronization result in unprecise trajectory estimation. The originality of our approach is the use of a three dimensional Kalman filter to predict 3-D position and to smooth the fingertip trajectory. The predicted 3-D position is projected in the two images, and a local search is performed for the fingertip detection.

## 2   Finger Detection

### 2.1   Hand Segmentation

Hand segmentation is the first important step. Fast and robust segmentation is needed, without assumptions on the background color. In previous experiments, the classical background subtraction method has proved to be too much sensitive to shadows and illumination variations, even in a controlled environment.

Skin color detection is now commonly used in both hand and face segmentation. Many approaches have proved their efficiency, with different color spaces or learning techniques [9]. We have chosen to detect skin color pixels in the YCbCr color space, with the fast and simple approach presented in [10]. Figure 1.(b) shows that the result is convincing, even if some skin pixels are not detected on the right part of the hand. In order to reduce the noise from the binary silhouette, a median filter is applied, then a morphological filtering, and finally a connected components labeling to remove the non-hand regions and to fill holes in the hand blob.

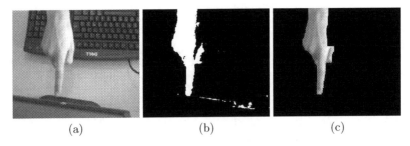

(a)                    (b)                    (c)

**Fig. 1.** Hand segmentation: (a) original image, (b) silhouette obtained from CbCr thresholding and (c) final silhouette after filtering and connected components labeling

## 2.2 Fingertip Detection

When the finger enters in the cameras field of view, it is necessary to detect accurately the fingertip position in order to initialize the tracking. As we consider the case of pointing gesture, we assume that only one finger is pointing and so the fingertip is the point located at the extremity of the hand region.

With the hand silhouettes obtained from the previous stage, we describe the boundary of the hand region by a succession of points $P(i) = (x(i), y(i))$. The fingertip is the point of the boundary that maximizes the distance from the center of gravity of the hand region. The center of gravity is obtained with the computation of the geometrical moments.

However this measure is not very precise, depending on the hand orientation. Hence we refine the fingertip detection with the curvature of the boundary with the method presented in [7]. The k-curvature is given by the angle between the vectors $[P(i-k)P(i)]$ and $[P(i)P(i+K)]$. The fingertip is the point with the stronger curvature.

# 3 Three Dimensional Tracking

With the position of the fingertip in each of the two images, one can compute its 3-D position. However the 3-D positions are not precise for several reasons: unprecise detection of the fingertip due to a bad segmentation, discretization of the images (one pixel error on the fingertip localization can represent several millimeters in 3-D), temporal shift between the acquisition of the two images (the two cameras are not synchronized).

Furthermore it is not necessary to treat the whole image whereas we know the finger position. Thus the research of the fingertip can be reduced to a small window, thanks to the tracking of the finger and the prediction of its position with the preceding pair of images. The goal of the temporal tracking is thus to facilitate the localization of the finger and to smooth the trajectories.

## 3.1 Kalman Filter

Our approach is based on a Kalman filter [11] in three dimensions, with the fingertip's location and velocity. We assume that the movement is uniform and the velocity is constant, the frame interval $\Delta T$ being short. The state vector $\mathbf{x}_t$ is defined as:

$$\mathbf{x}_k = (x(k), y(k), z(k), v_x(k), v_y(k), v_z(k))^T$$

where $(x(k), y(k), z(k))$ is the position and $(v_x(k), v_y(k), v_z(k))$ the velocity of the fingertip in frame $k$. The state vector $\mathbf{x}_k$ and the observation vector $\mathbf{z}_k$ are related by the following equations:

$$\mathbf{x}_{k+1} = A\,\mathbf{x}_k + \mathbf{w}_k$$
$$\mathbf{z}_k = H\,\mathbf{x}_k + \mathbf{v}_k \qquad (1)$$

with $\mathbf{w}_k$ and $\mathbf{v}_k$ the process and measurement noises, assumed to be independent white gaussian noises, A the state transition matrix and H the observation matrix:

$$A = \begin{pmatrix} 1 & 0 & 0 & \Delta T & 0 & 0 \\ 0 & 1 & 0 & 0 & \Delta T & 0 \\ 0 & 0 & 1 & 0 & 0 & \Delta T \\ 0 & 0 & 0 & 1 & 0 & 0 \\ 0 & 0 & 0 & 0 & 1 & 0 \\ 0 & 0 & 0 & 0 & 0 & 1 \end{pmatrix}$$

$$H = \begin{pmatrix} 1 & 0 & 0 & 0 & 0 & 0 \\ 0 & 1 & 0 & 0 & 0 & 0 \\ 0 & 0 & 1 & 0 & 0 & 0 \end{pmatrix}$$

Writing $\mathbf{x}_k$ and $\mathbf{x}_k^-$ the *a posteriori* and *a priori* state estimates, $P_k$ and $P_k^-$ the *a posteriori* and *a priori* estimate error covariances, $Q$ the process noise covariance, $R$ the measurement noise covariance, and $K_k$ the Kalman gain, one obtains the following equations:

Prediction equations:

$$\mathbf{x}_k^- = A\mathbf{x}_{k-1}$$
$$P_k^- = AP_{k-1}A^T + Q \tag{2}$$

Update equations:

$$K_k = P_k^- H^T (HP_k^- H^T + R)^{-1}$$
$$\mathbf{x_k} = \mathbf{x_k}^- + K_k(\mathbf{z_k} - H\mathbf{x_k^-})$$
$$P_k = (I_6 - K_k H)P_k^- \tag{3}$$

*Parameters Setting.* The three components are supposed to be independent, thus the covariance matrices are diagonal. As we assume constant velocity in our model, which may not be always true, the process noise covariance is supposed to be important on the velocity component whereas it is weak in the position one.

The measurement noise covariance is calculated with a sequence of images where the finger remains fixed. We obtain $Var(X, Y, Z) = (0.31, 2.39, 15.06)$, which shows that the measurement error is more significant on component Z than on X and Y.

## 3.2   Developed Algorithm

Figure 2 summarizes the different stages of the treatment: starting from the computation of the 3-D position with a pair of images, one can predict the 3-D position corresponding to the following pair of images. The predicted 3-D position is projected in the two images to obtain a 2-D prediction of the fingertip position. Then the research of the fingertip in each image can be reduced to a

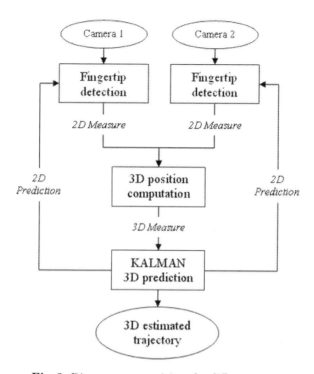

**Fig. 2.** Diagram summarizing the different stages

neighborhood of the predicted fingertip position. The size used for the research window is $80 \times 80$ pixels.

The detection of the finger is then carried out with the method described in Sec. 2. Finally, the epipolar constraint is checked to ensure the good detection of the fingertip in the two images. However, because of the non-synchronisation, a little error is admitted in the epipolar constraint checking.

## 4    Results

We use two common webcams, with $352 \times 288$ image resolution. Images are transmitted by USB connection, with a MJPEG compression which introduces noise on the images. Moreover, the two cameras are not synchronized, which can induce a small difference in position between two images, and can result in an oscillation in the finger trajectory: during the time interval between the two frame grabbings, the finger can have moved, depending on the velocity of movement. Consequently, the triangulation is skewed, mainly on the depth dimension (corresponding to the optical axis of the cameras).

### 4.1    Example: Case of a Circle

In order to be able to measure computation errors of the 3-D position, it is necessary to know the ground truth, which is often difficult in stereovision. In our configuration the reconstruction error is found mainly on the component $Z$, corresponding to the depth (direction of the optical axes). Thus we are interested in a plane trajectory, a circle realized on the desk, which corresponds to the plane $z = 0$ (Fig. 3). As the trajectory is plane, standard deviation of component Z can easily be computed to compare the reconstruction errors.

We can see on Fig. 4.(a) the estimated 3-D trajectory of the circle, as well as measurements in dotted lines. The reconstruction error is more important on the $Z$ component, corresponding to the depth. Figure 4.(b) reveals that the Kalman filter smoothes the component Z, in this case the standard deviation on the depth is reduced from 9.77 to 5.46.

## 4.2   Velocity Influence

The velocity of the movement influences the reconstruction error. Indeed, the faster is the movement, the more the finger can have moved between the acquisition of the two images, which results in a more significant error. Table 1 illustrates this with the study of two plane trajectories (circle and square), treated in real time (30 Hz).

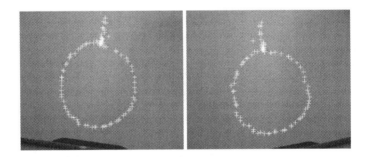

**Fig. 3.** Left and right images with a circle trajectory and detected fingertip positions

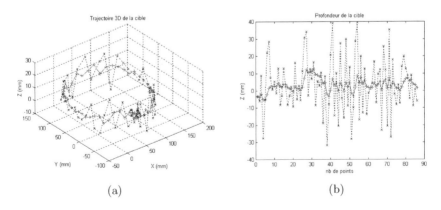

(a)                                    (b)

**Fig. 4.** (a) 3-D trajectory with a circle gesture and (b) component Z, corresponding to the depth dimension (measures in dotted lines, estimations in full lines)

These trajectories have been realized at three different velocities, thus a faster trajectory is made up of a lower number of points. The standard deviation on component Z is then computed to compare the reconstruction errors.

In both cases we see that the standard deviation increases with speed, and the standard deviation is weaker for the trajectory estimated by the filter of Kalman than for measurements. We also see that the reconstruction error is smaller for the square, the linear movement being better adapted to the model than the circular one.

**Table 1.** Evolution of the standard deviation on the depth according to the speed of realization of the movement

| Trajectory | Velocity | Number of points | Std dev Mesures | Std dev Estimation |
|---|---|---|---|---|
| Circle | slow | 306 | 9.7673 | 5.4587 |
| | medium | 189 | 11.3158 | 8.3916 |
| | fast | 108 | 14.7552 | 10.8265 |
| Square | slow | 290 | 10.4771 | 4.8718 |
| | medium | 185 | 11.1463 | 4.4337 |
| | fast | 106 | 12.2786 | 6.0401 |

## 5 Conclusion

We presented a three dimensional finger tracking system based on a Kalman filter, which performs robust detection thanks to the reduction of the fingertip research to a small window and the reduction of the estimation error with the smoothing of the 3-D trajectories. The system runs in real time on real data, on a 2.6 GHz PC. With adapted detection method, other applications are possible, like people or vehicles tracking. To improve the system, the computation of the research window width could be adapted to the movement velocity. We also plan to extend the tracking to multiple fingers and to deal with occlusion problems.

## References

1. Pavlovic, V., Sharma, R., Huang, T.: Visual interpretation of hand gestures for human-computer interaction : A review. IEEE trans. on Pattern Analysis and Machine Intelligence **19** (1997)
2. Wu, A., Shah, M., da Vitoria Lobo, N.: A virtual 3d blackboard: 3d finger tracking using a single camera. In: Proc. of the IEEE Int. Conf. on Automatic Face and Gesture Recognition. (2000)
3. Hung, Y., Yang, Y., Chen, Y., Hsieh, I., Fuh, C.: Free-hand pointer by use of an active stereo vision system. In: Proc. of the IEEE Int. Conf. on Pattern Recognition, Brisbane (1998) 1244–1246
4. Crowley, J., Berard, F., Coutaz, J.: Finger tracking as an input device for augmented reality. In: IEEE Int. Workshop on Automatic Face and Gesture Recognition, Zurich (1995) 195–200

5. Martin, J., Durand, J.B.: Automatic handwriting gestures recognition using hidden markov models. In: Proc. of the IEEE Int. Conf. on Automatic Face and Gesture Recognition. (2000)
6. Oka, K., Sato, Y., Koike, H.: Real-time fingertip tracking and gesture recognition. IEEE trans. on Computer Graphics and Applications **22** (2002) 64–71
7. Segen, J., Kumar, S.: Human-computer interaction using gesture recognition and 3d hand tracking. In: Proc. of the IEEE Int. Conf. on Image Processing. (1998)
8. Jojic, N., Huang, T., Brumitt, B., Meyers, B., Harris, S.: Detection and estimation of pointing gestures in dense disparity maps. In: Proc. of the IEEE Int. Conf. on Automatic Face and Gesture Recognition. (2000)
9. Phung, S., Bouzerdoum, A., Chai, D.: Skin segmentation using color pixel classification: analysis and comparison. IEEE trans. on Pattern Analysis and Machine Intelligence **27** (2005)
10. Chai, D., Ngan, K.: Face segmentation using skin-color map in videophone applications. In: IEEE Trans. on Circuits and Systems for Video Technology. Volume 9. (1999)
11. Welch, G., Bishop, G.: An introduction to the kalman filter. Technical report (1995)

# Multistage Face Recognition Using Adaptive Feature Selection and Classification

Fei Zuo[1], Peter H.N. de With[1,2], and Michiel van der Veen[3]

[1] Faculty EE, Eindhoven Univ. of Technol.,
5600MB Eindhoven, The Netherlands
[2] LogicaCMG Eindhoven, The Netherlands
[3] Philips Research Labs Eindhoven
F.Zuo@tue.nl
http://vca.ele.tue.nl/people/Zuo.html

**Abstract.** In this paper, we propose a cascaded face-identification framework for enhanced recognition performance. During each stage, the classification is dynamically optimized to discriminate a set of promising candidates selected from the previous stage, thereby incrementally increasing the overall discriminating performance. To ensure improved performance, the base classifier at each stage should satisfy two key properties: (1) *adaptivity* to specific populations, and (2) *high training and identification efficiency* such that dynamic training can be performed for each test case. To this end, we adopt a base classifier with (1) dynamic person-specific feature selection, and (2) voting of an ensemble of simple classifiers based on selected features. Our experiments show that the cascaded framework effectively improves the face recognition rate by up to 5% compared to a single stage algorithm, and it is 2-3% better than established well-known face recognition algorithms.

## 1 Introduction

In recent years, automatic face recognition has aroused great interest in both industry and academia. However, face identification in unconstrained real-life situations still remains a difficult problem, which is caused by

1. *Complex face distributions*: Due to the large variations in illumination, expression and poses, faces images from one person form a highly complex cluster in the image space, which may even be mingled with clusters from other persons, thereby causing great difficulties in discrimination.
2. *Small sample size problem*: In many real-life scenarios, we have too few training images to characterize high-dimensional feature spaces. This causes instability of many popular classification algorithms, which require a good approximation of the sample distribution w.r.t. the true-class distribution.

For face identification, we need to find the most 'similar' person from a face gallery given a probe face. We use a classification function $A$ to predict the face identity $k$, given a certain face representation (denoted as feature vector $x$),

J. Blanc-Talon et al. (Eds.): ACIVS 2005, LNCS 3708, pp. 17–25, 2005.
© Springer-Verlag Berlin Heidelberg 2005

thereby giving $A(x) = k$. A considerable part of existing work on face recognition uses a fixed classification function $A$ for all persons (e.g. PCA, LDA, Bayesian or Neural network) with a fixed feature representation $x$ (e.g. image-based or Gabor-wavelet based) [8]. However, using a fixed classification function and feature representation is not optimal for *completely* discriminating all persons, especially for large face databases. We propose a multistage face recognition technique that is suited for large databases and provides higher recognition accuracy. At each stage, we select a cluster of candidates with highest similarity rankings and adapt $A$ and/or $x$ to this specific population. Basically, two schemes can be used for this purpose:

1. Faces in the gallery can be *pre-clustered* during the training stage, and classification can be optimized within each cluster. In [3], this is exploited for a two-stage SVM-based face classification. However, this is a static method with no adaptation to the test data, and can be problematic with cases located near the cluster boundary.
2. The adaptation can be performed *dynamically* for each probe face during the identification. This requires iterative online training and can be computationally prohibitive for some algorithms.

In this paper, we propose a cascaded identification framework with efficient dynamic classification. During each stage in the cascade, we select a subset of person-specific discriminative features w.r.t. the specific population. Based on the selected features, a pool of simple classifiers are used to locate the most similar face in the gallery. The adaptation procedure is extremely efficient and can be readily applied in a cascaded framework.

The remainder of the paper is organized as follows. Section 2 provides a detailed illustration of the proposed cascaded recognition framework. Section 3 introduces an efficient based classifier to be used in the cascaded framework. Section 4 presents the experimental results and Section 5 gives the conclusions.

## 2   Cascaded Face Recognition Framework

In a cascaded face-recognition framework, a series of classifiers are used to gradually reject unlikely candidates in the database until the best-match is found. Within one stage, a classifier is customized for a selected set of candidates, which leads to improved discriminating capability for this stage.

At each processing stage, according to the outputs of each classifier, a similarity ranking of the face candidates is derived and promising candidates with high rankings are passed to subsequent classifiers for refined classification. Within each stage, the feature representation $x$ and classification function $A$ are dynamically optimized for the remaining candidates. By this incremental classification optimization w.r.t. the probe face, the best candidate is expected to float up to the highest ranking position. The ranking and selection mechanism is visualized in Fig. 1. In order to achieve effective and efficient cascaded recognition, the classification scheme at each stage should satisfy the following conditions.

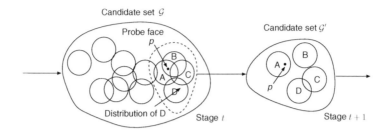

**Fig. 1.** Two stages in the cascaded face recognition

1. **Adaptivity.** The classification at each stage in the cascade should be able to adapt to the selected population $\mathcal{G}$. In other words, the classification function $A$ and/or the feature representation $x$ is dependent on $\mathcal{G}$. Classification schemes such as the 'nearest neighbor' rule based on fixed-distance metrics, are not adaptive, thereby not leading to *effective* cascaded identification.
2. **High training and identification efficiency.** Since the candidate selection and classifier adaptation have to be performed during the process of the identification, the training and identification should be as efficient as possible. Classification schemes involving space transformations (e.g. PCA, LDA or intra-space Bayesian) or complex optimization procedures (e.g. SVM, Neural networks) require high computation cost and would severely degrade the efficiency of the system, if applied in a cascaded manner.

In the following, we propose a classification scheme with adaptive feature selection and classification. The adaptivity is ensured by the following two aspects: (1) adaptive representation $x$ by person-specific feature selection, and (2) statistical dependence of the corresponding classification function $A(x)$ on the current population. Furthermore, the training and identification procedures are extremely efficient and do not introduce significant overhead.

## 3 Efficient Classification Using Person-Specific Classifiers

### 3.1 Person-Specific Feature Selection by Maximum Marginal Diversity

It has been advocated in literature that not all feature components $x_i$ ($1 \leq i \leq D$) of feature vector $x$ are equally important in a discriminant point of view. It has been shown in [9] and [10] that by applying a careful feature selection, similar or better recognition accuracy can be achieved with a much smaller number of features. Furthermore, using dynamic feature selection provides feature adaptivity in a cascaded recognition framework. However, the computation cost of popular feature selection techniques (e.g. Adaboost and SFFS) is too high to be used for dynamic online training.

Motivated by [6], we propose a fast feature selection scheme favoring those features with Maximum Marginal Diversity (MMD). Different from [6], where

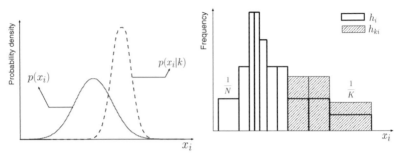

**Fig. 2.** Left: Marginal diversity of feature $x_i$ for person $k$. Right: Feature selection using equi-probability histograms.

the features are selected based on maximum discrimination between all classes, we aim to select a subset of features $\mathcal{F}_k$ ($\mathcal{F}_k \subset \mathcal{F}$), such that $\mathcal{F}_k$ provides optimal discrimination especially for class (person) $k$. Our experimental evidence shows that this one-versus-all selection offers a significantly better performance than using the approach from [6]. Following the same principle of MMD, we give the guideline for selecting the best feature set for class $k$.

**Principle 1.** *The best feature set characterizing class $k$ should contain those features with large marginal diversities. The marginal diversity $MD_k(x_i)$ of feature $x_i$ in class $k$ is defined as the Kullback-Leibler (KL) divergence between the class-$k$ conditional probability density of $x_i$ ($p(x_i|k)$) and the probability density of $x_i$ ($p(x_i)$) for all classes, thus*

$$MD_k(x_i) = \int p(x_i|k) \log \frac{p(x_i|k)}{p(x_i)} dx_i. \tag{1}$$

According to Principle 1, the best features for class $k$ should have a class-conditional density that is distant (by KL criterion) from the total distribution of all classes. These are the most discriminating and informative features that distinguish person $k$ from other people in the population examined.

Similar to [6], we select $P_k$ features with the largest marginal diversities to form a customized feature set for person $k$. This can be easily implemented by *estimating* $p(x_i|k)$ and $p(x_i)$ by histograms. Generally, $p(x_i)$ can be fairly reliably estimated, while the estimation of the class-conditional density $p(x_i|k)$ often suffers from the small sample size problem. This problem is solved by the following proposal.

***Estimation Property.*** *Suppose we use an unequally spaced $N$-bin histogram $h_i$ to represent $p(x_i)$, where each bin is equally probable (see Fig. 2). Further suppose that the samples of person $k$ span $K$ of these bins ($K \leq N$). It is assumed that the samples from $k$ have an equal probability to fall into one of the $K$ bins. This is justified due to the lack of sufficient samples to reliably estimate $p(x_i|k)$. Histogram $h_{ki}$ is used to characterize distribution $p(x_i|k)$. In this case, Principle 1 favors those $x_i$ with smaller $K$. This can be easily seen, because by applying the above assumptions to Eq. (1), it follows that*

$$MD_k(x_i) = \sum_j h_{ki}(j) \log \frac{h_{ki}(j)}{h_i(j)} = \log \frac{N}{K}. \tag{2}$$

In [7], a closely related approach called reliable component scheme is used to select a set of *reliable* features for biometric authentication. It can be regarded as a
special case of the feature selection based on the previously presented estimation
property, where $N = 2$ and features are selected[1] with $K = 1$.

   In our experiments with only 2-3 training images per person, we found that
a finer quantization (larger $N$) does not necessarily lead to better recognition
performance. Our experiments on the FERET face database show that the best
average performance is achieved when $N = 2$ or 3, while using $N = 3$ leads to a
slightly better performance than using $N = 2$.

   It can be easily seen that the person-specific feature selection based on the
maximum marginal diversity (MMD) conforms to adaptivity, since the total distribution $p(x_i)$ is dependent on specific populations. Furthermore, our specific
feature selection process also improves the identification efficiency, because normally only 30-50% of all available features are selected and used.

## 3.2   Classification Based on a Pool of Simple Classifiers

Assume that we have selected a 'good' feature subset for each person at a certain
stage, denoted as $\mathcal{F}_k$ for person $k$, let us now discuss the design of an effective
yet efficient classifier based on these features.

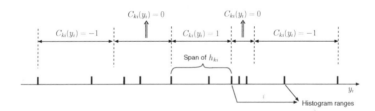

**Fig. 3.** A simple classifier for class-specific identification

   Given the total histogram distribution $h_i$, person-$k$ distribution $h_{ki}$ and an
arbitrary probe sample feature vector $\boldsymbol{y}$, and suppose that $y_i$ falls into the $u$-th
bin of the total histogram $h_i$, then we define a simple classifier $C_{ki}$ based on the
feature with index $i$ ($i \in \mathcal{F}_k$) as:

$$C_{ki}(y_i) = \begin{cases} 1, & \text{if } u \text{ is covered by } h_{ki}, \\ 0, & \text{if } y_i \text{ is of } p \text{ percentile distance to } h_{ki}, \\ -1, & \text{otherwise.} \end{cases} \tag{3}$$

$C_{ki}$ can be seen as a voting expert, which bases its output on the proximity
between $y_i$ and $h_{ik}$. The region close to the classification boundary is usually

---

[1] In [7], the class mean is used as a reference for selecting reliable features, while the
class median is used in our case according to our estimation property.

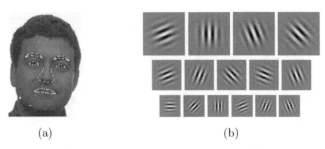

(a)                                    (b)

**Fig. 4.** (a) Face image with automatically extracted fiducial feature points. (b) Gabor convolution kernels with various frequencies and orientations.

ambiguous, therefore, we define a 'marginal region' where the classifier outputs zero to indicate uncertainty (see Fig. 3).

For all selected features $x_i$ for person $k$, we derive a pool of simple classifiers $C_{ki}(x_i)$. The 'similarity' between an arbitrary sample feature vector $\boldsymbol{y}$ and person $k$ is based on the outputs from all these simple classifiers, so that

$$C_k(\boldsymbol{y}) = \frac{\sum_{i \in \mathcal{F}_k} C_{ki}(y_i)}{|\mathcal{F}_k|}, \tag{4}$$

To find the best-match of $\boldsymbol{y}$ within a gallery of $M$ persons, we need only to find person $k_m$, such that $C_{k_m}(\boldsymbol{y}) = \max\{C_k(\boldsymbol{y})|1 \leq k \leq M\}$.

### 3.3   The Cascaded Recognition Algorithm

In the following, we present the multi-stage face recognition algorithm using MMD-based feature selection (Section 3.1) and pooled classification (Section 3.2).

**Table 1.** Cascaded face recognition algorithm

---

**Algorithm**
**Input:** A gallery set containing $M_0$ persons (with identity set $\mathcal{G}_0$). Probe face $p$.
**Output:** The identity of $p$.
1.   let $M = M_0$ and $\mathcal{G} = \mathcal{G}_0$.
2.   **for** $s = 1$ to $STAGES$
3.           **for** $k = 1$ to $M$
4.                   select a set of features $\mathcal{F}_k^{(s)}$ for person $k$ with maximal marginal diversity based on statistics on $\mathcal{G}$.
5.                   compute similarity measure $C_k(p)$ based on $\mathcal{F}_k^{(s)}$ and classification rule as defined in Eq. (3).
6.           select $M'$ candidates with highest similarity with $p$.
7.           let $M = M'$, and let $\mathcal{G}$ contain only the selected $M'$ identities.
8.   **return** the best-match selected from the last stage.

---

## 4   Experiments

***Data Preparation.*** We used a subset of the FERET face database [11] for our experiments. The subset contained 1167 face images of 237 persons. We automatically extracted 51 fiducial points for each face [5]. For each fiducial point $p = (x, y)^T$, we derived a corresponding Gabor jet by convolving a small image patch around the fiducial point with a set of Gabor kernels of various frequencies and orientations. The adopted Gabor kernels [2] are defined as:

$$\phi_m(p) = \frac{k_m^2}{\sigma^2} \exp\left(-\frac{k_m^2 p^2}{2\sigma^2}\right) \left[\exp(j(k_m \cdot p)) - \exp\left(-\frac{\sigma^2}{2}\right)\right], \text{ where}$$

$$k_m = \begin{pmatrix} k_v \cos\varphi_\mu \\ k_v \sin\varphi_\mu \end{pmatrix}, k_v = 2^{-\frac{v+2}{2}}\pi, \varphi_\mu = \mu\frac{\pi}{8}, m = 8v + \mu. \tag{5}$$

We used 5 frequencies and 8 orientations (thereby 40 kernels), and $v = 0, 1, ..., 4$, $\mu = 0, 1, ..., 7$. Therefore, for one face image, we obtained a Gabor-wavelet based feature vector $x$ with 2040 feature components (see Fig. 4).

For each test, we randomly selected two sample pictures per person as training images, and the rest were used as probe samples. The training images were selected such that they were captured on a different date from the test images. This simulates a typical real-life face recognition scenario, where we need to predict face identities given only training images captured in a different situation. Note that this is a more difficult scenario than commonly adopted partitioning strategies from literature used for the FERET dataset, such as *fafb*. To evaluate each algorithm, we performed 12 random tests, each of which adopted a different partition of the training and testing images.

***Performance of the Cascaded Face Recognition.*** To measure the performance gain by using the cascaded framework, we compared the single-stage (S-PSC, *STAGES*=1 in Table 3.3) and cascaded (C-PSC, *STAGES* = 3 in Table 3.3) classification schemes. The rank-$N$ performance statistics is depicted in Fig. 5(a). It can be seen that using the cascaded scheme improves the recognition rate by 4-5% in our experiments.

We also implemented a number of well-known face recognition algorithms in literature and compared our approach with them. The results are portrayed by Fig. 5(b), and all algorithms use the same Gabor representation. A brief summary of these algorithms is given as follows.

(1) **Cosine distance:** This is originally used by Wiskott *et al.* [2] as the similarity measure between two Gabor feature vectors.
(2) **Gabor-based PCA:** A Principle Component Analysis is performed on Gabor features. Here we use a reduced feature dimension of 400.
(3) **Regularized LDA:** We apply an R-LDA (Regularized LDA) as proposed by Lu *et al.* [4] to cope with the small sample problem. Here the regularization factor $\eta$ is set to 0.9.

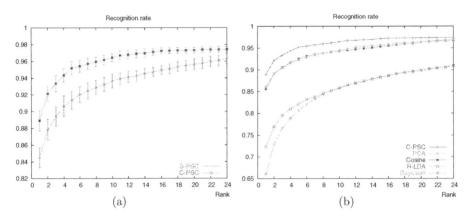

**Fig. 5.** (a) Performance of S-PSC and C-PSC (Points: average recognition rate. Error-bars: variance with one std. dev.) (b) Comparison with other recognition algorithms.

(4) **Bayesian (ML):** By directly modeling the intra-class distribution, we can derive a probabilistic similarity measure between Gabor feature vectors. This is similar to the Maximum Likelihood approach used by Moghaddam *et al.* [1].

From Fig. 5(b), we can see that in this experimental scenario, using the simple cosine distance already gives good performance. The Bayesian approach slightly outperforms cosine distance, with 0.6% improvement for rank-1 recognition rate. The rank-1 performance of the Bayesian approach is 1% better than the S-PSC. Note that using the C-PSC outperforms all other approaches. Furthermore, due to the simplicity of the training and matching procedure of PSC, the C-PSC scheme is very efficient and its computation cost increases linearly with the size of the face gallery. In our implementation of C-PSC, it takes 300ms for one match given the gallery size as specified above.

## 5   Conclusions

In this paper, we proposed a cascaded face recognition framework using a series of adaptive classifiers. During each stage, a refined classification is performed on a selective set of promising candidates, achieving an optimized discrimination for this specific group of people. We adopt a base classification scheme employing (1) dynamic feature selection, and (2) voting by an ensemble of simple classifiers. The scheme has inherent adaptivity and can be efficiently implemented. The experiments show that our proposed approach outperforms a number of well-known face recognition algorithms in a performance-critical test scenario.

## References

1. Moghaddam, B., Jebara, T. *et al.*: Bayesian face recognition. *Pattern Recognition*, Vol 33(11), pp. 1771-1782, November 2000.
2. Wiskott, L, Fellous. J.M. *et al.*, Face recognition by elastic bunch graph matching. *Intell. Biometric tech. in fingerprint and face recog.*, pp. 355-396, CRC Press, 1999.

3. Li, Z., and Tang X., Bayesian face recognition using Support Vector Machine and face clustering. *Proc. IEEE Int. Conf. CVPR*, vol 2, pp. 374-380, 2004.
4. Lu, J, Plataniotis, K.N., and Venetsanopoulos, A.N., Regularization studies on LDA for face recognition. *Proc. ICIP*, pp. 63-66, 2004.
5. Zuo, F., de With, P.H.N., Fast facial feature extraction using a deformable shape model with Haar-wavelet based local texture attributes, *Proc. ICIP*, pp. 1425-1428, 2004.
6. Vasconcelos, N., Feature selection by maximum marginal diversity: optimality and implications for visual recognition. *Proc. CVPR*, vol 1, pp. 762-769, 2003.
7. Tuyls, P., Akkermans, A.H.M. *et al.*, Practical biometric authentication with template protection. *To appear in Proc. AVBPA*, 2005.
8. Li, S.Z., and Lu, J., Face detection and recognition, *Emerging Topics in Computer Vision*, Prentice-Hall, 2004.
9. Zhang, L., and Li, S.Z., *et al.*, Boosting local feature based classifiers for face recognition. *Proc. CVPR Workshop*, pp. 87-87, 2004.
10. Gokberk, B., Irfanoglu, M.O., *et al.*, Optimal Gabor kernel location selection for face recognition, *Proc. ICIP*, pp. 677-680, 2003.
11. Phillips, P.J., and Moon, H., *et al.*, The FERET evaluation methodology for face recognition algorithms, *IEEE Trans. PAMI*, Vol.22, pp. 1090-1104, 2000.

# Fast Face Detection Using a Cascade of Neural Network Ensembles

Fei Zuo[1] and Peter H.N. de With[1,2]

[1] Faculty Electrical Engineering, Eindhoven Univ. of Technology,
5600MB Eindhoven, The Netherlands
[2] LogicaCMG Eindhoven, The Netherlands
F.Zuo@tue.nl
http://vca.ele.tue.nl/people/Zuo.html

**Abstract.** We propose a (near) real-time face detector using a cascade of neural network (NN) ensembles for enhanced detection accuracy and efficiency. First, we form a coordinated NN ensemble by sequentially training a set of neural networks with the same topology. The training implicitly partitions the face space into a number of disjoint regions, and each NN is specialized in a specific sub-region. Second, to reduce the total computation cost for the face detection, a series of NN ensembles are cascaded by increasing complexity of base networks. Simpler NN ensembles are used at earlier stages in the cascade, which are able to reject a majority of non-face patterns in the backgrounds. Our proposed approach achieves up to 94% detection rate on the CMU+MIT test set, a 98% detection rate on a set of video sequences and 3-4 frames/sec. detection speed on a normal PC (P-IV, 3.0GHz).

## 1 Introduction

Face detection from images (videos) is a crucial preprocessing step for a number of applications, such as object-based coding, biometric authentication and advanced human computer interaction. Furthermore, research results in face detection can broadly facilitate general object detection in visual scenes. Although tremendous effort has been spent on designing face detection techniques in the past decade, a performance trade-off still exists between the detection accuracy (robustness) and the operation efficiency. The direct use of low-level image features (e.g.color, shape) gives fast performance, but they are usually vulnerable to environment changes (e.g. illumination or imaging devices). Besides this, more advanced learning-based techniques, such as Support Vector Machines (SVM) [1] and Neural-Networks (NN) [2], provide superior performance with regard to varying face appearances. However, these algorithms often involve high processing complexity, which can be too costly for certain applications.

Among the robust face detectors mentioned above, the NN-based face detection technique proposed by Rowley *et al.* [2] is presently one of the best-performing techniques on face detection. In this work, a retinally connected neural-network examines small windows of an image, and decides whether each

J. Blanc-Talon et al. (Eds.): ACIVS 2005, LNCS 3708, pp. 26–34, 2005.
© Springer-Verlag Berlin Heidelberg 2005

window contains a face. The system achieves good detection performance even with a difficult test-set composed of low-quality scanned images. However, the primary drawback of the technique is the computation complexity (a reported example states 383 seconds for a 320×240 pixel image). Earlier, we examined in [4] a cascaded face detector, utilizing a color-based detector and a geometry-based detector as preprocessors to an NN-based detector, which effectively reduces the total computation cost. In this paper, we propose a homogeneous approach for face detection using a *cascade* of neural network *ensembles*, which yields improved robustness with similar computation cost to [4]. Furthermore, the proposed technique is highly efficient at the training stage. The design of the proposed detector is based on (1) construction of a coordinated *ensemble* of NNs for improved detection accuracy, and (2) construction of a *cascade* of NN ensembles for improved efficiency.

## 2   Architecture Component: A Neural Network Ensemble

For complex real-world classification problems such as face detection, the use of a single classifier may not be sufficient to capture the complex decision boundary between different image patterns. We propose a novel technique that trains an ensemble of neural networks in a specific order to boost the detection performance.

As shown in Fig. 1, our proposed classifier ensemble consists of two distinct layers: a set of sequentially trained component neural classifiers $\mathcal{H} = \{h_k | 1 \leq k \leq M\}$, and a decision network $g$. Each $h_k$ is a multi-layer back-propagation neural network with fixed topology, and $g$ is an independent neural network, which is trained to produce a nonlinear output composed from all component classifiers.

The training of each component classifier $h_k$ depends on the behavior of its previous classifiers. Given training face set $\mathcal{F}$, $h_k$ is only trained using a subset $\mathcal{F}_k$ ($\mathcal{F}_k \subset \mathcal{F}$), where $\mathcal{F}_k$ contains only face samples misclassified by its previous component classifiers. In this way, $\mathcal{F}$ is implicitly *partitioned* into several *disjoint* subsets, and each component classifier is trained specifically over a sub-region of the face space. Therefore, the learning difficulties are reduced for each component classifier. During the training of each $h_k$, we adopt the bootstrapping

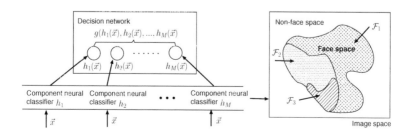

**Fig. 1.** The architecture of a neural network ensemble

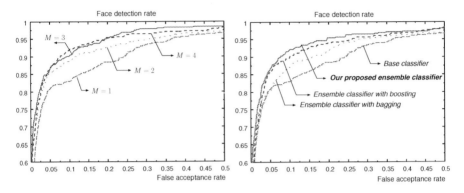

**Fig. 2.** Left: ROC curves of NN ensembles w.r.t. different M. Right: ROC curves of NN ensembles using different training strategies (all tested on $\mathcal{V}_f$ and $\mathcal{V}_n$).

technique from [2], which iteratively adds new false positives to the current non-face training set.

To verify the detection performance of an ensemble of NN classifiers, we train an NN ensemble with relatively simple base network topology. The trained ensemble will be used as the first-layer pruner in the final detection cascade (see Fig. 3). The training face set $\mathcal{F}$ consists of 6,304 highly variable face images, all cropped to the size of $24 \times 24$ pixels. We further build up a non-face repository with an initial set of 4,548 non-faces and 2,000 additional non-face scenery images for use in the bootstrapping procedure. For validation purposes, we use a separate test face set $\mathcal{V}_f$ consisting of 488 faces and a test non-face set $\mathcal{V}_n$ consisting of 23,573 non-faces. Each sample image is preprocessed to zero mean and unity standard deviation to reduce the interference of global illumination.

The base component network (denoted as *FNET-A*) is a three-layer network with locally connected neurons. It accepts a down-sampled $8 \times 8$ grid as its input, where each input element is an averaged value of a neighboring $3 \times 3$ block in the original $24 \times 24$ image. Each hidden unit in *FNET-A* is connected to a neighboring $4 \times 4$ block from the input layer. At the left of Fig. 2, we depict the ROC (Receiver Operating Characteristics) curves of ensembles with a different number of components. We can see that the detection performance of *FNET-A* ensembles consistently improves by up to three components, while adding more components does not yield significant improvements. Since using more classifiers inevitably increases the total computation cost, we can select $M$ for a given network topology with the best trade-off between the detection performance and the computation efficiency.

We also compare our proposed classifier ensemble with two other popular ensemble techniques, bagging and boosting [5], and the results are shown at the right of Fig. 2. Bagging uses a random resampling strategy where no correlation exists between the training sets used for different component classifiers. Our proposed approach shares a common feature with boosting in that both approaches sequentially train a set of interdependent classifiers. However, we implicitly per-

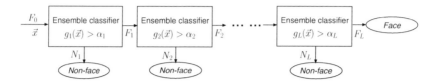

**Fig. 3.** A pruning cascade of neural ensembles

form a 'hard' partitioning of the feature space, which gives faster convergence during the training and results in fewer component classifiers. It can be seen from Fig. 2 that our proposed approach produces the best results.

## 3   Multi-net Cascade for Fast Face Detection

### 3.1   Formulation of a Pruning Cascade

In this section, we apply the cascading scheme to the neural classifier ensemble to optimize the detection efficiency. A pruning face detection cascade is basically a degenerated decision tree, with classifiers arranged by increasing complexity (see Fig. 3). Simpler ensemble classifiers are used at earlier stages in the cascade, which are able to reject a majority of non-face patterns, therefore boosting the overall detection efficiency. In the sequel, we introduce a formal notation framework in order to come to definitions of the detection accuracy and the operation efficiency. Afterwards, we propose an algorithm to jointly optimize the cascaded face detector for both accuracy and efficiency.

Let us now suppose $L$ classifier ensembles ($\mathcal{G} = \{g_i | 1 \leq i \leq L\}$) with increasing component complexity. The behavior of each classifier $g_i$ can be characterized by face detection rate $f_i(\alpha_i)$ and non-face acceptance rate $d_i(\alpha_i)$, where $\alpha_i$ is the output threshold for the decision network. We need to choose a set of values for $\alpha_i$, such that the performance of the cascaded classifier is optimized.

Suppose we have a detection task with a total of $T = F + N$ observations, where $F$ denotes the true number of faces and $N$ is the true number of non-faces. Initially, all observations are assumed to be faces. From Fig. 3, we can see that $F_0 = T$ and $F_{i-1} = F_i + N_i$ (for $1 < i \leq L$). At the $i$-th stage of the cascade, $F_{i-1}$ observations need to be classified, among which $F_i$ observations are classified as faces and $N_i$ observations are rejected as non-faces. Furthermore, it is easy to see that

$$F_i = f_i(\alpha_1, \alpha_2, ..., \alpha_i)F + d_i(\alpha_1, \alpha_2, ..., \alpha_i)N, \qquad (1)$$

where $f_i(\alpha_1, \alpha_2, ..., \alpha_i)$ and $d_i(\alpha_1, \alpha_2, ..., \alpha_i)$ represent the detection rate and false acceptance rate, respectively, of the sub-cascade formed *jointly* by the 1-st to $i$-th ensembles. An *optimal* cascade should achieve both high detection accuracy and operation efficiency (a more accurate specification comes later).

**Table 1.** A summary of the network topology employed in the detection cascade

| Network | Structure |
|---------|-----------|
| FNET-A | see Section 2. |
| FNET-B | 3 layers, 225 connections, with extended hidden neurons ($6 \times 1$ and $2 \times 3$) compared with FNET-A, each of which looks at a $2 \times 1$ (or $4 \times 3$) block from its lower layer. |
| FNET-C | 4 layers, 447 connections, with $24 \times 24$ pixels as inputs, two hidden layers ($2 \times 2$ and $8 \times 8$ neurons), each unit locally connected to a sub-block from its adjacent lower layer. |
| FNET-D | 4 layers, 2039 connections, enhanced version of FNET-B and FNET-C, with additional hidden neurons arranged in horizontal and vertical stripes. |
| FNET-E | 4 layers, 3459 connections, enhanced version of FNET-D allowing overlapping of locally connected blocks. |

**Detection Accuracy.** To ensure good detection accuracy for an $L$-layer cascade ($i = L$), the following cost function should be maximized

$$C_p(\alpha_1, ..., \alpha_L) = \max\{f_L(\alpha_1, ..., \alpha_L) \mid d_L(\alpha_1, ..., \alpha_L) < T_d\}, \qquad (2)$$

where $T_d$ is a threshold for the final false acceptance rate.

**Operation Efficiency.** Suppose the classification of one observation by ensemble classifier $g_i$ takes $t_i$ time. To classify $T = F + N$ observations by cascade $\mathcal{G}$, we need a total amount of time

$$C_e(\alpha_1, ..., \alpha_L) = \sum_{i=1}^{L} F_i t_i = \sum_{i=1}^{L} (f_i(\alpha_1, ..., \alpha_i)F + d_i(\alpha_1, ..., \alpha_i)N)t_i, \qquad (3)$$

where $f_0 = 1$ and $d_0 = 1$.

A possible combined optimization goal based on both Eq. (2) and Eq. (3) can be formulated as a weighted summation, hence

$$C(\alpha_1, ..., \alpha_L) = C_p(\alpha_1, ..., \alpha_L) - w \cdot C_e(\alpha_1, ..., \alpha_L). \qquad (4)$$

We use a subtraction for the efficiency (time) component to trade-off against accuracy. By adjusting $w$, the relative importance of desired accuracy and efficiency can be controlled. The direct optimization of Eq. (4) using exhaustive search is computationally prohibitive, especially when $L$ is large. In the following subsection, we will give a heuristic sub-optimal search for the trade-off between detection accuracy and operation efficiency.

### 3.2   Implementation of a Cascaded Face Detector

We build a five-layer cascade of classifiers with increasing order of topology complexity, which are summarized in Table 1. The first networks have fewer layers and use only low-resolution image representations, while they are computationally efficient. The subsequent networks have more layers and exploit finer details

**Table 2.** Backward parameter selection for the face detection cascade

| |
|---|
| **Algorithm** *Parameter selection for the detector cascade* |
| **Input:** $F$ test face patterns and $N$ test non-face patterns. A cascade $\mathcal{G}$ of $L$ neural ensemble classifiers. Maximally allowed false acceptance rate $\hat{d}$. |
| **Output:** A set of selected parameters $(\alpha_1^*, \alpha_2^*, ..., \alpha_L^*)$. |
| 1.   Select $\alpha_L^* = \mathrm{argmax}_{\alpha_L} f_L(\alpha_L)$, subject to $d_L(\alpha_L) \leq \hat{d}$. |
| 2.   **for** $k = L - 1$ to $1$ |
| 3.       Select $\alpha_k^* = \mathrm{argmax}_{\alpha_k} C(\alpha_k, \alpha_{k+1}, ..., \alpha_L)$. |

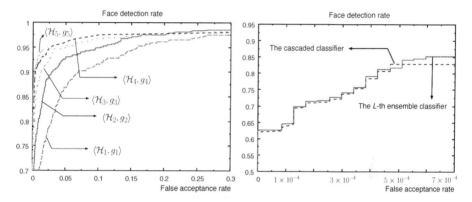

**Fig. 4.** Left: ROC curves of individual NN ensembles. Right: Comparison between the $L$-th ensemble classifier and the cascaded classifier (all tested on $\mathcal{V}_f$ and $\mathcal{V}_n$).

of the image. At the left of Fig. 4, we depict the ROC curves for individual neural ensemble classifiers for face detection.

Now we select the best set of parameters $(\alpha_1^*, \alpha_2^*, ..., \alpha_L^*)$ for both high detection accuracy and computation efficiency. Since the cascaded face detection rate $f_L(\alpha_1, ..., \alpha_L)$ is upper-bounded by $f_L(\alpha_L)$, we adopt an efficient sequential backward selection as shown in the algorithm of Table 2, which yields a sub-optimal solution to the parameter selection. The ROC curve of the resulting cascade is depicted at the right of Fig. 4, and the performance of the $L$-th ensemble classifier (individual performance) is also plotted for comparison. We can see that for a false acceptance rate below $5 \times 10^{-4}$, which is normally required for real-life applications, the cascaded detector keeps almost the same face detection rate as the most complex $L$-th stage classifier. However, the computation time drastically drops to less than 5%, as compared to the $L$-th stage classifier alone.

## 4   Application to Real-World Face Detection

In this section, we apply the obtained cascaded face detector in real-world applications with arbitrary images (videos) as input. For a given image, the detector needs to search for possible faces at every location and scale. This is similar to

**Table 3.** Comparison of different face detectors on CMU+MIT data set

| Detector | Detection rate | Num. of false positives |
|---|---|---|
| 1. Single neural network [2] | 90.9% | 738 |
| 2. Multiple neural networks [2] | 84.4% | 79 |
| 3. Bayes statistics [6] | 94.4% | 65 |
| 4. SNoW [7] | 94.8% | 78 |
| 5. AdaBoost [3] | 88.4% | 31 |
| 6. SVM [1] | 89.9% | 75 |
| 7. Our approach | 94.4% | 61 |

**Fig. 5.** Example detection results

the image pyramid structure in [2], with a scaling factor of 1.2. Furthermore, to facilitate fast illumination correction, we use a pair of auxiliary integral images as in [3] for fast processing of mean and variance of an image window.

To evaluate the detection accuracy, we first applied our detector on the well-known CMU+MIT test sets and compared our results[1] with reported results in Table 3. It can be seen that our approach is among one of the best performing techniques in terms of detection accuracy. We also applied our detector to a test set composed of various web images downloaded from Internet, and we achieved up to 93% detection rate. Some detection results are shown in Fig. 5. In addition, we built a video test set containing 20 sequences, including a number of standard MPEG test sequences and our self-made sequences capturing various indoor and outdoor scenes. A total of 98% detection rate is achieved.

We also evaluate the efficiency gain when using a cascade of neural classifier ensembles. For the CMU+MIT test sets, the five ensembles ordered for $i = 1, 2, ..., 5$ in the cascade reject 77.2%, 15.5%, 6.2%, 1.1% and 0.09% of all the background windows, respectively. For an image of size $320 \times 240$, using a cascade can significantly reduce the total computation of the final neural classifier ensemble by 99.4% (from several minutes to sub-second level). We also applied our face detector as a preprocessor in a live-video based surveillance system. With $320 \times 240$ frame resolution, we achieve 3-4 frames/sec. detection speed on a Pentium-IV PC. It is also worth noticing that our approach also offers the advantage of training efficiency. Normally less than 1 hour is required to train a complete detector cascade, including the parameter selection (for some advanced training [3], around 15 days are required for a complete detector cascade).

# 5   Conclusions

In this paper, we have presented a (near) real-time face detector using a cascade of neural network ensembles, with the following two advantages. First, we used a parallel ensemble technique within one component for improved detection accuracy. Experiments show that the proposed NN ensemble significantly outperforms a single network in accuracy (e.g. by up to 12%). Second, to reduce the total computation cost, a series of NN ensembles are cascaded into a chain by increasing complexity of base networks. Fast ensemble detectors are used first to quickly prune large background areas, while the subsequent ensemble detectors are only invoked for difficult cases that failed to be rejected by the previous layers. A special backward parameter selection algorithm is applied to generate a (sub)-optimal tuning of the cascade, so that both high detection accuracy and operation efficiency are obtained simultaneously. We have applied the proposed approach to real-world applications. Both high detection accuracy (94% detection rate on CMU+MIT sets) and efficiency (3-4 frames/sec. on video seqs.) are achieved.

---

[1] Techniques 3, 4, and 6 use a subset of the test sets excluding hand-drawn faces and cartoon faces (483 faces). We reported our results on 479 faces, excluding further 4 faces using face masks or having poor resolution.

# References

1. B. Heisele, T. Poggio, and M. Pontil, *Face detection in still gray images*, AI Memo 1687, MIT, 2000.
2. H. Rowley, S. Baluja and T. Kanade, *Neural network-based face detection*, IEEE Trans. PAMI, vol 20(1), pp. 23-28, 1998.
3. P. Viola and M. Jones, *Rapid object detection using a boosted cascade of simple features*, Proc. Int. Conf. CVPR, vol 1, pp. 511-518, 2001.
4. F. Zuo and P.H.N. de With, *Fast human face detection using successive face detectors with incremental detection capability*, Electronic Imaging (VCIP'03) Proc. SPIE, 5022, pp. 831-841, 2003.
5. R. Duda, P. Hart, and D. Stork, *Pattern classification*, 2nd Ed., Wiley interscience, ISBN: 0-471-05669-3, 2001.
6. H. Schneiderman and T. Kanade, *A statistical model for 3D object detection applied to faces and cars*, Proc. Int. Conf. CVPR, vol 1, pp. 746-751, 2000.
7. D. Roth, M.-H. Yang and N. Ahuja, *A SNoW-based face detector*, Adv. in NIPS, vol 12, pp. 855-861, MIT Press, 2000.

# Use of Human Motion Biometrics for Multiple-View Registration*

László Havasi[1], Zoltán Szlávik[2], and Tamás Szirányi[2]

[1] Péter Pázmány Catholic University,
H-1083 Budapest Práter u. 50/a., Hungary
Havasi@digitus.itk.ppke.hu
[2] Analogic and Neural Computing Laboratory, Hungarian Academy of Sciences,
H-1111 Budapest, Kende u. 13-17, Hungary
{Szlavik, Sziranyi}@sztaki.hu

**Abstract.** A novel image-registration method is presented which is applicable to multi-camera systems viewing human subjects in motion. The method is suitable for use with indoor or outdoor surveillance scenes. The paper summarizes an efficient walk-detection and biometric method for extraction of image characteristics which enables the walk properties of the viewed subjects to be used to establish corresponding image-points for the purpose of image-registration between cameras. The leading leg of the walking subject is a good feature to match, and the presented method can identify this from two successive walk-steps (one walk cycle). Using this approach, the described method can detect a sufficient number of corresponding points for the estimation of correspondence between views from two cameras. An evaluation study has demonstrated the method's feasibility in the context of an actual indoor real-time surveillance system.

## 1 Introduction

Registration between partially overlapping views of the same scene is a fundamental task in a number of applications involving multi-camera systems, such as stereovision, three-dimensional reconstruction, or object tracking/observation in surveillance systems. In the literature on computer vision, many examples in which the registration of different views has been achieved have been described, together with the associated problems. The existing methods can be divided into two groups: those which are still-image based, and motion-based ones. Still-image based algorithms, e.g. those used in [1][2][3][4], attempt to match static features in images, such as edges, corners, contours, color, shape etc. They are often used for image pairs with small differences, when the difference between features is negligible. However, they may fail at occlusion boundaries, within featureless regions, and if the chosen primitives or features cannot be reliably detected. The other group, the motion-based methods such as [5][6], try to find matchings between different views by analyzing the dynamics of the scene as recorded by the different cameras. In [5], the tracks of moving objects are the

---

* This work was supported by the NoE MUSCLE project of the EU.

J. Blanc-Talon et al. (Eds.): ACIVS 2005, LNCS 3708, pp. 35–43, 2005.
© Springer-Verlag Berlin Heidelberg 2005

basic features for the matching of the different views. In [6], a method is reported which finds co-motion point-pairs in the videos as recorded from the same scene by the different cameras. Both these methods assume that the objects of interest are moving on the ground-plane; and also that the cameras are far distant from the scene, so that the height of the moving objects is small enough for them to appear in the recorded videos as "moving blobs on the ground".

In practice, the existing algorithms can be used only in restricted situations. The reported methods focus on the solution of the view-registration problem in respect of outdoor scenes, and neglect the additional difficulties which tend to arise for indoor scenes. In case of indoor cameras, the still-image based methods may fail due to the variability of conditions: occlusions, changing illumination etc. Due to the larger size of the moving objects, the cited motion-based methods will also fail; the observed motions are not necessarily on the ground-plane – while for outdoor scenes, such an assumption can safely be made.

The aim of this paper is to present an algorithm which can resolve the above problems. Our method is based on the pedestrian-detection algorithm which we have described previously [12]; this algorithm extracts symmetry-patterns generated by walking humans, and can be used for the detection of motion direction, and of the leading leg of the walking subject. In our method the leading leg is the basic feature for the estimation of correspondences between the different views.

The remainder of the paper describes the algorithm in detail, and reports its performance using real image-data.

## 2  Walk Pattern Extraction

The methods proposed here are based on the detection of human motion-activity (namely, walking) in the scene. This task is a binary classification problem: the periodicity of human walking, together with the characteristic human shape of the target, provide key differences which enable us to distinguish pedestrians from the motion-patterns of other objects. For the detection of human walking patterns we have previously introduced a simplified symmetry-extraction algorithm [8], and have also described an effective method for the tracking and detection of human motion [10][11]. This approach uses the motion information contained in video sequences, so that the extracted symmetry-patterns consist of information about the spatio-temporal changes of a moving object. The main steps of the algorithm are:

- Background subtraction, change-detection
- Edge-map detection and symmetry computation (first level)
- Extension of symmetry computation up to level three (L3S)
- Temporal tracking using reconstructed masks
- Preprocessing for classification: re-sampling, reduction of dimensionality
- Non-linear classification: "walk" vs. "non-walk"

Sample results of the image-processing steps are shown in Figure 1, which illustrates the results of the algorithm steps up to the stage of symmetry-pattern extraction from the reconstructed masks. The details of the processing steps are described below.

## 2.1  Background Subtraction

An elementary method to reduce the computation cost of methods using motion information derived from static-position cameras is that of background subtraction (or change-detection). In our method, the filtered image does sometimes still contain some parts of background objects (Figure 1b); this is because we use a relatively simple method. The development of a general method for background subtraction is a challenging task [5][9].

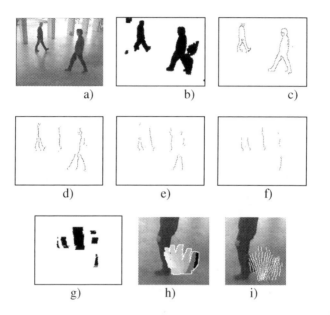

**Fig. 1.** Overview of pattern-extraction: a) Image from input sequence. b) Result of change-detection. c) Filtered Canny edge-map. d) First level symmetries. e) Second level symmetries. f) Third-level symmetries (L3S). g) Reconstructed masks from symmetries. h) Tracking, showing coherent masks in the sequence. i) Symmetry pattern.

We have therefore implemented a middle-way solution; the change-detection algorithm can be selected from two methods: either a simple running-average [11] in case of indoor scene (as used in Figure 1b); or a Gaussian-mixture model [10][9] in case of outdoor scene. Both methods have disadvantages, but the computation time for the background-estimation can be reduced to 1-5 milliseconds with the reduction of input image size. In our experimental trials most of the problems were caused by shadows and reflections, because the methods were evaluated using images from a camera system set up in an indoor space where the background "wall" is in fact a large expanse of window.

## 2.2  Simplified Symmetry Extraction

Our symmetry-detection method [8] is based on the use of morphological operators to simulate spreading waves from the edges. In our pedestrian-detection approach

[10][11], we simplify the algorithm by using only horizontal morphological operators – since in practice we essentially need to extract only vertical symmetries.

The symmetry operator normally uses the edge map, obtained by the Canny algorithm, of the original image masked with the estimated foreground (see Figure 1c). As illustrated in Figure 1, the symmetry concept can be extended by iterative operations. The symmetry of the Level 1 symmetry map (Figure 1d) is the Level 2 symmetry (Figure 1e); and the symmetry of the Level 2 map is the Level 3 symmetry (L3S), as shown in Figure 1f. There are two major advantages of this feature-extraction approach: the extracted symmetry-map reflects the structural properties of the object; and secondly, its computation is extremely fast, and hence it can be readily used in real-time applications.

### 2.3 Temporal Tracking

In general, a number of symmetry-fragments may be present in the image, which may have arisen from errors in change-detection or from the complexity of the background; for examples, see Figure 1f. However, even the existence of perfect symmetries in a single static image does not necessarily provide usable information about the image-content; for this, we track the changes of the symmetry fragments by using temporal comparisons. We have implemented an effective tracking method which uses reconstructed masks around the symmetries. Briefly, the algorithm generates a mask around the L3S fragments from their radii; such masks can be seen in Figure 1g. During tracking, the algorithm calculates the overlapping areas between symmetry masks in successive frames, and then constructs the symmetry-patterns of the largest overlapping symmetries frame by frame. An overlapping mask sequence can be seen in Figure 1h, and the symmetry pattern in Figure 1i. A detailed description of the tracking method can be found in our previous paper [11].

In our experiments, we found that the most critical factor is the image refresh rate: we found that a rate of at least 10 frames/second is required. However this requirement can be easily met, since the method described can run at 20-40 FPS on a simple desktop PC (the achievable rate depends on the number of tracked objects). Further information about the performance is presented in Section 5 below.

## 3   Detection and Biometric Extraction

The above-described symmetry patterns are represented by the upper and lower endpoints of the two sides (left and right) of the symmetry mask. In a real-life system it is important to be able to detect the relevant information even in cases where we do not assume an ideal scene (only one person in the image, static background, exact silhouette, separable figure and background). Our work focuses on human activities, so we decided to make use of the extracted symmetry patterns for human walk detection and biometrics determination (begin and end of walk pattern, leading leg in the walk cycle).

### 3.1 Classification With SVM in EigenWalks Space

The extended version of our detection method [11] operates in the eigenwalks space and utilizes the Support Vector Machine method (SVM) for pattern classification

[12]. In a preprocessing stage we re-sample the extracted symmetry patterns; this is because patterns depend both on the frame rate and the walking speed, so a pattern usually contains data from 6-15 frames. We perform this task using Bezier spline interpolation. Next the interpolated 3D points are rearranged into a row-vector with dimension 800 (this is because we compute 100 points for the coordinates (x,y) of every point). For dimension reduction, which is important in order to achieve a lower computational cost during classification, we utilize the Principal Component Analysis method (PCA). We consider the space spanned only by the 3 most significant eigenvectors that account for 93% of the variation in the training dataset: this is the Eigenwalk space. The human patterns lie on a non-linearly shaped manifold in the eigenspace. The classification process is carried out using a non-linear classification method, namely SVM with radial basis kernel function. In our tests, the correct-classification rate was found to be 92%.

## 3.2 Leading Leg Identification

The 2D motion vector on the image-plane, and the walker's gait-period, can be extracted directly from the detected patterns: we estimate the motion vector by fitting a regression line to the last half-trajectory of the lower two points of the pattern.

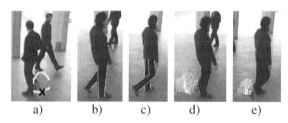

**Fig. 2.** a) An image showing the location of the derived symmetry-pattern (marked with white border; "x" marks a feature-point, see Section 4). b), c) Illustrations of our definition of "leading leg"; the "standing" or leading leg is the right leg in b), and the left leg in c) (legs highlighted manually). d), e) The detected patterns for the same steps as shown in b) and c); the 2D direction is bottom-left to upper-right (case 2 in Table 1).

In this section we present a method to determine, from one detected walk cycle, whether the leading leg is the right or the left leg. According to our terminology, the leading leg is the "standing" leg which at that instant carries the person's weight (see Figures 2b and 2c). Depending on the 3D walk-direction, and on which is currently the leading leg, one leg or the other practically obscures the visible area between the legs (Figure 2a). During a walk-cycle the ratio of the areas, together with the 2D direction on the image-plane, can be used to identify which is the leading leg. During one cycle, the left leg and right leg in turn are in the leading position. The above-described method can detect one step. To connect two successive steps as one walk-cycle, we calculate the 2D displacement vector of a detected step, and then search for another step in the estimated 2D position and at a time-point after a forecast walk-period. Table 1 summarizes the relationship between the leading leg and the ratio of surfaces from two successive patterns defined by:

$$ratio = \frac{area_t}{area_{t-1}} \tag{1}$$

A limitation of the described method is that it cannot identify the leading leg when the motion is parallel to the camera plane, since in such cases the areas are nearly equal (cases 3, 4 and 9, 10 in Table 1).

**Table 1.** Surface-area dependencies on the 2D walk-direction (6 of 8 possible cases) and the leading leg (Right, Left)

| Case | 2D Dir. | Leading leg | Ratio | Case | 2D Dir. | Leading leg | Ratio |
|------|---------|-------------|-------|------|---------|-------------|-------|
| 1 | ↗ | Right | $>1$ | 7 | ↖ | Right | $<1$ |
| 2 | | Left | $<1$ | 8 | | Left | $>1$ |
| 3 | → | Right | $\approx 1$ | 9 | ← | Right | $\approx 1$ |
| 4 | | Left | $\approx 1$ | 10 | | Left | $\approx 1$ |
| 5 | ↘ | Right | $<<1$ | 11 | ↙ | Right | $>>1$ |
| 6 | | Left | $>>1$ | 12 | | Left | $<<1$ |

## 4 Registering Two Views

An automatic registration method needs a feature selection and matching algorithm to select corresponding points between the views obtained from two cameras. In 3D motion-based camera calibration a major problem is to estimate the height of the motion above the defined ground-plane. In our case however, since we can detect the legs in motion, their lower point can conveniently be used for registering common points on the ground-plane.

The problem can be summarized as follows: given a set of points $x_i$ and a corresponding set of points $x'_i$, we need to compute the projective transformation (2D homography) that takes each element $x_i$ to $x'_i$. The problem is to compute a 3x3 matrix, H, such that:

$$x'_i = Hx_i \tag{2}$$

This computation can be accomplished in several ways; details can be found in [7]. To solve the problem, we need at least four point-correspondences.

To detect such corresponding points, we use our walk-detection and leading-leg identification methods. Both methods provide information which is useful in matching points between the two views: detected walk patterns must be concurrent in both views; and, likewise, the leading leg must be the same. In both views the central lower points of the detected walk-patterns are the feature points (e.g. the one marked with a black "x" in Figure 2a). The extraction of a feature point from one of the views is followed by searching for its pair in the other view. The algorithm searches for concurrent points by examining the timestamps of points, and for points which were detected during walk cycles with the same leading leg. Nevertheless, neither of these features is unique for person identification (in cases where more than one person is visible). This fact results in some outliers in the detected points. However, because the leading leg is a stronger feature for identification, there are fewer outliers than if we were to use only the concurrent condition. For the estimation of the transformation H that maps points of one camera scene onto the other, and for rejection of outliers from the set of candidate point-pairs, we have implemented both the simple DLT method, and its extension using the RANSAC algorithm [7].

## 5  Experimental Results

We evaluated the registration algorithm by using surveillance cameras placed in a public area located in the university building. The angle between the view-axes of the two cameras employed was nearly 90° (hence, to detect corresponding points using standard optical methods would be difficult). In our series of tests, the successfully detected and classified walk-patterns were 241 for the first camera, and 220 for the second camera. In our system the cameras are in principle synchronized, but there is a small temporal drift between the walk patterns generated by each camera; hence we define a permitted time-window for events which are classed as "concurrent". This time-window for concurrent checking was 5 frames. After such checking, there remained 46 concurrent corresponding points (S1 dataset) and 8 with the leading leg verified (S2 dataset). We found 15 invalid points in the S1 dataset. Table 2 summarizes the results of the simple DLT and the RANSAC+DLT methods applied to several combinations of the S1 and S2 datasets (cases 1 to 5). We assessed the accuracy of the computed transformations (rightmost column) using manually-selected control points.

**Table 2.** Experimental results on data from "Aula" cameras (RANSAC distance threshold is t=0.01)

| Case | Method | Input | Points | Correct points | Detected outliers | Average error (pixel) |
|------|--------|-------|--------|----------------|-------------------|------------------------|
| 1 | DLT | S2 | 8 | 8 | - | 6.4 |
| 2 | DLT | S1+S2 | 54 | 39 | - | 250.2 |
| 3 | RANSAC+DLT | S2 | 8 | 8 | 4 | 12.5 |
| 4 | RANSAC+DLT | S1+S2 | 54 | 39 | 25 | 7.8 |
| 5 | RANSAC+DLT | S1 | 46 | 31 | 28 | 6.2 |

Because of the near-orthogonal orientation of the two cameras used for the tests, the algorithm can rarely detect two successive walks for leading-leg identification, and therefore there are few points in the S2 dataset. Nevertheless, in case 1, all the points in S2 are correct points; and the simple DLT method can compute a good transformation. The DLT method fails when there are outliers (as for the S1+S2 dataset), and in this case (case 2) the position error is extremely high. In cases 4 and 5, the RANSAC algorithm has managed to reject the outliers from S1, and the DLT method then computes a good transformation. In case 3, RANSAC+DLT fails to give good accuracy because there are too few points in the S2 dataset [7].

**Fig. 3.** Transformation from the first-camera view (left) to the second (right): Detected corresponding points, and a synthetic line-trajectory

To summarize the test-results: the DLT method is fast enough to run in real-time, but it needs an input containing only "good" points (like our S2 dataset). On the other hand the RANSAC algorithm can successfully reject outlier points (such as contained in our S1 dataset) but it does require much more computing time (5-20 seconds).

## 6 Conclusions

A camera registration method has been presented which uses walk-parameters as features to identify corresponding points. The features we used  (concurrent walk-steps, and leading-leg identity) seem potentially to provide good data for the estimation of homography between two different camera views of the same scene. The registration method has been verified on an actual indoor camera surveillance system, and was able to provide real-time feature (walk) detection. The described method is an extension of our previous work [6], which investigated an automatic registration method used in an outdoor environment.

## References

1. S. T. Barnard, W. B. Thompson: Disparity analysis of images, IEEE Trans. PAMI, Vol. 2(4) (1980) 333-340
2. J. K. Cheng, T. S. Huang: Image registration by matching relational structures, Pattern Recog., Vol. 17(1) (1984) 149-159
3. J. Weng, N. Ahuja, T. S. Huang: Matching two perspective views, IEEE Trans. PAMI, Vol. 14(8) (1992) 806-825
4. Z. Zhang, R. Deriche, O. Faugeras, Q.-T. Luong: A robust technique for matching two uncalibrated images through the recovery of the unknown Epipolar Geometry, Artificial Intelligence Journal, Vol.78 (1995) 87-119
5. L. Lee, R. Romano, G. Stein: Monitoring activities from multiple video streams: establishing a common coordinate frame, IEEE Trans. PAMI, Vol. 22(8) (2000)
6. Z. Szlávik, L. Havasi, T. Szirányi: Estimation of common groundplane based on co-motion statistics, ICIAR'04, Lecture Notes in Computer Science, Vol. 3211 (2004) 347-353
7. R. Hartley, A. Zisserman: Multiple View Geometry in Computer Vision, Cambridge, Cambridge University Press (2003)

8.  Havasi L., Szlávik Z. (2004), Symmetry feature extraction and understanding, Proc. CNNA'04, pp. 255-260
9.  Stauffer C., Eric W., and Grimson L., Learning patterns of activity using real-time tracking, IEEE Trans. on PAMI, 22(8), (2000), 747-757.
10. L. Havasi, Cs. Benedek, Z. Szlávik, and T. Szirányi, „Extracting structural fragments of overlapping pedestrians", IASTED VIIP, (2004).
11. L. Havasi, Z. Szlávik, and T. Szirányi, „Pedestrian detection using derived third-order symmetry of legs", Kluwer, ICCVG, (2004).
12. L. Havasi, Z. Szlávik, T. Sziranyi: „Eigenwalks: Walk detection and biometrics from symmetry patterns", IEEE ICIP, (2005)

# Real Time Tracking of Multiple Persons on Colour Image Sequences

Ghilès Mostafoui, Catherine Achard, and Maurice Milgram

LISIF, case courrier 252,
4, place Jussieu, 75252 Paris Cedex 05
ghiles.mostafaoui@lis.jussieu.fr
{achard, maum}@ccr.jussieu.fr

**Abstract.** We propose a real time algorithm to track moving persons without any a priori knowledge neither on the model of person, nor on their size or their number, which can evolve with time. It manages several problems such as occlusion and under or over-segmentations. The first step consisting in motion detection, leads to regions that have to be assigned to trajectories. This tracking step is achieved using a new concept: elementary tracks. They allow on the one hand to manage the tracking and on the other hand, to detect the output of occlusion by introducing coherent sets of regions. Those sets enable to define temporal kinematical model, shape model or colour model. Significant results have been obtained on several sequences with ground truth as shown in results.

## 1 Introduction

Real time objects tracking is a difficult task which is present in a great number of applications on image processing, like human-machine interaction, civil and military monitoring, virtual reality, analysis of human movement or images compression. This difficulty is accentuated in environments without constraints where the system must be able to deal with significant variability of objects, variations of luminosity, occlusions and also with the segmentation problems.

There are many tracking algorithms yet proposed by several authors. Different strategies can be used for the tracking step, among them we can mention heuristic methods simple to implement [6], the JPDAF algorithm (Joint Probabilistic Data Association Filter) [2] which calculates the association probabilities of each measurement to a known and fixed number of targets or the Multiple Hypothesis Tracker (MHT) algorithm [12] that explores each way to match any region with any track. This probabilistic data association algorithm needs any initialisation and deals with an unknown and non-constant number of objects. Particle filters [8] have recently been introduced. They represent the state density by a set of particles, allowing working with multi-modal function. This technique has been initially developed for the tracking of one object but has been extended to several [7]. We can also mention the recent works of Comaniciu et al [3] which introduces the Mean-Shift.

For all these algorithms, different features can be used to model objects as kinematics [1], shape (silhouettes [4], 2d and 3d articulated models [14][9]) or appearance

J. Blanc-Talon et al. (Eds.): ACIVS 2005, LNCS 3708, pp. 44–51, 2005.
© Springer-Verlag Berlin Heidelberg 2005

models such as [13][11]. Naturally, the robustness of the tracking is increased using simultaneously different sources of information.

The real time tracking algorithm proposed in this article is not supervised, it requires any initialisation neither on the tracks models, nor on their number, which can evolve with time. It is achieved using simultaneously kinematics, shape and an appearance model of objects based on colour. The originality of this method consists in the introduction of a new concept: **elementary tracks**. Those will play a significant role in the tracking by tackling the problem of grouping regions to true trajectories (specially in bad segmentation conditions), and also, by managing the different interactions between the tracks (occlusions). The first step of the algorithm consists in a motion detection achieved by thresholding the difference between a reference image (background image) and the current image. This step, presented in section 2 is very sensitive to noise and then, is following by a Markovian relaxation. The so-obtained regions produce elementary tracks (section 3), which will be assigned to trajectories as describe in section 4. Results presented in section 5 show on real sequences with ground truth (benchmark data's suggested in the PETS2004 conference) that segmentation problems and occlusions are correctly managed.

## 2 Motion Detection

The motion detection is performed by subtracting to each image a reference one (created and updated automatically), called the background image. To reduce the noise on these difference images a Markovian relaxation is performed with the ICM algorithm (Iterated Conditional Modes) [5]. A labelling step ends the detection by producing regions that will be assigned to tracks. Before describing the assignment process, let us define these tracks and their model.

## 3 Definition of the Tracks

### 3.1 The Elementary Tracks

Let $R_i^k$ and $R_j^{k+1}$ two moving regions belonging to images $I_k$ and $I_{k+1}$. These regions are neighbouring and **connected** (in a graph theoretical meaning) if the area of their overlapping part (when projected in the same image) is not zero. We say that $R_i^k$ and connected by a **strong edge** (in a graph theoretical sense) if $R_i^k$ has a single neighbour (at time $k+1$) that is $R_j^{k+1}$ and if conversely $R_j^{k+1}$ has a single neighbour at time $k$, the region $R_i^k$. We so define an undirected graph $G$ where nodes are regions $R_i^k$ and edges are pairs $(R_i^k, R_j^{k+1})$ of connected regions (strong edge or not).

An **elementary track** is then a path in the graph $G$ composed by strongly connected regions $R_i^k$. It follows first that there is no branching node in an elementary track and second that an **elementary track** may have **no more than one region in the same image**. The association of regions to elementary tracks is considered as sure and will not be studied again. As example, regions shown on the figure 1 lead to five elementary tracks.

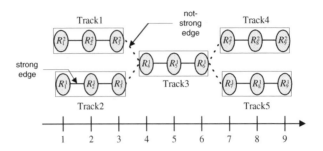

**Fig. 1.** Elementary tracks for a sequence of regions

This notion of elementary track is very important, as it constitutes the basic block to build true trajectories. Generally, a large number of elementary tracks is generated for an image sequence due to segmentation errors or occlusions. Actually, as any a priori knowledge is employed on the height of the persons, any threshold has been used on the size of regions. This leads to a great number of small regions which generate several elementary tracks. We prefer keeping them at this low level stage and waiting for higher-level information to perform an efficient reduction of tracks. Elementary tracks allow introducing coherent sets of regions, which could be modeled more globally than a single region (by temporal features as velocity for example). Also, they will make it useful to distinguish interactions between trajectories (occlusions) from segmentation problems. These elementary tracks have now to be merged in principal tracks representing the different trajectories.

### 3.2  The Principal Tracks

Let $ET_1$ and $ET_2$ be two elementary tracks. $ET_1$ and $ET_2$ are **connected** if there is a way constituted by not-strong edges (see Fig. 1) for going from $ET_1$ to $ET_2$. A **principal track** is then defined as a **set of connected elementary tracks**. Ideally, each principal track represents the trajectory of a person in the sequence. Note that **several regions** of the same image $I_k$ can now belong to the same principal track. In order to compare the tracks each other, we introduce below a model of track.

### 3.3  Model of Tracks

Each track $T_i$ (elementary or principal) is modeled at each time $k$ by its kinematical parameters, shape parameters and also by an appearance model.

   a) **Kinematical parameters** are composed by: the center of gravity $(gx^k, gy^k)$ of regions in the track, the velocity $(dx, dy)$ of the track and a weight $w$ which represents the probability of the track and is function of its temporal duration.

   The velocity is computed using gravity centers of regions as follow: let us consider a track $T_i$ present across times $k_0..k_n$ and its gravity centers $(gx^0...gx^n, gy^0...gy^n)$. We note $(Vx^k,Vy^k)=(gx^k - gx^{k-1}, gy^k - gy^{k-1})$ the velocities at each time $k$. This computational process is very fast but unfortunately, the speeds so obtained are very sensitive to segmentation problems. For example, we can see on figure 2 that $\vec{V2}$ is wrong due to the bad segmentation. For short tracks, this produces a high error rate on the average speed $(dx,dy)$.

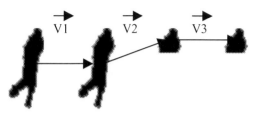

**Fig. 2.** The update process of velocity

To deal with this problem, velocity updating is performed by weighting each speed with a pertinence factor $m^k$ which is function of the area difference between two consecutive times (equation 1). When segmentation problems appear, areas present a big variation and $m^k$ will be small to penalise the corresponding velocity vector.

$$\begin{cases} dx = \sum_{k=1}^{n} m^k * Vx^k \\ dy = \sum_{k=1}^{n} m^k * Vy^k \end{cases}, \quad with \quad m^k = \exp\left\{\frac{-\left|(A^{k+1} - A^k)\right|}{\alpha}\right\} \Big/ \sum_{k'=1}^{n} \exp\left\{\frac{-\left|(A^{k'} + 1 - A^{k'})\right|}{\alpha}\right\} \quad (1)$$

$A^k$ is the area of the track at time $k$. $\alpha$ is a parameter used in the "softmax" to adjust the decrease of the exponential (we set it to 50). The average speed ($dx,dy$) so computed is assigned to all regions of the track (performing a speed smoothing).

   b) **The shape** is characterized by an ellipse of axes $2\sigma_x$ and $2\sigma_y$ where $\sigma_x$ and $\sigma_y$ are the horizontal and vertical standard deviations of pixels belonging to the track.

   c) **The appearance** is described by a color model and a vector of appearance probability $AP$. The color model is similar to this presented in [10]. The principle consists in projecting on the vertical axis, the color average of pixels belonging to the track. This 1D model describes a person with less precision than 2Dmodels [13] but is still representative of the general color of the person. It presents two main advantages compared to the 2D model: it is more robust against changes in the shape of the moving people (due to the projections) and its adjustment to the region is simplified (1D correlation) and more robust. Moreover, it makes it possible to reduce significantly the computational time.

The vector of appearance probability $AP$ represents the likelihood of the object being observed at each line of the color model. It will be used as a weighting during the computation of the distance between models of appearance. We have introduced all the notions used by the tracking algorithm which will be now described.


## 4   The Tracking Method

The tracking algorithm will consist on gathering connected elementary tracks in principal tracks, each one representing ideally the trajectory of a person.

   Let $PT_i^{k-1}$ $i=(1..N)$ the principal tracks present at the time $k-1$ and $ET_l^k$ ($l=1..M$), the elementary tracks present at the time $k$. Each elementary track $ET_l^k$ has to be associated to a principal track $PT_i^{k-1}$ (or to a new principal track).

Let $S_i^k$ the set of elementary tracks connected to the principal track $PT_i^{k-1}$ (and thus probably belonging to $PT_i^{k-1}$). Several cases can occur:

**a)**   If $S_i^k$ is empty then the track $PT_i^{k-1}$ is stopped.

**b)**   If $S_i^k$ contains one elementary track which is not connected to another principal track then parameters of the track $PT_i^{k-1}$ are updated at the time $k$

**c)**   If $S_i^k$ contains one or more elementary tracks connected to another track $PT_j^{k-1}$, we have to choose between the presence of an occlusion or a segmentation error. For that, we study the orientation of velocity vectors of the concerned principal tracks $PT_i^{k-1}$ and $PT_j^{k-1}$ by computing the error:

$$E(i,j) = F\left(\left|\theta_i - \theta_j\right|\right) \; with \begin{cases} F(\theta) = 1 & if \quad \theta < \varepsilon \\ F(\theta) = \exp\left(\dfrac{|\theta - \varepsilon|}{A}\right) & else \end{cases} \qquad \text{where } \theta \text{ is the cinematic orientation} \qquad (2)$$

In a heuristic way, $A$ was set to 18. The function $F(\theta)$ is used to clearly discriminate two tracks which have different orientations.

If $E(i,j)$ is higher than a threshold $S_{fo}$, an occlusion is detected between $PT_i^{k-1}$ and $PT_j^{k-1}$ and a new track called an "**occlusion track**" is created (the tracks $PT_i^{k-1}$ and $PT_j^{k-1}$ are obviously not destroyed to manage the exit of occlusion). If $E(i,j)$ *is bellow the* threshold, a segmentation error is detected and the track with the lower weight is destroyed while the other is updated.

**d)** If $S_i^k$ contains several elementary tracks which are not connected to another principal track, we can have an over-segmented person or two persons previously detected as one track and now separated (**split of the track**). The decision is still made by studying the velocity but here, we have to study the velocities in the future frames which are unknown. To solve this problem, we use elementary tracks and their velocities: using the k-means algorithm ($k=2$), we separate the elementary tracks in two classes with the kinematical direction as criterion. Let $\theta_{c1}$ and $\theta_{c2}$ the centers of these classes. If $F\left(\left|\theta_{c1} - \theta_{c2}\right|\right) < S_{fo}$, an over-segmentation is find and the track $PT_i^{k-1}$ is updated. In the other case, a split is detected. Between the two sets of elementary tracks, the most similar to the principal track $PT_i^{k-1}$ is assigned to this track. The second set will be assigned to a new track that corresponds to the second trajectory, after the splitting.

If the case of splitting in an **occlusion track**, an appearance model is computed for each of the two classes defined above. Those models will be compared to those of the tracks $PT_i^{k-1}$ and $PT_j^{k-1}$ that have created the occlusion. If both models do not belong to the same track and if shapes (ellipses) are coherent, then $PT_i^{k-1}$ and $PT_j^{k-1}$ are updated and the occlusion track is destroyed (end of the occlusion). Else, the occlusion is not broken.

## 5   Results

Our method was tested on a great number of sequences. We present here the results obtained on nine sequences from the *pets2004* conference. Their scenarios are varied

**Browse2** represents a person browsing and reading for a moment, **Browse4** a person browsing a desk, **Bww2** a person browsing and waiting, **Rsf** a person slumping on the floor, **Rff** a person falling down and staying immobile, **Mwt1** two people meeting and walking together, **Mws** two people meeting, walking together and splitting, **Mc** crowding of four people meeting, walking and splitting, **Fra1** two people meeting, fighting and runing away, **Fomd** two people meeting, fighting, one down, other runs away and **Lbox** a person putting a box on the floor. The main advantage of these sequences is their "ground truth" (number of people, localization of people... etc) that allows estimating numerically the quality of our results as follow: Let us consider an edge (strong or not) that connects two regions. Let $E1vt$ and $E2vt$ the labels (number of the tracks) of these regions given by the ground truth and $E1r$ and $E2r$ the labels resulting from our method. The edge is called positive if: ($E1vt=E2vt$ and $E1r=E2r$) or ($E1vt\neq E2vt$ and $E1r\neq E2r$), else it is negative. The table below summarizes the results obtained on all the sequences.

**Table 1.**

|  | Browse2 | Browse4 | Rsf | Lbox | Mwt1 | Mws | Mc | Fra1 | Fomd |
|---|---|---|---|---|---|---|---|---|---|
| NI | 875 | 1138 | 910 | 862 | 706 | 622 | 490 | 550 | 959 |
| NR | 3176 | 3654 | 3106 | 3515 | 1902 | 2005 | 995 | 3823 | 3056 |
| NPvt | 2 | 3 | 3 | 4 | 5 | 9 | 4 | 7 | 9 |
| NPr | 2 | 3 | 4 | 5 | 5 | 12 | 4 | 10 | 10 |
| NPvtI | 1.10 | 0.77 | 3.17 | 3.4 | 1.8 | 2.7 | 2.3 | 4.9 | 2.76 |
| NRI | 3.62 | 3.21 | 3.38 | 4.07 | 2.69 | 3.23 | 2.02 | 6.9 | 3.18 |
| NAP | 3169 | 3662 | 3108 | 3521 | 1885 | 1995 | 876 | 3815 | 3073 |
| NAN | 26 | 20 | 25 | 15 | 56 | 37 | 135 | 28 | 31 |

In addition to edges evaluation (number of positive and negative edges "**NAP**" and "**NAN**"), we compare the number of people found on these sequences (**NPr**) with that of the ground truth (**NPvt**). Some statistics of the sequences are also given in the table (**Ni**: number of images, **NR**: number of regions, **NPvtI**: average of the number of people by image, **NRI**: average of the number of regions by images). These statistics give, for each sequence, a global idea of the problems of over or under-segmentations and occlusions. Thus, by comparing NPvtI with NRI, we can notice the **significant number of over-segmentations** (on the sequence Browse4, a person is on average represented by four regions). This latter could be reduce by introducing a threshold on the size of regions, but as we didn't know a priori the height of the persons, we cannot set a priori this threshold. Thus, we have to manage all these over-segmentations and to correctly affect regions to tracks.

For all these sequences, no manual initialization was carried out and no threshold was changed (the algorithm has only one threshold used for the study of the kinematics of the tracks). In addition, no a priori information was introduced on the objects to track.

The results above show that our algorithm is able to track several people (two sequences comprise 9 persons), and to detect and manage the interactions between this persons (occlusions, under- or over-segmentations). Actually, we can note small errors on the evaluation of the number of persons on these difficult sequences, in spite of the lack of a priori knowledge and the number of over-segmentations.

We can nevertheless note a higher error rate for some sequences (*Mwt1* and *Mc*). These errors are generally produced by people who interact with nearly identical kinematical parameters. This makes difficult the occlusions and splitting detection. Moreover, for the *Mws* sequence, two people who are crossing have identical colorimetric characteristics. It explains the error of labeling after the separation of the persons (exit of occlusion). Generally, on these difficult sequences, the algorithm works correctly with a small number of negative edges (NAN) in front of the positive ones.

## 6 Conclusion

We have presented a real time and robust method for the tracking of moving objects using simultaneously kinematics, shape and an appearance model. In order to correctly manage the problems of occlusions and over-segmentations, we have introduced a new concept: elementary tracks. Those gather in a sure way (strong edges) some regions of the sequence. This allow to access to temporal models (model of shape, kinematics and appearance) which could not be defined for isolated regions. These elementary tracks are very useful to detect the beginning or the end of occlusion, or to manage over or under-segmentation. Experimental results carried out on various sequences with a ground truth were presented with a numerical evaluation of the performances of our system. This latter produces good results on these particularly difficult sequences. As we do not know a priori the height of the persons, we impose no criterion on the size of regions and have to deal with a great number of small regions (hands, feet, ...) which have to be assigned on real trajectories. Our perspectives consist in incorporating the tracking algorithm in a real application of person counting by introducing a priori knowledge on the tracked objects and the environment to increase the robustness of the system.

## References

1. C. Achard, G. Mostafaoui, M. Milgram, Object tracking based on kinematics with spatiotemporal blob, to appear in MVA2005
2. Y. Bar-Shalom, XR Li, Multitarget-Mulisensor tracking, Publisher: Yaakov Bar-Shalom, 1995.
3. D. Comaniciu, V. Ramesh, and P. Meer, Real-time tracking of non-rigid objects using mean shift, in Proc. IEEE Conf. on Computer Vision and Pattern Recognition, June 2000, pp. using silhouettes, International Conference on Pattern Recognition 1998, pp. 77-82.

4.  J. Denoulet, G. Mostafaoui, L. Lacassagne, A. Merigot, Robust Embedded Hardware im-
    plementation of Motion Markov Detection and hysteresis thresholding  in colors se-
    quences, to appear 142--151.
5.  I. Haritaoglu, D. Harwood, and L.S. Davis, Ghost: A human body part labelling system
    in CAMP2005
6.  I. Haritaoglu, D. Harwood, L.S. Davis, W4S : a real time system for detecting and track-
    ing people in 2,5D, European Conference Computer Vision, pages 877—892, 1998,
    Maryland.
7.  C. Hue, J.P. Le cadre, P. Perez, Tracking multiple objects with particle filtering, RR
    INRIA n° 4033, 2000.
8.  M. Isard, A. Blake, Condensation I conditional density propagation for visual tracking, Int.
    J. Computer Vision, 29, 1, 5--28, 1998.
9.  H. Moon, R. Chellappa, A. Rosenfeld, Tracking of Human Activities Using Shape-
    encoded Particle Propagation, ICIP2001 , vol 1, pp. 357-360
10. A. Mittal, L.S.Davis, $M_2$ Tracker : A Multi-View Approach to Segmenting and tracking
    people in a Cluttered Scene, IJCV(51), No. 3, February-March 2003, pp. 189-203.
11. S.Park, J.K.Aggarwal, Segmentation and tracking of interacting human body parts under
    occlusion and shadowing, Motion2002, pp.105-111
12. D.B. Reid, An algorithm for Tracking Multiple Targets, IEEE Trans. on Automatic Con-
    trol, Vol. AC-24, N° 6, pp 843-854, 1979.
13. A.Senior, Tracking People with Probabilistic Appearance Models, Pets2002, pp. 48-55
14. L.Wang, H.Ning, T.Tan, W.Hu, Fusion of static and dynamic body biometrics for gait
    recognition, ICCV 2003.

# A Study on Non-intrusive Facial and Eye Gaze Detection

Kang Ryoung Park, Min Cheol Whang, and Joa Sang Lim

Division of Media Technology, Sangmyung University,
7 Hongji-Dong, JongRo-Gu, Seoul, Republic of Korea
parkgr@smu.ac.kr

**Abstract.** To detect accurate human gaze position is vey difficult, but important problem for many applications. For that, it is requisite to detect the facial and eye movement accurately and fastly. So, we implemented a real-time gaze tracking system based on facial and eye movement. The performance of detecting facial features could be enhanced by Support Vector Machine and the eye gaze position on a monitor could be generalized by a multi-layered perceptron. And two gaze positions were geometically summed and final gaze position was acquired. Experimental results showed that the RMS error of gaze detection is about 2.4 degrees (1.68 degrees on X axis and 1.71 degrees on Y axis at the Z distance of 50 cm).

**Keyword:** Gaze Detection, Facial and Eye Movement.

## 1 Introduction

Gaze detection technology is applicable to the interface of man-machine interaction, such as the view control in three-dimensional simulation programs. Furthermore, it can help the handicapped to use computers and is also useful for those whose hands are busy doing other things[15]. The gaze detection researches can be classified into 4 categories. First one is that focused on 2D/3D head motion estimation[2][11]. Second one is that for the facial gaze detection[3-9][12][13][15] and the third one is the eye gaze detection[10][14]. And last one is that considering both head and eye movement has been researched. Ohmura and Ballard et al.[5][6]'s methods and Rikert et al.[9]'s method has the constraints that the user's Z distance should be measured manually and take much time to compute the gaze position. Gee et al.[7] and Heinzmann et al.[8]'s methods only compute gaze direction vector and do not obtain the gaze position on a monitor. In the methods of [12][13], a pair of glasses having marking points is required to detect facial features. The researches of [3][4][16] show the facial gaze detection methods and have the disadvantage that the gaze errors are increased in case that the eye movements happen. To overcome such problems, the research of [17] shows the facial and eye gaze detection, but uses only one wide view camera. In such case, the eye image resolution is too low and the fine movements of user's eye cannot be exactly detected. Wang et al.[1]'s method provides the advanced

J. Blanc-Talon et al. (Eds.): ACIVS 2005, LNCS 3708, pp. 52–59, 2005.
© Springer-Verlag Berlin Heidelberg 2005

approaches that combines head pose and eye gaze estimation by a wide view camera and a panning/tilting narrow camera. However, in order to compute the gaze position, their method supposes that they know the 3D distance between two eyes, that between both lip corners and the 3D diameter of eye ball. Also, they suppose there is no individual variation for the 3D distances and diameter. However, our preliminary experiments show that there are much individual variations for the 3D distances/3D diameter and such cases can increase much gaze errors. To overcome above problems, we propose the new method for detecting gaze position.

## 2 Localization of Facial Features in Wide View Image

In order to detect gaze position on a monitor, we first locate facial features in wide view images. To detect facial features robustly, we implement a gaze detection system as shown in Fig. 1. The IR-LED(1) is used to make the specular reflections on eyes. Due to the IR pass filter(2) in front of camera lens, the brightness of input image is only affected by the IR-LED(1) excluding external illumination. The reason of using IR-LED(1) of 880nm is that it does not make dazzling to user's eye. When a user starts our gaze detection system, the micro-controller(4) turns on the illuminator(1) synchronized with the even field of CCD signal and turns it off synchronized with the next odd field of CCD signal, successively[17]. From that, we can get a difference image between the even and the odd image and the specular reflection points on both eyes can be easily detected because their image gray levels are higher than other regions[17]. In addition, we use the Red-Eye effect and the method of changing Frame Grabber decoder value in order to detect more accurate eye position[17]. Around the detected corneal specular reflection points, we determine the eye candidate region of 30*30 pixels and locate the accurate eye (iris) center by the circular edge detection method. After that, we detect the eye corner by using eye corner shape template and SVM (Support Vector Machine)[17]. We get 2000 successive image frames for SVM training and additional 1000 images are used for testing from 100 persons. Experimental results show the classification error for training data is 0.11% and that for testing data is 0.2%. The classification time of SVM is 8 ms

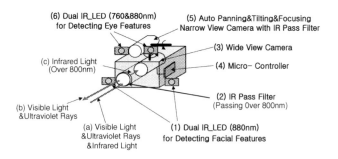

**Fig. 1.** The gaze detecting system

in Pentium-III 866MHz. After locating eye centers and eye corners, the positions of nostrils can be detected by anthropometric constraints in a face and SVM. In order to reduce the effect by the facial expression change, we do not use the lip corners. Experimental results show that RMS error between the detected feature positions and the actual positions are 1 pixel (of both eye centers), 2 pixels (of both eye corners) and 4 pixels (of both nostrils) in $640 \times 480$ pixels image. From those, we use 5 feature points (left/right eye corners of left eye, left/right eye corners of right eye, nostril center) in order to detect facial gaze position.

## 3   Computing Facial Gaze Position

Based on the detected 2D eye corner positions, we can pan/tilt the narrow view camera in order to capture the eye image. Here, the pan and tilting mechanism is hand-made by our research team with stepping motor. However, because the 2D feature positions are observed in the wide view camera and the panning/tilting should be performed in narrow view camera, the coordinate unification between the wide and narrow view camera using the camera parameters and the Z distance (between the wide view camera and the 3D eye corner positions) should be required in order to determine the accurate angle of panning/tilting as shown in Fig. 2(a). However, the accurate Z distance is difficult to be obtained with single wide view camera and we use the following method in order to determine the angle of panning/tilting. That is, the coordinate unification is required due to the coordinate discrepancy and we can preliminarily reduce the discrepancy by positioning the narrow view camera close to (above) wide view camera as shown in Fig. 2(a). In addition, conventional users tend to sit from 50 to 70 cm in front of monitor and such condition can restrict the coordinate discrepancy also as shown in Fig. 2(a). Of course, there can be individual variations for the user's sitting height, but there is also the limitation of sitting height considering the working comfort in the desktop computer environment. Considering such

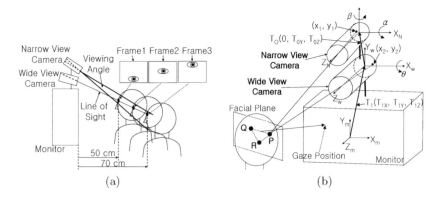

**Fig. 2.** Computing facial gaze position using wide and narrow view camera (a)Initial viewing angle of narrow view camera (b)Coordinate conversion among the narrow view camera, the wide view camera and the monitor

conditions, we determine the initial viewing angle of narrow view camera as 4.3 degree(from -2.15 to +2.15 degree, vertically) and we can obtain the magnified eye image of narrow view camera like Frame 1, 2, 3 (the diameter of iris is below 135 pixels at the Z distance of 50 cm) as shown in Fig. 2(a). From the Frame 1, 2, 3, we can detect more accurate 2D eye corner positions by the method as mentioned in section 2. Then, we compute the 3D eye corner positions using the narrow and wide view stereo camera as following. Supposing that P point, which is the left eye corner of right eye, is observed in both wide and narrow view camera as shown in Fig. 2(b), then we can obtain Eq. (1) [18].

$$X_{1,2} = \frac{x_{1,2} * (f_{1,2} - Z_{1,2})}{f_{1,2}}, Y_{1,2} = \frac{y_{1,2} * (f_{1,2} - Z_{1,2})}{f_{1,2}} \tag{1}$$

where $(x_1, y_1)$ is the observed 2D position in the narrow view camera, $(x_2, y_2)$ is the observed 2D position in the wide view camera and $f_1$, $f_2$ are the focal lengths of the narrow view and the wide view camera, respectively. In addition, $(X_1, Y_1, Z_1)$ is the 3D position of P point in the narrow view camera coordinate $(X_N, Y_N, Z_N)$ and $(X_2, Y_2, Z_2)$ is the 3D position of P point in the wide view camera coordinate $(X_W, Y_W, Z_W)$. Considering the coordinate conversion between the narrow and wide view camera [18] and Eq.(1), we can obtain the Z distance $(Z_2)$ as $Z_2 = A/B$.

Here, $A = y_2{}^*f_2 - y_1{}^*f_1{}^*f_2^2 + y_1{}^*f_2^2{}^*\cos\alpha{}^*\sin\beta{}^*x_2 + y_1{}^*f_2^2{}^*T_{0y}{}^*\sin\alpha - y_1{}^*f_2^2{}^*T_{0z}{}^*\cos\alpha{}^*\cos\beta + f_1{}^*f_2^2{}^*\sin\alpha{}^*\sin\beta{}^*x_2 - f_1{}^*f_2^2{}^*T_{0y}{}^*\cos\alpha - f_1{}^*f_2^2{}^*T_{0z}{}^*\sin\alpha{}^*\cos\beta$. $B = y_2 + y_1{}^*f_2{}^*\cos\alpha{}^*\sin\beta{}^*x_2 - y_1{}^*f_2^2{}^*\cos\alpha{}^*\cos\beta + f_1{}^*f_2{}^*\sin\alpha{}^*\sin\beta{}^*x_2 - f_1{}^*f_2^2{}^*\sin\alpha{}^*\cos\beta$.

Substituting the Eq. of $Z_2 = A/B$ into Eq. (1), we can obtain the 3D positions$(X_2, Y_2, Z_2)$ of feature point(P) in the wide view camera coordinate $(X_W, Y_W, Z_W)$. For that, we should know the camera parameters like $(T_{0y}, T_{0z}, f_1, f_2)$ as shown in Eq. of $Z_2 = A/B$, whose parameters are not changed after initial camera setup. So, we perform the camera calibration procedures using calibration panel and parameter estimation method (Davidon-Fletcher-Powell method) [3][4][18][19].

From that, we can obtain the accurate camera parameters value $(T_{0y} = 55mm, T_{0z} = 11mm, f_1 = 42mm, f_2 = 8mm)$. In addition, we should know the parameters of panning/tilting angle of narrow view camera ($\alpha$ and $\beta$) in order to obtain the the Z distance $(Z_2)$. Those parameters are changed according to the panning/tilting operation of narrow view camera and we can know them from camera micom as shown in Fig. 1. That is, the camera micom checks the panning/tilting angle values periodically (30 Hz) and transmits them to the gaze detection S/W in PC via RS-232C communication. From above procedures, we can get the 3D positions$(X_2, Y_2, Z_2)$ of feature point(P) in the wide view camera coordinate $(X_W, Y_W, Z_W)$. Then, we perform the additional coordinate conversion between the wide view camera coordinate $(X_W, Y_W, Z_W)$ and monitor coordinate $(X_m, Y_m, Z_m)$ as shown in Fig. 2(b). For that, we should know the camera parameters like $(T_{1x}, T_{1y}, T_{1z}, \theta)$ and we can also obtain them by the camera calibration procedures [3][4][18][19]. Same rules are applied to the other

4 features points and we can obtain the 3D positions of 5 features (left/right eye corners of left eye, left/right eye corners of right eye, nostril center) in monitor coordinate $(X_m, Y_m, Z_m)$. For that, additional panning/tilting of the narrow view camera may be required in order to include the other feature points in the narrow view image and it takes little time as below 5 ms. The experimental results show that the RMS error of between the computed 3D positions of 5 features and the actual ones (measured by 3D position tracking sensor (Polhemus Fastrak [21]) is about 0.781 cm (0.41cm in X axis, 0.45cm in Y axis, 0.49cm in Z axis) for 50 person data. Then, we can determine one facial plane from the computed 3D positions of the 5 features and the normal vector (whose origin exists in the middle of the forehead) of the plane shows a gaze vector by head (facial) movements. The gaze position on a monitor is the intersection position between a monitor and the gaze vector as shown in Fig. 2(b).

## 4   Auto Zooming and Focusing of Narrow View Camera

As mentioned in section 3 and Fig. 2(a), we get the eye image in narrow view camera, but the eye image size inevitably becomes small (the diameter of iris is below 135 pixels at the Z distance of 50 cm) in order to overcome the coordinate discrepancy between the wide and narrow view camera. In order to compute more accurate eye gaze position, we should get more magnified eye image. So, we implement the zoom lens into our narrow view camera and perform auto zooming operation in narrow view camera. In addition, conventional narrow view camera has small DOF (Depth of Field) and there is the limitation of increasing the DOF with the fixed focal camera. So, we also implement the focus lens into our narrow view camera and perform auto focusing operation in narrow view camera in order to capture clear eye image. For auto zooming and focusing, the Z distance between the eye and the narrow view camera is required and we can obtain the accurate Z distance $(Z_1)$ by the same method mentioned in section 3.

## 5   Localization of Eye Features in Narrow View Image

After we get the zoomed/focused eye image (the diameter of iris is about 200 pixels), we perform the localization of eye features again as shown in Fig. 3. J. Wang et al.[1] uses the method that detects the iris outer boundary by elliptical fitting. However, the upper and lower regions of iris outer boundary tend to be covered by eyelid and inaccurate iris elliptical fitting happens due to the lack of iris boundary pixels. In addition, their method computes eye gaze position by checking the shape change of iris when a user gazes at monitor positions. However, our experimental results show that the shape change amount of iris is very small and it is difficult to detect the accurate eye gaze position with that. So, we use the positional information of both pupil and iris. Also, we use the information of shape change of pupil, which does not tend to be covered by eyelid. In general, the IR-LED of short wavelength (700nm $\sim$ 800nm) makes the high contrast between iris and sclera and that of long wavelength (800nm $\sim$

900nm) makes the high contrast between pupil and iris. Based on that, we use the IR-LED illuminator of multi-wavelength (760nm and 880nm) as shown in Fig. 1(6). As shown in Fig. 3(a) and (b), the shapes of iris and pupil are almost ellipse, when the user gazes at a side position of monitor and we use the canny edge operator to extract edge components and a 2D edge-based elliptical Hough transform. In order to detect the eye corner position, we detect the eyelid as shown in Fig. 3 using the region-based eyelid template deformation and masking method. Here, we use 2 deformable templates (parabolic shape) for upper and lower eyelid detection, respectively. Experimental results show that RMS errors between the detected eye feature positions and the actual ones are 2 pixels (of iris center), 1 pixel (of pupil center), 4 pixels (of left eye corner) and 4 pixels (of right eye corner). Based on the detected eye features, we select the 22 feature values ($f_1 \sim f_{11}$ are used in case that right eye image can be captured by narrow view camera as shown in Fig. 3 and $f_{12} \sim f_{22}$ are used in case that left eye image can be captured).

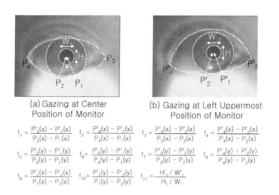

(a) Gazing at Center Position of Monitor       (b) Gazing at Left Uppermost Position of Monitor

$$f_1 = \frac{P'_3(x) - P'_1(x)}{P_3(x) - P_1(x)} \quad f_2 = \frac{P'_4(x) - P'_1(x)}{P_4(x) - P_1(x)} \quad f_3 = \frac{P'_3(x) - P'_2(x)}{P_3(x) - P_2(x)} \quad f_4 = \frac{P'_4(x) - P'_2(x)}{P_4(x) - P_2(x)}$$

$$f_5 = \frac{P'_3(y) - P'_1(y)}{P_3(y) - P_1(y)} \quad f_6 = \frac{P'_4(y) - P'_1(y)}{P_4(y) - P_1(y)} \quad f_7 = \frac{P'_3(y) - P'_2(y)}{P_3(y) - P_2(y)} \quad f_8 = \frac{P'_4(y) - P'_2(y)}{P_4(y) - P_2(y)}$$

$$f_9 = \frac{P'_1(x) - P'_2(x)}{P_1(x) - P_2(x)} \quad f_{10} = \frac{P'_1(y) - P'_2(y)}{P_1(y) - P_2(y)} \quad f_{11} = \frac{H'_1 / W'_1}{H_1 / W_1}$$

**Fig. 3.** The features for eye gaze detection from right eye

# 6   Detecting the Gaze Position on a Monitor

In section 3, we explain the gaze detection method only considering head movement. However, when a user gazes at a monitor position, both the head and eyes tend to be moved simultaneously. So, we compute the additional eye gaze position by the detected 22 feature values (as mentioned in section 5) and a neural network (multi-layered perceptron). For output function of neural network, we use a limited logarithm function, which shows better performance than that in case of using other functions, like a linear, sigmoid etc. The continuous output values of neural network represent eye gaze position on a monitor. After detecting eye gaze position, we can determine a final gaze position based on the vector summation of facial and eye gaze position.

## 7    Performance Evaluations

The gaze detection error of our method is compared to that of our previous methods[3][4][15][17]. The researches[3][4] compute facial gaze position not considering the eye movements. The research[15] calculates the gaze position by mapping the 2D facial feature position into the monitor gaze position by linear interpolation or neural network without 3D computation and considering eye movements. The method[17] computes the gaze positions considering both head and eye movements, but uses only one wide view camera. The test data are acquired when 95 users gaze at 23 gaze positions on a 19" monitor with instruction. The test data are different from the training data above mentioned. Here, the gaze error is the RMS error between the actual gaze positions and the computed ones. At the 1st experiment, the gaze errors are calculated in two cases as shown in Table 1. The case I and II show the gaze error about test data including only head movements and including both head and eye movements, respectively. In this case, we allow the range of head movement to be -21 to +21 degrees, horizontally and -16 to +16 degrees, vertically.

**Table 1.** Gaze error about test data (cm)

| Method | Linear interpol.[15] | Single neural net[15] | Combined neural nets[15] | [3] method | [4] method | [17] method | Proposed method |
|--------|--------|--------|--------|--------|--------|--------|--------|
| case I | 5.1 | 4.23 | 4.48 | 5.35 | 5.21 | 3.40 | 1.21 |
| case II | 11.8 | 11.32 | 8.87 | 7.45 | 6.29 | 4.8 | 2.11 |

Shown in Table 1, the gaze error of the proposed method is the smallest in any case. At the 2nd experiment, the points of radius 5 pixels are spaced vertically and horizontally at 1.5" intervals on a 19" monitor with monitor resolution of 1280×1024 pixels as such Rikert's research[9]. The RMS error between the real and calculated gaze position is 2.09 cm and it is superior to Rikert's method (almost 5.08 cm). Our gaze error is correspondent to the angular error of 1.68 degrees on X axis and 1.71 degrees on Y axis at the Z distance of 50 cm. In addition, we tested the gaze errors according to user's Z distance. The RMS errors are 2.07cm at 50cm, 2.07cm at 60cm, 2.11cm at 70cm and the performance of our method is not affected by the user's Z position change. Last experiment for processing time shows that our gaze detection process takes about 100ms in Pentium-III 866MHz and it is much smaller than Rikert's method (1 minute in alphastation 333MHz).

## 8    Conclusions

This paper describes a new gaze detecting method. Experimental results show that the RMS error of gaze detection is about 2.11 cm. In future works, we plan to develop the method to increase the auto zooming/focusing speed to decrease total processing time of gaze detection.

# Acknowledgement

This work was supported by Ministry of Education and Human Resources Development through Embedded Software Open Education Resource Center(ESC) at Sangmyung University.

# References

1. J. Wang and E. Sung, 2002. Study on Eye Gaze Estimation, IEEE Trans. on SMC, Vol.32, No.3, pp.332-350
2. A. Azarbayejani., 1993, Visually Controlled Graphics. IEEE Trans. PAMI, Vol.15, No.6, pp.602-605
3. K. R. Park et al., Apr 2000, Gaze Point Detection by Computing the 3D Positions and 3D Motions of Face, IEICE Trans. Inf.&Syst.,Vol.E.83-D, No.4, pp.884-894
4. K. R. Park, Oct 1999, Gaze Detection by Estimating the Depth and 3D Motions of Facial Features in Monocular Images, IEICE Trans. Fund., Vol.E.82-A, No.10, pp.2274-2284
5. K. OHMURA et al., 1989. Pointing Operation Using Detection of Face Direction from a Single View. IEICE Trans. Inf.&Syst., Vol.J72-D-II, No.9, pp.1441-1447
6. P. Ballard et al., 1995. Controlling a Computer via Facial Aspect. IEEE Trans. on SMC, Vol.25, No.4, pp.669-677
7. A. Gee et al., 1996. Fast visual tracking by temporal consensus, Image and Vision Computing. Vol.14, pp.105-114
8. J. Heinzmann et al., 1998. 3D Facial Pose and Gaze Point Estimation using a Robust Real-Time Tracking Paradigm. Proceedings of ICAFGR, pp.142-147
9. T. Rikert, 1998. Gaze Estimation using Morphable Models. ICAFGR, pp.436-441
10. A.Ali-A-L et al., 1997, Man-machine Interface through Eyeball Direction of Gaze. Proc. of the Southeastern Symposium on System Theory, pp.478-82
11. J. Heinzmann et al., 1997. Robust Real-time Face Tracking and Gesture Recognition. Proc. of the IJCAI, Vol.2, pp.1525-1530
12. Matsumoto-Y, et al., 2000, An Algorithm for Real-time Stereo Vision Implementation of Head Pose and Gaze Direction Measurement. the ICAFGR. pp.499-504
13. Newman-R et al., 2000, Real-time Stereo Tracking for Head Pose and Gaze Estimation. Proceedings the 4th ICAFGR 2000. pp.122-8
14. Betke-M et al., 1999, Gaze Detection via Self-organizing Gray-scale Units. the Proc. of IWRATFG. pp.70-76
15. K. R. Park et al., 2000. Intelligent Process Control via Gaze Detection Technology. EAAI, Vol.13, No.5, pp.577-587
16. K. R. Park et al., 2002. Gaze Position Detection by Computing the 3 Dimensional Facial Positions and Motions. Pattern Recognition, Vol.35, No.11, pp.2559-2569
17. K. R. Park, 2002, Facial and Eye Gaze detection. LNCS, Vol.2525, pp.368-376
18. R. C. Gonzalez et al., 1995, Digital Image Processing, Addison-Wesley
19. Steven C. Chapra et al., 1989, Numerical Methods for Engineers, McGraw-Hill
20. S. Whittaker and B.O'Connail, 1997, The role of vision in face-to-face and mediated communication. In K.E.Finn, A.J.Sellen, and S.B. Wilbur (Eds.), Video-mediated Communication, Lawrence Erlbaum Associates, Mahwah, NJ
21. http://www.polhemus.com

# Hidden Markov Model Based 2D Shape Classification

Ninad Thakoor[1] and Jean Gao[2]

[1] Electrical Engineering, University of Texas at Arlington, TX-76013, USA
[2] Computer Science and Engineering, University of Texas at Arlington, TX-76013, USA

**Abstract.** In this paper, we propose a novel two step shape classification approach consisting of a description and a discrimination phase. In the description phase, curvature features are extracted from the shape and are utilized to build a Hidden Markov Model (HMM). The HMM provides a robust Maximum Likelihood (ML) description of the shape. In the discrimination phase, a weighted likelihood discriminant function is formulated, which weights the likelihoods of curvature at individual points of shape to minimize the classification error. The weighting scheme emulates feature selection procedure in which features important for classification are selected. A Generalized Probabilistic Descent (GPD) method based method for estimation of the weights is proposed. To demonstrate the accuracy of the proposed method, we present classification results achieved for fighter planes in terms of classification accuracy and discriminant functions.

## 1 Introduction

Object recognition is classic problem of computer vision. Among others, object recognition based on shape is widely used. First step towards the design of a shape classifier is feature extraction. Shapes can be represented by their contour or region [11]. Curvature, chain codes, Fourier descriptors, etc. are contour based descriptors while medial axis transform, Zernike moments, etc. are region based features. Contour based descriptors are widely used as they preserve the local information which is important in classification of complex shapes.

Feature extraction is followed by shape matching. In recent years, dynamic programming (DP) based shape matching is being increasingly applied [8], [1]. DP approaches are able to match the shapes part by part rather than point by point, and are robust to deformation and occlusion. HMMs are also being explored as one of the possible shape modeling and classification frameworks [2], [3], [5]. Apart from having all the properties of DP based matching, HMM also provides a probabilistic framework for training and classification. HMM based shape classification approaches in [2], [3], [5] presented classification results for very dissimilar shapes. However, in practical situations shapes to be classified are generally very similar. To handle such situation modifications to existing approaches is mandatory.

The HMM approaches mentioned above apply maximum likelihood (ML) as their classification criterion. Due to good generalization property of HMM, applying ML criterion to similar shapes does not provide good classification. Also, ML criterion is evaluated using information from only one class and does not take advantage of information from the other classes. Generally shapes can be discriminated using only parts

J. Blanc-Talon et al. (Eds.): ACIVS 2005, LNCS 3708, pp. 60–67, 2005.
© Springer-Verlag Berlin Heidelberg 2005

of the boundaries rather than comparing whole boundary. ML does not provide such mechanism.

To overcome these shortcomings, we propose a weighted likelihood discriminant for shape classification. The weighting scheme emulates comparison of parts of shape rather than the whole shape. The weights are estimated by applying GPD method. Unlike ML criterion, GPD uses information from all the classes to estimate the weights. As GPD method is designed to minimize the classification error, the proposed classifier gives good classification performance with similar shapes.

This paper is organized as follows: The shape description phase of the proposed method is discussed in Section 2, while Section 3 formulates discriminative training with GPD. Experimental results are presented in Section 4 and the paper ends with the conclusions and suggestions for further research in Section 5.

## 2    Shape Description with HMM

Before we delve into details of the HMM topology used for shape description, we introduce the terminology used.

1. $S$, set of states. $S = \{S_1, S_2, \ldots, S_N\}$, where $N$ is number of states. State of HMM at instance $t$ is denoted by $q_t$.
2. $A$, state transition probability distribution. $A = \{a_{ij}\}$, $a_{ij}$ denotes the probability of changing the state from $S_i$ to $S_j$.

$$a_{ij} = P[q_{t+1} = S_j | q_t = S_i], \qquad 1 \leq i, j \leq N. \tag{1}$$

3. $B$, observation symbol probability distribution. $B = \{b_j(o)\}$, $b_j(o)$ gives probability of observing the symbol $o$ in state $S_j$ at instance $t$.

$$b_j(o) = P[o \text{ at } t | q_t = S_j], \qquad 1 \leq j \leq N. \tag{2}$$

4. $\pi$, initial state distribution. $\pi = \{\pi_i\}$, $\pi_i$ gives probability of HMM being in state $S_i$ at instance $t = 1$.

$$\pi_i = P[q_1 = S_i], \qquad 1 \leq i \leq N. \tag{3}$$

If $C_j$ is $j^{th}$ shape class where $j = 1, 2, \ldots, M$ and $M$ is total number of classes then for convenience, HMM for $C_j$ can be compactly denoted as,

$$\lambda_j = (A, B, \pi). \tag{4}$$

An in depth description about HMM can be found in [9].

For the approach proposed in this paper, the description phase employs HMM topology proposed in [2]. The curvature of the shape is used as the descriptor. The shape is filtered with large variance Gaussian filter to reduce the effect of noise in curvature estimation. The filtered shape is normalized to a fixed length to simplify comparison and its major eigen-axis is aligned horizontally to achieve an invariant starting point. Let the aligned shape be indicated by $D = \{D_n\}$ and $D_n = (x_n, y_n)$ for $1 \leq n \leq T$, where $T$ is the normalized length of the shape, and $D_n$ indicates coordinates of $n^{\text{th}}$ point of the shape. Finally, approximate curvature at each point is calculated as the turn angle at that point. The turn angle $\theta_n$ is treated as observation $O_n$ for HMM. Each shape class is modeled by a $N$-state ergodic HMM and observation symbol probability distribution, i.e., $b_j$ of each state is modeled as one-dimensional Gaussian distribution. Gaussian Mixture Model (GMM) [10] for $N$ clusters estimated from unrolled values of curvature is used to initialize $B$. Baum-Welch algorithm is then applied to estimate the parameters of the HMM $\lambda_j^N = (A, B, \pi)$. Optimum $N$ for the HMM is selected using Bayesian Inference Criterion (BIC). In [2] BIC is applied to GMM to select optimal $N$, but this gives optimal $N$ for GMM and not for HMM. In proposed approach, BIC is applied to HMM to ensure proper model selection. For HMM topology discussed, BIC can be written as,

$$\text{BIC}(\lambda_j^N) = \log P(O|\lambda_j^N) - \frac{N^2 + 2N - 1}{2} \log(T). \tag{5}$$

$N$ is selected to maximize $\text{BIC}(\lambda_j^N)$.

ML training approach described in this section utilizes information from only one class to build the models. Though other approaches, like Maximum Mutual Information (MMI), Generalized Probabilistic Descent (GPD), which use information of all the classes, have been proposed for model training. However, classification performance of properly designed and ML trained HMM cannot be improved significantly with MMI or GPD training of HMM [7]. Therefore in our paper, we will stay with optimally designed HMM and make our contributions in designing robust discriminant functions with minimum error. Hence Section 3.

## 3   Discriminant Function Formulation and Training

In this section, we formulate a minimum error classifier with weighted likelihood discriminant function. The weights introduced in the discriminant function are trained with GPD method. A detailed review of GPD based methods is given in [6].

### 3.1   Discriminant Function Selection

Consider observation sequence to be classified, $O = O_1 O_2 ... O_T$. After modeling this sequence with $j^{\text{th}}$ class HMM $\lambda_j = (A, B, \pi)$ and solving optimal path problem, optimum path is given by $Q^* = q_1^* q_2^* ... q_T^*$. The probability of observation sequence $O$ given the state sequence $Q^*$ and model $\lambda_j$ is given by,

$$P(O|Q^*, \lambda_j) = b_{q_1^*}(O_1) \cdot b_{q_2^*}(O_2) \ldots b_{q_T^*}(O_T). \tag{6}$$

Probability of state sequence $Q^*$ is given by,

$$P(Q^*|\lambda_j) = \pi_{q_1^*} \cdot a_{q_1^* q_2^*} \ldots a_{q_{T-1}^* q_T^*}. \tag{7}$$

Then probability of the both occurring simultaneously is given by,

$$\begin{aligned} P(O, Q^*|\lambda_j) &= P(O|Q^*, \lambda_j) \cdot P(Q^*|\lambda_j) \\ &= \pi_{q_1^*} b_{q_1^*}(O_1) \, a_{q_1^* q_2^*} b_{q_2^*}(O_2) ... a_{q_{T-1}^* q_T^*} b_{q_T^*}(O_T). \end{aligned} \tag{8}$$

Let $\Upsilon$ be defined as,

$$\Upsilon_{t,j} = \begin{cases} \log\{\pi_{q_1^*}b_{q_1^*}(O_1)\}, & t=1; \\ \log\{a_{q_{t-1}^*q_t}b_{q_t^*}(O_t)\}, & 2 \le t \le T. \end{cases} \tag{9}$$

Therefore, (8) can be expressed as,

$$\log P(O, Q^* | \lambda_j) = \sum_{t=1}^{T} \Upsilon_{t,j}. \tag{10}$$

Equation (10) can be used as discriminant for classification of the observation sequence $O$. This function gives equal importance to every point of the shape in shape classifications. Hence, we introduce a new discriminant function which weights the curvature likelihood of shape points according to their importance in classification. The new discriminant function, $g_j$ is given by,

$$g_j = \sum_{t=1}^{T} w_j(t).\Upsilon_{t,j}, \tag{11}$$

where $w_j$ is weighting function for class $C_j$. $w_j$ provides additional discrimination among the classes. These weights will be tuned by applying GPD method to minimize the classification error.

### 3.2   Weighting Functions

Weighting function at individual observation can be estimated by applying GPD to current formulation. But due to the large number of parameters (equal to $T$), the convergence of GPD will be slower and will need large number of observation sequences for training. As mentioned in Section 1, to discriminate between similar shapes, comparison between parts of their contour is sufficient. As a result, shape can be weighted segment by segment instead of being weighted pointwisely. Following this intuitive idea, weighting functions are chosen to be windows which can adapt their position, spread and height. Any smooth window function can be selected. Our approach uses weighting function given in (12), which is sum of $S$ Gaussian shaped windows.

$$w_j(t) = \sum_{i=1}^{S} p_{i,j} \cdot e^{-\frac{(t-\mu_{i,j})^2}{s_{i,j}^2}}. \tag{12}$$

Parameter $p_{i,j}$ governs the height, $\mu_{i,j}$ controls the position, while $s_{i,j}$ determines spread of $i^{\text{th}}$ window of $j^{\text{th}}$ class. In this case, we have only $3S$ parameters to estimate. The discriminant function can now be written as,

$$g_j = \sum_{t=1}^{T}\sum_{i=1}^{S} p_{i,j} \cdot e^{-\frac{(t-\mu_{i,j})^2}{s_{i,j}^2}} \cdot \Upsilon_{t,j}. \tag{13}$$

In the next subsection GPD method is applied to above formulation.

### 3.3   GPD Algorithm

To complete the formulation of GPD, we introduce misclassification measure for observation sequence of $j^{\text{th}}$ class as,

$$d_j = -g_j + \frac{1}{\eta}\log\left(\frac{1}{M-1}\sum_{k,k\neq j}e^{\eta\cdot g_k}\right) \tag{14}$$

and corresponding cost function as,

$$l_j = \frac{1}{1+e^{-\xi\cdot d_j}} \tag{15}$$

where $\eta$ and $\xi$ are positive constants which control the smoothness of the above function. The probabilistic descent re-estimation rule for parameters $\Lambda$ is given as,

$$\Lambda_{n+1} = \Lambda_n - \varepsilon U\nabla l_j. \tag{16}$$

For the proposed method, $U$ is chosen to be identity matrix and learning factor, $\varepsilon$ is chosen to be a small number compared to the dynamic range of the parameter. The re-estimation rules in iteration $n$, for $i^{\text{th}}$ window parameters of $k^{\text{th}}$ class when $C_j$ is the correct class are given by,

$$p_{i,k}^{n+1} = p_{i,k}^n - \varepsilon_p\cdot\frac{\partial l_j}{\partial p_{i,k}}, \tag{17}$$

$$\mu_{i,k}^{n+1} = \mu_{i,k}^n - \varepsilon_\mu\cdot\frac{\partial l_j}{\partial \mu_{i,k}}, \tag{18}$$

$$s_{i,k}^{n+1} = s_{i,k}^n - \varepsilon_s\cdot\frac{\partial l_j}{\partial s_{i,k}}, \tag{19}$$

for $1\leq i\leq S$, $1\leq k\leq M$.

Partial derivatives appearing in (17)-(19) can be calculated as,

$$\frac{\partial l_j}{\partial p_{i,k}} = \frac{\partial l_j}{\partial d_j}\cdot\frac{\partial d_j}{\partial g_k}\cdot\sum_{t=1}^{T}e^{-\frac{(t-\mu_{i,k})^2}{s_{i,k}^2}}\Upsilon_{t,k}, \tag{20}$$

$$\frac{\partial l_j}{\partial \mu_{i,k}} = \frac{\partial l_j}{\partial d_j}\cdot\frac{\partial d_j}{\partial g_k}\cdot\sum_{t=1}^{T}\frac{2p_{i,k}(t-\mu_{i,k})e^{-\frac{(t-\mu_{i,k})^2}{s_{i,k}^2}}}{s_{i,k}^2}\Upsilon_{t,k}, \tag{21}$$

$$\frac{\partial l_j}{\partial s_{i,k}} = \frac{\partial l_j}{\partial d_j}\cdot\frac{\partial d_j}{\partial g_k}\cdot\sum_{t=1}^{T}\frac{2p_{i,k}(t-\mu_{i,k})^2 e^{-\frac{(t-\mu_{i,k})^2}{s_{i,k}^2}}}{s_{i,k}^3}\Upsilon_{t,k}, \tag{22}$$

where,

$$\frac{\partial l_j}{\partial d_j} = \frac{\xi e^{-\xi\cdot d_j}}{(1+e^{-\xi\cdot d_j})^2}, \tag{23}$$

$$\frac{\partial d_j}{\partial g_k} = \begin{cases} -1, & j = k; \\ \frac{e^{\eta \cdot g_j}}{\sum_{k' \neq k} e^{\eta \cdot g_{k'}}}, & j \neq k. \end{cases} \quad (24)$$

Note that in above formulation $\Upsilon_{t,k}$ is treated as constant the HMM parameters are not affected by the change in $\Lambda$. The classification results for the proposed scheme are given in Section 4.

## 4  Experimental Results

The proposed classification scheme was verified with fighter aeroplane shapes. These fighter aeroplanes include Mirage, Eurofighter, F-14, Harrier, F-22 and F-15. Since F-14 has two possible shapes, one when its wings closed and another when its wings opened, total number of shape classes are seven and each class includes 30 shape samples. Shape database was created by taking digital pictures of die-cast replica models of these aeroplanes. Pictures were captured at 640×480 resolution, and were segmented using Spedge and Medge [4] color image segmentation algorithm. Contours of the segmented planes were used for training and testing of the classifier. Figure 1 shows the extracted shapes for different classes.

Shapes were filtered with Gaussian filter (standard deviation = 10) and shape length was normalized to 512 points. The normalized shapes were split randomly into training and testing samples. For one of the training samples of each class, HMM was built as explained in Section 2. Optimum number of HMM states were selected by applying BIC to models with 3 to 10 states. Sum of 20 Gaussian windows was used for formulation and training of the discriminant function. The window parameters were initialized to spread the windows uniformly over the shape. The training vectors were used to train the classifier with $\xi = 1$ and $\eta = 10$. Once the training was complete, testing samples were used to determine the classification performance. For comparison, ML classification was carried out with optimal HMM after application of BIC.

Table 1 gives classification results for ML classification (HMM-ML) and GPD based weighted likelihood classification (HMM-WtL) which was trained using 15 sam-

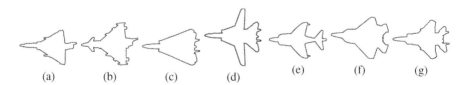

(a)          (b)          (c)          (d)          (e)          (f)          (g)

**Fig. 1.** Aeroplane shape classes: (a) Mirage, (b) Eurofighter, (c) F-14 wings closed, (d) F-14 wings opened, (e) Harrier, (f) F-22, (g) F-15

**Table 1.** Classification accuracy in %

| Class | Mirage | Eurofighter | F-14 Closed | F-14 Open | Harrier | F-22 | F-15 |
|---|---|---|---|---|---|---|---|
| HMM-ML | 79.42 | 78.14 | 79.28 | 52.57 | 78.28 | 68.71 | 62.57 |
| HMM-WtL | 99.33 | 98.66 | 98.66 | 99.33 | 100.00 | 100.00 | 100.00 |

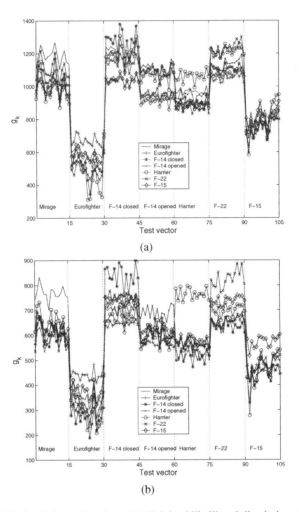

(a)

(b)

**Fig. 2.** (a) ML discriminant functions, (b) Weighted likelihood discriminant functions

ples per class. These results were averaged over 20 runs of the classifier design, each time with different combination of training samples.

Figure 2 shows the ML discriminant functions and weighted likelihood discriminant functions for the test vectors. The test vectors are grouped in sets of 15. Labels just above the x-axis indicate the correct class for the test vector and dotted lines separate the correct classes. For correct classification, discriminant function of correct class should be maximum. Difference between the discriminant function of correct class and the other classes is not clear in ML for all the classes. As a result, the classification accuracy is not satisfactory. For weighted likelihood discriminant, this difference is large and clearly separable. This large difference results into very high accuracy for the proposed classifier.

# 5    Conclusion and Future Work

In this paper, we proposed a weighted likelihood discriminant function for shape classification by the combination of GPD theory and HMM. A training algorithm based on GPD method to estimate the optimal weights with minimum classification error was formulated. The performance of the proposed shape classification scheme was tested on shapes of seven fighter planes. The classification accuracy is found to be 99.43% which is much higher than 71.3% of ML discriminant.

Though the shapes used for training and testing of the classifier exhibit some deformation (due to varying view points) and noise (due to automatic segmentation), a comprehensive analysis in presence of noise, occlusion and deformations needs to be evaluated by designing appropriate experiments. Currently, the number of weighting windows is selected manually and their parameters are initialized uniformly. A better initialization strategy like initializing them at curvature extremes can be employed.

# References

1. T. Adamek and N. E. O'Connor. A multiscale representation method for nonrigid shapes with a single closed contour. *IEEE Transactions on Circuits and Systems for Video Technology*, 14(5):742–753, May 2004.
2. M. Bicego and V. Murino. Investigating hidden markov models' capabilities in 2d shape classification. *IEEE Transactions on Pattern Recognition Machine Inteligence*, 26(2):281–286, Feb 2004.
3. J. Cai and Z.-Q. Liu. Hidden markov models with spectral features for 2d shape recognition. *IEEE Transactions on Pattern Analysis Machine Intelligence*, 23(12):1454–1458, Dec. 2001.
4. J. Gao, A. Kosaka, and A. Kak. Interactive color image segmentation editor driven by active contour model. *Proceedings of International Conference on Image Processing*, 3:245–249, Oct. 1999.
5. Y. He and A. Kundu. 2-d shape classification using hidden markov model. *IEEE Transactions on Pattern Analysis Machine Intelligence*, 13(11):1172–1184, Nov. 1991.
6. S. Katagiri, B.-H. Juang, and C.-H. Lee. Pattern recognition using a family of design algorithms based upon the generalized probabilistic descent method. *Proceedings of IEEE*, 86(11):2345–2373, Nov. 1998.
7. E. McDermott. *Handbook of Neural Networks for speech processing*, chapter 5, pages 159–216. Artech House, 2000.
8. E. G. M. Petrakis, A. Diplaros, and E. Milios. Matching and retrieval of distorted and occluded shapes using dynamic programming. *IEEE Transactions on Pattern Analysis and Machine Intelligence*, 24(11):1501–1516, Nov. 2002.
9. L. R. Rabiner. A tutorial on hidden markov models and selected application in speech recognition. *Proceedins of IEEE*, 77(2):257–286, Feb. 1989.
10. D. A. Reynolds and R. C. Rose. Robust text-independant speaker identification using gaussian mixture models. *IEEE Transactions on Speech and Audio Processing*, 3(1):72–83, Jan. 1995.
11. D. Zhang and G. Lu. Review of shape representation and description technique. *Pattern Recognition*, 37(1):1–19, Jan. 2004.

# A Fast Method to Detect and Recognize Scaled and Skewed Road Signs*

Yi-Sheng Liou[1], Der-Jyh Duh[1], Shu-Yuan Chen[1], and Jun-Wei Hsieh[2]

[1] Department of Computer Science and Engineering
{s889404, s909408}@mail.yzu.edu.tw, cschen@saturn.yzu.edu.tw
[2] Department of Electrical Engineering
shieh@saturn.yzu.edu.tw
Yuan Ze University, 135 Yuan-Tung Road, ChungLi, TaoYuan, Taiwan 320, R.O.C.

**Abstract.** A fast method to detect and recognize scaled and skewed road signs is proposed in this paper. The input color image is first quantized in HSV color model. Border tracing those regions with the same colors as road signs is adopted to find the regions of interest (ROI). Verification is then performed to find those ROIs satisfying specific constraints as road sign candidates. The candidate regions are extracted and normalization is automatically calculated to handle scaled and skewed road signs. Finally, matching based on distance maps is adopted to measure the similarity between the scene and model road signs to accomplish recognition. Experimental results show that the proposed method is effective and efficient, even for scaled and skewed road signs in complicated scenes. On the average, it takes 4–50 and 11 ms for detection and recognition, respectively. Thus, the proposed method is adapted to be implemented in real time.

## 1 Introduction

Road signs provide drivers useful information about roads. Proper usage of road signs can improve driving safety. Unfortunately, the objective of using road signs may not be accomplished if human drivers are careless or tired. To assist human in driving, automatic detection and recognition of road signs is an essential issue in driver support system.

The methods used for road sign detection can be divided into two groups according to gray level [1,2] or color images [3–14] are used. Because RGB color model is sensitive to lighting change. Other color models are used for color transformation, such as HSI [3,4,5,6], HSV [10,13,14], Color Formation Equations (CFE) [7], YUV [8] or combination of HSV and YUV [12]. Hue value is often used in pixel classifier to determine the color class of a pixel. The elementary shape features are extracted after color labeling has been executed. At this moment, the color labels can be used to detect the road signs by corner detection

* This work was partially supported by the National Science Council of Taiwan, R.O.C., under Grants NSC-92-2213-E-155-003.

J. Blanc-Talon et al. (Eds.): ACIVS 2005, LNCS 3708, pp. 68–75, 2005.
© Springer-Verlag Berlin Heidelberg 2005

[3], Hough transform [8], genetic algorithm [4,5], neural network [6,9], or color segmentation followed by geometrical analysis [7,10,11,13,14]. The region that are likely to contain a road sign are marked as candidates of road signs. The candidates are extracted and usually normalized to the same size as model images in the database before recognition. Normalized cross-correlation [5,8,2], template matching [7,9], neural network [1,3,4,13,14] and Laplace kernel classifier [10] can be used for road sign recognition.

The proposed method uses color and shapes for road sign detection and recognition. Rather than most existing methods incorporating models of various parameters into their database [1,3,7,10,2] to achieve rotation, scaling, and translation invariance, which causes computation burden of the system, our method proposes a color quantization method to identify color of road signs and geometric verification to detect road signs. Finally, skew normalization is adopted to handle scaled and skewed road signs and matching based on distance maps is performed for recognition. The proposed method is effective and efficient. In particular, it is simple and fast, thus can be easily implemented in real time.

The proposed method consists of two stages: detection and recognition. The outline of the proposed method is described briefly and shown in Fig. 1. Note that Steps 1 and 2 belong to the detection stage and Steps 3–5 belong to the recognition stage.

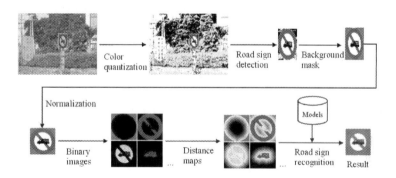

**Fig. 1.** Outline of proposed method for road sign detection and recognition

1. Color images captured by camera are used as input. HSV color model is adopted to quantize each pixel in the input image to one of eight labels (Red, Yellow, Green, Cyan, Blue, Magenta, Black, and White). The quantized image was then used for road sign detection and recognition.
2. Border tracing and ROI verification are used to detect road signs. The region inside the border that is found by border tracing is defined as a region of interest (ROI). The ROI satisfying the simple constraints on boundary rectangle and geometric constrains on road signs are designated as road sign candidates.

3. The bounding box enclosing the candidate region is extracted and its background is masked according to the border. The image is then normalized to $96 \times 96$ pixels using bilinear interpolation.
4. The normalized image was partitioned into eight binary images according to each quantized color. Distance map was then generated for each binary image.
5. Matching based on distance maps is used for road sign recognition. The scores are sorted and the road sign with highest score is classified as the recognition result.

This paper is organized as follows. Road sign detection is presented in Section 2. Road sign recognition is described in Section 3. Finally, the experimental results and conclusions are given in Sections 4 and 5, respectively.

## 2    Road Sign Detection

Road signs are designed using specific colors and shapes. Thus, color is a significant feature for road sign detection. Input color images are first quantized into eight colors in HSV color model as shown in Fig. 2.

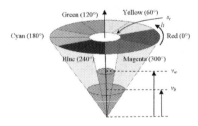

**Fig. 2.** Partition of HSV color space for color quantization

Where $v_b$, $v_w$, and $s_c$ are thresholds used in the color quantization. The quantization reduces the amount of image data. On the other hand, the quantization can simplify the processes of road sign detection and recognition by treating each of the eight color planes as a binary image.

Border tracing is used to find regions that have border color the same as road sign. A closed region with red border is found when the tracing is done. Regions smaller than $20 \times 20$ pixels are considered as noise and not processed further. Because the boundary rectangle of a road sign has a specific aspect ratio, a ROI that is not likely to be a road sign can be pruned by this simple constraint.

Further geometric constraints on road sign concerning that border pixels must be fitted to geometric equations representing road sign shapes. The details of geometric verification are described below.

1. The road sign shape represented by the geometric equation is called template. Template size is auto-adjusted by the boundary rectangle of ROI. Circular and triangle templates used in our study are shown in Fig. 3.
2. The problems that the distance and view angle between camera and scene road signs are varied can be solved by adjustable templates and rescale of ROIs.
3. The border pixels were rescaled by the aspect ratio of ROI to fit to the templates. The distance between the rescaled border pixels and the template are calculated.
4. Compute the number of border pixels consistent with template for which the distance is less than a threshold $e$. We set $e = \max(3, w/8, h/8)$, where $w$ and $h$ are width and height of ROI, respectively. The higher the ratio of fitted pixels is, the more possible the ROI is road sign candidate.
5. Color ratio in the center part of candidate are check to prune false alarm.

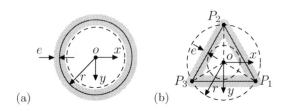

**Fig. 3.** Templates for geometric verification. (a) Circular template. (b) Triangular template.

In a summary, the geometric constraints are applied on the contour of border pixels. If more than 80% of rescaled border pixels fall in the gray area of templates in Fig. 3 and the color ratio of the ROI is sensible, the corresponding ROI is regarded as a candidate of road sign.

## 3    Road Sign Recognition

Matching based on distance maps is used for road sign recognition. The ROI of detected road sign found in the detection stage is pre-processed and normalized to be of the same size as model images in the database. The matching scores between the scene and model road signs are calculated and sorted. The model road sign with the highest score is designated as recognition result.

*Scene Image Pre-processing and Normalization.* The detected region in the quantized image contains the scene road sign and background. The background may interference consequent matching, thus, they are masked out by assigning Magenta to all the pixels outside the border (Fig. 4). In other words, Magenta means do not care in our system.

Since the distance and view angle between camera and scene road signs may be varied, road signs appearing in the image may have various scales and skews. To improve recognition accuracy, the boundary rectangle of the detected road sign are normalized to handle the scaled and skewed problems.

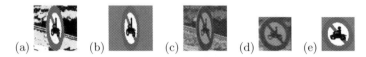

**Fig. 4.** Preprocessing and normalization. (a) Detected road sign (56 × 127 pixels), (b) detected road sign with background masked off, (c) extracted road signs, (d) normalized road sign (96 × 96 pixels), and (e) scene image for recognition.

*Matching Based on Distance Maps.* Both scene and model images are first partitioned into eight binary images according to each quantized label (Fig. 5). Median filter is then adopted to eliminate isolated noises in the binary images. Distance maps are then built for corresponding binary images. Similarity measure between the scene image and model images are calculated based on the distance maps. The values of similarity are sorted in the descending order, and the model with the maximum value of similarity is designated as the recognition result.

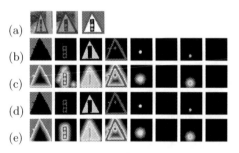

**Fig. 5.** Color planes and distance maps. (a) Original scene image, rescaled scene image and quantized scene image (b) original binary images, (c) inverse distance maps for original binary images, (d) median filtered binary images, and (e) inverse distance maps for median filtered binary images.

## 4     Experimental Results

The proposed method has been implemented on a PC equipped with AMD AthlonXP 2200+ CPU, 512 MB of main memory, running Windows XP operating system. The program was developed using Visual C++ language. Input color images were captured by Sony DSC-P1 digital camera on urban and country roads. The image is of JPEG file format with size 640 × 480.

To evaluate the performance of the proposed method, 134 images were taken as test images, in which there are 154 road signs. In particular, some scaled and skewed road signs were taken as shown in Fig. 6 to show that our method is insensitive to the variation in scale and skew.

**Fig. 6.** Road sign in the variations of scale and skew. Detected road signs are marked by rectangles.

Our method can detect road signs that are smaller that $20 \times 20$ pixels up to full image size in 4–50 ms. 145 road signs (94%) are correctly detected, nine road signs (6%) are missing and one false alarm. The 145 correctly detected road signs are shown in Fig. 7.

The 145 detected road signs are used to evaluate the performance of the proposed road sign recognition. The model database used for road sign recognition is shown in Fig. 8. The recognition accuracy of our method is 73.1%. On

**Fig. 7.** 145 correctly detected road signs

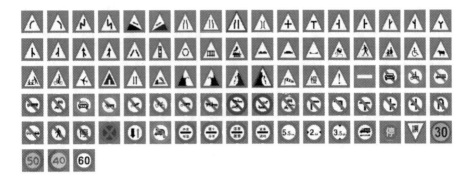

**Fig. 8.** Model database (88 images of size 96 × 96 pixels)

the average, our method can recognize a road sign in 11 ms, thus the proposed method is fast.

Moreover, to show both the color information and the skew correction are essential to the recognition accuracy. Three other versions of recognition methods were implemented for comparison. The first one is applied to gray level image and uses traditional cross-correlation [2] as matching function. This version is denoted as cross-correlation method. The other two are our method and the cross-correlation method without performing the skew normalization as described in Section 3. Examples of input images to our method and the cross-correlation method with and without performing normalization are shown in Fig. 9. The accuracy rates of our method and the other three versions are listed in Table 1. Note that our method has higher rate (73.1%) than the cross-correlation method does (68.3%). Thus, our method outperforms. On the other hand, no matters for color or gray versions, those methods without performing normalization have lower recognition rates. Thus, the skew normalization is necessary.

**Fig. 9.** Four version of images used for road sign recognition. (a) Normalized color image, (b) normalized gray image, (c) non-normalized color image, and (d) non-normalized gray image.

**Table 1.** Comparison of different versions of road sign recognition methods

| Method | Correct recognition |
|---|---|
| Our method | 106/145 (73.1%) |
| Cross-correlation | 99/145 (68.3%) |
| Our method without normalization | 82/145 (56.6%) |
| Cross-correlation without normalization | 70/145 (48.3%) |

# 5   Conclusions

In this paper, we propose an effective and efficient method for road sign detection and recognition even for skewed and scaled road signs in complicated scene. Color quantization is first employed to simplify the process of road sign detection and recognition. Verification on simple and geometric constraints and matching based on distance maps are performed to detect and recognize road signs, respectively. More important, normalization is adopted to handle scaled and skewed road signs. From the experimental results, we can find that the proposed method has high recognition accuracy and fast execution rate. For complicated scene, the recognition accuracy is 73.1% and on the average it takes 4–50 and 11 ms for detection and recognition, respectively.

# References

1. Douville, P.: Real-time classification of traffic signs. Real-Time Imaging **6** (2000) 185–193
2. Piccioli, G., Micheli, E.D., Parodi, P., Campani, M.: Robust method for road sign detection and recognition. Image and Vision Computing **14** (1996) 209–223
3. de la Escalera, A., Moreno, L.E., Salichs, M.A., Armingol, J.M.: Road traffic sign detection and classification. IEEE Trans. Ind. Electronics **44** (1997) 848–859
4. de la Escalera, A., Armingol, J.M., Mata, M.: Traffic sign recognition and analysis for intelligent vehicles. Image and Vision Computing **21** (2003) 247–258
5. de la Escalera, A., Armingol, J.M., Pastor, J.M., Rodríguez, F.J.: Visual sign information extraction and identification by deformable models for intelligent vehicles. IEEE Trans. Intelligent Transportation Systems **5** (2004) 57–68
6. Fang, C.Y., Chen, S.W., Fuh, C.S.: Road-sign detection and tracking. IEEE Trans. Vehicular Technology **52** (2003) 1329–1341
7. Lauzière, Y.B., Gingras, D., Ferrie, F.P.: A model-based road sign identification system. In: IEEE Conf. Computer Vision and Pattern Recognition. (2001) 1163–1170
8. Miura, J., Kanda, T., Shirai, Y.: An active vision system for real-time traffic sign recognition. In: IEEE Conf. Intelligent Transportation Systems. (2000) 52–57
9. Ohara, H., Nishikawa, I., Miki, S., Yabuki, N.: Detection and recognition of road signs using simple layered neural networks. In: IEEE Int. Conf. Neural Information Processing. (2002) 626–630
10. Paclík, P., Novovičová, J., Pudil, P., Somol, P.: Road sign classification using Laplace kernel classifier. Pattern Recognition Letter **21** (2000) 1165–1173
11. Ritter, W., Stein, F., Janssen, R.: Traffic sign recognition using colour information. Mathematical and Computer Modeling **22** (1995) 149–161
12. Shadeed, W.G., Abu-Al-Nadi, D.I., Mismar, M.J.: Road traffic sign detection in color images. In: IEEE Int. Conf. Electronics, Circuits and Systems. (2003) 890–893
13. Vitabile, S., Pollaccia, G., Pilato, G., Sorbello, F.: Road signs recognition using a dynamic pixel aggregation technique in the HSV color space. In: IEEE Int. Conf. Image Analysis and Processing. (2001) 572–577
14. Vitabile, S., Gentile, A., Sorbello, F.: A neural network based automatic road signs recognizer. In: IEEE Int. Conf. Neural Networks. (2002) 2315–2320

# Road Markings Detection and Tracking Using Hough Transform and Kalman Filter

Vincent Voisin[1,2], Manuel Avila[1], Bruno Emile[1], Stephane Begot[1],
and Jean-Christophe Bardet[1]

[1] Laboratoire Vision et Robotique,
IUT de l'Indre, 36000 Châteauroux, France
[2] Vectra Road Engineering, 78320 La Verrière, France
vincent.voisin@vectra.fr

**Abstract.** A lane marking tracking method using Hough Transform and
Kalman Filtering is presented. Since the HT is a global feature extraction algorithm, it leads to a robust detection relative to noise or partial
occlusion. The Kalman filter is used to track the roadsides which are
detected in the image by this HT. The Kalman prediction step leads to
predict the road marking parameters in the next frame, so we can apply
the detection algorithm in smaller regions of interest, the computional
cost is being consequently reduced.

## 1  Introduction

Many lane detection systems were developed in the past. Those systems can
mainly be classified into two main domains. The first ones are using 2D image
models for modelling road edge [1,5,7]. The second approach takes into account
the vehicle motion on the road and use 3D road models, those approaches lead to
a search space reduction of features [2,3]. Our approach comes from the second
category. Most of the lane detection systems aims at improve security and/or
control at the vehicle. The application field of our method is the road engineering
and management: we want to localize the lane markings. Nowadays the road
width measurement is done by a human operator, it is quite a slow and dangerous
task. Our algorithm leads to automatic measurement of the width installed in
our road survey vehicule. Then we approach the lane detection problem from
another point of view. We see that task in a more metrological way, we want
to measure locally the width and the orientation of the lane with accuracy. To
reach this goal, a wide angle camera is used with an important tilt angle. In
such configuration, we assume that lane markings are straight lines. So we use
a simple rectilinear model for the lane marking. It makes the detection easier
because of the small number of degrees of freedom, the risk of divergence is then
more efficiently controlled. The paper is organized as follows: in the section 2, we
describe the models that are used and the relationship between 3D road model
and image model, secondly we describe the different steps in the whole process
in section 3. Finally we present some results.

J. Blanc-Talon et al. (Eds.): ACIVS 2005, LNCS 3708, pp. 76–83, 2005.
© Springer-Verlag Berlin Heidelberg 2005

# 2   Models Description

Before describing in detail the algorithm, it is necessary to formalize the models that are used. First we describe roadsides are modeled in reference frame link to the vehicle in 2.1. Secondly we give the roadsides model in the image in 2.3 and then we give the geometrical relationship between the road markings reference frame and the image.

## 2.1   The Reference Frame

Some classical assumptions are used: the road is considered as flat, the optical axis is colinear to the direction of movement.

**Fig. 1.** The Reference Frame and a resulting image

The roadside parameters, that we will estimate, are expressed in the reference frame $R_v$ linked to the vehicle and described in figures 1 and 2. The origin, the $x_v$ and the $y_v$ axes are the vertical projection on the road of the optical center, the optical axis $y_c$ and the $x_c$ axis of the camera reference system, the $z_v$ axis is normal to the road. We can see in figure 1 a resulting image, the maximum viewing distance is about 10 meters.

## 2.2   Road Markings Model

Roadsides are modeled by lines, they are parameterized by four parameters : $d_l$ and $d_r$ the distances from respectively the left roadside and from the right one to the center of the reference frame $R_v$, and $\psi_l$ and $\psi_r$ the angles made by the roadsides and the $y_v$ axis (see figure 2). $(d_l, \psi_l, d_r, \psi_r)^T$ is the state vector $X$ that will be estimated.

## 2.3   Road Markings Image Model

The lines extraction is made by a Hough Transform [4] applied on binarized gradient image, during that step the lines in the image are expressed in polar coordinates:

$$\rho = u \sin \theta + v \cos \theta \tag{1}$$

Where $\rho$ is the perpendicular distance from the origin to the line and $\theta$ is the angle between the line and the $u$ axis (see figure 3).

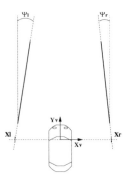

**Fig. 2.** The 3D Roadsides Model

### 2.4   Relationship Between Image and Road Markings Model

We have the following relationship, which is derived from the well-known pinhole camera model [6]:

$$\begin{cases} x = (\frac{u-cu}{f})(y\cos\theta_c + H\sin\theta_c) \\ y = \quad H\frac{f\cos\theta_c - (v-cv)\sin\theta_c}{(v-cv)\cos\theta_c + f\sin\theta_c} \end{cases} \qquad (2)$$

Where $(x, y)$ represent the coordinates in the $R_v$ reference system, $(u, v)$ are the pixel coordinates, $H$ is the height of the camera, $cu$ and $cv$ the image center coordinates, $f$ the focal length in pixels, and $\theta_c$ the camera tilt angle (see figure 1).

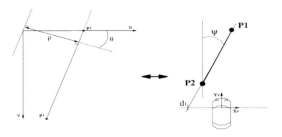

**Fig. 3.** Image to 3D reference frame transformation

When a line is detected in the image, relations (2) and (3) are used to compute the roadsides model parameters $d$ and $\psi$:

$$\begin{cases} d = x_1 - \frac{x_2-x_1}{y_2-y_1}x_1 \\ \psi = \arctan\frac{x_2-x_1}{y_2-y_1} \end{cases} \qquad (3)$$

Where $p1$, $p2$ are two points belonging to the detected line in the image and $P1 = (x_1, y_1, 0)^T$, $P2 = (x_2, y_2, 0)^T$ their projections in the roadsides reference frame (see figure 3). So for each line in the image defined by $\rho$ and $\theta$, the corresponding 3D parameters $d$ and $\psi$ can be computed.

## 2.5   ROIs Creation

The roadsides extraction is made in two Regions Of Interest (ROI), one for each side. That ROIs are computed from the predict state vector $X(k + 1|k)$ and his covariance matrix $P(k + 1|k)$ provided by the Kalman filter prediction step described in 3.2. We consider one roadside prediction for example $(d_l(k + 1|k)), \psi_l(k + 1|k))$ noted $(d_l, \psi_l)$ and the standard deviation $\sigma_{d_l}$ and $\sigma_{\psi_l}$ on that two parameters extracted from the predicted covariance matrix $P(k + 1|k)$. For that roadside, we define a region in $Rv$, delimited (see figure 4) by two lines parametrized by two couples (4), where $\alpha$ and $\beta$ are used to tune the ROIs sizes:

$$\begin{cases} (d_l + \alpha\sigma_{d_l}, \psi_l + \beta\sigma_{\psi_l}) \\ (d_l - \alpha\sigma_{d_l}, \psi_l - \beta\sigma_{\psi_l}) \end{cases} \tag{4}$$

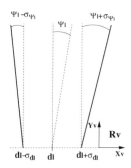

**Fig. 4.** ROI definition

The back projection of this region, by using the inverse computation of section 2.4, corresponds to an area in the Hough Space. The whole couple $(\rho, \theta)$ in this area corresponds to a ROI in the image. The roadside extraction process (see section 3.1) is computed in this ROI.

# 3   A Combined Kalman Filter and Hough Transform

## 3.1   Road Markings Extraction in ROI

The lane marking extraction is computed in the two ROIs one for each lane marking. We present the method for one ROIs, the process is the same for the other one.

**Edge Points Extraction.** Due to the small distance of view, the road edges are mainly vertical. So a horizontal gradient is sufficient for the extraction of road marking edges. Then we convolve ROIs with a 3*3 horizontal sobel filter.

**Lines Detection Using Hough Transform.** The Hough Transform (HT) is a very powerful global pattern detection method. The standard HT detects patterns that forms straight lines, but it can be generalized to a large number of patterns ( curves , circles, ...). The idea is that the HT changes the feature extraction problem to an easier peak detection problem.

Each line in an image can be parametrized in polar coordinate ( see relation 1 and figure 3 ). The whole couple of $(\rho, \theta)$ is named Hough Space or Parameters Space. The HT algorithm can be seen as a voting process, each non null point in the thresholded gradient image belonging to a line votes for all possible patterns that pass through that point. Votes are collected in a $[\rho, \theta]$ accumulator array, the maximum of this array corresponds to the most salient line. The interest of the HT is due to the fact that it is a global feature extractor which is very robust to noise or discontinuities. Then that operator appears to be ideal for localizing road markings that are intermittent or partially occluded. A HT is applied independently in each ROI, the way to compute this ROI is described in 2.5. Once the roadsides are detected in the image, we compute the 3D parameters with the process described in section 2.4.

## 3.2 Parameters Estimation with an Extented Kalman Filter (EKF)

Using an EKF allows to estimate recursively the road parameters and the corresponding covariance matrix by taking into account the vehicle motion. The whole algorithm is detailed in figure 6.

**Road Parameters Evolution Model.** The parameters for the next image can be easily estimated by a Kalman filter using vehicle motion. The parameters evolution is given by the following relation:

$$X(k+1|k) = f(X(k|k), U(k)) \tag{5}$$

$$\begin{cases} d_l(k+1|k) = d_l(k|k) + \delta_s \tan \psi_l(k|k) \\ \psi_l(k+1|k) = \psi_l(k|k) \\ d_r(k+1|k) = d_r(k|k) + \delta_s \tan \psi_r(k|k) \\ \psi_r(k+1|k) = \psi_r(k|k) \end{cases} \tag{6}$$

where $X(k+1|k)$ is the state vector prediction for the $k+1$ image, $X(k|k)$ is the current state and $\delta_s$ is the travelled distance. In fact this relation models a simple translation of the vehicle along the $y_v$ axis (see figure 5).

The state prediction is associated to the covariance prediction corresponding to this state:

$$P(k+1|k) = J_{X(k)} P(k/k) J_{X(k)}^T + Q \tag{7}$$

Where $P(k+1|k)$ is the predict covariance matrix, $P(k|k)$ is the current covariance matrix, $Q$ is the process noise covariance matrix, and $J_{X(k)}$ is the jacobian of $f$ (see (5)).

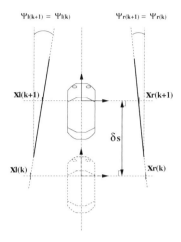

**Fig. 5.** Roadsides parameters evolution

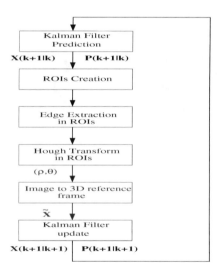

**Fig. 6.** Algorithm description

**ROIs Updating.** Thanks to the prediction of the state vector and his co-variance matrix we have an apriori knowledge of the roadside location. So the roadside extraction process describe in section 3.1 is done in two ROIs defined by $X(k+1|k)$ and $P(k+1|k)$, the ROIs processing is described in section 2.5. So the Kalman filter prediction step leads to reduction of the computational cost of the roadside extraction in the images. Then road markings are extracted in the ROIs and a road parameter measurement $\tilde{X} = (\tilde{d}_l, \tilde{\psi}_l, \tilde{d}_r, \tilde{\psi}_r)^T$ is computed.

**Kalman Filter Updating.** This measurement is used for updating the Kalman filter. This phase consists in calculating a new vector $X(k+1|k+1)$ and a new covariance matrix $P(k+1|k+1)$ deduced from the measurement $\tilde{X}$ and the previous state $X(k+1|k)$ and $P(k+1|k)$:

$$\begin{cases} X(k+1|k+1) = X(k+1|k) + K(k+1)(\tilde{X} - CX(k+1|k)) \\ P(k+1|k+1) = (I_4 - K(k+1)C)P(k+1|k) \end{cases} \tag{8}$$

– $K(k+1)$ is the Kalman gain. It is defined as follows:

$$K(k+1) = P(k+1|k)C^T[CP(k+1|k)C^T + Q]^{-1} \tag{9}$$

– $C$ is the measurement matrix:

$$\tilde{X} = CX = I_4 X \tag{10}$$

## 4   Results

We have applied our algorithm to a 1900 image sequence. Figure 7 shows typical images with surimposed detected lines.

**Fig. 7.** Results

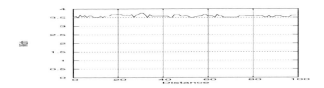

**Fig. 8.** Estimated width on a 100 meters road with a constant width

We have also tested our algorithm on a 100 meters road with a nearly constant width (3.6m)(see figure 8). The lane width was computed using results of the algorithm. We obtain a coarse standard deviation on algorithm width measurement $\sigma = 0.2m$ (5% of the measure).

The main drawback is a wrong detection problem. The very simple low level feature extraction (horizontal sobel filter) leads to the detection of:

– edges that don't belong to a road marking,
– dash road marking instead of continuous marking when the centerline is composed by a continous and a dash marking.

# 5    Conclusion and Future Works

We described in this paper an algorithm which succeeds in locating roadsides using an onboard camera. It has the ability to estimate the roadside location and the orientation with respect to the camera. Those information are very useful for road engineering applications. Future work will be mainly focused on:

- a more reliable low level feature extraction to get rid of wrong detections,
- using proprioceptive information (gyrometer) in the Kalman evolution model,
- coupling algorithm with a GPS receiver to locate the road markings in a global reference frame.

# References

1. M. Bertozzi and A. Broggi, "Gold: a parrallel real-time stereo vision system for generic obstacle and lane detection," *IEEE Transactions on Image Processing*, pp. 62-81, January 1998.
2. R. Chapuis, J. Laneurit, R. Aufrère, F. Chausse, T. Chateau, "Accurate Vision Based Road Tracker," *Intelligent Vehicules Symposium* , Versailles, Juin 2002.
3. E. D. Dickmanns, R. Behringer, C.Brudigam, F.Thomanek and V. von Holt, "An all-transputer visual Autobahn-autopilot/copilot," *International Conference on Computer Vision*, pp.608-615, Berlin, May 1993.
4. R. O. Duda and P. E. Hart, "Use of the Hough transformation to detect lines and curves in pictures," *Communications of the ACM*, Vol. 15, pp. 11-15, January 1972.
5. D. A. Pomerleau, "RALPH: Rapidly adapting lateral poistion handler," *IEEE Symposium on Intelligent Vehicles*, Detroit, Michigan (USA), September 25-26 1995.
6. E. Trucco and A. Verri, "Introductory techniques for 3-d computer vision," *Prentice Hall*,1998.
7. Y. Wang, D. Schen and E. K. Teoh, " Lane detection using Catmull-rom spline," *Intelligent Vehicules Symposium*, Vol. 1, pp. 51-57, Stuttgart, October 28-30 1998.

# Selective Color Edge Detector Based on a Neural Classifier

Horacio M. González Velasco, Carlos J. García Orellana,
Miguel Macías Macías, and Ramón Gallardo Caballero

Department of Electronics and Electromechanical Engineering,
University of Extremadura, Av. de la Universidad, s/n. 10071 Cáceres - Spain
horacio@nernet.unex.es

**Abstract.** Conventional edge detectors are not very useful for generating an edge map to be used in the search of a concrete object with deformable models or genetic algorithms. In this work, a selective color edge detector is presented, which is able to obtain the edges in the image and determine whether or not those edges are originated in a concrete object. The system is based on a multilayer perceptron neural network, which classifies the edges previously detected by the multidimensional gradient (color images), and is trained using some images of the searched object whose edges are known. The method has been successfully applied to bovine livestock images, obtaining edge maps to be used for a boundary extraction with genetic algorithms technique.

## 1 Introduction

Edge detection in both grayscale and color images is a well-known operation in digital image analysis. Edges define the limits of the objects, so they can be used to interpret the scene. However, when outdoors-taken images are considered, there are usually many *secondary objects* and textures in the background, thus generating many edges in the image. This is an important drawback when you are trying to detect a concrete object in the foreground of the image, considering its boundary. Particularly, when you are using boundary extraction techniques based on genetic algorithms search [1,2,3] and deformable models [4,5], the process is driven by a *potential image*, obtained by an edge detection, and it is very important for the performance of those boundary extractors that the edge maps do not contain many more edges than those corresponding to the searched object.

In this work, a selective color edge detector is defined, similar to that described in [6] for grayscale images. This system is based on a multilayer perceptron neural network, that determines whether or not an given edge of an edge map obtained from the color image using a conventional method (in our case the multidimensional gradient defined by Cumani [7]) is originated in the searched object. Such a classification is carried out considering some parameters that describe two rectangular windows at both sides of the edge pixel, in

---

J. Blanc-Talon et al. (Eds.): ACIVS 2005, LNCS 3708, pp. 84–91, 2005.
© Springer-Verlag Berlin Heidelberg 2005

the direction of the gradient (see fig. 2). Particularly, simple statistical parameters (mean and variance) and PCA parameters has been used to describe the windows, comparing the results obtained with both systems.

The method has been used as a part of a boundary detection system for cattle images, in which genetic algorithms and deformable models search is applied [8]. The final aim of this boundary detection is to extract the contour of the animal in the picture, to be used later as the base of a morphological assessment system.

In the following section the proposed selective edge detector is described. Later, in sections 3 and 4, the input parameters for the classifier and the training of the neural network are considered. Finally, in section 5, results from our concrete application of the method are presented, while in section 6 there is a brief discussion about the method and its possible improvements.

## 2   Selective Edge Detector

As described in the introduction, our selective edge detector for color images is based on a multidimensional gradient calculation and a neural network classifier. Although several previous papers can be found regarding the use of neural networks techniques applied to edge detection (e.g. [9]), they in general focus on the enhancement step, trying to obtain a good detector in a classical sense (absence of false positives and false negatives, and precision in the location of the edge pixels). However, it is not our interest to detect edges by means of the neural network, but to *select* those that serve for the subsequent processing step, once detected.

In fig. 1 an outline of the system is represented, whose operation can be described in four steps:

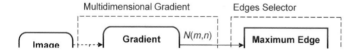

**Fig. 1.** Outline of the selective edge detector proposed. The image and the directions map of the multidimensional gradient appear as inputs to the NN classifier because they are needed to define the windows and calculate the parameters.

1. **Calculation of the *multidimensional gradient*:** In this step we include the two first stages of a conventional edge detector: smoothing and enhancement [10]. As we are dealing with color images, the multidimensional gradient defined by Cumani [7] has been used, considering the CIELAB color space. As a result we obtain the module of the gradient, that must be followed by a nonmaximum suppressor, with which best–located one–pixel–width edges are obtained. Besides, we obtain the directions (of the gradient) map, which is used later.

2. **Extraction of a *maximum edge map*:** Since there could be, a priori, weak and strong edges in the contour we wish to extract, we are interested in classifying all those pixels that are detected as edge, whatever their strength. Thus, the pixels to be classified will be determined by thresholding the nonmaximum suppressor output image $N(m, n)$, using for the threshold a low value. This is called *maximum edge map* $E(m, n)$. In our application, we used a threshold low enough to permit at least 95% of the pixels of $N(m, n)$ without zero value to be considered as edges, rejecting the 5 % of weaker detected ones, which likely correspond to noise introduced in the image capture process. An example is shown in fig. 3(b).

3. **NN processing:** Once the edge pixels to be classified are determined, a set of $P$ parameters (see section 3) is calculated for each one, related to its position and the color profile around it in the original image. Those parameters are used as inputs for a multilayer perceptron, with one hidden layer and two neurons at the output, which provides the membership to each class: $y_c(m, n)$ for correct edges and $y_e(m, n)$ for erroneous ones. The grey-level image $N'(m, n)$ has then a value proportional to $y_c(m, n) - y_e(m, n)$ for those pixels detected as edges, and 0 for the rest. Therefore, pixels with larger values correspond with correct edges, and vice versa, so by the thresholding process, the "more correct" edges will be obtained. To carry out the training of the selector, $K$ images $I_k(m, n)$ with $k \in \{1, \cdots, K\}$ (where $I_k(m, n) \in [0, 1]$) are used, for which their corresponding reference edge maps $R_k(m, n)$ are available. In those maps only the edges corresponding to the object can be found ($R_k(m, n) = 1$ for edge pixels, and 0 otherwise)

4. **Final thresholding:** This stage, placed outside the selector (see fig. 1), is responsible for pointing out as edges those pixels of $N'(m, n)$ with larger intensity (correct edges). For the threshold, a value such that the number of edge pixels in $M(m, n)$ is similar to the average number of edges in the reference images $R_k(m, n)$ is proposed.

Regarding this process, two aspects of the neural network classifier require further explanation: parameters used as input and the training process.

## 3   Input Parameters for the Classifier

In our previous paper [6] we applied a selector with a similar structure to grey-scale images, differing in the first step (we did not need a multidimensional

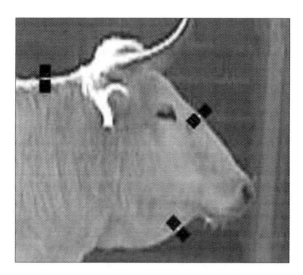

**Fig. 2.** In this figure, examples of edge pixels (white) and the windows of $7 \times 7$ size in the direction orthogonal to the edge (black) are presented. Observe that one of the windows is always located within the object and has a uniform color.

gradient) and in the parameters used to characterize the edges. The system worked quite well, so we thought that including color information would improve significantly the performance.

Imagine that the searched object has a uniform color. Then, a good method to identify whether or not an edge belongs to the object consist of analyzing the color profile in the direction orthogonal to the edge, where two regions with different colors must be observed: on one side the area corresponding to the object, and on the other, the area corresponding to background. For that reason, we propose to define two rectangular windows in the direction orthogonal to the edge, located on each side of it (fig. 2), and characterize those windows with a set of parameters. In this work two sets of parameters has been considered:

1. *Simple statistical parameters: mean and variance.* As we are processing color images, we calculate mean and variance for each color component, so we have a total of 12 parameters (3 components $\times$ 2 windows $\times$ 2 parameters) to describe an edge pixel. This parameters were used with relative success for grayscale images in [6].

2. *PCA calculated parameters.* In order to obtain the most significative parameters which describe the windows in a concrete problem, we propose to use a technique based on PCA. Considering a set of $K$ images representative of our problem (*PCA training set*, which can be the same set of images used for the training of the selector), we can divide the process in several steps:

   (a) First, we have to obtain a great number of windows, corresponding to the pixels detected as edges in the maximum edge maps of the training images. There are many of those pixels in each image (see fig. 3(b)), so the pixels to be considered must be selected. That selection can be made randomly, but most of the edge pixels will be detected for the background and not for the object we are trying to find. In order to have a representative number of windows originated in edge pixels of the object, we propose to guarantee that a given percentage of the windows are obtained from those pixels.

(b) The calculated windows can be converted in vectors by placing consecutively the rows for $L$, $a$ and $b$ components of the color space. With those vectors, the PCA can be calculated.

(c) In the new generated basis, we retain only the $Q$ most significative vectors. Therefore, we keep the matrix with the first $Q$ eigenvectors because they are needed later to calculate the first components of a given vector in the new basis.

(d) With that information, we can calculate the first $Q$ components in that basis for any window obtained from an edge pixel in any image (not necessarily in the training set). Therefore, we are describing each edge pixel with $2Q$ parameters (notice that we have 2 windows per edge pixel).

Furthermore, in those applications where the object of interest has a well–defined shape and a position that varies within certain limits, it is advantageous to use also as parameters the position of the pixel and the direction orthogonal to the edge, since finding edges of the object around certain positions and with a concrete direction should be expected.

## 4   Training of the NN

To train the neural network, prototypes for each of the two proposed clases are needed. Considering that we are classifying those pixels detected as edges, the prototypes extraction process for each training image will consist of three steps. First, for the image $I_k(m, n)$ a maximum edge map is obtained. Later, the set $P_{C,k}$ is defined which contains the $k$-th image pixels detected as edges that belong to the considered object (prototypes for the class of correct edges), and the set $P_{E,k}$ which contains the pixels detected as edges that do not belong to the object (prototypes for the class of erroneous edges). Finally, for each pixel of both sets, the parameters are calculated, to be used in the training of the network.

Once obtained the prototypes from all the $K$ images, the whole set of prototypes is split into three subsets: training, validation and test, and the process starts training one perceptron with very few neurons in the hidden layer. The training is carried out using the training subset and the RPROP algorithm described in [11], and stops when the number of misclassifications obtained over the validation set goes through a minimum. Later, we repeat this process by increasing the network size and we choose the new configuration as optimal if the number of misclassifications over the validation set is lower than the previous one.

# 5   Experiments and Results

The proposed selective edge detector was tested using outdoors-taken color images of bovine livestock in lateral position. All the animals were of the same breed, which has a uniform white color, and our aim was to obtain only the edges of the animal in the picture. From our whole database of images, $K = 45$ were selected and their references (positions of the edges of the animal) were generated by hand. Those 45 images were used to obtain examples for the PCA calculation, and also were used in the training process of the neural network, with both sets of parameters: simple statistical and PCA generated.

In order to calculate the parameters, we decided to work with windows of $7 \times 7$ pixels size (in $640 \times 480$ images). To obtain the PCA, 10.000 edge pixels were selected randomly from the maximum edge maps of the 45 images, guaranteeing that at least a 20 % of them were generated in the animal boundary. Therefore, we considered 20.000 vectors of 147 elements ($7 \times 7 = 49$ values $\times$ 3 color components). After the calculations, we retained the first $Q = 10$ eigenvectors of the covariance matrix to represent the data, thus considering a total of 23 parameters as inputs to the neural network (including the three parameters corresponding to the position of the pixel and the direction of the gradient). In the case of the mean and the variance, the number of total parameters was 15.

Regarding the training of the network (for both types of parameters), the 45 images were divided into three subsets: the prototypes obtained from 27 were used for training, those from 9 for validation and those from the other 9 for test. From all the generated prototypes, the training of the network was carried out using 60.000 from the training subset and 20.000 from the validation, uniformly distributed between classes. Later, the performance of the trained network was verified with 20.000 prototypes corresponding to the test subset, that were not involved in the training process.

Using this sets, networks were trained with a number of neurons in the hidden layer between 25 and 70, obtaining the best results with 50 neurons for the simple statistical parameters, and 65 for the PCA-generated parameters. In each configuration, more than 90 % of success rates where obtained for the class *correct edges*, considering the test subset. Also, more than 80 % was obtained for the class *erroneous edges*.

Once the NN was trained, the selective edge detector was applied to the 9 images of the test subset, with three different configurations: without edges selector, with the selector using simple statistical parameters, and with the selector using PCA parameters. In order to compare the effectiveness of those configurations, the figure of merit proposed in [6] was used. The first remarkable result is that, in all the cases (with edges selector), the percentage of improvement regarding the edge detector without selector is larger than 100 %, quite better improvements than those obtained with grayscale images [6]. Also, results for the PCA parameters are slightly better than those for simple statistical parameters (more than 10 % in some cases).

Regarding the computational cost, this method obviously demands more resources than conventional edge detectors. However, considering that the NN are

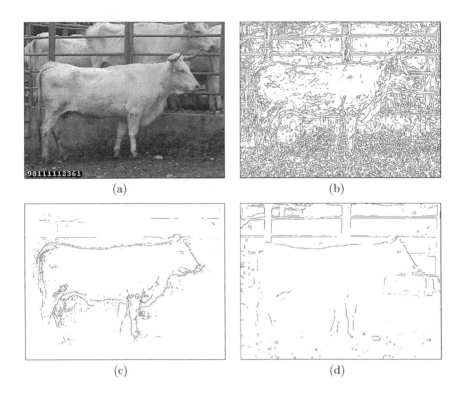

**Fig. 3.** In this figure, an example of bovine livestock image is presented, along with the maximum edge map (b) and the results obtained using the edge detector: (c) with selector (PCA parameters) and (d) without selector

not very large, and the parameters that describe the windows can be calculated easily, the increase in processing time is not critical. For our experiments, the process took always about 1 minute and a half.

Finally, in fig. 3(a) an example is presented, where the outputs of the detector, along with the original image, are shown. As can be seen, while in the results without selector many edges are observed due to the objects in the background, they disappear almost completely when the selector is applied. More examples of the application of the selective edge detector to images of bovine livestock, including other positions, can be consulted in [12]

## 6    Conclusions

In this work, a selective color edge detector has been presented that can be used to obtain, from a concrete image, only those edges that has learned in its training process, discarding the rest. This kind of system is very useful to obtain edge maps to be used later to drive a deformable models or genetic algorithms contour search. The results of applying the system to bovine livestock images have shown that the method is quite effective, and performs better when considering color images, and when the windows at both sides of the edge pixels are described with many parameters.

The main drawback of this edge detector is the requirement of having reference images for a *training set* of images, needed to generate prototypes for the supervised training of the neural classifier and for the generation of the PCA to determine the parameters which describe the windows. Nevertheless, if we are using parametric shape models for the subsequent boundary extraction, as PDM [1,13], the labeling of the points (which could be obtained with semi-automatic methods) can be used to define the reference images too, linking the points with lines. That was the case in our concrete application.

# References

1. Hill, A., Taylor, C.J.: Model-based image interpretation using genetic algorithms. Image and Vision Computing **10** (1992) 295–300
2. Toet, A., Hajema, W.P.: Genetic contour matching. Pattern Recognition Letters **16** (1994) 849–856
3. Toet, A.: Target detection and recognition through contour matching. Technical report, CALMA (Combinatorial Algorithms for Military Applications) project (1994)
4. Kass, M., Witkin, A., Terzopoulos, D.: Snakes: Active contour models. Journal of Computer Vision **1** (1988) 321–331
5. Cohen, L.D., Cohen, I.: Finite-element methods for active contour models and balloons for 2-d and 3-d images. IEEE Tran. on Pattern Analysis and Machine Intelligence **15** (1993) 1131–1147
6. González, H.M., García, C.J., Macías, M., López, F.J., Acevedo, M.I.: Neural–networks–based edges selector for boundary extraction problems. Image and Vision Computing **22** (2004) 1129–1135
7. Cumani, A.: Edge detection in multispectral images. CVGIP: Graphical Models and Image Processing **53** (1991) 40–51
8. González, H.M., García, C.J., Macías, M., Acevedo, M.I.: GA techniques applied to contour search in images of bovine livestock. Lecture Notes in Computer Science **2084** (2001) 482–489
9. Wong, H.S., Caelli, T., Guan, L.: A model-based neural network for edge characterization. Pattern Recognition **33** (2000) 427–444
10. Parker, J.R.: Algorithms for image processing and computer vision. John Wiley (1996)
11. Riedmiller, M., Braun, L.: A direct adaptive method for faster backpropagation learning: the RPROP algorithm. In: Proc. IEEE International Conference on Neural Networks. (1993) 586–591
12. Department of Electronics and Electromechanical Engineering (Univ. of Extremadura): (Application of GA and Deformable Models Techniques to Contour Extraction in Bovine Livestock Images: Results) Url: http://nernet.unex.es/cows/.
13. Cootes, T.F., Hill, A., Taylor, C.J., Haslam, J.: The use of active shape models for locating structures in medical images. Image and Vision Computing **12** (1994) 355–366

# Recovering the Shape from Texture Using Lognormal Filters

Corentin Massot and Jeanny Hérault

Laboratory of Images and Signals, Grenoble, France
corentin.massot@lis.inpg.fr

**Abstract.** How does the visual cortex extract perspective information from textured surfaces? To answer this question, we propose a biologically plausible algorithm based on a simplified model of the visual processing. First, new log-normal filters are presented in replacement of the classical Gabor filters. Particularly, these filters are separable in frequency and orientation and this characteristic is used to derive a robust method to estimate the local mean frequency in the image. Based on this new approach, a local decomposition of the image into patches, after a retinal pre-treatment, leads to the estimation of the local frequency variation all over the surface. The analytical relation between the local frequency and the geometrical parameters of the surface, under perspective projection, is derived and finally allows to solve the so-called problem of recovering the shape from the texture. The accuracy of the method is evaluated and discussed on different kind of textures, both regular and irregular, and also on natural scenes.

## 1 Extraction of Perspective in Natural Scenes

How does the visual system extract a perspective information from natural scenes images? Based on the actual knowledge on the processing of the visual system, we present an algorithm which is dedicated to the extraction of the orientation and the shape of a surface which supports a texture. A texture is a pattern distributed more or less regularly on a surface and having different frequency and orientation components (figure 1).

**Fig. 1.** Examples of studied textures: regular grid, texture from Super *and al* ([1]), meshes of a sweater from Clerc *and al* ([2]), sunflowers field

Since the beginning of the 90's, the use of the spectral information has conducted to several efficient algorithms of extraction of the shape from the texture.

J. Blanc-Talon et al. (Eds.): ACIVS 2005, LNCS 3708, pp. 92–99, 2005.
© Springer-Verlag Berlin Heidelberg 2005

Some methods [3], [4] are able to deal with regular textures, exhibiting at least two discret orientation components; other methods [1], [2], [5] do not make any assumption on the spectral components and manage to obtain results on irregular textures. This last kind of texture is difficult to analyse due to the presence of important non-sationnarities in the image (for example in the sunflowers field, the change in size of the flowers or the presence of a person create local non-stationnarities).

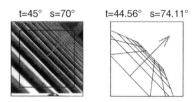

**Fig. 2.** Example of result obtained from our approach on one texture of the figure 1; on the left, the true angles (t: tilt, s: slant) are indicated and on the image the estimated normal to the plane is drawn; on the right the estimated angles are indicated and the image represents the equivalent inclinated grid

Our aim is to develop a model based on the biological visual processing. The main mechanisms of the primary visual system are now well identified [6]. The retina performs a set of pre-treatments leading to the separation between the shading and the texture information [7]. Each region of the space is analysed through a large set of receptive fields, overlapping each other. The signal is then transmitted to the primary visual area V1, where a set of simple and complex cells is associated to each receptive field and perform a sampling of the signal according to the frequencies and the orientations. These cells are organised into macro-columns of local orientation and frequency components. The response of the complex cells is classically modelised as a gabor-like bandpass filtering of the energy spectrum associated to the region of the studied visual space.

The projection of an image from the real world on a surface induces affine deformations (gradients) of the texture covering the surface. Even in static monocular vision the system is able to recover the three-dimensionnal characteristics of the image. In this paper a new technique allowing to recover the shape from the texture gradients analysis, based on the presented simplified model of the visual system, is described. It is based on the decomposition of an homogeneous texture into a set of local patches (similarly to the V1 macro-columns organisation). Section 2 presents a new kind of log-normal filters, better adapted than the Gabor filters to the simulation of the cortical cells. They are used to realise the spectrum sampling. These filters allow to develop a technique to estimate the local frequency which takes into account the whole set of frequency scales available after the cortical filtering. Section 3 presents the model of perspective projection and the relation between the local frequency variation and the geometrical parameters of the surface. Section 4 describes the final obtained algorithm and show different results on textures, both regular and irregular, and on natural scenes.

## 2  Log-Normal Filters and Local Frequency Estimation

Gabor filters are usually used to modelise the cortical cells. Their main advantage is to be localised both in space and frequency but they are not separable in frequency and orientation. In addition they are not symetrical when expressed on a log-polar scale and they have a non-null transmission at $f = 0$ which can lead to spurious responses in low frequencies ([8]). We present here new *log-normal* filters which are better suited to our problem and represent a better approximation of the cortical cells response.

### 2.1  Log-Normal Filters

The expression of these new filters is based on the log-normal law:

$$|G_{i,j}(f,\theta)|^2 = A\frac{1}{f^2}exp\left(-\frac{1}{2}\left(\frac{ln(f/f_i)}{\sigma_r}\right)^2\right).cos^{2n}(\frac{\theta-\theta_j}{2}) = |G_r.G_\theta|^2$$

where $G_{i,j}$ is the transfert function of the filter, $f_i$, the central frequency, $\theta_j$, the central orientation , $\sigma_r$, the frequency bandwidth, $n$ controls the orientation bandwidth. $A$ is a normalisation factor such as $||G_{i,j}(f,\theta)||^2 = 1$ and $A = \frac{2^{2n}}{2\pi C_{2n}^n}\frac{1}{\sigma_r\sqrt{2\pi}}$. Finally $G_r$ and $G_\theta$ represent respectively the radial and the angular component of the filter; these filters are then separable in frequency and orientation.

First row of the figure 3 presents log-normal filters in cartesian and log-polar coordinates. Contrary to the Gabor filters, log-normal filters are insensitive to the continuous component whatever the chosen frequency bandwidth. These filters are assymetrical in log-polar coordinates, similarly to the responses of the cortical complex cells ([6]). Second row of figure 3 presents a log-normal filters bank. It is possible to observe the good coverage and the regularity of the sampling, specially in log-polar coordinates.

### 2.2  Estimation of Mean Local Frequency

In this section we present a method allowing to estimate the mean frequency at a given position in the image. Let's take the frequency component of a log-normal filter at the central frequency $f_i$:

$$G_i^2(f) = \frac{1}{f^2}exp\left(-\frac{1}{2}\left(\frac{ln(f/f_i)}{\sigma_r}\right)^2\right)$$

Similarly to Knutsson *and al* [9], the ratio between two adjacent filters tuned at $f_i$ and $f_{i+1}$ is expressed by:

$$\frac{G_{i+1}^2(f)}{G_i^2(f)} = exp\left(-\frac{1}{2\sigma_r^2}[(ln(f/f_{i+1})^2 - (ln(f/f_i))^2]\right)$$

$$= \left(f/\sqrt{f_if_{i+1}}\right)^{\frac{ln(f_{i+1}/f_i)}{\sigma_r^2}}$$

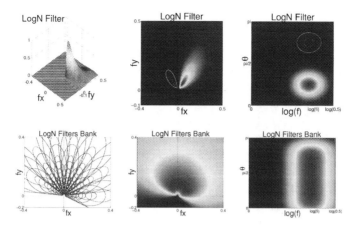

**Fig. 3.** First row: log-normal filters, left: 3D representation; middle and right: filter and contours representing 50% and 90% of the maximum energy in cartesian coordinates on the frequency plane and in log-polar coordinates. Second row: log-normal filters bank, left: contours of the filters of the bank; middle and right: filters bank in cartesian coordinates on the fequency plane and in log-polar coordinates.

Taking $\sigma_r^2 = ln(f_{i+1}/f_i)$, we finally obtain:

$$G_{i+1}^2(f) = \frac{f}{\sqrt{f_i f_{i+1}}} G_i^2(f) \quad (2)$$

So as to extract an information on the scale independantly of the local orientations, we consider frequency tuned band filters (FBF) which result from the summation over all the orientations $j$ of the responses of the filters tuned at the same central frequency $f_i$ on the energy spectrum of the image $S(f,\theta)$:

$$C_i = \int_f G_i^2(f) \int_\theta S(f,\theta) \sum_j G_j^2(\theta) f\,df\,d\theta \quad \text{thus using (2)}$$

$$\frac{C_{i+1}}{C_i} = \frac{1}{\sqrt{f_i f_{i+1}}} <f> \quad (3)$$

The ratio between two adjacent FBF gives equation 3 and represents an estimation of the mean local frequency for the band centered at the $i$th central frequency of the filters bank (narrow band estimation). Finally summing on the whole set of estimations (wide band estimation) we get:

$$<f> = \sum_i \frac{C_i}{\sum_i C_i} <f>_i \quad (4)$$

It has to be noticed that this method takes into account the different estimations over the whole set of available central frequencies which makes it robust to scale variation between the different studied textures. Moreover this method is based on the separation between the frequency and the angular information which allows to independantly use the frequency information without any assumption nor perturbation due to the orientation information contained in the analysed texture. This method is simple and efficient as it is only based on the first order combination of different filters and can be well identified to a *feedforward* process in the early visual system which is not the case with other similar methods such as [1] or [5].

## 3   Geometry and Estimation of the Orientation of Plane Surfaces

### 3.1   Perspective Projection

We consider a perspective projection model for the transformation from the three-dimensionnal world to the bi-dimensionnal plane of the image. Figure 4 presents the coordinates system of the projection model. $(x_w, y_w, z_w)$ represents the world coordinates, $(x_s, y_s)$, the surface coordinates and $(x_i, y_i)$, the image coordinates. $d$ (resp. $zw0$) represents the image coordinate of the image (resp. of the surface) on the $z_w$ axis. $\tau$ (*tilt*) represents the angle between $x_i$ and the projection of the normal $z_s$ at the surface on the image plane. $\sigma$ (*slant*) is the angle between $z_w$ and the normal of the surface at $zw0$. Its value falls between 0 and $\pi/2$.

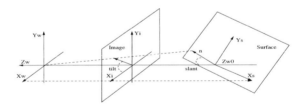

**Fig. 4.** Model of the perspective projection

The relation between the coordinates $(x_s, y_s)$ of the surface and the coordinates $(x_i, y_i)$ of the image is expressed by (see also [1]):

$$\begin{bmatrix} x_s \\ y_s \end{bmatrix} = \frac{\begin{bmatrix} (cos(\sigma)\ 0) \\ 0\ \ \ 1 \end{bmatrix} \begin{bmatrix} (cos(\tau)\ sin(\tau)) \\ -sin(\tau)\ cos(\tau) \end{bmatrix} \begin{bmatrix} x_i \\ y_i \end{bmatrix}}{a_i} = \frac{A}{a_i} \begin{bmatrix} x_i \\ y_i \end{bmatrix} \quad (5)$$

with $a_i = \dfrac{-sin(\sigma)sin(\tau)x_i + cos(\tau)sin(\sigma)y_i + dcos(\sigma)}{d + zw0}$ corresponding to a zoom factor according to the spatial position $(x_i, y_i)$, noted $x_i$ ( similarly we note

$f_i$ the vector $(f_{ix}, f_{iy})$. Around the optical axis, the energy spectrum of the image, $I_i(f_i)$ , is associated to the surface one, $I_s(f_s)$, by:

$$I_i(f_i) = \int_{x_i} i_s(x_s) e^{(-j2\pi x_i^t f_i)} dx_i = \int_{f_s} I_s(f_s) \int_{x_i} e^{j2\pi x_i^t (\frac{A^t}{a_i} f_s - f_i)} dx_i df_s$$

Supposing a constant illumination with the projection, we obtain $i_i(x_i) = i_s(x_s)$ with $x_s = \dfrac{A}{a_i} x_i$. Taking $a_i$ constant within a limited region centered around $x_i$, the change of variable $f_s \rightarrow a_i A^{-t} f_i$ gives:

$$I_i(f_i, x_i) = \int_{f_s} I_s(f_s) \delta(\frac{A^t}{a_i} f_s - f_i) df_s \qquad \text{thus} \qquad f_i = \frac{A^t}{a_i} f_s \quad (6)$$

Equation 6 gives the relation between the frequency $f_i$ of the image and the frequency $f_s$ of the surface (first order approximation).

## 3.2   Estimation of the Orientation of Plane Surfaces

So as to link the frequency variation with the orientation of the surface covered by an homogeneous texture, the presented method only requires a local station-narity assumption (weak stationnarity). The frequency variation on the image is then considered as to be uniquely due to the inclination in depth of the surface. From equation 6, the local frequency variation of the image $f_i$ is expressed by:

$$df_i = -\frac{\nabla^t a_i dx}{a_i^2} A^t f_s = -\frac{\nabla^t a_i dx}{a_i} f_i \quad (7)$$

In polar coordinates, the image frequency can be expressed by $f_i = v_i [cos(\varphi_i) \ sin(\varphi_i)]^t$. Equation 7 gives:

$$df_i = dv_i [cos(\varphi_i) \ sin(\varphi_i)]^t + v_i [-sin(\varphi_i) \ cos(\varphi_i)]^t d\varphi_i$$
$$= -\frac{\nabla^t a_i dx}{a_i} v_i [cos(\varphi_i) \ sin(\varphi_i)]^t \quad (8)$$

If we consider the gradient $df_i$ following the direction of $\varphi_i$, multiplying by $[cos(\varphi_i) \ sin(\varphi_i)]^t$ Equation 8 becomes:

$$\frac{dv_i}{v_i} = -\frac{\nabla^t a_i dx}{a_i} \qquad \text{thus} \qquad dln(v_i) = \frac{-sin(\sigma)}{a_i} [-sin(\tau) \ cos(\tau)][dx_i dy_i]^t$$

We finally deduce that, for an homogeneous and locally stationnary texture, the tilt angle corresponds to the direction of the frequency gradient and the slant angle is proportionnal to the gradient norm of the log-frequencies with the relation:

$$tan(\sigma) = \left( \frac{d}{d + zw0} \frac{1}{|dln(v_i)|} - ([-sin(\tau) \ cos(\tau)][x_i y_i]^t/d) \right)^{-1} \quad (9)$$

# 4  Final Algorithm and Results

The final algorithm can be devided into the following steps:

1. Retinal prefiltering of the image and decomposition into patches (for example: patch size of $96X96$ pixels with an overlapping step of 8 pixels).
2. Extraction of the log-normal filters coefficients (for example: using a $7X7$ filters bank), normalisation by simaler orientation band and summation over the whole set of orientations obtaining the FBF.
3. Combination of the responses using equation 3 and final combination with equation 4 so as to obtain an estimation of the local mean frequency over the whole image.
4. Computation of the local frequency gradients, extraction of tilt and slant angles and final averaging.

Figure 5 presents the results obtained on different textures and on natural scenes. We obtain a precision nearly to $3°$ for the tilt angle and to $5°$ for the slant angle which is comparable to the precision obtained by other methods such as [1] and [5]. The method gives also robust estimations on irregular textures.

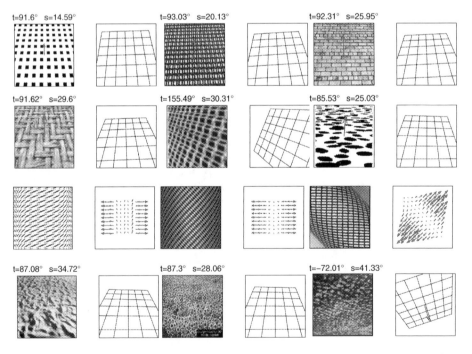

**Fig. 5.** Results obtained on regular and irregular textures and on natural scenes; the presentation is the same as figure 2

# 5   Conclusions

In this paper we have presented a new kind of log-normal filters which are separable allowing to obtain a simple, efficient and robust method of the estimation of the local mean frequency in an image. A complete algorithm performing the analysis of the shape of a surface using the texture information has been presented and evaluated on different kind of textures, both regular and irregular, and on natural scenes. The obtained precision is comparable to similar but more complex methods and can be identified to an early processing in the visual system. This precision can be improved using robust regularisation techniques.

# References

1. Super, B.J. and Bovik, A.C.: Planar surface orientation from texture spatial frequencies. Pattern Recognition **28** (1995) 729–743
2. Clerc, M. and Mallat, S.: The texture gradient equation for recovering shape from texture. IEEE Trans. PAMI **24** (2002)
3. Malik, J. and Rosenholtz, R.: Computing local surface orientation and shape from texture for curved surfaces. International Journal of Computer Vision **23** (1997) 149–168
4. Ribeiro, E. and Hancock, E.R.: Shape from periodic texture using the eigen vectors of local affine distortion. IEEE Trans. PAMI **23** (2001)
5. Hwang, W.L., Lu, C.S. and Chung, P.C.: Shape from texture estimation of planar surface orientation throught the ridge surfaces of continuous wavelets transform. IEEE Trans. on Image Processing **7** (1998)
6. Spillmann, L. and Werner, J.S.: Visual Perception: The Neurophysiological Foundations. Academic Press Inc. (1990)
7. Beaudot, W.H.: The neural information in the vertebra retina : a melting pot of ideas for artificial vision. Unpublished PhD thesis, tirf laboratory, Grenoble, France (1994)
8. Wallis, G.: Linear models of simple cells: Correspondence to real cell responses and space spanning properties. Spatial Vision **14** (2001) 237–260
9. Knutsson, H., Westin, C.F. and Granlund, G.: Local multiscale frequency and bandwidth estimation. IEEE International Conference on Image Processing (ICIP'94), Austin, Texas (1994)

# Affine Normalization of Symmetric Objects⋆

Tomáš Suk and Jan Flusser

Institute of Information Theory and Automation,
Academy of Sciences of the Czech Republic,
Pod vodárenskou věží 4, 182 08 Prague 8, Czech Republic
{flusser, suk}@utia.cas.cz
http://www.utia.cas.cz

**Abstract.** A new method of normalization is used for the construction of the affine moment invariants. The affine transform is decomposed into translation, scaling, stretching, two rotations and mirror reflection. The object is successively normalized to these elementary transforms by means of low order moments. After normalization, other moments of normalized object can be used as affine invariant features of the original object. We pay special attention to the normalization of symmetric objects.

## 1 Introduction

Affine moment invariants as features for object recognition have been studied for many years. They were introduced independently by Reiss [1] and Flusser and Suk [2], who published its explicit forms and proved their applicability in simple recognition tasks. In their work, they decomposed the affine transform into translation, anisotropic scaling and two skews. The systems of invariants were derived by direct solving Cayley-Aronhold differential equation [2], by tensor method [3] or, equivalently, by graph method [4]). The invariants are in form of polynomials of moments.

The normalization performs an alternative approach to deriving invariants. First, the object is brought into certain "normalized" or "canonical" position, which is independent of the actual position of the original object. In this way, the influence of affine transformation is eliminated. Since the normalized position is the same for all objects differing from each other just by affine transform, the moments of normalized object are in fact affine invariants of the original one. We emphasize that no actual spatial transformation of the original object is necessary. Such a transformation would slow down the process and would introduce resampling errors. Instead, the moments of normalized objects can be calculated directly from the original one using the normalization constraints. These constraints are often formulated by means of low-order moments.

The idea of normalization was successfully used in [5], but only normalization to rotation was considered in that paper. Affine normalization was firstly

---

⋆ This work has been supported by the grants No. 201/03/0675 and No. 102/04/0155 of the Grant Agency of the Czech Republic.

© Springer-Verlag Berlin Heidelberg 2005

described in [6], where two different affine decompositions were used (XSR decomposition, i.e. skew, anisotropic scaling and rotation , and XYS decomposition, i.e. two skews and anisotropic scaling). However, this approach leads to some ambiguities, which were studied in [7] in detail.

Pei and Lin [8] presented a method similar to ours. Their paper contains detailed derivation of the normalization to the first rotation and to anisotropic scaling, but they do not consider the problems with the symmetric objects and with the mirror reflection. This is a serious weakness because in many applications we have to classify man-made or specific natural objects which are very often symmetrical. Since many moments of symmetrical objects are zero, the normalization constraints may be not well defined.

Shen and Ip [9] used so called generalized complex moments computed in polar coordinates and analyzed their behavior in recognition of symmetrical objects. Heikkila [10] used Cholesky factorization of the second order moment matrix to define the normalization constraints.

We present a new, simpler way of normalization to the affine transformation, which is based both on traditional geometric as well as complex moments. The method is well defined also for objects having $n$-fold rotation symmetry, which is its main advantage.

## 2    Normalization of the Image with Respect to the Affine Transform

The affine transform
$$x' = a_0 + a_1 x + a_2 y,$$
$$y' = b_0 + b_1 x + b_2 y \tag{1}$$

can be decomposed into six simple one-parameter transforms and one non-parameter

Horizontal and vertical translation :
$$u = x - x_0$$
$$v = y$$

$$u = x$$
$$v = y - y_0$$

Scaling :
$$u = \omega x$$
$$v = \omega y$$

First rotation :
$$u = x \cos \alpha - y \sin \alpha$$
$$v = x \sin \alpha + y \cos \alpha$$

Stretching :
$$u = \delta x$$
$$v = \frac{1}{\delta} y$$

Second rotation :
$$u = x \cos \rho - y \sin \rho$$
$$v = x \sin \rho + y \cos \rho$$

Mirror reflection :
$$u = x$$
$$v = \pm y. \tag{2}$$

Any function $F$ of moments is invariant under these seven transformations if and only if it is invariant under the general affine transformation (1). The ordering of these one-parameter transforms can be changed, but the stretching must be between two rotations.

Each of these transforms imposes one constraint on the invariants. Traditional approach to the problem of affine invariants consists on expressing constraints in form of equations. Affine invariants are then obtained as their solutions.

Here we bring the object into normalized position. The parameters of the "normalization transforms" can be calculated by means of some object moments. Below we show how to normalize the object with respect to all seven one-parameter transforms.

## 2.1   Normalization to Translation and Scaling

We can easily normalize the image with respect to translation just by shifting it such that its centroid

$$x_c = \frac{m_{10}}{m_{00}}, \qquad\qquad y_c = \frac{m_{01}}{m_{00}}. \tag{3}$$

is zero. Practically, this is ensured by using central moments

$$\mu_{pq} = \int_{-\infty}^{\infty} \int_{-\infty}^{\infty} (x - x_c)^p (y - y_c)^q f(x,y)dxdy, \tag{4}$$

instead of geometric moments

$$m_{pq} = \int_{-\infty}^{\infty} \int_{-\infty}^{\infty} x^p y^q f(x,y)dxdy. \tag{5}$$

The normalization to the scaling is also simple. The scaling parameter $\omega$ can be recovered from $\mu_{00}$

$$\omega = 1/\sqrt{\mu_{00}}. \tag{6}$$

The scale-normalized moments are then defined as

$$\nu_{pq} = \mu_{pq}/\mu_{00}^{\frac{p+q+2}{2}}. \tag{7}$$

## 2.2   Normalization to the First Rotation and Stretching

Normalization to the rotation can advantageously be done by complex moments. Complex moment is defined as

$$c_{pq} = \int_{-\infty}^{\infty} \int_{-\infty}^{\infty} (x + iy)^p (x - iy)^q f(x,y)dxdy, \tag{8}$$

where $i$ denotes imaginary unit. Each complex moment can be expressed in terms of geometric moments $m_{pq}$ as

$$c_{pq} = \sum_{k=0}^{p} \sum_{j=0}^{q} \binom{p}{k} \binom{q}{j} (-1)^{q-j} \cdot i^{p+q-k-j} \cdot m_{k+j,p+q-k-j} \cdot \tag{9}$$

We can use normalized complex moments computed from the normalized moments $\nu_{pq}$ to get translation and scaling invariance.

When rotating the image, its complex moments preserve their magnitudes while their phases are shifted. More precisely,

$$c'_{pq} = e^{i(p-q)\alpha} c_{pq}, \tag{10}$$

where $\alpha$ is the rotation angle measured counterclockwise.

The simplest normalization constraint is to require $c'_{pq}$ to be real and positive. This is always possible to achieve (provided that $c_{pq} \neq 0$) by rotating the image by angle $\alpha$

$$\alpha = -\frac{1}{p-q} \arctan\left(\frac{\Im(c_{pq})}{\Re(c_{pq})}\right), \tag{11}$$

where $\Re(c_{pq})$ and $\Im(c_{pq})$ denote real and imaginary parts of $c_{pq}$, respectively.

Generally, any non-zero $c_{pq}$ can be used for this kind of normalization. Because of stability, we try to keep its order as low as possible. Since $c_{10}$ was already used for translation normalization, the lowest moment we can employ is $c_{20}$. It leads to well known "principal axes normalization", where the angle is given as

$$\alpha = -\frac{1}{2} \arctan\left(\frac{\Im(c_{20})}{\Re(c_{20})}\right) = -\frac{1}{2} \arctan\left(\frac{2\mu_{11}}{\mu_{20} - \mu_{02}}\right). \tag{12}$$

If the $c_{20}$ is zero, we consider the object is already normalized and set $\alpha = 0$.

Normalization to stretching can be done by imposing an additional constraint on second order moments. We require that $\mu'_{20} = \mu'_{02}$. The corresponding normalizing coefficient $\delta$ is then given as

$$\delta = \sqrt{\frac{\mu_{20} + \mu_{02} - \sqrt{(\mu_{20} - \mu_{02})^2 + 4\mu_{11}^2}}{2\sqrt{\mu_{20}\mu_{02} - \mu_{11}^2}}} \tag{13}$$

(this is well defined because $\mu_{20}\mu_{02} - \mu_{11}^2$ is always non-zero for non-degenerate 2-D objects).

After this normalization the complex moment $c'_{20}$ becomes zero and cannot be further used for another normalization.

The moments of the normalized image to the first rotation and stretching can be computed from the moments of the original by means of (9) and (10) as

$$\mu'_{pq} = \delta^{p-q} \sum_{k=0}^{p} \sum_{j=0}^{q} \binom{p}{k}\binom{q}{j} (-1)^k \sin^{p-k+j}\alpha \cos^{q+k-j}\alpha \, \nu_{k+j,p+q-k-j} . \tag{14}$$

## 2.3   Normalization to the Second Rotation

Normalization to the second rotation is a critical step, namely for symmetric objects. We propose a normalization by one complex moment, which must be of course nonzero. However, many moments of symmetric objects equal zero. The selection of the normalizing moment must be done very carefully, especially in a discrete case where some moments which should be theoretically zero may appear in certain positions of the object as nonzero because of quantization effect.

Let us consider an object having $n$–fold rotation symmetry. Then all its complex moments with non-integer $(p - q)/n$ equal zero. To prove this, let us rotate the object around its origin by $2\pi/n$. Due to its symmetry, the rotated object must be the same as the original. In particular, it must hold $c_{pq}^{rot} = c_{pq}$ for any $p$ and $q$. On the other hand, it follows from eq. (10)) that

$$c_{pq}^{rot} = e^{-2\pi i(p-q)/n} \cdot c_{pq}.$$

Since $(p - q)/n$ is assumed not to be an integer, this equation can be fulfilled only if $c_{pq} = 0$. Particularly, if an object has circular symmetry (i.e. $n = \infty$), the only nonzero moments can be $c_{pp}$'s.

The moment we use for normalization is found as follows. Let us consider a set of complex moments $\{c_{pq} | p > q, p+q \leq r\}$ except those moments which were used in previous normalization steps. We sort this set according to the moment orders and, among the moments of the same order, according to $p - q$. We get a sequence of complex moments $c_{21}, c_{30}, c_{31}, c_{40}, c_{32}, c_{41}, c_{50}, c_{42}, c_{51}, c_{60}$, etc. The first nonzero moment in this sequence is selected for normalization. (In practice, "nonzero moment" means that its magnitude exceeds some threshold.) If all the moments in the sequence are zero, we consider the object circular symmetric and no normalization is necessary.

Thanks to the proper ordering of moments, $c_{21}$ is always selected for non-symmetric objects. For symmetric objects the order of the selected moment is kept as low as possible. This is a favorable property of the method because low-order moments are more robust to noise than the higher-order ones.

Once the normalizing moment is determined, the normalizing angle $\rho$ is calculated similarly as (11)

$$\rho = -\frac{1}{p - q} \arctan\left(\frac{\Im(c_{pq})}{\Re(c_{pq})}\right). \tag{15}$$

Finally, the moments of the object normalized to the second rotation are calculated by means of a similar formula as in the case of the first rotation

$$\tau_{pq} = \sum_{k=0}^{p}\sum_{j=0}^{q} \binom{p}{k}\binom{q}{j}(-1)^k \ \sin^{p-k+j}\rho \ \cos^{q+k-j}\rho \ \mu'_{k+j,p+q-k-j}, \tag{16}$$

but here the moments normalized to the first rotation and stretching $\mu'_{pq}$ must be used on the right-hand side.

The moments $\tau_{pq}$ are new affine moment invariants of the original object. Note that some of them have "prescribed" values due to normalization, regardless of the object itself:

$$\tau_{00} = 1, \ \tau_{10} = 0, \ \tau_{01} = 0, \ \tau_{02} = \tau_{20}, \ \tau_{11} = 0, \ \tau_{03} = -\tau_{21}. \tag{17}$$

All other moments (and also $\tau_{20}$ and $\tau_{21}$) can be used as features for invariant object recognition.

## 2.4  Normalization to Mirror Reflection

Although the general affine transform (1) may contain mirror reflection, normalization to the mirror reflection should be done separately from the other transformations in (2) for practical reasons. In most affine deformations occurring in practice, any mirror reflection cannot be present in principle and we want to classify mirrored images into different classes (in character recognition we certainly want to distinguish capital S and a question mark for instance). Normalization to mirror reflection is not desirable in those cases.

If we still want to normalize objects to mirror reflection, we can do that, after all normalization mentioned above, as follows. We find the first non-zero moment (normalized to scaling, stretching and both rotations) with an odd $q$-index. If it is negative, then we change the signs of all moments with odd $q$-indices. If it is positive or if all normalized moments up to the chosen order with odd $q$-indices are zero, no action is required.

## 3  Numerical Experiments

To illustrate the performance of the method, we carried out an experiment with simple patterns having different number of folds. In Fig. 1 (top row), one can see six objects whose numbers of folds are 1, 2, 3, 4, 5, and $\infty$, respectively. In the middle row you can see these patterns being deformed by an affine transformation with parameters $a_0 = 0$, $a_1 = -1$, $a_2 = 1$, $b_0 = 0$, $b_1 = 0$, and $b_2 = 1$. For the both sets of objects the values of the normalized moments were calculated as described in Section 2. The moment values of the original patterns are shown in Table 1. The last line of the table shows which complex moment was used for the normalization to the second rotation. The moment values of the transformed patterns were almost exactly the same – the maximum absolute error was $3 \cdot 10^{-11}$, which demonstrate an excellent performance of the proposed method even if the test objects were symmetric.

In the bottom row of Fig. 1 the normalized positions of the test patterns are shown. We recall that this is for illustration only; transforming the objects is not required for calculation of the normalized moments.

The last line of Table 1 illustrates the influence of spatial quantization in the discrete domain. Theoretically, in case of the three-point star we would need to use $c_{30}$, in case of the five-point star $c_{50}$ should be used, and the circle would not require any normalization. However, in the discrete domain the symmetry is violated. That is why the algorithm selected other moments for normalization.

In the second experiment, we tested the behavior of the method in a difficult situation. The cross (see Fig. 2 left) has four folds of symmetry, so one would expect to choose $c_{40}$ for the normalization to the second rotation. However, we deliberately set up the proportions of the cross such that $c_{40} \doteq 0$. Since in the discrete domain it is impossible to reach exactly $c_{40} = 0$, we repeated this experiment three times with slightly different dimensions of the cross. The cross deformed by an affine transform is shown in Fig. 2 right. In all three cases

**Table 1.** The values of the normalized moments of the test patterns. (The values were scaled to eliminate different dynamic range of moments of different orders.) The complex moment used for the normalization to the second rotation is shown in the last line.

| moment | Letter F | Compass | 3-point star | Square | 5-point star | Circle |
|---|---|---|---|---|---|---|
| $\tau_{30}$ | -0.5843 | 0 | 0.6247 | 0 | -0.0011 | 0 |
| $\tau_{21}$ | 0.2774 | 0 | 0.1394 | 0 | 0.0024 | 0 |
| $\tau_{12}$ | 0.5293 | 0 | -1.2528 | 0 | -0.0038 | 0 |
| $\tau_{40}$ | 1.3603 | 1.013 | 1.4748 | 1.2 | 1.265 | 1 |
| $\tau_{31}$ | -0.0766 | 0 | -0.0002 | 0 | -0.0068 | 0 |
| $\tau_{22}$ | 0.9545 | 0.9371 | 1.4791 | 0.6 | 1.2664 | 0.9999 |
| $\tau_{13}$ | 0.1270 | 0 | -0.0001 | 0 | 0.0106 | 0 |
| $\tau_{04}$ | 1.0592 | 0.8972 | 1.48 | 1.2 | 1.2641 | 1 |
| | $c_{21}$ | $c_{31}$ | $c_{21}$ | $c_{40}$ | $c_{21}$ | $c_{40}$ |

**Fig. 1.** The test patterns: the originals (top row), the distorted patterns (middle row), the patterns in the normalized positions (bottom row)

**Fig. 2.** The cross: the original (left) and distorted (right)

the method performed very well. A proper non-zero moment was selected for normalization ($c_{51}$ once and $c_{40}$ twice) and the values of the normalized moments of the original and deformed crosses were almost the same.

## 4   Conclusion

We presented a new way of image normalization with respect to unknown affine transform. In addition to simplicity, the main advantage of the method is their ability to handle symmetric as well as non-symmetric objects. Unlike the Shen and Ip's method [9], which was also developed for symmetric objects and has been considered as the best one, our method does not require prior knowledge of the number of folds. This is a significant improvement because its detection (either by autocorrelation or by polar Fourier analysis) is always time-consuming and sometimes very difficult.

The experiments in the paper show the performance of our method on artificial binary images to demonstrate the main features of the method. In practice, the method can be applied without any modifications also to graylevel images regardless of their symmetry/non-symmetry. The only potential drawback of our method is that in certain rare situations it might become unstable, which means that a small change of the image results in a significant change of its normalized position. This is, however, a common weakness of all geometric normalization methods.

Once the image has been normalized, its moments can be used as affine invariants for recognition. Comparing to traditional affine moment invariants [2], [3], the presented method has a big theoretical advantage. The construction of the invariants is straightforward and their structure is easy to understand. Thanks to this, we can immediately resolve the problem of finding minimum complete and independent set of invariants. For the invariants [2] and [3], this problem has not been resolved yet. Here, each moment which was not used in normalization constraints, generates just one affine invariant. Independence and completeness of such invariants follow from the independence and completeness of the moments themselves. Using minimum complete and independent set of invariants yields maximum possible recognition power at minimum computational cost.

# References

1. T. H. Reiss, "The revised fundamental theorem of moment invariants," *IEEE Trans. Pattern Analysis and Machine Intelligence*, vol. 13, pp. 830–834, 1991.
2. J. Flusser and T. Suk, "Pattern recognition by affine moment invariants," *Pattern Recognition*, vol. 26, no. 1, pp. 167–174, 1993.
3. T. H. Reiss, *Recognizing Planar Objects using Invariant Image Features*, vol. 676 of *LNCS*. Berlin: Springer, 1993.
4. J. Flusser and T. Suk, "Graph method for generating affine moment invariants," In: *Proceedings of the 17th International Conference on Pattern Recognition. ICPR 2004. (Kittler J. ed.)*, pp. 192-195, 2004.
5. Y. S. Abu-Mostafa and D. Psaltis, "Image normalization by complex moment," *IEEE Trans. Pattern Analysis and Machine Intelligence*, vol. 7, pp. 46–55, 1985.
6. I. Rothe, K. Susse and K. Voss, "The method of normalization to determine invariants," *IEEE Trans. Pattern Analysis and Machine Intelligence*, vol. 18, pp. 366–376, 1996.
7. Y. Zhang, C. Wen, Y. Zhang and Y. C. Soh, "On the choice of consistent canonical form during moment normalization," *Pattern Recognition Letters*, vol. 24, pp. 3205–3215, 2003.
8. S. C. Pei and C. N. Lin, "Image normalization for pattern recognition," *Image and Vision Computing*, vol. 13, pp. 711–723, 1995.
9. D. Shen and H. H. S. Ip, "Generalized affine invariant image normalization," *IEEE Trans. Pattern Analysis and Machine Intelligence*, vol. 19, pp. 431–440, 1997.
10. J. Heikkila, "Pattern matching with affine moment descriptors," *Pattern Recognition*, vol. 37, pp. 1825–1834, 2004.

# Object Recognition Using Local Characterisation and Zernike Moments

A. Choksuriwong, H. Laurent, C. Rosenberger, and C. Maaoui

Laboratoire Vision et Robotique - UPRES EA 2078,
ENSI de Bourges - Université d'Orléans,
10 boulevard Lahitolle, 18020 Bourges Cedex, France
anant.choksuriwong@ensi-bourges.fr
http://www.bourges.univ-orleans.fr/rech/lvr/

**Abstract.** Even if lots of object invariant descriptors have been proposed in the literature, putting them into practice in order to obtain a robust system face to several perturbations is still a studied problem. Comparative studies between the most commonly used descriptors put into obviousness the invariance of Zernike moments for simple geometric transformations and their ability to discriminate objects. Whatever, these moments can reveal themselves insufficiently robust face to perturbations such as partial object occultation or presence of a complex background. In order to improve the system performances, we propose in this article to combine the use of Zernike descriptors with a local approach based on the detection of image points of interest. We present in this paper the Zernike invariant moments, Harris keypoint detector and the support vector machine. Experimental results present the contribution of the local approach face to the global one in the last part of this article.

## 1 Introduction

A fundamental stage for scene interpretation is the development of tools being able to consistently describe objects appearing at different scales or orientations in the images. Foreseen processes, developed for pattern recognition applications such as robots navigation, should allow to identify known objects in a scene permitting to teleoperate robots with special orders such as "move towards the chair".

Many works have been devoted to the definition of object invariant descriptors for simple geometric transformations [1], [2]. However, this invariance is not the only one desired property. A suited structure should indeed allow to recognize objects that appear truncated in the image, with a different color or a different luminance, on a complex background (with noise or texture). Amongst the available invariant descriptors, the Zernike moments [3], [4] have been developed to overcome the major drawbacks of regular geometrical moments regarding noise effects and presence of image quantization error. Based on a complete and orthonormal set of polynomials defined on the unit circle, these moments help in

J. Blanc-Talon et al. (Eds.): ACIVS 2005, LNCS 3708, pp. 108–115, 2005.
© Springer-Verlag Berlin Heidelberg 2005

achieving a near zero value of redundancy measure. In [5], a comparative study shows the relative efficiency of Zernike moments face to other invariant descriptors such as Fourier-Mellin ones or Hu moments. Nevertheless, Zernike moments can fail when objects appear partially hidden in the image or when a complex background is present.

In order to improve the performances of the method, we propose to combine the Zernike moments with the keypoints detector proposed by Harris [6]. The Zernike moments will then be calculated in a neighborhood of each detected keypoint. This computation is more robust face to partial object occultation or if the object appears in a complex scene.

In the first part of this article, the Zernike moments and Harris keypoints detector are briefly presented. The method we used for the training and recognition steps, based on a support vector machine [7], is also described. Experimental results, computed on different objects of the COIL-100 basis [8], are then presented permitting to compare the performances of the global and local approaches. Finally, some conclusions and perspectives are given.

## 2   Developed Method

### 2.1   Zernike Moments

Zernike moments [3], [4] belong to the algebraic class for which the features are directly computed on the image. These moments use a set of Zernike polynomials that is complete and orthonormal in the interior of the unit circle. The Zernike moments formulation is given below:

$$A_{mn} = \frac{m+1}{\pi} \sum_x \sum_y I(x,y)[V_{mn}(x,y)] \tag{1}$$

with $x^2 + y^2 \leq 1$. The values of $m$ and $n$ define the moment order and $I(x,y)$ is a pixel gray-level of the image $I$ over which the moment is computed. Zernike polynomials $V_{mn}(x,y)$ are expressed in the radial-polar form:

$$V_{mn}(r,\theta) = R_{mn}(r)e^{-jn\theta} \tag{2}$$

where $R_{mn}(r)$ is the radial polynomial given by:

$$R_{mn}(r) = \sum_{s=0}^{\frac{m-|n|}{2}} \frac{(-1)^s (m-s)! \, r^{m-2s}}{s!(\frac{m+|n|}{2} - s)! \, (\frac{m-|n|}{2} - s)!} \tag{3}$$

These moments yield invariance with respect to translation, scale and rotation. For this study, the Zernike moments from order 1 to 15 have been computed (it represents 72 descriptors).

## 2.2  Harris Keypoints Detector

Lots of keypoints detectors have been proposed in the literature [9]. They are either based on a preliminary contour detection or directly computed on grey-level images. The Harris detector [6] that is used in this article belongs to the second class. It is consequently not dependant of a prior success of the contour extraction step. This detector is based on statistics of the image and rests on the detection of average changes of the auto-correlation function. Figure Fig.1 presents the interest points obtained for one object extracted from the COIL-100 basis and presented under geometric transformation. We can observe that not all points are systematically detected. However, this example shows the good repeatability of the obtained detector.

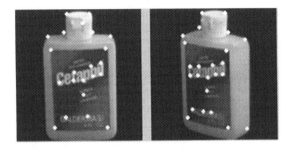

**Fig. 1.** Keypoints detection for the same object under different geometric transformations

The average number of detected keypoints is around 25 for the used images. In the local approach, the Zernike moments are computed on a neighborhood of each detected keypoint (see figure Fig.2).

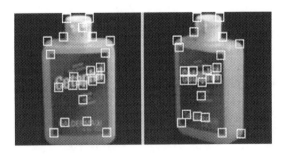

**Fig. 2.** Detected keypoints and associated neighborhood

## 2.3  Training and Recognition Method

Suppose we have a training set $\{\mathbf{x}_i, \mathbf{y}_i\}$ where $\mathbf{x}_i$ is the invariant descriptors vector described previously ($\mathbf{x}_i$ is composed of $N_{KP_i} {}^* N_{ZM}$ values, with $N_{KP_i}$ corresponding to the keypoint number of image $i$ and $N_{ZM}$ the number of Zernike moments depending on the chosen order) and $\mathbf{y}_i$ the object class. For two classes problems, $y_i \in \{-1, 1\}$, the Support Vector Machines implement the following algorithm. First of all, the training points $\{\mathbf{x}_i\}$ are projected in a space $\mathcal{H}$ (of possibly infinite dimension) by means of a function $\Phi(\cdot)$. Then, the goal is to find, in this space, an optimal decision hyperplane, in the sense of a criterion that we will define shortly. Note that for the same training set, different transformations $\Phi(\cdot)$ lead to different decision functions. A transformation is achieved in an implicit manner using a kernel $K(\cdot, \cdot)$ and consequently the decision function can be defined as:

$$f(\mathbf{x}) = \langle w, \Phi(\mathbf{x}) \rangle + b = \sum_{i=1}^{\ell} \alpha_i^* y_i K(\mathbf{x}_i, \mathbf{x}) + b \qquad (4)$$

with $\alpha_i^* \in R$. The value $w$ and $b$ are the parameters defining the linear decision hyperplane. We use in the proposed system a radial basis function as kernel function. In SVMs, the optimality criterion to maximize is the margin, that is the distance between the hyperplane and the nearest point $\Phi(\mathbf{x}_i)$ of the training set. The $\alpha_i^*$ allowing to optimize this criterion are defined by solving the following problem:

$$\begin{cases} \max_{\alpha_i} \sum_{i=1}^{\ell} \alpha_i - \frac{1}{2} \sum_{i,j=1}^{\ell} \alpha_i \alpha_j y_i K(\mathbf{x}_i, \mathbf{x}_j y_j) \\ \text{with constraints,} \\ 0 \le \alpha_i \le C \,, \\ \sum_{i=1}^{\ell} \alpha_i y_i = 0 \,. \end{cases} \qquad (5)$$

where $C$ is a penalization coefficient for data points located in or beyond the margin and provides a compromise between their numbers and the width of the margin (for this study $C = 1$). Originally, SVMs have essentially been developed for the two classes problems. However, several approaches can be used for extending SVMs to multiclass problems. The method we use in this communication, is called *one against one*. Instead of learning $N$ decision functions, each class is discriminated here from another one. Thus, $\frac{N(N-1)}{2}$ decision functions are learned and each of them makes a vote for the affectation of a new point $\mathbf{x}$. The class of this point $\mathbf{x}$ becomes then the majority class after the voting.

## 3  Experimental Results

The experimental results presented below correspond to a test database composed of 100 objects extracted from the Columbia Object Image Library (COIL-100) [8]. For each object of the gray-level images database, we have 72 views (128*128 pixels) presenting orientation and scale changes (see figure Fig. 3).

**Fig. 3.** Three objects in the COIL-100 database presented with different orientations and scales

We first used different percentages of the image database in the learning set (namely 25%, 50% and 75%). For each object, respectively 18, 36 and 54 views have been randomly chosen to compose the learning set. The Zernike moments from order 1 to 15 (that is to say 72 descriptors) have been computed on a 11*11 pixels neighborhood of each detected keypoint of these images. We present for each experiment the recognition rate of the neighborhood of a keypoint. In this experiment, we tuned the parameter of the Harris detector in order to have about 25 keypoints for each object sample. In fact, this step has been repeated 10 times in order to make the results independent of the learning base draw. Table 1 presents the results obtained for the global and local approaches. We can note that, the largest the learning basis is, the highest the recognition rate is. The best results are obtained with the local approach.

In order to measure the influence of the neighborhood size on the recognition rate, we tested four windowing size (7*7 pixels, 11*11 pixels, 15*15 pixels, 19*19 pixels). For this experiment the learning basis was constituted by 50% of the

**Table 1.** Recognition rate for different database sizes

| Size of training database | 25% | 50% | 75% |
|---|---|---|---|
| Global approach | 70.0% | 84.6% | 91.9% |
| Local approach | 94.0% | 94.1% | 97.7% |

images database (36 views for each object). Table 2 presents the results obtained in each case. Results show that we obtain the best recognition rate with a window size equal to 15*15 pixels.

**Table 2.** Influence of the neighborhood size on the recognition rate

| Neighborhood size | 7*7 | 11*11 | 15*15 | 19*19 |
|---|---|---|---|---|
| Recognition rate | 91.2% | 94.1% | 98.6% | 97.3% |

In order to evaluate the robustness of the proposed approach, we created 75 images for each object corresponding to alterations (see figure Fig. 4): 10 with an uniform background, 10 with a noisy background, 10 with a textured background, 10 with an occluding black box, 10 with an occluding grey-level box, 10 with a luminance modification and 15 with gaussian noise adding (standard deviation: 5, 10 and 20).

**Fig. 4.** Alterations examples

We kept the same Harris parameters setting and used for the local approach with a window size of $11 \times 11$ pixels. Figure Fig. 5 presents an example of detected keypoints and associated neighborhood face to three alterations (textured background, occluding box and noise adding).

Table 3 presents the results of robustness for the global and local approaches with different sizes of neighborhood. We used the whole database for the learning

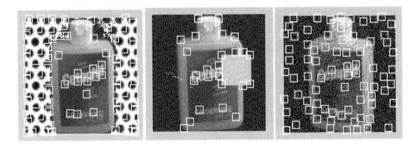

**Fig. 5.** Detected keypoints and associated neighborhood for three alterations (textured bakground, occluding box and noise adding)

**Table 3.** Robustness of the proposed approach face to alterations

|  | Global | Local 7x7 | Local 11x11 | Local 15x15 | Local 19x19 |
|---|---|---|---|---|---|
| uniform background | 31.8 % | 83.1 % | 85.7 % | **86.2%** | 86.1 % |
| noise background | 34.9 % | 62.5 % | 63.0 % | **63.5%** | 62.6 % |
| textured background | 7.5 % | 54.3 % | 54.9 % | 55.1 % | **56.8 %** |
| black occluding | 74.7 % | 78.0 % | 78.5 % | 79.1 % | **80.2 %** |
| gray-level occluding | 71.2 % | 79.4% | 80.3 % | 80.9 % | **81.2 %** |
| luminance | **95.9 %** | 87.7 % | 88.35 % | 80.0 % | 89.8 % |
| noise ($\sigma = 5$) | **100 %** | 70.5 % | 73.0 % | 73.4 % | 73.1 % |
| noise ($\sigma = 10$) | **100 %** | 68.3 % | 69.9 % | 70.1 % | 69.4 % |
| noise ($\sigma = 20$) | **100 %** | 62.2 % | 62.5 % | 62.9 % | 61.2 % |

phase and we try to recognize altered objects. These results show the benefit of the local approach except to noise adding and luminance modification. In this case, a lot of keypoints are extracted due to the presence of noise. The local approach is then penalized.

## 4    Conclusion and Perspectives

We present in this paper a study on object recognition by using Zernike moments computed in the neighborhood of Harris keypoints. Experimental results show the benefit of using the local approach face to the global one. We studied the influence of the neighborhood size for object recognition. The neighborhood of size $15 \times 15$ pixels is for us a good compromise between recognition rate and robustness to alterations.

Perspectives of this study concern first of all the computation of the recognition rate. The percentage of well-labeled keypoints is actually taken into account. In order to improve the method, the recognition of an object could be realized by determining the majority vote of the image keypoints. We finally plan to apply the proposed approach for the navigation of mobile robots.

# References

1. A. K. Jain, R.P.W. Duin and J.Mao: Statistical Pattern Recognition: A Review. IEEE Transactions on Pattern Analysis and Machine Intelligence **22(1)** (2000) 4–37
2. M. Petrou and A. Kadyrov: Affine Invariant Features from the Trace Transform. IEEE Transactions on Pattern Analysis and Machine Intelligence **26(1)** (2004) 30–44
3. A. Khotanzad and Y. Hua Hong: Invariant Image Recognition by Zernike Moments. IEEE Transactions on Pattern Analysis and Machine Intelligence **12(5)** (1990) 489–497
4. C.-W. Chong, P. Raveendran and R. Mukundan: Mean Shift: A Comparative analysis of algorithms for fast computation of Zernike moment. Pattern Recognition **36** (2003) 731-742
5. A. Choksuriwong, H. Laurent and B. Emile: Comparison of invariant descriptors for object recognition. To appear in proc. of ICIP-05 (2005)
6. C. Harris and M. Stephens: A combined corner and edge detector. Alvey Vision Conference (1988) 147–151
7. C. Cortes and V. Vapnik: Support Vector Networks. Machine Learning **20** (1995) 1–25
8. http://www1.cs.columbia.edu/cave/research/softlib/coil-100.html
9. C. Schmid, R. Mohr and C. Bauckhage: Evaluation of interest point detectors. International Journal of Computer Vision **37(2)** (2000) 151–172

# Natural Scene Classification and Retrieval Using Ridgelet-Based Image Signatures

Hervé Le Borgne and Noel O'Connor

Centre for Digital Video Processing, Dublin City University, Dublin 9, Ireland
{hlborgne, oconnor}@eeng.dcu.ie

**Abstract.** This paper deals with knowledge extraction from visual data for content-based image retrieval of natural scenes. Images are analysed using a ridgelet transform that enhances information at different scales, orientations and spatial localizations. The main contribution of this work is to propose a method that reduces the size and the redundancy of this ridgelet representation, by defining both global and local signatures that are specifically designed for semantic classification and content-based retrieval. An effective recognition system can be built when these descriptors are used in conjunction with a support vector machine (SVM). Classification and retrieval experiments are conducted on natural scenes, to demonstrate the effectiveness of the approach.

## 1 Introduction and Related Works

For the last 15 years, several fields of research have converged in order to address the management of multimedia databases, creating a new discipline usually called *Content-Based Image Retrieval (CBIR)* [1]. One of the key-issues to be addressed, termed the *semantic gap*, is the disparity between the information extracted from the raw visual data (pixel) and a user's interpretation of that same data in a given retrieval scenario [2]. Automatic image categorization can help to address this issue by hierarchically classifying images into narrower categories, thereby reducing search time. Some successes have been reported for particular problems, using various image processing and machine learning techniques. In [3], the dominant direction of texture, estimated via a multiscale steerable pyramid allows identification of pictures of cities and suburbs. In [4], *indoor/outdoor* classification was achieved using color (histogram), texture (MSAR) and frequency (DCT) information. In [5], the authors hierarchically discriminate *indoor* from *outdoor*, *city* from *landscape*, and *sunset* from *forest* and *mountain* using color histograms, color coherence vectors, DCT coefficients, edge histograms and edge direction coherence vectors. However, none of these approach take into account the particular statistical structure of a natural scene, although this has been widely studied in the literature. One of the most noticeable properties states that the average power spectrum of natural scenes decreases according to $1/f^\alpha$, where $f$ is the spatial frequency and $\alpha$ is approximatively 2 [6]. As a first approximation, this was considered true regardless of direction in the spectrum. Nonetheless, some studies have refined this assertion [7,8]. Natural scenes with

J. Blanc-Talon et al. (Eds.): ACIVS 2005, LNCS 3708, pp. 116–122, 2005.
© Springer-Verlag Berlin Heidelberg 2005

small perceived depth, termed *closed* scenes, do have a spectrum of $1/f^2$ in all directions, but when the depth of the scene increases, the presence of a strong horizontal line corresponding to the horizon enhances vertical frequencies. The latter type of images are termed *open* scenes. Moreover, images representing human constructions, termed *artificial*, contain a lot of horizontal and vertical lines and this reflected in the corresponding frequencies.

In [8], it was shown that some image categories can be defined, corresponding to an approximate depth of the scene (congruent to semantic), according the shape of their global and local spectrums. These properties were first used to address the semantic gap in [7], by classifying *landscapes* and *artificial scenes* using Gabor filters. In a similar vein, we exploit this statistical structure to address the semantic gap for natural scenes, using the ridgelet transform that is optimally designed to represent edges [9]. The main contribution of this work is to propose a method that reduces the size and the redundancy of this ridgelet representation, by defining both global and local signatures that are specifically designed for semantic classification and content-based retrieval. Section 2 presents the ridgelet transform and the associated proposed global and local signatures. Experimental results for image classification and retrieval using these descriptors are presented in section 3, with conclusions drawn in section 4.

## 2    Image Representation

### 2.1    Ridgelet Transform

Given an integrable bivariate function $f(x)$, its continuous ridgelet transform (CRT) is defined as [9]:

$$CRT_f = \int_{\mathbb{R}^2} \psi_{a,b,\theta}(\mathbf{x}) f(\mathbf{x}) d\mathbf{x} \tag{1}$$

where the bidimensional ridgelets $\psi_{a,b,\theta}(x)$ are defined from a unidimensional wavelet $\psi(x)$ as:

$$\psi_{a,b,\theta}(\mathbf{x}) = a^{-1/2} \psi \left( \frac{x_1 cos\theta + x_2 sin\theta - b}{a} \right) \tag{2}$$

where $a$ is a scale parameter, $b$ a shift parameter, and $\mathbf{x} = (x_1, x_2)^T$. Hence, a ridgelet is constant along the line $x_1 cos\theta + x_2 sin\theta = const$ and has the shape of the wavelet $\psi(x)$ in the perpendicular direction.

Finding a discrete form of the ridgelet transform is a challenging issue. The key point for this is to consider the CRT of an image as the 1-D wavelet transform of the slices of its Radon transform. We used the method developed in [10], based on the pseudopolar Fourier transform that evaluates the 2-D Fourier transform on a non-Cartesian grid. This transform is used to compute the Radon transform, and support several nice properties, such as invertibility, algebraic exactness, geometric fidelity and rapid computation for images of size $2^n \times 2^n$. Code for this is provided in the Beamlab package [11].

The ridgelet transform of an image corresponds to the activity of a mother ridgelet at different orientations, scales and spatial localizations. At a given orientation, there are $2^n$ localizations at the highest scale, $2^{n-1}$ at the next lowest scale, and so on. For an image of size $2^n \times 2^n$, this results in a response of size $2^{n+1} \times 2^{n+1}$. The challenge is therefore to create a signature for the image from these responses, that leads to a reduction of the size of the feature whilst preserving relevant information useful for discrimination.

## 2.2   Global Ridgelet Signature

The global ridgelet signature $(Rd_{glb})$ is extracted by averaging the ridgelet responses over all spatial locations. This is motivated by the reported possibility of defining semantic categories of natural scenes according to their global statistics [8]. Since ridgelets are computed on square images, we extract the largest square part of the image and reduce it to an image of size $2^n \times 2^n$. Keeping one coefficient for each of the $2^{n+1}$ orientations and $n - 1$ scales results in a signature of size $(n - 1) * 2^{n+1}$. Since the sign of the activity simply corresponds to contrast direction, the average of the absolute value of the activity is computed.

## 2.3   Local Ridgelet Signature

For this descriptor, the image is divided into $4 \times 4 = 16$ non-overlapping areas, and the ridgelet transform of each area is computed. Because of the same constraints as for the global signature, each area has actually a size $2^n \times 2^n$ pixels. It has been shown that narrower categories can be defined by such local statistics [8]. A local template is designed to compute the signature for each area. It defines 10 regions on which a measure of activity is computed, as shown on figure 1. Other local templates were designed but can not be presented in this paper due to space constraints. There are two regions at the lower frequencies and four at the middle and higher frequencies centered around $0°$, $45°$, $90°$ and $135°$. For each region, we compute the activity as the average absolute value of the ridgelet response divided by the standard deviation over the region. This gives 10 coefficients for each local signature i.e. 160 coefficients for the local ridgelet signature $(Rd_{loc})$.

## 2.4   Support Vector Classifier (SVC)

Support vector classifiers (SVC) [12] are commonly used because of several attractive features, such as simplicity of implementation, few free parameters required to be tuned, the ability to deal with high-dimensional input data and good generalisation performance on many pattern recognition problems.

To apply a support vector machine (SVM) to classification in a linear separable case, we consider a set of training samples $\{(x_i, y_i),\ x_i \in \mathcal{X},\ y_i \in \mathcal{Y}\}$, with $\mathcal{X}$ the input space, and $\mathcal{Y} \triangleq \{-1, +1\}$ the label space. In the linear case, we assume the existence of a separating hyperplane between the two classes, i.e a function $h(\boldsymbol{x}) = \boldsymbol{w}^\top \boldsymbol{x} + b$ parameterized by $(\boldsymbol{w}, b)$, such that the sign of this function when applied to $x_i$ gives its label. By fixing $\min_i |h(x_i)| = 1$, we chose

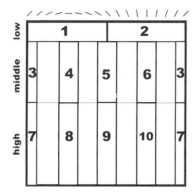

**Fig. 1.** Template defining 10 regions for the local signature. Rows represents the scales and columns are the orientations.

the normal vector $w$ such that the distance from the closest point of the learning set to the hyperplane is $1/\|w\|$. When training data is not linearly separable, a more complex function can be used to describe the boundary. This is done by using a kernel to map non-linear data into a much higher dimensional feature space, in which a simple classification is easier to find. In the following we use the LibSVM implementation [13] with a polynomial kernel of degree 1 to 4.

## 3    Experimental Results

In this section the performance of our ridgelet signatures for image classification and retrieval are compared to that of descriptors defined in the MPEG-7 visual standard [14]: *Edge histograms* (EH), *Homogeneous texture* (HT) based on a Gabor filter description, *Color Layout* (CL) and *Scalable Color*.

### 3.1    Scene Classification

Our test corpus consists of 1420 images of different sizes collected from both the web and professional databases[1] and are divided into four classes: *cities, indoor, open* and *closed* scenes. As explained in section 1, *open/closed* scenes refer to images of natural scenes with large/small perceived depth (i.e. with/without a horizon). Image signatures were computed as explained in section 2.2 and three sets of experiments were performed (Table 1). First, each class was classified against the others (Exps. $N°1\ldots4$). Then, *artificial* (consisting of both *cities, indoor*) versus *natural* (consisting of both *open, closed*) discrimination was investigated (Exp. $N°5$) as well as the intra-class classification within these classes (Exps. $N°6$, $N°7$). The final set of experiments investigated *cities* versus *natural* classification and the associated intra-class classification (Exps. $N°8\ldots10$). All experiments were repeated 10 times with randomly chosen learning and testing

---

[1] www.corel.com - www.goodshoot.com

**Table 1.** Percentage of correct classification for our signature and MPEG-7 descriptors (see part 3 for notations). Results are the average (± standard deviation) classification rate for 10 cross-validations.

| Exp. $N°$ | Experiment | $Rd_{glb}$ | $Rd_{loc}$ | EH | HT | CL | SC |
|---|---|---|---|---|---|---|---|
| 1 | Cities Vs other | 64.5(±3.9) | **77.2**(±4.2) | 67.0(±3.4) | 63.3(±4.5) | 59.5(±2.6) | 62.1(±4.0) |
| 2 | Closed Vs other | 60.4(±4.2) | 55.6(±1.8) | **73.6**(±3.1) | 59.6(±3.7) | 62.5(±5.1) | 62.9(±5.0) |
| 3 | Indoor Vs other | 71.1(±2.7) | 74.6(±2.1) | **79.4**(±2.2) | 72.2(±3.3) | **79.6**(±2.2) | 75.6(±3.4) |
| 4 | Open Vs other | 75.9(±3.6) | **93.0**(±1.3) | 78.2(±3.2) | 73.6(±3.9) | 65.4(±4.0) | 66.0(±3.1) |
| 5 | Artificial Vs Natural | 74.6(±1.7) | 72.8(±1.6) | **82.5**(±1.4) | 71.6(±2.8) | 64.3(±3.2) | 67.7(±3.3) |
| 6 | Indoor Vs Cities | 69.1(±2.0) | **88.1**(±1.4) | 71.9(±2.0) | 69.4(±3.2) | 83.3(±2.7) | 74.8(±2.2) |
| 7 | Open Vs Closed | 71.0(±2.6) | **91.8**(±0.9) | 72.9(±3.0) | 66.8(±2.4) | 65.3(±2.0) | 61.3(±3.8) |
| 8 | Natural Vs Cities | 73.2(±1.7) | **78.3**(±2.3) | **79.0**(±2.1) | 69.4(±2.5) | 57.5(±3.5) | 63.6(±4.3) |
| 9 | Open Vs Cities | 83.7(±2.2) | **96.5**(±1.0) | 85.3(±1.5) | 76.5(±2.7) | 60.0(±2.7) | 66.5(±1.9) |
| 10 | Closed Vs Cities | 70.1(±2.2) | 74.6(±1.3) | **78.2**(±1.8) | 70.5(±3.3) | 66.8(±1.9) | 68.9(±2.3) |

**Table 2.** Average precision for our signature and MPEG-7 descriptors (see part 3 for notations). It shows the average (± standard deviation) over 10 repetitions with different learning databases.

| Class | Size | $Rd_{glb}$ | $Rd_{loc}$ | EH | HT | CL | SC |
|---|---|---|---|---|---|---|---|
| city | 322 | 35.1(±3.7) | **48.1**(±4.8) | 32.8(±3.4) | 25.1(±4.2) | 25.7(±2.9) | 30.4(±3.4) |
| closed | 355 | 19.6(±1.3) | 24.3(±2.5) | **37.8**(±6.0) | 25.5(±2.8) | 32.3(±3.2) | 31.2(±2.7) |
| indoor | 404 | 36.6(±2.9) | 42.2(±4.5) | **52.4**(±4.0) | 38.5(±5.3) | 41.1(±2.3) | 41.6(±5.5) |
| open | 339 | 46.6(±5.4) | **66.8**(±3.9) | 54.7(±4.9) | 39.6(±5.4) | 34.9(±2.8) | 30.5(±2.6) |
| car | 136 | 18.2(±3.2) | **32.4**(±4.6) | 29.5(±7.0) | 10.7(±2.9) | 12.1(±1.6) | 10.4(±1.7) |
| doors | 100 | 43.9(±6.0) | 14.4(±4.2) | **74.8**(±5.9) | 19.6(±6.9) | 16.3(±3.5) | 10.7(±2.5) |
| firework | 100 | 41.7(±6.6) | 62.7(±5.7) | **68.2**(±9.0) | 55.0(±19.1) | 36.7(±13.2) | 34.3(±8.9) |
| flower | 100 | 11.6(±2.8) | 07.9(±2.4) | 21.7(±6.6) | 17.9(±7.4) | 10.2(±3.7) | **28.6**(±11.2) |
| sailing | 100 | 08.7(±1.3) | 21.7(±3.1) | 19.1(±4.1) | 6.4(±2.4) | 14.9(±5.3) | **24.2**(±8.1) |

databases without overlap (cross-validation). The size of the learning database was fixed to 40 images, but larger sizes gave similar results.

Experimental results are presented in Table 1. To discriminate one class from the others, $Rd_{loc}$ performs best for *cities* and *open*, while EH is better for *indoor* and *closed*. Color descriptors (CL and SC) have the worst performance, except for *indoor* for which all results are quite close, confirming the results of [4] that illustrated the importance of color descriptors for indoor/outdoor discrimination. In the *artificial* versus *natural* experiment, EH perform best, though $Rd_{loc}$ has significantly better results than any other descriptor in the intra-class experiments ($N°6$, 7). EH and $Rd_{loc}$ have similar results for *natural* versus *cities* classification ($N°8$). EH is slightly better in experiment $N°9$ but $Rd_{loc}$ outperforms all others in discriminating *open* scenes from *cities* ($N°10$).

### 3.2 Scene Retrieval

In order to estimate the retrieval performance of our signatures, the test corpus was extended to 1952 images using images from five smaller categories. Each of these new categories are characterized by the presence of an object: *door, firework, flower, car, sailing*. Objects are presented in a scene context that is congruent with their semantic: fireworks are in the sky, sailing activities on the sea, door on a building, cars on a road and flowers in a *closed* natural scene.

In practice, images are sorted according to their distance from the hyper-plane calculated by the SVC. Retrieval performances are usually estimated by the probability of detecting an image given that is relevant (*recall*) and the probability that an image is relevant given that it is detected by the algorithm (*precision*). However, precision generally decreases according to the number of images detected while recall increases. Thus, precision is a function of recall ($p(r)$) and a trade-off must be chosen. The average value of $p(r)$ over $[0 \ldots 1]$ defines the *average precision* and measures retrieval performance taking into account both recall and precision.

Retrieval experiments were repeated ten times with different learning data-bases, and the average performance (measured by *average precision*) are shown in Table 2. For scenes with global characteristics (first four rows), the ridgelet signature performs well for *open* and *cities* but less so for *closed* and *indoor*. In this latter case, results for $Rd_{loc}$ are similar to that of the color descriptors. Retrieval experiments for scenes containing a specific object (last five rows) demonstrate that $Rd_{loc}$ is among the best results for three categories (*car, firework, sailing*) but has poor results for *flowers* and *doors*. In this latter case, $Rd_{glb}$ has quite good performance though still significantly poorer than that of EH.

## 4   Concluding Remarks

In this paper, we proposed a new representation of natural images, based on a ridgelet description. Two image signatures were designed, allowing both global and local analysis. When used in conjunction with a support vector machine, these descriptors can be used to classify natural scene categories. The proposed descriptors also exhibit good performance in retrieval of scenes containing specific categories of objects. Future work will focus on defining other local signatures to address the shortcomings of this approach for specific categories, and combination between global and local approach.

## Acknowledgements

Part of this work was supported by the European Commission under contract FP6-001765 aceMedia (URL: http://www.acemedia.org). Authors are also supported by Enterprise Ireland and Egide that fund the Ulysse research project ReSEND (FR/2005/56).

## References

1. Santini, S.: Exploratory image databases : content-based retrieval. Academic press, London (2001)
2. Smeulders, A.W.M., Worring, M., Santini, S., Gupta, A., Jain, R.: Content-based image retrieval at the end of the early years. IEEE trans. on Pattern Analysis and Machine Intelligence **22** (2000) 1349–1380
3. Gorkani, M., Picard, R.: Texture orientation for sorting photos "at a glance". ICPR-A **1** (1994) 459–464
4. Szummer, M., Picard, R.: Indoor-outdoor image classification. In: IEEE international workshop on content-based access of images and video databases,. (1998) Bombay, India.
5. Vailaya, A., Jain, A., Zhang, H.J.: On image classification: City images vs. landscapes. Pattern Recognition **31** (1998) 1921–1936
6. Ruderman, D.: The statistics of natural images. Network: computation in neural systems **5** (1994) 517–548
7. Oliva, A., Torralba, A., Guérin-Dugué, A., Hérault, J.: Global semantic classification of scenes using power spectrum templates. In: Challenge of Image Retrieval, Springer-Verlag (1999) Newcastle, UK.
8. Torralba, A., Oliva, A.: Statistics of natural images categories. Network: Computation in Neural Systems **14** (2003) 391–412
9. Candès, E., Donoho, D.: Ridgelets: the key to high-dimensional intermittency? Phil. Trans. Royal Society of London A **357** (1999) 2495–2509
10. Averbuch, A., Coifman, R.R., Donoho, D.L., Israeli, M., Waldn, J.: Fast slant stack: A notion of radon transform for data in a cartesian grid which is rapidly computable, algebraically exact, geometrically faithful and invertible. SIAM Scientific Computing (2001)
11. Donoho, D., Flesia, A., Huo, X., Levi, O., Choi, S., Shi, D.: Beamlab 2.0. website (2003) http://www-stat.stanford.edu/ beamlab/.
12. Vapnik, V.: The Nature of Statistical Learning Theory. NY:Springer-Verlag (1995)
13. Chang, C., Lin, C.: LIBSVM: a library for support vector machines. (2001) Software available at www.csie.ntu.edu.tw/~cjlin/libsvm.
14. Manjunath, B., Ohm, J.R., Vasudevan, V., Yamada, A.: Color and texture descriptors. IEEE trans. circuits and systems for video technology **11** (2001) 703–715

# Multi-banknote Identification Using a Single Neural Network

Adnan Khashman[1] and Boran Sekeroglu[2]

[1] Electrical & Electronic Engineering Department, Near East University, North Cyprus
amk@neu.edu.tr
[2] Computer Engineering Department, Near East University, North Cyprus
bsekeroglu@neu.edu.tr

**Abstract.** Real-life applications of neural networks require a high degree of success, usability and reliability. Image processing has an importance for both data preparation and human vision to increase the success and reliability of pattern recognition applications. The combination of both image processing and neural networks can provide sufficient and robust solutions to problems where intelligent recognition is required. This paper presents an implementation of neural networks for the recognition of various banknotes. One combined neural network will be trained to recognize all the banknotes of the Turkish Lira and the Cyprus Pound; as they are the main currencies used in Cyprus. The flexibility, usability and reliability of this Intelligent Banknote Identification System (IBIS) will be shown through the results and a comparison will be drawn between using separate neural networks or a combined neural network for each currency.

**Keywords:** Neural Networks, Pattern Recognition, Image Processing, Multi-Banknote Identification.

## 1 Introduction

We, humans, excel at recognizing patterns and consequently identifying objects. Our ability to recognize objects is related to the intelligent processor within our brains, in addition to the process of learning overtime. This natural intelligence has been a target for researchers in Artificial Intelligence lately [1]. The idea is to develop machines with intelligence similar to that of our own. Even better, is to develop artificially intelligent machines that recognize pattern in a similar way as we do [2]. An example of our ability to recognize patterns is our recognition of banknotes without the need to "read" the number written on a banknote. This happens after we use banknotes for sometime (training time for our natural neural networks!). Once our brains learn the values of the banknotes, all we need would be to have a quick look and recognize the value.

IBIS (Intelligent Banknote Identification System) was designed to simulate the above using neural networks and pattern recognition [3]. Separate neural networks were developed to recognize different international banknotes [4].

J. Blanc-Talon et al. (Eds.): ACIVS 2005, LNCS 3708, pp. 123 – 129, 2005.
© Springer-Verlag Berlin Heidelberg 2005

The work presented within this paper aims at developing a *single* neural network with a *combined output* for two different international currencies; namely the Cyprus Pound and the Turkish Lira. The back propagation learning algorithm is implemented using an input layer with 100 neurons, one hidden layer with 30 neurons and one combined output layer with nine neurons.

A comparison will be drawn between using separate neural networks for each currency [5] and using a single neural network with a combined output for all currencies. Training and generalizing run times will be considered for the purpose of comparison.

## 2 The Banknotes

There are four banknotes of the Cyprus Pound (1CYP, 5CYP, 10CYP and 20CYP) and five banknotes of the Turkish Lira (500,000TL, 1,000,000TL, 5,000,000TL, 10,000,000TL and 20,000,000TL). The images of these banknotes are of size (550x256) pixels that are acquired using a scanner. Each banknote has different characteristics and patterns on its both sides (front and back).

These banknotes are organized into two sets: a training set and a generalizing (testing) set. The training set will include four Cypriot banknotes and five Turkish banknotes; each with front and back images resulting in a total of 18 images of the different banknotes (Fig.1 shows examples of front and back images of Turkish Lira and Cyprus Pound). The generalizing set will comprise nine old and soiled *(noisy)* banknotes of the same values; similarly resulting in 18 images for testing. The complete set of images used for training is shown in Fig. 2 and Fig. 3.

| (a) 1,000,000 TL Front | (b) 1,000,000 TL Back |
| (c) 1 CYP Front | (d) 1 CYP Back |

**Fig. 1.** Example of images of front and back of the Banknotes

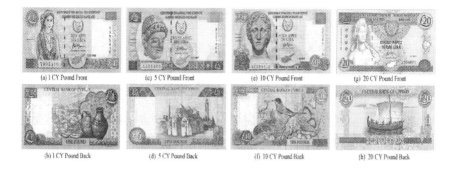

**Fig. 2.** Cyprus Pound Banknotes

**Fig. 3.** Turkish Lira Banknotes

## 3   Image Processing and Data Preparation

In the data preparation phase, image processing is applied to the banknotes prior to training the neural network. The "average pixel per node" approach is used to reduce the number of inputs to the network thus improving its training and generalization time. This is achieved via image segmentation and averaging using the following equations:

$$Seg_i = \left( \sum P[x, y] \right) / D \qquad (1)$$

where *Seg* denotes the segment number, *P* denotes the pixel value and *D* is the total number of pixels in each segment;

$$D = \left( TP_x.TP_y \right) / S \qquad (2)$$

where *TP* denotes the *x* and *y* pixel size of image and *S* is the total segment number.

Prior to training the neural network, scanned banknote images are converted to grayscale. A window of size (256x256) pixels is centered upon the image and the patterns within the window are cropped. This square segment of the banknote image is then compressed to (128x128) pixels. In order to reduce the training and generalization time of IBIS, a square window of size (100x100) pixels is extracted and the average pixel per node approach is applied using segments of 10x10 pixels. This results in 100 values that uniquely represent each banknote. The next phase will be training a single neural network to recognize the various banknote images.

## 4   Training the Neural Network

A 3-layer neural network using the back propagation learning algorithm is used for learning. The input layer has 100 neurons, the hidden layer has 30 hidden neurons and the output layer has 9 neurons. The neural network's topology can be seen in Fig. 4.

During this learning phase, initial random weights of values between –0.3 and 0.3 were used. The learning rate and the momentum rate; were adjusted during various experiments in order to achieve the required minimum error value and meaningful learning. An error value of 0.005 was considered as sufficient for this application. Table 1 shows the final parameters of the trained neural network.

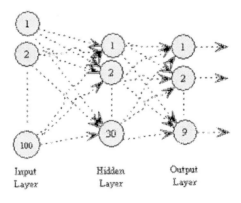

**Fig. 4.** Neural Network Topology

**Table 1.** Trained neural network final parameters

| | |
|---|---|
| Input Layer Nodes | 100 |
| Hidden Layer Nodes | 30 |
| Output Layer Nodes | 9 |
| Learning Rate | 0.0099 |
| Momentum Rate | 0.50 |
| Minimum Error | 0.005 |
| Iterations | 4241 |
| Training Time | 91 seconds |

## 5  Results

The Intelligent Banknote Identification System (IBIS) is implemented using the C-programming language. The first phase of data preparation using image processing is implemented prior to training or eventually generalizing the neural network in the second phase. Once the neural network learns the various patterns (banknotes), IBIS can be run with one neural network forward pass to recognize the banknote. A general block diagram of IBIS can be seen in Fig. 5.

IBIS was trained using 18 images of clean new banknotes. The results of generalizing the neural network using these clean banknotes was 100% as would be expected. However, to generalize the single neural network, 18 old used (noisy) banknotes were

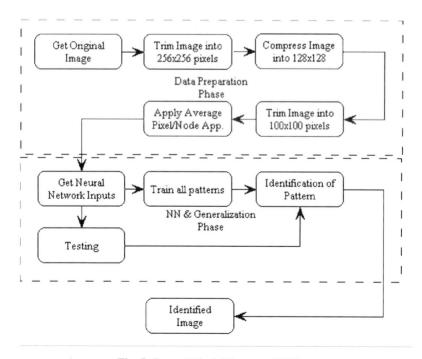

**Fig. 5.** General Block Diagram of IBIS

used. The difference between the banknotes used for training and for generalization would be the difference in the pixel values of the scanned images of the banknotes. It's thought that using real-life samples of banknotes would be more realistic while providing a robust way of testing the efficiency of the neural network in identifying noisy patterns. IBIS ability to recognize "noisy" patterns (i.e. old used banknotes) was also tested and returned 90% recognition rate for both currencies.

**Table 2.** Efficiency and Time Cost for Single versus Separate neural networks

| Pattern Set | Separate Neural Networks | | Single Neural Network | |
|---|---|---|---|---|
| | Training | Generalizing | Training | Generalizing |
| Training Time (seconds) | 130.4 | - | 91 | - |
| Generalizing Time (seconds) | - | 0.05 | - | 0.05 |
| Recognition Ratio | 100 % | 95 % | 100 % | 90 % |
| Total Efficiency | 97.5 % | | 95 % | |

Table 2 shows a comparison between the system presented within this paper (using a single neural network with combined output for both currencies) and the previously developed system [5] using two separate neural networks for each currency. An overall recognition ratio of 95% for the single network is considered sufficient considering the reduction in time cost. Training time reduction from 130.4 seconds to 91 seconds justifies the slight reduction (2.5%) in total efficiency when comparing the combined out network with separate output network. Generalizing (run) time based on a single forward pass of the neural network resulted in similar time cost of 0.05 seconds.

# 6  Conclusion

In this paper, an intelligent system for recognizing multi-banknotes of different currencies was presented. The system (IBIS) recognizes banknotes using patterns within the banknotes. Based on "average pixel per node" approach, IBIS provides training / generalization input data for the neural network. The currencies used for the implementation of IBIS were the Turkish Lira and the Cyprus Pound which are; commonly used currencies in Cyprus. The developed system may also be successfully used with any banknote of different currencies once the neural network is trained on these currencies.

The developed system uses a single neural network with a combined output for the recognition of the different banknotes in the different currencies. A training time of 91 seconds with generalization (run) time of 0.05 seconds shows a fast efficient intelligent system for recognizing multi-banknotes.

A comparison between using a single neural network and separate neural networks for different currencies has shown that a single network with combined output returns marginal reduction in time cost with a minimal reduction in recognition ratio.

Future work would include the implementation of IBIS using a single neural network for the recognition of more currencies such as the Euro, US Dollar and the new Turkish Lira (YTL) which will be used alongside the current TL during the year 2005. Finally, intelligent machine recognition of Euro banknotes and classification of which European Union country they originate from depending on the different patterns on the banknotes will also be considered.

## References

1. Koramtiperis P., Manoufelis N., Prafolis T.B.: Architecture Selection for Neural Networks, International Joint Conference on Neural Networks, The 2002 IEEE World Congress, Hawaii, May 12-17 (2002) 1115-1120
2. Azimi–Badjadi M., Salazar J., Robinson M.: Multi-Aspect Target Discrimination using Hidden Markov Models, , IEEE Transactions on Neural Networks, Vol 16. No:2 March (2005) 447-459
3. Khashman A. and Sekeroglu B.: Banknote Recognition using Neural Networks and Image Processing, Proceedings of the 2nd International Symposium on Electrical, Electronic and Computer Engineering, NEU-CEE'2004, IEEE Turkey Section, Nicosia, North Cyprus, March (2004) 272-275
4. Khashman A. and Sekeroglu B.: IBIS: Intelligent Banknote Identification System, Proceedings of the International Conference on Computational Intelligence ICCI'2004, IEEE Turkey Section, Nicosia, North Cyprus, (May 2004) 118-121
5. Khashman A. & Sekeroglu B.: Intelligent Banknote Identification System, Proceedings of the 9th World Multiconference on Systemics, Cybernetics and Informatics (WMSCI 2005), Orlando, USA, to be published in July( 2005)

# A New Voting Algorithm for Tracking Human Grasping Gestures

Pablo Negri, Xavier Clady, and Maurice Milgram

LISIF - PARC, UMPC (Paris 6),
3 Galilee 94200 Ivry-sur-Seine, France
pablo.negri@lisif.jussieu.fr
{clady, maum}@ccr.jussieu.fr

**Abstract.** This article deals with a monocular vision system for grasping gesture acquisition. This system could be used for medical diagnostic, robot or game control. We describe a new algorithm, the Chinese Transform, for the segmentation and localization of the fingers. This approach is inspired in the Hough Transform utilizing the position and the orientation of the gradient from the image edge's pixels. Kalman filters are used for gesture tracking. We presents some results obtained from images sequence recording a grasping gesture. These results are in accordance with medical experiments.

## 1 Introduction

In gesture taxonomy [1], manipulative gestures are defined as ones that act on objects inside an environment. They are the subject of many studies in the cognitive and medical communities. The works of Jeannerod [2,3] are the references in this domain. These studies are frequently carried out to determine the influences of psychomotor diseases (Parkinson [4], cerebral lesions [5], etc.) on the coordination of grasping gestures. A typical experiment involves numerous objects, generally cylindrical, of varying size and position placed on a table. Subjects grasp the objects following a defined protocol. Active infrared makers are placed on the thumb, the index finger and over the palm. Vision systems, such as Optotrack, track the markers to record the trajectory performed during the test, in order to measure the subject responses to the stimulus.

In this paper, we propose a low-cost and less restrictive vision system, requiring only one camera and a computer. Many applications could be envisioned with this device, for example medical assistance [4,5], as natural human-computer interface (see [6] for more information on natural HCI) to control arm robots for grasping tasks [7], or virtual games.

We follow the experimental protocol described in [2,3,5,4]. The system is composed of a layout according to the specification of the Evolution Platform (EP), made of eight colored circles placed in a known geometry (see fig. 1). The hand in a grasping configuration (the index opposite to the thumb) moves in a horizontal plane with constant height (Z-axis). The camera is static and

J. Blanc-Talon et al. (Eds.): ACIVS 2005, LNCS 3708, pp. 130–137, 2005.
© Springer-Verlag Berlin Heidelberg 2005

placed sufficiently far away in order to capture a complete view of the EP; with this configuration, we can consider the differences in Z-axis between hand points negligible. The 3D position of the finger are calculated with these assumptions and an iterative estimation of the camera pose [8] (see fig. 2).

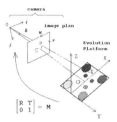

**Fig. 1.** Camera view of the Evolution Platform

**Fig. 2.** Systems of reference for the camera and platform

In the next section, we describe the procedures to extract the finger positions in the image. Once a subregion of the image has been determined with a background subtraction algorithm, a skin color distance image is calculated for the extraction of the oriented edges of the hand. These edges were used in an original algorithm, the Chinese Transform (CT), for the segmentation and localization of the fingers. This approach is inspired from the Hough Transform. This algorithm allows the extraction of finger segments. Section 3 concerns the gesture tracking. We use a Kalman filter adapted to segment tracking. A simplified hand model makes it possible to determine the hand parameters generally used to analyze the grasping gesture. Section 4 presents some results obtained with our system. We conclude this article with some perspectives.

## 2   Detection of Hand and Fingers

### 2.1   Image Preprocessing

During the initial phase of the image preprocessing we used background subtraction to localize a sub-region in the image where the hand could be. We applied Stauffer and Grimson's Gaussian Mixture Model (GMM) method [9]. In our approach, we use the chrominance of the color space $YC_bC_r$ instead of the $RGB$ color space used by Stauffer and Grimson [9]. This permit us to ignore shadows of the hand. From this background subtraction, we obtain a binary image of the foreground pixels representing moving objects. We defined a search window including all the foreground pixels, which offers the advantage of reduced computing time for the following operations.

Secondly, the search window in the color image is converted to a skin color distance image. We emphasize the pixels with skin color chrominances, giving the maximum values in the skin color distance image. The converted $RGB$ image, $I$, into the $YC_bC_r$ color space is referred to as $I_{ybr}$. Next, we calculate the inverse distance to the skin color, subtracting the chrominance channels $b$ and $r$ from $I_{ybr}$ with the experimental values $b_{skin}$ and $r_{skin}$ respectively.

$$\overline{I_b} = |I_{ybr}(b) - b_{skin}|$$
$$\overline{I_r} = |I_{ybr}(r) - r_{skin}|$$
$$\overline{I_{br}} = \sqrt{\overline{I_b} + \overline{I_r}}$$

Finally, we obtained a skin color distance image (see fig. 5), defined by :

$$I_{sk} = 1 - \frac{\overline{I_{br}}}{max(\overline{I_{br}})}$$

## 2.2    The Chinese Transformation

The Chinese Transformation (CT) takes its name from Zhongguo, usually translated as *Middle Kingdom*, the mandarin name for China. The CT is a voting method: two points having opposite gradient directions vote for their mid-point. This method has the same basic principle as Reisfeld [10].

In the example of figure 3, two edge points $e_1$ and $e_2$ obtained from an image of an ellipse $I_e$, were defined with two parameters: the normal vector, $n_i$, and the position in the image, $p_i(x, y)$, with $i = \{1, 2\}$. Each normal vector was represented by the orientation of the gradient at this point. $p_{12}$ was the segment drawn between the two points with $p_v$ its mid-point.

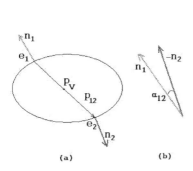

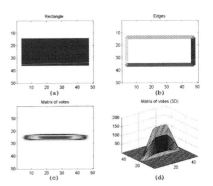

**Fig. 3.** (a) shows two edge points of the image with their normal vectors, (b) shows the two normal vectors superposed forming an angle $\alpha$

**Fig. 4.** Example of the CT for a rectangle. (a) original image, (b) oriented edges, (c) and (d) votes array in 2D and 3D spaces.

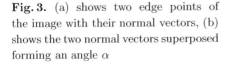

Superposing $e_1$ over $e_2$, we can compare their orientations. We say that $e_1$ and $e_2$ have opposite orientations if the angle $\alpha_{12}$ formed between $n_1$ and $-n_2$ satisfies the condition:

$$\alpha_{12} < \alpha_{threshold} \qquad (1)$$

Then, the CT votes for $p_v$, the mid-point point of $p_{12}$ if:

$$|p_{12}| < d \qquad (2)$$

We create and increment an accumulator (votes array) with all the couples satisfying the conditions (1) and (2).

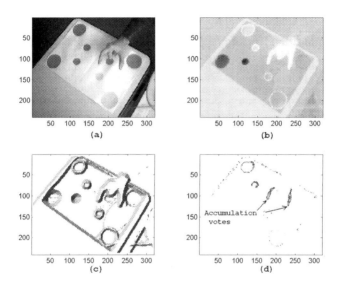

**Fig. 5.** Illustrations of Chinese Transform. (a) Original image, (b) Skin color distance image, (c) Oriented gradient image: each orientation is represented by a different color in the image, (d) Votes array.

The Fig. 4 is an example of the CT algorithm applied to a rectangle. The Fig. 4.a represents the original image. The Fig. 4.b shows the contour of 4.a and we can see the different orientations of the gradient in different colors. In practice, we sample the gradient orientations in $N = 8$ directions; this operation fixes a practical value for $\alpha_{threshold}$. The choix of this value depends on the application. With lower values there will be more pairs of voting points, increasing computing time. With higher values, we obtain much less voting points, losing information. The votes array (see Fig. 4.c and 4.d) is the result of applying the CT for all the edge points of Fig. 4.a with $d = 35$.

In our application, we take advantage of the form of the index finger and thumb (the two fingers forming the grip). Their parallel edges satisfy the distance and gradient direction conditions. The accumulation zones founded in the votes array can define the fingers regions (Fig. 5.d). A special function implementing a few variants of Hough Transform for segments detection is applied to the votes array (fig. 6). Each region's point votes, in the Hough space, with a value

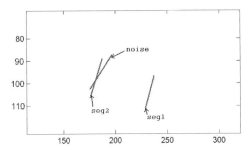

**Fig. 6.** The segments resulting from the CT

proportional to the quantity of votes in the accumulator. The resulting segments represent the finger regions.

Results of the CT can be compared with the morphological skeleton algorithm. But this method employs regions and has to deal with their usual defaults: holes presence, contour's gaps, partial occlusion, etc. The CT works around these problems with a statistical voting technique. In addition, it should be noted that CT could be useful in other contexts like detection of axial symmetries or the eyes localization in face images [11].

## 3   Gesture Tracking and Representation

Kalman filters [12] adapted to the segments makes it possible to both track the finger segments and eliminate the false alarms.

### 3.1   Segments Tracking

The objective is the tracking of segments belonging to the fingers in a sequence of images. This segments were obtained from the votes array of the Chinese Transformation and the application of the Hough Transformation. The parameters identifying each segment are (see fig. 7): $P_m(x_m, y_m)$, mid-point coordinates, $l$ and $\theta$, respectively the length and the angle of the segment.

Our system is made of three independent Kalman filters. Two scalar filters for the length and the orientation, and one vectorial filter for the position. If we consider constant speed, the state vectors are:

$$X^{P_m} = \begin{pmatrix} x_m \\ \dot{x}_m \\ y_m \\ \dot{y}_m \end{pmatrix} \qquad X^l = \begin{pmatrix} l \\ \dot{l} \end{pmatrix} \qquad X^\theta = \begin{pmatrix} \theta \\ \dot{\theta} \end{pmatrix}$$

We track all the segments in the image sequence. There are false alarms, but they disappear in the successive images. We keep and track the segments corresponding to the fingers. These segments follow the Kalman conditions and the constraints on the grip model.

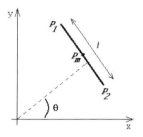
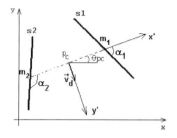

**Fig. 7.** Segment model                     **Fig. 8.** Grip model

## 3.2  Grip Tracking

From two fingers segments, we model a grip (see Fig. 8) with the following parameters: $p_c$, mid-point of the segment $m_1m_2$; $\Theta_{pc}$, angle that defines the inclination of the grip; $v_d$, unit vector which defines the grip's orientation and $l_{12}$, length of the segment $m_1m_2$.

We add two other parameters: the orientations $\alpha_1$ and $\alpha_2$ of the segments $s_1$ and $s_2$, calculated after a change of coordinate axis, from the $(x, y)$ (see fig. 8.a) axis into the $(p_c, x', y')$ axis related to the grip (see fig. 8.b).

The new state vectors for the grip tracking are: $X^{p_c}$, $X^{\Theta_{pc}}$, $X^{\alpha_1}$, $X^{\alpha_2}$ and $X^{l_{12}}$. This representation was inspired from the studies on grasping gestures from [2,3,5,4]. We can easily observe the principal variables used in these studies: inter-distance between fingers (grip aperture), positions and orientations of the hand related to the scene (and to the objects), etc. In addition, we can define an articulatory model of the grip. By considering its geometrical model inversion, we can simulate a robotized representation of the grip in an OpenGL virtual environment.

## 4  Results

We apply the CT in a video sequence, taked from a webcam at 14 frames/second, composed of three stages. The first stage shows a hand going to grasp an imaginary object in the corner of the EP (see Fig. 9). The next stage shows the subject's hand puting the imaginary object down in the opposite corner of the EP. The final stage is the hand returning to the initial position. Here, we present only the result obtained for the stage 1.

Results of the CT on the first stage are shown in Fig. 10. In Fig. 10.a we can see all the segments recorded along the first 38 frames from the sequence. In the Fig. 10.b, the trajectory of the $p_c$ point is shown. The grip aperture and hand velocity curves for the stage 1 are showed in Fig. 10.c and Fig. 10.d, respectively. According to Jeannerod, the arm mouvement to the target-object location of a normal subject is divided into 2 phases: a high-speed phase corresponding to the 75% of the movement of approach towards the object and a final low-speed phase [3]. In fig. 10.d we notice the first phase until the frame 15 characterized by a great acceleration and an increase in the distance inter fingers (fig. 10.c). Then,

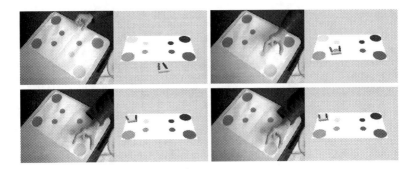

**Fig. 9.** This figure shows a picture sequence of the stage 1. On the left picture, we can see the camera view and, on the right image, the OpenGL environment with a virtual grip reproducing simultaneously the gesture.

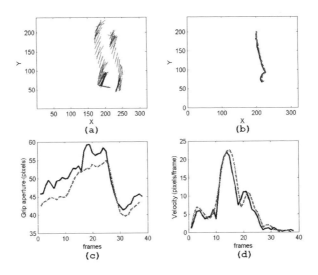

**Fig. 10.** Results for the stage 1: (a) all the segments. (b) trajectory of the point $p_c$. (c) distance between fingers (d) velocity of the hand. This figure show in dot points the hand labeled data for the curves (b), (c) and (d).

there are a deceleration of the hand while approaching to the object, reaching the final hand grip aperture.

This information can be used by the specialists in order to measure the patient's ability. They can also be useful for medical diagnostics.

## 5   Conclusion and Perspectives

Our goal was the tracking of the grasping gestures in a video sequence to detect psychomotor diseases. This article presented a system for the acquisition and analysis of the human grasping gestures. It used a new method for fingers detection and localization, called Chinese Transform. This technique is a voting method inspired by Hough Transform. Kalman filters were used for gesture tracking. The obtained results were in accordance with observations of medical studies [2,3].

The next steps of our works will be oriented in the determination and the prediction of the grip points on an object. For that, we will have to analyze the gesture related to the intrinsic (form, size, etc) and extrinsic (position, orientation) object characteristics.

# References

1. Pavlovic, V., Sharma, R., Huang, T.S.: Visual interpretation of hand gestures for human-computer interaction: A review. PAMI **19** (1997) 677–695
2. Jeannerod, M.: Intersegmental coordination during reaching at natural visual objects. Attention and performance (Long J, Baddeley A, eds) (1981) 153–168
3. Jeannerod, M.: The timing of natural prehension movements. Journal of Motor Behavior (1984) 16:235–254
4. Castiello, U., Bennet, K., Bonfiglioli, C., Lim, S., Peppard, R.: The reach-to-grap movement in parkinson's disease: response to a simultaneous perturbation of object position and object size. Computer Exp. Brain Res (1999) 453–462
5. Hermdrfer, J., Ulrich, S., Marquardt, C., Goldenberg, G., Mai, N.: Prehension with the ipsilesional hand after unilateral brain damage. Cortex (1999) 35:139–161
6. Turk, M., Kolsch, M.: Perceptual Interfaces. In: Emerging Topics in Computer Vision. Prentice Hall PTR (2005)
7. Triesh, J., von der Malsburg, C.: Classification of hand postures agains complex backgrounds using elastic graph matching. Image and Vision Computing **20** (2002) 937–943
8. Oberkampf, D., DeMenthon, D., Davis, L.: Iterative pose estimation using coplanar feature points. Computer Vision and Image Understanding **63** (1996) 495–511
9. Stauffer, C., Grimson, W.: Adaptive background mixture models for real-time tracking. In: CVPR. Volume 2., Fort Collins, Colorado (1999) 22–46
10. Reisfeld, D.: Generalized Symmetry Transforms: Attentional Mechanisms and Face Recognition. PhD thesis, Tel Aviv University (1994)
11. Milgram, M., Prevost, L., Belaroussi, R.: Multi-stage combination of geometric and colorimetric detectors for eyes localization. In: ICIAP, Cagliari, Italie (2005)
12. Kalman, R.: A new approach to linear filtering and prediction problems. Transactions of the ASME - Journal of Basic Engineering (1960) 35–45

# Gender Classification in Human Gait
# Using Support Vector Machine

Jang-Hee Yoo[1], Doosung Hwang[2], and Mark S. Nixon[3]

[1] ETRI-Information Security Research Division,
161 Gajeong-Dong, Yuseong-Gu, Daejeon 305-700, South Korea
jhy@etri.re.kr
[2] Department of Computer Science, Dankook University,
San#29, Anseo-Dong, Cheonan, Chungnam 330-714, South Korea
dshwang@dankook.ac.kr
[3] School of Electronics and Computer Science, University of Southampton,
Southampton SO17 1BJ, UK
msn@ecs.soton.ac.uk

**Abstract.** We describe an automated system that classifies gender by utilising a set of human gait data. The gender classification system consists of three stages: *i*) detection and extraction of the moving human body and its contour from image sequences; *ii*) extraction of human gait signature by the joint angles and body points; and *iii*) motion analysis and feature extraction for classifying gender in the gait patterns. A sequential set of 2D stick figures is used to represent the gait signature that is primitive data for the feature generation based on motion parameters. Then, an SVM classifier is used to classify gender in the gait patterns. In experiments, higher gender classification performances, which are 96% for 100 subjects, have been achieved on a considerably larger database.

## 1 Introduction

The study of human gait has generated much interest in fields including biomechanics, clinical analysis, computer animation, robotics, and biometrics. Human gait is known to be one of the most universal and complex of all human activities. It has been studied in medical science [5, 10], psychology [6], and biomechanics [15] for decades. In computer vision, automated person identification by gait has recently been investigated [11]. The potential of gait as a biometric has further been encouraged by the considerable amount of evidence available, especially in medical [10, 14] and psychological studies [6]. As a biometric, human gait may be defined as a means of identifying individuals by the way they walk. Using gait has many advantages over other biometrics such as fingerprints, most notably that it is non-invasive and can be used at a distance. Various approaches [2, 11] for the classification and recognition of human gait have been studied, but human gait identification is still a difficult task.

On the other hand, gender classification could play an important role in automatic gait recognition if the number of subjects is large, as it would split the number of subjects to be searched [2]. In study by Kozlowski and Cutting [8], they examined

J. Blanc-Talon et al. (Eds.): ACIVS 2005, LNCS 3708, pp. 138–145, 2005.
© Springer-Verlag Berlin Heidelberg 2005

recognising the gender of walker from moving light displays (MLDs) involving 3 male subjects and 3 female subjects all about the same height. Their results showed that humans were able to correctly identify gender using full body joint markers at 63% correctness on average, which is just better than chance (50%). In a later study, Mather and Murdoch [9] showed that frontal or oblique views are much more effective than a side view for gender discrimination, and emphasised that male subjects trend to swing their shoulders more while female subjects tend to swing their hips, the results improved to an accuracy of 79%.

In this paper, we propose an automated gender classification system in human gait using Support Vector Machine (SVM). The large amount of human gait data was collected from DV cameras, and the human body and its contour is extracted from the image sequences. A 2D stick figure is used to represent the human body structure, and it is extracted from body contour by determining the body points. To extract the body points, joint angles of each segment are extracted from gait skeleton data by linear regression analysis, and gait motion between key-frames is described by tracking the moving points of locomotion. The body segments and moving points are basically guided by topological analysis with anatomical knowledge. Also, the features based on motion parameters are calculated from sequence of the stick figures, and then an SVM classifier is employed to classify gender in the gait patterns.

## 2 Extracting Human Gait Motion

In computer vision, motion analysis of the human body usually involves segmenting, tracking and recovering the human body motion in an image sequence. Fig. 1 shows the system architecture used within this study. Here, a simplified 2D stick figure with six joint angles [16] is used to represent the human body structure for recovering and interpreting the human movement. Also, the horizontal centre of mass in the upper body is used as a gait symmetry point to detect the gait cycle. According to biomechanical analysis [15], the upper body's speed varies a little, being fastest during the double support phases and slowest in the middle of the stance and swing phases. Hence, the centre of mass of the upper body will keep the maximum distance from front foot at initial contact, end of terminal stance or terminal swing, and it has minimum distance from the front foot at end of mid-stance or mid-swing.

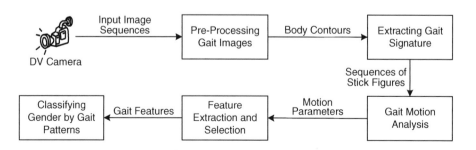

**Fig. 1.** Overview of Gender Classification System

## 2.1  Human Gait Database

The SOTON database [12] developed by the ISIS Research Group is one of the recent databases within the DARPA Human ID at a Distance program. An image sequence in the database contains only a single subject walking at normal speed and was acquired at 25 fps with 720×576 colour pixels from good quality progressive scan DV cameras. All subjects in the database are filmed fronto-parallel (where the walking path is normal to the camera view) or at an oblique angle. Each subject has at least four image sequences and each image sequence contains at least one gait cycle, together with background and other supporting data. The most recent version of the SOTON database contains more than 100 different subjects and was mostly acquired from young and healthy university students during the summer.

  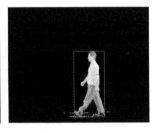

(a) Sample Image        (b) Background Subtraction        (c) Object Detection

**Fig. 2.** Background Subtraction and Object Detection

Fig. 2(a) shows sample image from the SOTON indoor database. As can be seen in the figure, a chroma-key laboratory was constructed to allow controlled lighting conditions. Due to the nature of both the capture and colour data in the database, the use of a colour specific extraction is possible. That is, human body extraction from the image sequences can be easily achieved through background subtraction as shown in Fig. 2(b). After that, the histogram projection profiles are analysed to estimate the position of a human body as shown in Fig. 2(c), and the body region is verified by prior knowledge such as size and shape. Thresholding and morphology are then used to extract the contour of a detected human body. Here, a thresholding method based on similarity measures between the background and the object image is used. Finally, the body contour is extracted by subtraction followed by dilation and erosion.

## 2.2  Extracting Gait Signature

The analysis of human motion often requires knowledge of the properties of body segments. To extract body points in a contour image, a skeleton data with body segment properties is used. For a body height $H$, an initial estimate of the vertical position of the neck, shoulder, waist, pelvis, knee and ankle was set by study of anatomical data to be $0.870H$, $0.818H$, $0.530H$, $0.480H$, $0.285H$, and $0.039H$, respectively [1]. The gait skeleton can be simply calculated by two border points of each body part $p$ with a range constraint. The angles $\theta_p$ of body part $p$ from skeleton data can be approximated by using the slope of the lines in linear regression equation. Also, each body point (position) can be calculated by

$$x_p, y_p = \left[ x_i + L_p \cos(\phi + \theta_p) \quad y_i + L_p \sin(\phi - \theta_p) \right] \tag{1}$$

where $\phi$ is the phase shift, $x_i$ and $y_i$ are the coordinates of a previously established position, and $L_p$ is the length of body segments guided by anatomical knowledge [1].

Now we can extract a 2D stick figure with the nine body points from the skeleton data of each body segment. The body points are clearly extracted around three double supports [14], but the points around single support appear less well defined than those for the double support. Thus, a motion tracking method between double supports is used to extract body points at the lower limbs. To track knees and ankles, the left-most skeleton points around the knee region and the right-most skeleton points around the ankle region are considered. In addition, functional or physical constraints are used to improve the robustness of the method. For example, during the gait cycle, the other foot is in contact with the floor (and does not move forwards), and the crossover of the two legs is performed on two single supports during one gait cycle.

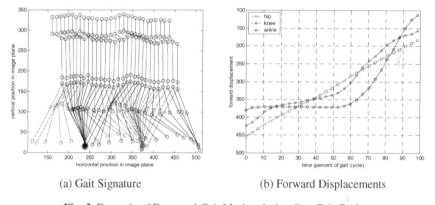

(a) Gait Signature                    (b) Forward Displacements

**Fig. 3.** Example of Extracted Gait Motion during One Gait Cycle

The extracted stick figures from an image sequence are shown in Fig. 3(a), and its forward displacement at hip, knee, and ankle shown in Fig. 3(b). The gait signature can be defined as a sequence of the stick figures obtained from gait silhouette data during one gait cycle. Here, the forward displacement of joints is consistent with medical data [5, 10, 14], and it is an important component for showing quality of the extracted gait signature. Also, the stick figure model is the most effective and well-defined representation method for kinematic gait analysis. Moreover, the stick figure is closely related to a joint representation, and the motion of the joints provides a key to motion estimation and recognition of the whole figure.

### 2.3  Feature Extraction and Selection

In the previous section, the gait signature is represented by a sequence of the simplified stick figure with 8 sticks and 6 joint angles, and gait motion can be describing the motion in a compact form as sequence of the joint parameters. Namely, each gait signature can be characterised by the body segments (the sticks) and joint angles. The joint angles of the hip, knee and ankle have been considered as the most important kinematics of the lower limbs. By definition [15], the joint angles are measured as one joint relative to another, so the relative angles in each joint are computed from the extracted angle values. In normal walking, the trunk of a human body can be considered to be almost vertical. Thus, the relative hip angle ($\theta_{hip}$) is the same as that of the extracted value ($\theta_H$), and the knee angle can be calculated from the extracted hip angle ($\theta_H$) and knee angle ($\theta_K$) as $\theta_{knee} = \theta_H - \theta_K$.

Kinematic analysis of human gait usually characterises the joint angles between body segments and their relationship to the events of the gait cycle [14, 15]. In addition, the trajectories of the gait signature contain many kinematic characteristics on human movement. The kinematic characteristics include linear and angular position, their displacements and the time derivatives, notably the linear and angular velocities and accelerations. Here, the kinematic parameters are obtained from the joint angles, which are interpolated by $4^{th}$-order trigonometric polynomials [16], during one gait cycle. In general, the kinematic parameters are time series data during the gait cycle, thus mean and standard deviation values of the time series can be used as gait features. Moreover, moments [4] are used to generate the features, which are invariant to translation and scaling of the hip and knee angles. The hip-knee cyclograms [4] represent the movement of nearly the entire body, thus they can be representative of the subject's gait pattern.

The trajectories of gait signature also contain the general gait parameters such as stride length, cycle time (or cadence) and speed and provide a basic description of the gait motion [14]. These parameters present essential quantitative information about a human gait and give a guide to the walking ability of subject. In addition, each parameter may be affected by such factors as age, sex, height, muscle strength, etc. The period of the gait is determined by number of frames during one gait cycle in image sequence, and the frame rate of the SOTON database was 1/25 seconds. The cycle time and the gait speed are given by

$$cycle\_time(\text{sec}) = gait\_period(\text{frames}) / frame\_rate(\text{frames} / \text{sec}) \qquad (2)$$

$$speed(\text{m/sec}) = stride\_length(\text{m}) / cycle\_time(\text{sec}) \qquad (3)$$

where the stride length can be directly estimated from the physical dimensions of the image plane. Namely, the stride length is determined by the coordinates of the forward displacements of the gait signature during one gait cycle.

To classify the gender in the human gait, a total of 26 parameters are considered as gait features. These are including general (temporal and spatial) parameter, kinematic parameters, and moments. The gait features may contain information that is redundant or superfluous, in which case it is usually required to select a subset to reduce extraneous noise. This process of removing irrelevant and redundant features is known as feature selection. Here, a statistical distance measure that distribution of subjects or classes in the feature space is employed. That is, inter-class separation due to mean-difference with respect to the class covariances is measured by a variation of the Bhattacharyya distance [3]. As a result, 19 important features are selected from these feature sets. The selected feature set includes most of general parameters, the joint angles, dynamic of the hip angles, the correlation coefficient between the left and right leg angles, and the centre coordinates of the hip-knee cyclogram.

## 3   Gender Classification by SVM

In gender classification, 100 different subjects (84 males and 16 females) with seven gait signatures of each subject, a total of 700 gait signatures ($\approx$19,534 images), are used. A total of the 400, 100, and 200 feature vectors extracted from the gait signatures are used for training, cross validation and testing. Support vector machines (SVMs) and neural network are employed as classifiers for this gender classification task in a way of 10-fold cross validation (CV).

### 3.1   Support Vector Machines

Support vector machines can perform binary classification and regression estimation tasks. Given a set of two-class labelled data $(x_i, y_i)$, $i = 1, 2, .., n$ and $y_i = \pm 1$, an SVM learns a separating hyper-plane <w, x> + $b = 0$, where $x_i \in R^n$, $w \in R^n$, and $b \in R$. In the linear hyper-plane, the SVM looks for a discriminating plane that maximises the margin by minimising $\|w\|^2/2$, subject to $y_i$(<w, $x_i$> + $b$) $\geq 1$ for all $i$. In the linear non-separable case, the optimal separating hyper-plane can be computed by introducing slack variables $\xi_i = 1, 2, .., n$ and an adjustable parameter $C$ and then minimising

$$\|w\|^2/2 + C\sum_i \xi_i, \text{ subject to } y_i\left(\langle w, x_i \rangle + b\right) \geq 1\text{-}\xi_i, \text{ and } \xi_i \geq 0 \text{ for all } i. \tag{4}$$

Lagrange multiplier $\alpha_i$ is used for solving the non-separable case by introducing the dual optimisation. The separating hyper-plane of linear function is not adjustable in many practical cases and takes the kernel function $K(\bullet)$ such that $K(x_i, x_j) = \phi(x_i) \cdot \phi(x_j)$. This $\alpha_i$ can be computed by solving the quadratic optimisation problem as

$$\min \quad W(\alpha) = -\sum_{i=1}^n \alpha_i + \frac{1}{2}\sum_{i,j=1}^n \alpha_i \alpha_j y_i y_j K(x_i, x_j)$$

$$\text{s.t} \quad \sum_{i=1}^n \alpha_i y_i = 0 \text{ and } 0 \leq \alpha_i \leq C, \text{ for all } i \tag{5}$$

Support vectors are the training examples with $\alpha_i > 0$. Specifically unbounded support $x_{usv}$ vectors [7] are with $0 < \alpha_i < C$ and bound support vectors with $\alpha_i = C$. The parameters of the separating hyper-plane are

$$w = \sum_{i=1}^n \alpha_i y_i x_i \text{ and } b = y_{usv} - \langle w, x_{usv} \rangle. \tag{6}$$

In the present study, the implementation of the SVM is based on the working set selection strategy of SVM$^{light}$ and there kernels of linear (<$x_i$, $x_j$>), polynomial ((<$x_i$, $x_j$> + 1)$^p$) and radial basis function (exp(-$\|x_i - x_j\|^2 / p^2$)) are chosen.

### 3.2   Experimental Results

The two feature vectors of each subject are used for test and the five are used for training and cross-validation. The experimental results are summarised in Table 1. The accuracy is the average by the number of SVs, classification rate and computational cost of all experiments with change in the kernel parameter $p$. The computational cost is measured by FLOP (floating point operation). The test result of 19 selected features is a little higher than that of 26 original features. The average accuracy of polynomial kernel ($p = 6$) was the best with around 100.0% for training, 95.0% for CV and 96.0% for testing in the 19 features. The error rate of the linear kernel was lower than that of other kernels in terms of classification rate and computational cost. The result shows that polynomial kernel is better than linear or RBF (Radial Basis Function) kernel [13] in this gender classification task.

**Table 1.** Experimental Results of 10-fold Cross Validation Test

| Kernel | $P$ | fts | SVs | Classification rate (%) | | | FLOP |
|---|---|---|---|---|---|---|---|
| | | | | Training | CV | Testing | |
| Lin. | | 26 | 121.1±4.2 | 94.4±0.5 | 92.4±3.2 | 93.9±1.7 | 54.2±11.8 |
| | | 19 | 140.9±6.2 | 93.4±0.4 | 91.2±3.2 | 94.6±1.2 | 67.2±15.2 |
| Poly. | 2 | 26 | 64.1±2.3 | 100.0±0.0 | 95.8±1.8 | 94.4±0.9 | 1.6±0.5 |
| | | 19 | 57.4±3.4 | 100.0±0.0 | 95.4±3.3 | 96.1±0.7 | 1.9±1.3 |
| | 6 | 26 | 68.3±4.3 | 100.0±0.0 | 94.0±4.8 | 93.9±0.7 | 0.9±0.4 |
| | | 19 | 63.8±3.2 | 100.0±0.0 | 95.6±2.7 | 95.7±0.7 | 1.0±0.7 |
| RBF | 1.5 | 26 | 137.6±4.6 | 96.8±0.3 | 94.4±2.8 | 95.7±0.9 | 4.1±0.4 |
| | | 19 | 133.7±5.1 | 96.8±0.5 | 93.6±2.8 | 96.5±0.6 | 4.7±1.1 |
| | 2.0 | 26 | 145.6±6.6 | 96.2±0.4 | 93.8±3.2 | 95.4±0.9 | 3.5±0.7 |
| | | 19 | 143.3±4.4 | 95.8±0.4 | 94.2±2.2 | 96.7±0.3 | 4.0±0.9 |

A 3-layer feed-forward neural network with resilient back-propagation learning algorithm was also tested for comparative study. The average accuracy with the 10-fold cross validation was 98.0% for training, 93.0% for CV and 92.0% for testing with the network topology of 19×28×2. The overall result is that SVM outperformed neural network in the given task. Naturally we seek to extend the technique in terms of biometric application capability as well as classifying gender for a large number of subjects in future. Notwithstanding this, the gender classification task can clearly handle a large number of subjects successfully. By this, these results show that people can be identified according to gender by their walking pattern. This accords with earlier psychological suggestions, and buttressing other similar results.

## 4    Conclusions

We have described an automated gender classification system using computer vision and machine learning techniques. To achieve this, the gait signature has been extracted by combining a statistical approach and topological analysis guided by anatomical knowledge. In the gait signature, the motion parameters were calculated, and the gait features based on the motion parameters were extracted, and the SVM and neural network classifiers were used to analyse the gender discriminatory ability of the extracted features. The results of SVM with polynomial kernel have produced very good classification rates which were 96% for 100 subjects on average. As such, the automated gender classification system not only accords with psychological analysis in the results it can produce, but also confirms distinctiveness by gender - as earlier suggested in psychological studies. There is interest in gait analysis for medical purposes as its convenience will also benefit analysis of children and elderly. Further, there is opportunity for greater realism in biometrics, though this will doubtless require more sophisticated features and modelling strategies.

# References

1. Dempster, W. T., and Gaughran, G. R. L.: Properties of Body Segments Based on Size and Weight. American Journal of Anatomy, **120** (1967) 33-54
2. Foster, J. P., Nixon, M. S., and Prügel-Bennett, A.: Automatic Gait Recognition using Area-based Metrics. Pattern Recognition Letters, **24**(14) (2003) 2489-2497
3. Fukunaga K.: Introduction to Statistical Pattern Recognition. 2$^{nd}$ eds. Academic Press, San Diego (1990)
4. Goswami A.: A New Gait Parameterization Technique by Means of Cyclogram Moments: Application to Human Slop Walking. Gait and Posture, **8**(1) (1998) 15-26
5. Inman, V. T., Ralston, H. J., and Todd, F.: Human Walking. Williams & Wilkins, Baltimore (1981)
6. Johansson, G.: Visual Perception of Biological Motion and a Model for Its Analysis. Perception and Psychophysics, **14**(2) (1973) 201-211
7. Joachims, T.: Learning to Classify Text Using Support Vector Machines. Dissertation, Kluwer (2002)
8. Kozlowski, L. T., and Cutting, J. T.: Recognizing the Sex of a Walker from a Dynamic Point-Light Display. Perception and Psychology, **21**(6) (1977) 575-580
9. Mather, G., and Murdoch, L.: Gender Discrimination in Biological Motion Displays based on Dynamic Cues. In Proceedings of the Royal Society of London, Vol.**B** (1994) 273-279
10. Murray, M. P., Drought, A. B., and Kory, R. C.: Walking Patterns of Normal Men. Journal of Bone and Joint Surgery, **46A**(2) (1964) 335-360
11. Nixon, M. S., Cater, J. N., Grant, M. G., Gordon, L., and Hayfron-Acquah, J. B.: Automatic Recognition by Gait: Progress and Prospects. Sensor Review, **23**(4) (2003) 323-331
12. Shutler, J. D., et al: On a Large Sequence-based Human Gait Database. In Proceedings of Recent Advances in Soft Computing, Nottingham, UK (2002) 66-71
13. Shin, M., and Park, C.: A Radial Basis Function Approach to Pattern Recognition and Its Applications. ETRI Journal, **22**(2) (2000) 1-10
14. Whittle, M. W.: Gait Analysis: An Introduction. 3$^{rd}$ eds. Butterworth Heinemann (2002)
15. Winter, D. A.: The Biomechanics and Motor Control of Human Gait: Normal, Elderly and Pathological. Waterloo Biomechanics, Ontario (1991)
16. Yoo, J. H., and Nixon, M. S.: Markerless Human Gait Analysis via Image Sequences. In Proceedings of the ISB XIX$^{th}$ Congress, Dunedin, New Zealand (2003)

# An Alternative Fuzzy Compactness and Separation Clustering Algorithm

Miin-Shen Yang[1,*] and Hsu-Shen Tsai[2]

[1] Department of Applied Mathematics, Chung Yuan Christian
University Chung-Li 32023, Taiwan
msyang@math.cycu.edu.tw
[2] Department of Management Information System, Takming College
Taipei 11451, Taiwan

**Abstract.** This paper presents a fuzzy clustering algorithm, called an alternative fuzzy compactness & separation (AFCS) algorithm that is based on an exponential-type distance function. The proposed AFCS algorithm is more robust than the fuzzy c-means (FCM) and the fuzzy compactness & separation (FCS) proposed by Wu et al. (2005). Some numerical experiments are performed to assess the performance of FCM, FCS and AFCS algorithms. Numerical results show that the AFCS has better performance than the FCM and FCS from the robust point of view.

**Keywords:** Fuzzy clustering algorithms; Fuzzy c-means (FCM); Fuzzy compactness & separation (FCS); Alternative fuzzy compactness & separation (AFCS); Exponential-type distance; Robust; Noise.

## 1 Introduction

Cluster analysis is a method for clustering a data set into most similar groups in the same cluster and most dissimilar groups in different clusters. It is a branch in statistical multivariate analysis and an unsupervised learning in pattern recognition. Since Zadeh [14] proposed fuzzy sets that produced the idea of partial memberships to clusters, fuzzy clustering has been widely studied and applied in a variety of substantive areas (see Baraldi and Blonda [1], Bezdek [2], Hoppner et al. [7] and Yang [12]). In fuzzy clustering literature, the fuzzy c-means (FCM) clustering algorithm and its variations are the most used methods.

Because the clustering results obtained using FCM are roughly spherical with similar volumes, many fuzzy clustering algorithms such as the Gustafson-Kessel (G-K) algorithm (Gustafson and Kessel [5]), the minimum scatter volume (MSV) and minimum cluster volume (MCV) algorithms (Krishnapuram and Kim [8]), the unsupervised fuzzy partition-optimal number of classes (UFP-ONC) algorithm (Gath and Geva [4]), Lp-norm generalization (Hathaway et al. [6]) and more generalized-type FCM (Yu and Yang [13]) were proposed to extend the FCM. However, most of these algorithms are based on a within-cluster scatter matrix with a compactness measure. Recently, Wu et al. [11] proposed a novel fuzzy clustering algorithm, called the fuzzy compactness & separation (FCS) algorithm. The FCS objective function is based on a

J. Blanc-Talon et al. (Eds.): ACIVS 2005, LNCS 3708, pp. 146–153, 2005.
© Springer-Verlag Berlin Heidelberg 2005

fuzzy scatter matrix so that the FCS algorithm can be derived by minimizing the compactness measure and simultaneously maximizing the separation measure. Wu et al. [11] had also shown that FCS is more robust to noise and outliers than FCM. Although FCS actually arose its insensitivity to noise and outliers to some extents, it somehow depends on the adjustment of the weighting exponent $m$ and its parameters. On the basis of our experiments, we find that FCS and AFCM [10] still lacks enough robustness to noise and outliers, especially for unequal-sized-cluster data sets.

In this paper we use an exponential-type distance based on the idea of Wu and Yang [10] to modify the FCS objective function. We then propose a clustering method, called the alternative FCS (AFCS) clustering algorithm. Since the exponential-type distance is more robust than the Euclidean distance. The proposed AFCS algorithm can improve the weakness found in the FCS and AFCM. The remainder of this paper is organized as follows. In Section 2 the proposed AFCS clustering algorithm is presented and its properties are also discussed. Numerical examples are given and comparisons are made between FCM, FCS, AFCM and AFCS in Section 3. Finally, conclusions are made in Section 4.

## 2   The AFCS Algorithm

Let $X = \{x_1, \cdots, x_n\}$ be an s-dimensional data set. Suppose $\mu_1(x)$, ..., $\mu_c(x)$ are the fuzzy c-partitions where $\mu_{ij} = \mu_i(x_j)$ represents the degree that the data point $x_j$ belongs to the cluster $i$, and $\{a_1, \cdots, a_n\}$ are the cluster centers. Then the FCM objective function is defined as follows:

$$J_{FCM}(\mu, a) = \sum_{j=1}^{n} \sum_{i=1}^{c} \mu_{ij}^m \left\| x_j - a_i \right\|^2$$

where the weighting exponent $1 < m < +\infty$ presents the degree of fuzziness . Recently, Wu et al. [11] proposed the fuzzy compactness & separation (FCS) algorithm based on a fuzzy scatter matrix by adding a penalized term to the FCM objective function. The FCS objective function is defined as follows:

$$J_{FCS}(\mu, a) = \sum_{j=1}^{n} \sum_{i=1}^{c} \mu_{ij}^m \left\| x_j - a_i \right\|^2 - \sum_{j=1}^{n} \sum_{i=1}^{c} \eta_i \mu_{ij}^m \left\| a_i - \overline{x} \right\|^2$$

where the parameter $\eta_i \geq 0$. It is clear that $J_{FCS} = J_{FCM}$ when $\eta_i = 0$. The update equations that minimize the FCS objective function are as follows:

$$\mu_{ij} = \left( \left\| x_j - a_i \right\|^2 - \eta_i \left\| a_i - \overline{x} \right\|^2 \right)^{\frac{-1}{m-1}} \Big/ \sum_{k=1}^{c} \left( \left\| x_j - a_k \right\|^2 - \eta_k \left\| a_k - \overline{x} \right\|^2 \right)^{\frac{-1}{m-1}} \quad \text{and}$$

$$a_i = \frac{\sum_{j=1}^{n} \mu_{ij}^m x_j - \eta_i \sum_{j=1}^{n} \mu_{ij}^m \overline{x}}{\sum_{j=1}^{n} \mu_{ij}^m - \eta_i \sum_{j=1}^{n} \mu_{ij}^m}, \quad \eta_i = \frac{(\beta/4) \min_{i \neq i} \left\| a_i - a_i \right\|^2}{\max_k \left\| a_k - \overline{x} \right\|^2}, 0 \leq \beta \leq 1.0 .$$

We see that the FCM and FCS objective functions both use the Euclidean distance $\|\cdot\|$. Wu and Yang [10] had claimed that the Euclidean distance is sensitive to noisy data points. They then proposed an exponential-type distance and extended the FCM to the alternative FCM (AFCM) algorithm. Next, we propose an exponential-distance FCS along with the Wu and Yang's approach. We call it the alternative FCS (AFCS) clustering algorithm. Thus, the proposed AFCS objective function $J_{AFCS}$ is created as follows:

$$J_{AFCS}(\mu, a) = \sum_{j=1}^{n} \sum_{i=1}^{c} \mu_{ij}^{m}(1 - \exp(-\alpha \|x_j - a_i\|^2)) - \sum_{j=1}^{n} \sum_{i=1}^{c} \eta_i \mu_{ij}^{m}(1 - \exp(-\alpha \|a_i - \bar{x}\|^2))$$

where $\eta_i$ and $\alpha$ are parameters. By minimizing the AFCS objective function $J_{AFCS}$, we have the following update equations:

$$\mu_{ij} = \frac{\left[(1 - \exp(-\alpha \|x_j - a_i\|^2)) - \eta_i(1 - \exp(-\alpha \|a_i - \bar{x}\|^2))\right]^{\frac{-1}{m-1}}}{\sum_{k=1}^{c}\left[(1 - \exp(-\alpha \|x_j - a_k\|^2)) - \eta_k(1 - \exp(-\alpha \|a_k - \bar{x}\|^2))\right]^{\frac{-1}{m-1}}} \qquad (1)$$

$$a_i = \frac{\sum_{j=1}^{n} \mu_{ij}^{m} \exp(-\alpha \|x_j - a_i\|^2)x_j - \eta_i \sum_{j=1}^{n} \mu_{ij}^{m} \exp(-\alpha \|a_i - \bar{x}\|^2)\bar{x}}{\sum_{j=1}^{n} \mu_{ij}^{m} \exp(-\alpha \|x_j - a_i\|^2) - \eta_i \sum_{j=1}^{n} \mu_{ij}^{m} \exp(-\alpha \|a_i - \bar{x}\|^2)} \qquad (2)$$

In fuzzy clustering, we restrict the fuzzy c-partitions $\mu_{ij}$ in the interval $[0,1]$. However, the $\mu_{ij}$ in the update equation (1) might be negative for some data point $x_j$ so that we need to make some restrictions on it. For a given data point $x_j$, if $1 - \exp(-\alpha \|x_j - a_i\|^2) \le \eta_i(1 - \exp(-\alpha \|a_i - \bar{x}\|^2))$ then $\mu_{ij} = 1$, and $\mu_{i^{'}j} = 0$, for all $i^{'} \ne i$. That is, if the exponential-distance between the data point and the $i$th cluster center is smaller than $\eta_i(1 - \exp(-\alpha \|a_i - \bar{x}\|^2))$, these data points will then belong exactly to the $i$th cluster with membership value of one . Each cluster in AFCS will have a crisp boundary such that all data points inside this boundary will have a crisp membership value $\mu_{ij} \in \{0,1\}$ and other data points outside this boundary will have fuzzy membership value $\mu_{ij} \in [0,1]$. Each crisp boundary, called a cluster kernel, will form a hyper-ball for the corresponding cluster. Figure 1 shows a two-cluster data set in which each cluster contains a cluster center and a cluster kernel.

The volume of each cluster kernel is decided by the term $\eta_i(1-\exp(-\alpha\|a_i - \overline{x}\|^2))$. In our AFCS, crisp and fuzzy membership values co-exist. These are similar to Özdemir and Akarun [9] and Wu et al. [11]. To guarantee that no two of these c cluster kernels will overlap, $\eta_i$ should be chosen as follows:

$$\eta_i = (\beta/4)\min_{i \neq i}\left(1-\exp(-\alpha\|a_i - a_i\|^2)\right)\Big/\max_k\left(1-\exp(-\alpha\|a_k - \overline{x}\|^2)\right)$$

where $0 \leq \beta \leq 1$. In general, $\alpha$ could be chosen as $\alpha = (\sum_{j=1}^{n}\|x_j - \overline{x}\|/n)^{-1}$.

Note that the value $(1/4)(1-\exp(-\alpha\|a_i - a_i\|^2)^{1/2}$ is a half the distance between cluster centers $a_i$ and $a_i$. Thus, equation (3) should guarantee that no two of these c cluster kernels will overlap. If $\beta = 1.0$, then the AFCS algorithm will cluster the data set using the largest kernel for each cluster. If $\beta = 0$, then the AFCS algorithm will cluster the data set with no kernel and will be equivalent to the AFCM algorithm proposed by Wu and Yang [10]. Thus, the proposed AFCS clustering algorithm is summarized as follows:

### The AFCS algorithm

Step 1: Fix $2 \leq c \leq n$ and fix any $\varepsilon > 0$.

Give initials $\mu^{(0)} = (\mu_1^{(0)}, \cdots, \mu_c^{(0)})$ and let $s = 1$.

Step 2: Compute the cluster centers $a^{(s)}$ with $\mu^{(s-1)}$ using (2).

Step 3: Update $\mu^{(s)}$ with $a^{(s)}$ using (1).

Step 4: Compare $\mu^{(s)}$ to $\mu^{(s-1)}$ in a convenient matrix norm $\|\cdot\|$.

IF $\|\mu^{(s)} - \mu^{(s-1)}\| < \varepsilon$, STOP

ELSE $s=s+1$ and return to step 2.

Let us first use the data set shown in Fig.1. We find that the clustering results from AFCS well separate the data into two clusters with symbols, cross "+" and circle "○", and also with two cluster kernels. We then run the AFCM and AFCS algorithms for the data set with $m = 2$ and $\beta = 0.05, 0.1$ and $0.5$. The results are shown in Fig. 2. We find that the clustering results from AFCS will have very similar clustering results as AFCM when the parameter $\beta$ in AFCS is small. However, the kernel volume for each cluster in AFCS will grow bigger when the parameter $\beta$ in AFCS is larger as shown in Fig. 2. In fact, the cluster kernel volumes will increase when $\beta$ in AFCS increases. Finally, we mention that the proposed AFCS is considered by replacing the Euclidean distance in FCS with an exponential-type distance. On the other hand, we can see that AFCS is a generalization of AFCM by adding a penalized term.

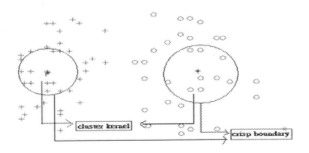

**Fig. 1.** Clusters obtained by AFCS

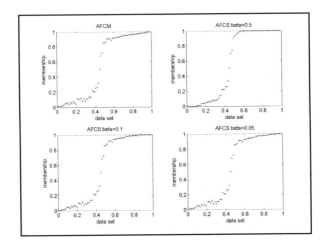

**Fig. 2.** Membership functions of AFCM and AFCS

## 3  Examples and Numerical Comparisons

In this section we use some numerical examples to compare the proposed AFCS algorithm with FCM, AFCM and FCS. These algorithms are implemented under the same conditions with the same initial values and stopping rules.

*Example 1.* First, we use a popular clustering problem with two clusters (see Ref. [3]) in that there are two great different cluster numbers for two clusters. The data set is given in Fig. 3. According to our experiments, Figs. 3(a)~(c) show that FCM and FCS with $m = 2$ and $\beta = 0.1$, $\beta = 0.2$ do not give good enough clustering results where one cluster is with the symbol of cross "+" and another cluster is with the symbol of circle "○". Obviously, FCM and FCS couldn't tolerate these unequal-sized clusters in the data set when the weighting exponent $m = 2$. However, if we set $m = 6$ for FCM and FCS, we find that FCS does give good enough clustering results with $m = 6$, $\beta = 0.1$ (see Fig. 3(f)), but FCM does not give good clustering results either (see Fig. 3(d)). Overall, FCS with a larger $m$ value gives good clustering results for the unequal-sized-cluster data set. According to Figs. 3(g) and (h), AFCM and AFCS actually give good clustering results when $m = 2$. That means, AFCM and AFCS presents less sensitivity to the weighting exponent $m$ than FCM and FCS.

Next, we add an outlier with the coordinate (30, 0) into the data set for our experiments. The clustering results from FCS, AFCM and AFCS are shown in Fig. 4. Even though the weighting exponent $m = 6$ or $m = 8$ is given, the FCS clustering results are obviously affected by this outlier where the outlier becomes a cluster alone so that the original two clusters are incorporated into one cluster as shown in Figs. 4(a)~(c). In Figs. 4(d)~(f), the results show that AFCM may be also affected by this outlier even though the $m$ value is large. On the contrary, Figs. 4(g)~(i) show that AFCS are not affected by the outlier when $m = 6$, $\beta = 0.7$.

***Example 2.*** According to Wu and Yang (2002), the AFCM is good for the unequal sample size data set. In this example, we make the comparisons of AFCS with AFCM and FCS. We add an outlier with the coordinate (10, 0) to the data set as shown in Fig. 5. The clustering results of AFCM, FCS and AFCS are shown in Figs. 5(a)~(f), respectively. Figs. 5(a)~(c) show that AFCM and FCS are affected by this outlier. Figure 5(d) shows that FCS with a large $m$ value is also affected by the outlier. Figure 5(f) shows that our proposed AFCS with a large $m$ value can detect unequal sample size clusters and is not affected by the outlier.

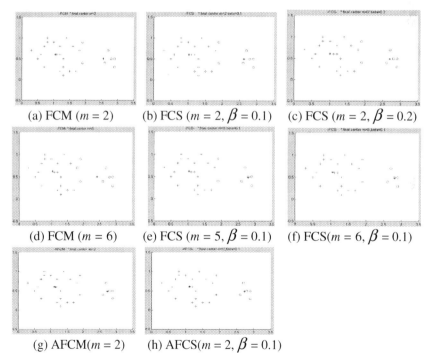

(a) FCM ($m = 2$)    (b) FCS ($m = 2$, $\beta = 0.1$)    (c) FCS ($m = 2$, $\beta = 0.2$)

(d) FCM ($m = 6$)    (e) FCS ($m = 5$, $\beta = 0.1$)    (f) FCS($m = 6$, $\beta = 0.1$)

(g) AFCM($m = 2$)    (h) AFCS($m = 2$, $\beta = 0.1$)

**Fig. 3.** FCM, FCS, AFCM and AFCS clustering results for unequal sample size data set without outlier

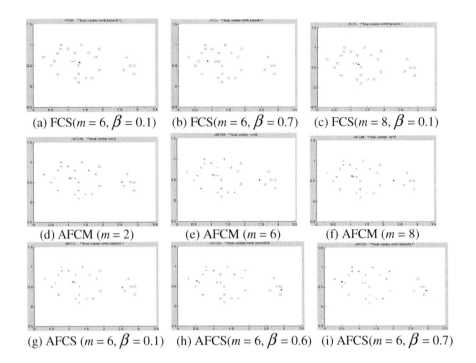

(a) FCS($m = 6$, $\beta = 0.1$)    (b) FCS($m = 6$, $\beta = 0.7$)    (c) FCS($m = 8$, $\beta = 0.1$)

(d) AFCM ($m = 2$)    (e) AFCM ($m = 6$)    (f) AFCM ($m = 8$)

(g) AFCS ($m = 6$, $\beta = 0.1$)    (h) AFCS($m = 6$, $\beta = 0.6$)    (i) AFCS($m = 6$, $\beta = 0.7$)

**Fig. 4.** FCM, FCS, AFCM and AFCS clustering results for unequal sample size data set with an outlier (30, 0)

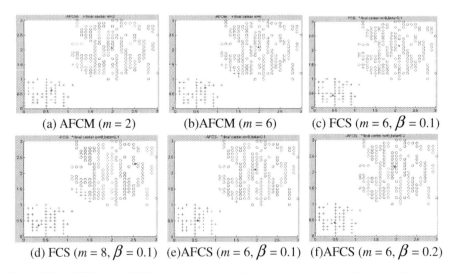

(a) AFCM ($m = 2$)    (b)AFCM ($m = 6$)    (c) FCS ($m = 6$, $\beta = 0.1$)

(d) FCS ($m = 8$, $\beta = 0.1$)    (e)AFCS ($m = 6$, $\beta = 0.1$)    (f)AFCS ($m = 6$, $\beta = 0.2$)

**Fig. 5.** FCS, AFCM and AFCS clustering results for unequal sample size data set with an outlier (10, 0)

# 4 Conclusions

In this paper, we proposed a clustering algorithm, called AFCS, using an exponential-type distance. Each cluster obtained by the AFCS will have a cluster kernel. Data points that fall inside any one of the c cluster kernels will have crisp memberships and be outside all of the c cluster kernels that have fuzzy memberships. The crisp and fuzzy memberships co-exist in the AFCS. Numerical examples show that, although FCS could tolerate unequal-sized clusters and is robust to outlier to some extent, but it needs to adjust the weighting exponent m to a larger number. On the other hand, FCS and AFCM are affected by an outlier for the unequal-sized-cluster data sets. However, the proposed AFCS clustering algorithm can overcome the above drawbacks. Overall, AFCS actually works better than FCM, AFCM and FCS.

# References

1. A. Baraldi and P. Blonda, A survey of fuzzy clustering algorithms for pattern recognition part I and II, IEEE Trans. Systems, Man and Cybernetics-part B 29 (1999) 778-801.
2. J.C. Bezdek, Pattern Recognition with Fuzzy Objective Function Algorithms, Plenum Press, New York, 1981.
3. R.O. Duda and P.E. Hart, Pattern Classification and Scene Analysis, Wiley, New York, 1973.
4. J. Gath and A.B. Geva, Unsupervised optimal fuzzy clustering. IEEE Trans. Pattern Anal. Mach. Intell. 11 (1989) 773-781.
5. D.E. Gustafson and W.C. Kessel, Fuzzy clustering with a fuzzy covariance matrix. In: Proc. IEEE Conf. Decision Contr., San Diego, CA, pp. 761-76, 1979.
6. R.J. Hathaway, J.C. Bezdek and Y. Hu, Generalized fuzzy c-means clustering strategies using $L_p$ norm distances, IEEE Trans. Fuzzy Systems 8 (2000) 576-582.
7. F. Hoppner, F. Klawonn, R. Kruse and T. Runkler, Fuzzy Cluster Analysis: Methods for Classification Data Analysis and Image Recognition, Wiley, New York, 1999.
8. R. Krishnapuram and J. Kim, Clustering algorithms based on volume criteria, IEEE Trans. Fuzzy Syst. 8 (2000) 228-236.
9. D. Özdemir and L. Akarun, A fuzzy algorithm for color quantization of images, Pattern Recognition 35 (2002) 1785-1791.
10. K.L. Wu and M.S. Yang, Alternative c-means clustering algorithms, Pattern Recognition 35 (2002) 2267-2278.
11. K.L. Wu, J. Yu and M.S. Yang, A novel fuzzy clustering algorithm based on a fuzzy scatter matrix with optimality tests, Pattern Recognition Letters 26 (2005) 639-652.
12. M.S. Yang, A survey of fuzzy clustering. Mathematical and Computer Modeling 18(11) (1993) 1-16.
13. J. Yu and M.S. Yang, Optimality test for generalized FCM and its application to parameter selection, IEEE Trans. Fuzzy Systems 13 (2005) 164-176.
14. L.A. Zadeh, Fuzzy sets. Information and Control 8 (1965) 338-353.

# Fuzzy Linguistic Rules Classifier
# for Wooden Board Color Sorting

Emmanuel Schmitt[1,2], Vincent Bombardier[1], and Raphaël Vogrig[2]

[1] Automatic Research Center of Nancy – CRAN, UMR 7039, Faculté des Sciences,
Boulevard des Aiguillettes, BP 239, 54506 Vandoeuvre-lès-Nancy Cedex, France
{emmanuel.schmitt, vincent.bombardier}@cran.uhp-nancy.fr
[2] Luxscan Technologies, Z.A.R.E. Ouest, L-4384 Ehlerange, Luxembourg
{schmitt, vogrig}@luxscan.lu

**Abstract.** This article exposes wood pieces classification method according to their color. The main difficulties encountered by the Company are primarily in the color recognition according to a certain graduality, and the decision to take on all the board with the different sides. These problems imply the use of flexible/robust model and the use of an "intelligent" information management delivered by the sensors. In order to improve the current system, we propose to integrate a method, whose principle is a fuzzy inference system, itself built thanks to fuzzy linguistic rules. The results obtained with our method show a real improvement of the recognition rate compared to a bayesian classifier already used by the Company.

## 1 Introduction

The wood product industry is placed in a highly competitive market. One task that lumber or wood product suppliers are currently faced with is the matching boards according to their color properties. For example, the face of higher quality wooden cabinets should be uniform in color. In general, the color grading procedure is highly subjective and requires human intervention. In order to reduce overhead costs and improve product quality, companies are looking to state-of-the-art technology. One relatively low-cost solution that may be applied to improve the color grading process involves adding a sensor to existing industrial wood scanners specifically designed to capture the color properties of the wood. However, colors are not easily quantified and sensor data in its raw form does not suffice to make decisions with regard to the color properties of boards that have been scanned. To address the issue of color classification, this paper introduces a novel approach to the robust classification of board color by incorporating sensor data into a new fuzzy classification system.

The work described here has been motivated by a collaborative effort between academia and industry. The Automatic Research Center of Nancy (CRAN) is the academic partner and Luxscan Technologies, an aggressive start-up company based in the Luxembourg is the industrial partner. Because the algorithms developed in this work are to be implemented into production systems, the ability to process boards and sort them according to their color properties in real time is crucial. In general, production lines may reach speeds of 180 meters of board length per minute. The

J. Blanc-Talon et al. (Eds.): ACIVS 2005, LNCS 3708, pp. 154–161, 2005.
© Springer-Verlag Berlin Heidelberg 2005

sensors intended for this application return data at a rate of 1500 lines per second where each line is composed of 900 pixels. Hence the method described here must be capable of processing at least 1,350,000 pixels per second. Figure 1 gives an overviews of the scanning and decision making system that has been developed for this work.

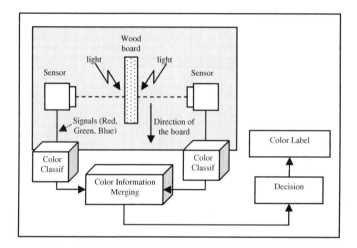

**Fig. 1.** Vision system

In this article, we present an improvement of the color classification module of this vision system. We only detail here the board classification according to the color of only one of these faces. In the next step of the process, this color information will be merging with the other one provided by the other face, i.e. by the second sensor (see figure 1). Finally, the vision system supplies a color label for the wooden board, in accordance with the industrial classification. In our case, we must distinguish different color classes according to the considered wood specie and customer wishes. So this study has been realized on red oak separated on 6 classes: Dark Red, Red, Light Red, Dark Brown, Brown and Light Brown. These colors don't correspond to a precise wavelength; they are defined according to the customer perception.

The first section of this article concerns the way to obtain the characteristic vector that we use to make the color recognition. The second part explains the Fuzzy Reasoning method used to make the color classification. Finally, we expose the results obtained with our Fuzzy Linguistic Rules Classifier, compared to the current classification based on bayesian classifier, and used by the Company.

## 2   Characteristic Vector Extraction

### 2.1   Color Characterization

Two aspects are essential to characterizing color: the reference color space and the characteristic vector. One of the most common color spaces denoted RGB, organizes the color information of an image into its red, green, and blue components. However, the International Commission on Illumination (CIE) does not recommend its use because the color components are not independent of one another. Other popular color spaces include the Lab and HSV (Hue, Saturation, Value (intensity)) spaces. Many studies on color space selection have been conducted elsewhere, i.e. [5][13]. After conducting several internal tests on various sets of wood samples, we decided to work in the Lab space because it provides the best color discrimination in our case. Moreover, this colorimetric reference space better represents colors seen by humans.

The choice of lighting is another important parameter for our study. The intensity, spectral density, and time variance of light, as well as ambient temperature, all have a significant effect on how colors are perceived. Extensive testing has been performed in order to determine parameters for how these features influence color perception. For example, a red piece of wood may be classified as brown if the temperature varies by just 5°C. Further discussion of these parameters is limited in order to protect the partner's intellectual property. Finally, we decided to work with white, non-neon lighting and process image data in the Lab space to obtain the best distribution of colors to sort.

## 2.2   Size of the Region of Interest

The manufacturing process allows us to only take an image from the side of the board. An example of obtained images is shown in the figure 2.

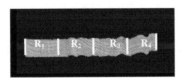

**Fig. 2.** Side image with 4 processing ROIs

For our application, we need to split the image in several Region Of Interest (ROI) to manage the color transition in a better way. Indeed, the board color is not really constant along the entire side. The wood is not a homogeneous material. It exists lots of variations in a board according to its color or its grain. Especially, if there are two or more colors on the processed board, we can classify it in a specific category. So, we propose to split the images in several ROI and we apply our classification method on each. The results, which will be presented further in this article, allow taking into account the importance of the ROI size. Its size must be large enough to be independent from the wood texture, but it must not be too large to avoid the confusion of two separated colors. A too large ROI also increase the processing time. Effectively, one of the main constraints for our system is the processing time, which is very small when we consider the quantity of information to manage on a whole board. Considering that the used sensors acquire 1500 lines per second, the time constraint for a 300 lines ROI must not exceed 0.2 s.

In the same way, it is necessary to characterize a color with simple characteristic vector. We choose one of the simplest attribute responding to the calculation time criterion: the average. So, we have defined the characteristic vector V with the expression (1) for each processed ROI. We could use additional information through the standard deviation of the different components, but, as said before, the wood is not a homogeneous material. A light wood board can have a dark grain and a dark board can have a light grain. For these two cases, the standard deviations will be the same. The size of 300 lines was selected after a study of ROI size impact in processing time between 50 lines and 450 lines.

$$V = \begin{pmatrix} m_L \\ m_a \\ m_b \end{pmatrix} . \tag{1}$$

where $m_i$ represent the mean value of the variable i ( i = {L,a,b} ).

# 3  Methodology of Color Classification

The second step for the color labeling is the classification method. Other methods were used to classify wooden boards according to color [9] [10]. But the color perception is a subjective concept in the image processing. It does not exist crisp boundary between the different colors, which we would like to classify. That's why we decide to use a method based on the fuzzy sets theory [11]. This theory allows keeping the subjectivity notion in the taken decisions. Fuzzy logic is an interesting tool to obtain repeatability in the colors recognition, because the colors can be regarded as intrinsically fuzzy [3]. Other methods based on 3D-color-representation [12] have been tested, but the results are not correct on unknown samples of wood. There are a lot of methods using Approximate Reasoning on numerical data. We have chosen to work with fuzzy logic concept and especially to use fuzzy linguistic rules based mechanisms. The main reason is the potentiality of human interpretation of the generated models from such a method.

## 3.1  Fuzzy Inference System (SIF)

The method for colors classification must allow using numerical information provided by the sensors. In fuzzy rules, we can use two different reasonings. The abductive reasoning allows obtaining information on the input X from the output variable Y; and the deductive reasoning allows deducing the output Y from input values X. In our case, we use the Modus Ponens, which corresponds to the second case. The generated rules can be classified in two categories: conjunctive and implicative rules. This dichotomy is explained also in a "cultural" point of view. For the implicative rules, the reasoning is governed by the knowledge. The more information we will have on the product, the more the results will be precise. In our case, we are located in the low level part of the image processing, so we don't have enough rich information to use this kind of rules. In fact, the conjunctive rules result from the data analysis field. That's why we have chosen a conjunctive parallel rules mechanism.

Two main models can be used to build such parallel mechanism: Larsen model and Mamdani model [3]. The difference between them is made according to the T-Norm choice for implicative operator. Finally, we have chosen an inference mechanism based on Larsen model, because the *Product* is more adapted than the *Minimum*

T-Norm in our case. In fact, by using the Product, we allow a non-linear splitting of input variables spaces [2]. After this premises processing, we combine the different partial results with a disjunction operator (T-Conorm): the **Maximum**. In our case, we don't want to generate a composition law but use a pseudo-implication of Larsen [3]. The output of our Fuzzy Linguistic Rule Classifier is a fuzzy vector providing the different membership degree of a sample to the different defined color classes. Finally, to take a decision, we affect the processed sample to the class with the maximum membership degree. The membership functions (figure 3) are constructed thanks to the expert knowledge. In fact, we split the representation space of the different attributes (L, a, b-averages) according to the color distribution. This processing engine is very adapted to this kind of data analysis problem [6]. The interest of our method is the calculation speed and the certainty to obtain coherent and non-redundant rules. There are many methods, which supply automatically fuzzy rules from a data set [1][5]. We decided, thanks to the criteria previously evoked, to use the technique developed by Ishibuchi, Nozaki and Tanaka [16]. The inference engine works as illustrated by the scheme of figure 3. The different parts of the algorithm are exposed in section 3.2.

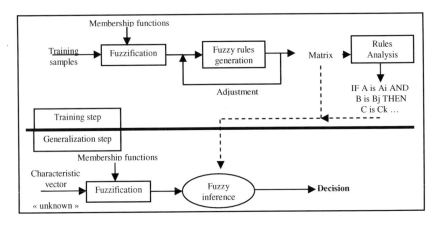

**Fig. 3.** Module of color recognition

In the section 4, we present a comparison between our method and a method much more traditional, which does not take into account the gradual aspect of the color, and our classification methodology [2].

## 3.2  Fuzzy Linguistic Rules Classifier

This mechanism is divided in three steps: the input fuzzification, the fuzzy generation rules and their adjustment.

Input attributes fuzzification: this part consists to split the characteristic vector parameters in several terms. We qualify these terms with a word in natural language. By example, the intensity of a color can be "light", "medium" or "dark". The decomposition number is currently realized empirically thanks to wood expert knowledge. Thanks to these words, we can thus generate linguistic rules.

Fuzzy rules generation: this part consists in generating fuzzy rules, like "IF... THEN...". These rules are obtained according to a training samples set.

If we consider two input attributes and one output color, the associated fuzzy rule is:

$$\text{"\textit{IF} } x_1 \text{ \textit{is} } A_i \textit{ AND IF } x_2 \text{ \textit{is} } A_k \textit{ THEN } y_1 \text{ \textit{is the color} } C_n.\text{"}$$

with   $x_1$ and $x_2$ the input parameters

$y_1$ the output data

$A_i$ and $A_k$ the fuzzy subsets

$C_n$ the color class n

Fuzzy rules adjustment: this part corresponds to the iterative step of the algorithm. In fact, we adjust the splitting of parameters representation spaces according to the training samples set. The base of fuzzy rules is under the form of a numerical matrix made up of the attributes, output classes to be recognized and a confidence degree. This degree associated to each rule, can be compared to a relevance degree of the rule in agreement with the input data. The results provided by our recognition module are similarity degrees [8] with the output classes. In other words, we are interested with the resemblance of our object to identify with the nearest color class.

## 4   Comparative Results with a Bayesian Classifier

To compare our method to a bayesian classifier, we selected 350 color samples for the training step and 1000 color samples for the identification step. The chosen colors are those specified in the introduction. We firstly compare the results provided by using a 300-lines-ROI. We have also tried to show the importance of the ROI's definition (cf. section 2.2) and the processing time for the two compared methods. The results shown in table 1 expose the enhancement that the use of fuzzy classification method gives. The increase of the generalization rate is promising and proves a good capacity for extrapolating in case of an unknown sample. For a use in an industrial environment, the generalization recognition rate is still too low, but all the products could not be classified according the color. Thus, the "unknown" pieces can be kept for other uses.

**Table 1.** Recognition rate on the training samples set

|  | Bayesian Classifier | Fuzzy Classifier |
|---|---|---|
| Training Recognition Rate | 77.20% | 91.10% |
| Generalization Recognition Rate | 72.48% | 83.89% |

### 4.1   Impact of the ROI Size in Color Recognition Rates

In this section, we want to show the influence of the ROI size in order to choose the better one for our application. Table 2 presents the results in generalization for different ROI size and the two tested methods.

The results concerning the different ROI size are also important. If the zone size is too small, the recognition rates are not the betters in generalization. To the opposite, by exceeding a certain threshold, we don't improve any more the identification rates.

**Table 2.** Recognition rates on the generalization samples set for different ROI sizes

| | Bayesian Classifier | | | | Fuzzy Approximate Classifier | | | |
|---|---|---|---|---|---|---|---|---|
| ROI size (in line) | 50 | 15 0 | 30 0 | 45 0 | 50 | 15 0 | 3 00 | 45 0 |
| Recognition Rate (in %) | 69. 19 | 71. 24 | 72. 48 | 72. 37 | 72. 41 | 77. 20 | 8 3.89 | 82. 97 |

With this generalization samples set, the best ROI size is 300 lines in the board length. As said in section 2.2, we process the images by ROIs. This explains because, if a board has two colors on one side in the length, we will make an error on the color classification. We precise our process must allow the labeling of the global board color. If a board has two colors in its width, we use a specific decision technique to process the color variation.

### 4.2 Processing Time for Color Classification

The second aspect checked to validate our method is the processing time. As said before, our time constraint is about less than 0.2 s.

**Table 3.** Processing time for one ROI of 300 lines

| | Bayesian Classifier | Fuzzy Classifier |
|---|---|---|
| Processing time | 0.12 ms | 0.05 ms |

The results exposed in table 3 allow us to validate the time performance of our method. The given time results are computed for the classification step of one ROI. It doesn't take into account the calculation time for obtaining the characteristic vector. However, the remaining laxity is large enough.

## 5   Conclusion

The color perception in the wood is a very subjective concept. This paper presents a methodology to keep the human-like perception to classify the color. Our numeric model is constituted of fuzzy conjunctives rules activated in parallel and merged with disjunctive operator. This model is generated from the Ishibuchi-Nozaki-Tanaka algorithm, which replies at our system constraints. This study demonstrates the advantages of using fuzzy logic. This is checked through the improvement of the recognition rates and the decrease of the time consuming. The future works concern the use of our developed sensor. Indeed, by using the fuzzy logic, we have access to fuzzy information through the membership degree to the different color classes. That's why we would like to improve our system by integrating the fuzzy sensor concept [14]. After this part, we must work on the information fusion. This topic is very important in our case because we scan boards on the different sides. The system must take a global decision for all the board. And it is not evident when the board has, by example, two sides of different colors. Thanks to the fuzzy data, which can be given by our system, we could also work on the notion of fuzzy information fusion [6][15]. The taken decisions for the scanned wooden boards should be perhaps more realistic.

# References

1. Berthold, M.R.: Mixed fuzzy rule formation. Int. Jour. of Approximate Reasoning, Vol 32. (2003) 67-84
2. Bombardier, V., Lhoste, P., Mazaud, C. : Modélisation et intégration de connaissances métier pour l'identification de défauts par règles linguistiques floues. TS Traitement du Signal, vol. 31, n° 3, pp. 227-247, ISSN 0765-0019, 2004.
3. Bouchon-Meunier, B.: La logique floue et ses applications. (ed.) Addison-Wesley (1995)
4. Carron, T.: Segmentations d'images couleur dans la base Teinte-Luminance-Saturation : approche numérique et symbolique. Thèse doctorale. Université de Savoie (1995)
5. Cordon, O., Del Jesus, M.J., Herrera, F.: A proposal on reasoning methods in fuzzy rule-based classification systems. Int. Jour. of Approximate reasoning, Vol. 20. (1999) 21-45
6. Dubois, D., Prade, H.: Fuzzy rules in knowledge-based systems – Modelling gradedness, uncertainty and preference. An introduction to fuzzy logic application in intelligent systems. Kluwer, Dordrecht, (1992) 45-68
7. Dubois, D., Prade, H., Yager, R.R.: Fuzzy Information Engineering: A Guided Tour of Applications. (ed) Wiley, (1996)
8. Dubois, D., Prade, H.: The semantics of fuzzy sets. Fuzzy Sets and Systems, Vol. 90. (1997) 141-150.
9. Dubuisson, B.: Diagnostic, intelligence artificielle et reconnaissance des formes. (ed) Hermès, (2001)
10. Hanbury, A.: Morphologie Mathématique sur le Cercle Unité avec applications aux teintes et aux textures orientées. Thèse doctorale. Ecole Nationale Supérieure des Mines de Paris, (2002)
11. Kaufmann, A.: Introduction à la théorie des sous-ensembles flous. (ed.) Masson, (1975)
12. 12.Kline, D.E., Conners, R.W., Lu, Q., Araman, P.A.: Automatic color sorting of hardwood edge-glued panel parts. Hardwood Symposium Proceedings (1997).
13. Lu, Q.: A real-time system for color-sorting edge-glued panel parts. Master's thesis in preparation. Department of Electrical Engineering, Virginia Tech, Blacksburg, Virginia
14. Mauris, G., Benoit, E., Foulloy, L.: Fuzzy sensors: another view. Information Engineering (1997)
15. Mauris, G., Benoît, E., Foulloy, L.: Fuzzy Linguistic Methods for the Aggregation of Complementary Sensor Information. In: Bouchon-Meunier, B. (ed.): Aggregation and Fusion of Imperfect Information. A Sringer-Verlag Company, Physica-Verlag Heidelberg New York, Vol. 12 (1998)
16. Nozaki, K., Ishibuchi, H., Tanaka, H.: A Simple but powerful heuristic method for generating fuzzy rules from numerical data. Fuzzy sets and systems, Vol. 86. (1997) 251-270

# Image Pattern Recognition with Separable Trade-Off Correlation Filters[*]

César San Martín[1,4], Asticio Vargas[2], Juan Campos[3], and Sergio Torres[4]

[1] Department of Electrical Engineering, University of La Frontera,
Casilla 54-D, Temuco, Chile
csmarti@ufro.cl
[2] Department of Science Physics, University of La Frontera,
Casilla 54-D, Temuco, Chile
avargas@ufro.cl
[3] Department of Physics, University of Barcelona,
08193 Bellaterra, Barcelona, España
juan.campos@uab.es
[4] Department of Electrical Engineering, University of Concepción,
Casilla 160-C, Concepción, Chile
sertorre@udec.cl

**Abstract.** In this paper, a method to design separable trade-off correlation filters for optical pattern recognition is developed. The proposed method not only is able to include the information about de desirable peak correlation value but also is able to minimize both the average correlation energy and the effect of additive noise on the correlation output. These optimization criteria are achieved by employing multiple training objects. The main advantage of the method is based on using multiple information for improving the optical pattern recognition work on images with various objects. The separable Trade-off filter is experimentally tested by using both digital and optical pattern recognition.

**Keywords:** Filter design, Separable filter, Optical and digital image processing, Optical correlator.

## 1 Introduction

It has been shown that correlation filters are an effective avenue for object discrimination in imaging pattern recognition [1,2,3]. The method used in the design of a correlation filter can strongly impact in its capacity to identify objects in an image. The correlation filters can be classified according to the size of the training set to be used. If one target object is used the correlation filters can be designed following: The Classic Matched Filter (CMF) method [4], the Phase Only Filter (POF) method [5], and the Inverse Filter (IF) method [6]. For cases in which more than one training object is used, the filter receives the name of

---

[*] Financed by Fondo Nacional de Desarrollo Científico y Tecnológico Proyecto Fondecyt N° 1010532 and N° 1040946; Dirección General de Enseñanza Superior del Ministerio de Educación y Cultura Proyecto N° BFM2003-06273-C02-01 and Proyecto de Investigación Conjunta dentro del Programa de Cooperación Científica con Iberoamérica DURSI-CONICYT ACI2003-51.S.T acknowledges support by grant Milenio ICM P02-049.

J. Blanc-Talon et al. (Eds.): ACIVS 2005, LNCS 3708, pp. 162–169, 2005.
© Springer-Verlag Berlin Heidelberg 2005

synthetic discriminate function (SDF) [7] and some examples are: The Minimum Variance (MVSDF) filter, the Minimum Average Correlation Energy (MACE) filter, and the Trade-Off filter [8,9,10]. Each one of the mentioned filter, are designed to optimize some quality criteria [1]. For example, the CMF filter optimizes the signal to noise ratio (SNR) criteria; the MACE filter optimizes the Peak to Correlation Energy (PCE) criteria. The Trade-off filter proposed in [11] can optimize more than one quality criteria by means of a parameter $\beta$ that permits to control the degree of compromise between the chosen criteria.

Normally, to process two-dimensional images, 2D correlation filters are necessary generating therefore 2D operations. The design of separable two-dimensional digital filters is proposed by Twogood et al. [12]. They show an efficient technique to filter design and implementation of separable filters using 1D instead of 2D operations. Mahalanobis [13] proposes one-dimensional separable filters to process two-dimensional images, with the advantage of using less memory storage and only 1D digital processing techniques. A separable filter is one in which the separability property of the digital filters, $h(x, y) = h_c(x)h_r(y)$, is implemented. A procedure for deriving optimal separable filters is treated in [14] by using singular value decomposition method, which is applied using a Maximum Average Correlation Height (MACH) criterion.

Mahalanobis [13] has developed a design methodology of separable filters for one training image using only the PCE criteria. In this work, we improve the Mahalanobis methodology not only by taking into account two optimization criteria: the approach of minimizing the energy of the correlation and reduce the effect of noise, but also by including more than one training image. The foregoing has the advantage of designing one filter using multiple information, which can improve the pattern recognition work on images with various objects. On the other hand, it is well known that optical pattern recognition perform high speed correlation operations, and optical process permits parallelism in information. Therefore, we test the proposed method implementing the designed filters in an optical correlator to perform optical pattern recognition.

The paper is structured as follow. In Section 2 the proposed method is developed. Implementations of the method and experimental setup of an optical correlator are described in Section 3. Digital and optical pattern recognition results are presented and discussed in Section 4. The main conclusions are presented in Section 5.

## 2   Design of Separable Trade-Off Correlation Filters

Let us start considering $N$ $d \times d$ training images $x_i$ ($i = 1, ..., N$); let $h_r$ and $h_c$ be the filters of length $d$ that process the rows and the columns respectively. Also, let us consider the Fourier Transforms (FT) of $x_i$, $h_r$ and $h_c$ as $X_i(k, l)$, $H_r(l)$ and $H_c(k)$ respectively, with $k$ and $l$ the horizontal and vertical frequencies. Further, $u_i$ is the desired $i$th output of the correlator given by,

$$\sum_{k=1}^{d}\sum_{l=1}^{d} H_r(l)\, H_c(k)\, X_i^*(k, l) = u_i,$$

where * denoted the complex conjugated. The average correlation energy $E_{av}$ is expressed by

$$E_{av} = \frac{1}{N} \sum_{i=1}^{N} \sum_{k=1}^{d} \sum_{l=1}^{d} |H_r(l)|^2 |H_c(k)|^2 |X_i(k,l)|^2,$$

and the output noise variance $\sigma^2$ is given by

$$\sigma^2 = \sum_{k=1}^{d} \sum_{l=1}^{d} |H_r(l)|^2 |H_c(k)|^2 C(k,l),$$

where $C(k,l)$ is the power spectral density of noise with zero mean. Now, to design the Trade-off filters, we have to minimize the correlation plane average energy $E_{av}$ and minimize the effect of additive noise on the correlation output ($\sigma^2$) fulfilling the value of each $u_i$, this is:

To minimize the term:

$$(1-\beta)NE_{av} + \beta\sigma^2 = (1-\beta) \sum_{i=1}^{N} \sum_{k=1}^{d} \sum_{l=1}^{d} |H_r(l)|^2 |H_c(k)|^2 |X_i(k,l)|^2 +$$

$$\beta \sum_{k=1}^{d} \sum_{l=1}^{d} |H_r(l)|^2 |H_c(k)|^2 C(k,l), \tag{1}$$

subject to the condition:

$$\sum_{k=1}^{d} \sum_{l=1}^{d} H_r(l) H_c(k) X_i^*(k,l) = u_i, \tag{2}$$

where $\beta$ is the balance parameter of the Trade-off separable filter. Applying the Lagrange multipliers, it can be shown that the functional $\Phi$ is given by

$$\Phi = \sum_{k=1}^{d} \sum_{l=1}^{d} |H_r(l)|^2 |H_c(k)|^2 \left\{ (1-\beta) \sum_{i=1}^{N} |X_i(k,l)|^2 + \beta C(k,l) \right\} - 2 \sum_{i=1}^{m} \lambda_i \left( \sum_{k=1}^{d} \sum_{l=1}^{d} H_r(l) H_c(k) X_i^*(k,l) - u_i \right),$$

where $\lambda_i$ are coefficients introduced for satisfy (1) and (2). Now deriving the functional $\Phi$ with respect to $H_r$, and equaling it to zero, we obtain for $H_r(l)$

$$H_r(l) = \frac{\sum_{k} H_c^*(k) \sum_{i=1}^{N} \lambda_i X_i(k,l)}{\sum_{k} |H_c(k)|^2 \left\{ (1-\beta) \sum_{i=1}^{m} |X_i(k,l)|^2 + \beta C(k,l) \right\}} \tag{3}$$

This can be expressed in matrix notation as:

$$H_r(l) = \frac{\mathbf{h}_c^+ \left[ \sum_{j=1}^{m} \lambda_j \mathbf{x}_j(l) \right]}{\mathbf{h}_c^+ \mathbf{T}(l) \mathbf{h}_c} \tag{4}$$

where $\mathbf{h_c}$ is a column vector of the filter $H_c(k)$, $+$ indicates the transpose conjugated, $x_j(l)$ is a column vector formed with the $l$th column of each FT, i.e, equal to $\mathbf{x}_j(l) = [Xj(1,l), ..., Xj(d,l)]^+$ and $\mathbf{T}(l)$ is a diagonal matrix with the sum of the columns of the power spectral density of the input images plus the columns of the matrix $C(k,l)$ calculated by $\mathbf{T}_{j,j}(l) = \left\{ (1-\beta) \sum_{i=1}^{N} |X_i(j,l)|^2 + \beta C(j,l) \right\}$.

Replacing (4) in (2) one obtain

$$u_i = \sum_{l=1}^{d} \frac{\mathbf{h}_c^+ \left[ \sum_{j=1}^{N} \lambda_j \mathbf{x}_j(l) \right] \mathbf{x}_i^+(l) \mathbf{h_c}}{\mathbf{h}_c^+ \mathbf{T}(l) \mathbf{h_c}} \tag{5}$$

Now, if $\mathbf{u} = [u_1, u_2, ..., u_N]$ and $\mathbf{L} = [\lambda_1, \lambda_2, ..., \lambda_N]$, the equation (5) can be rewritten in matrix form as $\mathbf{AL} = \mathbf{u}$, and $\mathbf{A}$ is an $N \times N$ matrix such that each elements is calculated by

$$a(i,j) = \sum_{l=1}^{d} \frac{\mathbf{h}_c^+ \mathbf{x}_j(l) \mathbf{x}_i^+(l) \mathbf{h_c}}{\mathbf{h}_c^+ \mathbf{T}(l) \mathbf{h_c}}, \quad i = 1, ..., N; j = 1, ..., N. \tag{6}$$

Then replacing $\mathbf{L} = \mathbf{A}^{-1}\mathbf{u}$ in (4) allows the calculus of the filter $Hr(l)$ by means

$$H_r(l) = \frac{\mathbf{h}_c^+ \left[ \mathbf{X}^+(l) \mathbf{A}^{-1}\mathbf{u} \right]}{\mathbf{h}_c^+ \mathbf{T}(l) \mathbf{h_c}} \tag{7}$$

where $\mathbf{X}(l)$ is a $d \times N$ matrix formed by the $l$ column of the FT of the $N$ training images, i.e. $\mathbf{X}(l) = [\mathbf{x}_1(l), \mathbf{x}_2(l), ..., \mathbf{x}_N(l)]$. The value of $H_c(k)$ will come out from maximizing a functional in the way

$$J(\mathbf{h_c}, i, j) = \sum_{l=1}^{d} \frac{\mathbf{h}_c^+ \mathbf{x}_j(l) \mathbf{x}_i^+(l) \mathbf{h_c}}{\mathbf{h}_c^+ \mathbf{T}(l) \mathbf{h_c}} \tag{8}$$

whose solution for a given $l$ and $i = j$ is

$$\mathbf{h_c} = T(l)^{-1} \mathbf{x}_i(l).$$

In the most general case, we propose maximizing (8) with a filter with the same structure of the trade-off filter [3] solution, calculated by

$$\mathbf{h_c} = \mathbf{T}^{-1}\mathbf{X} \left( \mathbf{X}^+\mathbf{T}^{-1}\mathbf{X} \right)^{-1} \mathbf{u} \tag{9}$$

where $\mathbf{T}$ is the mean of the $\mathbf{T}(l)$ matrix and $\mathbf{X}$ are the mean of $\mathbf{X}(l)$ for all $l$. Moreover, the $H_r(l)$ filter is obtained from (7).

Next, we implement this method to design separable trade-off filter and perform both digital and optical pattern recognition. Further, the optical experiments are made with an optical convergent correlator and the behavior of filters is measured.

## 3   Optical Implementation

The convergent optical correlator used in this experiment is shown in Fig. 1. In this figure, a monochromatic source of light ($\lambda$= 632.8nm) at point O illuminates the correlator, and $L_1$ and $L_2$ are lenses. The input scene $x(m,n)$ is introduced in the image plane. The optical Fourier transform of $x(m,n)$ is obtained in the filter plane by means of the $L_1$ lens. In such plane, the trade-off separable filter $H^*(k,l)$ is set. Finally in the correlation plane the optical correlation $(c(m,n))$ between the input scene and the Fourier transform of the filter $(H^*(k,l))$ is obtained by means of $L_2$ lens. A CCD camera captures the intensity plane and it is send to a computer to save it as a bitmap image to be analyzed. The filter was synthesized by digital holographic techniques using Lee's codification method [15] and implemented in a plastic substrate. Also, in this figure the $(m,n)$ coordinate represents the spatial domain and $(k,l)$ represents the spatial frequency domain.

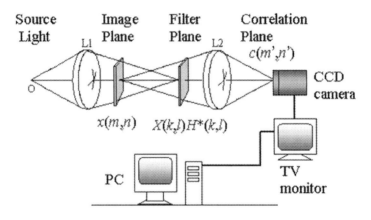

**Fig. 1.** Setup of optical convergent correlator. $O$ is a monochromatic source light, $L_1$ and $L_2$ are lenses, the Fourier transform of the input image $x(m,n)$ is obtained in the filter plane. Finally the correlation is captured by a CCD camera. The separable filter is introduced in the filter plane.

To quantify the recognition ability, we use the discrimination capability (DC) criteria given by [16]

$$\mathrm{DC} = 1 - \frac{\max\left\{\left|c_f^2\right|\right\}}{\max\left\{|c_o^2|\right\}} \qquad (10)$$

where $c_o$ and $c_f$ are the correlation peak values of the object to be recognize and to be discriminated against, respectively. DC values near to 1 indicate a good discrimination, and near to zero value indicates a poor discrimination.

## 4    Results

In this section, we present results obtained with the separable trade-off filter. The training objects are shown in Fig. 2a. They correspond to three angular positioned faces of two people. The input images have $256 \times 256$ pixels in gray scale. The separable trade-off filter is adapted to have a compromise between robustness to noise ($\beta = 0$) and sharpness of the correlation peaks ($\beta = 1$) criteria. This parameter exhibits a nonlinear behavior for both quality criteria, and we use a balance parameter of $\beta = 0.999$ [16]. The filter is designed to recognize three angular position faces in the left column of Fig. 2a, labelled with 0, 2 and 4 respectively; and to reject the faces of the right column of Fig. 2a, labelled with 1, 3 and 5 respectively. In this case, we obtain the DC values for each face of Fig. 2a from

$$\text{DC\_i} = 1 - \frac{\max\left\{\left|c_{f-i}^2\right|\right\}}{\max\left\{\left|c_o^2\right|\right\}}, \quad i = 0, 1, 2, 3, 4, 5 \tag{11}$$

where DC_i is the DC values of (10) applied for the object $i$. $c_{f-i}$ is the maximum of the correlation obtained for object $i$ and $c_o$ is the correlation peak for the reference object. We have selected the faces 0, 2 and 4 of input image (Fig. 2a) as reference objects for the calculus of DC_i. For a good discrimination, the DC_i values for $i = 1$, 3 and 5, must be near to one, and DC_i for $i = 0$, 2 and 4, must be near to zero.

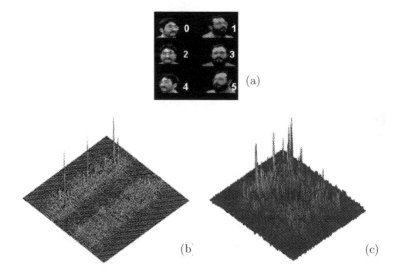

**Fig. 2.** a) Original input scene. A trade-off separable correlation filter has been designed for recognition of the objects 0, 2 and 4, and rejection of the 1, 3 and 5 objects. b) and c) 3-D intensity correlation planes obtained by numerical and optical experiments results respectively.

In Fig. 2b and Fig 2c, 3-D graphs of intensity correlation planes are shown. Numerical result of the intensity correlation plane obtained with the separable filter is shown in Fig. 2b. It can be clearly seen that the maximum peaks are in the position of the object to be recognized. In Fig. 2c, an experimental result by using an optical correlator is presented. We can observe that the correlation peaks are located at position of object 0, 2 and 4. However, the values of the correlation peaks corresponding to the objects 1, 3 and 5 are much higher than the numerical results. The noise in the optical results is higher than in the numerical results.

**Table 1.** Numerical DC_$i$ values obtained with trade-off separable filter for each object of Fig. 2a. The reference objects used are 0, 2 and 4 of Fig. 2a.

| Reference | DC_0 | DC_1 | DC_2 | DC_3 | DC_4 | DC_5 |
|---|---|---|---|---|---|---|
| Object 0 | 0,000 | 0,966 | 0,036 | 0,945 | -0,018 | 0,923 |
| Object 2 | -0,038 | 0,965 | 0,000 | 0,943 | -0,057 | 0,920 |
| Object 4 | 0,018 | 0,967 | 0,054 | 0,946 | 0,000 | 0,924 |

The performance of the designed separable trade-off filter is shown in tables 1 and 2. In Table 1 the values obtained by numerical simulation of DC_$i$ for the input image of Fig. 2a are shown, when the objects 0, 2 and 4 are used as reference. It is clear that the filter is having the ability to perform a correct classification of the objects. We can note that the values of DC for 0, 2 and 4 objects are near to zero, this means similar peaks values between objects indicating a good recognition. On the other hand, the rejection for 1, 3 and 5 objects with values near to one indicates low cross correlation peaks values. In Table 2 the experimental values obtained by means of an optical correlator are presented. It can be clearly seen that the parameters DC_1, DC_3 and DC_5 present lower values than the ones obtained with numerical results. However, the ability to perform a correct classification is maintained. In fact, the correlations with the objects to be rejected are at least 50% lower than the correlation with the objects to be detected.

**Table 2.** Experimental DC_$i$ values obtained with trade-off separable filter for each object of Fig. 2a. The reference objects used are 0, 2 and 4 of Fig. 2a.

| Reference | DC_0 | DC_1 | DC_2 | DC_3 | DC_4 | DC_5 |
|---|---|---|---|---|---|---|
| Object 0 | 0,000 | 0,717 | -0,063 | 0,562 | -0,042 | 0,518 |
| Object 2 | 0,059 | 0,734 | 0,000 | 0,588 | 0,020 | 0,547 |
| Object 4 | 0,040 | 0,729 | -0,020 | 0,580 | 0,000 | 0,538 |

## 5   Conclusions

In this work a methodology for the design of separable trade-off filters is presented. The design methodology is based in two criteria: the correlation plane energy and the signal to noise ratio on the correlation output. The aim of the filter is to be useful in cases when more than one object have to be recognized. Our results show a good performance of the separable filter designed for digital pattern recognition, exhibiting that the procedure of reducing to 1-D processing is an efficient processing alternative reducing memory storage. In optical pattern recognition, our results show that the performance of the separable trade-off filter has a similar behavior, but the noise is higher than in the numerical experiments. The proposed method will be evaluated with a larger and statistically more significant data set in the future.

# References

1. B. V. K. Vijaya Kumar and L. Hassebrook:Performance measures for correlation filters. App. Opt.**29**(20), (1990), 2997–3006.
2. D. Casasent and G. Ravichandran: Advanced distortion-invariant minimum average correlation energy (MACE) filters, App. Opt. **31**(8), (1992) 1109–1116.
3. J. Campos, F. Turon, L.P. Yaroslavsky and M. J. Yzuel: Some filters for reliable recognition and localization of objects by optical correlators: a comparison. International Journal of Optical Computing, John Wiley Sons Ltda.,**2**,(1991) 342-365.
4. A. Van der Lugt: Signal detection by complex spatial filtering. IEEE Trans. on Information Theory,**10**, (1964), 139-145.
5. J. L. Horner and P. Gianino: Phase-only matched filter App. Opt., **23**, (1984) 812-816 .
6. G. G. Mu, X. M. Wang and Z. Q. Wang: Amplitude compensated matched filtering, Appl. Opt., **27**, (1988) 3461-3463.
7. Casasent, David: Unified synthetic discriminant function computational formulation. Appl. Opt., **23**, (1984) 1620-1627.
8. B. V. K. Vijaya Kumar: Tutorial survey of composite filter designs for optical correlators. Appl. Opt., **31**. (1992) 4774–4801.
9. Ph. Rfrgier: Mthodes pour corrlation optique, in Reconnaissance des Formes et Reseaux Neuronaux, Revue Technique Thomson-CSF, **22**(4), (1990) 649–734 .
10. Ph Rfrgier: Filter design for optical pattern recognition: multicriteria optimization approach. Opt. Lett, **15**, (1990) 854-856.
11. Ph Rfrgier: Optimal trade-off filter for noise robustness, sharpness of the correlation peaks, and Horner efficiency. Opt. Lett., **32**, (1993) 1933-1935.
12. Twogood, Richard E., Mitra, Sanjit K: Computer-aided design of separable two-dimensional digital filters. IEEE Trans. on Acoustics, Speech, and Signal Processing, **2**, (1977) 165-169.
13. A. Mahalanobis: Correlation Pattern Recognition in Compressed Images. Opto-electronic Information Processing: Optics for Information System, P. Rfrgier, B. Javidi, C. Ferreira and S. Vallmitjana, Eds., **40** CR81,(2001) 126–147.
14. McFadden, F.E.: Optimal separable correlation filters. Proc. of SPIE, **4726**, (2002) 82-92.
15. W. H. Lee: Binary computergenerated holograms. Appl. Opt., **18**. (1979) 3661–3669.
16. A. Vargas, J. Campos, C. San Martn, N. Vera: Filter Design of Composite Trade-off Filter with Support regions to obtain invariant pattern recognition with defocused images, Optics and Laser in Engineering **40**. (2003) 67–79.

# Approximation of Linear Discriminant Analysis for Word Dependent Visual Features Selection

Hervé Glotin[1], Sabrina Tollari[1], and Pascale Giraudet[2]

[1] Laboratoire Sciences de l'Information et des Systèmes-LSIS CNRS UMR6168
[2] Département de Biologie,
Université du Sud Toulon-Var,
F-83957 La Garde cedex, France
{glotin, tollari, giraudet}@univ-tln.fr

**Abstract.** To automatically determine a set of keywords that describes the content of a given image is a difficult problem, because of (i) the huge dimension number of the visual space and (ii) the unsolved object segmentation problem. Therefore, in order to solve matter (i), we present a novel method based on an Approximation of Linear Discriminant Analysis (ALDA) from the theoretical and practical point of view. Application of ALDA is more generic than usual LDA because it doesn't require explicit class labelling of each training sample, and however allows efficient estimation of the visual features discrimination power. This is particularly interesting because of (ii) and the expensive manually object segmentation and labelling tasks on large visual database. In first step of ALDA, for each word $w_k$, the train set is split in two, according if images are labelled or not by $w_k$. Then, under weak assumptions, we show theoretically that Between and Within variances of these two sets are giving good estimates of the best discriminative features for $w_k$. Experimentations are conducted on COREL database, showing an efficient word adaptive feature selection, and a great enhancement (+37%) of an image Hierarchical Ascendant Classification (HAC) for which ALDA saves also computational cost reducing by 90% the visual features space.

**Keywords:** feature selection, Fisher LDA, visual segmentation, image auto-annotation, high dimension problem, word prediction, CBIR, HAC, COREL database, PCA.

## 1 Introduction

The need for efficient content-based image retrieval has increased in many application areas such as biomedicine, military, and Web image classification and searching. Many approaches have been devised and discussed over more than a decade. While the technology to search text has been available for some time, the one to search images (or videos) is much more challenging. Most of image content based retrieval systems require the user to give a query based on image concepts, but in general he asks semantic queries using textual descriptions. Some systems aim to enhance image word research using visual information

J. Blanc-Talon et al. (Eds.): ACIVS 2005, LNCS 3708, pp. 170–177, 2005.
© Springer-Verlag Berlin Heidelberg 2005

[13]. Anyway, one needs a fast system that robustly auto-annotates large un-annotated image databases. The general idea of image auto-annotation systems is to associate a class of 'similar' images with semantic keywords, e.g. to index by few keywords a new image according to a reference train set. This problem has been pursued in various approaches, such as neural networks, statistical classification, etc. One major issue in these models is the huge dimension number of visual space, and "it remains an interesting open question to construct feature sets that (...) offer very good performance for a particular vision task" [1].

Some recent works consider user feedback to estimate the most discriminant features. This exploration process before or during classification, like in Active Learning, requiers a lot of manual interactions, many hundreds for only 10 words [6]. Therefore these methods can't be applied to large image databases or large lexicons. In this paper we propose to answer to the previous question by automatically reducing the high dimensional visual space to the most efficient usual features for a considered word. The most famous method of dimensionality reduction is Principal Components Analysis (PCA). But PCA does not include label information of the data. Although PCA finds components that are useful for representing data, there is no reason to assume that these components must be useful for discriminating between data in different classes. But where PCA seeks direction that are efficient for representation, Fisher Linear Discriminant Analysis (LDA) seeks ones that are efficient for discrimination ([3] pp 117).

Indeed recent works in audio-visual classification show that LDA is efficient under well labelled databases to determine the most discriminant features, reducing the visual space [4,10,7]. Unfortunately, most of the large image databases are not correctly labelled, and do not provide a one-to-one relation between keywords and image segments (see COREL image sample with their caption in Fig. 1). Consequently usual LDA can't be applied on real image databases. Moreover because of the unsolved visual scene segmentation problem (see Fig. 1), real applications or training of image auto-annotation systems from web pages, would require a robust visual features selection method from uncertain data. Therefore, we present a novel Approximation of LDA (ALDA), in a theoretical and practical analysis. ALDA is simpler than usual LDA, because it doesn't need explicit labelling of the training samples for generating a good estimation of the most discriminant features. ALDA first stage consists, for each word $w_k$, to split train set in two, according if images are labelled by $w_k$ or not. Then, under weak assumption, we show that for a given $w_k$, Between and Within variances, between these two sets, are giving good estimates of the best discriminative features. Experimentations are illustrating features dependency to each word, and significant classification enhancements.

## 2   LDA Approximation and Adaptive Visual Features

Major databases are not manually segmented and segment-labelled, thus given a set of training images $\Phi = \{\phi_j\}_{j \in \{1,...,J\}}$ and a lexicon $\lambda = \{w_k\}_{k \in \{1,...,K\}}$, each image $\phi_j$ is labelled with some words of $\lambda$ (e.g. $\phi_j$ has a global legend constructed with $\lambda$ as shown in Fig. 1). In order to extract visual features of each object included in each $\phi_j$, one can automatically segment each image in many areas called blobs. Unfortunately, blobs generally do not match with the shape of each object. Even if they do, there is no way to relate each blob to the corresponding word.

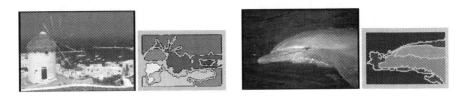

**Fig. 1.** Examples of an automatic segmentation (Normalized Cuts algorithm [11]) of two COREL images [1]. Image caption are (left image) "Windmill Shore Water Harbor" and (right) "Dolphin Bottlenosed Closeup Water". Each blob of each image is labelled by all words of its image caption. Notice also that dolphin is split in two parts as many as other objects after the Normalized Cuts algorithm.

Nevertheless, we show below that despite the fact that each word class $w_k$ is not associated to a unique blob, and vice-versa, one can estimate for each $w_k$ which are the most discriminant visual features. To this purpose we need to define four sets: $S$, $T$, $T_G$ and $G$. Let be $S$ the theoretical set of values of one feature $x$, calculated on all the blobs that are *exactly* representing the word $w_k$. We note for any feature set E, $c_E$ its cardinal, $\mu_E$ the average of all $x_i$ values of $x \in E$, $v_E$ their variance. Let be $T$ the set of $x$ values *of all blobs included in all images labelled* by $w_k$ (of course $T$ includes $S$). Let be $T_G$ such that $T = T_G U S$, with empty intersection between $T_G$ and $S$. We assume $c_{T_G} \neq 0$ (otherwise each image labeled by $w_k$ contains only the corresponding blobs).

Let be $G$ the set containing all values of $x$ from all blobs contained in images that are not labelled by $w_k$. In the following, we only assume the weak assumption (hyp. 1) $\mu_{T_G} = \mu_G$ *and* $v_{T_G} = v_G$, which is related to the simple assumption of context independency provided by any large enougth image database. We note $B_{DE}$ (resp. $W_{DE}$) the Between variance (resp. the Within variance) between any sets D and E. The usual LDA is based on the calculation, for each feature $x$ of the theoretical discrimination power $F(x; w_k) = \frac{1}{1+V(x;w_k)}$ where $V(x; w_k) = \frac{W_{SG}}{B_{SG}}$. We show below that $\hat{V}(x; w_k) = \frac{W_{T_G}}{B_{T_G}}$ is a good approximation of $V(x; w_k)$, and that if one apply $V$ to ordinate all $x$ for a given word $w_k$, then this order is the same by applying $\hat{V}$, at least for the most discriminant features $x$. Therefore the selection of features whith higher theoretical discriminative powers $F$ can be carried out from the calculation of practical $\hat{F}(x; w_k) = \frac{1}{1+\hat{V}(x;w_k)}$ values.

Let $p_S = \frac{c_S}{c_T}$ and $q_S = 1 - p_S = \frac{c_T - c_S}{c_T} = \frac{c_{T_G}}{c_T}$. We have $\mu_T = q_S.\mu_{T_G} + p_S.\mu_S$. Therefore:

$$\mu_T = q_S.\mu_G + p_S.\mu_S. \tag{1}$$

Let derive $v_T$ with $v_S$, $v_G$, and for any $x \in T$, the probability $p_i$ of event '$x = x_i$':

$$v_T = \sum_{x_i \in T} \left( x_i - \mu_T \right)^2 p_i \quad = \sum_{x_i \in T} \left( x_i - q_S.\mu_G - p_S.\mu_S \right)^2 p_i$$

$$= \sum_{x_i \in T_G} \left( (x_i - \mu_G) + p_S(\mu_G - \mu_S) \right)^2 p_i + \sum_{x_i \in S} \left( (x_i - \mu_S) + q_S(\mu_S - \mu_G) \right)^2 p_i$$

$$= \sum_{x_i \in T_G} (x_i - \mu_{T_G})^2 p_i + 2p_S(\mu_G - \mu_S) \sum_{x_i \in T_G} (x_i - \mu_G)p_i + p_S^2(\mu_G - \mu_S)^2 \sum_{x_i \in T_G} p_i$$

$$+ \sum_{x_i \in S} (x_i - \mu_S)^2 p_i + 2q_S(\mu_S - \mu_G) \sum_{x_i \in S} (x_i - \mu_S)p_i + q_S^2(\mu_S - \mu_G)^2 \sum_{x_i \in S} p_i$$

$$= q_S.v_{T_G} + 2p_S(\mu_G - \mu_S)\left( \sum_{x_i \in T_G} x_i.p_i - \mu_G \sum_{x_i \in T_G} p_i \right) + p_S^2(\mu_G - \mu_S)^2 q_S$$

$$+ p_S.v_S + 2q_S(\mu_S - \mu_G)\left( \sum_{x_i \in S} x_i.p_i - \mu_S \sum_{x_i \in S} p_i \right) + q_S^2(\mu_S - \mu_G)^2 p_S$$

$$= q_S.v_G + 2p_S(\mu_G - \mu_S)(q_S.\mu_{T_G} - \mu_G.q_S) + p_S^2.q_S(\mu_G - \mu_S)^2$$

$$+ p_S.v_S + 2.q_S.(\mu_S - \mu_G).(p_S.\mu_S - \mu_S.p_S) + q_S^2.p_S(\mu_S - \mu_G)^2$$

$$\text{then } v_T = q_S.v_G + p_S.v_S + p_S.q_S.(\mu_G - \mu_S)^2 \tag{2}$$

We are now able to derive and link $B_{TG}$ and $B_{SG}$:

$$B_{TG} = \frac{c_T}{c_T + c_G}\left( \mu_T - \frac{c_T.\mu_T + c_G.\mu_G}{c_T + c_G} \right)^2 + \frac{c_G}{c_T + c_G}\left( \mu_G - \frac{c_T.\mu_T + c_G.\mu_G}{c_T + c_G} \right)^2$$

$$= \frac{c_T}{c_T + c_G}\left( \frac{c_G.\mu_T - c_G.\mu_G}{c_T + c_G} \right)^2 + \frac{c_G}{c_T + c_G}\left( \frac{c_T.\mu_G - c_T.\mu_T}{c_T + c_G} \right)^2$$

$$B_{TG} = \frac{c_T.c_G(\mu_T - \mu_G)^2}{(c_T + c_G)^2} \tag{3}$$

$$= \frac{c_T.c_G.(q_S.\mu_G + p_S.\mu_S - \mu_G)^2}{(c_T + c_G)^2} = \frac{c_T.c_G.p_S^2(\mu_S - \mu_G)^2}{(c_T + c_G)^2} = \frac{c_G.c_S^2.(\mu_S - \mu_G)^2}{c_T.(c_T + c_G)^2}.$$

Similary to Eq. (3) we have: $B_{SG} = \dfrac{c_S.c_G.(\mu_S - \mu_G)^2}{(c_S + c_G)^2}.$ \hfill (4)

Thus from Eq. (4) and (5): $B_{TG} = \dfrac{c_S.(c_S + c_G)^2}{c_T.(c_T + c_G)^2}.B_{SG}.$ \hfill (5)

We also derive the Within variances $W_{TG}$ and $W_{SG}$:

$$W_{TG} = \frac{c_T.v_T + c_G.v_G}{c_T + c_G} \quad = \frac{c_T.(q_S.v_G + p_S.v_S + p_S.q_S.(\mu_G - \mu_S)^2) + c_G.v_G}{c_T + c_G}$$

$$= \frac{(q_S.c_T + c_G).v_G + p_S.c_T.v_S + p_S.q_S.c_T.(\mu_G - \mu_S)^2}{c_T + c_G}$$

$$\text{then } W_{TG} = \frac{(c_T - c_S + c_G).v_G + c_S.v_S + p_S.q_S.c_T.(\mu_G - \mu_S)^2}{c_T + c_G}. \tag{6}$$

By definition $W_{SG} = \dfrac{c_S.v_S + c_G.v_G}{c_S + c_G}$, so $v_G = \dfrac{c_S + c_G}{c_G}.W_{SG} - \dfrac{c_S.v_S}{c_G}$.

$$W_{TG} = \frac{(c_T - c_S + c_G).\left(\frac{c_S + c_G}{c_G}.W_{SG} - \frac{c_S.v_S}{c_G}\right) + c_S.v_S + p_S.q_S.c_T.(\mu_G - \mu_S)^2}{c_T + c_G}$$

$$= \frac{(c_T - c_S + c_G).(c_S + c_G)}{c_G.(c_T + c_G)}.W_{SG} - \frac{c_S.(c_T - c_S)}{c_G.(c_T + c_G)}.v_S + \frac{c_S.(c_T - c_S)}{c_T.(c_T + c_G)}.(\mu_G - \mu_S)^2. \tag{7}$$

$$\hat{V}(x; w_k) = \frac{\frac{(c_T - c_S + c_G).(c_S + c_G)}{c_G.(c_T + c_G)}.W_{SG} - \frac{c_S.(c_T - c_S)}{c_G.(c_T + c_G)}.v_S + \frac{c_S.(c_T - c_S)}{c_T.(c_T + c_G)}.(\mu_G - \mu_S)^2}{\frac{c_S.(c_S + c_G)^2}{c_T.(c_T + c_G)^2}.B_{SG}}$$

$$= \frac{c_T(c_T - c_S + c_G)(c_T + c_G)}{c_G.c_S(c_S + c_G)} \frac{W_{SG}}{B_{SG}} + \frac{(c_T - c_S)(c_T + c_G)}{c_S.c_G}\left(1 - \frac{c_T}{c_G} \frac{v_S}{(\mu_G - \mu_S)^2}\right)$$

$$\text{thus } \hat{V}(x; w_k) = A(w_k).V(x; w_k) + B(w_k).\left(1 - C(x; w_k)\right) \tag{8}$$

where $A$ and $B$ are positive constants independent of $x$, only depending on number of blobs in sets $T$, $S$, $G$ (experimentations on COREL database show that for all words, A and B are close to 10). Therefore, for any given word $w_k$, $\hat{V}(x; w_k)$ is a linear function of $V(x; w_k)$ if $C(x; w_k)$ is negligible in front of 1. This is the case if (hyp. 2) $\frac{c_T}{c_G}$ is small, which is true in COREL database since it is close to 0.01 for most words, and never exceeds 0.2 (actually one can build any database such that $C_T \ll C_G$) and (hyp. 3) $v_S$ is tiny in front of $(\mu_G - \mu_S)^2$ which is the case when $x$ is a reasonably good feature to discriminate $G$ and $S$ (e.g. $w_k$ is represented by a rather stationnary feature value different from the mean contextual value). Then order of $\hat{V}$ and $V$ values are the same. Finally, for each word $w_k$, even without knowing which blob of the image it labels, one can estimate the most discriminant features by simply ranking $\hat{F}$ values. Thereby, in order to estimate how many and which of the $\mathcal{X}_n, n \in \{1,.., \delta\}$ features are really discriminant for each word $w_k$, we simply sort by decreasing order all the $\hat{F}(\mathcal{X}_n; w_k)$, and calculate $N < \delta$ where $\delta$ is the dimension number of visual space and $N$ is defined by: $\sum_{n=1}^{N} \hat{F}(\mathcal{X}_n; w_k) = \frac{\sum_{n=1}^{\delta} \hat{F}(\mathcal{X}_n; w_k)}{2}$. Thus $\mathcal{X}_1, .., \mathcal{X}_N$ are considered as the $N$ best discriminative features for $w_k$.

## 3   Experimentations on COREL Image Database

To test the efficiency of ALDA, extensive experiments are done on the COREL[1] images database [9] made of 10 000 images with approximately 100 000 segments

---

[1] We thank K. Barnard and J. Wang for providing COREL image database.

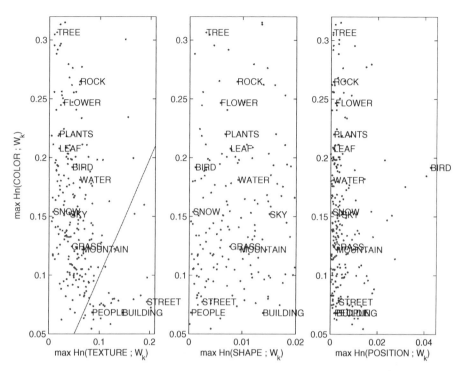

**Fig. 2.** Maximum values of normalised estimated discrimination power $Hn(x; w_k) = \hat{F}(x; w_k) / \sum_x \hat{F}(x, w_k)$ for COLOR, TEXTURE, SHAPE, and POSITION features sets for the 14 most frequent words of the database (other words are represented by a simple dot). Results are intuitively correct: TREE, ROCK, FLOWER, PLANTS are mostly discriminated by color; while BUILDING and STREET are more discriminated by texture. SHAPE is in average not very competitive in comparison to COLOR, neither POSITION. BIRD is the word the most discriminated by POSITION, indeed most of COREL images with a bird represent a bird in the image center.

preprocessed by K. Barnard and al. [1]. Each image is labelled by an average 3.6 words from a lexicon of 267 different words, and has an average of 10 visual segments ('blobs') from the Normalized Cuts algorithm [11], which somehow produces small ones. Each blob is described by a set of $\delta = 40$ features listed below by their dimension index. Firstly POSITION and SHAPE: (1,2) horizontal and vertical blob's position; (3) the proportion of the blob in its image; (4) ratio of bold's area to the perimeter squared; (5) moment of inertia; (6) ratio of the blob's area by its convex hull. COLOURS (7,..,24) are represented by the average and standard deviation of (R,G,B), (r,g,S) and (L,a,b). TEXTURES (25,..,40) are extracted by gaussian filters [1].

## 3.1    F Estimation for COLOR, TEXTURE, SHAPE and POSITION

We run ALDA on 6 000 COREL images, and measure for each word the maximum value of $\hat{F}$ for SHAPE, COLOR or TEXTURE features sets. These values represented in Fig. 2 for the 14 most frequent words are intuitively correct and show the word dependence of ALDA. The repartition analysis, over words of all the 6 000 images of the train set, of selected $N$ best features are respectively 3% for POSITION, 8% for SHAPE features, 65% for COLOR features, 24% for TEXTURE features. COLOR features are confirmed to be the most discriminant ones (see also Fig. 2). The simple TEXTURE features (16 gaussian filters) are better than the SHAPE ones, certainly because blobs' segmentation are imprecise (see Fig. 1).

## 3.2   Hierarchical Ascendant Classifications Improved by ALDA

To demonstrate ALDA efficiency on a classification task, we now run on COREL a Hierarchical Ascendant Classifications (HAC) of visual features into word categories [12]. As in [2], we measure the system performance using the Normalised Score $NS = sensi. + specif - 1$ [1,8]. Compared to the raw visual input space, good results have been obtained reducing HAC visual features inputs to ALDA $N$ best discriminant features as previously defined end of section 2 (method called NADAPT0.5). NS values for HAC on the 40 usual visual dimensions or word adaptive features are shown in Fig. 3.

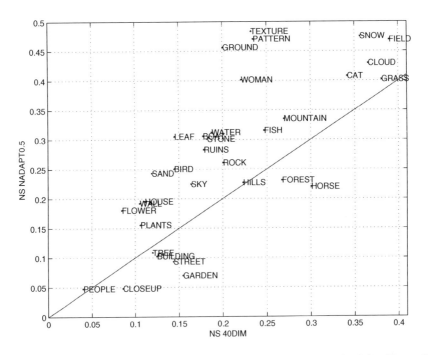

**Fig. 3.** Word visual consistency representation for 40DIM method (in X-coordinate) and for NADAPT0.5 method (in Y-coordinate). NADAPT0.5 method gives better results than 40DIM except for *closeup, garden, street, forest, horse.*

Classification of the 3 000 images of the test set shows a gain of $+37\%$ of NS, and simultaneously an average over all words of a dimension reduction from $\delta = 40$ to 4 best features (see [12] for more details on the HAC experiments).

## 4   Conclusion

In this paper we present ALDA based on an approximation of the Fisher LDA. We shown that, under weak assumptions (hyp. 1 to 3), ALDA estimates $N$ best features which enhance HAC task, while reducing by 10 the visual space dimension. The main contributions on this paper are summarized as follows: (a) For the first time a theoretical demonstration of ALDA is given in the first section. (b) We implement ALDA on a reference image database and we analyse word dependant features sets constructed using ALDA. (c) We integrate ALDA in a simple HAC model, leading to significant improvements. Further auto-annotation experiments are currently being done on COREL with a bayesian system (DIMATEX model [5]), yielding to promising first results.

## References

1. K. Barnard, P. Duygulu, N. Freitas, D. Forsyth, D. Blei, and M. Jordan. Matching words and pictures. In *Jour. of Machine Learning Research*, volume 3, 2003.
2. K. Barnard, P. Duygulu, R. Guru, P. Gabbur, and D. Forsyth. The effects of segmentation and feature choice in a translation model of object recognition. *Computer Vision and Pattern Recognition*, pages 675–682, 2003.
3. R. Duda, P. Hart, and D. Stork. *Pattern Classification*. Wiley, 2000.
4. J. Luettin G. Potamianos and C. Neti. Hierarchical discriminant features for audio-visual LVCSR. In *Proc. of IEEE Int. Conf. ASSP*, 2001.
5. H. Glotin and S. Tollari. Fast image auto-annotation with visual vector approximation clusters. In *IEEE EURASIP Content-Based Multimedia Indexing*, 2005.
6. P. Gosselin and M. Cord. A comparison of active classification methods for content-based image retrieval. In *Proc. CVDB04 with SIGMOD04*, Paris, 2004.
7. Q. Liu, R. Huang, H. Lu, and S. Ma. Face recognition using kernel based Fisher discriminant analysis. In *Proc. of Automatic Face & Gesture Recognition*, 2002.
8. F. Monay and D. Gatica-Perez. On image auto-annotation with latent space models. In *Proc. ACM Int. Conf. on Multimedia (ACM MM)*, pages 275–278, 2003.
9. H. Muller, S. Marchand-Maillet, and T. Pun. The truth about corel - evaluation in image retrieval. In *The Challenge of Image and Video Retrieval (CIVR02)*, 2002.
10. C. Neti, G. Potamianos, J. Luettin, I. Matthews, H. Glotin, and D. Vergyri. Large-vocabulary audio-visual speech recognition: A summary of the J. Hopkins Summer 2000 Wksp. In *IEEE Wksp. Multimedia Signal Process.*, 2001.
11. J. Shi and J. Malik. Normalized cuts and image segmentation. *IEEE Transactions on Pattern Analysis and Machine Intelligence*, 22(8):888–905, 2000.
12. S. Tollari and H. Glotin. Keyword dependant selection of visual features and their heterogeneity for image content-based interpretation. Technical Report LSIS.RR.2005.003, LSIS, Similar content submitted to ACMMM2005 2005.
13. S. Tollari, H. Glotin, and J. Le Maitre. Enhancement of textual images classification using segmented visual contents for image search engine. *Multimedia Tools and Applications*, 25(3):405–417, march 2005.

# Estimation of Intensity Uncertainties for Computer Vision Applications*

Alberto Ortiz and Gabriel Oliver

Department of Mathematics and Computer Science,
University of the Balearic Islands, Spain
{alberto.ortiz, goliver}@uib.es

**Abstract.** The irradiance measurement performed by vision cameras is not noise-free due to both processing errors during CCD fabrication and the behaviour of the electronic device itself. A proper characterization of sensor performance, however, allows accounting for it within image processing algorithms. This paper proposes a robust algorithm named $R^2CIU$ for characterizing the noise sources affecting CCD performance with the aim of estimating the uncertainty of the intensity values yielded by vision cameras. Experimental results can be found at the end of the paper.

## 1 Introduction

As it is well known, vision cameras measure the spatial distribution of light incident on a light-sensitive device (typically a CCD) and produce, accordingly, bidimensional descriptions of this distribution known as images. Due to both processing errors during CCD fabrication and the behaviour of the electronic device itself, the measurement process is, however, not noise-free. In contrast with geometric calibration, for which lots of algorithms have been published, the characterization of this noise for vision cameras (i.e. radiometric calibration) has been rarely studied. Perhaps, the paper by Healey and Kondepudy is one of the most detailed studies on the subject which can be found [1]. Their calibration algorithm is based on their own camera noise model and estimates the gain, the charge-independent non-spatial noise, the camera dark current and the photoresponse non-uniformity. After the paper by Healey and Kondepudy, Tarel [2] proposed several experiments for estimating the charge-independent non-spatial noise, the dark current and the joint effect of the fixed pattern array and the shadowing introduced by the camera optics due to the effect known as vignetting [3]. Finally, Gevers and Stokman [4] make use of a simplified camera noise model consisting of electronic gain, shot noise and dark current for error propagation inside an image segmentation framework.

On the basis of the camera noise model of [1], this paper describes how to determine intensity uncertainties on the basis of the estimates computed by a new robust algorithm for radiometric camera calibration called $R^2CIU$ (*Robust Radiometric Calibration and Intensity Uncertainty estimation*). It is based on uniform reflectance cards and, contrary to [1] and [2], does not intend to estimate spatial noise pixel by pixel, which is not

---

* Partially supported by project CICYT-DPI2001-2311-C03-02 and FEDER funds.

J. Blanc-Talon et al. (Eds.): ACIVS 2005, LNCS 3708, pp. 178–185, 2005.
© Springer-Verlag Berlin Heidelberg 2005

essential to compute intensity uncertainties, but focuses on the corresponding distribution parameters, making the estimation procedure simpler, but, at the same time, robust since all the image cells are involved in the computation of the estimates. Finally, the material presented in this paper is the continuation of a work which started in [5].

The rest of the paper is organized as follows: section 2 presents the image formation model assumed in this work; next, section 3 describes the procedures to estimate the distribution parameters of the different noise sources involved; the determination of the uncertainty for digital intensity levels is discussed in section 4; section 5 provides the calibration results obtained for a real CCD camera and illustrates the computation of intensity uncertainties; finally, section 6 concludes the paper.

## 2   Camera Operation Model

Ideally, the number of electrons accumulated at a given collection site or image cell $(i, j)$ for colour band $c$, $I^c(i, j)$, can be expressed as:

$$I^c(i, j) = T \int_\Lambda \left( \int_y \int_x E(x, y; \lambda) S_r(x, y) \eta(\lambda) \, dx \, dy \right) \tau^c(\lambda) d\lambda, \qquad (1)$$

where: (i) $(x, y)$ are continuous coordinates on the sensor plane, (ii) $\Lambda$ represents the set of wavelengths $\lambda$ within the visible spectrum, (iii) $T$ is the integration or *exposure time*, $E(x, y; \lambda)$ is the irradiance incident at point $(x, y)$ over the collection site, (iv) $S_r(x, y)$ is the *spatial response* of the collection site, (v) $\eta(\lambda)$ is the ratio of electrons collected per incident light energy (a form of the so-called *quantum efficiency*), and (vi) $\tau^c(\lambda)$ is the *filter transmittance* for colour channel $c$.

Assuming a non-attenuating propagation medium and ignoring the blurring and low-pass filtering effects of the point-spread function of the optics in a properly focused camera, $E(x, y; \lambda)$ and the corresponding scene radiance $L(p; \lambda)$ are related as $E = (\pi/4) (d/f)^2 (\cos\varphi)^4 L$, where $d$ is the effective diameter of the lens (i.e. its aperture), $f$ is the focal distance and $\varphi$ is the angle between the optical axis and the straight line that, passing through the lens nodal point, connects $(x, y)$ with the scene point $p$ [3]. The quantity $f/d$ is the so-called *F-number*.

Several sources of noise can affect the performance of CCD-based imaging systems, preventing them from measuring actual irradiance values. According to [1], the digitized signal corresponding to pixel $(i, j)$ can be stated as a random variable $D^c(i, j) = \mu^c(i, j) + N^c(i, j)$ as follows:

$$D^c(i, j) = \overbrace{(K(i, j) I^c(i, j) + \mu_{dc}(i, j)) A^c}^{\mu^c(i,j)} + \overbrace{\underbrace{(N_S^c(i, j) + N_{dc}(i, j)) A^c}_{N_c^c(i,j)} + \underbrace{N_R A^c + N_Q}_{N_f^c}}^{N^c(i,j)}, \quad (2)$$

where: (i) $K$ represents a random variable of (spatial) mean $E_I[K] = 1$ and (spatial) variance $\text{Var}_I[K]$ expressing the site-to-site non-uniformities among image cells due to processing errors during CCD fabrication, also called *photo-response non-uniformity* (PRNU); (ii) $N_S^c$ is the so-called *shot noise*, representing the uncertainty in the number of electrons collected at a given image cell, which is, in turn, distributed as a Poisson random variable of variance $KI^c$; (iii) $\mu_{dc}$ is the expected *dark current* generated by thermal energy at every collection site, and therefore expresses the *dark current non-uniformity* across image cells (DCNU), while $N_{dc}$ corresponds to the uncertainty in the number of dark electrons, the *dark current shot noise*, whose variance is $\mu_{dc}$; (iv) $N_R$ is the zero-mean noise introduced by the charge-to-voltage output amplifier of the camera; (v) $N_Q$ is a uniform random variable defined over the interval $[-1/2, 1/2]$ accounting for the *quantization noise*; and (vi) $A^c$ is the camera gain for colour channel $c$. In (2), $N^c$ represents non-spatial zero-mean additive noise, where $N_e^c$ depends on the number of collected electrons while $N_f^c$ does not.

# 3   Estimation of the Camera Noise Model Parameters

This section presents a set of techniques for estimating the parameters of the camera noise model expressed in equation 2. They are based on the use of a constant reflectance matte calibration card covering the whole field of view of the camera. If the card is not bent anyway and is uniformly illuminated, $I^c(i, j)$ of equation 2 should be approximately constant across the image in absence of camera lens imperfections. Under those circumstances, equation 3 results:

$$D^c(i, j) = (K(i, j)I^c + \mu_{dc}(i, j)) A^c + (N_S^c(i, j) + N_{dc}(i, j)) A^c + N_R A^c + N_Q . \quad (3)$$

## 3.1   Estimation of the PRNU and the DCNU Distribution Parameters

Let us assume that several images of the calibration card with the same camera and lighting parameters are taken and averaged pixel by pixel to produce image $\mu_{D^c}$. As discussed in [6,7], the non-spatial noise $N^c$ tends to vanish in the average pixel values $\mu_{D^c}(i, j)$. If, in turn, the average across the whole image of the $\mu_{D^c}(i, j)$ values is taken, then equation 4 results for $E_I[\mu_{D^c}]$, taking into account that $E_I[K] = 1$:

$$E_I[\mu_{D^c}] = I^c A^c + E_I[\mu_{dc}]A^c . \quad (4)$$

Next, given the independence between the PRNU and the DCNU and after the averaging of the $D^c(i, j)$ values, the (spatial) variance of the $\mu_{D^c}(i, j)$ values can be approximated by equation 5:

$$\text{Var}_I[\mu_{D^c}] = \text{Var}_I[K] (I^c)^2 (A^c)^2 + \text{Var}_I[\mu_{dc}] (A^c)^2 , \quad (5)$$

which, using equation 4, transforms into equation 6:

$$\text{Var}_I[\mu_{D^c}] = \text{Var}_I[K] (E_I[\mu_{D^c}] - E_I[\mu_{dc}]A^c)^2 + \text{Var}_I[\mu_{dc}] (A^c)^2 . \quad (6)$$

According to equation 6, points $(E_I[\mu_{D^c}], \text{Var}_I[\mu_{D^c}])$ lie in a parabola from whose parameters the (spatial) variance of $K$ and $\mu_{dc}$, together with $E_I[\mu_{dc}]$, can be estimated. Such points can be obtained from several sets of images of the calibration card taken at different values of $I^c$. These images can be easily generated changing, from set to set, the camera optics aperture (i.e. the F-number) or placing neutral-density (ND) filters in front of the camera.

## 3.2   Estimation of Camera Gain and Charge-Independent Non-spatial Noise

Further manipulation of equation 3 allows estimating the camera gain $A^c$ and the variance of the noise independent of the number of electrons stored at collection sites $N_f^c$. To perform this calculation, the (temporal) variance of the intensity level in a certain image cell between exposures, $\sigma_{D^c}^2(i,j)$, will be determined (i.e. several images of the calibration card under exactly the same imaging conditions are taken and the variance image $\sigma_{D^c}^2$ is considered). In such a case, the variation comes from the shot noises $N_S^c$ and $N_{dc}$, and from $N_f^c$. On the basis of the independence between the different noise sources, $\sigma_{D^c}^2(i,j)$ is given by:

$$\sigma_{D^c}^2(i,j) = [K(i,j)I^c + \mu_{dc}(i,j)](A^c)^2 + (\sigma_f^c)^2, \tag{7}$$

where $(\sigma_f^c)^2$ is the variance of $N_f^c$. Now, taking the (spatial) mean of the $\sigma_{D^c}^2(i,j)$ values and using equation 4, equation 8 results:

$$E_I[\sigma_{D^c}^2] = A^c E_I[\mu_{D^c}] + (\sigma_f^c)^2. \tag{8}$$

Therefore, according to equation 8, pairs $(E_I[\mu_{D^c}], E_I[\sigma_{D^c}^2])$ lie in a straight line whose slope and intercept with the $E_I[\sigma_{D^c}^2]$ axis coincide with, respectively, $A^c$ and $(\sigma_f^c)^2$. These pairs can be obtained taking several sets of images so that $I^c$ changes from set to set, as previously discussed, and computing the (spatial) average of the pixel-by-pixel (temporal) mean and variance of the images within every set.

# 4   Determination of Intensity Uncertainties

Let us assume a plane card of constant reflectance and uniformly illuminated is imaged by the camera. The goal is to quantify the variation which could be found in the resulting image with respect to the noiseless digital intensity value $I^c A^c$ which would result in a perfect camera. Clearly, every noise source contributes to the final uncertainty value. These contributions have already been expressed somewhere within section 3. From the independence of the noise sources, the total uncertainty is given by the sum in quadrature of the different contributions [1]. In this way, equation 9 provides, in the form of *expected value* ± *uncertainty* [8], an approximation of the final digital value returned by the camera, $D^c$, for every possible digital intensity level, $I^c A^c$.

$$D^c = (I^c A^c + E_I[\mu_{dc}]A^c) \pm t\sigma_I^c \tag{9}$$

$$\sigma_I^c = \sqrt{\mathrm{Var}_I[K](I^c A^c)^2 + \mathrm{Var}_I[\mu_{dc}](A^c)^2 + (I^c A^c)A^c + E_I[\mu_{dc}](A^c)^2 + (\sigma_f^c)^2}$$

For a given $t$, equation 9 relates every possible intensity value $I^c A^c$ with an interval of values $[D_a^c, D_b^c]$ where the corresponding digital value returned by the camera can lie with a certain probability. Resorting to the Chebyshev inequality[1], $t = 2, 3$ and 4 represent that the measurement $D^c$ will lie inside $[D_a^c, D_b^c]$ with, respectively, probabilities of 75.00%, 88.89% and 93.75% [9]. If, besides, the Poisson distributions associated to

---

[1] For a random variable $X(\mu, \sigma)$, $P(|X - \mu| \geq k\sigma) \leq 1/k^2, k > 0$.

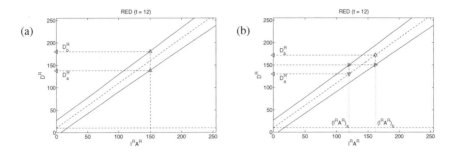

**Fig. 1.** (a) Uncertainty curves which derive from equations 9 after a proper calibration of the camera and a certain value of $t$, for the red colour channel. (b) Confidence interval $[D_a^R, D_b^R]$ corresponding to a certain measurement $D^R$. (In both plots, the dashed horizontal straight line at the bottom corresponds to $\mathrm{E}_I[\mu_{dc}]A^R$, while the slanted dashed line between the two uncertainty curves is $D^R = I^R A^R + \mathrm{E}_I[\mu_{dc}]A^R$).

the shot noises are approximated by Gaussian distributions, and the remaining noise sources are assumed Gaussian, the noise distribution results to be normal, and, therefore, the previous probabilities for $t = 2, 3$ and 4 increase, respectively, up to 95.45%, 99.73% and 99.99%. By way of example, figure 1(a) shows uncertainty curves (solid lines) for the red colour channel of a hypothetical camera.

Note that, however, equation 9 goes from the noiseless intensity values to the measurements produced by the camera, although only the latter are effectively available. Therefore, the relationship must be reversed to be useful: i.e. given a measure $D^c$, an interval of possible noiseless intensities, $[(I^c A^c)_a, (I^c A^c)_b]$, must be looked for (see figure 1(b)). $(I^c A^c)_a$ and $(I^c A^c)_b$ can be easily obtained reversing equation 9 to get equation 10, which involves a second degree polynomial in $I^c A^c$:

$$\alpha (I^c A^c)^2 - \beta (I^c A^c) + \gamma = 0$$
$$\alpha = \left(1 - t^2 \mathrm{Var}_I[K]\right) \qquad \beta = \left(t^2 A^c + 2(D^c - \mathrm{E}_I[\mu_{dc}]A^c)\right) \tag{10}$$
$$\gamma = (D^c - \mathrm{E}_I[\mu_{dc}]A^c)^2 - t^2 \left(\mathrm{Var}_I[\mu_{dc}](A^c)^2 + \mathrm{E}_I[\mu_{dc}](A^c)^2 + (\sigma_f^c)^2\right)$$

Once $(I^c A^c)_a$ and $(I^c A^c)_b$ are known for a certain $D^c$, a confidence interval $[D_a^c, D_b^c]$ can be calculated for $D^c$ by means of $D_a^c = (I^c A^c)_a + \mathrm{E}_I[\mu_{dc}]A^c$ and $D_b^c = (I^c A^c)_b + \mathrm{E}_I[\mu_{dc}]A^c$ (see figure 1(b)).

## 5   Experimental Results

This section reports the calibration results for a JAI CV-M70 progressive scan colour CCD camera with linear response and 8 bits per colour channel and pixel. The rest of the calibration setup hardware consisted of 400 W halogen illumination and a COMET Matrox frame grabber. Matte white calibration cards were used, although the particular reflectance is not relevant provided that it is approximately uniform throughout the image area. Besides, intensity uncertainties are also derived and illustrated.

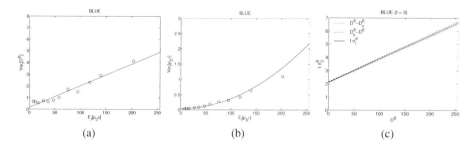

(a)                              (b)                              (c)

**Fig. 2.** (a) Estimation of camera gain and charge-independent non-spatial noise. (b) Estimation of the PRNU and the DCNU distribution parameters by means of parabolas sharing the first coefficient across colour channels. (c) Estimation of intensity uncertainties for the blue colour channel.

**Estimation of noise distribution parameters.** Both spatial and charge-independent non-spatial noise distribution parameters were measured by means of 12 sets of images of the calibration card, each set corresponding to a different lens aperture. Besides, each set of images consisted of 100 frames. For every set, pixel-by-pixel mean and variance images $\mu_{D^c}(i,j)$ and $\sigma^2_{D^c}(i,j)$ were calculated, which, in particular, allowed reducing the non-spatial noise $N^c(i,j)$ in images $\mu_{D^c}(i,j)$ at about only 10% of their original magnitude [6,7], improving, thus, the calculation of $E_I[\mu_{D^c}]$ and $Var_I[\mu_{D^c}]$ (see equation 6). Moreover, the 12 different values of $I^c$ led to the generation of 12 pairs $(E_I[\mu_{D^c}], Var_I[\mu_{D^c}])$ and $(E_I[\mu_{D^c}], E_I[\sigma^2_{D^c}])$ for estimating, respectively, the PRNU and the DCNU distribution parameters and the gain and charge-independent non-spatial noise of the camera under calibration.

With this set of images, camera gain $A^c$ and the variance of the charge-independent non-spatial noise $(\sigma^c_f)^2$ were estimated for every colour channel $c$ following the procedure outlined in section 3.2. The resulting estimates were $A = (A^R, A^G, A^B) = (0.0046, 0.048, 0.074) \pm (0.0012, 0.0016, 0.0018)$ and $\sigma_f = (\sigma^R_f, \sigma^G_f, \sigma^B_f) = (0.79, 0.59, 0.51) \pm (0.04, 0.06, 0.06)$, while the correlation coefficients for all three colour channels resulted to be (0.963,0.963,0.976). By way of illustration, figure 2(a) shows the fitting corresponding to the blue colour channel.

On the other hand, $Var_I[K]$, $E_I[\mu_{dc}]A^c$ and $Var_I[\mu_{dc}](A^c)^2$ were measured following the procedure described in section 3.1, but ensuring an only $Var_I[K]$ value resulted for the three colour channels because the internal organization of the camera under calibration was based on an only CCD. In this case, the estimates were $\sqrt{Var_I[K]} = 0.0057 \pm 0.0001$, $\sqrt{E_I[\mu_{dc}]}A = (0.00, 0.00, 0.00) \pm (0.01, 0.01, 0.01)$ and $\sqrt{Var_I[\mu_{dc}]}A = (0.20, 0.17, 0.20) \pm (0.00, 0.00, 0.00)$, while the correlation coefficients resulted to be (0.998,0.994,0.994). Figure 2(b) shows the fitting parabola for the blue colour channel.

**Determination of intensity uncertainties.** By way of illustration of the computation of the intensity uncertainties, figure 2(c) plots the uncertainties corresponding to the blue colour channel. The averaged parameters between the two executions of R$^2$CIU have been used. In the plot, $D^B - D^B_a$ and $D^B_b - D^B$ are shown, together with $t\sigma^B_I$, for

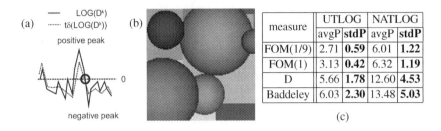

Fig. 3. (a) Selection of zero-crossings in UTLOG. (b) Noisy image. (c) Comparison results.

$t = 3$. Although little difference can be observed among them in the figure, they turned out to be relevant (i.e. larger than 0.5) for $t > 7$.

**Example of application.** To illustrate the use of the estimates produced by R²CIU, an edge detection task based on detecting LOG zero-crossings is next presented. In this case, uncertainties are used to devise a strategy for adaptive thresholding which will be called UTLOG (*Uncertainty-based Thresholding for LOG zero-crossings*). In particular, a detected LOG zero-crossing is classified as relevant if the positive and negative peak LOG values along the direction of detection are larger than $t$ times the respective uncertainties. Those uncertainties are calculated using standard uncertainty propagation rules, by which, if the output of the LOG operator is calculated as $f = \sum_x D^k(x)m(x)$, where $m(x)$ would be the LOG mask constants, then $\delta(f) = \sqrt{\sum_x \delta(D^k(x))^2 m^2(x)}$ [8]. By way of example, see figure 3(a), where only the zero-crossing under the circle would be considered relevant.

In order to study the performance of UTLOG, and, by extension, the usefulness of the estimated uncertainties, UTLOG was compared with a non-adaptive method which will be called NATLOG (*Non-Adaptive Thresholding for LOG zero-crossings*) in which LOG zero-crossings was selected by requiring negative and positive LOG peaks above a global threshold independent of the intensities involved. The goal of the experiment consisted in determining the optimum value of the only parameter of each algorithm for each image of a series of noisy synthetic images. A lower standard deviation of the optimum values found would mean, in this experiment, a larger easiness for finding the proper value and, thus, a larger adaptivity.

The comparison was performed over a set of 100 synthetic images involving spheres and planes of different reflectances (see Fig. 3(b) for an example) to which noise was added according to the camera noise parameters estimated in section 5. Besides, up to four empirical discrepancy evaluation measures were used to find the optimum values: the often-cited Pratt's Figure of Merit (FOM) with (1) $\alpha = 1/9$ and (2) $\alpha = 1$; (3) the discrepancy percentage (D); and (4) the Baddeley measure, which was found the best evaluation technique in a recent survey [10] which also involved, among others, Pratt's FOM and D. In this way, the result of the experiment did not depend on the optimization strategy employed. As for the range of values considered for the respective parameters, for UTLOG, $t \in [1..15]$, while for NATLOG, global integer thresholds between 1 and 30 were considered.

The quantitative results of the experiment appear in figure 3(c), where $stdP$ is the aforementioned standard deviation, while $avgP$ is the corresponding average. As can be observed, $stdP$ is quite lower for UTLOG than for NATLOG in all cases. Besides, column $avgP$ indicates, for UTLOG, that $t$ from 2-3 to 6-7 work well most times, while for NATLOG the global threshold interval seems to widen so as to cover values between 6 and 17, confirming, thus, the higher adaptivity of UTLOG thanks to the incorporation of intensity uncertainties in the thresholding.

# 6   Conclusions

An algorithm called $R^2CIU$ for radiometric camera calibration has been proposed. It allows estimating the distribution parameters of the noise sources of the camera noise model proposed by Healey and Kondepudy in [1]. The fact that all the pixels of the captured image can participate in the estimation makes $R^2CIU$ a robust estimator of the noise model parameters. It has also been shown how, with the previous estimates, intensity uncertainties can be determined and an example of application in an edge detection task has been presented to show how to incorporate those uncertainties in computer vision algorithms. Some experimental results have proved the usefulness of the uncertainties estimated. Other more sophisticated vision algorithms also using those uncertainties can be found in other papers published by the authors (for instance [11]). See [12] for more experimental results data and a more detailed presentation.

# References

1. Healey, G., Kondepudy, R.: Radiometric CCD Camera Calibration and Noise Estimation. PAMI **16** (1994) 267–276
2. Tarel, J.P.: Une Méthode de Calibration Radiométrique de Caméra à Focale Variable. In: Proc. 10ème Congrés AFCET, Reconn. des Formes et Intell. Artificielle, RFIA. (1996)
3. Horn, B.: Robot Vision. MIT Press (1986)
4. Gevers, T., Stokman, H.: Robust Photometric Invariant Region Detection in Multispectral Images. IJCV **53** (2003) 135–151
5. Ortiz, A., Oliver, G.: Estimation of Scene Lighting Parameters and Camera Dark Current. In: Frontiers in Artificial Intelligence and Applications. Volume 100., IOS Press (2003) 199–210
6. Holst, G.: CCD Arrays, Cameras, and Displays. 2nd edn. SPIE press (1998)
7. Janesick, J.: Scientific Charge-Coupled Devices. SPIE Press (2001)
8. Taylor, J.: An Introduction to Error Analysis. University Science Books (1997)
9. Lindgren, B.: Statistical Theory. 4th edn. Chapman & Hall (1993)
10. Fernandez-Garcia, N., et al.: Characterization of empirical discrepancy evaluation measures. PRL **25** (2004) 35–47
11. Ortiz, A., Oliver, G.: A Physics-Based Colour Edge Detector. In: Frontiers in Artificial Intelligence and Applications. Volume 113., IOS Press (2004) 201–208
12. Ortiz, A., Oliver, G.: $R^2CIU$: Robust Radiometric Calibration and Intensity Uncertainty estimation. Technical Report A-1-2005, Departament de Matemàtiques i Informàtica (Universitat de les Illes Balears) (2005)

# A Wavelet Statistical Model for Characterizing Chinese Ink Paintings

Xiqun Lu

College of Computer Science, Zhejiang University, Hangzhou, 310027, P.R. China
xqlu@cs.zju.edu.cn

**Abstract.** This paper addresses a wavelet statistical model for characterizing Chinese ink painting styles. The distinct digital profile of an artist is defined as a set of *feature-tons* and their distribution, which characterize the strokes and stochastic nature of the painting style. Specifically, the feature-tons is modeled by a set of high-order wavelet statistics, and the high-order correlation statistics across scales and orientations, while the feature-ton distribution is represented by a finite mixture of Gaussian models estimated by an unsupervised learning algorithm from multivariate statistical features. To measure the extent of association between an unknown painting and the captured style, the likelihood of the occurrence of the image based on the characterizing stochastic process is computed. A high likelihood indicates a strong association. The research has the potential to provide a computer-aided tool for art historians to study connections among artists or periods in the history of Chinese ink painting art.

## 1 Introduction

To analyze a large collection of paintings from different artists and to compare different painting styles is an important problem for not only computer scientist, but also for the art community. With advanced computing and image analysis techniques, it may be possible to use computers to study more paintings and in more details than a typical art historian could. Computers can be used to extract nuance features and structures from images efficiently, and these numerical features can be applied to compare paintings, artists, and even painting schools.

In this paper, a wavelet statistical model is presented to study collections of Chinese ink paintings. The distinctive digital profile of an artist is defined as a set of feature-tons and their statistical distributions. The feature-tons and their distribution are learned from thousands of multivariate statistical features by using an unsupervised clustering algorithm. The multivariate statistical feature is modeled by a set of high-order wavelet statistics, and the high-order correlation statistics across scales and orientations, while the feature-ton distribution is represented by a finite mixture of Gaussian models. Simulation experience is conducted on a database of high resolution photographs of Chinese ink paintings. The algorithm presented here has the potential to provide a computer-aided tool for art historians to study connections among artists or periods in the history of Chinese ink painting art.

J. Blanc-Talon et al. (Eds.): ACIVS 2005, LNCS 3708, pp. 186–193, 2005.
© Springer-Verlag Berlin Heidelberg 2005

## 1.1 Major Challengers

Unlike natural color images, Chinese ink paintings are in monochromic ink and sometimes do not even possess gradually changing tones. In terms of image content, there is little to compare among these paintings, because most of them depicted mountains, trees, rivers/lakes, and so on. So Chinese ink paintings demand unconventional image analysis techniques. An important aspect of Chinese ink paintings art historians often examine when studying and comparing different paintings is the characteristic stroke used by artists.

In this paper, we first divide an input image into 64×64 blocks, and we assume that each block in a Chinese ink painting contains a single fine style element. Because the fundamental idea behind the wavelet transform is to analyze the image at several different scales, block-based features are extracted from each training image based on the wavelet decomposition. In order to reduce the sensitivity to the variations in digitization and the image content, only the high-order statistics of the high frequency wavelet coefficients, which reflect the changes in pixel intensity rather than the absolute intensity, are used for the feature vector of each block. Here the feature vector extracted from each block is assumed to have been generated by one of a set of alternative random sources, so finite mixture models are used to fit the multivariate feature vectors.

## 1.2 Related Works

Research problems in concern and methodologies used in this paper are related to several technique fields, among which include computer vision, image retrieval and statistical image modeling. Instead of a broad survey, we try to emphasize some work most related to what we proposed.

For a general introduction to digital imagery of cultural heritage materials, see [1]. In [2], a statistical model based on 2-D multiresolution HMMs is proposed to the problem of automatic linguistic indexing of image retrieval. Almost the same technique is proposed in [3] to study the different styles of Chinese ink paintings. They constructed 2-D HMMs based on the wavelet decomposition to capture properties of the painting strokes, and the learned mixture of 2-D multiresolution HMMs profile the style of an artist. In [4] a region-based image categorization method using an extension of Multiple Instance Learning (MIL) is proposed. Each image is represented as a collection of regions obtained from image segmentation using the k-means algorithm. In their method, each image is mapped to a point in a bag feature space, which is defined by a set of instance prototypes learned with the Diverse Density function.

Although our statistical framework for profiling Chinese ink paintings was motivated by those ideas proposed in [3] and [4], it has several important distinctions from those previous works. First we will not create a mixture of 2-D multiresolution HMMs for each image as described in [3]. We divided the training images into blocks, and high-order wavelet statistics, and the correlation statistics across scales and orientations are extracted as a feature vector. Each feature vector is considered as an instance which is assumed to be generated by a finite mixture multivariate Gaussian Models. All of these feature vectors are clustered to form a set of feature-tons. However an important issue in mixture modeling is the selection of the number of components, we adopt the modified Minimum Message Length Criterion proposed in [5] to deal with the above problem, and the estimation and the model selection can be seamlessly integrated into a single algorithm. This is the biggest difference between our method and the approach proposed in [4] which is based on an extension of Multiple Instance Learning (MIL). The obtained clustered feature-tons and their distribution can be used to profile the latent style for an artist.

## 2   Multivariate Statistical Feature Extraction

First we divide the training images into blocks. The wavelet transform is used to extract statistical features from these blocks. One reason for this utility is that such decompositions exhibit statistical regularities that can be exploited. The decomposition is based on separable quadrature mirror filters. As illustrated in Fig.1, this decomposition splits the frequency space into multiple scales and orientations. This decomposition is accomplished by applying separable low-pass and high-pass filters along the image row and column, generating a vertical, horizontal, diagonal and low-pass subband. Subsequent scales are created by subsampling the low-pass subband by a factor of 2 and recursively filtering. The vertical, horizontal, and diagonal subbands at scale $i=1, 2, \ldots, n$ are denoted as $v_i(x,y)$, $h_i(x,y)$ and $d_i(x,y)$, respectively.

As we know that the mean and the variance of the subband coefficients are highly correlated to the content of the input image. In order to reduce sensitivities to variations in digitization and the image content, only the high-order statistics (skewness, and kurtosis) of the subband coefficients at each orientation and at scales $i=1, 2, \ldots, n$ are used. These statistics characterize the local coefficient distributions. As described in [3], the subband coefficients are correlated to their spatial, orientation, and scale neighbors. In order to capture the high-order correlations across different scales, these coefficient statistics are augmented with a set of statistics based on the errors in an optimal linear predictor of coefficients magnitude.

For the purpose of illustration, consider first a horizontal band, $v_i(x,y)$, at scale i. A linear predictor for the magnitude of these coefficients in a subset of all possible neighbors may be given by

$$|V_i(x, y)| = w_1|V_i(x-1, y)| + w_2|V_i(x+1, y)| + w_3|V_i(x, y-1)| + w_4|V_i(x, y+1)| + w_5|V_{i+1}(2x,2y)|$$
$$+ w_6|V_{i+1}(2x+1,2y)| + w_7|V_{i+1}(2x+1,2y)| + w_8|V_{i+1}(2x+1,2y+1)| \tag{1}$$

where $w_k$ denotes weights, and $|\bullet|$ denotes magnitude. The predictor coefficients ($w_1, \ldots, w_8$) are determined as follows: The column vector $\vec{v}$ contains the coefficient magnitudes of $v_i(x,y)$, and the rows of the matrix $Q$ contains the chosen neighboring coefficient magnitudes of $v_i(x,y)$. The linear predictor takes the form

$$\vec{V} = Q\vec{w} \tag{2}$$

where the column vector $\vec{w} = (w_1, \cdots, w_8)^T$. The predictor weights are determined by minimizing the quadratic error function:

$$E\{\vec{w}\} = [\vec{V} - Q\vec{w}]^2 \tag{3}$$

**Fig. 1.** A 3-level wavelet decomposition of a painting by Zeng Fan

This error function is minimized by differentiating with respect to $\vec{w}$:

$$dE\{\vec{w}\} / d\vec{w} = 2Q^T[\vec{V} - Q\vec{w}] \tag{4}$$

Setting the above equation to zero and yield

$$\vec{w} = (Q^TQ)^{-1}Q^T\vec{V} \tag{5}$$

Once the set of the predictor weights are determined, additional high-order statistics are collected from the errors of the final predictor. The entire process is repeated for each orientation, and at each scale i=1, 2, ..., n-1. For a n-level wavelet decomposition, the coefficient statistics consists of 6n values, and the prediction error statistics consist of another 6(n-1) values, for a total of 6(2n-1) statistics. These statistics represent the local statistical feature vector of a block.

## 2   Probabilistic Framework for Profiling Chinese Ink Paintings

Let $\mathbf{Y}=[Y_1, ..., Y_{30}]^T$ be a 30-dimensional random variable (here we apply the 3-level wavelet decomposition to each block), with $\mathbf{y} =[y_1, ..., y_{30}]^T$ representing one particular feature vector generated by $\mathbf{Y}$. It is assumed that $\mathbf{Y}$ follows a N-component finite mixture distribution if its probability density function can be written as:

$$p(\mathbf{y} \mid \boldsymbol{\theta}) = \sum_{m=1}^{N} \alpha_m p(\mathbf{y} \mid \theta_m) \tag{6}$$

where $\alpha_1, ..., \alpha_N$ are the mixing probabilities, each $\theta_m$ is the set of parameters defining the m*th* component, and $\boldsymbol{\theta}=\{\theta_1, ..., \theta_N, \alpha_1, ..., \alpha_N\}$ is the complete set of parameters needed to specify the mixture. Of course, being probabilities, the $\alpha_m$ must satisfy

$$\alpha_m \geq 0, \text{ m=1, ..., N, and } \sum_{m=1}^{N} \alpha_m = 1 \tag{7}$$

In this paper, we assume that all the components are multivariate Gaussian models. Given a set of k independent and identically distributed feature vector samples $Y=\{y(1), ...,y(k)\}$, the log-likelihood corresponding to a N-component mixture is

$$\log p(Y \mid \boldsymbol{\theta}) = \log \prod_{i=1}^{k} p(y(i) \mid \boldsymbol{\theta}) = \sum_{i=1}^{k} \log \sum_{m=1}^{N} \alpha_m p(y(i) \mid \theta_m) \qquad (8)$$

It is well known that the maximum likelihood (ML) estimate

$$\hat{\boldsymbol{\theta}}_{ML} = \arg \max_{\theta} \{\log p(Y \mid \boldsymbol{\theta})\} \qquad (9)$$

cannot be found analytically.

At the beginning we can let N be some arbitrary large value and infer the structure of the mixture by letting the estimates of some of the mixture probabilities be zero. This is equal to pruning the mixture models. The inference criterion adopted from [5] is used as the number of clusters selection criterion

$$L(Y, \boldsymbol{\theta}) = \frac{M}{2} \sum_{m:\alpha_m>0} \log(\frac{k\alpha_m}{12}) + \frac{N_{nz}}{2} \log \frac{k}{12} + \frac{N_{nz}(M+1)}{2} - \log(Y \mid \boldsymbol{\theta}) \qquad (10)$$

where M is the number of parameters specifying each component, i.e. the dimension of $\theta_m$, and $N_{nz}$ denotes the number of non-zeror-probability components.

The usual choice of obtaining ML estimation of the mixture parameters is the EM algorithm. EM is an iterative procedure which finds local maxima of $\log p(Y \mid \boldsymbol{\theta})$. The EM algorithm is based on the interpretation of Y as incomplete data. For finite mixtures, the missing part is a set of k labels $Z = \{z(1), ..., z(k)\}$ associated with the k training feature vectors, indicating which component generated each features. Each label is a binary vector $z(i) = [z(i)_1, ..., z(i)_N]$, where $z(i)_m = 1$ and $z(i)_p = 0$, for $p \neq m$, means that feature $y(i)$ was generated by the *mth* multivariate Gaussian model. The complete log-likelihood is

$$\log p(Y, Z \mid \boldsymbol{\theta}) = \sum_{i=1}^{k} \sum_{m=1}^{N} z(i)_m \log[\alpha_m p(y(i) \mid \theta_m)] \qquad (11)$$

Based on the above mentioned inference criterion, the EM algorithm produces a sequence of estimates of $\{\hat{\boldsymbol{\theta}}(t), t = 0,1,2,\cdots\}$, while at the same time to choose the number of non-zero-probability components $N_{nz}$ by alternatively applying two steps:

*1) E-step*: Computes the conditional expectation of the complete log-likelihood, given Y and the current estimation of $\hat{\boldsymbol{\theta}}(t)$. Since $\log p(Y, Z \mid \boldsymbol{\theta})$ is linear with respect to the missing data Z, we simply have to compute the conditional expectation $W \equiv E[Z \mid Y, \hat{\boldsymbol{\theta}}(t)]$, and plug it into $\log p(Y, Z \mid \boldsymbol{\theta})$. The result is the so-called Q-function:

$$Q(\boldsymbol{\theta}, \hat{\boldsymbol{\theta}}(t)) = E[\log p(Y, Z \mid \boldsymbol{\theta}) \mid Y, \hat{\boldsymbol{\theta}}(t)] \qquad (12)$$

Since the elements of Z are binary, their conditional expectations are given by

$$w(i)_m \equiv E[z(i)_m \mid Y, \hat{\boldsymbol{\theta}}(t)] = \Pr[z(i)_m = 1 \mid y(i), \hat{\boldsymbol{\theta}}(t)] = \frac{\hat{\alpha}_m(t) p(y(i) \mid \hat{\theta}_m(t))}{\sum_{j=1}^{N} \hat{\alpha}_j p(y(i) \mid \hat{\theta}_j(t))} \qquad (13)$$

where the last equality is simply the Bayes Theorem ($\alpha_m$ is the a prior probability that $z(i)_m = 1$, while $w(i)_m$ is the a posterior probability that $z(i)_m = 1$, after observing $y(i)$). In the initialization, we set $\hat{\alpha}_m(0) = 1 / N_{nz}$ ( m = 1, 2, ..., $N_{nz}$).

*2) M-step:* Here the EM algorithm to minimize the cost function in (10), with $N_{nz}$ fixed, has the following M-step:

$$\hat{\alpha}_m(t+1) = \frac{\max\{0, \sum_{i=1}^{k} w(i)_m - \frac{M}{2}\}}{\sum_{j=1}^{N} \max\{0, \sum_{i=1}^{k} w(i)_j - \frac{M}{2}\}} \tag{14}$$

for m = 1, 2, ..., $N_{nz}$.

$$\bar{\mu}_m(t+1) = \frac{\sum_{j=1}^{k} y(j) p(y(j), w(j)_m \mid \theta_m(t))}{\sum_{i=1}^{N_{nz}} \sum_{j=1}^{k} p(y(j), w(j)_i \mid \theta_i(t))} \tag{15}$$

$$C_m(t+1) = \frac{\sum_{j=1}^{k} (y(j) - \mu_m(t+1))^2 p(y(j), w(j)_m \mid \theta_m(t))}{\sum_{i=1}^{N_{nz}} \sum_{j=1}^{k} p(y(j), w(j)_i \mid \theta_i(t))} \tag{16}$$

for m: $\hat{\alpha}_m(t+1) > 0$. In the initialization, $N_{nz}$ is a large number, and randomly choose $N_{nz}$ feature vectors as the initial center (mean) vectors of the initial $N_{nz}$ clusters from the all input training feature vectors. The initial covariance matrices of the components are initialized to diagonal matrices proportional to 1/10 of the mean variance along all the axes.

Where $w(i)_m$ is given by the E-step equation. The $\theta_m$s corresponding to components for which $\hat{\alpha}_m(t+1) = 0$ become irrelevant. Notice in (8) that any component for which $\alpha_m = 0$ does not contribute to the likelihood. An important feature of the M-step defined by (14) is that it performs component annihilation, thus being an explicit rule for moving from the current value of $N_{nz}$ to a smaller one. Hence the estimation of $\{\hat{\theta}(t), t = 0,1,2,\cdots\}$ and the model selection $N_{nz}$ can be seamlessly integrated into a single algorithm.

## 3 Experimental Results

In the experiments, we start with $N_{nz}=N$, where N is much larger than the true/optimal number of mixture components, hence this algorithm is robust with respect to initialization.

We develop a distinct latent style profile for Tao Shi (1641-1724) who was an outstanding Chinese ink painting artist especially for his "mountains-and- waters" works. In order to capture the comprehensive painting style of Tao Shi, 21 representative paintings of Tao Shi are used as the training images to estimate the number of textons and their distributions. A total 4892 feature vectors are obtained in the feature extraction stage. In the initial stage of clustering, we set the maximum number of clusters as 200, and the minimum number of clusters as 10.

Fig. 2 shows the initial stage of clustering. After the unsupervised clustering algorithm, only the 22 clustered textons are obtained, and the 22 textons and their distributions are used as the digital latent style of the artist. The final estimation is indicated in Figure 3.

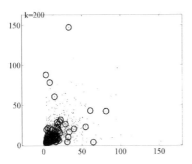

**Fig. 2.** Initialization with $N_{nz}=200$    **Fig. 3.** The final estimation with $N_{nz}=22$

To estimate the association of an unknown painting to the captured style, first it is converted to a set of multiresolution feature vectors as described in Section 2. Given the set of the feature-tons of the training feature space $\mathbf{m}_1, \ldots, \mathbf{m}_N$ and their distribution, all the obtained multivariate features $\mathbf{t}_1, \ldots, \mathbf{t}_{test}$ of the testing image are classified to the corresponding feature-tons as following:

$$lable_i = \arg\min_j d_{ij} = \left\| \mathbf{t}_i - \mathbf{m}_j \right\|_2^2 \tag{17}$$

and compute the center of each cluster as following:

$$\vec{m}_i^T = \frac{1}{N_i} \sum_{label(t_j)=i} \mathbf{t}_j \tag{18}$$

where $N_i$ is the number of the testing feature vectors in the *ith* cluster. The testing feature space T can be constructed as:

$$T_1 : \quad \vec{m}_{label_1}^T \qquad T_2 : \quad \vec{m}_{label_2}^T \cdots \qquad T_M : \quad \vec{m}_{label_M}^T \tag{19}$$

Note here the dimension of the training feature space N may not equal to the dimension of the testing feature space M (M≤N). Some of the clusters may be empty.

The likelihood of the unknown painting related to the captured style of the artist can be computed using the posterior probability of the trained mixture models:

$$p(\vec{m}_{label_1}^T, \vec{m}_{label_2}^T, \cdots \vec{m}_{label_M}^T \mid \boldsymbol{\theta}) = \sum_{i=1}^{M} \alpha_{label_i} p(\vec{m}_{label_i}^T \mid \theta_{label_i}) \tag{20}$$

This probability framework of estimation is to replace the "hard" decision by a "soft" decision. This statistical framework provides a computer-aided technique to Chinese ink paintings characterization.

In order to examine the accuracy of the learned 22 mixture Gaussian models, we choose 20 images painted by Tao Shi, and 20 images by Xiaoming Li, and another 20 images by an imitator of Tao Shi – Xinya Chen as the test images. The 20 testing paintings of Tao Shi are different from the paintings that used for the training. Table I gives the classification results. In this preliminary experiment we can see that our method is somehow better than the method proposed in [3].

Xiaoming Li used a very different Chinese ink painting skill from Shi, so the classification result is very good. However Xinya Chen is a skillful imitator of Tao Shi, sometimes even people can not tell the difference between the work painted by Shi and the painting by Chen. The stroke style of Chen is very similar to that of Shi. The method proposed in [3] can hardly tell the difference between the works of Chen and those of Shi. However our method is better than the method proposed in [3]. From the results shown in Table I our statistical framework can be extended to provide a computer-aided technique to Chinese ink painting authentication.

**Table 1.** The classification result obtained by the mixture Gaussian models. Each row lists the average classification accuracy of classify an artist paintings to Tao Shi.

| Percent (%) | Our Method | Method in [3] |
|---|---|---|
| | Shi | Shi |
| Shi | 83% | 72% |
| Li | 0 | 3% |
| Chen | 45% | 68% |

## 4 Conclusions

In this paper, a wavelet statistical model is developed to capture complex dynamic styles of Chinese ink paintings. The style profile of an artist is represented by a set of statistical feature-tons and their distribution. Local dynamics are captured by first- and high-order wavelet statistics, and the correlation statistics across scales and orientations, while the global style are modeled by a finite mixture of Gaussian models estimated by an unsupervised learning algorithm from multivariate features. The mechanisms behind our approach and the scheme proposed in [3] should be explored and compared extensively in the future work.

## References

1. Chen C., Wactlar H., Wang J. Z., Kiernan K.: Digital imagery for significant cultural and historical materials - an emerging research field bridging people, culture, and technologies, International Journal on Digital Libraries, Special Issue: Towards the New Generation Digital Libraries: Recommendations of the US-NSF/EU-DELOS Working Groups (2005)
2. Li J., Wang J. Z.: Automatic linguistic indexing of pictures by a statistical modeling approach, IEEE Trans. On Pattern Analysis and Machine Intelligence, Vol.25. (2003) 1075-1088
3. Li J., Wang J. Z.: Studying digital imagery of ancient paintings by mixtures of stochastic models, IEEE Trans. On Image Processing, Vol.13.(2004) 340-353
4. Chen Y., Wang J. Z.: Image categorization by learning and reasoning with regions, Journal of Machine Learning Research, Vol.5 (2004) 913-939
5. Figueiredo M. A. T., Jain A. K.: Unsupervised learning of finite mixture models, IEEE Trans. On Pattern Analysis and Machine Intelligence, Vol.24 (2002) 381-396

# Image Formation in Highly Turbid Media by Adaptive Fusion of Gated Images

Andrzej Sluzek[1] and Tan Ching Seong[2]

[1] Nanyang Technological University, School of Computer Engineering,
Blk N4, Nanyang Avenue, Singapore 639798
assluzek@ntu.edu.sg
[2] Singapore Institute of Manufacturing Technology,
71 Nanyang Drive, Singapore 638075
cstan@SIMTech.a-star.edu.sg

**Abstract.** A visibility enhancement technique for highly-scattering media (e.g. turbid water) using an adaptive fusion of gated images is proposed. Returning signal profiles produced by gated imaging contain two peaks: the backscattering peak followed by the target-reflected peak. The timing of the backscattering peak is determined by the laser pulse parameters, while the location of second peak depends on the target distance. Thus, a sequence of gated images ranged over a variety of distances can be used to visualize scenes of diversified depths. For each fragment of the scene, the gated image containing the maximum signal strength (after ignoring the backscattering peak) is identified to form the corresponding fragment of the fused image. This unique capability of capturing both visual and depth information can lead to development of fast and robust sensors for vision-guided navigation in extremely difficult conditions.

## 1 Introduction

Visibility in highly scattering media (e.g. turbid water) is severely degraded because imaging devices capture not only the signal reflected from observed objects, but also a large amount of radiance scattered toward a device by the medium. No significant enhancement can be achieved by illuminating the scene with a high-intensity light source, as this proportionally increases the scattering noise and the overall SNR (signal-to-noise ratio) remains unaffected. Although certain improvements in image quality are possible by post-processing, the target-reflected radiance and the scattered radiance are generally inseparable at "traditional" capturing devices.

The alternative method is to capture images with devices that can discriminate between reflected and scattered signals. Range-gated imaging (e.g. [1], [2], [3], [4]) is such a technique. A gated imaging system basically consists of a pulsed laser (usually, the pulses are diverged into a conical shape) a high-speed gated camera and the control and synchronization circuitry. The principles of operation are explained in Fig.1. Projected laser pulses reflect from objects and return to a camera with electronically controlled (gated) shutter. If the gate opening is synchronized with the head of the pulse reflected from an object, and closing is synchronized with the pulse tail, the camera captures the image of this object (and possible other objects within the same range).

J. Blanc-Talon et al. (Eds.): ACIVS 2005, LNCS 3708, pp. 194–201, 2005.
© Springer-Verlag Berlin Heidelberg 2005

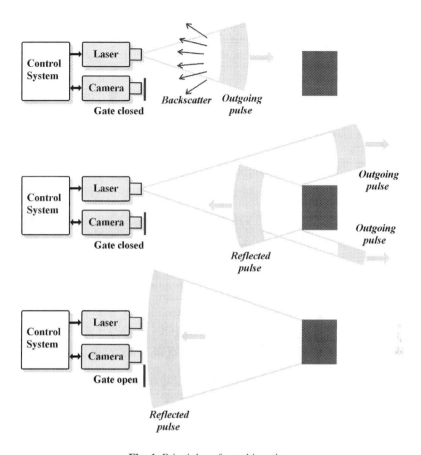

**Fig. 1.** Principles of gated imaging

Reflections from more distant objects do not return before the shutter closes (i.e. such objects are invisible) while reflections from front objects return before the shutter opens (i.e. such objects become dark shadows as no reflected signal is received at those areas). As an illustration, a non-gated image is compared to two gated images (ranged to different depths) in Fig. 2. These images are captured in low-turbidity medium.

Additionally, the amount of backscattering noise is minimized in gated images as most of the backscattered signal (produced by the layer between the camera and the target) returns when the shutter is closed. Thus, if the distance to observed targets is correctly estimated, gated imaging can produce in turbid media images of much better quality (and at longer ranges) than "traditional" devices. It is claimed (see [5]) that visual penetration of turbid media is 3-6 times deeper for gated imaging systems than for their non-gated counterparts. As an example, Fig. 3 shows a test object captured in highly turbid water by a non-gated camera and a gated one.

In more realistic scenarios, the observed scenes may contain numerous objects at diversified distances. To effectively use gated images in such unpredictable

**Fig. 2.** A non-gated image (left) and two gated images captured at different ranges. Note the contribution of ambient light to the gated images.

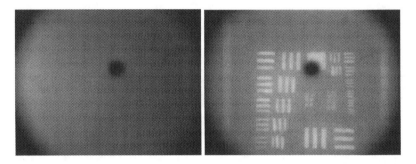

**Fig. 3.** A non-gated image (left) and a gated one (right) captured in a highly turbid medium. The gated image is ranged to the actual distance to the object.

conditions (in high-turbidity media, in particular) novel methods of image formation should be developed. This paper presents theoretical foundations and preliminary experimental results for such a method. The method would be particularly useful in short-range problems, (e.g. autonomous navigation in turbid waters, visibility enhancement in heavy smoke, etc.). Section 2 of the paper briefly overviews a model of short-range gated imaging and highlights the most significant properties of the model. The image formation by fusion of gated images is subsequently discussed in Section 3, including exemplary experimental results. In Section 4, the obtained results are concluded and further developments of the methods are proposed.

## 2  Model of Short-Range Gated Imaging

The radiation returning to a camera after illuminating the scene by a laser pulse is an additive composition of backscattering noise and target-reflected signals. The actual profile of the returning signal depends on the pulse duration, the medium turbidity, and on the target reflectivity and its distance to the camera. Although the detail model of this phenomenon is very complex (e.g. [6]), under simplifying assumptions the returning backscattered signal can be modeled as a convolution (with fixed upper limit) of the emitted pulse profile $P_0(t)$ with the kernel $S(r)$ representing optical properties of the medium. If the assumed duration of the laser pulse is $2t_0$, and an opaque target is placed at $r_0$ distance, the formula for the backscattering noise is:

$$P_{BSN}(t) = \int_{v(t-2t_0)/2}^{vt/2} S(r)P_0(t - 2r/v)dr \quad \text{for } t \leq (2r_0/v + 2t_0 + \tau) \tag{1}$$

The target reflected signal can be modeled as:

$$P_S(t) = B \cdot P_0(t - 2r_0/v) \quad \text{for } 2r_0/v < t \leq 2r_0/v + 2t_0 \tag{2}$$

where **B** jointly represents the target reflectivity and optical properties of the medium. In Eqs (1) and (2) **v** is the speed of light in the medium. More analytical results and further discussions on the model limitations are available in [7].

As an illustration, model-predicted profiles (the light intensity returning to the camera - arbitrary units used) are given in Fig. 4. They are computed (for various water turbidities) for a target at 1.8m distance illuminated by 9ns laser pulses.

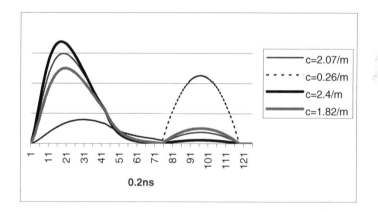

**Fig. 4.** Light intensity profiles returning to the camera computed for a 1.8m opaque target illuminated by a 9ns laser pulse in water of various turbidity levels (attenuation **c**)

The actual profiles measured for the same scene are shown in Fig. 5. The measured profiles and their modeled counterparts are qualitatively similar, but some differences (due to the model simplification) can be noticed. For example, the backscattering peaks (the left peaks in Figs 4 and 5) in the measured profiles are delayed with respect to the modeled peaks (especially in high turbidities). This is because the backscattering signal is modeled using only single-scattering photons. In turbid media, a large portion of that signal is formed by multiple-scattered photons that are additionally delayed before returning to the camera. Moreover, the shape of reflected signal peaks (the right peaks in Figs 4 and 5) is not modeled accurately (the assumed profile of the laser pulses may differ from the actual pulse profile).

Fig. 6 presents the modeled profiles for a similar scene (in high-turbidity conditions) illuminated by pulses of various durations (all pulses carry the same energy).

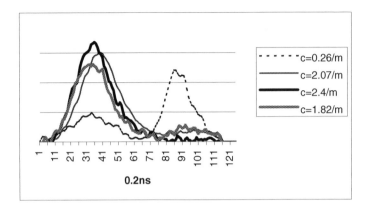

**Fig. 5.** Light intensity profiles returning to the camera measured for a 1.8m opaque target illuminated by a 9ns laser pulse in water of various turbidities (attenuation *c*)

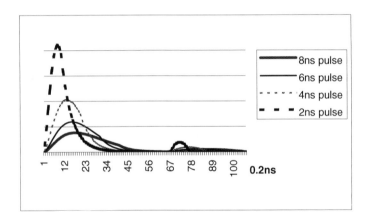

**Fig. 6.** Light intensity profiles returning to the camera for high turbidity water (c=2.2/m) with a target at 1.5m. The laser pulses of 2, 4, 6 and 8ns (carrying the same energy) are used.

Figs 4 to 6 show that the backscattering noise forms a peak in the returning signal before $2t_0$ time (the duration of the laser pulse). Afterwards, the noise rapidly diminishes and eventually terminates at approx. $2r_0/v+2t_0$ time (where $r_0$ is the target distance and $v$ is the light speed). The peak's magnitude is proportional to the turbidity level. Although the model predicts that for higher turbidities the backscattering peak appears earlier, this effect is not observed in the measured profiles (as explained earlier). The reflected signal peak always starts at the moment corresponding to the target distance, and the width of the target peak is determined by the duration of laser pulses.

In scenes with several targets at various distances, the backscattering part of profiles will be similar for the whole scene. The target-reflected peak, however, will be differently shifted in various parts of the scene.

A gated image is formed by integration of a returning signal profile from $t_1$ (gate opening) to $t_2$ (gate closing). Figs 4-6 clearly explain that a high-quality image can be obtained when the gating period $<t_1, t_2>$ coincides with the target-reflected peak. The effects of incorrect and correct timing of gate opening are shown in Fig. 3 (more details on gating period optimization are given in [6] and [7]).

## 3 Fusion of Gated Images

Scenes containing multiple objects at diversified distances cannot be visually represented by a single gated image that depicts only a narrow "slice" of the scene. Nevertheless, a sequence of gated images timed to various depths contains enough information to visualize the scene over a wide range of distances, even in turbid media. Therefore, a fusion of gated images is the most natural approach to improve visibility in high-turbidity conditions. However, the method would be efficient only if the pieces of visual data are relevantly extracted from individual gated images to form the fused image.

Assume that for each location $(x,y)$ within the formed image, the returning signal profile $P_{x,y}(t)$ can be approximated (using a sequence of gated images of gradually increased range). For low-turbidity media, the target-reflected peak is always much higher than the backscattering peak (see selected profiles in Figs 4 and 5) so that for any $(x,y)$ coordinate of the fused image intensity should be selected as maximum of the returning profile:

$$f(x, y) = \max_{t \in <0,T>} P_{x,y}(t) \tag{3}$$

where $<0; T>$ is a period of time over which the returning profile (i.e. a sequence of gated images) has be captured/reconstructed.

The method works well (more in [8]) but in low turbidities there is no real need for gated imaging since sufficient quality can be achieved by non-gated imaging (i.e. by integration of the whole returning signal). In high turbidities (when there is the actual need for gated imaging) the backscattering peaks dominate (see Fig. 6) and images fused by "choose max" approach are mostly formed of noise. Thus, their quality is not better than the quality of non-gated images., Fig. 7 compares an exemplary fused image to an image than averages (integrates) the returning profile.

**Fig. 7.** A clear water image (left) and images in highly turbid water obtained by averaging the returning profile (center) and by "choose max" fusion of gated images (right)

The same method, nevertheless, can be more successful if the search for the profile maximum is limited to $<2t_0+\Delta; \; T>$ period (where $2t_0$ is the pulse length and $\Delta$ is a short additional increment). Most of the backscattering noise returns before $2t_0+\Delta$ moment (see Fig. 6) so that the maximum value found in the remaining part of the profile corresponds to the target reflections (except for the areas with no target, where only backscattering noise of rather small magnitude is detected). Fig. 8 shows how this method works for an exemplary complex scene. The figure contains three gated images, the resulting fused image and the corresponding non-gated.

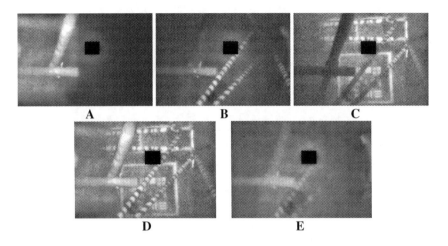

**Fig. 8.** Images captured in high-turbidity water. (A, B, C) – selected gated images; (D) – the image fused from a sequence of gated images; (E) – the corresponding non-gated image.

A disadvantage of the method is its inability to capture objects at very short distances (so that the reflected peak overlaps the backscattering peak)). It can be corrected, however, by using shorter illumination pulse (if shorter range is needed). For example, the minimum distance for a 4ns pulse is approx. 0.5m (in water) or 0.7m (in air) that is acceptable for typical prospective applications.

A more advanced version of the method would be a detail analysis of the returning profiles in order to detect the second peak (or at least a bulge) that would indicate the target reflection. If the second peak is not detected, the formed fused image remains black (i.e. the signal at that location would be assumed backscattering noise only). The method would also generate the range information since the timing of detected peaks corresponds to the target distance. In this advanced method, even targets at very short distances and targets of very low reflectivity would be identified (providing the receiver's gated camera is sensitive enough). Our experiments have shown feasibility of this approach, but the available equipment does not fully satisfy the method's requirements. In the conducted experiments, we reconstructed the returning profiles by subtracting consecutive gated images differing by very short (1ns) gating time increments. The system parameters (in particular, fluctuations of the laser pulses and the dark noise of the camera) have not been found satble enough for the accurate reconstruction of the profiles. There are, however, promising emerging technologies (e.g.

[9], [10]) that may possibly be used to overcome the current limitations. This would eventually lead to development of unique sensors capable of capturing both visual and depth information with extremely high speed, high reliability in turbid media and over a wide range of distances (including very short distances).

## 4 Conclusions

The paper presents a method for good quality visualization of complex scenes in highly turbid media. The theory is supported by exemplary experimental results. The experiments have been conducted in the Robotics Research Centre of NTU using a gated imaging system developed around a 3m water tank (with controllable level of turbidity). In most cases, a laser illuminator producing 9ns pulses carrying 18mW energy was used with a gated camera of 14ns minimum gating time. In some experiments, a high-sensitivity camera of 0.2ns gating time was used with a low-energy laser (to prevent the camera damage). Additionally, a specialized FPGA-based device has been developed to test the automatic on-line control of parameters (e.g. gating delays, laser triggering) and to perform in real-time the fusion of gated images. Details of the device are reported in [11].

In the future, we plan to further develop the digital control module (using high capacity and high speed FPGA) and to integrate a more compact gated imaging system (with additional improvements of its optical path). The theory supporting the experimental results is continuously developed as well.

## References

1. Witherspoon, N.H., Holloway, J.H. Jr.: Feasibility testing of a range gated laser illuminated underwater imaging system. SPIE Proc., Vol. 1302, Ocean Optics X (1990) 414–420.
2. Swartz, B.A.: Laser range gated underwater imaging advances. Proc. IEEE Oceans'94, Brest, Vol II (1994) 722–727.
3. Fournier, G.R., Bonnier, D., Forand, J.L., Pace, P.W.: Range gated underwater laser imaging system. Optical Engineering, Vol. 32 (1993) 2185-2189.
4. McBride, W.E. III, Weidermann, A.D.: Meeting navy needs with the generic lidar model. SPIE Proc., Vol. 3761, Airborne and In-Water Underwater Imaging (1999) 71-81.
5. Laseroptronix (http://www.laseroptronix.se/gated/gatsys.html).
6. Tan, C.S.: The backscattering phenomena on range-gated imaging in short-range turbid media. PhD thesis, NTU Singapore (2005).
7. Tan, C.S., Sluzek, A., Seet, G., He, D.M.: Model of gated imaging in turbid media. Optical Engineering, accepted (2005).
8. Sluzek, A., Czapski, P.: Image enhancer for an underwater LIDAR imaging system, Proc. ACIAR'2003, Bangkok, (2003) 107-110.
9. DeWeert, M. J., Moran, S. E., Ulich, B. L., Keeler, R. N.: Numerical simulation of the relative performance of streak tube, range gated, and PMT-based airborne imaging lidar systems with realistic sea surface," SPIE Proc., Vol. 3761, Airborne and In-water Underwater Imaging (1999) 115-129.
10. Areté Associates (http://www.arete.com/stil.shtml).
11. Fujishima, H.: Range-gated image enhancer system: FPGA implementation for real-time performance, SCE 03-471, NTU Singapore (2004).

# Multi-object Digital Auto-focusing Using Image Fusion*

Jeongho Shin, Vivek Maik, Jungsoo Lee, and Joonki Paik

Image Processing and Intelligent Systems Lab., Department of Image Engineering,
Graduate School of Advanced Imaging, Multimedia, and Film,
Chung-Ang University, Seoul 156-756, Korea
paikj@cau.ac.kr

**Abstract.** This paper proposes a novel digital auto-focusing algorithm using image fusion, which restores an out-of-focus image with multiple, differently out-of-focus objects. The proposed auto-focusing algorithm consists of (i) building *a prior* set of point spread functions (PSFs), (ii) image restoration, and (iii) fusion of the restored images. Instead of designing an image restoration filter for multi-object auto-focusing, we propose an image fusion-based auto-focusing algorithm by fusing multiple, restored images based on prior estimated set of PSFs. The prior estimated PSFs overcome heavy computational overhead and make the algorithm suitable for real-time applications. By utilizing both redundant and complementary information provided by different images, the proposed fusion algorithm can restore images with multiple, out-of-focus objects. Experimental results show the performance of the proposed auto-focusing algorithm.

## 1 Introduction

A demand for digital multi-focusing techniques is rapidly increasing in many visual applications, such as camcorders, digital cameras, and video surveillance systems. Multi-focusing refers to a digital image processing technique that restores multiple, differently out-of-focused objects in an image. Conventional focusing techniques, such as manual focusing, infra-red auto-focusing, through the lens auto-focusing, and semi-digital auto-focusing, cannot inherently deal with multi-focusing function. Multi-focusing can be realized with fully digital auto-focusing based on PSF estimation and restoration.

In this paper, a novel digital auto-focusing algorithm using image fusion is proposed, which restores an out-of-focus image with multiple, differently out-of-focus objects. When an image contains two or more objects, the proposed auto-focusing algorithm can restore all of out-of-focus objects by restoring the image without PSF estimation and fusing several partially restored images. For image restoration, we

---

* This work was supported by Korean Ministry of Science and Technology under the National Research Laboratory Project, by Korean Ministry of Information and Communication under the Chung-Ang University HNRC-ITRC program, and by the Korea Research Foundation Grant funded by Korean Government (MOEHRD)(R08-2004-000-10626-0).

J. Blanc-Talon et al. (Eds.): ACIVS 2005, LNCS 3708, pp. 202–209, 2005.
© Springer-Verlag Berlin Heidelberg 2005

build *a prior* set of PSFs and restore the out-of-focus image with the generated set of PSFs. These multiple restored images are then fused to form an in-focus image with maximal focus information.

The rest of the paper is organized as follows. Existing techniques and problem formulation are described in section 2. The proposed algorithm is described in section 3. Simulation results and comparisons are shown in section 4. Finally, concluding remarks are outlined in section 5.

## 2   Existing State-of-the-Art Methods

The image restoration problem has been faced in many ways. NAS-RIF [2], for example, involves minimizing a cost function while NLIVQ (nonlinear interpolative vector quantization) [3] and ARMA methods [4, 5], are borrowed from data compression field. Although both ARMA model and nonparametric approaches can provide acceptable focusing results under a set of assumptions, computational complexity due to numerical optimization and non-trivial number of iterations for convergence makes the corresponding system unrealizable as a commercial product.

A practically realizable AF technique was proposed under assumption that the PSF of the image formation system is isotropic or symmetric in every direction [6]. Since this technique doesn't involve an iterative procedure for identifying ARMA-model's coefficients. It can be applied to real-time applications, such as a digital auto-focusing and a low-cost video surveillance system. While this technique has requires significantly reduced hardware and computational overhead, it loses accuracy due to the inaccurate approximation of the isotropic PSF [6, 7].

Our work starts from the consideration found in [4, 5], which propose complete blind restoration system. In [8], analyzed images are subdivided in to sub-blocks and an edge detection algorithm, via gradient analysis, is applied. PSF is computed based on the average 1-D step response along the orthogonal direction of detected edges. Finally, a constrained least square filter is generated using the PSF.

## 3   Proposed Auto-Focusing Algorithm

The proposed auto-focusing algorithm uses the following three procedures to obtain a good restored image: (i) building *a prior* set of PSFs (ii) regularized iterative restoration, and (iii) fusion of the restored images.

### 3.1   Prior PSF Estimation

The discrete approximation of an isotropic PSF is shown in Fig. 1. As shown in Fig. 1, many pixels are located off concentric circles within the region defined as

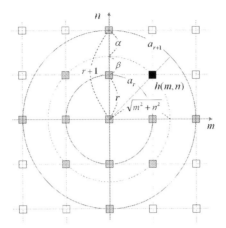

**Fig. 1.** The geometrical representation of a 2D isotropic discrete PSF: The gray rectangles represent inner pixels of the PSF and the empty ones are outer pixels of the PSF

To estimate a prior set of PSF's the Gaussian width of the intensity distributions are used. The Gaussian PSF is given by

$$G_\sigma(x) = \frac{1}{2\pi\sigma^2} \exp\left[\frac{-x^2}{2\sigma^2}\right].$$  (1)

As can be seen in (1) Gaussian PSF can often be approximated with standard deviation parameter $\sigma$: In our experiment we develop 100 prior PSF's for varying values of $\sigma$. The range of values for sigma was chosen to be from [0.04, 4.0] with a fixed step increment of 0.04 for each PSF. This approximation of 2D discrete PSF is available to the popular isotropic blurs, such as Gaussian out-of-focus blur, uniform out-of-focus blur, and x-ray scattering. The optimal PSF's were selected using the out-of-focus estimate by calculating the distance between the unit step function and a luminance profile across the edge of the restored with various PSF's as

$$d^{(k)} = \left\| s^{(k)} - u \right\|_2 = \left( \sum_{i=1}^{N} \left| s_i^{(k)} - u_i \right|^2 \right)^{1/2}, \quad for \ k = 1, 2, \cdots, K.,$$  (2)

where $s^{(k)}$ represents the restored edge profile with the $k^{th}$ pre-estimated PSF in the selected AF region, and $u$ the unit step function. Here, $N$ denotes the number of points in the edge profile and $k$ is an index for a PSF in the set of $K$ members. The optimal PSF can be determined by choosing the $k^{th}$ PSF with minimum distance as

$$\arg\min\{d^{(k)}\}, \ for \ k = 1, 2, \cdots, K.$$  (3)

### 3.2   Constrained Least Square Image Restoration

In this paper we present the CLS filter, which restores the out-of-focus image with the prior estimated set of PSF's. Regularization methods play an important role in solving out-of-focus problem with prior knowledge about the solution. Constrained least square image restoration is most suitable for multi-focusing because: (i) knowledge about the solution can be incorporated into the restoration process, (iii) the solution process can be monitored as it progresses, and (iv) constraints can be used to control the effects of noise [8].

The image degradation model is given as

$$y = Hx, \tag{4}$$

where $y$, $H$, and $x$ respectively represent the observed image, the degradation operator, and the original image. The corresponding regularization results in minimization of

$$f(x) = \|y - Hx\|^2 + \lambda \|Cx\|^2. \tag{5}$$

In (5), $C$ represents a high-pass filter, and $\|Cx\|$ represents a stabilizing functional whose minimization suppresses high frequency components due to noise amplification. The regularization parameter $\lambda$ controls the fidelity to the original image and smoothness of the restored image. In order to derive the closed-form solution in the frequency domain, we can rewrite (5) as

$$f(x) = y^T y - y^T Hx - x^T H^T y + x^T H^T Hx + \lambda x^T C^T Cx, \tag{6}$$

By setting

$$\frac{\partial}{\partial x} f(x) = 0, \tag{7}$$

we have

$$Tx = b, \tag{8}$$

where,

$$T = H^T H + \lambda C^T C \text{ and } b = H^T y. \tag{9}$$

The solution of equation (8) can be given as

$$x = T^{-1} b. \tag{10}$$

on condition that matrix $T$ is nonsingular. Even if $T$ is nonsingular, it is not easy to compute its inverse because the size of the matrix is usually very large. By using the property that the two-dimensional DFT matrix can diagonlize any doubly block circulant matrix, we can easily compute the solution of (8) in the frequency domain. By multiplying the two-dimensional DFT matrix of (10) on the left-hand side by $F$, using (9) and the orthogonal property of the DFT matrix, we have

$$Fx = F\left(H^T H + \lambda C^T C\right)^{-1}\left(F^* F\right)H^T y = \left\{F\left(H^T H + \lambda C^T C\right)F^*\right\}^{-1}\left(FH^T F^*\right)(Fy), \tag{11}$$

which can be rewritten as

$$\tilde{x} = \left( \tilde{H}^T \tilde{H} + \lambda \tilde{C}^T \tilde{C} \right)^{-1} \tilde{H}^T \tilde{y}, \tag{12}$$

where $\tilde{C}$ and $\tilde{C}^T$ represent the diagonal matrices whose diagonal elements are equal to the row-ordered vector of the two-dimensional DFT of $c(m, n)$ and its conjugate, respectively. Because all matrices in (12) have been diagonalized, the two-dimensional DFT of $x$ can be computed using scalar multiplications and divisions, such as, for $k, l = 0, 1, \ldots, N - 1$,

$$X(k, l) = DFT\{x(m, n)\} = \frac{DFT\{h(m, n)\}^*}{\left| DFT\{h(m, n)\} \right|^2 + \lambda \left| DFT\{c(m, n)\} \right|^2} DFT\{y(m, n)\}, \tag{13}$$

where $DFT\{\cdot\}$ represents the $(k, l)$ th coefficient of the two-dimensional DFT. Finally, the solution for x is obtained from the inverse transform as

$$F^* \tilde{x} = F^* F x = x. \tag{14}$$

In (13), if the regularization parameter $\lambda$ is equal to zero, the solution is equivalent to that achieved by the inverse filter. On the other hand, a nonzero $\lambda$ can control the amount of smoothness in the solution. The frequency-domain implementation of regularization in equation (13) is also called the *Constrained Least Squares filter*.

### 3.3 Focus-Based Image Fusion

In order to produce the final restored image we need to fuse the images restored using prior training PSF's. In order to apply the fusion algorithm, the focus measure at a point $(i, j)$ is computed as the sum of modified Laplacian values, in a small window around $(i, j)$, that are greater than a threshold value,

$$F(i, j) = \sum_{x=i-N}^{i+N} \sum_{y=j-N}^{j+N} M_k(x, y) \, for M_k(x, y) \geq T_1. \tag{15}$$

where $M_k$ refers to the laplacian value for the $k^{th}$ restored image given by,

$$M_k(i, j) = \left| 2I(i, j) - I(i-1, j) - I(i+1, j) \right| + \left| 2I(i, j) - I(i, j-1) - I(i, j+1) \right|, \tag{16}$$

In contrast to auto focusing methods, we typically use a small window of size, i.e. $N = 1$. The arbitrary threshold value in the range [0, 30], provides acceptable results in most cases. A typical problem that can occur with any type of image fusion is the appearance of unnatural borders between the decisions regions due to overlapping blur at focus boundaries. To combat this, soft decision blending can be employed using smoothing or low pass filtering of the saliency parameter. In this paper Gaussian smoothing has been used for obtaining the desired effect of blending. The reconstruction process, operates on each level of the pyramid of the original images in conjunction with sum modified Laplacian to generate the composite image C. The reconstruction process iteratively integrates information from the lowest to the highest level of the pyramid as follows:

$$L_{ck} = M_k.L_{Ak} + (1 - M_K)L_{Bk},$$ (17)

$$C_k = L_{ck} + w[C_k + 1] \uparrow 2.$$ (18)

Where $C_k$ represents the reconstructed image from level $N$, the lowest level, to level $k$ and $\uparrow 2$ refers to the expand process. The expansion process consists of doubling the width and height of the image by introducing columns and row in the original and then convolving the resulting image by the $w$ filter. This creates weighted decision regions where a linear combination of pixels in the two images A and B are used to generate corresponding pixels in the fused image C. Then we have,

$$L_{ck} = \begin{cases} L_{Ak}, \tilde{M}_k < l, \\ L_{Bk}, \tilde{M}_k > h, \\ \tilde{M}_k.L_{Ak} + (1 - \tilde{M}_k)L_{Bk}, otherwise. \end{cases}$$ (19)

where $\tilde{M}_k$ is now a smoothed version of its former self.

## 4   Experimental Results

In order to demonstrate the performance of the proposed algorithm, we used real images with one or more differently out-of-focused objects from background. Experiments were performed on a 256-level image of size 640x480. Here, each image contains multiple objects at different distances from the camera. Thus one or more objects naturally become out of focus when the image is taken. Fig 2(a) represents image with low depth of field, where focus is on the objects near from the camera lens. Each test image was restored using four different optimal PSF's. The final restored images is obtained by fusion of the multiple restored images. Fig 2 shows the result of fusion based restoration applied to two images having different depth of focus. The resulting composite merges the portions that are in focus from respective images. Fig 2(b), (c), (d), (e) represents the images restored using different prior estimated PSF's. Fig 2(e) is the final restored image formed by fusion of 2(c), (d), (e) and (f). The above set of results illustrates the effectiveness of the proposed fusion based algorithm and how it can effectively used to overcome the out-of-focus blur in images.

**Fig. 2.** Experimental results: (a) The source image, (b)-(e) restored image using *a prior* set of PSFs, and (f) the restored image based on image fusion

## 5  Conclusions

In this paper, we proposed a novel digital auto-focusing algorithm using image fusion is proposed, which restores an out-of-focus image with multiple, differently out-of-focus objects. For the realization of the digital auto-focusing, we used a set of prior estimated PSF's, regularized restoration, and fusion. Although the proposed algorithm is currently limited to space invariant, isotropic PSFs, it can be extended to more general applications by incorporating segmentation based multiple PSF estimation and spatial adaptive image restoration.

# References

[1] H. C. Andrews and B. R. Hunt, *Digital Image Restoration*, Prentice-Hall, New Jersey, 1977.

[2] S. K. Kim, S. R. Park, and J. K. Paik, "Simultaneous Out-of-Focus Blur Estimation and Restoration for Digital AF System," *IEEE Trans. Consumer Electronics*, vol. 44, no. 3, pp. 1071-1075, August 1998.

[3] M. Tekalp, H. Kaufman, and J. W. Woods, "Identification of Image and Blur Parameters for the Restoration of Noncausal Blurs," *IEEE Trans. Acoustics, Speech, Signal Proc.*, vol. ASSP-34, no. 4, pp. 963-972, August 1986.

[4] M. Tekalp and H. Kaufman, "On Statistical Identification of a Class of Linear Space-Invariant Image Blurs Using Nonminimum-Phase ARMA Models," *IEEE Trans. Acoustics, Speech, Signal Proc.*, vol. 36, no. 8, pp. 1360-1363, August 1988.

[5] K. Katsaggelos, "Maximum Likelihood Image Identification and Restoration Based on the EM Algorithm," *Proc. 1989 Multidimensional Signal Processing Workshop*, September 1989.

[6] J. Biemond, F. G. van der Putten, and J. Woods, "Identification and Restoration of Images with Symmetric Noncausal Blurs," *IEEE Trans. Circuits, Systems*, vol. 35, no. 4, pp. 385-393, April 1988.

[7] M. Subbarao, T. C. Wei, G. Surya, "Focused image recovery from two defocused images recorded with different camera settings", *IEEE Transactions on Image Processing*, vol. 4, No.12, pp. 1613 –1628, Dec. 1995.

[8] Kubota, K. Kodama, K. Aizawa, "Registration and blur estimation method for multiple differently focused images", *IEEE Proc. Int. Conf. Image Processing*, vol. 2, pp. 515 -519, 1999.

# Cognition Theory Based Performance Characterization in Computer Vision

Wu Aimin[1,2], Xu De[1], Nie Zhaozheng[3], and Yang Xu[1]

[1] Dept. of Computer Science & Technology, Beijing Jiaotong Univ., Beijing, China 100044
[2] Beijing Key Lab of Intelligent Telecommunications Software and Multimedia,
Beijing Univerisity of Posts and Communications, Beijing China 100876
[3] Dongying Vocational College, Shandong, China 257091
wuaimin@sohu.com, xd@computer.njtu.edu.cn

**Abstract.** It is very difficult to evaluate the performance of computer vision algorithms at present. We argue that visual cognition theory can be used to challenge this task. In this paper, we first illustrate why and how to use vision cognition theory to evaluate the performance of computer vision algorithms. Then from the perspective of computer science, we summarize some of important assumptions of visual cognition theory. Finally, some cases are introduced to show effectiveness of our methods.

## 1 Introduction

Since the early 1980s, much work has been done to challenge performance characterization in computer vision, but only a little success has been made. We indeed agree with that the theoretical analysis and the empirical evaluation can ultimately address the complicated evaluation problem, but L. Cinque et al in [8][10] explicitly pointed out: "we realize that many difficulties in achieving such a goal may be encountered. We believe that we still have a long way to go and therefore must now principally rely on human judgment for obtaining a practical evaluation; for some specific applications we feel that this is doomed to be the only possibility." The visual cognition theory mainly investigates the principles of human vision system, such as seeing what, seeing where, how to see, so in this paper we will discuss in detail why and how to apply visual cognition theory to performance characterization of computer vision algorithms.

## 2 Algorithms Evaluation and Visual Cognition Theory

Three self-evident truths and two propositions will be discussed, which can illustrate that algorithm evaluation of computer vision requires visual cognition theory.

**Truth 1: Assumptions in computer vision algorithms have to be made, and unsuitable assumptions must lead to poor results.**

All models of computer vision algorithm are certainly not accurate description of real world in a strict sense [1-5], so some assumptions are unavoidable. Bowyer et al argue that performance of computer vision algorithm will decrease or even fall when

J. Blanc-Talon et al. (Eds.): ACIVS 2005, LNCS 3708, pp. 210–218, 2005.
© Springer-Verlag Berlin Heidelberg 2005

complexity increases, so they suggest that the selection and measurement of the basic assumptions must be an essential part of algorithm development [11].

Additionally, T. Poggio in [12] argues that most of computer vision issues are inverse optical problems and most of inverse problems are ill-posed. The most important criterion for ill-posed problems is the physical assumption plausibility [13,pp.75, 104]. So it is very important to extract and validate the assumptions of algorithms, which can be used to evaluate computer vision algorithms at the theoretical level. If the assumptions used by algorithm are unsuitable for a given application, the results produced by this algorithm must be poor.

**Truths 2: Each algorithm used by human vision system is the best and most general, so the assumptions used by these algorithms must be physical plausibility.**

**Proposition 1: To obtain optimal results for a given tasks, assumptions used by computer vision algorithm should be same as (or similar to) those employed by human vision system.**

According to Marr's vision theory, each process should be investigated from three independent and loosely related levels: computational theory, representation and algorithm, and hardware implementation. From the perspective of information processing, the most critically important level is the computational theory [13,pp.10-12], whose underlying task is to find and to isolate assumptions (constraints) that are both powerful enough to define a process and generally true for the real world [13, pp.22-28]. These assumptions (constraints) are often suggested by everyday experience or by psychophysical (vision cognition theory) [13, pp.331].

Additionally, Computer vision problem in theory is similar to human vision problem, both of which are the process of discovering from images what is present in the world, and where it is [13, pp.1][14, pp.1-11]. The human eye and camera surely have the same mechanism from the perspective of optical imaging [14, pp.2][15, pp.1], so we can surely make use of principles of human vision to build a strong computer vision system [14, pp.19-20]. Therefore, in term of Truths 2, and above discussions, the Proposition 1 should be reasonable right.

**Truths 3: One of main tasks of visual cognition theory is to find the assumptions used by Human Vision System.**

**Proposition 2: Visual cognition theory can be used to judge whether assumptions of an algorithm are suitable for given tasks, which can be further used to evaluate the algorithm.**

Using Truths 3, Proposition 1, and Truth 1, the Proposition 2 can be easily logical proved right.

Above discussions extensively illustrate that visual cognition theory can be used to evaluate computer vision algorithm both for theoretical evaluation and for empirical evaluation. These ideas are paraphrased into the ***Principle of Qualitative Evaluation for Computer Vision Algorithm:***

**For a given task, if the assumptions used in computer vision algorithm are not consistent with assumptions of visual cognition theory (human vision system), the performance of this algorithm must be poor.**

Fig.1 shows three main steps to use this principle. The step 1 extracts assumptions used by the computer vision algorithm. The difficulty is that assumptions of many algorithms are so rarely explicitly expressed that we often have to infer them. The step 2 judges whether these assumptions are consistent with assumptions of visual cognition theory. The set of assumptions of cognition theory and their applicable tasks are build offline before evaluation (see Section 3). The step 3 reports the result of evaluation, which is divided into three categories: *Good* if all assumptions match, *Fair* if some assumptions match, and *Poor* if no assumption match.

**Fig. 1.** Three main steps to use the Principle of Qualitative Evaluation for Computer Vision Algorithm. The set of assumptions is built offline in advance.

## 3   The Set of Assumptions

Most of assumptions of visual cognition theory come from [13-21], which are reorganized and reedited from the perspective of computer science.

**a. Both eye and brain** [14, pp.128-136][15, pp.1-13]: Human has a plenty of knowledge about physical world and how they behave, which can be used to make inferences. *Structured knowledge constraints*: If we want to design a general-purpose vision machine, we must first classify and structure knowledge about real world for it.

**b. Abstract & classification principle** [21, pp.1]: we use three principles of construction to understand the physical world: (1) identifying the object and its attributes, e.g. a tree and its size; (2) identifying the whole and its components, e.g. a tree and its branches; (3) identifying different classes of object, e.g. the class of trees and the class of stones.

**c. Brain is a probability computer** [15, pp.9-13]: Brain makes hypotheses and checks them, then makes new hypotheses and checks them again until making the best bet, during which all knowledge can be made use of. Eyes and other senses within a short time would rather provide evidence for brain to make hypotheses and to check them than give us a picture of world directly. Mechanism of inference is classified into unconscious inference and conscious inference [19, pp.1-16]. *Methodology constraint:* probability method may be better for computer vision problems.

**d. See world by object not pattern** [20]: Human eye receives patterns of energy (e.g. lightness, color), but we see by object not pattern. We do not generally define object by how it appears, but rather by its uses and its causal relations. Once we know what the object is, we must know its shape, size, color and so on. *Object constancy constraints:* Physical object exists continuously, uniquely, and constantly, though time is flying [13, pp.205].

**e. Do we have to learn how to see?** [15, pp.136-169] The inheritance only forms the basis for learning, so that we have to learn much knowledge and ability for the sake of seeing. *Computer learning constraint:* we should continuously help computer with learning by active hands-on exploration to relate the perception to conception, as do it for a baby.

**f. The law of Gestalt** [14, pp.113-123][17, pp.106-121]. The Grouping principle can be further summarized into five principles: (a) the principle of proximity, (b) the principle of similarity, (c) the principle of good continuation, (d) the principle of closure tendency, and (e) the principle of common fate. The Figure-ground segregation principle means that (1) in ambiguous patterns, smaller regions, symmetrical regions, vertically or horizontally oriented regions tend to be perceived as figures; (2) The enclosed region will become figure, and the enclosing one will be the ground; (3) The common borders are often assigned to the figure; (4) Generally, the ground is simpler than the figure.

**g. Simultaneous contrast** [13, pp.259-261] [15, pp.87-92]: Human eyes don't detect the absolute energy of brightness, lightness, color, and motion, but their difference that is directly proportional to the background energy (e.g. Weber's Laws). *Threshold constraint:* a differential value is better than absolute one. *Compensation constraint:* brightness, lightness, color, and motion should be compensated according to the background energy.

**h. Constancy world** [14, pp.15-52]: According to the knowledge of geometrical optical imaging, the retinal image is different from the objects' outline, and the retinal image continually varies as human moves, but the object looks the same to us, which is called Constancy. There are size constancy, color constancy, brightness constancy, lightness constancy, shape constancy, motion constancy, and so on.

**i. The principle of modular design** [13, pp.99-103]: Each system (e.g. vision, touch etc.) of the perception and each channel (e.g. seeing color and seeing movement of vision) of different system work independently. Sometimes, different systems and different channels may make inconsistent conclusions, which force the brain to make a final decision. *Multi-channel constraint, Information encapsulation constraint:* have been applied to Object-Oriented analysis and design by computer community [21]. Furthermore, one channel (e.g. color) of vision system may affect or even mask another channel (e.g. shape), which is called *visual masking effects.*

**j. Two eyes and depth clues** [14,pp.53-90] [15, pp.61-66]: Two eyes share and compare information, so they can perform feats that are impossible for the single eye, e.g. the 3-D perception from two somewhat different images. Depth perception cues include retinal disparity, convergence angle, accommodation, motion parallax and pictorial information (occlusion, perspective, shadow, and the familiar sizes of things). *Depth perception constraint: in order to yield definite depth perception, all clues must work collectively.*

**k. Brightness is an experience** [15, pp.84-97]: Brightness is a function not only of the intensity of light falling on a given region of retina at a certain time, but also of the intensity of light falling on other regions of retina, and of the intensity of the light that the retina has been subject to in the recent past. In the dark, the mechanisms of dark-adaptation trade eye's acuity in space and time for increase in the sensitivity *(The continuity of brightness change constraint).* The brightness can be reflected by shading and shadow, which can indicate objects' information (e.g. *Top-down light source constraint).*

**l. Two seeing movement systems** [14, pp.17-202] [15, pp.98-121]: One is the image/retina system that passively detects the movement. Another is the eye/head movement system that positively seeing movement. When searching for an object, the eyes move in a series of small rapid jerks *(Motion discontinuous assumption)*, but when following an object, they move smoothly *(Motion continuous assumption)*. The eyes tend to suggest that the largest object is stationary *(Motion reference frame constraint)*. Persistence and apparent movement imply *continuity, stability and uniqueness constraints*.

**m. RGB is not the whole story** [15, pp.121-135]: Only mixing two, not three, actual colors can give a wealth of colors. The mixture of three primary colors (e.g. RGB) can't produce some colors that we can see, such as brown, the metallic colors. Color is a sensation. It depends not only on the stimulus wavelengths and intensities, but also on the surrounding difference of intensities, and on whether the patterns are accepted as objects *(Color computational constraint)*.

**n. Topological rules in visual perception** [18, pp.100-158]: Local homotopy rule: we tend to accept an original image and its transformed image as identical, if the image is made a local homotopy transformation within its tolerance space. The same is true for the homeomorphism rule, homeomorphism and null-homotopy rule in cluster, the object superiority effect, and the configurable effect.

**o. The whole is more than the sum of its parts** [13, pp.300-327] [16][17, pp.176]: The same parts (primitive) with different relations may construct different objects. It is possible to match a number of objects with a relatively small number of templates, because it may be easier to recognize parts (primitives) with relatively simper probability methods.

**p. Marr's underlying physical assumptions** [13, pp.44-51]: (1) existence of smooth surface in the visible world, (2) hierarchical spatial organization of a surface with a different scale, (3) similarity of the items generated at the same scale, (4) spatial continuity generated at the same scale, (5) continuity of the loci of discontinuities, and (6) continuity of motion of an rigid object.

**q. Edge perception and edge type** [14, pp.49-50]: The vision system only picks up luminance difference at the edge between regions, and then assumes that the difference at the edge applies throughout a region until another edge occurs. Furthermore vision system divides the various edges into two categories: lightness edge and illumination edge. The perceptual lightness value at the edges is only determined by lightness edge.

From other psychological literatures, we can extract more assumptions such as object rigidity assumption, Gauss distribution assumption, and smooth assumption, etc.

# 4  Case Studies

## 4.1  The Problems of Optical Flow

The optical flow problems were discussed by Horn [22] and Verr [23]. Their results are consistent with the judgments based on our principle, shown in Table 1, which is also harmony with the conclusion of McCane's experiments in [9].

**Table 1.** the discussion about optical problem. Note: (k) in the table refers to k<sup>th</sup> assumption in Section 3.

| Problem | Assumptions | Suitable | Result |
|---|---|---|---|
| Determining the optical flow | Flat surface | Suit (p) | Some suit Fair |
| | Uniform incident illumination | Ill-Suit (k, q) | |
| | Differentiable brightness | Suit (k) | |
| | Smooth optical flow | Suit (p, l) | |
| Recovering 3-D structure | Motion field equals to optical flow field | Ill-suit (l) | Poor |

## 4.2 Waltz's Line Drawings [13, pp.17-18]

When all faces were planar and all edges were straight, Waltz made an exhaustive analysis of all possible local physical arrangement of these surfaces, edges, and shadows of shapes (Structured knowledge constraint and Abstract & classification principle in Section 3 a, b). Then he found an effective algorithm to interpret such

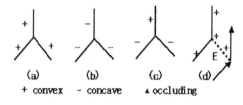

+ convex    − concave    ▲ occluding

**Fig. 2.** The ideas behind Waltz's theory

actual shapes. Fig.2 shows that some of configurations of edges are physically plausibility, and some are not. The trihedral junctions of three convex edges (a) or the three concave edges (b) are plausibility, whereas the configuration (c) is impossible. So the direction of edge E in (d) must be the same type as (a). This example shows the power of physical assumption plausibility.

## 4.3 Attention Mechanism

L. Itti et al define a set of linear "center-surround difference" operator (Simultaneous Contrast in Section 3 g) to reproduce the attention mechanism of primate visual system (visual masking effects in Section 3 i). However, it is only a bottom-up guidance

**Table 2.** Attention models and their assumptions for object recognition or scene analysis. Note: (a) in the table refers to a<sup>th</sup> assumption in Section3.

| Model | Assumptions | Suitable | Result |
|---|---|---|---|
| L. Itti model | Center-surround difference | Simultaneous Contrast: suit (g) | Some suit Fair |
| | Only bottom-up | Structured Knowledge constraints: ill-suit (a) | |
| | Only focus on one element | Masking effects: suit (i) | |
| V.Naval-pakkam model | L. Itti model & Distribution of background | All suit (a, g, i) | Good |
| A. Oliva model | L. Itti model & Task graph (Top-down) | All suit (a, g, i) | Good |

of attention without using any prior knowledge. V. Navalpakkam et al proposed to use a task graph to describe the real world entities and their relationships as Top-down control [25]. A. Oliva et al used the distribution of background of scenes as knowledge constraints [26]. Both V. Navalpakkam model and A. Oliva model employed *Structured knowledge constraints* (Section *3 a)*, so the effect and performance of their model are better than that of pure bottom-up attention model.

### 4.4 Comparison with CVIR Experiments

Many researchers have compared the performance of Content-based Visual Information Retrieval (CVIR) algorithms in an experimental way [27, 57-305], listed in Table 3. It is inherent consistency between these experimental results and the judgments of our principle.

**Table 3.** comparisons between experimental results and those by our methods about CVIR algorithms. Note: NH=normal histogram; CH=cumulative histogram; EDH= edge direction histogram; Wavelet MM= wavelet Modulus Maxima; Local M= Local Motion detection; L&GM= Local motion detection after Global Motion compensation; (d) in the table refers to $d^{th}$ assumption in Section 3.

| Feature | Method name | Experimen-tal Result | Assumptions | Suitable | Our Result |
|---------|-------------|----------------------|-------------|----------|------------|
| Color | NH | Poor | Color is linear | Ill-suit (m) | Poor |
|  | CH | Fair | Color is non-linear | Suit (m) | Fair |
| Shape | EDH | Fair | Brightness changes in boundary | Suit (k, q) | Fair |
|  | Wavelet MM | Good | Brightness changes in boundary, Multi-size & Multi-channel, and Gauss distribution. | All Suit (k, q, i) | Good |
| Color & Shape | CH | Fair | Color is nonlinear | Suit (m) | Fair |
|  | EDH | Fair | Brightness changes in boundary | Suit (k, q) | Fair |
|  | NH & EDH | Good | Brightness changes in boundary & Color is nonlinear | Suit (m, k, q) | Good |
| Mo-tion | LocalM | Poor | Absolute motion | Ill-suit (g) | Poor |
|  | L&GM | Fair | Relative motion | Suit (g, l) | Fair |

## 5    Conclusion and Further Work

The preliminary study strongly suggests that vision cognition theory can be used to evaluate computer vision algorithms. In this paper, we propose the Principle of Qualitative Evaluation for computer vision algorithms. To easily use this principle, we summarize some important assumptions of psychology. Further works include: 1) to model users under the integrated framework to automatically define the ground truth; 2) to explore cognition-based methods for empirical performance characterization; 3) to find more psychological assumptions and their applicable tasks. After all, our ultimate aim is to evaluate the usefulness of a computer vision system for end users.

## Acknowledgement

This work was supported by the Beijing Jiaotong University Research Project under Grant No. 2004SM013.

## References

1. R. M. Haralick, "Computer Vision Theory: The Lack Thereof," *Computer Vision Graphics and Image Processing*, vol. 36, no. 2, pp. 272-286, 1986.
2. R. M. Haralick, "Performance Characterization in Computer Vision," *Computer Vision, Graphics and Image Processing: Image Understanding,* vol. 60, no. 2, pp. 245-249,1994.
3. R. M. Haralick, "Comments on Performance Characterization Replies," *Computer Vision, Graphics, and Image Processing: Image Understanding,* vol. 60, no. 2, 264-265, 1994.
4. W. Foerstner, "10 Pros and Cons Against Performance Characterization of Vision Algorithms, " *Proc. ECCV Workshop on Performance Characteristics of Vision Algorithms,* Apr., 1996.
5. N. A. Thacker, "Using Quantitative Statistics for the Construction of Machine Vision Systems," *Keynote presentation given to Optoelectronics, Photonics and Imaging 2002,* Sept., 2002.
6. M. Heath, S. Sarkar, et al, "A Robust Visual Method for Assessing the Relative Performance of Edge Detection Algorithms," *IEEE Trans. PAMI,* vol. 19, no. 12, pp. 1338-1359, Dec. 1997.
7. H. Müller, W. Müller, et al, "Performance Evaluation in Content--Based Image Retrieval: Overview and Proposals," *Pattern Recognition Letters,* vol. 22, no. 5, pp. 593--601, 2001.
8. Min C. Shin, D. B. Goldgolf, and K. W. Bowyer, "Comparison of Edge Detector Performance Through Use in an Object Recognition Task, " *Computer Vision and Image Understanding,* vol. 84, pp. 160-178, 2001.
9. B. McCane, "On Benchmarking Optical Flow," *Computer Vision and Image Understanding,* vol. 84, pp.126–143, 2001.
10. L. Cinque, C. Guerra, and S. Levialdi, "Reply On the Paper by R.M. Haralick," *Computer Vision, Graphics, and Image Processing: Image Understanding,* vol. 60, no. 2, pp. 250-252, Sept., 1994.
11. K. W. Bowyer and P. J. Phillips, "Overview of Work in Empirical Evaluation of Computer Vision Algorithms," In *Empirical Evaluation Techniques in Computer Vision,* IEEE Computer Press, 1998.
12. T. Poggio, et al "Computational Vision and Regularization Theory," *Nature,* 317(26), pp 314-319, 1985.
13. D. Marr, *Vision,* Freeman, 1982.
14. Rock, *Perception,* Scientific American Books, Inc, 1984.
15. R. L. Gregory, *Eye and Brain,* Princeton university press, 1997.
16. Biederman, "Recognition-by-Components: A Theory of Human Image Understanding," Psychological Review, vol. 94, pp. 115-47, 1987.
17. K. Koffka, *Principle of Gestalt Psychology,* Harcourt Brace Jovanovich Company, 1935.
18. M. Zhang, *Psychology of Visual Cognition,* East China Normal University Press, 1991.
19. Rock, *The Logic of Perception,* MIT Press, 1983.
20. D. M. Sobel, et al, "Children's causal inferences from indirect evidence: Backwards blocking and Bayesian reasoning in preschoolers," *Cognitive Scienc*e, vol. 28, pp. 303–333, 2004.

21. P. Coad and E. Yourdon, *Object-Oriented Analysis,* Yourdon Press, 1990.
22. B. K. P. Horn, et al, "Determining Optical Flow," *Artificial Intelligence*, vol.17, pp.185-203, 1981.
23. Verr, et al , "Motion Field and Optical Flow: Qualitative Properties, " *IEEE Trans. PAMI,* vol. 11, pp. 490-498, 1989.
24. L. Itti, C. Koch, and E. Neibur, "A Model of Saliency-based Visual Attention for Rapid Scene Analysis," *IEEE Trans. PAMI*, vol. 20, no. 11, 1998.
25. V. Navalpakkam and L. Itti, "A Goal Oriented Attention Guidance Model," *Lecture Notes in Computer Science,* vol. 2525, pp. 453-461, 2002.
26. Oliva, A. Torralba, M. Castelhano, and J. Henderson, "Top-down Control of Visual Attention in Object Detection," *International Conference on Image Processing,* 2003.
27. Y. J. Zhang, Content-based Visual Information Retrieval, Science Press, Beijing, 2003.

# Morse Connections Graph for Shape Representation

David Corriveau[1,*], Madjid Allili[2], and Djemel Ziou[1]

[1] Université de Sherbrooke, Département d'informatique,
Sherbrooke, Qc, J1K 2R1, Canada
{david.corriveau, djemel.ziou}@usherbrooke.ca
[2] Bishop's University, Department of Computer Science,
Lennoxville, Qc, J1M 1Z7, Canada
mallili@ubishops.ca

**Abstract.** We present an algorithm for constructing efficient topological shape descriptors of three dimensional objects. Given a smooth surface $S$ and a Morse function $f$ defined on $S$, our algorithm encodes the relationship among the critical points of the function $f$ by means of a connection graph, called the *Morse Connections Graph*, whose nodes represent the critical points of $f$. Two nodes are related by an edge if a connection is established between them. This graph structure is extremely suitable for shape comparison and shape matching and inherits the invariant properties of the given Morse function $f$.

## 1 Introduction

Due to the recent improvements in laser scanning technology, vast amounts of 3D models are easily produced and archived. The World Wide Web enables access freely or commercially to these digital archives. Thus, it becomes imperative to develop efficient methods for comparison and matching of 3D shapes to enable automatic 3D shape retrieval. One of the central issues in shape comparison and shape matching is the representation of shapes by means of descriptors [1]. To represent a shape we characterize it in terms of descriptors so that it is possible to reconstruct the shape to a certain degree of precision from such descriptors. Typically, the descriptors measure several shape characteristics of statistical, geometrical, and topological nature. In our approach, we focus on topological descriptors since they provide information that can remain constant despite the variability in appearance of objects due to noise, deformation and other distortions.

In this paper, we introduce a new topological descriptor for shape representation based on classical Morse theory. More precisely, given a smooth surface $S$ and a Morse function $f$ defined on $S$, our algorithm encodes the relationship among the critical points of the function $f$ by means of a graph whose nodes represent the critical points of $f$. Two nodes are related by an edge if a connection is established between them. That is, if the intersection of their stable and

---

* This research is supported by NSERC.

unstable manifolds is not empty (details will be given in section 2). We call this graph the *Morse Connections Graph*. The graph structure is extremely suitable for shape comparison and shape matching. The role of the function is to measure different characteristics of the 3D object while the graph is used to synthesize the regions of topological interest of the object and the relationships between them. Different Morse functions with specific invariant properties can be used for the same object to provide graph structures inheriting the same invariant properties.

The following section presents a background on Morse theory and pertaining to the definition of the *Morse Connections Graph*. In section 3, we will give details about the algorithms used to compute the *Morse Connections Graph*. Finally, we will present some computational results.

## 2    Morse Connections Graph

Morse theory [2,3] has become a fundamental technique for investigating the topology of smooth manifolds. The basic results in this theory prove that the topology of a smooth manifold is very closely related to the critical points of a smooth function on the manifold.

In the sequel $\mathcal{M}$ denotes a smooth compact, connected $n$-dimensional manifold without boundary. A smooth function $f : \mathcal{M} \to \mathbb{R}$ is a Morse function if all its critical points, i.e., points $p \in \mathcal{M}$ where the differential $Df$ vanishes are non degenerate in the sense that near such a point $p$, there exists a local coordinate system $(x_1, \ldots, x_n)$ in which the determinant of the Hessian of $f$ at $p$

$$H_f(p) = \left( \frac{\partial^2 f}{\partial x_i \partial x_j} \right)$$

does not vanish. A second order invariant is associated with each non degenerate critical point $p$, which Morse called the *index* of $f$ at $p$ and denoted $\lambda(p)$, and which is defined as the number of negative eigenvalues of the Hessian $H_f(p)$. The index $\lambda(p)$ corresponds to the dimension of the unstable manifold $W^u(p) = \left\{ q \in \mathcal{M} \mid \lim_{t \to -\infty} \psi(t, q) = p \right\}$, where $\psi : \mathbb{R} \times \mathcal{M} \to \mathcal{M}$ denotes the negative gradient flow associated with $f$ on $\mathcal{M}$. The unstable manifold $W^u(p)$ is homeomorphic to an open cell of dimension $\lambda(p)$. In a similar way, the stable manifold is defined as $W^s(p) = \left\{ q \in \mathcal{M} \mid \lim_{t \to \infty} \psi(t, q) = p \right\}$. By contrast, the stable manifold is homeomorphic to an open cell of dimension $\dim(\mathcal{M}) - \lambda(p)$. In addition, we denote by $\mathcal{M}_t$ the submanifold of $\mathcal{M}$ (also called the lower level set of $f$) consisting of all points of $\mathcal{M}$ at which $f$ takes values less than or equal to $t$, i.e. $\mathcal{M}_t = \{ p \in \mathcal{M} \mid f(p) \leq t \}$.

A fundamental result in this theory, called the Morse Lemma [3], asserts that $f$ has a quadratic form representation near critical points and allows to prove that a Morse function defined on a compact manifold admits only finitely many isolated critical points.

Finding the critical points (including degeneracies) on a discretization requires adequate tools. For this reason, we use the Conley index theory [4] which is a topological version of the Morse index theory and better suited for dynamical systems in the presence of perturbations due to noise and approximation. Briefly, this theory is used to study invariant sets (sets containing the critical points) and their type (minimum, saddle, maximum). An invariant set is a set of points of $\mathcal{M}$ that remains constant over the time parameter for the flow associated to $f$. Computing the invariant sets directly is a difficult task, so instead the theory considers isolating neighborhoods of the invariant sets. The index is defined as the rank of the relative homology type [5,6] of the isolating neighborhood with respect to its exit set, that is the set of points whose trajectory exits the set in the forward time. When the homology groups [5,6] are non-trivial, the index indicates that the isolating neighborhood contains an invariant set.

First, we track the potential invariant regions of the gradient flow associated with $f$ and use the Conley index to confirm the presence of nonempty invariant sets. Then, we decompose the surface into regions of homogeneous flow [7] better known as stable and unstable manifolds. Figure 1 illustrates the decomposition of the torus into the stable and unstable manifolds of its critical points for a given Morse function (here the height function). In this example, there are four critical points $p, q, r$ and $s$. The stable manifold of $p$ is the whole surface without the inner bold and the upper dashed loops. $W^s(q)$ and $W^s(r)$ are respectively the inner bold loop and the upper dashed loop. Finally, the stable manifold of $s$ is made of the isolated critical point $s$. The unstable manifolds decomposition of the torus for the same height function is similar and shown in figure 1.

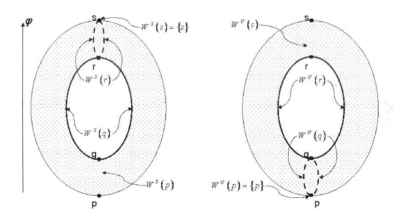

**Fig. 1.** Stable and unstable manifolds for the height function on the torus

## 2.1  Morse Connections Graph

In this section, we present how the *Morse Connections Graph* is defined. Readers familiar with the Reeb graph [8,2] will observe some similarities. The Reeb graph considers sections of the shape $\mathcal{M}$, where each section is formed by the set of points contained between two consecutive lower level sets $\mathcal{M}_t$ and $\mathcal{M}_{t-\epsilon}$ for some small $\epsilon$. As $t$ will change, the Reeb graph will record any change occurring in the topology of two consecutive sections. For a $2D$ shape embedded in a $3D$ space, the Reeb graph will track the loops of the different sections and record any time when a loop will appear, disappear or when any two loops will merge or split. These changes in the topology of the sections are in fact related to the presence of critical points of $f$. Since the critical points of $f$ are directly related to changes in the topology of the loops, the *Morse Connections Graph* will have the same nodes as the Reeb graph. The difference will be in the way the arcs between those nodes are established. In the Reeb graph, an arc is created between two nodes when the associated loops belong to the same connected component. For the *Morse Connections Graph*, an arc is created between two nodes when there exists a connection as defined lower.

Let's consider the flow $\psi$ associated to the function $f$. All non-critical points of $f$ will lie on a unique trajectory. This trajectory is said to start at a critical point $p$ when going backward in time, the limit of the trajectory goes to $p$. Similarly, the trajectory will end at a critical point $q$ when going forward in time, the limit goes to $q$. Let's say that for a given regular point $r$, its trajectory is starting and ending at the critical points $p$ and $q$. Clearly, the point $r$ will belong to the unstable manifold of $p$, $W^u(p)$, since it gets away of $p$ as the $t$ parameter of the flow increases. Similarly, the point $r$ will belong to the stable manifold of $q$, $W^s(q)$, since it gets closer to $q$ as the $t$ parameter of the flow increases. Thus we say that this trajectory is connecting the critical points $p$ and $q$, because the flow will gradually progress from $p$ to $q$ as the parameter $t$ will increase. It is this kind of connection characterized by the *Morse Connections Graph*. For this purpose, we came with the following definition of a connection.

**Definition 1.** *Let $p$ and $q$ be two critical points of a Morse function $f : \mathcal{M} \to \mathbb{R}$. We say there is a* connection *from $p$ to $q$, denoted $p \rightsquigarrow q$, if $W^u(p) \cap W^s(q) \neq \emptyset$.*

For a given flow $\psi$, all regular points of $\mathcal{M}$ belong to a unique trajectory. So when $W^u(p) \cap W^s(q) \neq \emptyset$, it means there exists a point of $\mathcal{M}$ belonging to a trajectory starting from $p$ and ending at $q$, thus connecting the critical points $p$ and $q$. From this notion, we define the *Morse Connections Graph* as follows.

**Definition 2.** *The* Morse Connections Graph *is defined as $MCG_f = (V_f, E_f)$, where*

$$V_f = \{critical\ points\ of\ f\} \quad and$$
$$E_f = \{(p_i, p_j) \in V_f \times V_f \mid p_i \rightsquigarrow p_j\}.$$

Possible degeneracies of the critical points are not a problem because the definitions are formulated on the intersection of stable and unstable manifolds, which can always be computed wether a critical point is degenerate or not. Also, to obtain a more accurate representation shapes, labels can be assigned to the nodes and edges. For the nodes, we can assign the critical value and the index of the critical point. For the edges, we can assign the type of connection by

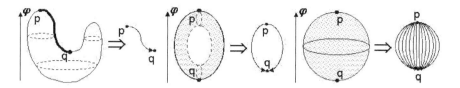

**Fig. 2.** The types of connections can be used as a label for the edges of the *Morse Connections Graph*

computing the homology type (connected components, holes, voids) of $W^u(p) \cap W^s(q) \cup \{p, q\}$. Figure 2 illustrates three different kinds of connections.

Computing the *Morse Connections Graph* requires finding efficient ways to compute the critical points and their connections, that is their stable and unstable manifolds. The following section will detail efficient algorithms for computing them. We state some results that will serve to validate these algorithms. In the example of figure 1, the stable and unstable manifolds of the critical points of $f$ seem to form a partition on the points of $\mathcal{M}$, since they cover the whole space and have an empty intersection. Indeed, the following two results show that the stable and unstable manifolds do form a partition of $\mathcal{M}$.

**Theorem 1.** *Let $p$ and $q$ be two distinct critical points of a Morse function $f$. Then $W^u(p) \cap W^u(q) = \emptyset$ and $W^s(p) \cap W^s(q) = \emptyset$.*

Suppose that $W^s(p) \cap W^s(q) \neq \emptyset$. It means $\exists r \in \mathcal{M}$ such that $r \in W^s(p)$ and $r \in W^s(q)$. This is equivalent to say that $p = \lim_{t \to \infty} \psi(t, r) = \lim_{s \to \infty} \psi(s, r) = q$. But $p$ and $q$ are distinct by hypothesis. Thus, $W^s(p) \cap W^s(q) = \emptyset$. Similar reasoning for $W^u$ □

**Theorem 2.** *Let $\{p_1, \ldots, p_k\}$ be the set of all critical points of a Morse function $f$. Then $\bigcup_{i=1}^{k} W^u(p_i) = \bigcup_{i=1}^{k} W^s(p_i) = \mathcal{M}$.*

Suppose that $\bigcup_{i=1}^{k} W^s(p_i) \neq \mathcal{M}$. Then, $\exists q \in \mathcal{M}$ such that $q \notin \bigcup_{i=1}^{k} W^s(p_i)$. Since $q$ lies on a distinct trajectory, let $p_q = \lim_{t \to \infty} \psi(t, q)$ be the stationary ending point (critical point) of the trajectory on which $q$ is lying. Thus, by definition, $q \in W^s(p_q)$. But, by hypothesis, $q \notin \bigcup_{i=1}^{k} W^s(p_i)$ which is a contradiction. Thus $\bigcup_{i=1}^{k} W^s(p_i) = \mathcal{M}$. Similar reasoning for $W^u$ □.

To end this section, we illustrate the difference between the Reeb graph and the *Morse Connections Graph*. In the example of figure 3, the Reeb graph connects the points $r$ and $q$ because they belong to the same connected component.

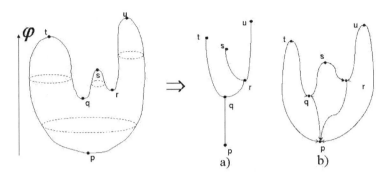

**Fig. 3.** Reeb graph (a) and *Morse Connections Graph* (b) for the height function

It is possible to come up with more examples where the Reeb graph connects two critical points because they belong to the same connected component but are located arbitrarily far from one another. In our opinion, the *Morse Connections Graph* is better suited for shape representation.

## 3    Implementation Details

Our algorithm takes a cellular complex and a smooth function defined on it as input. The following data members are defined for the cells of highest dimension.

**Cell**:

- *id*: unique identifier of the cell.
- *val*: cell's value of the function $f$.
- *flow, invFlow*: identifier of the next cell by iterating one step in direction (or inverse direction) of the flow $\psi$.
- *idWu, idWs*: let *idWu, idWs* be identifiers of critical cells. This cell belongs to $W^u$ (*idWu*) and $W^s$ (*idWs*).

The main algorithm is composed of the following steps:
*ComputeMCG()*

1. Initialization.
2. Compute critical cells.
3. Compute stable and unstable manifolds.
4. Determine Connections.

**First Step:** This step initializes data members of all cells of the complex. To each cell , we assign a unique identifier and its value by the function $f$. Also, we compute the flow (and inverse flow) with respect to $f$, meaning we find the next cell lying on the same trajectory in forward time (and reverse time). We perform a smoothing of $f$ by a gaussian kernel to average the main direction of the flow. Once the main direction is determined, we select the nearest cell in this direction and assign that cell's identifier to the *flow* data member. Similar for *invFlow*. Finally, *idWu* and *idWs* are initialized to an invalid cell identifier.

**Second Step:** In this step, we used the Conley index [4] to determine the critical cells but any preferred method could be used. It is not required to test for all cells. We measured the rate of change of the angle made by the flow vector and a reference axis. The cells for which this rate of change varies more than a threshold are considered as potentially critical and only those cells are tested by the Conley index to see wether or not they are critical. When a critical cell $c$ is found, we assign $c.idWu = c.idWs = c.id$.

**Third Step:** This step orders the cells by increasing value of $f$ which takes $\Theta(n \log n)$ time. The stable manifolds is computed in linear time as follows.

```
For all cells "c" by increasing value of c.val
    if(c.idWs != c.id)    // if c is not critical
        c.idWs = Cell(c.flow).idWs;
```

The function *Cell(id)* returns the cell referenced by the *id* identifier. Since the cells lying on a trajectory of the flow are traversed by decreasing values of $f$,

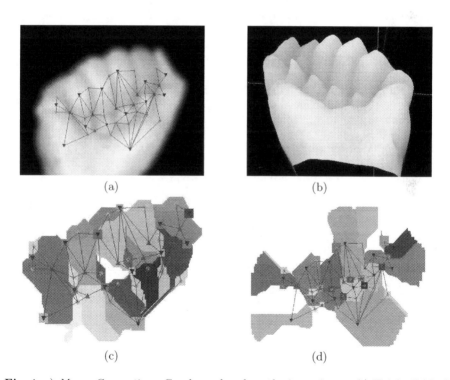

(a)     (b)

(c)     (d)

**Fig. 4.** a) *Morse Connections Graph* overlayed on the input image. b) Height field of the input image. c-d) Respectively the stable and unstable manifolds decompositions.

we always assign the stable manifold identifier of a cell that has been processed. For the unstable manifolds, we use the decreasing order and the inverse flow.

**Fourth Step:** Finally, we need to establish the connections between the critical points for which the intersection of their stable and unstable manifolds is not empty. This is easily done in linear time by scanning all cells $c$ and connecting $Cell(c.idWu)$ to $Cell(c.idWs)$ because $c$ is lying on a trajectory starting at $Cell(c.idWu)$ and ending at $Cell(c.idWs)$.

In figure 4, we illustrate an example of the *Morse Connections Graph* obtained for a two dimensional shape. We chose to use the smoothed pixel intensities of an image as a 2D surface and the height function for $f$ because this example allows us to view the *Morse Connections Graph* overlayed on the shape in an more convenient way. Also, we show the associated stable and unstable manifolds decompositions. Some *less significant* critical points have been ignored, which explains why the two decompositions don't cover the whole surface.

In conclusion, we introduced the *Morse Connections Graph* for shape representation. For a given Morse function, this graph will represent its critical points and their connections. The *Morse Connections Graph* and the Reeb graph are similar but differ in the way of establishing the connections. We believe that this difference allows the *Morse Connections Graph* to give a better representation of the shape. In a future work, we plan to test this tool for a real life application.

# References

1. Allili, M., Corriveau, D., Ziou, D.: Morse Homology Descriptor for Shape Characterization. 17th International Conference on Pattern Recognition **4** (2004) 27–30
2. Fomenko, A., Kunii, T.: Topological Modeling for Visualization. Springer-Verlag, Tokyo, ISBN: 4-431-70200-8 (1997)
3. Milnor, J.: Morse Theory. Princeton University Press, Princeton, NJ, ISBN: 0-691-08008-9 (1969)
4. Mischaikow, K.: The Conley Index Theory: A Brief Introduction. Banach Center Publications **47** (1999)
5. Munkres, J.R.: Elements of Algebraic Topology. Addison-Wesley, ISBN: 0-201-04586-9 (1984)
6. Kaczynski, T., Mischaikow, K., Mrozek, M.: Computational Homology. Volume 157 of Appl. Math. Sci. Series. Springer-Verlag, New York, ISBN: 0-387-40853-3 (2004)
7. Thom, R.: Sur une partition en cellules associée à une fonction sur une variété. Comptes Rendus de l'Académie de Sciences **228** (1949) 973–975
8. Shinagawa, Y., Kunii, T.: Constructing a Reeb Graph Automatically from Cross Sections. IEEE Comp. Graph. and Appl. **11** (1991) 44–51

# A Quantitative Criterion
# to Evaluate Color Segmentations
# Application to Cytological Images

Estelle Glory[1,2,3], Vannary Meas-Yedid[2], Christian Pinset[3],
Jean-Christophe Olivo-Marin[2], and Georges Stamon[1]

[1] Laboratoire des SIP-CRIP5, Université Descartes-Paris 5, 75006 Paris
[2] Laboratoire d'Analyse d'Images Quantitatives, Institut Pasteur, 75015 Paris
[3] Celogos, 25 rue du Dr Roux, 75015 Paris, France
{eglory, vmeasyed, cpinset, jcolivo}@pasteur.fr
stamon@math-info.univ-paris5.fr

**Abstract.** Evaluation of segmentation is a non-trivial task and most often, is carried out by visual inspection for a qualitative validation. Until now, only a small number of objective and parameter-free criteria have been proposed to automatically assess the segmentation of color images. Moreover, existing criteria generally produce incorrect results on cytological images because they give an advantage to segmentations with a limited number of regions. Therefore, this paper suggests a new formulation based on two normalized terms which control the number of small regions and the color heterogeneity. This new criterion is applied to find an algorithm parameter to segment biological images.

## 1   Introduction

A segmentation process subdivides an image into regions in order to extract the objects of interest from the scene. Many algorithms for segmenting color images have been developed and reported in literature [1][2]. The problem is difficult and there does not exist a universal solution to solve it. For these reasons, the performance evaluation of color segmentations is very important for comparing them. Segmentation results are usually assessed visually and qualitatively, but it would be better to use an objective and quantitative method. In spite of the development of color segmentation algorithms, their evaluations are relatively limited. In 1996, Zhang has surveyed evaluation methods for image segmentation [3] but most of them are applied on gray-level images.

In section 2, empirical methods able to quantify the quality of color segmentations are reviewed. Section 3 presents an improvement of the Borsotti's criterion, based on more robust requirements. Finally, we show in section 4 the validation and an application to find appropriate parameter for thresholding cytological images.

J. Blanc-Talon et al. (Eds.): ACIVS 2005, LNCS 3708, pp. 227–234, 2005.
© Springer-Verlag Berlin Heidelberg 2005

## 2    Empirical Methods To Evaluate Color Segmentations

*Analytical* methods directly examine the algorithm by analyzing their properties, whereas *empirical* methods evaluate the result of the segmentations on given data sets. Most of the algorithms are not analytically defined, thus Zhang concluded that empirical methods are preferable [3]. Two categories of empirical approaches can be distinguished. The first one, so-called unsupervised, is based on desirable properties of well segmented images, according to the human visual interpretation. The second one, so-called supervised, requires a segmentation of reference or *a priori* knowledge (e.g. number of objects, shape, reference colors ...). Here, in the absence of reference segmentations we seek an empirical evaluation. Haralick and Shapiro defined qualitative criteria of segmentation quality in [4].

### 2.1    Liu and Yang's Evaluation Function

Liu and Yang [5] have suggested an elegant quality measure that does not require any user parameter. The proposed criterion is based on two characteristics: (1) segmented regions should respect color homogeneity, (2) for the same number of misclassified pixels, the segmentation with limited number of created regions is preferable. Translated into mathematical expressions, the authors have suggested the $F(I)$ function:

$$F(I) = \frac{1}{1000.A}\sqrt{R}\sum_{i=1}^{R}\frac{e_i^2}{\sqrt{A_i}} \qquad (1)$$

$I$ is the segmented image, $A$ the size of the image and $R$ the number of regions in the segmented image. $A_i$ and $e_i$ are respectively, the area and the average color error of $i$th region. $e_i^2$ is defined as the sum of the Euclidean distance of the RGB vectors between the original image and the mean color of the segmented region, for each pixel belonging to the region $i$.

The average color error is significantly higher for large regions than for small ones, thus, $e_i^2$ is scaled by the factor $\sqrt{A_i}$. The term $\sqrt{R}$ is a global measure which penalizes the segmentation generating too many regions (e.g. small regions). Small values of $F(I)$ correspond to segmentations of good quality.

### 2.2    Borsotti's Evaluation Function

Borsotti et al. [6] have observed that Liu's criterion penalizes the presence of many small regions only by the global measure $\sqrt{R}$. When the average color error of small regions is close to zero, the function tends to evaluate very noisy segmentations favorably. Thus, Borsotti et al. have proposed a new expression $Q(I)$:

$$Q(I) = \frac{1}{10000.A}\sqrt{R}\sum_{i=1}^{R}[\frac{e_i^2}{1+log(A_i)} + (\frac{R(A_i)}{A_i})^2] \qquad (2)$$

This formulation includes a new term in the sum: $(\frac{R(A_i)}{A_i})^2$. It is designed to penalize the numerous small regions, where $R(A_i)$ represents the number of regions having an area which is equal to $A_i$. Moreover, the denominator of $e_i^2$ has been modified to $1 + log(A_i)$ in order to obtain a stronger penalization of small non-homogeneous regions.

# 3   The Revised Evaluation Functions

Borsotti's method is commonly used to evaluate color segmentations. Nevertheless, as the Liu's criterion, the Borsotti's criterion has the undesirable property of reaching a minimum value when the only segmented region is the entire image. More generally, these two criteria favor segmentations with a limited number of regions.

## 3.1   Increases of Robustness Against One-Region Segmentation

The drawback above is due to the global term $\sqrt{R}$ which involves an *a priori* knowledge on the number of objects in the scene, by penalizing too many regions. To prevent the under-segmentation sensitivity, the factor $\sqrt{R}$ has been removed [7]:

$$Q1(I) = \frac{1}{10000.A} \sum_{i=1}^{R} \left[ \frac{e_i^2}{1 + log(A_i)} + \left( \frac{R(A_i)}{A_i} \right)^2 \right] \tag{3}$$

Moreover, we propose to compute $e_i^2$ in a uniform color space (*Luv* or *Lab*) because the Euclidean distance corresponds to the visual interpretation [8]:

$$e_i^2 = \sum (p_{iL} - \mu_{iL})^2 + (p_{iu} - \mu_{iu})^2 + (p_{iv} - \mu_{iv})^2 \tag{4}$$

The figure 1 shows how $Q1$ criterion ranks segmentation roughly consistently with a human expert.

## 3.2   A Normalized Criterion

The elimination of the $\sqrt{R}$ term makes the criterion $Q1$ more sensitive to noisy segmentations (Fig. 2). When there are small noisy regions, the term $\left( \frac{R(A_i)}{A_i} \right)^2$ should compensate the small values of color heterogeneity, but the range of values of these two terms are too different to be compared. Thus, we normalize each term before adding them.

**Color Heterogeneity.** The normalization of the color heterogeneity term, $h$ consists of dividing the sum of the region heterogeneity by the heterogeneity of the entire image. One is added to the denominator to avoid the null value of a uniform color image.

$$h = \frac{\sum_{i=1}^{R} \frac{e_i^2}{1+log(A_i)}}{\frac{e^2}{1+log(A)} + 1} \tag{5}$$

(a) stained cytological image

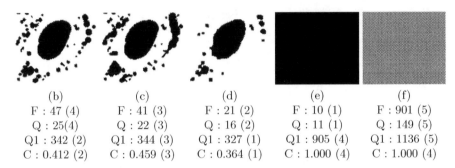

| (b) | (c) | (d) | (e) | (f) |
|-----|-----|-----|-----|-----|
| F : 47 (4) | F : 41 (3) | F : 21 (2) | F : 10 (1) | F : 901 (5) |
| Q : 25(4) | Q : 22 (3) | Q : 16 (2) | Q : 11 (1) | Q : 149 (5) |
| Q1 : 342 (2) | Q1 : 344 (3) | Q1 : 327 (1) | Q1 : 905 (4) | Q1 : 1136 (5) |
| C : 0.412 (2) | C : 0.459 (3) | C : 0.364 (1) | C : 1.000 (4) | C : 1.000 (4) |

**Fig. 1.** A cytological image where the cell nucleus is stained in blue and vacuoles in red (a). Five segmentations are proposed and ranked by a human expert: segmentation (b) is better than (c), followed by (d), while (e) and (f) are both bad segmentations. In fact, (e) is a non-segmented image and (f) is an over-segmented image where there are as many regions as pixels. Values and ranks computed by Liu's ($F$), Borsotti's ($Q$), $Q1$ and $C$ criteria are reported below each segmentation.

$e^2$ is the color heterogeneity computed on the entire image. $h$ is close to 1 for a one-region segmentation but it is not necessarily the upper limit (Fig. 1e). At the opposite, $h$ vanishes for an over-segmention (Fig. 1f).

**Number of Small Regions.** The range of values of the normalized term $n$ is defined between $\frac{1}{A}$ for an over-segmentation and 1 for an under-segmentation:

$$n = \frac{\sum_{j=A_{Min}}^{A_{Max}} \frac{R(A_j)}{A_j^2}}{R} \tag{6}$$

where, $A_{Min}$ and $A_{Max}$ are the area of the smallest and the largest segmented regions.

**The Proposed Formulation.** With the previous definitions of $h$ and $n$, the normalization by the size of the image is implicit. As $h$ and $n$ have comparable ranges of values, the formulation of $C$ is the sum of these two terms:

$$C(I) = \frac{\sum_{i=1}^{R} \frac{e_i^2}{1+log(A_i)}}{\frac{e^2}{1+log(A)} + 1} + \frac{\sum_{j=A_{Min}}^{A_{Max}} \frac{R(A_j)}{A_j^2}}{R} \tag{7}$$

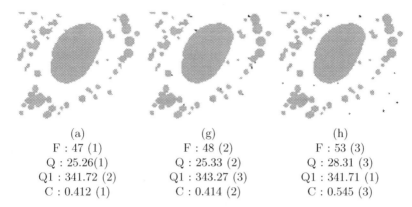

|           (a)           |           (g)           |           (h)           |
|:-----------------------:|:-----------------------:|:-----------------------:|
|       F : 47 (1)        |       F : 48 (2)        |       F : 53 (3)        |
|      Q : 25.26(1)       |      Q : 25.33 (2)      |      Q : 28.31 (3)      |
|     Q1 : 341.72 (2)     |     Q1 : 343.27 (3)     |     Q1 : 341.71 (1)     |
|      C : 0.412 (1)      |      C : 0.414 (2)      |      C : 0.545 (3)      |

**Fig. 2.** From the segmentation of the figure 1a, pixels have been artificially added, either by joining the existing regions (g) or by creating independent small regions (h). We can note that criterion $Q1$ incorrectly favors segmentation (h) whereas criterion $C$ correctly favors segmentation (a).

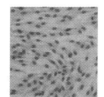

(a) original color image

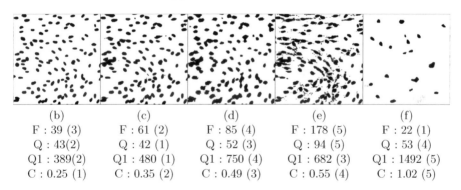

|         (b)         |         (c)         |         (d)         |         (e)          |         (f)          |
|:-------------------:|:-------------------:|:-------------------:|:--------------------:|:--------------------:|
|     F : 39 (3)      |     F : 61 (2)      |     F : 85 (4)      |     F : 178 (5)      |     F : 22 (1)       |
|      Q : 43(2)      |     Q : 42 (1)      |     Q : 52 (3)      |     Q : 94 (5)       |     Q : 53 (4)       |
|     Q1 : 389(2)     |    Q1 : 480 (1)     |    Q1 : 750 (4)     |    Q1 : 682 (3)      |    Q1 : 1492 (5)     |
|    C : 0.25 (1)     |    C : 0.35 (2)     |    C : 0.49 (3)     |    C : 0.55 (4)      |    C : 1.02 (5)      |

**Fig. 3.** Validation on an image where nuclei are stained in magenta with the Giemsa dye. Five segmentations are sorted by a human observer in this sort b,c,d,e,f. Scores and relative ranks of criteria are shown under the corresponding segmentation. The $C$ criterion ranks segmentations as the human observer does.

According to this criterion, segmentations of figures 1 and 2 are ranked as by the human expert, except for the segmentation (d) (Fig. 1). This first place is due to the high color homogeneity and the absence of small regions which give a $C$ low value. Therefore, this rank is objectively correct but not in this application where interpretation involves other characteristics. Globally, $C$ retains all the merits of $Q1$ and Borsotti's functions while overcoming their limitations.

# 4    Experimental Results

## 4.1    Validation of The Criterion

The proposed criterion has been validated on thirty images extracted from three cytological applications:

- blue/red staining cell nuclei and vacuoles (Fig. 1a),
- Giemsa dye, which stains the nuclei in magenta (Fig. 3a),
- peroxydase dye, which stains the cytoplasm in brown (not shown).

According to the human evaluation, $C$ ranking results are similar or better than those of Liu or Borsotti (Fig. 3).

**Table 1.** Threshold values of twenty images. Five experts have been consulted and the number of experts who have preferred this segmentation is reported in brackets. For an image, the sum of experts can exceed five because multiple selections are allowed when the quality is equivalent.

| Image name | C threshold | Ridler's threshold | Otsu's threshold |
|---|---|---|---|
| 10 0005 | 152 (3) | 161 (1) | 162 (2) |
| 10 0006 | 150 (4) | 162 (1) | 163 (3) |
| 10 0007 | 163 (4) | 169 (4) | 171 (5) |
| 32 0758 | 147 (5) | 164 (0) | 166 (0) |
| 51 0044 | 153 (4) | 161 (2) | 163 (0) |
| 54 0780 | 143 (5) | 152 (0) | 154 (0) |
| 54 0868 | 136 (5) | 156 (0) | 158 (0) |
| 55 0352 | 123 (5) | 148 (0) | 151 (0) |
| 58 0397 | 135 (5) | 150 (0) | 153 (0) |
| 58 1116 | 164 (5) | 168 (0) | 170 (0) |
| 58 1787 | 147 (5) | 175 (0) | 177 (0) |
| 87 0091 | 161 (5) | 168 (0) | 170 (0) |
| 92 0748 | 123 (5) | 137 (0) | 140 (0) |
| 93 0150 | 78 (5) | 98 (0) | 101 (0) |
| 93 0318 | 120 (5) | 158 (0) | 160 (0) |
| 96 0203 | 149 (5) | 155 (0) | 157 (0) |
| 134 0270 | 142 (5) | 152 (0) | 154 (0) |
| 135 0594 | 133 (5) | 146 (0) | 147 (0) |
| 148 0004 | 168 (5) | 173 (1) | 175 (1) |
| 149 0145 | 138 (4) | 165 (1) | 168 (0) |

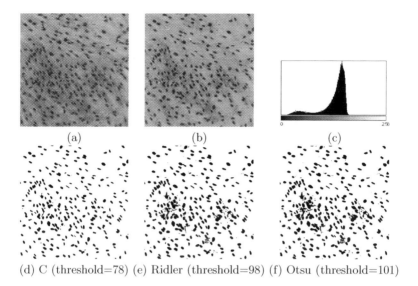

(d) C (threshold=78) (e) Ridler (threshold=98) (f) Otsu (threshold=101)

**Fig. 4.** (a)The original color image 93 0150, (b) the normalized green component and (c) the associated histogram. The second row shows the segmentations obtained with (d) the C criterion, (e) Ridler's threshold (f) Otsu's threshold. Colored nuclei are more distinguishable in segmentation (d).

### 4.2   Application to Segment Cytological Images by Thresholding

The $C$ criterion, defined to evaluate the segmentation quality, can also be used to determine an optimal parameter value for a segmenting algorithm. The example shown in this paper is related to a threshold value. First, the color image is transformed into gray level images (e.g. components of color spaces). Then, all threshold values in the range of gray-levels are tested and resulting segmentations are evaluated by $C$. Finally, the segmentation corresponding to the smallest value of $C$ is selected as the best result.

The normalized green component (Fig. 4a and 4b) has been chosen because magenta and green are complementary colors. Moreover, the luminosity variations are eliminated by the normalization (previous studies [7][11]). If there is no *a priori* knowledge on the color projection, each color component has to be computed.

Results are compared with the segmentations obtained with Ridler's [9] and Otsu's [10] thresholding algorithms (Table 1). In order to validate the relevance of the proposed method, five experts in cytology were independently consulted to select the best segmentation among the three values of threshold. These results shows that our method is clearly superior to Otsu and Ridler's methods on these cytological images (Fig. 4).

## 5   Conclusion

To compare different segmentations, it is useful to evaluate their quality without adjusting parameters. Liu and Borsotti have proposed parameter-free functions which quantify the performance of color segmentations. To prevent the drawback of Borsotti criterion, this paper suggests a new formulation based on normalized terms that does not favor the under-segmentations of cytological images. The two terms control the color heterogeneity of segmented regions and the number of small regions. The validation has been performed on thirty cytological color images. The proposed criterion can also be used to select the parameter value of a segmentation algorithm that produces the best segmentation. In this paper, the choice of a threshold value is described and validated by expert in cytology. We can also use this criterion to determine the color space or the algorithm that gives the most efficient results. In future work, we will validate the proposed criterion on different types of images.

## Acknowledgments

We thank G. Derocle, N. Potin, L. Lesage, K. Gajek and A. Papodoulos for their expert evaluations of the segmentations.

## References

1. Pal, N. R., Pal, S.K.: A review on image segmentation techniques. Pattern Recognition **26-9** (1993) 1277–1294
2. Cheng, H. D. , Jiang, X. H., Sun, Y., Wang, J.: Color image segmentation: advances and prospects. Pattern Recognition **34-12** (2001) 2259–2281
3. Zhang, Y.J.: A survey of evaluation methods for image segmentation. Pattern Recognition **29-8** (1996) 1335–1346
4. Haralick, R. M., Shapiro, L.G.: Survey: image segmentation techniques. Vision Graphics and Image Processing **29** (1985) 100–132
5. Liu, J., Yang, Y.-H.: Multiresolution color image segmentation. Analysis and Machine Intelligence **16-7** (1994) 689–700
6. Borsotti, M., Campadelli, P., Schettini, R.: evaluation of color image segmentation results. Pattern Recognition Letters **19** (1998) 741–747
7. Meas-Yedid, V., Glory, E., Morelon, E., Pinset, Ch., Stamon, G., Olivo-Marin, J.-Ch.: Automatic color space selection for biological image segmentation. Proceedings of ICPR **3** (2004) 514–517
8. Sangwine, S.J, Horne, R.E.N.: The colour image processing Handbook. Ed. Chapman and Hall (1998) 67–89
9. Ridler, T.W., Calvard, S.: Picture thresholding using an iterative selection method. IEEE Trans. System, Man and Cybernetics **8** (1979) 630–632
10. Otsu, N.: A threshold selection method from gray-level histograms. IEEE Trans. on System, Man and Cybernetics **9-1** (1979) 62–66
11. Glory, E., Faure, A., Meas-Yedid, V., Cloppet, F., Pinset, Ch., Stamon, G., Olivo-Marin, J-Ch.: A quantification tool to analyse stained cell cultures. Proceedings of ICIAR **9-1** (2004) 84–91

# A Novel Region-Based Image Retrieval Algorithm Using Selective Visual Attention Model[1]

Songhe Feng[1,2], De Xu[1], Xu Yang[1], and Aimin Wu[1]

[1] Dept. of Computer Science & Technology, Beijing Jiaotong Univ., Beijing, China 100044
[2] Beijing Key Lab of Intelligent Telecommunications software and Multimedia,
Beijing university of posts and communications, Beijing, China 100876
songhe_feng@163.com, xd@computer.bjtu.edu.cn

**Abstract.** Selective Visual Attention Model (SVAM) plays an important role in region-based image retrieval. In this paper, a robust and accurate method for salient region detection is proposed which integrates SVAM and image segmentation. After that, the concept of salient region adjacency graphs (SRAGs) is introduced for image retrieval. The whole process consists of three levels. First in the pixel-level, the salient value of each pixel is calculated using an improved spatial-based attention model. Then in the region-level, the salient region detection method is presented. Furthermore, in the scene-level, salient region adjacency graphs (SRAGs) are introduced to represent the salient groups in the image, which take the salient regions as root nodes. Finally, the constructed SRAGs are used for image retrieval. Experiments show that the proposed method works well.

## 1 Introduction

Modeling human visual process is crucial for image understanding that is able to produce consistent results to human perception. The human visual system is able to reduce the amount of incoming visual data to a small but relevant amount of information for higher-level cognitive processing [5]. Selective attention is the process of selecting and gating visual information based on saliency in the image itself.

Several computational visual attention models have been proposed for simulating human visual attention [1] [2]. The model in [1] considered three low-level features (color, intensity and orientation) on different scales to compute the center-surround differences. To decrease the computational complexity, [2] only considered the color contrast in LUV space.

However, most of these models are used for salient region detection and object recognition, little work has been done to extend these benefits for image retrieval, and existing region-based image retrieval method rarely consider the attention model [8]. So in this paper, a novel region-based image retrieval algorithm using selective visual attention model is proposed. First in the pixel-level, the salient value of each pixel is calculated using an improved spatial-based attention model. Then in the region-level,

---

[1] This work was supported by the Beijing Jiaotong Univerisity Research Project under Grant No.2004SM013.

J. Blanc-Talon et al. (Eds.): ACIVS 2005, LNCS 3708, pp. 235–242, 2005.
© Springer-Verlag Berlin Heidelberg 2005

in contrast to existing salient region detection methods, we use a maximum entropy-based method to determine the salient regions after computing the saliency value of each segmented region. Furthermore, in the scene-level, the concept of salient region adjacency graphs (SRAGs) is introduced to represent the salient groups in the image, which use the salient regions as root nodes. Finally, the constructed SRAGs are used for image retrieval.

The rest of this paper is organized as follows. The detail of salient region detection method is proposed in Section 2. Then, the Salient Region Adjacency Graphs are constructed and the image retrieval strategy is discussed in Section 3. Experimental results are reported in Section 4. Finally, conclusions will be presented in Section 5.

## 2 A Novel Salient Region Detection Method

Selective visual attention model has been applied in multimedia area such as scene analysis and object recognition [1] [3]. It has been recognized that detection of region attracting user attention is much helpful in many applications such as region-based image retrieval [2]. Since the motivation of this paper is image retrieval, salient region detection is the basis of our work. In contrast to existing salient region detection methods which only consider the saliency map, in this paper, we combine the selective visual attention model with image segmentation method. The novelty of the combination lies in that it provides a robust and reliable method for salient region detection especially when there exists more than one salient region in the image.

In order to fulfill the proposed method, we first compute the saliency value by an improved selective visual attention model on pixel-level. Then, after combining image segmentation method, a maximum entropy-based algorithm is used to determine the salient regions. The details are described in this section below.

### 2.1 Pixel-Level Saliency Value Computing

There are already several different selective visual attention model existed including two most popular ones [1] [2]. Itti's method [1] consider three low-level features (color, intensity and orientation) on different scales, but it brings about high computational complexity. Ma's method [2] only consider the color contrast for computational simplicity, but it may not be robust for the cases where color is not the most useful feature to detect saliency. In addition, Sun's method [5] computes the grouping-based saliency map, but how to define the grouping is a difficult problem. So here we propose a simple but effective saliency value computing method on pixel-level which combines the above three models.

The saliency value is computed on three resolution scales of the image ($1, 1/2$, and $1/4$) separately. For a given color image, suppose $x$ is a given pixel in $M \times N$ image, $w_x$ is a size of $d \times d$ window centered at $x$ for the computation of contrast. In our algorithm, we take $d = 3$. Then we compute the feature contrast between $x$ and other pixels in $w_x$. Many features can attract human's attention. Here we follow [1] and [5]'s method which considering color, intensity, and orientation features. So the saliency value for the pixel $x$ can be calculated as:

$$S_x = \sum_{y \in W_x} \left( \alpha S_{CI}(x, y) + \beta S_o(x, y) \right) \tag{1}$$

where $y$ is the pixel belong to $W_x$, $S_{CI}(x, y)$ and $S_o(x, y)$ denote the color-intensity contrast and orientation contrast between $x$ and $y$. Here, $\alpha$ and $\beta$ are the weighting coefficients and here be set to 1 for simplicity. (See [5] for details)

After that, we use a Gaussian filter to remove the noise points: $\hat{S}_x = S_x \otimes G_x$, where $G_x$ is a gaussian filter with the standard deviation $\sigma = 1$. The same work can be done on other two resolution scales.

After all the three-level saliency values are computed, we combine the results to form the final saliency value on the original resolution scale. The examples of salient value computing on pixel-level are given in Fig.1.

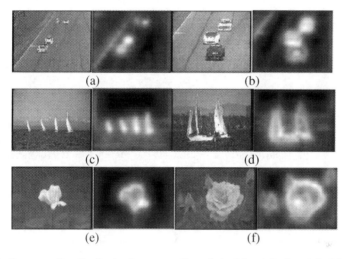

(a)                    (b)

(c)                    (d)

(e)                    (f)

**Fig. 1.** Some results of salient value computing of pixel-level. Left: original image. Right: its saliency map. (a)-(b) Racecar. (c)-(d) Sailing. (e)-(f) Flower.

## 2.2 Region-Level Salient Region Detection

After obtaining the saliency value on pixel-level, the next step is to compute the salient regions. Detection of salient regions in images is useful for object-based image retrieval and browsing applications. Some methods based on the selective visual attention model have been used for this task. Most of these works are based on the saliency map with seeded region growing method. However, since saliency map is a blur map, how to choose the seeds for region growing is a difficult problem. Besides, the number of salient regions is various according to different circumstances. To avoid such problems, in this paper, we combine the classic region segmentation method and pixel-level saliency value to detect salient regions.

### 2.2.1 Image Region Segmentation Using K-Means Clustering Method

To reduce the computational cost, the image is transformed from color level to gray level firstly. The K-means clustering image segmentation algorithm [9] is then used to obtain the segmented homogeneous regions.

### 2.2.2 Salient Region(s) Detection Using Maximum Entropy-Based Algorithm

After the image is segmented into homogeneous regions, salient region(s) have to be detected. Previous works for salient region detection assume that only one salient region exist in the image. However, this assumption won't be robust for the cases where there are more than one salient region in the image. In this paper, a robust salient region(s) detection method using maximum entropy-based algorithm is proposed. The maximum entropy-based algorithm has been proved to be efficient for image threshold selection in [7]. Here we use this principle for salient region detection.

For each segmented region $R_i$ in the image $I$, the region saliency value $S_{R_i}$ and region average saliency value can be calculated as follows:

$$S_{R_i} = \sum_{x \in R_i} s_x \qquad AVS_{R_i} = \frac{S_{R_i}}{AREA(R_i)} \tag{2}$$

where $s_x$ denotes the saliency value of pixel $x$. $AREA(R_i)$ denotes the area of $R_i$ and $i \in [1...N]$ where $N$ is the number of regions in the image $I$.

First, in order to remove some regions which have a large area but with the low region average saliency, we bring a threshold $t$. If the region which average saliency value is below $t$, then it should be removed from the salient regions candidates.

Then, suppose the scope of saliency value for each region is between $[1...L]$. The threshold to determine the salient regions is calculated as follows:

$$T = \arg\max_{T} \left( -\sum_{u=1}^{T} \frac{N_u}{\sum_{v=1}^{T} N_v} \log \frac{N_u}{\sum_{v=1}^{T} N_v} - \sum_{u=T+1}^{L} \frac{N_u}{\sum_{v=T+1}^{L} N_v} \log \frac{N_u}{\sum_{v=T+1}^{L} N_v} \right) \tag{3}$$

where $N_u$ is the number of regions with saliency value $u$, $L$ is the total number of saliency value levels and $T$ is the threshold.

After the threshold is determined, the salient regions are defined as the set of regions whose saliency value is above the threshold $T$. So the salient regions of an image can be denoted as: $\left\{ R_i \middle| S_{R_i} \geq T \ \& \ AVS_{R_i} \geq t \right\}$. The examples can be seen in Fig. 2.

**Fig. 2.** Some results of extracted salient regions which combining SVAM with image segmentation

# 3 Image Retrieval Based on Salient Regions

Existing computational models of visual attention are mainly spatial-based. However, some researchers have proposed the object-based visual attention model. The mainly difference between object-based and spatial-based visual attention model lies in that the former holds that visual attention can directly select discrete objects while the latter holds that attention only select continuous spatial areas of the visual field. Since it's difficult to build a pure object-based visual attention model, [5] defined the grouping to integrate object-based and spatial-based attention. Here we construct the Salient Region Adjacency Graphs (SRAGs) to achieve the integration between spatial-based and object-based visual attention.

## 3.1 Scene-Level Salient Region Adjacency Graphs Construction

Psychological experiments have shown that, human shift the attention from one salient object to another salient object. However, existing selective visual attention model can only simulate the shift from one salient region to another salient region. There exists the essential difference between object and region. Some existing methods [6] try to use so called attention window to represent the object or salient region, but how to define the size of the attention window has no general way. Although perfect object extraction is impossible from region-based segmentation, object is defined as a group of the related regions according to Gestalt rules, so here we propose the Salient Region Adjacency Graphs (SRAGs) to denote the salient groups.

Region Adjacency Graph (RAG) is an effective way to represent an image because it provides a "spatial view" of the image. [4] proposed a BRAG and Sub-graph Isomorphism mechanism for image retrieval. The RAG is decomposed into several small graphs, called Basic RAGs. The decomposed graphs are used to compare the similarity between two images. However, they construct Basic RAGs for each segmented regions without considering the saliency value of the regions. So the computational cost would be very high.

Here we propose an improved method to construct Salient Region Adjacency Graphs (SRAGs). Each Salient Region Adjacency Graph is constructed which only uses salient region as root node. This method is based on two considerations: on one hand, each SRAG can denote the concept of "salient group" which is useful to simulate human's selective visual attention model; on the other hand, using SRAG for image retrieval can effectively reduce the computation cost.

## 3.2 Image Retrieval Method Based on Salient Region Adjacency Graphs

After all the salient region adjacency graphs (SRAGs) are constructed well, we use an improved sub-graphic isomorphism algorithm proposed by [4] for the matching.

First, the SRAGs of the input image and all reference SRAGs in the database are constructed and ordered by the root node's salience value. In other words, we put the SRAGs in descending order according to the saliency value of each root node (salient region).

Second, we propose a matching strategy using exhaust search method. Assume the input image $A$ has $m$ SRAGs denoted as $\{A_i | i = 1...m\}$ and the image in the database $B$ has $n$ SRAGs denoted as $\{B_j | j=1...n\}$. Besides, both of them have put their SRAGs in order according to the root node's saliency value. The distance between them are calculated as:

$$DISTANCE \ (A,B) = \frac{1}{m} \sum_{i=1}^{m} \min_{j=1...n} \{w_r \times dist\left(A_i^r, B_j^r\right) + w_b \times dist\left(A_i^b, B_j^b\right)\} \qquad (4)$$

where $dist\left(A_i^r, B_j^r\right)$ is the distance between two root nodes (salient regions) which separately belong to $A_i$ and $B_j$. $dist\left(A_i^b, B_j^b\right)$ is the distance between the branch nodes derived from the root nodes . $w_r$, $w_b$ are the weighting of root node distance and branch nodes distance. In the experiment we set $w_r$ to 0.9, while $w_b$ to 0.1 respectively. Here we use HSV color features to represent the regions and the Euclidean distance is considered to measure the difference between two regions. The most similar $k$ images can be obtained using above methods.

## 4   Experimental Results

To evaluate the performance of the proposed method, we choose 2035 images from 18 categories of the Corel Photo Gallery as our test image database. In current experiment, we choose a subset of the database which includes 500 images from ten selected categories. The selected ten categories are: flower, sunset, racecar, butterfly, forest, boat, animal, mountain, waterfall and factory. Since the proposed algorithm is based on visual attention model, so most selected images contain salient region(s).

Precision and Recall are used as the basic evaluation measures. Precision is the ratio of the number of correct images to the number of retrieved images. Recall is the ratio of the number of correct images to the total number of correct images in the database. They are defined as follows:

$Precision\,(N) = \dfrac{C_N}{N}$ and $Recall\,(N) = \dfrac{C_N}{M}$ where $N$ is the number of retrieved images, $C_N$ the number of relevant matches among all $N$ retrievals, and $M$ the total number of relevant matches in the database.

Fig. 3 shows part of query results with the proposed method where flower and sunset categories are selected.

We test the proposed method using different query images and retrieval numbers, we also fulfill a region-based image retrieval method which consider all the segmented regions for comparison. And the average precision and recall rates are seen in Fig. 4.

In our experiment, we found that the flower and sunset categories can achieve better results than factory and forest categories since the former two categories have salient regions or objects while the latter two have clutter scenes. However, the proposed method still achieves improvements. The comparison between the proposed method and other region-based image retrieval methods is still under experiment.

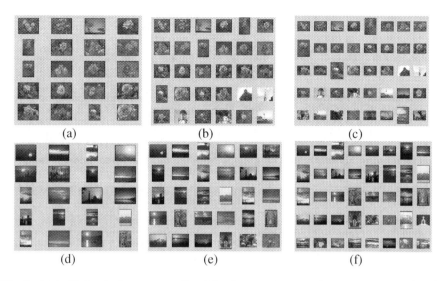

**Fig. 3.** (a) to (f) denote the query results of the flower category and sunset category using the proposed method where retrieved numbers N are 20,30, and 40. The query images of flower and sunset categories are on the top-left of (a) and (d), respectively.

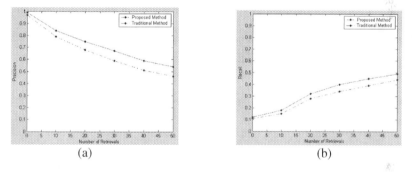

**Fig. 4.** (a) and (b) denote the average precision and recall rates of ten categories. The traditional method used here is region-based image retrieval method which doesn't consider the salient regions.

## 5 Conclusion

This paper presents a new region-based image retrieval algorithm based on the selective visual attention model (SVAM). The proposed method combines the SVAM with image segmentation method to extract salient regions. The advantage of the combination lies in that it provides a robust and accurate way for the salient regions extraction especially when there exists more than one salient region in the image. After the salient regions are chosen, the concept of salient region adjacency graphs (SRAGs) is proposed to represent the salient groups. Finally, the image retrieval method is presented based on the salient region adjacency graphs. Experimental results have proved the proposed method. However, the proposed method can be further improved in the future. For example, a better image segmentation method is needed for the basis of salient region detection. How to represent the objects in the image is a crucial and interesting issue.

# References

1. L. Itti., C. Koch., E. Niebur.: A Model of Saliency-Based Visual Attention for Rapid Scene Analysis. *IEEE Trans on* Pattern Analysis and Machine Intelligence, Vol. 20, No.11, pp. 1254-1259, 1998.
2. Yu-Fei Ma., Hong-Jiang Zhang.: Contrast-based Image Attention Analysis by Using Fuzzy Growing. ACM Multimedia 2003, pp. 374-381.
3. Dirk Walther., Ueli Rutishauser., Christof Koch., Pietro Perona.: On the usefulness of attention for object recognition. ECCV 2004, pp. 96-103.
4. Ruey-Feng Chang., Chii-Jen Chen., Chen-Hao Liao.: Region-based Image Retrieval Using Edgeflow Segmentation and Region Adjacency Graph. *Proc. of IEEE International Conference on Multimedia & Expo* 2004, TaiPei, Taiwan, June 27-30, 2004, pp.1883-1886.
5. Yaoru Sun., Robert Fisher.: Object-based visual attention for computer vision. *Artificial Intelligence*, vol. 146, pp. 77-123, 2003.
6. ByoungChul Ko., Soo Yeong Kwak., Hyeran Byun.: SVM-based Salient Region(s) Extraction Method for Image Retrieval. *IEEE Int. Conf. on Pattern Recognition,* 2004.
7. H. D. Cheng., Y. H. Chen., X. H. Jiang.: Thresholding Using Two-Dimensional Histogram and Fuzzy Entropy Principle. *IEEE Trans on* Image Processing, Vol. 9, No. 4, pp. 732-735, 2000.
8. Feng Jing., Mingjing Li., Hong-Jiang Zhang., Bo Zhang.: An Efficient and Effective Region-Based Image Retrieval Framework. *IEEE Trans on* Image Processing, Vol. 13, No. 4, pp. 699-709, MAY 2004.
9. Tekalp A M.: Digital Video Processing. Prentice-Hall, 1995.

# Region Analysis of Business Card Images Acquired in PDA Using DCT and Information Pixel Density

Ick Hoon Jang[1], Chong Heun Kim[2], and Nam Chul Kim[3]

[1] Kyungwoon University, Dep. of Electronic Engineering, Gumi 730-850, Korea
ihjang@ikw.ac.kr
[2] LG Electronics Co., Ltd., Products Research Institute, Gumi 730-820, Korea
BalUpZillot@lge.com
[3] Kyungpook Nat'l University, Dep. of Electronic Engineering, Daegu 702-701, Korea
nckim@ee.knu.ac.kr

**Abstract.** In this paper, we present a method of region analysis for business card images acquired in a PDA (personal digital assistant) using DCT and information pixel (IP) density. The proposed method consists of three parts: region segmentation, information region (IR) classification, and character region (CR) classification. In the region segmentation, an input business card image is partitioned into $8 \times 8$ blocks and the blocks are classified into information blocks (IBs) and background blocks (BBs) by a normalized DCT energy. The input image is then segmented into IRs and background regions (BRs) by region labeling on the classified blocks. In the IR classification, each IR is classified into CR or picture region (PR) by using a ratio of DCT energy of edges in horizontal and vertical directions to DCT energy of low frequency components and a density of IPs. In the CR classification, each CR is classified into large CR (LCR) or small CR (SCR) by using the density of IPs and an averaged run-length of IPs. Experimental results show that the proposed region analysis yields good performance for test images of several types of business cards acquired in a PDA under various surrounding conditions. In addition, error rates of the proposed method are shown to be 2.2–10.1% lower in region segmentation and 7.7% lower in IR classification than those of the conventional methods.

## 1   Introduction

Business cards have been widely used by career men as a means of an advertisement. Recently as one's own p.r. is regarded as of great importance, the class of business card users is being extended to common people. Accordingly, people get more business cards of others and need efficient management of them instead of carrying all of them. Up to now people usually manage business cards by putting it in a book of business cards directly or making a note of its information in a memo pad. A hand-held PDA widely used in recent days can easily obtain an image of a business card by digitizing it with its built-in camera. It can also

J. Blanc-Talon et al. (Eds.): ACIVS 2005, LNCS 3708, pp. 243–251, 2005.
© Springer-Verlag Berlin Heidelberg 2005

recognize characters in an image and store the recognized characters. So such a management of the information of a business card using the PDA may be more efficient.

Business cards are generally composed of characters such as logotype, name, affiliation, address, phone number, e-mail address, etc., pictures such as photograph, symbol mark, line, etc., and background. So if a region analysis that divides a business card image into CRs, PRs, and BRs is performed, then any following processing for business card management may be much more efficient. Until now many region analysis methods have been proposed. Most of the methods are for document images [1]–[10]. In [4]–[6], a document image is first partitioned into blocks, the blocks are then classified into IBs containing characters or pictures and BBs using a block activity, and the image is finally divided into IRs and BRs. As a block activity, variance of a block [4], edge information in a block [5], or DCT energy in a block [6] is used. In addition, a document image is first binarized as IPs and BPs, and then divided into IRs and BRs using a run-length smoothing [1] or projection profiles of the binarized image [7]. Besides, an IR is classified into CRs and PRs by using adjacency of character strings [8], repetition of character strings [9], or distribution of IPs in its binarized region [10]. In [11], an extraction of text lines for business card images acquired in scanners has been proposed.

Since document images are usually acquired by high resolution scanners, they usually have regular illumination and intensity distributions in their local regions are nearly uniform. They also have many character strings of regular positions and pictures somewhat isolated from their adjacent characters. On the other hand, business card images acquired in a PDA with its built-in camera usually have lower resolution. In addition, they may often have irregular illumination and shadow due to acquisition under unstable hand-held situation. So their intensity distributions in local regions may not be uniform but severely varied. Moreover, they have low average density of characters and sizes of their characters may often vary in a few lines of irregular positions, and often have pictures lie close to their adjacent characters. Thus the performance of region analysis on business card images acquired in a PDA using the conventional region analysis methods for document images may be deteriorated. In this paper, we present a method of region analysis for business card images acquired in a PDA considering the characteristics of business card images.

## 2 Proposed Region Analysis

### 2.1 Region Segmentation Using DCT

In the region segmentation, an input image is first partitioned into blocks and the blocks are classified into IBs and BBs based on a block activity using DCT. We determine the block size as $8 \times 8$ by considering the averaged density and size of characters in business card images and define the block activity as the block energy with the absolute sum of low frequency DCT coefficients in the block. We also normalize the block energy by the RMS (root mean square) of block signal, which is for compensation of the severe intensity variation in local regions. Thus the block activity of the $k$th block can be written as

$$E_N^k = \frac{1}{\sqrt{\frac{1}{64}\sum_{i=0}^{7}\sum_{j=0}^{7}\left(x_{ij}^k\right)^2}}\sum_{\substack{u=0 \\ u+v\leq 3 \\ (u,v)\neq(0,0)}}^{7}\sum_{v=0}^{7}|D_{uv}^k| \tag{1}$$

where $x_{ij}^k$ and $D_{uv}^k$ denote the intensity value of pixel $(i,j)$ and the DCT coefficient of frequency $(u,v)$ at the $k$th block, respectively. So the classification of the $k$th block using (1) can be represented as

$$\text{Decide IB if } E_N^k \geq Th_E; \text{ otherwise decide BB} \tag{2}$$

where $Th_E$ denotes a threshold. In this paper, $Th_E$ is determined as the average of $E_N^k$ over the entire image. After the block classification, the input image is then segmented into IRs and BRs by region labeling on the classified blocks.

Figure 1(a) shows an ordinary $640 \times 480$ business card image with complex background acquired in a PDA. Figure 1(b) shows the result image of block classification for the image of Fig. 1(a). Gray parts represent IBs and black ones BBs. As shown in Fig. 1(b), we can see that most of the blocks are well classified. However, there are some isolated IB regions in the upper left part which are actually BB regions. The isolated IB regions are eliminated in the region labeling. Figure 1(c) shows the result image of the elimination of isolated IB regions for the image of Fig. 1(b). From Fig. 1(c), one can see that almost all of the isolated IB regions are eliminated so that the image is well segmented into IRs and BRs.

### 2.2   Information Region Classification Using DCT and Information Pixel Density

Among IRs, CRs usually have strong edges in horizontal and vertical directions. On the contrary, PRs do not have such strong edges. They also have higher energies in their low frequency bands and higher IP densities in their blocks compared to the CRs. Based on these characteristics, the IRs are classified into CRs and PRs. In the IR classification, the segmented IRs are first partitioned into blocks of $8 \times 8$ size for locally adaptive classification which may be advantageous for discriminating CRs from PRs. The energy of horizontal edges in each block is computed only with DCT coefficients of horizontal frequency components. Similarly, the energy of vertical edges is also computed. The energy of low frequency components is computed with several low frequency DCT coefficients. Thus the energy of edges in horizontal and vertical directions at the $k$th block in the $m$th segmented IR, $EE^{m,k}$, and the energy of low frequency components, $EL^{m,k}$, can be represented as

$$EE^{m,k} = \sum_{u=1}^{7}|D_{u0}^{m,k}| + \sum_{v=1}^{7}|D_{0v}^{m,k}| \tag{3}$$

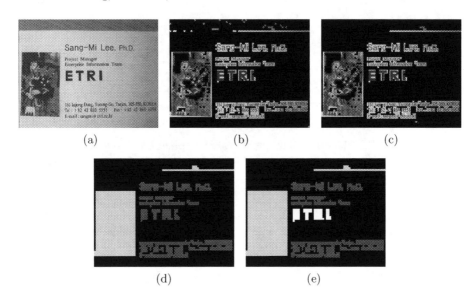

**Fig. 1.** An ordinary business card image with complex background and the results of the proposed region analysis. (a) Original image, (b) block classification, (c) elimination of isolated IB regions, (d) IR classification, and (e) CR classification.

$$EL^{m,k} = \sum_{\substack{u=0 \\ u+v\leq 2 \\ (u,v)\neq(0,0)}}^{7} \sum_{v=0}^{7} |D_{uv}^{m,k}| \tag{4}$$

where $D_{uv}^{m,k}$ denotes the DCT coefficient of frequency $(u,v)$ at the $k$th block in the $m$th segmented IR. Next, considering CRs have high energy of edges in horizontal and vertical directions and PRs have high energy of low frequency components, the ratio of the energy of edges $EE^{m,k}$ to the energy of low frequency components $EL^{m,k}$ is computed at the $k$th block and the ratio is then averaged over the entire $m$th segmented IR as

$$RE^m = \left\langle \frac{EE^{m,k}}{EL^{m,k}} \right\rangle \tag{5}$$

where $< \cdot >$ denotes the average of the quantity.

In order to compute the density of IPs in a segmented IR, each IR is binarized with a threshold by Otsu's threshold selection method [12]. In a binarized IR, black pixels are IPs and white ones are BPs. Then the density of IPs in the $m$th segmented IR is given as

$$DIP^m = \frac{NIP^m}{NIP^m + NBP^m} \tag{6}$$

where $NIP^m$ and $NBP^m$ denote the number of IPs and that of BPs in the $m$th segmented IR, respectively.

Using the ratio of energy $RE^m$ and the density of IPs $DIP^m$, the $m$th segmented IR is classified into CRs and PRs as

$$\text{Decide CR if } RE^m \geq Th_R \text{ and } DIP^m \leq Th_D; \text{ otherwise decide PR} \qquad (7)$$

where $Th_R$ and $Th_D$ denote thresholds. In this paper, $Th_R$ is determined as the average of $RE^m$ over the entire image and $Th_D$ is experimentally determined. Hollows and holes in each PR are filled using the run-length smoothing method in [1]. Figure 1(d) shows that the map image of the result of IR classification. Dark gray parts represent CRs, bright gray ones PRs, and black ones BRs. We have given the result of IR classification as the region map image to discriminate the CRs from PRs. As shown in Fig. 1(d), one can see that the IRs are well classified into CRs and PRs.

### 2.3 Character Region Classification Using Information Pixel Density and Run-Length

Among characters in business card images, logotypes are usually larger than the other characters such as name, affiliation, address, phone number, and e-mail address. Logotypes are sometimes modified, so they may give little information. Logotypes usually have higher densities of IPs and have longer run-lengths of IPs compared to the other characters. Based on these characteristics, the CRs are classified into LCRs and SCRs. For the CR classification, we define the average run-length of IPs in the $n$th CR as

$$RL^n = \langle HL_i^n \rangle + \langle VL_j^n \rangle \qquad (8)$$

where $HL_i^n$ and $VL_j^n$ denote the maximum run-length of IPs at the $i$th horizontal line and that at the $j$th vertical line in the $n$th CR, respectively. Using the density of IPs in (6) and the average run-length of IPs in (8), the $n$th CR is classified into LCR or SCR as

$$\text{Decide LCR if } DIP^n \geq Th'_D \text{ and } RL^n \geq Th_L; \text{ otherwise decide SCR} \qquad (9)$$

where $Th'_D$ and $Th_L$ denote thresholds. In this paper, $Th'_D$ and $Th_L$ are experimentally determined. Hollows and holes in each LCR are also filled using the run-length smoothing method in [1]. Figure 1(e) shows that the map image of the result of CR classification. White parts represent LCRs, dark gray ones SCRs, bright gray ones PRs, and black ones BRs. As shown in Fig. 1(e), one can see that the CRs are well classified into LCRs and SCRs.

## 3 Experimental Results and Discussion

To evaluate the performance of the proposed region analysis, test images of several types of business cards were acquired using a PDA, iPAQ 3950 by Compaq, with its built-in camera, Nexicam by Navicom, under various surrounding conditions. In the business cards, there are ordinary business cards, special business

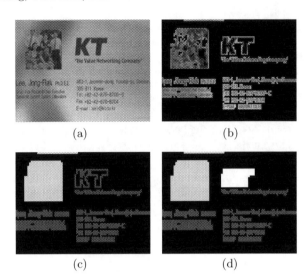

(a)                           (b)

(c)                           (d)

**Fig. 2.** An ordinary business card image having shadows in its left part and the results of the proposed region analysis. (a) Original image, (b) region segmentation, (c) IR classification, and (d) CR classification.

cards of textured surfaces, and special business cards with patterns in their surfaces. The surrounding conditions can be divided into good condition and ill condition containing irregular illumination, shadow, and complex backgrounds.

Figures 2 and 3 show a $640 \times 480$ ordinary business card image having shadows in its left part and a special business card image with patterns in its surface and their results of the proposed region analysis. One can see that the proposed method yields good results of region segmentation, IR classification, and CR classification. Experimental results have shown that the proposed method yields similar results on other test business card images.

Next, we evaluated error rates of region segmentation. To do this, we produced standard region segmented images for 100 test business card images. In the way, each test image is manually segmented into IRs and BRs and the map image of the IRs and BRs is produced. Its original image is partitioned into $8 \times 8$ blocks and the blocks are classified as IBs and BBs. A block is classified as IB if 10% or more pixels in the block belong to an IR of its region map image. Otherwise, the block is classified as BB. After the block classification, a standard region segmented image is produced by region labeling on the classified blocks. The error rate of region segmentation for the test image is evaluated by comparing its region segmented image with its standard region segmented one.

The error rate of region segmentation for a test image is defined as $\varepsilon_S = (\varepsilon_{IB} + \varepsilon_{BB})/2$, where $\varepsilon_{IB}$ and $\varepsilon_{BB}$ denote the error rate of IB and that of BB, respectively. The $\varepsilon_{IB}$ and $\varepsilon_{BB}$ are defined as $\varepsilon_{IB} = N_{MIB}/N_{IB}$ and $\varepsilon_{BB} = N_{MBB}/N_{BB}$, where $N_{IB}$ and $N_{BB}$ denote the number of IBs and that of BBs in the standard region segmented image, respectively. The $N_{MIB}$ and $N_{MBB}$ denote the number of mis-segmentated IBs and that of mis-segmented BBs in

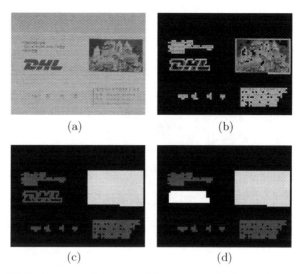

(a)                                              (b)

(c)                                              (d)

**Fig. 3.** A special business card image with patterns in its surface and the results of the proposed region analysis. (a) Original image, (b) region segmentation, (c) IR classification, and (d) CR classification.

**Table 1.** Comparative error rates of region segmentation for the conventional region segmentation methods in [4]–[6] and the proposed region segmentation method

| Type of business card | Surrounding condition | Variance % | Edge information % | DCT energy % | Proposed % |
|---|---|---|---|---|---|
| Ordinary | Good | 15.0 | 12.7 | 11.5 | 11.4 |
| | Ill | 24.9 | 16.7 | 15.2 | 12.6 |
| Special | Good | 22.8 | 22.6 | 16.0 | 15.3 |
| | Ill | 35.3 | 28.5 | 23.7 | 18.3 |
| Average | | 24.5 | 20.1 | 16.6 | 14.4 |

the region segmented image, respectively. Table 1 shows comparative error rates of region segmentation for the conventional region segmentation methods in [4]–[6] and the proposed region segmentation method. As shown in Table 1, we can see that the proposed method gives 14.4% average error rates of region segmentation so that it yields 2.2–10.1% performance improvement for the test images. Besides, the performance of our method is especially better on the special business card images under ill surrounding conditions.

In addition, we evaluated error rates of IR classification. To do this, standard IR classified images for test business card images was produced in such a way of the production of standard region segmented images. The error rate of IR classification is defined as $\varepsilon_C = N_{MIR}/N_{IR}$, where $N_{IR}$ and $N_{MIR}$ denote the number of IRs in the standard IR classified image and that of mis-classified IRs in the IR classified image. Table 2 shows the comparative error rates of

**Table 2.** Comparative error rates of IR classification for the conventional IR classification method in [10] and the proposed IR classification method

| Type of business card | Surrounding condition | Region | Method in [10] % | Proposed % |
|---|---|---|---|---|
| Ordinary | Good | CR | 8.4 | 2.8 |
| | | PR | 11.8 | 5.9 |
| | Ill | CR | 11.4 | 5.7 |
| | | PR | 18.7 | 6.7 |
| Special | Good | CR | 13.6 | 4.9 |
| | | PR | 16.7 | 5.6 |
| | Ill | CR | 13.7 | 6.0 |
| | | PR | 16.3 | 11.1 |
| Average | | | 13.8 | 6.1 |

IR classification for the conventional IR classification in [10] and the proposed IR classification method. As shown in Table 2, we can see that the proposed method gives 6.1% average error rate of IR classification so that it yields 7.7% performance improvement for the test images.

## Acknowledgement

This work was supported in part by Samsung Electronics Co., Ltd.

## References

1. Drivas, D., Amin, A.: Page segmentation and classification utilising bottom-up approach. Proc. IEEE ICDAR'95 (1995) 610–614
2. Sauvola, J., Pietikäinen, M.: Page segmentation and classification using fast feature extraction and connectivity analysis. Proc. IEEE ICDAR'95 (1995) 1127–1131
3. Wang, H., Li, S.Z., Ragupathi, S.: Document segmentation and classification with top-down approach. Proc. IEEE 1st Int. Conf. Knowledge-Based Intelligent Electronic Systems 1 (1997) 243–247
4. Chen, C.T.: Transform coding of digital image using variable block DCT with adaptive thresholding and quantization. SPIE 1349 (1990) 43–54
5. Bones, P.J., Griffin, T.C., Carey-Smith, C.M.: Segmentation of document images. SPIE 1258 (1990) 66–78
6. Chaddha, N., Sharma, R., Agrawal, A., Gupta, A.: Text segmentation in mixed-mode images. Proc. IEEE Twenty-Eight Asilomar Conf. Signals, Systems and Computers 2 (1994) 1356–1361
7. O'Gorman, L.: The document spectrum for page layout analysis. IEEE Trans. Pattern Anal. Machine Intell. 15 (1993) 1162–1173
8. Li, X., Oh, W.G., Ji, S.Y., Moon, K.A., Kim, H.J.: An efficient method for page segmentation. Proc. IEEE ICIPS'97 2 (1997) 957–961
9. Lee, S.W., Ryu, D.S.: Parameter-free geometric document layout analysis. IEEE Trans. Pattern Anal. Machine Intell. 23 (2001) 1240–1256

10. Yip, S.K., Chi, Z.: Page segmentation and content classification for automatic document image processing. Proc. IEEE Int. Symp. Intelligent Multimedia, Video and Speech Processing (2001) 279–282

11. Pan, W., Jin, J., Shi, G., Wang, Q.R.: A system for automatic Chinese business card recognition. Proc. IEEE ICDAR'01 (2001) 577–581

12. Otsu, N.: A threshold selection method from gray-level histograms. IEEE Trans. Syst., Man, Cybern. **SMC-9** (1979) 62–66

# Design of a Hybrid Object Detection Scheme for Video Sequences

Nikolaos Markopoulos and Michalis Zervakis

Department of Electronic and Computer Engineering,
Technical University of Crete, Chania, Greece
{nikolasmark, michalis}@danai.systems.tuc.gr
http://www.ece.tuc.gr/

**Abstract.** A method is presented for extracting object information from an image sequence taken by a static monocular camera. The method was developed towards a low computational complexity in order to be used in real-time surveillance applications. Our approach makes use of both intensity and edge information of each frame and works efficiently in an indoor environment. It consists of two major parts: background processing and foreground extraction. The background estimation and updating makes the object detection robust to environment changes like illumination changes and camera jitter. The fusion of intensity and edge information allows a more precise estimation of the position of the different foreground objects in a video sequence. The result obtained are quite reliable, under a variety of environmental conditions.

## 1 Introduction

Traditionally, the most important tasks of surveillance and monitoring safety are based on human visual observation; however, an autonomous system able to detect anomalous or unexpected situations can help a human operator, even if it cannot or should not replace his/her presence.

One of the goals of surveillance systems is to locate objects in the observed scene by a static camera. The result is a binary mask that indicates the presence or absence of a foreground object for each pixel in the image. Moving objects and objects that do not belong to a predefined background generate changes in the image intensity. Many authors have presented approaches towards surveillance and automatic object detection. In most papers background subtraction is used. Jabri, Duric and Wechsler [8] introduce confidence maps of the intensities of an image in order to represent the results of background subtraction. Fengliang and Kikuo [10] present a method where gray and depth images are used to enhance reliability of the method. In [1] multiple constrains like motion vectors, temporal edges from frame differences and color are used. The work in [4] attempts to combine statistical assumptions with high-level information regarding moving objects, apparent objects and shadows derived in the processing of previous frames. These methods are quite effective under certain conditions, but most of

J. Blanc-Talon et al. (Eds.): ACIVS 2005, LNCS 3708, pp. 252–259, 2005.
© Springer-Verlag Berlin Heidelberg 2005

them are not designed and are inappropriate for real time implementation as their computational complexity is quite high.

This paper describes a robust object detection method for surveillance systems, monitoring indoor environments. The first problem to be addressed is the localization of the objects of interest inside the scene. It is very difficult to design a unique, general and accurate detection scheme for objects of interest in all possible surveillance applications. Our approach develops two detection schemes, one based on the intensity difference of the current image of the sequence to the background and the other based on the color edges of the current image. The latter scheme is influenced by the former as to limit its search area in the regions of interest defined by intensity differences. Merging both methods provides a robust algorithm for detecting objects of interest. An updating of the background image is performed in parallel, in order to make the system illumination adaptive.

The proposed method will be used in surveillance systems using a panoramic view taken from several cameras within the EC funded project with the acronym OPTAG [12]. The paper structure proceeds as follows. Section 2 presents the object detection scheme proposed, whereas section 3 presents the issues related to background estimation and updating. Examples are presented in section 4.

## 2   Object Detection

The object detection approach of this work is based on subtracting frames from an "empty room" as it has the advantage of detecting moving objects, objects that temporarily stopped moving, or still objects which do not belong to the predefined background. Due to similarities between the object and background intensities, objects are often split into pieces at regions of such similarities. In order to alleviate this problem, we use detailed edge information from such regions in the frame under consideration, in order to enhance local region contrast and enable the discrimination between object and background.

Overall, we propose the sequential use of abrupt temporal changes between frame and background and smoother spatial changes in local regions of the frame considered. The local regions are defined as *regions of interest* for edges by the first process.

### 2.1   Object Detection Using Area

Image substraction is a fast and a low computational cost method to obtain foreground objects from a scene. The current image is subtracted by a stationary one, modeling the background. By thresholding this difference we obtain a binary image of the areas belonging to the foreground. A further labeling process defines compact objects (blobs), as well as their bounding box. If $B(x, y)$ is the background image and $I_i(x, y)$ any single frame, then the blobs result from the difference image $D_i(x, y)$ which is calculated by thresholding as:

$$D_i(x, y) = \begin{cases} 0 \text{ if } |B_i(x, y) - I_i(x, y)| \leq threshold \\ 1 \text{ if } |B_i(x, y) - I_i(x, y)| > threshold \end{cases} \quad (1)$$

Unfortunately perfect background and a still camera models do not exist which often results in noisy difference images with incomplete blobs like the ones shown in Fig. 1. False positive and false negative detection is usually experienced, resulting in grain noise on both the object and background regions. In order to reduce

(a) Background          (b) Current image          (c) Subtracted

**Fig. 1.** Simple differentiating method (thresholded)

noise and produce thicker homogenous areas we propose a three step approach. First the absolute value of the difference is calculated. Then a two-dimensional $3 * 3$ averaging filter is applied to smooth the image and reduce random noise. Finally, thresholding provides the areas not belonging to the background and a final filtering process removes the remaining grain noise (scattered noise pixels and areas of 10 or less connected pixels). If a low threshold is chosen, then the probability of false negatives corresponding to noise, shadows and reflections rises. A further refinement step labels the objects of interest and creates the bounding boxes of the extracted blobs. The areas of the blobs and their corresponding bounding boxes are used as a priori information for edge detection, as presented in the next section (Sec. 2.2).

At this point it is worth mentioning that the previous step operates on intensity rather than color information for deriving area differences. The reason for that is efficiency, besides the side effect of reducing computational complexity. Indeed, in several tests,the additional information gained from color-level subtraction was found to be negligible. Besides the fact that the intensity of an image embodies most area variations, it is also more prune to noise and camera jitter dependencies. Color information is introduced in association with the next stage, for edge detection within the specified bounding boxes.

## 2.2   Object Detection Using Edges

In figure 1 it is shown that the object detection based only on the area of the image differences (current image and background) is often not reliable enough to detect and define compact objects. In order to generate homogenous blobs of the actual object, the image difference must be supplemented by additional information that does not rely on the intensity of an image. Many authors have proposed to use the static and the moving edges of an image to introduce such intensity invariant information [8],[10]. The presented method makes only use of the static edges. The aperture problem and the lack of speed of the objects supersede the use of moving edges.

For the process of edge detection, there are several methods that can efficiently extract spatial edges from an image (Sobel, Canny, Prewitt, etc.). Sobel is a simple, fast and efficient edge detector in terms of accuracy and susceptibility to noise. The Sobel approach detects edges using the Sobel approximation to the derivative. It returns edges at those points where the gradient of the image $I_i$ is maximum. The Sobel edge detector uses two convolution kernels, one to detect changes in vertical contrast and one to detect horizontal contrast. Other edge detectors, such as the Canny, may have good or even better performance, but their complexity and time delay make them less appealing for real time applications.

The edge detector in our approach operates only within the bounding boxes of interest defined by the previous step (section 2.1 in the current frame, but considers differentiation in a color space; we use RGB in our application. The information obtained by superimposing the edges of each color band is up to 10% more than just using the intensity values of an image [9]. The contours provided by the edge detector are postprocessed with simple morphological techniques. The following flowchart demonstrates the steps for postprocessing of edges detected using the Sobel operator (Fig. 2). At first, the edges of image $I_i$ are

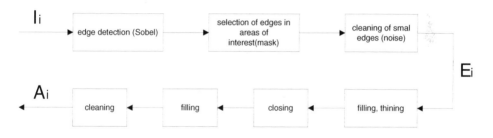

**Fig. 2.** Flowchart of the postprocessing steps using edges

computed within the bounding boxes of objects derived from the thresholded difference image (Sec. 2.3). A cleaning step is necessary in order to remove small-extent edges. The thinning block is then used to avoid merging of neighboring edges that possibly trigger different objects. Line filling and morphological closing are used in order to produce homogenous areas and a final cleaning step is employed to remove any remaining small regions. The closing step enables the definition of areas enclosed by closed lines and derives area patterns from line patterns as demonstrated in figure 2.3 (b) and (c). The final result $A_i$ (as in Fig. 2), has the form of compact regions similar to those in section 2.1.

One major difference from many other methods that use contours to enhance the reliability of the extracted data, is that we do not extract edges of the background. This makes the proposed process quite immune to camera jitter. Notice that comparison of background edges in successive frames would indicate displaced edges in the case of camera jitter, with a high possibility of misinterpreting them as object edges and triggering false negative detection. Besides, our process of edge detection is only applied at selected local regions, which drastically speeds up the algorithm.

## 2.3   Merging of the Area and Edge Methods

In previous sections we presented two procedures of detecting objects or parts of objects from a scene using simple, robust and fast algorithms. A fusion of the results of these procedures completes the hybrid method introduced in this paper and can overcome the deficiencies of each method alone. The proposed approach comprises the following steps: reference image acquisition (background), sample image acquisition (current frame), calculation of the difference image, spatial thresholding of the difference image into a binary image, morphological post-processing of the binary image to remove pixel noise, bounding box creation of the detected blobs. In parallel an edge detection in and around the area of interest (blobs) obtained from the differentiating method is performed (within the bounding boxes). The last step is the superimposition of areas from the thresholded difference and the morphologically processed edge regions (Fig. 3). The derived regions (blobs) from area and edge processing (Sec. 2.1 and 2.2) are combined as $Y_i = max\{A_i, D_i\}$. $Y_i$ is the resulting binary image final form of blobs that can be labeled and used in subsequent tracking.

Although the differential approach is a good method to obtain areas of interest, the method is complemented by the edges of the image providing a robust and partially illumination invariant method.

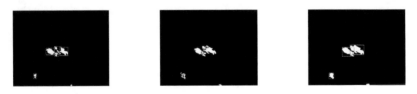

(a) Thresholded image dif-    (b) Morphological proces-    (c) Superimposition of a)
ference                       sed edges                     and b)

**Fig. 3.** Merging steps

## 3   Background Estimation and Updating

The maintenance of a background image is an important part of all object detection methods. An ideal background maintenance system would be able to handle problems like lightning changes or camera jitter [2],[3]. The use of the background enables the discrimination and detection of temporarily stationary objects like left bags and luggage.

## 3.1   Background Estimation

In [5] it is proposed to estimate an initial background image using a large number of pictures and the median filter operating in the temporal axis. The assumption is that the pixel stays in the background for more than half of the frames used for the estimation.

$$B_{x,y} = median(I_{1(x,y)}, \ldots I_{n(x,y)}) \tag{2}$$

where $B$ is the background image, $I$ is the frame image and $n$ is the number of frames to be used for the approximation of the background.

## 3.2   Background Updating

To avoid false object detection (false negatives) that may be caused by slight but steady lightning changes, a knowledge-based background updating algorithm is proposed in [8]. The background image that has been given or estimated with the background estimation algorithm has to be updated in regular time intervals. Using the knowledge of the detected objects in a scene (Sec. 2), it is possible to define a selective update, which computes a new background value only if a point is not marked as an object pixel.

Two different types of backgroundupdating were considered:

- The *blobs algorithm* uses the blobs of the detected objects and updates according to equation 3 the background around these blobs. The background covered by the blobs is not updated and remains equal to the last updated background.
- The *bounding box algorithm* behaves like the blob algorithm with the slight difference that the background around the computed bounding rectangle of each object is updated. In this case the updated area is smaller than ideally, excluding the entire bounding box rather than the object itself, but the implementation is simpler.

In both cases wider boundaries are chosen in order to avoid calculating shadows or similar background colored objects in the updated image. The blobs algorithm appears to be the better, as more background can be updated in each step. Moreover, it is not dependent on object orientation compared to the bounding box algorithm.

The new background is the weighted average between the current background objects and the old background.

$$B_j = (1 - \alpha)B_{j-1} + \alpha I_i \tag{3}$$

where $B_j$ is the $j$th updated background image ($j = i \bmod K$), $I_i$ is the current image, and $\alpha$ ($0 \le \alpha \le 1$) is a scalar representing the importance of the current data and the learning rate of the model. $K$ controls the update frequency of the background to avoid the updating for every frame.

## 4   Results Evaluation

The object detection approach presented in this paper was tested in several video sequences provided by a public site of the CAVIAR project[11]. The evaluation of object detection is difficult to present without being able to observe the sequences and the corresponding detected objects. The definitions of sensitivity and specificity fail to describe the efficiency of the detector presented, as they fail to encode the occurrence of occluded or split detected objects. For this purpose, we provide a table (Tab.1) that lists the number of expected objects, the number of merged objects , the number of split objects and the false negatives that are recorded in the sequences. The objects in each sequence denote number of objects in all frames of the sequence. The number of the false negatives is experienced in the first two sequences that reflect slowly moving objects, due to the fact that these objects influence the background updating scheme presented in chapter 3.1. A more efficient method for background estimation would

(a) Image with objects        (b) Intensity diff. blobs    (c) Hybrid technique blobs

**Fig. 4.** Resulting blobs

probably eliminate this effect. The results indicate that our method is effective in detecting objects even in dense scenes, even though it slightly suffers form merging or splitting in occlusion (as in the Walk2 sequence). This performance can be drastically improved through efficient tracking of labels, which is not implemented in this work.

Figure 4 shows two persons to be extracted and the results using a simple thresholding and the presented hybrid algorithm. The hybrid solution detects the two persons correctly as a whole blob with slight wider boarders which are due to the dilation operation applied.

**Table 1.** Detection results

| Sequence | Objects | Merged | Split | FN |
|---|---|---|---|---|
| Left Bag | 1300 | 1 (0.08%) | 3 (0.23%) | 30 (2.30%) |
| Walk1 | 1050 | 165 (15.71%) | 4 (0.38%) | 80 (7.62%) |
| Walk2 | 1500 | 300 (20.00%) | 500 (33.33%) | 3 (0.20%) |

# 5   Conclusion

The proposed method allows a robust and accurate detection of moving and temporarily stationary objects that not belong to the stationary background. The key strength of this method is the hybrid object detection based on the merging of two different detection approaches. The first approach employs intensity differences from a frame to the background and the other uses the color edges of that frame. The utilization of edges provides additional information in areas where the substraction scheme might fail. The background updating scheme employed allows detection independent of gradual changes in light conditions and forms the a priori step for correctly extracting the desired regions of interest. Extensions to the proposed method involve linking with a tracking algorithm, which could handle occlusions in the range of the surveillanced area.

# References

1. Ismail Oner Sebe, Object-Tracking I—Using Multiple Constraints, EE392J, Digital Video Processing, Standford University, 2002.
2. Kentaro Toyama, John Krumm, Barry Brumitt, Brian Meyers,Wallflower: Principles and Practice of Background Maintenance,Microsoft Research Redmond, 1999.
3. Young-Kee Jung, Kyu-Won Lee, Yo-Sung Ho, Content-Based Event Retrieval Using Semantic Scene Interpretation for Automated Traffic Surveillance, IEEE Transactions on Intelligent Transpotation Systems, Vol.2, No.3, September 2001.
4. Rita Cucchiara, Constantino Grana, Massimo Piccardi, Andrea Prati, Detecting Moving Objects, Ghosts, and Shadows in Video Streams, IEEE Transactions on Pattern Analysis and Machine Intelligence, Vol25, No.10, October 2003.
5. Sen-Ching S. Cheung and Chandrika Kamath, Robust techniques for background subtraction in urban traffic video, Center for Applied Scientiffic Computing Lawrence Livermore National Laboratory, Livermore, Canada
6. C.E. Liedtke, *Mustererkennung Vorlesungs Manuskript*, Hannover, Germany: Universitaet Hannover, 1999.
7. Matrox Image Libraty 7.5 User Guide, Matrox Electronic Systems Ltd., 2003.
8. S. Jarbi and A. Rosenfeld, Detection and Location of People in Video Images Using Adaptive Fusion of Color and Edge Information, Department of Computer Science, George Mason University, Fairfax.
9. Alex Leykin and Florin Cutzu, Differences of edge properties in photographs and paintings, Dept of Computer Science Indiana University Bloomington, USA.
10. Fengliang Xu and Kikuo Fujimura, Human Detection Using Depth and Gray Images, Ohio State University, Honda Research Institute USA, 2003.
11. CAVIAR project (Context Aware Vision using Image-based Active Recognition, http://homepages.inf.ed.ac.uk/rbf/CAVIAR).
12. OPTAG project (Improving airport Efficiency, Security and Passenger Flow by Enhanced Passenger Monitoring FP6-2002-Aero No.502858).

# Interactive Object-Based Retrieval Using Relevance Feedback

Sorin Sav, Hyowon Lee, Noel O'Connor, and Alan F. Smeaton

Centre for Digital Video Processing,
Dublin City University, Glasnevin, Dublin 9, Ireland
sorinsav@eeng.dcu.ie

**Abstract.** In this paper we present an interactive, object-based video retrieval system which features a novel query formulation method that is used to iteratively refine an underlying model of the search object. As the user continues query composition and browsing of retrieval results, the system's object modeling process, based on Gaussian probability distributions, becomes incrementally more accurate, leading to better search results. To make the interactive process understandable and easy to use, a custom user-interface has been designed and implemented that allows the user to interact with segmented objects in formulating a query, in browsing a search result, and in re-formulating a query by selecting an object in the search result.

## 1 Introduction

Automatic segmentation and indexing of objects such as persons, cars or buildings, represents one of the most active research areas in content-based image and video retrieval [1]. However, considering the interest in the problem and the variation of approaches and effort currently undertaken in this direction [2] [3] , progress is slow and performance accurate enough to be used in real applications still seems to be a distant goal. In the task of automatically segmenting and indexing objects in image/video content, the main difficulty is the diverse manifestations of an object in the image/video regardless of the object's inherent visual features such as colour, shape and texture. Factors such as different lighting conditions and camera angles and occlusions make the actual segmentation of an object extremely difficult, even before it can be accurately labeled. Considering this problem, one workaround solution we have been exploring is to use relevance feedback to take a human user's judgements on object definitions into account in retrieving objects. There is a long history of experimentation and successful use of relevance feedback in text-based information retrieval. This has included short-term modelling of a user's information need by dynamically updating the user's query formulation in mid-search as well as long-term modelling of user's needs by profiling his/her interests over time leading to personalisation. This has also been successfully applied to content-based retrieval [4][5].

In this paper, we present an interactive, object-based search system that uses a novel query formulation mechanism and makes use of the user's query

J. Blanc-Talon et al. (Eds.): ACIVS 2005, LNCS 3708, pp. 260–267, 2005.
© Springer-Verlag Berlin Heidelberg 2005

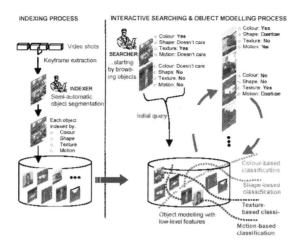

**Fig. 1.** System Overview showing off-line indexing and interactive searching

formulations as automatic feedback to the system in order to develop and refine the modeling of segmented objects in the database. As query formulation is the key element for getting feedback from the user in our approach, the system we have built incorporates a user interaction strategy at the front-end in which a user can efficiently and easily interact with segmented objects in video keyframes. The approach allows the user to highlight any segmented objects, select them, and then to use them for subsequent query formulation. The novelty of this work lies in using query formulations from users as implicit relevance feedback in developing more accurate object classes, the use of object matching in retrieval and the fact that we have built a system for users to interact with.

The remainder of the paper is organised as follows: in Section 2 we give an overview of the system explaining how objects are segmented and stored in the database and how user query formulation is used in an interactive session to refine object modelling in the database for subsequent retrieval. Section 3 describes the video object retrieval mechanism. Experimental results are presented in Section 4. Section 5 concludes the paper and outlines our plans for extending the system's capability and further refining the user-interface.

## 2   System Overview

Our system processes one object from each keyframe taken from each shot in the video and stores these in the database to be used in the retrieval process during an interactive search session (see Figure 1). We use keyframes automatically extracted from the TRECVid 2003 [6] test corpus, as well as images from the well known Corel test corpus.

For each keyframe, a semi-automatic object segmentation process was used to accurately segment one main object in the image. The segmentation tool

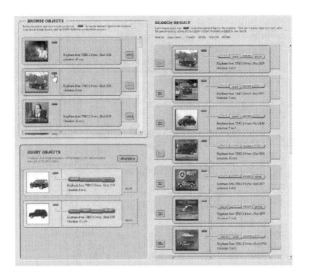

**Fig. 2.** User interface after two iterations of query composition using objects

used was previously reported in [7]. It allows fast and accurate automatic segmentation based on a small amount of user interaction that is easy to perform.
The output can be iteratively refined in order to obtain very accurate object
segmentations.

Once segmented, each object is automatically indexed by colour, shape and
texture using the following well known MPEG-7 descriptors [8]: dominant colour
descriptor, the compactness moment of the shape and the texture browsing descriptor. The motion feature as depicted in Figure 1 is not currently incorporated into the working system but the user-interface we have designed includes
all four features for smoother upgrading of the underlying system in the near
future. This completes the offline object segmentation and indexing process.
Determining similarity among objects for retrieval purposes is done during interactive search without pre-computation as the system progressively receives
more information from the user.

Query formulation is the core user interaction required to achieve more accurate search through iterative refinement of object modeling. Relevance feedback
occurs each time a user formulates a query to search for objects. Figure 2 shows
a screen from our interface after two iterations of query formulation and viewing
of search results.

In Figure 2, after selecting an object, the user can then specify which low-
level features (colour, shape or texture) of the specified object s/he is interested
in. Each of the feature buttons toggles between positive, negative or neutral
preferences for each feature.

## 3    Retrieval Using User Query Formulation as Relevance Feedback

The initial query composed by the user is analysed in terms of the three low-level features (colour, shape and texture) and the degree of similarity between the query object's features and other objects in the database is computed. During interactive search, as more and more query formulation is conducted, the set of objects making up the input query becomes quite complex as it contains many objects, each of which represent positive or negative indications of the three features of the object the user is searching for. We assume the positive samples to be modeled by a mixture of Gaussian probability distribution functions (PDF) at feature level. Accordingly, each feature distribution is independently modeled as a Gaussian mixture, an assumption which is commonly used for image retrieval [9]. The feature vectors are modeled as a mixture of Gaussian distributions of the form:

$$f(X_i|\Phi) = \sum_{j=1}^{k} \pi_j f_j(X_i|\theta_j) \ . \tag{1}$$

where:

$$f(X_i|\theta_j) = \frac{1}{(2\pi)^{\frac{d}{2}}|\sum_j|^{\frac{1}{2}}} e^{-\frac{1}{2}(X_i-\mu_j)^T \sum_j^{-1}(X_i-\mu_j)} \ . \tag{2}$$

is the probability density function for cluster $j$, $\theta_j = (\mu_j, \sum_j)$ is the set of parameters for density function $f_j(X_i|\theta_j)$, $\mu_j$ is the mean of cluster $j$, $\pi_j$ is the mixing proportion of cluster $j$ subject to the condition $\pi_j \geq 0$ and $\sum_{j-1}^{k} \pi_j = 1$ where $k$ is the number of components. $X_i$ is the vector for either colour, shape or texture, $\Phi = (\pi_1, \pi_2...\pi_k, \theta_1, \theta_1...\theta_k)$ is the set of all parameters. Here $f(X_i|\Phi)$ is the probability density function given the colour, shape or texture, of the labelled object $X_i$ for each of the three features of a query object labelled by the user.

As the number of components in the mixture becomes larger, the model tends to follow the real distribution of the positive samples' features more accurately. However, maintaining and operating using a large model is increasingly difficult and therefore there is a need to restrain the model size. The model is built on the sample objects indicated by the user and unlabeled data. A minimum description length (MDL) constraint is used to ensure that the Gaussian mixture has the minimum number of components that correctly classifies the labeled (user indicated) set of objects without including a significant number of negative samples (model outliers). The number of components in the mixture is increased, when the user indicates new samples, only if the following expression is true:

$$\alpha[\log f(X|\Phi)^{(t+1)} - \log f(X|\Phi)^{(t)}] > \beta(N^{(t)} - N^{(t+1)}) \ . \tag{3}$$

where $t$ is the number of Gaussian components in the mixture, $log f(X|\Phi)$ is the log-likelihood function and $N$ is the number of negative samples (outliers) contained within the modelled PDF. The $\alpha$ and $\beta$ parameters are system weighting factors currently set to: $\alpha = 0.23$, $\beta = 0.07$.

The estimation-maximisation (EM) algorithm [10] is employed to estimate the PDF in the feature space in connection with the MDL constraint given by (3). The maximization is performed by the following iteration:

$$E[z_{ij}] = p(z_{ij} = 1|X, \Phi_{(t)}) = \frac{\pi_j^{(t)} p_j(X_i|\Phi_j^{(t)})}{\sum_{s=1}^{k} p_s(X_i|\Phi_s^{(t)})\pi_s^{(t)}} \ . \tag{4}$$

$$\pi_j^{(t+1)} = \frac{1}{N}\sum_{i=1}^{N} E[z_{ij}], \mu_j^{(t+1)} = \frac{1}{N\pi_j^{(t+1)}}\sum_{i=1}^{N} E[z_{ij}]X_i \ . \tag{5}$$

$$\Sigma_j^{(t+1)} = \frac{1}{N\pi_j^{(t+1)}}\sum_{i=1}^{N} E[z_{ij}](X_i - \mu_j^{(t+1)})(X_i - \mu_j^{(t+1)})^T \ . \tag{6}$$

where $E[z_{ij}]$ is the expected value of the probability that the data belongs to cluster $j$, and $\sum_{i=1}^{N} E[z_{ij}]$ is the estimated number of data points in class $j$. At each iteration, the model parameters are re-estimated to maximize the model log-likelihood, $f(X|\Phi)$, until convergence.

At each retrieval iteration, the Mahalanobis distance [11] from each Gaussian feature cluster to the existing objects in the database is computed as a measure of similarity (a minimum distance classifier) and the objects in the database are presented to the user as a ranked list in descending order of the cumulative similarity score $S(x)$ where each feature is weighted in direct proportion to the number of its positive samples indicated by the user. The Mahalanobis distance is expressed as:

$$r^2 = (x - \mu_i)^T \Sigma_i^{-1}(x - \mu_i) \ . \tag{7}$$

where $x$ is the vector for either colour, shape or texture, $\mu_i$ is the mean vector, and $\Sigma_i^{-1}$ is the diagonal covariance matrix for each of the colour and shape clusters. The weighting scheme favors the feature more often indicated as positive because its repeated occurrence suggests a larger incidence of similar objects in the database. The cumulative similarity score is expressed as:

$$S(x) = \lambda_{colour} S_{colour}(x) + \lambda_{shape} S_{shape}(x) + \lambda_{texture} S_{texture}(x) \ . \tag{8}$$

where $S_{feature}$ is the Mahalanobis distance for the given feature, and $\lambda$ is computed as:

$$\lambda_k = \frac{P_k}{P_k + P_l + P_m} \ . \tag{9}$$

with $k, l, m$ being the features colour, shape and texture.

## 4   Experimental Results

In order to evaluate the performance of the system we designed a retrieval experiment using 12 classes of objects, each class containing 50 objects. The objects classes used are: balloon, boat, butterfly, car, eagle, flower, horse, motorcycle, people, plane, shark, tiger.

Experiments were performed with an expert user selecting an initial query object and providing negative/positive feedback. For each query iteration a positive example was added in the query formulation, a negative example was added every second iteration. The query session for each object class was conducted for 5 iterations, therefore for each object class 5 positive examples and 2 negative examples were provided over 5 iterations. The mean precision-recall curves obtained are shown in Figure 3. Since representing 12 curves on the same graph becomes confusing, we present the precision-recall curves grouped on four sub-images for every three classes taken in alphabetical order. In order to provide a easy comparison between object classes, each sub-image contains the mean precision versus recall curve computed by averaging the results over the entire 12 classes.

The precision-recall curves show a relatively slow decay with increasing recall. The optimal values seem to be located around values of recall of 15-25

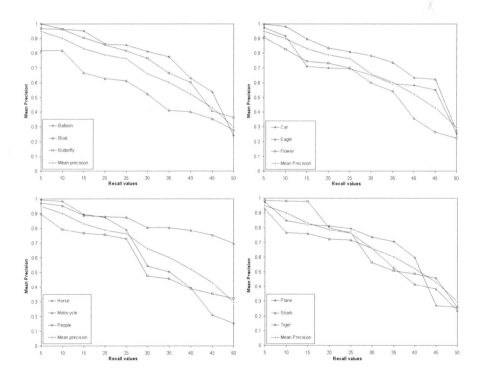

**Fig. 3.** Mean precision vs recall curves for 12 object classes

images/objects out of 50 objects per class, which seems to prove the effectiveness of the presented system. However, it is premature to generalise before performing comparisons against other retrieval systems on a common test set and with multiple users in the retrieval loop.

## 5   Conclusions and Future Work

In this paper we introduced an object-based video search system that features interactive query formulation using colour, shape and texture of an object. Iterative query/browsing incrementally improves object modelling in the database. The actual segmentation of objects from keyframes was supervised in order to provide accurate object sets and to better illustrate our retrieval approach in which the matching among objects (i.e. relating all similar objects in the database) can be helped using the user's query formulation history as feedback.

In its present form our system may not to be suitable for a realistic context, but the point of developing it was to demonstrate how an object-based query formulation mechanism could be realised to help dynamically refine the object model in the database and enhance retrieval.

We are working on several improvements including making object segmentation from each keyframe fully-automatic. Segmenting more than one object from each keyframe is also targeted for future work. Currently, a keyframe from a shot is used to segment objects: however, a more complete solution would be to use all frames within the shot, which could further provide additional information on the object based on its movement and trajectory.

## Acknowledgments

The support of the Enterprise Ireland Informatics Initiative is gratefully acknowledged. Part of this work was supported by Science Foundation Ireland under grant 03/IN.3/I361.

## References

1. Smeulders, A.W., Worring, M., Santini, S., Gupta, A., Jain, R. Content-Based Image Retrieval at the End of the Early Years. IEEE Transactions on Pattern Analysis and Machine Intelligence, vol. 22, pp. 1349-1380, 2000.
2. Smith, J.R., and Chang, S.F,. VisualSEEK: a fully automated content-based image query system. ACM Multimedia, Boston, November, 1996.
3. Carson, C., Thomas, M., Belongie, S., Hellerstein, J.M., Malik, J. Blobworld: A System for Region-Based Image Indexing and Retrieval. Proceedings of the Third International Conference on Visual Information and Information Systems, 1999.
4. Rui, Y., Huang, T. S. and Mehrotra S. Content-based image retrieval with relevance feed-back in Mars. Proceedings of IEEE International Conference on Image Processing ICIP, 1997.
5. Yan, R., Hauptmann, A. and Jin, R. Multimedia Search with Pseudo -Relevance Feedback. Proceedings of International Conference on Image and Video Retrieval CIVR 2003, Urbana, IL, July 24-25, 2003.

6. http://www-nlpir.nist.gov/projects/trecvid
7. O'Connor, N., Adamek, T., Sav, S., Murphy, N. and Marlow, S. QIMERA: A Software Platform for Video Object Segmentation and Tracking. Proceedings of the 4th Workshop on Image Analysis for Multimedia Interactive Service (WIAMIS 2003), London, U.K., April 9-11, 2003.
8. Salambier, P. and Smith, J.R. MPEG-7 Multimedia Descriptions Schemes. *IEEE Transactions on Circuits and Systems for Video Technology*, Vol. 11, pp. 748-759, June 2001.
9. Qian, F., Li, M., Zhang, L., Zhang, H.J. and Zhang, B. Gaussian mixture model for relevance feedback in image retrieval. Proceeding of IEEE International Conference on Multimedia and Expo, Lausanne, Switzerland, August, 2002.
10. Moon, T.K. The Expectation-Maximisation Algorithm. IEEE Signal Processing Magazine, November, 1996.
11. Fessant, F., Aknin, P., Oukhellou, L., and Midenet, S. Comparison of supervised self-organizing maps using Euclidian or Mahalanobis distance in classification context. Proceedings of the 6th International Work Conference on Artificial and Natural Neural Networks (IWANN2001), Granada, Spain, June 13-15, 2001.

# Pseudo-stereo Conversion from 2D Video

Yue Feng[1] and Jianmin Jiang

[1] IEEE Student Member, EIMC, University of Bradford, UK, BD7 1DP
{Y.feng1, J.jiang1}@Bradford.ac.uk

**Abstract.** In this paper, we propose a fast and effective pseudo-stereo conversion algorithm to transform the conventional 2D videos into their stereo versions. As conventional 2D videos do not normally have sufficient true depth information for stereo conversion, we explore the principle of extracting the closest disparity to reconstruct the stereo frame pair, where a simple content-based approach is followed. The proposed algorithm features in: (i) original 2D video frame is taken as the reference frame; (ii) closest disparity information is extracted by a texture-based matching inside a library of stereo image pairs; and (iii) the extracted disparity is then used to reconstruct the right video frame to complete the pseudo-stereo conversion. Our experiments show that certain level of stereo effect has been achieved, where all test video clips are publicly available on the Internet for the convenience of repetition of our proposed work.

## 1 Introduction

Along with series initiatives in high resolution digital TV, 3D TV has long been identified as a possible breakthrough for the next generation TV technologies. Research on stereoscopic video processing attracts considerable attention in the published literature [1~5]. A stereo pair of video sequences, recorded with a difference in the view angle, enables viewers to have 3D perception of the scene by exposing to each eye the respective image sequence. This creates an enhanced 3D feeling and increased 'telepresence' in teleconferencing and several other applications, such as medical and digital entertainment. Several industrial companies have exhibited their 3D glass-free display systems, which provide significant help in terms of eliminating the burden of wearing glasses, and thus generate a potential for another wave of research and development in 3D TV. The remaining bottleneck, however, is on the side of media content production, in which switching from 2D media production to 3D media production is implicated with both timing and costs. As a result, the success of the future 3D TV system will have to be dependent on the availability of sufficient 3D video materials, and the need for 3D content can only be partially satisfied with newly produced 3D recordings. To resolve this problem, one cost effective alternative is to develop new techniques to convert existing 2D video materials to their 3D versions, from which the work described in the paper is motivated.

The 2D video material is not totally the same as the stereoscopes [15, 16], where stereo vision builds correspondence between a pair of images acquired from two well positioned cameras but the 2D video material is only captured by monocular camera. In [6~9], it has been reported that, the depth or disparity value can be estimated by

J. Blanc-Talon et al. (Eds.): ACIVS 2005, LNCS 3708, pp. 268–275, 2005.
© Springer-Verlag Berlin Heidelberg 2005

knowing the information such as the camera focal length and the direction of the moving objects, but these reported algorithms are not suitable for general video sequences which may lack such information. Here in this paper, we describe our recent work on algorithm development for creating a 3D effect for conventional 2D videos without any knowledge of focal length or the moving direction of the object. As the 3D effect is created by estimation and inference on segmented video objects by the principle of extracting closest disparity, we coin such a 3D conversion as pseudo-stereo to identify its feature that the stereo effect is created without any stereo information. Therefore, there is no issue like whether the disparity retrieved is correct or not, as long as the added disparity enables construction of the right frame and provide users a convincing stereo viewing experience. Considering the fact that human visual perception is tolerant, there exists large scope for disparity estimation.

The rest of the paper is organized in two further sections. Section 2 mainly describes the 3D conversion algorithm design, and Section 3 report experimental results to evaluate the proposed algorithm. Finally, some concluding remarks are also included in the same section.

## 2 Design of Pseudo-stereo Conversion Algorithm

To explore the principle of extracting the closest disparity achieve the best possible 3D effects for the proposed pseudo-stereo conversion of existing 2D videos, we design our algorithm to include: (i) pre-processing of stereo image pairs to establish a library of disparities; (ii) segment 2D videos into foreground objects and background regions; (iii) search the library for the best match of visual content to identify the closest disparity; (iv) reconstruct right video frame to create pseudo-stereo video frame pair and complete the proposed conversion. Detailed description of each element inside our proposed system is organized into the following subsections.

### 2.1 Disparity Extraction in Stereo Pairs

With a set of stereo image pairs, we extract their disparity maps and segment them into a range of object regions corresponding to the disparity extracted. Such pre-processing of stereo image pairs enables us to establish a library of disparity maps and their corresponding object regions. Depending on the specific application, the size of such library would require to cover as many textured regions as possible to cope with the encountered 2D videos. In our proposed system, we used about 500 stereo image pairs to establish such a library. The size of the library can be easily increased without affecting the processing speed since its establishment is mainly off-line and has no effect upon the process of pseudo-stereo conversion.

To extract disparity maps from a given stereo image, we adopted one of the most recent and powerful dense-stereo algorithms [1], where a dynamic programming algorithm, minimizing a combined cost function for two corresponding lines of the stereoscopic image pair is used. Its specific implementation can be summarized as follows:

Given a pair of stereo image, we take the left image as the reference, and search the right image for correspondence pixel-by-pixel and line-by-line. Due to the fact that we limit our pseudo-stereo conversion to those stereos with parallax geometry, the search area for each left pixel $pl=(i_L, j_L)$ in the right image can be constrained within the same line and the searching range can be determined by minimum and maximum allowed disparity. As a result, the coordinates along i for each pixel can be ignored in the search process. The following cumulative cost function is minimized while searching through the right image.

$$C(j_r) = \min_{d(p_r)} \{ C(j_r - 1) + c(p_r, d_{p_r}) \}$$ (1)

where C(.) stands for a cost function, which takes into consideration the displaced frame difference (DFD) and the smoothness of the resulting vector field, $Pr$ is the pixel on the right image, and $dp_r=(i_l-i_r, j_l-j_r)$ is the disparity value that produces the minimum cost at the position of $j_r$.

The cost function $c(pr, dpr)$ is defined by

$$c(p_r, d_p) = R(p_r) DFD(p_r, d_p) + SMF(p_r, d_p)$$ (2)

Where $R(Pr)$ is a reliability function (weighting): in high texture and edge area, dp estimation is reliable $R(p)$ should be larger, making DFD more influential. In homogeneous area $dp$ estimation is not reliable, hence $R(Pr)$ should be smaller, making $SMF(p, d)$ more influential. To detect edges and high texture area, the technique similar to [8] is used, which is based on intensity variance or gradients.

The second term of (2) is the absolute difference of two corresponding image intensity blocks, which is defined as follows:

$$DFD(p_r, d_{p_r})$$ (3)

$$= \sum_{(X,Y) \in \beta} \| I_r(i_r + X, j_r + Y) - I_l(i_l + X, j_l + Y) \|$$

where $\beta$ is a rectangular window with the size of $(2N+1)*(2N+1)$ pixels.

$$SMF(d_{Pr}) = \sum_{n=1}^{N} \| d_{Pr} - d_n \| R(d_n)$$ (4)

where $d_n=1, 2, ... N$, are disparity vectors neighboring $dpr$. $R(d)$ (reliability function) aims to attenuate the contribution of unreliable vectors to the smoothing function.

After the disparity vectors are found, we also applied a consistence check to ensure that the disparity extracted represents the true disparity inside the stereo image pair. This is done by reversing the search direction, i.e., from right to left to see if the disparity generates the minimum cost value inside left image. Specifically, the process consists of: (i) a set of points of interest is defined by selecting pixels with left or right image projections located on depth and luminance edges. That is, edge points and depth points are selected as the points of interests, in which the edge points are selected by edge detection algorithm based on gradient, and the depth points are selected by disparity estimation. Alternatively, we can also take every point for the consistence check, which takes longer time to complete the process. Since this operation is of the off-line nature, this alternative would not make any difference upon the overall system performance. (ii) For each of the point, the disparity estimation produces left-to-right (LR) disparity fields. They need to be checked (consistence) by a right-to-left matching process, which is essentially the following condition:

$$d^{(rl)}(p_r) = -d^{(lr)}(p_r + d^{(rl)}(p_r))$$ (5)

After the condition is satisfied, the correspondence between $pr=(i_r, j_r)$ (the pixel in the right image) and $pl=(i_l, j_l)$ (the pixel in the left image) can be established. (iii) If the consistence check fails, (i.e. the above condition is not satisfied), disparity estimation needs to be corrected by a correction process as outlined below.

For each pair of pixels satisfying: $p_r = p_l + d^{(lr)}(p_l)$, the new corrected disparity should be calculated as follows:

$$d'^{(rl)} = \frac{d^{(rl)}\sigma_{lr}^2 - d^{(lr)}\sigma_{rl}^2}{\sigma_{lr}^2 + \sigma_{rl}^2} \tag{6}$$

and the corrected disparity error variance is given by:

$$\sigma_d^2 = \frac{\sigma_{lr}^2 \sigma_{rl}^2}{\sigma_{lr}^2 + \sigma_{rl}^2} \tag{7}$$

where $\sigma_{lr}^2$ and $\sigma_{rl}^2$ are the variances of the disparity estimates $d^{(lr)}$ and $d^{(rl)}$ respectively, which are calculated by:

$$\sigma(P_r, d_{P_r}) = \frac{1}{N^2} \sum_{k=-N}^{N} \sum_{l=-N}^{N} \left( I_r(i_r + k, j_r + l) - I_l(i_l + k, j_l + l) \right)^2 \tag{8}$$

An illustration of such disparity extraction is shown in Figure-1 part (a) and (b).

(a)                    (b)                    (c)

**Fig. 1.** (a) The left image of 'tsukuba'; (b) its disparity map; (c) its texture map

## 2.2 Library of Disparity Maps

By analyzing the stereo image pairs in terms of their disparity maps extracted from the previous section, it is discovered that each disparity region is generalized by an object region with similar texture characteristics. This leads to a further division of those disparity maps and the stereo image pairs into their object regions, where similar texture is illustrated. As a result, the library of disparity maps can be established in terms of object regions with consistent texture rather than the entire stereo image pairs. Note the object regions referred here are different from those semantic video objects as specified in MPEG-4. The major difference here is that our object regions may not necessarily coincide with those object perceived by human viewers. Rather, our object regions are derived by the criteria of texture smooth and consistency.

As all the stereo image pairs have their disparity map or correspondence being established, we can easily obtain the object segmentation based on the disparity values [2]. The results will be the object and background regions, respectively. In order not to accumulate the error into the next step, we further apply texture smooth check to derive regions, within which both disparity and texture are relatively smooth. And then, a post-processing algorithm based on the size of the segmented regions will be applied here to improve the accuracy, the details will be discussed later.

To examine the texture of the internal region, we adopted a simple binary texture representation technique [8]. This technique can be replaced by any other texture features such as those proposed in MPEG-7 etc. As a matter of fact, we are in the process of investigating other texture features including other content descriptors to see if any improvement can be achieved.

Given a pixel x, the binary texture representation compares its value with its eight neighboring pixels and produces a texture indicator by the following equation:

$$b_i = \begin{cases} 1 & if \ x \geq y_i \\ 0 & otherwise \end{cases} \quad i \in [0,7] \tag{9}$$

where the eight bits $b_0...b_7$(one byte) formulates an indicator for the texture information of the pixel $x$.

If the object region has $N$ pixels, we would have $N$ texture indicators. By counting the occurrence of each byte value, which is within [0, 255], we can produce a histogram for each segmented region, and this histogram can be used as a key to characterize the texture feature of the segmented region. This process also produces a texture map for the object and background region, respectively. Thus, the histogram and texture results will be stored in terms of object and background set in respect to the segmentation results. One example of such texture map is illustrated in Figure-1 (c).

### 2.3   Disparity Estimation for 2D Video Frames

As 2D videos do not normally have sufficient true depth information for stereo conversion, it becomes extremely difficult to extract their disparity values to reconstruct their stereo version. However, there exist some possibilities to estimate their disparity via processing other cues such as motion, content features including color and shape of the moving objects etc. In our work, we focused on texture match with those inside the library of disparities to allocate the closest possible disparity to similar texture regions inside the 2D video frames and complete the conversion of 2D to 3D.

To enable the search inside the library via texture features, we need to process the 2D video frames and segment them into regions, where texture feature can be extracted with reasonable consistency. Among many reported segmentation techniques in the published literature [10,13, 14], the seeded region-growing technique (SRG) in [10] remains to be the most suitable candidate for our purposes since we are looking for not only object segmentation, but region segmentation where texture consistency is maintained. One of the results via such SRG is shown in Figure-2.

Similar to the processing of those stereo image pairs in establishing the library of disparities, a texture map is constructed for each segmented region inside the 2D video frames, and the texture histogram is used as the indexing key to search for the best possible match of the segmented region inside the library of disparities. Given a set of texture histograms inside the library, $M = \{H_1^{3D}, H_2^{3D},... \}$, the best match of the texture map $H_{match}$ is obtained by:

$$H_{match} = \min_{H_i^{3D} \in M} \left( Difference \ (H^{2D}, H_i^{3D}) \right) \tag{10}$$

and $$Difference \ (H^{2D}, H_i^{3D}) = \sum_{k=0}^{255} \sqrt{(h_k^{2D} - h_k^{3D})^2} \tag{11}$$

where $H^{2D} = \{h_0^{2D}, h_1^{2D}, .... h_{255}^{2D}\}$ and $H_i^{3D} = \{h_0^{3D}, h_1^{3D}, ...h_{255}^{3D}\}$ stand for the texture histogram for 2D video frames and the $i$th texture histogram inside the disparities library.

To improve the accuracy of the matched disparity of the candidate region, one possible way is to put in a pre-processing algorithm before the matching algorithm above, which is the same as the one mentioned in section 2.1. As the different spatial positions of the object and background regions in the real world plane, the disparity characteristics of them represented in the same image plane will be dissimilar, which makes the disparity value of the foreground object region is normally bigger than the background ones. We first distinguish the foreground object regions with the background in the segmentation results and store them into object group and background group, respectively. Secondly, considering the big objects may be matched with the small objects in the library, we decompose each group into three sub-groups based on their size, that is:

$$\frac{size_{region}}{size_{frame}} = \begin{cases} (0,0.3] \rightarrow group\ 1 \\ (0.3,0.6] \rightarrow group 2 \\ (0.6,1] \rightarrow group\ 3 \end{cases} \quad (12)$$

where $size_{region}$ and $size_{frame}$ are the number of pixels in object region and the frame, respectively. The details will be discussed in the following section. This preprocessing also needs to be added into the preprocessing of the stereo image pair part.

Corresponding to $H_{match}$, its disparity map for the matched region inside the library can be retrieved. In principle, this retrieved disparity map can be allocated to the region of the 2D video frame. As the two matched regions may not have exactly the same size, further processing is required. To illustrate the concept, we use two ways to allocate the disparity values to the region inside the 2D video frame to complete its pseudo-stereo conversion. One is to simply use the average disparity values inside the matched region, and the other is to use the resized true disparity value.

## 3   Experimental Results and Conclusions

To evaluate the effectiveness of the proposed algorithm, we applied three publicly video clips to carry out the experiments. (The clips can be found though the web address of http://www-2.cs.cmu.edu/~cil/v-images.html.) To enable stereo viewing and assessment of the stereo effect inside the converted video sequences, we take each original video frame as reference (left) frame, and reconstruct a right frame according to the disparity values estimated from previous section [2,11,12]. And then, a pseudo-stereo frame will be created by writing the red component of the left frame and the green component of the right frame into its red and green layer, respectively. And the blue layer will be set as zeros. As a result, the final converted pseudo-stereo video can only be viewed with those red and green glasses. The disparity map is constituted by different intensity regions which represent the degree of the disparity between the left and right frame from the distance of the image reference plane to the world reference plane. Thus, the brighter the region is, the more it closes to the camera. The final results are illustrated in Figure-3, in which (b) uses the resized true disparity values to generate the final result (e), compared with (a, c) use the averaged disparity values.

**Fig. 2.** (a) Segmented object in 'slient'; (b) Segmented object region in 'Miss America'

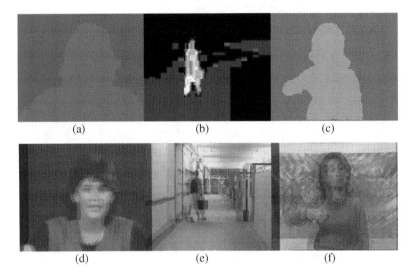

**Fig. 3.** (a~c) Disparity map of three video frames. (d~f) Converted colorful pseudo-stereo frames for (a~c).

In this paper, we proposed a pseudo-stereo conversion algorithm to convert conventional 2D videos into their stereo versions to explore the possibility of providing rich sources of 3D visual content out of conventional 2D videos. The work is important in the sense that present visual content production is dominated by two dimensional and 3D media production is very limited. While the proposed algorithm achieves certain level of stereo effect, there exist potential for further research and improvement, which can be identified as: (i) evaluation of all the available texture features is needed to ensure that the matched texture produces a matched disparity map; (ii) other cues need to be investigated and integrated into the process of disparity estimation for the 2D video conversion. In summary, our work described in the paper has initiated a new horizon for pseudo-stereo conversion of 2D videos along the direction of content-based approach, where promising results have been achieved and significant potential also exists for further research and development.

# References

1. Dimitrios Tzovaras, Ioannis Kompatsiaris, Michael G. Strintzis, "3D object articulation and motion estimation in model-based stereoscopic video conference image sequence analysis and coding", Signal Processing: Image Communication 14(1999) 817-840

2. Ping An; Chaohui Lu; Zhaoyang Zhang;, 'Object segmentation using stereo images', Communications, Circuits and Systems, 2004 International Conference on Volume 1, 27-29 June 2004 Page(s):534 - 538 Vol.1

3. N. Grammalidis, S. Malassiotis, D. Tzovaras, M. G. Strintzis, 'Stereo image sequence coding based on three-dimensional motion estimation compensation', Signal Processing: Image Communication 7 (Augest 1995) 129-145.

4. J.Liu, R.Skerjanc, 'Stereo and motion correspondence in a sequence of stereo images', Signal Processing: Image Process. 3 (September 1995) 589-609.

5. A. Tamtaoui, C. Labit, 'Constrained disparity motion estimators for 3DTV image sequence coding', Signal Processing: Image communication 4 (Nov. 1991) 45-54.

6. Y. L. Murphey, J. chen, J. Crossman, J. Zhang, P. Richardson, L. Sieh, 'Depth Finder, A Real-time Depth Detection System for Aided Friveing', Proceedings of the IEEE intelligent vehicles symposium 2000 Dearborn (MI), USA, OCT 3-5, 2ooo.

7. H. Guo and Y. Lu, "Depth Detection of Targets in a Monocular Image Sequence," 18th Digital Avionic Systems Conference, 1999.

8. Feng G.C. and Jiang J. "Image extraction in DCT domain" IEE Proceedings: Vision, Image and Signal Processing, Vol 150, No. 1, pp 20-27, 2003.

9. Honig, J.; Heit, B.; Bremont, J.' Visual depth perception based on optical blur', Image Processing, 1996. Proceedings. International Conference on, Volume: 1, 16-19 Sept. 1996 (721 – 724) vol.1

10. Adams, R.; Bischof. L; "Seeded region growing", Pattern Analysis and Machine Intelligence, IEEE Transactions on Volume 16, Issue 6, June 1994 Page(s):641 - 647

11. G. Fielding, M. Kam, 'Disparity maps for dynamic stereo', Pattern Recognition 34 (2001) 531-545.

12. U.R. Dhond, J.K. Aggarwal, Structure from stereo: a review, IEEE Transaction Systems Man Cybernet. 19 (6) (1989) 1489}1510.

13. Eftychis Sifakis; Ilias Grinials; Georgios Tziritas; Video Segmentation Using Fast Marching and Region Growing Algorithms; EURASIP journal on applied signal processing 2002: 4, 379-388

14. Chantal Revol, Michel Jourlin; A new minimum variance region growing algorithm for image segmentation; Pattern Recognition Letters 18(1997) 249-258.

15. Wildes, R.P.;' Direct recovery of three-dimensional scene geometry from binocular stereo disparity', Pattern Analysis and Machine Intelligence, IEEE Transactions on Volume 13, Issue 8, Aug. 1991 Page(s):761 - 774

16. Kanade, T.; Okutomi, M.; 'A stereo matching algorithm with an adaptive window: theory and experiment' Pattern Analysis and Machine Intelligence, IEEE Transactions on Volume 16, Issue 9, Sept. 1994 Page(s):920 - 932

# An Automated Facial Pose Estimation Using Surface Curvature and Tetrahedral Structure of a Nose

Ik-Dong Kim[1], Yeunghak Lee[2], and Jae-Chang Shim[1]

[1] Dept. of Computer Engineering, Andong National Univ.,
388 Songcheon-Dong, Andong, Kyungpook, 760-749, Korea (R.O.K)
{kid7, jcshim}@andong.ac.kr
[2] SEECS Yeunganam Univ.,
214-1 Dae-dong, Kyongsan-si, Kyungpook, 712-749, Korea (R.O.K)
annaturu@yumail.ac.kr

**Abstract.** This paper introduces an automated 3D face pose estimation method using the tetrahedral structure of a nose. This method is based on the feature points extracted from a face surface using curvature descriptors. A nose is the most protruding component in a 3D face image. A nose shape that is composed of the feature points such as a nasion, nose tip, nose base, and nose lobes, and is similar to a tetrahedron. Face pose can be estimated by fitting the tetrahedron to the coordinate axes. Each feature point can be localized by curvature descriptors. This method can be established using nasion, nose tip, and nose base. It can be applied to face tracking and face recognition.

## 1 Introduction

The interests and expectations of biometric identification have been greatly increased recently as a more accurate identification system is required for various security matters. A face recognition system can be used without any physical contact − not like other biometric recognition systems, for example, fingerprint or iris recognition − therefore, people feel more comfortable when they use the face recognition system. So far, 2D-intensity face images have been mostly used for existing face recognition, but the images are too sensitive when illumination varies[1], which can affect the result of a recognition. For this reason, 3D face recognition[3-7] has been studied to overcome the weakness of a 2D-based recognition system. 3D range images are less sensitive to illumination variance than 2D images. The accuracy of features extracted from face images directly affects the results of face recognition[2]. Facial pose also affects the result of the feature extraction and the face recognition process. This should be considered in the pre-processing stage.

Many researchers use 2D intensity images and color images in pose estimation[8-16]. They are based on color and template matching[8-9], pattern classifier based estimation[10], graph matching method[11-12], feature and template based matching[13-15], and trained view based matching[16]. Eye parallel measure, or the geometrical structure of eyes and nose, is often used to estimate the pose. But 2D-based pose estimation is affected by illumination. Some others have researched about pose with 3D images and features[4, 17, 18]. 3D-depth images can give more robust and

J. Blanc-Talon et al. (Eds.): ACIVS 2005, LNCS 3708, pp. 276−283, 2005.
© Springer-Verlag Berlin Heidelberg 2005

abundant information than intensity images for pose estimation. Lee et al.[4] calculated orientation angles using the similarity of the left and right sides of the nose tip and the modified centroid and moments. Morency et al.[18] created a face model from intensity images and depth images and estimated a pose based on the trained eigenspace for every view.

This paper proposes a simple feature-based facial pose estimation method. The nose is the most protruding component of a face. We hypothesize the human nose is a tetrahedral structure that is composed of five vertices: nasion, nose tip, left and right nose lobes, and nose base. It is also assumed that the nose base point is at the center of the two nose lobes. In Fig. 1, if $\overrightarrow{N_n N_b}$ is not parallel to the y-axis or $\overrightarrow{N_b N_t}$ is not parallel to the z-axis, we assume that the tetrahedron is in an oriented state.

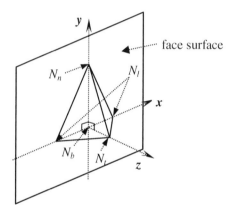

**Fig. 1.** Tetrahedral structure of a nose($N_n$: nasion, $N_b$: nose base, $N_t$: nose tip, $N_l$: nose lobes)

Surface curvature is the most robust feature descriptor in a 3D surface image. Every vertex of the tetrahedron can be extracted after analyzing maximum, minimum, and Gaussian curvatures on a face surface. Among those feature points, only three points, nasion, nose tip, and nose base, are used in this face pose estimation.

## 2  Data Acquisition

The sample data were collected with 4DCulture's 3D face scanner[19] which uses the laser triangulation principle. The laser triangulation method has higher precision than other 3D registration methods. This scanner has a profiler that projects a horizontal laser slit ray and moves it from the top of the head to the neck. At the same time, a CCD camera captures a three-second silhouette image that contains a laser profile. The scanner can only get a laser profile of the face by attaching an optical filter ahead of the CCD camera, and it removes noise and finds center profile from the input images. Then it creates 3D range image by merging center profiles extracted from each frame. The 3D face image consists of 320×400 range data that are stored in $2\frac{1}{2}$D. Robust and superior recognition could be possible using 3D features because 3D images that contain depth information are more invariant in different lighting conditions.

## 3  Nose Feature Extraction Using Surface Curvature

In this section, we extract a nose and nose feature points around the nose. Original 3D face images have some noise because of laser speckle noise at the acquisition stage. We preprocessed the input image with a 5×5 average filter to remove the noise. If face surface is a polynomial-like equation (1), it can be solved from Sahota's expansion[20].

$$Z(x, y) = a_{20}x^2 + a_{11}xy + a_{02}y^2 + a_{10}x + a_{01}y + a_{00} . \tag{1}$$

Sahota et al. calculated coefficients of (1) by least square error fit, and calculated maximum( $\kappa_1$ ) and minimum( $\kappa_2$ ) curvatures by defining the polynomial into the first and second differential forms. Gaussian curvature( $\kappa_3$ ) is the product of maximum and minimum curvatures. After calculating the maximum curvature ( $\kappa_1$ ), the binary image of $\kappa_1$ can be created by Eq. (2). After calculating the minimum curvature ( $\kappa_2$ ), the binary image of $\kappa_2$ can be created by Eq. (3).

$$B\kappa_1 = \begin{cases} 255, & \kappa_1 \geq 0.1 \\ 0, & otherwise . \end{cases} \tag{2}$$

$$B\kappa_2 = \begin{cases} 255, & \kappa_2 \geq 0.1 \\ 0, & otherwise . \end{cases} \tag{3}$$

$$B\kappa_3 = \begin{cases} 255, & 0.03 \leq \kappa_3 \leq 1.0 \\ 0, & otherwise . \end{cases} \tag{4}$$

Generally, a human face has some intersecting points of $\kappa_1$ and $\kappa_2$, especially in nasion, nose base, and nose lobes. We can extract the nose region, (d) in Fig. 2, by analyzing the blobs of the difference image (that is, the binary image of the $B\kappa_2$ image subtracted from the $B\kappa_1$ image based on the Table 1). Among them, the blob that meets the constraints is chosen as a nose. Fig. 3 presents the resulting image in every step for the nose blob extraction processes.

**Table 1.** Constraints for a nose candidate blob     (unit : pixel)

| Features | Value |
|---|---|
| Width | minimum(35) and maximum width(70) |
| Height | minimum(35) and maximum height(70) |
| | width+10 < height |
| Etc. | $uw$(width of upper side) < $lw$(width of lower side) |
| | $10 \leq |uw - lw| \leq 40$ |

Three feature points, nasion, nose tip and nose base, contribute to pose estimation and are localized by analyzing Gaussian curvature based on Eq. (4) around the nose.

The nose tip( $N_t$ ) is the CoG(Center of Gravity) of the largest Gaussian curvature area in the nose. The nasion( $N_n$ ) is the CoG of the nearest and largest Gaussian curvature area from the nasion seed point( $N_n'$ ) which is the center of the nose on the upper side. The nose base( $N_b$ ) is the CoG of the nearest and largest Gaussian curvature area from the nose base seed point( $N_b'$ ) which is the center of the nose on the lower side.

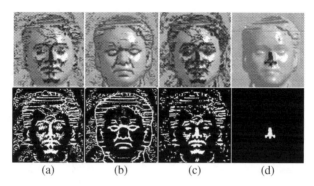

(a)            (b)            (c)            (d)

**Fig. 2.** Nose localization (a) maximum curvature image(upper) and its binary image(lower), (b) minimum curvature image(upper) and its binary image(lower), (c) maximum curvature image overlapped by minimum curvature image(upper) and difference image of the $B\kappa_2$ from the $B\kappa_1$ (lower), (d) extracted nose region overlapped on 3D face image(upper) and binary nose region image(lower)

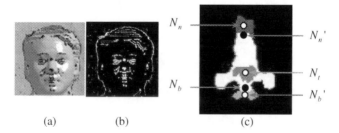

(a)            (b)                    (c)

**Fig. 3.** Nose feature extraction (a) 3D rendering image of Gaussian curvature areas(black), (b) Binary image of Gaussian curvature areas(white), (c) Nasal feature points around the nose

## 4   Pose Estimation Using Tetrahedral Structure of a Nose

Those three feature points which were extracted in section 3 are used to estimate a pose. The novel pose estimation method analyzes the geometrical orientation of the tetrahedral structure of a nose. The z-axis orientation is estimated first, and then the pose estimation of the y and x-axis are followed in sequence.

## 4.1  Yaw (z-Axis)

The orientation about z-axis can be estimated with nasion( $N_n$ ) and nose base( $N_b$ ) as shown in Fig. 4 (a). The angle of orientation, $\theta_z$ , is calculated by Eq. (5). It is more reasonable than the Hesher's[21] case that calculates angle using nasion and nose tip.

$$
\begin{aligned}
\overrightarrow{N_h} &= N_b^{'}(y) - N_n(y) \\
\overrightarrow{N_{bd}} &= N_b^{'}(x) - N_b(x) \\
\theta_z &= \tan^{-1}\left(\frac{\overrightarrow{N_{bd}}}{\overrightarrow{N_h}}\right).
\end{aligned}
\tag{5}
$$

$N_n^{'}$ is nasion on the input image and $N_n$ is nasion on the ideal image. The $x$ and the $y$ are coordinate values of each feature point. After calculating the $\theta_z$ , face image can be compensated by inverse matrix transform for better pose estimation along the y- and x-axis. $\overrightarrow{N_{bd}}$ is the distance of the $x$ coordinates between $N_b{'}$ and $N_b$ .

## 4.2  Pitch (y-Axis)

The orientation about the y-axis can be estimated with nose base( $N_b$ ) and nose tip( $N_t$ ) as shown in Fig. 4 (b). The angle of orientation, $\theta_y$ , is calculated by Eq. (6). $N_t{'}$ is the nose tip on the input image and $N_{tz}^{'}$ is the foot of perpendicular from $N_t{'}$ to $\overrightarrow{N_b N_n}$ .

$$
\begin{aligned}
\overrightarrow{N_t N_{tz}} &= N_t^{'}(x) - N_{tz}^{'}(x) \\
\overrightarrow{N_b N_{tz}} &= N_{tz}^{'}(z) - N_b^{'}(z) \\
\theta_y &= \tan^{-1}\left(\frac{\overrightarrow{N_t N_{tz}}}{\overrightarrow{N_b N_{tz}}}\right).
\end{aligned}
\tag{6}
$$

## 4.3  Roll (x-axis)

The orientation about the x-axis can be estimated with nasion( $N_n$ ) and nose base( $N_b$ ) as shown in Fig. 4 (c). The angle of orientation, $\theta_x$ , is calculated by Eq. (7).

$$
\begin{aligned}
\overrightarrow{N_{Td}} &= N_b^{'}(z) - N_b(z) \\
\overrightarrow{N_{Th}} &= N_n(y) - N_b^{'}(y) \\
\theta_x &= \tan^{-1}\left(\frac{\overrightarrow{N_{Td}}}{\overrightarrow{N_{Th}}}\right).
\end{aligned}
\tag{7}
$$

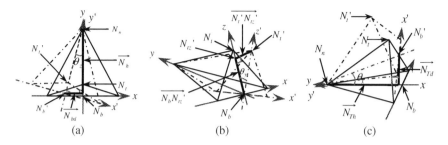

**Fig. 4.** Orientation calculation (a) Yaw(z-axis), (b) Pitch(y-axis), (c) Roll(x-axis)

# 5 Experiments

3D facial pose images for experiments were scanned by 4D Culture's face scanner based on the laser triangulation principle. The proposed pose estimation method was tested about 41 orientated images. Yaw and Pitch angles have 7 poses from -30° to +30° in every 10°. And Roll has 5 poses from -20° to +20° in every 10°. The distance between face and camera was 1.0m. Face segmentation was not executed before feature extraction. The Fig. 5 (a) shows the input pose images and (b) presents the results of pose compensation images after pose estimation by the proposed algorithm.

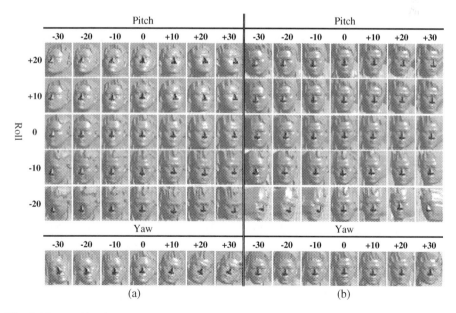

**Fig. 5.** The resulting images of the proposed pose estimation algorithm. (a) Before pose estimation, (b) Pose compensation after pose estimation

In most cases, proposed pose estimation and compensation were done successfully. But some cases were not, because of feature extraction errors.

The eigenface-based face recognition method was also studied. The 80 frontal 3D face images of the ANU3DFACE-1 database were chosen as sample data. From these, 40 images were used as learning data; the other 40 were used as test data. Each image was normalized by nose size, and segmented into 80×80 new face image which had nose tip in center. We grouped the recognition result into four groups. The result are presented in Fig. 6. The Euclidian distances of face matching are sorted in ascending order. We ranked the result as Rank 2, 4, 6, and 8. After pose estimation and pose compensation, the classification result was improved. The experiment with Rank 6 can classify about 93% correctness.

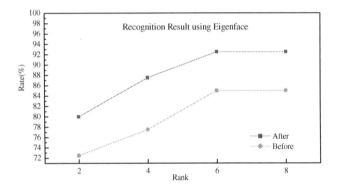

**Fig. 6.** The result of face recognition based on the eigenface method between before and after orientation compensation by the proposed algorithm

# 6 Conclusion

This paper proposed a new feature-based pose estimation method for robust 3D face recognition. Pose estimation must be preceded before matching, for better accuracy in face recognition. We hypothesized a nose, which is the most outstanding feature in 3D face, as a tetrahedral structure. The structure, composed by feature points such as nasion, nose tip, nose base, and nose lobes, is similar to a tetrahedron. The three feature points, nasion, nose tip, and nose base, which contribute to pose estimation, were extracted by surface curvature descriptors such as maximum, minimum, and Gaussian curvatures.

We calculated the orientation of the face by analyzing the geometrical feature vectors composed by vertices of the tetrahedron against coordinate axes. We experimented with this method below the orientation of 30°. Face pose can be estimated with only three feature points. This pose estimation method can be applied to face recognition and pose tracking systems. For further work, the method for the orientation above 30° is required to be studied.

# References

1. R. Chellappa, C. L. Wilson, and S. Sirohey. Human and machine recognition of face: A survey, *Proceedings of the IEEE*, Vol. 83, No. 5(1995) 705-740
2. A. Nikolaidis and I. Pitas, Facial feature extraction and determination of pose, *Pattern Recognition*, Vol. 33 (2000) 1783-1791
3. J. C. Lee and E. Milios, Matching range image of human faces, *Third International Conference on Computer Vision* (1990) 722-726
4. Y. H. Lee, K. W. Park, J. C. Shim, T. H. Yi, 3D Face Recognition using Statistical Multiple Features for the Local Depth Information, *16th International Conference on Vision Interface* (2003)
5. Fujiwara, On the detection of feature points of 3D facial image and its application to 3D facial caricature, *International Conference on 3-D digital Imaging and Modeling*(1999).
6. G. Gordon, Face Recognition based on depth maps and surface curvature, *SPIE Geometric methods in Computer Vision*, San Diego, Vol. 1570 (1991)
7. H. T. Tanaka, M. Ikeda and Hchiaki, Curvature-based face surface recognition using spherical correlation, *Third IEEE International Conference on Automatic Face and Gesture Recognition* (1998) 372-377
8. T. Fromherz, P. Stucki and M. Bichsel, A Survey of Face Recognition, MML Technical Report, No. 97.01, Dept. of Computer Science, University of Zurich (1997)
9. D. Beymer, Face Recognition Under Varying Pose, *Proc. IEEE Conf. Computer Vision and Pattern Recognition* (1994) 756-761
10. S. Birchfield. Elliptical head tracking using intensity gradients and color histograms, *IEEE Conference on Computer Vision and Pattern Recognition* (1998) 232-237
11. N. Oliver, A. Pentland, and F. Berard, Lafter: Lips and face real time tracker, *Computer Vision and Pattern Recognition* (1997)
12. J. Ng and S. Gong, Composite support vector machines for detection of faces across views and pose estimation, *Image and Vision Computing*, Vol. 20, No. 5-6 (2002) 359-368
13. A H. Gee, and R. Cipolla, Determining the gaze of faces in images, *Image and Vision Computing*, Vol. 12, No. 10 (1994) 639-647
14. N. Kruger, M. Potzsch, T. Maurer, and M. Rinne, Estimation of face position and pose with labeled graphs, In *British Machine Vision Conference*, Edinburgh (1996) 735-743
15. A. Lanitis, C. J. Taylor, and T. F. Cootes, A unified approach to coding and interpreting face images, In *IEEE International Conference on Computer Vision*, Cambridge, Massachusetts (1995) 368-373
16. A. Pentland, B. Moghaddam, and T. Starner, View-based and modular eigenspaces for face recognition, In *IEEE Conference on Computer Vision and Pattern Recognition*, Seattle, (1994) 84-91
17. T. S. Jebara, 3D Pose Estimation and Normalization for Face Recognition, Department of Electrical Engineering McGill University (1996)
18. L. P. Morency, P. Sundberg, T. Darrell, Pose Estimation using 3D View-Based Eigenspaces, *IEEE International Workshop on Analysis and Modeling of Faces and Gestures* (2003) 45
19. 3D Face Scanner, 4DCulture Co., http://www.4dculture.com/
20. Peet, F. G., and T. S. Sahota, Surface Curvature as a Measure of Image Texture, *IEEE Tran. on Pattern Analysis and Machine Intelligence*, Vol. 7, No. 6 (1985) 734
21. C. Hesher and G. Erlebacher, Principal Component Analysis of Range Images for Facial Recognition, *Proceedings of CISST*, Las Vegas (2002)

# Dynamic Pursuit with a Bio-inspired Neural Model

Claudio Castellanos Sánchez[1,2] and Bernard Girau[1]

[1] LORIA INRIA-Lorraine - Neuromimetic Intelligence team,
Campus Scientifique BP 239, 54506 Vandœuvre-lès-Nancy, France
[2] Scholarship of the National Council of Science and Technology (CONACyT), México
{castella, girau}@loria.fr

**Abstract.** In this paper we present a bio-inspired connectionist model for visual perception of motion and its pursuit. It is organized in three stages: a causal spatio-temporal filtering of Gabor-like type, an antagonist inhibition mechanism and a densely interconnected neural population. These stages are inspired by the neural treatment and the interactions of the primary visual cortex, middle temporal area and superior visual areas. This model has been evaluated on natural image sequences.

## 1 Introduction

The estimation of motion is a cognitive task enclosed in the perception-action loop of autonomous systems interacting with dynamic real-world environments. In these systems, connectionist models bring their power of generalization and their robustness to noise. Their intrinsic parallelism combined with local processings offer various areas of research for the development of real-time embedded models of perception-action.

In the field of autonomous robotics, the pursuit of an object in a dynamic environment involves complex tasks and reduced computing times. Several bio-inspired models exist to propose solutions to this problem by modelling the primary visual cortex (V1), the middle temporal area (MT) [8] and the middle superior temporal area (MST) [5,12]. We propose here a bio-inspired connectionist model that integrates the inter- and intra-interactions of the V1, MT, MST and superior visual areas for this cognitive task. Our model is based on our motion perception model proposed in [2], as well as on the focus and attention model of [11,7] in which neural sub-populations emerge. Our global model includes three modules: a spatio-temporal filtering based on Gabor spatial filters, a strongly localized inhibition mechanism based on antagonism criteria [2], and the emergence of a single target in a dynamic environment through the evolution of a densely interconnected neural population.

We first propose a rapid survey of the motion perception model we proposed in [2] and of the attention model of [11,7]. We then present their coupling and finally we describe the evaluation of this coupled model on several real image sequences.

## 2 A Connectionist Model for Motion Perception and Pursuit

Our neural model is based on the local and massively distributed processing defined in [2], where we have proposed a retinotopically organized model of the following perception principle: local motion informations of a retinal image are extracted by neurons

J. Blanc-Talon et al. (Eds.): ACIVS 2005, LNCS 3708, pp. 284–291, 2005.
© Springer-Verlag Berlin Heidelberg 2005

in the primary visual cortex, V1, with local receptive fields restricted to small spatial interaction areas; these neurons are densely interconnected for excitatory-inhibitory interactions.

In this paper we extend these two-modules of model by coupling it to a third module based on a bio-inspired model of focus and attention also developed in our team.

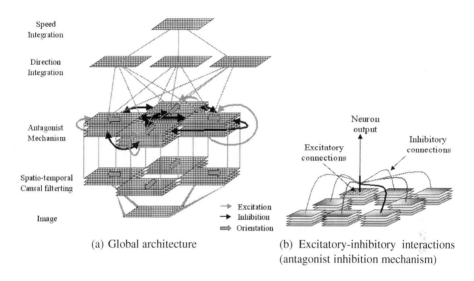

(a) Global architecture

(b) Excitatory-inhibitory interactions (antagonist inhibition mechanism)

**Fig. 1.** General architecture of our model for motion perception [2]

The first two main stages of the model (see figure 1(a)) will be described in this section: the causal spatio-temporal filtering and the antagonist inhibition mechanism. The biological foundations and the mathematical details will not be discussed in this paper (see [2]). The additional third module will be presented in subsection 2.4.

## 2.1 Causal Spatio-Temporal Filtering

The first stage of the model depicted in figure 1(a) performs a causal spatio-temporal filtering. It models the magnocellular cells seen as motion sensors that depend on the gradient of image intensity and on its temporal derivatives [6,4,3]. This filtering is performed in two steps: a spatial filtering and a causal temporal processing [2,10].

For the spatial filtering, Gabor filters are implemented as image convolution kernels in $\Theta$ different directions. It is represented in figure 1(a) for $\Theta = 4$ orientations (though we usually work with $\Theta = 8$).

Then the causal temporal processing involves the computation of a temporal average of Gabor filters for each direction and for a set of search places that correspond to $V$ assumed different speeds of each pixel. In other words, for each given assumed direction and speed, they reinforce the local motion with the average of the Gabor filters applied to past images an assumed past places. This principle is valid under the strong hypothesis of a high enough sampling frequency to ensure a local motion detection and an immediate constant local speed.

The computations described in this subsection have been parallelized and implemented on FPGA circuits for real-time embedded motion perception [10].

## 2.2   Antagonist Inhibition Mechanism

The second stage of the model of [2] (figure 1(a)) emulates an antagonist inhibition mechanism by means of excitatory-inhibitory local interactions in the different oriented cortical columns of V1 [1] in order to strengthen the coherence of the motion areas.

In this mechanism each neuron receive both excitation and inhibition signals from neurons in a neighborhood or influence range to regulate its activity. In figure 1(b) we show the excitatory and inhibitory local interactions where neurons interact in a close neighborhood centered around the neuron under consideration. The strong interactions in this mechanism change the internal state of neurons and, consequently, their influence range, which generates a dynamic adaptive process.

As in usual excitatory-inhibitory neural models, the weighted connections to and from neurons have modulated strength according to the distance from one another. Nevertheless, we call it an antagonist inhibition mechanism because the inhibitory connections among neurons regulate downwards the activity of opposing or antagonist neurons, i.e. neurons that do not share a common or similar orientation and speed. On the other hand, excitatory connections increase the neuron activity towards the emergence of coherent responses, i.e. grouping neuron responses to similar orientations and speeds through an interactive process.

Then, the updating of the internal state of a neuron is

$$
\begin{aligned}
\eta \frac{\delta H(x,y,T)}{\delta T} = & -A \cdot H(x,y,T) \\
& +(B - H(x,y,T)) \cdot Exc(x,y,T) \\
& -(C + H(x,y,T)) \cdot Inh(x,y,T)
\end{aligned}
\tag{1}
$$

where $-A \cdot H(\cdot)$ is the passive decay, $(B - H(\cdot)) \cdot Exc(\cdot)$ the feedback excitation and, $(C + H(\cdot)) \cdot Inh(\cdot)$ the feedback inhibition. Each feedback term includes a state-dependent nonlinear signal $(Exc(x,y,T)$ and $Inh(x,y,T))$ and an automatic gain control term $(B - H(\cdot)$ and $C + H(\cdot)$, respectively). $H(x,y,T)$ is the internal state of the neuron localised in $(x,y)$ at time $T$, $Exc(x,y,T)$ is the activity due to the contribution of excitatory interactions in the neighborhood $\Omega^{\Theta_E}_{(x,y)}$ and $Inh(x,y,T)$ is the activity due to the contribution of inhibitory interactions in the neighborhood $\Omega^{\Theta_I}_{(x,y)}$. Both neighborhoods depend on the activity level of the chosen neuron in each direction. $A$, $B$ and $C$ are the real constant values and $\eta$ is the learning rate. For more details on the excitation and inhibition areas see [2].

Let $\rho$ be the influence range of neuron $(x,y)$ in this stage. This neuron receives at most $\rho^2$ excitatory connections from neurons with the same direction and speed and at most $(V \cdot \Theta - 1) \cdot \rho^2$ inhibitory connections from other close neurons.

At this level, each pixel corresponds to $\Theta \cdot V$ different neurons that encode informations of directions and speeds. Their integration is performed in a intermediate stage named velocity integration.

## 2.3    Velocity Integration

In [2], the results of the antagonist inhibition mechanism are integrated thanks to a winner-take-all process defined by

$$\hat{H}(x,y,t) = max_{v \in V} \left( \sum_{\theta} H_{(\theta,v)}(x,y,T) \cdot \vartheta_{\theta} \right) \tag{2}$$

where $\hat{H}(x,y,t)$ is the winner neuron and $\vartheta_{\theta}$ is the unit vector in direction $\theta$. $H_{(\theta,v)}(x,y,T)$ is the final result of the antagonism mechanism in direction $\theta$ and for a supposed speed $v$. Then we search the maximum of the vector sum on all directions of each supposed speed. $T$ and $t$ are the epoch in the antagonism mechanism and the time in the images sequence, respectively. This stage corresponds to both parts labeled *integration* in figure 1(a).

Until there, the model keeps entirely local and distributed with motion areas being relatively coherent in orientation and speed, but without a global response. Next subsections describe our coupled model that extracts a global response using the bio-inspired attention model of [7,11].

## 2.4    Visual Attention

The third module of our model consists of a neural population which interactions target the emergence of attention. The output of the second module (antagonist inhibition) is coupled to the input of the attention module. Before describing this coupling, we will present the main principles of the attention model. See [7,11] for the mathematical and implementation details.

**Distributed Model for Visual Attention.** This bio-inspired model is based on the interactions between the superior visual areas (V4, Inferotemporal -IT- and the Frontal Eye Field -FEF-), and some other ones (superior colliculus, pulvinar nuclei and thalamus). The authors propose a model of interactions between eight different maps and their interactions within each map with the application of the Continuum Neural Field Theory 2D [9].

Figure 2 describes the eight maps of this model and the neuron required to switch attention. Three processing levels may be found: in the first level (attention emergence) only one activity bubble of close neurons may emerge in the neural population of the input, visual and focus maps. In the second level (attention fixation) the FEF and memory maps sustain the bubble activity and localisation that can keep track of this stimulus if another one takes back focus. In the last level (attention switching) the striatum, GPI, thalamus and inhibition maps combined with the reward neuron make the necessary interactions to switch attention (supervised mode).

Some of these maps use lateral interactions (see figure 2): each neuron is completely connected to the other ones in the same map. The communication between different maps of this model is based on the principle of local receptive field.

In the maps that use lateral interactions, the internal state of each neuron in a map $A$ with adjacent map $\hat{A}$ is updated according to

$$\tau\frac{\partial u(x,y,t)}{\partial t} = -u(x,y,t) + \int_A w_A((x,y)-(\bar{x},\bar{y}))f(u(\bar{x},\bar{y},t))dxdy$$
$$+ \int_{\hat{A}} s((x,y),(\hat{x},\hat{y}))I(\hat{x},\hat{y},t)d\hat{x}d\hat{y} + h \tag{3}$$

where $u(x,y,t)$ is the membrane potential of the neuron in position $(x,y)$ at time $t$. $f(\cdot)$ represents the mean firing rate, $I(\hat{x},\hat{y},t)$ is the neuron input $(\hat{x},\hat{y})$ at time $t$ in map $\hat{A}$. $w_A((x,y)-(\bar{x},\bar{y}))$ is the lateral connection weight function in map $A$, given by

$$w_A((x,y)-(\bar{x},\bar{y})) = Bexp\left(\frac{|(x,y)-(\bar{x},\bar{y})|^2}{b^2}\right) - Cexp\left(\frac{|(x,y)-(\hat{x},\hat{y})|^2}{c^2}\right) \tag{4}$$

and $s((x,y),(\hat{x},\hat{y}))$ is the adjacent connection weight function of neuron $(\hat{x},\hat{y}) \in \hat{A}$ to neuron $(x,y) \in A$ defined by

$$s((x,y)-(\hat{x},\hat{y})) = Bexp\left(\frac{|(x,y)-(\hat{x},\hat{y})|^2}{b^2}\right) \tag{5}$$

with $B,C,b,c \in \Re_+^*$.

In the maps without lateral interactions, the internal state of each neuron in a map $A$ with adjacent map $\hat{A}$ is updated according to

$$\tau\frac{\partial u(x,y,t)}{\partial t} = -u(x,y,t) + \int_{\hat{A}} s((x,y),(\hat{x},\hat{y}))I(\hat{x},\hat{y},t)d\hat{x}d\hat{y} + h \tag{6}$$

Each map send its results to the next maps applying equation 6 according to figure 2. The free parameters have been chosen as reported [11].

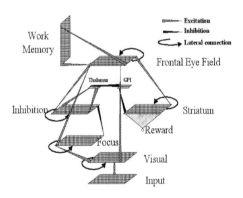

**Fig. 2.** General architecture of the visual attention model [11]

**Coupling of Both Models.** The attention model recovers the most salient characteristics in the image by means of the application of a Gaussian filter focused on a specific colour, i.e. this model was designed to focus attention on objects with predefined colour patterns. Then, this preprocessing step generates outputs in [-1,1] and it compresses the image to $40 \times 40$ pixels.

But it is not always possible to search for a predefined color in real scenes to follow an object. Our model supplies an instantaneous image of the moving objects without any immobile object. Then coupling this attention model with our motion perception model cancels the restriction of searching only for predefined color.

Following the architecture of figure 1(a), both stages labeled "integration" now use a strong winner-take-all process defined by

$$\overline{H}(x,y,t) = \frac{1}{\xi_{CN} \cdot \eta_{CN}} \sum_{\xi_{CN} \times \eta_{CN}} max_{\theta \in \Theta, v \in V} H_{(\theta,v)}(x,y,T) \tag{7}$$

where $\xi_{CN}$ and $\eta_{CN}$ define the receptive field size required to reduce the number of outputs of our antagonist inhibition module to a size that may be handled by the attention module.

Next section illustrates the motion perception and pursuit performed by the whole coupled model when applied to real image sequences.

## 3   Results

The free parameters of our model were set according to the suggestions in [2,11]. We chose three real image sequences of video surveillance. They include various numbers of RGB images, but all images are the same size: $384 \times 288$, and they are first grey-scaled. Sequence ABrowse has 1043 images, AFight and BFight both have 551 images.

Figure 3 show four images of one chosen part for three different image sequences. The pursuit results for each chosen part of each sequence are shown in the last column.

The first real image sequence, named "ABrowse", may be split into four parts: (1) two persons are walking; (2) only one person is walking; (3) there is no motion; (4) one person is walking until the sequence is stopped. The first part is shown in the first row of figure 3.

The second real image sequence, named "AFight", may be split into five parts: (1) three persons are walking; (2) two persons are walking; (3) only one person is walking; (4) two persons are walking, approaching face to face, arguing and then striding towards different directions; (5) three persons are moving at the bottom of the image. The fourth part is very complex because two persons are arguing and the attention is always drawn towards the first one. This fourth part is shown in the second row of figure 3.

Finally, the third real image sequence, named "BFight", may be split into three parts: (1) there are four persons but only one is walking; (2) one person is walking, followed by another person coming from a different direction, then the second person joins the first one and they argue; (3) both persons stride towards opposite directions, and then join together a little further away. The second part is shown in the third row of figure 3.

In the first part of sequence ABrowse two persons are walking: one makes the big movements and remain in the center of the scene while the other one goes on walking. Our system always pursuits the last one. In the fourth part of sequence AFight two persons walk, argue and stride towards different directions but our system always pursuits the first one. Finally, in the second part of sequence BFight two persons walk, join and argue: even if the first one is smaller than the other one our system pursuits the first one.

Initial image          Intermediate 1          intermediate 2          Final image          Pursuit path

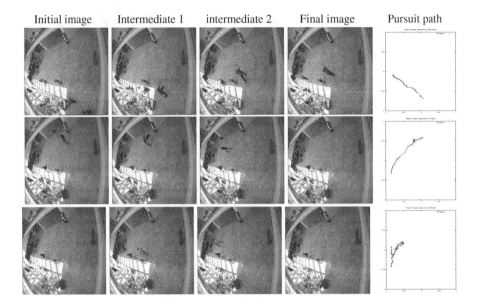

**Fig. 3.** Real image sequences used in this work: ABrowse, AFight and BFight, respectively in each row, and, from left to right, four images of each sequence and their pursuit path

In the three cases our system always focuses on the first moving person that holds attention of the memory map (to pursuit the other persons, one could use the supervised attention switching system of the model).

## 4   Conclusion and Discussion

This work is based on a coupling of two bio-inspired models developed in our connectionist research team: the first one performs motion perception, the second one makes it possible to focus attention. The whole model is fully inspired by the visual cortex system, the superior motor areas, and their relations.

Our model consists of three modules: a low-level analysis to detect local motions, then to detect coherent moving areas, and a high-level analysis for the emergence of focused attention. These modules are gathered into a densely interconnected bio-inspired model that uses weighted excitatory and inhibitory connections. Most excitatory interactions correspond to feed-forward receptive fields, whereas most inhibitory ones correspond to lateral interactions.

Our first experiments show that our model is able to detect moving persons or objects and to pursue them in an environment where other persons or objects move. The system appears as robust enough to avoid the loss of the original target. It is able to pursue objects in quite complex scenes without any predefined information. Nevertheless, in very complex scenes, this system may switch attention towards far more salient targets. Our current works aim at strengthening the focus stability at two levels: in the V1 model (including the antagonist inhibition mechanism) and in the superior cortical model (attention mechanism).

Other bio-inspired models perform object pursuit [5,8,12]. Our goal is to build a whole model using only local, highly distributed, and densely interconnected excitatory and inhibitory connections.

Our current works finalize our three-module model by introducing feedback connections from the third module towards the antagonist inhibition process module. Such backward interactions bring us closer to the cortex architecture, and it is able to strengthen the emergence of a robust pursuit of a moving target in a dynamic environment.

# References

1. Frédéric Alexandre. *Une modélisation fonctionnelle du cortex: la Colonne Cortical. Aspects visuels et moteurs.* PhD thesis, Henri Poincaré, Nancy, France, 1990.
2. Claudio Castellanos Sánchez, Bernard Girau, and Frédéric Alexandre. A connectionist approach for visual perception of motion. In Leslie Smith, Amir Hussain, and Igor Aleksander, editors, *Brain Inspired Cognitive Systems (BICS 2004)*, pages BIS3-1 1–7, September 2004.
3. P. Hammond and J. Reck. Influence of velocity on directional tuning of complex cells in cat striate cortex for texture motion. *Neuroscience Letters*, 19:309–314, 1981.
4. W. T. Newsome, M. S. Gizzi, and J. A. Movshon. Spatial and temporal properties of neurons in macaque mt. *Investigative Ophtalmology and Visual Science Supplement*, 24:106, 1983.
5. Christopher Pack, Stephen Grossberg, and Ennio Mingolla. A neural model of smooth pursuit control and motion perception by cortical area mst. Technical Report CAS/CNR-TR-99-023, Department of Cognitive and Neural Systems and Center for Adaptive Systems, 677 Beacon St, Boston, MA 02215, September 2000.
6. D. Pollen and S. Ronner. Phase relationships between adjacent simple cells in the visual cortex. *Science*, 212:1409–1411, 1981.
7. N. Rougier and J. Vitay. Emergence of attention within a neural population. *Accepted to Neural Networks*, 2005.
8. Eero P. Simoncelli and David J. Heeger. A model of neural responses in visual area mt. *Vision Research*, 38(5):743–761, 1998.
9. J. G. Taylor. Neural 'bubble' dynamics in two dimensions: foundations. *Biological Cybernetics*, 80(6):393–410, 1999.
10. César Torres Huitzil, Bernard Girau, and Claudio Castellanos Sánchez. Digital implementation of a bio-inspired neural model for motion estimation. In *International Joint Conference on Neural Networks 2005*, pages –, August 2005.
11. J. Vitay, N. P. Rougier, and F. Alexandre. A distributed model of spatial visual attention. In S. Wermter and G. Palm, editors, *Neural Learning for Intelligent Robotics*. Springer-Verlag, 2005.
12. Richard S. Zemel and Terrence J. Sejnowski. A model for encoding multiple object motions and self-motion in area mst of primate visual cortex. *The Journal of Neurosciences*, 18(1):531–547, 1998.

# Scene-Cut Processing in Motion-Compensated Temporal Filtering

Maria Trocan and Béatrice Pesquet-Popescu

ENST, Signal and Image Processing Department,
46, rue Barrault, 75634 Paris, France
{trocan, pesquet}@tsi.enst.fr

**Abstract.** Motion-compensated temporal filtering (MCTF) is a powerful technique entering scalable video coding schemes. However, its performance decreases significantly if the video signal correlation is poor and, in particular, when scene-cuts occur. In this paper we propose an improved structure for MCTF by detecting and processing the scene-cuts that may appear in video sequences. It significantly reduces the ghosting artefacts in the temporal approximation subband frames, providing a higher quality temporal scalability, and dramatically improves the global coding efficiency when such abrupt transitions happen.

## 1 Introduction

The 3-D subband schemes $(t + 2D)$ exploit the temporal interframe redundancy by applying an open-loop temporal wavelet transform over the frames of a video sequence. Temporally filtered subband frames are further spatially decomposed and can be encoded by different algorithms such as 3D-SPIHT [1] or MC-EZBC [2].

A weakness of the existing $t + 2D$ video codecs is related to the way the temporal filtering behaves near scene changes. Usually, the input video signal is partitioned into GOPs and temporally filtered without checking the correlation between the GOP frames. Moreover, the sliding window implementation of the temporal filtering is done using frames from adjacent GOPs in the processing of the current GOP. When the input signal involves complex motion transitions, and especially scene-cuts, this can translate into inefficient prediction/update operations, leading to poor quality results and also to reduced temporal scalability capabilities.

Several attempts to avoid the artefacts related to these abrupt changes have already been proposed for *hybrid* coding, such as the scene-cut detection and content-based sampling of video sequences [3] or video segmentation using encoding cost data [4], alleviating but not completely solving this problem.

In this paper we present a motion-compensated temporal transform coding scheme, specifically adapted to the detection and processing of the uncorrelated shots of the input video sequence. After the scene-cuts are detected, we encode each set of frames between two consecutive scene-cuts separately, by adapting

J. Blanc-Talon et al. (Eds.): ACIVS 2005, LNCS 3708, pp. 292–299, 2005.
© Springer-Verlag Berlin Heidelberg 2005

the temporal filtering to cope with arbitrary number of frames in a shot. An advantage of our scheme is that scene-cuts once eliminated, MCTF efficiency is maximal, as for highly-correlated video signals. The problem is related to border effects, and therefore is much easier to cope with in case of Haar MCTF. However, it has been shown [5,6,7] that the use of longer bidirectional filters, like the 5/3 filter bank, can take better advantage of the temporal redundancy between frames. Existing methods for adaptive GOP structure in the MCTF framework [8,9] basically detect changes and limit the number of temporal decomposition levels based on a measure of unconnected pixel percentage. However, compared with our approach, this technique does not make a strict correspondence between the scene cut and the GOP boundary. Our proposed approach varies the GOP size only on the frames previous to the transition, and these frames are encoded in several GOPs of power of two sizes. In this way, the scene cut does not span any GOP. We present therefore our scene-cut processing method in the framework of 5/3 MCTF, but our proposal can be adapted to other temporal filters.

The paper is organized as follows: in the next section, we recall the classical motion-compensated 5/3 temporal transform and present the method proposed in this framework for scene-cuts detection and processing. Section 3 illustrates by experimental results the coding performance of the proposed scheme. We conclude in Section 4.

## 2   Scene-Cut Detection and Processing

The MCTF approach consists in a hierarchical open-loopsubband motion- compensated decomposition. Let us denote by $x_t$ the original frames, $t$ being the time index, and by $h_t$ and $l_t$ the high-frequency (detail) and low-frequency (approximation) subband frames, respectively. For the 5/3 filterbank implemented in lifting form, the operators allowing to compute these subbands are bidirectional, and the equations have the following form (see also Fig. 1):

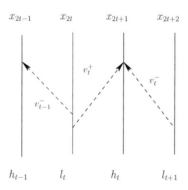

**Fig. 1.** MCTF with bidirectional predict and update lifting steps

$$\begin{cases} h_t = x_{2t+1} - \dfrac{1}{2}\big(\mathcal{F}(x_{2t}, \boldsymbol{v}_t^+) + \mathcal{F}(x_{2t+2}, \boldsymbol{v}_t^-)\big) \\ l_t = x_{2t} + \dfrac{1}{4}\big(\mathcal{F}^{-1}(h_{t-1}, \boldsymbol{v}_{t-1}^-) + \mathcal{F}^{-1}(h_t, \boldsymbol{v}_t^+)\big) \end{cases} \tag{1}$$

where $\mathcal{F}(x_t, \boldsymbol{v}_t)$ is the motion prediction operator, compensating the frame $x_t$ by projection in the direction of the motion vector field $\boldsymbol{v}_t$, and $\boldsymbol{v}_t^+$, $\boldsymbol{v}_t^-$ are the forward and backward motion vectors predicting $x_{2t+1}$, respectively . The notation $\mathcal{F}^{-1}(h_t, \boldsymbol{v}_t)$ corresponds to the compensation of the $h_t$ frame in the opposite direction of the motion vector field $\boldsymbol{v}_t$. Indeed, in general the motion prediction is not an invertible operator. Unconnected and multiple connected pixels are processed as detailed in [10].

When the input sequence involves complex motion transitions, this can translate to inefficient prediction/update operations, leading to poor quality results and temporal scalability capabilities, as illustrated in Fig.2. One can remark in particular the energy of the detail frames, which need to be encoded, and also the poor visual quality of the approximation frame, very penalizing for temporal scalability.

In the following, we suppose the scene-cuts have been detected, and we present the algorithm used for change detection at the end of this section.

First, the temporal filtering needs to be changed in order not to filter over a scene-cut. The second modification is related to the encoding of the last group of frames (GOF) before the scene-cut.

To this end, both the predict and update steps have to be modified near the end of the first scene, as illustrated in Fig. 3. For sequences processed homogeneously, the temporal subbands resulting from the MCTF are encoded by GOFs of $2^L$ frames, where $L$ is the number of temporal decomposition levels that were performed. When a scene-cut occurs in a sequence, the GOF just before the change will have in general a different number of frames. If we denote its number of frames by $A_n$ and write this number as:

$$A_n = (a_0 a_1 \ldots a_{L-1})_2 = \sum_{l=0}^{L-1} a_l 2^l,$$

then we shall decompose the GOF in smaller GOFs, in decreasing order of their size: $a_l 2^l$, $l \in \{0, \ldots, L-1\}$, $a_l \in \{0, 1\}$, which will be filtered and encoded separately. This also corresponds to changing the number of temporal decomposition levels and filtering operations for these sub-GOFs. Indeed, we can do only $l$ temporal decomposition levels for a sub-GOF of size $2^l$, $l < L$. Moreover, the prediction across the scene-cut is inhibited, as well as the usage of the reverse motion vector field over the same transition, during the update step. After the scene-cut, the normal filtering with "sliding window" is started, the effect of the scene cut being only a slight modification of the filters to take into account the induced border effects.

Now that we have explained the modifications in filtering and coding in order to take into account scene changes, we turn to the detection of such transitions.

**Fig. 2.** Approximation (a) and detail (b) frames in a GOF without scene-cut. Approximation (c) and detail (d) frames when the GOF contains a scene-cut (first part: "foreman" sequence, second part: "mobile" sequence).

Several criteria for scene-cut detection have been proposed in the literature, like: the variation of the relative energy of the displaced frame difference (DFD) along the sequence [11], the energy and angle distribution of the motion vector fields in consecutive frames [12], by keeping track of the percentage of the unconnected pixels, estimated after motion estimation [13] or using unsupervised segmentation and object tracking [14].

For our simulation we have used, as detection criteria, the variation of the relative energy of the DFD along the sequence. If the displaced frame difference between two successive frames is computed as:

$$d_t = DFD(x_t, x_{t+1}) = x_{t+1} - \mathcal{F}(x_t, \boldsymbol{v}_t) \qquad (2)$$

then the variation of the relative energy of the DFD is computed as:

$$\Delta_{2t} = \frac{d_{2t}^2}{d_{2t-1}^2} \qquad (3)$$

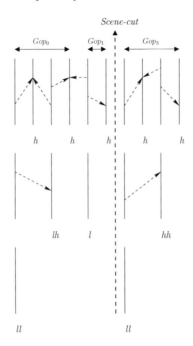

**Fig. 3.** Scene-cut processing over two temporal levels for a 10-frames video shot

When the input signal is highly-correlated, the variation of the relative energy of the DFD along the sequence is almost constant (i.e. $\Delta \approx 1$). We say a scene-cut is detected when the variation of relative energy has a rapid change. For appropriately chosen parameters $\tau_1$ and $\tau_2$, we say that the scene-cut occurs after the frame $x_{2t+1}$ when:

$$
\begin{cases}
|\Delta_{2t} - 1| < \tau_1 \\
|\Delta_{2t+1} - 1| > \tau_2
\end{cases}
\tag{4}
$$

## 3   Experimental Results

For simulations, we considered a high-definition video sequence (HD format: 1920×1280, 60 fps) from the "Erin Brockovich" movie, containing 180 frames and 3 scene-cuts: after the $44^{th}$, the $80^{th}$ and respectively, the $161^{th}$ frame. Moreover, in order to work on a representative set of test sequences, we also built several test sequences obtained by concatenating parts of the standard CIF sequences at 30 fps: Foreman and Mobile (i.e.: MF_18 × 16 - video file containing the first 18 frames from Mobile and the next 16 frames from Foreman, FM_16 × 16 - with the first 16 frames from Foreman, followed by the first 16 frames from Mobile). The aim was to test all possible configurations for the number of frames in the GOF previous to the scene-cut. In order to detect the abrupt scene transitions, the values of $\tau_1$ and $\tau_2$ were empirically determined as being equal to 0.1 and

0.4, respectively. These parameters ensured that all the scene-cuts were detected and no false alarms appeared for the considered sequences. Sequences with fade or dissolve transitions can be processed with the described MCTF scheme, but the detection method should be replaced with an appropriate one, as described in [15].

The target number of decomposition levels for motion-compensated 5/3 temporal filtering is $L = 4$. The coding procedure is based on the MC-EZBC codec and the used motion estimation algorithm is a Hierarchical Variable Size Block Matching (HVSBM) one. The motion vectors have been estimated with $1/8^{th}$ pixel accuracy and the temporal subbands were spatially decomposed over 4 levels with the biorthogonal 9/7 wavelet. The encoding of the entire YUV sequence was performed, but the results are further expressed only in terms of average YSNR.

**Table 1.** PSNR results of 5/3 MCTF with and without scene-cut processing for "Erin Bronckovich" - (HD, 60fps, 180 frames)

| YSNR (dB) | 6000 kbs | 8000 kbs | 12000 kbs |
|---|---|---|---|
| SC-MCTF | 36.4227 | 36.8639 | 37.6387 |
| MCTF | 34.9281 | 35.7519 | 36.5217 |

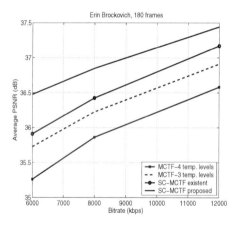

**Fig. 4.** Rate-distortion curves for 180-frames HD Erin Brockovich sequence

The importance of correctly processing the scene-cuts is illustrated in Fig. 4, Fig. 5 , as well as in the Tables 1-2, where the rate-distortion performances for 5/3 MCTF with (denoted in these tables by SC-MCTF) and without (simply denoted by MCTF) scene-cut processing are compared. It can be easily noticed that in all the cases our scheme performs better, achieving a gain between 0.5 dB and 2.0 dB over a classical MCTF. Results in Fig. 4 indicate that reducing the GOF size (from 16 to 8 frames) can alleviate the problem of scene-cuts by decreasing their influence, but a correct processing of these zones allows us

**Table 2.** PSNR results of 5/3 MCTF with and without scene-cut processing for the "MF_18x16" and "FM_16x16" sequences

| MF_18x16 sequence (30fps) | | | | |
|---|---|---|---|---|
| YSNR (dB) | 512 kbs | 768 kbs | 1024 kbs | 1536 kbs |
| SC-MCTF | 30.1185 | 32.3141 | 33.7612 | 35.6489 |
| MCTF | 23.9811 | 28.5192 | 30.4135 | 32.8334 |
| FM_16x16 sequence (30fps) | | | | |
| YSNR (dB) | 512 kbs | 768 kbs | 1024 kbs | 1536 kbs |
| SC-MCTF | 30.3151 | 32.7043 | 34.1021 | 35.9510 |
| MCTF | 26.4706 | 30.3061 | 31.8275 | 33.8650 |

both to take advantage of the temporal correlation in homogeneous shots and to increase the coding efficiency. It can also be observed that our proposed technique outperforms the one described in [8,9].

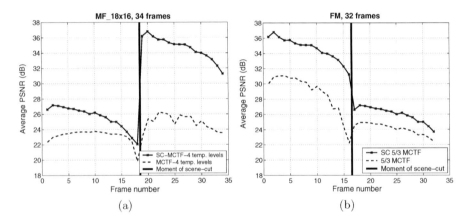

(a)                              (b)

**Fig. 5.** PSNR for the "MF_18x16" (a) and "FM_16x16" (b) sequences, with and without scene-cut processing. Scene-change after the $18^{th}$ and respectively, $16^{th}$ frame.

## 4   Conclusion and Future Work

In this paper, we proposed an improved version of the 5/3 MCTF coding scheme, able to detect and process the scene-cuts appearing in video sequences. The lifting structure of the filters has been modified such that the filtering does not encompass the scene-cut. Moreover, the coding units were reduced to accommodate this change. As can be observed from the experimental results, our method gives an average YSNR gain of about 1.5 dB on the tested video sequences and higher for frames close to the scene-cut.

The presented method supposes the scene-change detection algorithm to be applied before starting the encoding process. In future work, we will focus on improvements allowing to process in one pass the video sequence, by performing the scene-cut detection during the encoding process.

# References

1. B.-J. Kim, Z. Xiong, and W.A. Pearlman, "Very low bit-rate embedded video coding with 3-D set partitioning in hierarchical trees (3D-SPIHT)," *IEEE Trans on Circ. and Syst. for Video Tech.*, vol. 8, pp. 1365–1374, 2000.
2. S. Hsiang and J. Woods, "Embedded image coding using zeroblocks of subband/wavelet coefficients and context modeling," in *ISCAS*, Geneva, Switzerland, 2000, pp. 589–595.
3. B. Shahraray, "Scene change detection and content-based sampling of video sequences," *SPIE*, vol. 2419, 1995.
4. R. L. De Queiroz, G. Bozdagi, and T. Sencar, "Fast video segmentation using encoding cost data," Tech. Rep., Xerox Corporation, 1999.
5. Y. Zhan, M. Picard, B. Pesquet-Popescu, and H. Heijmans, "Long temporal filters in lifting schemes for scalable video coding," doc. m8680, Klagenfurt MPEG meeting, July 2002.
6. J.-R. Ohm, "Complexity and delay analysis of MCTF interframe wavelet structures," doc. m8520, Klagenfurt MPEG meeting, July 2002.
7. D. Turaga and M. van der Schaar, "Unconstrained temporal scalability with multiple reference and bi-directional motion compensated temporal filtering," doc. m8388, Fairfax MPEG meeting, 2002.
8. Y. Wu and J.Woods, "MC-EZBC Video Proposal from RPI," Tech. Rep. MPEG04/M10569/S15, ISO/IEC JTC1/SC29/WG11, 2004.
9. P. Chen and J.Woods, "Bidirectional MC-EZBC with lifting implementation," *IEEE Trans.on CSVT*, vol. 14, pp. 1183–1194, 2004.
10. C. Tillier, B. Pesquet-Popescu, and M. Van der Schaar, "Weighted average spatiotemporal update operator for subband video coding," *ICIP*, Singapore,Oct. 2004.
11. Y. Tsaig, *Automatic Segmentation of Moving Objects in Video Sequences*, Ph.D. thesis, Department of Computer Science, School of Mathematical Sciences, Tel-Aviv University, Tel-Aviv 69978, Israel.
12. F. Porikli and Y. Wang, "Automatic video object segmentation using volume growing and hierarchical clustering," Technical Report TR2004-012, MERL-Mitsubishi Electric Research Laboratory, 2004.
13. J. Konrad and M. Ristivojevic, "Video segmentation and occlusion detection over multiple frames," *SPIE VCIP*, San Jose, 2003.
14. S.-C. Chen and M.-L. Shyu, "Video scene change detection method using unsupervised segmentation and object tracking," *ICME*, Tokyo, 2001.
15. B.T. Truong, C. Dorai, and S Venkatesh, "Improved fade and dissolve detection for reliable video segmentation," *Proceedings of the IEEE International Conference on Image Processing*, vol. 3, pp. 961–964, 2000.

# Image Indexing by Focus Map

Levente Kovács[1] and Tamás Szirányi[2]

[1] University of Veszprém, Dept. of Image Processing and Neurocomputing,
Egyetem u. 10, H-8200 Veszprém, Hungary
kla@vision.vein.hu
http://vision.vein.hu/~kla/
[2] Hungarian Academy of Sciences, Analogical Comp. Lab.,
Comp. and Automation Research Institute,
Kende u. 15, H-1111, Budapest, Hungary
sziranyi@sztaki.hu
http://www.sztaki.hu/~sziranyi/

**Abstract.** Content-based indexing and retrieval (CBIR) of still and motion picture databases is an area of ever increasing attention. In this paper we present a method for still image information extraction, which in itself provides a somewhat higher level of features and also can serve as a basis for high level, i.e. semantic, image feature extraction and understanding. In our proposed method we use blind deconvolution for image area classification by interest regions, which is a novel use of the technique. We prove its viability for such and similar use.

**Keywords:** indexing, blind deconvolution, focus map, CBIR.

## 1 Introduction

We present an image indexing method using regions of interest, i.e. focus maps, in which we extract focused areas of images and use the such extracted areas for image indexing. Then queries can be formulated, searching for images on which specified areas are in focus, or there is an object in focus on a selected image region. For the extraction of such areas we use blind deconvolution.

Blind deconvolution [1] is a well known method used in the field of linearly degraded image reconstruction [2] when we lack the knowledge about the original source image, the point spread function (PSF) - i.e. the blurring function - or the additive noise superimposed. This is the case when the original - noise-free, not blurred - image is not available, too hard to access, or even dangerous. Blind deconvolution is able to estimate both the PSF and the original image. Thus, in such cases blind deconvolution algorithms can be really useful and, depending on the parameter estimation techniques used and on the quality of the observed image, sometimes quite high quality restoration can be achieved. There are numerous applications of blind deconvolution in the fields of microscopy, astronomy, tomography [4,5,6,18], and in many other areas.

Reading the above, one could easily ask how could (blind) deconvolution be used for image classification and indexing. What may sound at first peculiar,

J. Blanc-Talon et al. (Eds.): ACIVS 2005, LNCS 3708, pp. 300–307, 2005.
© Springer-Verlag Berlin Heidelberg 2005

it may turn out to be quite the opposite. The estimation of possible blurring functions over an image, or blocks of an image in our case, can yield the data we need for focus map extraction. The main idea behind our approach is, that the calculated PSFs over blocks of an image can give information about the local blurriness or sharpness of the image, thus information about how important the respective image area could be in the context of the entire image.

There are many ways to accentuate parts of an image. A most obvious one is that if the focus of the image is centered on an object and the rest is out of focus or blurred, the attention will concentrate on the object in focus. Another artistic tool for object accentuation is when the photographer guides the attention by light-shadow plays e.g. when an object is intentionally shot with more light on, or the opposite, in shadows if wished to lower its importance. Usually being more in focus, having more contrast, having more light are some tools of emphasizing important objects/areas in a scene.

There exist approaches of determining depth maps and focused regions with the use of multiple images shot with different camera focus settings, like in [3], but in the area we target there are no such shots available but a single image.

In our approach, by performing localized blind deconvolution on arbitrary images and classification of the obtained local PSFs we obtain such segmentation images which we can use to extract the areas of interest. Then, we build a database of images and their obtained segmentations, on which queries will be made by two possible ways: by model images, where a model image is given and its segmentation is used as a mask for the search, or by hand-drawn query images, where one just draws blobs on a blank image to specify the places where important areas should be searched over the database.

In the following we will present the method in detail, perform some comparisons with other similar techniques, detail the query and search and provide results. We will also discuss possible applications of the technique. For example, in video contents indexing, one of the most important task is to find the central spot of an event, what is usually the best focused object. For example, with a group of people, there could be several skin-colored areas and moving bodies, but the central person can only be found by searching around the focus area among moving head-type objects.

## 2   Method Overview

Previously we have been investigating alternative ways of image and video classification, indexing and retrieval, like motion-based methods [16], camera depth maps with multifocus images [3] or painterly-rendering based strokes-series indexing [17]. Here we will detail our novel blind deconvolution based classification method and compare it to two other similar methods, classification based on autocorrelation and on edge content. The goals of these techniques is similar to what we wish to achieve, that is extract important image areas so as to be able to perform higher order queries. Such queries would be like specifying that we want to search for images on which the important areas are at places given on the query. That can mean searching by a model image for finding similarly arranged compositions, or by drawing a binary query image to specify where we want to see emphasized areas. Techniques for finding out whether an image or parts of an image are out of focus have practical uses [10,11] in photography. An overview of focus/sharpness methods is in [1,12]. However, we are dealing with the possible uses of blind deconvolution for indexing/search/retrieval purposes, where we do not have multifocus images at hand.

For our purpose, the basis of the region of interest extraction is locally performed blind deconvolution. The type of the used deconvolution is irrelevant, as long as it provides local PSF estimates. Thus, we chose the MATLAB implementation of the Lucy-Richardson [13,14] deconvolution for our tests.

## 2.1 Blind Deconvolution Based Classification

Blind deconvolution [1] is basically a blind image restoration method, where the noise content is neglected. Let the model of a degraded image be

$$f_O = \int_{-\infty}^{+\infty} \int_{-\infty}^{+\infty} f(\alpha, \beta) \cdot h(x - \alpha, y - \beta) d\alpha d\beta + n(x, y) \tag{1}$$

where $f_O$ is the observed image, $h$ is the impulse response of the linear degradation system and $n$ is the additive noise, with the simple form in discrete case being

$$f_O = f * h + n \tag{2}$$

The function $h$ is the so called point spread function (PSF) which can be conceived as blurring a white point on a black background with the blurring function of the channel (e.g. caused by the optics). The term is used to denote positive valued blurring functions. If we neglect the noise content (as we do in our case with the images in the database), blind deconvolution can be used to estimate the PSF which caused the blurring in the observed image. And this is what we use in out classification. Taking the logarithm of the degraded image Fourier spectra

$$ln(F_O) = ln(F) + ln(H) \tag{3}$$

we find the spectra of the original image (here unknown) and the PSF to be separable. Thus statistical estimation methods can be applied that are used in case of additive noise.

There exist quite a few methods for blind deconvolution calculation (see [1]). We use the blind deconvolution algorithm in MATLAB in our proof of concept code, which uses a maximum likelihood parameter estimation [7] process. Here, one seeks to maximize the Bayesian probability

$$P\{h * f|g\} = \frac{P\{g|h * f\} \cdot P\{f\} \cdot P\{h\}}{P\{g\}} \tag{4}$$

which is equivalent to maximizing $m = lnP\{g|h * f\} + lnP\{f\} + lnP\{h\}$.

The process of estimating the PSF of a degradation process is quite similar to the methods used for system identification and system control in electrical engineering tasks. Thus an analogy can be drawn between the two processes. The maximum likelihood estimation process is an approach to obtain the parameters of an autoregressive moving average model, in which the original image is modeled as a two dimensional autoregressive process, the PSF is a two dimensional finite impulse response linear system, and the degraded image itself is taken as an autoregressive moving average process. Thus, deconvolution is the parameter identification process, where in the end we obtain an estimation of the PSF. So as to reduce the complexity of the calculations, usually the estimation process is fed with an initial guess regarding the PSF ($h$). Since the process is more affected by the size of the initially guessed filter than it's values, the initial PSF is given as a two dimensional flat unit function.

The main steps of the classification process are as follows:

1. load image A
2. obtain local PSFs on image A in $n \times n$ blocks
3. for each obtained PSF calculate its distance from the average PSF of the whole image
4. classify blocks of the image on the basis of their distance from the average PSF

Block sizes are usually $32 \times 32$ or $16 \times 16$ pixels, distance calculation is done with mean square error being $MSE(A, B) = (1/n^2) \cdot \sum_{i=1}^{n}(A_i - B_i)^2$ and 3 to 10 classes are used.

The result of the above process is a mask image where important areas have a higher class. Important in this case can mean a variety of things. For example on an image where everything is blurred but the one object in focus, that object will have a higher class. On an image where everything is in focus, areas with better contrast or higher brightness will have a higher focus. In general, objects and areas with important features will be extracted. For an example see Figure 1. The classification is momentarily far from being realtime, mainly because of the unoptimized MATLAB code. The query performing program is written in C++ and has running times of around 30 seconds for 400 images on a 2800+ Sempron processor.

We compared our region extraction approach with two similar techniques, which are shortly described in the following.

**Fig. 1.** The Monarch image segmented with the blind deconvolution approach. Left: original, middle: local PSFs, right: segmentation.

**Autocorrelation Based Classification.** Autocorrelation based sharpness measures ([9,15]) are sometimes used in evaluating overall or local sharpness of an image. Autocorrelation of a continuous function $f$ is

$$Ac_f(\tau) = \int_{-\infty}^{+\infty} f(t) \cdot f(t - \tau)dt \qquad (5)$$

which in the case of discrete space images is the convolution of an image (or block of image in our case) with itself. and indicates how well neighboring pixels correlate. Practically, in-focus images contain many small correlated areas, having high central peaks (or one peak in case of full image autocorrelation). An important property of autocorrelation calculation is that the Fourier transform of autocorrelation is the energy of the signal itself, that is $F(Ac_f) = |F(f)|^2$, which means we can use a fast, Fourier-space computation. In the end, areas with higher autocorrelation responses will have a higher class.

**Edge Content Based Classification.** Edge content and/or gradient based sharpness measures ([8,15]) are also used for local and global sharpness measures. These are very fast, but not quite robust methods, and are based on the idea that image edges (quite important structure features) are very sensitive to being out of focus (i.e. blur). The measure of edge blurriness can thus be a measure of image or image area sharpness. The technique we use here is an edge content based classification, where blocks of an image are classified based on the edge count of the respective block. The more edge content an area has, the higher its class will be.

### 2.2 Comparison

On Figure 2 comparisons of the above three approaches are presented (our blind deconvolution based classification, autocorrelation based and edge content

**Fig. 2.** Comparisons of classifications with the autocorrelation (2nd column), edge content (3rd column) and blind deconvolution (4th column) based methods.

based) by example pairs of input images and their segmentations. The reason why the blind deconvolution based classification is better is that it works quite well with many types of images, be that focused with blurred background, focused on the whole image and so on, while depending on edge content can give false results when the whole image is in focus, or when too much texture is on the image. Depending on autocorrelation can also give false responses when there are large homogeneous areas or lots of fine details.

## 3   Indexing, Search and Retrieval

As we described earlier, the result for the classification using blind deconvolution is segmentation data containing class information for blocks of the images. These segmentation data are stored along with the input images and later the queries are performed on them. Currently we have gathered a dataset with  400 real life images, different in size, type, contents, topic, containing images about nature, people, streets, buildings, cityscapes, etc. First these images are processed for classification. Then, queries can be performed. A query can be a model image or a user-drawn query image.

We consider "good" such answers to a query, which have a similar structure of interest regions as the model image (or mask) had. Thus, e.g. in the topmost query in Figure 3 the query image has a somewhat large query region in the upper right corner, and response images also have similar regions in their middle-upper right regions. In the second example, the same is true for middle-upper regions.

In the first case, a model image is given, its classification is obtained similarly as on the database images, and the generated class mask is used as a query on the database. If the query image differs in size from the actual image in the database to which is currently compared to, then the database image's class mask is transformed in size to match the query mask (the other way around was also tested, yielding the same results, so we sticked with this version). The masks are compared using mean square error distance. At the end the results are sorted in increasing of the obtained errors, and the first 10 images are given as response. Trials show a high average good response.

In the second case, the user draws a binary mask (basically blobs) on a blank image. The drawn image is taken as a query mask and will be compared to the database's masks in binary mode (if there are higher class areas where the user has specified, a positive answer is given). The 10 most similar images are given as responses.

Figure 3 presents queries-responses for both of the above query modes.

*Notes, Conclusions.* In the above, we have shown the viability of using local blind deconvolution for local PSF estimation for image classification purposes. The benefits of using this method over others for area of interest extraction are that it provides a higher order image feature extraction than basic sharpness measures, it gives good results in a broad spectrum of image types from partially blurred to totally in focus. Our near future work concerns an implementation of

**Fig. 3.** Three query-response examples (upper two: with model image, bottom: hand-drawn mask). In each case the upper left is the query image and its segmentation, and the first 7 responses (in the last case a binary hand-drawn mask is used, and all the responses are given.

a localized deconvolution implementation with better convergence control. We presented a feature extraction that is also crucial for video understanding. The possible uses of this method are numerous, we are also working on some, which involve higher order feature tracking in video based on the presented technique.

*Acknowledgements.* Our work has been supported by the Hungarian Ministry of Economy and Transport and the European Union in the frameworks of the ECOP/GVOP AKF388 and the NoE MUSCLE project.

# References

1. Kundur, D., Hatzinakos, D.: Blind Image Deconvolution. IEEE Signal Processing Magazine (1996) May 43–64
2. Pratt, W.K.: Digital Image Processing. 3rd Edition. John Wiley & Sons (2001) 241–399
3. Czúni, L., Csordás, D.: Depth-Based Indexing and Retrieval of Photographic Images. VLBV 2003, Lecture Notes in Computer Sciene: Visual Content Processing and Representation (2003) 76–83

4. Jefferies, S.M., Schulze, K., Matson, C.L.m Stoltenberg, K., Hege, E.k.: Blind Deconvolution In Optical Diffusion Tomography. Optical Express 10 (2002) 46–53
5. Jefferies S. M., Schulze, K. J., Matson, C. L., Giffin, M, Okada, J.: Improved Blind Deconvolution Methods for Objects Imaged through Turbid Media. AMOS Technical Conference, Kihei HI (2002)
6. Dey, N., Blanc-Faud, L., Zimmer, C., Kam, Z., Olivo-Marin, J.C., Zerubia, J.: A Deconvolution Method For Confocal Microscopy With Total Variation Regularization. Proceedings of IEEE International Symposium on Biomedical Imaging (2004)
7. Chong-Yung Chi, Wu-Ton Chen: Maximum-Likelihood Blind Deconvolution: Non-White Bernoulli-Gaussian Case. IEEE Trans. on Geoscience and Remote Sensing (1991), 29, 5
8. Dijk, J., van Ginkel, M., van Asselt, R.J., van Vliet, L.J., Verbeek, P.W.: A New Sharpness Measure Based on Gaussian Lines And Eedges. Proceedings of ASCI2002 (2002) 39–73
9. Santos, A., Ortiz de Solorzano, C., Vaquero, J.J., Pena, J.M., Malpica, N., Del Pozo, F.: Evaluation Of Autofocus Functions In Molecular Cytogenetic Analysis. Jourlan of Microscopy (1997), 188, 3 264–272
10. Shaked, D., Tastl, I.: Sharpness Measure: Towards Automatic Image Enhancement. Hewlett-Packard Laboratories Technical Report HPL 2004-84 (2004)
11. Lim, S.H., Yen, J., Wu, P.: Detection of Out-Of-Focus Digital Photographs. Hewlett-Packard Laboratories Technical Report HPL 2005-14 (2005)
12. Pech-Pacheco, J.L., Cristobal, G., Chamorro-Martinez, J., Fernandez-Valdivia, J.: Diatom Autofocusing in Brightfield Microscopy: A Comparative Study. Proceedings of ICPR 2000 (2000), 3, 314–317
13. Lucy, L.B.: An Iterative Technique For Rectification of Observed Distributions. The Astronomical Journal (1974) 79, 6, 745–754
14. Richardson, W.H.: Bayesian-Based Iterative Method of Image Restoration. JOSA (1972) 62, 55–59
15. Batten, C.F., Holburn, D.M., Breton, B.C., Caldwell, N.H.M.: Sharpness Search Algorithms for Automatic Focusing in the Scanning Electron Microscope. Scanning: The Journal of Scanning Microscopies (2001) 23, 2, 112–113
16. Hanis, A., Szirányi, T.: Measuring the Motion Similarity in Video Indexing. Proceedings of 4th Eurasip EC-VIP-MC, Zagreb (2003)
17. Kato, Z., Ji, X., Szirányi, T., Tóth, Z., Czúni, L.: Content-Based Image Retrieval Using Stochastic Paintbrush Transformation, Proceedings of ICIP 2002 (2002)
18. Szirányi, T., Nemes, L., Roska, T.: Cellular Neural Network for Image Deconvolution and Enhancement: A Microscopy Toolkit Proceedings of IWPIA (1995) 113–124

# Distance and Nearest Neighbor Transforms of Gray-Level Surfaces Using Priority Pixel Queue Algorithm

Leena Ikonen and Pekka Toivanen

Laboratory of Information Processing, Department of Information Technology,
Lappeenranta University of Technology, P.O.Box 20, 53851 Lappeenranta, Finland
{leena.ikonen, pekka.toivanen}@lut.fi

**Abstract.** This article presents a nearest neighbor transform for gray-level surfaces. It is based on the Distance Transform on Curved Space (DTOCS) calculated using an efficient priority pixel queue algorithm. A simple extension of the algorithm produces the nearest neighbor transform simultaneously with the distance map. The transformations can be applied for example to estimate surface roughness.

## 1 Introduction

Nearest neighbor, or nearest feature transforms, are closely related to distance transforms, and should preferably be achieved using the same algorithm. In the case of binary images, distance transforms can be derived from nearest neighbor transforms, but not vice versa [8]. Distance transformations were among the first image processing algorithms. Rosenfeld [10] presented a sequential local transformation algorithm for calculating distances in binary images in 1966, and similar chamfering techniques have been applied widely in the field, e.g., [1], [9], [13]. The transformations propagate local distance values across the image with a mask operation, which may have to be iterated several times to achieve globally optimal distances for gray-level images.

Alternatives to chamfering include ordered and recursive propagation [9], and pixel queue algorithms [11], [16]. The recursive propagation proceeds like a depth first search, while ordered propagation and pixel queue algorithms are applications of breadth first search. The efficiency of the depth first search is highly dependent on the propagation order, and breadth first approaches eliminate some of the repetition of distance calculations caused by finding shorter paths later on in the transformation. Gray-level distance transforms with varying local distances can be calculated correctly with ordered or recursive propagation, if neighbors of updated pixels are reprocessed. However, this is very inefficient for gray-level distance transforms of complex surfaces with highly curved paths. The ordered propagation seems to be more efficient in calculating the Distance Transform on Curved Space (DTOCS) [13] than the chamfering approach, but the priority pixel queue algorithm, which corresponds to a best first search, clearly outperforms both in large complex images [4]. A priority pixel queue

J. Blanc-Talon et al. (Eds.): ACIVS 2005, LNCS 3708, pp. 308–315, 2005.
© Springer-Verlag Berlin Heidelberg 2005

idea by Verwer [15] is implemented with bucket sorting, which is applicable only with integer distances. Bucket sorting is also utilized in the transformation algorithm by Cuisenaire and Macq [3], where Euclidean distance values are obtained by gradually increasing the propagation neighborhood. The priority queue algorithm for calculating the geodesic time by Soille [12] also enumerates all possible distance values. The priority value is increased with one when no pixels with the current priority value are found in the queue. As the geodesic time sums gray-values along digital paths, the distance values can become very large, which also means a lot of priority values must be tested. Our minimum heap based transformation is applicable for any positive distances, including floating point distance values, and processes only distance values, which are needed. The priority queue approach enables easy implementation of the nearest neighbor transform, which can be calculated simultaneously with the distance transform. The unified distance transformation algorithm by Paglieroni [8] also calculates the nearest neighbor and distance transformation simultaneously using horizontal and vertical scans in a parallel architecture.

This article is organized as follows. The distance transforms are presented in Section 2 and the pixel queue transformation algorithm in Section 3. Section 4 presents the nearest neighbor transform, and Sections 5 and 6 some application ideas. Section 7 contains conclusions and discussion.

## 2   The Distance Transforms

The Distance Transform on Curved Space (DTOCS) calculates distances along a gray-level surface, when gray-levels are understood as height values. Local distances, which are summed along digital paths to calculate the distance transform values, are defined using gray-level differences:

$$d(p_i, p_{i-1}) = |\mathcal{G}(p_i) - \mathcal{G}(p_{i-1})| + 1 \tag{1}$$

where $\mathcal{G}(p)$ denotes the gray-value of pixel $p$, and $p_{i-1}$ and $p_i$ are subsequent pixels on a path. The locally Euclidean Weighted DTOCS (WDTOCS) is calculated from the height difference and the horizontal distance using Pythagoras:

$$d(p_i, p_{i-1}) = \begin{cases} \sqrt{|\mathcal{G}(p_i) - \mathcal{G}(p_{i-1})|^2 + 1} \,, & p_{i-1} \in N_4(p_i) \\ \sqrt{|\mathcal{G}(p_i) - \mathcal{G}(p_{i-1})|^2 + 2} \,, & p_{i-1} \in N_8(p_i) \setminus N_4(p_i) \end{cases} \tag{2}$$

The diagonal neighbors of pixel $p$ are denoted by $N_8(p) \setminus N_4(p)$, where $N_8(p)$ consists of all pixel neighbors in a square grid, and $N_4(p)$ of square neighbors. More accurate global distances can be achieved by introducing weights, which are proven to be optimal for binary distance transforms, to local distances in the horizontal plane. The Optimal DTOCS is defined in [5] as

$$d(p_i, p_{i-1}) = \begin{cases} \sqrt{|\mathcal{G}(p_i) - \mathcal{G}(p_{i-1})|^2 + a_{opt}^2} \,, & p_{i-1} \in N_4(p_i) \\ \sqrt{|\mathcal{G}(p_i) - \mathcal{G}(p_{i-1})|^2 + b_{opt}^2} \,, & p_{i-1} \in N_8(p_i) \setminus N_4(p_i) \end{cases} \tag{3}$$

where $a_{opt} = (\sqrt{2\sqrt{2} - 2} + 1)/2 \approx 0.95509$ and $b_{opt} = \sqrt{2} + (\sqrt{2\sqrt{2} - 2} - 1)/2 \approx$ 1.36930 as derived by Borgefors [1] by minimizing the maximum difference from the Euclidean distance that can occur between points on the binary image plane.

## 3   Pixel Queue Distance Transformation Algorithm

The DTOCS has previously been calculated with a mask operation, which has to be iterated several times before the distance map converges [13]. The larger and more complex the image surface is, the more iterations are needed, whereas the pixel queue approach slows down only slightly with increased surface complexity [4]. The efficient pixel queue algorithm eliminates repetition of local distance calculations by using a priority queue implemented as a minimum heap:

1. Define binary image $\mathcal{F}(x) = 0$ for each pixel $x$ in feature set, and $\mathcal{F}(x) = max$ for each non-feature $x$.
2. Put feature pixels to *priority queue* Q.
3. While Q not empty
    $p = dequeue(Q)$, $\mathcal{F}_q(p)$ was the smallest distance in Q.
    If $\mathcal{F}_q(p) > \mathcal{F}(p)$ (obsolete value), continue from step 3.
    $\mathcal{F}(p)$ becomes $\mathcal{F}^*(p)$ (value is final).
    For neighbors $x$ of $p$ with $\mathcal{F}(x) > \mathcal{F}^*(p)$
        Compute local distance $d(p, x)$ from original image $\mathcal{G}$.
        If $\mathcal{F}^*(p) + d(p, x) < \mathcal{F}(x)$
            Set $\mathcal{F}(x) = \mathcal{F}(p) + d(p, x)$
            $enqueue(x)$
        end if
    end for
end while

If the feature point sets are large and connected, it can be beneficial to enqueue only the feature boundary pixels in step 2. of the algorithm, but the same result is achieved as when enqueuing all feature pixels. The priority queue approach for calculating distances ensures that distance values are final when they are dequeued, and propagated further. Repeated enqueuings are possible if a new shorter path is found, but previous instances of the pixel in the queue can be eliminated based on obsolete distance values. The local distance calculation between two pixels is never repeated, as only pixels with final distance values can be source points, and pixel pairs, where the destination point already has a smaller distance value than the source point are also eliminated. The complexity of the pixel queue algorithm is in $\mathcal{O}(n \log n_q)$, where $n_q$ is the length of the queue, which varies throughout the transformation. Typically, $n_q \ll n$, so the algorithm is in practise near-linear [4].

## 4   Nearest Neighbor Transform

The nearest neighbor transform can be viewed as a discretized version of the Voronoi diagram dividing the image to polygons around the feature or site points, so that each pixel belongs to the region of the closest site. In fact, Voronoi diagrams can be used to calculate Euclidean distance transforms for binary images [2], including voxel images in arbitrary dimensions [7]. The nearest neighbor transform assigns to each pixel the identity of its nearest feature pixel. The nearest site is here determined according to DTOCS distances, i.e. distances along the varying height surface, but the same algorithm works for any distance transforms with non-negative distance values. As local distances based on gray-values can vary a lot, the nearest neighbor transform can result in any shapes of regions around each site.

The nearest neighbor transformation produces a tesselation image, which is initialized to zero at non-feature pixels, and to a unique seed value $1..n_f$ at each of the $n_f$ feature pixels. A simple extension of the priority pixel queue algorithm calculates the nearest neighbor transform simultaneously with the distance transform. When a pixel with a new distance value is enqueued, the corresponding pixel in the tesselation image gets the seed value of the pixel from which the distance value propagated. If the same pixel is enqueued repeatedly, the seed value is replaced with the new one. The final seed value identifies the feature pixel from which the propagation path of the final distance value originated. Points equally distant from two or more seed points will end up in the region from which the distance propagated first. A similar region growing algorithm for Voronoi tesselation of 3D volumes resolves collisions of neighboring regions using Euclidean distances [6], but in the DTOCS with curved paths, the Euclidean distance between the pixels does not correspond to the real distance the transformation approximates.

An example of a nearest neighbor transform can be seen in Fig. 1. The familiar 'Lena' image represents a varying height surface, and a nearest neighbor transform using an evenly spaced grid of seed points is calculated. The original image is shown with the seed points in Fig. 1 a), and the resulting nearest neighbor transform is shown in Fig. 1 b) with seed values marked on each region. As distances are calculated along the surface with the DTOCS, seed points in areas with more variation are surrounded by small regions (e.g. seed value 23).

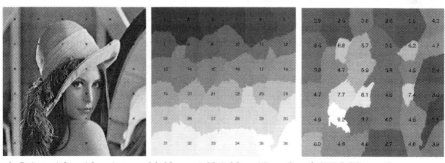

a) Orig. with grid points    b) Nearest Neighbor Transf.    c) DTOCS roughness map

**Fig. 1.** Nearest neighbor transform and roughness map from an even grid of points

In smooth areas distances can propagate further, covering more pixels. Region borders are more likely to appear near locations, where there are abrupt changes in gray-values, causing large local distances. This can be seen for example in regions 21, 16 and particularly 11, where the brim of Lena's hat is clearly visible. This suggests that the nearest neighbor transform could be applied to segmenting highly varying textures from smoother ones. The roughness map in Fig. 1 c) will be explained in Section 6.

## 5   Propagation Visualization

The nearest neighbor transform can be used to visualize propagation of distance values. The points in the feature set can be numbered as seed points for the nearest neighbor transform, and when the distance values propagate, the seed values propagate as well. When the distance map is final, the tesselation map shows from which feature point each distance value has propagated. On a varying image surface with several feature points, some feature seed values propagate only in a small area, or not at all, if distance values spread fast from points in the vicinity of the point. The order in which feature pixels are enqueued, and in which neighbors of the dequeued pixel are processed, affect the propagation order. Equal distances could be achieved along several different paths, but the seed values indicate via which points the values have in practise propagated.

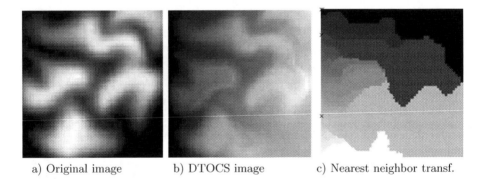

a) Original image          b) DTOCS image          c) Nearest neighbor transf.

**Fig. 2.** Example surface with its distance transform and propagation tesselation

Figure 2 shows a height map, its distance image and the propagation tesselation map, when the feature point set consists of all points in the leftmost column. The color of an area in Fig. 2 c) identifies the feature point from which the distance value has propagated. It can be seen that the number of different seed values propagating decreases towards the end of the distance transformation, i.e. when the highest distance values towards the right edge of the image are reached, only two different seed values are left of the original 128 feature point values used in the 128 * 128 surface image. The feature points with the three furthest spread seed values are marked with 'x' on the tesselation image.

# 6   Roughness Measurement

The distance and nearest neighbor transforms can be combined into a method estimating the roughness of a gray-level surface. Figure 1 c) shows an example of a roughness map, where the values marked on each region of the nearest neighbor transform indicate the average roughness of that region. The values are calculated as the average of normalized distance values within each region. The normalized values are obtained by dividing the curved DTOCS distances calculated from a grid of feature points with the corresponding straight distances. The straight distance, or chessboard distance, is simply the larger of the coordinate differences between the point in question and its nearest neighbor grid point. The more variation there is around the grid point, the larger are the normalized distances, and subsequently the roughness value of the region. An estimate of the global roughness of the image surface can be calculated as the average of all normalized distances. In future works, the method will be applied to measuring roughness of paper from microscopic gray-level images.

# 7   Discussion

The main contribution of this paper is the new nearest neighbor transform algorithm for gray-level surfaces based on the priority pixel queue distance transformation. The algorithm is very simple, and fast, as its complexity is near-linear. The nearest neighbor transform is calculated simultaneously with the distance transformation, and the value of a pixel is known to be final once it is dequeued. This means that intermediate results can be used in time critical applications, or if a complete distance transformation is not needed. For instance, if the distance transforms are used to find a route along a surface, as presented in [5], the transformation starts from the source point, and can be interrupted once the destination point is reached, that is, when the destination point is dequeued. Obviously, the path of the shortest distance could be recorderd during the distance transformation by storing the direction from which the distance propagates to each pixel, but only a single path would be found, whereas the Route DTOCS algorithm [5] finds points on any path. The nearest neighbor transform could also be utilized in some shortest path problems. The actual path is not found, but the nearest of several destinations can be selected by calculating the nearest neighbor transform with the alternative destinations as features, and then selecting the destination with the seed value, which the source point obtained in the transformation.

An application idea of using the distance and nearest neighbor transformations for surface roughness evaluation was also presented. Generally, the DTOCS is well suited for measuring the amount of variation in a gray-level image. The first application of the DTOCS involved selecting control points for image compression [14]. To store information from locations, where gray-levels change, the control points were selected from boundaries, at which the curved DTOCS distances normalized with the corresponding chessboard distances exceed a given threshold. The priority queue approach could produce the boundary in a straightforward manner by not enqueuing pixels after reaching the threshold. The implementation utilizing sequential DTOCS has to search for the boundary in the transformed image. In general, equal distance curves can be found easily with the priority queue approach, and also limiting the transformation to some maximum distance value is trivial, unlike in mask operations, where the whole image must be processed to be sure distance values are globally optimal.

The curved DTOCS paths are similar to paths formed in constrained distance transforms, see for instance [9], and in fact, the DTOCS can be used as a constrained distance transform. Constraint pixels are marked with values differing so much from other image areas, that paths to other pixels will generally not cross them. The same idea can also be implemented by multiplying the gray-level difference used in the local distance definition by a large factor. A maximum distance value can be set, so that the transformation finishes without calculating the distances to the constraint pixels, which otherwise would get huge values. The DTOCS can be applied in obstacle avoidance problems with several levels of obstacles, for example areas that can be crossed with a higher cost in addition to completely constrained areas. All accessible areas in an obstacle avoidance setting could be found by using the DTOCS or the nearest neighbor transform with a maximum allowed distance, and at the same time, the shortest path to the destination could be found in a navigation application.

# References

1. Gunilla Borgefors. Distance Transformations in Digital Images. *Computer Vision, Graphics, and Image Processing*, 34:344–371, 1986.
2. Heinz Breu, Joseph Gil, David Kirkpatrick, and Michael Werman. Linear time Euclidean distance transform algorithms. *IEEE Transactions on Pattern Analysis and Machine Intelligence*, 17(5):529–533, May 1995.
3. O. Cuisenaire and B. Macq. Fast Euclidean distance transformation by propagation using multiple neighborhoods. *Computer Vision and Image Understanding*, 76(2):163–172, November 1999.
4. Leena Ikonen. Pixel queue algorithm for geodesic distance transforms. In *Discrete Geometry for Computer Imagery (DGCI)*, pages 228–239, Poitiers, France, April 2005.
5. Leena Ikonen and Pekka Toivanen. Shortest routes on varying height surfaces using gray-level distance transforms. *Image and Vision Computing*, 23(2):133–141, February 2005.
6. C. A. Kapoutsis, C. P. Vavoulidis, and I. Pitas. Morphological iterative closest point algorithm. *IEEE Transactions on Image Processing*, 8(11):1644–1646, November 1999.
7. Calvin R. Maurer, Rensheng Qi, and Vijay Raghavan. A linear time algorithm for computing exact Euclidean distance transforms of binary images in arbitrary dimensions. *IEEE Transactions on Pattern Analysis and Machine Intelligence*, 25(2):265–270, February 2003.
8. David W. Paglieroni. Distance Transforms: Properties and Machine Vision Applications. *CVGIP: Graphical Models and Image Processing*, 54(1):56–74, January 1992.

9. Jim Piper and Erik Granum. Computing Distance Transformations in Convex and Non-convex Domains. *Pattern Recognition*, 20(6):599–615, 1987.
10. Azriel Rosenfeld and John L. Pfaltz. Sequential Operations in Digital Picture Processing. *Journal of the Association for Computing Machinery*, 13(4):471–494, October 1966.
11. Jaime Silvela and Javier Portillo. Breadth-first search and its application to image processing problems. *IEEE Transactions on Image Processing*, 10(8):1194–1199, 2001.
12. Pierre Soille. *Morphological Image Processing: Principles and Applications.* Springer-Verlag, 2 edition, 2003.
13. Pekka J. Toivanen. New geodesic distance transforms for gray-scale images. *Pattern Recognition Letters*, 17:437–450, 1996.
14. Pekka J. Toivanen, Ari M. Vepsäläinen, and Jussi P. S. Parkkinen. Image compression using distance transform on curved space (DTOCS) and Delaunay triangulation. *Pattern Recognition Letters*, 20:1015–1026, 1999.
15. Ben J. H. Verwer, Piet W. Verbeek, and Simon T. Dekker. An efficient uniform cost algorithm applied to distance transforms. *IEEE Trans. on Pattern Analysis and Machine Intelligence*, 11(4):425–429, April 1989.
16. Luc Vincent. New trends in morphological algorithms. In *Proc. SPIE/SPSE*, volume 1451, pages 158–170, 1991.

# Flow Coherence Diffusion. Linear and Nonlinear Case

Terebes Romulus[1,2], Olivier Lavialle[2], Monica Borda[1], and Pierre Baylou[2]

[1,2] Technical University of Cluj-Napoca,
15 C. Daicoviciu Street,
400020 Cluj-Napoca, Romania
{Romulus.Terebes, Monica.Borda}@com.utcluj.ro
[2] UMR 5131 ENSEIRB-ENITA-Université Bordeaux 1, Av. du Dr. Schweitzer,
33402 Talence, France
{lavialle, baylou}@tsi.u-bordeaux1.fr

**Abstract.** The paper proposes a novel tensor based diffusion filter, dedicated for filtering images composed of line like structures. We propose a linear version of nonlinear diffusion partial derivative equation, previously presented in [5]. Instead of considering nonlinearity in the image evolution process we are only including it at the computation of the diffusion tensor. The unique tensor construction is based on an adaptive orientation estimation step and yields a significant reduction of the computational complexity. The properties of the filter are analyzed both theoretically and experimentally.

## 1 Introduction

In recent years a lot of work was devoted in proposing efficient partial derivative equations (PDE) based image-filtering techniques. Increased precision, directionality, nonlinearity leading to the coexistence of complex complementary processes of smoothing and enhancement, strong anisotropic behavior, are only some key factors that lead to the expansion of this research area. Major contributions are related to the seminal works of Perona and Malik or Catte et al. on anisotropic diffusion filtering, Alvarez et al. on mean curvature motion like filters, Osher and Rudin on PDE shock filters and Weickert on tensor-driven diffusion processes. For a review of the domain and of its applications [9], [6] and the references therein can be consulted.

Within this framework the present paper proposes a new PDE dedicated for filtering images composed of line like structures. The method is essentially a tensor-driven anisotropic diffusion linear filter; the evolution equation we propose is linear and it represents a generalization of an original, nonlinear filter, previously published in [5]. Nonlinearity is included in a unique orientation estimation step, optimized for reducing the noise influence in the estimation of the diffusion directions. Some partial, intermediate results of this research are presented in [7].

The paper is organized as follows. In Section 2 we briefly review some concepts related to tensor driven diffusion processes. Section 3 is devoted to our novel diffusion equation. In Section 4, through a statistical approach, we prove the efficiency of our method, when compared with other anisotropic diffusion techniques.

J. Blanc-Talon et al. (Eds.): ACIVS 2005, LNCS 3708, pp. 316–323, 2005.
© Springer-Verlag Berlin Heidelberg 2005

## 2  Tensor Driven Anisotropic Diffusion

Anisotropic diffusion techniques are modeling the image filtering process through some divergence PDE that relates the time and spatial partial derivatives of a gray level intensity image $U(x,y,t)$ [3]:

$$\frac{\partial U}{\partial t} = div[c(U,x,y,t)\nabla U],  \tag{1}$$

The diffusivity function $c(.)$ controls the anisotropic smoothing process induced by the PDE. Although anisotropic behavior can be governed by scalar diffusivities, matrix like diffusion functions are allowing a more efficient and true separation of the filter behavior along distinct diffusion directions.

Matrix or tensor- driven diffusion is closely related to the work of Weickert in scale space analysis [8], [9]. The basic idea behind this class of filters is to steer the diffusion process along the eigenvectors of some diffusion matrix (a 2 x 2 square matrix for gray level images). Of particular interest for our work is the coherence-enhancing filter (CED) [8]. Starting from the classical structure tensor [2], [4]:

$$J_\rho(\nabla U_\sigma) = \begin{pmatrix} G_\rho * (\frac{\partial U_\sigma}{\partial x})^2 & G_\rho * \frac{\partial U_\sigma}{\partial x}\frac{\partial U_\sigma}{\partial y} \\ G_\rho * \frac{\partial U_\sigma}{\partial x}\frac{\partial U_\sigma}{\partial y} & G_\rho * (\frac{\partial U_\sigma}{\partial y})^2 \end{pmatrix},  \tag{2}$$

obtained by a pointwise Gaussian convolution of the smoothed image derivatives, a diffusion tensor is built by using an eigenvector like decomposition:

$$D(U_\sigma,x,y,t) = (\vec{v}_1 | \vec{v}_2) \begin{pmatrix} \alpha & 0 \\ 0 & f(\mu) \end{pmatrix} \begin{pmatrix} \vec{v}_1^T \\ \vec{v}_2^T \end{pmatrix}.  \tag{3}$$

Here $\vec{v}_1, \vec{v}_2$ are the eigenvectors of the structure tensor $J_\rho(\nabla U_\sigma)$. The two vectors are robust estimates of the mean orientation of the structures ($\vec{v}_2$) and of the orthogonal directions ($\vec{v}_1$), computed at a semi local scale $\rho$. Strong anisotropic behavior (e.g. smoothing action mainly only along edges) is achieved by imposing particular choices for the eigenvalues of (3). The constant $\alpha$ is typically chosen equal to $0.001$ whereas $f(\mu)$ is a function of a coherence measure $\mu$, defined to be the difference between the eigenvalues of (2) ($\lambda_1, \lambda_2$) :

$$\begin{cases} \mu = \lambda_1 - \lambda_2 \\ f(\mu) = \alpha + (1-\alpha)\exp(-C/\mu^2) \end{cases}.  \tag{4}$$

In each pixel of the image the modified tensor steers an anisotropic diffusion process:

$$\frac{\partial U}{\partial t} = div[D(U_\sigma, x, y, t)\nabla U].$$  (5)

Another classical technique, proposed also by Weickert, is the edge enhancing diffusion filter *(EED)*. The filter uses matrix diffusivity with diffusion axes computed as the directions of the gradient vectors and the orthogonal ones, defined for a smoothed version of the processed image $\vec{v}_1 \parallel \nabla U_\sigma$ and $\vec{v}_2 \perp \nabla U_\sigma$ [9].

In [5], [6] we proposed a method similar in spirit with the *CED*, but devoted for filtering images containing flow like structures that exhibit also numerous junctions and corners. When designing a specific filter one must take into account the topological changes introduced on the output image by the filtering process. In proposing our flow coherence diffusion filter *(FC)* we addressed the lack of sensitivity of the *CED*'s coherence measure to abrupt orientation changes. The single parameter of the *CED* that can be used for this purpose is the constant $C$ in equation (4). Nevertheless, since the *CED*'s coherence measure is contrast sensitive, increasing $C$ in order to lower smoothing intensity in the neighborhood of corners can also produce less effective filtering of low contrast oriented patterns. Based on these observations we proposed a coherence measure close to that used by Rao in orientation estimation [4]:

$$\mu = \frac{\sum\limits_{(i,j)\in W(x_0,y_0)} |\nabla U|_{i,j} \cos^2(\theta_{x_0,y_0} - \theta_{x_i,y_j})}{\sum\limits_{(i,j)\in N(x_0,y_0)} |\nabla U|_{i,j}}.$$  (6)

In (6) $|\nabla U|_{i,j}$ denotes the norm of the gradient vector in a pixel of coordinates $(x_i, y_j)$, $W(x_0, y_0)$ is a centered neighborhood of the pixel $(x_0, y_0)$ and $\theta_{x_i,y_j}$ - the orientation of $\vec{v}_2$ - is the smoothed orientation computed in the same pixel.

For unidirectional noisy patterns, provided that the influence of noise on the estimated orientation can be eliminated, (6) is local contrast independent. As far as junctions and corners are concerned, in $W(x_0, y_0)$ the dispersion of the smoothed orientations around the orientation of the central pixel is nonzero and, thus, these regions correspond to local minima of (6). Similarly to the *CED* we used a diffusion matrix to weight the smoothing intensity along the diffusion axes:

$$D(U_\sigma, x, y, t) = (\vec{v}_1 \mid \vec{v}_2) \begin{pmatrix} \alpha & 0 \\ 0 & \alpha + (1-\alpha)h_\tau(\mu) \end{pmatrix} \begin{pmatrix} \vec{v}_1^T \\ \vec{v}_2^T \end{pmatrix}.$$  (7)

In the direction of structures the intensity of the process is modulated by a nonlinear function that takes (6) as one of its parameters:

$$h_\tau(\mu) = \frac{\tanh[\gamma(\mu - \tau)] + 1}{\tanh[\gamma(1.0 - \tau)] + 1}.$$  (8)

$h_\tau(\mu)$ plays the role of a fuzzy corner and junction detector. Whereas regions exhibiting coherence values below the threshold $\tau$ are smoothed in an isotropic manner with an intensity given by the small positive constant $\alpha$, directional patterns are processed anisotropically since on these regions $h_\tau(\mu)$ has values close to 1 [5]. The evolution equation for the flow coherence diffusion filter was nonlinear, taking the form of equation (5).

## 3  Linear Flow Coherence Diffusion Filter

Nonlinearity is a common concept for all the filters presented in the previous section. When dealing with image processing applications nonlinearity is of course desirable since it allows adaptive processing of various regions of interest of an image.

However, from a computational point of view, for PDE based image processing nonlinearity is also the source of poor efficiency. The continuous models are transposed into numerical models by means of finite time and space differencing. The solution is then approximated using explicit or implicit schemes through time consuming iterative processes. Tensor driven approaches are computationally intensive; both discussed models (*CED* and *FC*) need the estimation at each diffusion step of a structure tensor, computed according to (3) or (7). Although the problem can be somewhat solved by using elaborate implicit schemes we are adopting a different approach and we are proposing a linear flow coherence diffusion model *(LFC)*:

$$\frac{\partial U}{\partial t} = div[D(U^0(x, y))\nabla U],$$

(9)

that uses a unique diffusion tensor, computed on the original noisy image:

$$U^0(x, y) = U(x, y, 0).$$

(10)

From a theoretical point of view it is clear that a linear diffusion filter based on the above two equations will lack the precision of a nonlinear filter and, consequently, nonlinearity must be included at some level of the design of the diffusion filter. Instead of using a nonlinear evolution model we are considering nonlinearity in the orientation estimation step. We design the orientation estimation step to be scale adaptive using the coherence measure (6) as a decision criterion. The subsequent steps used for the orientations estimation step are summarized as follows:

1) For each pixel we estimate the orientation $\theta$ of the eigenvector $\overrightarrow{v_2}$ that corresponds to the gradient autocorrelation matrix $M$, defined over a square rectangular window $W(x,y)$ centered on the pixel under study:

$$M = \frac{1}{N}\sum_{i=1}^{N}\nabla U_i^0\nabla U_i^{0T} = \begin{pmatrix} \frac{1}{N}\sum_{i=1}^{N}(\frac{\partial U^0}{\partial x})^2 & \frac{1}{N}\sum_{i=1}^{N}(\frac{\partial U^0}{\partial x})(\frac{\partial U^0}{\partial y}) \\ \frac{1}{N}\sum_{i=1}^{N}(\frac{\partial U^0}{\partial x})(\frac{\partial U^0}{\partial y}) & \frac{1}{N}\sum_{i=1}^{N}(\frac{\partial U^0}{\partial y})^2 \end{pmatrix}.$$

(11)

2) For each scale $N = card(W(x,y))$ and for each pixel of coordinates $(x_0, y_0)$ we compute a coherence measure based on (6) and defined over the support of $M$:

$$\mu_N (x_0, y_0) = \frac{\sum\limits_{(i,j)\in W(x_0,y_0)} |\nabla U|_{i,j} \cos^2(\theta_{x_0,y_0} - \theta_{x_i,y_j})}{\sum\limits_{(i,j)\in W(x_0,y_0)} |\nabla U|_{i,j}}, N = card(W(x_0, y_0)). \qquad (12)$$

3) The scale $N_{opt}$ for which the coherence $\mu_N (x_0, y_0)$ exhibits a maximum :

$$\mu_{N\,opt} (x_0, y_0) = \max_N \mu_N (x_0, y_0). \qquad (13)$$

is the optimal scale pixel of coordinates $(x_0, y_0)$; the estimated orientation $\theta$ of a structure that passes through $(x_0, y_0)$ is the one computed in step 1 at a scale $N=N_{opt}$.

We use the results of the adaptive orientation estimation step to assemble the diffusion tensor according to (7) and considering $\vec{v}_2 = (\cos\theta, \sin\theta)^t$ :

$$D(U^0(x, y)) = (\vec{v}_1 \mid \vec{v}_2) \begin{pmatrix} \alpha & 0 \\ 0 & \alpha + (1-\alpha)h_\tau(\mu_{N_{opt}}) \end{pmatrix} \begin{pmatrix} \vec{v}_1^T \\ \vec{v}_2^T \end{pmatrix}. \qquad (14)$$

For unidirectional patterns affected by uncorrelated, zero mean additive noise, by maximizing the size of the support we approach the assumptions from [2]: zero values for the spatial means of partial derivatives, computed both for noise and for the noise-signal products. As pointed out by Jahne in [2], under these conditions the orientation estimated using a structure tensor approach is highly robust with respect to noise and one is able to compute the orientation of the noise free image. The coherence measure will be close to 1 for these regions and, consequently, will induce efficient noise elimination through constant intensity unidirectional smoothing.

In the vicinity of junctions an orientation estimation technique based on the structure tensor tends to produce false orientations. In these areas the same algorithm minimizes estimation errors by favoring choices of small support windows that are including only gradient vectors belonging to a single directional texture.

## 4   Experimental Results

Comparing PDE based filters is not an easy task. Most of the models have a large number of parameters and the quality of the filtered results depends strongly on their choice. Disposing of an original and of a degraded image we opted for a full parameter search, trying to find a best filtered result that maximizes an objective measure. The experimental plan involves 15 synthetic images composed of directional patterns and degraded by Gaussian noise (Fig.1). As an objective measure we have chosen the classical *PSNR* since recent work in image quality assessment shows that it can be closely related to the subjective perception of the human visual system. The noise levels and the *PSNR* corresponding to the best result are shown on Table 1.

All the numerical filters were implemented using Weickert's nonnegative numerical scheme [6]. Both our methods provided superior results to those of the coherence enhancing filter and of the edge enhancing filter. Instead, the results corresponding to the linear and nonlinear versions of the flow coherence are very close. In order to investigate if the results are due to the particular choice of the test images or if they are representative for the performances of each method, we performed a non-parametric two-way rank analysis of variance (ANOVA) [1] (Table 2.)

**Table 1.** Quantitative measures for the study including 15 synthetic images

| Image | Noise levels PSNR[dB] | Best filtered results - PSNR[dB] | | | |
|-------|------------|----------|----------|----------|----------|
| | | **EED** | **CED** | **FC** | **LFC** |
| 1 | 16.66 | 24.662 | 25.67996 | 26.82621 | 26.9634 |
| 2 | 14.07 | 19.48746 | 20.81219 | 21.19285 | 21.16698 |
| 3 | 14.67 | 23.27541 | 23.49707 | 23.97254 | 24.24443 |
| 4 | 15.60 | 21.95431 | 22.65379 | 23.15798 | 23.16356 |
| 5 | 15.16 | 22.70581 | 22.64653 | 23.23814 | 23.25276 |
| 6 | 13.68 | 22.19151 | 22.50154 | 22.78201 | 22.75901 |
| 7 | 15.00 | 21.89273 | 23.74538 | 24.02237 | 24.42807 |
| 8 | 14.95 | 22.82565 | 22.96993 | 23.3488 | 22.937 |
| 9 | 14.64 | 23.89563 | 23.9439 | 24.46515 | 24.30819 |
| 10 | 14.39 | 21.39066 | 22.2376 | 22.79918 | 22.94494 |
| 11 | 14.85 | 23.0874 | 23.3992 | 23.9798 | 23.9383 |
| 12 | 16.10 | 24.0483 | 24.3268 | 24.6058 | 24.5806 |
| 13 | 13.27 | 20.027 | 21.0839 | 21.5093 | 21.4642 |
| 14 | 16.65 | 24.7 | 24.6496 | 25.0269 | 25.18447 |
| 15 | 14.14 | 23.5511 | 23.2455 | 23.5412 | 23.6359 |

**Table 2.** Two-way ANOVA results for the experimental plan

| Source of variance | Sum of squares | Degrees of freedom | Mean square | F | p |
|--------------------|----------------|--------------------|-------------|---|---|
| Total | 17995.00 | 59 | 305.00 | | |
| Between images | 16351.53 | 14 | 1145.83 | | |
| Between methods | 1289.27 | 3 | 388.91 | 20.76 | $2.09 \cdot 10^{-8}$ |
| Residual | 786.67 | 42 | 18.73 | | |

As the results from Table 2 are showing, more that 95 % of the variability between the obtained results is due to the processing methods and to the nature of the images. The two-way ANOVA design allows us to isolate and investigate only the method effect. The extremely low probability $(p=2.09 \cdot 10^{-8})$ associated to a Fisher-Snédécour test $(F=20.76)$ allows us to conclude that the processing method has a significant influence over the quality of the processed result.

We are also interested of building a hierarchy for the analyzed methods. The mean ranks, computed for each method over the 60 measurements from Table 1, are: $R_{EED}=24.4$, $R_{CED}=28.3$, $R_{FC}=34.73$, $R_{LFC}=36.7$. For comparing the three values we use the classical Student-Newman-Keuls post-hoc test [1]. Its critical values, computed for a 5% risk, are: 3.18 for comparing two consecutive ranks, 3.85 for three ranks and 4.24 for comparisons spanning four ranks. We conclude that both *LFC* and *FC* are better that the *CED* but no distinction can be done statistically between their performances. *CED* proves to be, globally, better than *EED*.

In terms of visual results we first show in Fig.1 the filtered results computed on a synthetic image processed by the analyzed methods (image number 14).

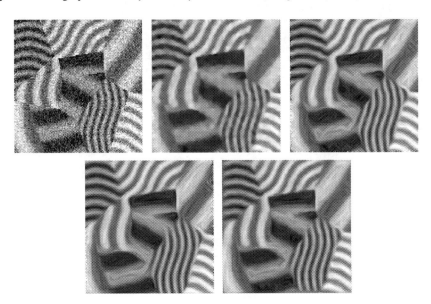

**Fig. 1.** Degraded image and filtered results. From top to bottom and left to right: degraded image, *EED* result, *CED* result, *FC* result, *LFC* result.

The behavior of the analyzed diffusion filters can be observed on the presented results. The edges are irregular and slightly blurred in the *EED* processed result; the effect is due to the less robust estimation of the diffusion axes. The *CED* best result is inferior with close to 0.5dB with respect to *FC* and *LFC*. The lower quality of the result is explainable by the fact that the *CED's* coherence measure is local contrast dependent and, consequently, the smoothing process intensity is lowered on large, region like images. Reduced sensitivity to semi-local contrast variations allows both *FC* and *LFC* to produce better results. In terms of complexity, the computational time was 0.6s/iteration for FC and of 0.07s/iteration for FCL (orientation estimation step included). The results are given for a 128x128 pixels image and were implemented on a Pentium 4, 1.5MHz processor PC.

Basically the same behavior can be observed when processing real images. We show such an image in Fig.2. The *CED* result is characterized by strong fluctuations on the oriented part of the image. The fluctuations cannot be eliminated since, in order to avoid geometric distortions, the filter must be stopped relatively quickly. The results between *FC* and *LFC* are different. We judge as the best result the one issued by processing the input image with the *LFC* filter since it exhibits a better homogeneity of the oriented background. The adaptive orientation step diminishes the sensibility of the filter with respect to the local signal energy and produces a more efficient smoothing. In terms of computational complexity the results are corresponding to 8s/iteration for *FC* and to 1.2s/iteration for *LFC* on a 429x319 pixels image.

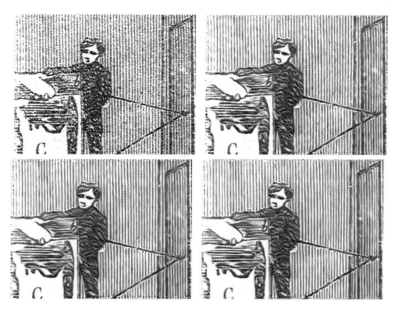

**Fig. 2.** Results on a real image. From top to bottom and left to right: original image, *CED* result *FC* and *LFC* results.

# References

1. Connover W. J., Imam R. L.: Rank transformations as a bridge between parametric and non-parametric Statistics. The American Statistician, 35, (1981) 124-129
2. Jahne, B.: Performance characteristics of low – level motion estimators in spatio-temporal images. DAGM Workshop Performance Characteristics and Quality of Computer Vision Algorithms, Braunschweig, Germany (1997)
3. Perona, P. and Malik, J.: Scale-space and edge detection using anisotropic diffusion. IEEE Transactions on Pattern Analysis and Machine Intelligence, 12/7 (1990) 629-639
4. Rao, A.: A taxonomy for structure description and classification: Springer-Verlag, Berlin Heidelberg New York (1990)
5. Terebes, R., Lavialle, O., Baylou, P, Borda M.: Flow Coherence Diffusion. In: Proceedings of the 2003 International TICSP Workshop on Spectral Methods and Multirate Signal Processing , Barcelona, (2003) 197-202
6. Terebes, R.: Diffusion directionnelle. Applications à la restauration et à l'amélioration d'images de documents anciens. Ph.D thesis 2819, Université Bordeaux 1 France (2004)
7. Terebes, R. Borda, M., Lavialle, O., Baylou, P., Pop, S., Adam, T.: Linear flow coherence diffusion. In: Proceeding of the 7th International Carpathian Control Conference ICCC2005, Miskolc (2005) 65-72
8. Weickert, J.: Coherence-enhancing diffusion filtering. International Journal of Computer Vision, 31 (1999) 111-127
9. Weickert, J.: A review of nonlinear diffusion filtering.In: B.ter Haar Romeny, L. Florack, J. Koenderink, M. Vierger (eds.), Scale Space Theory in Computer Vision, Lecture notes on Computer Science, vol. 1252, Springer-Verlag, Berlin Heidelberg New York (1997) 3–28

# Updating Geospatial Database: An Automatic Approach Combining Photogrammetry and Computer Vision Techniques

In-Hak Joo[1], Tae-Hyun Hwang[1], and Kyoung-Ho Choi[2]

[1] Electronics and Telecommunications Research Institute, Daejeon, Korea
[2] Mokpo National University, Dept. of Electronics Engineering, Mokpo, Korea
{ihjoo, hth63339}@etri.re.kr, khchoi@mokpo.ac.kr

**Abstract.** In this paper, we suggest an automatic approach based on photogrammetry and computer vision techniques to build and update geospatial database more effectively. Stereo image or video is spotlighted as a useful media for constructing and representing geospatial database. We can acquire coordinates of geospatial objects appearing in image frames captured by camera with mobile mapping system, but quite a lot of manual input are required. We suggest a change detection method for geospatial objects in video frames by combining computer vision technique and photogrammetry. With the suggested scheme, we can make the construction and update process more efficient and reduce the update cost of geospatial database.

## 1 Introduction

As the advent of newest application fields of information technology such as telematics or Location-Based Service(LBS), geospatial database becomes more and more important. The geospatial database usually has large volume and requires frequent update. Therefore, efficient construction and update method is an important issue in geospatial database. Recently, stereo image or video has been introduced as a construction tool for geospatial database. Because video is more perceptible than conventional "map", it is spotlighted as a useful media for constructing, representing, and visualizing geospatial database[1].

The video-based Geographic Information System(GIS) researched so far has been mainly realized by *mobile mapping system* that is a platform with S/W, H/W, and sensors such as cameras, Global Positioning System(GPS), and Inertial Navigation System(INS) integrated. Many mobile mapping systems are developed, usually in the form of sensor-equipped vehicle, and used till now [2]. It can acquire coordinate of geospatial objects (such as roads and buildings) appearing in images captured by camera, with *photogrammetry* used. With the stereo image and accurate position/attitude of camera, we can calculate 3-d coordinate of an object therein by pointing the object in two images.

However, when the mobile mapping system constructs coordinates of objects with video, it suffers from two problems: sensor inaccuracy and quite a lot of

J. Blanc-Talon et al. (Eds.): ACIVS 2005, LNCS 3708, pp. 324–331, 2005.
© Springer-Verlag Berlin Heidelberg 2005

manual input required. Enhancing accuracy of sensors is beyond the scope of this paper, and we will discuss about reducing manual input in this paper. To reduce the manual input time when we get objects' coordinates from images, we need automatic or semi-automatic recognition of objects from images.

In the previous researches about object detection from images captured by mobile mapping system or running vehicle along the roads, usually road lanes, road signs, or roadside facilities are handled. This is because there are many objects in such images, and because they have different characteristics and require different approaches for detection. The examples of researches are found in [3] where automatic extraction and identification of road sign is used for driver-assistance system, and in [4] for positioning road facilities. Other papers focus on the automatic road lane extraction that is used for automatic driving.

To detect objects from the image captured by mobile mapping systems, we consider (1)complicated recognition method is required because the images have many exceptive conditions that may bring actual problems in the recognition process; (2)recognition process cannot be entirely done by vision, but together with location information, sensor data, and photogrammetric calculation; and (3)the recognition process can be done in an automatic fashion.

In this paper, we suggest a method for constructing and updating geospatial objects based on photogrammetry and computer vision techniques, which is used together with a mobile mapping system to enhance the efficiency of the works.

## 2    Data Construction by Mobile Mapping System

Mobile mapping systems collect stereo video and position/attitude of cameras synchronized to each frame, from which we can calculate 3-d coordinate of object appearing in images by picking a pair of corresponding point in the images. We have developed a mobile mapping system called *4S-Van*[5], which we use as a platform for our suggestions. It is equipped by sensors such as GPS, INS, and cameras, as shown in Fig.1. The camera can capture stereo video of $640 \times 480$ resolution in 15 *frame/sec* frame rate.

The photogrammetry is a technology that can be applied to stereo image collected by mobile mapping system[6]. With position/attitude data for each

**Fig. 1.** 4S-Van: a mobile mapping system

frame accurately synchronized to time, pixel coordinates of a point(both left and right) can be converted into world coordinates. Conversely, world coordinates of a point can be converted to pixel coordinates of any frame. Details of two conversion functions are presented in [6], and abstractly expressed as

$$P = Intersection(p_l, p_r, C_l, C_r, A_l, A_r) \tag{1}$$

$$p_l = Resection(P, C_l, C_r, A_l, A_r) \tag{2}$$

where $P$ is 3-dimensional world coordinates, $p$ is pixel coordinates (each left and right frame; $p_l$ and $p_r$), $C$ is camera position(each left and right camera; $C_l$ and $C_r$), and $A$ is attitude of camera(each left and right camera; $A_l$ and $A_r$). With the two functions, world coordinates of geospatial object can be obtained from a given pair of pixel coordinates, and vice versa.

## 3   Automatic Construction and Update of Geospatial Database

Our basic approach is to apply object detection as a complimentary method for selecting a frame per object among all frames where input or update process should be done. The roles of detection method are (1)when we initially build geospatial database, it helps selecting frames where the manual input should be done; (2)when we update geospatial database, it detects only the changed road signs for which necessary actions are required. The detailed descriptions of processes for two cases will be shown in Sec.3.2 and Sec.3.3, respectively. The concept of the suggested system is illustrated in Fig.2.

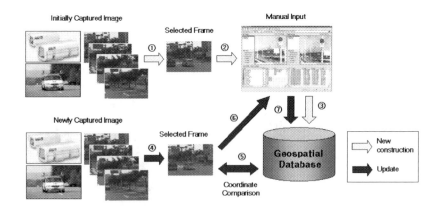

**Fig. 2.** The overview of the system

## 3.1  Detection Method

In this section, we present the detection method for road signs, which is used for construction and update of road signs. Processing the following steps, we automatically detect road signs that appear in stereo video frames.

**Clipping.** We assume that the road signs appear the upper half of image because the 4S-Van keeps to the right when running and the cameras look downward. So, in our experimental environment and camera configuration, the road sign seldom appear in the lower half of images. Therefore we clip the image from original $640 \times 480$ to $640 \times 240$ by clipping off the lower side of image.

**Resizing.** We down-sample the clipped image from $640 \times 240$ to $320 \times 120$ size for more efficient computations and reduction of noises of original image.

**Reducing ROI.** Because the entropy of region for road sign is higher than other regions, we exclude the low-entropy regions from Region Of Interest(ROI). First, image is converted to luminance image $L(x, y)$ as

$$L(x, y) = 0.3 \times R(x, y) + 0.6 \times G(x, y) + 0.1 \times B(x, y) \tag{3}$$

where $R(x, y)$, $G(x, y)$, $B(x, y)$ are three color components of the image. Next, $L(x, y)$ image is divided into fixed size($16 \times 16$) blocks. And for each block, an entropy is derived and quantified by using Picture Information Measure(PIM), which is defined as

$$PIM = \sum_{i=0}^{255} h(i) - max\left(h(i)\right) \tag{4}$$

where $i$ is gray value($0 \sim 255$) of each pixel and $h(i)$ is histogram of the gray value with regard to given block[7]. The PIM value for each image block is used as a indicative information about the image block. That is, busy and uniformly distributed image block has a large PIM value, while simple and non-uniformly distributed image block has low value. Because image block that corresponds to region of road sign has large PIM value, we can exclude blocks of small PIM value from ROI.

**Finding Candidate Regions.** To find candidate regions for road signs from the chosen ROIs, we calculate chromatic image. As the gray color has a low chromatic value while the others a high value, the chromatic image represents the inside part of the sign that has high color. The normalized errors for each color component with regard to (3) are defined as

$$e_R(x, y) = \frac{|L(x, y) - R(x, y)|}{L(x, y)} \, , \tag{5}$$

$$e_G(x, y) = \frac{|L(x, y) - G(x, y)|}{L(x, y)} \, , \tag{6}$$

$$e_B(x, y) = \frac{|L(x, y) - B(x, y)|}{L(x, y)} \, . \tag{7}$$

The values of (5), (6), (7) would be close to zero if the color is close to gray. Finally, the chromatic image $A(x, y)$ represents the maximum error, and is defined as

$$A(x, y) = max(e_R(x, y), e_G(x, y), e_B(x, y)) \tag{8}$$

which is used to choose ROIs with a given threshold[3].

**HSI Thresholding.** After extracting regions with high color, we convert RGB image to HSI image. Then we process filtering for image by

$$P(x, y) = \begin{cases} Red & \text{if } (H(x, y) < R_l \text{ or } H(x, y) > R_u) \text{ and } S(x, y) > T_S \\ Blue & \text{if } B_l < H(x, y) < B_u \text{ and } S(x, y) > T_S \\ 0 & \text{otherwise} \end{cases}$$

$$\tag{9}$$

where $H(x, y)$ is hue value (0∼360 degree) and $S(x, y)$ is saturation value (0∼1). The threshold values for (9) are determined by measuring hue and saturation values of road signs in our dataset. With (9) we can extract regions with colors that are similar to color of road sign.

**Labelling and Detection.** With the result image of HSI thresholding, we execute labelling process with flood-fill algorithm, to extract regions for road signs. With the assumption that the Minimum Bounding Rectangles(MBR) of target road signs have height/width ratio close to 1, we regard only the regions with 0.8∼1.2 ratio as regions for road sign. If there are multiple regions detected, we select the region whose MBR is the largest.

**Classification.** To classify the labelled regions, we use a simple neural network, because of the types of target road sign is limited. The processing result is passed through neural network for learning the type of road sign[8]. Used neural network is *Back Propagation Network* with 1 hidden layer, 24 feature vectors, and 24 outputs.

### 3.2 Construction of Road Sign Database

Because an object appears in several frames in most cases, we should consider avoiding duplicative input for the same object during scanning the frames. We should select a frame where the coordinate of an object will be actually calculated. This process needs an assumption that the calculation accuracy is higher when the object appears larger, which is from the experiments and accuracy test of 4S-Van data[5]. Another assumption is that the road signs are not so close to each other. That is, we ignore the case that two road signs appear closely in the same frame. With these assumptions, we select the target frame for manual input of each road sign and construct its coordinate. The whole process is done by scanning all frames and processing following steps for each frame. Note that we scan the frames reversely with regard to time, in order that the object appears larger in earlier frames, which is more convenient to process.

1. **detect all road signs**
2. **select the road sign whose region(MBR) is the largest**
3. **pick a pair of feature point of road sign**

4. calculate approximated 3-d coordinate
5. if the coordinate is near to one of the already constructed road sign (within the predefined threshold), discard it
6. else select it as target for input; process manual input

Once a frame for each road sign is selected(step 6), we should pick a pair of feature point manually to calculate accurate 3-d coordinate of the road sign. The calculation is done by photogrammetric operation (1), and our experiments with 4S-Van data shows that 3-d coordinate error of (1) is under $30cm$. Though picking a feature point of the road sign as input point can be done automatically, it is likely to bring erroneous result because determination of feature point is more inaccurate compared to manual input, unless it is an ideal condition. When the coordinate of each object is stored, necessary attributes such as kind of sign is also stored. In this stage, information for type of road sign can be automatically determined because the road sign is already classified from the image(Sec.3.1).

## 3.3    Update of Road Sign Database

Assuming that all coordinates of road signs have been already constructed, the database should be updated periodically to reflect the changes of road signs. It is obvious that most of road signs remain unchanged if the update period is short. So we detect changed objects and add/modify/delete them while take no action about unchanged objects, which means minimal manual operation. To do such job, we scan all frames and process following steps for each frame.

1. uncheck the flags of all road signs in database
2. for each frame of newly captured video,
   (a) detect all road signs
   (b) select the road sign whose region(MBR) is the largest
   (c) pick a pair of feature point of road sign
   (d) calculate approximated 3-d coordinate
   (e) if the coordinate is near to any road sign in database (within the predefined threshold), check the flag for the road sign
   (f) else select it as target for addition; process manual input
3. delete data of each road sign whose flag is unchecked

If the comparison (step 2e) succeeds, the object is regarded as unchanged, so there needs no update process about this object. Otherwise, it means the object detection and/or coordinate calculation yields too large error or the object is newly built. For both cases, user is required to recalculate and correct (or add) the coordinate of the object by manual process. The user should pick a pair of conjugate point from each of two images, which is because the accurate picking is important for accurate coordinate calculation. After processing all frames, we can also conclude that unchecked objects in the database no more exist; we simply remove the objects in the database.

However, there is always chance for misjudgement because of the unclarity and uncertainty of images, positioning accuracy, and threshold value. So, we should monitor and adapt the threshold value while processing video frames.

## 4    Result

We have implemented and tested the suggested method with the video frames captured by 4S-Van. The video has been captured for about $10km$ of road interval, with $640 \times 480$ resolution and $15\ frame/sec$ frame rate. The detection method has detected predefined road signs successfully. The observed error of 3-d coordinate without manual input is about $\leq 5m$ in our experimental environment. As expected, the error is larger than the error of manually calculated coordinate ($\leq 30cm$). Though the error is too large to calculate the coordinate where high accuracy is required, we can say that it is small enough to detect changed road signs and compare them with existing database.

Fig.3(a) shows an intermediate image for a frame where the region with (8) value $\leq 0.4$ is removed. The regions with high color component are extracted, such as red-colored road sign and yellow-colored road lanes. Fig.3(b) shows result of HIS thresholding where all colors other than red and blue is removed. Fig.3(c) shows the result of labelling where the candidate regions of road sign are extracted; a labelled region is zoomed at lower-left corner.

(a) Chromatic image

(b) Result of HIS thresholding

(c) Result of labelling

**Fig. 3.** Result images

## 5    Conclusion

In this paper, we suggest an automatic approach based on photogrammetry and computer vision techniques to build and update geospatial database more effectively. Though we can construct geospatial database by processing video frames captured by mobile mapping system, the cost of construction or update is still high because of large volume of video and required manual input. So we suggest a scheme of automatic change detection for geospatial database(road signs in this paper) to reduce manual process and make the construction/update process more efficient. To detect the road signs in image frames, image processing, computer vision technologies, and photogrammetry are combined and applied. With the suggested scheme, we can make the construction and update process more efficient and reduce the update cost of geospatial database.

The suggested approach suffers from the error come from synchronization of 4S-Van sensor and the unclarity and uncertainty of images. Methods for obtaining more exact sensor data and clear image will improve the performance of suggested method. Further, because only limited kinds of geospatial objects are handled by our suggestion, we should research about similar schemes for other types of geospatial objects as the future studies.

# References

1. In-Hak Joo, Tae-Hyun Hwang, and Kyung-Ho Choi, Generation of Video Metadata Supporting Video-GIS Integration, Proceedings of ICIP(International Conference on Image Processing) 2004, Oct 2004, Singapore.
2. Ron Li, "Mobile Mapping-An Emerging Technology for Spatial Data Acquisition'" Journal of Photogrammetric Engineering and Remote Sensing. Vol.63, No.9, 1997, pp.1085-1092
3. Arturo de la Escalera, Jose Maria Armingol, Jose Manuel Pastor, and Francisco Jose Rodriguez, "Visual Sign Information Extraction and Identification by Deformable Models for Intelligent Vehicles," IEEE Transactions on Intelligent Transportation Systems, Vol. 5, No. 2, Jun 2004.
4. Zhuowen Tu and Ron Li, "Automatic Recognition of Civil Infrastructure Objects in Mobile Mapping Imagery Using Markov Random Field," Proc. of ISPRS Conf. 2000, Amsterdam, Jul 2000.
5. Seung-Yong Lee, Seong-Baek Kim, Ji-Hoon Choi, and Jong-Hun Lee, "4S-Van: A Prototype Mobile Mapping System for GIS," Korean Journal of Remote Sensing, Vol.19, No.1, 2003, pp.91-97.
6. Paul R. Wolf and Bon A. Dewitt, "Elements of Photogrammetry: With applications in GIS," McGraw-Hill, 2000.
7. Shi-Kuo Chang, "Principles of Pictorial Information Systems Design," Prentice-Hall, 1989, pp.61-81.
8. H.schweitzer, J.W.Bell, and F. Wu, "Very Fast Template Matching," Lecture Notes in Computer Science 2353, 2002, pp.358-372.

# Affine Invariant Feature Extraction Using Symmetry

Arasanathan Anjulan and Nishan Canagarajah

Department of Electrical and Electronic Engineering,
University of Bristol, Bristol, UK
{A.Anjulan, Nishan.Ganagarajah}@bristal.ac.uk

**Abstract.** This paper describes a novel method for extracting affine invariant regions from images, based on an intuitive notion of symmetry. We define a local affine-invariant symmetry measure and derive a technique for obtaining symmetry regions. Compared to previous approaches the regions obtained are considered to be salient regions, of the image. We apply the symmetry-based technique to obtain affine-invariant regions in images with large-scale difference and demonstrate superior performance compared to existing methods.

## 1  Introduction

Content-based recognition of images from different imaging conditions is a difficult problem. An efficient solution will have several applications in Intelligent Content Based Retrieval (ICBR) systems. Local image features are shown to be useful in this venue, as they are robust to partial visibility and clutter. However, obtaining a limited number of regions to uniquely represent an image is not trivial. Two important points should be considered while obtaining these regions. The first one is that these regions should be invariant to different imaging conditions. A certain number of selected regions should be same in different images for good matching performance. Secondly, the chosen regions should be representative of the image in that they should come from visually important parts of the region.

Since the advent of the influential paper of Schimid and Mohr [13], many local region selection algorithms were published. Mikolajczyk and Schmid extended the earlier work of Schmid and Mohr into a scale invariant approach [6] and then to a fully affine invariant [7] region selection. They used Harris corner detector to select the regions in multi-scaled Gaussian smoothed images. However, the use of corners to find interest points may lead to the selection of non-planar regions affecting the affine invariance assumption of the region selection algorithms. Tuytelaars and Van Gool [16]used image edge and corner features to select affine-invariant regions. They used Harris corner detector and Canny edge detector to find corners and edges. Edge detection part reduces the stability of their algorithm as there is no perfect method for detecting same edges in different images. Later, they also selected regions with large intensity gradi-

J. Blanc-Talon et al. (Eds.): ACIVS 2005, LNCS 3708, pp. 332–339, 2005.
© Springer-Verlag Berlin Heidelberg 2005

ents along the boundaries [15]. They used the local intensity extrema points as the initial points, which sometimes reduces the performance of their algorithm.

Kadir and Brady [1] select scale invariant regions in images, based on entropy and later extended the approach to handle affine invariant regions [2]. Nonetheless, entropy calculation over regions is computationally intensive and it has been shown that the entropy based selection is not entirely robust to imaging conditions [9]. A fast and efficient algorithm is proposed by Matas [5][10] where grey scale image is iteratively thresholded until maximally stable regions are obtained. Lowe [3] searches in "scale-space" to extract interest regions and then uses the Scale Invariant Feature Transformation (SIFT) algorithm to obtain a robust scale-invariant descriptor of the selected regions. While his scale-space interest region selection method fails when there is a large affine transformation, the SIFT descriptor is widely used to describe the interest regions in many other region selection methods [9].

Symmetric regions are descriptor rich and can be highly discriminative. Near symmetric regions are common in natural images. Humans have strong sense of symmetry and symmetric regions make up a large number of "pop-up" areas of an image. Reisfeld [11] used generalised symmetry transform to obtain symmetric regions in natural and artificial images. He used a step by step multi-scale search approach. Resifeld and Yeshurun [12] applied the symmetry transform to obtain robust face features. Thomas Zielke and Brauckmann [17] applied a vertical symmetry detection algorithm in a car-following application. They used an intensity based method to find the vertical symmetry axis and then used directional filters to obtain edge symmetry. In a recent work, Loy and Zelinsky [4] used a fast radial algorithm to detect symmetric interest points. Shen [14] used the generalised complex moments to detect symmetry. But his approach is limited to isolated objects.

In this paper, we propose an interest point detection scheme where a number of near symmetric regions are chosen to represent the image. A selected region of high symmetry is approximated by an ellipse whose major axis or minor axis is the axis of symmetry. The selected regions are naturally salient parts in an image and the results show a superior performance compared to existing methods. The algorithm for finding symmetric regions is described in section 2. In section 3, we explain the experiments carried out to demonstrate the performance of symmetry regions in content-based image retrieval and compare the results to other interest point methods and conclusions are presented in section 4.

## 2   Proposed Approach

We define a measure of symmetry, based on the generalised symmetry transform of Resifeld [11]. This measure is used to find symmetry points, given a symmetry axis. Symmetry regions are obtained by fitting ellipses to the chosen symmetry points, as elliptical regions remain elliptical(with possibly different major, minor axis and eccentric angle) with affine transformation.

## 2.1  Symmetry Measure

Let $\mathbf{p}_i = (x_i, y_i)$ and $\mathbf{p}_j = (x_j, y_j)$ be two points which lie in equal distance from a symmetric axis (left hand figure in figure 1). The intensity gradient at point $\mathbf{p}_i$ is given by $\mathbf{g}_i = \{\frac{\partial}{\partial x} I(\mathbf{p}_i), \frac{\partial}{\partial y} I(\mathbf{p}_i)\}$. Here, $I(\mathbf{p}_i)$ is the image pixel value at point $\mathbf{p}_i$. The log-magnitude $(r_i)$ and the orientation $(\theta_i)$ are defined at the point $\mathbf{p}_i$ as

$$r_i = log(1 + \|\mathbf{g}_i\|) \tag{1}$$

$$\theta_i = \arctan(\frac{\frac{\partial}{\partial x} I(\mathbf{p}_i)}{\frac{\partial}{\partial y} I(\mathbf{p}_i)}) \tag{2}$$

Let the line passing through the points $\mathbf{p}_i$ and $\mathbf{p}_j$ makes an angle $\alpha_{ij}$ with the horizontal line. This is shown in figure 1. The Symmetry measure $C(i, j)$ between points $\mathbf{p}_i$ and $\mathbf{p}_j$ is defined as follows

$$P(i, j) = (1 - \cos(\theta_i + \theta_j - 2\alpha_{ij}))\cos(\theta_i - \theta_j) \tag{3}$$

$$C(i, j) = P(i, j)r_i r_j \tag{4}$$

The phase weight function $P(i, j)$ measures the symmetry between the two points. The first term, $(1 - \cos(\theta_i + \theta_j - 2\alpha_{ij}))$ will reach its maximum value 2 when maximum symmetry is achieved $(\theta_i - \alpha_{ij} + \theta_j - \alpha_{ij} = \pi)$ . This happens when the gradients at $\mathbf{p}_i$ and $\mathbf{p}_j$ are oriented in the same direction towards each other or against each other. Both of these situations are consistent with the intuitive notion of symmetry. The second term in the phase weight function is introduced to prevent high symmetry measure on straight edges. The gradient magnitude part $(r_i r_j)$ is used to prevent high symmetry in smooth regions and the logarithm of the magnitude is used to prevent the edge influence biasing the symmetry influence. Therefore high symmetric measure will be obtained in any symmetric points with high gradient value (symmetric edge points).

## 2.2  Symmetry Regions

Given a symmetric axis and a location in an image, we search for symmetric points (at equal perpendicular distance from the symmetry line) along the symmetry line. Candidate pair of points, with a symmetric measure that is above a threshold value and a local maximum compared to its neighboring pairs of points, are chosen (figure 1). The local maximum symmetry pair selection ensures the affine invariance. We searched up to a defined number (70 is used for all the experiments in this paper) of pixel distances from the symmetry line.

Once the symmetric points are chosen for a particular symmetric axis at a given location, we try to fit ellipses of different sizes and eccentricities whose major or minor axis lies in the symmetry axis such that it approximates the chosen symmetry points (right hand figure in figure 1).

In this work we have searched symmetry regions at 40 different orientations. At each orientation corresponding symmetry lines are placed in parallel( at a perpendicular distance of 1 pixel ) and possible symmetry regions are searched.

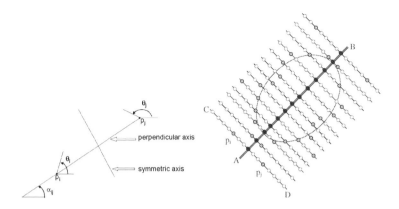

**Fig. 1.** Symmetry measure and symmetry regions.The left hand figure explains the terms used in the calculation of the symmetry measure of points $p_i$ and $p_j$. The right hand figure illustrates the process of obtaining a symmetry region given a set of symmetry points and the corresponding symmetry axis, $AB$. Here, $CD$ is one of the search line, perpendicular to the symmetry axis and $p_i$ and $p_j$ are the pair of symmetry points found on that line.

When an elliptic symmetry region undergoes an affine transformation, it will become another elliptic region with possibly, a different symmetric axis. As we are searching with 40 possible symmetric axis, our approach can handle large affine variations.

## 3   Results

The region selection algorithms needs to be robust against varying image conditions and affine variations. Their performance can be evaluated using two different criteria: repeatability of same regions in different images and the consistency of the region descriptors for matching.

We evaluate the performance of the symmetry-based region selection algorithm firstly on images transformed by scale and rotation and secondly for full affine deformation using the above two criteria. The performance is compared with two commonly used region selection algorithms proposed by Mikolajczyk and Schmid [7] and Matas [5]. The test image sets and the ground truth homography between them was obtained from www.robots.ox.ac.uk/ vgg/research/affine.

The symmetry-based elliptical regions are first chosen from images independently. The repeatability of same regions between two images is calculated by first mapping regions from one image to another using the provided homography and then estimating the error in the overlap. If the error is less than 40% the region is deemed as repeating in both images. The total repeatability between two images is calculated as the ratio of the number of repeated regions between the two images and minimum of the two total number of selected regions from the two images. More detailed explanation of these measures can be found in [7][9].

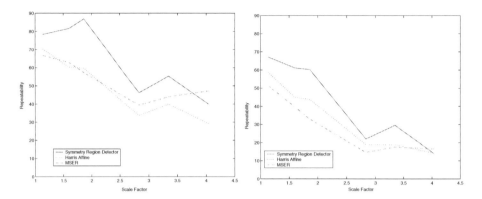

**Fig. 2.** Repeatability with scale variation. The left hand figure shows the repeatability of the regions with increasing scale factor. The right hand figure shows the consistency of the SIFT descriptor with increasing scale factor (The results in this figure are obtained by using the sample image set given in Fig 6).

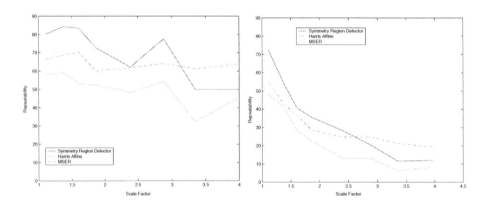

**Fig. 3.** Repeatability with scale variation. The left hand figure shows the repeatability of the regions with increasing scale factor. The right hand figure shoes the consistency of the SIFT descriptor with increasing scale factor. (The results in this figure are obtained by using the sample image set given in Fig 5).

Even though the repeatability criteria is useful in evaluating the performance of the region selection algorithm, a more practical measure, from the image matching algorithm's point of view, is the consistency of image descriptors of the same regions detected in different images. This is the second criteria we used to evaluate our algorithm. Scale Invariant Feature Transform (SIFT)[3] is used to obtain the region descriptors in our experiments, as SIFT is proved to be more robust than any other type of region descriptor [8].

The results are given in figures 2,3 and 4. In Figure 2, the variation of the repeatability is shown with the increasing scale factor between the two images. The images used in this test were taken at the same scene with a still camera, but

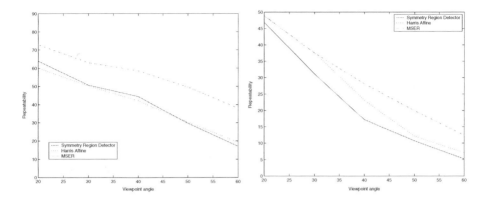

**Fig. 4.** Repeatability with viewpoint angle variation. The left hand figure shows the repeatability of the regions with increasing viewpoint angle. The right hand figure shows the consistency of the SIFT descriptor with increasing view point angle.

**Fig. 5.** Some of the repeated regions in two images taken in different zoom position and rotational angle

using different zooming positions. The first image is taken as the reference image and all other images varies by scale factors ranging from 0.2 to 4, compared to the first image. Figure 2(left hand) shows the repeatability of the regions and Figure 2(right hand) shows the consistency of the descriptors. It is clear from these results that the repeatability between the regions is good enough to identify the match of the images (taken at the same scene) even at a scale factor difference of 4. The results obtained using MSER and Harris Affine algorithms are also given for comparison. It is clear from Figure 2 that our algorithm outperforms the other two methods in large zoom conditions. The sample images used in this test are given in Figure 5 with some of the matched regions.

Figure 3 again shows the variation of the repeatability with increasing scale factor, but with different set of images. The sample images used in this experiment are given in Figure 6. Again the results show the superior performance of

**Fig. 6.** Some of the repeated regions in two images taken in different zooming position and rotational angle

our algorithm compared to existing methods. Figure 4 shows the performance of the algorithm with increasing viewing angle. The images used in this test were taken at the same scene using different camera viewing angles. Again the first image is taken as the reference image and all other images have viewing angle difference ranging from 10 to 60 degrees compared to the first image. Figure 4(left hand) shows the the repeatability of the regions and Figure 4(right hand) shows the consistency of the descriptors. The results obtained using MSER and Harris Affine algoritmhs are also given in the figure. Though the MSER algorithm gives better results in high view angle variation, our algorithm gives equally good results as the Harris Affine region detector.

## 4   Conclusion

A novel method for affine invariant region selection, based on a measure of symmetry, is proposed. The selected regions are nearly symmetric and obtained from visually important parts of the image. The proposed method is compared with some of the existing techniques for interest region selection. The results demonstrate that the symmetry based interest regions provide significantly improved performance, especially when there is large scale and rotational variations in the images. Future work will consider methods for improving the symmetry-based region selection technique to handle large view-angle changes.

## References

1. T. Kadir and M. Brady. Saliency, scale and image description. *Int. Journal of Computer Vision*, Vol 45, No 2, pages 83–105, November 2001.
2. T. Kadir, A. Zisserman, and M. Brady. An affine salient region detector. In *ECCV*, pages 228–241, 2004.
3. D.G. Lowe. Distinctive image features from scale-invariant key points. *Int. Journal of Computer Vision*, Vol 60, No 2, pages 91–110, November 2004.

4. G. Loy and A. Zelinsky. A fast radial symmetry transform for detecting points of interest. In *Proc. 7th European Conf. on Computer Vision*, pages 358–368, 2002.
5. J. Matas, O. Chum, M Urban, and T Pajdla. Robust wide baseline stereo from maximally stable extremal regions. In *BMVC*, pages 384–393, 2002.
6. K. Mikolajczyk and C. Schmid. Indexing based on scale invariant interest points. In *ICCV*, pages 525–531, July 2001.
7. K Mikolajczyk and C. Schmid. An affine invariant interest point detector. In *ECCV*, pages 128–142, 2002.
8. K. Mikolajczyk and C. Schmid. A performance evaluation of local descriptors. In *CVPR*, Vol 2, pages 257–263, 2003.
9. K. Mikolajczyk, T. Tuytelaars, C. Schmid, A. Zisserman, J. Matas, F. Schaffalitzky, T. Kadir, and L. Van Gool. A comparison of affine region detectors. Technical report, University of Oxford, 2004.
10. S. Obdrzalek and J. Matas. Local affine frames for image retrieval. In *CIVR*, pages 318–327, July 2002.
11. D. Reisfeld, H. Wolfson, and Y. Yeshurun. Context free attentional operators: the generalized symmetry transform. *Int. Journal of Computer Vision*, Vol 4, No 2 pages 119–130, March 1995.
12. D. Reisfeld and Y. Yeshurun. Robust detection of facial features by generalized symmetry. In *International Conference on Pattern Recognition*, pages 117–120, August 1992.
13. C. Schimid and M. Mohr. Local greyvalue invariants for image retrieval. *IEEE Trans. Pattern Analysis and Machine Intell.*, Vol 19, Issue 5, pages 530–535, May 1997.
14. D. Shen and H.S. Horace. Symmetry detection by generalized complex (gc) moments: A close-form solution. *IEEE Trans. Pattern Analysis and Machine Intell.*, Vol 21, No 5, pages 466–476 May 1999.
15. T. Tuytelaars and L. Van Gool. Content-based image retrieval based on local affinely invariant regions. In *Third Int'l Conf. on Visual Information Systems*, pages 493–500, 1999.
16. T. Tuytelaars and L. Van Gool. Wide baseline stereo based on local affinely invariant regions. In *BMVC*, pages 412–422, 2000.
17. T. Zielke, M. Brauckmann, and W. Von Seelen. Intensity and edge based symmetry detection with an application to car-following. *CVGIP: Image Understanding*, Vol58, Issue2, pages 177–190, September 1993.

# A Hybrid Color-Based Foreground Object Detection Method for Automated Marine Surveillance

Daniel Socek, Dubravko Culibrk, Oge Marques, Hari Kalva, and Borko Furht

Center for Coastline Security Technologies (CCST),
Department of Computer Science and Engineering,
Florida Atlantic University, Boca Raton FL 33431, USA

**Abstract.** This paper proposes a hybrid foreground object detection method suitable for the marine surveillance applications. Our approach combines an existing foreground object detection method with an image color segmentation technique to improve accuracy. The foreground segmentation method employs a Bayesian decision framework, while the color segmentation part is graph-based and relies on the local variation of edges. We also establish the set of requirements any practical marine surveillance algorithm should fulfill, and show that our method conforms to these requirements. Experiments show good results in the domain of marine surveillance sequences.

## 1 Introduction

Automatic detection of semantic visual objects within a digital image or video stream still represents one of the great challenges in computer vision. Although the problem of object detection within a video sequence (*foreground object detection*) is often treated separately from the image segmentation problem (*color-texture segmentation*), the two problems exhibit a strong conceptual similarity. In this paper, we present a framework that combines a foreground object detection approach and an image color segmentation technique in order to achieve better detection of semantic objects within a video sequence.

Common solutions to foreground object detection from a digital video are based on some form of background subtraction or background suppression [4,5]. These approaches work well when the camera is in a fixed position, and when there is no background movement (e.g., a footage taken by a stationary camera filming a highway toll plaza on a bright, sunny day). However, if the camera moves, or if the scene contains a complex moving background, the object detection and tracking becomes more difficult. In many real-world applications, such as marine surveillance, a scene can potentially contain both types of background: moving and stationary.

Object detection plays a crucial role in most surveillance applications. Without a good object detection method in place, the subsequent actions such as object classification and tracking would be infeasible. Our main goal was to obtain a robust marine surveillance object detection method that can successfully

J. Blanc-Talon et al. (Eds.): ACIVS 2005, LNCS 3708, pp. 340–347, 2005.
© Springer-Verlag Berlin Heidelberg 2005

overcome obstacles inferred by the presence of the complex, moving background. In our view, such algorithm should have the following properties in order to be of practical use:

1. *Determine potentially threatening objects within a scene containing a complex, moving background.* In marine surveillance applications, it is essential that the algorithm can deal with moving background such as flickering water surfaces and moving clouds, and still detect potential objects of interest.
2. *Produce no false negatives and a minimal number of false positives.* A surveillance application in general prefers no false negatives so that no potential threat is ever overlooked. On the other hand, having too many false positives would make potential postprocessing activities, such as object classification, highly impractical.
3. *Be fast and highly efficient, operating at a reasonable frame rate.* The object that poses a potential threat must be detected fast so that the appropriate preventive action can be taken in a timely manner. Furthermore, if the algorithm operates at an extremely small frame rate due to its inefficiency, some potential objects of interest could be overlooked.
4. *Use a minimal number of scene-related assumptions.* When designing an object detection method for marine surveillance, making the algorithm dependent upon too many assumptions regarding a scene setting would likely make the algorithm fail as soon as some of the assumptions do not hold.

To our knowledge, the existing literature does not offer an approach that exhibits all of the aforementioned properties. In this paper, we establish a hybrid method that essentially has such properties. We have slightly modified and extended two previously proposed general-purpose approaches, one for color-texture image segmentation and one for a foreground video object detection, and merged them into a hybrid method that is suitable for practical marine surveillance applications.

The paper is organized as follows. Section 2 briefly introduces related work, including the two methods used in our hybrid approach. The framework of our proposed algorithm is described in Section 3, with its experimental results given in Section 4. The last section concludes this paper.

## 2   Related Work

Some of the early methods for dealing with the instances of non-stationary background were based on smoothing the color of a background pixel over time using different filtering techniques such as Kalman filters [7,9], or Gabor filters [6]. However, these methods are not particularly effective for sequences with high-frequency background changes. Slightly better results were reported for techniques that rely on a Gaussian function whose parameters are recursively updated in order to follow gradual background changes within the video sequence [1]. More recently, this model was significantly improved by employing a Mixture of Gaussians (MoG), where the values of the pixels from background objects are described by multiple Gaussian distributions [2,12,15]. This model was considered promising since it showed good foreground object segmentation results for many outdoor sequences. However, weaker results were reported [8] for video sequences containing non-periodical background changes. This is the case for most of the marine sequences, which exhibit frequent background changes due to waves and water surface illumination, cloud shadows, and similar phenomena.

Voles *et al.* proposed a method suitable for object detection in maritime scenes based on anisotropic diffusion [14]. Unlike Gaussian filtering, anisotropic diffusion preserves well-defined edges and large homogeneous regions over poorly defined edges and small inhomogeneous regions. This approach performs well for horizontal and vertical edges, but it fails for other directions. In addition, unless simplified at the expense of performance, anisotropic diffusion is iterative and time consuming.

In 2003, Li *et al.* proposed a method for foreground object detection employing a Bayes decision framework [8]. The method has shown promising experimental object segmentation results even for the sequences containing complex variations and non-periodical movements in the background. In addition to the generic nature of the algorithm where no *a priori* assumptions about the scene are necessary, the authors claim that their algorithm can handle a throughput of about 15 fps for CIF video resolution, which is a reasonable frame rate for our purposes. Moreover, the algorithm is parallelizable at the pixel level, so that even better frame rates could be achieved if parallelization can be afforded. However, when we applied the algorithm to marine sequences, the object boundaries were not particularly accurate, and the segmented frames contained too many noise-related and scattered pixels. Furthermore, the adaptive threshold mechanism from [10] that was originally used by Li *at al.* performed poorly when fast large objects suddenly entered a scene. As a consequence, the algorithm produced instant flashing frames where most of the pixels were mistakenly classified as a foreground.

For removing these scattered noise pixels, Li *et al.* suggested applying morphological open and close operations [8]. Unfortunately, in doing so, small objects of interest could be lost or the boundaries of larger objects could be degraded and chopped, which could potentially change the outcome of the threat classification postprocess.

In general, the idea of combining the motion-related and texture-related information to improve the segmentation output is not new. In [11], Ross presented a method in which a duality of color segmentation and optical flow motion information was exploited. As a result, a better image segmentation is reported for a variety of natural images (frames) [11]. Ross also presented a comparative study of some of the relevant color-texture segmentation methods suitable for algorithmic synergy with the motion-related information. Among the candidates, the Felzenszwalb-Huttenlocher (F-H) [3] image segmentation algorithm was outstanding for its speed, its clear theoretical formulation, and its performance on natural images. The overview of F-H approach is presented in the following section.

# 3   Description of the Proposed Algorithm

The proposed hybrid background segmentation method has two distinct phases:
(i) primary foreground segmentation based on background modeling; and (ii)
post-processing based on color segmentation. A block diagram of the system is
shown in Fig. 1.

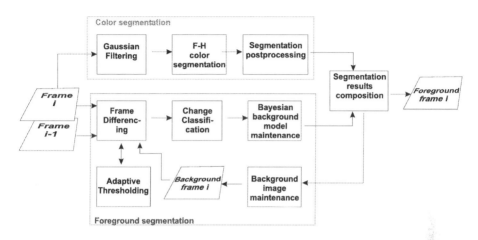

**Fig. 1.** Block diagram of the proposed foreground segmentation system

Primary foreground segmentation is based on a partial probabilistic model of
the background in conjunction with a more classical low-pass filtered background
image and a Bayesian decision framework for change classification proposed in
[8]. The approach relies on the assumption that for a scene obtained from a static
camera, there exist features, which can be used to discern whether a certain
pixel belongs to a background or a foreground object and on the idea that the
background can be modeled by probabilities of a certain feature value occurring
at a specific pixel. Furthermore the background is viewed as consisting of objects
that may be moving to an extent but are stationary in general, making it possible
to model it by a small number of feature values that occur at a specific pixel with
significant probability. This assumption is ground for computational feasibility
of the proposed approach.

The used Bayesian classifier is general in terms of allowing for the use of
different features to describe the stationary and movement characteristics of
the background [8]. The specific features employed in this project are the color
descriptors (RGB values) for the stationary background model and the color co-
occurrence descriptors (RGB values the pixel takes in two consecutive frames)
to describe the background movement.

The foreground segmentation algorithm (Fig. 1) has four main steps: change
detection, change classification, foreground segmentation and background model

learning and maintenance. The last step is addressed by two modules concerned with two distinct parts of the background model, as indicated in Fig. 1.

The initial stage of the algorithm is concerned with detecting the differences between the current frame and the background reference image kept (to detect the "stationary" differences) as well as the differences between two consecutive frames of the video sequence (to detect the movement). Once the differences are identified, they are used to determine whether the change is something consistent with the background or something that should be deemed foreground, based on the learned probabilistic model of the background. This is followed by a post-processing step used to enhance the effects of foreground segmentation by combining them with the results of color-based segmentation. The final step of the algorithm is the one in which background statistics are learned and the background image updated. In it, the information of how the pixels have been classified is used to gradually change the probabilities of significant feature values encountered to be able to accurately classify changes in the future. In addition to the probability learning process, knowledge of the background is stored by maintaining a reference background image updated through Infinite Impulse Response (IIR) filtering.

The Bayesian decision framework forms the change classification and part of the background model learning and maintenance step. The probabilistic model is used as the sole model for the movement of the background, however, it is only an extension of a more traditional IIR filter model. Therefore, for change detection, the post-processing in the third step and the background image filtering an arbitrary approach could be used. The original approach used automatic thresholding based on noise intensity estimation approach proposed in [10] for change detection while morphological open and close operations were used to enhance the foreground segmentation results. Our hybrid approach uses the original Bayesian classifier and the IIR filter based background image maintenance. However we found that automatic thresholding based on a Poisson distribution model for the spatial distribution of the noise [10] leads to better results in our application domain (the noise appeared more distinguished from the signal). In addition, we choose to enhance the results of the foreground segmentation based on color-based image segmentation algorithm, which, unlike the morphological operations, provides additional information. The authors of the original approach used feature binding to enhance the performance of the algorithm. We have not followed this practice, fearing reduced accuracy of segmentation.

The F-H algorithm [3], indicated by the top box in Fig. 1, uses a simple graph theoretic model that allows for the segmentation in $O(n \log n)$ time, $n$ being the number of image pixels. The F-H algorithm is based on a local variation (the intensity differences between neighboring pixels). Image segmentation was treated as a graph partitioning problem where for each given image, a graph $G = (V, E)$ is defined such that each vertex from $V$ corresponds to an image pixel, and each edge from $E$ corresponds to a connection between two neighboring pixels. Any given edge in $E$ carries a weight given by the intensity difference between pixels it connects. In such setting, image segmentation is equivalent to obtaining a partition of the graph $G$ into disjoint connected components. Given a measure of variation between two disjoint components (called *external variation*) and a measure of the inner variation of a single component (called *internal variation*) it is possible to evaluate a given segmented image, or equivalently a given graph partition. More precisely, a graph partition is over-segmented with too many components if the variation between two disjoint components is small relative to the internal variation of both components. On the other hand, a partition is under-segmented (not enough components) if there is a way to split some of its components and produce a partition which is still not over-segmented. The F-H algorithm essentially generates a partition that is optimal in the sense that it is neither over-segmented nor under-segmented. In this model, *internal variation* of a component is the maximum edge weight in any minimum spanning tree of that component, and the *external variation* between two components is the lowest edge weight connecting them. The threshold function $\tau(C) = k/|C|$ of a component $C$ controls the degree to which the external variation can be larger than the internal variations, and still have the components be considered similar. In our experiments, we have selected the input parameter $k = 100$.

The segment postprocessing for minimizing the number of segments by blindly merging the small segments with the larger neighboring ones, which was proposed by the authors [3], is far too dangerous to apply in marine surveillance applications since the small objects could disappear in the process. For that reason, we modified the postprocessing mechanism to work on a more sophisticated level. Namely, our modified postprocessing was based on the segment features consisting of the first and the second order color moments [13], calculated per each RGB channel. In many instances, better results were obtained when the features also included several bins counting very small vertical, horizontal, and diagonal edge weights within a segment.

## 4   Experimental Results

To test the approach a number of sequences extracted from a marine surveillance video has been used. The data used is real and pertinent to our problem domain. Frames include water-surface, sky, parts of solid ground and were captured by a stationary camera. The camera was occasionally moved slightly by wind.

Fig. 2 illustrates the enhanced performance of our approach in the case of a frame on which both algorithms perform comparably well. Better results were achieved through the use of color-based segmentation over those achieved by employing morphological operations. Primary motivation for the use of different thresholding approach was the inability of the original approach to adequately select the threshold in a number of specific frames, specifically when an object first enters the scene and when the camera is slightly moved by the wind. Fig. 3 illustrates the performance of the original thresholding approach for these two cases.

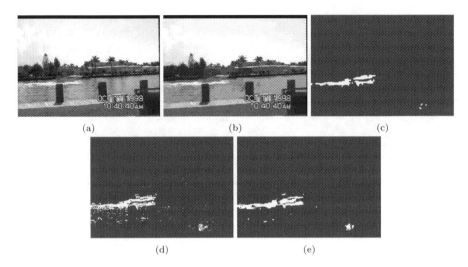

**Fig. 2.** The experiment performed on a video containing typical marine surveillance footage: (a) the original frame, (b) color segmentation results, (c) foreground obtained using the model described in [8] where morphological operators were used, (d) foreground obtained using new Poisson spatial noise distribution model-based thresholding without enhancement of the background segmentation results, and (e) with color segmentation-based enhancement

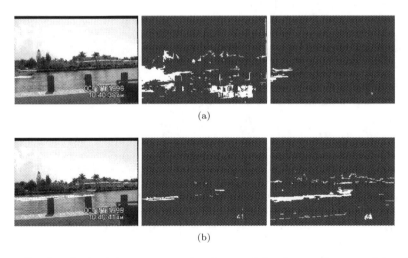

**Fig. 3.** Results obtained for representative frames: (a) a frame where an object first enters the scene (original frame and foreground obtained with the original and new approach, from left to right), (b) a frame where there a slight movement of the camera occurred (same layout as previous)

# 5   Conclusions

Object segmentation in the domain of marine surveillance is faced with the task of distinguishing between object of interest and complex moving background. We presented a hybrid method combining color-based single frame segmentation and change detection and classification based foreground segmentation. We evaluated the performance of the proposed method on a set of real marine surveillance sequences and presented a number of representative result frames.

# References

1. Boult, T.E., Micheals, R., Gao, X., Lewis, P., Power, C., Yin, W., Erkan, A.: Frame-rate omnidirectional surveillance and tracking of camouflaged and occluded targets. in Proc. of IEEE Workshop on Visual Surveillance (1999) 48-55
2. Ellis, T.J., Xu, M.: Object detection and tracking in an open and dynamic world. in Proc. of the Second IEEE International Workshop on Performance Evaluation on Tracking and Surveillance (PETS'01) (2001)
3. Felzenszwalb, P.F., Huttenlocher, D.P.: Image segmentation using local variation. in Proc. of Computer Vision and Pattern Recognition (CVPR'98) (1998) 98–104
4. Haritaoglu, I., Harwood, D., Davis, L.: $W^4$: Real-time survallance of people and their activities. IEEE Trans. Pattern Analysis and Machine Intelligence $22(8)$ (2000) 809–830
5. Heikkila, J., Silven, O.: A real-time system for monitoring of cyclists and pedestrians. in Proc. of the Second IEEE Workshop on Visual Surveillance (1999) 74–81
6. Jain, A.K., Ratha, N.K., Lakshmanan, S.: Object detection using Gabor filters. Journal of Pattern Recognition $30(2)$ (1997) 295–309
7. Karmann, K.-P., von Brandt, A.: Moving object recognition using an adaptive background memory. in "Timevarying Image Processing and Moving Object Recognition, 2", V. Cappellini (ed.), Elsevier Publishers B.V., Amsterdam, The Netherlands, (1990) 297-307
8. Li, L., Huang, W., Gu, I.Y.H., Tian, Q.: Foreground object detection from videos containing complex background. in Proc. of the Eleventh ACM International Conference on Multimedia (MULTIMEDIA'03) (2003) 2–10
9. Ridder, C., Munkelt, O., Kirchner, H.: Adaptive background estimation and foreground detection using Kalman-filtering. in Proc. of International Conference on Recent Advances in Mechatronics (ICRAM'95) (1995) 193–199
10. Rosin, L.R.: Thresholding for change detection. in Proc. of the Sixth International Conference on Computer Vision (ICCV'98) (1998) 274–279
11. Ross, M.G.: Exploiting texture-motion duality in optical flow and image segmentation. *Master Thesis*, Massachusetts Institute of Technology (2000)
12. Stauffer, C., Grimson, W.E.L.: Learning patterns of activity using real-time tracking. IEEE Transactions on Pattern Analysis and Machine Intelligence $22(8)$ (2000) 747–757
13. Stricker, M.A., Orengo, M.: Similarity of color images. in Proc. of SPIE Storage and Retrieval for Image and Video Databases III $2420$ (1995) 381–392
14. Voles, P., Teal, M., Sanderson, J.: Target identification in complex maritime scene. in Proc. of IEEE Colloquium on Motion Analysis and Tracking $15$ (1999) 1-4
15. Ya, L., Haizhou, A., Guangyou, X.: Moving object detection and tracking based on background subtraction. in Proc. of SPIE Object Detection, Classification, and Tracking Technologies $4554$ (2001) 62–66

# Image Registration Using Uncertainty Transformations

Kristof Teelen and Peter Veelaert

Hogeschool Gent, Dept. INWE, Schoonmeersstraat 52, B9000 Ghent, Belgium
{kristof.teelen, peter.veelaert}@hogent.be

**Abstract.** In this work we introduce a new technique for a frequently encountered problem in computer vision: image registration. The registration is computed by matching features, points and lines, in the reference image to their corresponding features in the test image among many candidate matches. Convex polygons are used to captivate the uncertainty of the transformation from the reference features to uncertainty regions in the test image in which candidate matches are to be found. We present a simple and robust method to check the consistency of the uncertainty transformation for all possible matches and construct a consistency graph. The distinction between the good matches and the rest can be computed from the information of the consistency graph. Once the good matches are determined, the registration transformation can be easily computed.

## 1   Introduction

Image registration is an important step in many computer vision applications [5]: visual inspection, medical imaging, video processing, remote sensing. Area-based registration methods, e.g. correlation-like methods, are among the most used techniques for registration, but also have several disadvantages, the inherent limitation to suit only local translation transformations, a high computational load when generalized to full rotation and scaling, and their sensitivity to intensity changes. There are also many feature-based registration methods: a first group uses invariant descriptors to match the most similar features; a second group exploits the spatial relationship between features, e.g. by graph matching or clustering. Our method performs feature matching by considering the consistency of spatial relations between features, i.e. by considering consistent uncertainty transformations, without using any local image information during the matching step.

The uncertainty transformations can cover affine transformations [4], but in this work the transformations are limited to translation and anisotropic scaling, as only these are necessary in the application described below. We use lines, next to points, as features, because lines offer the advantage of a more stable and repeatable detection under different circumstances. We propose a new and simple method to distinguish the best matching feature pairs and compute the parameters of the registration transformation. Our method differs from other techniques by its use of uncertainty polytopes and consistency graphs, based on principles and methods of digital geometry. To be precise, the uncertainty of the transformation parameters is modeled by polytopes. Furthermore, after computing the uncertainty transformation from one reference to one test image feature, we map all reference features into uncertainty regions according to the computed transformation. All candidate matches lying in the mapped uncertainty regions

J. Blanc-Talon et al. (Eds.): ACIVS 2005, LNCS 3708, pp. 348–355, 2005.
© Springer-Verlag Berlin Heidelberg 2005

give rise to consistent uncertainty transformations. All the consistent transformations are then gathered in a consistency graph. The best matches can be distinguished by computing the maximum clique of the consistency graph and can then be used to compute the image transformation. Checking the consistency of the uncertainty transformations by looking for a maximum clique in a consistency graph proves to be a fast and very robust method for feature matching.

Our registration method will be illustrated by an application in visual inspection. A camera system takes pictures of a sequence of objects and compares each picture to a reference image. Due to the mechanics of the camera and the lens system, the transformation of the real objects is not precisely known, and it is our job to recover the transformation from the reference image to each of the pictures of the sequence. We assume that the transformation is composed of translation and anisotropic scaling. Bounds on the maximal values of translation and scaling parameters can be deducted from the mechanics of the system. There is no a-priori knowledge about the contents of the pictures or their statistical properties, but we assume there is a sufficiently large number of detectable features available in the pictures.

The next section describes the feature detection problem in more detail. Our feature matching method, based on the consistency of uncertainty transformations, is presented in Section 3. The registration transformation can then be computed from the best matches as explained in Section 4. Finally we conclude in Section 5.

## 2   Feature Detection

Features are characteristic objects in an image, distinguishable from other, possibly similar, objects. Mostly single points are used, characterized by strong intensity or brightness changes. But points are often not that reliable as features in image sequences: a point present in one image, may be occluded in the next image, and illumination changes between subsequent images may cause a shift in the position of a feature point. In this work we apply two techniques to cope with these problems. First, we will not only use points but also line features as lines are expected to be more stable, as they are less affected by illumination changes and occlusion. Second, slight positional variations caused by the feature point detector can be accounted for by using uncertainty transformations: feature points are located in an a-priori determined region of interest, the uncertainty region.

Gray level corners are used as feature points, where a corner is defined as a junction point of two or more straight edges, i.e. L-corners and T-, Y- and X-junctions. Among the available corner detectors, we chose the Noble variant [2] of the Harris detector [1], because of its remarkable characteristics concerning accuracy and stability. Straight lines are used as a second feature. In this work, we only use horizontal and vertical line segments, because they nicely fit in the matching method discussed in the next section. We use a simplified Radon-method to extract straight lines from edge information.

The feature detection step is first performed on the reference image. A subset of typically $20 - 30$ features, containing a subset of the detected lines and/or feature points, is used in the remainder of our method. For each feature of the reference image, possible candidate matches are selected in a region of interest in the test image. Size and position of this region can be defined by predicting the location of the feature in the test image, e.g. depending on the movement of an object, and choosing maximum bounds on the parameters of the expected transformation. This is an important advantage of the proposed method: by considering only a subset of the features in the test image as valid candidate matches, a lot of computation time can be saved.

Figure 1 illustrates the feature detection step for the example application in visual inspection: a camera system compares a sequence of images during processing, e.g. Figure 1(b), to a reference image taken in advance (Figure 1(a)). The detected features in the reference image are shown in Figure 1(c). In this application, features are expected to appear in more or less the same position, so we expect a unity transformation, i.e. the position of the center of the rectangular region of interest for candidate feature points in the test image is the same as the position of the features in the reference image. Lines must meet two criteria to be accepted as candidate matches. First, candidate matching lines must be located in an interval, centered on the position of lines in the reference image, and second, lines in the reference and the test image must mutually overlap for a certain percentage (e.g. 50%); this implicitly assumes that lines must also be situated in an interval along the lines direction. The maximal deviation possible

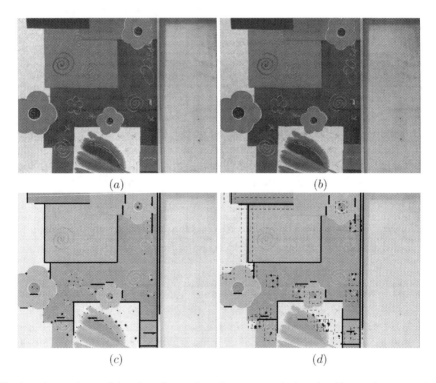

**Fig. 1.** Reference image $(a)$ and test image from the sequence during visual inspection processing $(b)$. The features in the reference image $(c)$ are detected before processing. The features in the sequence test image $(d)$ are then detected in a region of interest (dashed lines), the location of which is determined by the position of a selected subset of reference features.

within the region of interest is defined by the expected maximal value of translation and scaling parameters, determined by the mechanics of the system. Figure $1(d)$ shows the candidate matching line and point features for the selected subset of features (indicated by a star(*) in $(c)$). The regions of interest are indicated by a dashed line (for the line intervals only a few examples are shown for clarity).

## 3   Feature Matching

To register two different images, each of the detected features in one image must be matched with its corresponding feature in the other image, i.e. corresponding features must indicate the same object in each image. Our matching method is based on the theory of uncertainty transformations. We first discuss uncertainty transformations in more detail before continuing with the actual matching method.

### 3.1   Definition of an Uncertainty Transformation

Suppose an object can be mapped onto another object according to a certain transformation. In standard geometry this requires one-to-one relationships between a set of points on the first object (the source) and a set of points on the second object (the image). But what can be done if there is no exact knowledge about the correct location of an image point? The uncertainty about the position of the image point can be modeled by defining a set of possible image points, the uncertainty region in which the point must lie, without knowing its exact position.

In general, if $p$ is a point in $\mathbb{R}^2$, and $R$ a subset of $\mathbb{R}^2$, then we let $\mathcal{T}(p, R)$ denote the set of all transformations $T$ that map $p$ into $R$. To model the uncertainty of the image $(x', y')$ of a point $p = (x, y)$, we define the uncertainty region $R$ as a convex polygon bounded by $n$ halfplanes. In this work the following assumptions are made:

- The uncertainty regions $R$ are rectangles in the $x'y'$-plane, which are represented as the Cartesian product of two intervals: $R = I^r \times I^s$, with $I^r$ and $I^s$:

$$r_1 \leq x' \leq r_2$$
$$s_1 \leq y' \leq s_2. \tag{1}$$

- Transformations are composed of translations and anisotropic scaling in 2D:

$$x' = ax + e$$
$$y' = dy + f \tag{2}$$

with $a$, $d$, $e$ and $f$ the four parameters defining the transformation.

The uncertainty transformation $\mathcal{T}(p, R)$ is then described by two separate transformations mapping a coordinate into an interval, $T^x = T(x, I^r)$ and $T^y = T(y, I^s)$, which are found by substituting Eqs. (2) in (1), yielding for $T^x$ and $T^y$ respectively:

$$r_1 \leq ax + e \leq r_2$$
$$s_1 \leq dy + f \leq s_2. \tag{3}$$

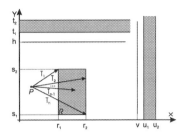

**Fig. 2.** The uncertainty transformation $\mathcal{T}(p, R)$ for a point $p$ to an uncertainty region $R$. A horizontal and vertical line and their uncertainty intervals.

This framework can easily incorporate horizontal and vertical lines, $y = h$ and $x = v$, with $h$ and $v$ constants. The images of lines after transformation (2) are again horizontal or vertical lines, $h'$ and $v'$, expected to be situated in an uncertainty interval $I^h$, $t_1 \leq h' \leq t_2$ or $I^v$, $u_1 \leq v' \leq u_2$, leading to the uncertainty transformations $\mathcal{T}^v$ and $\mathcal{T}^h$:

$$t_1 \leq dh + f \leq t_2$$
$$u_1 \leq av + e \leq u_2. \tag{4}$$

This notion of an uncertainty transformation can be extended to sets of points and lines. Consider the points $p_i = (x_i, y_i)$ in $\mathbb{R}^2$, the uncertainty regions $R_i \subseteq \mathbb{R}^2$ defined as the Cartesian product of two intervals $R_i = I_i^r \times I_i^s$, the vertical and horizontal lines $v_i$ and $h_i$ and the uncertainty intervals for the horizontal and vertical lines $I_i^h$ and $I_i^v$. Let $S^x$ be a finite set of elements $s_i^x$, in which $s_i^x$ is either a point coordinate $x_i$ or a vertical line $v_i$. Let $\mathcal{I}^r = \cup_i I_i^r, \mathcal{I}^v = \cup_i I_i^v, \mathcal{I}^x = \mathcal{I}^r \cup \mathcal{I}^v$, and let $f^x$ be a mapping that assigns each element $s_i^x$ of $S^x$ to its corresponding interval $I_i^x$ in the set $\mathcal{I}^x$. Clearly, we have $\mathcal{T}^x = \mathcal{T}(S^x, \mathcal{I}^x, f^x) = \cap_i \mathcal{T}(s_i^x, I_i^x)$. $\mathcal{T}^x$ can be represented as a convex polygon in a two dimensional space, one dimension for each transformation parameter. Similar definitions can be given for the uncertainty transformation $\mathcal{T}^y = \mathcal{T}(S^y, \mathcal{I}^y, f^y)$. Including rotations in the uncertainty transformations requires six parameters instead of four in (2), so the uncertainty transformation can then be represented as two convex polytopes in two 3D parameter spaces.

Suppose we consider another coordinate $s_k^x$ not in $S^x$. One can show that once a transformation polygon $\mathcal{T}^x$ is known, we can easily determine the uncertainty interval $I_k^x$ into which $s_k^x$ will be projected [3]. To be precise, let $s_k^x$ be a coordinate, and let $\mathcal{T}^x$ be a given polygon, then we let $I(s_k^x, \mathcal{T}^x)$ denote the uncertainty interval resulting from mapping $s_k^x$ by all transformations in $\mathcal{T}^x$; that is, $I(s_k^x, \mathcal{T}^x) = \{q \in \mathbb{R} : q = T(s_k^x) \text{ for some } T \in \mathcal{T}_x\}$. Moreover, one can show that $I(s_k^x, \mathcal{T}^x)$ is the convex hull of the points $T_v^x(s_k^x)$ where the transformation $T_v^x$ denote the vertices of the polygon $\mathcal{T}^x$.

### 3.2  Matching Problem

The feature matching problem consists of the selection of feature pairs corresponding to the same feature in both images among many candidate features. To match features we use the concept of uncertainty transformations.

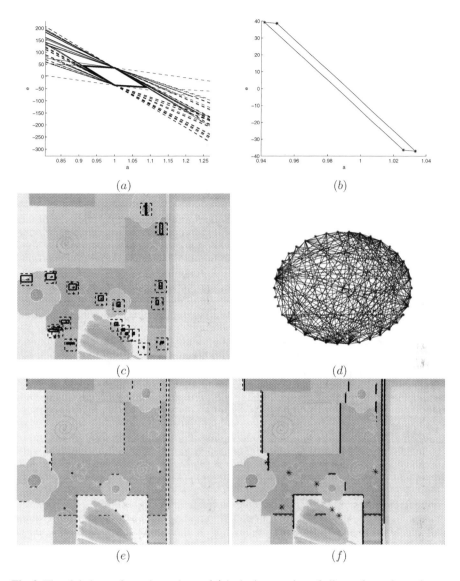

**Fig. 3.** The global transformation polygon $(a)$ is the intersection of all transformation polygons. The local transformation polygon in the $ae$-space $(b)$ for the lowest candidate matching feature point $q_{low}$ in the test image (see image $(c)$). All reference feature points are transformed according to the vertices of the transformation polygon in $(b)$, resulting in small projected uncertainty regions $(c)$ inside the regions of interest, indicated by dashed rectangles (the projected intervals for lines are left out for clarity). All candidate features lying in the uncertainty region will produce consistent transformations: the vertex in graph $G$ corresponding to $q_{low}$ will be connected with the vertices corresponding to the 'in-lying' feature points. The graph $G$ is obtained once the same steps are performed for all candidate feature points. By computing the maximum clique in $G$, the best matching pairs are obtained. The reference features of the matches are shown in $(e)$, and the best matches in the test image are indicated in $(f)$ by stars and solid lines (the position of reference line features is indicated by dashed lines).

First, the global transformation $\mathcal{T} = \mathcal{T}(S, \mathcal{R}, f)$, composed of $\mathcal{T}^x = \mathcal{T}(S^x, \mathcal{I}^x, f^x)$ and $\mathcal{T}^y = \mathcal{T}(S^y, \mathcal{I}^y, f^y)$, can be computed for the selected subset of features. The transformation uncertainty polygon $\mathcal{T}^x$ maps each feature $s_i^x \in S^x$ in the reference image into the uncertainty interval $I_i^x \in \mathcal{I}^x$ in the test image, in which $I_i^x$ is assigned as the interval of interest for the reference feature $s_i^x$ by the mapping $f^x$. $\mathcal{T}^x$ is the intersection of all $T_i^x = T(s_i^x, I_i^x)$ as can be seen in Figure 3($a$). Similar definitions can be given for $\mathcal{T}^y$.

Next a consistency graph $G$ is constructed. $G$ is an $r$-partite graph in which the $r$ parts correspond to $r$ uncertainty regions assigned to the reference features. The vertices $q_{ij}$ in each part of the graph are the candidate matches for the reference feature $s_i$, found in the uncertainty region $R_i(I_i^x, I_i^y)$. Each pair of candidate features in different parts is joined by an edge in $G$ provided their respective transformations are consistent. Although consistency can be checked by computing whether the intersection of each pair of uncertainty polygons is non-empty [4], here we present a computationally more efficient method. The algorithm to construct the consistency graph $G$ for all uncertainty transformations proceeds as follows:

```
For all candidate features qij,
    compute Tᵢⱼˣ = T(sᵢˣ, Iᵢⱼˣ) and Tᵢⱼʸ = T(sᵢʸ, Iᵢⱼʸ)
    For all reference features sₖ with k ≠ i,
        compute Iₖᵢⱼˣ = I(sₖˣ, Tᵢⱼˣ) and Iₖᵢⱼʸ = I(sₖʸ, Tᵢⱼʸ) with Iₖᵢⱼˣ ⊆ Iₖˣ, Iₖᵢⱼʸ ⊆ Iₖʸ
        For all candidate features qₖₗ with k ≠ i,
            If qₖₗˣ ∈ Iₖᵢⱼˣ and qₖₗʸ ∈ Iₖᵢⱼʸ,
                Tₖₗ = T(qₖₗ, Iₖ) is consistent with Tᵢⱼ
                ⇒ join the vertices (qᵢⱼ, qₖₗ) by an edge in G
        end
    end
end
end
```

For all candidate features, the local transformation $T_{ij}$ is computed for a reference feature $s_i$ mapped into a small region $R_{ij}(I_{ij}^x, I_{ij}^y)$ around $q_{ij}$. An example is given in Figure 3($c$), where the local transformation is computed for the lowest candidate match in the image, leading to the transformation polygon presented in Figure 3($b$). All other reference features $s_{k,k\neq i}$ are then mapped according to this local transformation $T_{ij}$, resulting in smaller uncertainty regions $R_{kij} \subseteq R_k$, as can been seen in Figure 3($c$). Transformations consistent with the used transformation can then be computed for each candidate $q_{kl}$ located in one of the regions $R_{kij}$. So each 'in-lying' candidate $q_{kl}$ is connected to $q_{ij}$ in the graph $G$. The final graph $G$ is shown in Figure 3($d$).

Each vertex in the consistency graph represents the uncertainty transformation from a reference to a test feature. For each transformation the graph shows which other transformations are consistent with it. The consistency checks for all the uncertainty transformations result in a very robust feature matching method. The best matching feature pairs can then be selected by looking for the maximum clique in the consistency graph, because the vertices within the maximum clique will be consistent with most other possible transformations. Figures 3($e$) and ($f$) show the best matching reference and test features.

# 4   Computation of the Registration Transformation

The final step in registering the test image with the reference image requires the computation of the registration transformation: one transformation mapping each reference feature as well as possible upon the best matching test image feature. Each uncertainty transformation can be represented as two polygons, one in the $ae$-, and one in the $df$-space. We recall that the global transformation polygon for a set of features is represented as the intersection of all polygons: $\mathcal{T}(S^x, \mathcal{I}^x, f^x) = \cap_i \mathcal{T}(s_i^x, I_i^x)$. Then the minimal size of the intervals $I_i^x$ in $\mathcal{I}^x$ can be computed for which transformations $\mathcal{T}(s_i^x, I_i^x)$ exist such that the intersection $\mathcal{T}(S^x, \mathcal{I}^x, f^x)$ is non-empty and contains at least one transformation [4]. Moreover, the intersection will contain exactly *one* point, i.e. the polygons will have one point in common, being a vertex of one of the polygons. To find the registration transformation it suffices to first compute the minimal size for the intervals. Then we look for the vertex lying in all polygons, which are computed for the intervals of the minimal size. If these computations are done in both parameter spaces ($ae$ and $df$), the transformations parameters $a$, $e$, $d$ and $f$, as defined in (2), for the registration transformation are obtained.

# 5   Conclusion

We presented a simple, fast and robust method for image registration. The registration transformation is based on a set of corresponding features in a reference and test image. To obtain more stable features, points as well as lines are used. Features in the reference image will typically have zero, one or many possible corresponding features in the test image, so for each reference feature the best corresponding candidate must be distinguished. Using only the features in uncertainty regions as possible candidates offers a gain in computation time, where the use of the consistency graph for uncertainty transformations proves to be a very robust method for feature matching. Our method seems to be fairly independent of the statistics of the image, i.e. the percentage of false positives and negatives and the positional error made by the feature detector. This statistical dependence, however, has not yet been examined in full detail and remains a subject for future research. All our experiments on real data, however, show that the correct transformation can be computed efficiently and robustly, even when the percentage of false negatives (e.g. 30%) or positives is very large (e.g. 300%).

# References

1. C. Harris and M. Stephens: A combined corner and edge detector, Proc. Alvey Vision Conf., Univ. Manchester (1988), 147-151
2. A. Noble: Finding Corners, Image and Vision Computing Journal, 6(2) (1988), 121-128
3. K. Teelen and P. Veelaert: Uncertainty of Affine Transformations in Digital Images, Proc. ACIVS (2004), 23-30
4. K. Teelen and P. Veelaert: Computing the uncertainty of transformations in digital images, Proc. SPIE Vision Geometry XIII (2005), 1-12
5. B. Zitova and J. Flusser: Image registration methods: a survey, Image and Vision Computing 21 (2003), 977-1000

# Majority Ordering and the Morphological Pattern Spectrum

Alessandro Ledda and Wilfried Philips

Ghent University, Telin-IPI, St. Pietersnieuwstraat 41, B-9000 Gent, Belgium
ledda@telin.UGent.be
http://telin.ugent.be/~ledda/

**Abstract.** Binary and grayscale mathematical morphology have many applications in different area. On the other hand, colour morphology is not widespread. The reason is the lack of a unique ordering of colour that makes the extension of grayscale morphology to colour images not straightforward. We will introduce a new *majority sorting scheme* that can be applied on binary, grayscale and colour images. It is based on the area of each colour or grayscale present in the image, and has the advantage of being independent of the values of the colours or grayvalues. We will take a closer look at the morphological pattern spectrum and will show the possible differences of the morphological pattern spectrum on colour images with the grayscale image pattern spectrum.

## 1 Introduction

### 1.1 Binary Morphology

*Mathematical morphology* [1] [2] is based on set theory. The shapes of objects in a binary image are represented by object membership sets. Object pixels have value 1, the background pixels have value 0. Morphological operations can simplify image data, preserving the objects' essential shape characteristics, and can eliminate irrelevant objects.

Binary mathematical morphology is based on two basic operations, defined in terms of a *structuring element* (short: *strel*), a small window that scans the image and alters the pixels in function of its window content: a *dilation* of set $A$ with strel $B$ ($A \oplus B$) enlarges the object (more 1-pixels will be present in the image), an *erosion* ($A \ominus B$) lets it shrink (the number of 1-pixels in the image diminishes) (see figure 1).

Mathematically, the basic operators are defined as:

$$\begin{aligned} dilation &: A \oplus B = \bigcup_{b \in B} T_b(A) \\ erosion &: A \ominus B = \bigcap_{b \in B} T_{-b}(A) \end{aligned} \qquad (1)$$

with $T_b(A)$ the translation of set $A$ over vector $b$. This formulation can be rewritten as equation 2, used for grayscale morphology.

Other operations, like the *opening* (an erosion followed by a dilation) and the *closing* (a dilation followed by an erosion), are derived from the basic operators.

J. Blanc-Talon et al. (Eds.): ACIVS 2005, LNCS 3708, pp. 356–363, 2005.
© Springer-Verlag Berlin Heidelberg 2005

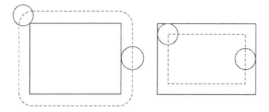

**Fig. 1.** The basic morphological operators. Solid line: original object; Dashed line: result object; Circle: structuring element. Left: *dilation*; Right: *erosion*.

## 1.2 Grayscale Morphology

The morphological theory can be extended to grayscale images with the *threshold* approach or with the *umbra* approach [2]. The latter permits the use of grayscale structuring elements but the resulting grayvalues after a morphological operation can be outside the original range. We will use the threshold approach.

For binary images, the union and intersection operation are used for the dilation and erosion, respectively. In the case of grayscale images (sets become functions), the union and intersection of sets are replaced by the maximum and minimum of grayvalues. For the dilation and erosion we now get:

$$dilation : (f \oplus g)(a) = \max\{f(b) \mid a - b \in g, b \in f\}$$
$$erosion : (f \ominus g)(a) = \min\{f(b) \mid b - a \in g, b \in f\} \tag{2}$$

where $f$ is the function representing the grayscale image and $g$ is the structuring element.

## 1.3 Colour Morphology

A colour image is represented in some colour space. The colours in such a colour space can be interpreted as vectors.

A frequently used space is the RGB space, used in computer systems. There are three colour bands (red, green and blue) that together represent the colours of the pixels in the image in the RGB-space.

There is no absolute ordering of the colour vectors, so the max- and min-operation can't be extended easily to vectors and therefore an extension to colour morphology is not straightforward. In order to be able to extent the principles of grayscale morphology to colour images, the colours in a colour image have to be ordered in some way [3] [4]. A way of doing this is to transform the vectors into scalars with a *lexicographical ordering scheme*, further explained in section 2.1. We also present a new technique (section 2.3) that not only can be applied to colour images, but also to binary and grayscale images.

## 1.4 The Pattern Spectrum

If we take a strel and use it to perform an opening on a binary image, some objects will disappear. If we take a bigger strel, then more elements in the image will vanish. In this way we can determine how the number of eliminated objects increases when the image is morphologically opened using strels $nB = B \oplus B \oplus \ldots \oplus B$ ($n$ times) of increasing size $n$. The resulting plot of the number of eliminated pixels versus the strel size $n$ is called the *pattern spectrum* (PS) [5].

The pattern spectrum is a histogram of the distribution of the sizes of various objects displayed in an image. Formally, it is defined as follows:

$$PS(A; B)(n) = \sharp[(A \circ nB) - (A \circ (n+1)B)], \; n \geq 0 \qquad (3)$$

where $\circ$ is the opening symbol and $\sharp$ is the count of pixels. Note that $0B = \{0\}$.

Notice that a different strel results in different pattern spectra, and thus in other values for the parameters.

The same equation can be used for grayscale images. The difference with the binary case is the count of pixels that is replaced by a count of decrease in grayvalues.

## 2   Methodology

### 2.1   Colour Morphology

First, we transform the RGB image into an HSL image. In the HSL space the colour channels are the *luminance* (the intensity), the *saturation* (the purity), and the *hue* (the primary colour).

We will use the double-cone HSL representation. The luminance $L$ has values between 0 and 1, the hue $H$ lies between $0°$ and $360°$. The saturation $S$ has values between 0 and 1 for $L = \frac{1}{2}$ and the maximum $S$ decreases linearly as $L$ goes to 0 or 1. At $L = 0$ and $L = 1$ the saturation can only be 0.

The ordering of the colours is done with a lexicographical ordering rule on the HSL-vector [4]. Putting $L$ as a criterion on the first line in the lexicographical ordering ($L$-ordering) gives a different ordering than using $S$ or $H$ on that line. In this paper we will use the lexicographical rules from [4] (the $H$-ordering uses a saturation-weighted hue).

The comparison of the hue values is the comparison between the acute angles of the hue values with a reference hue $H_0$. The choice of $H_0$ can be arbitrary or calculated in function of the image content (section 2.1).

**Vector Ordering.** According to [4], a morphological operation can be performed on an a colour image (in HSL space) by comparing the current pixel with the other pixels in the window of the structuring element. This operation can be quite intensive because a lot of comparisons have to be made. To avoid the recalculations of the order of one pixel compared to another, it is better to transform the HSL image into a scalar image, based on the lexicographical ordering.

A 24 bits RGB image will then be transformed into a 24 bits "grayscale" image. The most important rule in the lexicographical ordering occupies the highest 8 bits, the least important rule the lowest 8 bits. Each pixel gets some value between 0 and $2^{24} - 1$. As a result, equation 3 can be used.

**Origin of Hue.** A possible value for $H_0$ could be the hue that appears the most in the image. If the background is the most present in the image, then all hue values are referenced to the hue of the background.

We can also take the hue value of the average chromaticity vector as $H_0$ (also in [6]). To calculate this average, we transform each hue value, represented as a point on a circle with an angle $\theta$ and with radius $r = 1$, in its Cartesian coordinates. Then we average the vectors and transform this average vector back to polar coordinates. This gives us $H_0$: it is the average angle $\bar{\theta}$.

An alternative way to calculate the average hue value is to take the histogram of the hue in the image and then give the radius $r$ the value of the number of pixels with a certain hue. This approach is less accurate because the histogram consists of a certain number of bins, thus introducing a limited number of possible hue values, while the hue originally could have any value in its domain. This is not really a problem because for the vector ordering (section 2.1) the hue was also made discrete.

A less elegant method for the definition of the average hue is to perform a number of shifts of the hue histogram with a number of bins, because of the periodic character of the hue domain. The introduced shift is needed because, for example, a hue of $10°$ and $350°$ would give an average of $180°$, while we would expect $0°$. If it is shifted with $10°$, then the hue angles will be $20°$ and $0°$, so the average hue is $10°$ and minus the shift this would give us the correct result. We calculate the variance of every shifted spectrum, and finally calculate the average hue (using the same formulation as for the mean object size for the pattern spectrum (section 2.2)) from the histogram with the smallest variance. In the example, the variance of this shifted spectrum is smaller than the variance of the original.

## 2.2   The Pattern Spectrum

In the binary case, the pattern spectrum is a graph of how many pixels were removed because of the opening of the image with the increasing strel $(n+1)B$.

By extension, the pattern spectrum of a grayscale image tells how many of grayscale intensity disappeared. This is the sum of the decrease in grayvalue for each pixel. The number of graylevels gives an indication how dark the resultant image becomes after an opening.

In the case of colour images, the interpretation is more abstract. The principle is the same as the one for grayscale images, but we could now speak of a decrease in colour intensity. The pattern spectrum gives an indication of the change in colour after an opening. This change depends on the ordering used. For example, in the case of an ordering with saturation in the first ordering rule, the pattern spectrum values indicate how the saturation decreases.

From the pattern spectrum we can extract different parameters [5], [7] that provide statistical information about the content of the image:

- **Mean object size:** the mean strel size or mean area;
- **Average roughness:** the *entropy*, a quantification of the shape-size complexity;

- **Normalised average roughness:** the entropy divided by $\log_2(N_{max}+1)$;
- **B-shapiness:** a quantitative measure of the resemblance of the objects to the strel shape;
- **Maximal n** $(N_{max})$**:** the last bin (the highest $n$-value, when all image objects are sieved out) of the pattern spectrum histogram.

## 2.3   Majority Ordering by Total Area

In this section we propose a new type of sorting of the pixels, the *majority sorting scheme* (MSS). Instead of using the grayvalues or ordered colours, we count the number of pixels present in the image for each colour. All morphological operations are then performed on the newly obtained image, as if it is a grayscale image. See figure 2 for a visual example.

 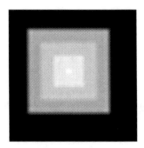

**Fig. 2.** Left: colour image; Right: MSS ordering map

The motivation comes from the fact that in general the background is most present in the image, that important colours (objects) are highly present and that details or noise are rare colours. These assumptions are at the same time the restrictions of this technique.

Colours with the same number of pixels will be treated equally, but it is possible to steer the area values by adding a constant to it, for example if a specific background colour has to be chosen. For the pattern spectrum we will treat such colours equally.

With the MSS, the pattern spectrum gives an indication of the change in colour (or grayvalue), where the least dominant colours disappear first.

A technical difficulty is the fact that quantisation of the number of colours or grayvalues is necessary. If too many different colours are present, then too many equal small areas will be detected, which cancels the effect of the area ordering. Therefore, in most cases a quantisation will have to be done, but not too drastic so that the useful colour differences in the image would be retained.

A suggested quantisation is to reduce the number of colours (for example using *peer group filtering* [8]) until this number is the same as (or a certain percentage of) the number of different levels in the majority sorted image.

Notice that the background has the biggest area, so the erosion and dilation operations should be switched, or the values of the areas must be switched.

This technique has several advantages:

- The technique can be used for binary, grayscale and colour images; also an extension to multispectral images is possible with the same majority ordering scheme;
- Colour images with only two colours will be treated as if it were binary images;
- The technique doesn't expect a specific colour space to work with;
- We don't have to define a value $H_0$ [6];
- The technique is quasi invariant for colour and grayscale transformations (e.g. $\gamma$-compensation); when all colours change in a new map of unique colours (the transformation is bijective), then there is no difference in the majority ordering;
- Using only one RGB colour band of a grayscale image will give the same results as the grayscale image itself.

## 3  Experimental

### 3.1  Objects of One Colour

If all objects in the image have the same colour, then the image can be seen as a binary image. Morphological operations will produce the results we expect with the majority sorting scheme and the lexicographical orderings. The pattern spectra are the same shape, so the spectral parameters will be identical.

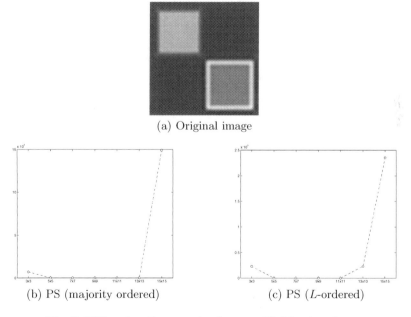

(a) Original image

(b) PS (majority ordered)          (c) PS ($L$-ordered)

**Fig. 3.** Different pattern spectra for an artificial colour image

There are some exceptions, though. In the case of the $S$- and $H$-ordering, the comparison of the luminances (see [4]) is referenced to $L = \frac{1}{2}$, which means that there is no difference between colours with $L$ lying the same distance from $L = \frac{1}{2}$. Another effect can occur with the $H$-ordering: the ranking of the background colour can be higher than that of the object colour. The object on a background is then regarded as a hole in an object. The choice of $H_0$ is important in this case. These effects are not present in the case of the pattern spectrum of the majority ordered image.

## 3.2   Objects of More Colours

Figure 3 shows two objects with a small edge. This could be the effect of blurring of the image.

The majority sorted spectrum shows a peak at a lower bin, which indicates pixels that don't specifically belong to a big object. In this case these are the pixels from the blurring ring.

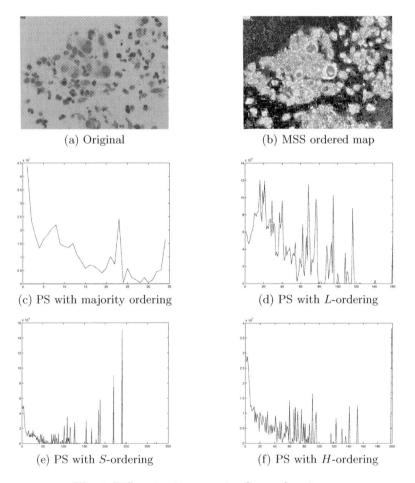

(a) Original                    (b) MSS ordered map

(c) PS with majority ordering        (d) PS with $L$-ordering

(e) PS with $S$-ordering              (f) PS with $H$-ordering

**Fig. 4.** Different pattern spectra for a colour image

The *L*-ordered spectrum shows pixels that disappear after an opening with a $13 \times 13$ square strel. These are the values between the edges. This kind of feature can make the interpretation of the pattern spectrum difficult.

### 3.3   Real Images

Figure 4(a) shows a medical image. The pattern spectrum of the majority sorted image shows the most realistic graph (figure 4(c)). There are no objects 160 times the strel (a square with side 3) present, so the *L*-ordering doesn't produce a useful spectrum. The same problem is present with the other lexicographical orderings.

## 4   Conclusion

Grayscale morphology can be used on colour images, if the colours are ordered in some way. The use of the morphological pattern spectrum for colour images can be a big advantage in situations where important colour information is lost when the colour image is transformed to grayscale.

This ordering can be done with a lexicographical rule. But we also proposed a *majority sorting scheme* that orders the colours according to the count of pixels of that colour present in the image. This method has some advantages over the lexicographical ordering scheme.

## References

1. Serra, J.: Image Analysis and Mathematical Morphology. Volume 1. Academic Press, New York (1982)
2. Haralick, R., Shapiro, L.: 5. In: Computer and Robot Vision. Volume 1. Addison-Wesley (1992)
3. Peters II, R.: Mathematical morphology for angle-valued images. In: Proceedings of the SPIE, Nonlinear Image Processing VIII. Volume 3026. (1997) 84–94
4. Hanbury, A., Serra, J.: Mathematical Morphology in the HLS Colour Space. In: BMVC 2001, Manchester, UK (2001) 451–460
5. Maragos, P.: Pattern Spectrum and Multiscale Shape Representation. IEEE Transactions on Pattern Analysis and Machine Intelligence **11** (1989) 701–716
6. Hanbury, A.: Lexicographical order in the HLS Colour Space. Technical Report N-04/01/MM, Centre de Morphologie Mathématique Ecole des Mines de Paris (2001)
7. Banerjee, S., Sahasrabudhe, S.: C-factor: a morphological shape descriptor. Journal of Mathematical Imaging and Vision **4** (1994) 43–55
8. Deng, Y., Kenney, C., Moore, M., Manjunath, B.: Peer group filtering and perceptual color image quantization. In: Proceedings of IEEE International Symposium on Circuits and Systems. Volume 4. (1999) 21–24

# A New Reference Free Approach for the Quality Assessment of MPEG Coded Videos

Rémi Barland and Abdelhakim Saadane

IRCCyN-IVC, UMR n°6597 CNRS, Ecole Polytechnique de l'Université de
Nantes Rue Christian Pauc, La Chantrerie, BP50609, 44306 Nantes, France
{remi.barland, abdelhakim.saadane}@univ-nantes.fr

**Abstract.** Currently, the growing of digital video delivery leads to compress at
high ratio, the video sequences. Different coding algorithms like MPEG-4 introduce different artifacts (blocking, blurring, ringing) degrading the perceptual
video quality. Such impairments are generally exploited by the No-Reference
quality assessment. In this paper, we propose to use the principal distortions introduced by MPEG-4 coding to design a new reference free metric. Using the
frequency and space features of each image, a distortion measure for blocking,
blurring and ringing effects is computed respectively. On the one hand, the
blocking measure and on the other hand, a joint measure of blurring and ringing
effects are perceptually validated, which assures the relevance of distortion
measures. To produce the final quality score, a new pooling model is also proposed. High correlation between the objective scores of the proposed metric and
the subjective assessment ratings has been achieved.

## 1 Introduction

The field of digital video services has been quickly developed in the last few years,
based on the advances and progresses in digital signal compression technology. The
emergence of new technologies such as digital video broadcasting or streaming is the
perfect example of this current trend. However, these applications necessitate the use
of video sequences with high compression ratios and hence, the use of efficient coding algorithms. The different coding techniques like MPEG-1/2/4 introduce impairments producing an embarrassment for a human observer. To maximize the benefit
brought by an efficient compression technique, new techniques for assessing video
quality must be developed in parallel.

Subjective experiments represent the ideal approach for assessing video quality.
Organizations like the International Telecommunication (ITU) or the Video Quality
Expert Group (VQEG) propose some recommendations [1, 2], specifying the conditions of observations, the choice of observers, the test material, etc. However, these
subjective tests are very long, expensive and difficult to practice. The quality metrics
represent an alternative. Most of proposed video quality assessment approaches require the original video sequence as a reference. The most widely used objective
image quality metrics is Peak Signal-to-Noise Ratio (PSNR) and Mean Squared Error
(MSE). However, the predicted scores do not obtain a good correlation with subjective ratings: MSE and PSNR do not support fully the visual perception of a human

J. Blanc-Talon et al. (Eds.): ACIVS 2005, LNCS 3708, pp. 364–371, 2005.
© Springer-Verlag Berlin Heidelberg 2005

observer. Moreover, for many applications such as digital video broadcasting or streaming, the technical constraints (reception/transmission capacity) prohibit the exploitation of a reference video. The end user judges the video quality without comparing to the original video sequence. Therefore, the ability for assessing video quality using only the sequence, without a reference, turns out to be an important challenge for these applications.

A No-Reference (NR) approach generally seeks to assign quality scores, which are consistent with human perception using a prior knowledge about the types of video coding impairments. Considering the MPEG coded videos, the problem is simplified because there are a limited number of artifacts, which introduce an embarrassment for a human observer. The three most annoying distortions are the blocking, blurring and ringing effects. In [3], the authors propose a new distortion measure for each previously cited impairment. The pooling model is based on a linear combination of the three distortion measures and an additional feature, the bit rate. In [4], Caviedes et al. use three artifact measures, i.e. blocking, ringing and corner outlining (missing pixels belong to natural edges with strong contrast) measures. The three artifact measures are first normalized individually, then combined using Euclidean norm to form the reference free objective quality measure.

In this paper, the proposed method is to design separate models specifically tuned to certain type of distortion (blocking, blurring, ringing), and combine their results according to the impact of each type of impairment on the video quality. In the cases of ringing and blurring effects, two distinct measures are proposed: for the blurring effect, the distortion measure depends on all spatial information contained in each image of video sequence, while, for the ringing effect, only the local information is exploited. A joint measure of both of these distortions has been perceptually validated, using a database of JPEG-2000 compressed images. The same perceptual validation has been followed in the case of blocking effects. The difference comes from the nature of the image coder: only JPEG compressed images have been used. This step of the proposed metric demonstrates the efficiency of prediction of each distortion measure. A new pooling model is used in order to predict quality score. The performance of the proposed metric is evaluated using selected MPEG compressed video sequences in terms of different statistical coefficients with regard to subjective test data. The paper is organized as follows: section 2 describes the structure of the proposed quality assessment metric. Its performance evaluations are presented in Section 3 and conclusions are given in Section 4.

## 2   No-Reference Quality Metric

As mentioned in introduction section, at low bit rate, MPEG coding introduces visual impairments such as the blocking, blurring and ringing effects. Taking into account these observations, the proposed video quality metric (figure 1) is designed as follows: after a conversion in a perceptual color space of each image of the video sequence, the three distinct distortion measures of blocking ($BlM_i$), blurring ($BM_i$) and ringing ($RM_i$) effects are computed. Then, for each impairment, a temporal pooling is performed and at the last stage, a quality score is computed.

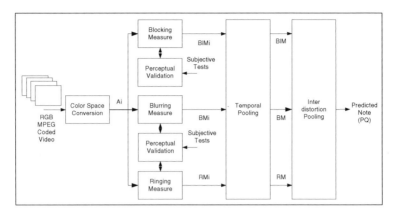

**Fig. 1.** Block diagram of the proposed NR quality metric

## 2.1  Color Space Conversion

In input of the proposed metric, the file format of the MPEG coded video is AVI RGB. Digital images coded in RGB color space cannot be used directly within a vision model, because the perception of color differences is highly no uniform. So, the first stage of the metric performs the conversion from RGB color space of each image of the MPEG compressed video to an opponent color space. This color space is inspired by the processing taking place in the human visual system, which presumably uses separate channels for black-white, red-green and blue-yellow information.

An image presented to the retina is sampled by cone photoreceptors maximally sensitive to Long (L cones), Middle (M cones), or Short (S cones) wavelengths. The RGB values are converted in LMS values by using transformations given in [5, 6]. Several opponent color spaces exist. In our lab, the Krauskopf color space [7] has been validated [8]. In this space, the decomposition into three components, called A, Cr1 and Cr2, corresponds to the three separate channels of the human visual system. Only the achromatic component ($A_i$) of each image of the video sequence is considered in this paper.

## 2.2  No-Reference Blocking Artifact Measure

Blocking effect is visually defined by a block structure in the video sequence, caused by the separated quantization of DCT coefficients of each block. In the literature, many algorithms measuring the blocking effect are proposed. A recent comparative study [9] has shown that the different approaches have the same performance. Hence, we have chosen a method, the Wang's metric [10] and we have tested its performance during a perceptual validation (see section 2.5). The key idea of Wang et al. is to model the blocky image as a non-blocky image interfered with a pure blocky signal. The blocking measure ($BIM_i$) is computed detecting and evaluating the power of the blocky signal.

## 2.3  No-Reference Blurring Artifact Measure

Blur in an image is due to the attenuation of the high spatial frequency coefficients, which occurs during the compression stage. Visually, the blurring effects correspond to a total distortion on the whole image, characterized by an increase of the spread of edges and spatial details. The structure of the NR blurring artifact measure is given by the figure 2.

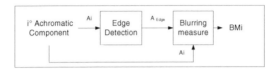

**Fig. 2.** NR blurring artifact measure

We measure the blurring artifact using spatial information and pixel activity. Let $I_A(i,j)$ the pixel $(i,j)$ intensity of $A_i$ component of size MxN pixels. The blurring measure ($BM_i$) is defined by (1):

$$BM_i = \frac{\sum_{i=1}^{M} \sum_{j=1}^{N} A'_{Edge}(i,j).I_A^2(i,j)}{\sum_{i=1}^{M} \sum_{j=1}^{N} A_{Edge}(i,j).I_A^2(i,j)} \cdot \frac{\frac{N(A'_{Edge})}{MxN}}{\frac{N(A_{Edge})}{MxN}} \tag{1}$$

Where $A_{Edge}$ is the binary image resulting from A edge detection. $A'_{Edge}$ is the $A_{Edge}$ opposite binary image. $N(A_{Edge})$ (respectively $N(A'_{Edge})$) is the number of non-null pixel values of $A_{Edge}$ (respectively $A'_{Edge}$).

The $BM_i$ formula is composed of two terms. The first one is defined by the ratio of activities between the areas of middle/low and high frequencies. The second one corresponds to the ratio of the occurrence probabilities of each area. The blurring measure follows the human visual perception: blurrier the image appears, bigger the blurring measure is.

## 2.4  No-Reference Ringing Artifact Measure

Ringing effect is caused by the quantization or truncation of the high frequency coefficients resulting from a coding based on DCT or Wavelet transform. This is also known as the Gibbs phenomenon. In the spatial domain, the ringing effect locally produces haloes and/or rings near sharp object edges in the picture. Before measuring this distortion, the areas around edges, called "ringing regions", must be identified. These are computed by using a binary "ringing mask" on the current image, resulting from the detection and the dilatation of strong edges (figure 3). The "ringing region" image ($A_{Ringing\ Mask}$) is computed by using a binary "ringing mask" on the current image. Then, a measure of ringing artifact is computed, defined by the ratio of regions activities of middle low and middle high frequencies, localized in these "ringing regions". Let $I_{ARM}(i,j)$ the pixel $(i,j)$ intensity of $A_{Ringing\ Mask}$ image of size MxN pixels. The ringing measure ($RM_i$) is defined by (2):

$$RM_i = \frac{\sum_{i=1}^{M} \sum_{j=1}^{N} A'_{RM\ Edge}(i,j).I^2_{A\ RM}(i,j)}{\sum_{i=1}^{M} \sum_{j=1}^{N} A_{RM\ Edge}(i,j).I^2_{A\ RM}(i,j)} \cdot \frac{\frac{N(A'_{RM\ Edge})}{N(Ringing\ Mask)}}{\frac{N(A_{RM\ Edge})}{N(Ringing\ Mask)}} \qquad (2)$$

Where $A_{RM\ Edge}$ is the binary image resulting from $A_{Ringing\ Mask}$ image edge detection. $A'_{RM\ Edge}$ is the combination (XOR operator) of $A_{RM\ Edge}$ opposite binary image and *Ringing Mask* binary image. $N(A_{RM\ Edge})$ (respectively $N(A'_{RM\ Edge})$ or $N(Ringing\ Mask)$) is the number of non-null pixel values of $A_{RM\ Edge}$ (respectively $A'_{RM\ Edge}$ or *Ringing Mask*) binary image.

The $RM_i$ formula looks like the $BM_i$ definition. However, only the information localized in ringing regions is exploited. Moreover, instead of considering the regions of low and high frequencies, only the areas of middle low and middle high frequencies are used for defining and computing the $RM_i$ formula terms.

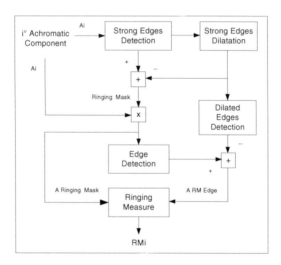

**Fig. 3.** NR ringing artifact measure

## 2.5  Perceptual Validation

Before optimizing the pooling model, the distortion measures must be tested. This perceptual validation consists in assessing the performance of each algorithm on an image database. Blocking effect is the most annoying distortion of JPEG coding, while, ringing and blurring are the two most notorious impairments of JPEG-2000 coding. Hence, in the experiments, we use two different image databases [11], which consist of 29 original high-resolution 24-bits/pixel RGB color images (typically 768x512) and their compressed versions with different compression ratios (227 images in each database). The bit rates used for compression are in the range of 0.03 to 3.2 bits per pixel, chosen such that the resulting distribution of quality scores is roughly uniform over the entire range. Each database is divided randomly into two sets: 14 training images and 15 testing images, together with their compressed versions.

In order to quantify the performance of a quality metric, VQEG propose some statistical tools [2]: the Pearson linear correlation for the accuracy, the Spearman rank order correlation for the monotonicity, the outliers percentage for the consistency and the Kappa coefficient for the agreement. The Table 1 illustrates the results of these performance tests for the blocking measure on the one hand and a joint measure of ringing and blurring effects [12], on the other hand.

**Table 1.** Perceptual validation of NR blocking, blurring and ringing measures

| | Pearson correlation | Spearman Correlation | Outlier ratio | Kappa coefficient |
|---|---|---|---|---|
| Blocking measure | 0.96369 | 0.92908 | 3.43% | 0.72206 |
| Joint measure of ringing and blurring effects | 0.89637 | 0.8716 | 6.20% | 0.47957 |

Accuracy is the ability of a metric to predict subjective scores with a minimum average error. The two obtained linear correlations between subjective and objective scores justify this prediction accuracy. Monotonicity is another important attribute. Spearman rand order correlations test for agreement between the rank orders of MOS and model predictions. This correlation method only assumes a monotonic relationship between the two quantities. With Spearman rank-order correlation coefficients equal to 0.8716 and 0.92908, the degree of monotonicity of each distortion measure can be considered as good. The outlier analysis evaluates an objective model's ability to provide consistently accurate predictions for all types of compressed images and not fail excessively for a subset of images, i.e., prediction consistency. The two image quality metrics obtain a small outlier percentage (6.2% and 3.43%), which means that the two prediction models are consistent. The Kappa coefficient is a measure of agreement. Usually, a Kappa coefficient superior to 0.4 is a good value; so the two metrics obtain a good agreement between subjective and predicted scores. All performance tests proposed by VQEG are satisfied, which demonstrates the efficiency of each distortion measure.

## 2.6 Pooling

The proposed pooling model is composed of two parts: the first one consists of a temporal pooling for each artifact, while, the second one defines an inter distortion pooling. For each artifact, the temporal pooling of blocking (BlM), blurring (BM) and ringing (RM), respectively are computed by Minkowski summation. Then, the final predicted quality score for an entire video sequence can be obtained by a linear combination of temporal distortion measures:

$$PQ = a_1.BlM + a_2.BM + a_3.RM + a_4.BlM.BM + a_5.BM.RM \qquad (3)$$

Where $a_i$, i=1..5 are the weights to be optimized. The three first terms of the final pooling model correspond to the distortion caused by each artifact, while the others define the combined actions of blocking/blurring and blurring/ringing effects.

## 3  Experiments and Results

The proposed video quality metric is tested using a video database. This set consists of 35 video sequences derived from 7 original scenes. These clips contain a wide range of entertainment content from TV news to sport event. Each original video sequence is compressed using XVID coder (a free MPEG-4 coder) at five different bit rates ranging from 1.6Mbps to 5 Mbps. Subjective ratings of the compressed videos are obtained using psychophysical experiment and following the recommendation ITU-T BT.500.10 [13]. In our experiment, the database is divided randomly into two sets: 4 training videos and 3 testing videos, together with their compressed versions.

The weights $a_i$ of the pooling model are estimated from training videos using minimal mean squared error estimate between quality predictions and subjective scores. Then, the proposed trained quality metric is validated on the test database. The quality predictions resulting from this assessment are compared with human scores. The performance of the proposed metric is assessed using the statistical tools recommended by VQEG (table2).

**Table 2.** Performance measures of the reference free video quality metric

|  | Pearson correlation | Spearman Correlation | Outlier ratio | Kappa coefficient |
|---|---|---|---|---|
| Proposed metric | 0.8931 | 0.89996 | 8.429% | 0.42117 |

In spite of the simplicity of the proposed algorithm, the proposed metric demonstrates its efficiency in the video quality prediction. The different performance metrics of VQEG recommendations are satisfied. Moreover, this quality metric is only based on research of distortions resulting from the achromatic component of each image of a video sequence. So, if the impairments of two chromatic components were considered, the performances of quality prediction would be improved.

## 4  Conclusions

In this paper, we have presented a new reference free quality metric for assessing the quality of MPEG compressed video sequences. The proposed method is based on the exploitation of separate models specifically tuned to certain type of distortion (blocking, blurring, ringing). Each algorithm of impairment measure is previously validated with subjective ratings, which assures the efficiency of the proposed approach. Our future works aim to improve the prediction performance exploiting some properties of the human visual system.

## References

1. ITU-T Recommendation P.910, *Subjective video quality assessment methods for multimedia application.* 1999, ITU: Geneva, Switzerland.
2. Rohaly, A.M., P. Corriveau, J. Libert, et al. *Video Quality Experts Group: current results and future directions.* in *Proceedings of Visual Communications and Images Processing.* 2000.

3.  Cheng, H. and J. Lubin, *Reference free objective quality metrics for MPEG coded video.* Visual Communications and Image Processing, 2003.
4.  Caviedes, J. and J. Jung. *No-reference metric for a video quality control loop.* in *World Multi-Conference on Systems Cybernetics and Informatics Broadcasting Convention.* 2001.
5.  Judd, D.B., *Report of U.S. Secretariat Committee on Colorimetry and Artificial Daylight.* 1951, Bureau Central de la CIE.
6.  ITU-R Recommendation BT.709-4, *Parameter values for the HDTV standards for production and international programme exchange.* 2000, ITU: Geneva.
7.  Williams, D.R., J. Krauskopf and D.W. Heeley, *Cardinal directions of color space.* Vision Research, 1982. **22**: p. 1123-1131.
8.  Bédat, L., *Aspects psychovisuels de la Perception des Couleurs. Application au Codage d'Images Couleurs Fixes avec Compression de l'Information.*, in *Université de Nantes, IRESTE.* 1998: Nantes.
9.  Pan, F., X. Lin, S. Rahardja, et al., *A locally adaptive algorithm for measuring blocking artifacts in images and videos.* Signal Processing Image Communication, 2004. **19**: p. 499-506.
10. Wang, Z., A. Bovik and B. Evans. *Blind measurement of blocking artifacts in images.* in *IEEE International Conference on Image Processing.* 2000.
11. Sheikh, H., Z. Wang, L. Cormack, and A. Bovik, *LIVE Image Quality Assessment Database.* http://live.ece.utexas.edu/research/quality.
12. Barland, R. and A. Saadane. *Reference Free Quality Metric for JPEG-2000 Compressed Images.* in *International Symposium on Signal Processing and its Applications.* 2005. Sydney, Australia.
13. ITU-R Recommendation BT.500-10, *Methodology for the subjective assessment of the quality of television pictures.* 2000, ITU: Geneva.

# Reduced-Bit, Full Search Block-Matching Algorithms and Their Hardware Realizations

Vincent M. Dwyer, Shahrukh Agha, and Vassilios A. Chouliaras

Department of Electronic and Electrical Engineering, Loughborough University,
Loughborough, Leicestershire, UK
v.m.dwyer@lboro.ac.uk

**Abstract.** The Full Search Block-Matching Motion Estimation (FSBME) algorithm is often employed in video coding for its regular dataflow and straightforward architectures. By iterating over all candidates in a defined Search Area of the reference frame, a motion vector is determined for each current frame macroblock by minimizing the Sum of Absolute Differences (SAD) metric. However, the complexity of the method is prohibitively high, amounting to 60-80% of the encoder's computational burden, and making it unsuitable for many real-time video applications. One means of alleviating the problem is to calculate SAD values using fewer bits (Reduced-Bit SAD), however the reduced dynamic range may compromise picture quality. The current work presents an algorithm, which corrects the RBSAD to full resolution under appropriate conditions. Our results demonstrate that the optimal conditions for correction include a knowledge of the motion vectors of neighboring blocks in space and/or time.

## 1   Introduction

In order to meet power consumption requirements for battery powered (or hand-held) real-time visual communication applications, Motion Estimation (ME) algorithms [1, 2] are generally implemented at a coding stage. The notion behind the approach is that temporal redundancy in a video sequence may be used to compress the video data. The prevailing methods over recent years use block-matching algorithms [3], which compute motion vectors on a block-by-block basis, and generally out-perform other alternatives, such as the pel-recursive algorithm [4].

The block-matching algorithm divides the current frame $\mathbf{F_c}$ into non-overlapping square blocks, of $N \times N$ pixels, which are matched to blocks of the same size within a pre-defined Search Area of a reference frame $\mathbf{F_r}$. For most ME algorithms, the Search Area is taken to be a square of size $(N+2p)^2$ centered around the block of interest. All pixels within the same current frame macroblock are assigned the same motion vector $\mathbf{mv}$. $N$ is most commonly taken equal to 16, while the value of $p$ is generally fixed by whatever processing power is available. A wide variety of Motion Estimation algorithms have been proposed, however the gold standard is the Full Search Block-Matching Motion Estimation (FSBME) algorithm. The Full-Search algorithm compares a current frame macroblock with all similar sized blocks in the Search

J. Blanc-Talon et al. (Eds.): ACIVS 2005, LNCS 3708, pp. 372 – 380, 2005.
© Springer-Verlag Berlin Heidelberg 2005

Area of the reference frame. As a result it will always find the best fit, and the most appropriate motion vector, for a given value of $p$. Additionally the dataflow is regular and the silicon architectures are relatively straightforward. However, in order to encode, say, a CIF-sized video at 30 fps, billions of arithmetic operations per second are required together with a memory bandwidth of the order of GByte/s [5, 6]. Consequently, if the Search Area (effectively the value of $p$) is large, it is not feasible to use the FSBME algorithm and meet the low power constraints of today's processor technologies [7].

Fast Motion Estimation algorithms can give reduced computational complexity, as well as advantages for VLSI design in area and power consumption [e.g. 5, 6 and references therein]. However, the reduced computational complexity has often to be offset by losses in visual quality and/or by irregularities in dataflow, making it difficult to achieve efficient VLSI implementations [5, 6]. The result is that most hardware designs attempt to develop faster or lower power strategies while still employing the Full Search method. Such, also, is the aim of this paper.

The figure of merit which is used to determine the 'best match' between blocks in the current and reference frames is usually a distance metric, and is typically the Sum of Absolute Difference (SAD) value, between the pixel values of the current frame macroblock (MB) and those of the candidate MBs in the Search Area of the reference frame. Taking the reference frame as the immediately preceding frame, we have

$$SAD(m,n) = \sum_{i,j=1}^{16} |s(i,j,k) - s(i+m, j+n, k-1)| \tag{1}$$

Occasionally this sum is termed the Mean Absolute Difference (or MAD) value.

For a $16 \times 16$ macroblock, SAD values are calculated over the ranges $-p \le m \le p - 1$ and $-p \le n \le p-1$. The motion vector for the block is determined as that pair of $(m,n)$ values which produce the lowest SAD. In eqn. (1), $s(i,j,k)$ is the (8-bit luminance) pixel value at $(i,j)$ in frame $k$. With the FSBME method, all $16 \times 16$ macroblocks in the Search Area are candidates [3], making the search for the best fit naturally computationally burdensome. Even with $p$ as small as to 8 this still corresponds to 256 candidates, while, in general, larger $p$ values are required to increase the PSNR.

One means of reducing the computation is to use one of the Fast Motion Estimation algorithms such as the Three Step Search [8, 9], or one of the many other 'fast' methods which may be found, for example, in reference [5, 6 and 10] and references therein. These methods base the definition of the candidate set on current results, which increases the design complexity, disturbs the dataflow and makes dedicated hardware implementations very difficult [5, 6].

The standard means of assessing the accuracy of these algorithms is through the use of the Peak-Signal to Noise Ratio (PSNR), usually defined as the fractional RMS error between the predicted and true frames, expressed on a dB scale. To be considered realistic, fast algorithms really need to be within a fraction of a dB of the FSBME value. In order to preserve dataflow regularity, and at the same time to reduce computational complexity, we have recently employed a full-search algorithm using Bit Truncation, which uses eqn. (1) based on a reduced number of bits [11, 12], and provides an RBSAD (Reduced-Bit Sum of Absolute Difference) metric [13, 14]. The downside of the method is the reduced dynamic range it imposes. With an 8-bit SAD, the pixel luminance values occupy the entire integer range [0, 255] while, with a 4-bit RBSAD, the resolution in these values is naturally reduced, since the step-size is increased from one to 16. Potentially this leads to an increased error matrix and consequently a lower bit-rate, or a higher quantization error, and a reduction of visual quality. In practice, however, PSNR values for the two methods are very close for many real sequences, as may be seen in Table 1. which shows the maximum difference between PSNR values at full resolution (FSBME) and with RBSAD, for a variety of sequences. Indeed, the only case studied in which the maximum and/or average PSNR values are significantly worse using a 4-bit RBSAD is the 'Claire' sequence for which the average PSNR values (with full and reduced resolution) are both already large.

It is possible to correct the RBASD value to full resolution by adding the term [12]

$$\lambda(m,n) = \sum_{i,j=1}^{16} \varepsilon_{i,j}(m,n)\left(s(i,j,k)_{\langle 3:0\rangle} - s(i+m,j+n,k-1)_{\langle 3:0\rangle}\right) \tag{2}$$

Here the subscript $\langle 3:0\rangle$ refers to the lower four bits of the pixel values, and $\varepsilon_{i,j}(m,n)$ is the sign of $s(i,j,k)_{\langle 7:4\rangle} - s(i+m,j+n,k-1)_{\langle 7:4\rangle}$, unless it is zero, when $\varepsilon_{i,j}(m,n)$ defaults to the sign of $s(i,j,k)_{\langle 3:0\rangle} - s(i+m,j+n,k-1)_{\langle 3:0\rangle}$. To implement this correction consequently requires the signs of the absolute difference values at the base of the adder tree, and their zero flag output, to be saved. This corresponds to a slight increase in the, generally large, on-chip memory requirement for the processing elements which perform the Motion Estimation. There is also a slight overhead in the overall size of the adder tree. An adder tree required to calculate an 8-bit SAD, is generally slightly smaller than the sum of that required for a 4-bit (RB)SAD and that required to calculate the correction term, eqn. (2). However it is clear that the power savings can be significant. The main question for investigation, and the focus of this work, is:- Under what conditions should this correction (to full resolution) be applied to obtain the best results?

## 2     Corrected-RBSAD Algorithm

We restrict our study to those cases in which the RBSAD is poor. We wish to generate an algorithm which maintains the advantages of reduced bits (power and speed) but avoids some of the disadvantages. This means that our study will necessarily revolve around the 'Claire' sequence. The difference between the average PSNR for the full resolution and with reduced bits (using 4-bits) is around 1.5dB for the sequence, with a maximum value of 2.86dB. This difference is plotted for the first one-hundred frames of the sequence in Fig.1., and is clearly too large for the RBSAD method to be considered as an alternative to the FSBME in this case. The problem relates to the fact that 'Claire' is a head and shoulders sequence, with little motion for many MBs. Consequently there can be several good matches and the RBSAD method naturally can have difficulty in selecting the best [12]. Indeed the RBSAD calculation will not be able to distinguish between any candidate blocks for which, for example, the RBSAD calculation is equal to zero, and this still leaves a wide range of possible SAD values. However any lack of motion may be tested for, through the temporal and/or spatial correlation of motion vectors between and within frames. In order to determine when the RBSAD metric should be used and when correction to full resolution should be applied, we consider the following seven algorithms which implement these notions:

I.     **if** (RBSAD = 0) **then** apply correction

II.    **if** ($mv_T$ = 0) **then** apply correction in range of mv's given by = [-1,1] × [-1,1]

III.   **if** ($mv_S$ = 0) **then** apply correction in range = [-1,1] × [-1,1]

IV.    **if** ($mv_S$ = 0 or $mv_T$ = 0) **then** apply correction in range = [-1,1] × [-1,1]

V.     **if** (RBSAD = 0) **then** apply correction

       **and if** ($mv_S$ = 0) **then** apply correction in range = [-1,1] × [-1,1]

VI.    **if** (RBSAD = 0) **then** apply correction

       **and if** ($mv_T$ = 0) **then** apply correction in range = [-1,1] × [-1,1]

VII.   **if** (RBSAD = 0) **then** apply correction

       **and if** ($mv_T$ = 0 **or** $mv_S$ = 0) **then** apply correction in range = [-1,1] × [-1,1].

**Table 1.** Maximum PSNR values corresponding to full and reduced resolution

| Sequence | Mom | Foreman | Fog | Snow Fall | SnowLane | Claire |
|---|---|---|---|---|---|---|
| FSBME | 35.86 | 28.46 | 32.28 | 26.82 | 30.16 | 46.15 |
| RBSAD | 35.58 | 28.37 | 31.76 | 26.70 | 30.09 | 43.29 |

**Table 2.** Average corrected-PSNR values, % corrected calculations and % power saving

| Algorithm | Average PSNR | Average % corrections | % Power saving |
|---|---|---|---|
| FSMBE | 41.49 | 100 | 00.0 |
| RBSAD | 40.27 | 0 | 50.0 |
| I | 40.61 | 23 | 38.5 |
| II | 41.11 | 3 | 48.5 |
| III | 41.27 | 3 | 48.5 |
| IV | 41.47 | 3 | 48.5 |
| V | 41.37 | 25 | 37.5 |
| VI | 41.27 | 25 | 37.5 |
| VII | 41.47 | 25 | 37.5 |

Under Algorithm I, the correction to the full resolution metric is applied whenever the RBSAD is equal to zero [11]. Our results show that RBSAD metric performs less well for head-and-shoulder sequences like 'Claire' which are mostly reasonably static.

However, such sequences have high spatial and temporal correlation which can be used to generate potential conditions for the application of the correction.

Algorithm II makes use of the temporal correlation between frames. Here $mv_T$ is the motion vector of the corresponding macroblock in the previous frame (i.e. in the same position). The notion is that if the block did not move in the previous frame then it is unlikely to move far in the current frame so that the correction should be applied in the nine cases $m = -1, 0, +1$ and $n = -1, 0, +1$ (although this could be extended to $-2, -1, 0, +1, +2$, etc.). Algorithm III assumes that a degree of spatial correlation exists, where $mv_S$ is the motion vector of the macroblock to the left (or above, if no such MB exists) of the current macroblock in the same frame. Algorithm IV utilizes both spatial and temporal correlation, and is a simple hybrid of Algorithms II and III. Likewise Algorithm V is a hybrid of Algorithms I and III, Algorithm VI is hybrid of Algorithms I and II and Algorithm VII is hybrid of Algorithms I and IV.

The average corrected-PSNR values obtained as a result of application of these algorithms on the 'Claire' sequence (using the first 100 frames), along with the average percentage of cases for which corrections are applied, are given in Table II. It is clear that, for this sequence, those algorithms that involve a correction criterion based on the spatial and/or temporal redundancy in the video clip offer the best power savings and require the lowest number of corrections. The power saving calculation is a relatively simplified version. Assuming a fraction $(1 - \alpha)$ of full resolution calculations are performed at full power P, and the remainder, a fraction $\alpha$, are calculated at power P/2 (i.e. 4-bits), then the fractional power dissipated relative to FSBME is $(1 + \alpha)/2$. In truth a full SAD calculation, in the current model, requires slightly more than P, say $P(1 + \beta)$, where $\beta$ is small but may be readily calculated for any given architecture.

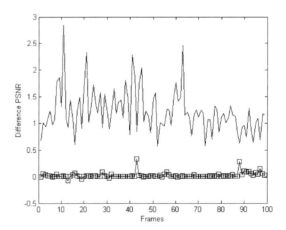

**Fig. 1.** PSNR differences for Claire sequence

Fig. 1. shows PSNR differences for the 'Claire' sequence. The solid curve represents the difference between FSBME and RBSAD, whereas the squares indicate the difference between FSBME and the corrected-RBSAD using Algorithm IV. Note that the maximum PSNR difference has fallen from 2.86 dB to around 0.35 dB. While Algorithm IV generates the best results for the 'Claire' sequence there will be occasions when reducing the SAD calculation to the ranges $m = -1, 0, +1$ and $n = -1, 0, +1$ will be too restrictive, as a result it is recommended that Algorithm VII, which also calculates SAD values for those cases in which RBSAD = 0, should be applied in general. Alternatively the range $\{-1, 0, +1\}$ could be widened to, for example, $\{-2, -1, 0, 1, +2\}$.

## 3    General Form of Hardware

Motion Estimation hardware is generally designed around the concept of the processing element (PE), a number of which work in parallel to perform the calculations. The RBSAD calculation for a MB is done on a row by row basis, taking one row of 16 (4-bit) pixel values from each of the current and reference frames. The general form of the processing element (PE) envisaged here is depicted in Fig. 2., along with the memory used in the hardware architecture for the motion estimation process. The PE is divided into two blocks; the left-hand block (as depicted here) contains an absolute difference unit (AD), with 16 carry trees to calculate signs and 16 × four-bit subtracters, and an adder tree containing fast adders. As the tree requires only small adders (16 × 4-bit adders, 8 × 5-bit adders, 4 × 6-bit adders, 2 × 7-bit adders and 1 × 8-bit adder) simple ripple adders can be used, which are as fast as other choices, for such small bit numbers [15], but consume less power and occupy a smaller silicon area.

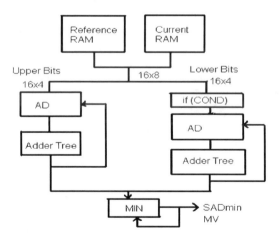

**Fig. 2.** A general form of processing element

The right-hand block in Fig. 2., which will calculate the correction term for the SAD value due to the lower four bits, i.e. $\lambda(m,n)$, is very similar to left-hand block, the major difference being the addition of a condition unit, so that the adders and subtracters will only be enabled when the appropriate algorithmic condition is met. Under Algorithm I, and any hybrids containing it, the left-hand block and right-hand (or $\lambda$-) block will run in a pipelined fashion, the $\lambda$-block running if the RBSAD has been calculated to zero, while under other algorithms the blocks may run in parallel as the truth of the condition is known before the start of the calculation. An SAD metric will then take sixteen clock cycles to be executed, using a single row of sixteen pixels at a time. Using the FSBME method, or the corrected-RBSAD method, the best match of a current frame macroblock to a similar macroblock in a search area of $16 \times 16$ macroblocks, will take $16 \times 16 \times 16$ clock cycles.

The hardware implementation for Algorithm I, i.e. the condition RBSAD(7:4) = 0, was considered in ref [11]. The other algorithmic conditions ($mv_T = 0$ and $mv_S = 0$) are equally simple, but require registers at the output of each processing element to store the *zero condition* of the spatial and/or temporal motion vectors. These algorithms also require a number of memory locations within the processing element to store the sign and zero information required by the $\lambda$-block. The functional block which calculates $\lambda(m,n)$ is almost identical to that which calculates RBSAD, one difference being in the selection of the inputs in the absolute difference unit, which only depends upon the sign of $s(i,j,k)_{<7:4>} - s(i,j,k-1)_{<7:4>}$ in the RBSAD calculation but is slightly more complicated for the correction term $\lambda(m,n)$. The power implications for such a scheme are obvious as whenever the algorithmic condition is not met, the $\lambda$-block is disabled.

A second, but not inconsiderable, power saving, which results from this architecture, is through memory reads from on-chip memory. If the data is stored in two *separate* memory blocks as it is written to the on-chip memory, with the upper four bits in one block and the lower four bits in another, then most calculations will only require reads from the upper block. Only when the algorithmic condition is met, will reads from both memory blocks will be necessary. The purpose of this paper is to investigate what are the most appropriate conditions to apply correction.

We have considered a number of test sequences, Table I. These involve most types of motion seen in typical sequences and so are representative of what might be expected in real video clips. The hardware essentially executes the code as follows:

```
If(condition) then Output := SAD(7:0)
else if(not(correcting)) Output := RBSAD(7:4)
    else Output := xFFFF;
    end;
end;
```

where we have used the notation that RBSAD(7:4) is an SAD calculation based on using the top four bits (7:4) of the luminance pixel values. Note that if the 'correcting' flag is set the RBSAD minimization is halted and only correct SAD values are used to calculate the motion vectors. Note also that, for those sequences for which the RBSAD calculation produces an accurate PSNR value, almost no corrections are applied.

## 4    Conclusions

In this paper we have considered an alternative implementation to the conventional Full Search Block-Matching Motion Estimation (FSBME) method for the estimation of Motion Vectors for video encoding [11, 12]. The present method is based around the general good performance of the method of Bit Truncation in which (typically) the upper four bits are used in the Sum of Absolute Difference calculation [13, 14]. It is clear that, if the method can be applied without loss in picture quality, there is significant room for improvement in power performance. Here we have considered various combinations of conditions under which the RBSAD value could be corrected to the full resolution. The sequence requiring correction is the standard 'Claire' sequence, for which uncorrected bit-truncation of the SAD calculation performs significantly less well than full resolution FSBME.

The best performing algorithms are those retaining some temporal memory (the zero condition for the motion vector of the same MB in the reference frame) and/or spatial memory (the zero condition for the motion vector of neighboring current frame MBs). Using both spatial and temporal correlation, Algorithm IV has the additional advantage that it can handle sudden scene changes, which destroy temporal correlation.

The majority of standard architectures, based on a bit slice design and a single processing element per current frame MB, can easily be adapted to implemented these algorithms. The algorithms show a significant improvement in accuracy towards the FSBME method but with most of the power and time savings of the Reduced-Bit SAD method. While Algorithm IV is best for the 'Claire' sequence it is likely that Algorithm VII, which generates a super-set of Algorithm IV, should be applied in general.

## References

[1]  ISO/IEC JTC1/SC29/WG11-1313-1, Coding moving pictures and associated audio, 1994.

[2]  CCITT SG XV, Recommendation H.261 – Video codec for audiovisual services, 1990.

[3]  J R Jain and A K Jain, Displacement measurement and its application in interframe image coding, IEEE Trans Commun, **COM-29** 1799-1808 (1981).

[4]  A Netravali and J D Robbins, Motion compensated television coding: Part I, Bell Syst. Tech J., **58** (1979) 629-668.

[5]  P M Kuhn, Fast MPEG-4 Motion Estimation: Processor based and flexible VLSI implementation, J. VLSI Signal Processing **23** (1999) 67-92.

[6]  P M Kuhn, G Diebel, S Herman, A Keil, H Mooshofer, A Karp, R Mayer and W Stechele, Complexity and PSNR-comparison of several fast Motion Estimation algorithms for MPEG-4, SPIE **3460**, Applications of Digital Image Processing XXI, San Diego, USA, (1998) 486 – 499.

[7]  V G Moshnyaga, A new computationally adaptive formulation of block-matching Motion Estimation, IEEE Trans. Cir. Sys. Video Technol. **11**, (2001) 118-124.

[8]  T Koga, K Lumina, A Hirano, Y Lijima and T Ishiguro, Motion compensated interframe coding for video conferencing, Proc NTC **1981**, G5.3.1-5.

[9]  H Jong, L Chen and T Chieuh, Accuracy improvement and cost reduction of three-step search block matching algorithm for video coding, IEEE Trans. Cir. Sys. Video Tec. 4, (1994) 88-91.

[10]  R Srinivasan and K Rao, Predictive coding based on efficient Motion Estimation, IEEE Trans. Commun., **38** (1990) 950-953.

[11]  V M Dwyer, S Agha and V Chouliaras, Low power full search block matching using reduced bit sad values for early termination, Mirage 2005, Versailles, France, March 2-3, 2005.

[12]  S Agha, V M Dwyer and V Chouliaras, Motion Estimation with Low Resolution Distortion Metric, submitted Elec Letters, 2005.

[13]  Y Baek, H S Oh and H K Lee, An efficient block-matching criterion for motion estimation and its VLSI implementation, IEEE Trans Cons Electr., **42** (1996) 885-892.

[14]  S Lee, J-M Kim and S-I Chae, New Motion Estimation algorithm using an adaptively quantized low bit-resolution image and its VLSI architecture for MPEG2 video encoding, IEEE Trans. Cir. Sys. Video Tec.**8**, (1998) 734-744.

[15]  A.Th. Schwarzbacher, J.P. Silvennoinen and J.T.Timoney, Benchmarking CMOS Adder Structures, Irish Systems and Signals Conference, Cork, Ireland, pp 231-234, June 2002.

# Lossy Compression of Images with Additive Noise

Nikolay Ponomarenko[1], Vladimir Lukin[1], Mikhail Zriakhov[1],
Karen Egiazarian[2], and Jaakko Astola[2]

[1] Dept of Receivers, Transmitters and Signal Processing, National Aerospace University,
17 Chkalova St, 61070 Kharkov, Ukraine
lukin@xai.kharkov.ua
[2] Institute of Signal Processing, Tampere University of Technology,
FIN-33101, Tampere, Finland
{karen, jta}@cs.tut.fi

**Abstract.** Lossy compression of noise-free and noisy images differs from each other. While in the first case image quality is decreasing with an increase of compression ratio, in the second case coding image quality evaluated with respect to a noise-free image can be improved for some range of compression ratios. This paper is devoted to the problem of lossy compression of noisy images that can take place, e.g., in compression of remote sensing data. The efficiency of several approaches to this problem is studied. Image pre-filtering is shown to be expedient for coded image quality improvement and/or increase of compression ratio. Some recommendations on how to set the compression ratio to provide quasioptimal quality of coded images are given. A novel DCT-based image compression method is briefly described and its performance is compared to JPEG and JPEG2000 with application to lossy noisy image coding.

## 1 Introduction

Image compression nowadays is an area of very intensive investigations. Basically, most efforts are spent on design and implementation of techniques and algorithms for compression of noise-free images [1]. However, compression of noisy images is also an important subject, especially for such applications as data coding in remote sensing [2,3], monitoring systems [4,5], medical imaging [6], etc. Lossless image compression for the considered applications is usually unable to satisfy practical needs due to noise presence and other reasons. The achievable compression ratio (CR) is commonly only slightly larger than unity. This makes lossy compression the basic tool in noisy image coding.

Furthermore, lossy compression being applied to noisy images provides one more benefit. Simultaneously with decreasing a compressed image size with respect to original image, lossy compression performs noise reduction [2-9]. This effect is useful since noise in images does not contain any valuable information about sensed terrain or imaged scene. Thus, noise retaining while compressing an image is absolutely unnecessary. Moreover, in performance analysis of techniques for noisy image lossy compression it is common to use image compression quality criteria that "compare" a compressed image not to original noisy one but to a noise-free image [4-8]. The most often used quantitative criterion derived in aforementioned way is peak signal-to-

J. Blanc-Talon et al. (Eds.): ACIVS 2005, LNCS 3708, pp. 381–386, 2005.
© Springer-Verlag Berlin Heidelberg 2005

noise ratio (PSNR) (although some other criteria can be also taken into account [3,10]). However, such PSNR can be obtained for only test, artificially noised images when one has the corresponding noise-free images (let us further denote it as $PSNR_{nf}$). And for real life noisy images, PSNR for compressed data can be calculated only with respect to original noisy images (such PSNR is denoted below as $PSNR_{or}$).

Note that different methods can be used as a basis for noisy image lossy compression, namely, DCT-based [4-7], wavelet-based [2,3,8,9], vector quantization [10] and fractal ones [11]. Moreover, special additional means can be applied for improving coder efficiency like noisy image pre-filtering [8] or pre-processing [6], decompressed image restoration or post-processing [4,7], etc. Depending upon this, different techniques can provide the best performance. Dependence of coder performance on image properties, noise type and statistical characteristics should be mentioned as well. Thus, our first goal was to carry out a brief analysis of performance for few compression techniques for images corrupted by additive Gaussian noise. In particular, a technique recently proposed by us [12] has been considered.

Another problem analyzed below is how to reach a quasi-optimal quality of compressed noisy image. JPEG2000 coder is designed in a way to provide required CR and, thus, it is well suited for communication and multimedia applications. But in remote sensing applications, the main requirement is to provide the quality of compressed image appropriate for further interpretation, whereas the requirement to ensure maximally reachable CR is of less importance. The authors of [4] have shown the existence of such point of dependence of $PSNR_{nf}$ on CR for which $PSNR_{nf}$ is maximal (called "the optimal operation point") but they have not given strict recommendations how to reach it. In Section 3 we are addressing to this problem.

## 2  Performance Analysis of the Considered Techniques

Commonly wavelet and DCT based image compression techniques provide better trade-off between PSNR and CR than fractal and vector quantization methods [1]. Thus, let us concentrate on consideration of JPEG and JPEG2000. Besides, we analyze the performance of recently proposed DCT based technique [12]. It differs from the standard JPEG by three modifications. First, image is divided into 32-by-32 size blocks (instead of 8-by-8 in JPEG). Second, DCT coefficients in each block are divided into bit planes and complex probability models for data coding are used. And third, DCT based post-processing (de-blocking) of decompressed images with setting hard threshold equal to a half of quantization step applied at compression stage is used [13]. Due to these modifications, the proposed coder called AGU (accessible from http://www.cs.tut.fi/~karen/agucoder.htm) can outperform JPEG2000 in the sense of better PSNR for a given CR. Besides, AGU produces much smaller blocking artifacts in comparison to the standard JPEG and provides few dBs better PSNR in the case of noise-free image compression [12].

Our experiments have been conducted on Lenna and Barbara 512x512 grayscale images. Noisy images have been created by adding a zero mean Gaussian noise to them with two variances $\sigma^2$ equal to 50 and 200. CR was expressed in bits per pixel (bpp). Besides, we have studied two approaches: compression of noisy images without pre-processing and image coding with pre-filtering by means of spatially invariant

DCT based filter with hard thresholding (according to recommendation [14] threshold is set to $2.7\sigma$). Therefore, in aggregate, six compression techniques have been exploited: JPEG, JPEG2000, AGU, and these techniques with pre-filtering denoted as F-JPEG, F-JPEG2000, and F-AGU, respectively. The dependencies of $PSNR_{or}(bpp)$ for all methods behave in traditional [4,6,7] and similar manner, i.e. $PSNR_{or}$ reduces with bpp decreasing.

Behavior of dependencies $PSNR_{nf}(bpp)$ is more interesting. They are presented in Figures 1 and 2. For techniques JPEG, JPEG2000, AGU the plots are similar to those ones presented in papers [4,6,7]. When CR increases (bpp reduces) $PSNR_{nf}$ first remains almost unchanged or grows (up to optimal operation point) and then drops down.

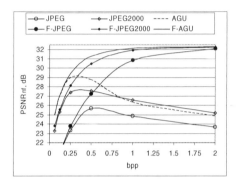
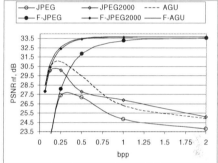

**Fig. 1.** Dependencies $PSNR_{nf}$ (bpp) for different compression methods for the test images Barbara (left) and Lena (right) for $\sigma^2=200$

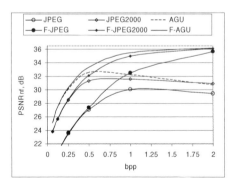
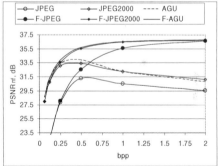

**Fig. 2.** Dependencies $PSNR_{nf}$ (bpp) for different compression methods for the test images Barbara (left) and Lena (right) for $\sigma^2=50$

Note that for both test images and both noise variances JPEG2000 and AGU outperform JPEG for all range of bpp variation. In the neighborhood of optimal operation point the values of $PSNR_{nf}$ for AGU are 0.5...1.5 dB better than for JPEG2000. For the test image Lena (for the same $\sigma^2$) better (larger) values of $PSNR_{or}$ are observed than for the test image Barbara, especially in the neighborhoods of optimal operation points. Certainly, if $\sigma^2$ is smaller, better $PSNR_{or}$ are provided.

Behavior of dependencies $PSNR_{nf}$(bpp) for the techniques F-JPEG, F-JPEG2000, and F-AGU differs from that one for the techniques JPEG, JPEG2000, AGU. First of all, for large bpp $PSNR_{nf}$(bpp) for F-JPEG, F-JPEG2000, F-AGU are larger than for JPEG, JPEG2000, AGU, respectively. Only for very small bpp these curves practically coincide. This means that pre-filtering allows considerably better compression of noisy images than direct application of coding to original noisy images. Second, the dependencies $PSNR_{nf}$(bpp) for F-JPEG, F-JPEG2000 do not have maxima that are observed in optimal operation points for JPEG, JPEG2000, and AGU. If pre-filtering is applied, $PSNR_{nf}$ reduces with bpp decreasing. However, for bpps corresponding to optimal operation points for techniques JPEG, JPEG2000, and AGU the values of $PSNR_{nf}$ for F-JPEG, F-JPEG2000 and F-AGU are anyway about 0.5...1.5 dB larger than for the corresponding method if pre-filtering is not applied. Again, the results for F-JPEG2000 and F-AGU are better than for F-JPEG. And for F-AGU, $PSNR_{nf}$ can be up to 1.5 dB larger than for F-JPEG2000.

We have compared the method F-AGU to compression technique with pre-filtering described in [5] for original image SNR=10 dB (image Lena). For bpp 0.25...0.5 F-AGU provides about 2 dB better $PSNR_{nf}$. Also, the performance of the proposed technique F-AGU has been compared to the method [6] for additive noise variance 100 and the test image Lena of size 256x256 pixels. For bpp 0.25...0.5 (and this is the neighborhood of optimal operation point) F-AGU produces approximately 3 dB better results due to more efficient pre-filtering and coding.

## 3    Determination of Optimal Operation Point

As it was mentioned in Introduction, for a real life situation one is unable to calculate $PSNR_{nf}$ (since noise-free image is not at disposal). Thus, the question arises how to get to optimal operation point. Note that for different $\sigma^2$ and test images optimal operation point is observed for different bpp although for given $\sigma^2$ and test image it practically coincides for all considered methods (JPEG, JPEG2000, and AGU). For example, for $\sigma^2=200$ the corresponding maximal $PSNR_{nf}$ is observed for bpp$\approx$0.5 for the test image Barbara and for bpp$\approx$0.25 for the test image Lenna (see Fig.1). Similarly, for $\sigma^2=50$ the maximal $PSNR_{nf}$ takes place for bpp$\approx$0.75 for the test image Barbara and for bpp$\approx$0.5 for the test image Lenna (see Fig.2).

Recall that in the process of image compression a quantitative measure available for calculation (controllable) is $PSNR_{or}$ and it can be evaluated for either noise-free or noisy image. By joint analysis of the plots $PSNR_{nf}$(bpp) and $PSNR_{or}$(bpp) we have noticed that maximal $PSNR_{nf}$ (for methods without pre-filtering) was observed for such bpp when $PSNR_{or}$ becomes equal to $T=10\log_{10}(255^2/\sigma^2)$ or $20\log_{10}(255/\sigma)$. Really, for $\sigma^2=200$ one has T=25.12dB and for $\sigma^2=50$ T=31.12dB.

Let us now consider the plots presented in Figure 3. As can be seen, when the curve $PSNR_{or}$(bpp) crosses the level T, the maximal $PSNR_{nf}$ are provided for the corresponding compression technique. Thus, only two question remain unanswered – how to set T and how to determine the "moment" the curve $PSNR_{or}$(bpp) crosses the level T.

The answer to the first question is simple. In some practical cases $\sigma^2$ can be a priori known and T is easily calculated. If $\sigma^2$ is a priori unknown, it can be pre-estimated using some blind technique of noise variance evaluation (see, for example, [15]). Then, using the obtained estimate $\sigma^2_{est}$ instead of the true value of $\sigma^2$ one gets $T=10\log_{10}(255^2/\sigma^2_{est})$. The method [15] provides the accuracy of the estimate $\sigma^2_{est}$ about few percent. Thus, T can by estimated with an error no large than 0.5 dB.

The answer to the second question is mainly "technical". One possible approach is to apply iterative procedure. As the first step, determine $PSNR_{or}$ for original noisy image to be compressed for some a priori set bpp if JPEG2000 coder is used as the basis or for some preset quantization step if DCT based coders are applied (JPEG or AGU). If the obtained initial $PSNR_{or-1}$ is larger than T, then at the next step one has to decrease required bpp for JPEG2000 coder or to increase quantization step (QS) for DCT based coders. If the obtained initial $PSNR_{or-stl}$ is smaller than T, then opposite actions has to be carried out. In this way, sooner or later, at some i-th step of iteration procedure one comes to one of the following two situations: $PSNR_{or-i-1}>T> PSNR_{or-i}$ or $PSNR_{or-i-1}<T< PSNR_{or-i}$ where $PSNR_{or-i}$ denotes the $PSNR_{or}$ obtained at the i-th step. If coding procedure parameters (bpp for JPEG2000 or QS for DCT based coding) are saved for each step, then the bpp or the QS required for providing optimal operation point can be determined by using, for example, linear interpolation of the curves PSNR(bpp) or PSNR(QS). In this manner, the final values of bpp or QS are obtained and compression is performed using them.

Such verbal description leaves space for considering what can be reasonable parameters of the corresponding procedure for minimizing the number of iterations or for providing required accuracy (one direction of the future research). But it is clear that such procedure can be easily realized automatically. Our experience shows that 3...6 iterations are often enough.

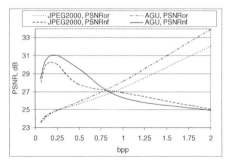 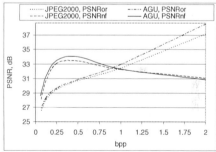

**Fig. 3.** Dependencies $PSNR_{nf}$(bpp) and $PSNR_{or}$(bpp) for JPEG2000 and AGU for the test image Lena corrupted by additive noise with $\sigma^2$=200 (left, T=25.12dB) and $\sigma^2$=50 (right, T=31.12dB)

# 4 Conclusions

We have shown that image pre-filtering can be useful for further lossy compression of noisy images. The recently proposed DCT based coder AGU can outperform JPEG2000 based coder for the considered application. The way to optimally select CR for providing the best quality of compressed images is described.

# References

1. Salomon, D.: Data Compression. The Complete Reference. 3 rd edn. Springer (2004)
2. Wei, D., Odegard, J.E., Guo, H., Lang, M., Burrus, C.S.: Simultaneous Noise Reduction and SAR Image Data Compression Using Best Wavelet Packet Basis. Proceedings of International Conference on Image Processing, V. 3 (1995) 200-203
3. Mittal, M.L., Singh, V.K., Krishnan, R.: Wavelet Transform Based Technique for Speckle Noise Suppression and Data Compression for SAR Images. Proceedings of the Fifth International Symposium on Signal Processing and Applications (1999) 781-784
4. Chan, T.C.L., Hsung, T.C., Lun, D.P.K.: Improved MPEG-4 Still Texture Image Coding under Noisy Environment. IEEE Transactions on Image Processing, V. 12, 5 (2003) 500-508
5. Kim, S.D., Jang, S.K., Kim, M.J., Ra, J.B.: Efficient Block-based Coding of Noisy Images by Combined Pre-filtering and DCT. Electronic Letters, V. 35, 20 (1999) 1717-1719
6. Al-Shaykh. O.K., Mersereau, R.M.: Lossy Compression of Noisy Images. IEEE Transactions on Image Processing, V. 7, 12 (1998) 1641-1652
7. Al-Shaykh. O.K., Mersereau, R.M.: Restoration of Lossy Compressed Noisy Images. IEEE Transactions on Image Processing, V. 8, 10 (1999) 1348-1360
8. Sabelkin, M.V., Ponomarenko, N.N.: MM-Band Radar Image Wavelet Compression with Prefiltering. Proceedings of Kharkov Symposium on Millimeter and Sub-millimeter Waves MSMW, V. 1 (2001) 280-282
9. Chang, S.G., Yu, B., Vetterli, M.: Adaptive wavelet thresholding for image denoising and compression. IEEE Trans. on Image Processing, V. 9, 9 (2000) 1532-1546
10. Venkatraman, M., Kwon, H., Nasrabadi, N.M.: Object-Based SAR Image Compression Using Vector Quantization. IEEE Trans. on Aerospace and Electronic Systems, V. AES-36, 4 (2000) 1036-1046
11. Koh, S.S., Kim, C.H.: Fractal Image Coding Based on the Accurate Estimation of Image Parameters from Noise Image. Proceedings of IEEE International Conference on Multimedia and Expo, (2001) 1159-1162
12. Ponomarenko, N.N., Lukin, V.V., Egiazarian, K.O., Astola, J.T.: DCT Based High Quality Image Compression, accepted to Scandinavian Conference on Image Analysis (2005)
13. Egiazarian K., Helsingius M., Kuosmanen P., Astola J.: Removal of blocking and ringing artifacts using transform domain denoising. Proc. of ISCAS'99, V. 4 (1999) 139 – 142
14. Egiazarian K., Melnik V., Lukin V., Astola J.: Local transform-based denoising for radar image processing. Proc. SPIE Nonlinear Image Processing and Pattern Analysis XII, V. 4304 (2001) 170-178
15. Ponomarenko N.N., Lukin V.V., Abramov S.K., Egiazarian K.O., Astola J.T.: Blind evaluation of additive noise variance in textured images by nonlinear processing of block DCT coefficients. Proc. of IS&T/SPIE International Conference on Image Processing: Algorithms and Systems, SPIE V. 5014 (2003) 178-189

# Latency Insensitive Task Scheduling for Real-Time Video Processing and Streaming

Richard Y.D. Xu[1] and Jesse S. Jin[2]

[1] Faculty of Information Technology, University of Technology,
Sydney Broadway NSW 2007 Australia
richardx@it.uts.edu.au
[2] School of Design, Communication & I.T, The University of Newcastle,
Callaghan NSW 2308, Australia
jesse@newcastle.edu.au

**Abstract.** In recent times, computer vision and pattern recognition (CVPR) technologies made automatic feature extraction, events detection possible in real-time, on-the-fly video processing and streaming systems. However, these multiple and computational expensive video processing tasks require specialized processors to ensure higher frame rate output. We propose a framework for achieving high video frame rate using a single processor high-end PC while multiple, computational video tasks such as background subtraction, object tracking, recognition and facial localization have been performed simultaneously. We show the framework in detail, illustrating our unique scheduler using latency insensitive tasks distribution and the execution content parameters generation function (PGF). The experiments have indicated successful results using high-end consumer type PC.

## 1 Introduction

As personal computers keep an upward trend on processing capacity, more and more average computer users begin to enjoy the benefits of real time video processing and streaming.

Until recently, most video streaming application requires minimal processing to the captured frames. These processing tasks are limited to video compression, changing resolutions and frame rates. For this reason, this type of video processing scheduling only takes into consideration of information in video bit-stream domain (video frame size, frame rate, type of codec), and the information of video content is being ignored. For example, in Tanenbaum et al. [1], the author proposed two algorithms for hard real-time deadline scheduling. These scheduling policies are generated according to video types, frame size and rates but not to the video frame content.

In recent times, with the aid of advanced CVPR technologies, video is not merely used as output streaming data, it is also being used as inputs to feature extraction and event detection algorithms in many intelligent application. These applications are found in the areas of pervasive computing [2], human computer interaction (HCI), and recently in intelligent lecture streaming. Examples are Xu et al. [3] and Shi et al. [4], where the authors have designed real-time learning video streaming based on the

J. Blanc-Talon et al. (Eds.): ACIVS 2005, LNCS 3708, pp. 387–394, 2005.
© Springer-Verlag Berlin Heidelberg 2005

automatic events occurred in the live classroom using CVPR techniques including background subtraction, object and human tracking, pre-trained object recognition and human identification.

Many of such systems require specialized hardware to achieve real-time processing and high resolution frame output, such as video feature extraction in Bianchi [5], and multi-processors cluster computers used in Klimeck *et al.* [6]. Many literatures can also be found to use parallel computer vision algorithms on single processor; however, most of these works are concentrating on single CVPR algorithm rather than a set of them running simultaneously. The examples can be found at Ben-Ezra *et al.* [7] and François *et al.* [8].

## 2   Properties of Real-Time CVPR Video Processing

For vast majority of computer users, neither special hardware is feasible nor will the application only contain single CVPR algorithm. However, there are some properties that these video processing tasks exhibit where we can explore these properties to allow execution using inexpensive hardware and produce high frame rate streaming output.

### 2.1   Task Priority Latency Sensitivities

In real time application, each video task has different levels of sensitivities to time delays. Such as video capture, compression and streaming task are highly sensitive to latency, as each frame must be processed and delivered in real time with minimum fluctuation in quality. On the other hand, most video detection tasks can allow longer delays in processing. For example, an object recognition task that takes 1 more second in processing is considered equally useful in many consumer type applications. The latency sensitivities for common real-time CVPR tasks are listed in table 1:

**Table 1.** Video task time latency sensitivity

| Tasks | Latency sensitivity |
|---|---|
| Object Recognition | Insensitive |
| Face identification | Insensitive |
| Object Tracking | Sensitive, but minor delays is tolerable, if objects or camera has slow motions |
| Background Subtraction | Sensitive |
| Video capture, compression, streaming | Sensitive |

Ideally, if processor is powerful enough, all required processing tasks can achieve completion regardless of its time-delay sensitivities, as illustrated in fig 1.a. However, in most PC application, the CPU has much lower processing capacity, if tasks are executed sequentially, then the time sensitive task may be delayed, shown in fig 1.b.

A logical approach is to distribute the latency insensitive tasks among each video frame processing, shown in fig 1.c.

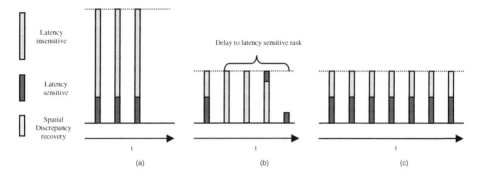

**Fig. 1.** Allocation of video task: a) Ideal case: processor is powerful enough that all tasks can complete on time. b) Processing tasks sequentially, delay latency sensitive tasks.   c) Task allocation using our method, spatial discrepancy recovery task is used for some latency task to recover discrepancy between a processed and current video frame (this is not elaborated in this paper).

## 2.2  Content Dependant Execution

Unlike traditional video scheduling, the processing times required for CVPR type video task is not only dependant on the data bit domain alone (size, codec etc). It is also dependant on other factors relating to both video frame content features and the nature of individual task. The processing times may vary dramatically from frame to frame. For example, a complete object recognition matching algorithm may have processing times ranging from 500ms to 2800ms at different frame of same video clip in our experiment.

Therefore, in order to 'place' portions of the video processing accurately and fairly into each frame delivery as shown in fig 1.c, an execution time prediction method is required. This predication is derived from video frame content features for individual task. In most times, unlike uncorrelated images, consecutive video frame's contents do not vary significantly; therefore, video task execution time can be estimated temporally as well as spatially. In addition, the execution time history (histograms) for video frames containing similar features should also be accountable to the time predication algorithm.

By considering these properties we therefore, have formulated our unique video task scheduling policy and mechanism to run video task in multi-threads. We claim it is an efficient and adaptive method for scheduling latency insensitive and computational video tasks.

We have noticed that there is a lack of attention for a systematic approach to schedule multiple CVPR video tasks in real-time streaming application in the current literature. This is primarily due to the relative short time period since CVPR has been applied to real-time streaming using PCs. We will illustrate our attempts in this article, where we divide the scheduling system logically into two layers: the *scheduling policy* and *scheduling implementation* layer as shown in Fig. 2. This paper concentrates on the scheduling policy layer where the rest of this paper is organized as each subcomponent resulted from our research.

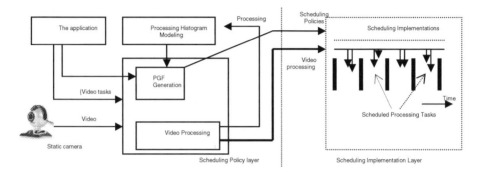

**Fig. 2.** Framework system diagram

The Processing History Modeling subsystem considers the PGF parameters being generated and produces a predication base on the histogram with similar parameter values. This is discussed in section 3. The PGF Generation subsystem is to systematically generate parameters to predicate the execution time of each video task. This subsystem accounts for property indicated in section 2.2, and will be discussed in detail in section 4.

## 3   Execution Time Histogram Modeling

### 3.1   Histogram Training

The task execution times are recorded and used to approximate later tasks execution times. The recording and modeling have done in both online and offline fashion:

Offline training is required before first real-time streaming session begins. This is because initially, the system has no knowledge of user hardware specification and hence there is no modeling information to begin with. During offline training, the user is required to perform certain artificial video events. These tasks include moving training objects in front of the camera for object tracking task; and holding a photo (which is printed from the system training library) steady in front of the video camera for recognition task execution time calculation.

Online execution time histogram modeling is a real-time continuous updating process. As soon as a video task is completed, its execution time is being recorded and modeled. These data is then used for later sessions.

### 3.2   Histogram Modeling

As shall be seen in Section 4, it is difficult to formulate the relationships directly between the parameters being generated with the video task execution time. Therefore, we have used histogram to model the execution times.

It is both intuitive and experimentally proven that video frame generates similar parameters has similar processing times. Therefore, in both training methodologies, for each video task, there is a hash table and sets of Gaussian model fittings associated. The hash table's dimension is governed by the numbers of parameters required for each video task. Each hash table index contains ranges of parameters values. The detail of parameter generation is stated in the Section 4.

For video processing tasks has same (or similar) parameters, the executions time will contain variances. A Gaussian model is hence used which corresponds to a hash table entry that has relatively higher number of counts, as shown in Fig 3. When video task's parameters are being generated, the counting for the corresponding hash table entry is incremented. At the same time, the exact parameters values are used to update its Gaussian model fitting. This is very similar to algorithm used in Wren [9], where a similar methodology is applied to video background subtraction training. Our predication on processing completion time in current video frame is always based on the mean of the corresponding Gaussian fittings in the histogram.

The hash tables and associated Gaussian fittings are initially populated with values being generated from the pre-session (offline) training. Its values are being updated as more processing and streaming sessions to occur.

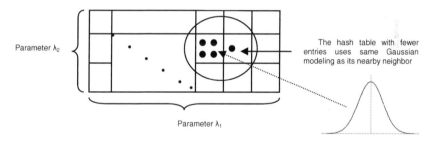

**Fig. 3.** Hash table for video task execution time modeling in parameter space

# 4   Parameters Generation Function

Before execution histogram can be modeled as stated in the previous section, we must accurately determine the set of parameters from video processing tasks results to each video frame. We have therefore proposed our unique execution time parameters generation function (PGF) specific to individual video task (algorithms) being incorporated into a real-time video streaming system.

The scheduler is based on our current streaming application, where we used various video processing and CVPR algorithms. These tasks include object tracking, object recognition, background subtraction and face detection. Therefore, we have devised a unique PGF for each task. To illustrate its novelty, we will present the PGFs for tracking and recognition task, which corresponds to temporal and spatial parameter generation respectively.

In the first step, in order to accurately assess the execution time, we have applied off the shelf profiling software to determine the part of program which accounts for more than 80% of the computation using several training video sequence. Parameters correspond to the executions of this portion of program is used.

## 4.1 Temporal Predication

To illustrate the temporal predication method, we illustrate a PGF for tracking, where our method is based on kernel based mean shift [10].

For mean shift tracking, the intuitive parameters would be $\lambda_x$, $\lambda_y$ corresponding to the elliptical shape of the region containing the tracked object. This is calculated via the adaptive bandwidth from the previous video frame. Also for mean shift tracking similarity measure, $\lambda_{barta}$ is used to represent the maximized Bhattacharyya coefficients used in mean shift process. Therefore, the execution parameter space contains $\{\lambda_x, \lambda_y, \lambda_{barta}\}$.

The parameters values of the current video frame are derived temporally (past video processing) using common Kalman filtering predication for tracking region variation.

## 4.2 Spatial Predication

To illustrate the temporal predication method, we illustrate a PGF for object recognition, where our method is based on recently popular Scale Invariant Feature Transform (SIFT) [11]. We have identified that the algorithm is most computational expensive at the key point's localization and the descriptor generations in most of cases.

We have formulated to use $\lambda_{smooth}$ and $\lambda_{keys}$ as the parameters. $\lambda_{keys}$ represents the number of key points. $\lambda_{smooth}$ represents how "smooth" the current video frame is. $\lambda_{smooth}$ is determined from points counting from binary threshold image of the Difference of Gaussian ($DoG$) response of the current video frame.

$$DoG = G(x, y, k\sigma_1) * I(x, y) - G(x, y, k\sigma_2) * I(x, y)$$

where $G$ is the Gaussian kernel derivative and $I$ is the current video frame. $\sigma_1$ and $\sigma_2$ are the first two variable variances used in the Gaussian kernel. Therefore, for smoother image, the smaller value of $\lambda_{smooth}$ is, which indicates less computation is required for completing rest of stable feature generation for object recognition tasks using current video frame.

## 4.3 Minimum Overhead PGF

The above two examples also illustrates the idea of generating most parameters from the initial part of computations of the actual video processing task rather than having a separate parameter generation function. For example, $\{\lambda_x, \lambda_y, \lambda_{barta}\}$ are required to compute mean shift object tracking even there is no execution scheduler or PGF being used. Kalman filtering is the only overhead, which is low in computation.

## 5   Empirical Result

We have tested our work using live static video camera and a single high-end PC for processing. Each video task is running in different thread according to our scheduling policies. We have achieved high frame output while the predication using PGF contains moderate variances.

We have record the test result in table 2; the input video is 640*480 resolutions and processed video is at 320 * 240 resolutions. We have applied three latency insensitive tasks, object tracking, object recognition and facial detection using Viola *et al.* [12]. The latency sensitive tasks include background subtraction and video compression using MPEG-4 codec. We have turn off all other applications to ensure maximum CPU availability.

The results are promising, in both cases, we have achieved high frame rate around 20 FPS, while the latency insensitive tasks have successfully being scheduled in a delayed but satisfactory rate. The objection recognition has performed at about 2 second period. Tracking and facial detection has been performed around 5 and 3 per second respectively.

**Table 2.** Number of completed tasks

| # of task | Video 1 | Video 2 |
|---|---|---|
| Total play time | 30 | 54 |
| processed output frame | 634 | 1032 |
| FPS | 21.13 | 19.11 |
| Completed SIFT | 14 | 23 |
| Completed Tracking | 162 | 248 |
| Completed Facial detection | 96 | 138 |

## 6   Discussion

We have presented in this paper an approach to schedule multiple content dependent video processing tasks on a single processor PC. This methodology can be used to resolve processing bottleneck, which the time delay sensitive task will be executed in priority while the latency insensitive tasks is not delayed excessively. This is achieved through an accurate predication model using our unique execution time parameter generation functions (PGF) and the execution histogram modeling.

Much work is required for fairer scheduling policies and researching more PGFs for other commonly used CVPR algorithms. We argue that most parts of our framework are still valid, if we are to apply this method in a multiprocessor environment.

## Acknowledgment

This project is supported by Australia Research Council SPIRT Grant (C00107116).

# References

[1] S. Tanenbaum, (2001) Chapter 7.4 Multimedia Process scheduling on Modern operating systems Prentice Hall, c2001. pp. 649

[2] S. Senda, K. Nishiyama, T. Asahi, K.Yamada, Camera-typing interface for ubiquitous information services, Proc Second IEEE Conference on Pervasive compeering 2004, pp. 366- 369

[3] R.Y.D. Xu, J.S.Jin, J.G. Allen, Framework for Script Based Virtual Directing and Multimedia Authoring in Live Video Streaming, Proc. 11th Intl Conf. Multi-Media Modelling, Melbourne, Australia, 2005, pp. 427-432

[4] Y. Shi, W. Xie, & G. Xu, Smart Remote Classroom: Creating a Revolutionary Real-Time Interactive Distance Learning System. Advances in Web-based Learning, 1st Int. Conf. Web-based Learning 2002,J. Fong et al. (Eds). Springer-Verlag, LNCS 2436, 130-141.

[5] M. Bianchi, AutoAuditorium (1998) A fully automatic, multi-camera system to televise auditorium presentations", Proc. of Joint DARPA/NIST Smart Spaces Technology Workshop, July 1998

[6] Gerhard Klimeck, Gary Yagi, Robert Deen, Myche McAuley, Eric DeJong, Fabiano Oyafuso "Near Real-Time Parallel Image Processing using Cluster Computers", International Conference on Space Mission Challenges for Information Technology (SMC-IT), Pasadena, CA July 13-16, 2003.

[7] M. Ben-Ezra, S. Peleg, M. Werman, "Real-Time Motion Analysis with Linear Programming," Computer Vision and Image Understanding, 78(1), April 2000, pp. 32-52.

[8] A. R. J. François, G. G. Medioni, "A Modular Software Architecture for Real-Time Video Processing", Proc. the Second International Workshop on Computer Vision Systems, 2001, pp 35 – 49

[9] C. Wren, A. Azarbayejani, T. Darrell, and A.P. Pentland, "Pfinder: real-time tracking of the human body," IEEE Trans. on Pattern Anal. and Machine Intell., vol. 19, no. 7, pp. 780–785, 1997.

[10] D. Comaniciu, V. Ramesh, P. Meer (2003): Kernel-Based Object Tracking, IEEE Trans. Pattern Analysis and Machine Intelligence, 25(5): 564-575, 2003.

[11] D. Lowe, Distinctive image features from scale invariant key points David G. Lowe, International Journal of Computer Vision, 60, 2 (2004), pp. 91-110.

[12] P. Viola, M. Jones, Fast and Robust Classification using Asymmetric AdaBoost and a Detector Cascade, *Neural Information Processing Systems* 14, Dec 2001

# Entropy Reduction of Foveated DCT Images[1]

Giovanni Iacovoni*, Salvatore Morsa*, and Alessandro Neri**

* Ericsson Lab Italy, Via Anagnina 203,
00040 Rome, Italy
{Giovanni.iacovoni, salvatore.morsa}@ericsson.com
** Applied Electronics Department, University of ROMA TRE,
Via della Vasca Navale 84, 00146 Rome, Italy
neri@ele.uniroma3.it

**Abstract.** This contribution addressees the problem of the theoretical assessment of the bit rate reduction that can be achieved through foveated image compression for codecs operating in the DCT domain. Modeling the image components as Compound Gaussian Random Fields (CGRFs), we extend the mathematical analysis of the DCT coefficient distributions reported in [1] to foveated images. As a general result, we demonstrate that the DCT coefficients of low pass filtered image blocks can be effectively modelled with Laplacian distributions. This property allows us to express the Shannon rate reduction achievable with foveated compression in a simple and compact form as function of the foveal filter coefficients. Experiments results used to validate the theoretical analysis are also included.

## 1 Introduction

The non-uniform distribution of photoreceptors in the human retina drastically limits the maximum spatial frequency that can be perceived by the human visual system in regions far away from the fixation point (the point on the image the subject is looking at). *Foveation* defines a relation between the maximum detectable spatial frequency for a human at a given point as function of the coordinates of the fixation point. This relation has been used in recent works, [2]-[5], in the field of image and video compression techniques. More precisely, foveation is used to low-pass filter the images according to the distance from the fixation point (the greater the distance the more the image is filtered). This allows achieving higher compression ratios than those attained when encoding uniform resolution images.

In this paper we analytically quantify the entropy reduction due to the above foveation process. To this aim, we start from the observation that any AC-DCT coefficient is Laplacian distributed [1]. We then show that after filtering the distribution is still Laplacian, with the original parameter modulated by the geometric mean of the filter coefficients.

After that we apply the Rate-Distortion theory yielding the Shannon lower bound for the entropic coding of Laplacian distributed variables.

---

[1] This work was carried out in the context of the research activities of CoRiTeL Consortium, Via Anagnina 203, 00040 Rome, Italy.

J. Blanc-Talon et al. (Eds.): ACIVS 2005, LNCS 3708, pp. 395–402, 2005.
© Springer-Verlag Berlin Heidelberg 2005

In section 2 all the above mentioned procedure is detailed. Section 3 provides a comparison of this analytical result with the numerical evaluation of the actual compression gain achieved through entropy coding of some examples of actual images.

## 2 Entropy Reduction

For the evaluation of the reduction of the bit rate achieved by the foveal filtering we assume as in [1] that each image component $\mathbf{Z}$ (e.g. luminance) is a Compound Gaussian Random Field (CGRF). Definition and properties of a CGRF can be easily derived from those of the Gaussian Random Fields, (see [6], [7]), recalling that the statistical properties of a non stationary zero mean Gaussian Random Field $\{Z[k,q]\}$ are completely determined by the covariance function

$$R_z(k_1,q_1,k_2,q_2) = E\left\{\left[z(k_1,q_1)\right]\left[z(k_2,q_2)\right]\right\}.$$

A CGRF is a doubly stochastic random field whose covariance function $R_z(k_1,q_1,k_2,q_2)$ is the realization of a stationary process, so that, when conditioned to $R_z(k_1,q_1,k_2,q_2)$, it reduces to a classical GRF. For instance, the conditional first order distribution of $\{Z[k,q]\}$ takes the form:

$$p_Z\left[z(k,q);s^2(k,q)\right] = \frac{1}{\sqrt{2\pi}s(k,q)}\exp\left\{-\frac{\left[z(k,q)\right]^2}{2s^2(k,q)}\right\} \qquad (1)$$

where we put $s^2(k,q) = R_z(k,q,k,q)$.

In order to derive the statistical properties of the DCT coefficients, let us partition the original image into square blocks of $N$x$N$ pixels and let us denote with $\mathbf{Z}^{(i,j)}$ the 2D array corresponding to the $(i,j)$ block. Let us denote with $\mathbf{D}$ the one-dimensional DCT operator and with $\mathbf{Y}^{(i,j)} = \mathbf{D}\mathbf{Z}^{(i,j)}\mathbf{D}^T$ the DCT of the $(i,j)$ block.

The linear relationship between $\mathbf{Y}^{(i,j)}$ and $\mathbf{Z}^{(i,j)}$ implies that $\mathbf{Y}^{(i,j)}$ is a CGRF with covariance function:

$$\sigma_{i,j}^2(n,m) = \sum_{k_1=0}^{N-1}\sum_{q_1=0}^{N-1}\sum_{k_2=0}^{N-1}\sum_{q_2=0}^{N-1} D_{n,k_2}D_{n,k_1} \times$$

$$\times R_z(iN+k_1, jN+q_1, iN+k_2, jN+q_2)D_{q_1,m}^T D_{q_2,m}^T. \qquad (2)$$

Thus, according to [1], the DCT coefficient $y^{(i,j)}(m,n)$ of block $(i,j)$ has the following conditional p.d.f.

$$p_Y\left[y^{(i,j)}(m,n)/\sigma_{i,j}^2(m,n)\right] = \frac{\exp\left\{-\dfrac{\left[y^{(i,j)}(m,n)\right]^2}{2\sigma_{i,j}^2(m,n)}\right\}}{\sqrt{2\pi\sigma_{i,j}^2(m,n)}}. \qquad (3)$$

Thanks to the central limit theorem, the first order distribution of DCT coefficients still holds even when $\mathbf{Z}$ deviates from Gaussianity.

As observed in [1], statistical analysis applied to real world images show that the first order distribution of $\sigma_{i,j}^2(n,m)$ is "somewhere between exponential and half gaussian". Consequently, averaging of (3) with respect to $\sigma_{i,j}^2(n,m)$ yields that the the pdf's of the AC transform coefficients is well approximated by a Laplacian model, having zero mean and variance $1/\lambda(m,n)$, i.e.

$$p_Y\left[y^{(i,j)}(m,n)\right] = \frac{\sqrt{2\lambda(m,n)}}{2}e^{-\sqrt{2\lambda(m,n)}\left|y^{(i,j)}(m,n)\right|}. \tag{4}$$

To quantify the entropy reduction for a single DCT coefficient subjected to foveation, we observe that image filtering can be directly modelled in the DCT domain. As demonstrated in [8], the DCT of the filtered signal is given by the product of the DCT of the input signal and the FFT of the filter impulse response. Thus, denoting with $H_{Fov}^{(i,j)}(m,n)$ the coefficients of the frequency response of the foveal filter applied to block $(i,j)$, the DCT coefficients $I_{Fov}^{(i,j)}(m,n)$ of the foveated block are given by $I_{Fov}^{(i,j)}(m,n) = H_{Fov}^{(i,j)}(m,n) I^{(i,j)}(m,n)$. We remark that this property can be directly used for real time implementation of foveal filtering in transcoders operating in the transformed domain.

This property also implies that the conditional p.d.f of the filtered DCT coefficient $I_{Fov}^{(i,j)}(m,n)$ conditioned to the pixel variance inside the block is still approximately Gaussian, i.e.:

$$p(I_{Fov}^{(i,j)}(m,n)/\sigma^2(m,n)) = \frac{e^{-\frac{\left[I_{Fov}^{(i,j)}(m,n)\right]^2}{2\left[H_{Fov}^{(i,j)}(m,n)\right]^2\sigma^2(m,n)}}}{\sqrt{2\pi}\left|H_{Fov}^{(i,j)}(m,n)\right|\sigma(m,n)}. \tag{5}$$

Considering now as in [1] the case of exponentially distributed pixel variance we have

$$p(I_{Fov}^{(i,j)}(m,n)) = \int_{-\infty}^{\infty} \frac{e^{-\frac{\left[I_{Fov}^{(i,j)}(m,n)\right]^2}{2\left[H_{Fov}^{(i,j)}(m,n)\right]^2\sigma^2}}}{\sqrt{2\pi}\left|H_{Fov}^{(i,j)}(m,n)\right|\sigma}\lambda(m,n)e^{-\lambda(m,n)\sigma^2}d\sigma^2$$

$$= \frac{\sqrt{2\lambda(m,n)}}{2\left|H_{Fov}^{(i,j)}(m,n)\right|}\exp\left\{-\sqrt{2\lambda(m,n)}\frac{\left|I_{Fov}^{(i,j)}(m,n)\right|}{\left|H_{Fov}^{(i,j)}(m,n)\right|}\right\}. \tag{6}$$

It can be easily verified that similar result applies for half-Gaussian distributions.

Thus, after filtering the marginal distribution of each AC DCT coefficient is Laplacian with parameter

$$\mu_{m,n}^{(i,j)} = \sqrt{2\lambda_{Fov}^{(i,j)}(m,n)} \tag{7}$$

where:

$$\lambda_{Fov}^{(i,j)}(m,n) = \frac{\lambda(m,n)}{\left[H_{Fov}^{(i,j)}(m,n)\right]^2}. \tag{8}$$

We remark that in this case, the field of DCT coefficients has statistical properties that varies with the DCT coefficient indexes as well as with block. Nevertheless, the Laplacian behaviour still implies that the uniform mid-step quantizer is the optimal one (see [9]).

Thus, assuming the Mean Squared Error (MSE) as the distortion metric, the rate related to the AC coefficients has to satisfy the Shannon lower bound condition ([10])

$$R_{in}(D) \geq \frac{1}{2} N_{Tot} \log_2 \frac{2e}{\pi 2 \tilde{\lambda}_{in} D} \tag{9}$$

with

$$\tilde{\lambda}_{in} = \left[ \prod_{i=1}^{M_h} \prod_{j=1}^{M_v} \prod_{m=1}^{N} \prod_{n=1}^{N} \lambda(m,n) \right]^{\frac{1}{N_{Tot}}} \tag{10}$$

where $D$ is the distorsion due to quantization, $N_{Tot}$ is the number of pixels in the image, $M_h$ and $M_v$ are the number of horizontal and vertical blocks respectively. Relationship (9) can also be written as

$$R_{in}(D) = \frac{1}{2} \log_2 \frac{e}{\pi \lambda_{in} D} + \Delta_{in}. \tag{11}$$

Similarly, after filtering we have

$$R_{Fov}(D) \geq \sum_{i=1}^{M_h} \sum_{j=1}^{M_v} \sum_{i=1}^{N} \sum_{i=1}^{N} \frac{1}{2} \log_2 \frac{e}{\pi \lambda_{Fov}^{(i,j)}(m,n) D} \tag{12}$$

or equivalently

$$R_{Fov}(D) \geq \frac{1}{2} N_{Tot} \log_2 \frac{e}{\pi D} + \frac{1}{2} \log_2 \frac{1}{\prod_{i=1}^{M_h} \prod_{j=1}^{M_v} \prod_{m=1}^{N} \prod_{n=1}^{N} \lambda_{Fov}^{(i,j)}(m,n)} \tag{13}$$

In the two above relationships we implicitly assumed that the distortion $D$ can be considered the same before and after the foveation process. This is always true when $R>1$ (see [10]).

Thus, denoting with $\tilde{\lambda}_{Fov}$ the geometrical mean of the foveal frequency response, i.e.

$$\tilde{\lambda}_{Fov} = \left[ \prod_{i=1}^{M_h} \prod_{j=1}^{M_v} \prod_{m=1}^{N} \prod_{n=1}^{N} \lambda_{Fov}^{(i,j)}(m,n) \right]^{\frac{1}{N_{Tot}}} = \left[ \prod_{i=1}^{M_h} \prod_{j=1}^{M_v} \prod_{m=1}^{N} \prod_{n=1}^{N} \frac{\lambda(m,n)}{\left| H_{Fov}^{(i,j)}(m,n) \right|^2} \right]^{\frac{1}{N_{Tot}}} \tag{14}$$

we finally have

$$R_{Fov}(D) \geq \frac{1}{2} N_{Tot} \log_2 \frac{e}{\pi \tilde{\lambda}_{Fov} D}. \tag{15}$$

Let us notice that

$$\frac{\tilde{\lambda}_{Fov}}{\tilde{\lambda}_{in}} = \frac{1}{\left[\displaystyle\prod_{i=1}^{M_h}\prod_{j=1}^{M_v}\prod_{m=1}^{N}\prod_{n=1}^{N}\left|H_{Fov}^{(i,j)}(m,n)\right|^2\right]^{\frac{1}{N_{Tot}}}} \cdot \tag{16}$$

In other words $\lambda_{Fov} = k\,\lambda_{in}$ with

$$k = \frac{1}{\left[\displaystyle\prod_{i=1}^{M_h}\prod_{j=1}^{M_v}\prod_{m=1}^{N}\prod_{n=1}^{N}\left|H_{Fov}^{(i,j)}(m,n)\right|^2\right]^{\frac{1}{N_{Tot}}}} \cdot \tag{17}$$

Since relationship (15) can also be rewritten as:

$$R_{Fov}(D) = \frac{N_{Tot}}{2}\log_2\frac{e}{\pi\tilde{\lambda}_{Fov}D} + \Delta_{Fov} \tag{18}$$

we finally have

$$\Delta R = R_{in} - R_{Fov} = -\frac{N_{Tot}}{2}\log_2 k + \Delta_{in} - \Delta_{Fov}$$

$$= \sum_{i=1}^{M_h}\sum_{j=1}^{M_v}\sum_{m=1}^{N}\sum_{n=1}^{N}\log_2\left|H_{Fov}^{(i,j)}(m,n)\right| + \Delta_{in} - \Delta_{Fov} . \tag{19}$$

Eq. (19) gives the entropy reduction that can be achieved by foveal coding.

From a practical point of view the degree of approximation involved when computing $R_{in}$ (for instance not perfect laplacianity, and so on) is the same as for $R_{Fov}$, so that it is reasonable to assume that $\Delta_{in}$ is the same order of magnitude of $\Delta_{Fov}$.

## 3   Experimental Results

To verify the accuracy of Eq. (19) we have compared the entropy reduction predicted by the theoretical analysis with the empirical compression gain evaluated by coding both the original image and its foveated counterpart.

The empirical model for the maximum detectable frequency $f_c$ is [5]:

$$f_c(x,y,x_f,y_f,V) = \frac{1}{1 + 13.75 * \tan^{-1}(\dfrac{d-R}{V})}, \tag{20}$$

where $d$ is the euclidean distance between the current point $(x, y)$ and the fovea point $(x_f, y_f)$ on the image, $V$ is the viewing distance and $R$ is the radius of the fovea region (which is unfiltered by the eye). $R$ comes from the need of modelling a "flat unfiltered zone" in the digital domain. The value of $R$ depends on $V$. The test images are filtered according to the following foveation process where the fovea is placed in the center of each image: first, we apply the DCT transform to every 8x8 block of the images; then, we filter the images in the DCT domain [8] using 8 different 7-taps filters whose cut off frequencies decrease as the distance of the block from the fovea increases. Filter generation is done using *Matlab* function *fircls* (as in 2) with normalized cut off frequencies ranging from 0.125 to 1, with a step of 0.125. The radius of fovea used in the experiments is equal to 32 pixels.

**Table 1.** Comparison of bit reductions for the DCT coefficients in $(x,y)$ position for three test images: computed and given by (19): a) "Lena" b) Baboon and c) Bridge

| "Lena" | Empirical | Theoretical |
|--------|-----------|-------------|
| (1,2)  | 704       | 777         |
| (2,2)  | 1396      | 1554        |
| (1,3)  | 3143      | 3294        |
| (5,6)  | 10236     | 11326       |
| (8,8)  | 8944      | 9431        |

(a)

| "Baboon" | Empirical | Theoretical |
|----------|-----------|-------------|
| (1,2)    | 720       | 777         |
| (2,2)    | 1675      | 1554        |
| (1,3)    | 3260      | 3294        |
| (5,6)    | 20147     | 22404       |
| (8,8)    | 24102     | 25060       |

(b)

| "Bridge" | Empirical | Theoretical |
|----------|-----------|-------------|
| (1,2)    | 812       | 777         |
| (2,2)    | 1675      | 1554        |
| (1,3)    | 3494      | 3294        |
| (5,6)    | 16281     | 17744       |
| (8,8)    | 14059     | 14653       |

(c)

We apply the following process to both the original and the foveated version of the test images: first we extract the DCT coefficients in the same position from each block and, after quantization (we choose the quantization factor Q=1), we code them using optimised Huffman tables [11].

The bit reductions due to foveation for luminance of three test images (Baboon, Bridge and Lena) obtained with this processing are shown for some DCT coefficients in the first column of Table 1. The second column contains the correspondent entropy reduction predicted by Eq. (19). The considered images have a size of 512x512 pixels.

Regardless of the order of the considered DCT coefficient, the tables show that the error resulting from formula (19) is around 10% in the worst case. These discrepancies are mainly due to the unavoidable violation of the assumption of perfect Laplacian distribution of DCT coefficient of the original image. Besides, the entropy gain cannot exceeds the number of bits needed to code the DCT coefficient in the original image. Therefore, whenever the latter is less than the entropy gain predicted by (19) the second column of the table gives just the number of bits needed to code the DCT coefficient of the original image.

## 4   Conclusions

We have proposed a compact formula for the entropy reduction that can be achieved through foveated image compression for codecs operating in the DCT domain. Compared to real compression gain there are minor discrepancies discussed in Section 3.

However, care must be employed when applying the above results since they strongly depend on the assumption that the quantization distortion $D$ doesn't change when foveation is applied. Further studies will develop an analysis to assess the validity of that assumption.

The extension of the entropy reduction to the whole image is straightforward, considering that the DC coefficient is never filtered.

## References

1. E.Y. Lam, J.W. Goodman, "A Mathematical Analysis of the DCT Coefficient Distribution for Images", *IEEE Trans. Image Processing*, vol.9, no. 10, pages 1661- 1666, Oct. 2000.
2. H. R. Sheikh, S. Liu, B. L. Evans and A. C. Bovik, "Real-Time Foveation Techniques For H.263 Video Encoding Software*", 2001 IEEE Int. Conf. on Acoustics, Speech, and Signal Processing*, vol 3, vol. 3, pp. 1781-1784, May 2001.
3. Z. Wang, L. G. Lu, A. C. Bovik, "Foveation Scalable Video Coding with Automatic Fixation Selection", *IEEE Trans. Image Processing*, vol. 12, no. 2, Feb. 2003
4. L. Itti, "Automatic Foveation for video compression using a neurobiological model of visual attention", *IEEE Trans. Image Processing*, vol. 13, no. 10, Oct 2004
5. W. S. Geisler, J. S. Perry "A real-time foveated multi-resolution for low-bandwidth video communication", *Proc. SPIE*, vol. 3299, pp. 294-305, 1998.
6. Kung Yao, "A Representation Theorem and Ist Applications to Sperically-Invariant Random Processes", *IEEE Trans. On Information Theory*, pages 600- 608, Vol. IT-19, No. 5, Semptember 1973.
7. B. Picinbono, "Sperically Invariant and Compound Gaussian Stochastic Processes", *IEEE Trans. On Information Theory*, pages 77- 79, Vol. IT-16, No. 1, January 1970.

8.  B. Chitprasert and K.R. Rao, "Discrete cosine transform filtering", *Signal Processing*, vol.19, no. 3, Apr. 1990.
9.  T. Berger, "Optimum Quantizers and Permutation Codes", *IEEE Trans. Info. Theory*, vol. IT-18, no.6, Nov. 1972
10. Netravali, B. Haskel, *Digital Pictures: Representations, Compression, and Standards (Applications of Communications Theory)*, Plenum Pub. Co., 1995.
11. http://www.ux.his.no/~karlsk/proj99

# Flexible Storage of Still Images
# with a Perceptual Quality Criterion

Vincent Ricordel, Patrick Le Callet, Mathieu Carnec, and Benoit Parrein

Image and Video Communication Team, IRCCyN UMR CNRS 6597,
Ecole Polytechnique de l'Université de Nantes,
La Chantrerie, BP 50609, 44306 Nantes Cedex 3
vincent.ricordel@polytech.univ-nantes.fr

**Abstract.** The purpose of the paper is to introduce a new method for
flexible storage of still images. The complete design of the system is
described with the scalable encoding, the distortion computation, the
bits allocation strategy, and the method for the memory management.
The main improvement is the full exploitation of a perceptual metric
to assess precisely the introduced distortion when removing a layer in
a scalable coding stream. Experimental results are given and compared
with a system which uses the PSNR as distortion metric.

## 1   Introduction

In the paper we focus on the problem of digital still image storage. The problem
occurs when the total memory size is limited, the amount of data to be stored
is large and the quality of the decoded images must be high. Basic memory
systems store each image, by granting each item a fixed share of the memory (see
fig 1 [a]). The maximal number of stored images is thus limited. An improvement
of these systems is usually based on the image encoding in order to minimize
the compressed image size and to save a bigger memory area. The classical
"flexible" storage implementation [1] aims at improving both these aspects : the
image encoding and the storage process.

More precisely, the flexible method takes avantage of the scalability concept
which provides a way to separate the image quality in several accessible layers.
Then it is possible to keep the most significant image layers and to remove
the least significant image layers already stored in the memory area. An optimal
flexible allocation of storage capacity is performed with the use of flexible storage
because : ($i$) the available storage capacity is fully exploited, ($ii$) the number
of images to store is variable and can be changed at anytime, ($iii$) the highest
possible quality is preserved when a new image is stored. While a basic system
stores only necessary layers to get the minimal acceptable quality, a flexible
system allows to store extra layers up to the best quality. Figure 1 [b] shows
the advantages of the flexible storage principle with respect to a basic scheme.
We can see that the allocated image size is distributed according to a quality
criterion, which allows having little quality difference between the stored images.

J. Blanc-Talon et al. (Eds.): ACIVS 2005, LNCS 3708, pp. 403–410, 2005.
© Springer-Verlag Berlin Heidelberg 2005

The use of a memory whose size is fixed but with the properties associated to the flexible memory may have a lot of applications in image database storage or digital still cameras.

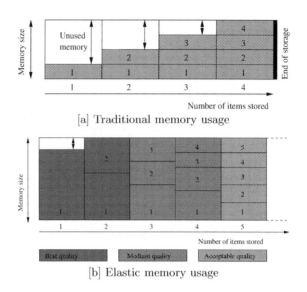

[a] Traditional memory usage

[b] Elastic memory usage

**Fig. 1.** Elastic memory principle

## 2    System Overview

Figure 2 illustrates the general structure of the system. To deliver a compressed version with several layers for each image, we use as scalable encoding scheme the standard JPEG2000 with quality scalability mode i.e. Signal to Noise Ratio (SNR) scalability. Storage a new image is achieved using a process of memory allocation. This implies a rate *vs.* distortion tradeoff to insert some new image layers by remaining the most relevant ones of the previous stored images. To measure the distortion, we have to use a quality criterion that must produce objective quality scores in good correlation with human judgment. Usually, PSNR is computed as a quality criterion. Unfortunatly, it is too poorly correlated with human judgement. We prefer to use a perceptual criterion. To present the entire process, the extraction and decoding steps are included in the figure 2 for the final image visualisation even if they are not specific to flexible memory. The following subsections detail more precisely the system overview.

### 2.1    The JPEG2000 Quality Layers

The SNR scalability included in JPEG2000 is based on a rate / distortion optimization, called Post Compression Rates Distortion (PCRD-opt), included in the algorithm Embedded Coding with Optimal Truncation (EBCOT). This stage carried out after the contextual arithmetic coding is a rate allocation to various layers of quality which are separated between them by truncation points. Within an image, layers are hierarchically ordered which means that a layer might be exploited only if the first layers are available. From a practical point of view, the JPEG2000 header provides the set of truncation points between layers. So, it is easy to reach the associated rate of each layer and to remove unnecessary layers according to the hierarchical order. For this purpose, we have elected to take the JP2000 stream as it comes without modifying the rate / distortion process. This leads to define the optimal size of the layers for each image independently for our system.

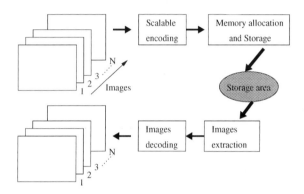

**Fig. 2.** Flexible storage implementation

## 2.2   Perceptual Distortion

By the past we have developped several criteria based on human vision model for still color image quality assessment. Here, we use a reduced reference quality criterion that is well suited for distortions stemming from JPEG 2000 compression [2]. This criterion is divided into two steps. At first, a reduce description is built for both original and distorted image by extracting features in a psychovisual space. Then, the two reduced descritions are compared to produce the quality score.

To build the reduced description of an image, we project it in a psychovisual space. This is achieved through different functions including perceptual colorspace transformation (Krauskopf'one [3]), contrast sensitivity function, perceptual channels decomposition and masking effect functions. These different steps lead to a subband representation for the achromatic component (17 subbands) and to two images for the chromatic components. The next step, feature extraction is achieved only on the subbands of the achromatic component but taking into account the chromatic data. We select locations, called "characteristic points", in the subband representation in order to extract features on them. These points are located on concentric ellipses, centered on the image center. We choose a fixed number of points per ellipse so these points are more concentrated in the image center (which generally gathers the objects of interest). At last, we extract several features on each characteristic point. First, a linear structure is extracted by a "stick growing algorithm". This structure is described by its orientation, its size (length and width), its maximum contrast amplitude. We also extract the mean values of achromatic and chromatic components computed on a circular neighboorhood of radius 5 pixels around the structure. All these features for all the characteristic points constitute the reduced description of the image.

The computation of an image quality from the reduced description of its reference and its distorted version, is also achieved in several steps. First, we produce for each characteristic point a correspondence coefficient per feature which indicates the similarity between the feature values of the distorted and the reference image. Then these coefficients are combined locally to produce a local similarity measure. The global similarity measure is defined as the mean of the local similarity measures. Finally, the objective quality score is produced using a linear transformation of the global similarity measure. Parameters of this linear transformation can be adapted to a particular distortion system. Here we use parameters adapted for JPEG2000. With this criterion [1], we get a value of 0.95 for the correlation coefficient between objective quality score and human judgment on the JPEG2000 images of the LIVE database [4].

### 2.3   Memory Management

The bit allocation problem occurs in order to share the memory between the compressed images. It consists in minimizing the global distortion $D$ subject to the constraint that the global rate $R$ is under the memory size $R_d$. For each JPEG2000 stream corresponds a set of layers. Let be $j$ the stream index, and $i$ the layer number. $d_{i,j}$ and $r_{i,j}$ are respectively the distortion and the rate for the $j$-th stream with $i$ layers (note that $i$ can be different for each stream). If there are $M$ streams, we assume that the problem is:

$$\min D = \min \sum_{j=0}^{M-1} d_{j,i} \text{ subject to } R = \sum_{j=0}^{M-1} r_{j,i} \leq R_d \tag{1}$$

A combination of $M$ streams involves a point $(R, D)$ in the distortion / rate space, all the combinations produce a cluster. The problem becomes the determination, on the cluster convex hull, of the point whose rate is just lower than $R_d$. In order to reduce the complexity the Lagrange-multiplier method is introduced to solve:

$$\min(D + \lambda \times R) \Longleftrightarrow \sum_{j=0}^{M-1} \min(d_{i,j} + \lambda \times r_{i,j})$$

The complexity decreases because the reduction of distortion is now achieved separately from each stream. The general form of the algorithm is:

---

[1] The implementation is available freely (http://www.dcapplications.t2u.com).

1. The convex hull $d(r)$ for each stream is directly computed, by storing the distortion / rate point corresponding to each layer;

2. The point on the global convex hull is determined, its rate is just below $R_d$. For this second step, the algorithm proposed by Shoham [5] is particularly adapted. It is based on the computation of singular values of the Lagrange-multiplier $\lambda$. Precisely a singular value of $\lambda$ is the slope of the line that pass through two consecutive points of the convex hull. So from a first point on the hull, by successive computations of singular values, we get the global convex hull.

In practice a first point is $(R_{max}, D_{min})$ where $D_{min}$ equals to the sum of the distortions when considering each stream with all its layers, the corresponding rate $R_{max}$ is then maximal. Removing the $i$-th layer of the $j$-th stream implies an increase in distortion and a decrease in rate, and we get:

$$\lambda_{i,j} = \frac{\Delta d_{i,j}}{\Delta r_{i,j}} = \frac{d_{i-1,j} - d_{i,j}}{r_{i,j} - r_{i-1,j}}$$

The successive singular values of $\lambda$ are obtained by ordering the $\lambda_{i,j}$ in a decreasing manner and by considering all the streams.

The first step consists in computing a new distortion / rate curve for each new compressed image to store: respecting the layers order and the rates from JPEG2000 PCRD-opt, but using our perceptual metric. As a consequence the new $d^*(r)$ curves are not necessary convex and the previous bit allocation process has to be adapted to our problem.

As long as the memory is not full, the compressed images are stored with all their layers so with the best quality. When the physical storage area becomes full, the goal is to remove the layers which induce the largest decrease in rate and the smallest increase in distortion. For each new image addition in the memory, the basic allocation method steps are:

1. calculate the set of $\lambda^*_{i,j} = \Delta d^*_{i,j}/\Delta r_{i,j}$ and store them in a list conserving the layers order of the jpeg stream. This list will be used as a "FILO", where the first accessible item corresponds to the lambda of the last jpeg layer;

2. considering the FILO lists of the jpeg streams already stored and the FILO list of the new compressed image:

until the rate criterion of equation 1 is satisfied, find successively the smallest accessible item $\lambda^*$, remove it from its list and delete the corresponding jpeg layer;

We impose another constraint such as the system guarantees a minimal quality to the stored images. Thus it is forbidden to continue to remove a layer of a jpeg stream once this threshold is reached. In practice for the allocation method, the corresponding lambdas are simply retired from the list relative to the suppressible layers. Obviously when the memory is full with compressed images having reached all this threshold of minimal quality, it is impossible to add another picture (without erasing completely beforehand a stored jpeg stream).

# 3   Experimental Results

A first use consists of the insertion of six 512x512 colour images in the flexible memory with the perceptual quality criterion. The JPEG2000 coding is made from the Kakadu library[2] functions. The setup fixes a max rate to 1 bpp, a initial layers number to 9 and a perceptual score threshold to 4 for a memory size of 100 kB. Table 1 illustrates the various stages of the operation while indicating to each new insertion (ni): the number of layers, the perceptual score, the number of extra layers for each image inserted as well as the use of the memory in term of flexibility (a number of releasable bytes corresponding to the total number of extra layers) and of availability compared to the inserted images set. The first 3 insertions of 'Lena', 'Peppers' and 'Air-Force Plane' do not pose any problem because the memory is sufficient: no quality layers are removed. If one preserves in the state the whole of the layers only 1.8 % of the memory is available. On the other hand, one has a budget of around 50 kB (half of the memory) compared to the acceptable perceptual score. The insertion of a new image generates the optimization of the memory by suppression of extra layers ('Lena' loses 2 layers, 'Peppers', 'Air-Force' and 'Barbara' 1 layer). The budget of 20 kB is sufficient for the insertion of the House image which extracts all the extra layers of the other images except Lena which preserves 2 extra layers. These last bring a very significant quality compared to the bytes used. It does not allow the insertion of the sixth image ('Fruits') taking into account the thresholds of the flexible memory. For the 5 images stored, the perceptual scores are quite homogeneous.

**Table 1.** Basic usage of flexible storage with successive new insertions (ni) of five images

| Inserted images | # layers | Percept. score | Extra layers | Extra bytes | Availability (%) |
|---|---|---|---|---|---|
| Lena (ni) | 9 | 5 | 4 | 22030 | 67.2 |
| Lena | 9 | 5 | 4 | 36200 | 34.5 |
| Peppers (ni) | 9 | 5 | 2 | | |
| Lena | 9 | 5 | 4 | 50251 | 1.8 |
| Peppers | 9 | 5 | 2 | | |
| Air-Force (ni) | 9 | 4.89 | 2 | | |
| Lena | 7 | 4.91 | 2 | 19729 | 7.7 |
| Peppers | 8 | 4.77 | 1 | | |
| Air-Force | 8 | 4.58 | 1 | | |
| Barbara (ni) | 8 | 4.60 | 1 | | |
| Lena | 7 | 4.91 | 2 | 7932 | 0.8 |
| Peppers | 7 | 4.30 | 0 | | |
| Air-Force | 7 | 4.10 | 0 | | |
| Barbara | 7 | 4.58 | 0 | | |
| House (ni) | 7 | 4.03 | 0 | | |

---

[2] avalaible at http://www.kakadusoftware.com

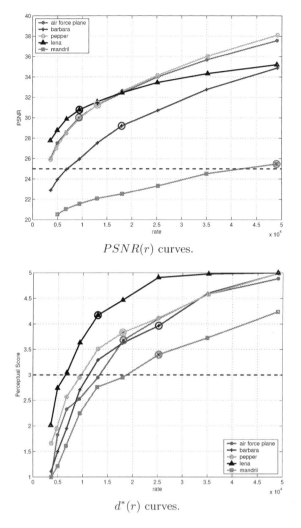

$PSNR(r)$ curves.

$d^*(r)$ curves.

**Fig. 3.** Distortion / rate curves obtained when storing 5 images in the flexible memory. The circles mark the retained points after bit allocation.

The goal of this second test set is the comparison with a PSNR based scheme. Five images of the previous data set are stored. The setup is the same as before, except: the coding max rate is 1.5 bpp, and the quality threshold is 25 dB for a PSNR and 3 for a perceptual distortion use. This parameters are choosen for increasing the extra layer number and for highlighting our results when storing the image 'Mandril'. The curves of the figures 3 (for which, after bit allocation, the choosen $PSNR(r)$ or $d^*(r)$ points are marked by circles) show indeed that for this high frequency image, the classical distortion gives low PSNR values and no layer can be removed. Our perceptual metric produces objective distortion measures: some layers can be deleted from the 'Mandril' stream without visual artifacts, and the saved bits give more rate to store the other images with a homogeneous visual quality.

## 4 Conclusion

We have introduced a new method for the flexible storage of still images. The method is based on the use of a perceptual metric which produces objective quality scores when coding the images with JPEG2000. An overview of the system is given. The perceptual distortion computation and the memory management are detailed. Results are given with a basic usage and a PSNR comparison. They show how the objective quality evaluation allows to share more efficiently the bits between the stored layers of the JPEG2000 streams.

## References

1. Van Der Vleuten, R., Kleihorst, R., Hentschel, C.: Flexible storage of images with application to digital cameras. In: Proc. of Int. Conf. on Image Proc. ICIP, Thessaloniki, Greece (2001) 1097–1100
2. Carnec, M., Le Callet, P., Barba, D.: An image quality assessment method based on perception of structural information. In: Proc. of Int. Conf. on Image Proc. ICIP, Singapore (2004)
3. Krauskopf, J., Williams, D., D.W., H.: Cardinal directions of color space. Vision Research **22** (1982) 1123–1131
4. Sheikh, H., Wang, Z., Cormak, L., A.C., B.: Live image quality assessment database. http://live.ece.utexas.edu/research/quality (2003)
5. Shoham, Y., Gersho, A.: Efficient bit allocation for an arbitrary set of quantizers. IEEE Transactions on Acoust. Speech Signal Processing **36** (1988) 1445–1453

# Image De-Quantizing via Enforcing Sparseness in Overcomplete Representations

Luis Mancera and Javier Portilla*

Visual Information Processing Group,
Department of Computer Science and Artificial Inteligence,
Universidad de Granada
{mancera, javier}@decsai.ugr.es

**Abstract.** We describe a method for removing quantization artifacts (*de-quantizing*) in the image domain, by enforcing a high degree of sparseness in its representation with an overcomplete oriented pyramid. For this purpose we devise a linear operator that returns the minimum L2-norm image preserving a set of significant coefficients, and estimate the original by minimizing the cardinality of that subset, always ensuring that the result is compatible with the quantized observation. We implement this solution by alternated projections onto convex sets, and test it through simulations with a set of standard images. Results are highly satisfactory in terms of performance, robustness and efficiency.

## 1 Introduction

Spatial quantization is part of the image capture with digital devices. Usually artifacts (false contours and suppression of low-contrast texture) are close or even below the visibility threshold, but they become evident in a number of situations. For instance when stretching the local luminance range for detail inspection, or when de-convolving quantized blurred images, mostly if there is little random noise. It is also a useful step for local features extraction (e.g., luminance gradient) sensitive to those artifacts, for interpolating iso-level curves in topographic or barometric maps, or for using a reduced number of bits per pixel when there are not enough resources to perform image compression.

Surprisingly enough, de-quantizing in the image domain has received little attention in scientific literature (exceptions are [1,2]). In contrast, transform quantization has been widely treated, especially in the context of post-processing compressed images (de-blocking), usually under orthogonal or bi-orthogonal transforms (e.g., [3,4,5]), but also under overcomplete transforms (e.g., [6,7]). In this work we propose to enforce a certain characterization of sparseness in the overcomplete wavelet domain as the base criterion of the restoration, always ensuring that the estimated image is compatible with the quantized observation. The solution is formulated as belonging to the intersection of two convex sets [8].

---

* Both authors funded by grant TIC2003-1504 from the Ministerio de Ciencia y Tecnologia. JP is under the "Ramon y Cajal " program.

J. Blanc-Talon et al. (Eds.): ACIVS 2005, LNCS 3708, pp. 411–418, 2005.
© Springer-Verlag Berlin Heidelberg 2005

## 2   Image Model

Linear representations based on multi-scale band-pass oriented filters (*wavelets*) are well-suited for representing basic properties of natural images, such as scale-invariance and the existence of locally oriented structures. Natural images typically produce *sparse* distributions of their wavelet coefficients. This means that the energy of the image is mostly concentrated in a small proportion of coefficients [9,10]. It has also been observed that overcomplete representations 1) may produce sparser distributions than critically sampled wavelets [11]; and 2) being translation invariant, they typically provide better results for image processing (e.g., [12,13]). For this work we chose the steerable pyramid [14], an oriented overcomplete representation whose basis functions are rotated and scaled versions of each other. In addition to marginal statistics in the wavelet domain, many authors have exploited the dependency existing among neighbor coefficients (e.g., [15,16,17,18]). We have considered this dependency when selecting significant coefficients, in Section 4.1.

## 3   Enforcing Sparseness

Most degradation sources decrease the sparseness of the wavelet coefficients (e.g., [19,20]). In an attempt to recover the high-sparseness condition of the original, we devise an operator which increases the image sparseness by preserving a given subset of *significant* coefficients while minimizing the global L2-norm. Now we describe this operator for overcomplete representations.

Let $\mathbf{x} \in \mathbb{R}^N$ be an image and $\mathbf{x}' = \mathbf{\Phi}\mathbf{x}$ its overcomplete representation. $\mathbf{\Phi}$ is an $M \times N$ matrix ($M > N$) with each row $\phi_j$ representing an analysis function. We assume that $\mathbf{\Phi}$ preserves the L2-norm, $\|\mathbf{\Phi}\mathbf{x}\| = \|\mathbf{x}\|$, and that it has perfect reconstruction, $\mathbf{\Psi}\mathbf{\Phi}\mathbf{x} = \mathbf{x}$, where $\mathbf{\Psi} = (\mathbf{\Phi}^T\mathbf{\Phi})^{-1}\mathbf{\Phi}^T$ is the pseudoinverse of $\mathbf{\Phi}$. Given an index set $G$ of what we consider the $M'$ most significant coefficients of $\mathbf{x}'$ (see Section 4.1), we define $\mathbf{\Phi}_G$ as the $M' \times N$ matrix formed by all $\phi_j$ row vectors such that $j \in G$. Our sparseness-enforcing operator for that set is:

$$\tilde{\mathbf{x}}(G, \mathbf{x}) = \arg \min_{\mathbf{z} \in \mathbb{R}^N} \|\mathbf{z}\| \text{ s.t. } \mathbf{\Phi}_G \mathbf{z} = \mathbf{\Phi}_G \mathbf{x}. \tag{1}$$

Naming $\mathbf{\Psi}_G$ the pseudoinverse of $\mathbf{\Phi}_G$, previous equation is equivalent to $\tilde{\mathbf{x}}(G, \mathbf{x}) = \mathbf{\Psi}_G\mathbf{\Phi}_G\mathbf{x}$. We call $\mathbf{S}_G = \mathbf{\Psi}_G\mathbf{\Phi}_G$. Note that, when $rank(\mathbf{\Phi}_G) = N$ the Equation (1) has a trivial solution, $\mathbf{x}$. Thus, for $\mathbf{S}_G$ to be of interest, we choose $M' < N$. However, note that $\mathbf{\Psi}_G$ is not trivial to compute. In practice we have applied the method of alternated projections (POCS), that states that iterative orthogonal projections onto a number of intersecting convex sets converge strongly to their intersection. We have used two convex sets: 1) the set of vectors of coefficients having the same values as $\mathbf{x}$ for the indices in $G$, $V(G, \mathbf{x}) = \{\mathbf{z}' \in \mathbb{R}^M : z'_j = \phi_j\mathbf{x}, \forall j \in G\}$; and 2) the set of admissible vectors of coefficients, $A(\mathbf{\Phi}) = \{\mathbf{z}' \in \mathbb{R}^M : \exists \mathbf{x}^0 \in \mathbb{R}^N : \mathbf{z}' = \mathbf{\Phi}\mathbf{x}^0\}$. The orthogonal projection onto the first set is achieved by setting the coefficients with indices in $G$ to their original values, leaving the rest unchanged: $P_{V(G,\mathbf{x})}^\perp(\mathbf{z}') = \mathbf{D}(G)\mathbf{x}' + (\mathbf{I}(M) - \mathbf{D}(G))\mathbf{z}'$, where $\mathbf{x}' = \mathbf{\Phi}\mathbf{x}$, $\mathbf{I}(M)$ is the $M \times M$ identity matrix and $\mathbf{D}(G)$ is a $M \times M$ diagonal matrix such that $d_{ii} = 1$ if $i \in G$ and $d_{ii} = 0$ otherwise. For the other set, the orthogonal projection consists of inverting the transform and applying it again: $\mathbf{P}_{A(\mathbf{\Phi})}^\perp \mathbf{z}' = \mathbf{\Phi}\mathbf{\Psi}\mathbf{z}'$. The solution $\tilde{\mathbf{x}}(G, \mathbf{x})$ can be expressed as the inverse transform of the minimum L2-norm vector belonging to the intersection of both sets. So [1]: $\tilde{\mathbf{x}}(G, \mathbf{x}) = \mathbf{S}_G\mathbf{x} = \mathbf{\Psi}\lim_{n\to\infty}(\mathbf{P}_{A(\mathbf{\Phi})}^\perp P_{V(G,\mathbf{x})}^\perp)^n(\mathbf{0})$. Since $P_{V(G,\mathbf{x})}^\perp(\cdot)$ is an affine orthogonal projector, superindex $n$ indicates the number of iterative compositions of the functions within the brackets, not a power.

## 4 Image De-Quantizing

Left panel of Figure 1 shows a joint histogram of the coefficients for a subband of quantized *Boat* image vs. those of the original. It is normalized in amplitude by columns to express the probability of the observed given the original. We can see that low-amplitude coefficients are severely damaged whereas high-amplitude coefficients are just slightly damped and contaminated with noise of nearly constant variance. Right panel shows the same joint histogram, but normalized by rows and transposed, so now it expresses an empirical measurement of the posterior density of the original given the observation. We can also discriminate an inner region, for which the posterior density is complicated, and an outer region, where the original can be reliably estimated from the observation.

### 4.1 Selecting Significant Coefficients

According to the right panel of Figure 1, it seems natural to choose a threshold to discriminate the inner from the outer region. Discarding the effect of the prior density, it is also reasonable to choose, for each subband $k$, a threshold $\lambda_k^\alpha$ proportional to the standard deviation of the noise caused by the quantization in that subband, $\sigma_k$. That is, $\lambda_k^\alpha = \alpha\sigma_k$ with $\alpha \in \mathbb{R}^+$, where $\sigma_k$ can be estimated analytically from the analysis functions, assuming that quantization noise is white and uniform in density. However, a more reliable estimate can be obtained through simulations, by measuring the variance for a set of quantized standard images, and averaging these measurements (our choice). Once we have estimated every $\sigma_k$ for a certain quantization process, we can sweep the proportionality factor $\alpha$ from $0$ to $\infty$ to control the cardinality of $G$, as a sparseness index of $\tilde{\mathbf{x}}(G, \mathbf{x})$. We have obtained better results for this task by considering that a coefficient is significant if *any* coefficient within its neighborhood, including itself, surpasses the amplitude threshold $\lambda_k^\alpha$. For this work we have used a $5 \times 5$ spatial neighborhood. Naming $I_k^0$ the set of indices of subband $k$ and $N(\cdot)$ the neighborhood set for a given index, the set of significant coefficients of $k$ is:

$$I_k(\alpha) = \{i \in I_k^0 : i \in N(j); \forall j \in I_k^0 : |\phi_j\mathbf{x}| \geq \alpha\sigma_k\},$$

and the total set of significant indices is: $G(\alpha) = \bigcup_{k=1}^K I_k(\alpha)$.

---

[1] We have greatly accelerated convergence by using a linear prediction technique.

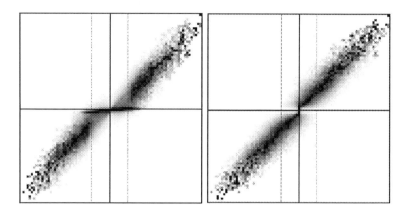

**Fig. 1.** Normalized joint histograms of the coefficients of a subband from a quantized image and from the original image. *Left*: degradation model (original in abscissas). *Right*: Posterior density (quantized in abscissas).

## 4.2 Global Problem Formulation

Let's consider an index set $G(\alpha)$ and let $q(\mathbf{x}) = \mathbf{y}$ be a quantization process. When applying our sparseness-enforcing operator, it exists the possibility that $q(\mathbf{S}_{G(\alpha)}\mathbf{x}) \neq \mathbf{y}$. We must ensure that the final estimation belongs to $Q(\mathbf{y}) = \{\mathbf{x} \in \mathbb{R}^N : q(\mathbf{x}) = \mathbf{y}\}$, the compatibility set for $\mathbf{y}$. On the other hand, it is easy to check that $\mathbf{S}_{G(\alpha)}$ is the orthogonal projector onto the set $C(G(\alpha)) = \{\mathbf{x} \in \mathbb{R}^N : \exists \mathbf{x}^0 \in \mathbb{R}^N \text{ s.t. } \mathbf{x} = \mathbf{S}_{G(\alpha)}\mathbf{x}^0\}$, which represents the set of *sparsified* images obtained with the set of indices $G(\alpha)$. This is a linear subspace. Its dimensionality is the cardinality of $G(\alpha)$, which decreases as $\alpha$ increases. As we are looking for the smallest possible set of significant coefficients, we search for the highest $\alpha$ such that $C(G(\alpha))$ still includes at least one image compatible with $\mathbf{y}$:

$$\hat{\alpha} = \sup\{\alpha \in \mathbb{R}^+ : C(G(\alpha)) \bigcap Q(\mathbf{y}) \neq \emptyset\}. \tag{2}$$

Calling $T(\alpha, \mathbf{y}) = C(G(\alpha)) \bigcap Q(\mathbf{y})$, we choose our final estimate to be the element of $T(\hat{\alpha}, \mathbf{y})$ closest to the observation $\mathbf{y}$: $\hat{\mathbf{x}} = P^{\perp}_{T(\hat{\alpha}, \mathbf{y})}(\mathbf{y})$, where $P^{\perp}_{T(\hat{\alpha}, \mathbf{y})}$ is a (non-linear) orthogonal projection function. In contrast with most estimators used in restoration, this preserves all the information carried by the observation.

## 4.3 POCS-Based Solution

As $Q(\mathbf{y})$ and $C(G(\alpha))$ are both convex sets, we can compute our estimation for a given $\alpha$, noted $\hat{\mathbf{x}}^{\alpha}$, through alternated orthogonal projections. The orthogonal projection onto $Q(\mathbf{y})$ can be defined as $\mathbf{z} = P^{\perp}_{Q(\mathbf{y})}(\mathbf{x})$, with

$$z_i = \begin{cases} x_i, & y_i - \frac{\delta_i}{2} < x_i \le y_i + \frac{\delta_i}{2} \\ y_i - \frac{\delta_i}{2} + \epsilon, & x_i \le y_i - \frac{\delta_i}{2} \\ y_i + \frac{\delta_i}{2}, & y_i + \frac{\delta_i}{2} < x_i \end{cases}$$

where $\delta_i$ are each quantization interval width and $\epsilon \in \mathbb{R}^+$ (ideally infinitesimal) is an artifice to achieve empty intersection between adjacent closed intervals. Therefore, our estimation for a given $\alpha$ is: $\hat{\mathbf{x}}^\alpha = \lim_{n\to\infty}(P^\perp_{Q(\mathbf{y})}\mathbf{S}_{G(\alpha)})^n\mathbf{y}$. We use a line search to find the highest factor $\hat{\alpha}$ for which previous limit converges.

### 4.4   An Efficient Approximated Solution

We have verified two very positive facts. First, that the factor $\hat{\alpha}$ closely match the LSE hand-optimized factor in simulations. Second, that $\hat{\alpha}$ is remarkably constant for different images (typically ranging between 4 and 5), under the same linear representation and the same quantization. Thus we have used, instead of a different $\hat{\alpha}$ each time, an averaged value computed off-line for a collection of standard images. Doing that, we save around one order of magnitude in computation time (which becomes close to 10 s. for $256^2$ images and to 50 s. for $512^2$, with our MATLAB implementation using a 3.4 Ghz Pentium IV CPU), whereas decrease in Signal-to-Noise Ratio is only around 0.10 dB. We note that when the average factor is higher than the optimal value, $Q(\mathbf{y})$ and $C(G(\alpha))$ do not intersect, and then POCS provides a LS-optimal solution.

## 5   Results and Discussion

We have tested our method on a set of ten 8-bit grayscale standard images, of $256^2$ pixels (*Lena, Peppers, Cameraman, Einstein, House*) and $512^2$ (*Barbara, Boat, Goldhill, Plane, Windmill*). We have used the steerable pyramid [14] with 6 scales and 4 orientations. Figure 2 shows the increase in Signal-to-Noise Ratio (ISNR) of the processed images w.r.t. the observations for a range of quantization bits. Improvement is remarkable, especially in the medium range. There is a sudden descent in performance in the fine quantization range that we have not completely explained yet.

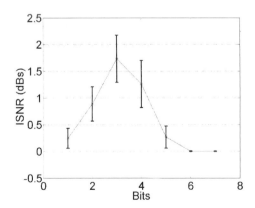

**Fig. 2.** Increment in SNR (ISNR), expressed as $10 \cdot log_{10}(\sigma_q^2/\sigma_r^2)$, where $\sigma_q^2$ and $\sigma_r^2$ are the MSE for observation and estimation, respect., and for several quantization bits

416    L. Mancera and J. Portilla

**Table 1.** Results of our method for 3 and 4 bit quantization, showing the increment w.r.t. the original in Signal-to-Noise-Ratio (in dB) and also in the Structural Similarity Index (×100) [21]

| Bits | Metric | Ref. | Barbara | Boat | Lena | Peppers |
|------|--------|------|---------|------|------|---------|
| 3 | ISNR | 28.74 | 2.29 | 2.24 | 1.93 | 2.01 |
|   | ISSIM | 80.53 | 7.29 | 6.03 | 6.71 | 7.48 |
| 4 | ISNR | 34.77 | 1.91 | 0.86 | 1.54 | 1.38 |
|   | ISSIM | 90.10 | 3.70 | 0.85 | 3.24 | 3.05 |

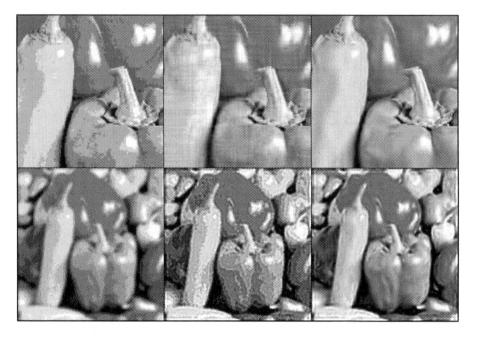

**Fig. 3.** Some visual results. *Left*: Observation. *Center*: Comparison method. *Right*: Our method. See text for details.

Table 1 shows numerical results for quantization using 3 and 4-bits. We also include the increase in the Structural Similarity Index (SSIM) [21], a perceptually-inspired metric taking values in the range [0,1]. First column shows the averaged PSNR/SSIM values of the observation (SSIM values multiplied times 100). There is a very significant improvement under both metrics. First row of Figure 3 shows a cropped result using 3 bits. We have implemented a method (central panel) to help us as a reference, based on a similar strategy than [2]: a gradient-descent in the L2-norm of the output of a high-pass (Laplacian) filter applied to the image, each time projecting the updated image onto the compatibility set $Q(\mathbf{y})$. Our result (right panel) is 1.30 dB above, confirming once again that sparseness-based solutions are more powerful than classical

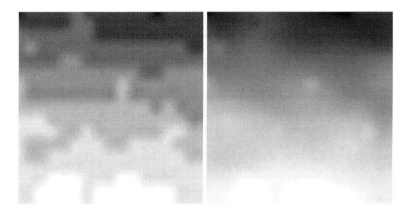

**Fig. 4.** *Left.* Detail of the sky of a real 8-bits photographic picture (amplified contrast). *Right.* Same detail in the picture after processed by our method.

smoothness-based approaches. Second row shows another example. The same image is blurred with a Gaussian kernel ($\sigma_b = \sqrt{2}$), corrupted with noise ($\sigma_n = 2$) and then quantified with 3 bits. Central panel shows the results from a general purpose maximum-likelihood semi-blind deconvolution method (**deconvblind** in MATLAB), passing the Point Spread Function as argument but not the variance of the noise. Right panel shows the deconvolution after de-quantizing the observation. The suppression of artifacts is very noticeable (1.18 dBs ISNR, 0.13 ISSIM). It is remarkable that we have obtained for the image in the right panel the same SSIM (0.70) w.r.t. the original as for the result of applying the deconvolution directly to the unquantized blurred and noisy image. Figure 4 shows removal of low-contrast artifacts in a 8-bit image.

To conclude, we have presented an automatic sparseness-based practical tool for removing pixel quantization artifacts which provides close to LS-optimal results. We still have to further investigate the causes for the drop in performance on the fine quantization range.

# References

1. Desolneux, A., Ladjal, S., Moisan, L., Morel, J.M.: Dequantizing Image Orientation. IEEE Trans. Image Proc. **11**, 10, (Oct 2002) pp. 1129-1140.
2. Chan, Y.H., Fung, Y.H.: A Regularized Constrained Iterative Restoration Algorithm for Restoring Color-Quantized Images. Elsevier Sig. Proc., **85**, pp. 1375-1387, 2005.
3. Paek, H., Kim, R., Lee, S.: On the POCS-based Postprocessing Technique to Reduce the Blocking Artifacts in Transform Coded Images. IEEE Trans. Circuit and Syst. for Video Tech., **8**, 3, (Jun 1998), pp. 358-367.
4. Mateos, J., Katsaggelos, A.K., Molina, R.: A Bayesian Approach to Estimate and Transmit Regularization Parameters for Reducing Blocking Artifacts, IEEE Trans. Image Proc., **9**, 7, (2000), pp. 1200-1215.

5. Li, X.: Improved Wavelet Decoding via Set Theoretic Estimation. Images. IEEE Trans. Circuit and Syst. for Video Tech., **15**, 1, (Jan 2005), pp. 108-112.
6. Xiong, Z., Orchard, M.T., Zhang, Y.: A Deblocking Algorithm for JPEG Compressed Images Using Overcomplete Wavelet Representations. IEEE Trans. Circuit Syst. Video Tech., **7**, 2, (Apr 1997), pp. 433-437.
7. Goyal, V.K., Vetterli, M., Thao, N.T.: Quantized Overcomplete Expansions in $\mathbb{R}^n$: Analysis, Synthesis and Algorithms. IEEE Trans. Inf. Theory, **44**, 1, (1998), pp.16-31.
8. Youla, D.C.: Generalized Image Restoration by the Method of Alternating Orthogonal Projections. IEEE Trans. Circuits and Syst., **CAS-25**, 9, (Sep 1978).
9. Mallat, S.G.: A Theory for multiresolution signal decomposition: The wavelet representation. PAMI, **11**, (Jul 1989, pp. 674-693.
10. Olshausen, B.A., Field, D.J.: Natural Image Statistics and Efficient Coding. Network Computation in Neural Systems, **7**, (1996), pp. 333-339.
11. Olshausen, B.A., Field, D.J.: Sparse Coding with an Overcomplete Basis Set: A Strategy Employed by V1?. Vision Res., **37**, 23, (1997), pp. 3311-3325.
12. Simoncelli, E.P., Freeman, W.T., Adelson, E.H., Heeger, D.J.: Shiftable Multi-Scale Transforms. IEEE Trans. Inf. Theory, **38**, 2, (Mar 1992), pp. 587-607.
13. Coifman, R.R., Donoho, D.L.: Translation Invariant De-noising. Lecture Notes in Statistics, **103** (1995) pp. 125-150.
14. Simoncelli, E.P.: The Steerable Pyramid: A Flexible Architecture For Multi-Scale Derivative Computation. 2nd IEEE Intl Conf. Im. Proc., **III**, pp.444-447, Oct 1995.
15. Shapiro, J.: Embedded Image Coding Using Zerotrees of Wavelet Coefficients. IEEE Trans. Signal Proc., **41**, 22, (Dec 1993), pp. 3445-3462.
16. Buccigrossi, R.W., Simoncelli, E.P.: Image Compression via Joint Statistical Characterization in the Wavelet Domain. IEEE Trans. Image Proc. **8**, 12, Dec 1999, pp. 1668-1701.
17. Pižurica, A., Philips, W., Lemahieu, I., Acheroy, M.: A joint inter- and intrascale statistical model for Bayesian wavelet based image denoising. IEEE Trans. Image Proc., **11**, 5, (May 2002), pp. 545-557.
18. Portilla, J., Strela, V., Wainwright, M.J., Simoncelli, E.P.: Image Denoising using Scale Mixtures of Gaussians in the Wavelet Domain. IEEE Trans. Image Proc., **12**, 11, (Nov 2003), pp. 1338-1351.
19. Rooms, F., Philips, W., Portilla, J.: Parametric PSF estimation via sparseness maximization in the wavelet domain. SPIE Conference "Wavelet Applications in Industrial Processing II" (Oct 2004), Philadelphia. Proc. SPIE **5607**, pp. 26–33.
20. Wang, Z., Wu, G., Sheikh, H.R., Simoncelli, E.P., Yang, E.H., Bovik, A.C.: Quality-Aware Images. IEEE Trans. on Image Proc., accepted, 2005.
21. Wang, Z., Bovik, A.C., Simoncelli, E.P.: Image Quality Assessment: from Error Visibility to Structural Similarity. IEEE Trans. Im. Proc. **13**, April 2004,pp.600-612.

# Reduction of Blocking Artifacts in Block-Based Compressed Images

G.A. Triantafyllidis, D. Tzovaras, and M.G. Strintzis

Informatics and Telematics Institute,
Thermi 57 001, Thessaloniki, Greece
Tel.: +30.2310.464160
gatrian@iti.gr

**Abstract.** A novel frequency domain technique for image blocking artifact reduction is presented in this paper. For each block, its DC and AC coefficients are recalculated for artifact reduction. To achieve this, a closed form representation of the optimal correction of the DCT coefficients is produced by minimizing a novel enhanced form of the Mean Squared Difference of Slope (MSDS), for every frequency separately. Experimental results illustrating the performance of the proposed method are presented and evaluated.

## 1 Introduction

The block based discrete cosine transform (B-DCT) scheme is a fundamental component of many image and video compression standards. Since blocks of pixels are treated as single entities and coded separately, correlation among spatially adjacent blocks is not taken into account in coding, which results in block boundaries being visible when the decoded image is reconstructed. Such so-called "blocking" artifacts, are often very disturbing, especially when the transform coefficients are subject to coarse quantization.

In this paper a new method is proposed for the reduction of the blocking effect in the B- DCT schemes. This method is applied only on the compressed data. The lowest DCT coefficients are recalculated by minimizing a novel enhanced form of the Mean Squared Difference of Slope (MSDS) [1], which involves all eight neighboring blocks. The minimization is constrained by the quantization bounds and is performed for every frequency separately. Thus, a closed form representation is derived, which predicts the DCT coefficients in terms of the eight neighboring coefficients in the subband-like domain.

The rest of this paper is organized as follows: Section 2 presents in detail the blocking artifact reduction algorithm by constrained minimization. Experimental results given in Section 3 evaluate visually and quantitatively the performance of the proposed methods. Finally, conclusions are drawn in Section 4.

J. Blanc-Talon et al. (Eds.): ACIVS 2005, LNCS 3708, pp. 419–426, 2005.
© Springer-Verlag Berlin Heidelberg 2005

## 2    Reduction of Blocking Artifact in the Frequency Domain

As noted, blocking effects result in discontinuities across block boundaries. Based on this observation, a metric called Mean Squared Difference of Slope (MSDS) was introduced in [1], involving the intensity gradient (slope) of the pixels close to the boundary of two blocks. Specifically, it is based on the empirical observation that quantization of the DCT coefficients of two neighboring blocks increases the MSDS between the neighboring pixels on their boundaries.

To better understand this metric, consider an $8 \times 8$ block $f$ of the input image and a block $w$ vertically adjacent to $f$. If the coefficients of the adjacent blocks are coarsely quantized, a difference in the intensity gradient across the block boundary is expected. This abrupt change in intensity gradient across the block boundaries of the original unquantized image is rather unlikely, because most parts of most natural images can be considered to be smoothly varying and their edges are unlikely to line up with block boundaries. From the above, it is clear that a reasonable method for the removal of the blocking effects is to minimize the MSDS, which is defined by:

$$\varepsilon_w = \sum_{m=0}^{7} [d_1(m) - d_2(m)]^2 \tag{1}$$

where $d_1(m)$ is the intensity slope across the boundary between the $f$ and $w$ blocks, defined by:

$$d_1(m) = f(m,0) - w(m,7) \tag{2}$$

and $d_2(m)$ is the average between the intensity slope of $f$ and $w$ blocks close to their boundaries, defined by:

$$d_2(m) = \frac{w(m,7) - w(m,6)}{2} + \frac{f(m,1) - f(m,0)}{2} \tag{3}$$

The ideas in the above discussion are applicable to both horizontal and vertical neighboring blocks. Specifically, if blocks $w$, $e$ denote the blocks horizontally adjacent to $f$, and blocks $s$, $n$ present the blocks vertically adjacent to $f$, then, the MSDS which involves both horizontal and vertical adjacent blocks (hereafter, $MSDS_1$) is given by:

$$MSDS_1 = \varepsilon_w + \varepsilon_e + \varepsilon_s + \varepsilon_n \tag{4}$$

where $\varepsilon_e$, $\varepsilon_s$ and $\varepsilon_n$ are defined similarly to (1-3).

We now extend the definition of MSDS by involving the four diagonally adjacent blocks. If $nw$ is a block diagonally adjacent to $f$, then, we define:

$$\varepsilon_{nw} = [g_1 - g_2]^2 \tag{5}$$

$$\text{where} \quad g_1 = f(0,0) - nw(7,7) \quad \text{and}$$

$$g_2 = \frac{nw(7,7) - nw(6,6)}{2} + \frac{f(1,1) - f(0,0)}{2} \tag{6}$$

If $nw$, $ne$, $sw$ and $se$ are the four blocks diagonally adjacent to $f$, the MSDS involving only the diagonally adjacent blocks (hereafter, $MSDS_2$) is:

$$MSDS_2 = \varepsilon_{nw} + \varepsilon_{ne} + \varepsilon_{sw} + \varepsilon_{se} \qquad (7)$$

where $\varepsilon_{ne}$, $\varepsilon_{sw}$ and $\varepsilon_{se}$ are defined in a manner similar to (5) and (6). Thus, the total MSDS (hereafter, $MSDS_t$) considered in this paper, involving the intensity slopes of all the adjacent blocks is:

$$MSDS_t = MSDS_1 + MSDS_2 \qquad (8)$$

The form of MSDS used in the proposed methods of [1,2] is $MSDS_1$, which, as mentioned above, involves only the horizontal and vertical adjacent blocks for its computation and thus does not use the intensity slopes of the four diagonally adjacent blocks. This implies that their methods cannot remove the specific type of blocking artifact called "corner outlier" [3], which may appear in a corner point of the $8 \times 8$ block.

In [2] a global minimization of the $MSDS_1$ is proposed for the reduction of blocking effects. However, since B-DCT schemes (such as JPEG) use scalar quantization (i.e., quantization of individual samples) for each frequency separately, a separate minimization of the contribution of the quantization of each particular coefficient to the blocking artifact is more appropriate than a global minimization. Global minimization would be more suitable if vector quantization (i.e., quantization of groups of samples or vectors) of the DCT coefficients were used, which is, however, not the case in B-DCT coding schemes. Consider also that, since DCT transform is very close to KL transform, the DCT coefficients are almost uncorrelated [4]. Thus, the modification of each DCT coefficient based on the minimization of MSDS which includes values of the low-pass, middle-pass and high-pass frequency coefficients is obviously not the best solution, and the minimization of $MSDS_t$ for each frequency separately is the appropriate procedure.

The new enhanced form of the $MSDS_t$ involving all eight neighboring blocks is used in this paper, and its local constrained minimization for each frequency, produces a closed-form representation for the correction of the DCT coefficients in the subband-like domain of the DCT transform. To achieve this, the form of $MSDS_t$ in the frequency domain is obtained, and all other frequencies apart from the one $(k, l)$ under consideration are set to zero. It was observed that only the first sixteen DCT coefficients (i.e., $0 \leq k, l \leq 4$) need to be recalculated by MSDS minimization, since the modification of the remaining coefficients does not improve significantly the reduction of the blocking artifacts (because of their poor contribution to MSDS [2]), while requiring nonnegligible extra computational load.

In the sequel, the $MSDS_t$ is calculated and minimized in the frequency domain.

## 2.1   Calculation of $MSDS_1$ in the Frequency Domain

Let $f(m, n)$ denote a $8 \times 8$ block of the input image and $F(u, v)$ denote its forward DCT, where $0 \leq m, n, u, v \leq 7$ and $(0,0)$ denotes the upper left corner pixel of the block as well as the first (DC) transform coefficient. Let $w$, $n$, $e$, $s$,

$nw$, $ne$, $sw$ and $se$ denote the eight blocks adjacent to $f$ in horizontal, vertical and diagonal directions and $W$, $N$, $E$, $S$, $NW$, $NE$, $SW$ and $SE$ denote their corresponding forward DCTs.

Following (2) and (3), the expression $d_1(m) - d_2(m)$ which is used for the calculation of $\varepsilon_w$ in (1) is:

$$d_1(m) - d_2(m) =$$

$$= f(m,0) - w(m,7) - \left(\tfrac{w(m,7)-w(m,6)}{2} + \tfrac{f(m,1)-f(m,0)}{2}\right) \tag{9}$$

where $0 \le m \le 7$. Let $G$ denote the discrete cosine transformation matrix (where the $u$th row of $G$ is the basis vector $C(u)\cos((2m+1)u\pi/16)$) and $G^T$ denote its transpose. Then, the $f$ block can be derived from the inverse DCT transform as follows:

$$\text{Inverse DCT} : f = G^T F G \tag{10}$$

Let $G_x$ and $G^y$ denote the $x$th row and $y$th column of the discrete cosine transformation matrix $G$. Using (10), $f(m,0)$ is easily seen to equal $G_m^T F G^0$. Likewise, the other terms of (9) can also be expressed in the frequency domain and (9) can be expressed as follows:

$$d_1(m) - d_2(m) = (G_m^T F G^0 - G_m^T W G^7) -$$

$$- \left(\tfrac{G_m^T W G^7 - G_m^T W G^6}{2} + \tfrac{G_m^T F G^1 - G_m^T F G^0}{2}\right) \tag{11}$$

Since,

$$G^1 = (-1)^u G^6 \quad \text{and} \quad G^0 = (-1)^u G^7 \tag{12}$$

where $u$ denotes the row number and $0 \le u \le 7$, expression (11) reduces to:

$$d_1(m) - d_2(m) =$$

$$= (1/2)G_m^T(3FG^0 - 3W(-1)^u G^0 - FG^1 + W(-1)^u G^1) = \tag{13}$$

$$= (1/2)G_m^T(F - (-1)^u W)(3G^0 - G^1)$$

Since $G$ is a unitary orthogonal transform, $\sum_{m=0}^{7} G^m G_m^T = I$, where $I$ is the identity matrix. Thus, adding the squares of (13) for all $m$ according to (1), the MSDS term $\varepsilon_w$ between the $f$ and $w$ blocks is produced:

$$\varepsilon_w = (1/4)(3G_0^T - G_1^T)(F - (-1)^u W)^T(F - (-1)^u W)(3G^0 - G^1) \tag{14}$$

The sum of the MSDS terms of the $f$ block corresponding to the four horizontally and vertically adjacent blocks can now be expressed as [2]:

$$MSDS_1 = \varepsilon_w + \varepsilon_e + \varepsilon_s + \varepsilon_n =$$

$$= (1/4)(3G_0^T - G_1^T)[(F - (-1)^u W)^T (F - (-1)^u W)$$

$$+(F - (-1)^u N)(F - (-1)^u N)^T + (E - (-1)^u F)^T (E - (-1)^u F) \tag{15}$$

$$+(S - (-1)^u F)(S - (-1)^u F)^T](3G^0 - G^1)$$

## 2.2   Calculation of MSDS$_2$ in the Frequency Domain

Using (6) the expression $g_1 - g_2$ which is used for the calculation of the MSDS term $\varepsilon_{nw}$ in (5) is found by:

$$g_1 - g_2 = f(0,0) - nw(7,7)-$$

$$-\left(\frac{nw(7,7)-nw(6,6)}{2} + \frac{f(1,1)-f(0,0)}{2}\right) \tag{16}$$

The above may be expressed in the frequency domain, using (10) as:

$$g_1 - g_2 = (G_0^T F G^0 - G_7^T N W G^7)-$$

$$-\left(\frac{G_7^T N W G^7 - G_6^T N W G^6}{2} + \frac{G_1^T F G^1 - G_0^T F G^0}{2}\right) \tag{17}$$

Using (12), eq. (17) reduces to:

$$g_1 - g_2 = \frac{3}{2}G_0^T(F - NW)G^0 - \frac{1}{2}G_1^T(F - NW)G^1 \tag{18}$$

Using (5), the MSDS term $\varepsilon_{nw}$ is now easily computed. Likewise, similar expressions are found for $\varepsilon_{ne}$, $\varepsilon_{sw}$ and $\varepsilon_{se}$, and from (7) the expression of the MSDS$_2$ in the frequency domain is immediately obtained.

## 2.3   Local Minimization of MSDS$_t$ for Each Frequency

We now set to zero all frequencies apart from frequency $(k, l)$. This implies that we set to zero all elements of the DCT matrices, involved in the expressions of MSDS$_1$ and MSDS$_2$ in the frequency domain, apart form the specific $(k, l)$ element. Thus, for the computation of MSDS$_1$ using (15), we set to zero all elements with frequencies $(i, j) \neq (k, l)$ of the matrices $F$, $W$, $E$, $S$ and $N$. If $p_i$ is the $i$th element of the vector $(3G^0 - G_1)$, the MSDS$_1^{kl}$ for the specific frequency $(k, l)$ is now easily derived from (15):

$$MSDS_1^{kl} = \frac{1}{4}(p_k^2(S_{k,l} - (-1)^k F_{k,l})^2 + p_k^2(F_{k,l} - (-1)^k N_{k,l})^2$$

$$+p_l^2(F_{k,l} - (-1)^k W_{k,l})^2 + p_l^2(E_{k,l} - (-1)^k F_{k,l})^2) \tag{19}$$

where the subscripts $k, l$ indicate the $(k, l)$th element of each matrix.

For MSDS$_2$, we also set to zero all frequencies apart from the frequency $(k, l)$. Then, if $a_i = (G^0)_i$, $b_i = (G^1)_i$, and using (5) and (18), we obtain for the MSDS term $\varepsilon_{nw}^{kl}$ computed only for the $(k, l)$ frequency the following expression:

$$\varepsilon_{nw}^{kl} = (\frac{9}{4}a_k^2 a_l^2 - \frac{3}{2}a_k a_l b_k b_l + \frac{1}{4}b_k^2 b_l^2)[F_{k,l} - NW_{k,l}]^2 \qquad (20)$$

For all four diagonal blocks, the $MSDS_2^{kl}$ for the specific frequency $(k,l)$ is:

$$MSDS_2^{kl} = \varepsilon_{nw}^{kl} + \varepsilon_{ne}^{kl} + \varepsilon_{sw}^{kl} + \varepsilon_{se}^{kl} =$$

$$(\tfrac{9}{4}a_k^2 a_l^2 - \tfrac{3}{2}a_k a_l b_k b_l + \tfrac{1}{4}b_k^2 b_l^2)[(F_{k,l} - NW_{k,l})^2 + \qquad (21)$$

$$(SW_{k,l} - F_{k,l})^2 + (SE_{k,l} - F_{k,l})^2 + (F_{k,l} - NE_{k,l})^2]$$

Setting the gradient of $MSDS_1^{kl}$ and $MSDS_2^{kl}$ to zero, we obtain the representation corresponding to the minimum $MSDS_t^{kl}$. Therefore, the imposition of

$$\frac{\partial(MSDS_t^{kl})}{\partial F_{k,l}} = \frac{\partial(MSDS_1^{kl} + MSDS_2^{kl})}{\partial F_{k,l}} = 0 \qquad (22)$$

results to:

$$2(p_k^2 + p_l^2)F_{k,l} + 4RF_{k,l} =$$

$$(S_{k,l} + N_{k,l})(-1)^k p_k^2 + (W_{k,l} + E_{k,l})(-1)^k p_l^2 \qquad (23)$$

$$+(NW_{k,l} + NE_{k,l} + SW_{k,l} + SE_{k,l})R$$

where $R = 9a_k^2 a_l^2 - 6a_k a_l b_k b_l + b_k^2 b_l^2$. Thus, (23) provides the following expression of the DCT coefficient at frequency $(k,l)$ in terms of its eight neighboring Laplacian corrected DCT coefficients in the subband-like domain:

$$F_{k,l} = \frac{(S_{k,l}+N_{k,l})(-1)^k p_k^2 + (W_{k,l}+E_{k,l})(-1)^k p_l^2}{2(p_k^2+p_l^2)+4R}$$

$$+\frac{(NW_{k,l}+NE_{k,l}+SW_{k,l}+SE_{k,l})R}{2(p_k^2+p_l^2)+4R} \qquad (24)$$

subject to:

$$F_{k,l}^L \leq F_{k,l} \leq F_{k,l}^U \qquad (25)$$

where $F_{k,l}^U$ and $F_{k,l}^L$ are the quantization upper and lower limit respectively.

Equation (24) subject to the constraint of equation (25) provides the correction of the $(k,l)$ DCT coefficient for the reduction of the blocking effect in B-DCT coded images (e.g. JPEG coded images).

## 3    Experimental Results

In this section, simulation results demonstrating the performance of the proposed technique are presented. For this purpose, several images of different characteristics were chosen and compressed using a JPEG picture.

In order to measure and evaluate the performance of our approach for blocking artifact reduction, the proposed constrained optimization method is applied

**Table 1.** A: $MSDS_t$ per block of the nonsmoothed reconstructed image, B: $MSDS_t$ per block of the reconstructed image processed by method [2], C: $MSDS_t$ per block of the reconstructed image processed by proposed method

| original image | bit per pixel | A | B | C |
|---|---|---|---|---|
| lenna | 0.4096 bpp | 3118 | 2980 | 2738 |
| $512 \times 512$ | 0.2989 bpp | 3898 | 3397 | 3082 |
| $MSDS_t$=1608 | 0.1942 bpp | 5413 | 4976 | 4537 |
| peppers | 0.4211 bpp | 2513 | 2311 | 2210 |
| $512 \times 512$ | 0.3137 bpp | 3013 | 2798 | 2595 |
| $MSDS_t$=2341 | 0.1989 bpp | 4467 | 3877 | 3419 |
| boat | 0.4988 bpp | 6145 | 5844 | 5334 |
| $512 \times 512$ | 0.3245 bpp | 7539 | 7008 | 6619 |
| $MSDS_t$=4393 | 0.2417 bpp | 8489 | 7823 | 7301 |

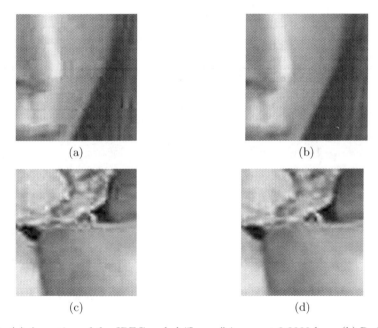

(a)

(b)

(c)

(d)

**Fig. 1.** (a) A portion of the JPEG coded "Lenna" image at 0.2989 bpp, (b) Reduction of blocking artifacts with the proposed method at 0.2989 bpp, (c) A portion of the JPEG coded "Peppers" image at 0.3137 bpp, (d) Reduction of blocking artifacts with the proposed method at 0.3137 bpp

to the test images. Commonly used metrics, such as the mean square error or signal to noise ratio were not employed, since they involve pixels of the entire image and not just the pixels near the block boundaries. Rather, the value of the $MSDS_t$ per block is used for the evaluation of our technique. The $MSDS_t$ is computed along each block boundary, considering a common boundary between two adjacent (vertical, horizontal or diagonal) blocks only once. Table 1 shows the image name, its size, the $MSDS_t$ of the original image (all in the first column), the coding rate (bits per pixel) and the value of the $MSDS_t$ per image block for the cases of the nonsmoothed reconstructed image, of the reconstructed image processed by method of [2] and finally for the case of the reconstructed image processed by the proposed algorithm.

As expected, in B-DCT coded images the value of $MSDS_t$ per block increases compared to the original images, due to quantization. Our approach shows a significant reduction of the $MSDS_t$ and clearly outperforms the method proposed in [2]. A visual illustration of the performance of our method, showing the JPEG reconstructed magnified portions of "Lenna" and "Peppers" images and the corresponding reconstructed portions of the images processed by the proposed method is shown in Fig. 1. These figures illustrate the efficiency of the proposed method.

## 4   Conclusions

When images are highly compressed using B-DCT transforms, the decompressed images contains bothersome blocking artifacts. This paper presented a novel algorithm applied entirely in the compressed domain, in order to reduce these blocking artifacts. A novel form of the criterion of Mean Squared Difference of Slope (MSDS) is also introduced involving all eight neighboring blocks. MSDS is then minimized for each frequency separately, producing a closed form for the correction terms for the DCT coefficients so as to achieve reduction of the blocking effect of coded images. Experimental evaluation of the performance of the proposed technique showed its ability to detect and alleviate blocking artifacts effectively.

## References

1. S. Minami and A. Zakhor, "An optimization approach for removing blocking effects in transform coding", *IEEE Trans. Circuits Syst. Video Technology*, vol. 5, pp 74-82, Apr. 1995.
2. G. Lakhani and N. Zhong, "Derivation of prediction equations for blocking effect reduction", *IEEE Trans. Circuits Syst. Video Technology*, vol. 9, no. 3, pp. 415-418, Apr. 1999.
3. Y.L. Lee, H.C. Kim, and H.W. Park, "Blocking effect reduction of JPEG images by signal adaptive filtering", *IEEE Trans. Image Processing*, vol. 7, pp. 229-234, Feb. 1998.
4. A.K. Jain, *Fundamentals of digital image processing*, Englewood Cliffs, NJ, Prentice Hall, 1989.
5. H. Paek, R.-C. Kim, and S.-U. Lee, "A DCT-based spatially adaptive post processing technique to reduce the blocking artifacts in transform coded images", *IEEE Trans. Circuits Syst. Video Technology*, vol. 10, no. 1, pp. 36-41, Feb 2000.
6. G.A. Triantafyllidis, D. Tzovaras and M.G. Strintzis, "Blockiness Detection in Compressed Data", *IEEE International Symposium on Circuits and Systems (ISCAS)*, Sydney, Australia, May 2001.
7. G.A. Triantafyllidis, D. Tzovaras and M.G. Strintzis, "Blocking Artifact Detection and Reduction in Compressed Data", *IEEE Trans. Circuits Syst. Video Technology*, Vol.12, No.10, pp.877-890, October 2002.

# FIMDA: A Fast Intra-frame Mode Decision Algorithm for MPEG-2/H.264 Transcoding*

Gerardo Fernández-Escribano, Pedro Cuenca, Luis Orozco-Barbosa, and Antonio Garrido

Instituto de Investigación en Informática de Albacete,
Universidad de Castilla-La Mancha, 02071 Albacete, Spain
{gerardo, pcuenca, lorozco, antonio}@info-ab.uclm.es

**Abstract.** The H.264 video compression standard provides tools for coding improvements of at least 2 dB, in terms of PSNR, and at least 50% in bit rate savings as compared with MPEG-2 video compression standard. It is expected that the H.264/MPEG-4 AVC will take over the digital video market, replacing the use of MPEG-2 in most digital video applications. The complete migration to the new video-coding algorithm will take several years given the wide scale use of MPEG-2 in the market place today. This creates an important need for transcoding technologies for converting the large volume of existent video material from the MPEG-2 into the H.264 format and vice versa. However, given the significant differences between the MPEG-2 and the H.264 encoding algorithms, the transcoding process of such systems is much more complex to other heterogeneous video transcoding processes. In this paper, we introduce and evaluate two versions of a fast intra-frame mode decision algorithm to be used as part of a high-efficient MPEG-2 to H.264 transcoder. In this work, we utilize an architecture of pixel domain video transcoding but we use the DC coefficient of the MPEG-2 DCT 8x8 blocks. Our evaluation results show that the proposed algorithm considerably reduces the complexity involved in the intra-frame prediction.

## 1 Introduction

Nowadays, the MPEG-2 video coding format [1] is being widely used in a number of applications from digital TV systems to video-on-demand services. The use of MPEG-2 technology represents billions of dollars of investment in the MPEG-2 infrastructure. During the last few years, technological developments, such as novel video coding algorithms, lower memory costs, and faster processors, are facilitating the design and development of highly efficient video encoding standards. Among the recent works in this area, the H.264 video encoding standard, also known as MPEG-4 AVC, occupies a central place [2]. The H.264 standard, jointly developed by the ITU-T and the MPEG committees, is highly efficient offering perceptually equivalent

* This work was supported by the Ministry of Science and Technology of Spain under CICYT project TIC2003-08154-C06-02, the Council of Science and Technology of Castilla-La Mancha under project PBC-03-001 and FEDER.

J. Blanc-Talon et al. (Eds.): ACIVS 2005, LNCS 3708, pp. 427–434, 2005.
© Springer-Verlag Berlin Heidelberg 2005

quality video at about 1/2 of the bitrates offered by the MPEG-2 format. These significant bandwidth savings open the market to new products and services, including HDTV services at lower bitrates. Furthermore, given the relatively early stage of video services in mobile phones, it will be one of the first market segments to adopt H.264 video. However, these gains come with a significant increase in encoding and decoding complexity [3].

While the H.264 video standard is expected to replace MPEG-2 video the coming years, a significant amount of research is needed for developing efficient encoding and transcoding technologies. The transcoding of MPEG-2 video to H.264 format is particularly interesting given the wide availability and use of MPEG-2 video nowadays. Furthermore, there is a clear industry interest in technologies facilitating the migration from MPEG-2 to H.264. The coexistence of these technologies until the complete adoption of H.264 creates a need for technologies to transcode from the MPEG-2 into the H.264 format and vice versa. However, given the significant differences between the MPEG-2 and the H.264 coding algorithms, transcoding is a much more complex task compared to the task involved in other heterogeneous video transcoding architectures [4-8].

The H.264 employs a hybrid coding approach similar to that of MPEG-2 but differs significantly from MPEG-2 in terms of the actual coding tools used. The main differences are: 1) use of an integer transform with energy compaction properties; 2) an in-loop deblocking filter to reduce block artifacts; 3) multi-frame references for inter-frame prediction; 4) entropy coding; 5) variable block size for motion estimation and 6) intra-frame prediction. The H.264 standard introduces several other new coding tools aiming to improve the coding efficiency [2].

In this paper, we focus our attention on the intra-frame prediction: one of the most stringent tasks involved in the encoding process. A complete overview of the H.264 can be found in [9]. The rest of the paper is organized as follows. Section 2 provides a brief overview of the intra-frame prediction process used by the H.264 encoding standard. In Section 3, we introduce a fast intra-frame prediction algorithm suitable for the transcoding of MPEG-2 into H.264. In Section 4, we carry out a performance evaluation of the proposed algorithm in terms of its computational complexity and rate-distortion results. Finally, Section 5 concludes the paper.

## 2   Intra-frame Prediction in H.264

H.264 incorporates into its coding process, an intra-picture prediction (defined within the pixel domain) whose main aim is to improve the compression efficiency of the intra-coded pictures and intra-MBs. Intra prediction can result in significant savings when the motion present in the video sequence is minimal and the spatial correlations are significant. Throughout the paper, we will illustrate the principle of operation of the intra-frame prediction modes as applied to the luminance and chrominance blocks.

While macro blocks (MB) of 16x16 pixels are still used, predicting a MB from the previously encoded MBs in the same picture is new in H.264. For *luminance component*, an MB may make use of 4x4 and 16x16 block prediction modes, referred to as Intra_4x4 and Intra_16x16, respectively. Recently, the Intra_8x8 block prediction mode has been added as part of the *Fidelity Range Extension* (FRExt) of the standard. There are nine 4x4 and 8x8 possible block prediction directions and four 16x16 block prediction directions. Figure 1 depicts the nine and four prediction directions for the 4x4, 8x8 and 16x16 prediction modes, respectively. For *chrominance component*, an MB makes use of 8x8 block prediction mode only. There are four 8x8 possible block prediction directions. The prediction directions for the 8x8 prediction mode (not shown in the figure) are similar to the ones used for the 16x16 prediction mode in the luminance component.

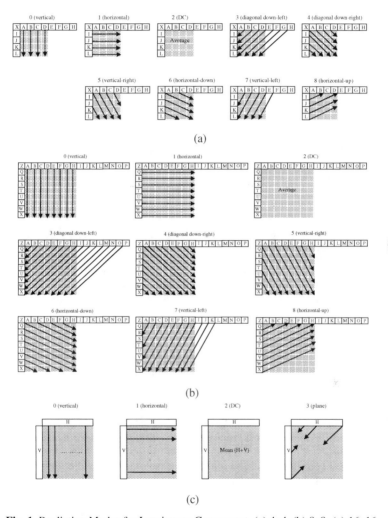

**Fig. 1.** Prediction Modes for Luminance Component. (a) 4x4. (b) 8x8. (c) 16x16.

These intra prediction modes include a directional prediction greatly improving the prediction in the presence of directional structures. With the intra-frame prediction, the I-pictures can be encoded more efficiently than in MPEG-2, which does not support intra-frame prediction.

For each MB, and for each color component (Y,U,V), one prediction mode and one set of prediction directions is kept. The H.264 encoder selects the best combination mode/direction by using the *Sum of Absolute Errors* (SAE). This implies that for each existing direction of each mode, the predictor within the pixel-domain is created from the boundary pixels of the current partition and the SAE costs are evaluated. The best combination of mode/direction is determined corresponding to the one exhibiting the minimum SAE cost. The residual is encoded using a 4x4 integer based transform. In the next section, we present a fast intra-frame mode decision algorithm suitable for transcoding video material from the MPEG-2 into the H.264 format. We achieve very high computational savings by accelerating the estimation process of intra-frame prediction of H.264 using the DC coefficient of the MPEG-2 DCT 8x8 blocks.

## 3  FIMDA: Fast Intra-frame Mode Decision Algorithm

Our approach simplifies the intra-frame prediction by making use of the DC coefficients available from the decoding process of the MPEG-2. However, due to the presence of three different sizes of blocks used by the H.264, namely 4x4, 8x8 and 16x16, and that the MPEG-2 standards use blocks of 8x8, the evaluation of the prediction mode involves and intermediate scaling process. In the following, we describe one by one the main steps of our algorithm.

### 3.1  Computation of the DC Coefficients of the Original Blocks

In an MPEG-2/H.264 video transcoder, once having decoded the MPEG-2 video, besides the uncompressed video, the DC coefficient of the 8x8 blocks (Y,U,V) is readily available to the H.264 video encoder. Since the MPEG-2 makes use of only 8x8 blocks, we need to devise a mechanism allowing us to properly compute the DC coefficients of the 4x4 and 16x16 blocks. Figures 2a and 2c depict the procedure for computing the DC coefficients of the four 4x4 blocks and the one associated to the 16x16 block. The DC coefficients of the 8x8 blocks are directly obtained by reusing the information coming from the MPEG-2 decoding process (Figure 2b).

As seen from Figure 2a, the process to obtain the four DC coefficients of 4x4 blocks involves first applying the inverse DCT to each 8x8 block of the decoded MPEG-2 picture. This step regenerates the 8x8 block in the space domain (pixel domain values are needed anyway). The process to obtain the DC coefficients in 4x4 blocks consists in the sum of all the pixel of the block divided by 4. In this case, we do not reuse the information of the DC coefficients of MPEG-2 8x8 blocks, because this solution is faster than other mechanisms, like the proposed in the paper [10]. For obtain the DC coefficients of the 8x8 blocks (see Figure 2b), no additional operation are required. This information is available in the decoded sequence.

Regarding the computation of the DC coefficient of the 16x16 block, this one can be obtained as follows,

$$DC_{16} = \frac{DC_8^1 + DC_8^2 + DC_8^3 + DC_8^4}{2} \qquad (1)$$

this is to say, by adding the four DC coefficients of the four corresponding 8x8 blocks and then dividing the result by two. Equation 1 is simply derived from the fact that the DC coefficient of an NxN block is nothing else but the mean value of all the pixels within the block. This conversion procedure is depicted in Figure 2c.

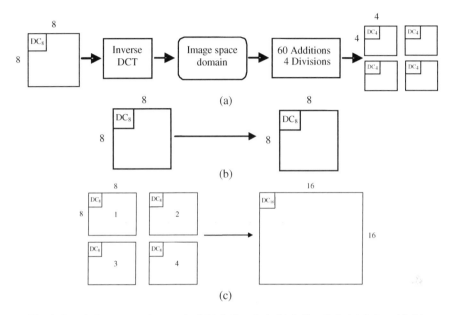

**Fig. 2.** Resolution conversion method (a) 8x8 to 4x4, (b) 8x8 to 8x8, (c) 8x8 to 16x16

### 3.2 Computation of the DC Coefficients of the H.264 Predictors

The computation of the DC coefficient of the intra luma and chroma block prediction directions of the H.264 standard is a straightforward procedure. Let's take the example of computing the Vertical Predictor (P0) involved in the 4x4 intra luma mode prediction. The predictor is created by copying the values of the upper border pixels into all the entries within the same column (see Figure 3). According to the DCT, the DC coefficient of the predictor is given by:

$$DC = a + b + c + d. \tag{2}$$

In this simple form, we are able to compute the DC coefficients of the Vertical Prediction. Similarly, this process can be applied for obtaining all the other predictors.

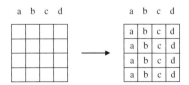

**Fig. 3.** Example of creation of a 4x4 predictor

### 3.3  Computation of the Prediction Mode and Predictors

The third step of our proposed algorithm consists in obtaining the prediction mode and predictors for each macroblock and for each color component. In order to obtain the overall best predictors over all the prediction modes for a given macroblock, we proceed as follows. In the case of the 16 x16 prediction mode, the best predictor is simply obtained by taking the one whose DC coefficient exhibits the lowest absolute (ABS) difference with respect to the DC coefficient of the original block. Similarly to the 16x16 prediction mode, for the 8x8 prediction mode, we determine the predictor whose DC coefficient exhibits the lowest absolute difference with respect to the DC coefficient of the original block for each one of the four 8x8 blocks of the macroblock. Similarly, for the 4x4 prediction mode, the best predictor is obtained for each one of the 16 4x4 blocks of the macroblocks. As a further feature allowing us to speed up this process, we only consider the use of the prediction directions 0, 1 and 2 (for all luma and chroma predictions modes). We base this choice by having studied a large number of images (more than 120.000 samples) available in the database reported in [11], these three predictors are used in more than 70% of the times with [12].

In this point, we evaluate the best prediction mode (4x4, 8x8 or 16x16 mode)  for coding a macroblock in two different ways: 1) **DC-ABS**. The prediction mode chosen will be the one which the accumulate errors is lowest. This accumulate error is the sum, in absolute value, of the differences between de DC coefficients of the original blocks and the DC coefficients of their respective prediction directions. 2) **DC-ABS pixel**. The prediction mode chosen will be the one which the accumulate error is lowest too. However, this accumulate error is now the sum, in absolute value, of the difference pixel by pixel between the original blocks and their respective prediction directions(in the pixel domain).

As we will show in the following section, the proposed algorithm will significantly reduce the number of operations involved in the calculation of the intra predictors when compared to the full estimation of the H.264 standard.

## 4  Performance Evaluation

In order to evaluate our Fast Intra-Frame Mode Decision Algorithm (FIMDA), we have implemented the proposed approach based on the H.264 reference software [12] (version 9.3). The metrics we have been interested are the computational cost and rate distortion function. Throughout our experiments, we have used various video sequences (in 4:2:0 format) exhibiting different spatial characteristics and different size formats (CCIR, CIF and QCIF). We use Q factors from QP=0 to QP=50 (corresponding to the full H.264 QP range). Every frame of each sequence was encoded as I-frame in order to obtain results for intra-frame prediction only.

Figure 4 shows the mean number of operations per MB used for the H.264 full estimation approach and for the two versions of our Fast Intra-Frame Mode Decision algorithm, showing the high gains on the reduction of computational complexity characterizing our proposed scheme.

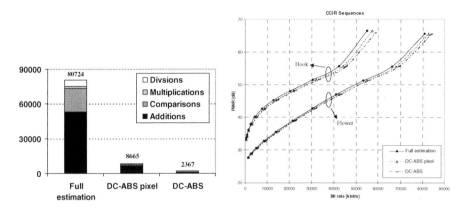

**Fig. 4.** Computational Cost: Operations per MB

**Fig. 5.** Rate Distortion Results. CCIR sequences

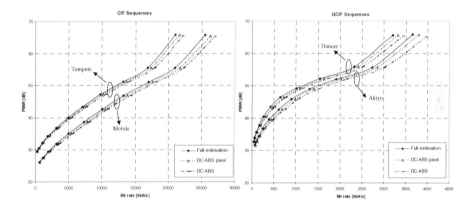

**Fig. 6.** Rate Distortion Results. CIF sequences

**Fig. 7.** Rate Distortion Results. QCIF sequences

Figures 5 to 7 show the RD results of applying the full estimation algorithm and our proposed intra-frame prediction algorithm to six different video sequences. As seen from the figures, the PSNR obtained when applying our algorithm deviates slightly from the results obtained when applying the considerable more complex full estimation procedure. As expected, the difference is less noticeable at lower bit rates: the blocking effect is more noticeable, i.e. the DC coefficient has a heavier weight. Based on the results depicted in Figures 5-7, depending on the image quality requirement, the use of the DC-ABS scheme may prove a viable solution when computational cost may be an issue.

## 5 Conclusions

In this paper, we have focused our attention on the intra-frame prediction: one of the most stringent tasks involved in the encoding process. In this work, we have studied two versions of a new fast intra-frame mode decision algorithm to be used in the implementation of MPEG-2 to H.264 transcoders. Our results show that the two versions of the proposed algorithm are able to maintain a good picture quality while considerably reducing the number of operations to be performed. Based on the results obtained, depending on the image quality requirement, the use of the DC-ABS scheme may prove a viable solution when computational cost may be a very important requirement. The proposed algorithm can be used as basis for a full low complexity transcoder applicable in the full QP range. Our future plans include reusing the information coming out from the MPEG-2 for speeding-up the inter frame prediction.

## References

1. ISO/IEC JTC11/SC29/WG11: Generic Coding of Moving Pictures and Associated Audio Information: Video, ISO/IEC 13818-2. May 1994
2. ITU-T RECOMMENDATION H.264: Advanced Video Coding for Generic Audiovisual Services. May 2003
3. Implementation Studies Group: Main Results of the AVC Complexity Analysis. MPEG Document N4964, ISO/IEC JTC11/SC29/WG11, July 2002
4. N. Bjork and C. Christopoulos: Transcoder Architectures for Video Coding. IEEE Trans. Consumer Electronics, vol. 44, no. 1, pp.88-98, Feb. 1998
5. A. Vetro, C. Christopoulos, and H.Sun: Video Transcoding Architectures and Techniques: An Overview. IEEE Signal Processing Magazine, vol. 20, no. 2, pp.18-29, March. 2003
6. S. Dogan and A. Sadka: Video Transcoding for Inter-Networks Communications. Chapter of Compressed Video Communications. John Wiley & Sons, pp.215-256, March. 2003
7. H. Kalva, A. Vetro, and H. Sun: Performance Optimization of the MPEG-2 to MPEG-4 Video Transcoder. SPIE Conference on Microtechnologies for the New Millennium, VLSI Circuits and Systems, May 2003
8. J.Bialkowski, A. Kaup and K. Illgner: Fast Transcoding of Intra Frames between H.263 and H.264. IEEE International Conference on Image Processing. October 2004
9. T. Wiegand, G. Sullivan, G. Bjontegaard, and A. Luthra: Overview of the H.264/AVC Video Coding Standard. IEEE Transactions on Circuits and Systems for Video Technology, Vol. 13, No. 7, pp.560-576. July 2003
10. T. Goto, T. Hanamura, T. Negami and T. Kitamura: A Study on Resolution Conversión Method using DCT Coefficients. International Symposium on Information Theory and its Applications. October 2004
11. http://sampl.eng.ohio-state.edu/~sampl/database.htm
12. Joint Video Team (JVT) of ISO/IEC MPEG and ITU-T VCEG, Referente Software to Comitee Draft. JVT-F100 JM9.3

# A New Rate-Distortion Optimization Using Structural Information in H.264 I-Frame Encoder

Zhi-Yi Mai[1], Chun-Ling Yang[1], Lai-Man Po[2], and Sheng-Li Xie[1]

[1] School of Electronic and Information Engineering, South China University of Technology, Guangzhou, Guangdong, 510640, China
[2] Department of Electronic Engineering, City University of Hong Kong, 83 Tat Chee Avenue, Kowloon Tong, Hong Kong, China
kathymaizy@yahoo.com.cn, eeclyang@scut.edu.cn, eelmpo@cityu.edu.hk

**Abstract.** Rate-distortion optimization is the key technique in video coding standards to efficiently determine a set of coding parameters. In the R-D optimization for H.264 I-frame encoder, the distortion (D) is measured as the sum of the squared differences (SSD) between the reconstructed and the original blocks, which is same as MSE. Recently, a new image measurement called Structural Similarity (SSIM) based on the degradation of structural information was brought forward. It is proved that the SSIM can provide a better approximation to the perceived image distortion than the currently used PSNR (or MSE). In this paper, a new rate-distortion optimization for H.264 I-frame encoder using SSIM as the distortion metric is proposed. Experiment results show that the proposed algorithm can reduced 2.2~6.45% bit rate while maintaining the perceptual quality.

## 1 Introduction

As the rapid development of digital techniques and increasing use of Internet, image and video compression plays a more and more important role in our life. The newest international video coding standard H.264 adopts many advanced techniques, such as directional spatial prediction in I-frame encoder, variable and Hierarchical block transform, arithmetic entropy coding, multiple reference frame motion compensation, deblocking etc. All these novel and advanced techniques make it provide approximately a 50% bit rate savings for equivalent perceptual quality relative to the performance of prior standards [1]. Except for the new techniques, the operational control of the source encoder is still a key problem in H.264, and it is still optimized with respect to the rate-distortion efficiency using Lagrangian optimization techniques, just like the prior standards, MPEG-2, H.263 and MPEG-4. In the R-D optimization function for H.264 intra prediction, distortion is measured as SSD between the reconstructed and the original blocks, which has the same meaning with MSE. Although Peak Signal-to-Noise Ratio (PSNR) and MSE are currently the most widely used objective metrics due to their low complexity and clear physical meaning, they were also widely criticized for not correlating well with Human Visual System (HVS) for a long time [2]. During past several decades a great deal of effort has been made to

J. Blanc-Talon et al. (Eds.): ACIVS 2005, LNCS 3708, pp. 435–441, 2005.
© Springer-Verlag Berlin Heidelberg 2005

develop new image quality assessment based on error sensitivity theory of HVS, but only limit success has been achieved by the reason that the HVS has not been well comprehended.

Recently a new philosophy for image quality measurement was proposed, based on the assumption that the human visual system is highly adapted to extract structural information from the viewing field. It follows that a measure of structural information change can provide a good approximation to perceived image distortion [3]. In this new theory, an item called Structural Similarity (SSIM) index including three comparisons is introduced to measure the structural information change. Experiments showed that the SSIM index method is easy to implement and can better corresponds with human perceived measurement than PSNR (or MSE). Thus, in this paper we propose to employ SSIM in the rate-distortion optimizations of H.264 I-frame encoder to choose the best prediction mode(s).

The remainder of this paper is organized as follows. In section II, the I-frame coding of H.264 and the idea of SSIM is summarized. The detail of our proposed method is given in section III. Section IV presents the experimental results to demonstrate the advantage of the SSIM index method. Finally, section V draws the conclusion.

## 2   H.264 I-Frame Encoder and SSIM

### 2.1   H.264 I-Frame Encoder

In H.264 I-frame encoder, each picture is partitioned into fixed-size macroblocks (MB) that cover a rectangular area of 16×16 samples of the luma component and 8×8 samples of each chroma component. Then each macroblock is spatially predicted using its neighbouring samples of previously coded blocks which are to the left and/or above the block, and the prediction residual is integer transformed, quantized and transmitted using entropy coding. The latest JVT reference software version (JM92) of H.264 [4] provides three types of intra prediction denoted as intra_16x16, intra_8x8 and intra_4x4. The intra_16x16 which supports 4 prediction modes performs prediction of the whole macroblock and is suited for smooth area, while the intra_8x8 and intra_4x4 which performs 8×8 and 4×4 block respectively support 9 prediction modes and are suited for detailed part of the picture. The best prediction mode(s) are chosen utilizing the R-D optimization[5] which is described as:

$$J(\mathbf{s}, \mathbf{c}, MODE \mid QP) = D(\mathbf{s}, \mathbf{c}, MODE \mid QP) + \lambda_{MODE} R(\mathbf{s}, \mathbf{c}, MODE \mid QP) . \qquad (1)$$

In the above formula, the distortion D($s,c$,MODE|QP) is measured as SSD between the original block $s$ and the reconstructed block $c$, and QP is the quantization parameter, MODE is the prediction mode. R($s,c$,MODE|QP) is the bit number coding the block. The modes(s) with the minimum J($s,c$,MODE|QP) are chosen as the prediction mode(s) of the macroblock.

### 2.2   Structural Similarity (SSIM)

The new idea of SSIM index is to introduce the measure of structural information degradation, which includes three comparisons: luminance, contrast and structure [3]. It's defined as

$$SSIM(\mathbf{x},\mathbf{y}) = l(\mathbf{x}, y) \cdot c(\mathbf{x},\mathbf{y}) \cdot s(\mathbf{x},\mathbf{y}) \ . \tag{2}$$

where $l(x, y)$ is Luma comparison, $c(x, y)$ is Contrast comparison and $s(x, y)$ is Structure comparison. They are defined as:

$$l(x, y) = \frac{2\mu_x \mu_y + C_1}{\mu_x^2 + \mu_y^2 + C_1} \ . \tag{3}$$

$$c(\mathbf{x}, \mathbf{y}) = \frac{2\sigma_x \sigma_y + C_2}{\sigma_x^2 + \sigma_y^2 + C_2} \ . \tag{4}$$

$$s(x, y) = \frac{(\sigma_{xy} + C_3)}{\sigma_x \sigma_y + C_3} \ . \tag{5}$$

where $x$ and $y$ are two nonnegative image signals to be compared, $\mu_x$ and $\mu_y$ are the mean intensity of image $x$ and $y$ respectively, $\sigma_x$ and $\sigma_y$ are the standard deviation of image $x$ and $y$ respectively, $\sigma_{xy}$ is the covariance of image x and y. In fact, without $C_3$, the equation (5) is the correlation coefficient of image $x$ and $y$, and $C_1$, $C_2$ and $C_3$ are small constants to avoid the denominator being zero. It's recommended by [3]:

$$C_1 = (K_1 L)^2, \ C_2 = (K_2 L)^2, \ C_3 = \frac{C_2}{2} \ . \tag{6}$$

where $K_1, K_2 \ll 1$ and L is the dynamic range of the pixel values (255 for 8-bit grayscale images). In addition, the higher the value of $SSIM(\mathbf{x},\mathbf{y})$ is, the more similar the image $x$ and $y$ are.

## 3   The R-D Optimization Using Structural Similarity in H.264

As the SSIM index method performs better as image quality measurement than MSE (SSD), we propose to replace the SSD with the SSIM index in the R-D optimization of H.264 I-frame encoder. The quality of the reconstructed picture is higher when its SSIM index is greater while the SSD performs the other way. Therefore the distortion in our method is measured as:

$$D(s, c, MODE|QP) = 1 - SSIM(s, c) \ . \tag{7}$$

where $s$ and $c$ are the original and reconstructed image block respectively.

Due to the change of distortion measure, the Lagrangian multiplier should be modified correspondingly. According to the relation between SSIM($s,c$) and R($s,c$,MODE|QP) and motivated by the theory in [6] and [7], the new Lagrangian multiplier in our algorithm is

$$\lambda_{MODE} = 1.11 * 2^{(QP-60)/5} .$$ (8)

where QP denotes the quantization parameter. Consequently, the new R-D cost function can be written as:

$$J(\mathbf{s}, \mathbf{c}, MODE \mid QP) = 1 - SSIM(\mathbf{s}, \mathbf{c}) + \lambda_{MODE} R(\mathbf{s}, \mathbf{c}, MODE \mid QP) .$$ (9)

Our new algorithm is using SSIM index instead of SSD as the distortion measure in RDCost_for_4x4IntraBlock, RDCost_for_8x8IntraBlock and RDCost_for_macro-blocks, but the decisions of finding the best mode for Intra_16x16 which uses Hadamard transform remain unchanged. The SSIM indexes of all types of prediction blocks are computed within 4×4 nonoverlapping square windows, while slide window, which is of 16×16, is used to compute the whole reconstructed image quality MSSIM (mean SSIM). Furthermore, the parameter setting here is chosen as follows: $K_1$=0.01, $K_2$=0.03, L=255.

## 4   Experimental Results

Experiments are carried out using several 8 bit/pixel grayscale images of various sizes. They are Apple, Claire, MissA and Salesman of 176×144, Bridge and Camera of 256×256, Airplane, Baboon, Lena and Sailboat of 512×512, Pentagon and Man of 1024×1024. All the modifications are based on the JVT reference software JM92 program [4]. Results in terms of total bits of the compressed image, MSSIM of the whole reconstructed image and the comparison between the two methods are listed in Table 1~3 under the Quantization Parameter (QP) equal to 10, 20 and 30 respectively.

**Table 1.** Simulation results with QP=10

| Image | H.264-JM92 | | Our method | | Comparison (%) | |
|---|---|---|---|---|---|---|
| | Bits | MSSIM | Bits | MSSIM | Bit decrement | MSSIM decrement |
| Apple | 53664 | 0.9980 | 50200 | 0.9973 | 6.45 | 0.07 |
| Claire | 39056 | 0.9976 | 37480 | 0.9973 | 4.04 | 0.03 |
| MissA | 42072 | 0.9965 | 40160 | 0.9959 | 4.54 | 0.06 |
| Salesman | 94760 | 0.9994 | 91800 | 0.9991 | 3.12 | 0.03 |
| Bridge | 335464 | 0.9997 | 327456 | 0.9995 | 2.39 | 0.02 |
| Camera | 227768 | 0.9976 | 218104 | 0.9968 | 4.24 | 0.08 |
| Airplane | 722888 | 0.9973 | 687392 | 0.9963 | 4.91 | 0.10 |
| Baboon | 1331024 | 0.9993 | 1294408 | 0.9990 | 2.75 | 0.03 |
| Lena | 874480 | 0.9982 | 835024 | 0.9973 | 4.51 | 0.09 |
| Sailboat | 1042040 | 0.9984 | 1003040 | 0.9978 | 3.74 | 0.06 |
| Man | 4068144 | 0.9986 | 3911080 | 0.9980 | 3.86 | 0.06 |
| Pentagon | 4589568 | 0.9991 | 4437472 | 0.9987 | 3.31 | 0.04 |

Results in Table 1 to 3 show that the proposed algorithm can achieve about 2.2~6.45% bits saving while maintaining almost the same MSSIM index. In order to illustrate the perceptual quality of the reconstructed image, this paper shows the original and reconstructed images with the largest MSSIM decreased in Figure 1, from which it's clear that the visual difference between the two reconstructed images using H.264 JM92 (Fig.1 b) and our proposed algorithm (Fig.1 c) can hardly be found. That means the new R-D optimization algorithm can achieve about 2.2~6.45% bit saving while maintaining almost the same perceptual quality.

**Table 2.** Simulation results with QP=20

| Image | H.264-JM92 | | Our method | | Comparison (%) | |
|---|---|---|---|---|---|---|
| | Bits | MSSIM | Bits | MSSIM | Bit decrement | MSSIM decrement |
| Apple | 16728 | 0.9889 | 15984 | 0.9879 | 4.45 | 0.10 |
| Claire | 17800 | 0.9941 | 17088 | 0.9934 | 4.00 | 0.07 |
| MissA | 16088 | 0.9898 | 15296 | 0.9885 | 4.92 | 0.13 |
| Salesman | 51984 | 0.9951 | 50192 | 0.9938 | 3.45 | 0.13 |
| Bridge | 209880 | 0.9968 | 203096 | 0.9958 | 3.23 | 0.10 |
| Camera | 108824 | 0.9818 | 104976 | 0.9802 | 3.54 | 0.16 |
| Airplane | 293744 | 0.9833 | 280152 | 0.9815 | 4.63 | 0.18 |
| Baboon | 821424 | 0.9928 | 789032 | 0.9907 | 3.94 | 0.21 |
| Lena | 366624 | 0.9813 | 349608 | 0.9790 | 4.64 | 0.23 |
| Sailboat | 548400 | 0.9858 | 524272 | 0.9834 | 4.40 | 0.24 |
| Man | 2039408 | 0.9859 | 1938360 | 0.9829 | 4.95 | 0.30 |
| Pentagon | 2595528 | 0.9906 | 2477960 | 0.9878 | 4.53 | 0.28 |

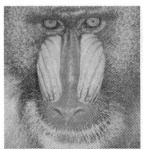  

(a) Baboon (original)    (b) Encoded by H.264 I-frame    (c) Encoded by our method
                         encoder with QP=30               with QP=30

**Fig. 1.** The reconstructed image by the two methods

**Table 3.** Simulation results with QP=30

| Image | H.264-JM92 | | Our method | | Comparison (%) | |
|---|---|---|---|---|---|---|
| | Bits | MSSIM | Bits | MSSIM | Bit decrement | MSSIM decrement |
| Apple | 5808 | 0.9762 | 5680 | 0.9731 | 2.20 | 0.32 |
| Claire | 8056 | 0.9829 | 7824 | 0.9812 | 2.88 | 0.17 |
| MissA | 6176 | 0.9718 | 5848 | 0.9681 | 5.31 | 0.38 |
| Salesman | 21416 | 0.9647 | 20528 | 0.9587 | 4.15 | 0.62 |
| Bridge | 97352 | 0.9714 | 92240 | 0.9647 | 5.25 | 0.69 |
| Camera | 48240 | 0.9561 | 46864 | 0.9512 | 2.85 | 0.51 |
| Airplane | 102904 | 0.9599 | 97920 | 0.9555 | 4.84 | 0.46 |
| Baboon | 361696 | 0.9457 | 343904 | 0.9368 | 4.92 | 0.94 |
| Lena | 102568 | 0.9468 | 98648 | 0.9420 | 3.82 | 0.51 |
| Sailboat | 173304 | 0.9362 | 163920 | 0.9306 | 5.41 | 0.60 |
| Man | 587952 | 0.9326 | 560816 | 0.9251 | 4.62 | 0.80 |
| Pentagon | 812728 | 0.9243 | 775392 | 0.9164 | 4.59 | 0.85 |

## 5  Conclusion

In this paper, we propose a new R-D optimization using the structural similarity (SSIM) instead of SSD for quality assessment in H.264 I-frame encoder. Experiments show that it can reduce approximately 2.2~6.45% bit rate while maintaining the same perceptual quality. The improvement of coding efficiency is not very large, but the new idea and the beginning results are inspiring. Thus, even better results maybe obtained by deeply studying. Furthermore, the proposed R-D optimization can be transplanted easily into motion estimation of inter frame coding.

## Acknowledgement

The work described in this paper was substantially supported by research projects from National Natural Science Foundation of China. [Project No. 60402015, No.60325310]

## References

1. Wiegand T., Sullivan G. J., Bjontegaard G., and Luthra A., "Overview of the H.264/AVC Video coding Standard," IEEE Trans. on CAS for video Technology, no.7, Vol. 13, pp.560-576, July 2003.
2. Wang Z., Bovik A. C., and Lu L., "Why is image quality assessment so difficult," in Proc. IEEE Int. Conf. Acoustics, speech, and Signal Processing, vol. 4, Orlando, FL, May 2002, pp.313–3316.
3. Wang Z., Bovik A. C., Sheikh H. R., and Simoncelli E. P., "Image quality assessment: from error visibility to structural similarity," IEEE Trans. Image Processing, vol. 13, no.4, pp. 600–612, Apr. 2004.

4. http://bs.hhi.de/~suehring/tml/download
5. Ma S.W., Gao W., Gao P., and Lu Y., "Rate control for advance video coding (AVC) standard," in Proc. ISCAS'03, vol.2, pp.II-892-II-895, May 2003.
6. Wiegand T. and Girod B., "Lagrangian multiplier selection in hybrid video coder control," in Proc. ICIP 2001, Thessaloniki, Greece, Oct. 2001.
7. Sullivan G. J. and Wiegand T., "Rate-Distortion Optimization for Video Compression", IEEE Signal Processing Magazine, vol. 15, no. 6, pp. 74-90, Nov. 1999

# BISK Scheme Applied to Sign Encoding and to Magnitude Refinement

Maria Bras-Amorós, Pere Guitart-Colom, Jorge González-Conejero,
Joan Serra-Sagristà, and Fernando García-Vílchez

Department of Information and Communications Engineering,
ETSE, Universitat Autònoma Barcelona, Spain
{Maria.Bras, Joan.Serra}@uab.es

**Abstract.** A shape-adaptive search is defined based on the BISK scheme and it is applied to sign encoding and magnitude refinement of images. It can be generalized to a complete bitplane encoder whose performance is comparable to that of other state-of-the-art encoders.

## 1 Introduction

Some competitive wavelet-based bitplane encoders, e.g. SPIHT [1] or SPECK [2], have no specific method to encode the sign of recently found significant coefficients nor the magnitude refinement bits; other encoders, e.g. JPEG2000 [3], EZBC [4], use an adaptive contextual arithmetic coder. From another perspective, Deever et al. [5] propose an alternative method that uses the wavelet transform properties to encode the transformed coefficients sign. Here we propose to adapt the notion of shape-adaptive coding [6] to define new methods to encode both the sign and the refinement bits of the coefficients.

The aim of shape-adaptive coding is to compress an image with a non-regular boundary assuming that both the encoder and the decoder know this boundary. Usually the image is located within a larger rectangular frame; pixels belonging to the image are named *opaque pixels*, pixels inside the frame but not belonging to the image are named *transparent pixels*. Some of the bitplane encoders used for shape-adaptive coding consist of well known regular-shape bitplane encoders, but treating only those bits corresponding to the opaque zone. This is the case of OB-SPIHT and OB-SPECK [7,8,9]. On the other hand, BISK [6,10] is a method based on SPECK, with the novelty that it alternates set partitioning with opaque zone shrinking. This shrinking step consists of reducing each partitioned subset to the minimum rectangular set containing all its opaque coefficients.

The approach we present here consists of encoding the sign bits and the refinement bits as if they were the coefficients of an irregular-shape image. For the case of sign encoding, from a whole image we consider opaques those coefficients that have been found significant in the last significance pass; then we encode the sign inside this opaque zone by using a BISK-based search. Similarly, to encode the refinement bits in a given bitplane, we split all the previously found significant coefficients in various opaque zones: two coefficients are placed in the same

J. Blanc-Talon et al. (Eds.): ACIVS 2005, LNCS 3708, pp. 442–451, 2005.
© Springer-Verlag Berlin Heidelberg 2005

opaque zone if all the first bits of their binary representation (up to the bitplane previous to the one currently being encoded) are the same; then, for each of these opaque zones we encode the refinement bits using the BISK-based search again.

Although the proposed methods for encoding the sign and the magnitude refinement bits may be considered independently and may be integrated to other bitplane encoders, the search scheme suggests a new complete wavelet transform-based bitplane encoder defined by a Repeated BISK-based search (REBISK). We will see that for some experiments, REBISK may give similar or even better results than other state-of-the-art encoders.

In Section 2 we define two-valued shape-adaptive search and describe both the classical method and the BISK-based search. In Section 3 we show how it can be applied to magnitude refinement and also to the significance pass. In Section 3.2 the two-valued shape-adaptive search is applied to sign encoding and the whole REBISK algorithm is stated. In Section 4 a performance comparison for REBISK, BISK, SPECK, SPIHT and JPEG2000 is provided.

## 2   Two-Valued Shape-Adaptive Search

The framework for the two-valued shape-adaptive search problem (TVSAS) is an irregular-boundary image with only two possible values ($1/0$ or $+/-$) where

```
procedure BBS(BF)                       procedure Partition(S,BF)
{                                       {
  if BF is empty then                     horizontal split S into S1 and S2:
    for each wavelet transf subband S       S1: size floor(y(S)/2) by x(S)
      SS=Shrink(S)                                #where
          #i.e. SS is the                         #y(S) is the n. of rows of S
          #minimal rectangle                      #x(S) is the n. of columns of S
          #containing S                   S2: size (y(S)-floor(y(S)/2)) by x(S)
      if SS is not empty                  Shrink(S1)
        append SS to BF                   Shrink(S2)

  append empty block to BF                if S1 is not empty then
                                            vertical split S1 into s1 and s2:
  S = extract first block of BF               s1: size y(S1) by floor(x(S1)/2)
  while S is not empty do                      s2: size y(S1) by (x(S1)-floor(y(S1)/2)
    if a in S                               Shrink(s1)
      emit 1                                Shrink(s2)
      Partition (S,BF)
    else                                  if S2 is not empty then
      emit 0                                vertical split S2 into s3 and s4:
      S = extract first element of BF         s3: size y(S2) by floor(x(S2)/2)
                                              s4: size y(S2) by (x(S2)-floor(y(S2)/2)
  while BF is not empty do                 Shrink(s3)
    S = extract first element of BF        Shrink(s4)
    Partition (S,BF)
}                                         for i from 1 to 4
                                          if si is not empty
                                            if a in si then
                                              emit 1
                                              if si is not a single coefficient
                                                append si to BF
                                            else
                                              emit 0
                                        }
```

**Fig. 1.** Functions used by the BISK-based search

the boundary is known by both the coder and the decoder. The aim is to define a coding method that determines the value of each point in the image. This is the case of determining the sign of recently found significant bits, or also the case of determining the refinement bits at a given bitplane.

We say *classical search* (CS) when referring to the method that scans the whole image in a predefined order and just sends the value of each point. On the other hand, we consider a *BISK-based search* (BBS). Suppose that the two possible values are $a$ and $b$, and that positions with value $a$ are to be determined.

We use a First-In-First-Out (FIFO) structure whose nodes are image blocks. This FIFO structure of blocks, named BF, may be either initialized to an empty FIFO, or to a FIFO containing somehow selected blocks. The blocks in BF have to be evaluated and, if needed, partitioned. After the partitioning, each of the resulting parts containing at least one $a$ is appended back to the BF. An empty block is inserted after the initial selected blocks to distinguish these blocks, which must be tested for significance, from those appended after partitioning a block (see Figure 3). Now, following the BISK scheme which alternates the SPECK block partitioning with the shrinking step, we can define the BBS procedure written down in Figure 1 and exemplified in Figure 3.

Notice that for the BBS, each block can be partitioned into 1, 2, 3 or 4 blocks, while for the original BISK, each block is partitioned into 1 or 2 blocks. The elements in each set of 1, 2, 3 or 4 bits denoting the significance of the corresponding blocks are encoded together to save bits using an *ad hoc* mapping.

## 3    TVSAS Applied to Encoding of Coefficients

### 3.1    Magnitude Encoding

**E–Sets and E–TVSAS.** Consider a wavelet transformed image as a set $I$ of coefficients. Let $min$, $med$ and $max$ be three values with $min \leqslant med \leqslant max$. Define the following subsets of $I$:

$E$–*opaques(min, med, max)*= $\{x \in I \mid min \leqslant |x| < max\}$.
$E$–*significants(min, med, max)*= $\{x \in I \mid med \leqslant |x| < max\}$.
$E$–*insignificants(min, med, max)*= $\{x \in I \mid min \leqslant |x| < med\}$.

Denote $E$–*TVSAS(min, med, max)* a TVSAS method that classifies E–significants and E–insignificants from the irregularly bounded set E–opaques. As examples of E–TVSAS methods, we consider:

$E$–*CS:* For each element in E–opaques, emit a 1 if it is in E–significants or a 0 otherwise.
$E$–*SBBS:* Determine the elements in E–significants among the ones in E–opaques by using the BISK-based search.
$E$–*IBBS:* Determine the elements in E–insignificants among the ones in E–opaques by using the BISK-based search.
$E$–*comb:* Shortest chain in $\{\ 0|E$–$CS,\ \ 10|E$–$SBBS,\ \ 11|E$–$IBBS\ \}$.

Following the same ideas, one can define the sets $E^+$-*opaques*, $E^+$-*signifi-cants*, and $E^+$-*insignificants* (respectively $E^-$-*opaques*, $E^-$-*significants*, and $E^-$-*insignificants*) containing the positive (respectively negative) values of the analo-gous E–sets. Then $E^+$-*TVSAS* and $E^-$-*TVSAS* methods can be defined as for E–sets.

**Significance Pass.** Let $MAX$ be the maximum absolute value among the coefficients in $I$ and threshold $T = 2^{\lfloor log_2(MAX) \rfloor}$. The following procedures are consecutive significance passes: E–TVSAS(0,T,2T), E–TVSAS(0,T/2,T), E–TVSAS(0,T/4,T/2),...

Notice that if E–SBBS is used as the E–TVSAS method, and at each step the structure BF is initialized with the insignificant blocks from the previous bitplane, these significance passes are approximately the significance passes of SPECK. The unique difference is that SPECK uses its $I$ sets while here we only consider rectangular sets.

**Refinement Passes.** An E–TVSAS(T, 3T/2, 2T) procedure after the sec-ond significance pass, namely E–TVSAS(0, T/2, T), gives the first magnitude refinement pass. Similarly, the three procedures E–TVSAS(T/2, 3T/4, T), E–TVSAS(T, 5T/4, 3T/2) and E–TVSAS(3T/2, 7T/4, 2T) after the third signifi-

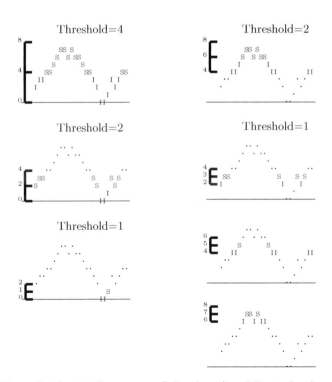

**Fig. 2.** E-sets for the significance pass (left column) and E-sets for the refinement pass (right column)

cance pass E–TVSAS(0, T/4, T/2) give the second magnitude refinement pass, and so on. Thus, the following algorithm yields a coding method for the absolute values in $I$.

```
for t from T to 1 by -1
   for min from 0 to 2T-2t by 2t
      E-TVSAS(min, min+t, min+2t);
```

Figure 2 shows the E–sets used for the significance pass and for the refinement passes.

### 3.2   Sign Encoding

As before, let $min$ and $max$ be two values with $min \leqslant max$ and define the subset $S\text{-}opaques(min,max)=\{x \in I \mid min \leqslant |x| < max\}$. We also denote $S\text{-}TVSAS(min,max)$ a TVSAS method that classifies the positive and negative values in the (irregularly bounded) set S–opaques(min,max). As S–TVSAS methods, we consider:

$S\text{-}CS$: For each element in S–opaques, emit a 1 if it is positive or a 0 otherwise.
$S\text{-}PBBS$: Determine the positive values in S–opaques by using the BISK-based search.
$S\text{-}NBBS$: Determine the negative values in S–opaques by using the BISK-based search.
$S\text{-}comb$: Shortest chain in $\{\ 0|S\text{-}CS,\ \ 10|S\text{-}PBBS,\ \ 11|S\text{-}NBBS\ \}$.

### 3.3   Image Coding

Now, the following algorithm yields a complete quality progressive image coding method.

```
for t from T to 1 by -1
   E-TVSAS(0, t, 2t);            /* Significance Pass */
   S-TVSAS(t, 2t);              /* Sign encoding      */
   for min from 2t to 2T-2t by 2t /* Refinement Pass  */
   E-TVSAS(min, min+t, min+2t);
```

The complete encoding algorithm that uses $E^+/E^-$–comb and S–comb as the E–TVSAS and S–TVSAS methods is named REBISK because of the Repeated E–BISK-based search.

## 4   Experimental Results

The lossy compression performance of REBISK is here compared to other coding systems for some images of the ISO/CCITT Corpus.

The ISO/CCITT Corpus is the corpus taken by the Joint Photographic Experts Group to evaluate the performance of classical JPEG encoding method on still images. It consists of 9 images (balloons, barbara1, barbara2, board, boats, girl, goldhill, hotel and zelda) of size 720×576. The original images have been

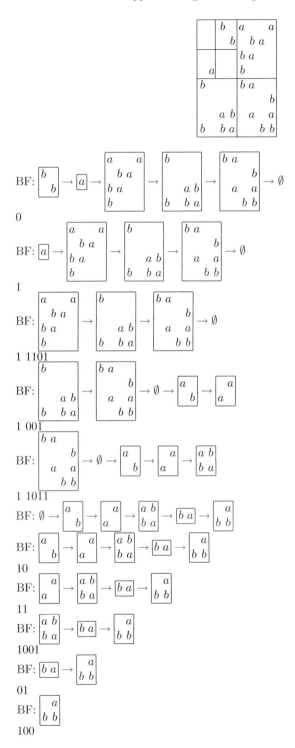

**Fig. 3.** Example of BISK based search. The positions with value $a$ are to be determined among the opaque positions of the irregular table at the top of the page.

**Table 1.** PSNR performance comparison (in dB) for boats

| Rate in bpp | REBISK | BISK | SPECK | SPIHT | JPEG2K |
|---|---|---|---|---|---|
| 0.0015 | 17.51 | 17.15 | 17.12 | 16.56 | 14.15 |
| 0.0026 | 19.38 | 18.52 | 18.43 | 18.35 | 14.15 |
| 0.0056 | 20.82 | 20.42 | 20.38 | 20.18 | 14.15 |
| 0.0137 | 22.72 | 22.53 | 22.50 | 22.38 | 21.56 |
| 0.0386 | 25.16 | 25.15 | 25.14 | 25.03 | 24.85 |
| 0.1029 | 28.13 | 28.18 | 28.17 | 28.14 | 28.17 |
| 0.2446 | 31.74 | 31.81 | 31.84 | 31.82 | 32.05 |
| 0.4958 | 35.69 | 35.79 | 35.82 | 35.81 | 36.14 |
| 0.9214 | 39.81 | 39.93 | 39.96 | 39.95 | 40.30 |

**Table 2.** PSNR performance comparison (in dB) for barbara2

| Rate in bpp | REBISK | BISK | SPECK | SPIHT | JPEG2K |
|---|---|---|---|---|---|
| 0.0019 | 16.39 | 16.08 | 16.08 | 15.97 | 13.68 |
| 0.0032 | 18.34 | 17.81 | 17.84 | 17.76 | 13.68 |
| 0.0062 | 19.55 | 19.37 | 19.38 | 19.13 | 13.68 |
| 0.0152 | 21.05 | 20.97 | 20.97 | 20.87 | 20.03 |
| 0.0442 | 22.73 | 22.73 | 22.74 | 22.62 | 22.61 |
| 0.1592 | 25.86 | 25.84 | 25.84 | 25.71 | 26.02 |
| 0.3784 | 30.05 | 30.01 | 30.05 | 29.98 | 30.59 |
| 0.7481 | 34.54 | 34.52 | 34.56 | 34.53 | 35.27 |
| 1.3126 | 39.10 | 39.15 | 39.19 | 39.17 | 39.78 |

**Table 3.** PSNR performance comparison (in dB) for girl

| Rate in bpp | REBISK | BISK | SPECK | SPIHT | JPEG2K |
|---|---|---|---|---|---|
| 0.0017 | 18.37 | 17.10 | 17.10 | 16.76 | 14.37 |
| 0.0028 | 20.16 | 19.03 | 19.10 | 19.09 | 14.37 |
| 0.0052 | 21.81 | 21.30 | 21.38 | 21.16 | 14.37 |
| 0.0120 | 24.02 | 23.85 | 23.86 | 23.74 | 21.91 |
| 0.0287 | 26.20 | 26.19 | 26.19 | 26.06 | 25.55 |
| 0.0744 | 29.11 | 29.14 | 29.15 | 29.08 | 28.97 |
| 0.1748 | 32.37 | 32.43 | 32.45 | 32.41 | 32.46 |
| 0.3811 | 35.95 | 36.02 | 36.05 | 36.03 | 36.21 |
| 0.7685 | 39.70 | 39.80 | 39.83 | 39.79 | 40.04 |

cut to images of size 512×512 (centered in the original image) with 8 bits per pixel resolution.

BISK, SPIHT and SPECK results are produced with QccPack [11], version 0.47. JPEG2000 results are produced with Kakadu [12], version v4.4. Both Qcc-Pack and Kakadu are employed with the default parameters, except for the

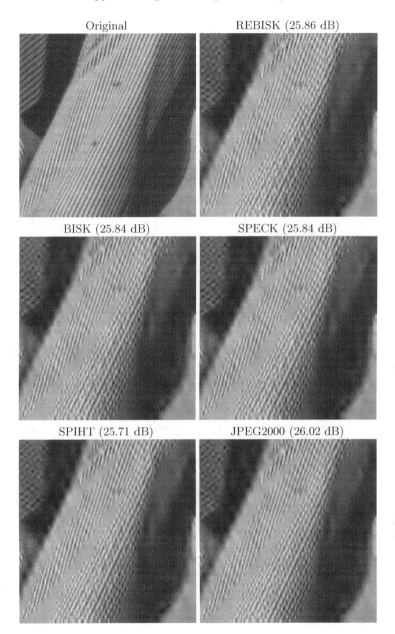

**Fig. 4.** Visual comparison for barbara2 at 0.16 bpp, compression factor about 50:1

type of DWT, the number of DWT levels and the transmission rate, selected accordingly. For all coding techniques, five levels of the 9/7 DWT are applied.

The distortion has been measured using the Peak Signal to Noise Ratio (PSNR), a measure accounting for the similarity between the original image

$I$ and the recovered image $I^*$, given in $dB$; for images with $B$ bit-depth resolution per pixel, $PSNR = 10\,log_{10}\frac{(2^B-1)^2}{MSE}$, where the Mean Square Error (MSE) is given by $MSE = \frac{1}{N_x}\frac{1}{N_y}\sum_i^{N_x}\sum_j^{N_y}(I_{ij}-I_{ij}^*)^2$.

Tables 1, 2 and 3 show the rate distortion performance of the different coding techniques when applied to boats, barbara2 and girl. The bit rates provided correspond to the bit budget spent by REBISK for each successive bitplane. Figure 4 allows to visually compare the reconstruction quality of the evaluated coding systems. The depicted area, whose size is 128 × 128, belongs to the rigth bottom corner of barbara2. The transmission rate is 0.1592 bpp, which corresponds to a compression factor of approximately 50:1.

## 5    Conclusions

In this paper we have introduced a new approach for encoding sign and refinement bits. Each refinement pass and each sign encoding procedure is seen as a two-valued shape-adaptive search. To proceed with each search we defined BISK-based schemes which combine the block partitioning of SPECK with the block shrinking of BISK. In addition, the significance pass can be treated also as a two-valued search and, in this way, the whole bitplane encoder REBISK has been defined by a repetition of the BISK-based scheme. For high compression ratios, REBISK provides better coding performance than other state-of-the-art coding techniques. For moderate bit rates (compression ratio 8:1 for 8 bpp images), REBISK is not as competitive as the other techniques, probably because it is the single technique not employing any adaptive arithmetic encoder. The behavior difference between high compression ratios and low compression ratios may be due to the advantage of the correlation between magnitudes having the same most significant bits up to a certain point, expected to be higher for the first bitplanes.

## Acknowledgements

This work has been partially supported by the Spanish Government MCYT Grant TIC2003-08604-C04-01 and by FEDER.

## References

1. Said, A., Pearlman, W.A.: A new, fast, and efficient image codec based on set partitioning in hierarchical trees. IEEE Transactions on Circuits and Systems for Video Technology **6** (1996) 243–250
2. Pearlman, W., Islam, A., Nagaraj, N., Said, A.: Efficient, low-complexity image coding with a set-partitioning embedded block coder. IEEE Transactions on Circuits and Systems for Video Technology **14** (2004) 1219–1235
3. Taubman, D., Marcellin, M.: JPEG2000: Image Compression Fundamentals, Standards, and Practice. Volume 642. Kluwer International Series in Engineering and Computer Science (2002)

 4. Hsiang, S.T.: Embedded image coding using zeroblocks of subband/wavelet co-efficients and context modeling. In: IEEE Data Compression Conference, IEEE (2001) 83–92
 5. Deever, A.T., Hemami, S.S.: Efficient sign coding and estimation of zero-quantized coefficients in embedded wavelet image codecs. IEEE Trans. Image Process. **12** (2003) 420–430
 6. Fowler, J.E.: Shape-adaptive coding using binary set splitting with K-D trees. In: IEEE International Conference on Image Processing. Volume 2., Singapore (2004) 1301–1304
 7. Minami, G., Xiong, Z., Wang, A., Mehrotra, S.: 3-D wavelet coding of video with arbitrary regions of support. IEEE Transactions on Circuits and Systems for Video Technology **11** (2001) 1063 – 1068
 8. Lu, Z., Pearlman, W.: Wavelet coding of video object by object-based SPECK algorithm. In: Proc. of SPC, Seoul, Korea (2001) 413–416
 9. Penedo, M., Pearman, W., Tahoces, P., Souto, M., Vidal, J.: Region-based wavelet coding methods for digital mammography. IEEE Transacions on Medical Imaging **22** (2003) 1288 – 1296
10. Rucker, J., Fowler, J.: Coding of ocean-temperature volumes using binary set splitting with K-D trees. In: IEEE International Geoscience and Remote Sensing Symposium. (2004)
11. Fowler, J.E.: QccPack: An open-source software library for quantization, compression, and coding. In Tescher, A., ed.: Applications of Digital Image Processing XXIII. Volume 4115., San Diego, CA, USA (2000) 294–301
12. Taubman, D.: Kakadu software. http://www.kakadusoftware.com/ (2000)

# Skeletonization of Noisy Images via the Method of Legendre Moments

K. Zenkouar, H. El Fadili, and H. Qjidaa

Faculté des science dhar el mehraz,
Département de physique, Lessi,
B.P. 1796 Fes Maroc
{Kzenkouar, el_fadili_hakim}@hotmail.com
qjidah@yahoo.fr

**Abstract.** This paper presents a new concept of skeletonization which produces a graph containing all the topological information needed to derive a skeleton of noisy shapes, the proposed statistical method is based on Legendre moment theory controlled by Maximum Entropy Principle (M.E.P.). We propose a new approach for estimating the underlying probability density function (p.d.f.) of input data set. Indeed the p.d.f. is expanded in terms of Legendre polynomials by means of the Legendre moments. Then the order of the expansion is selected according to the (M.E.P.). The points corresponding to the local maxima of the selected p.d.f. will be true points of the skeleton to be extracted by the proposed algorithm. We have tested the proposed Legendre Moment Skeletonization Method (LMSM) on a variety of real and simulated noisy images, it produces excellent and visually appealing results, with comparison to some well known methods.

## 1 Introduction

In the past several decades, a large number of skeletonization algorithms have been developed [1-5]. Of the many methods which can be used to generate these and other skeletal shape descriptors most can be put into four categories: iterative erosion of the shape boundary i.e. thinning [6], wave propagation from the boundary [7], detection of "local maxima" on a distance transform [8], and analytical methods, for simple shapes, following some form of function approximation, e.g. polygon approximation or spline fitting [9], [10]. These approaches present several advantages, however the main drawback of most of these methods is their noise sensitivity.

In this paper a novel skeletonization approach, is developed using a statistical method based on the estimation of probability density function p.d.f. where the skeleton is defined as the local maxima of this p.d.f.

Our proposed approach is based on the expansion of a multivariate function p.d.f. in terms of Legendre polynomials by means of Legendre moment. For this purpose the p.d.f. is approximated by a truncated series of polynomials. As the determination of the expansion order is a difficult problem in the framework of unsupervised classification we propose the determination of the optimal order for which the estimated p.d.f. has maximum entropy.

J. Blanc-Talon et al. (Eds.): ACIVS 2005, LNCS 3708, pp. 452–459, 2005.
© Springer-Verlag Berlin Heidelberg 2005

As the solution to this problem is mathematically too complexe to be tractable, we introduce an exhaustive search for the optimal order. We propose to estimate the p.d.f. for different orders and to select the optimal one as the one for which the entropy reaches a maximum according to the Maximum Entropy Principal M.E.P. [11-15]. This latter has been used for clustering, see for example [16] and for image restoration [17]. Having the optimal p.d.f., the true points of the skeleton are the local maxima of the p.d.f. extraction of the local maxima of the p.d.f. is carried out using the last phase of the proposed algorithm.

As a summary, our proposed LMSM skeletonization method based on the combination of the moment theory and MEP as a selection criterion, is composed of the three following steps:

1- Computation the p.d.f. using the Legendre moment.
2- Estimation of the optimal p.d.f. using MEP method.
3- Extraction of the local maxima of the optimal p.d.f. taken as the skeleton points.

The most important advantages of our method are the following:

1- No a priori information about the original image is required.
2- High robustness against noisy images.
3- The preservation of geometric properties of the original image.
4- Avoid preprocessing techniques which are time-consuming procedure.

The paper is organized as follows: the next section describes the basis of our statistical model, using Legendre moment. The maximum entropy principal is given in section 3. The details of our skeletonization algorithm is presented in section 4. Section 5 performs main results and performances of our skeletonization method. Finally section 6 deals with the summary of important results and conclusions of this work.

## 2 Statistical Modelisation Using Legendre Moment

### 2.1 Legendre Moments

The Legendre moments of order $(p+q)$ is defined for a given real image intensity function $f(x,y)$ as in [18]:

$$\lambda_{p,q} = \frac{(2p+1)(2q+1)}{4} \int_R \int_R P_p(x) \ P_q(y) \ f(x,y)dxdy \cdot \tag{1}$$

where $f(x,y)$ is assumed to have bounded support.

The aforementioned properties of the Legendre moments are valid as long as one uses a true analog image function. In practice, the Legendre moments have to be computed from sampled data, i.e., the rectangular sampling of the original image function $f(x,y)$, producing the set of samples $f(x_i,y_j)$ with a (M,N) array of pixels. The piecewise constant approximation of $f(x,y)$ in (1), proposed recently by Liao and Pawlak [19] yields the following approximation of $\lambda_{p,q}$ :

$$\hat{\lambda}_{p,q} = \sum_{i=1}^{M} \sum_{j=1}^{N} H_{p,q}(x_i, y_j) f(x_i, y_j) \quad \cdot \tag{2}$$

With the supposition that $f(x,y)$ is piecewise constant over the interval $[x_i - \frac{\Delta x}{2}, x_i + \frac{\Delta x}{2}] \times [y_j - \frac{\Delta y}{2}, y_j + \frac{\Delta y}{2}]$ and where

$$H_{p,q}(x_i, y_j) = \frac{(2p+1)(2q+1)}{4} \int_{x_i - \frac{\Delta x}{2}}^{x_i + \frac{\Delta x}{2}} \int_{y_j - \frac{\Delta y}{2}}^{y_j + \frac{\Delta y}{2}} P_p(x) P_q(y) dx dy \quad \cdot \tag{3}$$

represents the integration of the polynomial $P_p(x) P_q(y)$ around the $(x_i, y_j)$ pixel.

This approximation allows a good quality of reconstructed image by reducing the reconstruction error. $\hat{\lambda}_{p,q}$ Will be used for the estimation of the image function in the next section.

### 2.2 Estimation of the Probability Density Function

The image function reconstructed from $\hat{\lambda}_{p,q}$ up to a given order $\theta$ can be defined as:

$$\hat{f}_\theta(x_i, y_j) = \sum_{p=0}^{\theta} \sum_{q=0}^{p} \hat{\lambda}_{p-q} P_{p-q}(x_i) P_q(y_j) \cdot \tag{4}$$

The estimated probability density function p.d.f. for a given order $\theta$ denoted $\hat{p}_\theta(x_i, y_j)$ is obtained by normalizing $\hat{f}_\theta(x_i, y_j)$ [13], [15]:

$$\hat{p}_\theta(x_i, y_j) = \frac{\hat{f}_\theta(x_i, y_j)}{\sum_{x_i, y_j \in \Omega} \hat{f}_\theta(x_i, y_j)} \quad \cdot \tag{5}$$

where

$$\sum_{x_i, y_j \in \Omega} \hat{p}_\theta(x_i, y_j) = 1 \quad \cdot \tag{6}$$

and $0 \le \hat{p}_\theta(x_i, y_j) \le 1$, $\Omega$ is the image plane.

The estimated p.d.f. depends only on the expansion order $\theta$, a criterion for choosing this order is explained in the next paragraph according to the maximum entropy principal

## 3 Optimal Order Moments Selection Using MEP

We introduce the maximum entropy principle M.E.P. for the search of this optimal order, this automatic technique can estimate the optimal number of moments directly from the available data and does not require any a priori image information specially for noisy images.

Let $G_w$ be a set of estimated underlying probability density function for various Legendre moment orders $\theta$ :

$$G_w = \{\hat{p}_\theta / \theta = 1 \ldots \ldots \omega\} . \tag{7}$$

By applying the maximum entropy principle for noisy images, we deduce that among these estimates of the probability density function, there is one and only one probability density function denoted $\hat{p}_\theta^*(x_i, y_j)$ whose entropy is maximum [13],[17] and which represents the optimal probability density function, and then gives the optimal order of moments.

The Shannon entropy of $\hat{p}_\theta^*(x_i, y_j)$ is defined as:

$$S(\hat{p}_\theta) = - \sum_{x_i, y_j \in \Omega} \hat{p}_\theta(x_i, y_j) \log(\hat{p}_\theta(x_i, y_j)) . \tag{8}$$

and the optimal $\hat{p}_\theta^*$ is such that

$$S(\hat{p}_\theta^*) = MAX\{S(\hat{p}_\theta) / \hat{p}_\theta \in GW\} . \tag{9}$$

The process of determinating the optimal order $\theta$ consists in estimating the p.d.f. for different orders and selecting the optimal one as the one for which the entropy reaches maximum. The following is basic algorithm which consists in an exhaustive search to determine the optimal order which maximises $S(\hat{p}_\theta^*)$ :

1- Initialise $\theta$

2- Compute the p.d.f. $\hat{p}_\theta$ and its corresponding Shannon entropy $S(\hat{p}_\theta)$

3- If $\hat{p}_\theta$ is maximum, then $\theta$ is optimal and $\hat{p}_\theta = \hat{p}_\theta^*$, else $\theta = \theta + 1$ and go to 2.

Then, having $\hat{p}_\theta^*$, we assign to each point of the optimal p.d.f. $\hat{p}_\theta^*(x_i, y_j)$ defined by (5). In this case, the "good data" are the set of points belonging to the mode of $\hat{p}_\theta^*$. By extracting the local maxima of $\hat{p}_\theta^*$, we can determine the exact points of the skeleton. In the next section the details of our skeleton extraction algorithm is presented.

## 4 Skeleton Extraction Algorithm Using the Legendre Moment

We define the skeleton as the local maxima of the estimated probability density function selected in the previous section. The extraction of these local maxima allows us to determine the skeleton associated to the shape. The general idea of this algorithm consists of a successive points extraction presenting a local maxima of the selected optimal p.d.f..

The procedure consists in making a sweep mask of size 3x3 on all the image. The comparison of the p.d.f. estimated for the central pixel of the mask with its close eight neighbours following the eight directions, allows to confirm if this central pixel is a point of the skeleton or no.

Indeed two types of comparison are undertaken, a comparison following lines and columns and a comparison following the diagonal. A pixel is a point candidate if it presents a local maximum compared to its four neighbours following the lines and column direction (fig.1c ) or if it present a local maxima compared to its four neighbours following the diagonal direction (fig.1d).

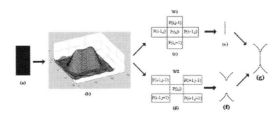

**Fig. 1.** Rectangle shape skeleton obtained by LMSM approach: a) rectangle shape, b) optimal p.d.f. corresponding to order 11, c) the mask w1 following lines and columns direction, d) the mask w2 following diagonal direction, e) extracted skeleton following lines and columns, f) extracted skeleton following the diagonal, g) resulting skeleton of the rectangle shape

## 5   Experimental Results

In this section, a comparison study is carried out on simulated and real images. The proposed LMSM skeletonization method is compared to Distance Transform and Parallel Thinning Algorithms.

To see the performance of the proposed skeletonization algorithm when applied to Hand-written characters, the LMSM is experimented with a hand-written word "moi" scanned and binarised on (100x100) image matrix (Fig.2a), then corrupted by an impulsive noise affected 10% of pixels (Fig.2b). Figure 1e illustrates the resulting skeleton generated by LMSM. The comparison of the skeletons generated by our method with distance transform and parallel thinning algorithm demonstrates clearly the high performance of the proposed skeletonization method against noise.

Figure 3 shows the performance and the potential of the proposed approach and its insensitivity to different noise values. The LMSM approach is applied to hand-written digit '3', '9' with image size 60x60 and '61' with image size (80x80), the presented figures show that our method performs well even with high noise levels.

Another example investigating the behaviour of the LMSM method is presented applied to a 'plane' scanned and binarized on 100x100 image matrix (Fig.4a) corrupted by an gaussian noise having a (Signal to Noise Ratio ) SNR=10db. The p.d.f. obtained by M.E.P. corresponding to optimal moment order is presented in Fig.4f. The skeleton obtained by our approach LMSM demonstrates the consistency of our algorithm against high level gaussian noise.

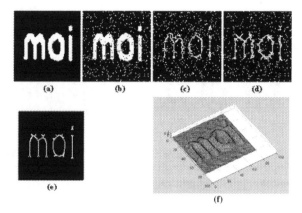

**Fig. 2.** Skeletonization of Hand-written word 'moi' by the proposed approach. a) original image. b) input noisy image with impulsive noise affecting 10% of pixels. c) skeleton obtained using the Distance Transform. d) skeleton obtained using the Parallel Thinning Algorithms. e) skeleton obtained using the proposed LMSM. f) estimated p.d.f. for optimal order 45.

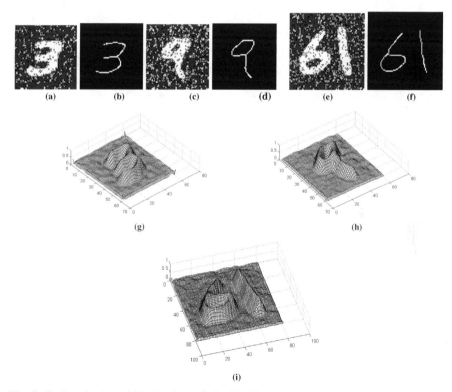

**Fig. 3.** Skeletonization of Hand-written digit '3', '9'and '61' by the proposed approach. The input noisy images, with impulsive noise affecting 15% of pixels (a), 25% of pixels (c), 35% of pixels (e), corresponding skeletons obtained with LMSM method for orders 27 (b), 30 (d), 38 (f) and obtained p.d.f. for those optimal orders.

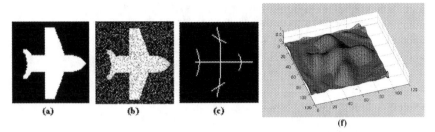

**Fig. 4.** Skeletonization of 'plane' shape by the proposed LMSM. a) original image and b) corresponding gaussian noisy image with SNR=10db. c) Skeleton for the noisy 'plane' shape by the proposed LMSM. f) estimated p.d.f. for optimal order 13.

## 6 Conclusion

In this work, we have proposed a statistical technique for skeletonization noisy images using the Legendre moment theory and the Maximum Entropy Principal. This skeletonization method based on the combination of the moment theory and M.E.P. are conceptually articuled into three steps. In the first one, the computation of p.d.f. using Legendre moment is carried out. In the second, the estimation of optimal p.d.f. is selected using M.E.P. criterion. Finally, the subset of local maxima pixels of the optimal p.d.f. are selected as belonging to the skeleton. The advantages of our algorithm is that no a priori information about the original image is required. Consequently, the practical implementation of the approach does not require any parameter setting. Through a comparative study with conventional methods, it performed quite well in experimental tests and the skeletonization has been greatly improved which demonstrates the robustness of the proposed approach against different and high noise levels.

## References

[1] L. Lam, S. W. Lee, and C. Y. Suen," Thinning Methodologies-A Comprehensive Survey," IEEE Trans. Pattern Anal. Machine Intell., Vol. 14, no 9, pp.869-885, September 1992.

[2] N. H. Han, C. W. La, and P. K. Rhee," An Efficient Fully Parallel Thinning Algorithm," in Proc. IEEE Int. Conf. Document Analysis and Recognition, Vol. 1, pp. 137-141 (1997).

[3] L. Huang, G. Wan, and C.Liu,"An Improved Parallel Thinnig Algorithm," ICDAR 2003,pp. 780-783.

[4] G. Borgefors, G. Ramella, G. Sanniti di Baja," Hierarchical Decomposition of Multi-scale Skeletons," IEEE Trans. On Pattern Analysis and Machine Intelligence, Vol. 23, No. 11, pp. 1296-1312, Nov. 2001.

[5] S. Svensson, I. Nystrom, G. Borgefors," On reversible skeletonization using anchor points from distance transforms," Int. Journal of Visual Communication and Image Representation, Vol. 10, pp. 379-397, 1999.

[6] C. J. Hildich. Linear skeletons from square cupboards. In B.Meltzer and D.Michie, editors, Machine intelligence IV, chapter 22, pages 403-420. Elsevier,New York, 1969.

[7]  H. Blum. Biological shape and visual science (part 1). Journal of Theoretical biology, 38(2):205-287, February 1973.

[8]  C.Arcelli and G. S. Di Baja. Feeding local maxima in a pseudo-Euclidian distance transform. Computer Graphics Vision and Image Processing, 43:361-367, 1988.

[9]  M. Brady and H. Asada. Smoothed local symmetries and their implementation. A.I. Memo 757, MIT, February 1984.

[10]  P. Saint-marc and G. Medioni. B-spline contour representation and symmetry detection. Technical Report IRIS #262, institute for robotics and intelligent systems, university of Southern California, Los Angeles, California 90089-0273, 1990.

[11]  E. T. jaynes, On the rationale of maximum entropy methods, Proceedings of the IEEE vol. 70, no. 9, Sept. 1982.

[12]  J. M. Van Campenout, and T. Cover, Maximum entropy and conditional probability, IEEE trans. on Information theory, vol. II, 27,no 4, Jul. 1988.

[13]  H. Qjidaa and L. Radouane, Robust line fitting in a noisy image by the method of moments, IEEE Trans. Pattern. Anal. Machine Intell. 21 (1999) 1216-1223.

[14]  J. M. Jolion, P. Meer, and S. Bataouche, Robust clustering with application in comptar vision, IEEE Trans. Pattern Anal. Machine Intell., Vol. 13, no 8, pp.791-802, Aug. 1991.

[15]  H. El Fadili, K. Zenkouar and H. Qjidaa, "Lapped Block Image Analysis Via the Method of Legendre Moments," EURASIP Journal on Applied Signal Processing, Vol. 2003, No.9, pp.902-913, 2003.

[16]  B. Gerardo and X. Liu, A Least biased fuzzy clustering method, IEEE Trans. Pattern. Anal. Machine. Intell, vol. 16, No. 9, pp. 954-960, Sept, 1994

[17]  X. Zhuang, R. M. Haralick and Y. Zhao, Maximum entropy image reconstruction, IEEE Trans. On Signal Processing. Vol. 39, no. 6, pp. 1478-1480, Jun. 1991

[18]  C. H. Teh and R.T. Chin, On image analysis by the methods of moments, IEEE Trans. Pattern Anal. Machine Intell. 10 (1988) 496-512.

[19]  S. X. Liao and Miroslaw Pawlak, On image analysis by moments, IEEE Trans. Pattern Anal. Machine Intell. 18 (1996) 254-266.

# The Hough Transform Application
# Including Its Hardware Implementation

Witold Zorski

Cybernetics Faculty,
Military University of Technology,
S. Kaliskiego 2, 00-908 Warsaw, Poland
wzorski@ita.wat.edu.pl

**Abstract.** This paper presents an application of the Hough transform to the tasks of identifying irregular patterns. The presented method is based on the Hough transform for irregular objects, with a parameter space defined by translation, rotation and scaling operations. The technique may be used in a robotic system, identification system or for image analysis, directly on grey-level images. An example application of the Hough transform to a robot monitoring within computer vision systems is presented. A hardware implementation of the Hough technique is introduced which accelerates the calculations considerably.

## 1  Introduction to the Hough Transform

The Hough transform was patented in 1962 as a method for detecting complex patterns of points in a binary image [4]. It introduced the possibility of determining a set of parameters circumscribing the searched pattern. The problem of complex pattern detection in an image is converted into one that searches for local maxima in a parameter space. This method has become very popular.

We may assume that the Hough transform is based on a representation of a given image $I$ into the **accumulator array** $A$, which is defined as follows

$$A : P \to N, \qquad \text{where } P = P_1 \times P_2 \times \cdots \times P_p. \tag{1}$$

The symbol $P_i \subset N$ determines the range of $i$-parameters of a $p$-dimensional space $P$. Determining array $A$ is conducted through the calculation of partial values for points of an object in image $I$ and adding them to the previous ones which constitutes a process of accumulation. Initially, all elements of array $A$ are set to zero.

This paper presents an application of the Hough technique to the tasks of irregular grey-level pattern recognition in the case of a robot monitoring within computer vision systems. It is based on the Hough transform with a parameter space defined by translation, rotation and scaling operations. A fundamental element of this method is a generalisation of the Hough transform for grey-level images. The Hough transform has been already described by the author in details [7]. Nevertheless a short introduction to the generalised form of the technique will be given in this paper too.

J. Blanc-Talon et al. (Eds.): ACIVS 2005, LNCS 3708, pp. 460–467, 2005.
© Springer-Verlag Berlin Heidelberg 2005

## 2  The Hough Transform for Irregular Objects

In 1981 Deans noticed [2] that the Hough transform for straight lines was a specific case of the more general Radon transform known since 1917, which is defined as (for function $I(x,y)$ in two-dimensional Euclidean space):

$$H(\rho,\alpha) = \int_{-\infty}^{\infty}\int_{-\infty}^{\infty} I(x,y)\delta(\rho - x\cos(\alpha) - y\sin(\alpha))dxdy , \qquad (2)$$

where $\delta$ is the delta function. This result shows that the function $I(x,y)$ is integrated along the straight line determined by the parametric equation $\rho = x\cos(\alpha) + y\sin(\alpha)$. The Radon transform is equivalent to the Hough transform when considering binary images (i.e. when the function $I(x,y)$ takes values $0$ or $1$). The Radon transform for shapes other than straight lines can be obtained by replacing the delta function argument by a function, which forces integration of the image along contours appropriate to the shape.

The existing algorithms usually apply to the Hough transform operation on binary images. The Radon transform is affirmed to be equivalent to the Hough transform only in the case of binary images. In the case of grey-level or colour images the issue becomes more complicated. Equations defining the Hough transform limit the application to binary images only. A set of transforms are applied which are aimed at converting the initial image into a binary image with minimal loss of information. In the case of analysing grey-level images, it is not always admissible to loose important information in the process of binarisation. Usually information loss is not harmful only in the case of images that include high contrast objects.

If we consider equation (2), which defines the Radon transform, we may state that there are no limitations on the value of function $I(x,y)$. It means that it may be applied directly to grey-level images. However, the following statement is raised: how do we modify the Hough transform for irregular patterns? The problem lies in the process of accumulation in the accumulator array (1).

## 3  Generalisation of the Hough Transform for Grey-Level Images

Let us first define the concept of a grey-level image, an object appearing in such an image and the concept of a grey-level pattern in a computer vision system.

**Definitions**
An **image with 256 grey levels** means a set of points, which have a value or "shade" from the set $\{0,...,255\}$. Such an image may be presented as follows

$$I_G : D \rightarrow \{0,...,255\}, \qquad \text{where } D = [1,...,W]\times[1,...,K] \subset N^2 . \qquad (3)$$

**Object** $b(I_G)$ in image $I_G$ is any fragment of that image which may be recorded in terms of

$$Q_G : D_Q \to \{0,\ldots,255\}, \quad \text{where} \quad D_Q \subset D = [1,\ldots,W] \times [1,\ldots,K] \subset N^2. \tag{4}$$

<u>Remark</u>: Identifying an object with an image fragment is a consequence of a set of values taken by function $I_G$.

**Pattern** $M_P$ means an image (square matrix) of size $N_P \times N_P$ which is as

$$M_P : D_P \to \{0,\ldots,255\}, \quad \text{where} \quad D_P = [1,\ldots,N_P] \times [1,\ldots,N_P] \subset N^2. \tag{5}$$

**The Hough transform** $H(x_T, y_T, \alpha)$ for grey-level image $I_G(x,y)$ in the process of identification of pattern $M_P$ is given by

$$H(x_T, y_T, \alpha) = \sum_{(x_i, y_i) \in M_P} h(x_i, y_i, x_T, y_T, \alpha), \tag{6}$$

where

$$h(x_i, y_i, x_T, y_T, \alpha) = 255 - \left| I_G(x_i', y_i') - M_P(x_i, y_i) \right|, \tag{7}$$

and the values $x_i'$, $y_i'$ are calculated from

$$\begin{cases} x_i' = x_r + (x_i - x_r)\cos(\alpha) - (y_i - y_r)\sin(\alpha) + x_T \\ y_i' = y_r + (x_i - x_r)\sin(\alpha) + (y_i - y_r)\cos(\alpha) + y_T \end{cases}. \tag{8}$$

The above equations relate to the schematic diagram given in Fig. 1.

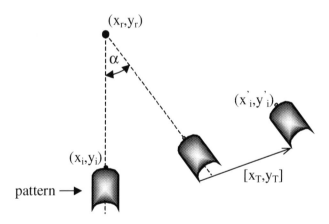

**Fig. 1.** Rotation and translation of pattern $M_P$ with respect to an arbitrary point $(x_r, y_r)$

As the above formulas show, the implementation of this definition of the Hough transform does not differ from the standard definition. However, it enables us to apply the method directly to grey-level images. The parameter space is defined by translation and rotation as $P = P_1 \times P_2 \times P_3 = [1,\ldots,W] \times [1,\ldots,K] \times [0,\ldots,L-1]$, and $A(w_0, k_0, l_0) = \max_{(w,k,l) \in P} A(w,k,l)$.

It is necessary to note that the local similarity function (7) can be introduced in a number of ways. The one proposed is not a unique possible solution, but directly suggests what to do in the case of grey-level images.

## An Example Result

Fig. 2 shows the initial image, identified pattern and content of accumulator array for the best angle of pattern rotation and the effect of the identification denoted by a circle in the initial image. The processing time took several seconds.

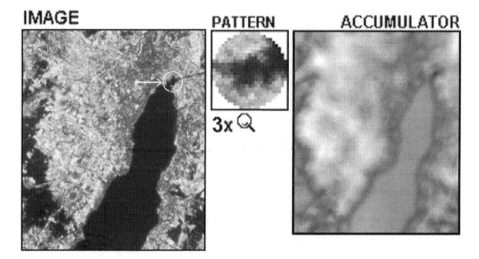

**Fig. 2.** Object location in a satellite image (the arrow points out calculated localisation)

Presented example confirms that the method provides correct results without binarisation of the initial image. The success rate achieved in a collection of dozens of images was over 80%. This method seems to be promising for any form of object identification; for example, in camera pictures, photos taken from aerospace vehicle or satellite and astronomical pictures.

## Application of the Histogram Function

To improve this elaborated method we wish to find a characteristic of the pattern that is invariant under rotation. The histogram is the obvious characteristic especially for diverse images (of 256 grey levels). The histogram of pattern $M_P$ is determined once only and compared with the histograms of fragments of image $I_G$, determined at all possible locations of the pattern $M_P$. A histogram of a grey-level image defines a function that maps for any grey level (from 0 to 255) the number of image pixels that have that level and may be denoted by

$$\Phi : \{0,...,255\} \rightarrow N . \tag{9}$$

**Algorithm** – **Histogram Analysis**

<u>Step 1</u>: Determine histogram $\Phi_p$ of the identified pattern $M_p$.

<u>Step 2</u>: Determine histograms $\Phi_{Q(i,j)}$ for all fragments $Q_G^{I_G(i,j)}$ of size $N_p \times N_p$ of image $I_G$ where $i = 1,..., W - N_p + 1$ and $j = 1,..., K - N_p + 1$.

<u>Step 3</u>: Compare the received histogram $\Phi_{Q(i,j)}$ with the histogram $\Phi_p$ using the following value

$$d_{(i,j)} = \frac{4}{\pi \cdot N_p^2} \sum_{k=0}^{255} \left| \Phi_{Q(i,j)}(k) - \Phi_p(k) \right|, \tag{10}$$

where the factor $\pi/4$ results from the relation of a circle area inscribed into a square.

<u>Step 4</u>: If $d_{(i,j)}$ is higher than a threshold value $d_{treshold}$ then it is excluded when calculating the accumulator array $A$.

This simple method reduces the complexity in terms of the calculation performed for the whole process (often by more than 50%).

## 4   The Use of the Hough Transform in a Robot Monitoring System

In a computerised robot monitoring system the identification of manipulated objects is carried out with the use of previously learned patterns.

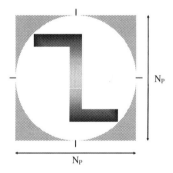

**Fig. 3.** Graphical illustration of pattern $M_p$

Fig. 3 shows the content of matrix $M_p$ for a hypothetical object. Elements in $M_p$ that are not taken into consideration in the process of identification are located outside the circle and marked grey. Such an approach is a result of the observation that these elements are not important when the pattern $M_p$ is rotated (see 10). However, **pixels marked white are very important for the process of identification**. This may be justified by the observation that the complement of object $b(M_P)$ to $M_P$ (i.e. "negative" $b(M_P)$) carries a lot of information about the object itself.

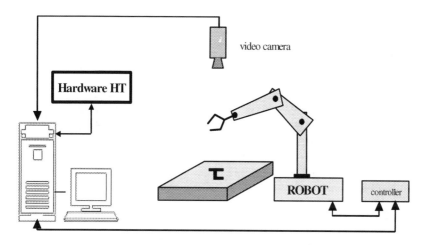

**Fig. 4.** Computer monitoring work station for a robot

The task is aimed at identifying (determining the location and rotation angle) a given object in the image of the scene (see Fig. 4). We assume that a given object is represented by the pattern $M_P$. Before we start to calculate the Hough transform, we must **scale** image I of a given scene **in a way determined by the scale of** $M_P$.

The task to identify pattern $M_P$ in image $I_S$ may be regarded as determining parameters $(w,k,\alpha)$ which uniquely describe its location $(w,k)$ and orientation $\alpha$ in a given image. In this sense the parameter space is defined as follows

$$P = P_1 \times P_2 \times P_3 = [1,...,W] \times [1,...,K] \times [0,...,L-1], \qquad (\Delta\alpha = \frac{2\pi}{L}). \qquad (11)$$

To identify pattern $M_P$ with an object in image $I_S$ the Hough transform of $A : P \to N$ must be calculated. As a result of this algorithm we obtain an accumulator array $A$. The most important thing is its maximum element

$$A(w_0,k_0,l_0) = \max_{(w,k,l) \in P} A(w,k,l). \qquad (12)$$

Parameters $w_0, k_0$ are the result of location $(w,k)$ of the object searched in the image and the angle of its rotation is $\alpha = l_0 \cdot \Delta\alpha$. It is necessary to establish the required threshold value for $A(w_0,k_0,l_0)$ and to take into account the possibility that the searched object in the analysed scene may not exist.

An example result obtained for this method is given in Fig. 5, which shows a scene observed by a robot camera and the result of analysis (location of the object and the accumulator array $A$). The processing time was a few seconds; $N_p=25$.

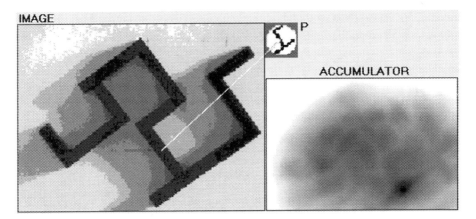

**Fig. 5.** Identification for the scene including objects connected to each other

# 5   Hardware Implementation of the Hough Technique [8]

This section describes a hardware implementation of the generalised Hough transform based on a powerful development board made by Altera®. The most important problem is the implementation of the function $H(x_T, y_T, \alpha)$ - see equation (6).

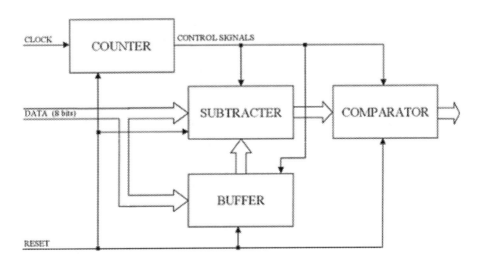

**Fig. 6.** Block diagram of the structure implemented for function $H(x_T, y_T, \alpha)$

The implemented structure has only one aim; to calculate the difference between the given fragment of the input image and the given pattern. The image fragment and the pattern are indicated by the arguments of function $H(x_T, y_T, \alpha)$. This means that the PC sends to the hardware co-ordinates $(x_T, y_T, \alpha)$ of the accumulator array and waits for the result, i.e. value of function $H(x_T, y_T, \alpha)$. This is a single cycle of the whole process of the accumulator array calculation which starts by sending signal RESET. Signal RESET clears the main elements of the implemented structure: COUNTER, BUFFER, SUBTRACTER and COMPARATOR. This is the initial step for the process and after that the device is ready to calculate accumulator array cells one by one. In order to describe precisely the basic cycle for the implemented structure the following algorithm will be useful.

**Algorithm**

<u>Step 0</u>: The APEX device receives (subsequent) co-ordinates $(x_T, y_T, \alpha)$ and indicates adequate fragment of the input image (by $x_T, y_T$) and adequate pattern (by $\alpha$).

<u>Step 1</u>: At the j-th step the BUFFER receives the j-th pixel (i.e. 8 bits) of the input image fragment and the SUBTRACTER receives the j-th pixel (i.e. 8 bits) of the pattern.

<u>Step 2</u>: The COUNTER sends the SUBTRACTER signal that begins the calculation process of the difference between the pixels. The obtained difference is added to the previous one stored in the SUBTRACTER.

<u>Step 3</u>: If there is any pixel of the pattern left, then $j := j + 1$ and go to step 1. If there is no more pixels of the pattern, the COMPARATOR receives value $H(x_T, y_T, \alpha)$ from the SUBTRACTER and compares it with the previous one.

<u>Step 4</u>: The COMPARATOR sends out value $H(x_T, y_T, \alpha)$ to the PC with information whether it is the temporary minimum or not.

# References

[1]   Ballard D. H.: *Generalizing the Hough Transform to Detect Arbitrary Shapes.* Readings in Computer Vision: Issues, Problems, Principles, and Paradigms. Los Altos, CA. 1987, pp. 714-725.

[2]   Deans S. R.: *Hough transform from the Radon transform.* IEEE Transactions on Pattern Analysis and Machine Intelligence, vol. 3, no. 2, 1981, 185-188.

[3]   Fu K. S., Gonzalez R. C., Lee C. S. G.: *ROBOTICS: Control, Sensing, Vision, and Intelligence.* McGraw-Hill, New York 1987.

[4]   Hough P. V. C.: *Method and means for recognizing complex patterns.* U.S. Patent 3,069,654, Dec. 18, 1962.

[5]   Jain A. K.: *Fundamentals of Digital Image Processing.* Prentice-Hall, New Jersey 1989.

[6]   Leavers V. F.: *Shape Detection in Computer Vision Using the Hough Transform.* Springer, London 1992.

[7]   Zorski W., Foxon B., Blackledge J., Turner M.: *Irregular Pattern Recognition Using the Hough transform.* Machine Graphics & Vision, 9, 2000, pp. 609-632.

[8]   Zorski W., Zak A., Turner M.: *Hardware Implementation of the Hough Technique for Irregular Pattern Recognition.* Proceedings of the 8th IEEE International Conference MMAR 2002, Vol.1, pp.561-566.

# A Bayesian Approach for Weighting Boundary and Region Information for Segmentation

Mohand Saïd Allili and Djemel Ziou

Sherbrooke University, Faculty of Science,
Department of Computer Science, Sherbrooke, J1K 2R1, Quebec, Canada
{MS.Allili, D.Ziou}@Usherbrooke.ca

**Abstract.** Variational image segmentation combining boundary and region information was and still is the subject of many recent works. This combination is usually subject to arbitrary weighting parameters that control the boundary and region features contribution during the segmentation. However, since the objective functions of the boundary and the region features is different in nature, their arbitrary combination may conduct to local conflicts that stem principally from abrupt illumination changes or the presence of texture inside the regions. In the present paper, we investigate an adaptive estimation of the weighting parameters (hyper-parameters) on the regions data during the segmentation by using a Bayesian method. This permits to give adequate contributions of the boundary and region features to segmentation decision making for pixels and, therefore, improving the accuracy of region boundary localization. We validated the approach on examples of real world images.

## 1 Introduction

Image segmentation is one of the most studied topics in computer vision and still is the focus of many recent researches. It is considered as a basic operation for many applications based on image content analysis, such as medical image processing, object recognition and tracking. The goal of the segmentation is to divide an image into distinct homogeneous regions, or underlying structures, delimited by smooth boundaries. To distinguish between different regions, image features such as the gray level, color or texture are the mostly used. Yet, most of the segmentation techniques are based on two main properties of the image: the similarity between pixels inside the regions (homogeneity) and the discontinuity of the features in the regions boundaries (contrast).

To enforce the precision and the robustness of the segmentation, several methods integrated boundary and region features in the segmentation, where an excellent survey on the exiting methods was presented in [7]. Two main approaches were investigated in the field. The first approach relies on fusing the results of initial boundary and region segmentations by exploiting their dual information to improve the final segmentation [5,8]. The boundary information can be used especially to refine the result of region-based methods, that might over-segment the image or yield poor localization of the region boundaries. The

J. Blanc-Talon et al. (Eds.): ACIVS 2005, LNCS 3708, pp. 468–475, 2005.
© Springer-Verlag Berlin Heidelberg 2005

second approach to combine region and boundary information, that is the concern of this paper, consists of embedding the boundary and region features to provide a unified segmentation process. Here, the boundary and region features are used jointly to provide a new decision criterion for the segmentation. This aims to bring accuracy to the segmentation which is critical for many image-based domains, like surveillance or diagnosis in medical images.

In this field, active contours segmentation has emerged in a very suitable way to combine region and boundary information. Active contours embodies various good properties, like the smoothness of the region contours and the ability to combine easily boundary and region information into one objective function [4,11]. Yet, this combination is subject to free hyper-parameters that fix the contribution of each feature in pixel segmentation decision making. Most of methods set the hyper-parameters to equal values in order to give equivalent contributions for the used features. However, even if the boundary and region information are complementary in their nature, they differ in their objectives. Region information is based on the homogeneity of features and boundary information is based on the discontinuity of the same features. According to this, local ambiguities for the segmentation may arise if boundary and region information do not agree in the segmentation decision. These ambiguities arise essentially when a contour encounters abrupt illumination changes or a local texture. In the first case, the homogeneity of the region changes even if the object remains the same; that is, the real region boundaries are not reached yet. In the second case, the strength of the gradient response can stop the evolution of the contour even if the the real region boundary is not reached. One suitable solution for the problem resides in calculating adaptively the hyper-parameters in order to control the contributions of the region and boundary features in the segmentation.

In the present paper, we investigate such an approach to estimate adaptively the hyper-parameters that fix the contribution of boundary and region features. Specifically, we combine the boundary and region segmentations, where the contribution of each feature is based on the neighboring information of each pixel. We reformulate the segmentation by maximizing the joint probability of boundary and region segmentation. By assuming the hyper-parameters locally constant, a local segmentation map is derived for each pixel neighborhood and the hyper-parameters are, then, estimated by maximizing the Bayesian evidence of the local segmentation map. We show on various examples that the approach overcomes the conflicts induced by local texture and illumination changes.

This paper is organized as follows: In section (2), after stating the problem, we present the model combining region and boundary information. This is followed by the treatment for estimating adaptive hyper-parameters for segmentation. In section (3), some examples of the approach are presented and commented. The paper ends with a conclusion and some perspectives.

## 2    Problem Statement and Formulation of the Model

Let $I$ be an image that is defined on the domain $\Omega = \mathcal{Z}^+ \times \mathcal{Z}^+$, where $\mathcal{Z}^+$ denotes the set of positive integers. For simplicity, we assume the domain of the image $I$ is composed of the region $R$ and a complementary background $R^c$, where each region is described by its mean parameter. We aim to track the foreground region by a deformable contour $C$, which is formulated by the following energy functional:

$$E(C, \theta_1, \theta_2) = \alpha \underbrace{\oint_C (1 - |(D(s) \cdot N(s))|)ds}_{E_b}$$

$$+ \beta \underbrace{\left[ \int\int_R (I - \theta_1)^2 dx dy + \int\int_{R^c} (I - \theta_2)^2 dx dy \right]}_{E_r} \qquad (1)$$

The first term of the functional (1) represents the boundary information, where $s$ is the arc-length parameter. The vector $N$ designates the unit normal to the curve $C$, while $D$ is the local direction of the edge. In an intensity image, $D$ is the gradient vector of the image and in multi-valued image, the vector will correspond to the direction of the strongest first order directional derivative [6]. In the second term of the functional (1), $\theta_1$ and $\theta_2$ represent respectively the mean parameter of the region $R$ and the background $R^c$. To understand the meaning of each term in the functional (1), the first term vanishes when the normal of the curve is aligned with image gradient vector (see figure (1), where the absolute value permits to take into account only the direction of the vectors and not their sense. That is, the boundary term is insensible to whether the contour lies in the dark or the bright part of a region boundary. The second term of the functional minimizes the Euclidian distance between the regions data and its mean. $\alpha$ and $\beta$ are the hyper-parameters that control the contribution of the energy terms. Following the Euler-Lagrange minimization, we obtain the following motion equation for the curve $C$:

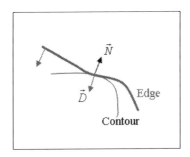

**Fig. 1.** An example of alignment of the curve normal with the image gradient vector

$$\frac{d\boldsymbol{C}}{dt} = \left(\alpha[\kappa - sign(\boldsymbol{D} \cdot \boldsymbol{N})div(\boldsymbol{D})] - \beta[(I - \theta_1)^2 - (I - \theta_2)^2]\right)\boldsymbol{N} \qquad (2)$$

Where $\kappa$ is the curvature of the curve $\boldsymbol{C}$ and $sign()$ is the function that returns the sign of its operand. The operator $div$ denotes the divergence of a vector. To have adaptive region parameters in the segmentation, the updating of the mean parameters is obtained by minimizing the functional (1) according to the parameters $\theta_1$ and $\theta_2$. This is performed by using Euler-Lagrange equations and leads to the following functions:

$$\theta_1 = \frac{\int\int_R I(x,y)dxdy}{\int\int_\Omega dxdy}, \theta_2 = \frac{\int\int_{R^c} I(x,y)dxdy}{\int\int_\Omega dxdy} \qquad (3)$$

By setting the hyper-parameters to $\alpha = \beta = 0.5$ in equation (2), we give equivalent contribution for the region and boundary terms. However, since the objective of the boundary and region information is different, local conflicts may arise for the decision making of pixel membership, when the the interior of a region contains spurious edges induced by texture or illumination changes. The objective of this work is to give each term of the energy functional a contribution when the conditions are favorable to play its expected and exact role. Namely, when the contour is situated inside a region, it is natural for the homogeneity information to prevail over the boundary information. The vice-versa should happen when the contour is in the vicinity of a region boundary.

## 2.1 Adaptive Estimation of the Hyper-Parameters $\alpha$ and $\beta$

Coming back to the energy functional (1), to derive the hyper-parameters estimation we re-write, firstly, the segmentation as the maximization of a probability function. That is, we consider the expected segmentation as the posterior probability of the contours localization with respect to boundary and region energies $E_b$ and $E_r$, weighted respectively by the hyper-parameters $\alpha$ and $\beta$ . The formulation of this is given as follows:

$$\min_{\boldsymbol{C},\Theta}[E] \equiv \max_{\boldsymbol{C},\Theta}[p(\boldsymbol{C}/E_b, \alpha)p(\boldsymbol{C}/E_r, \beta)] \qquad (4)$$

$$= \max_{\boldsymbol{C},\Theta}[\alpha\exp\{-\alpha \cdot E_b\}\beta\exp\{-\beta E_r\}] \qquad (5)$$

Here, $\Theta$ denotes the set of region statistical parameters $\{\theta_1, \theta_2\}$. In function (5), we have formulated the boundary and region segmentation probabilities by using two exponential distributions. The exponential distribution come out as a natural and suitable choice for the segmentation probability distribution. Firstly, as the segmentation is given by minimizing the energy functional, the exponential distribution reflects this fact by giving the maximum probability for segmentation when the boundary and region energies are minimized. Secondly, for practical regards, the unknown hyper-parameters $\alpha$ and $\beta$ play now the role of scale parameters for the boundary and region segmentation pdfs, which are statistically well defined and easy to deal with. To make the segmentation independent of the hyper-parameters, a correct Bayesian treatment is to integrate them out over any prediction. That is, the evidence of the contours localization that defines the segmentation is given by the following integrals:

$$P(C/E_b, E_r) = \int_0^\infty \int_0^\infty p(C, \alpha, \beta/E_b, E_r) d\alpha d\beta$$

$$\propto \int_0^\infty \int_0^\infty p(E_b, E_r/\alpha, \beta, C) p(\alpha, \beta, C) d\alpha d\beta$$

$$\propto \int_0^\infty \int_0^\infty p(E_b/C, \alpha) p(E_r/C, \beta) p(C/\alpha, \beta) p(\alpha, \beta) d\alpha d\beta \quad (6)$$

where the third line comes out by assuming the independence of the boundary and region information. This permits to separate the likelihoods of the region and boundary segmentations in the integral. Furthermore, we assume the independence of the hyper-parameters $\alpha$ and $\beta$ that will yield separate priors; that is, $p(\alpha, \beta) = p(\alpha)p(\beta)$.

The calculation of the above integrals requires choosing specific priors for the hyper-parameters. Since we assume that no information is available in advance about the hyper-parameters, one proper choice is to use non-informative priors. Noting that $\alpha$ and $\beta$ represent scale parameters imposes for the priors to be scale invariant [2,9], the appropriate priors are given by:

$$P(\alpha) \propto \alpha^{-1}, P(\beta) \propto \beta^{-1} \quad (7)$$

Thus far, the formulation in function (6) relies on the assumption that the hyper-parameters $\alpha$ and $\beta$ have the same value for the pixels lying on the contour at a given time in the segmentation. As the membership decision is made independently for each pixel according the pixel boundary and region information, one should calculate specific hyper-parameters for each pixel. In our work, we assume a configuration where the hyper-parameters are constant in a local neighborhood $N_{\mathbf{x}}$ surrounding each pixel $\mathbf{x} = (x, y)$. We define a neighborhood by a square window centered at the pixel in concern and having $m$ pixels in each side ($m$ is an odd number), see figure (2). The local hyper-parameters are denoted by $\alpha_l$

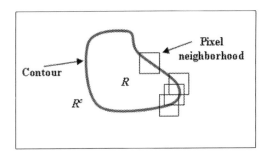

**Fig. 2.** An illustration of the neighborhood system used to calculate the hyper-parameters

and $\beta_l$ and we refer to the boundary and region energies in the local area respectively by $N_{\mathbf{X}}(E_b) = \sum_{\mathbf{x} \in N(\mathbf{X})} E_b(\mathbf{x})$ and $N_{\mathbf{X}}(E_r) = \sum_{\mathbf{x} \in N(\mathbf{X})} E_r(\mathbf{x})$. Then, we can write the following local segmentation probability function:

$$p(C(\mathbf{x})/E_b, E_r, \alpha_l, \beta_l) = \prod_{\mathbf{x} \in N(\mathbf{X})} p(C/E_b(\mathbf{x}), \alpha_l) \times p(C/E_r(\mathbf{x}), \beta_l)$$

$$= (\alpha_l \beta_l)^M \cdot \exp\{-\alpha_l N_{\mathbf{X}}(E_b) - \beta_l N_{\mathbf{X}}(E_r)\} \qquad (8)$$

According to the integral (6), we can derive for each pixel the probability of the localization of the contour, based the boundary and region information. This is given by the following:

$$P(C/N_{\mathbf{X}}(E_b)) = \int_0^{\infty} p(N_{\mathbf{X}}(E_b)/C, \alpha_l) d\alpha_l$$

$$= \int_0^{\infty} (\alpha_l)^{M-1} \exp\{-\alpha_l N_{\mathbf{X}}(E_b)\} d\alpha_l = \frac{\Gamma(M)}{(N_{\mathbf{X}}(E_b))^M} \qquad (9)$$

and in the same manner, we calculate for $\beta$:

$$P(C/N_{\mathbf{X}}(E_r)) = \frac{\Gamma(M)}{(N_{\mathbf{X}}(E_r))^M} \qquad (10)$$

Now by putting into logarithm, then summing and differentiating equation (9) and (10), we obtain:

$$\nabla log(P(C/N_{\mathbf{X}}(E_b), N_{\mathbf{X}}(E_r))) = M^2 (\nabla log(N_{\mathbf{X}}(E_b)) + \nabla log(N_{\mathbf{X}}(E_r))) \quad (11)$$

Note that the differentiation is performed according to the contour. Now, by performing the same differentiation to function (5), we obtain:

$$\nabla log(P(C/E_b, E_r) = \alpha \nabla E_b + \beta \nabla E_r \qquad (12)$$

and by comparing equations (11)and (12) term to term, we obtain the values of $\alpha$ and $\beta$ as following:

$$\hat{\alpha} = (N_{\mathbf{X}}(E_b))^{-1}, \hat{\beta} = (N_{\mathbf{X}}(E_r))^{-1} \qquad (13)$$

The obtained results for the values $\alpha$ and $\beta$ sound natural and expected in various regards and can be interpreted as follows. The increasing of some features energy functional should penalize its segmentation probability and decrease the corresponding hyper-parameters to diminish the feature contribution. Moreover, we can view the hyper-parameters as measuring the local variance of the energy functional in the vicinity of a pixel. That is, by adapting this variance to data, one diminishes the overlapping region between the region and boundary probability segmentation and, therefore, eliminate ambiguities in the membership decision making.

## 3   Experiments and Discussion

To validate the above model, we conducted experiments that relates to the segmentation of two region images. To allow automatic topology changes for the curves, the implementation of the curve evolution is based on the level-set narrow-band algorithm [1,10]. In the examples, we initialized the contour manually inside the object to be segmented from the image background. In figure (3), we show three examples for contour evolution, where the initializations are shown in the first row for all the examples. In the second row (b), the contours were evolved by using the Geodesic active contours model [3] that uses solely the boundary information ($\alpha = 1, \beta = 0$). In the examples, the contour was stopped by pixels showing a contrast due to a change of illumination (see the elephant) or texture (see the bird). These results are due to the absence of region information to distinguish, by global homogeneity, between the tracked region and the background. By converse, using only the regions information to evolve the contours ($\alpha = 0, \beta = 1$) resulted in a poor alignment of the final contours with the regions boundaries (see the third row(c)). In the fourth row (d), we show the evolution of the contours by using adaptive hyper-parameters. Clearly, the final contours were aligned with the real region boundaries, while the overall homogeneity of the regions was preserved. These results can be explained as fol-

**Fig. 3.** Three examples of image segmentation by using respectively: (b) ($\alpha = 1, \beta = 0$), (c) ($\alpha = 0, \beta = 1$), (d) adaptive hyper-parameters and (e) equivalent hyper-parameters ($\alpha = 0.5, \beta = 0.5$). The contour initializations are shown for each image in the row (a). For all the segmentations, the parameter $m$ is fixed to 7 pixels.

lows: By using only the region information, the contour can be stopped by false boundaries induced by change of illumination, see the elephant example. Since the boundary information contributes at these parts of the image, the contours surpassed the false edges and the included pixels in the region contributed to update the statistical parameters of the regions. This naturally augments the membership score for the shadowed pixels to the tracked region. Finally, we show in the last row (e) a combination of the energy and boundary information by using an arbitrary weighted sum, where ($\alpha = 0.5, \beta = 0.5$). Clearly, conflicting situations arise in parts there is change of illumination or an appearance of texture. Instead of giving a priority to only one of the features, the boundary and region modules act simultaneously on the contours, which arises in opposite forces that pushed away the contour from the real region boundaries (see the elephant and bird examples).

## 4  Conclusion

In the present work, a novel framework was proposed to the integration of the boundary and region information in image segmentation. Based on active contours model, a method is proposed to calculate adaptively the hyper-parameters weighting the boundary and region information. The method showed its performance through various examples where the accuracy and robustness of the segmentation was significantly enhanced. In future work, an improvement of the approach can be obtained by combining texture and color features to describe the regions.

## References

1. D. Adalsteinsson and J. Sethian: A Fast Level Set Method for Propagating Surfaces. Journal of Computational Physics, 118:269-277, 1995.
2. C. Bishops: Neural Networks for Pattern Recognition. Clarendon Press. Oxford, 1995.
3. V. Caselles, R. Kimmel and G. Shapiro: Geodesic Active Contours. IJCV, 22:61-79, 1997.
4. A. Chakraborty and J.S. Duncan: Game-Theoretic Integration for Image Segmentation. IEEE Trans. PAMI, 21(1):12-30, 1999.
5. C. Chu and J. Aggarwal: The Integration of Image Segmentation Maps Using Region and Edge Information. IEEE Trans. PAMI, 15(12):1241-1252, 1993.
6. C. Drewniok: Multispectral Edge Detection: Some Experiments on Data From Landsat-TM. IJRS, 15(18):3743-3765, 1994.
7. J. Freixenet, X. Munoz, D. Raba, J. Marti and X. Cuffi: Yet Another Survey on Image Segmentation: Region and Boundary Information Integration. ECCV, 408-422, 2002.
8. J. Hadon and J. Boyce: Image Segmentation by Unifying Region and Boundary Information. IEEE Trans. PAMI, 12(10):929-948, 1990.
9. P.M.Lee: Bayesian Statistics, an Introduction. Second edition, Arnold, 1997.
10. S. Osher and J. Sethian: Fronts Propagating With Curvature-Dependant Speed: Algorithms Based on Hammilton-Jacobi Formulations. Journal of Computational Physics, 22:12-49, 1988.
11. N. Paragios and R. Deriche: Unifying Boundary and Region-based Information for Geodesic Active Tracking. IEEE Conf. CVPR, 2:300-305, 1999.

# A Fast Sequential Rainfalling Watershed Segmentation Algorithm

Johan De Bock, Patrick De Smet, and Wilfried Philips

Ghent University, Belgium
jdebock@telin.UGent.be

**Abstract.** In this paper we present a new implementation of a rain-falling watershed segmentation algorithm. Our previous algorithm was a one-run algorithm. All the steps needed to compute a complete water-shed segmentation were done in one run over the input data. In our new algorithm we tried another approach. We separated the watershed algorithm in several low-complexity relabeling steps that can be performed sequentially on a label image. The new implementation is approximately two times faster for parameters that produce visually good segmentations. The new algorithm also handles plateaus in a better way. First we describe the general layout of a rainfalling watershed algorithm. Then we explain the implementations of the two algorithms. Finally we give a detailed report on the timings of the two algorithms for different parameters.

## 1 Introduction

Image segmentation is the process of partitioning a digital image in meaningful segments, i.e. segments that show a certain degree of homogeneity. Image segmentation can be interpreted and implemented in many ways. The division into edge detection and region growing algorithms could be a rough classification of segmentation algorithms. The watershed transform can be attributed properties of both classes, i.e. it tries to find the homogeneous closed regions by using an edge indication map as input. In case of intensity segmentation, the edge indication map can be created by calculating the gradient magnitude of the input image. The watershed transform then regards the edge indication map as a topographic landscape in which "valleys" correspond to the interior of segments, whereas the "mountains" correspond to the boundaries of segments. The watershed algorithm derives the "mountain rims" from the landscape and those mountain rims then delineate the segments in the image.

Watershed algorithms can be divided in two classes depending on the method that is used to extract the mountain rims from the topographic landscape. The first class contains the flooding watershed algorithms. These algorithms extract the mountain rims by gradually flooding the landscape. The points where the waterfronts meet each other constitute the mountain rims. This process is displayed chronologically in Fig. 1. A well-known example of this class is the discrete Vincent-Soille flooding watershed algorithm [1,2]. The second class contains the

J. Blanc-Talon et al. (Eds.): ACIVS 2005, LNCS 3708, pp. 476–482, 2005.
© Springer-Verlag Berlin Heidelberg 2005

rainfalling watershed algorithms. These type of algorithms will be discussed in this paper. Examples of this class are the algorithms described in [3,4] and our previous algorithm [5]. In Sect. 2 we describe the general layout of a rainfalling watershed algorithm. In Sect. 3 we explain the implementations of our two rainfalling watershed algorithms. First we will describe the implementation of our previous algorithm [5]. All the steps needed to do a complete watershed segmentation were done in one run over input data, hence the name one-run algorithm. Next we will describe the implementation of our new algorithm. We separated the watershed algorithm in several low-complexity relabeling steps that can be performed sequentially on a label image, hence the name sequential algorithm. We give a detailed report on the timings of the two algorithms for different parameters in Sect. 4. Finally we draw some conclusions in Sect. 5.

**Fig. 1.** Chronological stages in the flooding process

## 2   General Layout of a Rainfalling Watershed Algorithm

A rainfalling watershed algorithm exploits a different concept (compared to the flooding watershed) to extract the mountain rims. For each point on the topographic landscape an algorithm tracks the path that a virtual droplet of water would follow if it would fall on the landscape at that point. All droplets or points that flow to the same local minimum constitute a segment. This concept is depicted in Fig. 2 for the two-dimensional case. The lowest mountains (weakest edges) can be suppressed by drowning them. All the mountains below a certain drowning threshold will not be taken into account. This is shown in Fig. 3.

In the implementation, the rainfalling concept is carried out by calculating the steepest descent direction for each pixel. The directions are limited to the pixels neighboring the central pixel. For a four-neighborhood configuration this results in searching for the lowest neighboring pixel, for an eight-neighborhood configuration we have to take into account an additional $1/\sqrt{2}$ factor for the diagonal directions. A visualization of the steepest descent directions for an image of $10 \times 10$ pixels is given in Fig. 4 (eight-neighborhood). The pixels marked with a circle in the middle are pixels from where there is no descent possible. Hence, they are the local minima of the topographic landscape. Every group of pixels that is connected by the same tree of arrows leading to a local minimum must now make up one segment.

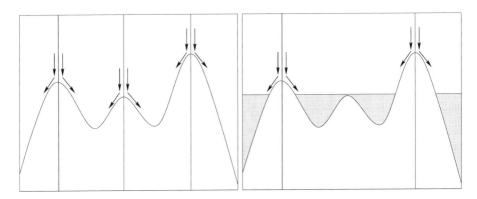

**Fig. 2.** Rainfalling concept          **Fig. 3.** Drowning threshold

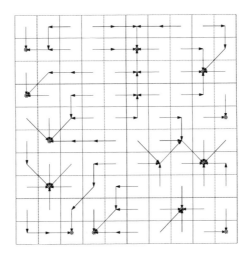

**Fig. 4.** Steepest descent directions

## 3    Description of the Rainfalling Watershed Implementations

The input matrix $G$ for both algorithms is the floating point gradient magnitude of an image containing $n$ pixels. The drowning threshold $dt$ and the neighborhood $nbh \in \{4, 8\}$ are the two input parameters. The drowning threshold can also be expressed by the relative drowning threshold $rdt$, this is $dt$ divided by the maximum value of $G$. The output data for both cases is a segment label image $S$, i.e. an image with for each pixel a label of the segment to which the pixel belongs.

First we describe our previous one-run rainfalling watershed segmentation algorithm which has been available publicly. The main data structures are:

- The segment label image, a matrix $S$ of labels. $S$ is initialised in the following way: for each $i$ the algorithm sets $S(i) := i$, with $i$ being the one-dimensional index into $S$, in video scanning order (from left to right, top to bottom).
- An array $P$ of pointers to pixels. For each segment, $P$ contains a singly linked list of pixels belonging to that segment. To be more precise, $P(i)$ gives the next pixel in the list of pixels of the segment to which pixel $i$ belongs. The start of the list of pixels of the segment with label $i$ is given by $P(i)$. The last pixel $i$ of a list is indicated by $P(i) := -1$. $P$ is initialised with $-1$ indicating that initially each pixel is a separate segment.

The only operation that will be applied on these two data structures is the $merge(labela, labelb)$ operation. This operation will merge the segments with $labela$ and $labelb$ by relabeling one of the two segments with the other label in $S$. $P$ is needed to efficiently locate the pixels with a certain label during the relabeling process. After the relabeling, the lists in $P$ of the two segments are updated by linking the tail of one list with the head of the other list.

The algorithm visits all pixels $i$ in $G$ in video scanning order. If the central pixel $i$ is below $dt$ then all neighboring pixels $nb$ (depending on $nbh$) are investigated; if $nb$ is below $dt$ then the algorithm executes $merge(S(i), S(nb))$. If the central pixel is above $dt$ then the steepest descent direction (depending on $nbh$) is calculated. If there is a steepest descent pixel (direction) $steepest$ then the algorithm executes $merge(S(i), S(steepest))$. By applying these merge operations the algorithm ensures that after investigating the last pixel, $S$ is in the desired state. Every group of pixels that is connected by the same tree of arrows will now have the same unique label (cfr. Fig. 4).

Now we describe our new sequential rainfalling watershed segmentation algorithm. The main data structures are:

- The segment label image, a matrix $S$ of pointers to pixels, or labels depending on the interpretation.
- The local minima image, a matrix $M$ of labels. $M$ is initialized with 1.

In the first step the algorithm visits all pixels $i$ in $G$ in video scanning order. If the central pixel $i$ is below $dt$ then $S(i) := i$. If the central pixel is above $dt$ then the steepest descent direction (depending on $nbh$) is calculated. If there is no steepest descent (local minimum) then $S(i) := i$. If there is a steepest descent pixel $steepest$ then $S(i) := steepest$ and $M(i) := 0$. The visual interpretation of the state of $S$ after the first step is shown in Fig. 4. After the first step $M$ indicates the locations of the local minima (the pixels below $dt$ are included here).

In the second step the pointers in $S$ are propagated until each pixel points to one of the local minima. For each pixel $i$ the algorithm repeats $next := S(next)$ starting with $next := i$ until it reaches a local minimum, i.e. until $next = S(next)$, then the algorithm sets $S(i) := next$. This step thus implements the tracking of the virtual droplet described above.

In the third step the algorithm applies a connected components algorithm directly on the local minima image $M$. This connected components algorithm assigns a different label to each separately connected group of local minima. This step is necessary to be able to merge the connected local minima.

In the final step the algorithm incorporates the new labels given by the connected components algorithm by doing the following relabeling: for each pixel $i$ the algorithm sets $S(i) := M(S(i))$. $S$ is now in the desired state.

Assuming that the labels and pointers all take up 4 bytes, then the one-run algorithm uses approximately $8n$ bytes and the sequential algorithm uses approximately $9n$ bytes. These $n$ bytes extra are used up by the connected components algorithm.

Theoretically these two implementations are identical, except for the handling of plateaus. A plateau is a group of connected local minima above the drowning threshold. In the sequential algorithm these plateaus are handled by the connected components step. Consequently, the individual pixels of the plateau are merged to one segment. In the one-run algorithm these plateau pixels will not be merged and therefore will form individual segments. If the topographic landscape is created by calculating the gradient magnitude of the input image, then linear gradients in the input image will result in plateaus in the landscape. Perceptually it is more appropriate to segment a linear gradient into one segment instead of individual pixel segments.

## 4   Results

To compare the performance of our two rainfalling watershed algorithms, we tested them on the well-known test image PEPPERS 512x512. The algorithms were implemented in C, compiled with gcc 3.4.2 with optimization parameter -O3 and run on an Intel Pentium 4 2.8 GHz. To obtain very accurate and reliable timings, we measured the time needed to execute 1000 watershed runs. The results for one watershed run are displayed in Fig. 5 for an eight-neighborhood configuration and Fig. 6 for a four-neighborhood configuration. We can see that the new implementation is approximately two times faster for parameters that

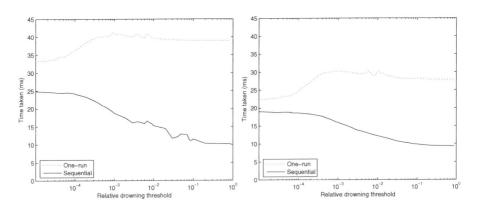

**Fig. 5.** PEPPERS 512x512, $nbh = 8$      **Fig. 6.** PEPPERS 512x512, $nbh = 4$

**Fig. 7.** PEPPERS 512x512, segmented with $rdt = 0.001$, $nbh = 8$

produce visually good segmentations. An example segmentation result is given in Fig. 7. The difference in computation time can be explained by the more efficient merging of a group of connected pixels below the drowning threshold. The difference clearly shows when we test the algorithms on the specific test pattern depicted in Fig. 8. The one-run algorithm needs 48.9 ms to segment the pattern, the sequential algorithm only needs 11.6 ms. Almost all pixels in this pattern are below the drowning threshold, thus the running time is almost completely dominated by the part that merges the connected pixels below the drowning threshold.

**Fig. 8.** Test pattern

For a comparison of our one-run algorithm with a Vincent-Soille based flooding watershed algorithm we refer to our previous paper [5]. That paper showed that the one-run algorithm is significantly faster than the flooding watershed algorithm.

## 5    Conclusion

In this paper we presented a new implementation of a rainfalling watershed segmentation algorithm. We separated the rainfalling watershed algorithm in several low-complexity relabeling steps that can be performed sequentially on a label image. The new algorithm handles plateaus in a better way and is approximately two times faster than our previous implementation for parameters that produce visually good segmentations. This is mostly due to the more efficient merging of a group of connected pixels below the drowning threshold. With execution times of approximately 20 ms (for images of size 512x512), this algorithm can be used to perform real-time video segmentation with a normal PC.

## References

1. Vincent, L., Soille, P.: Watersheds in digital spaces: An efficient algorithm based on immersion simulations. IEEE Transactions on Pattern Analysis and Machine Intelligence **13** (1991) 583–598
2. Soille, P.: Morphological Image Analysis: Principles and Applications. Springer (1999)
3. Beucher, S.: Segmentation d'images et morphologie mathématique. PhD thesis, School of Mines (1990)
4. Moga, A., Cramariuc, B., Gabbouj, M.: A parallel watershed algorithm based on rainfalling simulation. In: Proc. 12th European Conf. Circuit Theory and Design. Volume 1. (1995) 339–342
5. De Smet, P., Pires, R.: Implementation and analysis of an optimized rainfalling watershed algorithm. In: Proc. Electronic Imaging, Science and Technology, Image and Video Communications and Processing. (2000) 759–766

# Optimum Design of Dynamic Parameters of Active Contours for Improving Their Convergence in Image Segmentation

Rafael Verdú[1,*], Juan Morales[1], Rafael Berenguer[2], and Luis Weruaga[3]

[1] Department of Information Technologies and Communications,
Technical University of Cartagena, 30202, Cartagena, Spain
{rafael.verdu, juan.morales}@upct.es
[2] Department of Technical Sciences, Catholic University of Murcia,
30107, Murcia, Spain
rberenguer@pdi.ucam.edu
[3] Commission for Scientific Visualization, Austrian Academy of Sciences,
Donau-City Strasse 1, 1220, Vienna, Austria
luis.weruaga@oeaw.ac.at

**Abstract.** Active contours are useful tools for segmenting images. The classical formulation is given in the spatial domain and is based on a second order system. The formulation based on a frequency-domain analysis offers a new perspective for studying the convergence of the snake. This paper addresses an analysis and optimization for a snake-based segmentation algorithm. The study allows us to choose optimum values of the system dynamic parameters in the design of the active contour for improving its speed of convergence in a segmentation problem.

## 1 Introduction

The effectiveness of active contours in image processing for segmenting images is well known. The classical formulation [1] is given in the spatial domain and it is based on a second order linear system. Rigidity and elasticity are the static parameters and mass and damping the dynamic parameters for its characterization. Apart from the original formulation, several variants of deformable models have been proposed [2,3]. In [4], the original formulation is translated into the frequency domain which leads to a simple formulation and design, offering an important computational saving in comparison to the original one.

The basic principle behind active contours is the ability to draw a smooth parametric curve constrained to internal and external requirements, in an adaptive way by means of an iterative mechanism. As any adaptive system, the iterations required by the contour to delineate the target is of importance [5]. The speed of convergence depends specially on the second order dynamic parameters and on the distance between attracted nodes [6]. This paper uses the

---

* This work is partially supported by the Spanish *Ministerio de Ciencia y Tecnología*, under grant TIC2002-03033.

J. Blanc-Talon et al. (Eds.): ACIVS 2005, LNCS 3708, pp. 483–490, 2005.
© Springer-Verlag Berlin Heidelberg 2005

frequency based formulation in order to study the convergence of the snake in the iterative adjustment of this contour until it outlines the tracked object. It also shows the analysis for choosing the optimum values of the dynamic parameters in the design of the active contour for improving its speed of convergence in a segmentation problem.

## 2   Frequency Based Formulation

A snake is a time varying contour $\mathbf{v} = v(s,t)$ whose shape is governed by an energy functional of internal and external forces,

$$E(\mathbf{v}) = S(\mathbf{v}) + P(\mathbf{v}). \tag{1}$$

The internal deformation energy is defined as

$$S(\mathbf{v}) = \frac{1}{2} \int_0^L \alpha(s) \left| \frac{\partial \mathbf{v}}{\partial s} \right|^2 + \beta(s) \left| \frac{\partial^2 \mathbf{v}}{\partial s^2} \right|^2 ds. \tag{2}$$

The term of external energy $P(\mathbf{v})$ comprises the effect of external forces like the gradient of an image or the internal nonlinear forces like those that keep the contour length constant. For the practical implementation of the minimization of the energy functional, the parametric domain $0 < s < L$ is divided into subdomains and $\mathbf{v}$ is divided into snake elements, which are constructed by means of a shape function $f(s)$ and a shape parameter vector $\mathbf{u}(t)$. This is achieved by the Lagrange equations of motion and leads to the second order differential equation

$$\mathbf{M} \frac{d^2 \mathbf{u}(t)}{dt^2} + \mathbf{C} \frac{d\,\mathbf{u}(t)}{dt} + \mathbf{K}\,\mathbf{u}(t) = \mathbf{g}(\mathbf{u}(t)), \tag{3}$$

where $\mathbf{K}$ is the stiffness matrix, $\mathbf{M}$ and $\mathbf{C}$ are respectively the mass and damping matrices, and $\mathbf{g}$ is the external forces vector, whose value is determined by the position of the contour at time $t$ [1]. The stiffness matrix $\mathbf{K}$ is assembled according to the shape function $f(s)$ and to the rigidity and elasticity values. All the previous elements confer the snake its dynamic and shape characteristics.

Although from a general point of view $\mathbf{K}$ is a symmetric banded square matrix, in several applications, tension and rigidity ($\alpha(s)$ and $\beta(s)$) are $s$-independent and take the same values for all snake elements. This simplification of the model opens up the possibility to formulate the minimization of energy functional (2) in the frequency domain[4].

### 2.1   Closed Contours

The frequency-based formulation is applicable initially to closed contours, which can be considered as periodic signals, the period being the contour length. Let us define the following signals: $\hat{v}(s)$ is a periodic signal of period $L$ defined by $\hat{v}(s) = \mathbf{v}$, $0 \leq s < L$; $\hat{u}(s)$ is the periodic version of $u(s)$, defined as follows

$$u(s) = \sum_{n=0}^{N-1} u_n \, \delta(s - s_n),$$ (4)

where $N$ is the number of nodes of the snake, $u_n$ is the value of the $n$-th node, and $s_n$ are their positions (in a closed snake, $s_n = nL/N$). $\mathcal{U}(\Omega)$ is the Fourier transform of $u(s)$. The snake is closed and can be represented by the periodic signal defined by $\hat{v}(s) = \hat{u}(s) * f(s)$, where $*$ denotes linear convolution on the $s$ domain and $f(s)$ is the shape function, which determines the type of interpolation among the snake nodes. Since it was assumed that $\alpha$ and $\beta$ are $s$-independent, the energy functional (2) can be written as

$$S = \frac{\alpha}{2} \int_0^L |\hat{y}_1(s)|^2 \, ds + \frac{\beta}{2} \int_0^L |\hat{y}_2(s)|^2 \, ds,$$ (5)

where $\hat{y}_a(s) = \partial^a \hat{v}(s)/\partial s^a$. By using Parseval's rule, equation (5) can be expressed in the frequency domain

$$S = \frac{L}{2} \sum_{k=-\infty}^{\infty} \alpha \, |d_1(k)|^2 + \beta \, |d_2(k)|^2.$$ (6)

where $d_a(k)$ is the Fourier series of $\hat{y}_a(s)$. Then

$$S = \frac{1}{2L} \sum_{k=-\infty}^{\infty} |\mathcal{U}(\Omega)|^2 \, |\mathcal{K}_s(\Omega)|\Big]_{\Omega=k\frac{2\pi}{L}},$$ (7)

where

$$\mathcal{K}_s(\Omega) = \left(\alpha \, |\Omega|^2 + \beta \, |\Omega|^4\right) |\mathcal{F}(\Omega)|^2.$$ (8)

where $\mathcal{F}(\Omega)$ is the Fourier transform of the shape function $f(s)$. According to (4), $\mathcal{U}(\Omega)$ is a periodic spectrum of period defined in the frequency interval $[0, 2\pi\frac{N}{L}]$, and then (7) can be further simplified as

$$S = \frac{1}{2L} \sum_{k=0}^{N-1} |\mathcal{U}(\Omega)|^2 \, |\mathcal{K}(\Omega)|\Big]_{\Omega=k\frac{2\pi}{L}},$$ (9)

where

$$\mathcal{K}(\Omega) = \sum_{k=-\infty}^{\infty} \mathcal{K}_s(\Omega - k\frac{N}{L}2\pi).$$ (10)

From the previous statement it is clear that the energy functional has been translated into a frequency and also a discrete domain, and $N$ frequency-based values contain the relevant information. Given this discrete scenario in both spatial and frequency domain, let us translate (9) to the discrete space, i.e., $s_n \to n$, which implies $\Omega \to \omega$, $\omega$ being the frequency counterpart of $n$. Equation (9) becomes

$$S = \frac{1}{2N} \sum_{k=0}^{N-1} |U(\omega)|^2 |K(\omega)| \Big]_{\Omega = k\frac{2\pi}{L}}, \tag{11}$$

where $K(\omega)$ is called the frequency stiffness spectrum

$$K(\omega) = \sum_{k=-\infty}^{\infty} \left( \alpha |\Omega|^2 + \beta |\Omega|^4 \right) |\mathcal{F}(\Omega)|^2 \Big]_{\Omega = \omega - 2\pi k}. \tag{12}$$

Thus by taking the derivative in (11) respect each of the $N$ relevant values of $U(\omega)$, we obtain the Lagrange equation of motion of the snake formulated in the frequency domain

$$M \frac{\partial^2 U(\omega, t)}{\partial t^2} + C \frac{\partial U(\omega, t)}{\partial t} + U(\omega, t) K(\omega) = G(\omega), \tag{13}$$

where $M$ and $C$ are the mass and damping of the time-based second-order differential system, and are considered invariant throughout the snake. $G(\omega)$ is the Fourier transform of the external forces. Note that in (13) only values of $\omega$ that are multiples of $2\pi/N$ are relevant. The implementation of (13) is feasible by assuming a time step $\Delta t$, which leads to the discrete-time implementation where $\xi$ is discrete time, $b = 2M/\Delta t^2 + C/\Delta t$ and $c = -M/\Delta t^2$. The explicit equation of the snake motion is

$$(b + c + K(\omega)) U_\xi(\omega) = b U_{\xi-1}(\omega) + c U_{\xi-2}(\omega) + G_\xi(\omega), \tag{14}$$

This equation can be translated to the space-domain as

$$\eta^{-1}(\eta + k[n]) \circledast u_\xi[n] = b\, u_{\xi-1}[n] + c\, u_{\xi-2}[n] + \eta^{-1} g_\xi[n], \tag{15}$$

where $\eta = M + C$ is the global mass, $b = 1 + (1 + \gamma)^{-1}$ and $c = -(1 + \gamma)^{-1}$ are the second-order dynamic parameters, $\gamma = C/M$ is the damping-mass ratio, and $\circledast$ denotes circular convolution between equal length discrete sequences.

The spectrum $K(\omega)$ is the frequency kernel of the deformable model, and its discrete-space counterpart $k[n]$ corresponds to the first column (or row) of the stiffness matrix $\mathbf{K}$ from the original snake formulation [1]. Note that (15) is equivalent to the equation of motion of the original formulation: there the pseudo-inverse of the stiffness matrix is the kernel of the process, and, if the stiffness parameters are assumed to be spatial-invariant, the resulting matrix is circulant, that is, each column is constructed by shifting in one element the previous one. A circulant matrix is the algebraic representation of a circular discrete convolution.

## 3   Segmentation Process

In a classical problem of segmentation with active contours, at a certain point of the process, some nodes are "attached" to some high energy regions and the rest of the nodes are free. This scenario can be expressed as a non-uniform interpolation problem by reshaping (15) into

$$z_\xi[n] = b\, u_{\xi-1}[n] + c\, u_{\xi-2}[n], \tag{16}$$

$$y_\xi[n] = z_\xi[n] + (x_\xi[n] - z_\xi[n]) \sum_{k=-\infty}^{\infty} \delta[n - N_k], \tag{17}$$

$$u_\xi[n] = h[n] * y_\xi[n], \tag{18}$$

where $x_\xi[n] = \eta^{-1} g_\xi[n]$, $N_k$ are the positions of the nodes attracted by the external forces and $h[n]$ is the pseudo-inverse kernel of $k[n]$, i.e., its Fourier transform is

$$H(\omega) = \frac{\eta}{\eta + K(\omega)}. \tag{19}$$

Assuming initially for the analysis $N_k = kN$ and initial repose, then $X_\xi(\omega) = X_\xi(\omega - k\omega_0)$ with $\omega_0 = 2\pi/N$, $U_\xi(\omega) = Q_\xi(\omega)X_\xi(\omega)$, and equations (16)-(18) can be translated into the frequency domain,

$$Q_\xi(\omega) = b\, H(\omega)Q_{\xi-1}(\omega) + c\, H(\omega)Q_{\xi-2}(\omega) \tag{20}$$

$$-H(\omega)\frac{b}{N}\sum_{k=0}^{N-1} Q_{\xi-1}(\omega - k\omega_0) - H(\omega)\frac{c}{N}\sum_{k=0}^{N-1} Q_{\xi-2}(\omega - k\omega_0) + H(\omega).$$

Equation (20) shows that for a given $\omega$, the equivalent filter $Q_\xi(\omega)$ depends on its own values at frequencies equal to $\omega + k\omega_0$. By considering frequencies $\omega = i\omega_0 + \Delta\omega$ $(i = 0, ..., N-1$, and $|\Delta\omega| \le \omega_0/2)$, (20) yields to

$$\mathbf{q}_\xi = \mathbf{h} + \mathbf{H}\, (b\, \mathbf{q}_{\xi-1} + c\, \mathbf{q}_{\xi-2}), \tag{21}$$

where $\mathbf{q}_\xi = [Q_\xi(\Delta\omega), Q_\xi(\omega_0 + \Delta\omega), \ldots, Q_\xi((N-1)\omega_0 + \Delta\omega)]^T$, $\mathbf{h}$ defined accordingly, and matrix $\mathbf{H}$ is

$$\mathbf{H} = \mathrm{diag}(\mathbf{h}) - \frac{1}{N}\mathbf{h}\,[1 \overset{N}{\cdots} 1]. \tag{22}$$

In the steady state ($\xi = \infty$), equation (21) leads to $\mathbf{q} = (\mathbf{I} - \mathbf{H})^{-1}\mathbf{h}$, which describes the equivalent kernel in the steady state. The inverse process, that is, drawing kernel $H(\omega)$ from a desired final situation $Q(\omega)$ has no easy explicit formulation. Generally speaking, $Q(\omega)$ depends on the stiffness parameters, and on the overall mass $\eta$ (19). This means that for constant $\eta$, the solution reached in the steady state is the same regardless of the ratio damping-mass $\gamma$, however, the speed of the snake toward that final situation does depend on $\gamma$ [6].

## 3.1   Convergence Analysis

Subtraction of the final value in the recursion (21), that is, $\mathbf{r}_\xi = \mathbf{q}_\xi - \mathbf{q}_\infty$, gives rise to the linear difference equation that describes the residual evolution of the active contour

$$\mathbf{r}_\xi = b\,\mathbf{H}\,\mathbf{r}_{\xi-1} + c\,\mathbf{H}\,\mathbf{r}_{\xi-2}. \tag{23}$$

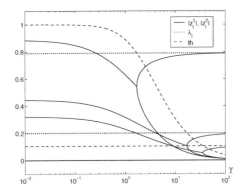

**Fig. 1.** Variation of $|z_i^1|, |z_i^2|$ and $|\lambda_i|$ with $\gamma$. The absolute value of the poles of the vibration modes are plotted in solid line, the eigenvalues of matrix **H** are plotted in dotted line, and, in dashed line, the threshold $th = (1 + \gamma)/(1 + \frac{1}{2}\gamma)^2$.

Matrix **H** can be expressed as $\mathbf{H} = \mathbf{LDL}^{-1}$, **D** being a diagonal matrix of eigenvalues $\lambda_1, ..., \lambda_N$, and **L** a matrix whose columns are the corresponding unitary orthogonal eigenvectors, $\mathbf{v}_i$. Then, (23) becomes

$$\mathbf{c}_\xi = b\, \mathbf{D}\, \mathbf{c}_{\xi-1} + c\, \mathbf{D}\, \mathbf{c}_{\xi-2}, \tag{24}$$

where $\mathbf{c}_\xi = \mathbf{L}^{-1}\mathbf{r}_\xi$. The decoupled difference equation (24) can be analyzed in the Z-plane domain. Then, solving the decoupled quadratic equations provides the poles of the vibration modes,

$$z_i^{1,2} = \frac{b\lambda_i}{2} \pm \frac{1}{2}\sqrt{b^2\lambda_i^2 + 4c\lambda_i}, \tag{25}$$

Depending on the sign of the discriminant, $\Delta_i = b^2\lambda_i^2 + 4c\lambda_i$, the resulting orthogonal mode can be underdamped ($\Delta < 0$), critical damped ($\Delta = 0$) or overdamped ($\Delta > 0$).

The fastest speed of the slowest mode is reached when the poles associated to the largest eigenvalue meets the critical damping condition and then

$$\gamma_0 = 2\lambda_{max}^{-1}\left(1 - \lambda_{max} + \sqrt{1 - \lambda_{max}}\right). \tag{26}$$

Figure 1 describes the behavior of the eigenvalues and the associated poles. Note that when the eigenvalue is bigger than threshold, the corresponding complex poles evolve into two real poles. Simulation parameters are $N = 4$, $\alpha = 0$ and $\beta = 1$ and finite differences.

### 3.2   Complexity Analysis and Optimum Parameters

When the eigenvalues are near the unity, it is difficult to appreciate differences between their system velocities. Another way to express the speed of convergence is by means of the system complexity, defined as

$$N_e = (1 - \lambda_{max})^{-1} \tag{27}$$

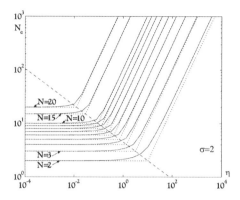

**Fig. 2.** Variation of system complexity $N_e$ with the global mass $\eta$ for different values of the largest gap in the node set $N$

where $\lambda_{max}$ is the largest eigenvalue of matrix $\mathbf{H}$ (22). Figure 2 contains, in solid line, the relation between mass $\eta$ and method complexity $N_e$ for different values of largest gap between attracted nodes $N$. Each curve is confined by two asymptotic lines (in dotted line), defined by

$$N_e = N \tag{28}$$

$$\log_{10}(N_e) = \log_{10}(\eta) + \sigma \ (\kappa_1 \log_{10}(N) + \kappa_2) \tag{29}$$

where $\kappa_1 = 1.97$, $\kappa_2 = -0.95$ and $\sigma$ is the derivative order ($\sigma = 2$ is equivalent to $\alpha{=}0$, $\beta{=}1$ in the original formulation). The crossing point between both asymptotes is described then by the following equation

$$\log_{10}(\eta_0) = (1 - \sigma\kappa_1) \log_{10}(N) - \sigma\kappa_2 \tag{30}$$

**Table 1.** Algorithm for the optimum design of dynamic parameters of active contours

$$
\begin{aligned}
\eta &= N^{(1-\sigma k_1)} 10^{(-\sigma k_2)} \\
N_e &= max \left\{ N, \eta N^{(\sigma k_1)} 10^{(\sigma k_2)} \right\} \\
\lambda &= 1 - 1/N_e \\
\gamma &= 2\lambda^{-1}((1 - \lambda) + \sqrt{1 - \lambda}) \\
b &= 1 + (1 + \gamma)^{-1} \\
c &= - (1 + \gamma)^{-1} \\
\mathbf{K} &= \alpha\,\mathbf{K}_\alpha + \beta\,\mathbf{K}_\beta \\
\mathbf{H} &= \eta\,(\eta + \mathbf{K})^{-1}
\end{aligned}
$$

**repeat**
$\quad\quad \mathbf{u} = DFT^{-1}\{\mathbf{H}\,(b\,\mathbf{U}_\xi + c\,\mathbf{U}_{\xi-1})\} + \eta^{-1}\mathbf{g}_\xi$
$\quad\quad \mathbf{U}_{\xi-1} = \mathbf{U}_\xi$
$\quad\quad \mathbf{U}_\xi \ = DFT\{\mathbf{u}\}$
**until** $\|\mathbf{U} - \mathbf{U}_\xi\| < tol$

Then, given a non uniformly distributed dataset, the algorithm would start by detecting the length of the largest gap in the dataset, then the optimum mass value is computed according to (30), and from there $N_e$ is obtained and then the necessary second order system parameters: $\lambda$, $\gamma$, $b$ and $c$. This optimum snake algorithm is described in Table 1.

## 4  Conclusions

The final contour shape of the segmentation is dependent on the sum of mass and rigidity, $\eta$, and is independent of the damping-mass ratio $\gamma$. The value of mass $\eta$ used to achieve a certain interpolation degree is theoretically infinite, or at least very high. From a practical point of view, given $\eta$ and $N$, one would be interested in setting $\gamma$ so that the snake achieves its maximum speed of convergence.

According to the previous results, the fastest interpolating snake could be based on using such a low value of mass $\eta$ that corresponds to a low value of method complexity $N_e = N$. The mass of the inflexion point (30), $\eta_o$, achieves a fair final interpolation, but if a finer segmentation is required, the mass value has to be increased. An increase in an order of magnitude in $\eta$ implies the same increase in $N_e$ and this could give rise to an prohibitive slow convergence.

## References

1. J. Liang, T. McInerney, and D. Terzopoulos, "United snakes," *ICCV*, 1999.
2. V. Caselles, R. Kimmel, and G. Sapiro, "Geodesic active contours," *ICCV*, 1995.
3. D. Terzopoulos, *Deformable models: classic, topology-adaptive and generalized formulations*, pp. 21–40, Geometric Level Set Methods. Springer-Verlag NY, 2003.
4. L. Weruaga, R. Verdú, and J. Morales, "Frequency domain formulation of active parametric deformable models," *IEEE Trans. PAMI*, pp. 1568–1578, Dec. 2004.
5. L. Weruaga, J. Morales, L. Núñez, and R. Verdú, "Estimating volumetric motion in human thorax with parametric matching constraints," *IEEE Trans. Medical Imaging*, vol. 22, no. 6, pp. 766–772, June 2003.
6. R. Verdú, J. Morales, R. González, and L. Weruaga, "Convergence analysis of active contours in image segmentation," *IEEE ICIP*, pp. 2749–2752, 2004.

# Moving Objects Segmentation Based on Automatic Foreground / Background Identification of Static Elements

Laurent Isenegger, Luis Salgado, and Narciso García

Grupo de Tratamiento de Imágenes,
E. T. S. Ingenieros de Telecomunicación – Universidad Politécnica de Madrid - Spain
{lis, lsa, ngs}@gti.ssr.upm.es

**Abstract.** A new segmentation strategy is proposed to precisely extract moving objects in video sequences. It is based on the automatic detection of the static elements, and its classification as background and foreground using static differences and contextual information. Additionally, tracking information is incorporated to reduce the computational cost. Finally, segmentation is refined through a Markov random field (MRF) change detection analysis including the foreground information, which allows improving the accuracy of the segmentation. This strategy is presented in the context of low quality sequences of surveillance applications but it could be applied to other applications, the only requirement being to have a static or quasi static background.

## 1 Introduction

One of the key steps of many segmentation algorithms is the background's estimation process. Various characteristics of the sequence can be used with different levels of complexity. In [1], exclusively temporal correlation is used to detect the background pixels; motion analysis is introduced in [2] while other works use edge information associated, for example, with color analysis [3] to detect moving objects. Currently, the algorithm, proposed in [4], is very popular, using a mixture of gaussians for each pixel to represent the distribution of its value along the sequence.

All these processes are often used to extract moving objects on static background. Nevertheless, the results applying directly this strategy are quite limited in specific situations. This is the case of the sequences where motionless objects are located in foreground. Moving objects are hidden by the foreground static elements, and the segmentation algorithms can not extract the detected objects. The detection of these foreground static elements would highly improve segmentation and tracking performances, allowing occlusion prediction. Additionally, another limitation comes from the computational requirements, which have to be reduced for many applications.

To overcome the above mentioned limitations, a new segmentation strategy, incorporating automatic detection of static elements in foreground is presented in this paper. It is designed to deal with low quality images, keeping at the same time a reasonable computational cost. A detection of static elements and a coarse segmentation, including a morphological analysis are performed based on a modified version of the

J. Blanc-Talon et al. (Eds.): ACIVS 2005, LNCS 3708, pp. 491–498, 2005.
© Springer-Verlag Berlin Heidelberg 2005

algorithm presented in [4]. These operations, which are the most computational demanding ones in our strategy, are carried out one every P frames of the sequence (key frames). The result of this process is used to separate the scene foreground and background combining: (i) static differences based analysis of the moving objects areas; (ii) segmentation of the reference image based on a basic region growing strategy. This coarse segmentation for the key frames is refined through a Bayesian algorithm using Markov Random Fields (MRF) [6] with multi-resolution differences [1]. For the images between key frames, tracking information obtained through a Kalman filter [5] is used to predict the evolution of the moving objects areas and segment them accordingly with the MRF strategy.

## 2   System Description

A block diagram of the proposed segmentation algorithm is presented in figure 1. The input is a sequence $I$ of images, where $I_n$ is the image at the instant n, and $I_{n;t}$ the pixel indicated by the vector $\mathbf{t}$ of coordinates $(x,y)$ in $I_n$. First, a simplified version of the algorithm developed in [4] followed by a morphological analysis, is applied on one of every P frames to create reference images $I_n^{ref}$ (i.e. images gathering only the static elements of the environment without any moving object), and perform a first coarse segmentation of the moving objects $S_n$. These results are used in a background/foreground segmentation phase composed of two steps: a pixel-based analysis and the introduction of contextual information using a region-growing strategy.

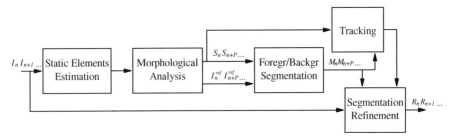

**Fig. 1.** Block diagram of the proposed algorithm

A tracking process through a structured Kalman filter [5] allows to reduce the final area of search of the moving object. Finally, the segmentation refinement is performed by a Bayesian algorithm using MRF [6] with multi-resolution differences [1]. The result of the algorithm is a multilevel mask image $R_n$ where each pixel is labeled either as "background", "foreground", or "belonging to a moving object". The following sections describe in detail each processing block.

### 2.1   Static Elements Estimation

The aim of the estimation of static elements is to create a low resolution mask indicating which pixels of the analyzed image are static. To detect the static elements, a modified version of the method presented in [4], is used. It is based on a combination of several gaussians for each pixel to model the distribution of its gray level value along the sequence. It offers a good trade-off between computational costs, adaptability to slow illumination changes, and robustness with respect to the noise. To reduce the computational requirements and the noise in the images, operations are carried out on subsampled versions of the images filtered using a bilinear filter to limit aliasing.

**Matched Component Identification.** For each pixel t, the distribution of its gray level values $f(I_{n;t})$ is modeled as a mixture of $K$ $(3 \leq K \leq 5)$ gaussians:

$$f\left(I_{n;t}\right) = \sum_{i=1}^{K} \omega_{n;t;i} * \eta\left(t; \mu_{n;t;i}; \sigma_{n;t;i}\right) \tag{1}$$

where $\omega_{n;t;i}$ represents the weighting factor associated to the i-th component, with the condition $\Sigma_i \omega_{n;t;i} = 1$, and $\eta$ $(t; \mu_{n;t;i}; \sigma_{n;t;i})$ is the i-th gaussian component with mean value $\mu_{n;t;i}$ and standard deviation $\sigma_{n,t,i}$. For each input pixel $I_{n;t}$, it is determined which one of the $K$ gaussians, the so called 'matched component', corresponds to the current pixel's value: The gaussian $i$ is considered as the 'matched component' if $\mid I_{n;t} - \mu_{n-1;t;i} \mid < M * \sigma_{n-1;t;i}$ with $M$, being a threshold defining a certain accepted deviation. Once identified the 'matched component', its values are updated as:

$$\omega_{n;t;i} = \left(1 - \alpha\right) * \omega_{n-1;t;i} + \alpha$$
$$\mu_{n;t;i} = \left(1 - \alpha\right) * \mu_{n-1;t;i} + \alpha * I_{n;t} \tag{2}$$
$$\sigma_{n;t;i}^{2} = \left(1 - \alpha\right) * \sigma_{n-1;t;i}^{2} + \alpha * \left(I_{n;t} - \mu_{n-1;t;i}\right)^{2}$$

where $\alpha$ is a parameter defined by the user $(0 < \alpha < 1)$, that influences directly the update rate of the background. In this approach, the updating process is significantly simplified through the use of $\alpha$ instead of $\rho$ (proposed in [4], complex and computationally intensive to estimate) with good results. The other $(K-1)$ gaussians keep the same values $\mu_{n;t;i}$ and $\sigma_{n,t,i}$ but their weighting factors are updated through:

$$\omega_{n;t;i} = \left(1 - \alpha\right) * \omega_{n-1;t;i} \tag{3}$$

If none of the gaussians corresponds to the 'matched component', the gaussian with the lower value of the weighting factor is replaced by a new gaussian with a mean value fixed to the pixel value (i.e. $\mu_{n;t;i} = I_{n;t}$), an initial standard deviation $\sigma_0$ quite high and an initial low value of the weighting factor $\omega_0$, then normalized.

**Pixel Classification.** This processing phase classifies each reference image pixel as either static (belonging to a background or foreground object) or dynamic (belonging to a moving object). For each pixel **t**, if the 'matched component' determined in the previous phase is one of the gaussians associated to the pixel when it represents a static element, the processed pixel is considered as a static element.

To determine the gaussians representing static elements, the K gaussians are first ranked by decreasing values of $\omega_{n;t;i}/\sigma_{n;t;i}$: as low variance and high weighting factor are typical characteristics of static elements, the number N of gaussians $(N \leq K)$ representing a static element is determined with the following criterion:

$$N = \underset{k}{\arg\min} \left( \sum_{i=1}^{k} \omega_{n;t;i} > T \right) \tag{4}$$

where $T$ is a threshold defined by the user ($0< T <1$). It gives the opportunity to represent a static element with several components, which would result very useful in case of small repetitive movements of the background (quasi-static background ).

This reference image mask can be computed for each one of the images in the sequence. Nevertheless, this operation has a high computational cost and it is only required when extremely fast changes appear in the sequence. This is not the case in most of the applications, so this process is only carried out on $I$ every $P$ frames of the sequence (key frames). For the examples provided in this work, $P=4$. Moreover, it must be stressed that the proposed strategy is able to deal with large lighting variations, only requiring a certain adaptation period to the new scene characteristics.

### 2.2 Morphological Analysis

The low quality of the highly compressed images provided by the cameras in this application, increases the number of wrong pixel classifications. A pixel labeled erroneously as static, generates an error in the updated reference image, while a pixel labeled erroneously as dynamic only delays its correct update in the reference image. Therefore, a morphological analysis is carried out which favors the re-classification of static pixels as dynamic when neighboring pixels are classified as dynamic. A filter is applied on every pixel classified as static in the image: if a certain portion of the pixels in the connected neighborhood are considered as dynamic elements (two in our implementation), the analyzed pixel classification will be changed to dynamic. Then, a dilation expands the regions associated to the moving objects to avoid errors appearing mainly in the limits of the detected object masks. After these operations performed on subsampled images, the full-resolution mask gathering the static and dynamic pixels is obtained through pixel duplication.

Based on this full-resolution mask, the update of the reference image is carried out as follows: if pixel **t** in the mask is labeled as static, the pixel **t** in the reference image is set to the current pixel's value ($I_{n;t}^{ref} = I_{n;t}$), and the coarse segmentation removes this pixel ($S_{n;t}=0$ ); otherwise, the pixel **t** in the reference image keeps the same gray level value than in the previous reference image ($I_{n;t}^{ref} = I_{n-P;t}^{ref}$ ), and in the coarse segmentation, the pixel is set to the current's pixel value ($S_{n,t}=I_{n,t}$). It should be stressed again that the update of the characteristics of the gaussians is performed for every image, while pixel classification, reference image creation, and the coarse segmentation are only carried out for the key frames.

### 2.3 Background / Foreground Segmentation

The aim of this processing phase is the identification of the background and foreground static elements using the reference image $I_n^{ref}$ and the coarse segmentation $S_n$. It is carried out by a pixel-based analysis using static differences, and the introduction of contextual information with a region growing strategy. Finally, a multi-level mask $M_n$ is created where pixels are labeled either as belonging to the"background" or "foreground" areas.

**Pixel-Based Analysis Using Static Differences.** It performs an identification of the static elements belonging to the background and those belonging to the foreground.

For the first reference image computed $I_I^{ref}$, all its pixels are considered as belonging to the foreground. For each new updated reference image $I_{n+P}^{ref}$, for every pixel **t** classified as dynamic in $S_{n+P}$, the static difference $|I_{n+P:t}^{ref} - S_{n+P:t}|$ is computed and compared with a threshold. If the value is above the threshold, it means that this difference is too high to be only due to the noise present in the images, and therefore **t** is likely being visited by a moving object. This implies that the moving object is occluding the static element represented in the reference image, and therefore the pixel in the reference image belongs to the background. For the pixels whose static difference are below the threshold, and for those considered as static elements after the morphological analysis, they keep the same label as in the previous computed mask.

**Contextual Information Based on Gray Level Values.** The pixel-based analysis introduced previously constraint the correct background/foreground identification to those pixels visited by a moving object. Effectively, if no moving objects visit a pixel, it will be considered as foreground even if there is no evidence. To relax this constraint, a region analysis on the reference image is incorporated. It is based on a simple region growing strategy - the single linkage region-growing [7] algorithm - with a homogeneity criterion based on pixel gray level differences below a threshold. After, a median filter is used to eliminate isolated regions in the segmented reference image.

For each segmented region in the reference image, if a certain portion of the pixels are already labeled as "background", the entire homogeneous region is labeled as background. The computational cost of these operations depends on the number of regions in the segmented image, directly related to the threshold value used in the region-growing strategy. This threshold has been set to 5 in our implementation as it keeps fine details in the reference image, while it reduces the computational cost.

     (a)           (b)           (c)

**Fig. 2.** Separation of background / foreground before (a) and after (b) the introduction of contextual information

Figures 2.(a) shows an image from a surveillance sequence where moving objects are passing in front of a shopping window full of sales advertisements in the foreground. The result after the pixel based analysis previously introduced is presented in (b). It can be observed that the bottom-left area is full of pixels which can not be classified as background (although they are par of it) because no moving object visits them. The introduction of contextual information increases the number of regions that are now considered background (as it can be seen in (c)), although this region based analysis imply some loss of detail as, for example, part of the "e" on the shop window glass is now considered as part of the background.

## 2.4  Tracking

Up to now, all the information extracted about the location of moving objects is relative to the key frames for which the first coarse segmentations are built (..., $S_{n-2P}$, $S_{n-P}$, $S_n$). The segmentation refinement described in the next section is applied to those moving objects detected, removing previously the static foreground regions identified. For those intermediate images ($I_{n-P+1}$,...,$I_{n-1}$,$I_{n+1}$....) for which no coarse segmentation is created, the same final segmentation algorithm is applied but restricted to the image areas covered by the moving objects predicted bounding boxes.

Prediction is achieved through a structured Kalman filter [5], based on the centroid of the moving objects position computed in the previous coarse segmentations ($S_{n-2P}$, $S_{n-P}$, $S_n$). The location of the moving objects bounding boxes in the intermediate images are predicted by the regions speed and acceleration provided by the Kalman filter: The last bounding box computed with a coarse segmentation is moved in the direction and amplitude described by speed and acceleration vectors of its centroid. A segmentation refinement is applied to the image area covered by the predicted bounding boxes having eliminated those pixels identified as foreground static elements.

## 2.5  Segmentation Refinement

This step is to segment accurately the moving objects in the sequence. The segmentation strategy proposed in [1] is applied using a MRF change detection operating on a combination of static and dynamic differences at different resolutions: a static difference image is computed as the difference between the reference image and the frames under analysis ($|I_n-I_n^{ref}|$); a dynamic difference image is computed as the difference between the two consecutive frames ($|I_n-I_{n-1}|$) to profit of the motion information. Then, the sum of these differences is used in the change detection.

**Change Detection.** The change detection is based on the relationship between the neighborhood of the pixel analyzed and a threshold v(j) defined as follows:

$$v(j) = t_s + 16*B + 4*B*j \qquad (5)$$

where $t_s$ is the so-called 'anchor threshold', $B$ is called 'potential value', and the variable $j$ represents the number of 'changed pixels' in a 3*3 window centered at the pixel analyzed [6]. The values of the threshold v(j) and the sum of the differences previously computed are compared: If the sum is above the threshold, the current pixel belongs to a moving object; otherwise, the pixel is labeled as 'background'. To reduce the computational cost, this strategy is applied on low resolution images.

**Refinement.** To obtain the final segmentation at full resolution, direct interpolation based on pixel duplication is carried out on the previous results, followed by a re-segmentation, applying the same change detection strategy but constrained to the contours of moving objects and foreground static elements: the areas where accuracy in the segmentation is lost due to the projection process. Finally, pixels corresponding to foreground static elements are removed from the segmentation.

# 3   Results

The proposed system has been used in surveillance applications where the acquisition device must be located within the premises. So, the camera is placed in the upper corner of the shop window as it can be seen in figure 3.(a). Besides avoiding the use of public domain areas, the location offers the advantage of physical protection. The acquired image has three different areas according to their distance to the camera: the moving objects to be analyzed, the background and the slogans on the glass (foreground), that occlude meaningful parts of the moving objects.

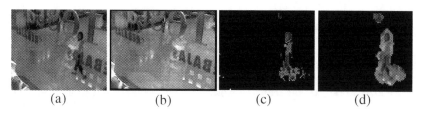

(a)                    (b)                    (c)                    (d)

**Fig. 3.** Results of estimation of static elements

After several tests conducted of different environment conditions, the following values were selected to generate the best reference image with the most appropriate update rate: $K=3$; $M=2,5$; $\alpha = 0,03$; $\sigma_0 = 2,5$; $\omega_0 =0,03$ and $T=0,6$. Moreover, the use of a relative low value (0,6) for the threshold $T$ usually reduces the representation of the static component to just one gaussian.

The application of the proposed scheme of estimation of static elements to the image of the figure 3.(a) is displayed in figures 3.(b)-(d). Figure 3.(b) shows the computed reference image $I_n^{ref}$. Figure 3.(c) and (d) present the detected moving object areas before and after the morphological analysis. They show the improvement of the coarse segmentation result, so that the whole moving object is segmented, and the number of wrong classified pixels is reduced.

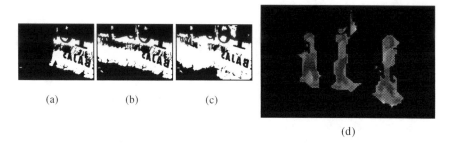

(a)              (b)              (c)

(d)

**Fig. 4.** Processing phases results

The foreground/background segmentation process is shown in figure 4.(a)-(c) To get these results, $ts$ is experimentally set to 55 and $B$ to 2,2. Figures 4.(a)-(c) display the identified foreground pixels (in black) at three different instants. In the first image (a), most of the static elements are considered foreground: only those visited by a moving object are correctly segmented (right side of the image). In (b) and (c), the correct identified areas have increased as most of the image pixels have been visited by a moving object. Figure 4.(d) presents the final segmentation results at different instants in the sequence. This final segmentation improves very significantly the coarse segmentation exposed in figure 3.(d). Although some parts of the moving object are hidden by the foreground detected areas, the resulting segmentation, even if broken into non-connected areas, is considered to belong to the same moving object. Occlusion detection is applied to keep temporal coherence of the detected moving regions.

## 4   Conclusions

A new moving objects segmentation strategy incorporating the automatic identification of the static elements in the foreground has been presented. Several tests have been conducted on different scenarios showing its usefulness and examples of one of these tests have been presented here. It must be stressed that the unique requirement is the presence of a static background, or at least a quasi static one with a change rate slower than the reference image refresh rate. Although average quality of the sequences is far from good, it shows typical scenarios for this type of surveillance. The proposed algorithm is being upgraded to provide better tracking accuracy, and achieve a more precise refinement block.

## Acknowledgements

This work has been partialy supported by the Plan Nacional de Investigación Científica, Desarrollo e Innovación Tecnológica of the Spanish Government under project TIN2004-07860-C02

## References

1. José M. Cobo, Luis Salgado, and Julián Cabrera, "Adaptative segmentation for gymnastic exercises based on change detection over multi-resolution combined differences" *Int. Conf. on Image Processing ICIP 2003,* p.337-340, 2003.
2. D. Farin, Peter H. N. de With, and W. Effelsberg, "Robust background estimation for complex video sequences", *Int. Conf. on Image Processing ICIP 2003.,* p.145–148, 2003.
3. S. Jabri, Z. Duric, H. Wechsler, A. Rosenfeld, "Detection and location of people in video images using adaptive fusion of color and edge information", *Int. Conf. On Pattern Recognition ICPR 2000,* Vol. 4, p. 4627, 2000.
4. W. E. L. Grimson y C. Stauffer, "Adapt. background mixture models for real-time tracking", *ICPR* , Vol. 1, p. 22–29, 1999.
5. Dae-Sik Jang, Seok-Woo Jang, and Hyung-Il Choi, "Structured Kalman filter for tracking partially occluded moving objects", IEEE Int. Workshop on Biologically Motivated Computer Vision p. 248-257, May 2000
6. T. Aach, and A. Kaup, "Bayes. algor. for adapt. Change detect. in image seq. using Markov Random Fields", *Signal Proc.: Image Communications,* vol.7, no. 2, pp. 147-160, 1995.
7. R. M. Haralick, and L. G. Shapiro, "Computer and Robot Vision", Addison-Wesley Publishing Company, 1992.

# Γ-Convergence Approximation to Piecewise Constant Mumford-Shah Segmentation

Jianhong Shen[*]

University of Minnesota, Minneapolis, MN 55455, USA
jhshen@math.umn.edu
http://www.math.umn.edu/~jhshen

**Abstract.** Piecewise constant Mumford-Shah segmentation [17] has been rediscovered by Chan and Vese [6] in the context of region based active contours. The work of Chan and Vese demonstrated many practical applications thanks to their clever numerical implementation using the level-set technology of Osher and Sethian [18]. The current work proposes a Γ-convergence formulation to the piecewise constant Mumford-Shah model, and demonstrates its simple implementation by the iterated integration of a linear Poisson equation. The new formulation makes unnecessary some intermediate tasks like normal data extension and level-set reinitialization, and thus lowers the computational complexity.

## 1 Introduction: The Mumford-Shah Segmentation Model

The Mumford-Shah segmentation model [17] is built upon a generic image model into which the edge feature is explicitly incorporated as in [10]. Consider the following image generation model:

$$\Gamma \longrightarrow u \xrightarrow{\oplus n} u_0,$$

where in the reverse order, $u_0$ denotes an observed image, $n$ an additive Gaussian noise field, and $u$ piecewise smooth (or cartoonish) image patches consistent with a given edge layout $\Gamma$.

From Bayesian point of view [10,16], segmentation is to estimate the posterior probability

$$p(\Gamma, u \mid u_0), \quad \text{or equivalently,} \quad p(u_0 \mid u, \Gamma)p(u, \Gamma)/p(u_0).$$

In the Markovian setting [7], the joint prior can be expressed by

$$p(u, \Gamma) = p(u \mid \Gamma)p(\Gamma).$$

Thus by putting aside the constant $p(u_0)$ and working with the energy function (or the *logarithmic likelihood function*) $E = -\log p$, one obtains the structure of the Mumford-Shah model up to an ineffectual constant:

$$E[\Gamma, u \mid u] = E[\Gamma] + E[u \mid \Gamma] + E[u_0 \mid u, \Gamma].$$

[*] Research is supported by the NSF (USA) under the grant number DMS-0202565.

J. Blanc-Talon et al. (Eds.): ACIVS 2005, LNCS 3708, pp. 499–506, 2005.
© Springer-Verlag Berlin Heidelberg 2005

The *full* Mumford-Shah model [15,17] is in fact explicitly expressed by:

$$E[\Gamma, u \mid u] = \sigma \text{length}(\Gamma) + \beta \int_{\Omega \backslash \Gamma} |\nabla u|^2 dx + \lambda \int_{\Omega} (u - u_0)^2 dx,$$

where $dx = dx_1 dx_2$ denotes the area element of a 2-D domain $\Omega$. The model has become a classic and been studied by numerous researchers (e.g., the monograph [15]).

For images made of piecewise *homogeneous* stochastic patches, only their constant averages can be identified as the cartoonish pieces, i.e.,

$$u(x) \equiv C_i, \qquad x \in \Omega_i, \quad \text{and} \quad \Omega_i \in \pi(\Omega \mid \Gamma).$$

Here the notation $\pi(\Omega \mid \Gamma)$ denotes the partitioning of the entire image domain $\Omega$ given an edge layout $\Gamma$, or the collection of *connected components* of $\Omega \backslash \Gamma$ topologically speaking. The original Mumford-Shah model is then reduced to the piecewise constant model, or simply, the *reduced* Mumford-Shah model:

$$E[(C_i's), \Gamma \mid u_0] = \sigma \text{length}(\Gamma) + \lambda \sum_{\Omega_i \in \pi(\Omega \mid \Gamma)} \int_{\Omega_i} (u(x) - C_i)^2 dx.$$

Mathematically this reduced model is a proper asymptotic limit of the full Mumford-Shah model, as discussed in the original paper of Mumford and Shah [17], or Chan and Shen [5]. Recently in the award-winning paper [6,21] (2003 Best Paper of IEEE Signal Processing Society), Chan and Vese rediscovered this model in the context of region based active contours. As in [6], we shall mainly focus on the 2-phase model to illustrate our primary contributions:

$$E[C_+, C_-, \Gamma \mid u_0] = \sigma \text{length}(\Gamma) + \lambda \int_{\Omega_+} (u(x) - C_+)^2 dx + \lambda \int_{\Omega_-} (u(x) - C_-)^2 dx,$$

$$(1)$$

where $\Gamma$ partitions $\Omega$ into the interior $\Omega_+$ and exterior $\Omega_-$. As remarkably demonstrated by Chan and Vese [6,21], such a 2-phase model has already witnessed numerous intriguing applications in astronomy and medicine.

Chan and Vese have successfully implemented the above model using the level-set computing technology invented and continuously advanced by Stan Osher and James Sethian [18]. Multiphase frameworks have also been developed by Chan and Vese [21], and lately by Lie, Lysaker, and Tai [13].

The current work is complementary to the above level-set approach. Inspired by the $\Gamma$-convergence approximation to the full Mumford-Shah model developed by Ambrosio and Tortorelli [1], we propose a new $\Gamma$-convergence formulation of the reduced Mumford-Shah model, and its robust and fast computational implementation. As in [1], the new formulation overcomes the fundamental theoretical and computational difficulties resulting from the free-boundary nature of the Mumford-Shah model (both the full and the reduced). The computation is reduced to the iterated integration of a linear Poisson equation, which can be easily and efficiently implemented in Matlab in a uniform code, without extra intermediate processing steps (e.g., normal extension and reinitialization in the level-set approach) [21].

The organization of the paper goes as follows. Section 2 briefly reviews the essence of the Γ-convergence approximation to the full Mumford-Shah model. In Section 3, we introduce our new Γ-convergence approximate model to the reduced (i.e., piecewise constant) Mumford-Shah model. Efficient computational schemes and examples of generic test images are presented in Section 4.

## 2    Γ-Convergence Approximation to the Full M.-S. Model

Γ-convergence has its rigorous mathematical definition in metric spaces [1]. The intuition in the current context could be easily revealed by phase-field modelling in superconductors, as in the the the works of Ginzburg and Landau [11]. We now briefly explain the core idea in terms of approximation theory, which will then naturally bring out the new model.

In the Γ-convergence setting [1,8,14], a curve Γ (in 2-D) is instead represented by a 2-D function $z = z_\epsilon(x_1, x_2) \in [0, 1]$, depending upon a small scale parameter $\epsilon$. The energy associated with such a *phase field* $z$ is defined as

$$L_\epsilon[z] = \int_\Omega \epsilon |\nabla z|^2 dx + \int_\Omega \frac{(1-z)^2}{4\epsilon} dx.$$

Since $\epsilon \ll 1$, under any finite energy bound, the second term demands the phase field $z = z_\epsilon(x_1, x_2)$ to be as close to 1 as possible almost everywhere on the image domain $\Omega$.

Suppose in addition that along some narrow bands (intended to be the $\epsilon$-neighborhoods of a curve $\Gamma$) the field $z$ sharply drops down to zero. The graph of $z$ then looks like a canyon along its valley line $\Gamma$. The entire Γ-convergence machinery is built upon the following remarkable approximation result:

$$L_\epsilon[z] \simeq \text{length}(\Gamma). \tag{2}$$

Rigorous mathematical analysis is more involved but a qualitative glimpse is not too far beyond the level of Advanced Calculus as presented below.

Applying the generic inequality $2AB \le A^2 + B^2$, one has

$$L_\epsilon[z] \ge \int_\Omega |\nabla z||z - 1| dx = \frac{1}{2} \int_\Omega |\nabla w|, \qquad w = (1-z)^2,$$

where the graph of $w = (1-z)^2$ looks like a set of walls. Most contributions to the integral come from a narrow band along $\Gamma$ since $w$ is flat away from it. With smooth $\Gamma$, the narrow tubular neighborhood can then be parameterized by the tangential (arc length) and normal coordinates $s$ and $n$. Since $w$ remains almost constant along the tangential direction, we have $|\nabla w(s, n)| \simeq |\partial w/\partial n|$, and

$$\frac{1}{2} \int_\Omega |\nabla w| \simeq \int_\Gamma \int_{-\epsilon}^{\epsilon} \frac{1}{2} \left| \frac{\partial w}{\partial n} \right| dn ds = \int_\Gamma \frac{1}{2} \text{TV}(w(s, \cdot)) ds.$$

For any fixed $s$, the total variation $\mathrm{TV}(w(s,\cdot))$ along the normal direction is ideally 2, since each shoulder of the wall contributes 1 (by ascending from 0 to 1 and then descending from 1 to 0). Hence we have shown qualitatively that

$$L_\epsilon[z] \geq \mathrm{length}(\Gamma).$$

Assisted with a suitable ordinary differential equation [1], one can further show that the lower bound can indeed be approached.

Notice that the above analysis crucially relies upon the assumption that $z$ does touch down to the zero along $\Gamma$. But the energy form $L_\epsilon[z]$ alone does not guarantee it. In Ambrosio and Tortorelli's approximation [1], it is explicitly enforced through the second term of the Mumford-Shah model:

$$E_\epsilon[z] = \sigma \left( \int_\Omega \epsilon |\nabla z|^2 dx + \int_\Omega \frac{(1-z)^2}{4\epsilon} dx \right) + \beta \int_\Omega z^2 |\nabla u|^2 dx + \lambda \int_\Omega (u - u_0)^2 dx.$$

Along the jump (edge) set $\Gamma$, $\nabla u$ is not classically defined, or remains very large (or expensive) even after discrete sampling or continuous blurring. Thus the second term forces $z$ to touch down to zero along $\Gamma$ to bound the total energy.

## 3    $\Gamma$-Convergence Form of the Reduced M.-S. Model

For the reduced (piecewise constant) Mumford-Shah model, the lack of the gradient term loses the control factor that forces the field $z$ to drop near edges. In the current paper, therefore, we propose a proper variation of Ambrosio and Tortorelli's original formulation for the full Mumford-Shah model [1]. As in Chan and Vese [6], we shall primarily focus on the 2-phase model, and multiphase extensions can be similarly accomplished as in Vese and Chan [21], and in particular, in the recent work of Lie, Lysaker, and Tai [13].

To explicitly enforce two-phase separation without turning to the gradient information $\nabla u$, we propose to replace the original phase field energy by

$$L_\epsilon[z] = \int_\Omega \left( 9\epsilon |\nabla z|^2 + \frac{(1-z^2)^2}{64\epsilon} \right) dx.$$

The range of $z$ is restricted within $[-1, 1]$. Since $\epsilon \ll 1$, a bounded energy will force $z = 1$ or $z = -1$ almost everywhere. Following the similar inequality in the preceding section, one has

$$L_\epsilon[z] \geq \frac{3}{4} \int_\Omega |\nabla z| |1 - z^2| dx = \frac{3}{4} \int_\Omega \left| \nabla \left( z - \frac{z^3}{3} \right) \right| dx \simeq \frac{3}{4} \int_\Gamma \int_{-\epsilon}^\epsilon \mathrm{TV}(w) dn ds,$$

where $w = w(z) = z(1 - z^2/3)$ is a monotone function on $z \in [-1, 1]$, and the local curvilinear coordinates have been applied along the transition medial line (where $z = 0$), as in the preceding section. Since $w(-1) = -2/3$ and $w(1) = 2/3$, one has $\mathrm{TV}(w(z(s,\cdot))) = 4/3$ locally along each $s$-normal line. Thus we have qualitatively established the lower bound:

$$L_\epsilon[z] \geq \mathrm{length}(\Gamma).$$

Further elaborate study shows that the hyperbolic tangent transition:

$$z(s,n) = \tanh\left(\frac{n}{24\epsilon}\right)$$

can approach the lower bound as $\epsilon \to 0$. Thus $L_\epsilon[z]$ well approximates the length of $\Gamma$.

In the ideal scenario of two *pure* phases, one then defines their associated regions separately:

$$\Omega_\pm = \{x \in \Omega \mid z = \pm 1\}.$$

The associated indicator functions are ideally given by

$$1_+(x) = \left(\frac{1+z}{2}\right)^2, \qquad 1_-(x) = \left(\frac{1-z}{2}\right)^2.$$

(The square is mainly for computational stability in case that $z$ strays away from $[-1,1]$.) Then,

$$\int_{\Omega_\pm} (u_0 - C_\pm)^2 dx = \int_\Omega \left(\frac{1\pm z}{2}\right)^2 (u_0 - C_\pm)^2 dx.$$

In combination, we thus propose to approximate the reduced Mumford-Shah model (1) by the following $\Gamma$-convergence energy:

$$E_\epsilon[z, C_+, C_- \mid u_0] = \sigma \int_\Omega \left(9\epsilon |\nabla z|^2 + \frac{(1-z^2)^2}{64\epsilon}\right) dx +$$
$$\lambda \int_\Omega \left(\frac{1+z}{2}\right)^2 (u_0 - C_+)^2 dx + \lambda \int_\Omega \left(\frac{1-z}{2}\right)^2 (u_0 - C_-)^2 dx. \tag{3}$$

One minimizes the energy by some optimal phase field $z$ and means $C_\pm$'s.

Notice that all the four terms involve the field function $z$, but only the last two contain the mean fields $C_\pm$'s. Denote the sum of the last two terms by the "conditional" energy $E[C_+, C_- \mid u_0, z]$ given any $z$. Then the standard property of weighted least square approximation explicitly yields the conditional optima.

**Theorem 1 (Optimal Means).** *Given any square integrable phase field $z$ on a finite domain $\Omega$, as long as $z$ is not constant, the optimal means $C_\pm$'s to a given image $u_0$ in terms of $E[C_+, C_- \mid u_0, z]$ are given by:*

$$C_\pm = C_\pm[z] = \frac{\int_\Omega (1 \pm z(x))^2 u_0(x) dx}{\int_\Omega (1 \pm z(x))^2 dx}. \tag{4}$$

On the other hand, by the direct method of Calculus of Variations using minimizing sequences [9], one can establish the existence of minimizers to (3).

**Theorem 2 (Existence of Optimal Phase Fields).** *Let $u_0$ be a square integrable image on a bounded domain $\Omega$. Then there exists an optimal triple $(z^*, C_+^*, C_-^*)$ which achieves the minimum energy of $E_\epsilon[z, C_+, C_- \mid u_0]$ among the admissible class of Sobolev phase fields [9].*

To compute an optimal minimizer, one could apply the conditional mean field formulae (4) to reduce the triple energy $E_\epsilon[z, C_+, C_- \mid u_0]$ to an energy solely depending upon $z$:

$$E_\epsilon[z \mid u_0] = E_\epsilon[z, C_+[z], C_-[z] \mid u_0].$$

But this energy is no longer quadratic in $z$ and complexities multiply due to the denominators involving $z$.

Thus in practice, one employs the *alternating minimization* technique prevailing in multivariable optimization problems [8,20]. For given $z^n$ at step $n$, one computes the optimal means $C_\pm^n = C_\pm[z^n]$ by the formulae (4), and then updates $z^n$ to $z^{n+1}$ by treating $C_\pm$'s as known and minimizing

$$E_\epsilon[z \mid u_0, C_+, C_-] = \sigma \int_\Omega \left( 9\epsilon |\nabla z|^2 + \frac{(1-z^2)^2}{64\epsilon} \right) dx +$$
$$\lambda \int_\Omega \left( \frac{1+z}{2} \right)^2 (u_0 - C_+)^2 dx + \lambda \int_\Omega \left( \frac{1-z}{2} \right)^2 (u_0 - C_-)^2 dx. \tag{5}$$

## 4    Fast and Robust Numerical Implementation; Examples

Computationally, the optimization problem (5) is solved via its Euler-Lagrange equation. Write $e_\pm = u_0 - C_\pm$ as the residuals on $\Omega_\pm$, which are independent of $z$ since $C_\pm$ are given. Let $\mu = \lambda/(4\sigma)$. Then the Euler-Lagrange equation of $E_\epsilon[z \mid u_0, C_+, C_-]$ is given by

$$0 = -9\epsilon\Delta z - \frac{(1-z^2)z}{32\epsilon} + \mu e_+^2(1+z) - \mu e_-^2(1-z), \tag{6}$$

with the Neumann adiabatic boundary condition. One further rewrites it to:

$$-9\epsilon\Delta z + \left( \frac{z^2}{32\epsilon} + \mu(e_+^2 + e_-^2) \right) z = \mu e_-^2 - \mu e_+^2 + \frac{z}{32\epsilon},$$

or simply $-9\epsilon\Delta z + R(z)z = f(z)$ with $R$ and $f$ denoting the corresponding terms. The latter can be solved iteratively by having the $z$'s in $R$ and $f$ frozen:

$$z_m \to z_{m+1} : \quad -9\epsilon\Delta z_{m+1} + R_m z_{m+1} = f_m, \tag{7}$$

where $R_m = R(z_m) \geq 0$ and $f_m = f(z_m)$. Thus at each step it suffices to solve this linear Poisson equation on $z_{m+1}(x_1, x_2)$, which can be implemented efficiently in Matlab due to many fast elliptic solvers. Our computational experiments show that even ordinary Guass-Jacobi type of iteration schemes [12] lead to fast and robust convergence, including starting from any random initial guess.

The following flow summarizes our entire algorithm:

$$\hookrightarrow z^n \xrightarrow{\text{by}(4)} [C_+^n, C_-^n] \to \left[ z_m^{n+1} \xrightarrow{\text{by}(7)} z_{m+1}^{n+1} \right] \to z^{n+1} \to$$

The examples in the next section have all been generated from this algorithm. Below we briefly discuss how to properly choose the parameters in the model.

(a) The $\Gamma$-convergence parameter $\epsilon$ should be in the order of $O(h)$, where $h$ denotes the grid scale of a discrete image domain, for example $\epsilon = 4h$.

(b) Generally $\sigma$ (or the tension parameter) is of order $O(1)$, while the fitting Lagrange multiplier $\lambda$ should be inversely proportional to the variance of the Gaussian noise embedded in the observed image $u_0$ [2,3,4,5,19].

In Figure 1, we have demonstrated the performance of our new model and algorithm on three generic test images: peppers, the Milky Way, and the Pathfinder on the Mars by NASA (USA). For the images of peppers and the Pathfinder, we have shown the $\Gamma$-convergence output $z$'s, while for the Milky Way in the middle, the zero level curve (i.e., the sharp transition curve) of the output $z$ has been superimposed upon the original image $u_0$. (The associated mpeg movies are available from the author upon request.) The numerical performance (e.g., topological merging and splitting) is comparable with Chan and Vese's level-set approach [6], while the computational complexity is substantially lower without intermediate tasks like normal extension and level-set reinitialization [6,18].

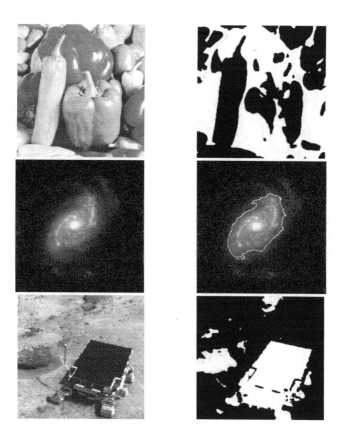

**Fig. 1.** Left: three generic images $u_0$'s: peppers, the Milky Way, and the Pathfinder landed on the Mars (NASA, USA); Right: the output $z$'s or their zero-level curves

# References

1. L. Ambrosio and V. M. Tortorelli. Approximation of functionals depending on jumps by elliptic functionals via $\Gamma$-convergence. *Comm. Pure Appl. Math.*, 43:999–1036, 1990.
2. T. F. Chan, S. Osher, and J. Shen. The digital TV filter and nonlinear denoising. *IEEE Trans. Image Process.*, 10(2):231–241, 2001.
3. T. F. Chan and J. Shen. Variational restoration of non-flat image features: models and algorithms. *SIAM J. Appl. Math.*, 61(4):1338–1361, 2000.
4. T. F. Chan and J. Shen. Mathematical models for local nontexture inpaintings. *SIAM J. Appl. Math.*, 62(3):1019–1043, 2001.
5. T. F. Chan and J. Shen. *Image Processing and Analysis: variational, PDE, wavelet, and stochastic methods*. SIAM Publisher, Philadelphia, 2005.
6. T. F. Chan and L. A. Vese. Active contours without edges. *IEEE Trans. Image Process.*, 10(2):266–277, 2001.
7. T. M. Cover and J. A. Thomas. *Elements of Information Theory*. John Wiley & Sons, Inc., New York, 1991.
8. S. Esedoglu and J. Shen. Digital inpainting based on the Mumford-Shah-Euler image model. *European J. Appl. Math.*, 13:353–370, 2002.
9. L. C. Evans. *Partial Differential Equations*. Amer. Math. Soc., 1998.
10. S. Geman and D. Geman. Stochastic relaxation, Gibbs distributions, and the Bayesian restoration of images. *IEEE Trans. Pattern Anal. Machine Intell.*, 6:721–741, 1984.
11. V. L. Ginzburg and L. D. Landau. On the theory of superconductivity. *Soviet Phys. JETP*, 20:1064–1082, 1950.
12. G. H. Golub and C. F. Van Loan. *Matrix Computations*. The Johns Hopkins University Press, Baltimore, 1983.
13. J. Lie, M. Lysaker, and X.-C. Tai. A binary level set model and some applications to Mumford-Shah image segmentation. *UCLA CAM Tech. Report*, 04-31, 2004.
14. R. March. Visual reconstruction with discontinuities using variational methods. *Image Vision Comput.*, 10:30–38, 1992.
15. J.-M. Morel and S. Solimini. *Variational Methods in Image Segmentation*, volume 14 of *Progress in Nonlinear Differential Equations and Their Applications*. Birkhäuser, Boston, 1995.
16. D. Mumford. *Geometry Driven Diffusion in Computer Vision*, chapter "The Bayesian rationale for energy functionals", pages 141–153. Kluwer Academic, 1994.
17. D. Mumford and J. Shah. Optimal approximations by piecewise smooth functions and associated variational problems. *Comm. Pure Applied. Math.*, 42:577–685, 1989.
18. S. Osher and J. A. Sethian. Fronts propagating with curvature-dependent speed: Algorithms based on Hamilton-Jacobi formulations. *J. Comput. Phys.*, 79(12), 1988.
19. L. Rudin, S. Osher, and E. Fatemi. Nonlinear total variation based noise removal algorithms. *Physica D*, 60:259–268, 1992.
20. J. Shen. Bayesian video dejittering by BV image model. *SIAM J. Appl. Math.*, 64(5):1691–1708, 2004.
21. L. A. Vese and T. F. Chan. A multiphase level set framework for image segmentation using the Mumford-Shah model. *Int. J. Comput. Vision*, 50(3):271–293, 2002.

# A Fully Unsupervised Image Segmentation Algorithm Based on Wavelet-Domain Hidden Markov Tree Models

Qiang Sun, Yuheng Sha, Xinbo Gao, Biao Hou, and Licheng Jiao

Institute of Intelligent Information Processing, Xidian University,
710071 Xi'an, China
qsun@mail.xidian.edu.cn

**Abstract.** A fully unsupervised image segmentation algorithm is presented in this paper, in which wavelet-domain hidden Markov tree (WD-HMT) model is exploited together with the cluster analysis and validity techniques. The true number of textures in a given image is determined by calculating the likelihood disparity of textures using the modified partition fuzzy degree (MPFD) function at one suitable scale. Then, possibilistic C-means (PCM) clustering is performed to determine the training sample data from different textures according to the true number of textures obtained. The unsupervised segmentation is changed into self-supervised one, and the HMTseg algorithm is used to achieve the final segmentation results. This algorithm is applied to segment a variety of composite texture images into distinct homogeneous regions and good segmentation results are reported.

## 1 Introduction

Image segmentation is an important and highly challenging task in many image analysis applications. In practice, texture plays an important role in low level image analysis. The problem of segmenting an image via textural information is referred to as texture segmentation, which deals with the identification of non-overlapping distinct homogeneous regions in a given image. The key step in texture segmentation is the feature characterization of textures within an image. As yet, a great variety of approaches have been presented to address this problem in the existing literature.

In this paper, wavelet-domain hidden Markov tree (WD-HMT) model is exploited to characterize the texture features on which the image segmentation is performed based. The WD-HMT models [1], pioneered by Crouse *et al.* as a type of wavelet-domain statistical signal models to characterize signals by capturing the inter-scale dependencies of wavelet coefficients, have gained more and more attention from signal and image processing communities due to its effectiveness in performing various tasks. On the basis of the WD-HMT model, a supervised multi-scale image segmentation algorithm, HMTseg [2], was developed by Choi *et al.* to address image segmentation problem. Meanwhile, HMTseg algorithm was modified to apply to synthetic aperture radar (SAR) image segmentation where a "truncated" HMT model [3] was proposed in order to alleviate the effect of speckle noise present at fine scales and a modified multi-scale fusion process was also provided to achieve better results.

J. Blanc-Talon et al. (Eds.): ACIVS 2005, LNCS 3708, pp. 507 – 514, 2005.
© Springer-Verlag Berlin Heidelberg 2005

More recently, a variety of unsupervised segmentation algorithms [4, 5, 6, and 7] have emerged to extend the supervised methodology to the unsupervised one based on the WD-HMT models. Zhen [4] integrated the parameter estimation and classification into one using a multi-scale Expectation Maximization (EM) algorithm to segment SAR images on the coarse scales. In [5], Song exploited HMT-3S model [8] and JMCMS approach [9] to provide another unsupervised segmentation algorithm, where K-means clustering was used to identify the corresponding training samples for unknown textures based on the likelihood disparity of HMT-3S. Subsequently, Sun adopted an effective soft clustering algorithm, possibilistic C-means (PCM) clustering to further improve the unsupervised segmentation performance. Alternatively, Xu *et al.* also extended the supervised HMTseg to an unsupervised algorithm, where the dissimilarity between image blocks was measured by the Kullback-Leibler distance (KLD) between the corresponding WD-HMT models, followed by a hierarchical clustering in the image blocks at the selected scale. It should be noted that all the unsupervised segmentation algorithms above are implemented under the assumption that the number of the textures in a given image is beforehand provided, which is unpractical for automatically segmenting images in many particular application areas, such as the content-based image retrieval where thousands of images need to be segmented without any *a priori* knowledge provided.

In this paper, we present a fully unsupervised image segmentation algorithm by combing the WD-HMT models with the cluster analysis, i.e. PCM clustering [10], and cluster validity (by the MPFD function [11]) techniques. Firstly, a global WD-HMT model is obtained using the EM training algorithm in consideration of the whole image to be segmented as one texture. This model contains information from all distinct regions, and the different goodness of fit between the global model and local texture regions exists. Secondly, the likelihood disparity is conducted at one suitable scale $J$ by the MPFD with the true number of textures in an image as the output. Thirdly, PCM clustering is used to determine the training sample data based on the true number of textures. Compared with the hard clustering approach, K-means clustering [5], PCM clustering, as one soft clustering method, can achieve reliable and stable clustering results. Finally, WD-HMT models for different textures are retrained with the extracted sample data, and the supervised segmentation procedures of the HMTseg algorithm [2] are carried out to achieve the final results.

# 2    Related Works

## 2.1    Wavelet-Domain Hidden Markov Tree Models

It is well known that the discrete wavelet transform (DWT) is an effective multi-scale image analysis tool because of its intrinsic multiresolution analysis characteristics, which can represent different singularity contents of an image at different scales and subbands. In Fig. 1 (a), one quad-tree structure of wavelet coefficients is shown, which demonstrates the dependencies of wavelet coefficients at three subbands.

For multi-scale singularity characterization, one statistical model, hidden Markov tree (HMT) model [1], was proposed to model this structure. The HMT associates with each wavelet coefficient a "hidden" state variable, which determines whether it is "large" or "small" (see Fig. 1 (b)). The marginal density of each coefficient is then modeled as one two-density Gaussian mixture model: a large-variance Gaussian for the large state and a small-variance one for the small state. Thus, the Gaussian mixture model (GMM) can closely fit the non-Gaussian marginal statistics of coefficient.

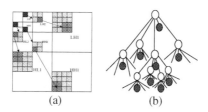

(a)                    (b)

**Fig. 1.** (a) Quad-tree structure of 2-D discrete wavelet transforms. (b) A 2-D wavelet-domain hidden Markov tree model for one subband. Each wavelet coefficient (black node) is modeled as a Gaussian mixture model by a hidden state variable (white node).

Grouping the HMT model parameters, i.e. state probabilities for the root nodes of different quad-trees, state transition probabilities and mixture variances, into a vector $\Theta$, the HMT can be considered as a high-dimensional yet highly structured GMM $f(w|\Theta)$ that approximates the joint probability density function of the wavelet coefficients $W$. For each coefficient, the overall pdf $f(w)$ of $W$ can be formulated as

$$f_W(w) = \sum_{m=1}^{M} p_S(m) f_{W|S}(w|S = m),\qquad(1)$$

where $M$ is the number of states and $S$ is the state variable. The HMT model parameters can be estimated using the iterative EM algorithm.

It should be noted that the HMT has one nesting structure that can match the multi-scale representation of an image shown in Figure 2(a). Each subtree of the HMT is also an HMT, with the HMT subtree rooted at node $i$ modeling the statistical characteristics of the wavelet coefficients corresponding to the dyadic square $d_i$ in the original image. In Figure 2 (b), we demonstrate the correspondence of quadtree structure of wavelet coefficients with the multi-scale representation of an image.

## 2.2 Supervised Image Segmentation

One Bayesian segmentation algorithm, HMTseg [2], was proposed to implement supervised image segmentation in which WD-HMT model is applied to characterize texture and a context vector is used to capture the dependencies of the multi-scale class labels.

Multi-scale segmentation obtains the dyadic image squares at different scales by recursively dividing an image into four equal sub-images. HMTseg can capture the feature of each dyadic square by WD-HMT model. More, contextual information is described by a vector $v^j$, which is derived from a set of dyadic squares at its parent scale. Denote a dyadic square and its class lable by $d_i^j$ and $c_i^j$ respectively, and $j$ is the scale index. Each context vector $v_i^j$ consists of two entries, the class label of the parent square and the dominat class label of the parent and its eight neighbors.

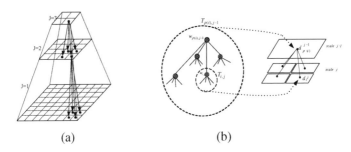

(a)                              (b)

**Fig. 2.** Multi-scale representation of an image (b) Correspondence of quadtree structure of wavelet coefficients with multi-scale representation of an image

The HMTseg algorithm relies on three separate tree structures: the wavelet transform quad-tree, the HMT, and a labeling tree [2]. As a complete procedure, it includes three essential ingredients, i.e. HMT model training, multi-scale likelihood computation, and fusion of multi-scale maximum likelihood (ML) raw segmentations.

1) Train WD-HMT models to characterize each texture using homogeneous training images. To obtain pixel-level segmentation, Gaussian mixture model (GMM) is used to train a pixel intensity pdf model.

2) Calculate the likelihood of each dyadic image square $d_i^j$ at each different scale. The conditional likelihoods $f(d_i^j | c_i^j)$ for each $d_i^j$ are obtained in this step.

3) Fuse multi-scale likelihoods using the labeling tree to form the multi-scale maximal a posterior (MAP) classification. Choose a suitable starting scale $J$ such that a reliable raw segmentation $c^J$ can be obtained at the scale. The contextual vector $v^{J-1}$ is calculated from the class labels $c^J$ of the $J$-th scale. Moreover, EM algorithm is applied to estimate $p(c_i^{J-1} | v_i^{J-1})$ by maximizing the likelihood of the image given the contextual vector $v^{J-1}$. In this step, each iteration updates the contextual posterior distribution $p(c_i | d_i, v_i)$. When the process of iteration converges, determine $c_i$ which maximizes the $p(c_i | d_i, v_i)$. The fusion is repeated in the next finer scale based on the contextual vector $v^{J-2}$ computed from $c^{J-1}$. Continue the multi-scale fusion across scales until the finest scale is reached.

## 3 Fully Unsupervised Segmentation Combining WD-HMT Models with Cluster Techniques

Fully unsupervised segmentation means identifying all the non-overlapping homogenous regions within an image without the knowledge on either the texture features or the number of textures. Our proposed segmentation algorithm consists of three phases: the determination of the true number of textures via the modified partition fuzzy degree (MPFD), the extraction of training sample data from different textures with the possibilistic C-means (PCM) clustering as well as the supervised segmentation mentioned above.

## 3.1 Determination of the True Number of Textures

Unlike most existing unsupervised texture image segmentation methods, the true number of textures in a given image, in this paper, is not assumed in advance, but determined using the likelihood results of image blocks at a certain suitable scale $J$ via an effective cluster validity approach, namely MPFD in [11], which could accurately find the optimal cluster number of numeric data set by combining the fuzzy partition entropy (FPE) and the partition fuzzy degree (PFD).

Let $X = \{x_1, x_2, \cdots, x_n\}$ denote as a data set, and $x_i = \left[ x_{i1}, x_{i2}, \cdots, x_{ip} \right]^T$ represent the $p$ features of the $i$-th sample. The fuzzy clustering can be represented as the following optimization problem

$$\min J_m(U, L) = \sum_{i=1}^{c} \sum_{j=1}^{n} u_{ij}^m d_{ij}^2, \quad subject\ to\ \sum_{i=1}^{c} u_{ij} = 1\ for\ all\ j. \tag{2}$$

In (2), $L = (\beta_1, \cdots, \beta_c)$ is a c-tuple of prototypes, $d_{ij}^2$ is the distance of feature point $x_j$ to prototype $\beta_i$, $n$ is the total number of feature vectors, $c$ is the number of classes, and $U = \left[ u_{ij} \right]$ is a $c \times n$ matrix, called fuzzy partition matrix. Here, $u_{ij}$ is the grade of membership of the feature point $x_j$ in cluster $\beta_i$, and $m \in [1, \infty)$ is a weighting exponent called the fuzzier, empirically taken as 2.

For a given cluster number $c$ and fuzzy partition matrix $U$, the fuzzy partition entropy (FPE) is defined as

$$H(U; c) = -\frac{1}{n} \sum_{i=1}^{c} \sum_{j=1}^{n} u_{ij} \log_a (u_{ij}), \tag{3}$$

and the definition of partition fuzzy degree (PFD) is

$$P_f(U; c) = \frac{1}{n} \sum_{i=1}^{c} \sum_{j=1}^{n} \left| u_{ij} - (u_{ij})_H \right| \quad with \quad (u_{ij})_H = \begin{cases} 1 & u_{ij} = \max_{1 \le i \le c} \{u_{ij}\} \\ 0 & otherwise \end{cases}, \tag{4}$$

where $(u_{ij})_H$ is the defuzzifying version of $U$.

Based on the expressions of FPE and PFD, the MPFD of a data set is denoted as

$$M_{pf}(U; c) = \frac{P_f(U; c)}{\tilde{H}(U; c)}, \tag{5}$$

where $\tilde{H}(U; c) = smoothing(H(U; c))$ is the smoothed FPE, typically obtained by the 3-point smoothing operator or median filter. The true number of textures can be found by the minimum of $M_{pf}(U; c)$ for the likelihood results of image blocks.

### 3.2  Extraction of Training Sample Data

The key step for a fully unsupervised segmentation is the extraction of sample data for training different textures to obtain their HMT models used for the following supervised procedure. The input is the true number of textures in an image, which has been obtained by the MPFD function above. Herein, an effective soft clustering algorithm, PCM clustering [10], is exploited to extract the sample data of different textures. PCM algorithm differs from the classical K-means and fuzzy C-means (FCM) algorithms since the membership of one sample in a cluster is independent of all other clusters in the algorithm. The objective function of the algorithm is given by

$$J_m(U,L) = \sum_{k=1}^{N} \sum_{l\in\Gamma_k} (u_{ij})^m \left\| f(y_{k,l}^{(J)}|\Theta) - f(y_k^{(J)}|\Theta) \right\|^2 + \sum_{k=1}^{N} \eta i \sum_{l\in\Gamma_k} (1-u_{ij})^m, \tag{6}$$

where $U, L$ and $m$ have the same meanings as (2), $\eta_i$ is a certain positive number, and $f(y_k^{(J)}|\Theta)$ is the likelihood mean of class $k$ at the suitable scale $J$, $f(y_{k,l}^{(J)}|\Theta)$ the likelihood of an image block $l$ regarding the class $k$. The $u_{ij}$ is updated by

$$u_{ij} = \cfrac{1}{1 + \left( \cfrac{\left\| f(y_{k,l}^{(J)}|\Theta) - f(y_k^{(J)}|\Theta) \right\|^2}{\eta_i} \right)^{\frac{1}{m-1}}}, \tag{7}$$

where $\eta_i$ is defined as

$$\eta_i = \cfrac{\sum_{j=1}^{N} u_{ij}^m \left\| f(y_{k,l}^{(J)}|\Theta) - f(y_k^{(J)}|\Theta) \right\|^2}{\sum_{j=1}^{N} u_{ij}^m}. \tag{8}$$

By PCM clustering, the resulting partition of data can be interpreted as degrees of possibility of the points belonging to the classes, i.e., the compatibilities of the points with the class prototypes, which is the key difference with the K-means and FCM clustering [10]. We refer the reader to [6] for the complete steps to extract the image sample data.

### 3.3  Supervised Segmentation Using HMTseg Algorithm

With the PCM clustering implemented at the scale $J$, reliable training samples for different textures can be extracted. Thereafter, HMT model parameters for different textures can be obtained through training of HMT models with the extracted sample data. Thus, the final results can be achieved HMTseg procedures in Section 2.2.

## 4   Experimental Results and Analysis

We tested our segmentation algorithm on several images of composite textures with size of $256 \times 256$ pixels. Textures from the Brodatz album [12] are used to constitute the composite texture images. Before segmentation, all the images are decomposed into four levels by Haar wavelet basis. The likelihood disparity is given by the MPFD function at the suitable scale $J = 4$, which is the coarsest scale with the size of $16 \times 16$. The number of cluster is assumed from 2 to 10, which is used to determine the true number of the textures in an image by finding the minimum of the $M_{pf}(U;c)$. Also, the PCM clustering is implemented at the scale $J$.

Fig. 3 shows four composite texture images, which are made up of 2, 3, 4 and 5 classes of homogeneous textures from the Brodatz album, respectively.

**Fig. 3.** Four composite texture images consisting of 2, 3, 4 and 5 textures

In Fig. 4, the plots on the determination of the true number of textures above are demonstrated. The minimum of $M_{pf}(U;c)$ indicates the true number of textures.

From left to right, all the true number of the four textures is correctly determined.

Fig. 5 gives the final segmentation results for the four composite textures using our fully unsupervised segmentation algorithm. The segmentation results are satisfactory on the whole, and only a few regions are misclassified.

## 5   Conclusions

In this paper, we have developed a fully unsupervised segmentation algorithm by characterizing the texture features using WD-HMT models, determining the number of textures by the MPFD function, and extracting their sample data with PCM clustering. Experimental results demonstrate that the proposed method can detect correctly the number of textures and give effective segment results on the composite textures.

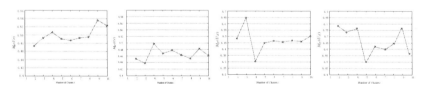

**Fig. 4.** Plots of the $M_{pf}(U;c)$ vs. $c$ to determine the true number of the four texture images

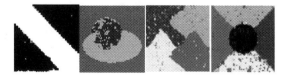

**Fig. 5.** Segmentation results for the textures in Fig. 3 with the proposed algorithm

# References

1. Crouse, M.S., Nowak, R.D., Baraniuk, R.G.: Wavelet-Based Signal Processing Using Hidden Markov Models. IEEE Trans. on Signal Processing. 46 (1998) 886–902
2. Choi, H., Baraniuk, R.G.: Multi-scale Image Segmentation Using Wavelet-Domain Hidden Markov Models. IEEE Trans. on Image Processing. 10 (2001) 1309–1321
3. Venkatachalam, V. , Choi, H. , Baraniuk, R.G.: Multi-scale SAR Image Segmentation Using Wavelet-Domain Hidden Markov Tree Models. In Proc. of SPIE, 4053 (2000) 1605–1611
4. Zhen, Y., Lu, C.C.: Wavelet-Based Unsupervised SAR Image Segmentation Using Hidden Markov Tree Models. In Proc. of ICPR. 2 (2002) 729–732
5. Song, X.M., Fan, G.L.: Unsupervised Bayesian Image Segmentation Using Wavelet-Domain Hidden Markov Models. In Proc. of ICIP. 2 (2003) 423–426
6. Sun, Q., Gou, S.P., Jiao, L.C.: A New Approach to Unsupervised Image Segmentation Based on Wavelet-Domain Hidden Markov Tree. In Proc. of International Conference on Image Analysis and Recognition, 3211 (2004) 41–48
7. Xu, Q., Yang, J., Ding, S.Y.: Unsupervised Multi-scale Image Segmentation Using Wavelet Domain Hidden Markov Tree. In Proc. of the 8th Pacific Rim International Conferences on Artificial Intelligence. 3157 (2004) 797–804
8. Fan, G.L., Xia, X.G.: Wavelet-Based Texture Analysis and Synthesis Using Hidden Markov Models. IEEE Trans. on Circuits and Systems. 50 (2003) 106–120
9. Fan, G.L., Xia, X.G.: A Joint Multi-Context and Multi-scale Approach to Bayesian Image Segmentation, IEEE Trans. on Geoscience and Remote Sensing. 39 (2001) 2680–2688
10. Krishnapuram, R., Killer, J.M.: A Possibilistic Approach to Clustering. IEEE Trans. on Fuzzy System. 1 (1993) 98–110
11. Li, J., Gao, X.B., Jiao, L.C.: A new cluster validity function based on the modified partition fuzzy degree. In Proc. of Rough Sets and Current Trends in Computing. 3066 (2004) 586–591
12. Brodatz, P.:Textures: A Photographic Album for Artists & Designers. Dover Publications, Inc., New York, 1966

# A Clustering Approach for Color Image Segmentation

F. Hachouf[1] and N. Mezhoud[2]

[1] Laboratoire d'automatique et de robotique,
Département d'électronique, université Mentouri Constantine,
Route d'Ain El Bey , 25000 Constantine, Algérie,
Tél : 213-62-04-25-54, Fax : 213-31- 80-90-13
fhachouf@wissal.dz
[2] Laboratoire LIRE, équipe vision,
Département d'informatique, université Mentouri Constantine,
Route d'Ain El Bey , 25000 Constantine, Algérie
mezhoud@wissal.dz

**Abstract.** This paper describes a clustering approach for color image segmentation using fuzzy classification principles. The method uses classification to group pixels into homogeneous regions. Both global and local information are taken into account. This is particularly helpful in taking care of small objects and local variation of color images. Color, mean and standard deviation are used as a data source. The classification is achieved by a new version of self-organizing maps algorithm . This new algorithm is equivalent to classic fuzzy C-mean algorithm (FCM) whose objective function has been modified. Code vectors that constitute centers of classes, are distributed on a regular low dimension grid. In addition, a penalization term is added to guarantee a smooth distribution of the values of the code vectors on the grid. Tests achieved on color images, followed by an automatic evaluation revealed the good performances of the proposed method.

## 1 Introduction

Image segmentation is an important step in image analysis and pattern recognition. It is the first essential step in low level vision. Segmentation is a process of partitioning an image into some non-intersecting regions such that each region is homogeneous, but the union of any two adjacent regions is not [1], [2], [3], [4]. It is applied in a variety of domains. The choice of segmentation technique depends widely on images and domain application. Literature concerning color segmentation methods is not as rich as that of gray level images. Human eye can distinguish thousand of color nuances but only about twenty gray levels. Often an object that is not extracted in gray levels, can be extracted while using the color information. Generally, monochromatic segmentation techniques are extended to color images. However, all these techniques have advantages and inconvenients. Most method of segmentation are combination of classic techniques and/or fuzzy logic notions, neural networks, genetic algorithms etc... [5].

J. Blanc-Talon et al. (Eds.): ACIVS 2005, LNCS 3708, pp. 515–522, 2005.
© Springer-Verlag Berlin Heidelberg 2005

Clustering methods are often associated to fuzzy approaches to cope with ambiguity and uncertainty in images. Fuzzy C-means algorithm (FCM) is the most widely used fuzzy partitioning method[6]. FCM restriction is   the clusters number which  must be known a priori.

Artificial neural networks (ANN) are applied in different domains. Parallel processing   and linear features that they offer make the ANN used a lot in classification and clustering. Self organizing maps of Kohonen (SOM) is a powerful tool for partitioning data [7]. SOM have the property of preserving the topology of data as well as the relation of distance between them. The space of data is projected on a regular grid whose dimension constitutes the number of clusters for the FCM.

In this work, we propose a hybrid segmentation method. It is based on a global information produced by fuzzy clustering in  which the number of clusters is optimized by self-organizing map algorithm, and a local information given by  the mean and the standard deviation. Objective function of fuzzy C-mean algorithm has been modified so that code vectors are distributed on a regular low dimension grid and, by the addition of a penalization  term to guarantee an uniform distribution of code vectors [8].

For color images, $I_1I_2I_3$ is the color space chosen because it offers a better quality of segmentation than the others [9]. The obtained results are evaluated using three automatic functions proposed in [10].

The present study is organized as follows. In section 2, the proposed method is described. The optimisation algorithm of the new objective function is presented. Section 3 will be devoted to the application of the proposed method to color images and to evaluation results. They are compared to results provided by SOM and FCM algorithms. Conclusion and perspectives of our work are developed.

## 2  Proposed Approach

### 2.1  Color Space

Color is perceived by humans as a combination of tristimuli R (red), G (green) and B (blue) which are usually called primary colors. Components R, G, B are highly correlated. So, RGB system is suitable  for visualization but not good for color scene segmentation and analysis [11], [12]. Several color spaces are built from RGB system by linear or no linear transformations (YIQ , YUV, $I_1I_2I_3$, HSI,  Nrgb, CIE (L*u*v*) or CIE(L*a* b*), XYZ) . Each space has its advantages and inconvenients [5]. Selecting the best color space is still one of the difficulties in color image segmentation. In this work, we have chosen $I_1I_2I_3$ space. In [9], $I_1I_2I_3$ have been compared to other spaces. It has been proven that $I_1I_2I_3$ is more efficient in terms of quality of segmentation and the computational complexity of the transformation. The three components $I_1I_2I_3$ are given by :

$$I_1=(R+G+B)/3 .$$
$$I_2=(R-B)/2 .$$
$$I_3=(2G-R-B)/4 . \hspace{2cm} (1)$$

For color images, every pixel will be characterized by its color given by $(I_1 + I_2 + I_3)$.

## 2.2  Parameters

Classic spatial clustering techniques use only the color of the pixel [3]. Cluster analysis does not use any spatial information. Often, clustering approaches are combined to other methods like region growing and spatial linkage techniques [6]. In the suggested approach, two parameters are considered that characterize local spatial information: the mean and standard deviation. This latter measures the contrast in a local region. It informs on the degree of homogeneity of this region [1].

For a pixel $P_{ij}$ standard deviation is calculated on a window $w_{ij}$ of size d x d and centered at (i,j).

$$v_{ij} = \left[ \frac{1}{d^2} \sum_{p=i-\frac{d-1}{2}}^{i+\frac{d-1}{2}} \sum_{q=j-\frac{d-1}{2}}^{j+\frac{d-1}{2}} (g_{pq} - \mu_{ij}) \right]^{1/2}. \tag{2}$$

where $0 \leq i, p \leq M-1$, $0 \leq j, q \leq N-1$
d : odd integer > 1
M x N : image size
$g_{ij}$ : gray level of pixel $P_{ij}$ at (i,j).
$\mu_{ij}$ is the mean of the gray levels within dxd window $w_{ij}$ and calculated as :

$$\mu_{ij} = \frac{1}{d^2} \left[ \sum_{p=i-\frac{d-1}{2}}^{i+\frac{d-1}{2}} \sum_{q=j-\frac{d-1}{2}}^{j+\frac{d-1}{2}} g_{pq} \right]. \tag{3}$$

Thus, The new self organizing network is composed of an orthogonal grid of N cluster units, each associated to five internal weights for data which are : $I_1$, $I_2$, $I_3$, mean and standard deviation.

## 2.3  Smoothly Distributed Fuzzy C-Means

Process of the proposed segmentation is inspired of FCM modified version which represents a new self organizing map [8]. It consists in minimizing an objective function given by :

$$\min_{u,v} \left\{ \sum_{i=1}^{n} \sum_{j=1}^{c} U_{ji}^m \| X_i - V_j \|^2 + \vartheta tr(VDV^t) \right\} \tag{4}$$

$\vartheta > 0$ represents a parameter that will guarantee smoothness of spatial distribution of the code vectors on the grid. Smoothness is necessary to ensure an ordered mapping, cf Fig. 1

D : Laplacian-like operator Matrix

$$D = 1/4 \begin{bmatrix} 2 & -1 & 0 & -1 & 0 & 0 & 0 & 0 & 0 \\ -1 & 3 & -1 & 0 & -1 & 0 & 0 & 0 & 0 \\ 0 & -1 & 2 & 0 & 0 & -1 & 0 & 0 & 0 \\ -1 & 0 & 0 & 3 & -1 & 0 & -1 & 0 & 0 \\ 0 & -1 & 0 & -1 & 4 & -1 & 0 & -1 & 0 \\ 0 & 0 & -1 & 0 & -1 & 3 & 0 & 0 & -1 \\ 0 & 0 & 0 & -1 & 0 & 0 & 2 & -1 & 0 \\ 0 & 0 & 0 & 0 & -1 & 0 & -1 & 3 & -1 \\ 0 & 0 & 0 & 0 & 0 & -1 & 0 & - & 2 \end{bmatrix}$$

| $V_1$ | $V_2$ | $V_3$ |
|-------|-------|-------|
| $V_4$ | $V_5$ | $V_6$ |
| $V_7$ | $V_8$ | $V_9$ |

**Fig. 1.** 3x3 grid containing c=9 code vectors

V : Code vectors matrix, tr : Trace of square matrix, $T$ : vector or matrix transpose.

In this case, centers of the clusters are calculated as :

$$V_j = \frac{\sum_{i=1}^{n} U_{ji}^m X_i + \vartheta \overline{V}_j}{\sum_{i=1}^{n} U_{ji}^m + \vartheta} \tag{5}$$

Code vectors updating reflects SOM characteristic that will be influenced by the data values and the nearest code vector in the grid.

Referring to Fig. 1, $\overline{V}_i$ are calculated as follow:

$$\begin{cases} \overline{V}_1 = (V_2 + V_4)/2 \\ \overline{V}_2 = (V_1 + V_3 + V_5)/3 \\ \overline{V}_5 = (V_2 + V_4 + V_6 + V_8)/4 \end{cases}$$

The following algorithm finds a solution that converges to a local minimum of the functional in eq. (4)

1. Initialise V randomly. Initialise U randomly satisfying the constraints:

$$\begin{cases} 0 \leq U_{ji} \leq 1 \\ \sum_{j=1}^{c} U_{ji} = 1 , \forall i \end{cases} \tag{6}$$

2. set $\vartheta > 0$.
3. set $m > 1$
4. For $i=1\ldots n$, and $j=1\ldots c$, compute

$$U_{ji} = \frac{1}{\sum_{k=1}^{c} \dfrac{\|X_i - V_j\|^{2/(m-1)}}{\|X_i - V_k\|^{2/(m-1)}}} \tag{7}$$

5. For $j=1...c$, compute     $$V_j = \frac{\sum_{i=1}^{n} U_{ji}^{m} + \vartheta \overline{\mathcal{N}_j}}{\sum_{i=1}^{n} U_{ji}^{m} + \vartheta} \qquad (8)$$

until convergence

6. Stop when the overall difference in the $U_{ji}$' between the current and the previous iteration is smaller than $\varepsilon$; otherwise go to step 4.

Algorithms based on clustering principle are very sensitive to initial conditions [8]. Therefore, the local minimum to which the algorithm converges depends on initial values of clusters centers. To reach the global minimum, a strategy developed in [13] is used. It consists in iterating stages 5 and 6 of the algorithm for a linear decrease of the fuzzy parameter m between two values $m_2$ and $m_1$.

## 3    Results Evaluation and Discussion

The suggested method can be used for any RGB images acquired with any captor because of the use of a special data structure. We have not applied any pre-process to uniformize the color scale but image histograms of the three components RGB are used. The used statistics are efficient for various acquisition conditions but they would more efficient if the window size is larger than 3x3 and taking into account spatial consideration. The proposed method has been applied on a large variety of monochromatic and color images example : peppers and house (Fig.3a and Fig. 4a). We have used different types of color images taken from the GDR-ISIS and Berkeley databases. For the defuzzification process, we have considered the decision by maximum membership. A pixel is assigned to a cluster $i$ if its membership degree to this cluster is largest and superior to a threshold $\beta$.

The proposed method has been compared to FCM and SOM algorithms. However, ITU is used and developed for video quality evaluation. In this work, still images and three evaluation functions of region color segmentation proposed in [14] and improved in [10] are used.

$$F(I) = \frac{1}{1000(N.M)} \sqrt{R} \sum_{i=1}^{R} \frac{e_i^2}{\sqrt{A_i}} \qquad (9)$$

$$F'(I) = \frac{1}{10000(N.M)} \sqrt{\sqrt{\sum_{A=1}^{Max}[R(A)]^{1+1/A}} \sum_{i=1}^{R} \frac{e_i^2}{\sqrt{A_i}}} \qquad (10)$$

$$Q(I) = \frac{1}{1000(N.M)} \sqrt{R} \left[ \frac{e_i^2}{1+\log A_i} + \left(\frac{R(A_i)}{A_i}\right)^2 \right] \qquad (11)$$

Where I is the segmented image.

NxM : image size.

R : number of regions in the segmented image. $A_i$ area of the $i^{th}$ region.

$e_i$ : average color error of the $i$th region; $e_i$ is defined as the sum of the Euclidian distances between the RGB color vectors of the pixels of region $i$ and the color vector attributed to region $i$ in the segmented image . In the F function, the term $\sqrt{R}$ penalizes segmentations that form too many regions, the term $\sum_{i=1}^{R} e_i \bigg/ \sqrt{A_i}$ penalizes segmentations having non-homogeneous regions. Since the average color error of small regions is often close to zero, the function tends to evaluate very noisy segmentation favourably. Function F ' is the function F modified in such a way that small region contribute by the exponent (1+1/A). Q function is constructed to penalize both small regions and regions having a large color error.

Fig.2a          Fig.2b          Fig.2c          Fig. 2d

Fig. 3a          Fig. 3b          Fig. 3c          Fig.3d

Fig.2a , Fig. 3a. Original images, Fig. 2b, Fig. 3b. SOM algorithm segmentation, Fig.2c , Fig.3c. FCM algorithm segmentation, Fig.2d , Fig.3d. Proposed method segmentation

Two further modifications of F are made to obtain Q. The first term in the sum also differs from its corresponding in F. $\sqrt{Ai}$ has been replaced by $(1+\log Ai)$ to obtain a stronger penalisation of non-homogeneous regions. Smaller values of the criterion Q(I) produce more satisfactory segmentation results.

Table .1 shows that proposed method yields better results than FCM and SOM algorithms. Values given by the three functions agree with the human judgment. Indeed, images of Fig. 2b and Fig. 3b that are the result of the SOM present a very bad quality of segmentation compared to images of Fig. 2c and Fig. 3c that are

**Table 1.** Comparative study between SOM, FCM and the proposed approach

| Algorithms<br><br>Images | SOM<br><br>N=5 | FCM<br>m=1.5, c=6<br>ε= 0.00005 | Proposed Approach<br>$m_1$=2 ; $m_2$ =1.5, c=6<br>$\vartheta$=0,55<br>maxstep = 500 , maxiter<br>=100 |
|---|---|---|---|
| House | F=334889.43<br>F'= 190415.99<br>Q = 159512.35 | F = 166794.08<br>F' = 102630.91<br>Q = 96 549.56 | F = 11612.69<br>F' = 86804.42<br>Q = 51 244.16 |
| Peppers | F = 224180.38<br>F' =211711.31<br>Q =185800.28 | F = 145573.85<br>F' = 26917.19<br>Q = 11603.46 | F = 3254.17<br>F' =1876.67<br>Q = 1325.67 |

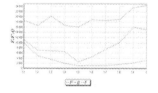 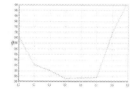 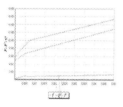

**Fig. 4.** Influence of m Parameter on color segmentation

**Fig. 5.** Influence of parameter $\vartheta$ on color segmentation

**Fig. 6.** Influence of parameter ε on color segmentation

segmented by FCM. Images of Fig. 2d and Fig. 3d are segmented by the proposed method. It is noticed a substantial clarity of the details on " peppers " image and a better segmentation of the house with regard to the two roofs, to the facade as well as the door. It is validated by values found by the Q function .

For each test image, we applied our segmentation algorithm, varying the input parameters ( such as the number of clusters C, fuzziness and smoothness parameters m and $\vartheta$ and convergence value $\mathcal{E}$ ). The plot of Fig.4 shows that the fuzzy parameter m varies between the two values $m_2$ and $m_1$ set to 2 and 1,5. Q function (Fig. 5) is minimal in the interval [0,5 0,7] of the domain of the smoothing parameter. Finally, quasi-constant shape of Q function (Fig. 6) shows that the segmentation is not very sensitive to the convergence threshold.

## 4 Conclusion

In this paper, we proposed a new approach for image segmentation. It is based on a new version of the algorithm of self-organizing maps of Kohonen, that consists in a modified version of fuzzy C-means. The new map preserves topological structure of the SOM and distances between data. Code vectors are forced to be very near from data and to change slowly on the grid ensuring an ordered mapping. These properties have been exploited for color image segmentation. Because of the strong correlation between R, G and B components, we used $I_1I_2I_3$ space which is more suitable for segmentation problems. The quality of the segmentation result is improved by identifying significant local information more efficiently. Optimal tuning of parameters has been realized by the study of variations of evaluation functions. These are automatic. They include no parameter to initialise and constitute in fact a good means to evaluate a color image segmentation .

Finally, the proposed fuzzy-neural  method presents a new approach in image segmentation, combining fuzzy set theory to manipulate uncertainty and ambiguity and neural networks for their robustness , to model the human cognitive activity.

In perspective to our work, we think that the method can be improved by introducing other homogeneity or texture parameters. These will be used in input layer of the SOM map. Markov fields associated to the proposed method would give an interesting results.

# References

1. Cocquerez , J. P.et Philipp, S. : Analyse d'images : filtrage et segmentation, Masson (1995)
2. Pal, S. K. et al. : A Review on Image Segmentation Techniques . Pattern Recognition, 29 (1993), 1277-1294
3. Haralick, R. M., Shapiro, L. G. : Image Segmentation techniques. Computer Vision Graphics Image Processing, 29 (1985) 100-132
4. Sahoo, P. K. et al. : A survey of thresholding techniques. Computer Vision Graphics Image Processing  41 (1988) 233-260
5. Cheng, H. D. et al.: Color Image Segmentation - Advances and Prospects. Pattern Recognition 34 (2001) 2259-2281
6. Cannon, R. L., Dave, J.V., Bezdek, J.C.: Efficient Imlementation of the Fuzzy C-means Clustering Algorithms. IEEE Trans. Pattern  Anal. Mach. Intell. 8 (2) (1986) 249-255
7. Kohonen, T. : The Self-Organizing Maps. Neurocomputing 21 (1998)  1-6
8. Pascual-Marqui, R. D. et al. : Smoothly distributed Fuzzy C-means -A   New Self-Organizing Map. Pattern Recognition 34 (2001) 2395-2402
9. Ohta, Y. I., Kanade, T. and  Sakai, T.: Color Information for Region Segmentation. Computer Graphics and Image Processing 13 (1980)  222-241
10. Borsotti, M. et al.: Quantative Evaluation of color image segmentation results. Pattern Recognition letters 19 (1998) 741-747
11. Pietikainen, M. et al.: Accurate color discrimination with classification based on feature distributions. International Conference on Pattern Recognition C (1996) 833-838
12. Littmann, E., Ritter, H.: Adaptive color segmentation – a comparison of neural and statistical methods. IEEE Trans. Neural Network 8 (1) (1997) 175-185
13. Graepel, T., Burger, M., Obermayer, K.: Self Organizing-Maps : Generalisation and new Optimisation techniques. Neurocomputing 21 (1998) 173-190
14. J. Lui, J.,Yang, Y. H. : Multiresolution color image segmentation. IEEE Trans. Pattern Anal. Mach. Intell. 16 (7) (1994) 689-700

# Affine Coregistration of Diffusion Tensor Magnetic Resonance Images Using Mutual Information

Alexander Leemans[1], Jan Sijbers[1], Steve De Backer[1], Everhard Vandervliet[2], and Paul M. Parizel[2]

[1] Vision Lab (Department of Physics), University of Antwerp, 171 Groenenborgerlaan, 2020 Antwerp, Belgium
{alexander.leemans, jan.sijbers, steve.debacker}@ua.ac.be
[2] Department of Radiology and Medical Imaging, University Hospital Antwerp 10 Wilrijkstraat, 2650 Edegem, Belgium
{everhard.vandervliet, paul.parizel}@uza.be

**Abstract.** In this paper, we present an affine image coregistration technique for Diffusion Tensor Magnetic Resonance Imaging (DT-MRI) data sets based on mutual information. The technique is based on a multichannel approach where the diffusion weighted images are aligned according to the corresponding acquisition gradient directions. Also, in addition to the coregistration of the DT-MRI data sets, an appropriate reorientation of the diffusion tensor is worked out in order to remain consistent with the corresponding underlying anatomical structures. This reorientation strategy is determined from the spatial transformation while preserving the diffusion tensor shape. The method is fully automatic and has the advantage to be independent of the applied diffusion framework.

## 1 Introduction

Image coregistration, also referred to as matching or warping, is the process of aligning images in order to relate corresponding features. The objective of any coregistration technique is therefore finding the transformation that maps these images into a common reference frame in which direct comparison is possible. For instance in medicine, it is often desirable to combine multiple data sets of the same patient (follow up), or even to merge intersubject information (control versus pathology). Only then, abnormalities can be quantified based on a statistical analysis of these multiple data sets.

Due to the rapid development of many image acquisition devices and the growing diversity of imaging modalities during the last decades, coregistration has become an important application in many fields of image analysis (e.g., multispectral classification in remote sensing, combining computer tomography (CT), positron emission tomography (PET), and magnetic resonance imaging (MRI), cartography, etc.). This diversity of images to be registered impedes the design of a universal method applicable to all registration tasks, resulting in an ever-increasing number of publications on the topic each year [1, 2, 3].

J. Blanc-Talon et al. (Eds.): ACIVS 2005, LNCS 3708, pp. 523–530, 2005.
© Springer-Verlag Berlin Heidelberg 2005

In this research, we focus on diffusion tensor magnetic resonance imaging (DT-MRI), a recently developed MRI technique that allows one to study brain connectivity in vivo and which is becoming an important diagnostic tool for various neuropathological diseases [4,5]. A technical overview regarding DT-MRI acquisition, theory, and data analysis can be found in [6].

In the work of Alexander *et al.*, a multiresolution elastic matching algorithm has been proposed using similarity measures of the diffusion tensor in order to manage DT-MRI data instead of scalar data [7]. Ruiz-Alzola *et al.* extended the intensity-based similarity coregistration to the tensor case and also proposed an interpolation method by means of the Kriging estimator [8, 9]. Their work is based on template matching by locally optimizing the similarity function. The work of Guimond *et al.* and Park *et al.* indicated the importance of channel information used for matching and introduced a multiple channel registration for tensor images by using, for example, all components of the tensor simultaneously in the registration process with successively updating the tensor orientation [10, 11]. Xu and colleagues applied the "Hierarchical Attribute Matching Mechanism for Elastic Registration" (HAMMER) approach, a high dimensional elastic transformation procedure, to DT-MRI data sets [12].

In this work, we developed a three-dimensional (3D) affine (rotation, translation, scale, and skew) DT-MRI coregistration technique based on the work of Maes et al. [13] using mutual information as a similarity measure. To preserve the orientational information of the diffusion tensor after affine transformation, an appropriate tensor reorientation must be applied in order to remain consistent with the alignment of the underlying anatomical structures. Current reorientation strategies (RS) for such an affine transformation, e.g. preservation of principal direction (PPD), require calculating several rotation matrices to reorient the diffusion tensor [14]. Here, a direct diffusion tensor reconstruction approach is developed without the need to calculate these rotation matrices, resulting in a lower computational cost.

## 2    Theory

### 2.1    Spatial Normalization

Mutual Information (MI) has already proven to be of high value for multimodality image registration since its development in the mid nineties and could be considered as the current *gold standard* [13, 15, 16]. For scalar images, the registration solution, i.e. the final transformation $\Phi$, is determined by maximizing the MI between the reference image $R$ and the source image $S$:

$$\Phi = \arg \max_{\phi} \mathrm{MI}[\phi(S), R] \quad , \tag{1}$$

where $\phi$ represents the affine transformation.

Specifically for DT-MRI, we apply a $k$-channel MI registration approach, where $k = 0, \ldots, K$ represents the number of Diffusion Weighted Images[1](DWI's):

---

[1] In our experiments, $K = 60$, where $k = 0$ represents the non-DWI.

$$\boldsymbol{\Phi}_k = \arg\max_\phi \mathrm{MI}\left[\phi(S_k), R_k\right] \quad, \tag{2}$$

where $R_k$ and $S_k$ denote the reference and source DWI's, respectively. It is important to note that the assumption is made that the DWI's, derived from a single acquisition, are already mutually aligned with the non-DWI, i.e.

$$\forall k = 1, \dots, K : \arg\max_\phi \mathrm{MI}\left[\phi(R_k), R_0\right] = \mathbf{1}$$
$$\forall k = 1, \dots, K : \arg\max_\phi \mathrm{MI}\left[\phi(S_k), S_0\right] = \mathbf{1} \quad, \tag{3}$$

where $\mathbf{1}$ represents the unity transformation.

From Eq. (2), the final transformation $\boldsymbol{\Phi}$ can be calculated as a weighted function of the transformations $\boldsymbol{\Phi}_k$ with the corresponding MI values as weighting factors, i.e.

$$\boldsymbol{\Phi} = \frac{1}{\Omega}\sum_{k=0}^{K}\omega_k\,\boldsymbol{\Phi}_k \quad\text{with}\quad \omega_k = \mathrm{MI}\left[\boldsymbol{\Phi}_k(S_k), R_k\right] \quad\text{and}\quad \Omega = \sum_{k=0}^{K}\omega_k \;. \tag{4}$$

Using Eq. (4) to calculate $\boldsymbol{\Phi}$, one can also obtain the registration precision $S_{\boldsymbol{\Phi}}$:

$$S_{\boldsymbol{\Phi}} = \sqrt{\frac{1}{\Omega K}\sum_{k=0}^{K}(\boldsymbol{\Phi} - \boldsymbol{\Phi}_k)^2} \quad, \tag{5}$$

which is a valuable measure to evaluate the quality of the registration technique.

## 2.2 Diffusion Tensor Reorientation

It is obvious that there are no difficulties in transforming scalar images. The image value from a specific voxel is transferred, via the spatial transformation, to the reference image, where *a posteriori* an interpolation method must be applied to reconstruct the reference grid. For rank one (and higher) tensors, a specific reorientation should be applied in order to keep the orientational information intact. For diffusion tensors (rank two), an extra condition is required, i.e. the shape should also be preserved [14].

Consider the real-valued symmetric diffusion tensor $\boldsymbol{D}$. After eigenvalue decomposition, $\boldsymbol{D}$ can be written as $\boldsymbol{D} = \boldsymbol{E} \cdot \boldsymbol{\Lambda} \cdot \boldsymbol{E}^t$, where the matrix $\boldsymbol{E}$ defines the orthonormal eigenvectors $\boldsymbol{e}_i$ and the diagonal matrix $\boldsymbol{\Lambda}$ represents the eigenvalues $\lambda_i$ of $\boldsymbol{D}$. Extracting the linear transformation matrix $\boldsymbol{\Phi}_L$ of $\boldsymbol{\Phi}$, the new eigenvectors $\boldsymbol{n}_i$ are calculated as follows:

$$\boldsymbol{n}_1 = \frac{\boldsymbol{\Phi}_L \boldsymbol{e}_1}{\|\boldsymbol{\Phi}_L \boldsymbol{e}_1\|} \quad, \quad \boldsymbol{n}_2 = \frac{\boldsymbol{\Phi}_L \boldsymbol{e}_2 - (\boldsymbol{n}_1{}^t\boldsymbol{\Phi}_L \boldsymbol{e}_2)\,\boldsymbol{n}_1}{\|\boldsymbol{\Phi}_L \boldsymbol{e}_2 - (\boldsymbol{n}_1{}^t\boldsymbol{\Phi}_L \boldsymbol{e}_2)\,\boldsymbol{n}_1\|} \quad, \quad \boldsymbol{n}_3 = \boldsymbol{n}_1 \times \boldsymbol{n}_2 \tag{6}$$

The reoriented diffusion tensor $\boldsymbol{D}_{\boldsymbol{\Phi}}$ can now be reconstructed as $\boldsymbol{D}_{\boldsymbol{\Phi}} = \boldsymbol{N} \cdot \boldsymbol{\Lambda} \cdot \boldsymbol{N}^t$, where the matrix $\boldsymbol{N}$ defines the transformed eigenvectors $\boldsymbol{n}_i$. Notice that the diffusion tensor shape is fully defined by the eigenvalue matrix $\boldsymbol{\Lambda}$ and is equal for $\boldsymbol{D}_{\boldsymbol{\Phi}}$ and $\boldsymbol{D}$.

# 3    Methods

## 3.1    Simulated DT-MRI Data

A recently developed mathematical framework is used to simulate DT-MRI data sets of WM neural fiber bundles, based on the corresponding diffusion related physical properties [17]. In summary, the synthetic DT-MRI data is constructed by first defining the fiber pathway, its corresponding width, Fractional Anisotropy (FA), mean diffusion (MD) and cross-sectional dependency of the fiber density [18]. Subsequently, these properties are translated in the eigenvalues and eigenvectors that define the diffusion tensor.

## 3.2    Experimental DT-MRI Data

Two in vivo DT-MRI data sets of the (healthy) human brain (male, 25y) were acquired on a 1.5 Tesla MR system (Fig. 1). Thereby, 60 axial slices with thickness of 2 mm were obtained covering the whole brain (voxel size of $2 \times 2 \times 2$ mm$^3$). A gradient configuration with 60 directions was used and additional acquisition parameters were as follows: $b$-factor $= 700$ s/mm$^2$, repetition time $=$ 8.3 s, echo time $= 108$ ms, and number of $b_0$ (no diffusion weighting) averages $= 10$. Further image processing of the DT-MRI data sets, i.e. calculation of the diffusion tensor and the direction color-encoded maps, was performed with 'ExploreDTI', a graphical toolbox for exploratory DT-MRI (available at http://www.dti.ua.ac.be) [19].

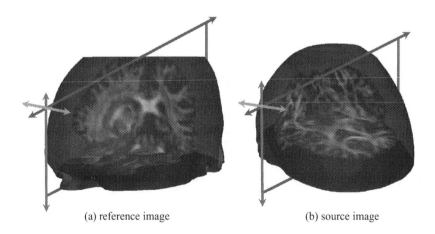

(a) reference image          (b) source image

**Fig. 1.** Two DT-MRI data acquisitions of the (same) brain under different orientations: (a) the reference image $R$ and (b) the source image $S$. The color-encoding in both images provides directional information, as indicated by the axes, of the underlying fiber orientation, which is assumed to be tangential to the local diffusion tensor.

# 4    Results

## 4.1    Coregistration of Simulated DT-MRI Data Sets

As shown in Fig. 2 (a,b,c), rotating a DT-MRI data set 90 degrees clockwise, as if considered to be scalar data, results in a loss of directional information of the underlying fiber tissue. Applying the RS corrects for both the shape and the predominant diffusion direction.

A second, less trivial example, is elucidated in Fig. 2 (d→g): a skew has been applied to the horizontal direction. After coregistration, a significant difference exists between the reoriented and non-reoriented diffusion tensor field.

Both qualitative results indicate that the proposed RS effectively reorients the diffusion tensor field, preserving the directional information of the underlying fiber direction.

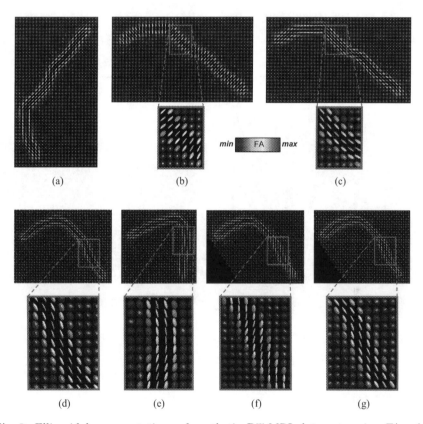

**Fig. 2.** Ellipsoidal representations of synthetic DT-MRI data sets using FA color-encoding. *Example 1:* (a) source image; (b) 90 degrees rotated (source) image without RS and (c) with RS. *Example 2:* the ground-truth data sets (d) reference image and (e) source image (=skewed reference image); the registered images *without* RS (f) and *with* RS (g).

## 4.2    Coregistration of Experimental DT-MRI Data Sets

Figure 3 shows the results when applying the registration method to experimental DT-MRI data. A specific part of the brain, i.e. the corpus callosum (CC), is zoomed in to properly visualize the (bidirectional) first eigenvector of both

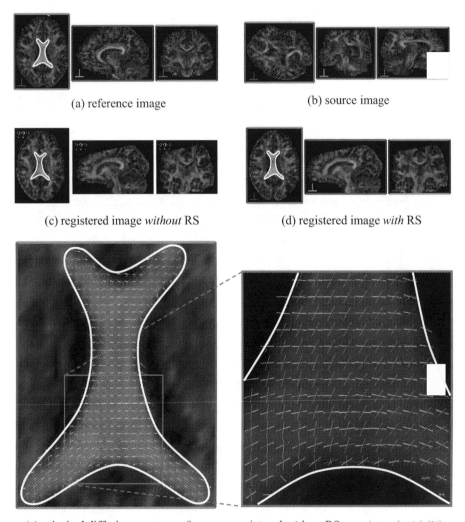

(a) reference image

(b) source image

(c) registered image *without* RS

(d) registered image *with* RS

(e) principal diffusion vectors: reference – registered *without* RS – registered *with* RS

**Fig. 3.** The experimental DT-MRI images (three orthogonal slices of the volume data): color-encoding again provides directional information, which is reflected by the colored axes (notice the question marks in (c) due to the unknown directional information). Note that in (e), the principal diffusion vectors of the registered image *with* RS are better aligned with the reference image, than when the RS is omitted.

the reference (red), the registered *without* RS (blue), and the registered *with* RS (orange) images. Although these results are qualitatively, they strongly indicate feasibility of the proposed coregistration technique to align experimental data.

## 5   Future Work

In this paper, we have presented qualitative results and feasibility of the new registration technique. The next step is providing quantitative results about the registration precision, accuracy, reproducibility, etc. Also deformable transformations, i.e. more than the 12 affine degrees of freedom, will be investigated.

## 6   Conclusions

A new 3D affine DT-MRI coregistration technique has been developed using a direct diffusion tensor reconstruction approach to preserve the underlying orientational information. This multi-channel matching method applies mutual information as a similarity measure for the multi-valued DT-MRI data sets. Simulations have been performed, demonstrating the applicability of the diffusion tensor shape preserving reorientation strategy. Also, an in-vivo coregistration example has been worked out, indicating feasibility of the proposed technique to register experimental data.

## Acknowledgements

This work was financially supported by the Institute for the Promotion of Innovation through Science and Technology in Flanders (IWT-Vlaanderen), Brussels. Jan Sijbers is a Postdoctoral Fellow of the F.W.O. (Fund for Scientific Research - Flanders, Belgium).

## References

1. Brown, L.: A survey of image registration techniques. ACM Computing Surveys **24** (1992) 326–376
2. Maintz, J., Viergever, M.: A survey of medical image registration. Medical Image Analysis **2** (1998) 1–36
3. Zitová, B., Flusser, J.: Image registration methods: a survey. Image and Vision Computing **21** (2003) 977–1000
4. Basser, P., Mattiello, J., Le Bihan, D.: MR diffusion tensor spectroscopy and imaging. Biophys J **66** (1994) 259–267
5. Mori, S., van Zijl, P.: Fiber tracking: principles and strategies - a technical review. NMR biomed **15** (2002) 468–480
6. Basser, P., Jones, D.: Diffusion-tensor MRI: theory, experimental design and data analysis - a technical review. NMR biomed **15** (2002) 456–467
7. Alexander, D., Gee, J.: Elastic matching of diffusion tensor images. Computer Vision and Image Understanding **77** (2000) 233–250

8. Ruiz-Alzola, J., Westin, C.F., Warfield, S., Alberola, C., Maier, S., Kikinis, R.: Nonrigid registration of 3D tensor medical data. Medical Image Analysis 6 (2002) 143–161

9. Ruiz-Alzola, J., Westin, C.F., Warfield, S., Nabavi, A., Kikinis, R.: Nonrigid registration of 3D scalar, vector and tensor medical data. In: Medical Image Computing and Computer-assisted Intervention. Volume 1935. (2000) 541–550

10. Park, H.J., Kubicki, M., Shenton, M., Guimond, A., McCarley, R., Maier, S., Kikinis, R., Jolesz, F., Westin, C.F.: Spatial normalization of diffusion tensor MRI using multiple channels. NeuroImage 20 (2003) 1995–2009

11. Guimond, A., Guttmann, C.: Deformable registration of DT-MRI data based on transformation invariant tensor characteristics. In: IEEE International Symposium on Biomedical Imaging (ISBI02), Washington, DC. (2002)

12. Xue, D., Mori, S., Shen, D., van Zijl, P., Davatzikos, C.: Spatial normalization of diffusion tensor fields. Magn Reson Med 50 (2003) 175–182

13. Maes, F., Collignon, A., Vandermeulen, D., Marchal, G., Suetens, P.: Multimodality image registration by maximization of mutual information. IEEE Trans. Medical Imaging 16 (1997) 187–198

14. Alexander, D., Pierpaoli, C., Basser, P., Gee, J.: Spatial transformations of diffusion tensor magnetic resonance images. IEEE Trans Med Imag 20 (2001) 1131–1139

15. Viola, P., Wells, W.: Multi-modal volume registration by maximization of mutual information. Med Image Anal 1 (1996) 35–51

16. Collingnon, A., Maes, F., Delaere, D., Vandermeulen, D., Suetens, P., Marchal, G.: Automated multimodality medical image registration using information theory. In: Proc. XIVth International Conference on Information Processing in Medical Imaging, Computational Imaging, and Vision. Volume 2082. (2001) 92–105

17. Leemans, A., Sijbers, J., Verhoye, M., Van der Linden, A., Van Dyck, D.: Mathematical framework for simulating diffusion tensor MR neural fiber bundles. Magn Reson Med 53 (2005) 944–953

18. Basser, P., Pierpaoli, C.: Microstructural and physiological features of tissues elucidated by quantitative-diffusion-tensor MRI. J Magn Reson B 111 (1996) 209–219

19. Leemans, A., Sijbers, J., Parizel, P.: A graphical toolbox for exploratory diffusion tensor imaging and fiber tractography. In: Section for Magnetic Resonance Technologists. (2005)

# Identification of Intestinal Motility Events of Capsule Endoscopy Video Analysis

Panagiota Spyridonos, Fernando Vilariño, Jordi Vitria, and Petia Radeva

Computer Vision Center, Universitat Autònoma de Barcelona,
08193 Bellaterra, Spain
{panagiota, fernando, jordi, petia}@cvc.uab.es
http://www.cvc.uab.es

**Abstract.** In this paper we introduce a system for assisting the analysis of cap-sule-endoscopy (CE) data, and identifying sequences of frames related to small intestine motility. The imbalanced recognition task of intestinal contractions was addressed by employing an efficient two-level video analysis system. At the first level, each video was processed resulting in a number of possible se-quences of contractions. In the second level, the recognition of contractions was carried out by means of a SVM classifier. To encode patterns of intestinal mo-tility a panel of textural and morphological features of the intestine lumen were extracted. The system exhibited an overall sensitivity of 73.53% in detecting contractions. The false alarm ratio was of the order of 59.92%. These results serve as a first step for developing assisting tools for computer based CE video analysis, reducing drastically the physician's time spent in image evaluation and enhancing the diagnostic potential of CE examination.

## 1 Introduction

Conventional endoscopic techniques for examining the small intestine (SI) are limited by its length (3.5-7.0 m) and by its complex looped configurations [1]. The current methods for imaging the SI include, primarily, barium X-rays and enteroscopy. How-ever, the diagnostic value of radiographic means for lesions such as angiodysplasias, and neoplasms is low [2]. On the other hand, direct visual inspection by enteroscopy, is highly invasive and is associated with discomfort and occasionally complications [3].

Capsule endoscopy (CE) is a new wireless endoscopy examination of the entire SI [1-4]. Moreover, CE is a technological invention designed to aid the gastroenterolo-gist in diagnosing SI diseases with higher sensitivity. The CE system is composed of the ingestible capsule, the data recorder, and the work station supplied with the ap-propriate image-visualization software. The capsule acquires two images per second and during a typical 8-hour examination, the recording device of the capsule stores about 50,000 images. After examination, images are downloaded to a PC workstation [4]. An expert physician is needed to inspect visually the video and to diagnose the presence (or absence) of abnormality.

However, the visualization of the whole study (video) is a burden and time con-suming procedure. In most of the cases the time it takes for a physician to review the capsule study is between one and two hours. This is quite a heavy load for the physi-

J. Blanc-Talon et al. (Eds.): ACIVS 2005, LNCS 3708, pp. 531–537, 2005.
© Springer-Verlag Berlin Heidelberg 2005

cian that renders the diagnostic task difficult and subject to variations in individual interpretation [5]. Subsequently, it would be particularly useful for physician to have an adjunctive tool able to short the reading time of a study and to automatically recognize sequences of frames meaningful for analysis.

Digital image processing and analysis techniques offer potential solutions to endoscopic images understanding and objective interpretation. Several researches have reported that endoscopic images carry rich information which, if quantified in terms of textural, color or other morphological features such as the lumen region, can allow the diagnosis of certain types of colon cancer [6-11]. However, as far as we know no preceding work has been reported on computerized analysis of CE data for the automatic identification of intestinal motility events.

In the present study, we introduce a CE video analysis system for detecting specific patterns related to intestine motility. The frequency and the type of contractions are of main interest and seemed to be correlated to the presence of several SI diseases [12]. The value of the proposed system relies on its ability to highlight special patterns of intestinal activity which might carry diagnostic information, reducing significantly the reading time of a CE study.

## 2  Material and Methods

Our clinical data consisted of a set of videos obtained by CE from six volunteers, in Digestive Diseases Dept., Hospital General "Vall D'Hebron" in Barcelona, Spain. The endoscopic capsule used, was developed by Given Imaging Limited, Israel [13]. Measuring 11x26 mm, the capsule contains 6 light emitting diodes, a lens, a color camera chip two batteries, a radio frequency transmitter, and an antenna. The capsule acquires two images per second at 256x256x24-bit resolution and transmits the data via radiofrequency to a recording unit located outside the body. Upon completion of the examination the data is transferred to the workstation for further visualization. Contractions were considered as dynamic events occurred in sequences of nine frames in the intestinal part between duodenum and cecum. Six videos were analyzed and labeled manually by an expert, specifying the time interval between duodenum and cecum and indicating the central frame in each sequence of contraction. Table 1 shows the number of frames per video registered between duodenum and cecum and the number of findings in this interval. Typical sequences of contractions are illustrated in Fig. 1. Each row corresponds with a contraction sequence. The contraction event occurs in the central frame.

**Table 1.** Number of frames and findings per video

|  | Number of frames for analysis | Number of findings |
|---|---|---|
| Video_1 | 29424 | 716 |
| Video_2 | 28783 | 487 |
| Video_3 | 27796 | 524 |
| Video_4 | 38865 | 718 |
| Video_5 | 17599 | 347 |
| Video_6 | 27156 | 911 |

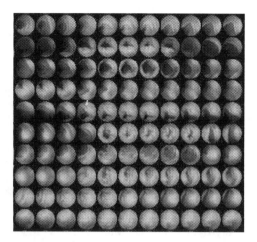

**Fig. 1.** Examples of sequences of intestinal contractions

The automatic recognition of contractions in a CE video is a highly skewed classi-fication problem on the order of 50 to 1(Table 1), which hardly can be tackled with a conventional direct classification process. Class imbalance is a well known issue for several real pattern recognition applications and has been addressed mainly by assign-ing distinct costs to training samples [14], by re-sampling the original dataset [15] or using cascade classifiers [16]. In this work, we addressed the imbalanced recognition task of small intestinal contractions by means of an efficient two-level video analysis process. At the first level of the system, each video was processed resulting in a num-ber of possible sequences of contractions, under the hypothesis that contractions might be described as a rapid closing and opening of the intestinal lumen and subse-quently could be characterized by a sharp variation of the grey-level intensity. The feature used to capture the intensity variation in a sequence was the locally normal-ized mean intensity of the image $I_N$ given by:

$$I_N = I - \bar{I} \tag{1}$$

where, $I$ is the mean grey-level intensity of the frame, and $\bar{I}$ is the averaged intensity estimated over a sequence of 9 frames:

$$\bar{I} = \frac{\sum_{i=1}^{9} I_i}{9} \tag{2}$$

This sequence length was chosen in accordance with the experts' assessment, in order to incorporate dynamic information for encoding the contraction event. Following this estimation, the intervals of sequential frames with positive $I_N$ were extracted from the whole series of the study. The frame with the maximum value $I_N$ in each interval was considered as the central frame of a possible sequence of contraction. An example is illustrated in Fig.2.

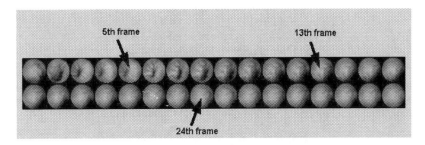

**Fig. 2.** Example of 32 sequential video frames; the indicated frames were selected during the first level of analysis as central frames of candidate sequences of contractions

In the second part of the system, the final recognition of contractions sequences was carried out by means of a support vector machine (SVM) classification algorithm [17]. To encode the patterns of intestinal motility a panel of textural and morphological features was extracted. Textural descriptors comprised features from first order statistics (mean value, standard deviation, skewness and kurtosis, estimated from the image histogram), second order statistics [18] (energy, entropy, inertia, local homogeneity, cluster shade, and cluster prominence), and Rotation Invariant Uniform Local Binary Units operator (LBPriu2) [19] applied in a circular symmetric neighbourhood P of radius R (P=16, R=2), using the eighteen bins histogram of the LBP$^{riu2}$ operator output (P+2=16+2). Morphological features of the intestinal lumen comprised measurements of blob area, blob shape (solidity), blob sharpness and blob deepness.

To estimate the lumen area, frames were processed by a Laplacian of Gaussian filter [20]. This filter has a high response at valleys that are dark regions surrounded of brighter regions. In our case, the region of interest in a frame was the lumen area. Dark areas were extracted by applying a greater-than-zero-threshold in the Laplacian image. The resulting binary image was superimposed to the Laplacian image. In the new image the blob sharpness was estimated by summing the pixel values of Laplacian image in the extracted objects. The object with the greater sum was selected as the blob area (Fig. 3). Blob deepness is the minimum of the Laplacian valley in the blob area.

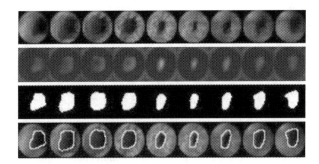

**Fig. 3.** Segmentation of blob area (top to down): original sequence of frames, estimated laplacian images, extracted blob areas, and blob contours superimposed to the original images

Following the feature extraction, each sequence was represented by a 37x9 dimensional feature vector. For feature reduction, a sequential forward selection method was used based on the performance of the system [21]. To evaluate the performance of the classifier, we used the leave-one-out technique. We run the classifier several times, and for each run all the videos except one were used for learning, and the one kept out was used for testing. For each video, the performance was evaluated in terms of sensitivity, specificity and False Alarm Ratio (FAR), taking into account the true and false positives and negatives as shown in Table 2. We used FAR as a false positive error measure since specificity by itself is not informative enough for skewed datasets. The sensitivity, specificity and FAR definitions used are the following: Sensitivity = TP/(TP+FN), Specificity = TN/(FP+TN), FAR= FP/(FP/TP+FN)

**Table 2.** Truth table

|  | **Manual Identification** | |
| --- | --- | --- |
| **System Identification** | *Contractions* | *Non-Contractions* |
| *Contractions* | True Positives  (TP) | False  Positives (FP) |
| *Non-Contractions* | False Negatives (FN) | True Negatives (TN) |

# 3  Results and Discussion

CE technology offers a safe, painless and effective method of diagnosing abnormalities in the SI. Current methods can be uncomfortable, or might be of limited diagnostic ability [2]. Although CE provides an excellent view of inaccessible parts of intestine, the amount of information registered during the capsule's transport time through the gastrointestinal tract is huge. Consequently, analyzing a CE study visually and qualitatively is a difficult and time consuming procedure, coupled with subjective interpretations. In the present study, we introduced a CE video analysis system based on computerized image analysis techniques. According to this system, data were analyzed in a cascade way in which redundant information was removed gradually. In this way, the reading time shorten significantly, without considerable loss of diagnostic information related to intestine motility. The detection of contractions is a primary feature, assessed visually by the experts during the CE visual inspection.

At the first level, the system reduced drastically the amount of data by removing 89.17% of them as redundant and missing 3.04% of the labeled findings (Table 3).

**Table 3.** First level processing of CE data

|  | Sequences passing 1st stage | Lost Conts. | Conts. | Non-Conts. |
| --- | --- | --- | --- | --- |
| **Video_1** | 3220/29424 (10.94%) | 26/716 (3.63%) | 690 | 2530 |
| **Video_2** | 3072/28783 (10.67%) | 25/487 (5.13%) | 462 | 2610 |
| **Video_3** | 3194/27796 (11.49%) | 11/524 (2.09%) | 513 | 2681 |
| **Video_4** | 4056/38865 (10.43%) | 15/718 (2.08%) | 703 | 3353 |
| **Video_5** | 1869/17599 (10.61%) | 7/347 (2.01%) | 340 | 1529 |
| **Video_6** | 2950/27156 (10.86%) | 30/911 (3.29%) | 881 | 2069 |
| **MEAN** | 10.83% | 3.04% | | |

At the second level the system refined the recognition of contractions by receiving only 10.83% of the initial data volume. The SVM classifier exhibited a performance of 75.81% in correct recognizing contractions and of 85.69 % in correct identifying non-contraction sequences (Table 4). The resulting best feature vector consisted of the following parameters: four morphological descriptors of the intestine blob (blob area, local normalized intensity, blob sharpness and blob deepness), and two textural features (energy and local homogeneity). The system yielded an overall sensitivity of 73.53% and an overall specificity of 98.76% (Table 5). However, in highly skewed classification problems with a very small number of positive instances the specificity by itself is a rather obscuring measure of performance [15]. For this reason we have used FAR, which is an indicative measure of the ability of the system to avoid false positives, taking into account the total number of existing contractions. The overall FAR of the system was of 59.92%. It means that in a practical case where the experts would have to analyze a video with 100 real contractions, our system would provide 60 false contractions and 74 real contractions. Now, the efforts of the physicians could be focused entirely in the analysis of these 134 sequences, discriminating between them which are the true and the false contraction sequences. This suppose a lot of save in visualization time, with acceptable performance values.

## 4   Conclusions and Future Work

The results from the present study might be promising in the development of assisting tools for computer based CE video analysis, reducing drastically the physician's time spent in image evaluation and enhancing the diagnostic potential of CE examination by introducing qualitative descriptors in diagnostic assessments. Further work is to be oriented to the problem of finding the optimal set of descriptors, deepening in the

**Table 4.** Second level processing of CE data

|         | TP  | TN   | FP  | FN  |
|---------|-----|------|-----|-----|
| Video_1 | 580 | 2082 | 448 | 110 |
| Video_2 | 319 | 2272 | 338 | 143 |
| Video_3 | 369 | 2395 | 286 | 144 |
| Video_4 | 575 | 2711 | 642 | 128 |
| Video_5 | 268 | 1343 | 186 | 72  |
| Video_6 | 610 | 1796 | 273 | 271 |

**Table 5.** Overall system performance in correct identifying sequences of SI contractions

|         | Overall sensitivity | Overall specificity    | Overall FAR         |
|---------|---------------------|------------------------|---------------------|
| Video_1 | 580/716 (81.00%)    | 28976/29424 (98.47%)   | 448/716 (62.56%)    |
| Video_2 | 319/487 (65.50%)    | 28445/28783 (98.82%)   | 338/487 (69.40%)    |
| Video_3 | 369/524 (70.41%)    | 27510/27796 (98.97%)   | 286/524 (54.58%)    |
| Video_4 | 575/718 (80.08%)    | 38223/38865 (98.34%)   | 642/718 (89.41%)    |
| Video_5 | 268/347 (77.23%)    | 17413/17599 (98.94%)   | 186/347 (53.60%)    |
| Video_6 | 610/911 (66.95%)    | 26883/27156 (98.99%)   | 273/911 (29.96%)    |
| **MEAN:** | **73.53%**        | **98.76%**             | **59.92%**          |

feature selection stage. In a parallel way, our group is focusing its efforts in the research for a better understanding of the intestinal contraction event, working altogether with the physicians in order to develop different paradigms. This represents a challenging line of work which we expect to be the target for future publications.

# References

1. Fireman, Z., Glukhovsky, A., Jacob, H., Lavy, A., Lewkowicz, S., Scapa, E.: Wireless Capsule Endoscopy. IMAJ. 4 (2002) 717-719
2. Schulmann, K.,Hollerbach, S., Kraus, K., Willert, J., Voleg, T., Moslein, G., Pox, C., Reiser, M., Reinacher-Schick, A., Schmiegel, W. : Feasibility and Diagnostic Utility of Video Capsule Endoscopy for the detection of Small Bowel Polyps in Patients with Hereditary Polyposis Syndromes. American Journal of Gastroenteroscopy. 100 (2002) 27-37
3. Waye, JD. : Small-intestinal endoscopy. Endoscopy. 33(1) (2001) 24-30
4. Rey, J-F., Gay, G., Kruse, A., Lambert, R.,: European Society of Gastrointestinal Endoscopy Guideline for Video Capsule Endoscopy. Endoscopy. 36 (2004) 656-658
5. Alder, D.G., Gostout, C.J.,: Wireless Capsule Endoscopy. Hospital Physician.(2003) 14-22
6. Tjoa, M.P., Krishman, S.M.,: Feature extraction for the analysis of colon status from the endoscopic images. Biomedical Engineering OnLine. 2 (2003)  3-17
7. Zheng, M.M., Krishman, S.M., Tjoa, M.P.: A fusion-based clinical support for disease diagnosis from endoscopic images. Computers in Biology and Medicine. Article in Press
8. Iakovidis, D.K., Maroulis, D.E., Karkanis, S.A., Papageorgas, P., Tzivras, M.: Texture Multichannel Measurements for cancer Precursors' Identification using Support Vector Machines. Measurement. 36 (2004) 297-313
9. Karkanis, S.A., Iakovidis, D.K., Maroulis, D.E., Karras, D.A., Tzivras, M.: Computer Aided Tumor Detection in Endoscopic Video using Color Wavelet Features. IEEE Transactions on Information Technology in Biomedicine. 7 (2003) 141-152
10. Boulougoura, M., Wadge,V, Kodogiannis, V.S., Chowdrey, H.S.: Intelligent Systems for Computer-Assisted Clinical Endoscopic Image Analysis. Proceedings of the 2nd IASTED Conference on Biomedical Engineering Innsbruck, Austria. (2005) 405-408
11. Kodogiannis, V.S., Chowdrey, H.S. : Multi-network Classification Scheme for Computer-Aided Diagnosis in Clinical Endoscopy. Proceedings of the International Conference on Medical Signal Processing (MEDISP) Malta. (2004) 262-267
12. Hansen, M.B.: Small Intestinal Manometry. Physiological Research. 51 (2002) 541-556
13. http://www.givenimaging.com
14. Karakoulas, G., Taylor, J.S. : Optimizing classifiers for imbalanced training sets. Proceedings of Neural Information Processing Workoshop NIPS'98. 253-259
15. Chawla, N.V. , Bowyer, K.W., Hall, L.O., Kegelmeyer, W.P.: SMOTE: Synthetic Minority Over-sampling Technique. Journal of Artificial Intelligence Research. 16 (2002) 321-357
16. Viola P., Jones, M.: Fast and Robust Classification using Asymmetric AdaBoost and a Detector Cascade: Advances in Neural Information Processing System 14, MIT Press, Cambridge, MA, (2002)
17. Vapnick, V.: Statitistical Learning Theory, John Wiley&Sons.
18. Theodoridis, S., Koutroumbas, K.: Feature Generation II. Pattern Recognition Academic Press (1998)
19. Ojala, T., Pietikainen, M.: Multiresolution Gray-Scale and Rotation Invariant Texture Classification with Local Binary Patterns. IEEE Transactions on Pattern Recognition Analysis and Machine Intelligence. 24(7) (2002) 971-987
20. Russ, J.C.: The Image Processing Handbook CRC Press. 2nd Edition. (1994)
21. Theodoridis, S., Koutroumbas K.: Feature Selection. Preprocessing. Pattern Recognition Academic Press (1998)

# A Likelihood Ratio Test for Functional MRI Data Analysis to Account for Colored Noise

Jan Sijbers[1], Arnold Jan den Dekker[2], and Robert Bos[2]

[1] University of Antwerp, Vision Lab, Groenenborgerlaan 171, U316, B-2020
Antwerpen, Belgium
[2] Delft University of Technology, Delft Center for Systems and Control, Mekelweg 2,
2628 CD Delft, The Netherlands

**Abstract.** Functional magnetic resonance (fMRI) data are often corrupted with colored noise. To account for this type of noise, many pre-whitening and pre-coloring strategies have been proposed to process the fMRI time series prior to statistical inference. In this paper, a generalized likelihood ratio test for brain activation detection is proposed in which the temporal correlation structure of the noise is modelled as an autoregressive (AR) model. The order of the AR model is determined from experimental null data sets. Simulation tests reveal that, for a fixed false alarm rate, the proposed test is slightly (2-3%) better than current tests incorporating colored noise in terms of detection rate.

## 1 Introduction

Functional magnetic resonance imaging (fMRI) is a noninvasive technique used to detect brain activity. By utilizing the fact that the magnetic resonance signal intensity is correlated with neural activity [1], fMRI can localize brain regions that show significant neural activity upon stimulus presentation. fMRI data sets typically consist of time series associated with the voxels of the brain. For each voxel, the significance of the response to the stimulus is assessed by statistically analyzing the associated fMRI time series. In this way, brain activation maps, or statistical parametric maps (SPMs), reflecting brain activity can be constructed.

Nowadays, the most common approach is to model the time series of fMRI data by a general linear model (GLM) disturbed by Gaussian distributed noise [2,3]. Potential time trends can be included in the linear model by adopting extra linear terms. The model contains one or more activation related parameters of interest as well as nuisance parameters. Statistical parametric maps (SPMs) are obtained by testing the significance of the activation related parameter(s) of the linear model using standard statistical tools such as the (two-sided) $t$-test (in the one parameter case) or the $F$-test (in the case of more than one parameters).

Current methods deal with temporally correlated noise by prewhitening the data based on the estimated correlation matrix of the noise [3]. This correlation matrix is estimated by fitting an autoregressive (AR) time series model to the residuals obtained after fitting the general linear model to the fMRI time series in least squares sense [4]. Since an estimate of the correlation matrix instead of

J. Blanc-Talon et al. (Eds.): ACIVS 2005, LNCS 3708, pp. 538–546, 2005.
© Springer-Verlag Berlin Heidelberg 2005

the (unknown) true correlation matrix of the noise is used for prewhitening the data, the assumption that the test statistic has a Student's $t$ distribution (upon which inference on the significance of the response is based) is only approximately valid. Obviously, this fact may harm the performance of the test.

In this paper, an alternative approach is proposed. This approach is also based on a general linear model with correlated noise modelled as an AR process, but, unlike the common GLM approach, it does not require a prewhitening step. Instead, statistical inference is based on the exact likelihood function (LF) that describes the statistics of the data including the temporal correlation structure of the noise. No approximations are made. The order of the AR process, which is fixed in the proposed test, is determined from practical null data sets (acquired in the absence of activity). The performance of the proposed tests is evaluated in terms of detection rate and false alarm rate properties.

The paper is organized as follows. In Section 2.1 and Section 3, statistical inference incorporating colored noise model is reviewed. Section 4 describes a novel approach for the construction of a statistical test that also accounts for colored noise. Simulation and experimental results are presented in Section 5.

## 2    Statistical Inference Incorporating Colored Noise

### 2.1    The Statistical Model of the fMRI Time Series

An fMRI time series $\boldsymbol{y} = (y_1, ..., y_n)^T$ (the superscript $T$ denotes matrix transposition) of equidistant observations can in general be modelled as [2,5]

$$\boldsymbol{y} = \boldsymbol{X}\boldsymbol{\theta} + \boldsymbol{v} \tag{1}$$

in which $\boldsymbol{X}$ is an $n \times m$ design matrix. It consists of $m$ columns that model signals of interest and nuisance signals such as potential drift. Furthermore, $\boldsymbol{\theta}$ is an $m \times 1$ vector of unknown parameters and $\boldsymbol{v}$ is an $n \times 1$ vector that represents stochastic noise contributions. The noise is modelled as a stationary stochastic AR process of order $p$ (i.e., an AR($p$) process):

$$v_t + \alpha_1 v_{t-1} + \alpha_2 v_{t-2} + \cdots + \alpha_p v_{t-p} = e \tag{2}$$

with $\boldsymbol{\alpha} = (\alpha_1, ..., \alpha_p)^T$ the vector of AR parameters and $e$ independent, zero mean Gaussian distributed white noise with variance $\sigma_e^2$. Let $\sigma_e^2 \boldsymbol{V}$ be the $n \times n$ covariance matrix of the AR process, i.e., $\sigma_e^2 \boldsymbol{V} = \mathbb{E}[\boldsymbol{v}\boldsymbol{v}^T]$ with $\mathbb{E}$ the expectation operator. For observations of stationary stochastic processes, the covariance matrix of the AR($p$) process $v_t$ may be written as

$$\sigma_e^2 \boldsymbol{V} = \sigma_v^2 \begin{pmatrix} \rho(0) & \rho(1) & \cdots & \rho(n-1) \\ \rho(1) & \rho(0) & \cdots & \rho(n-2) \\ \vdots & \vdots & \ddots & \vdots \\ \rho(n-1) & \rho(n-2) & \cdots & \rho(0) \end{pmatrix} \tag{3}$$

where $\rho(k) = \mathbb{E}[v_t v_{t+k}]/\sigma_v^2$ and $\sigma_v^2$ is the variance of $v_t$. Notice that it follows from this definition that $\rho(0) = 1$. The elements of the matrix $\boldsymbol{V}$ can be expressed in the AR parameters through the Yule Walker relations [6]:

$$\rho(k) + \alpha_1 \rho(k-1) + \cdots + \alpha_p \rho(k-p) = 0, \quad k > 0, \quad \rho(-k) = \rho(k). \quad (4)$$

Several authors have performed analyses that indicate that AR models give an accurate description of the actual temporal autocorrelation structure of the noise that contaminates fMRI data [4,7]. The validity of the model will be assessed using experimental data in section 5.1.

In this paper, the noise is assumed to be Gaussian distributed. Although magnitude MR data are known to be Rician distributed, the Rice distribution is nearly Gaussian at high SNR [8]. Hence, the test derived in this paper will only be valid for high SNR fMRI magnitude data (i.e., SNR>10).

## 2.2   Statistical Inference

In the next two sections, two-sided as well as one-sided hypothesis testing will be considered. If the test is two-sided, the null hypothesis $H_0$ that the task-related $i^{\text{th}}$ component $\theta_i$ of $\boldsymbol{\theta}$ equals zero is tested against the alternative hypothesis $H_1$ that $\theta_i \neq 0$. If it is known that $\theta_i > 0$ (under $H_1$), one may use a one-sided test in which $H_0$ that $\theta_i = 0$ is tested against $H_1$ where $\theta_i > 0$:

|                | $H_0$         | $H_1$                         |
|----------------|---------------|-------------------------------|
| one-sided test | $\theta_i = 0$ | $\theta_i > 0$ or $\theta_i < 0$ |
| two-sided test | $\theta_i = 0$ | $\theta_i \neq 0$             |

# 3   The Common GLM Approach

The widely used GLM approach consists of two steps. First, an estimate of the parameter vector $\boldsymbol{\theta}$ is obtained by least squares fitting of the model described by the right hand side of Eq. (1) to the data $\boldsymbol{y}$. A closed form expression of this so-called ordinary least squares (OLS) estimator is given by:

$$\widehat{\boldsymbol{\theta}}_{\text{OLS}} = (\boldsymbol{X}^T \boldsymbol{X})^{-1} \boldsymbol{X}^T \boldsymbol{y}. \quad (5)$$

Although not fully efficient, this estimator is unbiased [9]. Therefore, the residuals $\boldsymbol{y} - \boldsymbol{X}\widehat{\boldsymbol{\theta}}_{\text{OLS}}$ have zero expectation values and a correlation structure that is approximately equal to that of the noise $\boldsymbol{v}$. Assuming that the noise is generated by an AR($p$) model, the parameters of this model and hence the matrix $\boldsymbol{V}$ can be estimated from the residuals [3]. The estimated covariance matrix will be denoted as $\widehat{\boldsymbol{V}}$. Second, $\widehat{\boldsymbol{V}}^{-1}$ is used as weighting matrix in a generalized least squares (GLS) estimator of $\boldsymbol{\theta}$, which results in:

$$\widehat{\boldsymbol{\theta}}_{\text{GLS}} = \widehat{\boldsymbol{W}} \boldsymbol{X}^T \widehat{\boldsymbol{V}}^{-1} \boldsymbol{y} \quad (6)$$

where the $m \times m$ matrix $\widehat{\boldsymbol{W}} = (\boldsymbol{X}^T \widehat{\boldsymbol{V}}^{-1} \boldsymbol{X})^{-1}$ is an estimator of the covariance matrix of $\widehat{\boldsymbol{\theta}}_{\mathrm{GLS}}$ described by Eq. (6). Notice that estimator (6) is equivalent to applying the matrix $\widehat{\boldsymbol{V}}^{-1}$ to the model given by Eq. (1) before applying an ordinary least squares estimator. This is known as prewhitening of the data.

Finally, an estimator of $\sigma_e^2$ is given by

$$\widehat{\sigma_e^2} = \left(\boldsymbol{y} - \boldsymbol{X}\widehat{\boldsymbol{\theta}}_{\mathrm{GLS}}\right)^T \left(\boldsymbol{y} - \boldsymbol{X}\widehat{\boldsymbol{\theta}}_{\mathrm{GLS}}\right) /(n - m) \tag{7}$$

of which the statistics are not known exactly.

## 3.1   Statistical Inference

Brain activation can now be detected by testing the significance of the task-related parameter, say, $\theta_i$ of the linear model using standard statistical tools such as the $t$-test or the $F$-test. The Student's-$t$ test statistic is given by

$$T_t = \left[\widehat{\boldsymbol{\theta}}_{\mathrm{GLS}}\right]_i / \sqrt{\widehat{W_{ii}\sigma_e^2}} \quad , \tag{8}$$

where $\left[\widehat{\boldsymbol{\theta}}_{\mathrm{GLS}}\right]_i$ denotes the $i^{\mathrm{th}}$ element of $\widehat{\boldsymbol{\theta}}_{\mathrm{GLS}}$, $\widehat{\sigma_e^2}$ is given by Eq. (7), and $\widehat{W}_{ii}$ denotes the $i^{\mathrm{th}}$ diagonal element of the $m \times m$ matrix $\widehat{\boldsymbol{W}}$. The one-sided $t$-test decides $H_1$ if $T_t > \gamma$, whereas the two-sided $t$-test decides $H_1$ if $T_t < -\gamma$ or $T_t > \gamma$, with $\gamma$ a user specified, positive threshold. In practice, this threshold is chosen in function of a false positive rate that the user allows in case the null hypothesis $H_0$ is true. Approximately, the test statistic $T_t$ has a $t$ distribution with $n - m$ degrees of freedom (exact if $\boldsymbol{V}$ would be known) under $H_0$. Alternatively, one may use the test statistic

$$T_F = \left(\left[\widehat{\boldsymbol{\theta}}_{\mathrm{GLS}}\right]_i\right)^2 / \left(\widehat{W}_{ii}\widehat{\sigma_e^2}\right) \quad , \tag{9}$$

which has an approximate $F$ distribution with 1 and $n - m$ degrees of freedom (exact if $\boldsymbol{V}$ is known) under $H_0$. The $F$-test, which is a two-sided test, decides $H_1$ if $T_F > \gamma$, with $\gamma$ some user specified threshold.

## 4   Likelihood Based Tests

In this section, two new tests (a one-sided as well as a two-sided likelihood ratio test) for brain activation detection is presented with incorporation of colored noise. Thereby, the significance of the task-related parameter $\theta_i$ of the linear model is tested.

## 4.1   The Joint Probability Density Function of the Data

In order to use likelihood based tests, the joint probability density function (PDF) of the fMRI data $p(\boldsymbol{y}|\boldsymbol{\theta}, \boldsymbol{\alpha})$ is required. From Bayes' theorem, we have:

$$p(\boldsymbol{y}|\boldsymbol{\theta}, \boldsymbol{\alpha}, \sigma_e^2) = p(\boldsymbol{y}_p|\boldsymbol{\theta}, \boldsymbol{\alpha}, \sigma_e^2) \, p(\boldsymbol{y}_{n-p}|\boldsymbol{\theta}, \boldsymbol{\alpha}, \sigma_e^2, \boldsymbol{y}_p) \tag{10}$$

with $\boldsymbol{y}_p = (y_1, \ldots, y_p)^T$ and $\boldsymbol{y}_{n-p} = (y_{p+1}, \ldots, y_n)^T$. The second part of the right hand side is the conditional PDF of the observations $\boldsymbol{y}_{n-p}$ given that the initial observations $\boldsymbol{y}_p$ remain fixed at their observed values. Under the assumed AR model (2), where $e$ is Gaussian distributed, it may be written as [10]

$$p(\boldsymbol{y}_{n-p}|\boldsymbol{\theta}, \boldsymbol{\alpha}, \sigma_e^2, \boldsymbol{y}_p) = \left(\frac{1}{2\pi\sigma_e^2}\right)^{(n-p)/2} \times$$

$$\exp\left(-\frac{1}{2\sigma_e^2}\sum_{t=p+1}^{n}\{y_t - \boldsymbol{x}_t\boldsymbol{\theta} + \alpha_1(y_{t-1} - \boldsymbol{x}_{t-1}\boldsymbol{\theta}) + \ldots + \alpha_p(y_{t-p} - \boldsymbol{x}_{t-p}\boldsymbol{\theta})\}^2\right)$$

$$(11)$$

where $\boldsymbol{x}_t$ denotes the $t$-th row of the design matrix $\boldsymbol{X}$. The joint PDF of the data $\boldsymbol{y}_p$ may be written as [10]

$$p(\boldsymbol{y}_p|\boldsymbol{\theta}, \boldsymbol{\alpha}, \sigma_e^2) = \left(\frac{1}{2\pi\sigma_e^2}\right)^{p/2} \times$$

$$|\boldsymbol{V}_p|^{-1/2}\exp\left(-\frac{1}{2\sigma_e^2}(\boldsymbol{y}_p - \boldsymbol{X}_{1:p}\boldsymbol{\theta})^T\boldsymbol{V}_p^{-1}(\boldsymbol{y}_p - \boldsymbol{X}_{1:p}\boldsymbol{\theta})\right) \quad (12)$$

where $\boldsymbol{X}_{1:p}$ denotes the $p \times m$ matrix consisting of the first $p$ rows of the design matrix $\boldsymbol{X}$. $\boldsymbol{V}_p$ denotes the $p \times p$ covariance matrix of $\boldsymbol{v}_p = (v_1, \ldots, v_p)^T$ and $|\boldsymbol{V}_p|$ denotes the determinant of $\boldsymbol{V}_p$.

## 4.2   Statistical Inference

If we substitute the acquired data $\boldsymbol{y}$ in the expression for the joint PDF of the data (10), the resulting function is a function of the unknown parameters $(\boldsymbol{\alpha}, \boldsymbol{\theta}, \sigma_e^2)$ only. By regarding these parameters as variables, the LF $p(\boldsymbol{\theta}, \boldsymbol{\alpha}, \sigma_e^2; \boldsymbol{y})$ is obtained. Then, the generalized likelihood ratio (GLR) is given by [11]:

$$\lambda = \frac{\sup_{\theta_1, \ldots, \theta_{i-1}, \theta_{i+1}, \ldots, \theta_m, \boldsymbol{\alpha}, \sigma_e^2} p\left(\theta_1, \ldots, \theta_{i-1}, 0, \theta_{i+1}, \ldots, \theta_m, \boldsymbol{\alpha}, \sigma_e^2; \boldsymbol{y}\right)}{\sup_{\boldsymbol{\theta}, \boldsymbol{\alpha}, \sigma_e^2} p(\boldsymbol{\theta}, \boldsymbol{\alpha}, \sigma_e^2; \boldsymbol{y})} \quad . \quad (13)$$

The denominator of $\lambda$ is the LF evaluated at the maximum likelihood (ML) estimator under $H_0$, whereas the numerator of $\lambda$ is the LF evaluated at the ML estimator under $H_1$. From the GLR statistic, a one-sided as well as a two-sided likelihood ratio test can be constructed.

**Two-sided likelihood ratio test.** The generalized likelihood ratio test (GLRT) principle states that $H_0$ is to be rejected if and only if $\lambda \geq \lambda_0$, where $\lambda_0$ is some user specified threshold. It can be shown that, asymptotically (i.e., for $N \to \infty$), the modified GLR statistic

$$T_{LR} = 2\log\lambda \quad (14)$$

possesses a $\chi_1^2$ distribution, that is, a chi-square distribution with 1 degree of freedom, when $H_0$ is true [11].

**One-sided likelihood ratio test.** The signed likelihood ratio test statistic is given by [12]

$$T_{LR1} = \text{Sign}\left(\widehat{\theta}_i\right)\sqrt{2\log\lambda}. \tag{15}$$

The test decides $H_1$ if $T_{LR1} > \gamma$, with $\gamma$ some user specified threshold. Asymptotically, the test statistic $T_{LR1}$ has a standard normal distribution under $H_0$.

### 4.3   Computational Considerations

To obtain the likelihood ratio $\lambda$, the ML estimates of the unknown parameters under the null hypothesis $H_0$ and the alternative hypothesis $H_1$ have to be found. For that purpose, the LF has to be maximized with respect to the unknown parameters $(\boldsymbol{\alpha}, \boldsymbol{\theta}, \sigma_e^2)$. The noise variance $\sigma_e^2$ can be eliminated from this optimization problem since it can be shown that the value of $\sigma_e^2$ that maximizes the LF $p(\boldsymbol{\alpha}, \boldsymbol{\theta}, \sigma_e^2; \boldsymbol{y})$ with respect to $\sigma_e^2$ is given by

$$\sigma_e^2 = \frac{1}{n}\left[\sum_{i=1}^{p}\sum_{j=1}^{p}[\boldsymbol{V}_p^{-1}]_{ij}(y_i - \boldsymbol{x}_i\boldsymbol{\theta})(y_j - \boldsymbol{x}_j\boldsymbol{\theta}) + \right.$$
$$\left. \sum_{t=p+1}^{n}\{y_t - \boldsymbol{x}_t\boldsymbol{\theta} + \alpha_1(y_{t-1} - \boldsymbol{x}_{t-1}\boldsymbol{\theta}) + \ldots + \alpha_p(y_{t-p} - \boldsymbol{x}_{t-p}\boldsymbol{\theta})\}^2\right], \tag{16}$$

$[\boldsymbol{V}_p^{-1}]_{ij}$ being the $(i,j)$th element of $\boldsymbol{V}_p^{-1}$. Substituting (16) in (10) yields the so-called concentrated LF. The ML estimates $(\widehat{\boldsymbol{\alpha}}, \widehat{\boldsymbol{\theta}})$ of the parameters $(\boldsymbol{\alpha}, \boldsymbol{\theta})$ can now be found by maximizing the concentrated LF with respect to $(\boldsymbol{\alpha}, \boldsymbol{\theta})$, which is a nonlinear optimization problem that can be solved numerically.

## 5   Experiments

Experimental fMRI data sets were obtained from small animal as well as from human subjects. The experiments for the small animals (3 rats) were done on a 7T MRI system (SMIS, Guildford, UK) with an 80 mm aperture and self-shielded gradients. Images were taken with size $256 \times 128$, maximum gradient strengths $G_r = 0.017$ T/m, $G_p = 0.027$ T/m, $G_{sl} = 0.07$ T/m, and ramp time 100 $\mu s$. All human experiments were performed on a 1,5 T scanner with high-performance 40 mT/m gradients (Siemens Sonata, Erlangen, Germany). Subjects were three healthy volunteers (mean age 33 years). Gradient-recalled multi-shot EPI sequences (TE 50 ms, TR 3000 ms) were used with 30 slices covering the whole brain. The voxels dimensions were $3 \times 3 \times 3$ mm.

### 5.1   Order of the AR Model of fMRI Noise Structures

From the experimental fMRI null data, the order of the AR model was determined. Previous work by Woolrich et al. examined the necessary AR order from six null data sets. They concluded that AR(6) was sufficient for their data [4]. In our work, various null data sets were acquired from humans as well as from small animals. The null data were modelled with a second order polynomial model: $b_0 + b_1t + b_1t^2$ along with an AR($p$) model of which the order was estimated using Akaike's information criterion (AIC) [13], where a penalty factor of 3 instead of 2 was chosen [14]. Evaluation of AR order maps, constructed from these data revealed that an AR(3) model is conservative with enough freedom to accommodate even more complex AR processes than expected.

## 5.2   Simulation Experiments

For a fixed false alarm rate of 1%, the likelihood ratio tests proposed were compared to the GLM tests with respect to detection rate. The *false alarm rate* is the probability that the test will decide $H_1$ when $H_0$ is true. The *detection rate* is the probability that the test will decide $H_1$ when $H_1$ is true.

Simulation experiments were set up to detect brain activation. Thereby, a simple on-off activation scheme was used in which traces of 100 time-points were generated with period equal to 20 (10 on, 10 off). Also, small linear and quadratic trends were introduced that were modelled along with the baseline and activation pattern. The amplitude of the activation pattern was gradually increased from 0 till 0.6; the noise standard deviation was fixed to 1. For each simulation experiment, $10^4$ Monte Carlo simulations were run.

## 6   Results and Discussion

Typical results for the simulation experiments described in Subsection 5.2 are shown in Fig. 1. Fig. 1(a) shows the detection rate as a function of the amplitude of the activation pattern. Although results weakly depend on this amplitude, it may be concluded from the numerical outcomes that, for a fixed false alarm rate

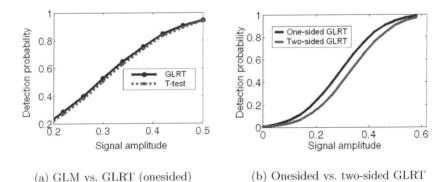

(a) GLM vs. GLRT (onesided)          (b) Onesided vs. two-sided GLRT

**Fig. 1.** Detection rates with a fixed false alarm rate of 1%

of 1%, the detection rate of the proposed one-sided GLRT is uniformly 2-3% better compared to the detection rate of the GLM test incorporating colored noise. Similar results were observed when comparing the two-sided tests.

Finally, Fig. 1(b) shows the results when comparing the one-sided test against the two-sided test in case the amplitude of the activation pattern was known to be positive. As expected, the one-sided test performs in that case over 10% better than the two-sided test.

## 7   Conclusions

In this paper, likelihood ratio tests for the detection of functional brain activity, one-sided as well as two-sided, have been presented. In contrast to the general linear model (GLM) tests, the proposed likelihood ratio tests allow direct incorporation of colored noise and do not require a prewhitening step. Simulation results showed that likelihood based detection results in systematic slightly improved detection probabilities compared to the currently popular GLM based tests.

## Acknowledgements

This work has been financially supported by the FWO (Fund for Scientific Research - Belgium). The authors like to thank A. Smolders and N. Van Camp for providing them with experimental fMRI null data.

## References

1. Cohen, M.S.: Real-time functional magnetic resonance imaging. Methods **25** (2001) 201–220
2. Friston, K.J., Holmes, A.P., Worsley, K.J., Poline, J.B., Frith, C.D., Frackowiak, R.S.J.: Statistical parametric maps in functional imaging: a general linear approach. Hum. Brain Mapp. **2** (1995) 189–210
3. Worsley, K.J., Liao, C.H., Aston, J., Petre, V., Duncan, G.H., Morales, F., Evans, A.C.: A general statistical analysis for fMRI data. NeuroImage **15** (2002) 1–15
4. Woolrich, M.W., Ripley, B.D., Brady, J.M., Smith, S.M.: Temporal autocorrelation in univariate linear modelling of fMRI data. NeuroImage **14** (2001) 1370–1386
5. Worsley, K.J., Friston, K.J.: Analysis of fMRI time-series revisited – again. NeuroImage **2** (1995) 173–181
6. Kay, S.M., Marple, S.L.: Spectrum analysis – a modern perspective. In: Proceedings of the IEEE. Volume 69. (1981) 1380–1419
7. Carew, J.D., Wahba, G., Xie, X., Nordheim, E.V., Meyerand, M.E.: Optimal spline smoothing of fMRI time series by generalized cross-validation. NeuroImage **18** (2003) 950–961
8. den Dekker, A.J., Sijbers, J.: Estimation of signal and noise from MR data. In: Advanced Image Processing in Magnetic Resonance Imaging. Volume 26 of Signal Processing and Communications. Marcel Dekker (2005) ISBN: 0824725425.

9. van den Bos, A.: 8: Parameter Estimation. In: Handbook of Measurement Science. Volume 1. Edited by P. H. Sydenham, Wiley, Chichester, England (1982) 331–377
10. Priestley, M.B.: Spectral analysis and time series. Academic Press, London (1981)
11. Kay, S.M.: Fundamentals of statistical signal processing: estimation theory. Prentice-Hall, Inc. (1993)
12. Rowe, D.B., Logan, B.R.: A complex way to compute fMRI activation. Neuroimage **23** (2004) 1078–1092
13. Ardekani, B.A., Kershaw, J., Kashikura, K., Kanno, I.: Activation detection in functional MRI using subspace modeling and maximum likelihood estimation. IEEE Trans Med Imaging **18** (1999) 246–254
14. Broersen, P.M.T.: Finite sample criteria for autoregressive order selection. IEEE Trans Sig Proc **48** (2000) 3550–3558

# Heuristic Algorithm for Computing Fast Template Motion in Video Streams*

Elena Sánchez-Nielsen[1] and Mario Hernández-Tejera[2]

[1] Department of Statistics, Operations Research and Computer Science,
University of La Laguna, 38271 La Laguna, Spain
enielsen@ull.es
[2] Institute of Intelligent Systems and Numerical Applications in Engineering,
Campus Universitario de Tafira, 35017 Gran Canaria, Spain
mhernandez@iusiani.ulpgc.es

**Abstract.** Many vision problems require computing fast template motion in dynamic scenes. These problems can be formulated as exploration problems and thus can be expressed as a search into a state space based representation approach. However, these problems are hard to solve because they involve search through a high dimensional space. In this paper, we propose a heuristic algorithm through the space of transformations for computing target 2D motion. Three features are combined in order to compute efficient motion: (1) a quality of function match based on a holistic similarity measurement, (2) Kullback-Leibler measure as heuristic to guide the search process and (3) incorporation of target dynamics into the search process for computing the most promising search alternatives. The paper includes experimental evaluations that illustrate the efficiency and suitability for real-time vision based tasks.

## 1 Introduction

Computing pattern or template motion in video streams is a critical task in pattern recognition and computer vision field with many practical applications such as vision based interface tasks [1], visual surveillance or perceptual intelligence applications [2]. Nowadays, three main issues must be addressed in order to compute effective target 2D motion: (1) indeterminate nature of shapes without any a priori specification of speed and trajectory, (2) dynamic changing environments and (3) real-time performance.

In this paper, it is proposed a fast algorithm to apply over a space of transformations for computing target 2D motion without any assumption of the speed and trajectory of the objects in unrestricted environments. The main contributions are focused on: (1) an A* heuristic search algorithm and (2) dynamic update of the search space in each image, whose corresponding dimension is determined by target dynamics. In addition to these contributions, the paper also contains a number of experimental evaluations and comparisons:

* This work has been supported by the Spanish Government and Canary Islands Autonomous Government under the Projects TIN2004-07087 and PI2003/165.

J. Blanc-Talon et al. (Eds.): ACIVS 2005, LNCS 3708, pp. 547–554, 2005.
© Springer-Verlag Berlin Heidelberg 2005

- A direct comparison of the performance of conventional searches [3] and the proposed A* search approach, demonstrating that the search approach proposed is faster.
- An analysis of the time required, illustrating that the time to track targets in video streams under unrestricted environments is lower than real-time requirements using general purpose hardware.

The structure of this paper is as follows: the problem formulation is illustrated in Section 2. In Section 3, the heuristic algorithm is described. Experimental results are provided in Section 4 and Section 5 concludes the paper.

## 2   Problem Formulation

For the sake of subsequent problem formulation, some definitions are introduced:

**Definition 1.** *Let* $T(k) = \{t_1, \cdots, t_r\} \subseteq \mathbb{R}^2$ *be a set of points that represent a template in step time k.*

**Definition 2.** *Let* $I(k) = \{i_1, \cdots, i_s\} \subseteq \mathbb{R}^2$ *be another set of points that denote an input image in step time k. It is assumed that each step time k corresponds to a new frame k of the video stream.*

**Definition 3.** *Let a bounded set of translational transformations be a set of transformations* $\mathbb{G} = [g_{xmin}, g_{xmax}] \times [g_{ymin}, g_{ymax}] \subseteq \mathbb{R}^2$ *and let* $g^c = (g_x^c, g_y^c)$ *denote the transformation that corresponds to the center of* $\mathbb{G}$*. It is defined as:* $g^c = \left( \left( \frac{1}{2} (g_{xmin} + g_{xmax}) \right), \left( \frac{1}{2} (g_{ymin} + g_{ymax}) \right) \right)$*, where (xmin, xmax) and (ymin, ymax) represent respectively the low and upper bounds of* $\mathbb{G}$ *in x and y dimension.*

**Definition 4.** *Let a bounded error notion of quality of match* $Q(g; T(k), I(k), \varepsilon)$ *be a measurement for computing the degree of match between a template* $T(k)$ *and a current input image* $I(k)$*, where the dependence of Q on T, I and/or $\varepsilon$ is omitted for sake of simplicity but without loss of generality. That is, the quality of match assigned to a transformation g is represented by the allowed error bound, $\varepsilon$, when template points are brought to image points using the transformation g. This quality of match function assigned to a transformation g is expressed as:*

$$Q(g) = \sum_{t \in T} \max_{i \in I} \|g(t) - i\| < \varepsilon \tag{1}$$

*where* $\| . \|$ *denotes a measurement of distance and* $g(t)$ *represents the result of applying the transformation* $g = (g_x, g_y)$ *to every point in template* $T(k)$*.*

Given a template $T(k)$, an input image $I(k)$ and an error bound $\varepsilon$, the template motion problem can be viewed as the search process in the space of transformations in order to find the transformation $g_{opt}$ that maximizes the quality of match $Q(g)$ between the transformed template $g(T(k))$ and the image $I(k)$:

$$g_{opt}(T(k), I(k), \varepsilon) = arg \max_{g \in \mathbb{G}} Q(g; T(k), I(k), \varepsilon) \tag{2}$$

# 3   Heuristic Search Algorithm

Formulation of problem solving under the framework of heuristic search is expressed through a *state space based-representation approach* [4], where the possible problem situations are considered as a *set of states*. The *start state* corresponds to the initial situation of the problem, the *final, goal* or *target state* corresponds to problem solution and the transformation between states can be carried out by means of *operators*. Next, the elements of the problem are described in order to formalize the heuristic search framework:

- *State*: each search state $n$ is associated with a subset $G_n \subseteq \mathbb{G}$. Each state is represented by the transformation $g^c$ corresponding to $G_n$.
- *Initial state*: is represented by a bounded set of translational transformations $\mathbb{G}$, which allow matching the current template position in the current scene.
- *Final state*: is the transformation that best matches the current template points $T(k)$ in the current image $I(k)$, according to $Q(g)$. The quality of function match assigned to a transformation $g$ is expressed in terms of the partial directed Hausdorff distance (see appendix) between $g(T(k))$ and $I(k)$:

$$Q(g) = h_q\big(g(T(k)), I(k)\big) < \varepsilon \qquad (3)$$

Where the parameter $q$ represents the $q^{th}$ quartile value selected according to expression 9 and $\varepsilon$ denotes that each point of $g(T(k))$ must be within distance $\varepsilon$ of some point of $I(k)$.

- *Operators*: are the functional elements that transform one state to another. For each current state $n$, the operators $A$ and $B$ are computed:
  - *Function A*. The current state is partitioned into four regions by vertical and horizontal bisections, that is, four new states.
  - *Function B*. The quality of function match (equation 3), is computed for each one of the new states generated, where $g(T(k))$ corresponds to $g^c(T(k))$.

Splitting each current state into four new states leads to the representation of the search tree to be a quaternary tree structure; where each node is associated to a $2^i \times 2^j$ region. To be precise, the heuristic search process is initiated by the association of $\mathbb{G}$ with the root of the search tree, and subsequently the best node at each tree-level $l$ is expanded into four new distinct and non-overlapping states. The splitting operation is finished when the quadrisection process computes a translational motion according to $Q(g)$ or all the regions associated with the different nodes have been partitioned in cells of unit size. Figure 1 illustrates the search process. Each one of the four regions computed are referred to as *NW, NE, SE* and *SW* cells. The best node to expand from these cells is computed using an A* approach [4], which combines features of uniform-cost search and heuristic search. The corresponding value assigned to each state $n$ is defined as:

$$f(n) = c(n) + h^*(n) \qquad (4)$$

Where $c(n)$ is the estimated cost of the path from the initial node $n_0$ to current node $n$, and $h^*(n)$ is the heuristic estimate of the cost of a path from node $n$ to the goal.

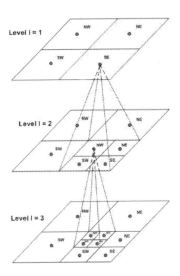

**Fig. 1.** Search tree: hierarchical partition of the space of states using a quadrisection process. The nodes at the leaf level define the finest partition

## 3.1   Heuristic Function h*(n) and Estimated Cost Function c(n)

The heuristic value h*(n) is estimated by means of evaluating the quality of the best solution reachable from the current state $n$. Desirability of the best state is estimated measuring the similarity between the distribution functions $P$ and $Q$ that respectively characterize the current and goal state. The definition of both functions is based on the quality of function match assigned to the target transformation, $g_{opt}$. Since the quality of function match is denoted by the partial directed Hausdorff distance, the function $P$ can be approximated by a histogram of distances $\{H_{g^c}\}_{i=1\cdots r}$, which contains the number of template points $T(k)$ at distance $d_j$ with respect to the points of $I(k)$, when the transformation $g^c$ of the current state $n$ is applied on $T(k)$. Figure 2a shows the function associated to $P$, when a transformation $g^c$ corresponds to $g_{opt}$. The distribution function $Q$ can be modeled by approximating $\{H_{g^c}\}_{i=1\cdots r}$ by an exponential function $f(n) = ke^{-an}$ such is illustrated in Figure 2b.

Given the distribution functions $P$ and $Q$, and let $R$ be the number of template points, the similarity between both distributions is measured using the Kullback-Leibler distance (KLD) [5]:

$$D(P\|Q) = \sum_{i=1}^{R} p_i log\frac{p_i}{q_i} \qquad (5)$$

According to [5], $D(P\|Q)$ has two important properties: (1) $D(P\|Q) \geq 0$; and (2) $D(P\|Q) = 0$ $iff$ $P = Q$. These properties show that when the template points do not match the input image points, the values of KLD will be non-zero and positive because the distributions are not similar, $P \neq Q$. On the other

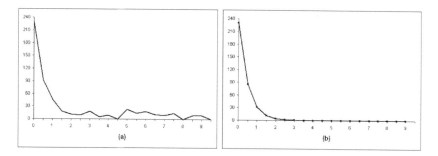

**Fig. 2.** Distribution functions: (a) $\{H_{g^c}\}_{i=1\cdots r}$ (b) $f(n) = ke^{-an}$, where $a = 1$. The horizontal axis represents distance values and the vertical axis denotes the number of transformed template points with $g^c$ at distance $d_j$ with respect to $I(k)$.

hand, if the template points match the input image points, then the value of KLD is equal or near zero.

An estimated cost function $c(n)$ is added to $f(n)$ in order to generate a back-tracking process when the heuristic function leads the search process towards no promising solutions. This term is based on the number of operators $A$ type applied from the initial state to the current state $n$.

### 3.2   Initial State Computation

The dimension $M \times N$ of $\mathbb{G}$ is computed by means of incorporating an alpha-beta predictive filtering [6] into the search algorithm. The parameters estimated by the filtering approach are represented by the 2D opposite coordinates of the bounding box that encloses the target shape and are expressed as a *four-dimensional* vector $\theta = [\theta_1, \cdots, \theta_4]^T$. The location and velocity vector are jointly expressed as a state vector $x = [\theta^T, \dot{\theta}^T]^T$. The state vector estimation using a constant velocity model is formulated as:

$$\hat{x}(k+1 \mid k+1) = \hat{x}(k+1 \mid k) + v(k+1)\left[\alpha \frac{\beta}{\Delta T}\right]^T \tag{6}$$

Since $v(k)$ represents a measure of the error of $\hat{z}(k+1)$, a decision rule focused on this uncertainty measurement can be obtained in order to compute the dimension of $\mathbb{G}$. Two main criteria are considered in the decision rule design. The first one is that small values of the innovation factor indicate low uncertainty about its estimate and therefore, a reduced size of $\mathbb{G}$. However, deviations of the target motion from the assumed temporal motion model involves higher uncertainty about the estimation and so, larger dimension of $\mathbb{G}$. The second criterion is that the dimension of $M \times N$ must be a $2^p \times 2^q$ value in order to assure that each terminal cell of $\mathbb{G}$ will contain a single transformation after the last quadrisection operation had been applied. Assuming these requirements, the dimension $M \times N$ of $\mathbb{G}$ is computed as:

$$M = \begin{cases} 2^{min}, \text{ if } w + 2^{min} \leq v_M(k) \\ 2^{max}, \text{ if } w + 2^{min} > v_M(k) \end{cases} \tag{7}$$

$$N = \begin{cases} 2^{min}, \text{ if } w + 2^{min} \leq v_N(k) \\ 2^{max}, \text{ if } w + 2^{min} > v_N(k) \end{cases} \tag{8}$$

Where $v(k) = (v_M(k), v_N(k))$, $2^{min}$, $2^{max}$ represent the nearest values to $v(k)$ and $w$ is calculated according to the expression: $w = \phi(2^{max} - 2^{min})$, where $\phi$ weights the influence of the difference between $2^{min}$ and $2^{max}$. The figure 3 and 4 show respectively the computation of $M \times N$ and the search algorithm. The bounds of $\mathbb{G}$ in each step $k$ are calculated as: $g_{xmin}(k) = g_x(k-1) - \frac{M}{2}$, $g_{xmax}(k) = g_x(k-1) + (\frac{M}{2}) - 1$, $g_{ymin}(k) = g_y(k-1) - \frac{N}{2}$, $g_{ymax}(k) = g_y(k-1) + (\frac{N}{2}) - 1$, where $(g_x(k-1), g_y(k-1))$ represents the solution transformation computed in previous step time $k - 1$.

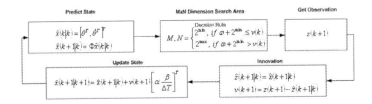

**Fig. 3.** Alfa-beta filtering stages and computation of $M \times N$ dimension of $\mathbb{G}$

*Input*
   $\mathbb{G}$: initial set of transformations.
   $\varepsilon$: distance error bound allowed when template points are brought to point's image using a transformation $g$.
   $D(P\|Q)$ : value of Kullback-Leibler distance.
   $\eta$ : number of operators of type $A$ applied from initial state to current state $n$.

*Algorithm*
   *Step 1)* Compute $M \times N$ dimension of $\mathbb{G}$
   *Step 2)* Find $g_{opt}$ that verify $Q(g) = h_q(g(T(k)), I(k)) < \varepsilon$:
      **While** $Q(g) > \varepsilon$ **Do**
         2.1) Split state $n$ into four new states $\{n\}_{i=1\cdots4}$
         2.2) Compute $Q(g_c) \leftarrow h_q(g_c(T(k)), I(k))$ for each $n_i$
         2.3) Expand the best $n_i$ according to $f(n) = c(n) + h^*(n)$:
            2.3.1) $h^*(n) \leftarrow D(P\|Q)$
            2.3.2) $c(n) \leftarrow c(n-1) + \eta$
      **End While**

**Fig. 4.** Heuristic algorithm for computing template motion

## 4   Experiments and Results

Thirty sequences have been used, achieving the same behavior for all of them on a P-IV 2.4 GHz. Particularly, sequences *"People" (855 frames)*, *"Hand" (512 frames), "Cars" (414 frames)* and *"Motorcycle" (70 frames)* are illustrated. The average size of each frame and template is respectively $280 \times 200$ and $170 \times 140$ pixels. Initial states evaluated correspond to: (1)*Fixed search area (A1)*: a 64x64 pixels 2D translations set ranging from (-32, -32) to (32, 32), (2)*Fixed search area with motion prediction (A2)*: a 64x64 pixels 2D translations set computed from the predicted target position and (3)*Adjustable search area (A3)*: the dimension of each initial state is computed according to expressions 7 and 8. The goal state is defined as the translation $g$ that verifies that 80% (parameter $q = 0.8$) of template points are at maximum 2 pixels distance ($\varepsilon = 2.0$) from $I(k)$. $\varepsilon$ is increased in one unit until a maximum value of 10 if no goal state is computed. Figure 5 illustrates three original sample frames of the sequences mentioned and the corresponding edge located template. No object is shown in the last frame of *Car* sequence because the object does not correspond to the target tracked.

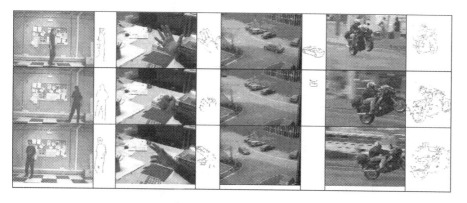

**Fig. 5.** Sample frames of *People, Hand, Car* and *Motorcycle* sequence

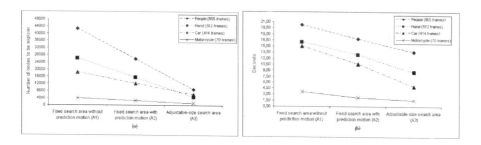

**Fig. 6.** Nodes explored and time required for processing the sequences

The performance of the approaches for computing initial search state is measured by means of the number of nodes explored and the time required for processing each sequence. The results of figure 6 show that the number of nodes to be explored are reduced considerably by incorporating a filtering approach into the search algorithm. On the other hand, the search proposed is faster than the conventional blind search strategy [3] at an average rate of three times better, allowing this way real time-performance using general purpose hardware. Average runtime for each frame of the sequences using the heuristic algorithm is 10 ms, clearly being lower than real-time restrictions (40ms).

## 5  Conclusions

This paper presents a heuristic algorithm that is lower than real-time requirements for computing template motion of arbitrary shapes in unrestricted environments. From the experimental study carried out, two conclusions have been obtained: (i) although abrupt motions cannot be predicted by an alpha-beta filtering, the algorithm was well adapted and (ii) color cue is required in those situations where the target shape is represented by a reduced set of sparse points.

## References

1. Turk, Mathew. Computer Vision in the Interface. *Communications of the ACM*, 47(1): 61 - 67, 2004.
2. Pentland, A. Perceptual Intelligence. *Communications of ACM*, 43(3): 35-44, 2000.
3. Rucklidge, W. Efficient computation of the minimum Hausdorff distance for visual recognition. Lecture Notes in Computer Science, n° 1173, Springer-Verlag, 1996.
4. Pearl, J. Heuristics. Intelligent Search Strategies for Computer Problem Solving. *Addison-Wesley Series in Artificial Intelligence*, 1984.
5. Cover, T. M., Thomas J.A, Thomas J.A. Elements of Information Theory. John Wiley & Sons Incs, 1991.
6. Bar-Shalom, Y., Xiao-Rong, Li. Estimation and Tracking: Principles, Techniques, and Software. Artech House, Boston, 1993.

## A    Partial Directed Hausdorff Distance

The *partial directed Hausdorff* distance between two sets of points $A$ and $B$ ranks each point of $A$ based of its distance to the nearest point in $B$ and uses the $q^{th}$ quartile value ranked point as the measure of distance. It is defined as:

$$h_q(A, B) = \underset{a \in A}{Q}^{th} \min_{b \in B} \|a - b\| \tag{9}$$

# Configurable Complexity-Bounded Motion Estimation for Real-Time Video Encoding

Zhi Yang, Jiajun Bu, Chun Chen, and Linjian Mo[*]

College of Computer Science, Zhejiang University,
310027 Hangzhou, P.R.China
{yangzh, bjj, chenc, molin}@zju.edu.cn

**Abstract.** Motion estimation (ME) is by far the main bottleneck in real-time video coding applications. In this paper, a configurable complexity-bounded motion estimation (CCBME) algorithm is presented. This algorithm is based on prediction-refinement techniques, which make use of spatial correlation to predict the search center and then use local refinement search to obtain the final motion field. During the search process, the ME complexity is ensured bounded through three configuration schemes: 1) configure the number of predictors; 2) configure the search range of local refinement; 3) configure the subset pattern of matching criterion computation. Different configuration leads to different distortion. Through joint optimization, we obtain a near-optimal complexity-distortion (C-D) curve. Based on the C-D curve, we preserve 6 effective configurable modes to realize the complexity scalability, which can achieve a good tradeoff between ME accuracy and complexity. Experimental results have shown that our proposed CCBME exhibits higher efficiency than some well-known ME algorithms when applied on a wide set of video sequences. At the same time, it possesses the configurable complexity-bounded feature, which can adapt to various devices with a wide range of computational capability for real-time video coding applications.

## 1 Introduction

With the rapid development of wireless network and consumer electronics, it is feasible to implement real-time video communication services on mobile devices such as *Pocket PCs* and *Mobile Phones*. However, the mobile devices are of various computational capability. Although specific algorithms can be designed to satisfy specific mobile device, it is not a cost effective way since there are so many different devices. Hence, it is desirable to design complexity-configurable algorithms to offer a good tradeoff between coding efficiency and the complexity. Moreover, in order to avoid delay and jitter in real-time video encoding, the encoder must possess the ability to encode the most complex compliant video frame

[*] The work was supported by National Natural Science Foundation of China (60203013), 863 Program (2004AA1Z2390) and Key Technologies R&D Program of Zhejiang Province (2005C23047 & 2004C11052).

J. Blanc-Talon et al. (Eds.): ACIVS 2005, LNCS 3708, pp. 555–562, 2005.
© Springer-Verlag Berlin Heidelberg 2005

within a relatively fixed interval. Therefore, complexity-bounded algorithms are taken into consideration.

Motion estimation (ME) plays an important role in video coding system [1] to reduce temporal redundancy between video pictures. Meanwhile, ME is the most time-consuming module of the encoder, e.g. full search ME consumes almost 80% of computing time. In order to implement real-time video coding applications, many fast ME algorithms have been developed to alleviate the heavy computation load, such as diamond search (DS) [2], hexagon-based search (HEXBS) [3] and some predictive algorithms [4][5]. However, despite of the significant speedups, ME still consumes the largest computational resources.

In order to further reduce the ME complexity, complexity-scalable ME algorithms [6][7] have been studied. It also provide a proper trade-off between motion accuracy and complexity such that it can adapt to the available computational resource dynamically. But the aforementioned fast MEs and complexity-scalable MEs do not ensure bounded complexity. Usually, more disordered motion leads to more complexity of ME. In the other words, these algorithms can not strictly ensure real-time encoding. The complexity-bounded ME (CBME) [8] achieve a constant complexity as there is no recursivity in the ME process and it is independent of any search window area size. However, it does not sufficiently make use of computational resources to maximize the ME accuracy.

In this paper, we propose a configurable complexity-bounded ME (CCBME) algorithm. This algorithm consists of two procedures. Firstly, making use of the spatial correlation to predict the search center; secondly, using fast ME algorithm to accomplish the local refinement search. During the search process, the number of predictors, the search range of local refinement and the subset pattern of matching criterion computation can be configured to ensure bounded complexity. The configurable schemes are analyzed with respect to the complexity and distortion. Through joint optimization based on the analyzed data, we obtain a near-optimal complexity-distortion (C-D) curve. According to the C-D curve, 6 effective configurable modes are selected to realize the complexity-configurable feature, which can achieve a good tradeoff between ME accuracy and complexity. Experimental results have shown that our proposed CCBME not only exhibits higher efficiency than some well-known ME algorithms such as DS [2], HEXBS [3] and CBME [8] , but also possesses the configurable complexity-bounded feature, which can adapt to various devices with a wide range of computational capability for real-time video coding applications.

The rest of the paper is organized as follows. The CCBME algorithm and joint optimization scheme are presented in *Section 2*. Experimental results and comparative analysis are shown in *Section 3*. In *Section 4*, we draw the conclusions and present the future works.

## 2    Configurable Complexity-Bounded Motion Estimation

The CCBME algorithm takes advantage of prediction-refinement techniques which use spatial correlation to predict the search center and then apply lo-

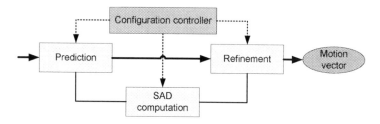

**Fig. 1.** Flowchart of configurable complexity-bounded motion estimation

cal refinement search to achieve the final motion vector (MV) (*Fig. 1*). Due
to simplicity and efficiency, the sum of absolute difference (SAD) is used as the
matching criterion in both prediction and refinement. The interesting problem is
how to achieve optimal computing resource allocation among the three modules
(prediction, refinement and SAD computation) for the given computational constraint while maximize the ME accuracy. Thus, configuration controller is added
to the CCBME algorithm to solve the problem. Next we present the detail.

## 2.1 Configurable Complexity-Bounded Prediction

The prediction is based on the hypothesis that motion fields varies slowly and
have spatial correlation. Therefore, we can choose a set of previously calculated
MVs as the candidate predictors to predict the MV of current block. After statistical analysis, zero MV (MV(0,0)) and four adjacent MVs (left, top, top-left
and top-right) make up of the candidate predictors and the one with the minimal
SAD is selected as the search center for next refinement search. It can be seen

**Table 1.** Prediction accuracy with different predictors according to full search results

| Sequence | 2 Predictors | 3 Predictors | 4 Predictors | 5 Predictors |
|----------|--------------|--------------|--------------|--------------|
| News | 88.92% | 91.62% | 91.92% | 92.53% |
| Foreman | 60.24% | 71.34% | 73.48% | 76.01% |
| Carphone | 51.29% | 63.49% | 65.90% | 69.87% |
| Mobile | 83.79% | 92.48% | 93.11% | 94.04% |
| Coastguard | 84.56% | 92.19% | 93.34% | 94.31% |

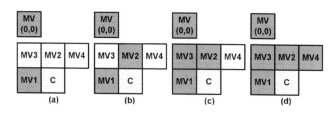

**Fig. 2.** Configurable complexity-bounded prediction: (a) two predictors ⟶ (d) five
predictors

from *Table 1* that different number of predictors leads to different prediction accuracy (predictive MV = final MV), also leads to different complexity. Therefore, we realize configurable complexity-bounded prediction through configuring different number of predictors. *Fig. 2* describes the scheme.

## 2.2   Configurable Complexity-Bounded Refinement

After prediction, the search center is equal or close to the final MV. We define the distance between predictive MV and the final MV by *Eqn. 1*.

$$D = \max\{|MV_{F_x} - MV_{P_x}|, |MV_{F_y} - MV_{P_y}|\} \tag{1}$$

Where $D$ denotes the distance; $MV_{F_x}$ and $MV_{F_y}$ denote the $x$ and $y$ components of final MV; $MV_{P_x}$ and $MV_{P_y}$ denote the $x$ and $y$ components of predictive MV. It can be seen from *Table 2* that the distance is below 4 with an acceptable high probability. So we adopt small diamond search (SDS *Fig. 3*) to accomplish the local refinement and limit the recursive step (*Fig.3 (b)*) up to 4 times. Well then, we realize the configurable complexity-bounded refinement search through configuring the recursive time.

**Table 2.** Probability within different distance

| Sequence | $D = 0$ | $D \leq 1$ | $D \leq 2$ | $D \leq 3$ | $D \leq 4$ |
|---|---|---|---|---|---|
| News | 92.22% | 95.92% | 97.34% | 98.20% | 98.62% |
| Foreman | 75.11% | 86.80% | 91.01% | 93.52% | 95.03% |
| Carphone | 66.87% | 83.15% | 88.42% | 92.66% | 95.43% |
| Mobile | 92.01% | 97.57% | 98.31% | 98.62% | 98.85% |
| Coastguard | 93.26% | 98.58% | 99.67% | 99.78% | 99.85% |

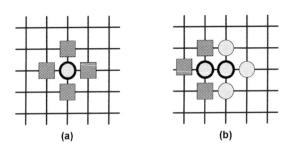

(a)                              (b)

**Fig. 3.** Small diamond search (a) first step (b) recursive step

## 2.3   Configurable Complexity-Bounded SAD Computation

In SAD computation, we use sub-sampling patterns to configure the complexity. Three sub-sampling patterns are chosen and different pattern results in different ME accuracy and complexity. So we realize the complexity configuration through selecting different sub-sampling patterns (*Fig. 4*) for matching criterion (SAD) computation.

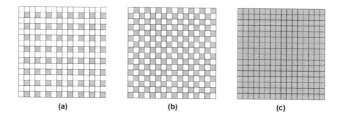

**Fig. 4.** SAD computation pattern (a) 1/4 (b) 1/2 (c) full computations

## 2.4    Joint Optimization Scheme

The joint optimization problem [9] is defined as: given the available computing resources, how to achieve efficient computing resource allocation among the
three aforementioned configurable complexity-bounded schemes such that the
ME accuracy is maximized? We define one full SAD computation as a complexity measurement unit (CMU). So the total cost of CMUs for one block ME can
be defined by *Eqn. 2.*

$$C = S(P + (a + bR))  \tag{2}$$

Where $C$ denotes the complexity (CMUs); $S$ denotes the SAD computation
pattern and $S$ equals 1/4, 1/2 or 1; $P$ denotes the predictor number and $2 \leq
P \leq 5$; $R$ denotes the refinement recursive time and $0 \leq R \leq 4$; $a = 4$ denotes
the complexity of first step in SDS (*Fig. 3 (a)*); $b = 3$ denotes the complexity of
recursive step in SDS (*Fig. 3 (b)*). Therefore, the complexity bound of one MV
search can range from 1.5 CMUs to 21 CMUs. The joint optimization problem
can be converted to *Eqn. 3.*

$$\min_{[s,p,r] \in S \times P \times R} D(s,p,r)  \quad subject \ to : C \leq C_{max}  \tag{3}$$

Where $D(s,p,r)$ denotes the distortion; $C_{max}$ denotes maximal constraint complexity; $s, p, r$ are configurable parameters. Directly setting parameters, there are
60 kinds of configuration choices. Through exhaustive statistical analysis (overall distortion data, mean square error (MSE), are measured by averaging five
video sequences: news, foreman, carphone, mobile and coastguard), we get the
near-optimal complexity-distortion (C-D) curve (*Fig. 5*) to achieve the preferable tradeoff between ME accuracy and complexity. Based on the C-D curve, 10
configuration modes marked by square are detected as follows: M1(1/4, 2, 0),
M2(1/4, 3, 0), M3(1/4, 4, 0), M4(1/4, 5, 0), M5(1/4, 5, 1), M6(1/4, 5, 2), M7(1/4,
5, 3), M8(1/4, 5, 4), M9(1/2, 5, 4), M10(1, 5, 4). From the *Fig. 5*, point A and
M8 have similar complexity-bound but significant difference in distortion; point
B and M5 have similar distortion but significant difference in complexity-bound.
This indicates that more complexity does not lead to less distortion. Therefore,
determining effective configurable modes will largely improve the performance.
Although all the aforementioned 10 modes are on the near-optimal C-D curve,

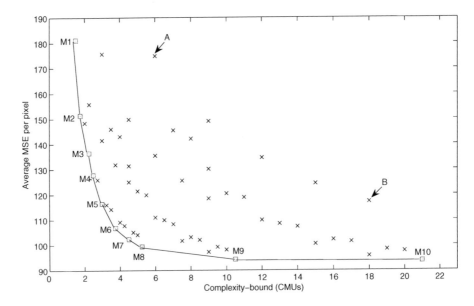

**Fig. 5.** Optimized complexity-distortion (C-D) curve

the slope is high from M1 to M5 and large distortion increase get little complexity reduction in return. Thus, we only preserve 6 configuration modes (M5 – M10) in our CCBME algorithm.

## 3    Experimental Results

Many experiments have been performed to evaluate extensively the performance of our proposed CCBME algorithm. The standard test sequences (*News, Foreman, Coastguard*) of CIF resolution are chosen as our test set. These sequences present different kinds of motion: small motion with fixed background, disordered motion and global motion. The experimental setup as follows: the distortion measurement of mean square error (MSE); the complexity measurement of CMUs (see *Section 2.4*); block-size of $16 \times 16$; search window size of $\pm 16$; frame rate of 30fps and 15fps respectively.

We compare the CCBME algorithm with some well-known fast ME algorithm such as DS [2], HEXBS [3] and CBME [8]. *Fig. 6* presents the results. It can be seen that DS, HEXBS and CBME have some limitation, e.g. for small motion scenario, DS performs better and for disordered or global motion scenario, CBME performs better. However, our proposed CCBME algorithm (on M10) outperforms these fast MEs in all kinds of motion scenarios while averagely saving 30% computing resources. Furthermore, through configuration from M5 to M10, the practical complexity of CCBME can range from 2CMUs to 14CMUs, resulting in an acceptable variation of distortion.

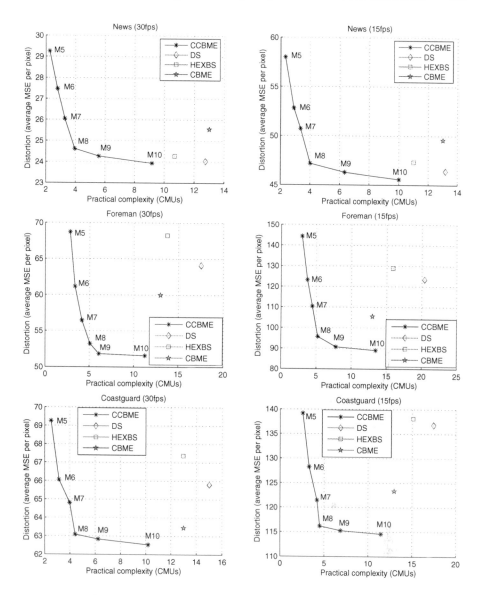

**Fig. 6.** Comparative evaluation of the CCBME algorithm

# 4    Conclusions and Future Works

Configurable complexity-bounded algorithms are useful for real-time video coding applications, especially on mobile devices. Since ME is an important and most time-consuming module in video encoding system, the paper propose a configurable complexity-bounded algorithm for ME. Through statistical analysis with respect to complexity and distortion, 6 effective configurable modes have been determined. The CCBME algorithm not only achieves a good tradeoff between ME accuracy and complexity, but also ensure bounded complexity for real-time video encoding. Good results have been observed in our experiments.

Although the CCBME algorithm strictly ensure the complexity bound, the practical complexity always less than the predefined bounded complexity due to early-termination scheme. In the other words, the computing resource is not sufficiently utilized. Moreover, the ME of motion-active area need more complexity than that of non-motion area. Therefore we believe that our CCBME algorithm can be improved by applying some resource adaptive allocation schemes, which will be taken into consideration in our future works.

# References

1. Sadka, A. H.: Compressed Video Communications, John Wiley & Sons Ltd. (2002)
2. Zhu, S., Ma, K.K.: A New Diamond Search Algorithm for Fast Block-Matching Motion Estimation, IEEE Transaction on Image Processing, Vol. 9, (2000), 287–290
3. Zhu, C., Lin, X., Chau, L.P.: Hexagon-based Search Pattern for Fast Block Motion Estimation, IEEE Transaction on Circuits and Systems for Video Technology, Vol. 12, (2002), 349-355
4. Chung, K.L., Chang, L.C.: A New Predictive Search Area Approach for Fast Block Motion Estimation, IEEE Transaction on Image Processing, Vol. 12, (2003), 648-652
5. Namuduri, K.R.: Motion Estimation Using Spatio-Temporal Contextual Information, IEEE Transaction on Circuits and Systems for Video Technology, Vol. 14, (2004), 1111-1115
6. Lengwehasatit, K., Ortega, A.: Computationally Scalable Partial Distance Based Fast Search Motion Estimation, Processing of International Conference on Image Processing, Vol. 1, (2000), 824-827
7. Mietens, S., de With, P.H.N., Hentschel, C.: Computational-Complexity Scalable Motion Estimation for Mobile MPEG Encoding, IEEE Transaction on Consumer Electronics, Vol. 50, (2004), 281-291
8. Chimienti, A., Ferraris, C., Pau, D.: A Complexity-Bounded Motion Estimation Algorithm, IEEE Transaction on Image Processing, Vol. 11, (2002), 387-392
9. Kwon, D., Agathoklis, P., Driessen, P.: Performance and Computational Complexity Optimization in a Configurable Video Coding System, IEEE Wireless Communications and Networking, Vol. 3, (2003), 2086-2089

# 3DSVHT: Extraction of 3D Linear Motion via Multi-view, Temporal Evidence Accumulation

J.A.R. Artolazábal and J. Illingworth

Center for Vision, Speech and Signal Processing,
University of Surrey, Guildford, UK
{j.artolazabal, j.illingworth}@surrey.ac.uk

**Abstract.** Shape recognition and motion estimation are two of the most difficult problems in computer vision, especially for arbitrary shapes undergoing severe occlusion. Much work has concentrated on tracking over short temporal scales and the analysis of 2D image-plane motion from a single camera. In contrast, in this paper we consider the global analysis of extended stereo image sequences and the extraction of specified objects undergoing linear motion in full 3D. We present a novel Hough Transform based algorithm that exploits both stereo geometry constraints and the invariance properties of the cross-ratio to accumulate evidence for a specified shape undergoing 3D linear motion (constant velocity or otherwise). The method significantly extends some of the ideas originally developed in the Velocity Hough Transform, VHT, where detection was limited to 2D image motion models. We call our method the 3D Stereo Velocity Hough Transform, 3DSVHT. We demonstrate 3DSVHT on both synthetic and real imagery and show that it is capable of detecting objects undergoing linear motion with large depth variation and in image sequences where there is significant object occlusion.

## 1 Introduction

Object recognition and motion estimation form two major areas of computer vision. Many methods have been developed to solve each of these problems in isolation but there has been less work on approaches that attempt to address both problems simultaneously. Object recognition via shape detection has been fairly successfully attempted using the Hough Transform[2], HT, and its variants, especially the Generalised Hough Transform[1], GHT. However, it is only fairly recently, in the Velocity Hough Transform[4], VHT, that the method has been extended to detect objects that simultaneously satisfy both a 2D shape model *and* a 2D image-motion model. The VHT clearly demonstrated the benefit of using both structural and temporal information simultaneously.

A significant limitation of the VHT method is that motion is only modeled in the 2D image plane. However, when an object travels in 3D then its perspective projection onto the image plane is a non-linear function of depth. This means that a uniform velocity linear motion in 3D does **not** project to a constant velocity 2D motion on the image plane. Hence, the VHT can fail in situations

J. Blanc-Talon et al. (Eds.): ACIVS 2005, LNCS 3708, pp. 563–570, 2005.
© Springer-Verlag Berlin Heidelberg 2005

where objects are close to the viewer and then move away in depth. In this paper we address this limitation for linear object motion by formulating a Hough Transform that adopts a novel motion parameterization based on the invariance properties of the cross-ratio of four scene points and their 2D projections. We also show how multi-view stereo and epipolar geometry can be incorporated to further constrain the Hough accumulation process and thereby improve the recognition process. We call our method the 3D Stereo Velocity Hough Transform and denote it by the mnemonic 3DSVHT.

In section 2 of the paper we present the central ideas of the method. We discuss the cross-ratio of a set of four points, its invariance under projection and how it can be calculated for specific 3D motion models. We then formulate a novel parameterization and show how individual pieces of image evidence can generate votes in a parameter space that encodes both shape and motion. We also discuss how evidence in one image of a stereo pair can restrict the votes generated by evidence in the other image of the pair. Section 3 presents results on both synthetic and real image sequences and compares the algorithm's performance to both the GHT and the VHT. Section 4 discusses conclusions and future work.

## 2   The 3D Stereo Velocity Hough Transform

### 2.1   Projective Invariance of the Cross Ratio

Consider a rigid object undergoing a constant velocity linear motion in 3D space, as depicted in figure 1. It can be readily seen that such 3D motion will cast a linear but non-constant velocity motion trajectory in 2D when projected to an image. The same idea applies to other linear 3D motions: *the parameters defining the 3D linear motion of an object cannot, in general, be directly applied to describe the 2D linear motion trajectories resulting from the perspective projection onto the image plane.* The reason for this lies in the properties of projective

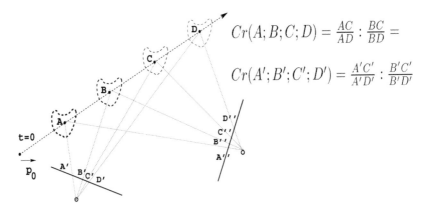

$$Cr(A;B;C;D) = \frac{AC}{AD} : \frac{BC}{BD} =$$

$$Cr(A';B';C';D') = \frac{A'C'}{A'D'} : \frac{B'C'}{B'D'}$$

**Fig. 1.** Plan view showing how a constant velocity 3D motion projects to a non-constant velocity in the 2D image planes of a stereo sensor

geometry, chiefly, in the fact that it preserves neither distances nor ratios of distances. However, the cross-ratio of four points, defined as a ratio of ratios of distances, is preserved under projection and is therefore a useful concept for understanding the relationship between 3D and 2D linear motions. Figure 1 gives a definition of the cross-ratio for four points, $(A, B, C, D)$, in 3D space and four points $(A', B', C', D')$ in the 2D image plane of a stereo pair. The values of the cross-ratio in the two cases must be the same. Hence if we can calculate the cross-ratio for 3D points in four time instants of a sequence from knowledge of a 3D motion model then we can test, using the equality of cross-ratios, whether four 2D image points seen at corresponding times in the image plane could be projections of that 3D motion. If the cross-ratios are equal and the image points lie on a linear trajectory then a vote can be added to a suitable Hough accumulator array.

## 2.2   3D Motion Models and the Cross Ratio

The position of the centre of mass, $P$, of an object under linear motion in 3D space is described by the vector equation:

$$P(t) = P_0 + m(a_1, a_2, \ldots, a_n, t) \tag{1}$$

where $P_0$ is the position for $t = 0$, and $m$ is a vector defining the 3D linear motion. In the case of linear motion a coordinate system can be chosen, (see figure 1), with its origin at $P_0$, and one of it's axis coinciding with the line of motion. With this new reference system, only one of the components of $P$ will be non-zero and this will hold all the information about the motion. Thus, equation (1) becomes a scalar one of the form:

$$P'(t) = m'(a'_1, a'_2, \ldots, a'_n, t) \tag{2}$$

where $m'$ will be a function of time as well as of $n$ parameters that define the motion along the axis. For uniform velocity linear motion only one parameter, $a'_1 = v$, is needed and that is a constant i.e. $P'(t) = vt$. For constant acceleration linear motion $P'(t) = ut + \frac{1}{2}at^2$ and hence two parameters are needed. For the sake of simplicity we will consider only constant velocity motion in this paper but all results can be generalized to the more complicated linear motion models.

Once a motion model has been defined it can be used to calculate the position of the object at four instances in time and the cross-ratio for the 3D motion can be calculated. For constant velocity motion the cross ratio is easily calculated given four time values. For example, for times $t = 1$, $t = 2$, $t = 3$ and $t = 4$ the cross ratio will be given by $Cr(t_1, t_2, t_3, t_4) = \frac{2v}{3v} / \frac{1v}{2v} = \frac{4}{3}$. Hence any 2D trajectories that are projections of this 3D motion must also have a cross-ratio, for these frames, equal to $\frac{4}{3}$.

## 2.3   Choice of Parameter Space and Voting Procedure

The basic idea behind all Hough like methods for shape or object recognition is that pieces of image evidence vote in a parameter space for all consistent possible instances of the object and its motion. Once the vote accumulation process has come to an end, local maxima define the position, shape and motion of the object. Hence, it is necessary to define a set of parameters that describe all possible object shape and motion instances as well as a mapping from an image observation to all consistent instances. In the current problem the choice of parameterization is complicated by the fact that the motion model is in 3D while the observations are in 2D. The choice of the parameters that form the shape sub-space is straightforward and we can typically use the location, scale and orientation parameters, $x_r, y_r, s$ and $\theta$ of the GHT. However, for the motion subspace we need a parameterization that relates observed 2D image positions to the 3D motion model via the cross-ratio. The calculation of the cross-ratio uses a subset of points from a motion trajectory and therefore it is natural to use parameters that encode such trajectories. A convenient choice is to take position of points in three arbitrarily chosen frames, $I_a, I_b, I_c$, and a subset of the 3D motion model parameters for this task. From these parameters the full motion trajectory can be calculated. However, equally important is that this parameterization facilitates a simple geometric construction that can be used generatively in the voting procedure to map a point image observation to feasible parameter values. Given evidence in the form of a point at location $p_i$ in the $i^{th}$ frame then only votes for trajectories that are both linear in 2D and where the cross ratio for the quadruple $(p_a, p_b, p_c, p_i)$ equals the cross ratio for the 3D motion model should be added to the Hough accumulator. The image data structure represented by $I_a, I_b, I_c$ can be efficiently used to generate only those quadruples that lie in a limited image region defined by the extremal values of $(p_a, p_b, p_c, p_i)$ and that also produce linear trajectories, thereby avoiding exhaustive enumeration and testing of all quadruples.

## 2.4  Exploiting Stereo Image Constraints

In section 2.1 we described how the cross-ratio can be used in the formulation of the HT to ensure that only 2D trajectories consistent with a 3D linear motion are accumulated. If calibrated stereo image pairs are available then points from each image sequence could be accumulated independently in a common parameter space. However, this does not use the stereo information that there are matching pairs of points across the images that correspond to projections of the same 3D scene point. When an image point votes for motion parameters (or in our encoding, possible trajectories), it conceptually maps out a hyper-surface, only one point of which corresponds to the correct value of the motion. Most of the votes generated are extraneous and could be regarded as noise. Reduction of these noise votes is one way to improve algorithm performance and can be achieved if possible stereo matches can be identified i.e. if two image points in different images of a stereo pair correspond to projections of the same 3D point then only the intersection of the two hyper-surfaces that they generate are candidates for the true motion parameters. The problem of course is to identify correct stereo matches and this is a very difficult problem. However, epipolar constraints geometrically restrict the possible set of matching points and can be used to limit

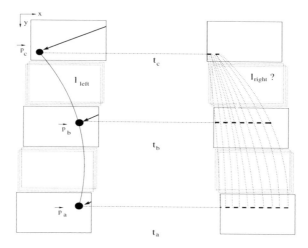

**Fig. 2.** Epipolar stereo constraints restrict the trajectories that can be generated by image evidence in the right image given a trajectory in the left image

the trajectories that a point in, say, a right image votes for given a trajectory that an image point in the left image has voted for. Figure 2 illustrates the idea for a sequence of rectified stereo images. If an image point in the left image votes for a trajectory denoted by $(I_a(x_1, y_1), I_b(x_2, y_2), I_c(x_3, y_3))$ then in the right image only trajectories characterized by $(I_a(x_4, y_4), I_b(x_5, y_5), I_c(x_6, y_6))$ with $y_4 = y_1$, $y_5 = y_2$, $y_6 = y_3$ and $x_4 \leq x_1$, $x_5 \leq x_2$, $x_6 \leq x_3$ are possible. Similar rules apply to left to right candidate matches.

## 3   Experimental Results

In this section we demonstrate the 3DSVHT algorithm on both real and synthetic stereo image sequences. The synthetic images are generated using the POVRAY ray-tracer and allow us to easily construct complicated, photo-realistic test data with known ground truth. The first, 50 frame image sequence considered contains three synthetic objects, a die, a duck and a cylinder topped by a cone. The sequence was engineered so that the objects had significant movement in depth (and hence change in observed scale), a range of velocities and underwent significant inter-occlusions. The sequence thereby represents a difficult image analysis task. The upper part of Figure 3 shows three frames from the right stereo camera with the contour of the detected duck overlayed. It can be seen that the object is well tracked. The lower part of Figure 3 shows two curves for the x and y coordinate of the duck over the full 50 frame sequence. The open circles are the duck's position as detected by the 3DSVHT while the dots show a line through the position determined by a standard GHT applied independently to each frame. The 3DSVHT closely follows ground-truth whereas the GHT results show that the GHT degrades catastrophically at points where the objects become occluded. This illustrates the benefits of temporal integration. In order to

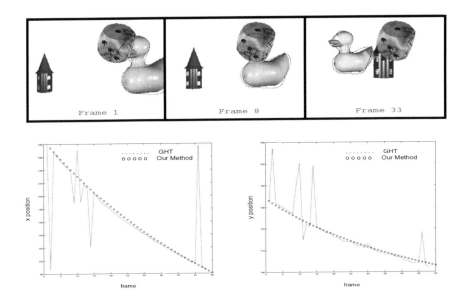

**Fig. 3.** Tracking results in a complicated synthetic image sequence

quantitatively compare the performance of our algorithm with similar existing
methods, we repeated the experiment reported in [4] and [3]. This consists of
a small circle moving with uniform velocity across the image plane. The circle
moves in the camera's fronto-parallel plane and does not move in depth. Hence,
a 2D rather than 3D motion is appropriate and the VHT can be applied to this
image sequence. The performance of the algorithm was tested for 76 sequences
each consisting of 11 frames. Sequences were distinguished by different values of
the circle's velocity or the amount of added image noise. The noise added to the
edge-map was simple "salt-and-pepper" noise. Examples of the edge images for
different values of noise can be seen in the upper part of figure 4 and are clearly
very challenging. The lower part of the figure shows a comparison between the
performance of the GHT, the VHT and the 3DSVHT as a function of noise.
The error measure used is the Euclidean distance between the position of the
detected ball and ground truth, averaged over the 76 sequences. It can be seen
that the VHT (which incorporates temporal integration) out-performs the GHT
but that the 3DSVHT (which utilizes both temporal integration and stereo) does
better than both GHT and VHT.

Finally, we have applied our algorithm to real data of a ball rolling at approximately constant velocity on a table. The camera view is such that the ball
is moving away from the viewer. The results of applying the GHT, the VHT
and the 3DSVHT are shown overlayed in the mosaic of images frames shown in
Figure 5. The ball location found by the GHT is shown as a square, the location
found by the VHT is shown by a diamond and the location determined by the
3DSVHT is denoted by a circle. The GHT fails badly in most frames as the images are too cluttered and produce too many extraneous edge points. The VHT

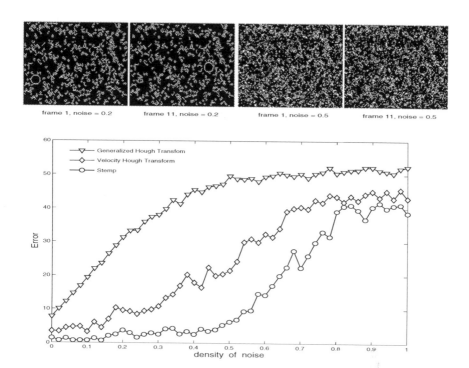

**Fig. 4.** Comparison of GHT, VHT and 3DSVHT tracking a small circle moving with constant 2D velocity in a noisy image sequence

**Fig. 5.** Results of GHT, VHT and 3DSVHT tracking a ball rolling on a table

tracks the ball for the first few frames but then fails as the 3D motion of the ball is not correctly captured by the 2D motion model. The 3DSVHT successfully tracks the ball throughout the sequence even when the scale of the ball changes significantly due to changes in depth.

## 4    Conclusions and Future Work

We have presented a novel Hough Transform technique that allows arbitrary shaped objects undergoing linear 3D motion to be tracked in long image sequences even in the presence of significant occlusion. It exploits properties of the cross-ratio of scene and image points to allow 2D evidence to be constrained to vote only for feasible 3D hypotheses. It can be applied to situations where existing methods such as the VHT fail. We have demonstrated the method on both synthetic and real image data and shown it outperforms both the GHT and the VHT.

## References

1. D. H. Ballard. Generalizing the hough transform to detect arbitrary shapes. *Pattern Recognition*, 13(2):111–122, 1981.
2. P.V.C Hough. Method and means for recongnizing complex patterns. *U.S Patent 3,069,654*, 1962.
3. Pelopidas Lappas, John N. Carter, and Robert I. Damper. Robust evidence-based object tracking. In *Pattern Recognition Letters*, volume 23, pages 253–260, 2002.
4. Jason M. Nash, John N. Carter, and Mark S. Nixon. Dynamic feature extraction via the velocity hough transform. *Pattern Recogn. Lett.*, 18(10):1035–1047, 1997.

# Fast Mode Decision and Motion Estimation with Object Segmentation in H.264/AVC Encoding

Marcos Nieto, Luis Salgado, and Julián Cabrera

Grupo de Tratamiento de Imágenes – E.T.S. Ingenieros de Telecomunicación,
Universidad Politécnica de Madrid, Spain
{mnd, lsa, jcq}@gti.ssr.upm.es

**Abstract.** In this paper we present a new and complete scheme of mode decision and motion estimation compliant with H.264/AVC encoding and decoding systems based on a moving object segmentation. It is particularly suited for applications, like surveillance, where a moving object segmentation is available. The knowledge of the moving object areas and background areas allows to reduce the set of modes permitted by the standard. This sub-set is selected in order to obtain a more accurately motion estimation for active objects and less intensive for quasi-static background. The number of comparisons needed to find the best motion vectors is reduced, conforming an encoding process simple and fast, compliant with the real time requirements of a surveillance application. An improved prediction of the motion vector is computed based on the result of the object segmentation. This avoids erroneous predictions to be carried out. Results will show that the number of comparisons needed to perform inter prediction is reduced by 60%-70% depending on the sequence, keeping the same image quality and bit-rate obtained without using segmentation.

## 1 Introduction

Some applications perform a moving object segmentation, like surveillance applications, where remote control centers carry out the supervision of the sequences. The transmission of the video data of this kind of applications is usually needed at real time conditions and with the minimum possible bit rate to allow remote storage.

The new international video coding standard H.264/AVC [1][2] is expected to improve features in video coding against earlier standards such as MPEG-2 or recent MPEG-4. It uses block motion estimation (ME) and compensation for exploiting temporal redundancy. This module is one of the most important parts of video coding related to rate-distortion and, on the other hand, the most computationally expensive operation of the encoder. H.264/AVC has been made with the purpose of achieving a higher coding efficiency by increasing the intensity of the ME process. In earlier standards, frames are divided into fixed size macroblocks (MB) which are the basic units of ME. H.264/AVC allows the subdivision of MB into smaller blocks, down to sizes of 4x4 pixels [1]. The encoder then may choose between large blocks with just a few motion vectors to transmit, or smaller blocks and more motion vectors. The standard specifies sub-partition modes permitted, those shown in the Fig. 1.

J. Blanc-Talon et al. (Eds.): ACIVS 2005, LNCS 3708, pp. 571–578, 2005.
© Springer-Verlag Berlin Heidelberg 2005

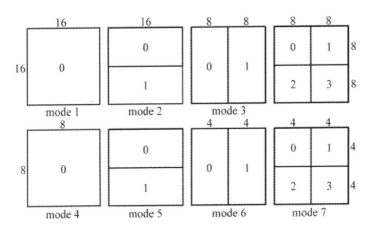

**Fig. 1.** Sub-partition block scheme of H.264/AVC

The decision is usually taken performing rate-distortion optimization criteria [3] applying the Lagrangian multiplier technique [4], by minimizing the function

$$J_m = D_{rec} + \lambda_m \cdot R_m \qquad (1)$$

where $D_{rec}$ is the sum of absolute difference (SAD) between current MB and its re-constructed MB after quantization, $\lambda_m$ is the Lagrangian multiplier and $R_m$ are the bits to encode MB header, motion vector difference (MVD) and residual DCT coefficients. This criterion provides the total coding cost for a MB (rate-distortion), so the encoder may just choose the mode that offers the minimum value of the function $J_m$.

Motion estimation is the most expensive part of encoding process, and even more in the case of H.264/AVC, as it combines tree structured motion compensation with multiple reference frames. Many efforts have been made to reduce this computational load by proposing different strategies. One of them is the development of fast ME algorithms that reduce the number of comparisons to do into the search area [5][6]. These strategies are usually combined with features like early termination that prevents from comparing useless candidates if a previous candidate offers a Sum of Absolute Difference (SAD) below a defined threshold [7][8]. Other works tend to use thresholds to combine strategies of fast ME algorithms with mode decision algorithms [9] based on detection of activity for each MB, studied as elemental ME unit.

However, in the case of surveillance applications, a more important reduction of the computational load is required for real time conditions. For these applications, where a moving object segmentation is available, this segmentation may be used to reduce the computational effort of the coding stage. The moving objects are areas of the image that need more computational effort at motion estimation, whereas the background may be encoded with a reduced sub-set of modes.

In this paper we propose a new scheme of mode decision based on a previous available object segmentation, suitable with H.264/AVC encoding and decoding systems, where MBs can be classified as belonging to moving objects or to the quasi-static background. The object becomes the global ME unit and, as it will be shown in next sections, its management permit to use safely the skip mode, which is the main difference with strategies based on processing MB as the elemental ME unit.

The advantage of the proposed scheme is that it does not need an accurate segmentation, so it is especially effective for those applications that carry out a coarse moving object segmentation.

## 2  Segmentation

Object segmentation can be exploited for mode decision and ME in H.264/AVC even when it is a standard that does not support transmission of segmentation information. As it will be described in next sections, segmentation masks identify MBs belonging to moving objects in the scene. Sub-division mode can be then selected in order to adapt smaller blocks to the object shape.

We propose a mode decision scheme based on the sub-division of MBs into smaller sizes, down to 4x4 pixels. Therefore, segmentation information is just needed at 4x4 block level. Though the proposed scheme can be employed with any segmentation algorithm, for the present paper we use the adaptive segmentation strategy proposed in [10] where segmentation is done at sub-sampled copies of the image, and then may be refined to pixel level at successive recurrent stages. We will use the results of the segmentation at the sub-sampled level, without refinement, where each pixel can be projected into a 4x4 block at the original image, fitting with minimum block-size permitted by H.264/AVC.

Moving object masks are used for the ME process, therefore no segmentation information is necessary at the decoder side. Absolute compliance with H.264/AVC decoding systems is then guaranteed when using segmentation information into ME process.

Fig. 2 (a) shows two examples of the segmentation mask obtained for studied sequences. One of them is *Hall Monitor* an example of a surveillance like sequence, whereas *Miss America* is a standard MPEG test sequence where the proposed scheme can be employed if a moving object segmentation is available. Black areas are the identified background while transparent areas are the grouped 4x4 blocks belonging to a moving object. The object shape is squared into block units that will be used in mode decision.

Next sections will highlight improvements achieved through the use of the segmentation results.

## 3  Mode Decision

Once the object segmentation is available, the mode decision is dramatically simplified. In this paper we propose an adaptive sub-set mode selection attending to MB type. Segmentation masks can be used to classify MBs in two main groups: object-MBs and background-MBs. As it is shown in Fig. 2 (b), object-MBs are those that contain at least one 4x4 block belonging to the segmented object. Black areas are background-MBs, those that do not contain 4x4 object-blocks.

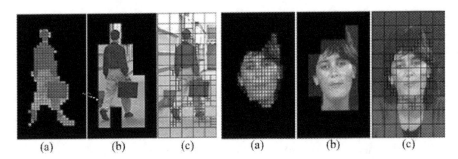

**Fig. 2.** *Hall Monitor* frame #45 and *Miss America* frame #113, zoom to moving object, (a): segmentation mask 4x4, (b): segmentation mask 16x16, interior MBs and boundary MBs, (c): subdivision mode obtained

### 3.1  Background-MBs

We propose to use skip mode for those background-MBs that in the immediately previous frame were background as well. For the case of quasi-static backgrounds the analysis of the complete set of modes is expected to be highly redundant because blocks show no motion or changes. For these MBs, experience shows that skip mode usually offers minimum cost at equation (1). Skip mode is a way of processing MBs, specified by the standard, where no bits are transmitted to the decoder (neither coded coefficients of difference values or MVs). The decoder identifies those MBs and builds the reconstructed MBs from MBs of the immediately previous frame, pointed by a motion vector prediction obtained from MVs of neighboring blocks [1]. Usually this prediction offers zero vector for static background, but non-zero vector is also allowed.

This mode reduces dramatically the bits to transmit, so the larger background area, the more compression achieved. Furthermore, the ME process for these MBs is done without new comparisons, so it can be assumed instantaneous.

Skip mode can not be used for background MBs that in the previous frame were object-MBs. The prediction would be erroneous and the decoder would display an artifact in the reconstructed sequence like the object leaves a trail behind it. In this case, the use of skip mode is complemented with Mode 1 (16x16) if at the rest of references frames there are at least one background-MB at the same position as the current MB, or with the complete analysis of modes if no background-MB can be found in the reference frames.

### 3.2  Object-MBs

The proposed mode decision for object-MBs firstly consists of classifying those MBs into two classes: boundary-MBs and interior-MBs. Boundary-MBs are those that contain background 4x4 blocks and moving object 4x4 blocks, while interior-MBs are the rest of object-MBs. The appropriate selection of the modes, attending to the shape of the objects, is based on the continuity of the objects between frames.

For boundary-MBs the mode decision is made by sub-dividing the MB into MB partitions and sub-MB partitions down to 4x4 pixels, adapting to the object shape as shown in Fig 2 (c). As it can be seen, the adaptation is oriented to separate background and object areas of a boundary-MB for ME process, so more detail is needed in areas where the boundary between object and background draws a complex shape, like feet, head or briefcase corners. The proposed sub-division algorithm is described as follows for each boundary-MB, and examples of selection are shown in Fig. 3:

a) Select mode 1 (16x16) if only one 4x4 block is of different type (object or background) than rest of blocks.

b) Select mode 2 (16x8) if subdividing the MB into 2 MB partitions of 16x8, at least seven 4x4 blocks of each MB partition are the same type and predominant type is different between MB partitions.

c) Select mode 3 (8x16) analogous to mode 2.

d) If modes 1, 2 and 3 are not selected, split MB into four 8x8 blocks, and for each MB partition, do:

  e) Select mode 4 (8x8) if all four 4x4 blocks in MB partition are the same type.

  f) Select mode 5 (8x4) if subdividing the MB partition into 2 sub MB partitions of 8x4, both 4x4 blocks of each sub MB partition are the same type and this type is different from the other sub MB partition.

  g) Select mode 6 (4x8) analogous to mode 5.

  h) Select mode 7 if no previous mode is selected.

Finally, the segmentation mask does not include changes or activity information about interior-MBs, so the full set of modes is analyzed for these MBs.

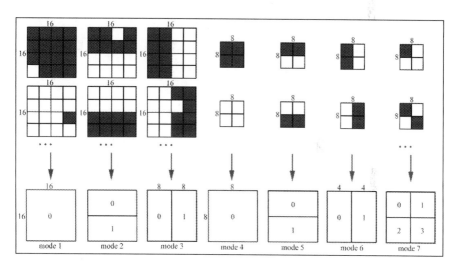

**Fig. 3.** Examples of the subdivision algorithm: White blocks are moving object blocks and black blocks are background blocks. Mode 7 is selected if no previous mode is chosen.

## 4 Motion Estimation

Another high efficient new feature in H.264/AVC is the prediction of the motion vector. Sub-dividing MBs into smaller blocks generates a huge amount of MVs to be transmitted (up to 16 per MB), that may significantly increase the output bit-rate while high prediction quality is achieved. Usually, it is expected that neighboring blocks obtain similar MVs, therefore a motion vector prediction (MVp) can be calculated from neighbors and the difference between MV and MVp is transmitted. Usually, this Motion Vector Difference (MVD) is very small; therefore less bits are needed for transmitting MV information. MVp is also used as the center of the search process at ME for each reference frame [1]. Therefore a good prediction might reduce the number of comparisons to be done in a sub-optimal ME algorithm with early termination [9].

Prediction errors may occur for those MBs whose neighbors-MBs do not belong to the same object. In order to overcome this problem, we propose to take advantage of segmentation information to improve MVp by just using the neighbors belonging to the same object. Therefore, an improved-MVp is generated, especially for boundary-MBs, where the current MB and some of its neighbors belong to different objects, and its MV may not fit with the motion of the object that the current MB belongs to.

All this process can be done without transmission of segmentation information to the decoder, that creates the common MVp. The encoder must send the MVD between MV and non-improved-MVp, while keep using improved-MVp as the center search for ME. Absolute compliance with H.264/AVC decoding systems is then guarantied.

**Table 1.** Comparison between proposed algorithm (Seg) and the complete analysis of modes (Normal) in PSNR, Rate and the computational reduction achieved

|  |  | PSNR | R (kbps) | AC | RF (%) |
|---|---|---|---|---|---|
| *Suzie* QCIF | Normal | 35.60 | 82.18 | 8374.2 | 35.9 |
|  | Seg. | 35.54 | 82.92 | 5365.5 |  |
| *Miss America* QCIF | Normal | 38.64 | 37.83 | 8486.2 | 83.9 |
|  | Seg. | 38.23 | 38.86 | 1362.9 |  |
| *Hall Monitor* CIF | Normal | 36.16 | 237.27 | 7732.1 | 97.2 |
|  | Seg. | 35.59 | 220.09 | 219.4 |  |
| *Trevor* QCIF | Normal | 35.62 | 78.03 | 8176.8 | 67.0 |
|  | Seg. | 35.57 | 80.77 | 2694.7 |  |

## 5   Results

Experimental tests have been made with the proposed algorithm implemented into the reference software model JM 9.2 [11]. Any fast ME algorithm may be used with the proposed mode scheme. For numerical results, in this work we have employed the default fast ME algorithm of the reference software model JM 9.2, called UMHexagonS [11].

A comparison between the full analysis of modes and the proposed scheme is reported for several sequences in Table 1. This table shows encoding tests with constant QP = 31 (Quantization Parameter). We have used the Baseline Profile, with three reference frames for P-SLICES, IDR each twelve frames and common 16-pixel Search Range.

**Fig. 4.** *Trevor* frame #131. (a): Original frame, (b): reconstructed with full analysis of modes, (c): reconstructed with proposed scheme, (d): Difference image with full analysis, (e): Difference image with proposed scheme.

In Table 1, AC value represents the average number of comparisons needed for a MB to perform inter-prediction. This number contains the total number of comparisons over all analyzed modes and all reference frames. The UMHexagonS algorithm is based on an early termination algorithm, so different values of AC are obtained for each sequence. RF value is the reduction factor achieved in AC by using the proposed scheme.

As it is shown, the proposed scheme ensures a PSNR and a bit rate similar to the one of common ME process in all cases while computational load is dramatically reduced in most cases. Best reduction is achieved for surveillance like sequences, for example, *Hall Monitor*, where there is a large background area and skip-mode is used with the related coding efficiency.

However, any type of sequence may be analyzed with the proposed scheme, like *Miss America*, *Suzie* or *Trevor* where results show little Rate Distortion deviation and computation reduction in function of the size of the moving object area delivered by the segmentation process.

Regarding subjective quality, Fig. 4 shows a frame for *Trevor* sequence, where (a) is the original frame and (b) and (c) are the reconstructed images with full analysis of modes and our proposed scheme respectively. Fig. 4 (d) and (e) shows the reconstruction error images where contrast has been increased for a better visualization. As it is shown, there are not significant perceptual differences between the two methods, mainly due to the fact that for perceptually relevant areas, like those composed by boundary MBs which define the object shape, an accurate estimation have been made with our approach as described in Section 3.

## 6   Conclusions

In this work we have presented an algorithm for fast mode decision and motion estimation over H.264/AVC for applications that carry out an object segmentation, such as surveillance applications. With this method, we allow these applications to use H.264/AVC and its coding efficiency reducing dramatically its associated computational load.

Our results have shown that best computational reductions are achieved for sequences with large background areas, like those typical obtained from surveillance applications, and neither quality nor bit rate are seriously affected.

Future works will focus on performing a fast mode decision scheme that performs its own segmentation masks without extra computational load, suitable for real time applications that need to reduce dramatically the computational load without losing the compression efficiency achieved with H.264/AVC.

## Acknowledgements

This work has been partially supported by the Plan Nacional de Investigación Científica, Desarrollo e Innovación Tecnológica of the Spanish Government under project TIN2004-07860-C02.

M. Nieto wishes to acknowledge the scholarship received by Cátedra Amena of the E.T.S. Ing. de Telecomunicación of the Universidad Politécnica de Madrid.

## References

1. T. Wiegand, G.J. Sullivan, "Overview of the H.264/AVC video coding standard," IEEE Transactions on Circuits and Systems for Video Coding, vol. 13, n. 7, pp. 560-576 July 2003.
2. Ian E. G. Richardson. "H.264 and MPEG-4 Video Compression. Video Coding for Next-generation Multimedia". Ed. Wiley 2003.
3. G. J. Sullivan and T. Wiegand, "Rate-distortion Optimization for Video Compression," IEEE Signal Processing Mag., vol. 15, no. 6, pp. 74-90, November 1998.
4. T. Wiegand and Bernd Girod, "Lagrange Multiplier Selection in Hybrid Video Coder Control", Proc. Int. Conf. on Image Processing, ICIP'01, Thessaloniki, Greece, vol. III, pp. 542-545, October 2001.
5. Tham, J.Y., Ranganath, S., Ranganath, M., Kassim, A.A., "A Novel Unrestricted Center-Biased Diamond Search Algorithm for Block Motion Estimation", IEEE Trans. On Circuits and Systems for Video Technology, vol. 8, no. 4, pp. 369-377, August 1998.
6. C. Zhu, X. Lin and L.P Chau, "Hexagon-Based Search Pattern for Fast Block Motion Estimation", IEEE Trans. On Circuits and Systems for Video Technology, vol. 12, no. 5, pp. 349-355, May 2002.
7. Gagan Bihari Rath and Anamitra Makur, "Subblock Matching-Based Conditional Motion Estimation With Automatic Threshold Selection for Video Compression", IEEE Trans. Circuits and Systems for Video Technology, vol. 13, nr. 9, pp. 914-924, September 2003.
8. Shi, Y.Q., Xia, X., "A Thresholding Multiresolution Block Matching Algorithm", IEEE Trans. On Circuits and Systems for Video Technology, vol. 7, no. 2, pp. 437-440, April 1997.
9. J. Lee and B. Jeon, "Fast Mode Decision for H.264 with Variable Motion Block Sizes," ISCIS 2003, Lecture Notes in Computer Science, vol. 2869, pp. 723-730, Nov. 2003.
10. José M. Cobo, Luis Salgado and Julián Cabrera, "Adaptive segmentation for gymnastic exercises based on change detection over multiresolution combined differences", Proc. Int. Conf. on Image Processing, ICIP'04, Singapore, pp. 337-340, October 2004.
11. H264/AVC Reference Software Model (JM_92): http://bs.hhi.de/~suchring/tml/index.html

# Non-rigid Tracking Using 2-D Meshes

Pascaline Parisot, Vincent Charvillat, and Géraldine Morin

IRIT-ENSEEIHT, 2 rue Camichel, F-31071 Toulouse, France
`firstname.name@enseeiht.fr`

**Abstract.** Mesh motion estimation is a tracking technique useful in particular for low bitrate compression, object-based coding and virtual views synthesis. In this article we present a new triangular mesh tracking algorithm preserving the mesh connectivity. Our method generalizes the rigid template tracking method proposed by Jurie and Dhome [5] to the case of non-rigid objects. Thanks to a learning step that can be done off-line for a given number of nodes, the tracking step can be performed in real time.

## 1 Introduction

The 2-D mesh motion compensation is an alternative solution to the classical block-based techniques. Dynamic 2-D meshes have been studied in different research areas: hierarchical and content-based design [13,10], hierarchical motion estimation, occlusion modeling and scalable coding. Historically designed for the low bitrate video compression, the 2-D mesh tracking is also adapted for the object segmentation, tracking, coding and motion generation [11,9,10].

Our method is a non-rigid generalization of the rigid Jurie and Dhome learning-based tracking method [5]. This method is achieved through two steps. The off-line step estimates, at each node, a linear relation between the gray levels differences and the parameters of the triangular mesh distortion. Then the tracking step iterates the following process: read gray levels differences and get the distortion parameters from the estimated linear relation. We express the distortion parameters in generalized barycentric coordinates in order to apply a mesh motion relative to the current frame. Our method gives results as good as those given by the Hexagonal Matching method [8] considered as one of the most reliable mesh tracking methods. Nevertheless our tracking step is of lower complexity and thus faster than the Hexagonal Matching one and could be used in real-time applications.

In section 2, we define the local transformations of a mesh and propose an optimization model. Then, in section 3, we give a state of the art on mesh tracking methods and present the key ideas of our work. In section 4, we detail our approach and give experimental results.

## 2 Notations: Mesh Transformations and Criteria

In mesh-based motion tracking, the frame distortion is modeled by a mesh distortion. In the case of triangulation, this motion model assumes a piecewise

J. Blanc-Talon et al. (Eds.): ACIVS 2005, LNCS 3708, pp. 579–586, 2005.
© Springer-Verlag Berlin Heidelberg 2005

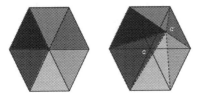

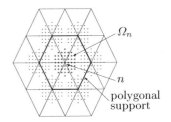

**Fig. 1.** Nodal transformation: initial mesh in solid lines (left and right), image and mesh distorted by a nodal transformation, mesh in dashed lines (right)

**Fig. 2.** Example of a sample pattern of the mesh. The sample pattern of the node $n$ is $\Omega_n$.

affine distortion of the image. This distortion can be parameterized either, for each triangle, by the six parameters of an affine transformation [8,1] or, for each node, by a displacement vector [6]. We use this second approach; so the mesh connectivity is intrinsically preserved.

To estimate these nodal transformations, we use the criterion $E_t$ based on the displaced frame difference:

$$E_t(\mu) = \sum_{p \in \Omega} (I_t(f(p; \mu)) - I_{ref}(p))^2, \qquad (1)$$

where $I_{ref}$ is the reference frame (generally, $I_0$ or $I_{t-1}$), $p$ a pixel of the image domain $\Omega$, $\mu$ the parameters vector and $f$ the piecewise affine transformation. We want to determine the vector $\mu_t$ that minimizes this criterion: $\mu_t = argmin_\mu E_t(\mu)$.

A global mesh transformation can be broken down into local transformations, that we call nodal transformations. These transformations are characterized by the displacement of only one node of the triangulation (see Fig. 1). The global criterion (1) can be broken down, like the global mesh transformation, into local criteria around each node $n$ of the mesh:

$$E_t(\mu, n) = \sum_{p \in \Omega_n} (I_t(f(p; \mu)) - I_{ref}(p))^2, \qquad (2)$$

where $\Omega_n$ is a set of pixels, not dense in our case (see Fig. 2). Then we determine the nodal transformation $T_{\Delta\mu}$, that is, the displacement vector $\Delta\mu$ of the node $n$ minimizing (2).

## 3   State of the Art and Key Ideas

In this section, we first explain the advantages and disadvantages of current mesh methods based on the criterion (1). Then, we describe the learning-based rigid tracking method that we shall generalize.

**Mesh Tracking:** Marquant *et al.* directly solve the global problem [6]. They linearize the non-linear least squares criterion (1) using the second order Taylor's expansion. Their method gives good results but is slow.

A pioneer algorithm, due to Brusewitz [3], divides the image into triangular patches and estimates a motion vector for each triangle vertex. A dense motion field is interpolated within each patch and the motion vectors are estimated (in the least squares meaning) from the optical flow equation. In contrast with this global method, Nakaya *et al.* [8] propose an Hexagonal Matching method: a two-step search optimizes the node motion vectors representing an affine motion compensation for each triangle. This method minimizes the prediction error defined on the hexagonal support of a nodal transformation. Because of the exhaustivity of the search, this method is expensive. However, it is considered as one of the most reliable mesh tracking methods. It will be used as a benchmark to validate our results.

Wang *et al.* propose a local closed-form solution based on a gradient descent to estimate the motion and minimize the criterion (1) [13]. Altunbasak *et al.* find locally optimal closed-form solutions to estimate the frame distortion using either node or patch approaches and either image gradients or dense motion vector fields [1]. Their method is less expensive than the Hexagonal Matching one but their results are not as good.

We use such local techniques and generalize the methods proposed by Hager and Belhumeur [4] and Jurie and Dhome [5] to the non-rigid mesh-based tracking.

**Learning-Based Tracking:** We first approximate the criterion $E_t(\mu, n)$ (eq. (2)) in the same way Hager and Belhumeur do for their own criterion [4]. Our local criterion $E_t(\mu, n)$ can be written: $E_t(\mu, n) = \| I_t(\mu) - I_0(0) \|^2$, where $I_t(\mu)$ is the vector $[I_t(f(p; \mu))]_{p \in \Omega_n}$ and $I_0(0) = [I_0(f(p; 0))]_{p \in \Omega_n} = [I_0(p)]_{p \in \Omega_n}$. Assuming a small disruption $\Delta\mu$ between two successive frames $I_t$ and $I_{t+\tau}$ (generally, $\tau = 1$), a first order expansion gives $I_{t+\tau}(\mu + \Delta\mu) \approx I_t(\mu) + M(\mu, t)\Delta\mu + \tau\nabla_t I_t(\mu)$, where the matrix $M(\mu, t)$ (noted $M$ below) is a jacobian matrix. Using the approximation $\tau\nabla_t I_t(\mu) \approx I_{t+\tau}(\mu) - I_t(\mu)$, the criterion is now $E_t(\Delta\mu, n) \approx \| M(\mu, t)\Delta\mu + I_{t+\tau}(\mu) - I_0(0) \|^2$. Solving $\nabla E_t(\Delta\mu, n) = 0$, with $\Delta I = I_{t+\tau}(\mu) - I_0(0)$, we obtain the linear relation:

$$\Delta\mu = A^t \Delta I, \text{ where } A^t = -(M^T M)^{-1} M^T. \tag{3}$$

This linear relation links $\Delta\mu$, a small disruption of the parameters $\mu$, and $\Delta I$, a gray levels difference sampled with $\Omega_n$.

As Jurie and Dhome [5], we assume that, at any time, we can express our problem in the reference frame $I_0$, solve it and then transfer the solution back to the frame $I_t$. As a consequence, $A$ is estimated only once (off-line) on the reference frame $I_0$ and thus is time independent. Our method requires the estimation of such a matrix $A$ at each node of the mesh.

## 4   Estimation of Transformations by Learning

We estimate the motion of one node $n$ at a time, that is, a nodal transformation. We first set the problem between two successive frames $I_{t-1}$ and $I_t$ and then show that this problem is equivalent to a problem between the reference frame $I_0$

and a frame $I_0'$. By expressing the displacement vector in generalized barycentric coordinates, we adapt this displacement found in the setting of $I_0$, to the frame $I_{t-1}$. This adaptation is necessary, since the node and its adjacent nodes have moved between $I_0$ and $I_{t-1}$.

## 4.1    Learning and Tracking Stages of a Nodal Transformation

The detailed explanation is based on the figure 3. To simplify, only one point of the sample pattern $\Omega_n$ is shown per triangle.

**The Problem:** The figure 3 (b-i) shows the frame $I_{t-1}$ with the right position of the mesh. We assume that, from $I_0$ to $I_{t-1}$, the image has been mapped by a piecewise affine transformation and that the tracking has been perfect. The frame $I_t$ is shown on the figure 3 (b-ii). This frame is the result of a nodal transformation $T_{\Delta\mu'}$ applied to the frame $I_{t-1}$. The position of the mesh is the one of the frame $I_{t-1}$.

Between these two situations on $I_{t-1}$ and $I_t$, reading the gray levels differences between $I_{t-1}$ and $I_t$ at each point $p$ of the sample pattern $\Omega_n$ (see Fig. 2), a vector $\Delta I$ can be computed: $\Delta I = [I_t(f(p; \mu_{t-1})) - I_{t-1}(f(p; \mu_{t-1}))]_{p\in\Omega_n}$.

We are seeking the vector $\Delta\mu'$, parameterizing the nodal transformation of the image, to accordingly transform the mesh. This displacement vector is predicted from $\Delta I$ thanks to the linear relation (3).

**The Corresponding Problem in the Reference Frame $I_0$:** Since the tracking is perfect at time $t-1$, that is $I_0(p) = I_{t-1}(f(p; \mu_{t-1}))$ for any $p$ in $\Omega_n$ (see Fig. 3 (a-i) and (b-i)), an image $I_0'$ following the frame $I_0$ can be generated such that:

$$\Delta I = [I_0'(p) - I_0(p)]_{p\in\Omega_n} = [I_t(f(p; \mu_{t-1})) - I_{t-1}(f(p; \mu_{t-1}))]_{p\in\Omega_n}. \quad (4)$$

If the image $I_0'$ is also a nodal transformation of $I_0$ (see Fig. 3 (a-i) and (a-ii)), denoted $T_{\Delta\mu}$, then we know how to simulate the same vector $\Delta I$ without generating the image $I_0'$. Instead of applying the nodal transformation to the frame $I_0$ and leaving the mesh and the sample pattern $\Omega_n$ unchanged, we apply the inverse nodal transformation[1] $T_{\Delta\mu}^{-1}$ to the mesh and $\Omega_n$ and leave $I_0$ unchanged (see Fig. 3 (a-iii)):

$$\Delta I = [I_0(T_{\Delta\mu}^{-1}(p)) - I_0(p)]_{p\in\Omega_n}.$$

Therefore any gray levels difference calculated between two successive frames can be generated on the reference frame $I_0$. Thus we can learn a link between the parameters of the nodal transformation and the gray levels differences. This learning stage is only based on the reference frame $I_0$ and the local criterion (2). From the simulation of numerous experiments $j$ ($j \in [1..J]$, where $J \approx 400$), consisting in applying disruptions $T_{\Delta\mu^j}^{-1}$ and then in collecting the induced $\Delta I^j$,

---

[1] Warning, the inverse nodal transformation $T_{\Delta\mu}^{'-1}$ is piecewise defined but with another support than $T_{\Delta\mu}$. That is why the edges are broken.

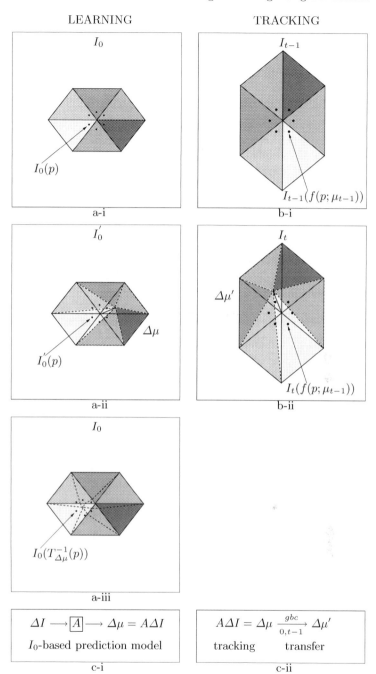

**Fig. 3.** Scheme showing the key ideas of our method

we estimate the best linear predictor in the least squares meaning (see eq. (3)). This predictor is indeed the learning matrix $A$ (see Fig. 3 (c-i)): $\Delta\mu = A\Delta I$.

**Interpretation in the Frame $I_t$:** The prediction $\Delta\mu$, that is the displacement vector of a node on the frame $I_0$ expressed in cartesian coordinates, is transferred to the vector $\Delta\mu'$ to take into account the distortion of the region to track between the frames $I_0$ and $I_{t-1}$.

To do this, we express $\Delta\mu$ in generalized barycentric coordinates (gbc) $\Delta\mu_{gbc}$. The base of these coordinates is the ordered vertices of the polygonal support (see Fig. 2). We use the Wachspress coordinates [12] because they are invariant by affine transformations and easy to compute [7]. We obtain $\Delta\mu'$ by expressing $\Delta\mu_{gbc}$ from the new position of the base in the frame $I_{t-1}$ (see Fig. 3 (c-ii)). This result is exact when the polygonal support has been affinely transformed, and, in practice, satisfactory for any conformable mesh transformation.

### 4.2    From Nodal Transformations to Global Mesh Distortion

To track global mesh distortion, during the learning stage, we compute a learning matrix $A_n$ for each node $n$ and, during the tracking stage, we implement the following relaxation algorithm:

---

Relaxation algorithm :
- For each node $n$,
  + calculate $\Delta I(n)$ (eq. 4)
  + using the gbc, determine $\Delta\mu'(n)$
  + calculate the criterion $E_t$ (eq. 1)
  End for
- Select the node $n$ that most decreases $E_t$
- While the gain on $E_t$ is bigger than a threshold loop
  + Move $n$ of $\Delta\mu'(n)$
  + Update :
    * the interest points of the polygonal support of $n$
    * the motion vectors of the nodes of the polygonal support and of $n$
    * the global criterion of the nodes of the polygonal support and of $n$
  + Select the node $n$ that most decreases $E_t$
  End loop

---

We have worked on "Miss America", "Foreman" and synthetic sequences. We have chosen a regular triangulation of 19 nodes centered on the faces. The sample pattern is shown on figure 2. The learnt displacements are all possible vectors with their coordinates between $-10$ and $10$ pixels.

**Synthetic Sequences:** The synthetic sequence illustrated on figure 4 (top) is obtained by non-rigid transformations [2] of the first image of the "Foreman" sequence. These non-rigid transformations are defined by a radial basis mapping using thin-plate spline basis functions and 19 kernels of non-rigidities. We assume that we perfectly know the motion of the mesh border nodes. The figure 5 shows

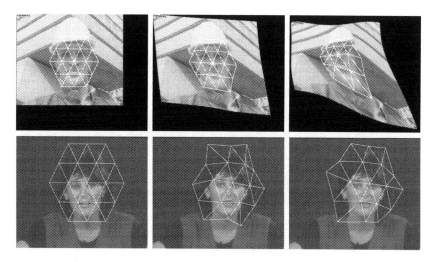

**Fig. 4.** Top: Synthetic video sequence of non-rigid deformations on "Foreman". Left: reference frame (frame 1) and its learning mesh. Middle: frame 13 and its mesh tracked by our method. Right: frame 43 and its mesh tracked by our method. Bottom: Video sequence "Miss America". Left: reference frame (frame 1) and its learning mesh. Middle: frame 78 and its mesh tracked by the Hexagonal Matching method. PSNR of 31.41 dB. Right: frame 78 and its mesh tracked by our method. PSNR of 30.40 dB.

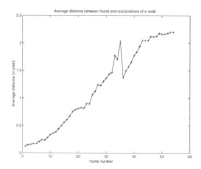

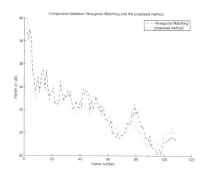

**Fig. 5.** Tracking on the synthetic sequence of non-rigid transformations on "Foreman": average distance between the found and real positions of a node

**Fig. 6.** Comparison between the Hexagonal Matching method and the proposed method on the video sequence "Miss America"

that our method well approximates these non-rigid transformations: the maximum average error per pixel is only of 2.2 pixels and is get on the last frame.

**Real Sequences:** The figure 4 (bottom) shows the results obtained on the "Miss America" sequence using the Hexagonal Matching (HM) method [8] and our method. The PSNR between the frame rebuilt from the estimated mesh localization and the corresponding frame in the sequence enables to quantify the tracking. The graph on figure 6 shows that our results are similar to the results of (HM). Moreover, our method is faster than (HM). In fact, for each node, the complexity of (HM) is $O(K_H P_H M_H^2)$ ($K_H$ being the number of iterations, $P_H$ the number of pixels in the polygonal support and $M_H$ the size of the search window). Our algorithm complexity is $O(PM^2)$ for the learning stage and $O(KP)$ for the tracking stage. Since $KP \approx K_H P_H$ in the tracking stage, our method is $M_H^2 \approx 200$ times less complex than (HM).

## 5 Conclusion

Our mesh tracking method based on a learning preserves the mesh connectivity. The results are similar to the ones of the Hexagonal Matching method which is recognized as one of the most efficient in terms of results accuracy [8,1]. Our method is simpler and quicker, which is due to the learning stage.

## References

1. Altunbasak, Y., Tekalp, A.M.: Closed-form connectivity-preserving solutions for motion compensation using 2-D meshes. IEEE Trans. on Image Proc. (sept. 1997) vol. 6, no. 9, pp. 1255-1269.
2. Bookstein, F.L.: Principal Warps: Thin-Plate Splines and the Decomposition of Deformations. IEEE Trans. on PAMI (june 1989) vol. 11, no. 6, pp. 567-585.
3. Brusewitz, H.: Motion compensation with triangles. Proc. 3rd International Workshop on 64 kbits/s Coding of Moving Video. (sept. 1990)
4. Hager, G.D., Belhumeur, P.N.: Efficient region tracking with parametric models of geometry and illumination. IEEE Trans. on PAMI (1998) vol. 20, no. 10, pp. 1025-1039.
5. Jurie, F., Dhome, M.: Hyperplane approximation for template matching. IEEE Trans. on PAMI (2002) vol. 24, no. 7, pp. 996-1000.
6. Marquant, G., Pateux, S., Labit, C.: Mesh-based scalable video coding with rate-distortion optimization. Visual Communications and Image Processing (june 2000) pp.967-976.
7. Meyer, M., Barr, A., Lee, H., Desbrun, M.: Generalized barycentric coordinates on irregular polygons. Journal of Graphics Tools archive (nov. 2002) vol. 7, pp. 13-22.
8. Nakaya, Y., Harashima, H.: Motion compensation based on spatial transformations. IEEE Trans. on CSVT (june 1994) vol. 4, no. 3, pp. 339-367.
9. Toklu, C.: Object-based Digital Video Processing using 2-D Meshes. PhD Thesis, Univ. of Rochester (1998)
10. Valette, A., Magnin, I., Prost, R.: Active mesh for video segmentation and objects tracking. Proc. IEEE ICIP'2001 (oct. 2001) vol. 2, pp. 77-80.
11. van Beek, P., Tekalp, A.M., Zhuang, N., Celasun, I., Xia, M.: Hierarchical 2-D Mesh representation, tracking and compression for object-based video. IEEE Trans. on Circ. Syst. for Video Tech. (1998) vol. 9, no. 2.
12. Wachspress, E.: A rational finit element basis. Academic Press (1975)
13. Wang, Y., Lee, O.: Active mesh-a feature seeking and tracking image sequence representation scheme. IEEE Trans. on Image Processing (sept. 1994) vol. 3, no. 5, pp. 610-624.

# An Offline Bidirectional Tracking Scheme

Tom Caljon, Valentin Enescu, Peter Schelkens, and Hichem Sahli

Vrije Universiteit Brussel - Interdisciplinary Institute for Broadband Technology,
Department of Electronics and Informatics (ETRO),
Brussels, Belgium
tcaljon@vub.ac.be

**Abstract.** A generic bi-directional scheme is proposed that robustifies
the estimation of the maximum-a-posteriori (MAP) sequence of states
of a visual object. It enables creative, non-technical users to obtain the
path of interesting objects in offline available video material, which can
then be used to create interactive movies. To robustify against tracker
failure the proposed scheme merges the filtering distributions of a forward tracking particle filter and a backward tracking particle filter at
some timesteps, using a reliability-based voting scheme such as in democratic integration. The MAP state sequence is obtained using the Viterbi
algorithm on reduced state sets per timestep derived from the merged
distributions and is interpolated linearly where tracking failure is sus-
pected. The presented scheme is generic, simple and efficient and shows
good results for a color-based particle filter.

## 1 Introduction

One component in our offline video content analysis application needs to track
objects within shots of all kinds of videos, possibly containing challenges such
as occlusion, lighting changes, moving cameras and cluttered backgrounds. The
idea is that prior to tracking, an operator selects the interesting objects in one
or more frames, called seeds, and can correct at any time during tracking, giving
rise to retracking in parts of the sequence using additional seeds. In specific cases
(such as face tracking) we envision to drop the necessity for human interaction
in favor of a slow but accurate detection algorithm every $n$ frames. Furthermore,
we do not want to equate offline processing to 'much slower than realtime': speed
still matters to remain usable. Intended use cases are the addition of interactivity
to video sequences (e.g. clicking on a soccer player to get his resume) and region
of interest coding.

Most trackers in literature are concerned with sequentially obtaining an estimate $\hat{x}_k$ of the real object state $x_k$ at timestep $k$, or the *filtering distribution*
$p(x_k|z_{1:k})$, given the newly arrived measurement (frame) $z_k$. Often dependent
modules exist that require such an estimate at each timestep, for example to
maneuver a robot or control a pan/tilt camera. Our application has no such
needs, and the quantity of interest is the state sequence (path) $x_{1:T}$ of the object.
Particle filters can be used to sequentially estimate $p(x_{1:k}|z_{1:k}) \; \forall k \in \{1, \ldots, T\}$,

J. Blanc-Talon et al. (Eds.): ACIVS 2005, LNCS 3708, pp. 587–594, 2005.
© Springer-Verlag Berlin Heidelberg 2005

at the real risk of early discarding the future best paths during resampling steps. Another approach is to randomly generate paths from the smoothing densities $\{p(x_k|z_{1:T})\}_{k=1}^T$ obtained using a smoothing particle filter[2]. Since the final result is supposed to be one state sequence, the technique presented in [3] is more appropriate: the object state space at each timestep $k$ is discretized to the $M$ most promising states, which correspond to the particles of the filtering density obtained by a particle filter. Next the $O(TM^2)$ Viterbi algorithm is run to find the maximum-a-posteriori state sequences.

The weakness of the latter technique is the employed particle filter: failure of this filter due to occlusion, clutter or illumination changes often means no particles are near the real object state at some timesteps, a deficiency that the Viterbi step can not correct for. A viable solution is to enhance the particle filter so that it will fail less, and this will likely come at the cost of less generic, carefully tuned models and increased complexity. Instead, the next sections show a generic complementary solution that makes use of additional seeds, also at the expense of extra processing. The main assumptions are that failure-prone intervals in the sequence occur only from time to time and that tracking before and after such intervals is feasible. We show good results for the proposed scheme in section 4, for experiments with a color-based particle filter on both synthetic and real world videos.

## 2    Particle Filters and the Viterbi Algorithm

Given a time-evolving system that is described by an unknown state vector $x_k$ at timestep $k$, particle filters[1] offer a sequential Monte Carlo style solution to finding the filtering distribution $p(x_k|z_{1:k})$, the distribution of the state given past noisy observations $z_{1:k} = \{z_1, \ldots, z_k\}$. This distribution is approximated by a cloud of samples (particles) $\{x_k^{(i)}\}_{i=1}^N$ with associated weights $\{\pi_k^{(i)}\}_{i=1}^N$: $p(x_k|z_{1:k}) = \sum_{i=1}^N \pi_k^{(i)} \delta(x_k - x_k^{(i)})$. One way to recursively maintain a weighted samples approximation is by selecting the most succesful particles at timestep $k$ and propagating them to timestep $k+1$ according to the state transition prior $p(x_{k+1}|x_k)$. In this case (sampling-importance-resampling filtering) the new weights are the likelihood of the observation given the state: $\pi_{k+1}^{(i)} = p(z_{k+1}|x_{k+1}^{(i)})$.

Independent of the scheme presented next, we performed experiments with a color-based particle filter with state vector $[x, y, w, h, \dot{x}, \dot{y}, \dot{w}, \dot{h}]$ that defines the bounding box around the tracked object, together with a change in each parameter. The state transition prior is a constant speed model, the likelihood $p(z_k|x_k)$ is the Bhattacharrya distance between the model histogram and the histogram of pixels inside $x_k$.

For more information, the reader is referred to [1] and [4].

The Viterbi algorithm is used to get the MAP state sequence $\hat{x}_{1:T}^{MAP}$ i.e. the sequence for which $p(x_1)p(z_1|x_1)\Pi_{k=2}^T p(x_k|x_{k-1})p(z_k|x_k)$ is maximized, given $M$ possible states $\{x_k^{(i)}\}_{i=1}^M$ at timestep $k$:

1. Initialize
   For $1 \leq i \leq M_1$ :
   $$\delta_1(i) = \log p(z_k|x_1^{(i)})$$
2. Find best path ($\delta$ is probability, $\psi$ is previous) for arriving in $x_k^{(j)}$
   For $2 \leq k \leq T$ :
   For $1 \leq j \leq M_k$ :
   $$\delta_k(j) = \log p(z_k|x_k^{(j)}) + \max_i\{\delta_{k-1}(i) + \log p(x_k^{(j)}|x_{k-1}^{(i)})\}$$
   $$\psi_k(j) = \arg\max_i\{\delta_{k-1}(i) + \log p(x_k^{(j)}|x_{k-1}^{(i)})\}$$
3. Choose best path
   $$i_T = \arg\max_i \delta_T(i)$$
   $$\hat{x}_T^{MAP} = x_T^{(i_T)}$$
4. Backtrack
   For $k = T - 1, \ldots, 1$
   $$i_k = \psi_{k+1}(i_{k+1})$$
   $$\hat{x}_k^{MAP} = x_k^{(i_k)}$$

Its complexity is $O(TM^2)$. In [3] it is argued that the possible states at timestep $k$ can correspond to the states in the approximation of $p(x_k|z_{1:k})$ by a particle filter.

## 3   Proposed Approach

We assume the shot under consideration consists of frames $1, \ldots, T$ and that only one object is tracked. If only one initialization is given (e.g. $x_1$), we default to the algorithm in [3]. An automatic detection algorithm may however generate extra seeds (e.g. $s$), as can an operator anticipating or observing tracking failure. Although not required, for simplicity we will assume $s = T$ in the remainder of this paper. In that case, tracking proceeds as follows:

1. One particle $x_1^{(1)} = x_1$ is inserted at timestep 1, with weight 1;
2. One particle $x_T^{(1)} = x_T$ is inserted at timestep $T$, with weight 1;
3. A particle filter sequentially estimates, forward in time using $p(x_k|x_{k-1})$
   $P_f = \{p_f(x_k|z_{2:k})\}_{k=2}^{T-1}$ starting from $\{(x_1^{(1)}, 1)\}$
4. A particle filter sequentially estimates, backward in time using $p(x_k|x_{k+1})$
   $P_b = \{p_b(x_k|z_{T-1:k})\}_{k=2}^{T-1}$ starting from $\{(x_T^{(1)}, 1)\}$
5. Combined particle representations are obtained (see section 3.1):
   $P_c = \{p_c(x_k|z_{2:T-1}) = f_{comb}(p_f(x_k|z_{2:k}), p_b(x_k|z_{T-1:k}))\}_{k=2}^{T-1}$
6. The Viterbi algorithm calculates the MAP-path from timestep 1 to $T$ using $x_1$, $x_T$ and the most probable states in $P_c$. In addition, interpolation is performed at timesteps where the hypotheses are considered faulty or marked faulty by the operator. See section 3.3.

The filtering processes for $P_f$ and $P_b$ are independent: failure is anticipated, so we do not want to corrupt the 'second opinion' of one particle filter by the possibly faulty output of the other.

## 3.1 Obtaining $P_c$

Inspired by the integration of cues in multiple-cue trackers, each $p_f$ and $p_b$ will be merged into the new probability density function $p_c$ according to a measure of reliability.

A popular integration approach by Triesch and von der Malsburg is *democratic integration*[6]. This scheme is originally used to unidirectionally track faces using a motion detection cue, a color cue, a prediction cue, a shape cue and a contrast cue. At each timestep $k$, each cue $i$ votes for each possible state. The vote weight depends on the similarity with a prototype for that cue and on an adaptive reliability measure for that cue. Spengler and Schiele integrate particle filters (`Condensation`) with democratic integration in [5]. Their technique boils down to particle filtering where the weight of each particle is a non-adaptive linear combination of the likelihoods of different cues.

Our integration method is based on a similar voting scheme i.e. after obtaining $P_f$ and $P_b$, we require that each

$$p_c(x_k|z_{2:T-1}) = r_f(k)p_f(x_k|z_{2:k}) + r_b(k)p_b(x_k|z_{T-1:k})$$

where $r_f(k)$ and $r_b(k)$ denote the reliability or confidence in $p_f(x_k|z_{2:k})$ and $p_b(x_k|z_{T-1:k})$ respectively. In our case, these reliabilities will bias the selection of particles from either $p_f$ or $p_b$ in section 3.2. A weighted sample representation of $p_c(x_k|z_{2:T-1})$ is $\{(x_{c,k}^{(i)}, \pi_{c,k}^{(i)})\}_{i=1}^{2N} =$

$$\{(x_{f,k}^{(1)}, r_f(k)\pi_{f,k}^{(1)}), \ldots, (x_{f,k}^{(N)}, r_f(k)\pi_{f,k}^{(N)}), (x_{b,k}^{(1)}, r_b(k)\pi_{b,k}^{(1)}), \ldots, (x_{b,k}^{(N)}, r_b(k)\pi_{b,k}^{(N)})\}$$

as

$$p_c(x_k|z_{2:T-1}) = \sum_{i=1}^{N} (r_f(k)\pi_{f,k}^{(i)})\delta(x_k - x_{f,k}^{(i)}) + \sum_{i=1}^{N} (r_b(k)\pi_{b,k}^{(i)})\delta(x_k - x_{b,k}^{(i)})$$

In contrast to a scheme that multiplies $p_f$ and $p_b$, the anticipated disagreement between $p_f$ and $p_b$ does not leave us with a (near) zero $p_c$ or, after normalization, with a $p_c$ having unrealistic modes (e.g. when $p_f$ and $p_b$ are Gaussians).

A straightforward choice for the reliabilities is $r_b(k) = r_f(k) = 0.5$. However, since the particle weights $\{\pi_{f,k}^{(i)}\}$ and $\{\pi_{b,k}^{(i)}\}$ have been separately normalized to sum to 1 by the particle filter, only the relative success between particles of the same particle set is retained. The relative success between particles of $p_b(x_k|z_{T-1:k})$ and $p_f(x_k|z_{2:k})$ is lost e.g. the particles of $p_b$ could all be spot on the real object state (all high likelihood) and the particles of $p_f$ could all have lost track (all low likelihood), without this being deducible from the normalized particle weights. Therefor, the definition of reliability as the sum of the likelihoods within a particle set solves this problem: if the non-normalized reliabilities are $r'_f(k) = \sum_{i=1}^{N} p(z_k|x_{f,k}^{(i)})$ and $r'_b(k) = \sum_{i=1}^{N} p(z_k|x_{b,k}^{(i)})$ then the weights for $p_c$ become

$$r_f(k)\pi_{f,k}^{(\cdot)} = \frac{r'_f(k)}{r'_f(k) + r'_b(k)}\frac{p(z_k|x_{f,k}^{(\cdot)})}{r'_f(k)} = \frac{p(z_k|x_{f,k}^{(\cdot)})}{r'_f(k) + r'_b(k)}$$

and $r_b(k)\pi_{b,k}^{(\cdot)} = \frac{p(z_k|x_{b,k}^{(\cdot)})}{r_f'(k)+r_b'(k)}$ i.e. each of $p_c$'s particles is now properly weighted relative to the total likelihood of all particles.

With these definitions, $r_f(k)$ and $r_b(k)$ respond to occlusion and loss of track in the expected way. However, another common cause of tracking failure, inability of a filter's likelihood function $p(z|x)$ to distinguish between the real object and distractors, will not cause the ideal response in the corresponding reliability. This weakness is often by design e.g. because a more accurate likelihood function would be too complex or hard to model. We try to compensate for such generically undetectable failures by assuming the odds of encountering them is proportional to the number of frames tracked. At the same time introducing dynamics for the reliabilities to manage their rate of change, the final reliabilities are calculated as follows: $\forall k \in \{2, \ldots, T-1\}$:

$$r_f(k) = \min(\max(r_f(k-1) + d(k) - p(k), 0), 1) \tag{1}$$
$$r_b(k) = 1 - r_f(k) \tag{2}$$

where:

$$d(k) = \frac{q_f(k) - r_f(k-1)}{\tau} \tag{3}$$

$$q_f(k) = \frac{q_f'(k)}{q_f'(k) + q_b'(k)} \tag{4}$$

$$q_f'(k) = \sum_{i=1}^{N} p(z_k|x_{f,k}^{(i)}), q_b'(k) = \sum_{i=1}^{N} p(z_k|x_{b,k}^{(i)}) \tag{5}$$

As in [6], $\tau$ should be configured to filter out high-frequency noise but still allow quick enough adaptation. $p(k)$ is penalty that should work in favor of $r_f(k)$ when $k$ is close to 1, and in favor of $r_b(k)$ when $k$ is close to $s$. In our experiments, $p(k)$ defaults to increasing linearly between $p(1) = -0.2$ and $p(T) = 0.2$.

## 3.2  Selecting a Reduced State Set

Given the $O(TM^2)$ complexity of the Viterbi algorithm, for each timestep $k \in \{1, \ldots, T\}$ we wish to retain only the $M < N$ distinct most promising states. The main concern is offering enough valid choice to Viterbi. The object states at timestep $k$ that are selected for the Viterbi algorithm are the $M$ distinct states from $\{x_{c,k}^{(i)}\}_{i=1}^{2N}$ that have the largest probability according to $p_c(x_{c,k}^{(i)}|z_{2:T-1})$.

## 3.3  Interpolated Maximum-a-Posteriori Path

We now have a drastically reduced set of possible object states $\{x_k^{(i)}\}_{i=1}^{M_k}$ at each timestep $k$, that has either been assigned by a user or a detection algorithm ($M_k = 1$), obtained using a particle filter ($M_k = M$) or obtained using both a forward particle filter and a backward particle filter as described above

($M_k = M$). Hence the MAP-sequence can be calculated using the Viterbi algorithm as described in section 2. The required likelihoods of these states for the Viterbi algorithm have already been calculated during filtering.

When loss of track (e.g. due to occlusion) occurs, often no possible object states are near the real object state. Many of these situations can be detected by inspecting $\max_i\{p(z_k|x_k^{(i)})\}$: if below a certain threshold (e.g. 0.1), loss of track at timestep $k$ is assumed. Additionally, the user can select intervals in which results are not acceptable. The Viterbi algorithm can easily be extended to then discard the available hypotheses at these timesteps and interpolate (e.g. linearly): given the current position of the algorithm is timestep $k$ and $k-(n+1)$ is the last timestep that had valid possible object states:

---

1. Find probability for linearly interpolated paths
   For $1 \leq j \leq M_k$ :
      For $1 \leq i \leq M_{k-(n+1)}$:
         Let $y_{i,j}^1, \ldots, y_{i,j}^n$ be the $n$ linearly interpolated states
         between $x_{k-(n+1)}^{(i)}$ and $x_k^{(j)}$
         $\delta_k(i,j) = \log p(z_k|x_k^{(j)}) + \delta_{k-(n+1)}(i) + \log p(y_{i,j}^1|x_{k-(n+1)}^{(i)})$
            $+ \log p(y_{i,j}^2|y_{i,j}^1) + \ldots + \log p(x_k^{(j)}|y_{i,j}^n)$
2. For $1 \leq j \leq M_k$ :
   $i_m = \arg\max_i \delta_k(i,j)$
   $\delta_k(j) = \delta_k(i_m, j)$
   Insert $\{y_{i_m,j}^1, \ldots, y_{i_m,j}^n\}$ between $x_{k-(n+1)}^{(i_m)}$ and $x_k^{(j)}$ using $\psi$

---

## 4   Experiments

Experiments were performed with the color based particle filter introduced in section 2. The first test sequence consists of 89 frames of a duck disappearing behind a tree early in the sequence, reappearing 20 frames later. Initializations were given in the first and last frame. $\tau$ is set to 1. Figure 1 shows the 200 particles of $p_f$ and $p_b$ and the reduced particle set for Viterbi (100 states) of $p_c$ at different timesteps. Both the forward and backward particle filter lose track at the time of disappearance, and $r_f$ behaves accordingly. The right states are selected for $p_c$. The occlusion is detected and no states are retained for the corresponding timesteps. Figure 1 shows that the MAP state sequences using states from either $P_f$ or $P_b$ are outperformed by the MAP path obtained using states from the combined probability density functions. The resulting path is interpolated at timesteps where the occlusion takes place.

For a challenging soccer sequence with distractors and occlusion, similar encouraging results were obtained using the same configuration (200 particles per tracker, 100 states retained, initialization in first and last frame). They are presented in figure 2. The PAL-resolution soccer sequence was tracked in both directions at 7 frames per second on a 2Ghz PC. Obtaining the states for Viterbi

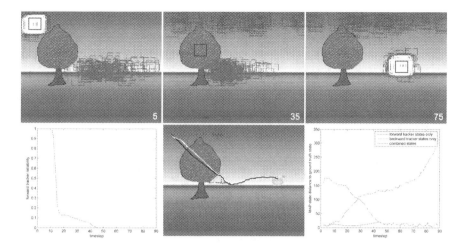

**Fig. 1.** Duck sequence. Top,red: forward tracker states. Top,green: backward tracker states. Top,white: retained states for Viterbi. Top,thick blue: true state. Bottom left: $r_f$. Bottom middle: MAP state sequences (same color assignments). Bottom right: state sequence distance to ground truth.

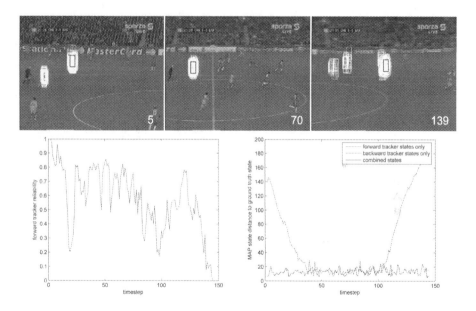

**Fig. 2.** Soccer sequence. Top,red: forward tracker states. Top,green: backward tracker states. Top,white: retained states for Viterbi. Top,thick blue: true state. Bottom left: $r_f$. Bottom right: state sequence distance to ground truth.

takes less than one second, the Viterbi algorithm itself 10 seconds. Simplifying the employed state transition prior $p(x_k|x_{k-1})$ for the Viterbi algorithm from the tracker's constant velocity model to a normal distribution over the distance between the centers of $x_k$ and $x_{k-1}$ reduces this time to 1 second, while still producing good results.

## 5   Conclusion

The presented scheme per timestep successfully selects a limited amount of states from the filtering distributions of a forward tracking particle filter and a backward tracking particle filter using a reliability-based voting scheme. This has the desirable effect of both speeding up the estimation of the maximum-a-posteriori state sequence so that it becomes interactively usable, and robustifying it by offering a second opinion, which is indispensable when the forward tracker fails. The Viterbi algorithm is well suited for this application, as it naturally allows to guide paths through states indicated by users. Further enhancements at the user interface level are possible, for example correction of the MAP-path by simple mouse clicks, preferably without retracking.

## Acknowledgments

This work is a result of the Advanced Media project, a joint collaboration between the Vrije Universiteit Brussel, VRT and IBBT. Peter Schelkens holds a post-doctoral fund with the Fund for Scientific Research Flanders (FWO).

## References

1. M. Arulampalam, S. Maskell, N. Gordon, and T. Clapp. A tutorial on particle filters for online nonlinear/non-gaussian bayesian tracking. *IEEE Transactions on Signal Processing*, 50(2):173–188, 2002.
2. A. Doucet, S. Godsill, and M. West. Monte carlo filtering and smoothing with application to time-varying spectral estimation. In *IEEE International Conference on Acoustics, Speech and Signal Processing*, volume II, pages 701–704, 2000.
3. S. Godsill, A. Doucet, and M. West. Maximum a posteriori sequence estimation using monte carlo particle filters. *Ann. Inst. Statist. Math.*, 52, 2001.
4. P. Pérez, C. Hue, J. Vermaak, and M. Gangnet. Color-based probabilistic tracking. In *ECCV*, pages 661–675, 2002.
5. M. Spengler and B. Schiele. Towards robust multi-cue integration for visual tracking. *Mach. Vis. Appl.*, 14(1):50–58, 2003.
6. J. Triesch and C. von der Malsburg. Self-organized integration of visual cues for face tracking. In *Proceedings of the Fourth International Conference on Automatic Face and Gesture Recognition*, pages 102–107, 28–30 2000.

# On the Performance Improvement of Sub-sampling MPEG-2 Motion Estimation Algorithms with Vector/SIMD Architectures

Vasilios A. Chouliaras, Vincent M. Dwyer, and Sharukh Agha

Department of Electronic and Electrical Engineering,
Loughborough University, UK
v.a.chouliaras@lboro.ac.uk

**Abstract.** The performance improvement of a number of motion estimation algorithms are evaluated following vector/SIMD instruction set extensions for MPEG-2 TM5 video encoding. Simulation-based results indicate a substantial complexity metric reduction for Full-Search, Three Step Search, Four Step Search and Diamond Search making the later three appropriate for execution on a high performance embedded VLSI platform. A simple model is developed to explain the simulated results, and a compound performance/power metric, the complexity-power-product (CPP), is proposed for algorithmic optimisation in vectorized applications for low-power, consumer devices.

## 1 Introduction

MPEG-2 [1, 2] is a popular, lossy video compression standard currently employed in many consumer products including DVD recorders, and digital, set-top boxes. This standard was introduced to support high-quality video at transmission rates from 4 to 80 Mbit/s, utilizing a dataflow similar to MPEG-1. The MPEG-2 codec is based on the discrete cosine transform (DCT), either of the residual data, obtained after performing motion estimation (ME) and compensation (MC) to remove redundancy between frames (inter-frame coding), or of the original luminance and chrominance data in removing redundancy within the same frame (intra-frame coding). Quantization then removes the high spatial frequency components to reduce the channel rate.

Full-Search Motion Estimation (FSME), the default method in the MPEG-2 TM5 implementation, exhaustively matches each macroblock in the *current* frame to all macroblocks, within a given search area, of a previous (*reference*) frame. It is clear however that, for portable real-time embedded applications, the power requirements are in direct conflict with the billions of arithmetic operations required by FSME per second, in order to sustain CIF-sized (352x288 pixels) real-time video encoding at 25 or 30 frames per second (fps).

Fig. (1) depicts processor requirements for real-time CIF video at 25 fps. These results were obtained by scaling architecture-level results (dynamic instruction count) by an average clocks-per-instruction (CPI) value of 1.5. This CPI value was chosen as characteristic of a 32-bit scalar CPU with a 2-way, 16KB instruction cache and a 4-way, 16KB write-through data cache when executing the MPEG-2 TM5 workload. Clearly the frequencies obtained are far too high to be realistic for FSME with

J. Blanc-Talon et al. (Eds.): ACIVS 2005, LNCS 3708, pp. 595–602, 2005.
© Springer-Verlag Berlin Heidelberg 2005

battery-powered devices. To reduce the ME complexity, a number of fast algorithms have been suggested [4-9]. A common factor in all ME methods is the computation of an error term that identifies how well the predicted macroblock maps to a reference macroblock. A software-based codec implementation should target all these data-parallel computations using both custom vector instructions and multithreaded processor designs, since such benefits can be utilized by all search methods. The current paper looks the benefits of vectorization.

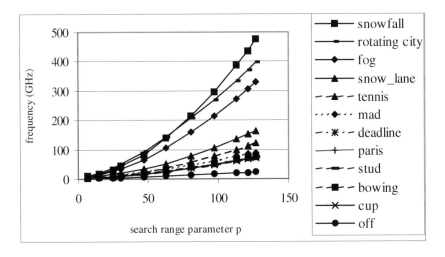

**Fig. 1.** Full-Search ME performance requirements for a variety of sequences

**Table 1.** Fractional DIC (see eqn (1)) for main ME functions for p in the range 2 and 62

| p | DIST1 | FDCT | FULLSEARCH | REMAINDER |
|---|-------|------|------------|-----------|
| 6 | 51.0 | 21.1 | 3.5 | 24.5 |
| 14 | 61.1 | 13.7 | 9.2 | 15.9 |
| 24 | 68.3 | 7.8 | 14.7 | 9.1 |
| 30 | 69.8 | 6.1 | 17.1 | 7.1 |
| 46 | 71.7 | 3.3 | 21.1 | 3.9 |
| 62 | 71.9 | 2.1 | 23.5 | 2.4 |

As shown in Table 1, the major complexity contributor in MPEG-2 TM5 is the inner loop of the ME function (DIST1) which computes the error of the current macroblock over all macroblocks in the search area. In particular, the DIST1 function complexity ranges from 52% to 73% of the unmodified reference software complexity for a search range of p = 6 to   p = 62 pels respectively. The forward-DCT computation (FDCT) is the next largest contributor to the complexity, but as shown in the table, its percentage complexity decreases with increasing search window size due to corresponding increase in the DIST1 contribution. The third greatest contributor to the complexity of the coder is the FULLSEARCH function itself, which is not discussed in this work as it has been the focus of numerous simulations in the past. Optimized (fast) ME algorithms, as mentioned above, significantly reduce the relative complexity contribution of FULLSEARCH as well as that of the whole video coder and are presented in the results section. In the current work we estimate performance improvement of such sub-sampling ME algorithms due to vector/SIMD instruction extensions. An approximate theoretical description of the complexity values obtained is developed which generates a possible performance evaluation metric appropriate to the optimization of data-parallel algorithms for embedded platforms.

## 2  Simulation Infrastructure, Results and Analysis

Simulations were performed on a modified version of the SimpleScalar toolset for instruction set architecture research [10]. The toolset consists of a C-compiler, assembler and linker, and a collection of an architectural- (no timing effects), and a single microarchitectural-simulator (including timing effects). The default sim-profile

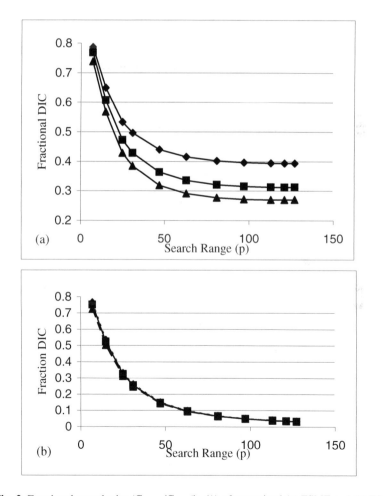

**Fig. 2.** Fractional complexity ($C_{DIST1}/C_{TOT}(k=1)$) of vectorized (a) FSME and (b) TSS

simulator was extended with additional processor state and additional instructions to transform that state. A scripting infrastructure was developed to automatically walk the algorithm optimization space and collect the performance metrics reported in this paper, using data-parallel extensions developed in [11].

Exhaustive simulations of the MPEG-2 TM5 video encoder were performed, for several sub-sampling ME methods, which were applied to twelve different video sequences, each consisting of 25 frames, for three vector register file lengths (VLMAX = 4, 8 and 16), using our simulation infrastructure. The complexity metric we have used here is the dynamic instruction count (DIC) of the executed algorithm. This metric is a direct measure of performance and does not relate to any particular CPU implementation. To correlate the metric to real-time (i.e. clock cycles), the micro-architectural metric of the average CPI can be used. The dynamic instruction count, multiplied by the average CPI and the clock period of the microarchitecture translates directly into time units. Utilizing this DIC metric, our results are applicable to a wide range of CPU architectures based on the principles of RISC processing.

Fig. (2a) depicts the dynamic instruction count of the vectorized full-search DIST1 function over search range and vector register length, and Fig. (2b) depicts the Three Step Search for the same metric. Other sub-sampling ME algorithms such as four step, three step search and diamond search follow a curve very similar to that in Fig. (2b). The data presented is relative to the dynamic instruction count of the unmodified (non-vectorized) full-search ME algorithm as it appears in the TM5 distribution.

Exploitation of DLP leads to a family of optimized video encoders that can be utilized in power-conscious, real-time devices. We observe the (expected) insensitivity of the sub-sampling ME algorithms over the search range (Fig. (2b)) which comes at a minimal loss of PSNR. This is attributed to the use of slow-moving video sequences which experience little and smooth motion across frames. The superiority of FSME is seen in fast-moving sequences such as 'Rotating City'.

## 3   Theoretical Analysis

Table1 reports the simulation results for the fractional Dynamic Instruction Count (DIC) of the various parts of the Full Search algorithm as a function of the search range in the reference frame. For macroblocks of size $N \times N$ pixels, and a search area of $(N+2p) \times (N+2p)$, the number of SAD calculations to be performed is $(2p+1)^2$. Naively, one expects part of the total DIC ($C_{TOT}$) to scale as $(2p+1)^2$, with the rest independent of p. For example, as the forward DCT occurs after the block matching completes it will be independent of search area, while clearly the DIC value for DIST1 will increase with p. Let us define complexity (DIC) measures for FULLSEARCH, DIST1, FDCT and the remaining functions REM as respectively $C_{FS}$, $C_{DIST1}$, $C_{FDCT}$ and $C_{REM}$, thus $C_{TOT} = C_{FS} + C_{DIST1} + C_{FDCT} + C_{REM}$. Similarly, let us define fractional values, with respect to $C_{TOT}$, of $C_{FS}*$, $C_{DIST1}*$, $C_{FDCT}*$ and $C_{REM}*$. From this naïve perspective we expect $C_{FDCT} + C_{REM}$ to be a constant independent of search area, c say. $C_{DIST1}$ can then be expressed in terms of these fractional values as

$$\frac{C_{DIST1}*}{C_{REM}*+C_{FDCT}*} = \frac{C_{DIST1}}{C_{REM}+C_{FDCT}} = \frac{1}{c}C_{DIST1} \tag{1}$$

and similarly for $C_{FS}$. Naturally $C_{FS}$ and $C_{DIST1}$ will be functionally dependent on the search range parameter $s = 2p+1$, and a plot against $s^2$ reveals their behaviour. Fig. 3 shows a plot of $C_{DIST1}/c$ values (table 1) against $s^2$ together with the straight line $1.9 + s^2/1100$, clearly the approximation is excellent except for the smallest window size, where the fit curve is slightly too high. Also shown is a plot of $C_{FS}/c$ values against $s^2$ together with the straight line $0.37s^2/1100$ and again, except at small window size, the fit is excellent. In addition, we expect $C_{FDCT}/C_{REM} = C_{FDCT}*/C_{REM}*$ to be a constant, $\alpha$ say. From table 1 it is clear that $\alpha \sim 1.16$ to an excellent approximation (values range from 1.14 to 1.17) and consequently this analysis shows that individual contributions to the total DIC, $C_{TOT}$, are approximately

$$C_{DIST1} = c\left(1.9 + \frac{(2p+1)^2}{1100}\right), \quad C_{FS} = 0.37c\frac{(2p+1)^2}{1100}, \quad C_{REM} = \frac{c}{2.16}, \quad C_{FDCT} = \frac{1.16c}{2.16} \qquad (2)$$

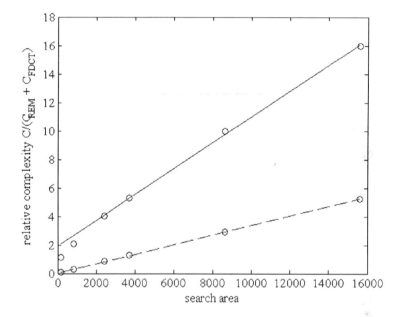

**Fig. 3.** Graph-based DIST1 and FULLSEARCH approximations

When the algorithm is vectorized, DIC values gain a functional dependence upon $k$, the multiplicity of datapaths with respect to the scalar version (or VLMAX). In the current implementation of TM5 we choose to disable the vectorized FDCT, while the FS function is characterized by thread-level parallelism (TLP), a complementary form of DLP, which is not exploited in this particular study. One expects that $C_{DIST1}$ will possess a section of code whose complexity decreases as $1/k$, while the REM instructions cannot be vectorized. For now let us assume that the split between those parts of DIST1 which can be vectorized ($k^{-1}$ dependence ) and those that cannot yields

$$C_{DIST1} = c\left(0.9 + \frac{1.}{k} + \frac{(2p+1)^2}{1100k}\right) \qquad (3)$$

which shall be justified later through Fig. 4.

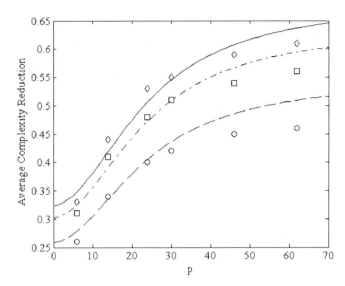

**Fig. 4.** Fractional complexity over search range and vector register file length

The f ractional reduction R in DIC on vectorizing is

$$R = 1 - \frac{C_{TOT}(k)}{C_{TOT}(1)} = \frac{\left(1 + \frac{(2p+1)^2}{1100}\right)\left(1 - \frac{1}{k}\right)}{2.9 + 1.37 \frac{(2p+1)^2}{1100}} \tag{4}$$

Fig. 4 shows a plot of R against (2p+1) for k = 4 (lower curve), 8 and 16 (upper curve) together with results taken from reference [3] which are shown as data points. It is likely that a better fit to these data points may be obtained by a more thorough investigation of the split in eqn (3). This is confirmed by the saturation values see in Fig. (2a) which are predicted in this model to be 0.40, 0.25 and 0.19 but which are measured to be 0.40, 0.31 and 0.26. A significant conclusion is that the DIC value for DIST1, and consequently the total DIC value, is bounded below by c(2.15 + $0.37s^2/275$) and no further increase in VLMAX will improve matters. There are also a number of downsides to increasing k, in particular more power will be dissipated in evaluating the DIST1 function with increased vector length. Indeed one might expect the total power for the calculation to increase linearly with k, say as

$$P(k) = P(1)(1 + (k-1)\Delta) \tag{5}$$

where P(1) is the scalar power dissipation (VLMAX = 1) and $\Delta$ (< 1) is the fractional rate of increase with vectorization. Thus one must effectively offsets DIC (and hence the operational frequency) against power dissipation.

A variety of optimization problems may now be set up to determine, for example, the best vector length for a given search range 2p+1. A figure of merit for such a purpose is the product of the total DIC and the overall power dissipation, CPP (the complexity-power product), which may be used in a manner similar to that of the area-delay product, used in optimizing circuit designs. For a given value of p (essentially PSNR) the CPP is $P(k)C_{TOT}(k)$, i.e.

$$CPP(k) = P(1)c\left(1.9 + \frac{1}{k} + \frac{(1+0.37k)(2p+1)^2}{1100k}\right)(1+(k-1)\Delta) \quad (6)$$

Clearly CPP(k) is large at both large and small k, with a minimum at intermediate value. Differentiating with respect to vector length, yields an optimum value $k_{opt}$ of

$$k_{opt}(s)^2 = \frac{1-\Delta}{\Delta}\left(\frac{1+s^2/1100}{1.9+0.37s^2/1100}\right) \quad (7)$$

Clearly $k_{opt}(s)$ is bounded above by $k_{opt}^{(max)} \to 1.64\sqrt{(1-\Delta)/\Delta}$ the value for very large search regions (s → ∞) and thus $k_{opt}(s) < k_{opt}^{(max)}$. When $\Delta = 0.2$, $k_{opt}^{(max)} = 3.25$ so that VLMAX should be taken as ~ 4 (i.e. 32 bits) while for $\Delta = 0.05$, $k_{opt}^{(max)} = 7.25$ leading to a VLMAX of 8 (i.e. 128 bits). For small search ranges (s < 32, p < 16) the optimum k value is roughly linear in s, $k_{opt}^{(max)} \sim (0.66 + 0.55(s/128))\sqrt{(1-\Delta)/\Delta}$. Now for $\Delta = 0.2$, $k_{opt}^{(max)} \sim 2$, leading to VLMAX = 2 (i.e. 16 bits).

The expression for $k_{opt}(s)$ illustrates, that an algorithm optimised with respect to CPP for a given search area, will become suboptimal if the Search Area is increased (in an attempt to increase PSNR for example). Eqn. (7) indicates how the vector length should be altered to accommodate such a change. If as above $\Delta = 0.2$, VLMAX should be set to 2 for small search areas, increasing to 4 as s increases. The analysis here is based largely on the results in [3] and in table 1, obtained by averaging over a large range of different types of video sequence. However these results are also valid for a wide number of individual standard video clips as discussed in ref [12].

### 3.1  IC for TSS, FSS and Other 'Fast' Algorithms

For fast algorithms, such as the Three Step Search (TSS), the dependence of DIC on window size is weak. From the same naïve perspective as above we expect that the vectorised-TSS DIC relative to the scalar value, $C_{TOT}^{TSS}(k)/C_{TOT}^{TSS}(1)$, should be

$$\frac{C_{TOT}^{TSS}(k)}{C_{TOT}^{TSS}(1)} = \frac{A_{TSS} + B_{TSS}/k}{A_{TSS} + B_{TSS}} = (1-\beta_{seq}) + \frac{\beta_{seq}}{k} \quad (8)$$

Here $B_{TSS}$ and $A_{TSS}$ represent those parts of the TSS algorithm which scale with $k^{-1}$ and are independent of it, respectively. $B_{TSS}$, $A_{TSS}$ and $\beta_{seq}$ are likely to be sequence dependent. Relative to the vectorized Full Search the TSS complexity varies as

$$\frac{C_{TOT}^{TSS}(k)}{C_{TOT}^{FS}(k)} = \frac{A_{TSS} + B_{TSS}/k}{c\left(1.9 + \frac{0.37(2p+1)^2}{1100} + \frac{1}{k}\left(1 + \frac{(2p+1)^2}{1100}\right)\right)} \quad (9)$$

In terms of DIC, it is expected that one gets a greater advantage from vectorizing the Full Search algorithm than is the case for the TSS (or other fast methods).

Consequently this ratio will increase with k, bounded above by the k → ∞ value. This again shows that vectorization is a process which has an optimum solution. This is considered in more detail in [12].

# 4  Conclusions

Exploitation of DLP, via vector/SIMD instruction set architecture extensions and the use of ME algorithms, is vital for real-time execution of the complex MPEG2-TM5 video encoder. CPU architects utilize architectural and/or trace-driven simulation to determine the optimal mix of microarchitecture (DLP) and algorithmic optimisations. This will converge to a local minimum in the design space, primarily reached via the optimization of a few complexity/microarchitectural metrics such as dynamic instruction count, average CPI or bus utilization. We advocate a complementary approach based around an analytical complexity model for the vectorized MPEG-2 application through extrapolating the architecture-level simulation data. As shown, the model matches the simulation results quite accurately for a search window range of between 8 and 64 pels. Subsequently, we proposed a new complexity metric, the complexity-power-product (CPP) to drive the optimization process without the need for prohibitively long, exhaustive simulation of the algorithmic and microarchitectural space. We continue to develop this model for the case of thread-level-parallelism (TLP) in order to explore the architecture/ microarchitecture space in a fraction of the time taken by simulation methodologies.

# References

[1]   T. Sikora, "MPEG Digital Video-Coding Standards," IEEE Signal Proc. **14** (1997) 82 -100.
[2]   Motion Picture Experts Group http://www.mpeg.org
[3]   V.A. Chouliaras, J.L. Nunez-Yanez, S. Agha, *'Silicon Implementation of a Parametric Vector Datapath for real-time MPEG2 encoding'*, paper 444-252, Proc. IASTED (SIP) 2004, Honolulu, Hawaii, USA.
[4]   J.R. Jain and A.K. Jain *"Displacement measurement and its application in interframe image coding"*, IEEE Trans. Comm., COM **29** (1981) 1799-1806.
[5]   M. Ghanbari, *"The cross-search algorithm for motion estimation"*, IEEE Trans. Comm., COM **38** (1990) 950-953.
[6]   R. Li, B. Zeng, and M.L. Liou *"A new three step search Algorithm for Block Motion Estimation"*, IEEE Trans. Circuits Syst. Video Technol., **4**, (1994) 438-442.
[7]   L-M Po and W-C Ma, *"A novel four step-search algorithm for fast block motion estimation"*, IEEE Trans. Circuits. Syst. Video Technol., **6**, (1996) 313-317.
[8]   L.K. Liu and E. Feig, *"A block based gradient descent search algorithm for block motion estimation in video coding"*, IEEE Trans. Circuits Syst. Video Techol., **6**, (1996) 419-422.
[9]   J.Y. Tham, S. Ranganath, M. Ranganath and A.A. Kassim, *"A novel unrestricted center-biased diamond search algorithm for block motion estimation"*, IEEE  Trans. Circuits Syst. Video Technol., **8**, (1998) 369-377.
[10]  SimpleScalar LLC http://www.simplescalar.com/
[11]  V.A. Chouliaras  J.L. Nunez, D.J. Mulvaney, F Rovati, D Alfonso, *'A Multi-standard Video coding accelerator based on a vector architecture'*, IEEE Trans. Cons. Electr., **51** (2004) 160-167.
[12]  V.M. Dwyer, V.A. Chouliaras and S. Agha, in preparation.

# A Dynamic Bayesian Network-Based Framework for Visual Tracking

Hang-Bong Kang and Sang-Hyun Cho

Dept. of Computer Engineering, Catholic University of Korea,
#43-1 Yokkok 2-dong Wonmi-Gu, Puchon City Kyonggi-Do, Korea
hbkang@catholic.ac.kr

**Abstract.** In this paper, we propose a new tracking method based on dynamic Bayesian network. Dynamic Bayesian network provides a unified probabilistic framework in integrating multi-modalities by using a graphical representation of the dynamic systems. For visual tracking, we adopt a dynamic Bayesian network to fuse multi-modal features and to handle various appearance target models. We extend this framework to multiple camera environments to deal with severe occlusions of the object of interest. The proposed method was evaluated under several real situations and promising results were obtained.

## 1 Introduction

Visual tracking in complex environments is an important task for surveillance, teleconferencing, and human computer interaction. It should be computationally efficient and robust to occlusion, changes in 3D pose and scale as well as distractions from background clutter. To meet these requirements, it is desirable to fuse multi-modal features efficiently. In addition, in order to monitor a site effectively, it is necessary to develop a tracking algorithm in multiple overlapping field of view camera environments.

Numerous visual tracking algorithms have been proposed. As the deterministic approach, Comaniciu et al. [1] proposed mean shift tracker which is a non-parametric density gradient estimator based on color distribution. The method can reliably track objects with partial occlusions. As the probabilistic approach, Isard et al. [2] proposed CONDENSATION algorithm, otherwise known as particle filtering, for visual tracking. Nummiaro et al. [3] proposed an adaptive color-based particle filter by extending CONDENSATION algorithm. It shows good performance in comparison with mean shifter tracker and Kalman filtering. As multi-modal feature-based tracking, Liu et al. [4] suggests a multi-modal face tracking method using Bayesian network. It integrates color, edge and face appearance likelihood models into Bayesian networks for robust tracking. For object tracking in multi-camera environments, Comaniciu et al. [5] proposed a flexible multi-camera system for real-time tracking. Kahn et al. [6] suggested a system for people tracking in multiple uncalibrated cameras. They use spatial relationships between camera fields of view to correspond with those between different views of the same person.

For our visual tracking, we adopt a dynamic Bayesian network based multi-modal features fusion and appearance target model handling. Dynamic Bayesian network

J. Blanc-Talon et al. (Eds.): ACIVS 2005, LNCS 3708, pp. 603–610, 2005.
© Springer-Verlag Berlin Heidelberg 2005

(DBN) provides a unified probabilistic framework in integrating multi-modalities by using a graphical representation of the dynamic systems. The proposed tracker has the following characteristics. First, multiple modalities are integrated in the dynamic Bayesian network to evaluate the posterior of each feature. Secondly, a memory-based appearance model is introduced to handle abrupt appearance changes. Finally, our proposed model is extended into overlapped multiple camera environments to deal with occlusions.

The paper is organized as follows. Section 2 discusses dynamic Bayesian network. Section 3 presents our proposed tracking method in single and multi camera environments. Section 4 shows experimental results of our proposed method in face tracking.

## 2   Dynamic Bayesian Network

The Dynamic Bayesian Network (DBN) provides a coherent and unified probabilistic framework to determine a target object state in each frame by integrating modalities such as the prior model of reference state and evidence in target object candidate.

### 2.1   Dynamic Bayesian Network

To construct DBN for visual tracking, we must specify three kinds of information such as the prior distribution over state variables $p(x_0)$, the transition model $p(x_n \mid x_{n-1})$ and the observation model $p(y_n \mid x_n)$. Fig. 1(a) shows an example of DBN for object tracking.

The transition model $p(x_n \mid x_{n-1})$ describes how the state evolves over time. In this paper, we only consider a first-order Markov process. The observation model $p(y_n \mid x_n)$ describes how the evidence variables are affected by the actual state of the object tracking. The target object candidate is evaluated as the posterior probability through the integration of multiple cues in DBN. In other words, the posterior probability of the candidate is evaluated as

$$p(x_n \mid y_n, x_{n-1}) \tag{1}$$

where $x_n$ and $x_{n-1}$ are the target object candidate and reference object state, respectively. $y_n$ is the evidence of low-level features such as color and edge information resulting from the target object candidate.

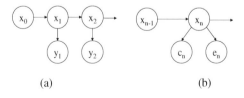

(a)                              (b)

**Fig. 1.** Dynamic Bayesian Network

As target models, color distributions are usually used because they achieve robustness against non-rigidity, rotation and partial occlusion. However, when the background color is similar to the object of interest, the color information only is not good enough to track object robustly. In this case, edge information is also useful to track object effectively. So, multi-modal object tracking is desirable for robust tracking. In our visual tracking, we use two features such as color and edge. This is shown in Fig. 1(b). As evidence variables in our framework, we use color likelihood $p(c_n \mid x_n)$ and edge likelihood $p(e_n \mid x_n)$ where $c_n$ and $e_n$ are the color and edge measurements at time $n$, respectively. The posterior probability like Eq. (1) is interpreted as

$$p(x_n \mid c_n, e_n, x_{n-1}) \propto p(c_n \mid x_n) p(e_n \mid x_n) p(x_n \mid x_{n-1}) \tag{2}$$

Here, we define sample state vector $x$ as

$$x = \{a, b, l_a, l_b, k\} \tag{3}$$

where $a, b$ designate the location of the ellipse, $l_a$, $l_b$ the length of the half axes and $k$ the corresponding scale change. The dynamic model can be represented as

$$x_n = A x_{n-1} + r_{n-1} \tag{4}$$

where $A$ defines the deterministic component of the model and $r_{n-1}$ is a multivariate Gaussian random variables.

The color likelihood $p(c_n \mid x_n)$ is defined as

$$p(c_n \mid x_n) = \left[ \frac{1}{\sqrt{2\pi}\sigma} e^{-\frac{1 - \sum_{u=1}^{m} \sqrt{p_i^{(u)} q^{(u)}}}{2\sigma^2}} \right] \tag{5}$$

where $p_i^{(u)}$ is the $i^{th}$ object candidate's color distribution and $q^{(u)}$ is color distribution of reference object.

We use the edge likelihood as the one proposed by Nishihara [7]. The edge likelihood is computed as

$$p(e_n \mid x_n) = \left( \frac{1}{N_p} \sum_j \left| n(j) \cdot g(j) \right| \right) \tag{6}$$

where $\{n(i)\}_{i=1,\dots,N_p}$ is the unit vector normal to the ellipse (object) at pixel j and $\{g(i)\}_{i=1,\dots,N_p}$ is the intensity gradient at perimeter pixel j of the ellipse, and $N_p$ is the number of pixels on the perimeter of an ellipse.

## 2.2  Appearance Model

To track object effectively, the tracking system should be able to adopt itself to suddenly changing appearances. For example, if there are significant differences between the reference model and the target object candidate in observation, object tracking might not be possible. These differences might occur due to changes in pose, illumination or occlusion between the moment when the reference model was built and the moment when the observation was made. However, people can track objects pretty well based on his memory or experiences regardless of occlusions or sudden appearance changes. So, we generate a model similar to people's short-term memory in order to deal with various appearance models [8].

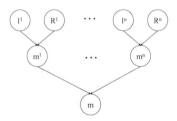

**Fig. 2.** Noisy-OR gate model for memory-based appearance representation

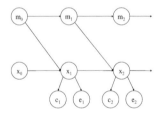

**Fig. 3.** Our Proposed Tracker

The posterior probability for target object candidate is The short-term memory consists of a set of reference object models and provides various reference models in determining target object candidate. To integrate memory function with DBN, we adopt noisy OR-gate model [9]. This is shown in Fig. 2. In this model, the state variable $m$ is determined from the nodes $I$ and $R$. The node $I$ shows causal inhibition and if $I$ is 1, the causality is inhibited. The inhibition of one cause is independent of the inhibition of another cause. The node $R$ represents the reference object model. We also assume accountability that an effect can happen only if at least one of its causes is present and is not being inhibited.

For example, if the reference model $R^i$ is not similar to target object candidate, the inhibition of reference model $I^i$ is on and one of other reference models in short-term memory is compared. The proposed approach is shown in Fig. 3, which integrated memory-based appearance models with DBN.

## 2.3  Approximate Inference in DBN

For approximate inference in DBN, we use particle filtering because it seems to maintain a good approximation to the true posterior using a constant number of samples [3]. In our proposed approach, the particle filtering method is executed as follows:

*Step 1: N samples are created by sampling from the prior distribution at time 0.*
*Step 2: Each sample is propagated forward by sampling from the transition model like* $p(x_n \mid x_{n-1}, m_{n-1})$.

*Step 3: Each sample is weighted by the log likelihood such as* $k_1 p(c_t \mid x_t) +$
$k_2 p(e_t \mid x_t)$ *where* $k_1, k_2$ *are the confidence weight of each likelihood.*

*Step 4: The population is re-sampled to generate a new population of N samples with weighted-sample-with-replacement.*

    evaluated through the integration of multiple cues using Bayesian Network. In other words, the posterior probability of the candidate is evaluated as

$$p(x_n \mid c_n, e_n, x_{n-1}, m_{n-1}) \tag{7}$$

where $x_n$ and $x_{n-1}$ are the target object state and previous object state, respectively. $m_{n-1}$ refers to the a set of reference appearance models in the short-term memory. $c_n$ and $e_n$ are the color and edge measurements, respectively. The posterior probability is interpreted as

$$p(x_n \mid c_n, e_n, x_{n-1}, m_{n-1}) \propto p(c_n \mid x_n) p(e_n \mid x_n) p(x_n \mid x_{n-1}) p(x_n \mid m_{n-1}) \tag{8}$$

# 3  DBN-Based Visual Tracking

In this Section, we will present how to implement our proposed tracking system in single camera and multi-camera environments.

## 3.1  Visual Tracking in Single Camera Environment

Our proposed tracker executes our particle filtering method. In other words, it selects the samples from the sample distribution of the previous frame, and predicts new sample positions in the current frame. After that, it measures the observation weights of the predicted samples. The weights are computed from color and edge likelihoods like Eq.(5) and Eq.(6), respectively. The confidence weights $k_i$ for each feature are learned from training data. The estimated target object state is computed by

$$E(x_n) = \sum_{i=1}^{N} (k_1 p(c_i \mid x_n^i) + k_2 p(e_i \mid x_n^i)) x_n^i \tag{9}$$

To update target model, we compute target update condition as

$$S(E(x_n), q_n) > T \tag{10}$$

where $S(E(x_n),q_n)$ is similarity between the estimated state $E(x_n)$ and target model $q_n$, $T$ is the target update threshold value. If this condition is satisfied, the update of the target model is performed by

$$q_n = (1-\alpha)q_{n-1} + \alpha p_{E(x_n)} \qquad (11)$$

where $\alpha$ weights the contribution of the estimate state histogram $P_{E(x)}$.

## 3.2 Visual Tracking in Multi-camera Environments

In multi-camera environments, each camera has limited overlapping field of views. If one object is detected in one camera, we try to find corresponding object in other cameras using epipolar geometry. We compute epipolar lines between cameras and the corresponding object's position is estimated along the epipolar lines. In the DBN framework, as shown in Fig. 4, we add epipolar variable P to DBN. For example, $p_n^{12}$ represents the epipolar line likelihood between camera 1 and camera 2.

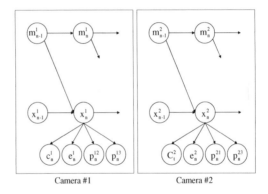

Camera #1                    Camera #2

**Fig. 4.** DBN in multi-camera environments

To track an object effectively in multiple camera environments, we detect the occlusion case in each camera. The occlusion is determined by computing Bhattacharyya coefficient between the target object and the reference object. In the case of occlusion, the Bhattacharyya coefficient is too small and we calculate the intersection points between epipolar lines to locate virtual target object. After that, if desirable target object is found at the estimated location, the tracking process in that camera resumes.

## 4   Experimental Results

Our proposed DBN-based visual tracking algorithm is implemented on a P4-2.4Ghz system with 320*240 image size. We made several experiments in a variety of environments to show the robustness of our proposed method.

In our experiment, we use three cameras (left, center, and right) which have limited overlapping FOVs. For face tracking, we detect a face from camera input using Viola and John's method [10]. For one pair of cameras, we compute epipolar lines. As shown in Fig. 5, the center camera target object is occluded by an unspecified object after a short time. Our proposed method resumes to track the target object well because our method maintains several appearance models using short-term memory. In Fig. 6, the error result of our method is analyzed by comparing the resulting tracks

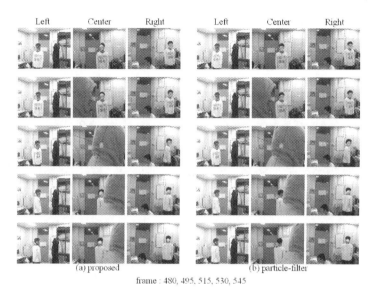

**Fig. 5.** Experimental Result (a)proposed method, (b) general particle filter method

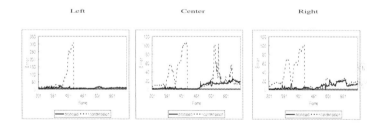

**Fig. 6.** Error result of sequence (solid line-proposed, dotted line-particle filter)

to the ground truth. The solid line shows the error result of our method and the dotted line shows the error result of general particle filter method.

## 5   Conclusions

In this paper, dynamic Bayesian network based visual tracking method is proposed. Dynamic Bayesian network provides a unified probabilistic framework to determine a target object state in each frame by integrating various modalities. For robust tracking, we implement a multi-modal tracking method that integrates color and edge and appearance information in multiple camera environments. We have presented results on realistic scenarios to show the validity of the proposed approach. Compared to other tracking algorithms, our proposed system shows a better and more robust tracking performance.

# References

1. Comaniciu, D. and Meer, P.:Real-Time Tracking of Non-Rigid Objects Using Mean Shift, proc. IEEE Conf. Computer Vision and pattern Recognition, vol 2. (2000) 142-149
2. Isard, M. Blake, A.: CONDENSATION – Conditional Density Propagation for Visual Tracking, International Journal on Computer Vision 1 (29), (1998) 5-28
3. Nummiaro, K., Koller-Meier, E. and Van Gool, L.: A Color-Based Particle Filter, First International Workshop on Generative-Model-Based Vision (2002) 53-60
4. Liu, F., Lin, X., Li, S. and Shi, Y.: Multi-Modal Face Tracking Using Bayesian Network, IEEE Workshop, AMFG 2003, (2003) 135-142
5. Comaniciu, D., Berton, F. and Ramesh V.: Adaptive Resolution System for Distributed Surveillance, Real-Time Imaging, Vol. 8, (2002) 427- 437
6. Kahn, S., Javed, O. and Shah, M.: Tracking in Uncalibrated Cameras with Overlapping Field of View, PETS (2001)
7. Nishihara, H., Thomas, H. and Huber, E.: Real-time tracking of People using stereo and motion, Proc. SPIE, vol. 2183, (1994) 266-273
8. Kang, H. and Cho, S.: Short-term Memory-based Object Tracking, LNCS 3212 , (2004) 597-605
9. Neapolitan, R.: Learning Bayesian Networks, Prentice Hall, (2004)
10. Viola, P., Jones, M.: Rapid Object Detection using a Boosted Cascade of Simple Features, Proc. CVPR '01, (2001)

# Background Modeling Using Color, Disparity, and Motion Information

Jong Weon Lee, Hyo Sung Jeon, Sung Min Moon, and Sung W. Baik

Sejong University, Center for Emotion and Robot Vision,
98 Kunja-dong, Kwangjin-ku,
Seoul 143-747, Korea
jwlee@sejong.ac.kr, cgibin@hanmail.net,
minloveu@hotmail.com, sbaik@sejong.ac.kr

**Abstract.** A new background modeling approach is presented in this paper. In most background modeling approaches, input images are categorized into foreground and background regions using pixel-based operations. Because pixels on the input image are considered individually, parts of foreground regions are frequently turned into the background, and these errors cause incorrect foreground detections. The proposed approach reduces these errors and improves the accuracy of a background modeling. Each input image is categorized into three regions in the proposed approach instead of two regions, background and foreground regions. The proposed approach divides traditional foreground regions into two sub-regions, intermediate background and foreground regions, using activity measurements computed from optical flows at each pixel. The other difference of the proposed approach is grouping pixels into objects and using those objects at the background updating procedure. Pixels on each object are turned into the background at the same rate. The rate of each object is computed differently depending on its category. By controlling the rate of turning input pixels into the background accurately, the proposed approach can model the background accurately.

## 1 Introduction

The background modeling has been an issue in the computer vision area, and the background modeling has been used as the first procedure for various applications such as security surveillance, motion analysis, and object tracking. Ren, Chua, and Ho model a background statistically for non-stationary camera [1]. Jabri, Duric, Wechsler, and Rosenfeld detect humans in video images using color and edge information [2]. Hong and Woo applied two color spaces for background subtraction [3]. The deformable shape model is used to track humans in [4], and color and disparity information is used for background estimation in [5].

Popular information used in the background modeling is color and disparity information [6]. Color and disparity information could be used together in a background modeling system to compensate drawbacks of systems using color or disparity information alone [6],[7]. Systems using only the disparity information have difficulties to detect objects located near the background, but these objects can be easily detected by

J. Blanc-Talon et al. (Eds.): ACIVS 2005, LNCS 3708, pp. 611–617, 2005.
© Springer-Verlag Berlin Heidelberg 2005

systems using the color information unless the objects are covered with the color similar to the background color. For objects camouflaged by the background, the disparity information could be used to detect them from the background as long as objects are not located near the background. Shadows also cause a problem to systems using the color information alone. Shadows of foreground objects are generally detected as foreground objects because the color of shadows frequently differs from the background color. The shadow problem can also be eliminated using the disparity information. The disparity information is also more robust than the color information to illumination changes in environment.

In this paper, we present a new background modeling approach that improves the quality of the background model using color, disparity, and motion information. Using motion information in the proposed approach, foreground regions detected using color and disparity information are further divided into two sub-regions, intermediate background and foreground regions.

The proposed approach divides input images into three regions; background, intermediate background, and foreground regions. Background regions are image areas of static objects in the environment such as floor, wall, and ceiling. Intermediate background regions are images of objects that are entered into the view of the camera and stayed for the given period without any movement. These objects could be cars in a parking lot and furniture at home. Image areas of moving objects are considered as foreground regions. Intermediate background and foreground regions, which are generally considered as the foreground regions by most background modeling approaches, are distinguished by the activities of pixels in the proposed approach. Pixels of foreground regions with little or no activities are considered as intermediate background regions, and other pixels are considered as foreground regions. The optical flow information is used to compute the activity of each pixel in the foreground regions. Pixels on these three regions affect differently. The background updating rates are computed differently for pixels in intermediate background and foreground regions.

The other difference of the proposed approach is grouping pixels into objects and using those objects at the background updating procedure. Pixels on each object are turned into the background at the same rate. The rate of each object is computed differently depending on its category. By applying the same background updating rate for pixels in the same object, the proposed approach improves the accuracy of the background model. The proposed approach prevents parts of the object become the background.

This paper is organized as follows. In section 2, components of the proposed approach are described. The experiments and their results are presented in section 3, and the conclusion is presented in section 4.

## 2   Proposed Approach

The system overview is shown in Figure 1. Two types of inputs, intensity and disparity images, are given to the system to model a background. Optical flows are computed from the intensity image at the first step. At the second step, three backgrounds are constructed from two input images, and foreground regions are segmented from intensity and disparity images. Intensity and disparity backgrounds are modeled using the Gaussian Mixture model. The third background, an optical flow background, is also modeled from the estimated optical flows. Foreground regions (**FGs**) are segmented from intensity and disparity images using intensity and disparity background models.

At the third step, foreground objects are detected. Since the disparity information is more robust to shadows and illumination changes, foreground objects are detected from the disparity foreground regions, and their area and boundary information is stored.

At the last step, the activities of foreground objects are estimated using the object information and the optical background model constructed in the second step. These activity measurements are the main inputs of the background invalidation procedure that categorizes foreground regions (**FGs**) into intermediate background (**IBs**) and foreground regions (**fgs**). Foreground regions (**fgs**) are regions that should not be turned into the background, so the proposed approach prevents them from turning into the background. The output of the background invalidation procedure is a binary mask that distinguishes pixels in **fgs** from pixels in **IBs**. For pixels in **fgs**, the value of the mask is 1, and 0 is given to pixels in **IBs**. The regions with value 1 will not affect the background model at all while pixels with value 0 will modify the background model.

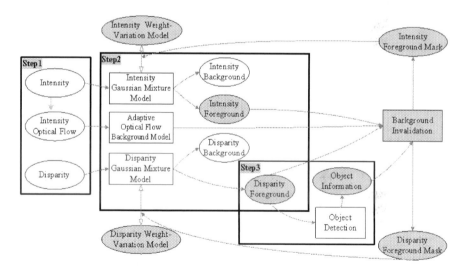

**Fig. 1.** System overview. The first, second and third steps are indicated with the rectangular boxes, and the fourth step is indicated with grey color. Regions with grey color are elements involved in the fourth step.

## 2.1 Intensity and Disparity Background Modeling

Intensity and disparity backgrounds are modeled using the adaptive background mixture models presented in [8]. A mixture of four Gaussian distributions is used to model the recent history of each pixel on intensity and disparity images. When the current pixel value is matched with one of the pixel's Gaussian distribution, the weight of that distribution is increased. If there is no matched Gaussian distribution, the Gaussian distribution with the lowest weight is replaced with a new Gaussian distribution. The mean and the weight of the new Gaussian distribution are the current pixel value and the weight of the replaced Gaussian distribution respectively. The reasons for using the weight of the replaced Gaussian distribution as the weight of the new Gaussian distribution are to keep the order of weights among four Gaussian distributions and to reduce computation time.

The background distribution is the distribution with the highest value of $w/\sigma$, where $w$ is weight and $\sigma$ is a standard deviation. The matching Gaussian distribution is selected by comparing the current pixel value $X_t$ with the mean value $\mu_{i,t}$ and the standard deviation $\sigma_{i,t}$ of the $i$th Gaussian in the mixture at time $t$, Equation 1.

$$\mu_{i,t} - \sigma_{i,t} < X_t < \mu_{i,t} + \sigma_{i,t} \tag{1}$$

## 2.2  Object Detection

In the object detection procedure, foreground pixels are grouped into regions, and their areas and boundaries are computed. Foreground pixels on the disparity image are first grouped into regions through the region growing procedure, which extends a region by connecting neighboring pixels with pixel values close to the pixel value of the considering pixel. After removing small regions, each remaining region is considered as one foreground object, and the area and the boundary of each foreground object are computed. The detected foreground objects are input to the next procedure, the background invalidation, that requires a object-based operation instead of a pixel-based operation. The object-based operation has advantage over the pixel-based operation. For the object-based operation, all pixels in the same object are turning into the background at the same rate, so the object-based operation prevents some pixels in the same object are turned into the background while other pixels in the same object are still remained as the foreground.

## 2.3  Background Invalidation

Ideally only background pixels should affect the background model. However, the background model is affected by foreground pixels with most existing background modeling systems. Harville, Gordon, and Woodfill tried to minimize this undesired behavior applying activity-based learning modulation in [6]. That system produced good results, but the system turned some pixels of foreground objects into the background as shown in the experiment section. This happens occasionally for the following two cases. Some pixels on foreground objects do not move much even though other pixels in the same foreground object have high activities. Then, these pixels are recognized as the pixels that could be turned into the background, and these pixels become the background when it stays stationary for the certain period. For examples, pixels in legs of a standing person could be turned into the background, because legs are not moved much while a person is standing and talking with other person. Similar errors are occurred for pixels moving into regions that have the similar pixel values. When a person wearing a T-shirt with a single color moves little bit while talking with other person, center pixels of the T-shirt are turned into the background. The pixel values at different frames are still fallen into the same Gaussian standard deviation even though the person is not stationary. This problem is caused because most existing background modeling approaches are based on individual pixels and are not based on the entire objects.

To overcome this problem, the background invalidation procedure is developed. In this procedure, the foreground regions (**FGs**) detected using the disparity information are categorized into intermediate background regions (**IBs**) and foreground regions (**fgs**) using object and the activity information. Pixels on **IBs** and **fgs** are affecting the background model differently. The background model is not modified by pixels the **fgs**, but pixels on the **IBs** modify the background model by updating the Gaussian distributions of the background model.

The activity history of each individual pixel is computed from the optical flow background. The activity history stores the history of activities of each individual pixel, and it is constructed by applying the adaptive background mixture models presented in [8] to optical flows of the intensity image. The activity $M$ is computed for each object using the activity history to determine whether that region belongs to the foreground regions (**fgs**) or the intermediate background regions (**IBs**). Objects with larger activity values than the threshold value are considered as **fgs** while other objects are considered as **IBs**. The activity $M$ is computed by Equation 2, which adds square of activity history values, $OF$, on the optical flow background in the object area $b_n$. $b_n(x, y)$ in Equation 2 indicates pixels in the $n$th object boundary at time $t$, and $\alpha$ in Equation 2 represents weighting between new optical flow at time $t$ on $n$th image position, $F_{n,t}$, and the previous activity history value, $OF_{n,t-1}$.

$$M_{n,t} = \sum^{b_n(x,y)} OF_{n,t}^{2}$$

$$OF_{n,t} = \alpha F_{n,t} + (1-\alpha)OF_{n,t-1}$$

(2)

The background invalidation procedure is applied to detected foreground regions, **fgs**. All pixels on **fgs** are masked as invalid, and those pixels are not considered for updating the background models. For pixels on **fgs**, previous Gaussian distributions are not modified at all. This prevents any pixel on foreground objects affecting the background model, so this procedure is considered as the object-based operation instead of the pixel-based operation.

## 3  Experiments

In these experiments, the presented approach is compared with the background modeling approach described in [6] and [8]. One scenario has been applied to both approaches, and their results are shown in Fig. 2.

The scenario of the experiments begins with two students talking about the classes in the lab. One student stands next to the other student who sits on a chair. After few moments, the student sat on the chair stands up to talk with the other student. The ideal background model constructed after the scenario is the background containing the chair and other stationary objects. Any pixels on two students should not affect the background model.

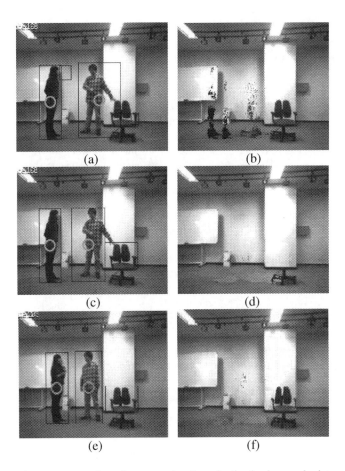

**Fig. 2.** Comparing two approaches, the approach using adaptive background mixture model and the proposed approach. The first row describes the results achieved from the comparing approach at frame 168. The second and third rows describe the results achieved from the proposed approach at frame 168 and 206 respectively. The first column is the captured image with object and activity marks, and the second column is the intensity background model construed using each method. The black rectangles indicate the objects, and the circles indicate the existence of activities.

When the comparing approach is applied to the video capturing the scenario, leg areas and middle areas of student regions are turned into the background incorrectly as shown in Fig. 2(b) even though any areas in student regions should not turn into the background. In contrast to this result, only few pixels in student regions are turned into the background using the proposed approach as shown in Fig. 2(d). At frame 168, only part of the chair became the background, and the entire chair became the background a little later, Fig. 2(f). When the chair is entered into the view, pixels in the chair regions are active and are invalidated in the invalidation procedure. This invalidation delays the chair to be turned into the background in the proposed approach compared with the approach described in [6] and [8]. Currently we are trying to solve this problem, but the solution has not been found yet.

# 4   Conclusion

In this paper, we improve the quality of the background model by categorizing the foreground regions (**FG**s) further into two sub regions, the intermediate background (**IB**s) and foreground regions (**fg**s) in the background invalidation procedure. This improvement is achieved by applying the object-based operation and the optical flow computation, which requires additional time to the system. The proposed approach is currently processing about ten frames per second. We think the required extra time is not serious because the processors are advanced rapidly. We believe that the proposed approach could be used soon for various applications that require real-time foreground detections such as surveillance, robot, and virtual reality.

## Acknowledgement

This paper was performed for the Intelligent Robotics Development Program, one of the 21$^{st}$ Century Frontier R&D Programs funded by the Ministry of Science and Technology of Korea.

## References

1. Y.Ren, C.Chua, and Y.Ho "Statistical background modeling for non-stationary camera," Pattern Recognition Letters, Vol. 24(1-3), 2003, 183-196
2. S.Jabri, Z.Duric, H.Wechsler, and A.Rosenfeld "Detection and Location of People in Video Images Using Adaptive Fusion of color and Edge Information," Proc. ICPR, Vol. 4, 2003, 4627-4631
3. D.Hong, and W.Woo "A Background Subtraction for a vision-based User Interface," Proc. ICICS-PCM 2003
4. L.Davis, "Tracking humans from a moving platform," Proc. ICPR, Vol 4, 2000, 171-178
5. G. Gordon, T. Darrell, M. Harville, J. Woodfill "Background estimation and removal based on range and color," Proc. CVPR, 1999, 459-464
6. M.Harville, G.Gordon, and J. Woodfill "Foreground Segmentation Using Adaptive Mixture Models in Color and Depth," Proc. IEEE Workshop on Detection and Recognition of Events in Video, 2001
7. C.Eveland, K.Konolige, and R.Bolles "Background Modeling for Segmentation of video-Rate Stereo Sequences," Proc. CVPR, 1998
8. C. Stauffer, W.E.L. Grimson. "Adaptive Background Mixture Models for Real-Time Tracking," Proc. CVPR, Vol.2, 1999, 246-252

# Video Denoising Algorithm in Sliding 3D DCT Domain

Dmytro Rusanovskyy and Karen Egiazarian

Institute of Signal Processing,
Tampere University of Technology, Finland
FirstName.LastName@tut.fi

**Abstract.** The problem of denoising of video signals corrupted by additive Gaussian noise is considered in this paper. A novel 3D DCT-based video-denoising algorithm is proposed. Video data are locally filtered in sliding/running 3D windows (arrays) consisting of highly correlated spatial layers taken from consecutive frames of video. Their selection is done by the use of a block matching or similar techniques. Denoising in local windows is performed by a hard thresholding of 3D DCT coefficients of each 3D array. Final estimates of reconstructed pixels are obtained by a weighted average of the local estimates from all overlapping windows. Experimental results show that the proposed algorithm provides a competitive performance with state-of-the-art video denoising methods both in terms of PSNR and visual quality.

## 1 Introduction

Digital images and video nowadays are essential part of everyday life. Often imperfect instruments of data acquisition process, natural phenomena, transmission errors and compression can degrade a quality of collected data. Presence of noise may sufficiently affect the further data processing such as analysis, segmentation, classification and indexing. Denoising is typically applied before any aforementioned image/video data processing. Herein, the problem of denoising of video corrupted by additive independent white Gaussian noise is considered.

Historically, first algorithms for video denoising operated in spatial or spatio-temporal domains [1]. Recent research on denoising has demonstrated a trend towards transform-based processing techniques. Processing in a transform domain (e.g. in DCT, DFT or wavelet domains) provides a superior performance comparing to the spatio-temporal methods due to a good decorrelation and compaction properties of transforms.

Wavelet-based video denoising was inspired by the results of the intensive work on the wavelet-based image denoising [3-5] initiated by Donoho's *wavelet shrinkage* approach [2]. Several multiresolution (*wavelet-based*) approaches were recently proposed to the problem of video denoising, see, e.g. [6] and [7].

Local adaptive *sliding window DCT* (SWDCT) image denoising method [8], [9] is a strong alternative to the wavelet-based methods. This paper gives an extension of it to SWDCT denoising of video. This extension is not a straightforward one. Video data in the temporal direction are not stationary due to a motion present in videos. Thus, two pixels located at the same spatial location of consecutive frames could be

J. Blanc-Talon et al. (Eds.): ACIVS 2005, LNCS 3708, pp. 618–625, 2005.
© Springer-Verlag Berlin Heidelberg 2005

uncorrelated. On the other hand, DCT is a good approximation of the statistically optimal Karhunen-Loeve transform in the case of highly correlated data [10]. Thus, a wise selection of local 3D data through the different frames should be performed before any application of a 3D DCT. One approach to this is to use a block matching technique to correlate 2D image blocks in sequential frames via minimization of some cost function (MSE or MAE). Full search or any of fast block matching schemes could be utilized here.

This paper is organized as following. In Section 2, the SWDCT image denoising approach is briefly described. A 3D-SWDCT video denoising algorithm is proposed in Section 3. In Section 4, denoising performance of the proposed algorithm is analyzed in comparison with the recent wavelet-based video denoising algorithms [6], [7], [13]. Conclusions are given in Section 5.

## 2  Sliding Window DCT Denoising of Images

Sliding window DCT denoising approach is well developed tool for image denoising, (see, e.g. [8] and [9]). In this section we will briefly describe its basic principles. SWDCT denoising scheme is graphically depicted in **Fig. 1**.

Suppose, we wish to recover unknown image $x(t)$ from noisy observations $y(t) = x(t) + n(t)$, where $t = (t_1, t_2)$ are coordinates in 2D space, $n(t)$ is an additive Gaussian noise $N(0, \sigma^2)$ with variance $\sigma^2$.

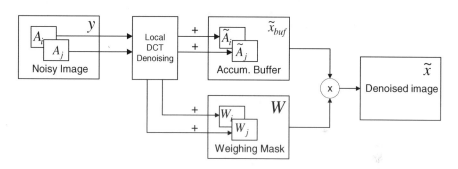

**Fig. 1.** A general SW-DCT image denoising scheme [9]

Noisy image $y(t)$ is locally processed in the overlapped blocks (windows) $\{A_i\}$. Running over the image each $A_i$ is separately filtered in the DCT domain (computing 2D DCT of $\{A_i\}$, thresholding obtained coefficients and applying an inverse 2D DCT to the result) to obtain a local estimate $\tilde{A}_i$. For every $\tilde{A}_i$ its "relevance" is reflected by a weight $W_i$ evaluated from the local DCT spectrum properties (selected to be a reciprocal of the number of remaining (nonzero) after a threshold DCT coefficients in the block). These estimates $\tilde{A}_i$ and weights $W_i$ are further accumulated in the buffer $\tilde{x}_{buf}$ and in the weighting mask $W$, respectively. Finally, every denoised image pixel

$\tilde{x}(t)$ is obtained by a weighted average of denoised local estimates of the same pixel from all overlapped estimates $\tilde{A}_i$.

The SWDCT denoising algorithm can be expressed by equations (1)-(4)

$$Y(w) = F\{A_i\},\tag{1}$$

$$\hat{X}(w) = T\{Y(w)\},\tag{2}$$

$$\tilde{A}_i = F^{-1}\{\hat{X}(w)\},\tag{3}$$

$$\tilde{x}(t) = W(t)\tilde{x}_{buf}.\tag{4}$$

where $F\{\ \}$ is a separable 2D forward DCT and $F^{-1}\{\ \}$ is its inverse, $w = (w_1, w_2)$ are coordinates of 2D DCT coefficients and $T\{\ \}$ is a hard thresholding function

$$\hat{X}(w) = \begin{cases} Y(w), & |Y(w)| \geq Thr \\ 0, & \text{else} \end{cases}.\tag{5}$$

The SW-DCT denoising assumes several tunable parameters, such as the local window size and sliding steps along the image directions. They can be user-specified [9] either adaptive to a local signal statistic [12] in order to achieve a better performance/complexity tradeoff.

## 3   Video Denoising Based on a 3D DCT

The SW-DCT denoising method is well developed for images. In the case of video, SW-DCT should be performed in the 3D space, and the use of a temporal redundancy of video can improve the filtering performance. Let us assume that SW-DCT operates in the spatial domain of each video frame as it is described above. In the temporal direction 1D sliding DCT can be similarly applied along the temporal axis. On the other hand, SW-DCT performance can be significantly improved, if the transform will operate over a highly correlated signal. However, pixels along the temporal axis may be uncorrelated due to dynamical nature of a video signal.

Due to this, we propose to perform a local 3D DCT denoising on an array $B_i$ (of size $L_h \times L_w \times L_t$) that is built from correlated 2D blocks $A_{i,k}$ (k – is an index of the current frame) taken from the $L_t$ consecutive frames. These $A_{i,k}$ blocks are selected using a block matching or similar technique [11]. Here, the full search or a fast block matching scheme via minimization of some cost function (MSE or MAD) can be employed.

A general scheme of the proposed algorithm for video processing is depicted in **Fig. 2.** A noisy sequence $y$ is processed locally in the 3D windows of size

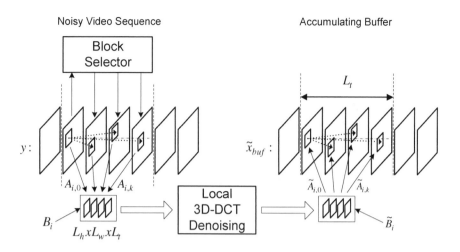

**Fig. 2.** A general block-diagram of proposed video denoising algorithm

$L_h \times L_w \times L_t$. An accumulating buffer $\tilde{x}_{buf}$ keeps $L_t$ consecutive frames. *Block selector* uses a sliding window $A_{j,0}$ in the $0^{th}$ frame of the buffer as a reference and searches in every sequential frame for the best match $\{A_{i,1}, ..., A_{i,k}; k = L_t - 1\}$ in terms of their correlation to $A_{i,0}$. These 2D blocks $A_{i,0}$ and $\{A_{i,1}, ..., A_{i,k} : k = L_t - 1\}$, are filled to the buffer $B_i$. Note here that it may appear that a block selector will fail to find, in some frame, a subblock $A_{i,k}$ that correlates with $A_{i,0}$. This could appear either due to a dynamic nature of a video or due to a global scene change. In order to prevent an error propagation further, block selection for the current $A_{i,0}$ should be terminated. In such a case a local 3DDCT denoising should be performed on a shorter in the temporal direction array $B_i$, in other words we implement an adaptive window size selection in the temporal domain. As a result, we have produced a 3D array $B_i$ filled with $L_t$ highly correlated 2D blocks $\{A_{i,0}, ..., A_{i,k}; k = L_t - 1\}$ which is now a subject of denoising. We retrieve a locally denoised estimate of $\tilde{B}_i$ as a result of hard-thresholding of the 3D-DCT coefficients of $B_i$ and accumulate it in the buffer $\tilde{x}_{buf}$. Amount of the retrieved estimates for a particular $\tilde{x}_{buf}(t)$ and statistical properties of the local DCT spectra define $W(t)$, as it was specified in Section 2.

After the current $L_t$ frames are processed, the sliding window shifts in the temporal direction and a new $L_{t+1}$ frame becomes to be involved in the denoising procedure. Described operations (namely, block matching, local denoising of $B_i$, accumulation of $\tilde{B}_i$ in $\tilde{x}_{buf}$) are recursively performed on a group of frames until the last frame of the sequence is processed. Finally, every pixel $\tilde{x}(t)$ is reconstructed from a coordinate-wise weighting of $\tilde{x}_{buf}(t)$ with a mask $W(t)$.

The computational complexity of the proposed algorithm is mostly depends on the computation of the 3D DCTs and a block matching procedure performed for every spatial block. If we assume that sizes of a local 3D DCT are $L$ in all directions, and the sliding parameters for both spatial coordinates are $P$, then the number of arithmetic operations per output sample for the transform part of the algorithm is

equal to $2 \cdot \mu \cdot \left( \dfrac{2L}{P^2} + 1 \right)$, where $\mu$ is a complexity of the 1D DCT. If $L = 8$ and

$P = 4$, this number is $4 \cdot \mu$. Few operations per output sample should be added to this in the case of application of a fast block matching procedure.

## 4   Experimental Results

To evaluate the performance of the proposed method, several standard test CIF and QCIF video sequences were used, see Tables 1 and 2. Original sequences were corrupted by an additive Gaussian noise with a standard deviations equal to 10, 15 and 20, and then processed with the denoising algorithm proposed in Section 3.

In our simulations we chose processing buffer $B_i$ to be of size of 8x8x8 due to existed and well developed software and hardware solutions for 8-point DCT [10]. Buffer $B_i$ was chosen to be sliding over a video data with the steps equal to 2 in both spatial directions and 1 in the temporal direction. The hard thresholding procedure was applied to all 3D-DCT coefficients of the buffer $B_i$ to get a locally denoised estimate $\tilde{B}_i$. Threshold value *Thr* in the Equation 5 was chosen to be equal to $2\sigma$ [8]. To select highly correlated $A_{i,k}$ blocks from 7 consecutive frames, we have used a fast block matching algorithm in the pixel domain (so called "logarithmic search" [11]) with a minimal absolute error (MAD) as a cost function. To prevent error propagation, an adaptive window size selection in temporal domain was performed. The block selection procedure was terminated for a particular $A_{i,0}$ if a correlated $A_{i,k}$ can not be found in the current frame. This improves a filtering performance especially in the presence of high motion or scene change. Furthermore, a selection algorithm that operates in the pixel domain and is based on MAD or MSE criteria may provide $A_{i,k}$ correlated rather with a noise pattern of the reference $A_{i,0}$ than with the original video signal. This could become a problem in video fragments with a very low signal to noise ratios, for example, dark flat regions corrupted with heavy noise. To suppress such false motion prediction we rejected (set to zero) motion vectors if MAD of a prediction is lower than a predefined threshold within the distance of $3\sigma$. In **Table 1,** a performance of our algorithm is compared with the results of wavelet-based denoising schemes of [6] and [7]. The average PSNR values presented in **Table 1** are computed over 40 ("Salesman") and 52 ("Tennis" and "Flower Garden") frames. The first four frames of processed sequences are excluded from PSNR calculation due to the recursive nature of the WRSTF algorithm [7] in order to make the comparison more objective.

**Table 1.** Video denoising, comparative results

| Video | Noise, $\sigma$ | Average PSNR, dBs | | | |
|---|---|---|---|---|---|
| | | Noisy | Soft3D [6] | WRSTF [7] | 3D SWDCT |
| "Tennis" | 10 | 28.16 | 31.86 | 32.41 | **33.34** |
| | 15 | 24.63 | 29.86 | 30.12 | **30.80** |
| | 20 | 22.15 | 28.58 | 28.68 | **29.52** |
| "Salesman" | 10 | 28.15 | 34.85 | 35.82 | **37.01** |
| | 15 | 24.72 | 33.29 | 33.91 | **34.83** |
| | 20 | 22.35 | 32.00 | 32.40 | **33.29** |
| "Flower" | 10 | 28.34 | 30.23 | 30.80 | **31.25** |
| | 15 | 24.88 | 27.71 | 28.19 | **28.62** |
| | 20 | 22.44 | 26.01 | 26.39 | **26.80** |

To compare performance of the proposed algorithm with the results reported in [13], we have applied our algorithm to "Miss America" and "Hall" video sequences corrupted with additive Gaussian noise (average PSNR of noisy video are 20 dBs). Results are shown in **Table 2**. Analysis of **Tables 1** and **2** demonstrates that our algorithm outperforms those from [6], [7] and [13]. **Fig 3.** and **4** give some examples of denoised frames to subjective judgment of visual quality of denoised video sequences.

(a)                                    (b)

**Fig. 3.** A fragment of the $30^{th}$ frame of the "Salesman" video sequence. (a) Noisy (PSNR of fragment 22.29 dBs). (b) Denoised with the proposed algorithm (PSNR of fragment 33.06 dBs).

(a)                                         (b)

**Fig. 4.** A fragment of the 30th frame of the "Flower" video sequence. (a) Noisy (PSNR of fragment 22.41dBs). (b) Denoised with the proposed algorithm (PSNR of fragment 26.39 dBs).

**Table 2.** Video denoising, comparative results

| Video | Average PSNR, dBs | | |
|---|---|---|---|
| | Noisy | Proposed in [13] | 3D SWDCT |
| "Miss America" | 20 | 34.1 | **34.9** |
| "Hall" | 20 | 29.1 | **31.8** |

Detailed information on the developed algorithm and video sequences processed by 3D-SWDCT are available from: http://www.cs.tut.fi/~rusanovs/.

## 5   Conclusions

A problem of denoising of video signals corrupted by an additive Gaussian noise is considered in this paper. A novel 3D DCT based video denoising algorithm is proposed. High filtering performance of the local 3D DCT based thresholding is achieved by a proper selection of video volume data to be locally denoised. A 3D DCT thresholding is performed on a group of highly correlated sliding in spatial directions 2D windows that are selected from the set of sequential frames. Weighted average of overlapped denoised estimates provides a final denoised video. We have tested the proposed algorithm on a group of standard video test sequences corrupted by an additive Gaussian noise with a variety of standard deviations. Results have demonstrated that the proposed algorithm provides competitive results with wavelet-based video denoising methods both in terms of PSNR and subjectively quality.

# Acknowledgements

This work has been financially supported by the Academy of Finland, Finnish Center of Excellence Programme 2000-2005, project no. 5202853, as well as EU project NoE FP6-PLT 511568-3DTV.

The authors would like to thank V. Zlokolica and I. Selesnick for providing processed video sequences resulting from applications of their denoising algorithms (presented in Table 1).

# References

1. J.C. Brailean, R.P. Kleihorst, S.Efstratiadis, A.K.Katsaggelos, R.L.Lagendijk, "Noise Reduction Filters for Dynamic Image Sequences: A Review", IEEE Proc, Vol. 83, no. 9, Sep, 1995
2. D.L.Donoho, "De-noising by soft-thresholding", *IEEE Trans. on Information Theory*, vol.41, no.3, pp.613-627, May 1995
3. L.Sendur, I.W.Selesnick, "Bivariage Shrinkage Functions for Wavelet-Based Denoising Exploiting Interscale Dependency", *IEEE Trans. on Signal Proc.*, vol. 50, n. 11, pp. 2745-2756, November 2002
4. R.Coifman,D.Donoho, "Translation Invariant de-noising", in Lecture Notes in Statistics: Wavelets and Statistics, vol. New York: Springer-Verlag, pp.125-150, 1995
5. N.Kingsbury, "Complex Wavelets and Shift Invariance", available by the URL: http://ece-www.colorado.edu/~fmeyer/Classes/ECE-5022/Projects/kingsbury1.pdf
6. W.I. Selesnick and K.Y. Li, "Video denoising using 2d and 3d dualtree complex wavelet transforms", in *Wavelet Applications in Signal and Image Processing (Proc. SPIE 5207), San Diego*, Aug. 2003.
7. V. Zlokolica, A. Pizurica, W. Philips "Wavelet Domain Noise-Robust Motion Estimation and Noise Estimation for Video Denoising " *First International Workshop on Video Processing and Quality Metrics for Consumer Electronics*, Scotssdale, Arizona, 23-25 January, 2005, USA
8. L. Yaroslavsky and K. Egiazarian and J.Astola, "Transform domain image restoration methods: review, comparison and interpretation", *TICSP Series #9*, TUT, Tampere, Finland, December 2000, ISBN 952-15-0471-4.
9. R. Öktem, L. Yaroslavsky and K. Egiazarian, "Signal and Image Denoising in Transform Domain and Wavelet Shrinkage: A Comparative Study", *in Proc. of EUSIPCO'98*, Sept. 1998, Rhodes, Greece.
10. K. Rao, P.Yip, *Discrete Cosine Transform: Algorithm, Advantages, Applications*, Academic Press, 1990.
11. R. J. Clarke, *Digital Compression of Still Images and Video*, Academic Press, 1995.
12. K. Egiazarian, V. Katkovnik, H. Öktem and J. Astola, "Transform-based denoising with window size adaptive to unknown smoothness of the signal", *In Proc. of First International Workshop on Spectral Techniques and Logic Design for Future Digital Systems (SPECLOG)*, June 2000, Tampere, Finland, pp. 409-430.
13. N. Gupta, E. Plotkin, M. Swamy, "Bayesian Algorithm for Video Noise Reduction in the Wavelet Domain", IEEE International Symposium on Circuits and Systems, ISCAS 2005, May 23-26, Kobe, Japan

# A Novel Histogram Based Fuzzy Impulse Noise Restoration Method for Colour Images

Stefan Schulte, Valérie De Witte, Mike Nachtegael, Dietrich Van der Weken, and Etienne E. Kerre

Ghent University, Department of Applied Mathematics and Computer Science, Krijgslaan 281 (Building S9), 9000 Gent, Belgium
Stefan.Schulte@UGent.be
http://fuzzy.ugent.be/

**Abstract.** In this paper, we present a new restoration technique for colour images. This technique is developed for restoring colour images that are corrupted with impulse noise. The estimated histograms for the colour component differences (red-green, red-blue and green-blue) are used to construct fuzzy sets. Those fuzzy sets are then incorporated in a fuzzy rule based system in order to filter out the impulse noise. Experiments finally show the shortcomings of the conventional methods in contrast to the proposed method.

## 1   Introduction

Reduction of noise in digital images is one of the most basic image processing operations. Recently a lot of fuzzy based methods have shown to provide efficient image filtering. Three of the most common noise types in the literature are additive, multiplicative and impulse noise. Impulse noise is usually characterized by some portion of image pixels that is corrupted, leaving the remaining pixels unchanged. Additive noise occurs when to each image pixel a value from a certain distribution is added, e.g. Gaussian distributed values. Multiplicative noise is generally more difficult to remove from images than additive noise, because the intensity of the noise varies with the signal intensity (e.g. Speckle noise).

The proposed method is developed to deal with impulse noise in digital colour images. For the modulation of impulse noise we refer to [1,2]. Conventional techniques, e.g. processing each component independently, do not take into account the correlation between the colour components causing some unwanted behaviour (artefacts). In this paper we describe a new method where we first estimate the original colour differences at a certain position. Afterwards we use these differences to filter out the impulse noise without destroying the dependencies between the colour components (i.e. the colour differences).

A lot of colour models exist to represent a digital colour image (denoted by $O$). We will use the well known RGB model. Colours in this model are represented by a three-dimensional vector, where each component is quantified to the range $[0, 2^m - 1]$ (mostly with $m = 8$). Therefore a digital colour image $O$ is usually represented by a two-dimensional array of vectors where an address $(i, j)$ defines a position in $O$, called a pixel or picture element.

J. Blanc-Talon et al. (Eds.): ACIVS 2005, LNCS 3708, pp. 626–633, 2005.
© Springer-Verlag Berlin Heidelberg 2005

## 2    Histogram Estimation

For each colour pigment we calculate the histogram of intensity values coming from the most likely corrupted impulse noise pixel pigments. This is realized by dividing the corrupted image (denoted by $A$) into several subimages of smaller size $x \times x$ (with $x = 3$ in this paper). Moreover, only the maximal and minimal intensity values of each subimage are stored into the histogram. The idea behind this is that impulse noise in a local window is usually identified by the minimal and maximal intensity values, because corrupted pixels are generally extremes compared with the other intensity values. Next, we use those histograms (denoted by $HIST^R$, $HIST^G$ and $HIST^B$ for the red, green and blue pigments respectively) to construct the fuzzy set $NOISE$. In fuzzy logic we represent such a fuzzy set by a proper membership function $\mu_{NOISE}$. A membership degree of one (zero) for a certain intensity value indicates that this intensity value will be considered as noisy (noise free) for sure. All the degrees between these two extremes indicate that there is some kind of uncertainty. For more background information about fuzzy logic we refer to [3]. The calculation of the membership degree for a certain intensity value $IV$ in the fuzzy set $NOISE$ is shown in Fig. 1. The horizontal axis in Fig. 1 indicates for a certain intensity value $IV$ the amount of stored pixels with this intensity value in the histogram. The vertical axis returns the corresponding membership degree in the fuzzy set $NOISE$. The parameters $a$ and $b$ are set to $a = \dfrac{\sum_{k=0}^{2^m-1} HIST(k)}{2^m - 1}$ and $b = 2 * a$, in order to incorporate the global histogram information for all the other intensity values.

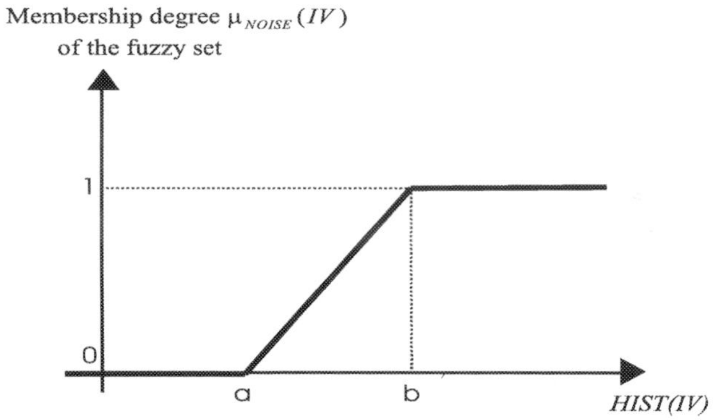

**Fig. 1.** The calculation of the membership degree $\mu_{NOISE}(IV)$ of the fuzzy set $NOISE$ for a certain intensity value IV

## 3    Filtering Method

Our new filtering method first calculates the differences between the colour pigments in an region around a central pixel. Next, we use this information to filter out the impulse noise.

## 3.1   Colour Component Differences Estimation

In contrast to many conventional techniques we use colour component differences. Therefore we introduce the following matrices:

$$M^{RG}(i,j) = A(i,j,1) - A(i,j,2)$$
$$M^{RB}(i,j) = A(i,j,1) - A(i,j,3)$$
$$M^{GB}(i,j) = A(i,j,2) - A(i,j,3)$$

(1)

where $A(i,j,1)$, $A(i,j,2)$, $A(i,j,3)$ are the red, green and blue component at position $(i,j)$ of the noisy input image $A$. Next, we transfer these matrices from the range $[-(2^m - 1), (2^m - 1)]$ to the range $[0,1]$. Afterwards we take into account three fuzzy sets, namely $SMALL$, $MEDIUM$ and $LARGE$, so that each matrix value can be mapped to a fuzzy variable with membership degrees in these three fuzzy sets. Windows of size $3 \times 3$ are used (in this paper) to scan across the normalized matrices of Expression 1. The elements of such a window used to scan for example across the normalized matrix $M^{RB}$ centred at $(i,j)$, are denoted as follows: $rb_1 = M^{RB}(i-1,j-1)$, $rb_2 = M^{RB}(i-1,j)$, $rb_3 = M^{RB}(i-1,j+1)$, $rb_4 = M^{RB}(i,j-1)$, $rb_5 = M^{RB}(i,j)$, $rb_6 = M^{RB}(i,j+1)$, $rb_7 = M^{RB}(i+1,j-1)$, $rb_8 = M^{RB}(i+1,j)$ and $rb_9 = M^{RB}(i+1,j+1)$. For each element of such a window three membership degrees in the corresponding fuzzy sets $SMALL$, $MEDIUM$ and $LARGE$ are calculated. This is realized by the membership functions: $\mu_{SMALL}$ shown in (2), $\mu_{MEDIUM}$ shown in (3) and $\mu_{LARGE}$ shown in (4).

$$\mu_{SMALL}(rb_k) = \begin{cases} 1 & \text{if } rb_k \le c_1 \\ \dfrac{1}{1 + \left(\dfrac{rb_k - c_1}{a_1}\right)^{2b_1}} & \text{if } rb_k > c_1 \end{cases} \quad k = 1,2,...,9 \quad (2)$$

$$\mu_{MEDIUM}(rb_k) = \dfrac{1}{1 + \left(\dfrac{rb_k - c_2}{a_2}\right)^{2b_2}} \quad k = 1,2,...,9 \quad (3)$$

$$\mu_{LARGE}(rb_k) = \begin{cases} \dfrac{1}{1 + \left(\dfrac{rb_k - c_3}{a_3}\right)^{2b_3}} & \text{if } rb_k \le c_3 \\ 1 & \text{if } rb_k > c_3 \end{cases} \quad (4)$$

$$k = 1,2,...,9$$

For the calculation of the parameters $a_k$, $b_k$ and $c_k$ (for $k = \{1,2,3\}$) we refer to [4].

Besides the three fuzzy sets above we also take into account a fourth fuzzy set that can be derived by the Fuzzy Rule 1. A pixel at position $(i,j)$ with membership degree 1 in this fuzzy set has a noise-free colour difference between the red and blue component. There also exist similar fuzzy sets for the red-green and the green-blue differences at position $(i,j)$.

**Fuzzy Rule 1.** *Defining the membership degrees in the fuzzy set $NOT\ NOISE$ for the red-blue difference at position (i,j):*

IF $\Big(A(i,j,1)\ is\ NOT\ NOISE\Big)$ AND $\Big(A(i,j,3)\ is\ NOT\ NOISE\Big)$

THEN $A(i,j,1) - A(i,j,3)\ is\ NOT\ NOISE$

In fuzzy logic we use involutive negators to represent negations. Here we use the standard negator ($NOT\ x = 1 - x$, where $x \in [0,1]$). For conjunctions and disjunctions we use triangular norms (roughly the equivalent of AND operations) and triangular co-norms (roughly the equivalent of OR operations), respectively. Two well known triangular norms (together with their dual co-norms) are the product (probabilistic sum) and the minimum (maximum). Here we will use the minimum and maximum. So the rule $\Big(A(i,j,1)\ is\ NOT\ NOISE\ \Big)$ AND $\Big(A(i,j,3)\ is\ NOT\ NOISE\ \Big)$ can be translated into:

$minimum\Big(\Big(1- \mu_{NOISE}(A(i,j,1))\Big), \Big(1- \mu_{NOISE}(A(i,j,3))\Big)\Big)$, which can be used to express the membership degree in the fuzzy set $NOT\ NOISE$ for the difference $(A(i,j,1) - A(i,j,3))$. This will be denoted by $\mu_{notNOISE}(A(i,j,1) - A(i,j,3))$.

Now we combine the previous three fuzzy sets $SMALL$, $MEDIUM$ and $LARGE$ with the fuzzy set $NOT\ NOISE$ to calculate three weights for each element of the window. This is realized by fuzzy rules. One example of such a rule is given by Fuzzy Rule 2 were the fuzzy weights $w_{rbk}^{SMALL}$ for the differences between red and blue pigments are calculated for the case $SMALL$. So finally we calculate three such weights for each element of the window: $w_{rbk}^{SMALL}$, $w_{rbk}^{MEDIUM}$ and $w_{rbk}^{LARGE}$.

**Fuzzy Rule 2.** *Defining the fuzzy weights for the fuzzy set SMALL:*

IF $\Big(rb_k\ is\ NOT\ NOISE\Big)$ AND $\Big(rb_k\ is\ SMALL\Big)$

THEN $w_{rbk}^{SMALL}\ is\ LARGE$

Once we have calculated the corresponding weights, we calculate three possible estimations for the difference red-blue at a certain position $(i,j)$. These three estimations are denoted as $\Delta_{SMALL}^{rbk}$, $\Delta_{MEDIUM}^{rbk}$ and $\Delta_{LARGE}^{rbk}$. They are calculated by the following fuzzy averaging:

$$\Delta_{SMALL}^{rbk} = \frac{\sum_{k=1}^{9} rb_k\ w_{rbk}^{SMALL}}{\sum_{k=1}^{9} w_{rbk}^{SMALL}}\ ;\ \Delta_{MEDIUM}^{rbk} = \frac{\sum_{k=1}^{9} rb_k\ w_{rbk}^{MEDIUM}}{\sum_{k=1}^{9} w_{rbk}^{MEDIUM}}\quad (5)$$

$$\Delta_{LARGE}^{rbk} = \frac{\sum_{k=1}^{9} rb_k\ w_{rbk}^{LARGE}}{\sum_{k=1}^{9} w_{rbk}^{LARGE}}$$

The final difference $\Delta^{rb}(i,j)$ between the red and blue pigment for a region around $(i,j)$ is one of the three estimations of Eq. 5, which is closest to some reference difference (denoted by $ref_{Delta}^{rb}(i,j)$). We used the following reference difference between the red and blue pigment for a position $(i,j)$:

$$ref^{rb}_{Delta}(i,j) = \frac{\sum_{k=1}^{9} rb_k \, \mu_{notNOISE}(rb_k)}{\sum_{k=1}^{9} \mu_{notNOISE}(rb_k)} \tag{6}$$

In the case where $\sum_{k=1}^{9} \mu_{notNOISE}(rb_k)$ is equal to zero the reference difference becomes the median of all $3 \times 3$ differences $rb_k$. After this step we have calculated three output differences $\Delta^{rg}(i,j)$, $\Delta^{rb}(i,j)$ and $\Delta^{gb}(i,j)$ for respectively the red-green, red-blue and green-blue differences at position (i,j). These output values are then transferred back to the interval $[-(2^m - 1), (2^m - 1)]$.

### 3.2   Noise Reduction

In this subsection we only explain the filtering step for the red component. The green and blue components are filtered analogously. We filter for example the red component of a noisy input image $A(i,j,1)$ at position $(i,j)$ if and only if $\mu_{NOISE}\big(A(i,j,1)\big)$ is greater than zero, because otherwise we know that this intensity value is noise free for sure. When we filter the red component at position $(i,j)$, then the final output becomes:

1. When $\mu_{NOISE}\big(A(i,j,2)\big)$ and $\mu_{NOISE}\big(A(i,j,3)\big)$ are both equal to 1, then the output $F(i,j,1)$ for the red component at position $(i,j)$ is equal to:

$$F(i,j,1) = \frac{\sum_{k=-1}^{+1} \sum_{l=-1}^{+1} (1 - \mu_{NOISE}(A(i+k,j+l,1))) \cdot A(i+k,j+l,1)}{\sum_{k=-1}^{+1} \sum_{l=-1}^{+1} (1 - \mu_{NOISE}(A(i+k,j+l,1)))}$$

2. When $\mu_{NOISE}\big(A(i,j,2)\big)$ is equal to 1 and $\mu_{NOISE}\big(A(i,j,3)\big) < 1$ then the output $F(i,j,1)$ for the red component at position $(i,j)$ is equal to: $F(i,j,1) = max(min((A(i,j,3) + \Delta^{rb}(i,j), 255), 0)$
3. When $\mu_{NOISE}\big(A(i,j,2)\big) < 1$ and $\mu_{NOISE}\big(A(i,j,3)\big)$ is equal to 1 then the output $F(i,j,1)$ for the red component at position $(i,j)$ is equal to: $F(i,j,1) = max(min(A(i,j,2) + \Delta^{rg}(i,j), 255), 0)$
4. Otherwise the output $F(i,j,1)$ for the red component at position $(i,j)$ becomes equal to: $F(i,j,1) = \frac{1}{2}\Big(A(i,j,2) + \Delta^{rg}(i,j)\Big) + \frac{1}{2}\Big(A(i,j,3) + \Delta^{rb}(i,j)\Big)$.

## 4   Experimental Results

In this section we will present some experimental results. We compared our method (entitled as Histogram based Fuzzy Reduction Method for Colour images (HFRMC)) with other well known fuzzy filters: DSFIRE [5] (dual step fuzzy inference rule by else-action), PWLFIRE [6] (piecewise linear FIRE), AWFM [7] (adaptive weighted fuzzy mean), HAF [4] (histogram adaptive fuzzy), FMF [8] (fuzzy median filter), IFCF [9] (iterative fuzzy control based filter), FSB [10] (fuzzy similarity filter), FIDRM [1,2] (fuzzy impulse noise detection and reduction method), FVRF [11] (fuzzy vector rank filter) and FCCF [12] (fuzzy

**Table 1.** PSNR results for the $(512 \times 512\text{-})$ *Lena* image for different impulse noise (salt and pepper) levels (5%, 10%, 20%, 30%, 40%) and different filters

| | PSNR (dB) | | | | | | PSNR (dB) | | | | |
|---|---|---|---|---|---|---|---|---|---|---|---|
| | 5% | 10% | 20% | 30% | 40% | | 5% | 10% | 20% | 30% | 40% |
| *Noise* | *18.3* | *15.2* | *12.2* | *10.5* | *9.2* | *Noise* | *18.3* | *15.2* | *12.2* | *10.5* | *9.2* |
| CSAM | 37.8 | 35.1 | 31.7 | 24.0 | 19.9 | TSM $(3 \times 3)$ | 36.8 | 33.2 | 28.1 | 23.1 | 18.5 |
| LUM | 33.1 | 31.1 | 28.2 | 23.2 | 18.5 | FSB | 34.5 | 33.4 | 29.3 | 23.5 | 18.9 |
| FVRF | 28.7 | 25.4 | 21.6 | 18.9 | 17.0 | FCCF | 31.7 | 30.4 | 27.0 | 22.0 | 18.1 |
| AWFM | 32.0 | 31.7 | 31.4 | 30.7 | 29.8 | IFCF | 34.0 | 32.6 | 29.4 | 25.7 | 22.1 |
| DSFIRE | 40.2 | 37.9 | 32.7 | 26.8 | 21.7 | PWLFIRE | 39.4 | 31.2 | 23.0 | 18.2 | 15.8 |
| FMF | 40.2 | 36.7 | 30.5 | 26.7 | 20.3 | HAF | 34.2 | 33.8 | 33.2 | 32.2 | 30.7 |
| HFRMC | *55.6* | *52.0* | *47.4* | *43.9* | *43.9* | FIDRM | 45.1 | 42.6 | 39.6 | 37.5 | 35.7 |

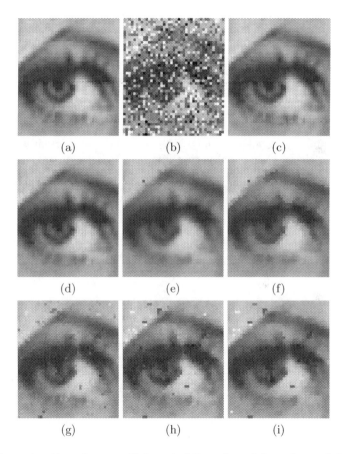

(a)    (b)    (c)

(d)    (e)    (f)

(g)    (h)    (i)

**Fig. 2.** The restoration of a magnified part of the coloured *Lena* image (a) corrupted with 30% salt and pepper noise (b). The applied methods are: (c) the proposed filter, (d) component based FIDRM, (e) component based HAF, (f) component based AWFM, (g) component based LUM (h), component based DSFIRE, (i) component based FMF.

credibility colour filter). Besides these fuzzy filters, we also used the CSAM [13] (conditional signal-adaptive median), TSM [14] (tri-state median filter) and the LUM [15] (lower-upper-middle filter) as non fuzzy filters.

As a measure of objective dissimilarity between a filtered image and the original one we use the peak signal to noise ratio (PSNR, Eq. 7 (expressed in decibels dB)):

$$PSNR(F,O) = 10\log_{10} \frac{3NMS^2}{\sum_{c=1}^{3}\sum_{i=1}^{N}\sum_{j=1}^{M} \left[O(i,j,c) - F(i,j,c)\right]^2} \tag{7}$$

where $O$ is the original image, $F$ the filtered image of size $NM$ and $S$ the maximum possible pixel value (with 8-bit integer values the maximum will be 255). Although the PSNR measure has his shortcomings with respect to expressing the quality of an image as observed by human beings, it is still widely used in the image processing community [16]. In order to get a clear idea of the performance with respect to the level of impulse noise, experiments have been carried out for 5%, 10%, 20%, 30% and 40% of impulse noise. This is illustrated in Table 1 where the numerical results for the well known test image *Lena* of size $512 \times 512$ are shown. It is clear that the newly proposed (HFRMC) method achieves the largest PSNR value. These numerical results are confirmed by the visual results shown in Fig. 2. The main improvements can be observed: in edge regions the proposed method does not introduce new colour artefacts and filters out many impulse noise pixels. Other well performing filters, as for example the FIDRM, introduce new colours artefacts as can be seen in Fig. 2. We also observe that the proposed method (HFRMC) preserves edge sharpness. Although this filter is designed for impulse noise only, the idea behind the proposed method can be used to preserve the colour information for other noise types as well. The disadvantage of the proposed method is that it will not reduce uniform impulse noise very well. But actually, this filter can be modified (i.e. changing the global histogram calculation into a local iterative detection method) to handle uniform impulse noise as well.

## 5    Conclusion

A new colour filter, which is based on fuzzy logic, has been presented. This filter is especially developed for reducing all kinds of fixed impulse noise from digital colour images while preserving the useful colour information. Visual observation confirms the numerical results expressed in PSNR values (Eq. 7), which illustrates that the proposed filter achieves convincing results for colour images.

## Acknowledgment

This work was financially supported by the GOA-project 12.0515.03 of Ghent University.

# References

1. Schulte, S., Nachtegael, M., De Witte, V., Van der Weken, D., Kerre, E.E.: A new two step color filter for impulse noise. Proceedings East West Fuzzy Colloquim (2004) 185-192
2. Schulte, S., Nachtegael, M., De Witte, V., Van der Weken, D., Kerre, E.E.: A fuzzy impulse noise detection and reduction method. IEEE Transactions on Image Processing, (accepted).
3. Kerre, E.E.: Fuzzy sets and approximate Reasoning. Xian Jiaotong University Press, Softcover (1998).
4. Wang, J.H., Chiu, H.C.: An adaptive fuzzy filter for restoring highly corrupted images by histogram estimation. Proceedings of the National Science Council - Part A **23** (1999) 630-643
5. Russo, F., Ramponi, G.: Removal of impulse noise using a FIRE filter. Third IEEE Intern. Conf. on Image Processing (1996) 975-978.
6. Russo, F.: Fire Operators for Image Processing. Fuzzy Set. Syst. **103** (1999)265-275
7. Lee, C.S., Kuo, Y.H.: Adaptive fuzzy filter and its application to image enhancement. IN: Kerre, E.E., Nachtegael, M. (eds.): Fuzzy Techniques in Image Processing, Vol. 52, Springer Physica Verlag, Berlin Heidelberg New York (2000) 172-193
8. Arakawa, K.: Median filter based on fuzzy rules and its application to image restoration. Fuzzy Set. Syst. **77** (1996) 3-13
9. Farbiz, F., Menhaj, M.B.: A fuzzy logic control based approch for image filtering. IN: Kerre, E.E., Nachtegael, M. (eds.): Fuzzy Techniques in Image Processing, Vol. 52, Springer Physica Verlag, Berlin Heidelberg New York (2000) 194-221
10. Kalaykov, I., Tolt, G.: Real-time image noise cancellation based on fuzzy similarity. IN: Nachtegael, M., Van der Weken, D., Van De Ville, D., Kerre, E.E. (eds.): Fuzzy Filters for Image Processing, Vol. 122 Springer Physica Verlag, Berlin Heidelberg New York (2003) 54-71
11. Androutsos, D., Plataniotis, K. N., Venetsanopoulos, A.N.: Colour image processing using vector rank filter. International conference on digital signal processing (1998) 614-619.
12. Vertan, C., Buzuloiu, V.: Fuzzy nonlinear filtering of color images. IN: Kerre, E.E., Nachtegael, M. (eds.): Fuzzy Techniques in Image Processing, Vol. 52, Springer Physica Verlag, Berlin Heidelberg New York (2000) 248-264
13. Pok, G., Liu, J.C., Nair, A.S.: Selective Removal of Impulse Noise Based Homogeneity Level Information IEEE Transactions on Image Processing **12** (2003) 85-92
14. Chen, T., Ma, K.K., Chen, L.H.: Tri-state median filter for image denoising. IEEE T. Image Process. **8** (1999) 1834-1838
15. Hardie, R.C., Boncelet, C.G.: LUM filters: a class of rank-order-based filters for smoothing and sharpening. IEEE T. Signal Proces. **41** (1993) 1834-1838
16. Van der Weken, D., Nachtegael, M., Kerre, E.E.: Using similarity measures for histogram comparison. Lecture Notes in Computer Science. **2715** (2003) 396-403

# Mirror Symmetry in Perspective*

Rudi Penne

Department Industrial Sciences and Technology, Karel de Grote-Hogeschool

**Abstract.** We assume the presence of mirror symmetry in the viewed scene. In this scene we consider planar point sets and their mirror reflections. We observe the existence of a homology that maps the image of such a planar point set to the image of its mirror reflection. We show how to compute the vertex and the axis of this homology. Finally, the homology is used to reduce image noise by "symmetrization".

## 1 Introduction

In our experiments we performed metric 3D reconstructions from images taken by one camera (monocular vision) in the presence of a plane mirror, [1]. The object features that we want to reconstruct or measure are put in such position that both the direct image and the reflected image are available. Obviously, mirror vision is a variant of stereo vision. The mirror reflection supplies the second view, and hence the depth information that is necessary for reconstruction. But it is not exactly the same. The second virtual camera that is induced by the mirror cannot be obtained by a rigid motion from the first camera due to the reflection. As a consequence the *epipolar geometry* degenerates ([2,3,4]), resulting into one epipole (the *mirror pole e*, Section 3) instead of two. The use of a mirror to obtain a second view has some crucial advantages over the classical stereo vision:

- The second view is captured by a camera that is identical to the first (up to mirror reflection). This means that both views can be perfectly calibrated by the same intrinsic camera parameters, as opposed to a situation with two cameras or even with one moving camera.
- In stereo vision the relative position of two cameras is specified by 6 parameters. In mirror vision we need only 3 parameters; they describe the position of the (only) camera relative to the mirror.
- We have induced a plane of symmetry in the viewed scene (the mirror). This symmetry gives a *homological constraint* on the direct and reflected images, which can be utilized to reduce pixel noise.

While the first two advantages have been exploited in [1], this articles focuses on the third one. The homological constraint is explained in Section 4 and is the basis of a *2D symmetrization* that goes beyond the method of [5]. The resulting correction of pixel noise significantly improves applications such as 3D measurements.

---

* This project was partially supported by a BOF-funds of the University of Antwerp.

J. Blanc-Talon et al. (Eds.): ACIVS 2005, LNCS 3708, pp. 634–642, 2005.
© Springer-Verlag Berlin Heidelberg 2005

## 2   A Symmetry Plane in the Pinhole Model

In the *pinhole model* the images of a camera are obtained by a pair $(C, \mathcal{R})$, consisting of a point $C$ (the *centre* of the camera) and a plane $\mathcal{R}$ (the *retinal plane* or *image plane*). More precisely, the camera image $m$ of a point $M$ in 3-space is obtained by projecting $M$ on $\mathcal{R}$ from $C$. We will use the *frontal* pinhole model, which means that the "screen" $\mathcal{R}$ separates the viewed objects from the centre $C$ ([2]). Notice that *nonlinear lens distortions* are not taken into account in the pinhole model.

Next, we assume the presence of a symmetry plane in the scene. This occurs for example if the viewed object is symmetric, as it is the case for certain buildings and for a lot of man-made objects. On the other hand, (perfect) plane symmetry can be forced by the placement of a mirror in the neighborhood of the photographed scene (Figure 2), as we did in our experiments. In the remainder of this article, the plane of symmetry will be called the *mirror*, denoted by $\mathcal{M}$. If the symmetry is induced by a mirror then we distinguish between the real feature point $M$ and its mirror reflection $M'$, and between the direct image $m$ of $M$ and the indirect (reflected) image $m'$. If rather $\mathcal{M}$ is a plane of symmetry of the viewed object then we use the same terminology, making an artificial distinction between the "real part" of the object and the "reflected part".

The (imagined) line $k$ where $\mathcal{R}$ and $\mathcal{M}$ meet, is called the *hinge* of the camera-mirror setting. We avoid situations with a camera parallel to the mirror, such that the hinge is a well-defined finite line. In the Euclidean space that represents the real world, we can define the *mirror angle* $\varphi \neq 0$, as the (positive) "sharp" angle between $\mathcal{R}$ and $\mathcal{M}$.

The plane $\mathcal{H}$ through the centre $C$ and perpendicular to the hinge $k$ is called the *horizontal plane*. Clearly, the horizontal plane contains the *optical axis* of the pinhole model (the line through $C$ and perpendicular to the retinal plane $\mathcal{R}$). The intersection $h$ of $\mathcal{H}$ with $\mathcal{R}$ is called the *horizon* of the image. Of course, the horizon contains the *principal point* $c$ in the image plane (the intersection of the optical axis with $\mathcal{R}$).

There is a certain point $e$ on the horizon that will be crucial in this paper, called the *mirror pole*. It is defined as the intersection of the line through $C$ and perpendicular to $\mathcal{M}$, and the retinal plane $\mathcal{R}$. In [4] $e$ is called the "epipole", while in [3] the authors refer to it as $VP$ (the "vanishing point").

## 3   The Pole Correction

The mirror pole $e$ can be considered as the vanishing point of each line perpendicular to the mirror $\mathcal{M}$. This fact is very useful. Indeed, let $m$ be the projection of a point $M$ into the image plane $\mathcal{R}$, and let $m'$ be the projection of the reflection $M'$ of $M$. In the sequel, $m$ will be called the *direct image* and $m'$ the *indirect* or *reflected image* of $M$. Because $e$ is the projection of the point at infinity of the line $MM'$, the three image points $m$, $m'$ and $e$ are collinear in $\mathcal{R}$. This condition is called the **mirror constraint**. It corresponds to the famous *epipolar constraint* of classical stereo vision ([6,7,2]). In our camera-mirror setting, the epipoles degenerate into one point: the mirror pole $e$ ([3,4]).

Once we are given two pairs $(m_1, m_1')$ and $(m_2, m_2')$ of direct and indirect images of some points $M_1$ and $M_2$ in 3-space, we can determine $e$ by

$$e = m_1 m_1' \wedge m_2 m_2'$$

To cope with noise it is preferable to have more of such pairs, and to determine $e$ by a least square approximation followed by a nonlinear optimization technique.

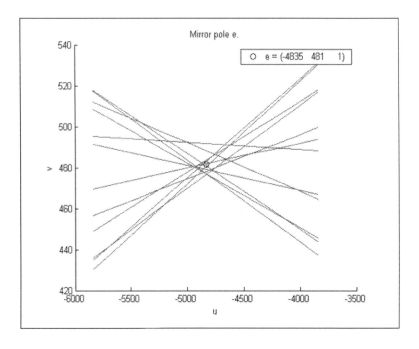

**Fig. 1.** In a noisy image the configuration of lines $mm'$ is not perfectly concurrent. The mirror pole $e$ has been obtained by a LSA.

Conversely, once we have detected the mirror pole $e$ we can use it to look for the indirect image $m'$ that corresponds to a given direct image $m$. Indeed, since $m'$ belongs to the line $em$, this narrows our search.

Let $(u_e, v_e)$ be the pixel coordinates of the mirror pole $e$. Each pair $(m, m')$ of a direct and a reflected image of a feature point $M$ gives one linear constraint for $u_e$ and $v_e$:

$$(v' - v)u_e + (u - u')v_e + u'v - uv' = 0 \qquad (1)$$

with $m(u, v)$ and $m'(u', v')$ the given pixel coordinates. For exact data two such equations (obtained from two feature points $M_1$ and $M_2$) suffice to solve for $e$ (assuming that the linear equations are linearly independent, which is equivalent to avoiding that $M_1 M_2$ is perpendicular to the mirror).

In real images the data are always corrupted, and we try to cancel out as much noise as possible by considering $n$ pairs $(m, m')$ with typically $n \geq 10$. Then we put $e$ equal to the least square approximation of the associated system of $n$ linear equations (1). If we normalize each such equation (1) by dividing by $\sqrt{(v' - v)^2 + (u - u')^2}$ then we can interpret this LSA geometrically as the point that globally minimizes the distances to the $n$ given lines $mm'$.

Once we fixed $e$ we can consider for each pair $(m, m')$ the unique line $\lambda^*$ through $e$ that minimizes

$$\delta = d(m, \lambda)^2 + d(m', \lambda)^2$$

In particular, using highschool calculus, we find $\lambda^* : y - v_e = a(x - u_e)$ with (putting $(u_1, v_1) = (u - u_e, v - v_e)$ and $(u_2, v_2) = (u' - u_e, v' - v_e)$):

$$a = \frac{v_1^2 + v_2^2 - u_1^2 - u_2^2 + \sqrt{(u_1^2 + u_2^2 - v_1^2 - v_2^2)^2 + 4(u_1 v_1 + u_2 v_2)^2}}{2(u_1 v_1 + u_2 v_2)}$$

This optimal line still leaves us with an error $\delta_e^*$ (which is only zero if $mm'$ contains $e$). The total deviation of the $n$ given pairs $(m, m')$ from the mirror constraint is the sum of all these errors:

$$\Delta_e = \sum_{(m, m')} \delta_e^*$$

which is a function in the coordinates $(u_e, v_e)$ of $e$. By means of a (nonlinear) numerical optimization procedure we minimize $\Delta_e$, starting at the LSA for $e$ that we found in the previous paragraph. In experiments we arrived at reliable, small values for $\Delta_e$.

Having computed an accurate position of $e$ we can correct the image data in order to force the mirror constraint. This is done by the orthogonal projection of the pair $(m, m')$ on the associated optimal line $\lambda^*$. We call this the *pole correction*. This procedure aims to reduce pixel noise by making the image data compatible with the presence of the plane symmetry (satisfying the mirror constraint). This strategy has the same spirit as the *2D data symmetrization* in [5]. There, the authors restrict to the case of "weak projection" (where the mirror pole lies at infinity in the image plane). In the next paragraph we will refine the process of data symmetrization one step further.

*Example 1.* In Figure 2 we show the direct and reflected images of a plane 5 by 5 grid. In a preprocessing phase we corrected radial distortion up to the second degree, resulting in the following lists of pixel coordinates (rounded up to units for display reasons):

$$\mathbf{grid} = \begin{array}{lllll} (784, 154) & (856, 216) & (932, 283) & (1016, 357) & (1106, 436) \\ (750, 264) & (819, 329) & (891, 398) & (971, 474) & (1056, 555) \\ (719, 367) & (784, 434) & (853, 506) & (929, 584) & (1009, 667) \\ (688, 466) & (750, 535) & (817, 609) & (889, 688) & (965, 772) \\ (660, 559) & (719, 629) & (783, 705) & (852, 786) & (923, 871) \end{array}$$

$$\mathbf{reflected\ grid} = \begin{array}{lllll} (355, 211) & (285, 277) & (219, 340) & (155, 400) & (95, 457) \\ (408, 295) & (337, 359) & (269, 421) & (204, 480) & (142, 536) \\ (464, 380) & (390, 444) & (320, 504) & (253, 561) & (189, 616) \\ (520, 468) & (444, 530) & (373, 588) & (304, 645) & (239, 698) \\ (578, 558) & (500, 618) & (427, 675) & (356, 730) & (289, 782) \end{array}$$

As a first guess for the mirror pole $e$, we minimize the sum of the squared distances from $e$ to the lines $mm'$ ($m$: direct image; $m'$: reflected image). We obtain $e_0 = (-1844.47, 505.41)$, leaving a residue of 109.715. Next, using $e_0$ as an initial value in the nonlinear minimization of $\Delta_e$, we get[1]

$$e = (-1752.03, 495.29)$$

with a residue of only 3.18.

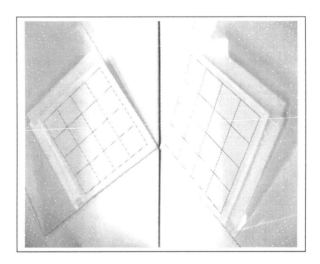

**Fig. 2.** The direct (right) and reflected (left) images of a 5 by 5 grid after the correction of radial distortion

---

[1] The computation has been performed by the function FindMinimum in Mathematica.

# 4    The Homological Constraint

Let $(M_1, M_2, M_3, \ldots)$ and $(M'_1, M'_2, M'_3, \ldots)$ be two corresponding sets of feature points under the given plane symmetry in the viewed scene. So, $M'_i$ is the mirror reflection of $M_i$. Further, we assume that the points $M_1, M_2, M_3, \ldots$ all lie in the same plane. Automatically, this is also true for the reflected points $M'_1, M'_2, M'_3, \ldots$. Typically, such a situation occurs for feature points $M_i$ on the same wall of a symmetric building, or on the same face of a symmetric polyhedral object. It also occurs when we photograph a planar pattern near a mirror for calibration purposes (Figure 2, [1]). In this case, the mirror symmetry implies a constraint on the image data that generalizes the previously described mirror constraint. This constraint seems to be missed by other authors ([5], [4], [3]). It gives rise to a useful 2D data symmetrization, more advanced than the pole correction.

Let $\mathcal{A}$ denote the plane that contains the feature points $M_1, M_2, M_3, \ldots$, and $\mathcal{A}'$ the plane that contains the mirror reflections $M'_1, M'_2, M'_3, \ldots$. We assume that $\mathcal{A} \neq \mathcal{A}'$. It is obvious that the line $a$ where these planes intersect lies on the mirror $\mathcal{M}$. The unique plane $\mathcal{C}$ through the camera centre $C$ and $a$ intersects the retinal plane $\mathcal{R}$ in the line $A$, that might be regarded as the image of the (virtual) line $a$. Further, the (sharp) angle between $\mathcal{A}$ and $\mathcal{M}$ is called $\alpha$, and the angle between $\mathcal{C}$ and $\mathcal{M}$ is called $\beta$.

The images of the points on $\mathcal{A}$ are mapped to the images of the points on $\mathcal{A}'$ by means of a homography $H$. Indeed, $H$ is the composition of the projectivity between $\mathcal{R}$ and $\mathcal{A}$ (from $C$), the mirror reflection (w.r.t. $\mathcal{M}$), and the projectivity between $\mathcal{A}'$ and $\mathcal{R}$. We can make a stronger statement: the mirror symmetry between two planes in 3D projects to a *homology* in the retinal plane. A homology is a homography $H$ that is characterized by a line $W$ of fixpoints (the *axis*), a fixpoint $v$ not on $W$ (the *vertex*) and a real number $\delta$ (the *modulus*). For every point $p \neq v$ in the projective plane the homological image $Hp$ is determined by

1. $p$ and $Hp$ are collinear with the vertex $v$
2. the line $pv$ intersects $W$ in a point $w$ such that the cross ratio

$$(v, w; p, Hp) = \delta$$

**Theorem 2.** *The images $m_1, m_2, m_3, \ldots$ of points in a plane $\mathcal{A}$ are mapped to the reflected images $m'_1, m'_2, m'_3, \ldots$ by a homology $H$ of $\mathcal{R}$. The mirror pole $e$ is the vertex of $H$, the line $A = \mathcal{A} \wedge \mathcal{A}'$ is the axis of $H$, and the modulus is given by*

$$\delta = \frac{\tan \alpha - \tan \beta}{\tan \beta + \tan \alpha}$$

*Proof.* The pencil of planes with axis $a = \mathcal{A} \wedge \mathcal{A}'$ is a one-dimensional projective system. Let $\mathcal{E}$ be the plane through $a$ and perpendicular to $\mathcal{M}$, and put $\delta$ equal to the cross ratio $(\mathcal{E}, \mathcal{C}; \mathcal{A}, \mathcal{A}')$.

If $M$ is an arbitrary point on $\mathcal{A}$ and if $M' \in \mathcal{A}'$ denotes its mirror reflection. The plane $\mathcal{D} = CMM'$ intersects $a$ in the point $D$, and intersects the pencil of planes through $a$ in a plane pencil of lines through $D$. Still

$$\delta = (\mathcal{E} \wedge \mathcal{D}, \mathcal{C} \wedge \mathcal{D}; \mathcal{A} \wedge \mathcal{D}, \mathcal{A}' \wedge \mathcal{D})$$

In $\mathcal{D}$, we can define a projectivity from the pencil through $D$ to the pencil through $C$ via the intersection by the line $MM'$. Notice that $MM'$ is parallel with $\mathcal{E} \wedge \mathcal{D}$, and so is $Ce$. We conclude that

$$\delta = (Ce, CD; CM, CM')$$

or, after intersecting by the retinal plane

$$\delta = (e, d; m, m')$$

where $d$ denotes the image of $D$ or, equivalently, $d = mm' \wedge A$.

Finally, if we put $S = CD \wedge MM'$ then we see that $\delta = \overline{SM}/\overline{SM'}$. If we put $M'' = MM' \wedge \mathcal{M}$ then $\overline{SM} = \overline{M''M} - \overline{M''S}$ and $\overline{SM'} = \overline{SM''} + \overline{M''M'}$, whence

$$\frac{\overline{SM}}{\overline{SM'}} = \frac{\tan \alpha - \tan \beta}{\tan \beta + \tan \alpha}$$

$\square$

If we fix a projective basis in the projective plane then we can express a homography $H$ by means of a 3 by 3 matrix, which is determined up to global scaling. By abuse of notation, this matrix will be denoted by $H$ too. In case $H$ is a homology, if $\overline{e}$ denotes a column vector of homogeneous coordinates of the vertex and if $\overline{a}$ denotes a column vector of line coordinates of the axis, then up to a scale factor $H$ is given by

$$H \sim I + \frac{(\delta - 1)}{\overline{e}^T \overline{a}} \overline{ea}^T$$

*Remark 3.* A homology $H$ has an eigenvalue of multiplicity 2, that can be put to 1 after rescaling of $H$; then the other eigenvalue equals the modulus $\delta$. The eigenvectors for eigenvalue 1 correspond to the points on the axis, the eigenvectors for eigenvalue $\delta$ to the vertex of the homology. We refer to [8] for more background on homologies.

## 5    Homological 2D Symmetrization

Let $m_1, m_2, m_3, \ldots$ be the images of the feature points $M_1, M_2, M_3, \ldots$. We can extract the pixel coordinates of these image points manually or automatically (e.g. using edge detection). In any case we encounter pixel noise (no perfect light or focus conditions, no infinite resolution, etc. . . ).

If the object points $M_1, M_2, M_3, \ldots$ belong to the same plane $\mathcal{A}$, and if moreover the reflected images $m_1', m_2', m_3', \ldots$ are available (object with plane of symmetry or presence of mirror) then we can exploit Theorem 2 to reduce the pixel noise significantly. We first compute the homology $H$ that approximately maps the direct images $m_i$ to the reflected images $m'_i$. Then we find the most likely (in some sense) corrections for $m_i$ and $m'_i$ that are compatible with $H$. This procedure is called *homological 2D symmetrization* and it is an improvement of the pole correction (Section 3) and the 2D symmetrization as described in [5], but it is restricted to coplanar object points.

We construct the homology $H$ by a separate computation of the vertex, the axis and the modulus. For each of these elements we look for the best candidates.

## Algorithmic Details:

1. Theorem 2 only guarantees the existence of a homology in the perfect pinhole model. Dealing with real data (and real lenses) nonlinear distortions cannot be ignored. Therefore, we first (partly) compensate for *radial* distortions by means of a standard procedure (e.g. [9]).
2. The vertex of the homology is the mirror pole $e$. Section 3 explains how an optimal choice for $e$ can be computed.
3. For each pair of directed images $(m_1, m_2)$ and reflected images $(m'_1, m'_2)$ of object points in the plane $\mathcal{A}$, the point of intersection $p_{ij} = m_1 m_2 \wedge m'_1 m'_2$ should belong to the axis $A$ (assuming a perfect, noise-free pinhole model). By linear regression we obtain an optimal choice for $A$ that minimizes the sum of squared distances to the different $p_{ij}$. Robust techniques are described in the literature to deal with outliers.
4. The homology $H$ now contains only one unknown, $\delta$. Finally, we find the most likely correction for the noisy data $m_1, m_2, \ldots, m'_1, m'_2, \ldots$ and the most optimal choice for $\delta$ by minimizing

$$\sum_i ||m_i^* - m_i||^2 + \sum_i ||Hm_i^* - m'_i||^2$$

*Example 4.* We pick up the example at the end of Section 3, concerning the 5 by 5 grid (Figure 2). The given (rounded) pixel coordinates have been first corrected from radial distortion. Since the 25 feature points are coplanar, we can apply the homology-method of the section. Recall we found an accurate location of the mirror pole, $e = (-1752.03, 495.29)$, serving as the vertex of the homology $H$. Next, for each pair $\{m_i, m_j\}$ of grid points we compute $p_{ij} = m_i m_j \wedge m'_i m'_j$, and obtain the axis $A$ of $H$ as the best linear fit for all these intersections $p_{ij}$:

$$A : y = 15.9978x - 9497.34$$

This yields the following matrix for the homology $H$ with unknown modulus $\delta$ (up to a global scalar):

$$H \sim \begin{pmatrix} 1 + 0.737183(-1+\delta) & -0.0460804(-1+\delta) & -437.641(-1+\delta) \\ -0.208398(-1+\delta) & 1 + 0.0130267(-1+\delta) & 123.719(-1+\delta) \\ -0.000420759(-1+\delta) & 0.0000263011(-1+\delta) & 1 + 0.24979(-1+\delta) \end{pmatrix}$$

Now we solve for a nonlinear numerical minimization of

$$\sum_i ||m_i^* - m_i||^2 + \sum_i ||Hm_i^* - m'_i||^2$$

with the 50 coordinates of $m_1^*, \ldots, m_{25}^*$ and $\delta$ as unknowns, using the given pixel coordinates and $\delta_0 = -1$ as initial values. We find the following optimal grid points:

(783.923, 153.503) (855.425, 216.264) (932.157, 283.486) (1015.76, 356.907)
(1106.25, 436.309) (750.405, 263.248) (818.542, 328.266) (891.668, 397.948)
(970.967, 473.637) (1056.37, 555.051) (718.516, 367.323) (783.579, 434.253)
(853.388, 506.064) (928.756, 583.681) (1009.51, 666.758) (688.437, 465.814)
(750.569, 534.509) (817.209, 608.262) (888.875, 687.556) (965.296, 771.992)
(659.624, 559.434) (719.093, 629.567) (782.844, 704.946) (851.158, 785.61)
(923.662, 871.102)

and $\delta = -1.68212$ (total residue $= 5.01767$). The reflected grid points are corrected by the homological images of the corrected (direct) grid points.

# References

1. Mertens, L., Penne, R., Kubica, M., Senft, D.: Metric 3d reconstruction from monocular vision by way of one plane mirror. Technical Report IWT2005-06, Karel de Grote-Hogeschool (2005)
2. Ma, Y., Soatto, S., Košecká, J.: An Invitation to 3-D Vision. Interdisciplinary Applied Mathematics. Springer-Verlag, New York (2004)
3. Mitsumoto, H., Tamura, S., Okazaki, K., Kajimi, N., Fukui, Y.: 3-D reconstruction using mirror images based on a plane symmetry recovering method. IEEE Trans. on Pattern Analysis and Machine Intelligence 14 (1992) 941–946
4. Huynh, D.: Affine reconstruction from monocular vision in the presence of a symmetry plane. In: Int. Conf. on Comp. Vision. Volume 1. (1999) 476–482
5. Zabrodsky, H., Weinshall, D.: Utilizing symmetry in the reconstruction of 3-dimensional shape from noisy images. In: Proc. ECCV-94 Conf. (1994) 403–410
6. Faugeras, O.: Three-Dimensional Computer Vision. A Geometric Viewpoint. MIT Press, Cambridge (1993)
7. Hartley, R., Zisserman, A.: Multiple View Geometry in Computer Vision. Cambridge University Press, Cambridge (2000)
8. Semple, J., Kneebone, G.: Algebraic Projective Theory. Oxford University Press (1952)
9. Devernay, F., Faugeras, O.: Straight lines have to be straight. Machine Vision and Applications 13 (2001) 14–24

# Impulse Noise Detection Based on Robust Statistics and Genetic Programming

Nemanja Petrović and Vladimir Crnojević

Faculty of Engineering, Trg Dositeja Obradovića 6,
21000 Novi Sad, Serbia and Montenegro
{petra, crnojevic}@uns.ns.ac.yu

**Abstract.** A new impulse detector design method for image impulse noise is presented. Robust statistics of local pixel neighborhood present features in a binary classification scheme. Classifier is developed through the evolutionary process realized by genetic programming. The proposed filter shows very good results in suppressing both fixed-valued and random-valued impulse noise, for any noise probability, and on all test images.

## 1 Introduction

Impulse noise presents a frequent problem in image processing. It emerges as a result of noisy sensors or transmission errors. Impulse noise suppression is required pre-processing stage, which cannot be efficiently done by employing simple linear filters. Therefore, a number of nonlinear and adaptive filtering techniques have been developed for this purpose.

Nonlinear techniques are mainly based on median or its modifications [1], which are robust estimators, immune to high levels of impulse noise. The major drawback of such algorithms is uniform application of particular filter across the entire image. Thus, besides noisy pixels, undisturbed pixels are also modified. Performances of these filters are enhanced by introducing an impulse detector and space-variant filtering, [2]-[8]. In this concept, each pixel is analyzed in context of its neighborhood, and decision is made whether the pixel is noise-free or corrupted. Accordingly, it will be left unchanged, or replaced by the estimated value, respectively. Adaptive filtering conducted through this procedure reduces distortion because most of the uncorrupted pixels are left unchanged. As a result, impulse detection becomes essential filtering stage. Constructing an impulse detector requires a trade-off between opposing demands for noise suppression and detail preservation [2]. Existing algorithms employ one [2], [4] or more [6], [8] thresholds which are compared to particular local neighborhood statistics in order to label pixel as noisy or noise-free.

In this work, a novel design of impulse noise detector is presented. It is based on the supervised learning paradigm and built as a binary classifier. Genetic Programming (GP) is relatively recent and fast developing approach to automatic programming [9]. In GP, solution to a problem is represented as a computer program in the form of a parse tree, consisting of primitive functions and terminals. It has been chosen among other learning algorithms due to its capability to fit extremely nonlinear

J. Blanc-Talon et al. (Eds.): ACIVS 2005, LNCS 3708, pp. 643–649, 2005.
© Springer-Verlag Berlin Heidelberg 2005

functions easily and mitigate influence of futile features. GP employs evolutionary principles of natural selection and recombination to search the space of all possible solutions in order to find the most satisfactory one.

This paper is organized as follows. The impulse noise model used in the paper is explained in Section 2 and design of a new impulse detector is presented in Section 3. Section 4 contains analysis of obtained results and finally, conclusions are drawn in Section 5.

## 2  Impulse Noise Model

A great variety of models for the image impulse noise exists today. Most of them have in common that percentage $p$ of image pixels are corrupted, while $1-p$ of pixels are left unchanged. Corrupted pixels have values equal to the maximum or minimum of the allowable dynamic range, which is well known salt-and-pepper noise model. Similarly, noisy pixels can be replaced by just one value chosen from available range. Although these models are mathematically very simple, they are far from being realistic. In this paper, besides the salt-and-pepper noise, we have used a more general noise model introduced recently [6], [7], [8]. In this noise model corrupted pixels can take arbitrary values within the dynamic range, i.e. [0,255] for gray-scale images, according to uniform probability distribution. Most of contemporary impulse noise filters are not capable of dealing with this noise model [10], [11]. In order to make a fair comparison between the impulse noise filters performance, both noise models have been included in testing. Besides, several filters included in comparison were originally designed for random valued impulse noise.

## 3  Impulse Detection

### 3.1  Robust Statistics

Let $x_{ij}$ and $y_{ij}$ denote pixels with coordinates $(i,j)$ in a noisy and a filtered image, respectively. If the estimated value of a particular noisy image pixel is $\varphi(x_{ij})$, then the filtered image is defined as:

$$y_{ij} = \varphi(x_{ij})M_{ij} + x_{ij}(1 - M_{ij}),\qquad(1)$$

where $M_{ij}$ is the binary noise map, containing ones at the positions detected as noisy and zeros otherwise. Noise map should be generated from some local neighborhood statistics. Let $W_K$ denote rectangular window centered at the position $(i,j)$, where the size of the window is $(2h + 1) \times (2h + 1)$ and $K=2h+1$. A set of pixels contained in the window $W_K$, centered at the position $(i,j)$, is defined as:

$$W_K(i, j) = \{x_{ij} \mid -h \leq i \leq h, -h \leq j \leq h, K = 2h+1\}.\qquad(2)$$

Median is a robust estimator of the location, reliable as long as the number of outliers i.e. noisy pixels in the given window $W_K$ is smaller than 50%. Similarly, MAD (median of the absolute deviations from the median) is well-known in robust statistics as a robust estimator of scale [12]. It is capable of estimating local variance even if up to 50% of pixels within window $W_K$ are noise impulses.

The absolute deviation from the median and MAD carry valuable information for detecting impulse noise. They are defined as follows:

$$d_{3x3}(i,j) = |x_{ij} - median(W_3(i,j))|, \tag{3}$$

$$d_{5x5}(i,j) = |x_{ij} - median(W_5(i,j))|, \tag{4}$$

$$MAD_{3x3}(i,j) = median|W_3(i,j) - median(W_3(i,j))|, \tag{5}$$

$$MAD_{5x5}(i,j) = median|W_5(i,j) - median(W_5(i,j))|. \tag{6}$$

These statistics are calculated for windows sizes 3x3 and 5x5, due to the fact that better robustness can be achieved by enlarging window size, at the expense of losing information about details. The absolute deviations from the median can indicate whether the currently analyzed pixel is corrupted. Larger deviation will suggest that the pixel is noisy and vice versa. However, if details are present in noise-free image, they can be mistakenly treated as noise. In order to avoid this, a robust estimate of local variance, obtained from MAD estimator, is used to make distinction between image details and impulse noise.

### 3.2 Genetic Programming

The output of a GP classifier is a numeric value that is translated into a class label. For binary classification case, this translation is usually based on the sign of a numeric value.

In the proposed design of a GP classifier, terminal set has four features and a number of randomly generated constants. Features are $d_{3x3}$, $d_{5x5}$, $MAD_{3x3}$ and $MAD_{5x5}$, as defined in (3)-(6). Features (3) and (4) are linearly normalized from range [0,255] to [-1,1] while features (5) and (6) are linearly normalized from range [0,127] to [-1,1]. Random constants are generated using uniform distribution within the range [-1,1].

Training set was built from standard test images *Lena* and *Goldhill*. Firstly, images were corrupted by a combination of fixed-valued and random-valued impulse noise. Secondly, features were calculated for all pixels in training images, and corresponding instances were labeled according to the following rule: 0 – noise-free pixel, 1 – corrupted pixel. At the end, the balanced training set was made by randomly selecting equal number of data points labeled as noise-free and corrupted.

Primitive function set consists of standard arithmetic *plus* and *minus* functions with two input arguments and *myif* function defined as:

$$myif(C_1, C_2, R_1, R_2) = \begin{cases} R_1, & C_1 \geq C_2 \\ R_2, & C_1 < C_2 \end{cases}, \tag{7}$$

where $C_1$, $C_2$, $R_1$ and $R_2$ are input arguments. These primitive functions are among the simplest, and *myif* function is of special importance. Its nonlinearity is suitable for modeling this type of problem, since it provides selection of different tree parts (R1, R2) based on values of input arguments C1 and C2.

A data point which represents a pixel is classified as noisy if the output of a GP classifier is positive, and it is classified as noise-free if the output is negative. Fitness function is defined as classification accuracy, i.e. number of correctly classified data points divided by total number of data points in the training set. According to this design, the best possible fitness is 100%.

The ramped half-and-half method was used for generating programs in the initial population and for the mutation operator [9]. The proportional selection mechanism and the reproduction, crossover and mutation operators were used in the evolutionary process. Size of initial generation is set to 200 and genetic programs are evolved for 50 generations. Maximum depth of a tree representing the genetic program is limited to 5, in order to avoid over-fitting and bloat.

### 3.3 Trained Classifiers

Five different GP classifiers were evolved on the same training set, starting from different initial populations. Let X1, X2, X3 and X4 denote normalized features, $d_{3x3}$, $d_{5x5}$, $MAD_{3x3}$ and $MAD_{5x5}$, respectively. Final classifier is made by majority voting over trained classifiers. Trained GP classifiers represented as strings are given bellow, and *Classifier 1* is presented in the form of a tree in Fig. 1.

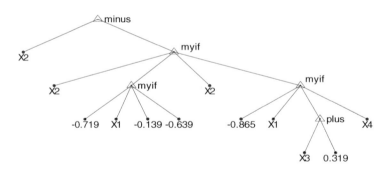

**Fig. 1.** *Classifier 1* represented in a tree form

*Classifier 1*
```
minus(X2,myif(X2,myif(-0.719,X1,-0.139,-0.639),X2,
myif(-0.865,X1,plus(X3,0.319),X4)))
```
*Classifier 2*
```
myif(minus(X1,plus(minus(-0.565,X2),-0.522)),myif(myif(X3,minus(X1,
X4),0.469,-0.459),X2,myif(X2,plus(X1,-0.255),myif(X1,-0.0299,
-0.565,-0.126),X4),-0.565),minus(X2,-0.755),plus(minus(X1,X4),
plus(minus(X1,X4),minus(X2,-0.755))))
```
*Classifier 3*
```
myif(X1,X4,plus(plus(plus(X2,0.713),minus(-0.814,-0.908)),
minus(X2,X4)),plus(plus(X1,0.713), plus(plus(X2,0.696),
minus(X2,X4))))
```

*Classifier 4*
```
minus(X2,myif(X1,-0.823,myif(-0.611,X1,X4,-0.823),
minus(X3,-0.351))))
```
*Classifier 5*
```
plus(myif(minus(X1,plus(X2,-0.093))),myif(plus(X2,-0.934),0.579,X4,
plus(X2,X4)),myif(X2,X4,0.794,X2),0.882),myif(X1,-0.637,0.794,
myif(X3,X1,X1,minus(-0.178,X3)))))
```

## 4 Results

The performance of the proposed filter has been compared with those of some existing detection based filters. Simulations were made on several standard grayscale test images (resolution 512×512) corrupted by salt-and-pepper and random-valued impulse noise. For each particular image and noise ratio, simulations were repeated a number of times and averaged results are given in Table 1, and Fig. 2. Quality measure used for evaluation was the peak SNR (PSNR). Filtered image has been generated according to Eq.(1), where simple 3x3 pixels median was used as the estimator $\varphi(x_{ij})$. Proposed filter is compared with SDROM [8], ACWMF [6], PWMAD [7], TSM [4] and PSM [10].

**Table 1.** Comparative results of impulse noise filters in PSNR. Test images are corrupted by 20% impulse noise.

| Filters | Random-valued Impulse Noise | | | | | | |
|---|---|---|---|---|---|---|---|
| | *Peppers* | *Bridge* | *Goldhill* | *Lena* | *Barbara* | *Boats* | *Airplane* |
| TSM [4] | 31.63 | 26.44 | 30.66 | 32.09 | 24.99 | 29.99 | 30.29 |
| PSM [10] | 27.48 | 25.64 | 27.22 | 27.50 | 24.40 | 27.15 | 27.64 |
| PWMAD [7] | 33.01 | 26.66 | 31.54 | 33.16 | 26.38 | 30.57 | 31.33 |
| ACWMF [6] | 32.10 | 26.63 | 31.15 | 32.61 | 25.35 | 30.50 | 30.97 |
| SDROM [8] | 31.57 | 26.58 | 30.81 | 32.06 | 24.90 | 30.20 | 30.61 |
| Proposed | 32.92 | 26.86 | 31.61 | 33.15 | 25.47 | 30.80 | 31.56 |
| Filters | Fixed-valued Impulse Noise | | | | | | |
| | *Peppers* | *Bridge* | *Goldhill* | *Lena* | *Barbara* | *Boats* | *Airplane* |
| TSM [4] | 25.81 | 23.95 | 25.70 | 26.01 | 23.05 | 25.56 | 25.51 |
| PSM [10] | 32.29 | 27.81 | 30.90 | 30.60 | 25.28 | 31.06 | 26.92 |
| PWMAD [7] | 31.45 | 26.83 | 30.87 | 31.80 | 24.99 | 29.97 | 30.27 |
| ACWMF [6] | 30.08 | 26.69 | 29.86 | 30.53 | 25.47 | 29.42 | 29.19 |
| SDROM [8] | 30.11 | 26.29 | 29.77 | 30.68 | 24.50 | 29.26 | 29.29 |
| Proposed | 31.83 | 27.13 | 31.18 | 32.44 | 25.50 | 30.61 | 31.01 |

Their performance comparison over noise ratios from 10% to 35% is given in Fig. 2. for test image *Airplane*, that was not included in the training set. It is interesting to observe that the proposed filter outperforms other filters in PSNR for both types of impulse noise. One can note that PSM filter shows better results for higher ratios of salt and pepper noise. However, unlike the proposed filter, PSM is implemented recursively. Multiple filtering with the proposed GP filter, or its recursive implementation, will significantly increase its performance for higher noise ratios.

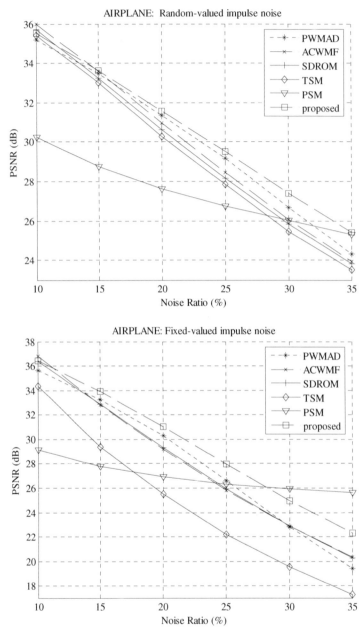

**Fig. 2.** Performance comparison of different filtering algorithms conducted on test image *Airplane* corrupted by various rates of random-valued and fixed-valued impulse noise

The efficiency of the proposed filter in processing different images has also been tested. Table 1 presents the comparison of PSNR results for images degraded by both kinds of impulses, where 20% of the pixels are contaminated in each image. The results have similar tendency for all images, where the proposed filter shows best results in most situations.

## 5  Conclusions

A new approach to the impulse detector design is presented. Trade-off between noise suppression and detail preservation is accomplished by using robust estimators of location and scale. Since these estimators are highly nonlinear, a genetic programming is used to combine them in order to find an optimal solution for the binary classification problem. Although presented approach requires training of the impulse detector, obtained GP trees are very simple and can be implemented easily on any platform. Simulations confirm that achieved generalization is excellent. In addition, in most cases results of the proposed filter were equal or better when compared to the results obtained with other filters. Moreover, it shows very good performance for both random- and fixed-valued impulse noises. Additional optimization of random constants within GP trees, and inclusion of more images in the training set, can lead to further improvement of the proposed filter performance.

## References

1. S.-J. Ko and Y.-H. Lee, "Center weighted median filters and their applications to image enhancement," *IEEE Trans. Circuits Syst.*, vol. 38, pp. 984–993, Sept. 1991.
2. T. Sun and Y. Neuvo, "Detail-preserving median based filters in image processing," *Pattern Recognit. Lett.*, vol. 15, pp. 341–347, Apr. 1994.
3. D. A. F. Florêncio and R. W. Schafer, "Decision-based median filter using local signal statistics," in *Proc. SPIE Symp. Visual Comm. Image Processing*, vol. 2038, Sept. 1994, pp. 268–275.
4. T. Chen, K.-K. Ma and L.-H. Chen, "Tri-state median filter for image denoising," *IEEE Trans. Image Processing*, vol. 8, pp. 1834–1838, Dec. 1999.
5. T. Chen and H. R. Wu, "Space variant median filters for the restoration of impulse noise corrupted images," *IEEE Trans. Circuits Syst. II*, vol. 48, pp. 784–789, Aug. 2001.
6. T. Chen and H. R. Wu, "Adaptive impulse detection using center-weighted median filters," *IEEE Signal Processing Lett.*, vol. 8, pp. 1–3, Jan. 2001.
7. V.Crnojevic, V.Senk, Z.Trpovski, "Advanced Impulse Detection Based on Pixel-Wise MAD", *IEEE Signal processing letters*, vol.11, no.7, July 2004.
8. E. Abreu, M. Lightstone, S. K. Mitra, and K. Arakawa, "A new efficient approach for the removal of impulse noise from highly corrupted images," *IEEE Trans. Image Processing*, vol. 5, pp. 1012–1025, June 1996.
9. J. R. Koza, "Genetic Programming: On the Programming of Computers by Means of Natural Selection", *Cambridge, MA: MIT Press*, 1992.
10. Z. Wang, D. Zhang, "Progressive Switching Median Filter for the Removal of Impulse Noise from Highly Corrupted Images", *IEEE Trans. on Circuits and Syst. II: Analog and Digital Signal Processing*, vol. 46, pp. 78-80, January 1999.
11. G. Pok, J. Liu, and A. S. Nair, "Selective Removal of Impulse Noise Based on Homogeneity Level Information," *IEEE Trans. Image Processing*, vol. 12, pp. 85–92, Jan. 2003.
12. P.Huber, Robust Statistics, *New York: Wiley*, 1981.

# FPGA Design and Implementation of a Wavelet-Domain Video Denoising System

Mihajlo Katona[1], Aleksandra Pižurica[2],
Nikola Teslić[1], Vladimir Kovačević[1], and Wilfried Philips[2]

[1] University of Novi Sad, Chair for Computer Engineering,
Fruškogorska 11, 21000 Novi Sad, Serbia and Montenegro
mihajlo.katona@krt.neobee.net
[2] Ghent University, Dept. Telecommunications and Information Processing,
Sint-Pietersnieuwstraat 41, B-9000 Ghent, Belgium
Aleksandra.Pizurica@telin.UGent.be

**Abstract.** Multiresolution video denoising is becoming an increasingly popular research topic over recent years. Although several wavelet based algorithms reportedly outperform classical single-resolution approaches, their concepts are often considered as prohibitive for real-time processing. Little research has been done so far towards hardware customization of wavelet domain video denoising. A number of recent works have addressed the implementation of critically sampled orthogonal wavelet transforms and the related image compression schemes in Field Programmable Gate Arrays (FPGA). However, the existing literature on FPGA implementations of overcomplete (non-decimated) wavelet transforms and on manipulations of the wavelet coefficients that are more complex than thresholding is very limited.

In this paper we develop FPGA implementation of an advanced wavelet domain noise filtering algorithm, which uses a non-decimated wavelet transform and spatially adaptive Bayesian wavelet shrinkage. The standard composite television video stream is digitalized and used as source for real-time video sequences. The results demonstrate the effectiveness of the developed scheme for real time video processing.

## 1 Introduction

Recently, several promising multiresolution (wavelet domain) video noise filters have been proposed. These can be categorized in *non-separable* spatio-temporal approaches utilizing a three-dimensional (3-D) wavelet representation [1], [2] and *separable* approaches that combine 1-D temporal filtering and 2-D spatial denoising in the wavelet domain [3,4]. Although these wavelet domain video filters were reported to outperform the more classical, single-resolution techniques, little research has been done so far towards their customization for hardware implementations and consequently, they are often considered as prohibitive for real-time applications.

Modern hardware solutions for digital signal processing algorithms increasingly employ Field Programmable Gate Arrays (FPGA). FPGAs accelerate the

J. Blanc-Talon et al. (Eds.): ACIVS 2005, LNCS 3708, pp. 650–657, 2005.
© Springer-Verlag Berlin Heidelberg 2005

execution of algorithms and offer a tremendous potential to improve performance through parallelization. While FPGA design of the orthogonal wavelet transform and related image compression tools (JPEG2000) has been well studied [5,6,7], only a few publications address FPGA design of other types of wavelet transforms or wavelet coefficient manipulations other than simple thresholding.

In this paper we efficiently customize one of the latest wavelet domain denoising filters [8] and implement it in FPGA's for real-time video denoising. Some additional details of the developed architecture can be found in [9], where we described the preliminary results of this research.

This paper is organized as follows. In Section 2 we describe the implemented algorithm and present its customization for real-time implementation. The real-time environment that is used in this study is described in Section 3. The conclusions are in Section 4.

## 2   Developed FPGA Design

Fig. 1 depicts the implemented video denoising scheme, which consists of the non-decimated 2-D wavelet transform, Bayesian wavelet shrinkage followed by the inverse wavelet transform and selective recursive temporal filtering.

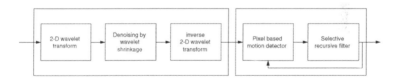

**Fig. 1.** The implemented denoising scheme

An important issue is whether to implement the floating-point arithmetic in FPGA and to use the original algorithm arithmetic or to convert the algorithm to the integer/fixed-point arithmetic. We use the fixed-point arithmetic which is less complex for a hardware implementation.

### 2.1   Non-decimated Wavelet Transform in FPGA's

While the implementations of the orthogonal wavelet transform have been extensively studied in literature [5,6,7] much less research has been done towards hardware implementations of the non-decimated wavelet transform. We design an FPGA implementation of the non-decimated wavelet transform using the algorithm *à trous* as it is described by Mallat and Zhong [10]. This algorithm replaces sub-sampling of the filtered signal by up-sampling the filters, where $2^{j-1}$ zeros ("holes", i.e., *trous* in French) are inserted between the filter coefficients at the decomposition level $j$.

We use the SystemC library [11] and a previously developed simulation environment [12,13] to develop a real-time model of the wavelet decomposition and composition [9]. The input value is 8 bit integer. We use the 16 bit arithmetic for wavelet decomposition and composition. The input 8 bits are placed at bit positions from 14 to 7. The output bits occupy the same positions (see Fig. 2).

| F | E | D | C | B | A | 9 | 8 | 7 | F | 5 | 4 | 3 | 2 | 1 | 0 |
|---|---|---|---|---|---|---|---|---|---|---|---|---|---|---|---|
| 0 | INPUT | | | | | | | | 0 | 0 | 0 | 0 | 0 | 0 | 0 |
| 0 | OUTPUT | | | | | | | | X | X | X | X | X | X | X |

**Fig. 2.** Input/Output data format

Our extensive simulations and tests demonstrate that this implementation results in a perfect reconstruction and gives practically the same results as a referent MATLAB code of the algorithm *à trous* [10]. At a number of input frames there were more than 97.13% errorless pixels with mean error of 0.0287. Analysis of those images at the level of bit representation, reveals that maximally 1 bit out of 16 was wrong. Moreover, the wrong bit may occur only on the least significant bit (LSB) position. If we take into account that input and output pixels are 8 bit places above first 6 LSB bits, we can ignore this error. This is depicted in Fig. 2.

## 2.2   FPGA Design of a Spatially Adaptive Wavelet Shrinker

We design FPGA architecture for a spatially adaptive wavelet denoising method of [8], which shrinks each wavelet coefficient according to the probability of presenting a "signal of interest" given the observed coefficient value and given a local spatial activity indicator (LSAI). In our implementation LSAI is the locally averaged coefficient magnitude within a 3x3 window and the signal of interest is defined as the noise-free component that exceeds in magnitude the noise standard deviation $\sigma$.

The analyzed denoising algorithm can be summarized as follows. Let $y_l$ denote the noise-free wavelet coefficient and $w_l$ its observed noisy version at the spatial position $l$ in a given wavelet subband. For compactness, we suppress here the indices that denote the scale and the orientation. The locally averaged coefficient magnitude is denoted by $z_l = \sum_{k \in N_l} |w_k|$, where $N_l$ is a square window centered at the position $l$. Further on, let $H_1$ denote the hypothesis "*the signal of interest is present: $|y_l| > \sigma$* " and let $H_0$ denote the opposite hypothesis "*the signal of interest is absent: $|y_l| \leq \sigma$*". The shrinkage estimator from [4] is

$$\hat{y}_l = \frac{\rho \xi_l \eta_l}{1 + \rho \xi_l \eta_l} w_l, \tag{1}$$

where

$$\rho = \frac{P(H_1)}{P(H_0)}, \quad \xi_l = \frac{p(w_l|H_1)}{p(w_l|H_0)} \quad \text{and} \quad \eta_l = \frac{p(z_l|H_1)}{p(z_l|H_0)}. \tag{2}$$

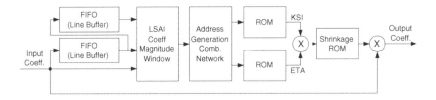

**Fig. 3.** Block schematic of implemented denoising architecture

and where $p(w_l|H_0)$ and $p(w_l|H_1)$ denote the conditional probability density functions of the noisy coefficients given the absence and given the presence of a signal of interest. Similarly, $p(z_l|H_0)$ and $p(z_l|H_1)$ denote the corresponding conditional probability density functions of the local spatial activity indicator. Under the Laplacian prior for noise-free data $p(y) = (\lambda/2)\exp(-\lambda|y|)$ we have [8] $\rho = \exp(-\lambda T)/(1 - \exp(-\lambda T))$. The analytical expressions for $\xi_l$ and $\eta_l$ seem too complex for the FPGA implementation. Based on an extensive experimental study, as we explain later in this Section, we efficiently implement the two likelihood ratios $\xi_l$ and $\eta_l$ as appropriate *look-up tables*, stored in two "Read-Only" Memories (ROM).

The developed architecture is presented in Fig. 3. One ROM memory, containing the look-up table $\xi_l$, is addressed by the coefficient magnitude $|w_l|$, and the other ROM memory, containing the look-up table $\rho\eta_l$ is addressed by LSAI $z_l$. For calculating LSAI, the coefficient values from the current line and from the previous two lines are averaged within a 3x3 window. The read values from ROM's are multiplied and the product $r$ is used to address another look-up table $r/(1+r)$, denoted as "shrinkage ROM". Its output (the shrinkage factor) is multiplied with the input coefficient to produce the denoised coefficient value.

The generation of the appropriate look-up tables for the two likelihood ratios resulted from our extensive experiments on different test images[1] and different noise-levels. Fig. 4 illustrates the likelihood ratio $\xi_l$ calculated from one test image at different noise levels. These diagrams show another interpretation of the well known threshold selection principle in wavelet denoising: a well chosen threshold value for the wavelet coefficients increases with the increase of the noise level. The maximum likelihood estimate of the threshold $T$ (i.e., the value for which $p(T|H_0) = p(T|H_1)$) is the abscissa of the point $\xi_l = 1$. Fig. 5 displays the likelihood ratio $\xi_l$, in the diagonal subband HH at third decomposition level, for 10 different frames with fixed noise standard deviations ($\sigma = 10$ and $\sigma = 30$). From a practical point of view, the difference between the calculated likelihood ratios for different frames is minor, especially for lower noise levels (up to $\sigma = 20$). Therefore we average the likelihood ratios over different frames and store these values as the corresponding look-up tables for several different noise levels ($\sigma = 5, 10, 15$ and $20$). In the denoising procedure, the user selects the input

---

[1] We used standard test images such as "Lena" and "Barbara", and frames from different standard test video sequences, such as "flower garden", "Miss America", "salesman", etc.

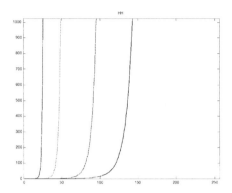

**Fig. 4.** Likelihood ratio $\xi_l$ for one test frame and 4 different noise levels ($\sigma$=5,10,20,30)

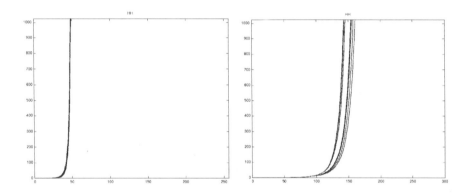

**Fig. 5.** Likelihood ratio $\xi_l$ displayed for 10 frames with fixed noise levels: $\sigma = 10$ (left) and $\sigma = 30$ (right)

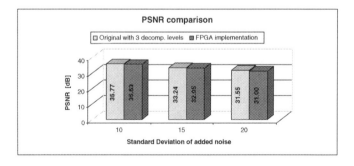

**Fig. 6.** Performance of the designed FPGA implementation in comparison with the original software version of the algorithm, which employs exact analytical calculation of the involved shrinkage expression

noise level, which enables addressing the correct set of the look-up tables. The performance loss of the algorithm due to simplifications with the generated look-up tables for different input noise levels is shown in Fig. 6. These results represent peak signal to noise ratio (PSNR) values averaged over frames of several different video sequences. For $\sigma=10$ the average performance loss was only 0.13dB (and visually, the differences are difficult to notice) while for $\sigma=20$ the performance loss is 0.55dB and is on most frames becoming visually noticeable, but not highly disturbing. For higher noise levels, the performance loss increases.

### 2.3 FPGA Design of a Selective Recursive Temporal Filter

A pixel based motion detector with selective recursive temporal filtering is quite simple for hardware implementation. Since we first apply a high quality spatial filtering the noise is already significantly suppressed and thus a pixel based motion detection is efficient. In case the motion is detected the recursive filtering is switched off.

Two pixels are needed for temporal filtering: one from the current field and another from the same spatial position in the previous field. We store the two fields in the output buffer and read the both required pixel values in the same cycle. If the absolute difference between these two pixel values is smaller than the predefined threshold value, *no motion* case is assumed and the two pixel values are subject to a weighted averaging, with the weighting factors defined in [4]. In the other case, when motion is detected, the current pixel is passed to the output. The block schematic in Fig. 7 depicts the developed FPGA architecture of the above described selective recursive temporal filter. In terms of computation accuracy, the only required adaptation of the original filter is the conversion from floating-point arithmetic to the integer arithmetic. We use the 8 bit arithmetic because the filter is located in the time domain where all the pixels are represented as 8 bit integers.

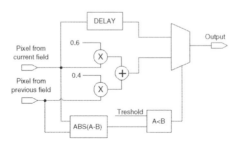

**Fig. 7.** Block schematic of implemented temporal filter

## 3   Evaluation in a Real-Time Environment

In our implementation we use the standard television broadcasting signal as a video signal source. A common feature of all standard TV broadcasting technologies is that the video sequence is transmitted in the analog domain (this

**Fig. 8.** A digital processing system for television broadcasting video sequences

excludes the latest DVB and HDTV transmission standards). Thus, before digital processing of television signals the digitalization is needed. Also, after digital processing the sequence has to be converted back to the analogue domain in order to be shown on a standard tube display. This pair of A/D and D/A converters is well known as a codec. The 8 bit codec, with 256 levels of quantization per pixel, is considered sufficient for preserving all details in the sequence. We use the PAL-B broadcasting standard and 8 bit YUV 4:2:2 codec. The hardware platform set-up consists of three separate boards: analog front-end (A/D conversion), processing board and analog back-end (D/A conversion) Each board corresponds to one of the blocks presented in Fig. 8:

The processing board consists of two Xilinx Virtex II FPGAs (XC2V6000-5) [14] and is equipped with plenty of SDRAM memory (6 banks with 32 bit access made with 256Mbit ICs). Additional implementation details are in [9].

An important practical issue is the specification of the following two parameters: estimated noise standard deviation $\sigma$ and the motion detection threshold. Currently we keep the motion detection threshold fixed and allow the choice of $\sigma$ from a set of predefined values. A future work will concentrate on estimating these parameters adaptively from the video sequence and on measuring the sensitivity of the scheme to these parameters.

An alternative real-time implementation of this algorithm may be based on commercially available DSP processors instead of FPGA. Indeed the approximation of the algorithm based on ROM tables as we proposed and speed-optimized programming in languages like C or C++ should significantly accelerate the software version of the algorithm. In this case, the profiling of the software implementation would be required to determine the DSP parameters, like the needed MIPS performance (MIPS - *Million Instructions Per Second*) and the ROM size, which are needed for real-time program running. However, it is not certain that a general purpose DSP processor could perform the non decimated wavelet transform of a television stream in real time due to a number of needed memory accesses for reading and writing the wavelet coefficients parallel with the accesses to the input and output buffers.

## 4    Conclusion

New trends in video technology and emerging wavelet domain video denoising methods require development of the appropriate real-time hardware architectures with FPGA's. This paper revealed technical details of one of such developments which has resulted in a real-time implementation of one of the latest wavelet domain denoising methods. We believe that some architectural design aspects presented in this paper should be interesting for future FPGA design of other, related wavelet domain denoising methods.

# References

1. Roosmalen, P., Westen, S., Lagendijk, R., Biemond, J.: Noise reduction for image sequences using an oriented pyramid thresholding technique. In: IEEE Conf. on Image Process. Lausanne, Switzerland (Sep. 1996) 375378
2. Selesnick, I., Li, K.: Video denoising using 2D and 3D dual-tree complex wavelet transforms. In: Wavelet Applications in Signal and Image Processing. Volume 5207 of SPIE Conf. (Aug. 2003) San Diego
3. Zlokolica, V., Pizurica, A., Philips, W.: Video denoising using multiple class averaging with multiresolution. In García, N., Martínez, J., Salgado, L., eds.: Proceedings of the 8th International Workshop, VLBV 2003. Volume LNCS 23849 of Visual Content Processing and Representation., Madrid, Spain, Springer (2003) 172–179
4. Pižurica, A., Zlokolica, V., Philips, W.: Noise reduction in video sequences using wavelet-domain and temporal filtering. In: Wavelet Applications in Industrial Processing. Proc. SPIE (2003)
5. Nibouche, M., Bouridane, A., Murtagh, F., Nibouche, O.: FPGA-based discrete wavelet transforms system. In Brebner, G., Woods, R., eds.: Field-Programmable Logic and Applications, Springer-Verlag (2001) 607–612
6. Wu, B.F., Hu, Y.Q.: An efficient VLSI implementation of the discrete wavelet transform usng embedded instruction codes for symetric filters. IEEE Transaction on Circuits and Systems for Video Technology **13 no. 9** (September 2003)
7. Dillen, G., Georis, B., Legat, J.D., Cantineau, O.: Combined line-based architecture for the 5-3 and 9-7 wavelet transform of JPEG2000. IEEE Transaction on Circuits and Systems for Video Technology **13 no. 9** (September 2003)
8. Pižurica, A., Philips, W.: Estimating the probability of the presence of a signal of interest in multiresolution single- and multiband image denoising. IEEE Trans. Image Processing (in press) (2005)
9. Katona, M., Pižurica, A., Teslić, V.Z.N., Philips, W.: Real-time wavelet domain video denoising implemented in FPGA. In: Wavelet Applications in Industrial Processing II. Volume 5607 of Proc. SPIE. (2004) 63–69
10. Mallat, S., Zhong, S.: Characterization of signals from multiscale edges. IEEE Trans. Pattern Anal. and Machine Intel. **14** (1992) 710–732
11. SystemC Version 2.0 Users Guide. www.systemc.org. (2002)
12. Katona, M., Teslic, N., Kovacevic, V., Temerinac, M.: Test environment for bluetooth baseband inegrated circuit development. In Milovanovic, B.D., ed.: TELSIKS 2001. Volume 2 of Telecommunication Technologies. (Septmeber 2001) 405–408
13. Katona, M., Teslic, N., Krajacevic, Z.: FPGA design with SystemC. In Napieralski, A., ed.: Mixed Design og Integrated Circuits and Systems. Volume 1 of MIXDES 2003. (Jun 2003) 220–223
14. Virtex II Platform FPGA: Complete Data Sheet. www.xilinx.com. (2004)

# Do Fuzzy Techniques Offer an Added Value for Noise Reduction in Images?

M. Nachtegael, S. Schulte, D. Van der Weken, V. De Witte, and E.E. Kerre

Ghent University, Dept. of Applied Mathematics and Computer Science,
Fuzziness and Uncertainty Modelling Research Unit,
Krijgslaan 281 - S9, 9000 Gent, Belgium
Mike.Nachtegael@UGent.be

**Abstract.** In this paper we discuss an extensive comparative study of 38 different classical and fuzzy filters for noise reduction, both for impulse noise and gaussian noise. The goal of this study is twofold: (1) we want to select the filters that have a very good performance for a specific noise type of a specific strength; (2) we want to find out whether fuzzy filters offer an added value, i.e. whether fuzzy filters outperform classical filters. The first aspect is relevant since large comparative studies did not appear in the literature so far; the second aspect is relevant in the context of the use of fuzzy techniques in image processing in general.

## 1 Introduction

Noise reduction is a well-known problem in image processing. The reduction of noise in an image sometimes is a goal itself, and sometimes is considered as a pre-processing step. Besides the classical filters for noise reduction, quite a lot of fuzzy inspired filters (i.e. filters that make use of techniques from fuzzy set theory) have been proposed during the past years. However, it is very difficult to evaluate the quality of this wide variety of filters, especially w.r.t. each other.

In this paper, we briefly explain the basic idea behind a "fuzzy" filter for noise reduction, we discuss the different classes of classical and fuzzy filters, and summarize the results of extensive comparative studies. The focus is on the filtering performance as such, i.e. we consider the reduction of noise as a goal itself. From these observations, it will be quite clear that fuzzy techniques for image noise reduction indeed have an added value in the field of image processing.

## 2 Noise Reduction Filters

### 2.1 Noise and Noise Reduction

Images can be contaminated with different types of noise, for different types of reasons. For example, noise can occur because of the circumstances of recording, the circumstances of transmission (damaged data), storage, copying, scanning, etc. Among the most common types of noise we find impulse noise (e.g. salt & pepper noise) and additive noise (e.g. gaussian noise).

J. Blanc-Talon et al. (Eds.): ACIVS 2005, LNCS 3708, pp. 658–665, 2005.
© Springer-Verlag Berlin Heidelberg 2005

The classical approach to reduce noise in a grayscale image mainly consists of replacing the grayvalue of a pixel with another value; the way in which the other value is determined depends on the filter that is applied. Quite often, all pixels are treated in the same way (the classical median filter is a typical example). It should be clear that this approach has some disadvantages. First, not all the pixels should be treated in the same way, because not all the pixels will be contaminated with noise in the same way. Secondly, one should try to find a more adaptive way to replace a pixel value (e.g. taking into account characteristics of a neighbourhood of the pixel).

A very important added value of fuzzy set theory is its ability to model and to reason with imprecision and uncertainty. Uncertainty is what occurs when processing an image for noise reduction, because of the fact that one can distinguish degrees of contamination of a pixel in an image. Fuzzy set theory allows to model and to work with this uncertainty, and to improve the quality of noise reduction. In general, a fuzzy filter for noise reduction uses both numerical information (just as classical filters) and linguistic information (modelled by fuzzy set theory; e.g. "small" and "large" values). This information is processed by fuzzy rules (approximate reasoning; e.g. "if most of the gradient values are large, then assume that the pixel is noisy"), resulting in a (defuzzified) filter output. The general scheme of fuzzy filters is shown in Figure 1.

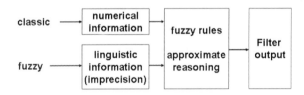

**Fig. 1.** Fuzzy filters use both numerical and linguistic information to process an image

## 2.2 Fuzzy Filters for Noise Reduction

The above observations have led to several proposals for noise reduction algorithms based on fuzzy set theory. The variety of available filters can ultimately be divided in three subclasses: (1) classical filters; (2) fuzzy-classical filters, i.e. fuzzy logic based filters that are a modification or extension of classical filters; (3) fuzzy filters, i.e. filters that are purely based on fuzzy logic and have no straightforward connection with classical filters. We have studied 38 different algorithms that were specifically designed for impulse noise and/or gaussian noise; the fuzzy-classical and fuzzy filters are accompanied by a reference for those readers who want more background information on them.

- **Classical filters:** MF (Median Filter), WF (Weighted Filter), AWF (Adaptive Weighted Filter), WIENER (Wiener Filter), GAUS (Gaussian Filter), EMF (Extended Median Filter).

- **Fuzzy-classical filters:** FMF (Fuzzy Median Filter, [1,2]), TMED (Symmetrical Triangle Fuzzy Filter with median center, [10]), ATMED (Asymmetrical Triangle Fuzzy Filter with median center, [10]), GMED (Gaussian Filter with Median Center, [10]), FIDRM (Fuzzy Impulse noise Detection and Reduction Method, [20]), WFM (Weighted Fuzzy Mean Filter, [11,12]), FWM (Fuzzy Weighted Mean, [2]), AWFM (first Adaptive Weighted Fuzzy Mean Filter, [11]), AWFM2 (second Adaptive Weighted Fuzzy Mean Filter, [12]), CK (Choi & Krishnapuram Filter, [3]), FDDF (Fuzzy Decision Directed Filter, [13]), TMAV (Symmetrical Triangle Fuzzy Filter with Moving Average Center, [10]), ATMAV (Asymmetrical Triangle Fuzzy Filter with Moving Average Center, [10]), DWMAV (Decreasing Weight Fuzzy Filter with Moving Average Center, [10]), GMAV (Gausian Fuzzy Filter with Moving Average Center, [10]), MPASS (Multipass fuzzy filter, [15,6]), FMMF (Fuzzy Multilevel Median Filter, [8,6]).
- **Fuzzy filters:** FIRE (Fuzzy Inference Ruled by Else-action Filter, [16]), DS-FIRE (Dual Step Fuzzy Inference Ruled by Else-action Filter, [17]), PWL-FIRE1 (first (non-adaptive) Piecewise Linear Fuzzy Inference Ruled by Else-action Filter, [18]), PWLFIRE2 (second (adaptive) Piecewise Linear Fuzzy Inference Ruled by Else-action Filter, [18]), IFCF (Iterative Fuzzy Control based Filter, [5]), MIFCF (Modified Iterative Fuzzy Control based Filter, [5]), EIFCF (Extended Iterative Fuzzy Control based Filter, [5]), SFCF (Smoothing Fuzzy Control based Filter, [4]), SSFCF (Sharpening Smoothing Fuzzy Control based Filter, [5]), GOA (Gaussian Noise Reduction Filter, [23]), HAF (Histogram Adaptieve Filter, [9]), FSB1 (first Fuzzy-Similarity-Based Noise Reduction Filter, [21,22]), FSB2 (second Fuzzy-Similarity-Based Noise Reduction Filter, [21,22]), FSB1R (first Recursive Fuzzy-Similarity-Based Noise Reduction Filter, [21,22]), FSB2R (second Recursive Fuzzy-Similarity-Based Noise Reduction Filter, [21,22]).

## 3    A Comparative Study

The evaluation of the 38 filters was carried out on two levels: numerical (based on the MSE values) and visual (based on visual inspection by humans). In order to get a clear idea of the performance w.r.t. the level of noise, experiments have been carried out for 10%, 20%, 30%, 50%, 70% and 90% of impulse noise and for gaussian noise with $\sigma = 25, 50, 75, 100$ and $125$. Furthermore, the experiments have been carried out on several images, such as the Lena image ($256 \times 256$), the Cameraman image ($256 \times 256$) and the Bridge image ($512 \times 512$). This resulted in a large amount of data, that was carefully examined. Due to space limitations, we limit ourselves here to the general conclusions, and some illustrative figures.

### 3.1    Reduction of Impulse Noise

The conclusions w.r.t. the numerical results can be summarized as follows:

- The FIDRM filter performs best for all levels of impulse noise. In the case of the Lena image it reduces the MSE by a factor 143 for low levels (10%) and by a factor 57 for very high levels (90%). For the other images these factors range between 68 to 77 and 37 to 40, respectively. These are remarkable results.

- For low noise levels (10%, 20% and 30%) the EMF filter nearly always is the second best performing filter (an exception is its forth place when the Lena image is corrupted with 30% impulse noise). Also the FMF filter has a good performance: it always belongs to the top-3 or top-4 of best performing filters. Other filters that perform good for low noise levels are the PWLFIRE2 filter (top-4 for 10% impulse noise), the AWFM2 filter (which performance increases when the noise rate gets higher), the HAF filter (same remark), the ATMED filter (top-5 for 20% impulse noise on the Cameraman image and for 30% impulse noise on the Bridge image), and the AWFM filter (top-5 for 30% impulse noise on the Cameraman and Lena images).
- For high noise levels (50%, 70% and 90%) the top-5 of best performing filters always consists of the same set, namely the FIDRM filter (always performs best), the AWFM2 filter (nearly always is the second best performing filter), and the HAF, ATMAV and AWFM filters.

In general, our conclusion based on the numerical evaluation of the filters is that the FIDRM filter outperforms the rest. For noise levels around 10% to 30% the

**Fig. 2.** The Lena image with 20% impulse noise, and the results of FIDRM (top right), EMF (lower left) and classical median filter (lower right)

EMF and FMF filters are respectable counterparts. For higher noise levels, it is clear that the AWFM2, HAF, ATMAV and AWFM filters constitute the top-5 of best performing filters. We can also clearly see that several filters are not designed to deal with impulse noise. For example, the classical WIENER and GAUS filters are specifically designed for gaussian noise and fail w.r.t. impulse noise.

The visual results of all best performing filters are in general very good for all considered noise levels. This confirms the good numerical performance of these filters. For all noise levels the HAF filter produces a more blurry picture than the FIDRM and AWFM2 filters; in other words, the FIDRM and AWFM2 filter have the property that they keep the sharpness of the image. For the lower noise levels (e.g. 30%), we also found that the FIDRM filter gives slightly sharper results than the AWFM2 filter, while for the higher noise levels (e.g. 70%) the AWFM2 filter gives slightly sharper results than the FIDRM filter. Figure 2 shows some visual results, including the best performing fuzzy filters and the classical median filter.

In summary, the numerical and visual experiments confirm each other: the FIDRM filter performs best for all noise levels, followed by the classical EMF filter for low noise levels, and the AWFM2 filter for high noise levels. These results show that the use of fuzzy techniques in image processing can have an added value. Indeed, except for the EMF filter all best performing filters belong to the class of fuzzy-classical or purely fuzzy filters.

## 3.2    Reduction of Gaussian Noise

The conclusions w.r.t. the numerical results can be summarized as follows:

- The GOA filter performs best for all levels of gaussian noise, for all 3 tested images. The GOA filter reduces the MSE by a factor 5 for low levels ($\sigma = 25$), and by a factor 8 to 12 for the higher noise levels. There is only one exception to this general observation: for $\sigma = 25$ in case of the bridge image, the GOA filter does not show up in the top-5 of best performing filters w.r.t. the reduction of MSE.

  From a numerical point of view these results are good. It should be noted that the reduction of MSE is more substantial for high levels of noise than for low levels of noise. Compared to the numerical results for impulse noise the reduction of MSE is less impressive, which without any doubt is due to the fact that gaussian noise is much more complex, and consequently much more difficult to remove than impulse noise.

- The MIFCF, SFCF and AWFM2 filters perform second to third best in case of low noise levels. The exact results differ depending on the used image; there is no general observation. For higher noise levels, these filters are not among the 5 best performing filters.

- The role of the second to third best performing filter for all noise levels above $\sigma = 25$ is taken over by the IFCF filter. For the Bridge image in particular, it always is the second best performing filter, followed by the EIFCF filter (which is a modified version of the IFCF filter) as third best performing filter. For the Lena and cameraman images, the EIFC filter is only the fifth best performing filter for the highest noise levels ($\sigma = 100, 125$). In general, it can also be observed that the relative difference in MSE-values between the GOA and the second to third best performing filters becomes greater for higher noise levels.

– The results regarding the fourth and fifth best performing filters are rather scattered for low noise levels, while they are quite pronounced for higher noise levels. For low noise levels ($\sigma = 25$), the FMF, EIFCF, AWFM2 and IFCF appear in the top-5. For slightly higher noise levels ($\sigma = 50$), the WF and DWMAV filters appear, together with the MIFCF and ATMAV filter. For the highest noise levels ($\sigma = 75, 100, 125$) it is quite clear from the experiments that the WF and DWMAV filters are the fourth to fifth best performing filters.

In general, our conclusion based on the numerical evaluation of the filters is that the GOA filter clearly outperforms the rest. It is difficult to select a group of other best performing filters, since the results depend too much on the processed image: for low noise levels the IFCF and EIFC filters turn out to be good, for high noise levels the WF and DWMAV filters generate quite stable results. The reduction of the MSE values is in all cases however less remarkable than in the

**Fig. 3.** The Lena image with $\sigma = 50$ (gaussian noise), and the results of GOA (top right), IFCF (lower left), and classical gaussian filter (lower right)

case of impulse noise, but this is not really surprising since gaussian noise is a much more complicated kind of noise.

The visual results for reducing gaussian noise are not as good as in the case of impulse noise. Nevertheless, the top-3 of best performing filters gives satisfying results for low noise levels; one can observe that the GOA filter produces a much nicer, although a bit blurrier, image. For values for $\sigma$ of 50 and higher, the results of the filters are not always satisfying. The GOA filter makes the images blurry (the higher the noise level, the blurrier the result after filtering), and the second and third best performing filters from a numerical point of view do not adequately reduce the noise. In particular, we notice the creation of small blocks in the images. Figure 3 shows some visual results, including the best performing fuzzy filters and the classical gaussian filter.

In summary, for low levels of gaussian noise the best performing filters give a good visual result, which is in accordance with the numerical observations. However, for higher levels of gaussian noise an honest conclusion is that the visual results could still be improved. This observation also leads to the conclusion that noise reduction filters, in the case of gaussian noise, should not only be evaluated based on numerical measures.

## 4   Conclusion

Our comparative study has revealed that the best performing filters, out of a total of 38 different classical and fuzzy filters, are based on fuzzy techniques. This conclusion holds for both impulse and gaussian noise, and illustrates the fact that fuzzy filters have resulted in an added value to the field of noise reduction.

Future research should, in our opinion, focus on the following three aspects: (1) the development of (fuzzy) filters for other types of noise (e.g. speckle noise) and mixed types of noise; (2) the extension of (fuzzy) filters to color and video images; cfr. [19] for a recent attempt; (3) a continued inventarization and comparison of noise reduction algorithms.

## References

1. Arakawa K., Median filter based on fuzzy rules and its application to image restoration, in: Fuzzy Sets and Systems, Vol. 77, 1996, pp. 3-13.
2. Arakawa K., Fuzzy rule-based image processing with optimization, in: Fuzzy Techniques in Image Processing (Kerre E.E. & Nachtegael M., editors), Springer-Verlag, 2000, pp. 222-247.
3. Choi Y., Krishnapuram R., Image enhancement based on fuzzy logic, in: IEEE Proceedings, 1995, pp.167-171.
4. Farbiz F., Menhaj M.B. & Motamedi S.A., Edge preserving image filtering based on fuzzy logic, in: Proceedings of the Sixth EUFIT conference (Aken, Duitsland), 1998, pp. 1417-1421.
5. Farbiz F. & M.B. Menhaj M.B., A fuzzy logic control based approach for image filtering, in: Fuzzy Techniques in Image Processing (Kerre E.E. & Nachtegael M., editors), Springer-Verlag, 2000, pp. 194-221.

6. Forero-Vargas M.G. & Delgado-Rangel L.J., Fuzzy filters for noise reduction, in: Fuzzy Filters for Image Processing (Nachtegael M., Van der Weken D., Van De Ville D. & Etienne E.E., editors), Springer-Verlag, 2002, pp. 3-24.

7. Grabisch M. & Schmitt M., Mathematical morphology, order filters and fuzzy logic, in: Proceedings of the Joint Conference of FUZZ-IEEE'95 and IFES'95 (Yokohama, Japan), 1995, pp. 2103-2108

8. Jiu J.Y., Multilevel median filter based on fuzzy decision, DSP IC Design Lab E.E. NTU., 1996.

9. Wang J.-H. & Chiu H.-C., HAF: An adaptive fuzzy filter for restoring highly corrupted images by histogram estimation, in: Proc. Natl. Sci. Counc. ROC(A), Vol. 23, No. 5, 1999. pp. 630-643.

10. Kwan H.K., Fuzzy filters for noise reduction in images, in: Fuzzy Filters for Image Processing (Nachtegael M., Van der Weken D., Van De Ville D. & Etienne E.E., editors), Springer-Verlag, 2002, pp. 25-53.

11. Lee C.S., Kuo Y.H. & Yu P.T., Weighted fuzzy mean filters for image processing, in: Fuzzy Sets and Systems, Vol. 89, 1997, pp. 157-180.

12. Lee C.S. & Kuo Y.H., Adaptive fuzzy filter and its application to image enhancement, in: Fuzzy Techniques in Image Processing (Kerre E.E. & Nachtegael M., editors), Springer-Verlag, 2000, pp. 172-193.

13. Mancuso M., De Luca R., Poluzzi R. & Rizzotto G.G., A fuzzy decision directed filter for impulsive noise reduction, in: Fuzzy Sets and Systems, Vol. 77, 1996, pp. 111-116.

14. Nachtegael M., Fuzzy morphological and fuzzy logical filtering techniques in image processing, Phd thesis, Ghent University, 2002 (in Dutch).

15. Russo F. & Ramponi G., A noise smoother using cascade FIRE filters, in: Proceedings of the 4th FUZZ-IEEE Conference, 1995, pp. 351-358.

16. Russo F. & Ramponi G., A fuzzy filter for images corrupted by impulse noise, in: IEEE Signal proceedings letters, Vol. 3, No. 6, 1996, pp. 168-170.

17. Russo F. & Ramponi G., Removal of impulse noise using a FIRE filter, in: IEEE Proceedings, 1996, pp. 975-978.

18. Russo F., FIRE operators for image processing, in: Fuzzy Sets and Systems, Vol. 103, 1999, pp. 265-275.

19. Schulte S., Nachtegael M., De Witte V., Van der Weken D. & Kerre E.E., A new two step color filter for impulse noise, in: Proceedings of the 11th Zittau Fuzzy Colloquium, 2004, pp. 185-192.

20. Schulte S., Nachtegael M., De Witte V., Van der Weken D. & Kerre E.E., A fuzzy impulse noise detection and reduction method, IEEE Transactions on Image Processing, accepted.

21. Tolt G. & Kalaykov I., Fuzzy-similarity-based noise cancellation for real-time image processing, in: Proceedings of the 10th FUZZ-IEEE Conference, 2001, pp. 15-18.

22. Tolt G. & Kalaykov I., Real-time image noise cancellation based on fuzzy similarity, in: Fuzzy Filters for Image Processing (Nachtegael M., Van der Weken D., Van De Ville D. & Etienne E.E., editors), Springer-Verlag, 2002, pp. 54-71.

23. Van De Ville D., Nachtegael M., Van der Weken D., Kerre E.E., Philips W. & Lemahieu I., Noise reduction by fuzzy image filtering, in: IEEE Transactions on Fuzzy Systems, Vol. 11, No. 4, 2003, pp. 429-436.

# Noise Reduction of Video Sequences Using Fuzzy Logic Motion Detection

Stefan Schulte[1], Vladimir Zlokolica[2], Aleksandra Pizurica[2],
Wilfried Philips[2], and Etienne Kerre[1]

[1] Ghent University, Department of Applied Mathematics and Computer Science,
Krijgslaan 281 (Building S9), 9000 Gent, Belgium
[2] Ghent University, Dept. of Telecommunications and Information Processing
(TELIN), IPI, Sint-Pietersnieuwstraat 41, 9000 Gent, Belgium
vzlokoli@telin.UGent.be, Stefan.Schulte@UGent.be

**Abstract.** In this paper we present a novel video denoising method
based on a fuzzy logic recursive motion detection scheme. For each pixel
a fuzzy quantity (motion confidence) is calculated, indicating the membership degree of the fuzzy set "motion". Next, this fuzzy quantity is
used to perform adaptive temporal filtering, where the amount of filtering is inversely proportional to the determined membership degree. Since
big motion changes reduce temporal filtering, a non-stationary noise will
be introduced. Hence a new fuzzy spatial filter is applied subsequently
in order to obtain the final denoised image sequence. Experimental results show that the proposed method outperform other state of the art
non-multiscale video denoising techniques and are comparable with some
multi-scale (wavelet) based video denoising techniques.

## 1 Introduction

Image sequences are often corrupted by noise, caused by e.g. bad reception of
television pictures. For certain applications such as television and surveillance,
these corruptions can often be approximated by an additive white Gaussian noise
model, which we consider in this paper.

Video denoising is generally achieved through some form of linear or nonlinear operation on a set of neighbouring pixels (in the spatio-temporal sense).
The defined spatio-temporal neighbourhood can be either defined through estimated motion trajectory (motion estimation and compensation) or by nearest
spatio-temporal neighbourhood (motion detection and exclusion). A thorough
review of noise reduction algorithms for digital image sequences is presented in
[1]. The best results for video denoising are generally obtained by motion compensated filtering. However, for some application such as for video sequences
with relatively big static background areas a less complex solution (e.g. motion
detection and exclusion filters) that performs comparable to more time consuming motion compensated filter is preferred for its simplicity. Nevertheless, for the
advantageous performance of the "motion detection-exclusion" video denoising
algorithm a reliable and noise-robust motion detection is required.

J. Blanc-Talon et al. (Eds.): ACIVS 2005, LNCS 3708, pp. 666–673, 2005.
© Springer-Verlag Berlin Heidelberg 2005

The disadvantage of the binary motion detection is the dependency of the selected threshold, which either detects false motion pixels due to noise (when the motion threshold is low) or detects not enough true motion pixels (when the motion threshold is high). Based on such motion detection output the algorithm decides if the pixel value will be filtered in temporal direction or not at, where the amount of filtering is fixed. This usually produces either motion blurring (case when not enough motion is detected) or impulse-like artefacts (some noise is also considered as motion).

In this paper a new noise reduction method of image sequences is presented, where the motion detection is based on fuzzy logic. This motion detector combines membership degrees appropriately using defined fuzzy rules, where the membership degrees are determined by a membership function. As an output the motion detector produces the membership degree in the fuzzy set "motion", which is expressed as a real number between the two extremes: zero (no motion for sure) and one (motion for sure). For each pixel, this membership degree is used to perform adaptive temporal filtering. The larger this degree the less temporal filtering will be applied. In such way we avoid temporal blurring and remove noise. Since the pixels undergoing motion will not be sufficiently filtered, we finally apply the proposed spatial filter. This fuzzy spatial filter is based on the GOA filter [2]. The general framework of the presented algorithm is illustrated in Fig. 1.

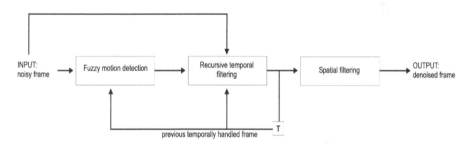

**Fig. 1.** Schema of the proposed algorithm

The paper is structured as follows: The details of the fuzzy motion detection are given in section 2. In section 3 the temporal and spatial filtering are discussed. Experimental results and conclusions are finally presented in section 4 and section 5, respectively.

## 2   Fuzzy Logic Motion Detection

In this section we investigate motion in noisy video sequences and propose the framework for the fuzzy logic based motion detection method. In the following, an image pixel will be denoted as $I(x, y, t)$, where $(x, y)$ and $t$ stand for the spatial and temporal coordinate of the image sequence $I$, respectively.

In order to determine motion detection from the input noisy sequences, we investigate the relative correlation of the absolute luminance differences $\Delta(x, y, t)$, defined as follows:

$$\Delta(x, y, t) = |I_{in}(x, y, t) - I_p(x, y, t - 1)| \tag{1}$$

in a small spatial 2D neighbourhood, where subindexes $in$ and $p$ stand for the input noisy frame and the previous temporally filtered frame, respectively. We assume that a certain pixel position being a part of a moving object if some spatial neighbours are part of this object too. Therefore, in order to detect motion for the current pixel position $(x, y, t)$, we also take into account the following eight differences: $\delta_1 = \Delta(x - 1, y - 1, t)$, $\delta_2 = \Delta(x - 1, y, t)$, $\delta_3 = \Delta(x - 1, y + 1, t)$, $\delta_4 = \Delta(x, y - 1, t)$, $\delta_5 = \Delta(x, y + 1, t)$, $\delta_6 = \Delta(x + 1, y - 1, t)$, $\delta_7 = \Delta(x + 1, y, t)$, $\delta_8 = \Delta(x + 1, y + 1, t)$. Specifically, the proposed motion detection is based on the following fuzzy rules:

**Fuzzy Rule 1.**

IF $\left( \Delta(x, y, t) \text{ is } LARGE \right)$ AND $\left( \text{ at least 3 of the } \delta_i\text{'s are } LARGE \right)$
THEN $I_{in}(x, y, t)$ is a $MOTION\ PIXEL$

**Fuzzy Rule 2.**

IF $\left( \Delta(x, y, t) \text{ is } SMALL \right)$ OR

$\left( \left( \Delta(x, y, t) \text{ is } LARGE \right) \text{ AND } \left( \text{ all } \delta\text{'s are } SMALL \right) \right)$ OR

$\left( \left( \Delta(x, y, t) \text{ is } LARGE \right) \text{ AND } \left( \text{ 7 of the 8 } \delta\text{'s are } SMALL \right) \right)$ OR

$\left( \left( \Delta(x, y, t) \text{ is } LARGE \right) \text{ AND } \left( \text{ 6 of the 8 } \delta\text{'s are } SMALL \right) \right)$

THEN $I_{in}(x, y, t)$ is a $NON\ MOTION\ PIXEL$

Because "LARGE" and "SMALL" are non-deterministic features, these terms are represented by fuzzy sets [3]. Fuzzy sets can be represented by membership functions. In the proposed algorithm we have used membership functions $\mu_{LARGE}$ (2) for the fuzzy set LARGE and $\mu_{SMALL}$ (3) for the fuzzy set SMALL, which are defined as follows:

$$\mu_{LARGE}(\Delta(x, y, t)) = \begin{cases} 0 & \text{if } \Delta(x, y, t) < a \\ \frac{\Delta(x,y,t) - a}{b - a} & \text{if } a \leq \Delta(x, y, t) \leq b \\ 1 & \text{if } \Delta(x, y, t) > b \end{cases} \tag{2}$$

$$\mu_{SMALL}(\Delta(x, y, t)) = \begin{cases} 1 & \text{if } \Delta(x, y, t) < a \\ 1 - \frac{\Delta(x,y,t) - a}{b - a} & \text{if } a \leq \Delta(x, y, t) \leq b \\ 0 & \text{if } \Delta(x, y, t) > b \end{cases} \tag{3}$$

where the parameters $a$ and $b$ are determined as a function of the estimated standard deviation, from the input noisy video sequence frame. For estimating noise level we have used the method proposed in [4].

In fuzzy logic, triangular norms and co-norms [5] are used to represent respectively the conjunction and the disjunction operators of Fuzzy Rule 1 and 2. Some well-known triangular norms (together with their dual co-norms) are the minimum (maximum) and the product (probabilistic sum) [5]. We use the product for the conjunction and the probabilistic sum for the disjunction operators.

Based on the Fuzzy Rules (1) and (2), we calculate the membership degree of the fuzzy set "motion pixel" ($M_{true}(x, y, t)$) and the membership degree of the fuzzy set "non motion pixel" ($M_{false}(x, y, t)$), respectively. Finally, the degree of motion confidence $\theta$ is determined in the following way: $\theta(x, y, t) = M_{true}(x, y, t)/(M_{true}(x, y, t) + M_{false}(x, y, t))$. The degree of motion confidence "one" indicates existence of motion for sure while the zero motion confidence degree indicates the total absence of motion. All degrees between these two extremes indicate that there is some kind of uncertainty.

## 3   Temporal and Spatial Filter

Using the output decision parameter - motion confidence, $\theta$ (section 2) for a certain position $(x, y, t)$, we perform recursive temporal filtering as follows: the larger the value $\theta(x, y, t)$ is the less we filter temporally (i.e. we do not take into account information from previously processed frames), because large $\theta(x, y, t)$-values indicate that pixel $(x, y, t)$ is part of an moving object. When $\theta(x, y, t)$-value is relatively small, we then use more information from the previously processed frame.

The temporal filtering method is presented in subsection 3.1, while the proposed fuzzy-logic based spatial filter for non-stationary noise is presented in subsection 3.2.

### 3.1   Temporal Filtering

Recursive temporal filtering is defined as follows:

$$I_p(x, y, t) = \alpha(x, y, t) I_{in}(x, y, t) + \left(1 - \alpha(x, y, t)\right) I_p(x, y, t - 1), \quad (4)$$

where the parameter $\alpha$ controls the amount of filtering. We define this parameter in terms of the motion confidence parameter $\theta$, as follows:

$$\alpha(x, y, t) = \frac{\alpha(x, y, t - 1)^2 + 2\sqrt{\theta(x, y, t)} - \alpha(x, y, t - 1)\sqrt{\theta(x, y, t)}}{2}, \quad (5)$$

where $\sqrt{\theta(x, y, t)}$ is an initial estimation based on the decision parameter $\theta$. With (5) we aim at introducing adaptation of temporal filtering in respect to the previous temporal recursion. Namely, the less filtering that was performed in the previous recursion the more we reduce the filtering in the current temporal recursion in order reduce the propagation of noise.

In order to adapt our algorithm to unsteady lighting conditions and sudden spatio-temporal changes of the noise levels, we estimate the standard deviation $\sigma$ of noise [6] for the first frame only and then adapt it through the sequence for each position $(x, y, t)$, separately (i.e. $\sigma(x, y, t)$). The evaluation of the local $\sigma(x, y, t)$ is performed by recursive averaging as explained in [6]. The higher the motion confidence, $\theta(x, y, t)$, the closer the current $\sigma(x, y, t)$ is to the previous value $\sigma(x, y, t-1)$, i.e. less temporal adaptation of local noise estimation will be performed. On the other hand, in cases when the determined motion confidence is relatively small the local noise estimation will be spatio-temporally updated in the 3D neighbourhood. It should be noted, that in case of recursive temporal filtering for regions not undergoing motion, the estimated local standard deviation will be relatively smaller in comparison to areas that are not being temporally filtered. This, however, is not a problem and even helps and enables efficient spatial filtering of spatially non-stationary noise, that we explain in subsection 3.2.

## 3.2   Spatial Filtering

The proposed spatial filter deals with the non-stationary noise left by the preceding temporal filter. The main idea of this filter is to use local fuzzy gradients for distinguishing between noise and edge elements. This method is inspired by the GOA [2] filter. The main difference is noticed by the usage of the fuzzy gradient values. In the proposed method these gradient values are used to derive weighting coefficients, where the GOA filter calculated a global correction term.

Consider a $3 \times 3$ neighbourhood of a pixel $(x, y, t)$. The gradient $\nabla_D I_p(x, y, t)$ is defined as the difference between the central pixel $(x, y, t)$ and its neighbour in the direction $D$; $D \in \{NW, W, SW, S, SE, E, NE, N\}$ (e.g. $\nabla_N I_p(x, y, t) = I_p(x, y-1, t) - I_p(x, y, t)$).

We assume that an edge passing through a certain pixel causes large gradient values perpendicular to the direction for the current pixel and for its two neigh-

**Table 1.** Pixels involved to calculate the fuzzy gradients: each direction $D$ (column 1) corresponds to a certain position (column 2) and column 3 specifies which pixels are considered w.r.t. that position in the calculation

| direction $D$ | position $(X, Y)$ | considered pixels | | |
|---|---|---|---|---|
| | | $(k_1, k_2)$ | centres | $(l_1, l_2)$ |
| NW | $(x-1, y-1)$ | $(-1, 1)$ | $(0, 0)$ | $(1, -1)$ |
| N | $(x-1, y)$ | $(0, -1)$ | $(0, 0)$ | $(0, 1)$ |
| NE | $(x-1, y+1)$ | $(-1, -1)$ | $(0, 0)$ | $(1, 1)$ |
| W | $(x, y-1)$ | $(-1, 0)$ | $(0, 0)$ | $(1, 0)$ |
| E | $(x, y+1)$ | $(-1, 0)$ | $(0, 0)$ | $(1, 0)$ |
| SW | $(x+1, y-1)$ | $(1, 1)$ | $(0, 0)$ | $(-1, -1)$ |
| S | $(x+1, y)$ | $(0, -1)$ | $(0, 0)$ | $(0, 1)$ |
| SE | $(x+1, y+1)$ | $(-1, 1)$ | $(0, 0)$ | $(1, -1)$ |

bouring pixels as well. For example, for an edge-structure in west-east (W-E) direction - $\nabla_N I_p(x, y, t)$, $\nabla_N I_p(x, y-1, t)$ and $\nabla_N I_p(x, y+1, t)$ are expected to be relatively big). By combining these three gradient values for each direction, in a fuzzy logic manner, we distinguish between local variations due to noise and due to edge structures. Table 1 gives an overview of the pixels that are involved in the calculation for every possible edge direction.

If two of the three gradient values for some direction are large in magnitude, we conclude that there is an edge in this direction. Consequently, we define the $D$th-direction fuzzy gradient value (positive) with Fuzzy rule 3:

**Fuzzy Rule 3.**

IF $\Big( \nabla_D I_p(x, y, t)$ *is positive large AND* $\nabla_D I_p(x + k_1, y + k_2, t)$ *is*

*positive large* $\Big)$ *OR*

$\Big( \nabla_D I_p(x, y, t)$ *is positive large AND* $\nabla_D I_p(x + l_1, y + l_2, t)$ *is*

*positive large* $\Big)$ *OR*

$\Big( \nabla_D I_p(x + k_1, y + k_2, t)$ *is positive large AND* $\nabla_D I_p(x + l_1, y + l_2, t)$ *is*

*positive large* $\Big)$

THEN $\nabla_D^{Fpos} I_p(x, y, t)$ *is positive large*

where an identical rule is defined for the negative fuzzy gradient value as well.

The product and probabilistic sum are used for the AND and OR operations, respectively. The corresponding membership functions are shown in Fig. 2 (a) and (b).

Finally, weighting coefficients $w$ in the proposed weighted averaging spatial filter are calculated for each of the eight neighbours around the central pixel $(x, y, t)$. This is realized by the following fuzzy rule:

**Fuzzy Rule 4.** IF $\nabla_D^{Fpos} I_p(x, y, t)$ *is small AND* $\nabla_D^{Fneg} I_p(x, y, t)$ *is small*

THEN $w(X, Y, t)$ *is large*

In case the negative and positive fuzzy gradient values for some direction $D$ are both small (i.e. when the membership degree in the fuzzy set "small" is large),

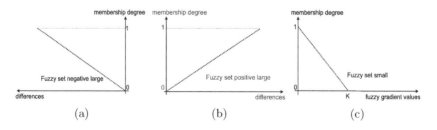

**Fig. 2.** Three membership functions: (a) negative large, (b) positive large and (c) small

we then suppose that the neighbour in direction $D$ w.r.t. the centre is similar to the centre. This indicates that no edge is present. Hence, the contribution of the corresponding pixel to the spatial filtering should be relatively large. This is done by introducing large weighting coefficient values in such cases and vice-versa in the opposite case.

The final output of the spatial filter is defined as follows:

$$I_{out}(x, y, t) = \frac{\sum_{k=-1}^{1} \sum_{l=-1}^{1} I_p(x+k, y+l, t) \cdot w(x+k, y+l, t)}{\sum_{k=-1}^{1} \sum_{l=-1}^{1} w(x+k, y+l, t)} \tag{6}$$

with $w(x, y, t) = 1$. The membership function "small" of the corresponding fuzzy set is shown in Fig. 2 (c) and it depends on the parameter $K$, where the parameter $K$ being proportional to the estimated $\sigma(x, y, t)$ (as explained in subsection 3.1) and is defined as $K = 3\sigma(x, y, t)/255$.

## 4    Experimental Results

The results of the proposed Fuzzy Motion Recursive Temporal-Spatial Filtering technique (FMRTSF) have been compared with several state of the art techniques for video denoising: (1) the motion and detail adaptive KNN filter [4], (2) the $\alpha$-trimmed filter [7], (3) the rational filter [8] and (4) the multi-class wavelet based spatio-temporal filter (MCWF) [9].

Table 2 illustrates the performance of the proposed method in comparison to the above mentioned methods, in terms of peak signal to noise ratio (PSNR). As seen from Table 2 the proposed Fuzzy Motion Recursive Temporal-Spatial algorithm outperforms single resolution techniques [4,8] and yields comparable results to more complex multi-scale techniques [9].

The main improvement of the spatial filter can be noticed in the reduction of the non-stationary noise while preserving the important image structures. Regions where the noise was filtered out temporally become sharper and regions

**Table 2.** The PSNR results for the processed sequences corrupted with Gaussian noise ($\sigma = 10$)

| | | PSNR (in dB) | | | |
|---|---|---|---|---|---|
| input sequence | Fuzzy MRTSF | adaptive KNN | $\alpha$ trimmed | rational | MCWF |
| Salesman | 34.2 | 32.5 | 29.4 | 30.6 | 33.0 |
| Deadline | 34.9 | 32.2 | 24.3 | 27.3 | 33.2 |
| Miss Am. | 36.8 | 35.3 | 35.1 | 35.2 | 35.9 |
| Trevor | 34.3 | 34.1 | 34.1 | 34.3 | 35.4 |
| Tennis | 31.5 | 30.5 | 22.5 | 26.5 | 31.3 |

with much non-stationary noise become smoother, whereby the visual performances increase (presented on: http://www.fuzzy.ugent.be/ACIVS05.html).

## 5   Conclusion

A novel fuzzy logic based recursive temporal - spatial filter has been presented in this paper. Fuzzy motion detection is followed by a recursive temporally filtering. Since the pixels undergoing motion will not be sufficiently filtered temporally, the spatial filtering is applied afterwards. This spatial filter is based on the GOA filter [2]. Further research could be aimed at improvement of the motion detection by local contrast enhancement and usage of color information.

## Acknowledgment

This work was financially supported by the GOA-project 12.0515.03 of Ghent University.

## References

1. Brailean, J. C., Kleihorst, R.P. and Efstratidis, S., Katsaggeleos, K.A., Lagendijk, R.L.: Noise reduction filters for dynamic image sequences: A Review. Proceedings of the IEEE **83** no. 9 (1995) 1272-1292
2. Van De Ville, D., Nachtegael, M., Van der Weken, D., Kerre, E.E., Philips, W.: Noise reduction by fuzzy image filtering. IEEE Transactions on Fuzzy Systems **11** (2001) 429-436
3. Kerre, E.E.: Fuzzy Sets and Approximate Reasoning. Xian Jiaotong University Press (1998)
4. Zlokolica, V., Philips, W.: Motion- and detail-adaptive denoising of video. Proc. SPIE Electronic Imaging 5298-47, January 2004, San Jose, California, USA
5. Klement, E.P, Mesiar, R., Pap, E.: Triangular Norms. Trends in Logic **8**, Kluwer Academic Pub. (2000)
6. Zlokolica, V., De Geyter, M., Schulte, S., Pizurica, A., Philips, W., Kerre, E.E.: Fuzzy logic recursive change detection for tracking and denoising of video sequences. Image and Video Communications and Processing (2005) 771-782.
7. Bednar, J., Watt, T.L.: Alpha-trimmed means and their relationships to median filters. IEEE Trans. on Acoustics, Speech and Signal Processing **32** (1984) 145-153
8. Cocchia, F., Carrato, S., Ramponi, G.: Design and real-time implementation of a 3-D rational filter for edge preserving smoothing. IEEE Transactions on Consumer Electronics **43** (1997) 1291-1300
9. Zlokolica, V., Pizurica, A., Philips, W.: Video denoising using multiple class averaging with multiresolution. Lecture Notes in Computer Science, Visual Content Processing and Representation (2003) 172-179

# A Restoration and Segmentation Unit for the Historic Persian Documents

Shahpour Alirezaee[1], Alireza Shayesteh Fard[2], Hassan Aghaeinia[3], and Karim Faez[3]

[1] Electrical Engineering Department, Islamic Azad University of Abhar, Abhar, Iran
[2] Electrical Engineering Department, Zanjan University, Zanjan, Iran
{Alirezae, Shayestehfard}@mail.znu.ac.ir
[3] Electrical Engineering Department, Amirkabir University of Technology, Hafez Ave., Tehran, Iran
{Alirezaee, Aghaeinia,faez}@aut.ac.ir

**Abstract.** This paper aims to provide a document restoration and segmentation algorithm for the Historic Middle Persian or Pahlavi manuscripts. The proposed algorithm uses the mathematical morphology and connected component concept to segment the line, word, and character overlapped in the Middle-age Persian documents in preparation for OCR application. To evaluate the performance of the restoration algorithm, 200 pages of the Pahlavi documents are used as experimental data in our test. Numerical results indicate that the proposed algorithm can remove the noise and destructive effects. The results also show 99.14% accuracy on the baseline detection, 97.35% accuracy on the text line extraction and removing other lines overlaps, and 99.5% accuracy for segmenting the extracted text lines to their components.

## 1 Introduction

Iranian languages are branch of "Iranian Indian" as well as "European Indian" languages. The Iranian Indian languages are divided into three distinct periods, "Ancient", "Middle-Age " and "Modern". This paper aims to provide a restoration algorithm for the Middle-age Persian or Pahlavi manuscripts.

The Middle Age Persian language has 16 characters and has a right to left direction. We are aiming to provide a restored and segmented document for the OCR applications. The major problems in the Middle-age Persian document are: 1) Noise and destructive effects, 2) Line, word and character intersections and overlaps. These effects have changed the Middle-age Persian to one of the most difficult Iranian languages.

Unfortunately the automatic recognition of the Pahlavi documents has not received any attention from the research community. This study is aiming to provide a document analysis system for restoring and segmenting documents to lines and words. The paper uses mathematical morphology and connected components concept to develop the restoration technique.

This paper has been organized as follows. The second section describes a typical document restoration and segmentation block. In this section, the essential document analysis blocks and our selected strategy are discussed in details. The third section presents the proposed algorithm. The numerical results are presented in the fourth section. Finally, the conclusions will be discussed in the last section.

J. Blanc-Talon et al. (Eds.): ACIVS 2005, LNCS 3708, pp. 674 – 680, 2005.
© Springer-Verlag Berlin Heidelberg 2005

# 2  Document Analysis

It is necessary to perform several document analysis operations prior to recognizing text in a scanned document. Some of the common operations performed prior to recognition are [2]-[5]: Thresholding, noise removal, line segmentation, the isolation of textual words, and character segmentation, and the isolation of individual characters. In the following the necessary steps for a typical document restoration and segmentation will be discussed.

## 2.1  Thresholding

The task of thresholding is to extract the foreground from the background. The histogram of gray-scale values of a document image typically consists of two peaks: a high peak corresponding to the white background and a smaller peak corresponding to the foreground. Therefore, the threshold gray-scale value is an "optimal" value in the valley between the two peaks. Several approaches have been developed on thresholding and many efficient algorithms have been proposed [6], [7].

In this study, methods such as Maximum Entropy Sum Method, Entropic Correlation Method and Renyi Entropy were selected [7]. The experimental results indicated that Renyi Entropy outperforms the other two techniques.

## 2.2  Noise Removal

Noise removal is a topic in the document restoration that has been dealt with extensively for typed or machine-printed documents. For handwritten documents, the connectivity of strokes has to be preserved. Digital capture of images can introduce noise from scanning devices and transmission media. Moreover, due to the old age of the documents under study many destructive effects such as moisture, dust, etc. haveaffected the quality of those texts. Smoothing operations are often used to eliminate the artifacts introduced during image capture. They are many noise removal and smoothing methods in the literature. The morphological operators have been used in this work [7], [8] and will be explained in the following.

They are two fundamental morphological operators, erosion and dilation. The erosion of A by B is defined as [7], [8]:

$$A \otimes B = \left\{ z \middle| (B)_z \subset A \right\} \tag{1}$$

When A is eroded by B, the latter is called a structuring element. Eroding an image by a structuring element B has the effect of 'shrinking' the image in a manner determined by B. Larger B causes more erosion effects on A. In this paper, we have used a $3 \times 3$ rectangle structure element as:

$$B = \begin{bmatrix} 1 & 1 & 1 \\ 1 & 1 & 1 \\ 1 & 1 & 1 \end{bmatrix} \tag{2}$$

The dilation of A by B, denoted $A \oplus B$, is defined as:

$$A \oplus B = \left\{ z \middle| (B)_z \bigcap A \neq \Phi \right\} \tag{3}$$

Dilation expands the image based on the structuring element characteristics.

Based on these two fundamental operators, many other functions have been defined, which opening and closing are the most important. Opening generally smoothes the contour of an object, breaks unwanted touching characters, and eliminates these degradations. Closing, as opposed to opening, generally fuses narrow breaks and long thin gulfs, eliminates small holes and fills gaps in the contour. Opening of the set A by structuring element B, denoted $A \circ B$, is defined as:

$$A \circ B = (A \otimes B) \oplus B \tag{4}$$

and similarly, the closing of set A by structuring element B, denoted $A * B$, is defined as:

$$A * B = (A \oplus B) \otimes B \tag{5}$$

Morphological smoothing operator is an opening followed by a closing. The net results of these two operations can remove (or attenuate) both bright and dark artifacts and noises. These operators are also capable of connecting undesired discontinuities caused in the previous stages as well as smooth the inner and outer contours.

### 2.3  Page to Line Segmentation

There are many techniques for Segmentation of handwritten text into lines [9], [10]. This can be accomplished by scanning the image horizontally to obtain the horizontal histogram profile and scanning at a different small angle and obtaining the histogram along this skewed line. The task is more difficult in the handwritten domain, where lines of text might be overlapping with the neighboring lines. In this paper we propose a line segmentation strategy, which has a good performance on the Middle-age documents.

### 2.4  Lines to Words and Characters Segmentation

Line separation is usually followed by a procedure that separates the text lines into words. The most approaches in the literature have focused on identifying physical gaps for word segmentation [9], [10]. These methods assume that gaps between words are larger than the gaps between the characters.

In contrast with the other handwritten texts, Pahlavi has some additional difficulties. Based on the Middle-age writing style, words, characters and their combinations are usually appeared with frequently overlaps. Therefore the gap between words is not a proper criterion for word segmentation. In this paper we have used the connected component approach [7] to solve the problem. Based on this idea, document lines are decomposed to many connected components. These components are characters or combination of connected characters. There are several connected component algorithms in the literature [7], [8], [10], [11], [12]. In this paper we have used the morphological method [7], [8], which will be presented in the following details.

Let Y represents a connected component contained in a set A and assume that a point P of Y is known. Then the following iterative expression in Eq.(6) yields all the elements of Y [7]:

$$X_k = (X_{k-1} \oplus B) \cap A \qquad (6)$$

where $X_0 = P$, and B is a suitable structuring element. If $X_k = X_{k-1}$, the algorithm has converged and we let $Y = X_k$. We have used simple rectangle structure element.

## 3 Proposed Document Analysis System

In the first step, thresholding is globally applied on the scanned page. Then the morphological smoothing is used for noise removal. In the next step, initial baseline candidates are extracted from the horizontal histogram maximas. In the initial step, many local peaks are extracted $\{l_1, l_2, ..., l_M\}$ which $l_i$ is the position of $i'th$ histogram peak. The most important task is to select some of these as the true baselines $\{l'_1, l'_2, ..., l'_N\}(N < M)$. We have used the clustering k-Means [13] to obtain this task. The clustering algorithm uses the histogram maximas to find potential position for the baselines $\{l'_1, l'_2, ..., l'_N\}$. Clustering of these baselines $\{l_1, l_2, ..., l_M\}$ yields the true baseline i.e. $\{l'_1, l'_2, ..., l'_N\}$. As can be seen in the next section, the applied procedure has a good performance for baseline detection. The other task of this block is line width estimation. We have applied the same procedure on the horizontal histogram minimas to find the best separation area for the successive lines. The result will be the best candidate for between line gaps. The average distance between these gaps (with illuminating the first and last lines) is considered as the line width and is called $2.\Delta$. In the next block an initial line candidate is extracted as:

$$Line_i = Input \_ page (l'_i - \alpha.\Delta : l'_i + \alpha.\Delta, :) \qquad (7)$$

$$i = 1, 2, ..., M , \alpha \in [1, 1.2]$$

which,

Input _ page : The original document page (not the thresholded image)

$l'_i$ : $i'th$ baseline position

$\alpha$ : The amount of line overlapping

$Line_i$ : $i'th$ extracted text line

As can be seen in Eq.(7), for more precision, line is extracted from the original image rather than the thresholded image Therefore this requires that the thresholding and noise removing process be repeated. In the next stage, morphological connected component detection is used for detecting the line components. The following steps has been used to extract all text components:

Step 1: Horizontally scan the page to find the starting
P point and set $X_0 = P$ and $k = 1$.

Step 2: Compute $X_k = (X_{k-1} \oplus B) \cap A$ and set
$$k = k + 1$$
Step 3: if $X_k \neq X_{k-1}$ go to step 2

Else, label $X_k$ as a component and remove it from the page image i.e
$$Line_i = Line_i - X_k$$
Step 4: If $Line_i \neq 0$ then go to step 1

Else, terminate

The results include the desired components or text line components as well as the undesired components or intersected upper and lower line components. These undesired components are generated from the overlapping part of neighbor lines, noise and thresholding effects. In this stage, the line pen width ( $pen\_width_i$ ) is estimated by the method of reference [14]. We have made a decision rule for discarding undesired components. The proposed decision making strategy uses the distance between component center of mass and baseline ( $dist_i$ ), as well as the component size ( $surf_i$ ):

$$dist_i = \|CM_i - l_i\| \tag{8}$$

And

$$surf_i = \sum C_i \tag{9}$$

These parameters are compared with " $\beta.\Delta$ " and " $pen\_width_i^2$ " as follows:

$$If \;\; (dist_i > \beta.\Delta) \vee (surf_i < pen\_width_i^2) \tag{10}$$
$$\Rightarrow \text{Discard this component}$$

$$\beta \in [.55 , 1]$$

Otherwise, the component will be sent to the recognition phase. The first condition checks the center of mess distance from baseline, if the distance is greater than $\beta.\Delta$ it means this component belongs to the adjacent lines. The second condition, checks the size of component with the smallest component in the Pahlavi text, which is a dot point. If this condition is satisfied the component is discarded.

## 4 Numerical Results

A set of 200 pages has been scanned from different volume of "The Pahlavi Manuscript Collections"[15]. The proposed document restoration has been tested on this database. Fig.1 shows the result of a sample page, which are respectively the original page, thresholded, noise removed image, and initial segmented lines. The results of the line segmentation have been presented in Fig.2 and Fig.3. We have also counted the number of misdetected text lines and connected components. In this way, the number of correct separated text lines and correct extracted components are divided by their total numbers.

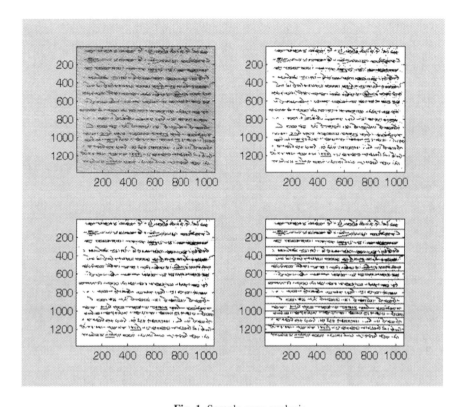

**Fig. 1.** Sample page analysis

**Fig. 2.** Second stage: line interference removal

**Fig. 3.** Third stage: character and connected component interference removal

# 5   Conclusions

In this paper, a document analysis system was proposed for the Middle-age Persian manuscript. Through this research, we are aiming to revitalize the Middle Persian and prepare those texts for OCR applications. The main idea of the proposed technique is based on the morphological analysis and connected component concept. The connected component properties were used to segment the line, word, and character overlapped Pahlavi documents. Performance of the algorithm was tested on 200 pages of the Pahlavi texts. The algorithm had a good success on document restoration and segmentation. Numerical results indicate that the proposed algorithm can remove the noise and destructive effects. The results also show 99.14% accuracy on the baseline detection, 97.35% accuracy on the text line extraction and removing other lines overlaps, and 99.5% accuracy for segmenting the extracted text lines to their components.

# References

1. West, E.W. : Pahlavi Texts, 5, 1860.
2. Jain, A.K., Yu, B. : Document Representation and Its Application to Page Decomposition, IEEE Trans. on Pattern Analysis and Machine Intelligence, 20(3), (1998) 294-308
3. Casey, R.G., Lecolinet, E. : A Survey of Methods and Strategies in Character Segmentation, IEEE Trans. on Pattern Analysis and Machine Intelligence, 18(7),1996.
4. Plamondon, R. ,Srihari, S.N. : On-line and Off-line handwriting Recognition,A Comprehensive Survey, IEEE Trans. on Pattern Analysis and Machine Intelligence, 22(1), 2000.
5. Arica, N., Yarman-Vural, F.T. : An Overview of Character Recognition Focused on Off-Line Handwriting, IEEE Trans. on Sys., Man., and Cybernetics, 31(2), 2001.
6. Sahoo, P.K., Soltani, S., Wong, A.K.C., Chen, Y.C. : A survey of thresholding techniques, Computer Vision, Graphics, and Image Processing, 41, (1998)233-260
7. Gonzalez, R.C. , Woods, R.E. :Digital image processing, second edition,2002.
8. Giardina, C.R., Dougherty, E.R., Morphological Methods in Image and Signal Processing, Prentice-Hall, Englewood Cliffs, New Jersey, 1988.
9. Mohaderan, U., Nagabhushanam, R.C.: Gap metrics for word separation handwritten lines, ICDAR, (1995)124-127.
10. Seni, G. , Cohen, E. : External word segmentation of off-line handwritten text lines, Pattern Recognition, 27(1), (1994)41-52
11. Ha, J., Haralick, R., Phillips, I. :Document Page Decomposi-tion by the Bounding-Box Projection Technique, ICDAR, (1995)119-122
12. Schomaker, L., Bulacu, M. : Automatic Writer Identification Using Connected-Component Contours and Edge-Based Features of Uppercase Western Script, IEEE Trans. on Pattern Analysis and Machine Intelligence, 26(6), 2004
13. Likas, A., Valassis, N., Verbeek, J.J.: The global k_means algorithm, Pattern Recognition, 36,(2003) 451-461
14. Schomaker,L., Bulacu,M. : Automatic Writer Identification Using Connected-Component Contours and Edge-Based Features of Uppercase Western Script, IEEE Trans. on Pattern Analysis and Machine Intelligence, 26(6), 2004.
15. Pahlavy Handwritten Documents, Asian Institute of Shiraz University, 1972.

# Cleaning and Enhancing Historical Document Images

Ergina Kavallieratou[1] and Hera Antonopoulou[2]

[1] Department of Information and Communication Systems Engineering,
University of The Aegean,
83200 Karlovassi, Samou, Greece
kavalieratou@aegean.gr
[2] Computer Technology Institute,
26500 Patras, Greece
antonopl@cti.gr

**Abstract.** In this paper we present a recursive algorithm for the cleaning and the enhancing of historical documents. Most of the algorithms, used to clean and enhance documents or transform them to binary images, implement combinations of complicated image processing techniques which increase the computational cost and complexity. Our algorithm simplifies the procedure by taking into account special characteristics of the document images. Moreover, the fact that the algorithm consists of iterated steps, makes it more flexible concerning the needs of the user. At the experimental results, comparison with other methods is provided.

## 1 Introduction

The binarization of images is a long investigated field with remarkable accomplishments. Some of them have also been applied to documents or historical documents. One of the older methods in image binarization is Otsu's [6], based on the variance of pixel intensity. Bernsen [1] calculates local thresholds using the neighbours. Niblack [5] uses local mean and standard deviation. Sauvola [7] presents a method specialised on document images that applies two algorithms in order to calculate a different threshold for each pixel. As far as the recent problem of historical documents is concerned, Leedham [3] compares some of the traditional methods on degraded document images while Gatos [2] builds up a new method by using a combination of existing techniques. These are also the cases of Shi[8] and Yan[9] applied to some historical documents from the US library of Congress. Leydier [4] works with coloured document images and implements a serialization of the k-means algorithm. Some of the above mentioned methods have also used specific filters or algorithms for the cleaning of the document as an additional module.

The historical documents suffer from bad storage conditions and poor contrast between foreground and background due to humidity, paper deterioration and ink seeking. Moreover, the fragility of those documents does not allow access to many researchers while a legible digitised version is more accessible.

In the next section, a description of the algorithm is given, while in section 3 the algorithm is analysed in detail. Some experimental results and a short comparison

J. Blanc-Talon et al. (Eds.): ACIVS 2005, LNCS 3708, pp. 681–688, 2005.
© Springer-Verlag Berlin Heidelberg 2005

with traditional binarization methods are described in section 4. Finally, our conclusions are provided in section 5.

## 2 Algorithm Description

As input, we assume greyscale historical document images where the tones of the foreground (characters, graphics, etc) outrange over the background (including spots, stains, wrinkles etc). As example, consider the historical documents of fig. 1. Our images are described by the equation:

$$I(x, y) = r, r \in [0,1] \tag{1}$$

where x and y are the horizontal and vertical coordinates of the image, and r can take any value between 0 and 1 while r=1 stands for white colour and r=0 stands for black colour. Our intention is to transform the intermediate grey tones to either black (r=0) for foreground or white (r=1) for background.

**Fig. 1.** Historical Documents before and after the application of our algorithm

The algorithm is based on the fact that a document image includes very few pixels of useful information (foreground) compared to the size of the image (foreground+background).

According to our experiments, rarely the black pixels exceed the 10% of the total pixels in the document. Taking advantage of this fact, we assume that the average value of the pixel values of a document image is determined mainly by the background even if the document is quite clear. This claim is supported from fig. 2, where are depicted the histograms of the above examples, respectively. In the same figure two thresholds, of our method and Otsu's method, as well as the average value in each case are given. It is obvious that the average value is always on the background side, considering either threshold.

Using this fact our method consists of two procedures that are applied alternately. In the first part the average colour value of the image is calculated and then subtracted from the image, while in the second part of the algorithm we perform histogram equalisation, thus the values of remaining pixels would expand and take up all of the greyscale tones. Briefly, the algorithm consists of the following steps:

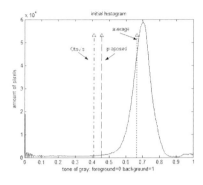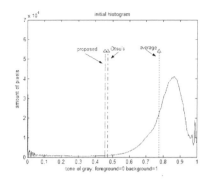

**Fig. 2.** The histograms of the corresponding documents of figure 1. The thresholds extracted with the proposed method (--), Otsu's method (-·) and the average value of the pixels (··).

1. Calculation of the average pixel value ($T_i$) of the image.
2. Subtraction of the $T_i$ from all the pixels of the image.
3. Histogram equalisation.
4. Repetition of steps 1-3 till the $T^0_i$-$T^0_{i-1}$<0.2, where $T^0_i$ the corresponding initial threshold for repetition i (see Eq. 6).
5. Binarization of the final image.

In the next section, we analyse each of the above steps giving the necessary mathematical formulas and examples.

## 3  Algorithm Analysis

Considering the equation (1) the calculation of the $T_i$, threshold used in i-th repetition for an MxN document image, is given by the formula:

$$T_i = \frac{\sum_x \sum_y I_i(x, y)}{MxN} \tag{2}$$

where $I_i(x,y)$ is the image at the i-th repetition. Eq. (2) is used in the subtraction, yielding $I_s$ before equalisation:

$$I_s(x, y) = 1 - T_i + I_i(x, y), \tag{3}$$

In each repetition, during the subtraction, a lot of pixels are moved to the side of the background and the rest of the pixels are fading. In fig. 3, the image that corresponds to the $T_1$ threshold of the document image 1b is shown as well as the image after the first subtraction.

After the subtraction step, we adjust the intensity of the image by using the histogram and extending the values to all the colour range from 0 to 1. Since the 1s (background) shouldn't be changed, and the rest of the pixel values should extend from 0 to 1, the relation we use for the equalisation is:

**Fig. 3.** (from left to right and up to down). a) the image that corresponds to the $T_1=0.7755$ threshold of the document image 1b, b) the image after the first subtraction and (c) the image after the first histogram equalisation.

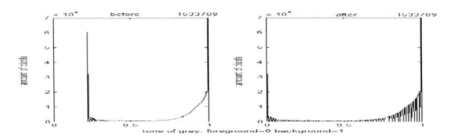

**Fig. 4.** The histograms of the document image of fig.1b before and after the first equalisation. Please note that the histograms have been scaled appropriately in order to show more detail. The maximum value is shown on the upper right corner.

$$I_i(x, y) = 1 - \frac{1 - I_s(x, y)}{1 - E_i} \qquad (4)$$

where $I_s$ is given by the equation (3) and $E_i$ is the minimum pixel value in the image $I_s$ during i-th repetition, just before the histogram equalisation. In fig. 4, it is shown the document image of fig.1b before and after the first histogram equalisation.

The whole procedure is repeated the necessary times till the document image is satisfactorily cleaned. The number of repetitions depends on the image and the intensity of any existent stains, crumples, lighting effects on the image. The terminal condition in our algorithm is the difference of two successive thresholds.

Combining the equations (3) and (4) we extract a relation between the final and initial image during a repetition of our algorithm:

$$I_i(x, y) = 1 - \frac{T_i - I_{i-1}(x, y)}{1 - E_i} \qquad (5)$$

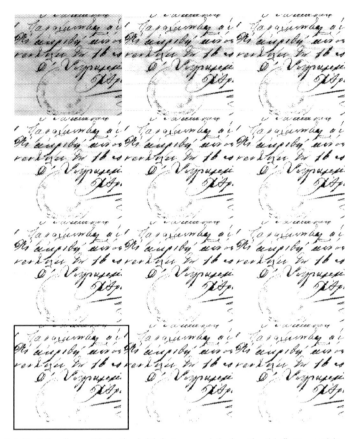

**Fig. 5.** A detail of the figure 1b in the initial stage and during the 11 first repetitions (from left to right and top to bottom). In rectangle, the suggested threshold result.

where $I_i$ is the image after the i-th repetition having used the corresponding thresholds $T_i$ and $E_i$ for the subtraction and equalisation in the repetition, as it has been described above. Thus, using the equation (5) and making the necessary replacements for n repetitions, the corresponding initial value $T^o$, in the initial histogram, of the final threshold $T_f$ will be:

$$T^{\,o} = T_f \cdot \prod_{i=1}^{n} E_i - \sum_{i=1}^{n} \prod_{j=1}^{i} E_j + \sum_{i=2}^{n} T_i \cdot \prod_{j=1}^{i-1} E_j + T_1 \tag{6}$$

The necessary amount of repetitions depends very much on the document. as well as on the required result, and it never exceeded the 20th repetition in our experiments (100 documents). However, the process after the first repetitions is very slow. Thus, we could say that more than one stage could be accepted. In fig. 5 is presented a detail of the figure 1b during the 11 first repetitions while in fig. 6 we show the first 15 corresponding thresholds on its histogram.

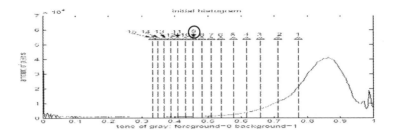

**Fig. 6.** The corresponding thresholds on the histogram of fig.1b. In circle, you can see the result according to the suggested threshold 3‰ of the document size.

Usually, such a procedure turns out a binary image. During our collaboration with historical researchers, we found out that they are more interested in cleaning the document in order to expose or print it but they prefer to keep the greyscale or coloured view of the document. However, in the adaptation of this algorithm for binarization, having already concluded to the right final stage, we binarize the image by turning all the pixels that are not already white (value 1) to black (value 0).

## 4   Experimental Results

Although the cleaning of historical documents is a great necessity, it is a relatively new field in research and there is no common database to be used for result valuation. In our research, we used a private archive with documents of 18th century that was the inspiration for this work. The archive was discovered recently in very bad condition and includes a lot of personal information. Thus, although it proved to be perfect for our work it is not allowed to be published in its majority. For that reason we will give just fragments of documents in our results.

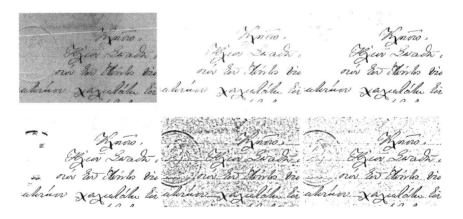

**Fig. 7.** Presence of background variance and baselines (from left to right and up to down) a) original b) proposed (greyscale) c) proposed (binary) d) Bernsen's e) Niblack's f) Otsu's

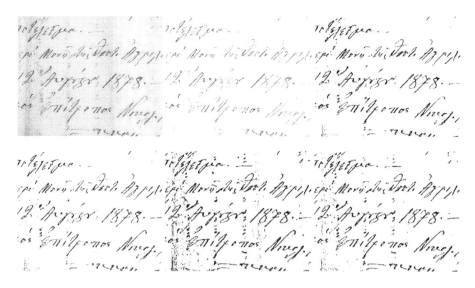

**Fig. 8.** Presence of background variance and transparency (from left to right and up to down). a) original b) proposed (grayscale) c) proposed (binary) d) Bernsen's e) Niblack's f) Otsu's.

As mentioned before in our experiments we used 100 document images in grey scale. In order to compare the results we used the methods described in [1,5,6,7]. Since those methods are used for binarization, we give the grey scale as well as the binary result of our method and the results of the other methods. Some results are shown in fig. 7-8, trying to demonstrate the performance of the proposed method in typical problems of historical documents like background variance stains and transparency.

Due to the simplicity of the algorithm, the computational cost is very low in comparison to other algorithms appropriate for document images.

## 5  Conclusion

In this paper we presented a method appropriate for the cleaning or binarization, if necessary, of historical document images. The method makes use of the fact that the pixels that compose the text in an historical document, usually, do not exceed the 10% of its size. This allowed us to build an algorithm that consists of two successive stages applied alternatively on the image. The results have been compared with other methods and are quite satisfactory.

The advantages of our algorithm is: simplicity, since it doesn't require any further pre-processing procedure and is based on a simple technique, low computational cost due to its simplicity, and robustness, since it gives the capability to the user to succeed the desirable result in greyscale or binarised final image.

It is in the interest of the authors to experiment by dividing and treating the image in areas, in order to deal with cases that the grey level of the desired text or graphics varies markedly, and possibly crosses over the grey level of background in other parts of the image.

## Acknowledgments

We would like to thank professor N.Papamarkos for providing the algorithms used for the comparison with other methods in our experiments, from his personal library http://ipml.ee.duth.gr/~papamark/demos.htm.

## References

[1] Bernsen, J."Dynamic thresholding of grey-level images", Proc. 8th International Conference on Pattern Recognition (ICPR8), pp 1251-1255, Paris, France, October 1986.

[2] Gatos B., Pratikakis I. and Perantonis S.J. "An adaptive binarisation technique for low quality historical documents". IAPR Workshop on Document Analysis systems (DAS'2004), Lecture Notes in Computer Science (3163), Florence, Italy, pp. 102-113.

[3] Leedham, G., S. Varma, A. Patankar, V. Govindaraju "Separating Text and Background in Degraded Document Images - A Comparison of Global Thresholding Techniques for Multi-Stage Thresholding" Proceedings Eighth InternationalWorkshop on Frontiers of Handwriting Recognition, pp. 244-249, September, 2002.

[4] Leydier Y., LeBourgeois F., Emptoz H., Serialized Unsupervised Classifier for Adaptative Color Image Segmentation: Application to Digitized Ancient Manuscripts, ICPR, pp 494-497, Cambridge, 23-26, 2004

[5] Niblack, W. "An Introduction to Digital image processing", pp 115-116, Prentice Hall, 1986.

[6] Otsu, N. "A threshold selection method from grey-level histograms". IEEE Trans. Systems Man Cybernet. pp. 62-66, 9 (1), 1979.

[7] Sauvola, J., Pietikainen, M., "Adaptive Document Image Binarization", Pattern Recognition, pp. 225-236, 33, 2000.

[8] Shi, Z., V. Govindaraju, "Historical Document Image Segmentation Using Background Light Intensity Normalization", SPIE Document Recognition and Retrieval XII, 16-20 January 2005, San Jose, California, USA.

[9] Yan, C., G. Leedham, " Decompose-Threshold Approach to Handwriting Extraction in Degraded Historical Document Images" Ninth International Workshop on Frontiers in Handwriting Recognition (IWFHR'04) pp. 239-244, Kokubunji, Tokyo, Japan, October, 2004

# Designing Area and Performance Constrained SIMD/VLIW Image Processing Architectures

Hamed Fatemi[1,2], Henk Corporaal[2], Twan Basten[2], and Richard Kleihorst[3], and Pieter Jonker[4]

[1] h.fatemi@tue.nl
[2] Eindhoven University of Technology,
PO Box 513, NL-5600 MB Eindhoven, The Netherlands
[3] Philips Research Laboratories,
Prof. Holstlaan 4, NL-5656 AA Eindhoven, The Netherlands
[4] Delft University of Technology,
Lorentzweg 1, NL-2628 CJ Delft, The Netherlands

**Abstract.** Image processing is widely used in many applications, including medical imaging, industrial manufacturing and security systems. In these applications, the size of the image is often very large, the processing time should be very small and the real-time constraints should be met. Therefore, during the last decades, there has been an increasing demand to exploit parallelism in applications. It is possible to explore parallelism along three axes: data-level parallelism (DLP), instruction-level parallelism (ILP) and task-level parallelism (TLP).

This paper explores the limitations and bottlenecks of increasing support for parallelism along the DLP and ILP axes in isolation and in combination. To scrutinize the effect of DLP and ILP in our architecture (template), an area model based on the number of ALUs (ILP) and the number of processing elements (DLP) in the template is defined, as well as a performance model. Based on these models and the template, a set of kernels of image processing applications has been studied to find Pareto optimal architectures in terms of area and number of cycles via multi-objective optimization.

## 1 Introduction

Recently, vision based human interfaces, robotic, inspection or surveillance systems have gained more and more importance, and real-time image processing is essentially necessary for these applications. Therefore, during the last decade, the exploitation of parallelism in applications has been increased [1].

Image processing operations can be classified as low-level (e.g. smoothing, sharpening and filtering), intermediate-level (e.g. Hough transform and object labeling) and high-level (e.g. position estimation and object recognition) [2]. Low-level operations and some medium-level operations can be implemented efficiently in single instruction multiple data (SIMD) processors to exploit data-level parallelism (DLP). High-level operations and some medium-level operations

J. Blanc-Talon et al. (Eds.): ACIVS 2005, LNCS 3708, pp. 689–696, 2005.
© Springer-Verlag Berlin Heidelberg 2005

can be mapped onto very long instruction word (VLIW) processors which exploit the instruction-level parallelism (ILP) [3].

During the last decade, many systems have been designed to exploit parallelism (DLP and ILP). Xetal [4] is an SIMD processor which includes 320 processing elements (PEs), each with one ALU. It is suitable for many low-level operations to exploit DLP. Trimedia [5] is a VLIW example; it can execute five operations per cycle. It is suitable to exploit ILP in high-level operations.

There are also some processors which combine DLP and ILP together, like Imagine [6], which includes eight PEs, with each PE including six ALUs. By increasing the number of PEs, it is possible to exploit more DLP in applications which leads to better performance (decrease in number of cycles). It is also possible to increase the potential for ILP by increasing the number of ALUs per PE, which again causes better performance. In both cases, the area (cost) of the architecture is increased. So, there is a trade-off between area and performance.

In this paper, the relationship between the number of processing elements and ALUs per PE, on the one hand, and the area and performance of the architecture, on the other hand, is studied. For this purpose, an area model based on the number of PEs and ALUs is defined, as well as a performance model. We use multi-objective optimization to find Pareto optimal architectures for several image processing kernels.

The paper is organized as follows. Section 2 explains the architecture on which our measurements are based. The area and performance models for this architecture are studied in Sections 3 and 4. The implementation of the kernels and the design-space exploration via multi-objective optimization are studied in Section 5. Conclusions and future work are discussed in Section 6.

## 2   Architecture

Fig. 1 shows the template (processor) which is used for our measurements. The template includes the following parts: Processing Elements (PEs); micro con-

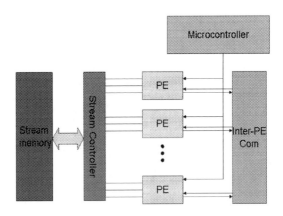

**Fig. 1.** SIMD Architecture Template (each PE can be a VLIW)

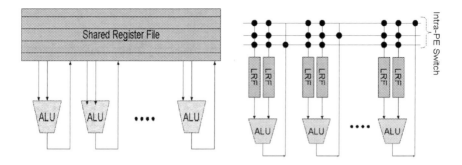

**Fig. 2.** PE with shared register file        **Fig. 3.** PE with local register file

troller unit; inter-PE communication unit; stream memory unit (including the stream controller).

Fig. 2 and 3 show the inside of a processing element which includes ALUs and register file(s). The number of ALUs is one of the template parameters determining the number of operations that can be performed at the same time by a single PE. Each ALU has two inputs and one output. Two kinds of register files can be used. One type is a shared register file. It means that each PE has one register file and each ALU is attached to this shared register file by three ports (two inputs and one output) (Fig. 2). Another kind of register file is the local register file. It means that each ALU input has a separate register file and there is an intra-PE switch that connects the ALU outputs to the inputs (Fig. 3). The stream controller unit is responsible for reading data (e.g. pixel values) from the stream memory and transferring it to the register files and vice versa. The size of the register file is also one of the template parameters. The micro controller unit has two parts: 1- the memory part for storing PE instructions and 2- the decoder for decoding PE instructions and sending them to PEs. The inter-PE communication unit is responsible for connecting PEs together to send/receive data among each other. This unit is an N*N switch (with N being the number of PEs). The stream memory unit is the connection between external memory and I/O (outside the template) and the PEs. It takes data from off-chip memory and sends it to the PEs via the stream controller and vice versa. Input and output data are stream based. Each PE iteratively reads elements from input streams and writes elements to the output streams. The stream memory contains N (the number of PEs) single ported memory banks and each PE is able to access its own part in parallel to other PEs. This implies that inter-PE communication requires a separate communication network (inter-PE communication unit) and cannot be done by the stream memory.

## 3   Area Model

In order to compare different parallel configurations, we developed an area model. We derive a formula for area, which is based on the number of ALUs (functional

**Table 1.** Parameters used in the area model

| Variable | Value | Description |
|---|---|---|
| N | - | Number of <subscript> (i.e., Npe= number of PEs) |
| A | - | Area of <subscript> (i.e., Ape= area of a PE) |
| b | 32 | Data width of the architecture |
| w | 1.86 | Wire pitch (typically 0.64 – 2μm/wire in a 0.18μm process) |

**Table 2.** Parameters of DSE

| Description | Values |
|---|---|
| Number of PEs in the template | 1,2,4,8,...1024- |
| Number of ALUs per PE | 1,2,3,4,.....10 |
| Type of register file | 1: shared & 2: local |
| Size of register file | 3,4,6,8,12,16....256 |
| Mem size of microcontroller | 256,512,.....2048 |

units) in each PE and the total number of PEs. This area model is meant to give an area estimation for the region containing the ALUs, PEs, micro controller and stream memory of the template. Template parameters are described in Table 1. The total area of the template is (in $mm^2$):

$$A_{total} = N_{PE} \cdot A_{PE} + A_{inter-PEcomm} + A_{stream-memory} + A_{micro} \quad (1)$$

The inter-PE communication unit allows each PE to send/receive data to/from other PEs. The area of this switch (assuming a wire limited design) grows quadratically with the number of PEs inside the template. The basic formula for the switch size is:

$$A_{inter-PEcomm} = N_{PE}^2 \cdot b^2 \cdot w^2 \quad (2)$$

To estimate the size of this switch, we used a wire pitch of 1.86 $\mu m$ to make enough room for power, ground, and noise shielding wires [7].

The PE area depends on the area of the ALUs, the register file and the intra-PE switch (in case of local register files). Based on the register file, the PE area can be calculated in two ways:

- PE with shared register file: In this case, the area includes the register file and the ALUs. For our estimation of the register file size, we borrow the model described by Rixner in [7]. In his model, the area of a register file is the product of the number of registers, the number of bits per register and the size of a single-bit register cell. The size of each register cell is a function of the width and height of the register cell without ports (estimated to be $w^2$) and the number of ports squared. As each ALU needs 3 ports (2 inputs and 1 output), the area of the register file is a function of the number of ALUs squared. The total area of a PE is:

$$A_{PE} = N_{register} \cdot b \cdot (3 \cdot N_{ALU})^2 \cdot w^2 + N_{ALU} \cdot A_{ALU} \quad (3)$$

- PE with local register files: In this case, the area includes the local register files, the ALUs and the intra-PE switch. Each ALU has two local register files with two ports (one input and one output). The area of a local register file is the product of the number of registers, the number of bits per register and the size of a single-bit register cell (with two ports). Regarding (2), the area of the intra-PE switch is proportional to the number of ALUs squared. Therefore, the area of a PE is:

$$A_{PE} = N_{register} \cdot 2 \cdot b \cdot A_{lrf\ bit} + N_{ALU} \cdot A_{ALU} + N_{ALU}^2 \cdot b^2 \cdot w^2 \quad (4)$$

Since every PE receives the same instruction, the micro controller size is constant as the DLP degree is increased. Even when the number of ALUs per PE increases, the code size does not change dramatically. The total number of operations remains roughly constant (assuming not too much speculative code). Only the number of NOP will increase (a well known VLIW problem). However, using NOP code compression will compensate for that. Therefore, the memory storage part of the microcontroller can remain constant, but the control logic and instruction decoders should be increased as we scale ILP:

$$A_{micro} = A_{micromemory} + A_{decoder} \cdot N_{ALU} \tag{5}$$

The area of the stream memory unit contains a constant part for the stream controller plus the product of the number of PEs, the number of ALUs per PE, the memory size for each ALU (when increasing the number of ALUs, more data storage is needed to keep them busy; we assume a constant memory size required per ALU), data width and the area of a 1-bit SRAM:

$$A_{stream-memory} = N_{PE} \cdot N_{ALU} \cdot b \cdot memory\ size\ per\ ALU \cdot A_{SRAM\ bit} + \\ A_{stream-controller} \tag{6}$$

## 4   Performance Model

For calculating the number of cycles of an application kernel, we used an adapted version of the Imagine tools. It is possible to simulate varying degrees of instruction-level parallelism by changing the number of ALUs in each PE. From the microcode file (output of the Imagine kernel compiler), we can directly determine the number of instructions in each basic block of a kernel. Furthermore, we know which of these blocks correspond to the kernel loop body and which are outside the loop. For kernels with one loop, we model its number of cycles as:

$$N_{cycle} = N_{loop-cycle} \cdot N_{loop-iter} + N_{nonloop-cycle} \tag{7}$$

$N_{loop-cycle}$ and $N_{nonloop-cycle}$ are extracted from the microcode file. The number of iterations ($N_{loop-iter}$) depends on $N_{data}$ (the amount of data sent to the kernel, e.g. image size) and $N_{PE}$, as expressed in the following formula.

$$N_{loop-iter} = \lceil \frac{N_{data}}{N_{PE}} \rceil \tag{8}$$

The cycle calculation is easily adapted to kernels with multiple loops.

## 5   Evaluation

In Sections 2, 3 and 4, we studied the template and the area/performance model related to it. In this section, the search for an optimal solution in terms of area and cycles is discussed.

## 5.1   Multi-objective Optimization

It is obvious that the number of cycles needed for the execution of a program can be decreased by increasing the number of PEs. By increasing the number of PEs, the area of the template is also increased (1). Therefore, improving the number of cycles leads to an increase in area and vice versa. To investigate this trade-off, we have used multi-objective optimization [8]. A general multi-objective optimization problem can be described as a vector function $f$ that maps a number of $m$ decision variables (in our case the template parameters; see Table 2) to a number of $n$ objectives (in our case area and performance). Formally:

$$
\begin{aligned}
&min/max\ \ Y = f(X) = (f_1(X), f_2(X), \ldots, f_n(X)) \\
&subject\ to : X = (x_1, \ldots, x_m), Y = (y_1, \ldots, y_n)
\end{aligned}
\tag{9}
$$

where $X$ is called the decision vector from the parameter space and $Y$ is the objective vector from the objective space. In our measurements, the objective vector consists of area and number of cycles. The set of solutions for a multi-objective optimization problem consists of all decision vectors for which the corresponding objective vectors cannot be improved in any dimension without degradation in another. These vectors are known as Pareto optimal. Mathematically, the concept of Pareto optimality is defined as follows. Assume, without loss of generality, a maximization problem and consider two decision vectors $a, b$. Then, $a$ is said to dominate $b$ if and only if:

$$
f_i(a) \geq f_i(b)\ \ \forall i = 1, \ldots, n \quad \bigwedge \quad f(a) \neq f(b)
\tag{10}
$$

All decision vectors which are not dominated by any other decision vector of a given set, are called non-dominated regarding to this set. The decision vectors that are non-dominated within the entire search space are Pareto optimal and constitute the so-called Pareto-optimal set.

## 5.2   Measurements

Table 2 shows the template parameters. Our design space has 13200 points and for finding Pareto points, we could still search the complete design space. It takes

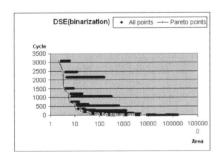

**Fig. 4.** DSE for binarization kernel

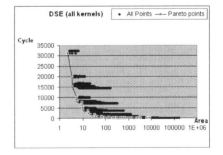

**Fig. 5.** DSE for merged kernels

around 10 minutes (on an Intel Pentium processor 1.70 GHZ) to perform this exhaustive search. The objective vector includes area and cycles for each point of the design space.

For measurement, we selected three of the most popular kernels from image processing applications [9] (color conversion, binarization, convolution, with image size 640 × 480). The result for binarization is shown in Fig. 4 (for the other kernels, results are similar). We used a normalized logarithmic scale for the horizontal axis. The big gaps in the figure are caused by changes in the number of PEs in the template. The Pareto points represent the trade-off between area and number of cycles.

In order to investigate the Pareto points for a *domain*-specific (i.e for all three kernels) architecture instead of an *application*-specific architecture, we merge these three kernels into one kernel (Fig. 5). The most interesting part of this graph is when the area is not much larger than 100 (larger chip area becomes too costly). Our measurements show the most interesting part is when the number of PEs is between 2 and 64 and the number of ALUs in each PE is between 1 and 4. More ALUs per PE causes an increase in the intra-PE switch area (needed for inter ALUs communication). All Pareto points turn out to have local register files, even if the PE contains only one ALU. The reason is that a shared register file needs (many) more ports (even for a single ALU, it needs three ports). By increasing the number of ALUs in a PE, it is possible to reduce the size of a local register file. For example in convolution, it is possible to reduce the size of each register file from 24 registers (PE with 1 ALU) to 8 (PE with 4 ALUs). The size of the microcontroller in all Pareto points is 256; it turns out that this is sufficient to store all kernels. By comparing these Pareto points, we can observe that specialized architectures (Pareto points of each kernel) do not perform much better than the generalized architectures (Pareto points of merged kernels) because of our limited design space. By adding other parameters to the template like inter-PE communication, specialized function units, etc., it is possible to observe the trade-off between specialization and generalization. This is a topic for our future research.

One of the ratios that can be used for comparing the Pareto points is per-formance per unit area. The optimal templates (better performance/area) have between 4 and 64 PEs and each PE has 1 or 2 ALUs. These Pareto points might be good candidates if the designer is interested in getting the most performance out of area.

# 6   Conclusions and Future Work

In this paper, we studied a suitable hybrid SIMD/VLIW processor for image processing kernels, regarding area and cycle numbers. The parameters which we studied are the number of ALUs, the number of PEs, the type of the register file, the size of the register file and the micro controller. To study this problem, area and performance models have been defined. For finding the Pareto-optimal solutions, we used multi-objective optimization. Regarding the design space, we used the full search method. By looking at the Pareto points in the design space, it is observed that most interesting points have 4-64 PEs, one or two ALUs per PE with local register files.

By increasing the number of PEs beyond 64, the area of the inter-PE communication unit dominates the area (2). For solving this problem, in the future, we will study other processor parameters such as the number of connections and the bandwidth between PEs. Furthermore, we will add parameters like the number of ports to the stream memory, special function units and the number of load/store units. This creates a larger design space. For finding Pareto points, in this extended space, we already developed a multi-objective optimization by using evolutionary algorithms (full search takes too much time). We also want to look at the delay (cycle-time) and energy of the template, and investigate a multi-processor template (combining multiple instances of our current template) for image processing applications.

# References

1. Caarls, W., Jonker, P., Corporaal, H.: Smartcam: Devices for embedded intelligent cameras. In: PROGRESS 2002, 3rd seminar on embedded systems, Proceedings, Utrecht, The Netherlands (24 October 2002) 1–4 (CD–ROM)
2. Komen, E.: Low-level Image Processing Architectures. PhD thesis, Delft University of Technology (1990)
3. Fatemi, H., Corporaal, H., Basten, T., Jonker, P., Kleihorst, R.: Implementing face recognition using a parallel image processing environment based on algorithmic skeletons. In: Proceedings of the 10th Annual Conference of the Advanced School for Computing and Imaging, Port Zelande, The Netherlands (June 2004) 351–357
4. Abbo, A., Kleihorst, R.: Smart cameras: Architectural challenges. In: Proceedings of ACIVS 2002 (Advanced Concepts for Intelligent Vision Systems), Gent, Belgium (2002) 6–13
5. TriMedia Technologies. (http://www.semiconductors.philips.com)
6. Khailany, B., Dally, W.J., Rixner, S., Kapasi, U.J., Mattson, P., Namkoong, J., Owens, J.D., Towles, B., Chang, A.: Imagine: Media processing with streams. IEEE Micro (April 2001) 34–46
7. Rixner, S., Dally, W.J., Khailany, B., Mattson, P., Kapasi, U.J., Owens, J.D.: Register organization for media processing. In: Proceedings of the 6th International Symposium on High-Performance Computer Architecture, Toulouse, France (Jan 2000) 375–386
8. Fonseca, C.M., Fleming, P.J.: An overview of evolutionary algorithms in multiobjective optimization. IEEE Micro **3** (1995) 1–16
9. Caarls, W.: Testbench algorithms for smartcam. Technical report, Delft University of Technology, The Netherlands (2003)

# Computing Stereo-Vision in Video Real-Time with Low-Cost SIMD-Hardware

Gerold Kraft[1] and Richard Kleihorst[2]

[1] Delft University of Technology, Delft, The Netherlands
[2] Philips Research Laboratories, Eindhoven, The Netherlands
Richard.Kleihorst@Philips.com

**Abstract.** The XETAL chip by Philips Electronics is a low-cost hardware-solution for image processing on pixel level. The architecture of XETAL focuses on a low-energy environment and it is therefore highly suited for integration into mobile vision and intelligent cameras. While hardware support for 2D-vision has reached the level of affordable state-of-the-art technology by thorough research, also real-time 3D-vision by stereo, based on the support by a low-cost and low-energy hardware, appears to be able to reach this level soon.

## 1   Introduction

A single image from an area-sensor maps the points of original 3D-scene onto a 2D-plane, parallel to the camera plane, leaving the third dimension ambiguous. However, depth can be reconstructed by registering at least two images from area-sensor, if they correspond to a stereoscopic geometry. Output of the stereo-reconstruction is a map of disparity values between the images. From calibration of the stereo setup, one can establish a mapping from disparities to physical depth measures.

Traditionally, and under focus of maximum robustness, only a small number of precisely measured key-feature points in the images are matched, producing a sparsely populated output map. In arbitrary scenes, it often poses a problem to identify valid key-features at a high level of image understanding, while low-level key-features are less descriptive and tend to produce cluttered output. To fill in missing data into sparse disparity maps is a second problem. Therefore, dense stereo mapping often gives more attractive results, where each position in the output grid has an unique disparity value assigned. The traditional approach to stereo *projects* the locations of matches onto the output grid. Therefore, accuracy in disparity-space remains preserved, but the technique can leave positions on the grid unexposed. In order to avoid such gaps in the output, dense disparity maps are *rendered*. However, the price is a loss of accuracy in disparity-space.

Dense output requires a gapless representation of the input. In its computationally simplest case [4], therefore intensity values at pixel positions are matched, e.g. by the Sum-of-Absolute-Differences (SAD) technique. However, noise in the disparity map will follow directly the pixel-noise of the imaging sensor. A pixel-to-pixel computed disparity map often will require post-filtering

J. Blanc-Talon et al. (Eds.): ACIVS 2005, LNCS 3708, pp. 697–704, 2005.
© Springer-Verlag Berlin Heidelberg 2005

or optimization. Successful registration of stereoscopic images requires the presence of local variance in the input. A most fundamental approach to reduce the matching error, it is therefore to register with a focus on image gradients instead of intensity values.

A final challenge to stereo it is to identify occlusions correctly, and, hence, to find correct correspondences in the images. Occlusions are naturally created around any 3D-object, because the stereo-geometry requires to image the object from different viewpoints. To one camera-view of a voluminous object parts of the surface remain occluded or hidden, while they are visible to the other view. Clearly, occlusions should not produce trustable matches in the stereo domain. However, due to noise they can appear falsely more trustable than the correct match, and possibly corrupt the disparity map at large. Correct identification of occlusions usually requires prior detailed knowledge about the geometry of objects in the scene. However, the problem also has been tackled with success by optimization approaches, like Dynamic Programming (DP), based on the basic assumption of smooth object surface only.

A fundamental constraint of stereo is that any correct reconstruction of image disparity is independent from position of reconstruction. E.g. a correct reconstruction of scene disparity to any left eye position will be identical to the projected reconstruction as seen from corresponding right eye position. Applying this constraint, the disparity map can be tested for occlusions by the so-called Left-Right-Check (LR-Check).

## 2   Previous Work

The authors of [1] give a detailed introduction into the hardware architecture of XETAL, from which, for reason of understanding, we summarize the following.

XETAL is a SIMD (Single Instruction Multiple Data) based processor for image-processing on pixel-level with one input channel accepting an intensity signal from a CMOS-sensor and RGB-color output channel. Input data from area sensors are processed sequentially by sensor scan-line, however data-parallel by

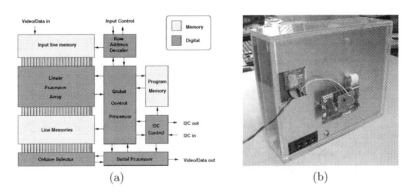

(a)                                    (b)

**Fig. 1.** (a) Architecture of XETAL, (b) XETAL Stereo Experimentation Box

pixel within each line. Valid input width is either 640 pixel following the VGA norm, or 320 pixel, according to the CIF-sensor format. The input is mapped to a linear array (Linear Processor Array, LPA) of Processor Elements (PE). In case of VGA-compatible input, each PE operates on two direct neighboring pixel in sequential fashion. Each PE has access to 32 ten bit wide signed integer data-words for local storage, which are organized into 16 double-words. Additionally, each PE has similar access to the 4 input and output channels. A single 10-bit data-word operates as the internal accumulator register of each PE. The computational core of any PE is based on a RISC (Reduced Instruction Set) architecture, executing each instruction exactly within 1 cycle. Current implementations of XETAL reach a maximum computational power of 12 Gops at 38 MHz cycle-speed, a typical value is 5 Gops at 16 MHz. The core of any PE allows integer-numerical operations like addition and signed scaling by coefficient for filtering operations as well local conditional testing and writing to memory. Each PE has access to own and the local memory of its two direct neighboring elements within 1 cycle. Hence, information easily can be shifted horizontally through the line. A Global Controller supervises the program-flow, decoding instructions from XETAL's program memory. An I2C-controller binds XETAL to any external host. A Serial Processor at the output, finally, enables XETAL to perform operations in dependency from global statistical values. It monitors for each output channel the maximum, minimum and average of all output pixel of the last line and makes this values available to the Global Controller. The narrow limits of memory require on XETAL a strong locality of operator in vertical direction, which is sequentially processed by the LPA. The operator's execution must finish within line-time, unless the operator can buffer intermediate results and it can be re-invoked on the buffer.

Based on the given architecture of XETAL, in [3] the authors discuss the implementation of a simple stereo method based on the sum of absolute intensity differences in the pixel grid. The stereo-system is weakly calibrated towards a parallel stereo-geometry, which allows to register sensor scan-lines directly as the representation of stereoscopic epipolar lines. Each PE computes the disparity for a pixel-position in the output line of the disparity map.

The authors found, that the video-time constraint and the operative limits of XETAL restrain their implementation of stereo-search to the small number of 19 disparity levels. In order to improve robustness, the authors propose to remove sensor-noise from the input channels by a low-pass filtering stage and base the SAD-estimator on a sliding window-technique. Noise in the output disparity map is removed by a minimum-filter, also correcting for inaccuracies of mechanical parallel sensor adjustment. Associating a low output disparity empirically with a low value for trust into the match, the authors propose to fill-in low-disparity areas by a heuristic method from surrounding higher disparities and the original intensity image. The authors have not implemented any minimization technique in order to reduce occlusion artifacts or a final occlusion test. We think, that knowledge and minimization of occlusions can improve the robustness of the proposed filling method.

The authors of [2] have implemented a similar dense stereo system on an alternative hardware, the IMAP VISION, which is developed by NEC. Similar to XETAL, it is a massive parallel hardware for image-processing. However, it is implemented as a set of multiple highly integrated IC's, and requires the energetic resources of a medium PC power-supply for operation. The pixel of video scan-lines are processed by a SIMD chain-ring. The SIMD-array consists of 256 eight-bit RISC PE, which are able to operate with register contents of direct neighboring PE. Major difference to XETAL is the costly memory architecture of the IMAP VISION. Each PE has a local storage of 1024 eight-bit data-words, which is accompanied by slower-clocked external memory of 64 kB per PE for means of video input, output and temporary storage. The memory architecture allows to run more complex imaging algorithms based on the lesser timing-constraint of video-frames. The computational power of the IMAP VISION is ranked to 10 Gops at 40 MHz cycle speed.

The stereo implementation of [2] also is founded on the computation of SAD values, but the greater memory resources of the IMAP VISION allowed the authors to implement dense stereo together with a minimization of occlusion artifacts using Dynamic Programming. After rectifying and transposing the input of a weakly calibrated stereo system, pairs of two PE compute complementary left and right disparity views for a pair of epipolar lines. 128 epipolar lines are processed data-parallel. Optimization by DP eliminates disparity outliers in each eye-view, and the consistency of the result is validated by a final LR-Check.

## 3    Stereo Method

We aim to a more robust and generic implementation of a stereo-method based on the pixel-grid to XETAL than that has been presented in [3]. We target to the near and medium-range depth-field, but we do not wish to limit the scene structure. Especially we do not require geometric knowledge of the scene. Though, we are bound by the capabilities and constraints of the XETAL hardware.

### 3.1    Input Formation

From external hardware, we expect to receive rectified grey-level input, i.e. pixel-noise and lens vignetting have been removed, the images have been warped in order to remove the geometrical lens-distortion and they are projected onto parallel eye planes. The rectification towards parallel eye-planes enables us to reduce the generic 2D stereo-search problem towards a 1D-search along parallel epipolar lines, which are represented by image scan-lines. Design and implementation of such external hardware currently is subject to a different project.

Because the architectural limits of XETAL do not allow to implement expensive optimization strategies to stereo-registration, we choose to enforce numerical robustness of the input. From intensity input we extract information about spatial variance by a Gaussian gradient filter in direction of the epipolar line. Such filters can be implemented very efficient on XETAL. From the gradient sub-channel we currently only input the magnitude information and ignore the

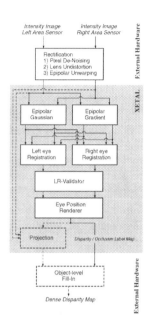

**Fig. 2.** Stereo Architecture

**Table 1.** Memory Usage

| Operation | Memory Words |
|---|---|
| Input Decode | 2 static |
| | 6 local |
| Input Vertical Filter N3 | 4 static |
| Matching and LR-Check | 12 static |
| | 2 local |
| Output Vertical Filter N3 | 4 static |
| Total | 22 static |
| | 6 local |
| | = 28 of 32 words |

gradient orientation, i.e. the sign. We sub-sample the level of the pixel intensity input from 10 to 4 bit information and eliminate noise from the intensity channel by a Gaussian averaging filter.

## 3.2 Stereo Registration

To estimate the depth of a 3D-point from its binocular stereoscopic projection, means to identify it's projection in one image, and, starting at this position in the second image as an initial guess, to *search* for its correspondence in that other image. The distance between both corresponding projections is called the disparity. For our setup and target depth field, we assume a negative lower disparity-bound of about $-1/20$ scan-line length and a positive upper disparity-bound of about $1/3$ scan-line length to search.

The stereo-matching algorithm expects pixel intensity and the epipolar gradient as two sub-channels of left and right eye input. We compute of both sub-channels the SAD, and combine the terms into a common value by weighted addition. Empirically we give higher priority to the gradient information because the intensity level of a pair of inexpensive area-sensors can vary much due to independent auto white-balancing. Still, the reduced intensity signal provides additional steering information to the matcher in ambiguous situations. From the input, the SAD-matching engine [3] renders a preliminary disparity map by convolving left and right eye positions and assigning an increasing disparity counter on each cycle if a new local minimum SAD value has been found. The rendering process is computationally more efficient for left-most eye and right-most eye output position than for any intermediate position as e.g. a virtual center position.

### 3.3   Output Validation

The preliminary disparity map for the left-eye also contains occlusions to the right eye, and vice versa. In order to remove this ambiguous information, we apply a disparity validation by a LR-check after the matching. In case we render the final disparity map for a right output position, occlusions are computed as inconsistent support of the left eye output to the very right eye output, and vice versa in opposite case.

While the LR-check takes the efficiently computed left and right preliminary disparity map as input, disparity validation still is computationally expensive because two SAD matching input-pipelines need to be executed. Second, one input channel needs to be projected to the domain of the other. While each projection-step by itself computationally is inexpensive, the validation must iterate as many times as disparity levels are found during the matching.

### 3.4   Robustness

There are three entry-points to the method, i.e. input, output and the registration, where improvements to the robustness of the method possibly can be added.

We remove noise in the grey-level input and preliminary disparity output by spatial filtering. However, it is not possible to implement filters in the temporal domain of image frames on XETAL.

As a possible improvement to the SAD-method one could evaluate the SAD-histogram of each position in the preliminary disparity map during the matching process. A high value of trust applies to candidate-matches which appear at the low edge of a high gradient slope. However, implementation of this proposal is very expensive on memory and little robust on itself.

Alternatively, the robustness of the SAD-method can be improved by relating the SAD-measures of the neighboring PE to each other at each step of the search. Currently we enforce both criteria at an off-line step by a LR-check.

- The pixel-distance of two valid match positions must be either 1 or equal to the difference of disparity levels. We can use this criteria to generate additional candidate matches.
- Two valid match-positions having a pixel-distance of 1 must have the same disparity level. We can use this criteria to rule-out candidate matches as potential occlusions.

Any simple implementation to the first criteria can be expected to have a very high computational cost. A more efficient solution is given by Dynamic Programming, which finds a global optimum-solution to both criteria while visiting each SAD-solution only once. A data-parallel evaluation of disparity levels has the least memory requirements for DP. The minimum requirements are 1 two-bit word for each pixel of the length of the scan-line, storing the minimum error path, and additionally about 10 temporary data-words with similar bit-width as the input, i.e. in total about 128 to 256 ten-bit data-words.

Unfortunately, the small amount of memory per PE is the strongest constraint on XETAL, prohibiting most of the proposed improvements.

## 4   Results

We implemented the stereo method on XETAL hardware and simulator. The hardware-solution is a closed architecture of stereo sensors, XETAL processor and display. In order to generate printable figures, we use the simulator. We are restricted 16 disparity levels per line-time (70 $\mu$s) by the limits on the instruction-count. In order to evaluate larger displacements, i.e. up-to 128 pixel, we sub-sample the video-frame in vertical direction by factor 8. To our experience, vertical resolution is less important in a horizontal stereo-setup than horizontal resolution. The input is sampled horizontally at 320 pixel per epipolar line, corresponding to the size of the LPA. Clocked at 16 Mhz, XETAL stereo-matches two sensor-lines of 320 pixel-positions in 556 $\mu$s with a maximum of 128 disparity-levels. With our current implementation we are using nearly the full memory resources of XETAL, as shown in Table 1. Figure 3 dis-

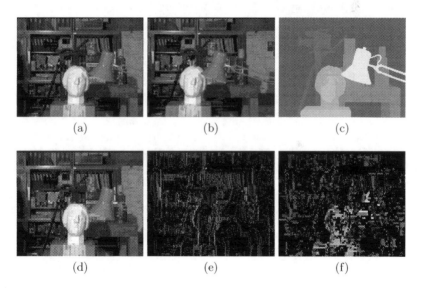

(a)          (b)          (c)

(d)          (e)          (f)

**Fig. 3.** Results (originals of this stereo test are courtesy of the University of Tsukuba): (a) rectified left eye input 4 bit intensity, (b) rectified right eye input 4 bit intensity, (c) center-eye ground truth disparity map, (d) left eye input vertically re-sampled factor 8, (e) left eye horizontal gradient magnitude, (f) left-eye stereo output after LR-validation

plays representative results of the stereo method using gradient and intensity input and a final LR-check. As XETAL registers left and right image on level of signal-processing, we obtain disparity information only for image positions with horizontal pixel-variance.

## 5 Conclusions

For reason of the enormous workload of image registration, massive parallel architectures are considered generally the most suited computational platform for stereo vision. On the base layer of signal-processing, i.e. the convolution of two 1D-signals, stereo vision is especially expensive on computation time. Implementation of this basic layer of stereo vision, completed with robustness-enhancing filters to input and output, is feasible with a low-cost SIMD hardware like XETAL. The widely applied approach to increase the robustness of a numerical vision-method, like stereo, by taking higher-order features of the scene into account, shows to be less suited for current implementations of low-cost SIMD hardware because its clear expense on memory. Approved methods for robust stereo-matching, like Dynamic Programming, can be expected to become implementable in near future to low-cost SIMD-hardware. On current low-cost SIMD-hardware with strong restrictions on memory, the robustness of the stereo-output can be improved by matching multiple sub-channels and a final validation of the disparity map by a LR-Check from different view-points.

## References

1. A.A. Abbo, R.P. Kleihorst, L. Sevat, P. Wielage, R. van Veen, M.J.R. Op de Beeck, and A. van der Avoird. A low-power parallel processor IC for digital video cameras. In *ESSCIRC'01 Proc. European Solid-State Circuits Conference*, 2001.
2. G. Kraft and P.P. Jonker. Real-time stereo with dense output by a SIMD-computed Dynamic Programming algorithm. In H.R. Arabnia, editor, *PDPTA'02 Proc. Int. Conf. on Parallel and Distributed Processing Techniques and Applications*, volume III, pages 1031–1036, Las Vegas, Nevada, USA, June 2002. CSREA Press, Las Vegas, Nevada, USA.
3. J. Smit, R. Kleihorst, A. Abbo, J. Meuleman, and G. van Willigenburg. Real time depth mapping performed on an autonomous stereo vision module. In *ProRISC Program for Research on Integrated Systems and Circuits*, pages 306–310, 2000.
4. H. Sunyoto, W. van der Mark, and D.M. Gavrila. A comparative study of fast dense stereo vision algorithms. In *IEEE Intelligent Vehicles Symposium*, pages 319–324, 2004.

# A Real-Time Iris Image Acquisition Algorithm Based on Specular Reflection and Eye Model

Kang Ryoung Park[1] and Jang Hee Yoo[2]

[1] Division of Media Technology, Sangmyung University, Seoul, Republic of Korea,
Biometrics Engineering Research Center
parkgr@smu.ac.kr
[2] Electronics and Telecommunications Research Institute (ETRI), 1 Kajeong-dong,
Yuseong-gu, Daejeon 305-350, Republic of Korea
jhy@etri.re.kr

**Abstract.** In conventional iris recognition camera, it is very difficult to capture the focused iris image at fast speed due to small range of DOF(Depth Of Field) in iris camera. So. we introduce a fast focusing method to capture user's focused iris image based on the corneal specular reflection and the human eye model. According to experimental results, we can reduce the focusing time of proposed method to be 450 ms on average.

## 1 Introduction

In conventional iris recognition camera, it is very difficult to capture the focused iris image at fast speed due to small range of DOF(the Z distance range in which focused iris images can be captured) in iris camera [1][5]. In previous researches and systems [2-4][8-15], they use the focusing method which has been used for general scene (landscape or photographic scenes) without considering the characteristics of iris image and their method cannot be applied to the focusing of iris recognition camera. So, the research [16] uses the method of checking the pixel difference in the region of corneal specular reflection(Here, specular means the brightest spot). However, they use only one illuminator for checking focus value and iris recognition. In such a case, the focus checking is impossible when the large specular reflection which happens on the surface of glasses hides that on a cornea. To overcome such problems, we propose a new method to capture user's focused iris image at fast speed based on the corneal specular reflection and the human eye model.

## 2 Proposed Focusing Method

### 2.1 Auto Focusing Algorithm Based on Corneal Specular Reflection

Iris is the region which exists between the sclera and the pupil as shown in Fig.1. Its main function is to contract or dilate the pupil in order to adjust the penetrated light volume into the retina. As shown in Fig.1, iris patterns are

J. Blanc-Talon et al. (Eds.): ACIVS 2005, LNCS 3708, pp. 705–712, 2005.
© Springer-Verlag Berlin Heidelberg 2005

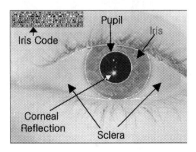

**Fig. 1.** Iris, sclera, pupil region and corneal specular reflection

highly detailed and unique textures that remain unchanged from 6 month of age to death. It shows the most highest pattern dimension. As mentioned before, in conventional iris recognition camera, it is very difficult to capture the focused iris image at fast speed due to small range of DOF(the Z distance range in which focused iris images can be captured) in iris camera. For focusing algorithm, we use the corneal specular reflection(SR) generated by IR-LED illuminator. In case that the Z position of user's eye is within the DOF, the size of SR can be minimized. On the other hand, in case that the Z position of user's eye is farther than DOF from camera, the size of SR can be increased and dark gray pixels exist in the edge of SR. And in case that the Z position of user's eye is nearer than DOF from camera, the size of SR can be also increased and dark gray pixels exist in the center of SR. Based on that information, we can determine the lens direction in case of defocusing. After determining the lens direction, the lens movement step should be also determined. Our experiments show that the size of the lens movement step can be determined based on the detected diameter of SR in image. Because our iris camera uses zoom lens, the captured iris diameter in image is maintained almost same size and the change of SR size in image is only caused by the optical defocusing(blurring). So, we can get the experimental relationship between the zoom (focus) lens position and the diameter of detected SR in image. According to our experiments (on 350 persons), such relationship proves to be almost identical to all the users and we can regard it as a standard relation generalized for all the user.

## 2.2   Compensating Focus Lens Position Based on Human Eye Model

In general, a human iris is positioned inside the cornea and the aqueous humor as shown in Fig. 2(a) [18]. The cornea and aqueous humor which surround iris and pupil act as a convex lens. As a result, the location and the size of the "projected image(PQ) of genuine iris " are different from those of the "genuine iris(P'Q')". In other words, when we see someone's iris of the eye, we see the refracted image(PQ) of the genuine iris(P'Q'). From that, we can see there exists some distance gap(L) between the position of corneal surface(on which specular reflection happens) and that of the projected iris image(PQ). As explained in section 2.1, we perform auto focusing and zooming by moving the camera lens

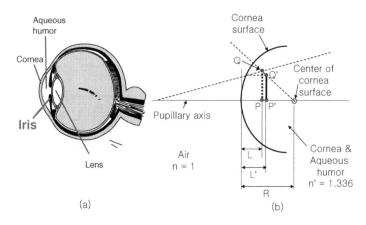

**Fig. 2.** A human eye structure and an equivalent eye model for obtaining the projected image of iris

in such a way that the size of the detected SR is minimized and it means our algorithm is operated by focusing the corneal specular reflection in other words. So, we should compensate the distance gap (L) because the projected iris(PQ) is positioned behind the cornea with the distance gap (L). Now, we explain the method of calculating the distance gap (L) based on a human eye structure and an equivalent eye model as shown in Fig. 2. According to the Gullstrand's eye model [19], the refractive index of cornea and aqueous humor is 1.336(n'), the radius of cornea is 7.8 mm(R) and the iris exists 3.6 mm(L') behind the cornea surface as shown in Fig. 2(b). From that, we can obtain the location(P) of the projected image of the iris from the Gaussian imaging formula written as $(n'/L' - n/L = (n'-n)/R)$. Here, n' and n are the refractive indexes of lens and air, respectively. In addition, L' and L are the locations of the object and the projected image, respectively. R is the radius of corneal surface (See Fig. 2(b)). From the Gauss lens formula and Gullstrand's eye model ($1.336/3.6 - 1/L = (1.336-1)/7.8$), we can obtain the distance gap (L = 3.05 mm) between the position of corneal surface and that of the projected iris image(PQ). So, in order to compensate such distance gap(3.05 mm) and focus actual iris region, we make the zoom (focus) lens be positioned closer to the eye by one more step (one step of lens corresponds to 5mm in our camera) compared to focusing corneal specular reflection.

## 2.3   Detecting Corneal Specular Reflection in Input Image

Now, we explain the method of detecting specular reflection in an input image. In order to detect the SR more easily, we use the method of changing the decoder value of frame grabber board. Due to the limitation of A/D converting range (from 0 to $2^8$-1), the conventional camera NTSC signal cannot be fully represented and some signal range may be cut off. In this case, the NTSC signal in high saturated range is represented as $255(2^8$-1) gray level in the input

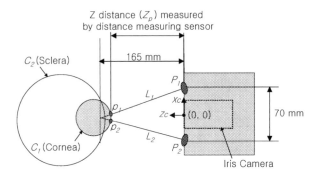

**Fig. 3.** Estimating the pixel distance between the genuine(corneal) SRs in even and odd field image

image and both the genuine SR on eye (cornea) and the other reflection region on facial skin or glasses surface may be represented as same gray level(255) in the input image. However, the NTSC analog level of SR on eye is higher than that of other region such as the reflection on facial skin. That is because the reflectance rate on cornea is greater than that on facial skin. So, if we change the decoder's brightness setting (making the input image darker), then the A-D converting range with decoder can be shifted to the upper range. In such case, there is no high saturated range and it is easy to discriminate the SR on eye and the other reflection. However, when a user with glasses tries to identify, large size of SRs or a lot of small imposter SRs generated by illuminator frequently happen on glasses surface. To overcome such problems, we use the successive On/Off scheme for IR-LED illuminators, in which IR-LED turns on and off, alternatively, synchronized with camera video signal. In our iris camera, we use two illuminators, which are positioned at left and right symmetrical to camera axis. So, one SR by left illuminator happens in even field and the other one does in odd field. Because we know the curvature of general human cornea(as explained in section 2.2) and the distance between left and right illuminators, we can estimate the distance between the genuine SRs in even and odd field image. However, the other SRs (that happens on the glasses surface or the scratches of glasses) have the tendencies not to exist with the pair characteristics (or having different size in even and odd field) or the distance between each SR may be greater than that between the genuine SRs on the cornea. That is because the curvature of glasses is much smaller than that of human cornea.

Here, we explain it in details. The Fig. 3 shows the relationship among the user's eye, illuminators and iris camera. In our iris camera, the distance between two illuminators ($P_1$ and $P_2$) is 70mm and they are positioned symmetrical to the camera axis ($Z_c$ axis in the Fig. 3). From that, we can get the 3D positions of $P_1$ and $P_2$ as (35, 0) and (-35, 0), respectively. In addition, two lights from illuminators are aligned to be intersected at the Z position of 165mm in our camera. The corneal ($C_1$) radius of the general user is known as about 7.8 mm as shown in Fig. 2(b) and the distance ($Z_p$) between the camera and the cornea surface is measured by distance measuring sensor. Based on that information, we can obtain two line equations of $L_1$ $(Z = -4.714X + 165)$ and $L_2$ $(Z = 4.714X + 165)$ in the coordinate $(X_c, Z_c)$. In addition, we can get the circle equation of $C_1$ $(X^2 + (Z - (Z_p + 7.8))^2 = 7.8^2)$. With two lines($L_1$, $L_2$) and circle equations($C_1$), we can obtain the X positions($X_1$, $X_2$) of $p_1$ and $p_2$ in the coordinate $(X_c, Z_c)$ and obtain the X distance $(D)$ between $p_1$ and $p_2$. With the calculated X distance $(D)$ and the perspective transform [6], we can estimate the X distance $(d)$ between two specular reflections in image like Eq. (1)

$$d = (D * f)/Z' \qquad (1)$$

where $f$ is camera focal length (we can get the value from camera micro-controller) and $Z'$ is the actual Z distance between the $p_1$ (or $p_2$) and the origin $(0,0)$ in the coordinate $(X_c, Z_c)$. With two lines($L_1$, $L_2$) and circle equations($C_1$), we can obtain $Z'$ $(Z' = Z_p + (7.8 - 7.8cos(sin^{-1}(D/(2*7.8)))))$. Of course, in case that the user does not align his eye into the camera optical axis $(Z_c)$ accurately, there can be some variations for $d$ in Eq. (1). However, such variations are very small according to our experiments (due to large Z distance of operating range of our iris camera (more than 100 mm) compared to small corneal radius (7.8 mm) and perspective transform) and we allow a little margin (+- 3 pixels) for $d$ in Eq. (1) to cover such variations. With the difference image of even and odd field image(in this case, we subsample each field of 640*240 pixels into that of 320*240 pixels in order to reduce processing time), we get an edge image by 3*3 sobel operator. From that, we detect the center and radius of the corneal SR by 2D gradient-based circle Hough transform [7]. With this scheme, we can detect the exact SR regions on cornea and move the zoom(focus) lens to the exact focusing position according to the SR size in image. From that, we can get the clear and focused eye image for iris recognition at very high speed.

## 3   Experimental Results

The evaluation tests were performed on 350 persons (175 persons without glasses and 175 persons with glasses). Each person tried to recognize 10 times and total 3500 trial data were acquired to measure the performance of our proposed algorithm. The test data includes the persons with an age between 23 and 60 years. In addition, we collected(rearranged) the test data according to the approaching speed of user; 1000 data at normal speed (from 5cm/sec to 15cm/sec), 1000 data at fast speed (more than 15cm/sec), and 1000 data at slow speed (below 5cm/sec). The reason why we collected data according to approaching speed is that it can affect the focusing time of camera lens. The remaining 500 data were collected in case that users approached to the camera not from the front but from the side. In the first experiment, we measured the processing time of detecting the SR in an input image and it takes a little processing time as 3 ms in Pentium-IV 1.8Ghz.

In the second experiment, we compared the performance of our focusing algorithm to those [8],[13],[14],[15] as shown in Fig. 4(a)(b). Fig. 4(a)(b) shows the

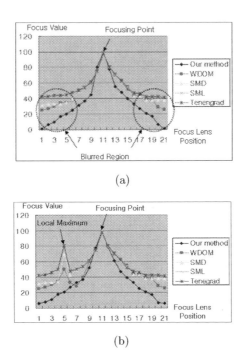

(a)

(b)

**Fig. 4.** Focus value vs. focus lens position (a)in case of users without glasses (b)in case of users with glasses

focusing performance by the curve of focus value vs. focus lens position. In general, if the curve is steep near a focusing point and in the blurred region, it is reported that the focusing algorithm shows good performance [15]. That is because if the slope near the focusing point is steep, the focus lens can reach the focused position fast and accurately. In addition, if the slope in the blurred region is also steep, the focus lens can determine its movement direction easily [15]. According to Fig. 4(a), our method shows the best focusing performance. In addition, other methods show the local maximums of focus value curve which make the focusing more difficult as shown in Fig. 4(b), but our method does not show any local maximum in focus value curve. In the third experiment, we compared the average focusing time. From the table 1, we can know our focusing method shows the best performance. In the fourth experiment, we measured the performances of our algorithm(with lens position compensation) in terms of recognition speed. The average recognition time (including focusing and iris recognition time) is 698 ms in case of the users without glasses and that is 1201 ms in case of that with glasses.

The reason that the recognition time is increased in the latter case is that large SR on glasses surface caused by illuminator hides the whole iris region sometimes. In such case, our system turns on the other illuminator (from left to right or from right to left) and the total recognition time is increased, consequently. In the fifth experiment, we measured the recognition rate and the results show the FAR(False Acceptance Error Rate) of 0% and the FRR(False

**Table 1.** The average focusing time (unit: ms)

| Method | Tenengrad [8] | SMD [13] | SML [14] | WDOM [15] | Our method without lens compensation | Our method with lens compensation |
|---|---|---|---|---|---|---|
| Users without glasses | 551 | 434 | 535 | 425 | 328 | 309 |
| Users with glasses | 1523 | 928 | 1411 | 890 | 628 | 601 |
| Average time | 1037 | 681 | 973 | 658 | 474 | 450 |

Rejection Error Rate) of 0.8%(28/3500 trials). The FRR is mainly caused by the large SR from glasses and most of them are recognized in second trial. Here, we used the iris recognition algorithm based on Daugman's method to measure the FAR and FRR [1]. In the sixth experiment, we tested the focusing time, recognition time and recognition rate according to the Z distance between user and the iris camera.

**Table 2.** The average focusing, recognition time and recognition rate according to Z distance

| Z distance | at 10 cm | at 12 cm | at 16 cm | at 20 cm | at 22 cm |
|---|---|---|---|---|---|
| Focusing time | 452 ms | 458 ms | 457 ms | 451 ms | 451 ms |
| Recognition time | 946 ms | 952 ms | 949 ms | 954 ms | 950 ms |
| False Acceptance Error Rate | 0 % | 0 % | 0 % | 0 % | 0 % |
| False Rejection Error Rate | 0.7 % | 0.79 % | 0.8 % | 0.79 % | 0.8 % |

From the table 2, we can know the focusing time, recognition time and recognition rate are almost same irrespective of the Z distance. In the last experiment, we tested the focusing time, recognition time and recognition rate by changing environmental lighting intensity(with fluorescent lamp).

**Table 3.** The average focusing, recognition time and recognition rate according to environmental illumination

| Illumination | 250 Lux. | 500 Lux. | 750 Lux. | 1000 Lux. | 1250 Lux. |
|---|---|---|---|---|---|
| Focusing time | 451 ms | 448 ms | 452 ms | 451 ms | 455 ms |
| Recognition time | 1220 ms | 1209 ms | 952 ms | 951 ms | 948 ms |
| False Acceptance Rate | 0 % | 0 % | 0 % | 0 % | 0 % |
| False Rejection Rate | 0.92 % | 0.83 % | 0.8 % | 0.79 % | 0.8 % |

From the table 3, we can know the focusing time, recognition time and recognition rate are almost same irrespective of the change of lighting intensity. To be notable, in case that the lighting intensity is below 500 Lux., the FRR and the recognition time is increased a little. That is because the pupil is dilated too much due to dark environmental light (iris region is contracted too much) and it causes False Rejection cases.

## 4   Conclusions

In this paper, we propose a new iris image acquisition method to capture user's focused iris image at very fast speed based on the corneal specular reflection and human eye model. From the experimental results, we can conclude our method can be applicable for the real-time iris recognition camera. In future works, we plan to estimate the user's motion and move the lens in advance to enhance the performance.

## Acknowledgement

This work was supported by a research grant from the ETRI, Korea.

## References

1. John G. Daugman, "High confidence visual recognition of personals by a test of statistical independence". IEEE Trans. PAMI., Vol. 15, No. 11, pp. 1148-1160, 1993
2. http://www.lgiris.com
3. http://www.iridiantech.com
4. http://www.panasonic.com/cctv/products/biometrics.asp
5. http://www.iris-recognition.org
6. Ramesh Jain, "Machine Vision", McGraw-Hill International Edition, 1995
7. D. Ioammou et al., "Circle Recognition through a 2D Hough transform and Radius Histogramming", Image and Vision Computing, vol. 17, pp. 15-26, 1999
8. Je-Ho Lee et al., "Implementation of a passive automatic focusing algorithm for digital still camera", IEEE Trans. on CE, vol. 41, no. 3, pp. 449-454, Aug. 1995.
9. H. Toyoda et al., "New Automatic Focusing System for Video Camera", IEEE Transactions on Consumer Electronics, vol. CE-32, no. 3, pp. 312-319, Aug. 1986
10. T. Haruki and K. Kikuchi, "Video Camera System Using Fuzzy Logic", IEEE Transactions on Consumer Electronics, vol. 38, no. 3, pp. 624-634, Aug. 1992
11. K. Ooi et al., "An Advanced Auto-focusing System for Video Camera Using Quasi Condition Reasoning", IEEE Trans. on CE, vol. 36, no. 3, pp. 526-529, Aug. 1990
12. K. Hanma et al., "Novel Technologies for Automatic Focusing and White Balancing of SolidState Color Video Camera", IEEE Trans. on CE, vol.CE-29, no. 3, pp.376-381, Aug. 1983
13. R. A. Jarvis, "Focus Optimization Criteria for Computer Image Processing", Microscope, vol. 24(2), pp. 163-180, 1976
14. S. K. Nayar and Y. Nakagawa, "Shape from Focus", IEEE Transactions on Pattern Analysis and Machine Intelligence, vol. 16, no. 8, pp. 824-831, Aug. 1994.
15. Kang-Sun Choi et al., "New Auto-focusing Technique Using the Frequency Selective Weight Median Filter for Video Cameras", IEEE Trans. on CE, Vol.45, No.3, pp.820-827, Aug. 1999
16. Y. Park et al., "A Fast Circular Edge Detector for the Iris Region Segmentation", LNCS, Springer Verlag, Vol. 1811, 2000, pp. 417-423
17. Sheng-Wen Shih, "A Novel Approach to 3-D Gaze Tracking Using Stereo Cameras", IEEE Transactions on Systems, Man and Cybernatics-Part B, Vol. 34, No. 1, Feb. 2004
18. Helmholtz and Hermann, Die Dioptrik des Auges Editor: Nagel W and Gullstrand A, Handbuch der physiologischen Optik, 1909
19. Y.L.Grand, "Light, Color and Vision", New York: Wiley, 1957

# An Image Sensor with Global Motion Estimation for Micro Camera Module

F. Gensolen[1,2], G. Cathebras[2], L. Martin[1], and M. Robert[2]

[1] STMICROELECTRONICS, ZI de Rousset, BP 2, 13106 Rousset, France
[2] LIRMM, Univ. Montpellier II / CNRS, 161 rue Ada, 34392 Montpellier, France
fabrice.gensolen@lirmm.fr

**Abstract.** We describe in this paper the building of a vision sensor able to provide video capture and the associated global motion between two consecutive frames. Our objective is to propose embedded solutions for mobile applications. The global motion considered here is the one typically produced by handheld devices movement, which is required for our purpose of video stabilization. We extract this global motion from local motion measures at the periphery of the image acquisition area. Thanks to this peculiar and "task-oriented" configuration, the resulting system architecture can take advantage of CMOS focal plane processing capabilities without sacrificing the sensor fill factor. Our approach is currently implemented in a CMOS 0.13μm technology.

## 1 Introduction

Our objective is to develop a smart CMOS image sensor for mobile systems (PDA, cell phone). Such handheld devices are very shake prone and often provide trembling video; also we focus in this paper on video stabilization. The best way to stabilize video is to perform an optical correction using gyro sensors and mobile optics/sensors, stabilizing directly the incidence of the light onto the focal plane. Nevertheless, this is a costly and burdening solution for embedded devices.

Another approach is completely electronic. It consists in analyzing the main displacement between two consecutive frames of the video, so called global motion or camera motion, in order to separate the intentional motion from the unwanted one. This last is then compensated, resulting in a video without jolts [1]. This is the stabilization scheme we have adopted. We focus in the present paper on the crucial global motion estimation stage of the processing.

Considering the signal processing architecture, such a motion estimation task can be realized as a post-processing of digital images coming from the imager (Fig. 1). In a time to market point of view, this is a very efficient way to implement an image processing on silicon. However, that means to process the huge amount of video data serially, which is very time and power consuming [2].

In this paper, we investigate another way to perform motion estimation task by reporting part of the processing at pixel level. This approach speeds up the processing time and alleviates the computing power by making use of parallelism of the pixels needed in image sensors for light spatial sampling. The main drawback of this kind of silicon integration is the increased area per pixel, which decreases the fill-factor and the image resolution. But we present and validate in this paper a new global motion

J. Blanc-Talon et al. (Eds.): ACIVS 2005, LNCS 3708, pp. 713–721, 2005.
© Springer-Verlag Berlin Heidelberg 2005

estimation technique based on local motion measures at the periphery of the image acquisition area. Thanks to this peculiar and "task-oriented" configuration, we take advantage of CMOS focal plane processing capabilities without sacrificing the sensor fill factor. Indeed, the silicon area has become the main contribution to the cost of image sensors, accounting for around 70% of the overall cost.

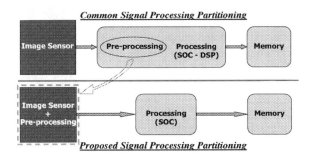

**Fig. 1.** Signal processing partitioning

We describe in section 2 our global motion estimation technique, based on peripheral local motion measures. Section 3 is dedicated to its validation by software implementation, and section 4 to the evaluation and the partitioning of the processing. Then we describe in section 5 the transfer of part of it onto focal plane, performing pixel level processing.

## 2   Global Motion Estimation

### 2.1   Principle and Basis

In order to describe the global motion between two consecutive frames, we make use of a four components parametric model, called similarity model. This model allows us to describe the main global movements perceived in the focal plane: that means rotations around the optical axis, zoom, and X-Y translations. Then, such a parametric motion can be ascribed to most of the pixels in an image. It is also a good tradeoff between complexity, noise sensitivity, and description of the inter frames movement.

Two kinds of motion are generally present in common video captures with handheld devices like cell phones: the one due to mobile elements in the scene, and the background one (Fig. 2). In our purpose of video stabilization, that is this last background movement which is of main interest as it informs directly about the camera/global motion.

Moreover we point out that the periphery of images are particularly interesting for this task. Indeed, this area of interest contain local motions that better constrain the global motion parameters. Also, these local motions are well distributed in the images and background is often on the periphery of images. Therefore, we only focus on this area to extract the desired global motion (Fig. 2).

 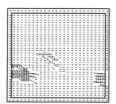

**Fig. 2.** Example of a scene, with the associated local motion vectors for a left panning of the camera. Edges on the right picture point out the area of interest.

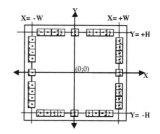

$$\begin{cases} Xj(t+dt) = \alpha * \cos\theta * Xj(t) + \alpha * \sin\theta * Yj(t) + Tx \\ Yj(t+dt) = -\alpha * \sin\theta * Xj(t) + \alpha * \cos\theta * Yj(t) + Ty \end{cases}$$

**Fig. 3.** Geometric system setting

## 2.2 Global Motion Estimation Procedure

Let us suppose that a picture "n" is transformed according to a geometric combination of a rotation , a zoom factor , and two translations Tx and Ty, in another picture "n+1": a pixel "j" with cartesian coordinates $(Xj(n), Yj(n))$ in frame "n" become the pixel with cartesian coordinates $(Xj(n+1), Yj(n+1))$ in frame "n+1". The system in Fig. 3 describes such a geometric transformation. Applying this transformation to all the points of the area of interest, that leads to the following linear over determined system:

$$P = K \times M \qquad (1)$$

Where P is the matrix positions $(Xj(n+1), Yj(n+1))$, K the matrix linking these positions to the ones of frame "n", composed of $(Xj(n), Yj(n))$ coordinates with "0" and "1", and M contains the four transformation parameters. These parameters are Tx, Ty, $\alpha.\cos\theta$, and $\alpha.\sin\theta$. Then knowing P and K, we are able to determine the four global motion parameters M thanks to an optimization process.

Matrix P is obtained summing original cartesian positions of pixels in frame "n" with local motions of this pixels between frame "n" and "n+1". The optimization operation is performed here in a least squares sense, and the resulting estimation can be written as [3]:

$$M = (K^T \times K)^{-1} \times K^T \times P \qquad (2)$$

## 3 Software Implementation

In order to validate our approach, we first evaluate the performances by software. Hence, we need to compute the local movement estimations at the periphery on the two consecutive images.

### 3.1 Local Motion Estimation

Several algorithms exist to perform local motion estimation, but one of the most efficient ways is to carry out pixel, or area, correspondence [4]. We have chosen two algorithms for extracting local motion vectors: the first is the well known full search block matching (FSBM), and the other comes from [5]. The last technique, called Census transform, consists in a local texture coding which results in a binary code for each pixel, that is then tracked from one frame into the next.

## 3.2  Performances

Using Matlab software, we have characterized our global motion estimation technique with respect to outdoor and indoor scenes. Firstly we built synthetic video sequences starting from a high resolution picture which we transformed and from which we picked a CIF one with a known displacement. Then we also grabbed real video sequences thanks to the same digital camera, providing a 15 im/s CIF video. Both synthetic and real sequences contain the same image texture. They have been captured in the same illumination conditions with various constant amplitudes of movement. These amplitudes are always lower than : 5% of the image size for translation, 3° for rotation, 2% for zoom. Both represent indoor and outdoor scenes. The indoor ones contain an environment of work with desks and chairs (lowly textured) and the outdoor ones are a nature environment with trees and a river (highly textured).

The inter frame global motion being unknown in real sequences, we apply the precise and robust algorithm developed by [6] in order obtain our reference motions (source code with makefiles are available on the IRISA website: http://www.irisa.fr/Vista/Motion2D/index.html). This algorithm is proven reliable in various applications like underwater vehicle positioning, or super-resolution, and car driving assistance.

We report in the following Table 1 the first results of our characterizations in terms of error percentage to the reference, or known, motion. As we can see, raw Census transform motion estimation gives lower results than block matching.

**Table 1.** First results on performances achieved with a software implementation of the global motion estimation (in terms of error percentage to the reference motion )

|  | Census 5*5 | Bloc matching |
|---|---|---|
| Synthetic outdoor | 5.8 % | 0.02 % |
| Real outdoor | 71 % | 12% |
| Synthetic. Indoor | 6.2 % | 0 % |
| Real indoor | 82 % | 15 % |

**Table 2.** Processing load of local motion estimation in elementary operations, and the associated ratio to the total computational load of the global motion estimation (with N=280 local motions on the periphery)

| Search area | FSBM 5×5 ~2×M²×S²×N | Census 5*5 |
|---|---|---|
| +/-16 pixels | ~15 232 068 op 99.92 % | ~4 394 495 op 99.73 % |
| +/- 12 pixels | ~8 736 042 op 99.87 % | ~3 369 087 99.65 % |
| +/- 8 pixels | ~4 032 002 op 99.31 % | ~ 2 330 367 99.49 % |

## 4  Towards a Vision System on Chip

Our final objective is to integrate the proposed technique to an image sensor. The main constraint, as discussed in the introduction of the paper is the silicon area. But the sensor has to perform the global motion estimation in real time and is dedicated to embedded devices, hence additional constraints have to be taken into account.

## 4.1  Complexity Analysis

In the hierarchy of vision sensor design flow, complexity analysis is the first step to optimize the digital hardware required.

Firstly we can point out that the lines number for all matrix involved in our technique can be half the original one, while keeping exactly the same estimation robustness. Indeed, let us suppose that we consider N positions of local motion estimations, the resulting over determined system of equation (1) contains 2N lines, as each position is described in the image plane by two coordinates.

Then if a local motion is erroneous, it constitutes a proportion of $2/2N=1/N$ of the system, which is the same proportion as if we consider only one of the two new coordinates $(1/N)$. Therefore we choose this last solution and we will involve in the global estimation only the coordinate parallel to the considered side of the image periphery. This is the same as computing one-dimensional motion estimation, and the overall processing load in terms of elementary operations number is half of the original one. We have quantified the total number of elementary operations to perform the global motion estimation, leading to $42N+207$ operations, where N is the number of local motion considered in the periphery of the image.

Let us now consider the local motion estimation processing load which constitutes the main part of the total load. Indeed, as described earlier, we compute local movement estimations thanks to matching algorithms, just as the well-used MPEG scheme. Unfortunately, these algorithms lead to highly regular low-level tasks, and a huge amount of data access through frame buffer is also required. In a typical video encoder for example, it accounts for as much as 60% of total CPU cycles [2]. In our case, FSBM and Census algorithms are both quadratic algorithms, with respective complexity of $2 \times M^2 \times S^2 \times N$ and $S^2 \times N$. Where $M \times M$ are blocks of pixels, S is the search area in pixels, and N the number of local movements considered. Let us consider that we perform one local motion measurement each 10 pixels of a SVGA frame, that means that $N=280$. In that case, it accounts for as much as the overall number of operations presented in the following Table 2.

## 4.2  Hardware Requirements and Partitioning

As pointed out in Table 2, local motion estimations accounts for around as much as 99% of the total processing load required to extract the global motion between two consecutive frames.

On the other hand, we can perform in CMOS technology numerous kinds of analog and/or mixed signal processing, as soon as the phototransduction [7], avoiding to perform the computation in the processing stage (Fig. 1). This computation saving being then allocated to higher level tasks as image segmentation for tracking for example. This is the processing partitioning that we propose, performing the peripheral local motion measurements at pixel level thanks to dedicated motion detectors, and adding the least square global motion estimation procedure to the processing hardware (Fig. 1). Therefore, the resulting vision sensor architecture is the one shown on the right in Fig. 4.

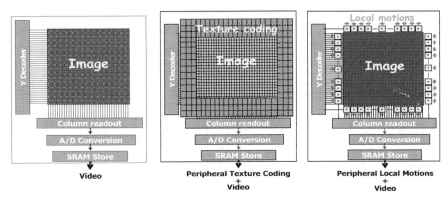

**Fig. 4.** Common image sensor architecture (left), and our two proposed achitectures (center and right). The prefered architecture is the right one.

## 5  Focal Plane Local Motion Measures

Focal plane signal processing performed in vision sensors are often elementary operations in order to keep relative simple pixels and preserve the sensor fill-factor while benefiting from the intrinsic massive parallelism of image sensors to obtain powerful computing architecture. It is also possible to design specific architectures dedicated to particular tasks.

Motion estimation is one of them, and several local motion detectors have been designed for this purpose [8]. Some of them are inspired from biology and constitute silicon models of elementary biological functions. Each of these smart pixels embeds additional electronics (around 20 transistors), leading to larger silicon area per pixel, hence lower resolution and higher cost compared to pixels dedicated only to the image acquisition (3 transistors). That is the main reason why these kind of smart pixels are not widely used in industry.

However, fixing our task of global motion estimation considering only the periphery of the image acquisition area avoids this antagonism between pixel level processing and silicon area required. Also, we propose in the following section two kinds of focal plane processing estimating the desired local motions. In the first solution we integrate a modified version of the census transform (center in Fig. 4), and in the second solution we propose the integration of the entire local motion estimations (right in Fig. 4).

### 5.1  Ternary Census Transform

We firstly consider the silicon integration of the census transform, which has been previously detailed in [9]. Then, based on our circuit characterizations, we have carried out further validations on the census transform. That brought us to introduce a new version of it, especially dedicated to a focal plane processing type, where no noise reduction is performed (due to silicon area saving). This new census transform has been shown to be more robust to fixed pattern noise due to CMOS process dispersions [10]. The resulting pixel architecture involves an hysteresis comparator to perform luminance comparisons between pixels, associated to a 3 transistors active pixel sensor (Fig. 5).

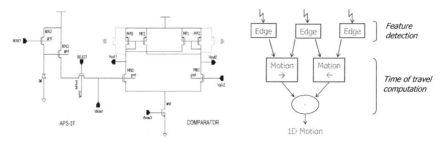

**Fig. 5.** Pixel architecture integrating the terna    **Fig. 6.** Local motion measurement census transform

Each pixel results in a 10×10μm² area, instead of 4×4μm² for pixels specialized in image acquisition only. Moreover, as explained in section 3, local motions are obtained performing pixel correspondence with neighbours. This implies to integrate not only a single line of ternary census pixels around the image, but several lines in order to be able to determine the magnitude of inter frame movements (b. in Fig. 4).

For a SVGA video module for example (sensor size which is currently on sale), the magnitude is about 3% of the image size, which equals about 21 pixels (in terms of image pixels size, i.e. 4×4μm² area). However in terms of ternary census pixels, it is equal to a displacement between 8 and 9 pixels in both directions. Therefore we need to integrate 2*9+1=19 lines of ternary pixels, increasing the image area by 22% of the original SVGA image acquisition area. This integration induces 50% saving of the overall computation load to perform global motion estimation (see Table 2).

It is important to point out that this silicon area proportion is more and more decreasing as the image sensor resolution grows (which is the actually evolution).

### 5.2 Local Motion Detector

As introduced at the beginning of this section, several motion detectors have been designed to measure local motions. We focus currently on the ones described in [11]. The main advantage of such a processing is the continuous time mode of measuring local motion. Indeed it avoids the problem of temporal aliasing [8]. The principle illustrated in Fig. 6 is to measure the time $\Delta t$ of travel of a spatial or temporal feature of the scene (an edge for example) between two photo elements distant of L, resulting in a crossing speed of :

$$V = \frac{L}{\Delta t}$$

This measure is asynchronous, that is why we are currently developing a technique to process a temporal integration over the inter frame period in order to synchronize our data with the video.

This elementary motion sensor is integrated in a 30×30µm² pixel. Moreover, thanks to the continuous time processing, only one line of such detectors are necessary, resulting in an increase in silicon area of 4% of the original SVGA image acquisition area. These local motion measurements induce around 99% saving of the overall computational load (see Table 2).

# 6  Conclusion

We have presented in this paper a new approach in performing video stabilization. The global motion required to fix this task is extracted from local motion estimations at the periphery of the image acquisition area. We performed a least-squares global motion estimation and local motion estimations with two pixel correspondence techniques: the Census transform and the block matching. The block matching technique gave us the best results, allowing to get a global motion estimation error of 12% of the true motion in real video sequences. Such an error is suitable for standard video captures but appears not precise enough in cases of large movements.

We have also described the building of a vision sensor able to provide video capture and the associated global motion. The main advantage of the proposed technique, in a vision system architecture point of view, is to perform each task of image acquisition and motion estimation independently, with the optimized focal plane processing. Indeed it avoids the sensible tradeoff between image pixel area and pixel level processing.

# References

1. C. Morimotto and R. Chellappa, "Fast Electronic Digital Image Stabilization", *in Proceedings of the 13th Int. Conf. on Pattern Recognition*, Aug. 1996, vol. 3, pp. 284-288.
2. P. M. Kuhn and W. Stechele, "Complexity analysis of the emerging MPEG-4 standard as a basis for VLSI implementation", *in Proceedings of the Int. Conf on Visual Communications and Image Processing*, San Jose, Jan. 1998, vol. SPIE 3309, pp. 498-509.
3. N.R. Draper and H. Smith, *"Applied Regression Analysis"*, 3rd Ed., John Wiley & Sons, New York, 1998.
4. F. Dufaux and F. Moscheni, "Motion estimation techniques for digital TV: a review and a new contribution", *in Proceedings of the IEEE*, vol. 83, Issue 6, June 1995, pp. 858-876.
5. R. Zabih and J. Woodfill, "Non-Parametric Local Transforms For Computing Visual Correspondance", *in 3rd European Conference on Computer Vision*, 1994, pp 151-158.
6. J.M. Odobez, P. Bouthemy, "Robust multiresolution estimation of parametric motion models", *Journal of Visual Communication and Image Representation*, December 1995, 6(4), pp.348-365.
7. C. Mead, "Analog VLSI and neural systems," *Addison-Wesley*, 1989.
8. R. Sarpeshkar, J, Kramer, G. Indiveri and C. Koch "Analog VLSI Architectures for Motion Processing: from Fundamental Limits to System Applications", *Proceedings of the IEEE*, Vol. 84, Issue: 7, , July 1996, pp. 969-987.
9. D. Navarro, G. Cathébras and F. Gensolen, "A block matching approach for movement estimation in a CMOS retina: principle and results," *proceedings of the European Solid-State Circuits Conference ESSCIRC'03*, 2003, pp. 615-618.

10. F. Gensolen, G. Cathebras, L. Martin, M. Robert, «Pixel level silicon integration of motion estimation», *IEEE workshop on Design and Diagnostic of Electronic Circuits and Systems*, Sopron, Hungary, April 2005.
11. J. Kramer, "Compact integrated motion sensor with three-pixel interaction", in IEEE trans. On Pattern Analysis ans Machine Intelligence, April 1996, vol. 18, Issue 4, pp. 455-460.

# Author Index

# Lecture Notes in Computer Science

For information about Vols. 1–3607

please contact your bookseller or Springer

||| || || ■ ||■||||||||| ||■||| ||| | || || ■ ||||| ||||| ■ |||